Urban Policymaking and Metropolitan Dynamics

A Comparative Geographical Analysis

Association of American Geographers

Comparative Metropolitan Analysis Project

Vol. 1 Contemporary Metropolitan America: Twenty Geographical Vignettes. Cambridge: Ballinger Publishing Company, 1976.

Vol. 2. Urban Policymaking and Metropolitan Dynamics: A Comparative Geographical Analysis. Cambridge: Ballinger Publishing Company, 1976.

Vol. 3. A Comparative Atlas of America's Great Cities: Twenty Metropolitan Regions. Minneapolis: University of Minnesota Press, 1976.

Vignettes of the following metropolitan regions are also published by Ballinger Publishing Company as separate monographs:

- Boston
- New York-New Jersey
- Philadelphia
- Hartford-Central Connecticut
- Baltimore
- New Orleans
- Chicago
- St. Paul-Minneapolis
- Seattle
- Miami
- Los Angeles

Supported by a grant from the National Science Foundation.

Urban Policymaking and Metropolitan Dynamics

A Comparative Geographical Analysis

John S. Adams, Editor
University of Minnesota

Ballinger Publishing Company • Cambridge, Massachusetts
A Subsidiary of J.B. Lippincott Company

This book is printed on recycled paper.

International Standard Book Number: 0-88410-426-5

Library of Congress Catalog Card Number: 76-25165

Printed in the United States of America

Library of Congress Cataloging in Publication Data

Main entry under title
Urban policymaking and metropolitan dynamics.
1. Cities and towns–United States–Addresses, essays, lectures.
2. Metropolitan areas–United States–Addresses, essays, lectures.
I. Adams, John S., 1938–
HT123.U748 301.36'3'0973 76-25165
ISBN 0-88410-426-5

List of Figures

List of Tables

Preface

This collection is the second volume of studies specially commissioned by the Comparative Metropolitan Analysis Project, a research program sponsored by the Association of American Geographers and supported by a grant from the National Science Foundation. The Project's overriding goal has been to provide an accurate comparative assessment of the progress made since the 1960s toward meeting human needs in America's twenty largest metropolitan regions.

The tension between uniqueness and generality among America's major cities has been accommodated by analyzing individual metropolitan regions in one part of the Project (Volume 1), specific metropolitan problems in another part (Volume 2), and by comparing the results of the regional and topical studies in *A Comparative Atlas of America's Great Cities* (Volume 3). No city's problems are exactly the same as any other city's. At the same time, neither are they wholly dissimilar. The same principle holds regarding workable solutions for urban problems. Whereas the policies and programs that would solve Atlanta's housing problems have elements in common with those that would work in New York City, they must also take on a character that responds to the individuality of the locality.

As the United States continues to mature, older metropolitan areas are in decline, new metropolitan regions are appearing, while parts of existing metropolitan regions are deteriorating both socially and physically. As federal, state, and municipal governments seek strategies for coping with the problems brought on by continued metropolitan growth and decay, the need for a comparative analysis of the American metropolitan experience has never been more urgent. The basic processes of urbanization and metropolitan evolution are common to all cities. Yet regional and temporal variations among American cities have caused urban processes to work themselves out in different ways, producing cities as distinctive as Baltimore and Los Angeles within the same nation. Programs and policies that fail to recognize and accommodate the individuality and the underlying similarities among the nation's metropolitan regions will certainly fail to yield maximum benefits.

Over the last decades geographers have made important progress toward understanding the use of urban space and the varied results of ongoing urban processes. The Comparative Metropolitan Analysis Project has applied these understandings to current metropolitan problems in the hope that its research results will stimulate greater concern with urban problems among geography teachers, students, and the lay public, and in the hope that its conclusions will assist the formulation of more effective urban policies. This volume is one step toward that goal. Each of the essays is a comparative geographical analysis of a set of metropolitan regions as they have been affected by a specific set of urban public policies and programs. As Brian Berry observes in his introductory chapter, the essays share in common the geographer's particular concern with *geography*—with the spatial structure of the metropolis, with the spatial patterns and dynamics of urban land use, with population distributions and social ecology, and with the physical geography of cities. They also share some of the perceptual persuasions that develop when a group of young, somewhat liberal scientists talk to each other. In their analysis, conclusions, and policy recommendations the authors speak clearly and forcefully, but it should be emphasized that they speak only for themselves.

In the review and editing of these essays and their accompanying artwork, I have been aided enormously by Ronald Abler and by the Project steering committee: Brian J.L. Berry, Chairman, Harvard University; John R. Borchert, University of Minnesota; Frank E. Horton, Southern Illinois University; James E. Vance, R., University of California at Berkeley; David Ward, University of Wisconsin at Madison; and J. Warren Nystrom, Executive Director, Association of American Geographers. Cartography and drafting was done by Sandra Haas, Robert Hyde, Ki-Suk Lee, Janeen E. McAllister, Kwai Shing Poon and Su Chang Wang in the Cartographic Laboratory of the University of Minnesota (Richard H. Skaggs, chairman), under the supervision of Ronald Abler and Ki-Suk Lee. For their above assistance and for the help of Project secretary Patricia A. Kelly I am profoundly indebted.

John S. Adams
Minneapolis, Minnesota
June 1976

Part 1

Introduction

Chapter 1

On Geography and Urban Policy

Brian J.L. Berry
Harvard University

Geographers have made few, if any significant contributions to the formulation or evaluation of urban policy, and the essays in this book are offered as one small step towards redressing the situation. In their powerlessness geographers are not, of course, unique; urban researchers in general lack influence and, frequently, respect. Indeed, when a senior staff member of the Department of Housing and Urban Development called together a small group "to review the fragmented, disjointed urban research scene, and to explore whether mechanisms could be instituted to improve the situation" three years ago, he said in his letter to this writer that "from the Federal point of view there are three questions: What do we now know? What do we need to know? and How can we find out?" His reflections were gloomy indeed:

> The knowledge crisis facing the policy-maker is very real because he cannot get adequately past Question Number One, 'What do we now know?' *The task of 'synthesis' is not being done.* Instead he confronts fragmentation, static rather than dynamic images under conditions of accelerating social and technological change, unexplained processes depicted as isolated facts, and the fact that his point of intervention and what would be the consequences of alternative actions are not given him by the knowledge community. Because Question Number One has not been answered, he is even more vulnerable on Question Number Two, 'What do we need to know?' He does not have a Mendeleevyan chart that by its gaps shows what must be sought. Instead, he confronts a host of competitive research proposals that relate to no universe of integrated knowledge, and generally do not even advance a hypothesis to relate the proposal to the existing body of knowledge. And further the research proposer is generally ignorant of the operational knowledge requirements of the policy-maker—because there is no scientific base of knowledge to which decisive appeal can be made. [Personal Communication]

He concluded that urban research in general is increasingly in ill-repute in leading government and private business circles because it has not only failed the first two questions, but crucially cannot identify the answer to Question Number Three, "How can we find out?" "Over 3 billion dollars have been spent in the last decade on social research, and because there was no critical test—and usually no prior hypothesis, we do not know what we are supposed to have learned by this immense effort" [*Ibid*].

Yet the blame does not entirely reside within academia. There is something more profound about the policymakers' all too frequent complaint that their consultants and advisers never answer the questions posed, but instead *tell them that the wrong questions are being asked.* As Philip S. Broughton commented in his foreword to Roy Lubove's *The Progressives and the Slums:*

> Our city governments and civic leaders have all too often engaged in dedicated efforts to find the right answers to wrong questions. Nowhere has this curious aberration had

> more devastating results than in land use planning and in the housing of people. . . . Only slowly have we begun to recognize that today's monumentally expensive urban redevelopment arises because we asked the wrong questions yesterday. . . . A re-examination of the questions we ask ourselves about our cities and our housing is overdue because the wrong answers have not merely cost city, state and federal money, but have helped change the character of our Republic. [pp. xii–xiii]

Somehow, effective bridges must be built between the world of policy and the research undertakings of the academic, and geographers must be numbered among those doing the bridge-building. Of course, what the urban policymaker normally is seeking is *a base of knowledge to which decisive appeal can be made.* The creation of such a knowledge-base is a research task worthy of any academic. Research undertaken to illuminate or influence policy issues of other kinds has an honorable and long tradition in the social sciences, going back at least as far as the economists' research on the Corn Laws. Such research has affected policy by providing information that enabled policymakers to estimate various parameters of a problem or to choose among competing hypotheses.

It is a mischaracterization to think of research as merely providing data or information however. *Perhaps the most important influence that good research can have on policy development is through its effect on the way policymakers look at the world.* It can influence what they regard as fact or fiction; the problems they see and do not see; the interpretations they regard as plausible or nonsensical; the judgments they make as to whether a policy is potentially effective or irrelevant or worse. Much of this influence occurs before a specific policy issue arises, in how people are educated before they become policymakers and what they have to read thereafter. The conceptions that a policymaker brings to a problem may loom large in importance relative to his efforts to learn about it by consciously surveying the state of relevant knowledge when confronted by a particular problem.

Influence also takes place as knowledge is marshaled in the course of the policy formation process, of course, and this means a central concern with *public policy analysis.* Expressed most generally, such analysis is the *future-oriented* inquiry into the optimum means of achieving social objectives. It encompasses studies designed to extend the range of social alternatives perceived by decisionmakers, and to suggest the long range and implicit consequences of various sets of value priorities. This may involve inquiry into alternative descriptions of the problem context, ways of conceptualizing the problem, sets of goals and objectives, courses of action for achieving selected objectives, predictions of probable outcomes of the courses of action considered (including alternative models), strategies for assuring preferred outcomes, and methods of appraising the implementation of a selected course of action. Increasingly explicitly, the evaluative function is expressed in such terms as "technology assessment," "systems analysis," "social accounting," "continuous appraisal" or some such designative terminology. Insofar as these concepts are applied to the analysis of major technological projects or to pressing social problems they clearly involve the assessment of the impact of the program's implementation on participants, values and institutions. Policy analysis thus means a *problem-oriented* approach as distinguished from a *disciplinary* approach, traditionally concerned, for the conventional organization of knowledge by academic disciplines and the continuing fragmentation of operating programs are not conducive to the problem-oriented approach. The educational and the research challenge must be faced if academics are to be effective participants in a world in which social change is increasingly being sought after by deliberate means. There is a commensurate challenge that the policymaker must address, for solutions to urban problems demand the careful, clear projection of policy objectives, program alternatives, and underlying economic and social forces, proceeding toward a solution through experimentation and feedback guided by theory and analysis with due allowance for the fact that most social problems are inherently complex. It is virtually impossible to analyze them neatly. Policy objectives tend to be diffuse and difficult to quantify. Program mechanisms are intricate and not easily controllable. Success is difficult to evaluate. While research can help in the design and improvement of programs, good policymaking requires art, judgment, and weighing of conflicting values. But is not the inherent difficulty that is implied the ultimate challenge to the academic's skill? The challenge cannot be met by withdrawal to the cloisters. What is needed from the research standpoint is both demonstrated competence of analysis and insight, and a willingness to engage in continuous dialogue with policymakers.

The Association of American Geographers' Metropolitan Analysis Project was formulated with such considerations in mind. Using the 1970 Census of Population and Housing as a base, the intent was to demonstrate geographers' research skills in a comparative analysis of the structure and change of the nation's 20 largest metropolitan regions, and of the progress that was made towards achieving the goals of the many urban programs that were developed during the 1960s. Among the products are *A Comparative Atlas of America's Great Cities,* published by the University of Minnesota Press, this volume, and its companion (also published by Ballinger Publishing Company), *Contemporary Metropolitan America: Twenty Geographical Vignettes.*

This volume comprises 12 geographical essays dealing with urban policymaking and metropolitan dynamics during the 1960s. Four essays are concerned with understanding and managing metropolitan environments in flux, five examine the nature and problems of urban programs, and three deal with metropolitan governance, urban political systems and electoral processes. The first group provides much new information and comparative information, the second focuses on comparative aspects of particular program areas and the third contends with program development and management in a federal system.

The essays have in common the geographer's particular concern with *geography*—with the spatial structure of the metropolis, with the spatial patterns and dynamics of urban land use, with urban population distributions and social ecology, and with the physical environment of cities. They do share many of the common perceptual problems that arise when a group of young, somewhat liberal, scientists talk to each other. Many of the essays, for example, take for granted that socioeconomic integration is a popularly supported national goal—forgetting that many groups remain highly conscious of class and status positions, and intensely protective of property. Yet few, gratifyingly, forget completely Yehezkel Dror's admonition (in *Public Policymaking Reexamined*) that

> much of the practical sterility . . . of the contemporary "modern sciences of society" . . . results from mistaken notions about whether "factual inquiry" should be, or even can be, divorced from social reality and social problems, from the construction of abstract theories, and from introspective contemplation . . . such notions lead to an unsophisticated disregard of the interdependence of "facts", "values", and "action" [p. vi]

even if occasionally, they are seemingly less aware of their own values than they are of those they are studying. And they do, in combination, provide a variety of valuable insights that should serve to refocus attention in urban policymaking from reactive attempts to "cure" particular problems perceived to exist in particular places, toward a realization of the interdependence of planned action and systemic response within the framework of urban regions viewed as complex dynamic spatial systems

UNDERSTANDING AND MANAGING METROPOLITAN ENVIRONMENTS IN FLUX

Charles S. Sargent, Jr., for example, in Chapter Two, looks at "Land Speculation and Urban Morphology." He argues that while we are well aware of *what* has been happening to the shape of the American city (rapid expansion) and *why* it is happening (shift to periphery, expanded transportation systems, communications improvements, the search for a better environment), we do not fully understand *how* it happens; i.e., we know little about the *processes* that lead to the development of the fringe, and therefore about the reasons for emergent urban morphology. One significant consequence is that we lack effective controls over land use. The shape of the city responds almost entirely to the operation of private market forces.

He finds that while some consider speculation in undeveloped or "raw" land a *derivative* of the land conversion process, it is in fact *fundamental;* a major force ranking with the extent and shape of the transportation network in determining the morphology of the city. It needs to be recognized as such. He therefore attempts (1) to clarify the relationship of raw land speculation to urban form; (2) to discover how land speculation may operate as an obstacle to attaining land use goals, especially on the fringe; and (3) to outline feasible land use controls and incentives that could change the impact of speculation in raw land upon the shape of the city.

In simplest form, he finds that the suburban land conversion process is a chain of independent yet closely linked actions undertaken by combinations of speculative agents. These agents may be categorized as:

- farmers—real, pseudo and marginal. For them all land has two values—for its agricultural returns and for its speculative value.
- intervening land owners. These are significant because there is a distinction between buildable land and buildable land offered for development.
- land developers. Their major role is not to speculate in land per se, but to develop it. The developer principally influences urban form by his role in determining the direction and shape of residential growth and by changing the scale and pattern of land ownership.

A number of catalysts in the land development and speculation process are identified. *Supporting* catalysts are those which both directly and indirectly finance speculation and development (banks, FHA, VA, etc.). The FHA, for instance, decided in favor of housing on the outskirts of cities, and suburbia is its monument. Internal revenue codes also favor speculation in land. Other catalysts are *permissive* (weakness of local government controls, expanding transportation and public service networks, the actions of land brokers). At the same time, there are relatively few physical constraints to land speculation today. The role of terrain, for instance, in influencing ultimate development has been weakened as the technology of land improvement and land fabrication develops.

The resultant form of the relatively free operation of speculative agents with willing catalysts and few constraints is commonly called "urban sprawl," an unsatisfactory term loaded with value judgments. Santa Clara County, California (San Jose, California SMSA), serves as a case study. Other cities are examined as well. Generally condemned, sprawl is rarely understood to be the *consequence of a process*. One should view the outward expansion of the city as the result of centrifugal economic and social forces and attitudes. As such it is a process amenable to change. Sprawl may indeed represent the optimal pattern for some activities. But if we seek to minimize the public and private costs that residential dispersion entails, influencing the free but far from invisible hand of raw land speculation is a necessity.

Sargent feels that we are slowly drawing away from a nineteenth century land ethic that the only function of land is to enable its owner to make money. Increasingly, land is viewed as a resource as well as a commodity. Nonetheless, existing land use controls are more cosmetic than structural in nature, able to only impose *standards* of development rather than have a major impact on the *location* of developments. Sargent looks at a number of conventional land use controls, but considers that there is really a single decision to be made: whether to control the impact of land speculation on urban form to the benefit of the general public, or whether to allow private interests to continue to direct the growth pattern of the American city as a by-product of serving their own goals. To date the momentum is still heavily in favor of the weak controls alternative. The future scenario this promises is one of an even more "disordered" urban landscape, higher costs of public services, continued environmental deterioration and the continued exclusion of the poor in general, and the black in particular, from many of the benefits of urban life.

Chapter Three looks at the opposite end of the housing spectrum—not at the speculative conversion of raw land at the periphery to urban uses, but at the abandonment of housing in the hearts of the nation's older central cities. Michael J. Dear's study, "Abandoned Housing," finds that abandonment is a contagious phenomenon. Once a deteriorated neighborhood experiences its first scattered abandonments, it is only a matter of time before a contagious abandonment takes hold and the wholesale abandonment of houses in the neighborhood begins. Very often, renewal or rehabilitation will not prevent further decay, since a pathological abandonment seems to occur, under which the process of abandonment is continuous.

At the national level, Dear finds that abandonment is currently confined to the cities of the Northeast and the Midwest, i.e., the larger, older cities. However, he also finds definite evidence of a potential for abandonment in the South and the West. In general, abandonment appears to be confined to the inner city and is associated with a loss of population, a concentration of low income households, cash flow problems for the landlord, and the lack of a management alternative to replace the landlord and real estate interests which are abandoning the inner city market. But he also finds that in the city of Philadelphia, although abandonment is prevalent in most of those areas which are subject to urban decay, it also has spread outside the areas of worst housing and now affects the whole inner ring of housing around the Philadelphia central business district. In one Philadelphia neighborhood, no less than 3.7 percent of the total of 10,000 residential structures were abandoned in 1969. By 1971 this proportion had risen to 4.6 percent. The pattern of abandonment in space involves an initial broad scattering of abandonments, followed by a later consolidation of the existing pattern. Less than 20 percent of abandonments are occurring in the worst housing units.

An explanation for abandoned housing, he feels, has to be sought on four separate levels. First, the principal force for abandonment is continuing suburbanization, which has caused a change in the traditional functions of the inner city. As yet, no "successor" function is in sight. Second, the localization of abandonment is largely associated with the normal process of urban decay. An abandonment due to "upgrading" occurs. However, another more virulent form of abandonment occurs outside areas of urban decay, primarily in association with the distribution of low income households. These are areas where confidence in the housing market has disappeared. A zone of potential abandonment is defined wherever property value is low or nonexistent. At a third level, the actual cause of the first abandonments appears to be various adverse events occurring within the zone of potential abandonment. Finally, abandonment seems to take on a dynamic of its own, largely independent of the forces which led to the initial abandonments.

He concludes that public policy toward abandoned housing ought to recognize the functional basis of abandonment (suburbanization), and the existence of an internal contagion dynamic, characteristic of the cycle of abandonment. Six specific policies to counter abandonment are suggested:

- the establishment of a public or quasi-public corporation with responsibility for the rehabilitation and reclamation of the inner city;
- the development of a community-agreed plan for inner city revitalization;
- the establishment of a public works labor force as the major "tool" of plan implementation;
- the development of specific antiabandonment policies, based upon recognition of abandonment as a contagious, cyclical process;
- the preparation of redevelopment plans for those areas which have been, or are about to be, abandoned; and
- the realignment of government housing subsidies into a housing allowance program.

These six policies, Dear feels, should be implemented together as a single policy package.

Between housing built on raw land at the periphery and abandoned neighborhoods is a vast array of private housing and many federally subsidized housing units. Located in certain sections of America's cities, these are the product of a bewildering tangle of legislation, programs, operating guidelines and application forms, a tangle that is scarcely understood by ordinary people, and which it is the purpose of Chapter Four—John Mercer's and John Hultquist's "National Progress Toward Housing and Urban Renewal Goals"—to clarify. Although the tangle has become more complex in recent years, thanks to the introduction of new programs, the bulk of the subsidized housing in the metropolitan areas that are examined (Atlanta, Chicago and Seattle) was produced by one program which is both long-standing and notorious—the Low Rent Public Housing Program, administered by local housing authorities. This program has undergone significant shifts in emphasis in recent years, including increasing amounts of construction to serve elderly Americans and an expansion of the less clustered, less intrusive Leased Housing Program.

There is one dominant spatial characteristic in many of the programs in all three cities and that is concentration. The overwhelming majority of units are located in the central city and, within those jurisdictions, they are generally clustered in certain neighborhoods, often black and low to moderate income in character.

Newer subsidy programs, though beset with scandals that caused their suspension, did generate an increasing amount of publicly assisted housing in suburban areas in a few short years, but even here, concentration in one or two municipalities tends to occur. The use of these newer programs for rental units or home-ownership seems to reflect developer experience. In an urban area characterized by single family units, the homeownership program attracted more developer interest, while the rental programs were more productive in those communities with strong apartment and rental submarkets.

Mercer and Hultquist quickly found that the Department of Housing and Urban Development and its predecessors had no effective locational policy to guide the spatial pattern of publicly assisted housing. Thus, the locational patterns which they have documented are the unanticipated result of a mix of (1) slum clearance activities, (2) private developer decisions concerning land costs and availability and project marketability, (3) landlord initiatives (in the case of leased housing) and (4) the distribution of need, especially with regard to housing for senior citizens.

They found that a thorough evaluation of the full range of impacts of federal housing policy still remains to be done, and this difficult task is a major challenge to policy analysts. The few studies that have been completed are unanimously critical of the high degree of spatial concentration of public housing, arguing that it produces a difficult and even dangerous residential environment for people, and one which is easily and readily stigmatized by nonresidents. The poor quality of local services in certain central city areas does nothing to balance the negative aspects of the projects themselves. The lack of directly assisted housing in the suburbs has serious implications for access to job opportunities and journey to work costs. The minimal and even substandard quality of many subsidized units does not make such units (let alone their occupants) attractive neighbors—"if we must have public housing, anywhere but next to me."

Thus, the authors argue that answers to "the housing problem" with which this nation has struggled for some 40 years (albeit with limited success) may lie in such redistributive programs as guaranteed annual incomes and housing allowances rather than in direct public housing construction. Specific recommendations that are made, based on an examination of the locational consequences of federal policy, or the lack of one, are modest but essential. An initial premise is that the American people are not likely to support or elect a government that believes in housing as a social good rather than an economic commodity. Therefore, no radical restructuring of the supply and pricing of housing is likely.

Because there is still a critical lack of information on the reality of the housing needs and aspirations of our people, the authors argue that the Department of Housing and Urban Development must vigorously support the documentation of such needs and aspirations. Secondly, basic information on all aspects between those concerned with the supply, administration and consumption of housing must be improved. Again, leadership is required, especially within the local community, with HUD assisting in the supply of technical information and cost-sharing.

The available data clearly show the existence of a dual housing market in publicly subsidized housing, paralleling that of the private market. The authors argue that this must be attacked immediately, and they recommend that mortgage lenders be required to develop a locationally integrated portfolio. They feel that if it can be shown that this can reduce "blockbusting," a practice that primarily benefits the speculators, and reduce the need for school busing, such a program may gain political and popular support.

To promote a less stratified and separate society and provide equality of access to various social and economic opportunities, they say that greater dispersal of assisted housing units must be achieved. They recommend an increased emphasis on the leased housing program, with greater incentives for landlords to participate. A form of the home ownership subsidy program with realistic cost limitations should be maintained and accelerated. For this to receive popular support, the issues of quality control and equitable treatment for noneligible households of similar income ranges must be confronted and resolved.

Small-scale public housing projects can also play a role in achieving the spatial dispersal which they advocate. Regional housing plans are useful in that they can reduce uncertainty and allow for a debate on the issues of public housing and its location–they should be vigorously pursued, say the authors.

Finally, and on a more general note, they say that those involved in housing and education must seek to dispel the myths and half-truths which sustain fear and prejudice. They feel that greater public awareness and understanding is a prerequisiste for equitable and democratic action.

From land use and housing Chapter Five turns to a consideration of "Progress Toward Environmental Goals for Metropolitan America." The nature of the nation's air, land, water and noise pollution problems is reviewed, the agreed-upon environmental quality standards that emerged from environmental control legislation in the late 1960s and early 1970s are outlined, and the progress made toward those goals in the limited period of time since enactment is evaluated. Some dramatic achievements can be cited, such as the cleaning up of the Willamette River in Oregon, but elsewhere achievements have been limited and further progress seems threatened by conflicting priorities brought on by the energy crisis. The nation's environmental policies run the gamut of planning approaches, from those that are clearly curative, reacting to and hoping to solve problems that already exist, to ventures in future problem avoidance, and all the way to careful systems analysis approaches directed at achieving positive goals for the future. But they also reveal the problems of planning in a government that is bureaucratically organized into parallel functional agencies, each with its own problems, goals, objectives and agencies, when the urban environments for which the plans are being made are complex systems that cut horizontally across what are, in fact, highly interdependent functional concerns of the line agencies.

THE NATURE AND PROBLEMS OF URBAN PROGRAMS

Such interdependence is the concern of Chapter Six, "Public School Goals and Parochial School Attendance in Twenty American Cities," by John S. Adams and Kathleen Molnar Brown, and, indeed, is the essence of the problems inherent in all urban programs.

Adams and Brown find that policy discussions in the field of public school education during the past decade have centered on how to raise more money and spend it more effectively and equitably, and on how to integrate public school classrooms to promote equality of educational opportunity. To a lesser degree the spotlight has been shared by questions of job protection for teachers, pay levels, work rules, neighborhood control of schools and the needs of children with special learning difficulties. But there has been comparatively less public discussion of the nature of general academic programs, their breadth or their effectiveness. Thus, as new funding programs and integration schemes get underway, sharply lower birth rates forecast drastically curtailed enrollments in the years ahead. Meanwhile, young households get older and relocate, emptying out school buildings in older high density inner city neighborhoods. But the major debates over school funding and school integration, and the public programs that followed, have usually been pursued without much attention either to those general trends or to the role of the nonpublic schools (mainly Catholic parish elementary schools) that operate over wide areas of many American cities, enrolling a significant fraction of elementary and secondary school children. The use of these schools raises a question of whether they prevent or promote the achievement of public goals for education. To be sure, the nonpublic schools help provide a pluralistic alternative in one important facet of child-rearing. They also provide competition to public school systems, although the consequences of this competition are hard to assess.

From one point of view school age children are clients to be served. From another viewpoint they provide the vital foundation needed to keep a school system in business. Thus, when nonpublic schools are available and used, they can help alleviate the budget crunch in public school districts where total enrollments are rising. Conversely, competition from nonpublic schools can threaten job security and upward mobility of public school personnel in districts with declining enrollments. They can provide an alternative to forced race-class integration of classrooms. They may also retard the out-migration of young white households from racially mixed neighborhoods. Perhaps. No one knows for sure. Whatever the case, the interests of the children are but one of several sets of interests considered in the public debate.

Adams and Brown thus begin by reviewing the major school finance and integration questions of the last decade, assessing national progress toward various goals, and conclude by describing patterns of nonpublic school attendance in 20 of the nation's largest cities, exposing some of the essential conflicts between short term public goals and longer term questions about the role of nonpublic schools in American urban neighborhoods. They find that after a decade of progress in education, a variety of issues remain unresolved. Professional educators feel the sting of limited financial resources, yet the vast majority of Americans report satisfaction with the schools. Public education's support by the property tax means that education does not automatically capture an ever-increasing share of national resources as do government activities funded by sales taxes or progressively structured income taxes. Thus, any decision to increase education's share of gross national product becomes a hotly contested issue in every local school district attempting to float a bond issue or increase its mill levy. Perhaps other classes of government expenditure should be subject to *more* political debate rather than yielding to the occasional pressure to make public education budgets less political. As enrollments decline, and as the share of the population without a direct stake in the school systems rises, political and electoral processes remain the best mechanisms for working out local conflicts with due sensitivity to the special needs of local settings.

While a controversy rages over the best ways to measure equality of educational opportunity, what really seems to matter is native intelligence and a family background that prepares a pupil to do well in school. Greater strides have been made in defining a judicially manageable standard of equity for the taxpayer who supports the schools. Attempts at fairness for the pupil must continue, but first must come equity within school districts. Differences between districts and between cities in teachers, students, plant, facilities and curriculum escape remedy because they currently defy analysis.

They find that the South made progress in racial integration of schools. Yet, as neighborhood public schools in the South have become more integrated, residential neighborhoods have simultaneously become steadily more segregated. If southern residential trends continue, southern cities, like their northern counterparts, will rely increasingly on busing to achieve school integration goals. Busing options are simpler in most southern cities because consolidated school districts usually cover entire counties. Balkanization of school districts in northern metropolitan areas prevents simple busing solutions to school segregation problems. District consolidation or cooperation based on court action or legislative bribe or mandate may speed up northern school integration. A permanent and fundamental solution based on residential integration of all minority groups appears substantially more remote than simple school integration.

Critics sometimes blame nonpublic schools for the racial isolation in many big city school systems. Adams and Brown conclude that this is usually an oversimplification that ignores the geographical patterns of race, class and residence inside large cities. Within most cities, blacks live in one set of neighborhoods and whites live elsewhere. In white neighborhoods, nonpublic schools thrive mainly in middle class Catholic areas, near major colleges and universities, and near military installations.

Nonpublic schools seem to persist and even thrive temporarily in certain racially mixed neighborhoods but the patterns of cause and effect are obscure. In racially changing neighborhoods the parochial schools are more white than the community and the public schools are more black. The parochial school is only a part of a many-sided community center, focused on the parish church, school, social center and often a political base. Catholic parishes will remain vigorous only if middle class families able and willing to exercise community leadership want to live in the neighborhood. On balance, they conclude, it is probably untrue that in the long run young Catholic families move into or remain in a neighborhood because of the parish life it offers. But in the short run, policies that (1) help make central city neighborhoods relatively more attractive for middle and upper middle class Catholic families compared to urban and suburban competitors may have the indirect effect of (2) stabilizing neighborhood and parish institutions and the viability of parochial schools.

Rising crime rates are one of the principal deterrents to achieving neighborhood stability in the nation's central cities. Thus, Gerald F.

Pyle turns his attention in Chapter Seven to "Geographic Perspectives on Crime and the Impact of Anticrime Legislation." He analyzes, from the policy impact point of view, the effects of current anticrime legislation in the United States in selected cities. The chapter begins with an examination of recent anticrime expenditures and the meaning of crime index statistics, and of variations in crime rates among the largest urban centers in the United States. Changing crime rates during the 1960s are compared to the period since 1970 in order to determine, at the national level, whether funding has had any impact on urban crime.

Two intraurban crime scenarios, one for Cleveland and one for Akron, are then developed to gain an understanding of variable distributions of major crimes within cities. Also, recent crime rates within these cities are compared with urban ecological indicators in an attempt to develop a clearer understanding of some of the causes of crime within cities. For example, some crimes, particularly those against the person, can be attributed to known poverty conditions within these cities. Other crimes, such as automobile theft and robbery, appear to be more directly related to opportunities made available to criminals. At the same time, more subtle dimensions are uncovered which explain some crime distributions as being related to subcultural conflicts between poverty youths and representatives of the law enforcement establishment.

The internal ecological crime-specific analysis of Akron and Cleveland looks at static statistical associations. An analysis of movements of crime suspects from place of residence to crime location is made within Akron in an attempt to identify more dynamic behavioral aspects of crime. For example, within Akron during 1971, suspects arrested for residential burglary of high income homes traveled from seven to nine times farther to commit these crimes than did those arrested for burglarizing homes in poverty areas. Yet another aspect of importance is the fact that, within Akron, patterns of arrest are biased toward middle and upper income neighborhoods in that arrest rates per crime are substantially higher for the latter areas than for poverty areas. Clearly, if this is an indication of what is happening in other cities, much work remains to be done in the areas of juvenile delinquency and police community relations.

In fact, when 12 major Law Enforcement Assistance Act (LEAA) funding categories are statistically tested against reported decreases in crime rates for the largest United States cities, two of the funding categories which appear to be manifesting a positive impact are police community relations and juvenile delinquency. In other words, while funds are being expended for a variety of purposes—for example hiring more police, buying more police equipment and developing more intricate communications and radar systems—the most effective programs appear to be the more subtle human-relations-oriented efforts. Such knowledge is important in the long run if we are to directly understand how to prevent and eliminate many crimes within cities, rather than simply developing more "effective" police.

Restructuring of anticrime programs is the principal thrust of Pyle's recommendations; the need for restructuring the health care delivery system in the United States is the theme of Chapter Eight—by Mary Megee.

Megee notes that the health care delivery system of the United States is one of the best in the world, and spectacular advances have been made in the control of numerous diseases, yet, during this period of rapid progress, services have developed unevenly throughout the nation, resulting in a high degree of technical sophistication in research and equipment in some areas and inadequacies in the delivery of minimum essential care in others. Many people and whole areas of the nation lack adequate medical attention. Serious illnesses often induce severe financial hardships, escalating costs of health care from both the private and public sectors.

She finds that the nation's health services system has retained an organization that, while it may have been adequate for the health needs of an earlier era, is woefully inadequate to meet current demands. In particular, it has failed to shift from the concept of curing sickness to one of maintaining health. Her essay thus is concerned with analyzing several phases of the health care delivery system of the United States with the goal of restructuring it in such a way as to expand its benefits, minimize prices of services, and achieve greater uniformity and effectiveness of coverage.

The main conclusions are the following:

1. There is an uneven distribution of diseases and deaths in the United States as measured

> by such dimensions of health as active cases or disease and numbers of deaths both on an intermetropolitan as well as an intrametropolitan basis.

Examination of data on an intermetropolitan level shows that those metropolitan areas with large black populations, though not necessarily the lowest median incomes per capita, had the largest number of deaths due to the largest number of major causes: Pittsburgh, Miami, New Orleans and Boston (seven major causes); St. Louis, Minneapolis-St. Paul, Cleveland and Houston (five major causes); and Hartford (four major causes). New York, of course, by virtue of sheer size, recorded the largest number of deaths in all categories, except accidents and suicides, where it was exceeded in each case by Los Angeles-Long Beach. At the same time, such metropolitan areas as Seattle (eight major causes), Washington, D.C. (six major causes), and Dallas-Ft. Worth and Los Angeles-Long Beach (five major causes each) showed lower than expected numbers of deaths for major causes. Three of these metropolitan areas had large black and/or Spanish heritage populations. Per capita median incomes varied from average to high, the latter in the case of Washington, D.C. However, on a macrometropolitan basis, strong positive relationships were not easily discernible or verifiable between such variables as mortality, income and race without greater in depth studies. On an intrametropolitan level, though, more direct positive relationships seem to exist on an areal basis. In the city of St. Louis in particular there is a very distinct and apparently high positive relationship between location of blacks, location of low incomes and occurrence of all the major causes of deaths and active cases of diseases.

> 2. There is a faulty allocation of resources, which is a major cause of inadequacies and inequalities in health services, resulting today in poor or substandard care for large segments of the population both on an inter- and intrametropolitan level.

Analysis shows that those metropolitan areas with a larger than expected supply of hospital facilities as measured in terms of beds are New Orleans, Miami, Minneapolis-St. Paul, St. Louis, Boston, Cleveland, Pittsburgh and Houston. This may be interpreted as supply exceeding demand, but without further in depth studies, these findings should be interpreted with care. Houston, for instance, represents a more than significant international hospital center, attracting patients from all over the world, particularly for heart and stroke surgery. The SMSA's which had fewer than expected numbers of beds were Washington, D.C. and San Francisco-Oakland. This can be interpreted as deficit of supply with respect to demand, and, secondarily, as a desirable shift in emphasis from hospital-based treatment to outpatient, office-based treatment and HMO (health maintenance organization) treatment.

On the demand side, such data as number of admissions, average daily census and patient days were analyzed to determine which of the metropolitan areas exceeded expectations and which were lower than expected. Those metropolitan areas with larger demand than expected for their sizes include Minneapolis-St. Paul, Houston, St. Louis, Boston, Miami, Pittsburgh and Baltimore. Those with smaller demand than expected include Hartford, Atlanta, Baltimore, Seattle, San Francisco-Oakland, Detroit and Los Angeles-Long Beach.

> 3. People cannot cope financially with the costs of health care without the substantial base of coverage now provided by both private and public insurance plans. An inadequate system is being overburdened and offers little prospect of materially improving the quality and quantity of medical services for the health of the American people.

Megee's analysis shows that Boston and Pittsburgh had larger than expected hospital expenses for their population sizes, while Hartford, Dallas-Ft. Worth, Seattle, Atlanta, St. Louis, Washington, D.C., Philadelphia and Detroit had fewer than expected expenses for their sizes.

She then turns to an investigation of health maintenance organizations, which can undoubtedly go a long way toward restructuring an archaic health delivery system in the United States, since they aim to provide maximum quality and quantity of benefits in the health care delivery field to all consumers and providers. They have increased since their inception in the 1920s. Passage of federal legislation in 1974 making health maintenance organizations the preferred method of medical care provides federal money to underwrite their development and is expected to produce rapid improvements in the quality, quantity and types of health care delivery systems within the next five years. At this time, these organizations are seen as a major vehicle in restructuring the health care delivery system.

However, Megee feels that these and related organizations are only stop-gap systems of health care. She feels that the obvious solution is a system of national health insurance or social medicine comparable to that of other countries. The HMOs and related types of programs seem to be an acceptable substitute mainly to the providers and to insurance companies, where more advantages accrue to these persons than to the consumers. Thus, HMOs are an advanced stage on the continuum of national health care, but they are not the end result. It is the providers, not the consumers, in the United States who are unable to accept the social medicine concept. The HMOs have been set up by the federal government, which bears an increasing burden of the total health expenditures in this country, and which justifiably has an interest in the restructuring of the health care delivery system, as an acceptable substitute for social medicine. It comes at a time when the public is not yet ready to accept what seems to be so radical a move, but which ultimately must be the outcome of all this interest, debate, legislation and government appropriation.

HMOs are but one example of the many federal institutions impacting on the nation's urban regions during the 1960s. Another example involves "The Federal Open Space Program" examined by Rutherford H. Platt in Chapter Nine. Platt looks at two specific programs instituted by Congress in the 1960s that offered matching grants to states and local governments to acquire and/or develop open space: The Open Space Land Program of the Department of Housing and Urban Development, and the Land and Water Conservation Fund administered by the Bureau of Outdoor Recreation of the Department of the Interior. He examines the origins and operation of the two programs, reviews their impact on the pattern of land use at various scales, and makes recommendations as to the policies and organization of federal open space assistance in the future. The operation and results of the two programs are analyzed with respect to: (1) the respective statutory capabilities and limitations of each; (2) the nature of the regional planning process by which federal funds are theoretically allocated; and (3) actual program activity as experienced nationally, at the state level and in three metropolitan areas that are included in the Comparative Metropolitan Analysis Project: Boston, Hartford and Chicago. He finds that these particular open space programs, while successful in numerous specific situations, have failed to fulfill their statutory purposes or to affect substantially the pattern or quality of urban development. Among reasons cited for this failure are: (1) that the programs were conceived as palliatives to "urban sprawl" and did not entail modification of other federal programs or policies which contribute to the problem; (2) that funding for both programs was modest in amount and precarious in reliability; (3) that available funds were diffused among nonurban as well as urban projects, and for development as well as acquisition; and (4) that in the absence of adequate performance standards and/or flexible federal participation ratios, grants in metropolitan areas favored wealthier and more peripheral municipal recipients.

At the time that federal initiatives have created opportunities for some, the needs of many other groups in society remain unmet. An example involves the "Housing and Transportation Problems of the Urban Elderly," the topic of Chapter Ten, by Stephen M. Golant. He argues that the factors underlying these problems are related both to the inevitable concomitants of human aging and to society's attitudes and responses to its older population. The evidence suggests that the incidence and magnitude of elderly housing and transportation problems vary among urban communities, and that it is essential that each make its own independent assessment of the housing and transportation status of its elderly population in order that existing needs can be translated into specific legislative programs. Relevant federal programs designed to meet these needs are found to be less than adequate, however, so he looks to the future rather than spending too much time in the past.

Golant thus recommends that, whatever form new federal housing programs assume, the older population should be identified as a distinctive needs group. A set of housing goals for the elderly population should be formulated and legislative programs and funding allocations provided to carry them out effectively.

The supply of low and moderate income housing designed to accommodate older persons has been insufficient, particularly in some regions and urban areas. Larger capital expenditures and larger, more flexible operating budgets are required. The role of the nonprofit sponsor as a developer of low and middle income housing for the elderly should be encouraged and facilitated. A variety of dwelling unit types which to varying degrees contain special architectural design features, extra security devices and congregate facilities, or are served by special community services, are required to serve a group of elderly with diverse and changing needs and personal resources. Because of the potentially crucial role played by managerial (superintendent) personnel of elderly housing in serving the needs of the elderly tenant, special care should be taken to insure that a sufficient supply of such well-trained personnel exists. The eligibility of "elderly" to enter low and moderate income federally or state-subsidized housing accommodations should be based not only on economic and chronological age definitions, but also on health and social needs criteria. Greater attention must be given to alleviating the problems of the older homeowner, either by policies enabling him to successfully remain in his independent living arrangements or, alternatively, by giving him greater assistance in the potentially difficult task of relocating to another form of residential accommodation. There should be improved cooperation and coordination between the variety of departments and agencies at various levels of government engaged in interdependent aspects of housing program development for the elderly. The decline of mass transit services should be arrested in order to insure adequate transportation for captive user groups such as the elderly. New transportation systems should incorporate design and operation features making them more accessible to the elderly. Efforts should be taken to insure that newly designed barrier-free transportation systems are not underused by the elderly who, in the course of utilization, must necessarily transfer from older connecting transportation lines. Existing urban mass transit systems should be supplemented by special transporation systems such as dial-a-bus or other forms of demand-responsive modes. In particular such services should be made available in neighborhoods with high concentrations of older persons and/or with elderly user groups with particularly severe accessibility problems. Coordination should be improved between departments at all governmental levels engaged in programs in which "transportation" is an integral component. Needs assessment studies should be initiated and continually updated to insure that those elderly are identified who most require improved transportation services. The evaluation of the benefits and costs of providing special vehicular services or better designed mass transit vehicles should consider indirect benefits resulting from improved transportation services, such as a reduction in the needs for special elderly housing programs, home delivery services, institutional and quasi-institutional accommodations or on the reduction of the psychological and economic burden of elderly on their families.

METROPOLITAN GOVERNANCE, POLITICAL SYSTEMS AND ELECTORAL PROCESSES

Golant's suggestions are highly specific and programmatic, but in Chapter Eleven, "Metropolitan Governance," Rex D. Honey argues that effective development of future urban programs is not simply a legislative matter, but will require more fundamental transformations of metropolitan political space. The quality of metropolitan governance, he feels, is an important policy arena confronting urban America. The social and economic organization of space has changed dramatically in American cities in this century. Simultaneously, demands on the public sector and expectations for public performance have risen. The political institutions for solving metropolitan problems have lagged behind social and economic reality. To shorten that lag, the federal government has encouraged metropolitan level decisionmaking. This encouragment has taken two forms: stipulations that metropolitan approval be obtained before federal funds are granted for many projects; and grants for the establishment and operation of metropolitan authorities. As a consequence of this federal cajoling, a layer of areawide authorities now oversees the governance of American cities. Several states have gone beyond the federal programs, further transforming the political organization of space within some metropolitan areas. The question is how effective these changes have been.

American metropolitan areas vary significantly in the strength of their metropolitan authorities and in the character of their metropolitan problems. Honey examines five areas, each a fairly young and rapidly growing metropolis with the heavy imprint of automobile age development. Each has experienced revolutions in the spatial organization of society and economy. Greater Miami possesses an urban county form of government, so it can marshall a concerted effort to solve problems within Dade County. Unfortunately, some of Miami's problems require broader solutions than the county's jurisdiction allows. The Twin Cities of Minneapolis and St. Paul have a metropolitan council serving as a governmental umbrella over a seven county area. The council has limited power and is not directly elected, but it has helped engender metropolitan consciousness and has proved a positive influence in regional affairs. Greater Atlanta also has an "umbrella" authority serving a seven county area. The Atlanta Regional Commission coordinates planning and special purpose district activity in the area. It is not as strong at the Twin Cities' Metropolitan Council, but it does guarantee that a metropolitan point of view will be heard. The other two areas studied, the San Francisco Bay Area and Greater Los Angeles, lack the focused metropolitan organizations serving the first three areas. The Bay Area has several areawide special purpose districts and a progressive council of governments, but coordination in the area is weak. In Los Angeles areawide cooperation and programs are even more weakly developed, thanks in part to the power of the county of Los Angeles.

Honey finds that continual improvement of the public sector in urban America demands more rational and effective governance, including metropolitan governance. To continue the strengthening of metropolitan governance he recommends that the federal government should: (1) continue and augment metropolitan review of local government applications for federal funds; (2) provide revenue-sharing for the metropolitan level; (3) establish more powerful areawide agencies in multistate metropolitan areas; and (4) implement national land use planning to prevent the coalescence of metropolitan development.

He finds the role of the states to be crucial because jurisdictions within a state are creatures of the state. The states he says, should: (1) provide financial assistance for metropolitan government; (2) strengthen regional planning by making local government membership in planning organizations compulsory; (3) increase the fluidity of political space by easing procedures for amalgamation, annexation and incorporation; (4) require periodic review of jurisdictions and duties; (5) control land development to prevent metropolitan coalescence; and (6) cooperate in multistate metropolitan areas.

Finally, he recommends that the people of each metropolis should strive for good governance by tailoring metropolitan authorities to match the social and economic organization of the metropolis. Honey's theme is extended, in Chapter Twelve, by David R. Reynolds, who asks whether there has been "Progress Toward Achieving Efficient and Responsive Spatial-Political Systems in Urban America." He finds that if any national goals pertaining to governance in metropolitan areas emerged in the past decade they were that political systems in urbanized areas should become more efficient, effective and accountable in their provision of public services. There is ample indirect evidence, he says, to suggest that the existence of a large number of politically independent governmental units in a metropolitan area is not prima facie evidence that simultaneously efficient, effective and accountable solutions to service provision problems cannot be found. However, the incidence of progress in achieving solutions, as demonstrated in three study areas (Los Angeles, Detroit and St. Louis) is locationally biased—it is primarily a suburban phenomenon. The benefits of Los Angeles' Lakewood Plan, Detroit area contracting, and county "modernization" and special district formation in St. Louis County are suburban. In the St. Louis, Detroit and Los Angeles areas, if any recent progress has been made, it has not been the result of any fundamental changes in the spatial organization of local governmental units themselves.

The internal spatial organization of most central city governments, he says, is simply not conducive to the effective articulation of local needs and demands, let alone to satisfying them. Where school district expenditures are concerned, increases in equity and effectiveness are traceable to increased state financial aid to school districts based on formulas designed to offset inequalities in abilities to pay. Attempts to effect such equity through the creation of very large school districts, such as the Los Angeles Unified School District, appear to be undesirable expedients, unless educational administrators can evolve more satisfactory systems of client accountability than they have heretofore. He concludes that continued improvement in the relations between existing governments, including further functional reorganization of service production and provision responsibilities, without spatial change, is insufficient and will continue to accelerate the decay of central cities.

Thus a more even geographical distribution of progress in achieving the goals of increased efficiency, effectiveness and accountability will necessitate a spatial reorganization of local governance. Existing central city governments, with financial assistance from the federal and respective state governments, should engage in spatial and administrative changes designed to enable groups of urban residents with common interests, tastes and needs to define and receive public goods and services more tailored to their collective needs. In order that this strategy be developed fully, it is essential, he says, that central cities permit, indeed encourage, the creation of self-initiated neighborhood or community subunits of government with broad authority to provide local services in general conformance with local tastes and needs. To provide an incentive for such change Reynolds therefore recommends (1) that a federally funded program be established to underwrite the "set up" costs of such subunits of government where revenue scarcity would otherwise prohibit their creation and (2) that each city or school district requesting federal funding for any project satisfy federal guidelines that would be the internal equivalent of A-95 review: namely, that the local government requesting funds make a reasonable attempt to assess the social impacts of its proposed expenditure. The implementation of a program authorizing the establishment of geographical subunits of city government could satisfy these requirements for review, provided that the subunits have been delegated some advisory or decisionmaking authority pertaining to the service function with which the expenditure proposal is concerned.

For the above strategy to be developed equitably, as well as fully, Reynolds feels that it is also essential that some mechanisms for generating revenues be found that will allow low income families to live where they want to without requiring the political units they choose to depend primarily on internal sources of funding. One source of revenue is state government. It is recommended that states begin to share more revenue with units of local government through formulas based upon the ability of residents in local units to pay. Since some states have been slow in moving in this direction, it is suggested that federal funding through grants-in-aid, state matching grants and revenue sharing be reduced or denied to any state failing to institute programs which decrease the dependency of cities and school districts on their internal sources of revenue.

Another source of aid is the federal government. Here he recommends that federal revenue sharing with cities be instituted on a more substantial basis and on one that is more likely to be perceived as permanent enough to represent a tenable solution to the problems of municipal finance in large cities.

The final chapter in the book explores the equity issue raised by Reynolds in another context, that of "Malapportionment and Gerrymandering in the Ghetto." In this essay, John O'Loughlin asks whether the Supreme Court's requirement that electoral districts have equal population (within 3 to 5 percent of the state average) and be as compact in shape as possible are being met. He finds a consistent reduction of the population deviations from the state average between 1958 and 1968; reapportionments which followed the Court's decisions that reduced underrepresentation in black districts but caused all city districts to become slightly underrepresented in 1968 than they were in 1958, due to a greater allocation of districts to the rapidly growing suburban areas; and ineffectiveness in producing compact districts. In general, he finds that black districts are slightly more compact than either white or changing districts. The reason why black districts are more compact, in all probability, lies in their being inner city in nature. Thus, black districts are not affected by the boundary indentations of the city limits, as are white districts. This aside, gerrymandering of districts at all electoral levels appears to be a continuing problem, but one that is difficult to prove.

Instead, O'Loughlin recommends that recourse be had to nonpartisan computer algorithms to solve the problem in an impartial and unbiased way.

OVERVIEW

The 1960s was a decade of major programs, of good intentions, and of broad and massive failures. Who, for example, could disagree with the noble intent of Title I, Section 101 of the *Demonstration Cities and Metropolitan Development Act of 1966* which directed the Department of Housing and Urban Development toward:

> . . . providing additional financial and technical assistance to enable cities of all sizes (with equal regard to the problems of small as well as large cities) to plan, develop, and carry out locally prepared and scheduled comprehensive city demonstration programs containing new imaginative proposals
> To rebuild or revitalize large slum and blighted areas;
> to expand housing, job, and income opportunities;
> to reduce dependence on welfare payments;
> to improve educational facilities and programs;
> to combat disease and ill health;
> to reduce the incidence of crime and delinquency;
> to enhance recreational and cultural opportunities;
> to establish better access between homes and jobs; and generally
> to improve living conditions for the people who live in such areas, and
> to accommodate these objectives through the most effective and economical concentration and coordination of Federal, State, and local public and private efforts to improve the quality of urban life.

Yet, one after another, these and other New Frontier and Great Society programs have fallen short of their objectives, or have had contrary results.

None of the changes has been as dramatic as those involving planners and planning in New York City—it is only a brief time since the November 25, 1969, *International Herald Tribune* reported with some amazement that a new concept and approach was coming to characterize American planning. The article noted that:

> After 31 years New York's Master Plan was finally released last week. . . . In 1938, when the city charter called for a comprehensive planning document, no one could have foreseen the fracas or even the kind of city the long awaited document is meant to guide. . . . At that time planning was an academic, Olympian exercise in ideal, long-range goals based on projections of statistical data in terms of physical land use and Utopian visions of the pushbutton "city of the future." This brand of planning has been updated in recent years by coloring a few of the foreground faces black. . . . Such proposals were destined to gather dust quietly while cities decayed and urban problems outstripped their textbook answers. Few, except planners, paid much attention to master plans at all. . . . But an extraordinary amount of attention is being paid to the newly unveiled "Plan for New York" . . . because it deals not in agreeable visions for the year 2000, but in specific, politically vulnerable programs and commitments. It advocates, for example, the total reform of welfare, the abolition of the Board of Education, and the encouragement of minority employment through the "leverage" of the city role in jobs, selective purchasing and industrial development programs. . . Unlike the plans of the past, this is not a long-range physical proposal. It deals with immediate priorities and possibilities, and its range of action is the next five to ten years. . . . New York's approach, still new in professional circles, is one toward which many cities and countries are moving. It is a social plan. It sets policies and goals and provides flexible guide-lines for city growth and change in terms of processes and people, not through diagrams of physical redevelopment. [p. 1]

Yet within five short years the New York Master Plan was discredited, and New York City on the verge of bankruptcy—the tip of an iceberg that is chilling many of the nation's central cities and administering the final coup de grace to many urban policies and programs.

What went wrong and why? First, it is clear from the essays presented in this book that the nature of urban change and the causes of urban problems were poorly understood. But what is not perceived by most of the authors is that change itself rendered ineffective many public policy instruments and finally that the policies themselves resulted in unresponsive juggernauts–bureaucratic superstructures and technocratic elites, substantially insulated from the political-electoral process, responsible for program development, implementation, self-congratulatory program evaluation *and their own survival.* More critical to such bureaucracies than program effectiveness are jobs and careers, and so the organizations develop a life of their own, feeding on the identification of yet more problems, the solutions for which require (of course) more money and staff. Massive programs, throwing untold millions of dollars at "problems," thus carried with them a built-in guarantee of the ineffectiveness and failures documented in what follows.

If there are lessons from all of this, one is that only with profound and incisive questioning of the real public benefits of programs that cannot and will not define what "effectiveness" and "efficiency" mean will research into the nature of urban change assume a meaningful role in public policymaking. Another is probably the need for "self-destruct" bureaucracies. And yet another is the plea for broader geographic participation in the urban policymaking process, because it is the changing dynamics of urban spatial systems that are the cause, the context and the consequence of urban problems, and of the opportunities for resolving them.

BIBLIOGRAPHY

Dror, Yehezkel. *Public Policymaking Reexamined.* San Francisco: Chandler Publishing Company, 1968.

Lubove, Roy. *The Progressives and the Slums.* Pittsburgh: University of Pittsburgh Press, 1962.

Part 2

Understanding and Managing Metropolitan Environments in Flux

Chapter 2

Land Speculation and Urban Morphology

Charles S. Sargent, Jr.
Arizona State University

INTRODUCTION

That the American city is rapidly expanding is readily apparent. Even the most casual of observers cannot fail to see the number of residential subdivisions, shopping centers and industrial parks on the edge of every major city. What is visually so overwhelming is also indicated, if less clearly, by the meager available data on the extent of rural lands subdivided or platted for urban uses as well as by the scope of annexations to existing cities and the increasing share of suburban versus central city population. A perusal of aerial photographs taken in various years, the examination of building permit data, even a comparison of old gasoline company street maps with new ones indicates and measures the extent, direction and changing form, or morphology, of the city. The expansion of urbanized areas in Greater Phoenix is typical of the rapid growth of many metropolitan areas in the last three decades (Figure 2-1).

The annexation of outlying areas into corporate city limits—a measure with severe limitations because all of the annexed land is rarely platted—also gives an indication of the spatial extent of urban growth. A study by Forstall shows that the total land area incorporated into the 290 larger cities of the United States doubled between 1950 and 1970, increasing from 7,610 to 15,588 square miles. In some of the smaller cities of 1950 the pace of annexation was stunning: from 1950 to 1970 Jacksonville, Florida, grew 25-fold; Nashville, Tennessee, 23-fold; Phoenix, 14-fold; both San Jose and Indianapolis, 8-fold.

In terms of population, about 75 percent of the nation's growth in the 1960s occurred within the boundaries of metropolitan areas as defined in 1960 and most of that growth was suburban. The share of the metropolitan population residing in the "suburban ring" rose from 40.8 million in 1950 to 59.6 million in 1960 and 75.6 million in 1970, a gain of 34.8 million for the 20 year period. In the same two decades, the central portions of the cities increased in population from 53.8 million to 63.8 million, a gain of but 10.0 million.

Indications are that entire metropolitan areas will eventually coalesce into "urban regions" as their fringe areas expand. The subdivisions of one city are already meeting the subdivisions of another in a number of places. At the same time, however, large undeveloped areas are left intact within the expanded urban fabric.

Both the process and the end product so described are commonly referred to as suburbanization or urban sprawl, a pattern typically characterized by scattered residential and commercial developments on the urban fringe—that large transitional zone around cities which displays great heterogeneity in land uses and an evolution toward more intensive land uses, particularly from agricultural fields to residential tracts. Population densities on the whole decrease as one moves outward from the older more developed portions of the city, a corollary in part of the increasing share of undeveloped

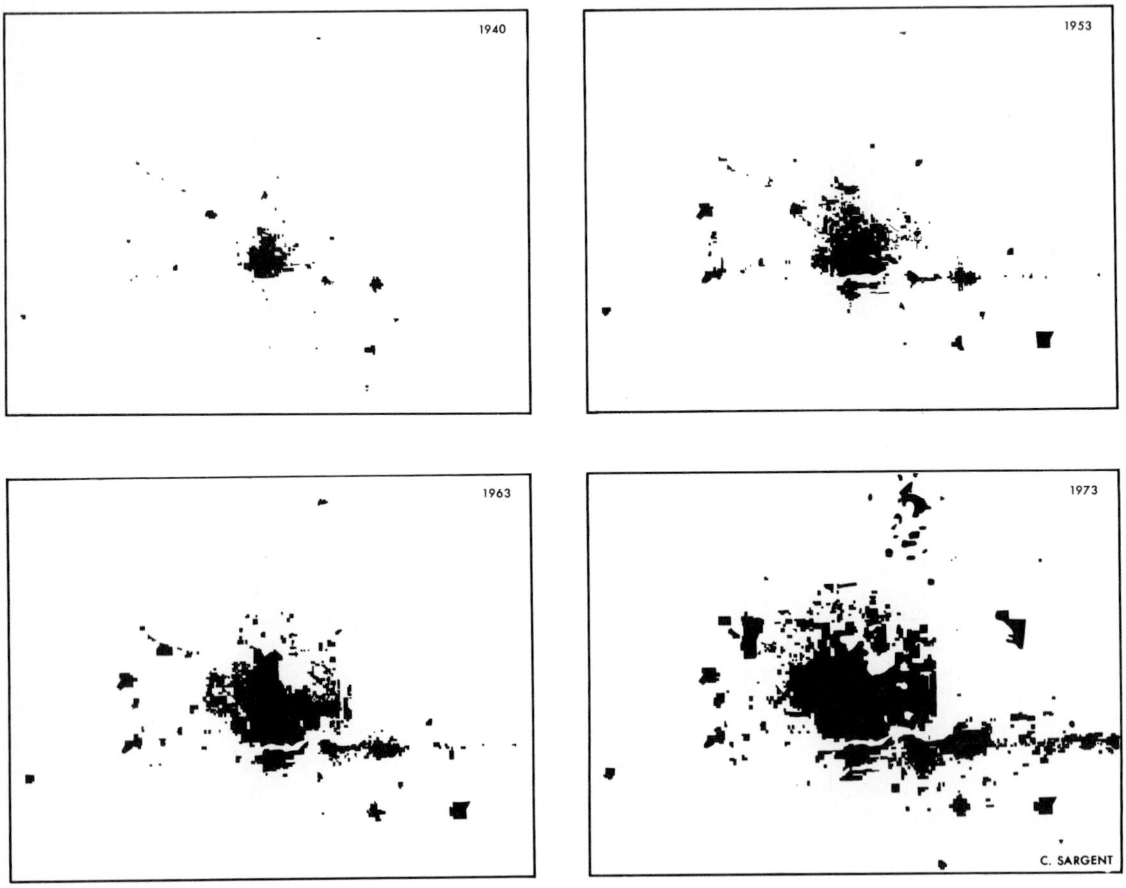

Figure 2-1. Expansion of Urbanized Areas in Greater Phoenix.

or raw land as one moves toward the periphery but also of the widespread development of the single family dwelling. Over time undeveloped areas have gradually filled in so that yesterday's fringe becomes today's fully developed suburb.

Forces Behind Suburban Expansion

The growth of the edge of the city is the consequence of many underlying forces. The rising share of national population that comes to reside in the major metropolitan areas is a principal demand factor. Concurrently, rising personal incomes have allowed many to move from older portions of the city to its periphery, widely viewed as a more desirable social and physical environment than the inner city with its deteriorated high density areas and inner city minorities. Transportation improvements, particularly the construction of boulevards and freeways since World War II, have also encouraged movement outward from the center. In an earlier period, the late nineteenth and early twentieth centuries, the evolution of widespread trolley networks played a similar though spatially more restricted role in dispersing population out of the center. In some cities, interurban rail services have been an important force in the expansion of cities.

The postwar decline of downtown stores, movie palaces and other businesses subsequent to the creation of outlying shopping centers and the gradual shift of doctors, dentists and their professional dependents from downtown professional buildings into outlying areas further increased the appeal of the periphery as did growing office and factory employment opportunities on the fringe. Over time, the periphery has come to offer virtually all the goods and services that urban dwellers require. This in turn has led to a greater focus on financial and general office activities in the central business district as retail activities declined.

House builders proved both willing and able to supply the demand of an increasing number of city dwellers for a more dispersed, low density environment in the metropolitan penumbra. Particularly after World War II they evolved mass methods of tract house construction that utilized advances in earth-moving equipment to facilitate the preparation of farmlands, hills and ravines, and adopted new materials and techniques in the construction of the popular detached single family "tract house." The conventional tract subdivision is now the norm, with an increasing number of mobile home parks and condominium apartment complexes. In recent years, a special form of the subdivision, the "planned communities and new towns" of single family houses and townhouses, have been sprouting like mushrooms on the urban fringe to supply a new "environment" to the more affluent.

An Inquiry Into Process

To comprehend the form of the city requires an understanding of the series of decisions made and the agents making them. Surprisingly, while we know *what* has been happening to the shape or morphology of the American city and *why*, we do not fully understand *how* it happens. As the National Academy of Sciences reported in 1972, we know relatively little about the individual processes that lead either to the development and use of raw land or to changes in the use of developed land. Clawson muses that we "understand the social, political, and legal aspects of current land settlement little better than did the contemporaries of nineteenth century westward expansion." While this is something of an exaggeration, it is true that significant studies of the land development process are still few in number.

To date there has been little systematic analysis of either the decisions or the promoters of urban development; as a consequence we have only fragmentary data from which to draw conclusions. And because we do not yet fully understand either the process of land conversion or the role that speculation in raw land as a form of behavior plays in that process, existing land use controls such as planning and zoning decisions typically are built upon an inadequate conceptual and legal foundation and inevitably prove less than adequate in execution.

It is not surprising, then, that the shape or morphology of the city responds almost entirely to market forces as influenced by the agents and catalysts of change. Indeed, to Peter Blake (and numerous others) ". . . just about the *only* factor that determines the shape of the American city today is unregulated private profit: profit from speculation with land, profit from manipulating land and buildings, and profit from the actual construction and subsequent lease or sale of buildings."

The Role of Land Speculation

Land speculation—the holding of real property for potential value increases—takes place throughout the city, but the two principal foci are the central city, where land prices have traditionally been highest and the pressures for urban renewal most intense, and the urban fringe, where the most land is available, new construction most common and the shape of the city most fluid. On the fringe—the focus of this study—residential development is the major land use and the leading edge of urban growth. There are many involved in land speculation on the city's edge: the farmers who hold raw land for speculative reasons; intervening (successive) landowners who buy and hold raw land, also for speculation; and developers interested in promoting both their raw land holdings and completed subdivisions. Analysis of these speculative agents, the forces that drive them, the catalysts that aid or constrain them and the nature of modifying influences is therefore viewed as a *sine qua non* to understanding the constantly changing form of the city and constitutes the organizing principle of this study.

While some consider speculation in undeveloped or "raw" land a *derivative* of the land conversion process, it is in fact a form of behavior *fundamental* to both the process of land conversion and the resultant form. It is a major force ranking with the transportation network, the availability of public facilities or zoning decisions in determining the morphology of the city. Its most obvious working is through the multitude of decisions made by speculators with respect to the release of land for development or its retention in its existing use.

Stories of fantastic increments in land values are the glamorous side of speculation in raw land and provide the raw material for books with engaging titles like "How I Made \$17½ Million in Real Estate—In My Spare Time." True, since World War II, land speculation has probably made more millionaires than any other form of business or investment, but it is the timing of land sales or the refusal to place land on the market at all that is the key to understanding speculation's impact upon urban form. Just as the holes help give form to a good Gruyere or Emmenthaler cheese, so does the reluctance of some speculators to sell raw land or the inability of some builders to buy it at the asking price help determine the form of the city by creating holes in the urban fabric.

There are many such holes; as defined by Manvel, unimproved land typically makes up about one-third of all privately held land in cities with populations exceeding 100,000 persons, and even most cities of over 250,000 have a considerable amount of undeveloped land. Earlier studies by Fisher, Hoyt, Cornick, Berkman, Fellman and others all indicate that the city has had extensive undeveloped, if platted, lands at least since the mid-nineteenth century. As Ward has summarized it, "at any given time, subdivided land prepared for sale occupied a more extensive and regular zone than did lots actually sold . . .". Raw land speculation clearly looms large in all explanations of the evolution of the urban fringe.

Scope of the Study

While some metropolitan areas are endowed with nearby vacationlands and the outer edge of the urban fringe may be so expansively viewed as to encompass summer cabins and cottages, the "second home" is not typically within the urban fringe. For this reason, although speculation in raw land is a key variable in understanding the evolution of *urbs in rure,* neither distant second home developments nor "Sunday suburbs," composed of the more adjacent retreats of city dwellers, concern us here. The three central goals of this essay are (1) to clarify the relationship of raw land speculation to urban morphology, (2) to discover how land speculation may operate as an obstacle to attaining the goal of optimal urban development and (3) to outline a number of feasible land use controls *and* incentives that could influence the impact of speculation in raw land upon urban form.

While not ignored, the ethnic and social ramifications of sprawl are purposefully not stressed, nor is the study intended to be a detailed critique of suburban life or the loss of agricultural land to housing; an examination of developers per se; or an in depth analysis of suburban land values, the problem of open space preservation or environmental quality. The central question is a direct one—what is the impact of raw land speculation upon the shape of the city and how does the process take place?

Study Areas

The principal criterion in the selection of study areas was to choose those that would most vividly give evidence of any impact of land speculation upon urban morphology. The best examples were found to be provided by cities that display most or all of the following preconditions:

- rapid population growth promoting high levels of effective demand for land on the periphery;
- an expanding transportation system that opens up or has the potential for opening up the "empty" periphery;
- a land-holding pattern that permits the easy acquisition of sufficiently large parcels of land for speculative actions;
- a location where neither legal nor physical restrictions upon land development effectively infringe upon individual speculative decisions and actions; and
- a "speculative mood" where confidence in continued growth and anticipation of future speculative gains in land is high.

Initially it was hoped that we would be able to provide comprehensive insight into the operation and impact of raw land speculation upon the urban morphology of four metropolitan areas that seem to meet all of the criteria: Atlanta, Los Angeles, San Jose and Phoenix. Unfortunately, the paucity of data and the almost total absence of studies that focus on the role of raw land speculation precluded such detailed analysis in the time allowed. Instead we must be content, as other studies must be, to use the often scattered and diffuse findings from these and other cities in an anecdotal form to gain insight into processes at work.

Sources

The expansion of the urban landscape onto surrounding farmlands, forests and deserts is widely viewed, rightly or wrongly, as a major environmental crisis and the extent, complexities, perplexities and problems of urban sprawl have constituted for some two decades one of the dominant themes of both the popular and the planning literature on the American city. In the last few years, nurtured by increasing concern for the environment and ecological considerations, a call for the creation of new, or the strengthening of existing, land use controls has surfaced.

But most reports and studies to date typically have described the urban fringe pattern (usually as "sprawl"), stressed design features (such as "planned unit developments") and outlined regulatory measures at the expense of the discovery and analysis of the processes that create the land use pattern. A number of studies examine the impact of urbanization upon agriculture. While a valuable and legitimate field of inquiry, the studies rarely include more than a superficial analysis of the processes behind urban fringe development. A few studies are also available that examine changing urban and suburban land values, but while valuable for indicating *why, how* and *how much* urban land values are rising, they too rarely consider the processes that relate land values to urban form.

Difficulty of access to many sources and the secrecy surrounding terms of purchase and sale, land costs, the use of options and other devices that influence both the timing and price of transactions and subsequent development are major handicaps to any study. Small wonder that few studies have even peripherally attempted to focus on the role of land speculation.

Research into decisionmaking, on the other hand, is now beginning to offer valuable insight into the motivations of both landowners and developers and continued work here holds considerable promise as more and better empirical data are incorporated into the essentially deductive models that have been formulated. Typical of the behavioral studies by Morrill, Kaiser and Weiss is the use of simulation models to understand what kind of settlement pattern is likely to emerge given certain key land development variables. By simulating the outward spread of the urban area, the intensity of development and the temporal rhythm of change, it is attempted with varying success to pinpoint major elements of the land development process.

Even here, though, the role of raw land speculation is still not adequately taken into account. In one major study of the suburban land conversion process by Chapin and Weiss, for instance, "the influence that large vacant tracts held out of development have on the land development patterns" was omitted due to time limitations despite awareness that the "tracts tied up in estates, land speculation schemes, and other restrictive holdings" function as barriers to development.

Finally, it should be noted that a number of studies have focused on solutions without attempting adequately to examine processes. Especially since about 1960 a number of White House task forces, congressional committees and public interest groups have attempted to develop elements of a national urban growth policy, with particular emphasis upon the conversion of land from rural to urban uses and the preservation of open spaces. Characteristically, these reports have sketched a similar range of solutions rather than examine the underlying dynamics affecting urban form, including raw land speculation. Still, it must be said that these reports have raised the national consciousness about urban problems, making the public increasingly aware that uncontrolled urban growth is not inevitable. One lesson of history is that future controls will likely continue to be of a superficial and cosmetic nature unless the underlying processes of urban land speculation are brought into sharper focus.

THE AGENTS OF LAND SPECULATION

The speculative alchemists of the medieval universities, we are told, were fascinated by the possible transmutation, with the aid of catalysts, of a base element such as lead into gold. Not surprisingly, all such attempts to transform common dross into a precious commodity met with failure. More successful have been the land speculators of the nineteenth and twentieth centuries, the alchemists of land use change whose base element—raw or undeveloped land—is as malleable as gold and whose catalysts for transformation are as strong, concentrated and effective as the inherent constraints upon change are weak and diffused. As a result, ordinary farmland, forest and desert on the edge of the city has for many decades been transformed and ultimately incorporated into the city, changing the city's form in turn. The result to date has been the modern "sprawling" American city, all of them very much alike in the *processes* affecting them, yet still very different in shape and detail because of their unique sites and situations, local transportation networks, history, architecture, disparities in population growth and dissimilar economic bases.

In its simplest form, the process of suburban land conversion can be viewed as a chain of independent yet closely linked actions undertaken by combinations of speculative alchemists who simultaneously manipulate the catalysts of raw land speculation and development and respond to the constraints imposed upon them. Each such speculative agent can alternately be viewed as an independent "profit center" that changes the nature and value of land through a wide range of decisions related to the retention, acquisition, sale or development of unimproved land.

Additions to the urban fringe are essentially speculative ventures but, in Higbee's words, "it is the lack of coordination of the decision to speculate which produces sprawl and not the speculation itself." Countless speculative decisions, based largely on the presumed profitability of holding land in "cold storage" for future appreciation rather than for immediate use, mean that there is a significant difference between buildable land and buildable land offered for development. The distinction, to Gold and Davidoff, is critical "where substantial tracts of land in fringe areas, and well-placed lots in central cities, are deliberately held out of the development process in expectation of a future rise in price." Sometimes, land is also withheld from development to allow future personal use; for purely emotional reasons, including a lack of interest; or to prevent certain types of "undesirable" uses—such as a housing tract adjacent to a private estate—from impinging on a more "desirable" land use. Still other reasons that privately held land might be kept from development include legal entanglements such as defective title, or tax considerations, parcel size unsuitable to development or an "unreasonable" asking price. Though the empirical evidence is meager, that which does exist leads us, like Clawson, to suspect that "the personal desires, projections, and preferences of present landowners must be a major factor responsible for some tracts developing while other intermingled ones do not."

Speculative Agents

To facilitate exposition it is convenient to categorize these speculative landowners—in terms of their relation to the land—as being either agriculturalists, intervening owners or land developers. The first two groups constitute the so-called "predevelopment" landowners; developers generally hold raw land only for a short time as a prelude to active development. It has been estimated by Schmid and Clawson that the total annual gain in land prices in converting from rural to suburban residential use may be on the order of $13.5 billion. About half of this probably goes to farmers, the other half to other speculators and dealers.

Agriculturalists As Speculators. Although some cities expand into forests and upon deserts and other "vacant" lands, it is more typical for the edge of the city to infringe upon outlying farmlands. The effect of urban expansion upon the farmer depends upon his commitment to agriculture, but few find it easy to resist becoming active land speculators, basing their actions on calculations of potential future capital gains as well as upon immediate returns from farming. The question then becomes: As the value of the land and the costs of holding it become increasingly related to the nearby city rather than to its agricultural value, how long will farmers continue to hold land before releasing it to a developer or to an intervening landowner? As illustrated in Figure 2-2, land values on the edge of an expanding urban area, as viewed by the farmer, are made up of two components—a value for agricultural use and a speculative value related to potential urban development. Near the city the value of land is more closely related to raw land speculation than to farming. With increasing distance from the city, the speculative value decreases and finally ceases at a distance [A] from the city where no urban development is anticipated even in the distant future.

Apart from the appeal of instant riches as a deterrent to continued farming, those who try to remain genuine commercial farmers on the urban fringe may find it difficult to carry out established farming practices. Plowing, crop-

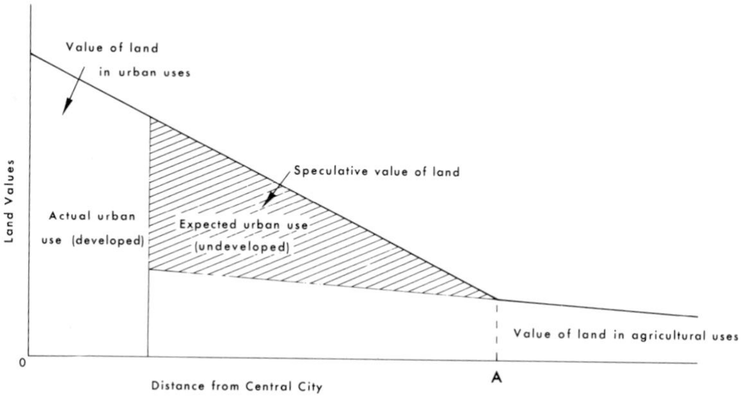

Figure 2-2. Components of Land Value.

dusting and other essential but noxious rural practices are commonly objected to by residents of nearby, new housing tracts. Increasing air pollution hurts some crops and vandalism of fields and orchards by juveniles further harasses the farmer and reduces his profit margin. Drainage problems caused by new construction, difficulties in reaching and farming small tracts, pressures to reduce livestock numbers and interference from residential construction are other problems that Sargent found plague the farmer. Rising taxes based on the enhanced value of the farmland for urban uses also increase operating costs; Krueger indeed calls many farmers little more than "urban drones in rural hives" because of their tax burden. However, as we will later note in detail, farmers in about half the states have been aided by the adoption of low tax assessments based on the existing agricultural rather than the potential urban value of their land. But it is still charged by some that assessors are often under the pressure of land speculators who have political influence to "put the squeeze" on farms so that owners will sell more quickly and at lower prices.

Another pressure for the release of farmland often comes from the younger members of the farm family, less closely tied to the land and less committed to rigors of rural life than their parents. Some farmers sell out in order to reestablish a larger farm farther from the city. In any case, there are few farmers today who are not aware of the potential value of their land and few will resist the bulldozer.

On the contrary, farmers are often in the vanguard of those who are fighting attempts by planning agencies to restrict urban sprawl. Witness, for example, the suburban sprawl moving closer to some of the horse farms on the edge of Lexington, Kentucky (Figure 2-3). Far from being distressed, a number of farmowners accept subdivisions amidst the equine estates and look forward to sale to developers and removal of the stables to more distant parts of the Bluegrass Country. A proposed "greenbelt" to hold in open space 210 square miles near Lexington was attacked as both "impractical" and not legally binding. On the other hand, we find that many farmers of Japanese descent in California have strong ties to the land and little willingness to sell out. Indeed, the internment of the California Japanese during World War II and the confiscation of some of their lands was in part motivated by the craving of others for their valuable properties. In Phoenix, the "Japanese gardens" are now a tourist attraction, as they represent the last major area of intensive fruit, vegetable and flower growing in the metropolitan area.

The great bulk of American farmers, however, are not genuine commercial farmers or ranchers, but rather what Higbee terms pseudo-farmers or marginal farmers. The former is so named because he derives the bulk of his income from off-farm sources, usually some form of employment in the nearby city. The farm is chiefly a residence and a speculative holding. The marginal farmer, undercapitalized and

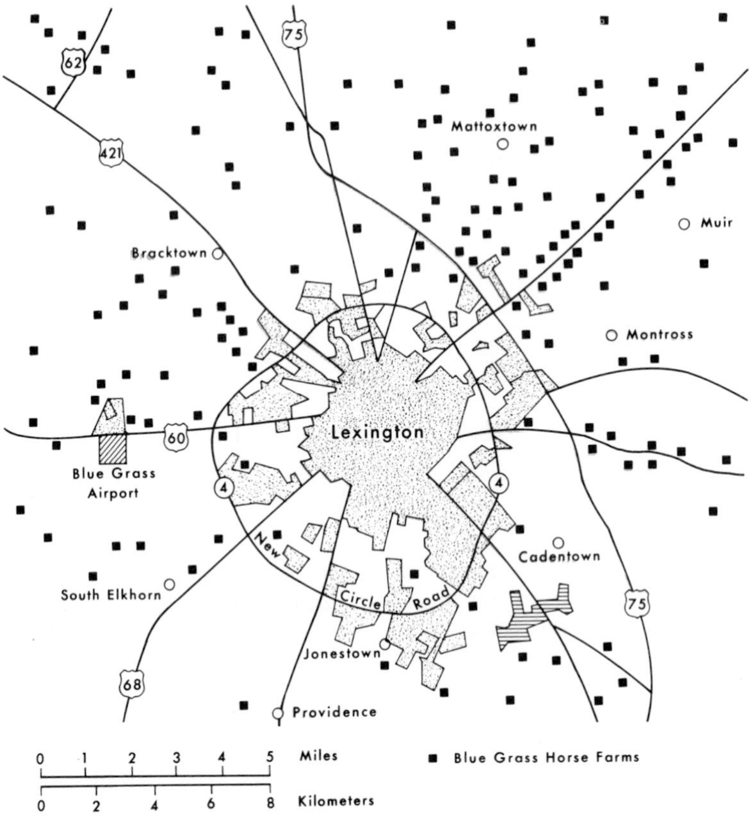

Figure 2-3. Urban Growth versus Horse Farms.

vulnerable to the vagaries of the marketplace, is always on the brink of becoming a pseudo-farmer. Both are highly susceptible to relinquishing their holdings.

Intervening Landowners. Much of the unimproved land held for speculative purposes on the urban fringe is in the hands of the nonfarmer—the urban land speculator who may lease his speculatively held land to a farmer for crops or grazing as a means of gaining some return until the land is deemed prime for urban uses. Others have drawn money from the Soil Bank program for not farming land they would not have farmed in any case. Still others do not utilize the land at all in the short run, treating the expenses of holding it as a tax loss to offset unrelated revenues.

Particularly in the highly urbanized northeast sector of the United States, some farm land on the fringe is held as estates for the truly affluent. Motivated by the beauty and openness of the land and a desire for isolation from urban problems, as well as by the promise of rising land values and either some income from the property or losses to permit a tax write-off, estate owners preserve open land until the costs of holding and/or the rewards of sale for development become too pervasive to resist.

Doctors, dentists, airline pilots, corporate executives and other high income persons are notable raw land speculators. In addition, syndicates of speculators assemble farm properties and an increasing number of investors are now buying shares in real estate investment trusts (REITs) which are similar to mutual funds except that they deal in real estate rather than stocks and bonds. While most REITs deal solely in mortgages, rapid rises in land values are the prod that moves others into the speculative market in raw land. In some high growth areas, such as southern California, small investment clubs have been engaged in land speculation for decades.

Some large institutional investors are also moving into both real estate speculation and land development. Industrial corporations also may engage in raw land speculation, for at the same time they purchase a farm for a suburban plant site there is a strong inducement to buy adjacent land for speculative purposes. Other corporations begin raw land speculation and development as a conscious effort to diversify their activities and boost earnings and end up as substantial landowners on the edge of the city (Figure 2-4).

Particularly in the environs of some of the younger, fast-growing Western cities there is still large-scale land ownership by either the state or the federal government. In these instances speculators and developers actively seek to acquire this land either through favorable purchases or land swaps. They are not without success, and pieces of the national patrimony are continually relinquished, ofttimes at either suspiciously low prices or through debatable swaps.

Land Developers As Raw Land Speculators. Although the speculative holding of raw land is not their principal purpose, most developers purchase more land than is immediately to be developed. In part the excess land is held as a hedge against a rise in prices; conversely, it is retained in order to enjoy gains from land value increases. The holding of raw land also helps

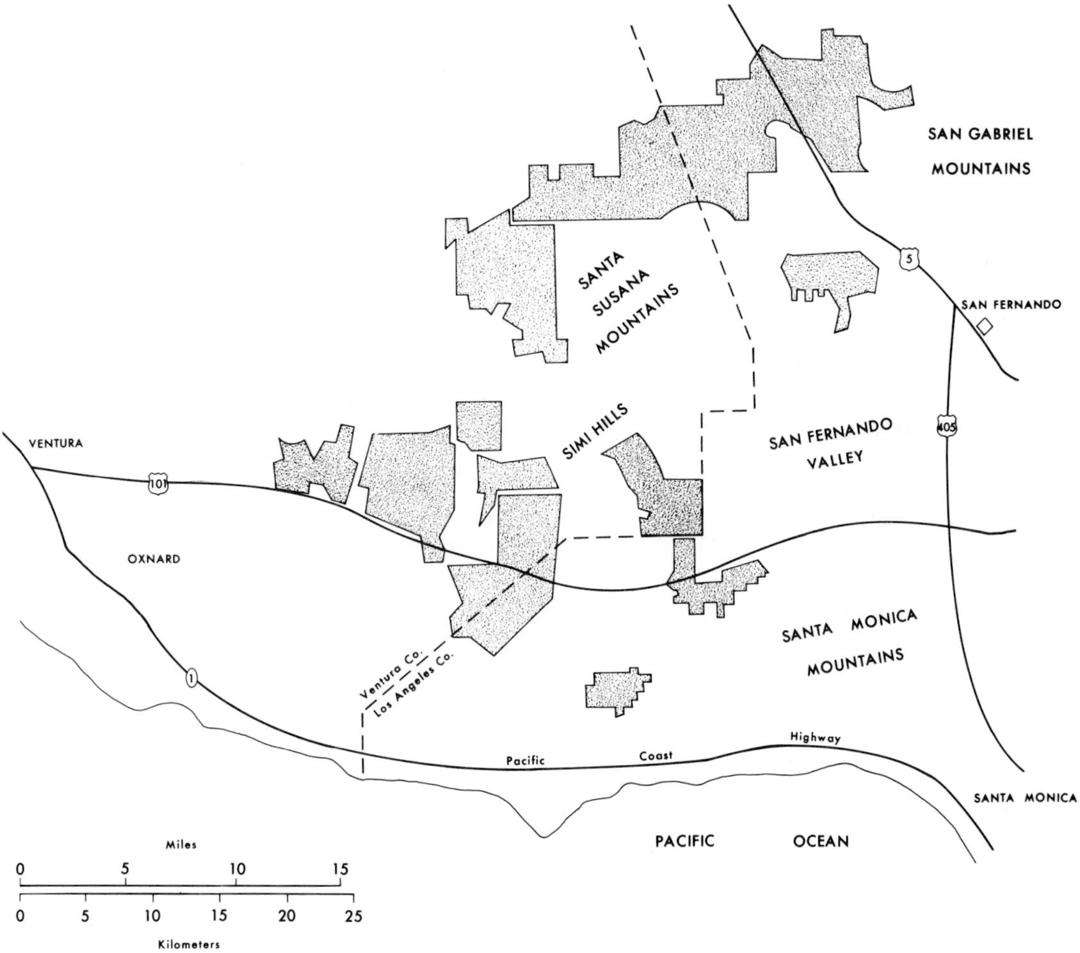

Figure 2-4. Large-Scale Corporate Land Holdings in the Western Los Angeles Urbanized Area.

assure continuous development with all of the production savings that this continuity permits. In a few instances, of course, too much land is acquired through faulty assessment of either the land's or the developer's potential. Poor judgment, of course, is not restricted to developers, but is also characteristic of intervening owners and farmers and points out that the "wrong move" should not be discounted as an influence on urban morphology.

Capital shortages and alternate uses for capital usually precludes long term large-scale speculative holdings by most developers. For the most part, land is acquired by developers pretty much as they wish to put it to use, but Milgram did find that about one quarter of the acreage in a North Philadelphia study area was purchased four or more years in advance. In Phoenix, one of the largest developers reportedly carries only a two or three year supply of land because of carrying costs and because of the higher return on capital invested in development rather than speculation in land. Our knowledge of the actual length of developer holding time is obscured, unfortunately, by the widespread use of options to purchase, long term agreements of sale, installment sales and other means of disguising effective control of the land.

The Developer's True Roles. Agriculturalists and intervening owners are the principal predevelopment landowners and they correspondingly make the decisions as to the retention or release of the great bulk of speculatively held raw land. But their actions are greatly influenced by the developer, who is the principal agent for expressing the demand by the general public for suburban locations. In terms of urban form, then, the developer plays two very significant roles: first as an assembler of land, and second as the creator of the actual subdivisions which give form to a number of earlier speculative decisions.

The selection and assembly of parcels of raw land held in numerous separate ownerships are, in much of the country, the most difficult tasks of the developer. They are also extremely significant operations since they affect urban morphology: more than by speculating in land, the developer influences urban form by determining the direction and shape of residential growth and by changing the scale and pattern of land ownership. As Mortimore has noted, any number of studies indicate that "the structure and pattern of land ownership . . . is an integral part of any settlement pattern" and that property lines constitute "an invisible skeleton for the growing body of the town." Thus, while the internal structure of individual tract developments and the character of the community are strongly influenced by the developer's engineer, who sketches lot sizes, street conformations and other details, and by the architect, who influences house types and dwelling placements within the range provided by prevailing subdivision controls, the *pattern* of urban fringe development is earlier determined by the interaction of land speculators (the supply side of the equation) with the developers (the demand side).

When available properties are considered too small for efficient development, assembly becomes particularly crucial; when available properties are too large for an individual developer there is the problem of partial acquisition. Today, for many developers, assembly is much more of a problem than land division. The problems imposed by the fragmentation of land ownership in suburban Washington, D.C., have been illustrated by Brodsky, difficulties that suggest why developers have attempted to gain ownership of the 10,000 acre Department of Agriculture farm at nearby Beltsville, Maryland. Urban military bases are another popular target, given the large consolidated acreages they encompass. On the other hand, relatively small parcels prove advantageous to small builders.

For large-scale developers, the reality of fragmented ownership, combined with higher land prices toward the urban center and isolated existing housing developments that would infringe upon a developer's "master plan," forces them to locate their "new towns" and "planned communities" toward the outer edge of the urban fringe. Like other large subdivisions, "new towns" such as Columbia, Maryland, Reston, Virginia, Jonathan, Minnesota, and Irvine, California, are all distant, but still within commuting range, of existing urban centers.

The assembly of land parcels into the large 7,000-12,000 acre holdings necessary for such large-scale developments is considerably easier in the western states. With a briefer time span of land occupancy and a more extensive pattern of land settlement, large western farms and ranches and large quantities of easily alienated public lands ease the assembly problem. Southern California, for example, still contains sizable remnants of the large *ranchos* and mission lands surveyed in the pre-1850 Mexican period that later became large private and corporate land holdings. Elsewhere in the west hundreds, even thousands, of acres near a city can be acquired from either a single or a relative handful of landowners.

The Preassembly Decisions. Before a developer purchases land various decisions must be made. One level of such decisions deals with the marketability of proposed housing types, an assessment that runs the gamut from "sophisticated" market analyses to highly personal impressions that "what sold before will sell again." In some fast-growing areas such as Washington, D.C., housing demand is so high that in fact almost *anything* can be sold. The larger developers, perhaps, tend toward more careful analysis than the smaller ones, but all analyses incorporate some combination of facts, judgments and value decisions: facts such as the socioeconomic characteristics of the market and the housing types in greatest demand; judgments about housing trends and interest rates; and value judgments such as what "environment" buyers are seeking. Thus, while Kaiser notes that the developer is no passive agent, but "imposes his own important location decision framework into the residential development process," Adams has found that the strategies of developers and the "mental maps," or spatial *Weltanschauung,* of housing consumers nonetheless "interact to reinforce one another's locational and directional biases."

Equal in importance to market factors are determinations of the physical, locational and "institutional" suitability and the cost of a site. Increasingly, as we have noted, the natural attributes of a site can be modified with modern earth-moving equipment, but excessive slope, poor drainage, depth to bedrock, unstable subsurfaces and similar considerations can adversely affect site potential. In some unfortunate instances they *should* have an adverse effect, but do not; in these instances, unscrupulous developers build on floodplains, unstable slopes or worse.

Proximity to paved roads and freeways, to shopping centers and to other residential tracts are important locational considerations to the developer, while the availability of utilities, parcel size and shape, the land's zoning potential, existing covenants and the absence of defective titles are institutional elements that must be taken into account. The price of land is an obvious consideration, but Weiss, Donnelly and Kaiser feel that developers "tend to react to relative land values rather than absolute land values." The incidence of high land costs ultimately rests with the consumer; the developer need only remain competitive.

Two inherently different approaches to site evaluation have been identified. The more traditional is the "contact approach" whereby the developer becomes aware of the availability of a specific site and then determines whether a market exists for the type of housing that could be put there. A newer technique is the "marketability approach" wherein a developer first identifies the demand and then seeks a site. While the latter approach seems to represent an emerging trend, the more traditional "contact" method still seems to be dominant.

Most developers, in reality, tend to "satisfice" rather than "optimize," to settle for a satisfactory return and location rather than insist upon an optimal set of conditions. Any tract that reasonably fits the development template may be suitable since other factors play the major role in profitability; the time and difficulty of finding the best tract may just not be worthwhile. A number of decisions are, in fact, made by default: typical is the desirable site that remains undeveloped because the developer and the landowner cannot agree on price or terms.

The typical development procedure before the post-World War II surge in housing was the subdivision of a parcel of land by a speculator or "subdivider" who staked lots, had the municipality install major utilities and sold the parcels to individual buyers who built as they would and could, usually contracting with an independent builder. Especially in the 1920s, numerous cities had miles of streets with expensive utilities in place but no houses. The wild expansion of the cities, in Warner's words "produced wildcat and premature subdivisions, overexpansion of residential sites, miles of sidewalks running through weed-covered vacant land, and clouded titles on thousands of vacant lots." Immediately after World War II a great many subdivisions were also poorly planned and hurriedly undertaken to take advantage of the expected housing boom. A number of these were also premature; one study in southwestern Michigan summarized by Clawson, Held and Stoddard concluded that over 40 percent could be so classified. Land in all these instances was being "forced" into urban uses and frozen there, unable to revert back to agricultural uses.

While it can still be shown today that rural land is being prematurely forced into development, the acquisition of land, dwelling construction, utility installations and local street improvements are now usually united in the hands of a single developer. Today, in excess of 75 percent of all builders build on their own land, which they either have purchased as improved lots or developed themselves. On the fringe of Indianapolis, for example, Sargent found that about two-thirds of the new homes are in identifiable subdivisions; the remaining one-third are on scattered single lots or small tracts along the major country roads. In Phoenix, even more of all new housing is in identifiable subdivisions.

Where the Money Is. While gains from speculation in raw land per se may sometimes be significant, the developer's gains normally come more from both the spread between raw land cost and finished site value and the spread between housing construction costs and ultimate sales price. There is, unfortunately, a paucity of basic data on prices, improvement costs and lot sizes, but a 1968 study by Schmid indicates that the spread between farmland values and finished lot prices is large and growing larger: the site value of developed lots for new single family homes advanced more than 300 percent between 1946 and 1964. At the same time, general price levels increased only 58 percent.

Though Schmid stresses that the data to estimate suburban land value appreciation above land and development costs are scarce, he reports that Federal Housing Administration data for 1964 show an 892 percent appreciation in the value of a finished lot above the farmland price. Data of the National Association of Home Builders for the same year showed an 1,875 percent appreciation, but this does not take improvement costs into account. On the average, FHA data indicate that land cost accounted for about 11 percent of the total value of a new house from about 1940 to 1955, up to about 19 percent by 1964. By 1972, it had reached 22 percent, a share comparable to the booming speculative period of the 1920s that preceded the general decline in land values in the 1930s.

Observations. As little as we know about the role of the developer in shaping the city, it is still more than we know about the preferences and the decisionmaking processes of speculative land holders, be they farmers, individuals, land syndicates, investment trusts or diversified corporations. All these agents constitute the major mechanism behind the constantly evolving shape of the city. Equally as important as understanding the initiators of change and their actions is an understanding of the instruments they utilize and the forces they control or to which they are subject.

CATALYSTS AND CONSTRAINTS

By definition, a catalyst is an agent which initiates or accelerates reactions but which itself remains virtually unchanged by the process. In the reactions unleashed by the modern speculative alchemists whom we have just discussed, these catalysts can be conveniently categorized as those which support raw land speculation and speculative developments and those which are permissive and reduce the frictions of raw land speculations.

Supportive Catalysts

A great many of the catalysts that financially nourish speculation and changes in the shape of the city are personified by banks, savings and loan associations, life insurance companies, and sundry federal agencies. Of particular interest to us are the *spatial* ramifications of their actions. It has been shown by Milgram, for instance, that while most investment decisions by banks et al. are largely determined by "market" criteria, a number of nonmarket, pseudoscientific or "customary" factors also enter the picture. For example, "if mortgage lenders generally regard North Philadelphia as a bad investment . . . this belief will largely determine the character and extent of the investments in that area regardless of the objective facts. . . . In Minneapolis, investments north and east of certain streets are taboo among mortgage lenders. . . ." Certain sections of Phoenix, Los Angeles, Atlanta or any other city are viewed with similar prejudice, helping to create and perpetuate an historical bias in the direction of growth. In financial circles this practice is referred to as "red-lining" of areas, placing them off-limits to significant levels of mortgage loans.

The federal government has indirectly nourished land speculation and influenced urban form at least since the Depression when a number of financing and loan insurance programs such as those of the Federal Home Loan Bank (1932) and Federal Housing Administration or FHA (1934) were created to revive the housing industry by augmenting the effective demand for new houses. With some reason it has been argued that, more than any single program, FHA insurance for single family homes has transformed the shape and social characteristics of American cities, especially since World War II. Suburbia is its monument, for hand in glove with its loan guarantees, the FHA decided that new housing should be built on the outskirts of the city, rather than within the cities themselves, if it was to have lower cost FHA-insured mortgages. Banks, savings and loan associations, and the Veterans Administration loan program, created under the 1944 "G.I. Bill of Rights," were all quick to adopt this spatial bias in their own loan policies. As a result, the mayor of San Jose, California, like others can in part credit residential sprawl in the American city to the FHA, which has facilitated insured loans for large developers of subdivisions. This, in tandem with tax codes that provide tax shelters in the suburbs and the unwillingness of public officials to "stand up" to developers, explains much of what has happened to San Jose and other cities since the mid-1940s.

Direct speculation in raw land has indeed been particularly favored by the structure of the internal revenue codes. In addition to the impetus given the suburban housing market by allowing the deduction of mortgage interest and property tax payments from taxable income (a subsidy going largely to middle and upper income groups), it is also profitable for many speculators with land in the path of urban growth to hold their land off the market in expectation of higher profits that will be taxed at favorable capital gains rather than regular income rates. These tax advantages, for example, are of great value to individuals in the higher tax brackets and tend to make them, as already noted, high bidders in the market for suburban land. Still other provisions allow tax-free exchanges of like land, thereby giving farmers, for instance, a substantial tax break if they exchange suburban fields with a developer for larger farmlands farther from the city.

The tax codes also encourage the time-phased or drawn out development of land rather than single phase development that would lump profits into but a few tax periods. Small wonder that most developers find it as important to get a good tax lawyer as an architect or engineer. In San Jose, to return to that classic case of rapid postwar growth, it has been calculated that the dollar break given landowners on capital gains exceeds the federal investment in city improvement programs. We should also note again that throughout the country local property tax rates are commonly much lower on unimproved land than on developed land, thus fostering raw land speculation by holding down the costs of land retention.

Land Prices. Rising land values are simultaneously a catalyst for continued, and a consequence of past, land speculation. The anticipation that land values will rise increases demand at the same time it restricts the supply of land since present owners hold for future gains. The paradox of the urban land market is not an absolute shortage of developable land but a constriction in available land as many speculators hold out for higher prices.

One consequence of this is that the supply of land in any one location is typically thin and the price high, bringing land in more distant, marginal locations into the market as speculative property and thereby expanding the urban fringe. For example, assuming that the more distant land is accessible and otherwise similar to more adjacent lands, rising land values will shift the land value curve upward so that land farther out takes on a speculative value (Figure 2-5). The land between A and B shifts into speculative holding *and* early development because it is cheaper than sites closer in.

As a general rule, raw land speculation is currently viewed as a reasonable investment if the land promises to double in value within seven years. This allows for a minimum 10 percent return on invested capital, enough to cover taxes, commissions and other fees and still leave a return at least comparable to earnings from tax-free municipal bonds. There is, of course, always the hope that land values will appreciate more rapidly than anticipated.

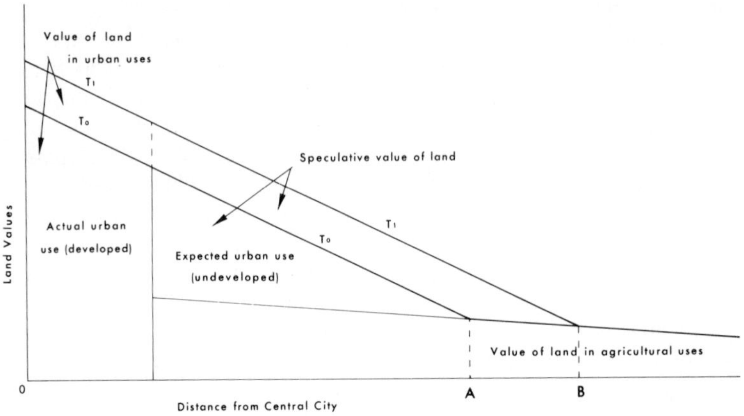

Figure 2-5. Land Values as a Function of Distance from the Central City.

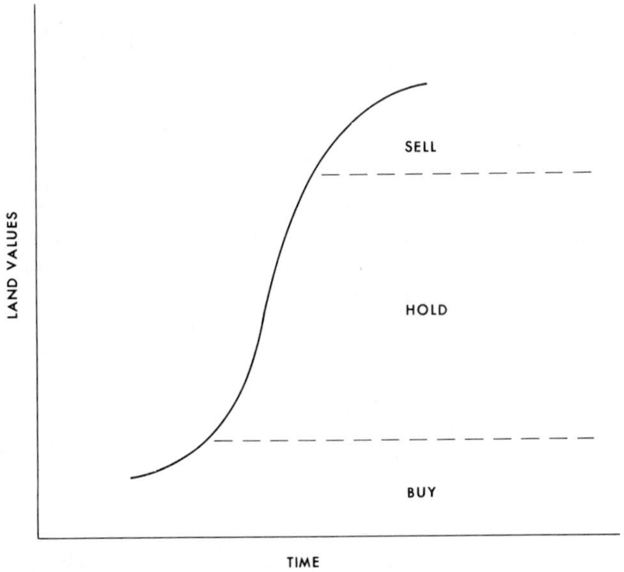

Figure 2-6. A Land Value Appreciation Curve.

In some rapid growth areas, such as the Santa Clara valley in California, investors are often advised to sell high value holdings that do not promise to double in value in five years, since lower priced raw land alternatives with the potential for rapid value rises are available. The advice, succinctly stated, is to buy relatively low priced land before it begins its steep value rise and sell it as the pace of appreciation slows down and results in a lower return on invested capital than is possible with cheaper land or other forms of investment (Figure 2-6).

Catalytic Commercial Sprawl. Raw land speculation on the fringe is also nourished by what Epstein has termed catalytic commercial sprawl—the creation of shopping areas on the periphery *before* the surrounding area is developed. The advantage to the developer is that a large shopping center can be built while land costs are still relatively low and a large 70 to 80 acre site can still be easily assembled. For raw land speculators, the very existence of the commercial center foretells a demand in the near future for land from residential developers who typically do not have a large stock of their own land.

Permissive Catalysts

A number of other catalysts pretty much give land speculation and development *carte blanche* in molding the shape of the urban periphery by reducing institutional constraints, by easing the frictions of distance and by lubricating the market mechanism that brings buyers and sellers together. Principal among these catalysts are permissive local government, expanding transportation and public utility networks, and the actions of land brokers.

Local Government. Perhaps the most important and certainly one of the most pervasive of the permissive catalysts to raw land speculation is the either open or covert advocacy of private speculative interests by individual members of city councils, county commissions and other governmental units. As Clawson, among others, points out, "land speculators and the 'Court House gang' are sometimes the same people or at least not unknown to one another," a cozy arrangement that can take much of the risk out of, and put profit into, land speculation. Particularly in many suburbanizing counties, few want to take part in local government and planning except those who have some direct financial gain from it. As a result, many officials are either landowners, developers, or the lawyers, architects or real estate people who represent their clients' interests.

Examples of abuses are many; a few will amply illustrate the point. In Fairfax County, Virginia, on the fast-growing fringe of Washington, D.C., members of the board of supervisors owned land and traded in land at the same time they took public actions that affected its value; several were eventually indicted and convicted of bribery and conspiracy in the approval of rezoning applications. In Chicago a high-ranking alderman pushed through the sale of a 148 acre tract near O'Hare airport to a land trust with which he had close associations, saw to it that prime city-owned land went to favored friends and exercised strong influence on the county tax board of appeals. In Phoenix, the vice chairman of the planning commission and an architect by profession designed a controversial hillside development that violates his own commission's hillside ordinance; the developer will seek a "variance" to permit construction. The chance ownership of land by local officials and their friends at proposed freeway interchanges, bridge approaches and other prime locations continually raises the specter of conflicting interests. On balance, strictly illegal acts are probably much less common than legal ones that nonetheless betray the public trust.

The very structure of local government is often enough to assure the precedence of private speculative interests over the public interest. It has been observed by many, including Wheaton, that local elected officials are primarily involved in their private activities rather than government and have little expertise in public matters. Many are also incapable of making tough decisions and avoid issues that might offend important local figures who are engaged in raw land speculation. They tend, in short, to accommodate speculators rather than to initiate or enforce controls upon them.

In dealing with developers, the local or county planning commission commonly abrogates its responsibility to *plan* and instead has its staff function to see whether a development proposal complies with *zoning* regulations. If it does not, the developer applies for a variance which is granted if the developer has the right political connections. Such connections are so commonplace that zoning controls and other regulations are not even taken seriously by speculators and developers; it is assumed they can be changed. Zoning maps, in fact, are almost routinely changed to favor one man and penalize another while having the superficial appearance of impartiality. "Not a few zoning maps have been drawn with such schemes in mind," notes Higbee, and ". . . some actually hobble a community just to steer economic growth where interested sponsors own the land." In Florida, Reilly tells us, "dizzyingly profitable deals have rested on 'understandings' about rezoning, dredge-and-refill permits (and) sewer hookups. . . ." All too often the planning and zoning commission is a money factory for the developer. The well-intentioned and sometimes well-conceived community master plans that the police power of zoning was meant to implement are typically reduced to little more than glossy, colorful handouts. Doubters of this need only compare past plans with present realities.

Some master plans, of course, are ill-conceived and the variance requested by developers may in fact constitute an enhancement of the urban area rather than its degradation. Typically there is the implicit assumption that the adopted comprehensive plan is a good plan; in reality that may not be the case. On the other hand, an adopted plan may be a good one. It also provides guidelines for both public and private investment decisions and should not be changed solely to suit the whim of individual interests.

An investigation of San Jose by the Stanford Environmental Law Society found that the city in its present form is largely the product of policies and practices pursued by aggressive city officials responsible only to a narrow range of private interests and concerned only with short-range goals. The problem in San Jose has been not a lack of government influence on growth, but altogether too much influence of the wrong kind. The city manager and the city council operated on the convenient assumption that unchecked and spatially uncontrolled growth per se was beneficial. The publisher of the widely read *Mercury* quite candidly admitted he wanted to replace the valley's famous and extensive orchards with people because "Trees don't read newspapers." Speculators and developers influenced the city government via the chamber of commerce and the newspaper, by promoting bond elections, and through direct participation in government.

Small wonder, then, that the county planning policy committee now finds that past urban development in and around San Jose has been uncoordinated, poorly located and ill-timed. It lays a good part of the blame squarely on local government for its uncritical accommodation of private interests. Collectively, the towns and county have, for example, grossly overzoned for commercial uses and thereby boosted the price of such land so high that many parcels will not be developed for a long time, creating pockets of "urban vacant" land, gaping holes in the urban fabric.

Farther south, in San Diego, it is widely acknowledged that developers have had a "stranglehold" on city hall and ignored the city's timetable for development. The Otay Mesa and Mira Mesa subdivisions, for example, have already become textbook examples of poor development and inadequate service provision as original master plans were emasculated by an endless stream of zoning variances and other speculator- or developer-engendered actions. Today there is some optimism that the new mayor will reduce such abuses; he at least campaigned on a platform that called for the authority and the tools to permit the city, rather than the developer, to determine the timing and location of new development. In fairness to the mayor should he fail, it must be pointed out that local government does not really have control over population growth, increasing wealth and mobility, and other forces that create the demand for homes on the periphery. Moreover, effectively to control the catalysts behind sprawl requires changes in policy and law at both the state and national level as prerequisites or companions to more effective local control.

Local governments on the outer fringes of metropolitan areas often have no zoning laws and subdivision regulations at all, let alone a general plan for development. Here, raw land speculation and development have a virtually free hand. Even within the city the almost inherent lack of coordination between the various governmental groups that are capable of influencing development helps guarantee a speculator-developer-directed growth pattern.

All in all, local, county, regional or state governments have the capacity to influence the pattern of land development only in an ad hoc and limited way and private motives typically reign over public interests. While these interests may be complementary at times, usually they are not, and it is the land speculator and developer who literally "win the field" thanks to coordinated effort, good contacts and strong pecuniary motivations. Whole sections of the urban fringe are much like a blank canvas, but what emerges has little chance of being a masterpiece given the hodgepodge of contributing artists. An analogy has been drawn by Reilly to a jacket produced over a number of years with sleeves, pockets and collar all designed by different tailors, and with no one responsible for fitting the parts together.

Transportation. The tie between urban transportation and urban form is a close one. Especially before the widespread introduction of the trolley the typical city was essentially mononuclear and compact in form, in large part because of the frictions of distance at a time when most people were pedestrians. Following the introduction of commuter trains in some larger cities and the widespread expansion of the electric trolley after about 1890 the star-shaped city emerged, a result of new residential and commercial development along the fixed routes (Figure 2-7). Later the automobile freed the periphery from these linear constraints and again changed the shape of the city, to what we know today. Now, of course, the city is no longer mononuclear but has important outlying commercial and industrial foci; population densities are significantly lower than in the earlier periods because of an accessibility to the large urban fringe. In 1920 the average density in cities over 100,000 was 6,580 persons per square mile; by 1960 that had dropped to 4,230 per square mile. If the present trend continues, by the year 2000 there will be about 3,700 per square mile, or almost half of the 1920 average! In brief, as transit shifted from individual (pedestrian) to mass (trolley and railroad movement) and then back to individual (automobiles), there were effects upon urban mobility, population densities and morphology. Proposed modern (mass) transit systems would again affect mobility, density and form.

The history of land speculation is replete with examples of landowners on the urban fringe who have actively sought or provided rail lines, trolley lines and roads in order to affect urban growth in their direction and thereby augment the value of their holdings. The trolley played the major role: indeed, as Vance has indicated, "in most parts of the United States the first large-scale land platting strictly for residential uses came with the trolley."

Faster, more comfortable, more dependable and with a greater frequency of service than the horse tram it replaced, the long, linear

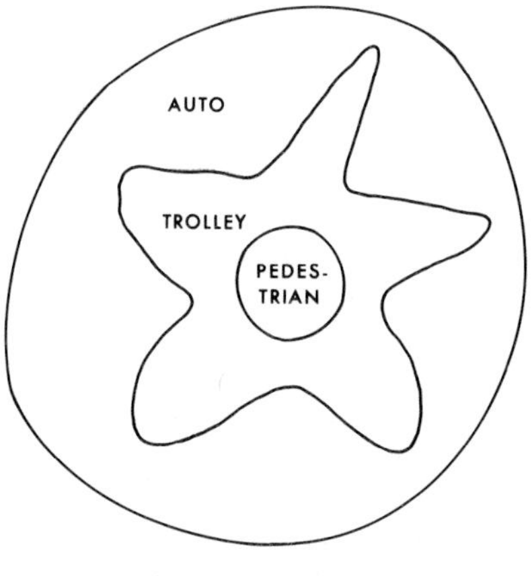

Figure 2-7. Transportation and City Form.

trolley lines opened up large expanses of the periphery of the city to speculation and development and at the same time made many vacant tracts closer to the center increasingly desirable for development. In a number of cities some trolley lines were built *primarily* to encourage raw land speculation and development, with the routing of the line dictated by the direction of the promoter's land holdings from the downtown. Not surprisingly, the peaks in residential building activity coincided with periods when access was being enhanced, generally prosperous time periods such as the 1920s when demand was high and money available for lot purchases and housing starts.

Today, highways and freeways have replaced the interurban railroad and trolley, but like these earlier transportation modes, they have great impact upon both the value of adjacent land and upon the location and timing of development. Studies indicate, for instance, that the value of land abutting new freeways can typically increase from two to 50 times in value. Any number of studies, as well as an alert eye, offer convincing evidence that developments follow existing or projected freeways, in the words of one large developer, "like fleas follow a dog."

While the major highways, boulevards and freeways most easily catch our attention, the urban fringe of most cities also possesses a relatively dense network of paved rural roads that provide access to undeveloped suburban properties. But precisely because the minor road opens virtually the entire periphery to potential development, there is a tremendous amount and variety of land available for development. This broadening of the land supply permits influences other than transportation—influences such as availability of public services, differentials in land prices, availability of tracts and physical features—to play a relatively more decisive role in the speculation and development process. The mode of transportation becomes, in time, less of a *determinant* of location and more of a *permissive* element.

Public Services. While there are few studies to suggest the impact of water and sewer lines on either land values or the timing of development, interviews of a cross-section of developers reported by the National Academy of Sciences suggest that the extension of utility trunk lines into the fringe enhances the value of suburban vacant land anywhere from two to seven times. Small wonder that landowners, in Clawson's words, "do not quietly wait for zoning or a new sewer line to drop a plum in their lap but shake the tree vigorously to help the decision drop where and when they want it."

Should local government prove reluctant to provide such utilities, special water and sewer districts can often be formed that have the power to issue bonds, levy taxes and acquire property by eminent domain. As Faltermeyer has pointed out, these "one-eyed governments" make decisions that can powerfully affect metropolitan growth and urban form while "pursuing their own myopic interests." Privately owned water companies are also established in some places and are typically purchased, in the long run, by a municipality and incorporated into the municipal network.

Another answer to the absence of public services is to release low density outlying areas from dependence upon them by utilizing independent systems. Drilled wells with automatic pumps replace the distant water lines while septic tanks replace the sewer and bottled gas the distant gas line. Inexpensive overhead electric and telephone lines are easily brought into the area if they are not already there. Rural fire departments offer a modicum of protection, as does the county sheriff.

Whether through the extension of existing municipal services or through their provision via special districts or private firms, the easy access to services facilitates the development of the fringe and therefore enhances raw land speculation. Land speculation and development also receives a fillip from the ease with which school districts can be expanded or created on the fringe. In California, for instance, the state department of education has supported sprawl by redistributing public funds to help school districts expand whenever and wherever localized land development occurs.

Land Brokers. At the same time raw land becomes more attractive for speculation and for development thanks to improved access and the availability of public services, the mechanism for its exchange is lubricated by the land broker. Nurtured primarily by commissions on sales, the broker is seldom a significant landowner in his own right, but a key catalyst to land speculation and development. His impact resides in his relatively comprehensive and current awareness of the land market—trends, prices, location of available parcels, alternate speculative opportunities—in contrast to the more imperfect awareness of the land market on the part of most farmers, intervening landowners and developers. In addition to bringing buyer and seller together he also counsels speculators on how to maximize speculative returns through the timing of sales that shift capital to more lucrative holdings. It is in part due to his actions that it is not uncommon for raw land to change hands five or six times before its ultimate development.

Performing a somewhat similar informational function are an increasing but still small number of land information services and property analysts. A few of the more comprehensive services, like Real Estate Today, Inc. in Atlanta, provide monthly information about the regional land market—location of sales, number and sales prices of raw land transactions—on a subscription basis to individuals, realtors, brokers and others. Aerial photo services sometimes offer similar information and financial advisory services also lubricate the investor's move into speculative land holding. A number of large Wall Street brokerage firms, for instance, have recently been setting up divisions to handle real estate services and to put together land syndicates. Private real estate research councils, such as the one that publishes the Northern California *Real Estate Report* offer much useful information about land trends.

Constraints to Raw Land Speculation

Common sense alone warns us to anticipate that there must be some constraints upon the free interaction between the land speculator and the catalysts outlined above. Just as the medieval alchemist could not change lead to gold, so can the modern raw land speculator not totally ignore or overcome all types of physical impediments, override all zoning and planning influences, or entirely control the location and timing of public service extensions. Still, most constraints have proven to be as weak as the land speculators and their catalysts for change have been strong.

Terrain. While at first glance it might seem fundamental, the influence of terrain upon the development capabilities of land has progressively decreased over time. The filling in of Boston's Back Bay or the waterfront of San

Francisco in the nineteenth century, and this century's draining and filling of Miami's swamps in the 1920s or the $10 billion, 30 year plan for urban development on part of the marshy 19,000 acres of the Hackensack Meadows across the Hudson from New York City indicate this declining role. Bayous on the edge of New Orleans and wetlands throughout the country are being drained and developed for residential tracts. Florida alone lost 169,000 acres of estuarine lands to dredging and filling from 1950 to 1969. The contouring of hills throughout the country is additional evidence of the increasingly minor role of adverse terrain conditions as land prices rise and available nearby land is harder to find.

Technology has played an important role in reducing terrain constraints as earth-moving equipment has gotten bigger, more powerful, more efficient and easier to operate and soils engineering more sophisticated. As *House and Home* pointed out to developers in 1960, "you can still dig, move and dump earth at 1930 prices" as a result of these improvements and therefore consider canyons, lagoons, swamps, ravines and steep slopes as suitable for development. One well-known developer, William Zeckendorf, Sr. was even quoted as saying the bulldozer was "the best invention we got out of the war."

The profitability of such projects is suggested by the transfer several years ago of 190 acres of valuable state-owned wetlands to a private developer at Ocean City, Maryland. The developer paid $100 an acre plus about $300,000 for mud he dredged from the adjacent bay to build up the low-lying property. He then subdivided the property into several hundred lots worth several million dollars. At the other physical extreme, expensive "pads" for houses are constructed on steep slopes in Los Angeles and Phoenix. Although they often create visual pollution because of extensive and long term scarring of the slopes, there are no effective ways to prohibit such developments and the fabricated lots are highly desired sites for showy, expensive homes. Where "land fabrication" is not feasible, it is sometimes possible to support hillside homes on stilts, as one finds along the slopes of the Santa Monica mountains between Los Angeles and the San Fernando Valley, and in Marin County, just to the north of San Francisco. Another technique in Los Angeles is the filling of canyons with refuse. Although the covered fills are not stable enough to themselves support housing, they do provide the land for open spaces such as golf courses and parks related to proposed residential developments.

The impact of terrain when it is not obvious is often simply ignored, and subdivisions are built on known floodplains or on soils unsuitable to development. Suburban Davidson County, surrounding Nashville, Tennessee, for instance, grew with virtually all the homes dependent upon septic tanks in limestone soil. Not surprisingly, the soil could not effectively absorb the waste and sewers had to be installed later at great expense. The costs incurred by the inundation of built-up floodplains and losses from mudslides are so well documented we need not discuss them here.

Still, the location of low density low and middle income tract development, which is the most areally extensive use of urban land *in toto,* is still sensitive to soil differences, slope, drainage and suitability for foundations and roads. The ideal is soils that require low grading costs, coarse soils for roads, and in some locations soils that permit septic tank drainage and low excavation costs. In many tracts, of course, excavation is minimal when a concrete slab is poured rather than a basement dug. No wonder farmland is so desirable.

Institutional Restraints. Other constraints to the free rein of land speculation on the edge of the city are more institutional than physical in nature.

One is the perception of some areas as inferior and even undesirable for residential development. Districts with relatively high percentages of minority group population are often viewed to be outside the principal growth corridors and are therefore less subject to the impact of high intensity raw land speculation. The major thrust of urban growth to the north rather than the south in Greater Atlanta, for example, can be in part explained in this way, as can the retarded growth of South Phoenix, or sectors of any number of other cities.

High interest rates can discourage the long term holding of land for speculation if other investment opportunities promise a higher return, and rising property taxes and other costs can also lessen the attractiveness of holding land. Also, increased "environmental" concern can constrain raw land speculation in spirit, if not in fact. The real, exaggerated or simulated anxieties of speculators and developers about municipally imposed moratoria on water and sewer connections or building permits, or concern about "militant environmentalists, who can play hob with an investment in raw land or in a land-development company" and other so-called "no-growth" attitudes and programs are universally assailed by speculators and developers. In reality, of course, almost all moratoria are short term and related to technical difficulties, such as an adequate present waste treatment capacity, rather than to a long run "no-growth" attitude. In any case, private interests commonly have enough "clout" to eventually overcome such constraints and to assure that speculatively held land and on-going and projected developments are not irreparably damaged or delayed.

FORM—THE PRODUCT OF PROCESS AND TIME

Speculation in land takes place throughout the city, but is particularly intensive in the very center and on the very edge. In the older, more central portions of the city it is expressed ultimately in the private and public urban renewal projects which are in part aimed at sustaining or rejuvenating the value of central city land. Most observe the impact of land speculation more clearly on the periphery of the city where land is transformed from orchard or field into tract developments, giving to the edge of the city a form commonly called "urban sprawl."

Like other value-laden, colorful epithets such as *slurb* (SLum + subURB), *scatteration* and *subtopia,* the term *sprawl* is seldom defined adequately: it is viewed by some as "urban growth exceeding all bounds," by others as "the scattering of urban settlement over the rural landscape" or "the transformation of farms into housing tracts," perspectives which recall the eighteenth century Physiocratic view that all value is derived from the land rather than from the "parasitic" city. Others have described it as "the gluttonous use of land," "a lack of continuity in expansion" or simply used the term rhetorically, condemning sprawl as "the scourge of the '50s and '60s."

To avoid analysis by cliché, it is best to return to a simple definition of sprawl as "scattered residential and commercial developments on the fringe of the urban area" and amend it in recognition that sprawl can take various forms and that it is part of a process—namely, the continuing evolution of an urban landscape—rather than something static. Sprawl is indeed a form of growth, for we see that the sprawl of the 1920s is the compact urban area of the 1970s. The question then is: How long is required for such compaction and what are the real costs of sprawl?

In reality, some sprawl is "compact" from its inception. The lowest order of sprawl and to many the least offensive, according to Harvey and Clark, is low density continuous development on the edge of the city (Figure 2-8). A second form, called ribbon development sprawl, is characterized by compact segments "which extend axially and leave the interstices undeveloped." Perhaps the most obvious form of sprawl is the "leap-frog" or "checkerboard" development of land, the settlement of "discontinuous, although possibly compact, patches of urban use."

Criticisms of Urban Sprawl

Critics of sprawl seem to be particularly offended by the checkerboard variety. One common complaint is that it leads to an inordinate decrease in the amount of land devoted to productive agricultural uses as parcels of land on the fringe are inefficiently used, left unused or otherwise "frozen" for future urban uses as the wave of development sweeps over the fringe. For reasons already discussed these parcels will be by-passed for larger, less expensive parcels farther out.

The high cost and forced timing of providing public services to a distant and thinly populated periphery is another commonly cited drawback to urban sprawl, and indeed a number of recent studies indicate that property tax returns may never pay in the long run for such services and that cities would be wise to buy and hold land as open space instead of allowing its development unless developers are required to provide all services, including parkland, space for schools and sewer lines larger than currently required for their own development.

Also significant are the high costs of police and fire protection. In some places so little service can be provided as to be virtually nonexistent. There is also the cost of providing and maintaining access to the fringe, and low density sprawl is widely viewed as one of the major barriers to a viable mass public transit system. It is, in fact, difficult to accept the

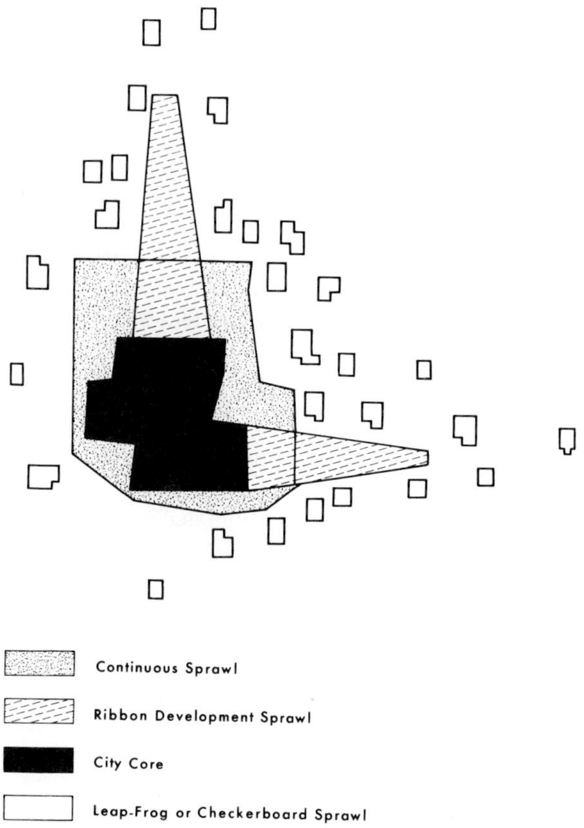

Figure 2–8. Forms of Urban Sprawl.

conclusions of the National Academy of Sciences report that sprawl may be an effective way of holding land from premature development or that subsequent "in-filling" may lead to lower total costs than would have been possible with more planned or orderly development.

While scattered development does indeed leave undeveloped open fields adjacent to new homes in the short run, these spaces ultimately disappear as the urban fabric eventually fills. Over the same period of time, the more distant outer edge of the city puts usable open space farther from the older, more densely settled portions of the city. Access to public lands is also made more difficult by developments which reduce the number of entry points to parks, forests and mountain preserves. In Phoenix, for example, the crowding of homes around the base and up the lower slopes of Camelback Mountain blocks many of the natural access routes to the publicly owned upper slopes just as access to many publicly owned beaches in Florida, California and Hawaii is impeded by intervening private property. Sprawl also affects the inner city by hastening the decline of "established" neighborhoods as the periphery attracts both commercial and residential expansion. In the process, covert housing discrimination on the fringe, "snob zoning" and income differentials tend to restrict the poor and racial minorities to inner city districts.

While sprawl may indeed be due in part to the survival of the frontier philosophy that "there is plenty more where that came from," it is also a fact that the countryside is not only receding from the heart of the city but that the subdivisions of one city are increasingly coming into contact with the subdivisions of another. And small wonder. Around the turn of this century a typical city expanded by about 10 acres for every 1,000 people added to its population. By 1930 about 30 acres were needed, and today 1,000 new residents consume over 200 acres. While Megalopolis, or "Boswash," is still far from being the continually built-up area from Boston to Washington that many suppose it to be, and while "Chipitts" (Chicago through Pittsburgh), "Sansan" (San Francisco-San Diego) and others are even further from coalescence, there are significant weddings taking place between suburbs of towns within portions of these growth corridors. While it is true that 70 percent of the nation's population lives on only 2 percent of the total land area, it is irrelevant that places like Wyoming have the room for an incalculable number of subdivisions. Few can make a living there, even in the foreseeable future.

Classic Sprawl

An instructive illustration of land speculation having an impact on urban form is provided by California's Santa Clara Valley. Situated at the southern end of San Francisco Bay, the valley is there about 20 miles wide, bounded on the east by the grass- and oak-covered Diablo range and on the west by the low redwood-covered Santa Cruz Mountains. The narrowing plain extends south about 25 miles to a point where the two ranges almost converge and then it widens again to a width of about 10 miles.

The rich alluvial soils at the northern end of the valley, an equable mean temperature of under 60 degrees and a growing season of about 300 days first brought commercial farming to the valley during the Gold Rush in the early 1850s. Farm towns slowly grew along the early stage routes, on a navigable slough on the bay's edge and along the railroad line (Figure 2-9). The towns of Palo Alto (Mayfield), Mountain View, Los Gatos, Alviso and Gilroy all date from this period. San Jose, the valley's major city, had been platted in proximity to the Santa Clara mission in 1777 while the area was still under Spanish control.

Both the agricultural base and the towns grew and diversified in the late nineteenth and early twentieth century. But by 1920 San Jose was still a small city of 40,000 and the whole county had but 100,000 population; as late as 1940 the corresponding figures were still only 69,000 and 175,000 (Figure 2-10). After World War II the economic base of the valley expanded rapidly, urban uses gobbled up agricultural land at a furious pace and county population rocketed to over a million by 1970 (Figure 2-11).

The impact of land speculation upon the evolving urbanized area is as undeniable as it is apparent. As the 1970 county master plan points out, "the county's rapid growth has brought with it a fever of land speculation . . . [and] in evolving from a sprinkling of rural towns to a metropolitan area, Santa Clara County played a leapfrog game of land development. Builders bypassed close-in land in favor of cheaper outlying parcels. The system of farm to market roads existing for many years afforded easy if inadequate access." Today, the freeway and arterial network is constantly being improved.

In addition, government policy at all levels facilitated scattered growth: FHA's mortgage insurance, the state's Subdivision Map Act, local government capital improvement programs and permissive zoning policy, as well as the ability of special districts to provide schools, fire protection, sewers and water. The Subdivision Map Act imposes regulations of design within subdivisions but sets neither restrictions nor guidelines for the location of the subdivisions themselves.

A survey in the early 1940s showed that Santa Clara County possessed 70 percent of the Class I or top grade farmland in the entire bay area; by the end of 1956 nearly one-third of that cultivable land was in nonagricultural use. By the early 1960s, developers had scattered their tracts over the entire northern valley; so random was the early growth that not a single square mile was said to have been untouched by at least one subdivision, an invasion that in effect held the remainder of the land as "hostage" for future urban development. Particularly susceptible were the extensive fruit and nut orchards; between 1954 and 1969 orchard acreage in the county dropped from 82,000 to 42,000 acres, vegetable acreage from 25,000 to 15,000 acres. Total cropland harvested declined from 148,000 to 42,000 acres and the total number of farms from 5,000 to 2,300. Newer developments are slowly moving onto the hillsides, but the danger of earthquakes and slumping makes developers wary of possible

Figure 2-9. Santa Clara County and Environs, 1869.

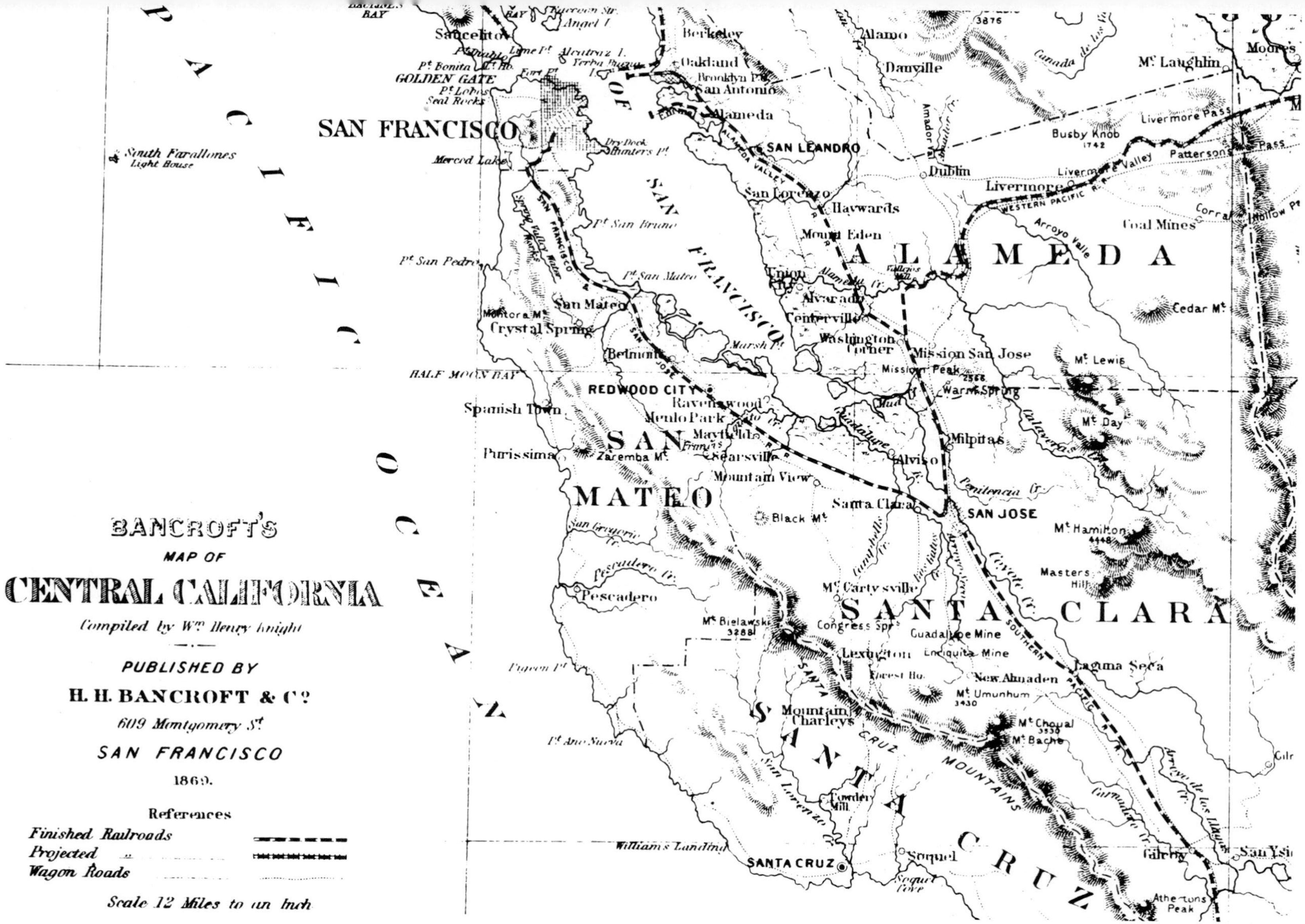

BANCROFT'S
MAP OF
CENTRAL CALIFORNIA
Compiled by Wm. Henry Knight
PUBLISHED BY
H. H. BANCROFT & Co.
609 Montgomery St.
SAN FRANCISCO
1869.
References
Finished Railroads
Projected "
Wagon Roads
Scale 12 Miles to an Inch
PACIFIC OCEAN
SAN FRANCISCO
South Farallones Light House
GOLDEN GATE
Saucelito
Pt. Bonita
Pt. Lobos
Seal Rocks
Merced Lake
Pt. San Pedro
HALF MOON BAY
Spanish Town
Purissima
Montora Mt.
Crystal Spring
San Mateo
Belmont
REDWOOD CITY
Ravenswood
Menlo Park
Mayfield
Searsville
Mountain View
Zaremba Mt.
SAN MATEO
San Gregorio Cr.
Pescadero Cr.
Pescadero
Pigeon Pt.
Pt. Ano Nuevo
Williams Landing
SANTA CRUZ
Soquel
Soquel Cove
San Lorenzo Cr.
Mountain Charleys
SANTA CRUZ MOUNTAINS
Mt. Bielawski 3288
Black Mt.
Santa Clara
SAN JOSE
Alviso
Milpitas
Mission San Jose
Mission Peak 2568
Warm Spring
Washington Corner
Centerville
Alvarado
Union City
Mount Eden
Haywards
San Lorenzo
SAN LEANDRO
Alameda
San Antonio
Brooklyn
Oakland
Berkeley
Alcatraz I.
Yerba Buena I.
Angel I.
Hunters Pt.
Pt. San Bruno
Pt. San Mateo
BAY OF SAN FRANCISCO
ALAMEDA
Alamo
Danville
Amador Val.
Dublin
Livermore
Livermore Valley
Livermore Pass
Busby Knob 1742
Mt. Laughlin
Pattersons Pass
Coal Mines
Corral Hollow
Arroyo Valle
WESTERN PACIFIC R.R.
Cedar Mt.
Mt. Lewis
Mt. Day
Calaveras Cr.
Penitencia Cr.
Mt. Hamilton 4448
Masters Hill
Coyote Cr.
SANTA CLARA
McCartysville
Congress Sprs.
Guadalupe Mine
Enriquita Mine
Lexington
New Almaden
Mt. Umunhum 3430
Mt. Choual 3530
Mt. Bache
Laguna Seca
SOUTHERN PACIFIC R.R.
Gilroy
Athertons Peak
Arroyo de los Llagas Cr.
San Ysidro

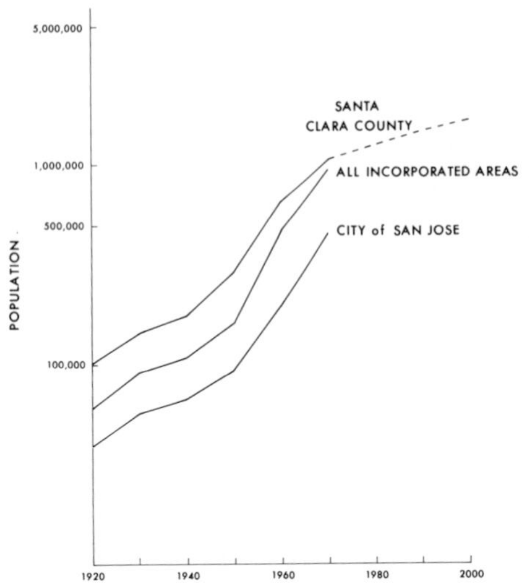

Figure 2-10. Population Growth of Santa Clara County.

future lawsuits. For this and other reasons the valley floor remains the main focus of development, and today, in the northern, more urbanized part of the valley, the "ranchers" enjoy a seller's market due to the shortage of available land.

As early as 1953 the county attempted to counter the loss of agricultural lands with exclusive agricultural zoning—or "greenbelting"—which prohibited subdivisions, factories and stores. The first land so zoned in 1954 was 744 acres of pear orchard, and by 1958, 400,000 acres were covered. The tax advantages of such zoning proved to be minimal, but covered farmers were not assessed for utility development, streets, etc. as they were in other parts of the valley.

In 1965 a new agricultural land preservation scheme was created upon passage of the California Land Conservation Act, or Williamson Bill, designed to help farmers resist development pressure by assessing taxes on the basis of current rather than potential use in return for an agreement to withhold farmlands from development for at least ten years. By June 1973, some 293,000 acres, or 35 percent of total county acreage, were covered; on these lands, the assessed value based on market value would be almost $33 million but it is actually only $7.7 million.

The major limitation of the Williamson Bill is that it was never intended as a device for assuring the permanent retention of agricultural or open land. Instead, it was designed as an interim measure to allow planners time to develop a land use plan and adequate land use controls and still be able to find lands that would be subject to them. Unfortunately, the controls still do not exist and, in addition, by payment of a penalty, the farmer is free to break the agreement and sell his land to a developer. For a number of ranchers it is simply a way to enjoy reduced taxes while holding land until an attractive developer offer materializes. Indeed, the Nader report on California, edited by Fellmeth, suggests that the act has been frequently misused, with much of the land covered under the act actually being land with little development potential, and with strong pressures prevailing on the county not to levy major penalties on ranchers who break the contract. The provisions of the act in reality amount to a substantial subsidy to major landowners by reducing their holding costs. The situation is even worse, says Reilly, in other states such as Florida, Maryland and New Jersey, and he suggests that all such tax relief programs, now in force in about half the states, should be reexamined to assure that public benefits match the substantial tax losses involved.

To William Whyte and many others, "nowhere has the collision between farm and city been so visible and ultimately destructive" as in Santa Clara County. But the processes are, of course, taking place throughout California and the United States. Despite rising wine prices there is growing urban pressure upon the vineyards of the Livermore Valley and the famous Napa and Sonoma valleys at the Northern end of San Francisco Bay. The walnut orchards of nearby Walnut Creek have proven, in Thompson's words, an "irresistible invitation to the residential subdivider [since] they generally offer level land with large, handsome shade trees and good access roads."

In the California "southland," a good share of Orange County's orchards have gone into urban uses, and urban development is in full swing in the San Fernando Valley to the northwest of downtown Los Angeles where small farms and orchards continue to be sold and subdivided. To the east, in Phoenix, whole sec-

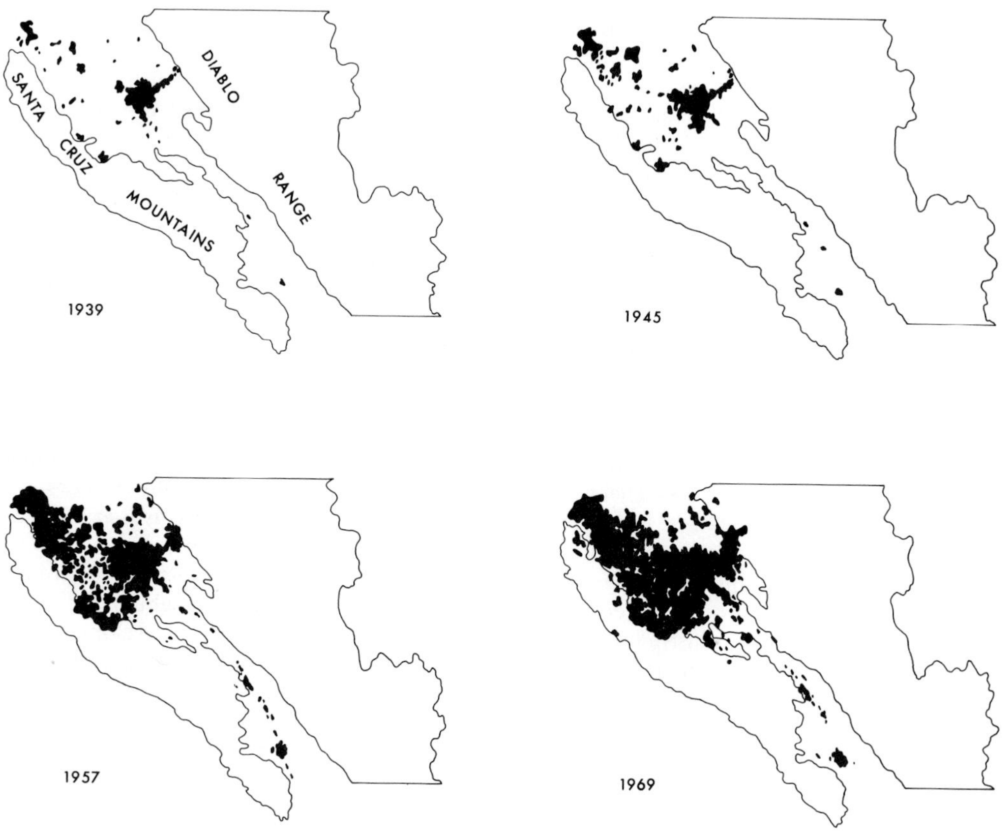

Figure 2-11. Urban Development in Santa Clara County, California.

tions of cotton and dairy lands as well as extensive tracts of desert rapidly go into housing tracts and shopping centers. We have already seen how developers are encroaching upon the horse farms of Lexington, to which we could add the farmlands outside Kansas City, Denver, Dallas or any number of other cities. In the southeast, Greater Atlanta increasingly sprawls out onto the gentle pine- and dogwood-covered Piedmont slopes and small farms of rural Georgia. Chapin and Weiss outline developments in a cluster of North Carolina cities, while Clawson examines the changing form of a number of cities in the Northeast.

Other Perspectives on Sprawl

A great many of those who can afford to, in terms of both monetary and time costs, are moving to the periphery. The detached single family house is still the norm although lot sizes seem to be decreasing and the suburban townhouse and condominium apartment are rapidly gaining in popularity. For those living on the fringe, freeways and car radios have eased the friction of distance while television has, in the words of Los Angeles architect William Pereira, "sweetened the sprawl" because it allows "unsophisticated people" to stay home for entertainment rather than depend on distant stages, theaters and amusement parks.

As Pereira's perception of the "unsophisticated" suggests, there is a sizable group with what Boyce calls a "strong Bohemian bias" for whom peripheral growth is anathema. Vance has characterized them as those "for whom the specialized social milieu of the professional intellectual is important. Artists, architects, designers, planners, musicians and writers, along with the secondary and tertiary occupations stemming from true creativity, all tend to generalize their individual views of the city from the need they experience for a closely settled ingroup of style and 'taste.'" To them, suburbs are "bad" or even "mentally degrading."

But what these sophists call sprawl, or worse, represents uncrowded, gracious living for former residents of older, more crowded neighborhoods and it is debatable whether these new suburbanites view the rise of adjacent subdivisions as abject environmental deterioration. It is all the more surprising, then, that the "sophisticates" have been successful in giving many people a sense of guilt about their choice of a suburban life. The trouble with most of the futuristic cities now on the drawing boards is that the cure to sprawl they promise is probably not very attractive to those who would have to live the high density life. There is no substantial evidence, in Boyce's words, that most people "dislike the suburbs . . . the spaciousness . . . and the automobiles they drive" or conversely, that they would prefer to live closer to the central business district, in denser surroundings or use mass transportation. Such "facts," Boyce says, are "difficult to substantiate and appear inconsistent with the realities of the situation." Even Paolo Soleri, advocate of high density, high rise "arcologies," apparently enjoys life on the low density desert fringe of Phoenix. Taliesin West, the western heart of the Frank Lloyd Wright school, is even farther out of town.

There is also increasing evidence that the optimum pattern for many activities may be dispersion rather than concentration and the evolution of outlying commercial and industrial cores, or "urban realms," further reduces dependence on the central city. As early as 1949 many saw that Los Angeles, now the prototype of the sprawling city, was achieving a pattern of self-sustaining outlying communities. In any case, it seems more objective to consider the outward expansion of the city not as a cancerous growth but as the result of centrifugal economic and social forces and attitudes. It is the result of definable processes which, fortunately, are amenable to change and spatial reorientation. As Harold Mayer sees it, "urban sprawl in itself is not undesirable; it is a manifestation of the urban way of life. . . . The problem is not to reduce urban sprawl but rather to reduce its frictions," avoiding at the same time what Higbee calls the "premature fractionation and haphazard spot development which destroys the whole cloth out of which a more rational and a more beautiful urban design otherwise might have been tailored at a later date."

A compromise solution might well be to restate the goal of continued urban growth as not necessarily the elimination of urban sprawl but the minimization of the public and private costs that do result in order to make sprawl more rational and better able to serve public needs. Influencing the free but not "invisible" hand of raw land speculation would be one of the necessary elements of such goal attainment.

Other Observations

One must obviously wonder to what degree the consumer, as the last link in the land development decision chain, actually influences the urban pattern: the consensus is that most consumers will accept most peripheral locations, so long as the frictions of distance do not overwhelm the advantages of suburban life. The actual choice of residential development sites is almost totally a developer decision that itself reflects the cost, nature, and availability of raw land; homebuyers have little real influence on which parcels are developed and are instead dulled by advertising, seduced by architectural gimmickry, attracted by the landscaping of "commons" and the proximity to an attractive, convenient shopping center, and reassured by the filtering out of undesirables through income and social segregation. It is hardly surprising to learn that the first known radio commercial, in 1922, was a ten minute introduction to the wonders of a real estate development in Queens County, New York. As with conventional tracts, the location of planned communities, including the so-called "new towns" is also a function more of the reality of raw land speculation and of developer profit guidelines than of the strength of easily manipulated consumer decisions.

If both consumer decisions and local government controls over the use of land are easily manipulated, one must either (1) accept it passively as the American system or (2) endeavor to bring the public interest more directly into the reckoning. Either position represents a policy decision. The first is an explicit if tacit approval of existing conditions; the second an explicit call for the creation of effective urban land development controls. Increasing attention is being given today to proposals along the entire spectrum outlined by these two policy extremes.

DIRECTING THE SHAPE OF THE CITY

Although raw land speculation may seem to be exhibiting unusually great vitality today, neither its quick pace, its motivations nor its techniques are as extraordinary as they might seem at first glance. Since the founding of the earliest settlements on the Atlantic coast in the seventeenth century, speculation has been an important element in the development of raw land in the United States and, according to Abernethy "was the most absorbing American enterprise during the later Colonial, the Revolutionary, and the early Republican periods—in those days, the country was run largely by speculators in real estate." A letter writer in 1783 noted, with considerable insight, that "If we review the rise and progress of private fortunes in America, we shall find that a very small proportion of them has arisen or been acquired by commerce, compared with those made by the prudent purchases and management of lands." Land, says Eichler and Kaplan was "a kind of blank check to be cashed as the country grew. Land grabbing became the avocation of many of the country's most prominent citizens," including George Washington, Benjamin Franklin and Patrick Henry.

A new phase began about 1800 as attention focused on "town creation," with speculators hiring agents and opening land offices to sell lots in new "planned communities." As Reps shows us, after about 1840 railroads became major developers of new towns as well, going so far as to set up model prefabricated buildings in some of them. By the mid-nineteenth century "city building" was a standard form of real estate speculation. At the same time speculative towns were being founded—some of which were destined to flourish, many others to stagnate or fail—raw land speculation *within* established cities and on their fringes began to play a role in the evolving shape of the city. Particularly in the late nineteenth and early twentieth centuries came the booms in speculative plattings that followed the introduction of the trolley and led to the creation of the "modern" suburb.

While the United States has never had a national land development policy in the modern sense of the term, we are nonetheless reminded by Gold and Davidoff that "the Headright System of the seventeenth century, the Northwest Ordinance of the eighteen century, and the Homestead Act of the nineteenth century testify to continuing governmental efforts [to utilize] the public land for socially beneficial purposes [and that] the social planning of land use, therefore, has early and ample precedent in American life." The fact that land speculators, including wealthy individuals and influential companies, gained title to immense tracts of the public domain amply illustrates that the libertarian social and economic theories guiding the distribution of the national patrimony were easily subverted to serve primarily private interests.

We are now slowly drawing away from the land ethic which evolved in the nineteenth century—that the only function of land was to enable its owner to make money. Today, Bosselman and Callies can instead call attention to a developing reaction, fostered by conservationists, that land should be viewed as a resource rather than a commodity. At the same time, however, because this nascent view "ignores the crucial importance of our constitutional right to own land and to buy and sell it freely," they feel it is essential to view land as *both* a resource and a commodity. On the other hand, the report of the Task Force on Land Use and Urban Growth, edited by Reilly, advocates a reinterpretation of the so-called "takings clause" of the Constitution, arguing that many Supreme Court precedents are now anachronistic and that the ownership of land carries no inherent right to its development.

Within the context of our twentieth century land use regulations, the idea that land is a resource as well as a commodity is a novel one. Planning and zoning ordinances, for instance, came to be widely accepted in the speculative 1920s by real estate interests precisely because their purpose was to maximize and maintain the value of land as a commodity. No attempt was made to conserve land for particular purposes or to direct it into a specific use; instead, the concern was to insure that land could not be used in such a way as to depreciate the value of neighboring land. Zoning, in short, was meant to protect land speculators from one another.

Today land speculators still advocate the "commodity" ethic and the "free market" mechanism that uses zoning as a tool of speculation. At the same time, they use the American flag as a patriotic blindfold and the specter of "socialism" or worse to screen out viable and proper, but unwanted, alternatives that might threaten self-serving interpretations of how the private enterprise system is meant to operate. The general public, politicians and government officials at all levels are deluged by the views and prejudices of speculators, developers and their agents as disseminated by lobby groups and friendly newspaper editors.

Ironically, at the same time both the public and politicians are implored to leave "the forces of the free marketplace" intact, speculators are actively engaged in promoting publicly financed transportation improvements, utility extensions into the periphery, favorable zoning decisions that will result in windfall profits and the acquisition of the public domain—either by favorable purchases or by land swaps. Somehow, it is deemed acceptable to call for public investment when it promises to serve private interests, but "un-American" to allow the public to protect its investment or recoup a share of the profits. Increasingly, however, the public is becoming aware of its heretofore abused rights, and development policies are being examined and proposed at the national, state and local level that will serve the public and preserve the national patrimony.

Proposed Controls—from Soft to Hard

We have already seen that existing land use controls—zoning ordinances and subdivision controls—do not have a significant effect upon the agents that determine the suburban land conversion process. Present controls in essence are much more cosmetic than structural, able to impose only standards of development rather than establish an "optimal" set of spatial relationships within the metropolitan area. Studies of the relationship of public policy to fringe area development typically conclude that the extent to which suburban growth has been guided toward public objectives is virtually nil. The usual consensus, however, is that "new policy mixes" and a better understanding of the process of suburban growth hold some hope for the future. The co-authors of one of the most recent volumes on land use, *Modernizing Urban Land Policy,* (ed. Clawson) are, for example, in substantial agreement that "if cities are to be developed or rebuilt to serve a broader constituency, there must be both procedural and substantive improvements in many urban land programs and a better coordination of public and private actions." Similar conclusions and recommendations are at the heart of numerous other reports.

The range of existing land use control proposals runs from the decidedly "soft" if important recommendation to establish systematic reporting of land transactions to the "hard" measures of property tax reformation, the public ownership of land in the path of development and the controlled timing of development.

Information Retrieval Systems. At the present time, opinion is a powerful agent in the land market both because land prices are a reflection of estimates of the future and because so little factual information exists about the present. Gaffney, for one, challenges us to try to find a simple statistic—like the number of lots subdivided annually, trends in land prices, the number of unrecorded and illegally subdivided urban sites, the acreages in various stages of urbanization, and so forth. As a consequence of the lack of such information billions of dollars worth of land exchanges hands without any party to the transaction really having enough facts adequately to support decisions. For lack of information, land that is ripe for development may remain vacant and vice versa, placing undue pressure on lands deemed to be in the "path" of urban growth and thereby further skewing the land development pattern, the shape of the city.

Public Service Provision as a Spatial Control. Since both raw land speculation and land development demonstrably follow either existing or proposed "urban umbilical cords"—notably the transportation and utilities ties—it is possible to control the expansion of the city through manipulating the location and/or availability of these lifelines. Refusing to extend water lines and trunk sewers or to improve roads until certain vacant lands on the periphery are developed could significantly affect the area of growth. To those who would be adversely affected by such controls this is decried as a no-growth policy: witness the present outcry from speculators and developers in response to an increasing number of short term building moratoria around the country that are required because of inadequate existing water and sewer capabilities.

Controls over transportation and utility extensions could promote whatever the community determines is "orderly growth" and strengthen local finances, sorely strained in most areas from having to match new subdivisions with parks, schools and public utilities. In Santa Clara County, for example, it has been proposed that cities provide streets and utilities selectively in order to control the timing and location of developments, ideally providing services only to areas near existing developments. In Ramapo, New York, permission for new developments is tied to the existence of a given level of services. In Phoenix, on the other hand, analysis in late 1973 of the 1974-1979 capital improvement program revealed that there are already 13 sewer lines in the program that conflict with the city's 1990 Comprehensive Plan and 11 other projects are "premature" in terms of the plan.

While this is not the context in which to outline all the advantages and drawbacks of any measure, restrictions on utility provision could mean that not enough land on the fringe would be available to meet actual housing needs, thus artificially boosting the value of developable land and increasing housing costs. Given the holes in most urban fabrics, this is unlikely. A second danger is that the influencing of local politicians and planning and zoning officials would probably be intensified. A third problem is pointed out by Clawson: "[T]he wisdom to plan public improvements in this way and the courage to enforce such plans would require a substantially higher level of performance than urban or metropolitan public service agencies typically now have." On balance, however, there is evidence that effective control over roads, utilities and other public services expansions would have a more positive than negative impact. Evidence from Europe, in particular, indicates that such controls can in fact work.

Tax Reforms. An administratively simpler tool for altering the impact of land speculation and directing land use would be to reduce or nullify the advantageous treatment currently accorded land speculators by both income and property tax codes. Not only could the capital gains provision, for example, be modified, but communities could also tax vacant land more heavily and structures less heavily. The supply of land actually sold is limited in part because the owners know that the tax cost of holding land is lower than the tax cost of holding other kinds of assets they might acquire with money they would get from selling the land. Tax codes, in short, operate to reinforce spatial assymetry in development by influencing the land retention decision.

Effective Planning Tools. At the very least there is a need to strengthen existing zoning ordinances and subdivision controls. As it now stands they are more an unsettling force than tools for orderly growth, since zoning favors are for sale, regulations are often so complicated and time-consuming as to be unenforceable and other agency decisions are often against the long run interests of the metropolitan region.

Some, such as Ledermann, an official of a builders' lobby, consider "planned area developments" and "clustering" as a "new approach" to the problem of sprawl. In reality, of course, these increasingly popular proposals—which allow a relatively free choice of building types and densities so long as the overall development meets required zoning densities—represent design changes, not structural, spatial controls on the location of developments. They do little or nothing to reduce either land speculation or the various forms of sprawl that accompany it. Indeed, just the opposite is sometimes the case, and Bosselman, for one, even fears that "the monotonous subdivision of the 1950's is being replaced by the monotonous planned unit development of the 1970's."

Public Land Assembly. While tax reforms offer some promise as a land use variable, it is very likely that even strengthened planning and zoning regulations and any restrictions on the provision of public services would be quickly subverted to the will of the agents of land speculation. Effective land use control thus suggests the need for some more "radical" departures from the present passive, permissive role of government. The West European experience, demonstrated by Great Britain, Germany and Sweden, indicates that public land assembly can be an effective land use control and also allow some recouping of publicly created land values that otherwise end in the pocket of the land speculator or developer as windfall or unearned gains.

The weight of existing evidence shows that true public control over raw land speculation and the pattern of land use is achieved only when a public agency can acquire land from present owners, hold it, and sell it at a time and in locations and quantities that foster orderly growth. All other controls can be evaded. One suggested mechanism for public land assembly and control is a system by which states (or state-chartered agencies) would buy land in the path of urban growth with the help of federal loans or grants; make detailed plans for its use; put in the streets, utilities and other public facilities; and then sell the land to private developers who would be obliged to adhere to the plan.

In Europe, public land acquisition is normally justified both as a control on urban sprawl and for its value in promoting the development of underutilized areas. In the United States, given the limited public awareness of the dominant and vested interests in the raw land market, there is widespread agreement that it is impossible to consider public land assembly a viable proposal at the present time. Yet, paradoxically, we do have public land assembly in central city urban renewal projects and this is accepted—even sought—because it *aids* private central city land speculation. It is in large part because public ownership of land on the periphery could reduce gains by special interests and instead profit the public that it is bitterly opposed. On the other hand, it would not be surprising to find, in the long run, that public land ownership on the edge of the city would become a tool of private speculation as it is in the central city.

Purchase of Development Rights. This land use control involves the public acquisition of the development rights to a parcel, giving compensation to the landowner for foregoing development. The public, in effect, pays for the assurance of continued open space. As a land use control tool it is, of course, far from revolutionary, since easements are widely used throughout the country.

The Reilly report, on the other hand, calls for an end to the landowner's traditionally presumed right to develop his property regardless of the cost to the public in scenic, ecological and cultural assets. Where orderly development is involved, the report notes, "a mere loss in land value should never be justification for invalidating the regulation of land use"—we must accept the reality that development rights are allocated to land by society, not by ownership, since the development potential of any land results from the actions of society.

Metropolitan Government. Whatever types of controls may be considered viable for a given area, the consensus is that the most effective level on which to implement them is the regional or metropolitan scale. Unfortunately, at the same time as cities have grown, numerous new local governments and special districts have been created. As a consequence, "the governmental process for dealing with growth has been scissored into bits and pieces," says the American Institute of Architects, and energy and resolve ". . . are dissipated in an almost infinite chain of separate and conflicting consents which have to be negotiated."

The underlying rationale behind metropolitan or regional government is the coordination of state, county and local government responses to urban expansion to provide the forum and focus for areawide land use controls. Far from being an authoritarian regional government, as critics charge, metro government, according to its advocates, would enhance "democracy" by putting regional decisions in the hands of a single group of officials who would act "in a fishbowl," under far closer public scrutiny than is possible with the existing potpourri of local governments and the special districts that few people even know exist.

On a more limited basis, Clawson has suggested growth coordination under planned development zones or suburban development districts whereby "various local government and private interests, subject to some regulation by the state, would be empowered to form special districts, with very wide powers over all aspects of the suburbanization process. Such powers would have a limited time duration and the districts would pass out of existence once an area were reasonably well settled." The basic notion is being tested in suburban Bucks County, Pennsylvania, where it is hoped to attract as much as possible of the county's anticipated growth to "planned development areas."

Whyte (among others) has called attention to the fact that there are many local efforts by private and public groups to control sprawl and save open space but that "each group is going at the problem from its special point of view, indeed without even finding out what the other groups are up to." The "quiet revolution in land use control" that Bosselman and Callies describe is the slow overthrowing of this *ancien régime,* this "feudal system under which the entire pattern of land development has been controlled by thousands of individual local governments." The tools of the revolution are new laws that share the common theme of incorporating some degree of state or regional participation in major decisions that affect the use of an increasingly limited supply of conveniently located and readily developable land.

Alternatives

There is really but a single decision to be made: Whether to control the impact of land speculation on urban form to the benefit of the general public, or to allow private interests to continue to direct the growth pattern of the American city as a *by-product* of serving their own goals. To date the momentum is still heavily in the direction of no effective controls with private interests dominant.

This continued imbalance between the impact of public and private interests is very likely in large measure due to the fact that the general public is only vaguely aware of the land use problem and of the forces and agents behind it and almost totally unaware of the alternatives available. Faltermeyer has found that not only does the majority of Americans not recognize the suburban explosion as a major physical and social occurrence—or, in his terms, "threat"—but that to many people "the steps to deal with that threat are certain to sound radical." Special interest groups actively keep this "radical" viewpoint instilled in the public mind by labeling controls as anathema to "everything that made this country great" and by ignoring or downgrading the positive contribution of public investments to urban growth and private profits. A number of politicians are closely tied to the private interests that oppose land use controls, but even intelligent and honest legislators, report Gold and Davidoff, "feel that if the need were urgent, the public outcry would be louder. And the public does not cry more, largely because it does not know positively that things could be helped rather easily."

Whether through sheer persistence or complicity, special interest groups commonly dominate the legislative processes that determine land use policy. Lobbying by land speculation and development interests, with their close ties to city councils and planning commissions and to state and national legislators assures the primacy of their viewpoint and, in most cases, the chosen policy is no policy at all or watered-down legislation designed to block truly effective programs.

The heavy hand of private interests is evident in a number of "independent," potentially respectable studies. Consider the following case of contrasts: While the American Institute of Architect's National Policy Task Force "would change the 'ground rules' that now shape, and distort the shape of American communities; create a new and useful scale for planning and building in urban areas; and commit the nation to a major land acquisition policy to guide development in and around key urban centers," the 1972 report of the Land Use Subcommittee of the Advisory Committee to the federal Department of Housing and Urban Development came to some strikingly different conclusions. The subcommittee, a number of whose members have either direct or indirect ties with real estate interests, seriously questions "general beliefs about both the impact of and the benefits accruing to the land speculator . . ." and suggests that because "land development problems—while important—are not yet crucial, this Committee is hesitant, based on its brief reconnaissance, to recommend 'national' policy for urban growth or land development." Calling the European experience "irrelevant," the committee doubted "that it would be possible to define a meaningful growth policy, given the heterogenic character of the nation's population and the resultant pluralism of its institutions."

Others admit to the role of raw land speculation in influencing urban form, but argue that there should be no controls imposed. One such study, by Elias and Gillies, viewing land as a commodity and founded on a number of debatable premises and examples, concludes that the control of land speculation and the acquisition of land by public bodies is not only unnecessary but even harmful. But critics of raw land speculation contend that speculation, contrary to supporting a land market, as Elias and Gillies imply, destroys the marketability of large areas of land by pricing them out of the reach of immediate users, limits competition by holding a large part of the land supply off the market, and even channels capital away from productive investment.

Conclusions

The consensus of the available literature on land use planning and control is that it would clearly be desirable to create public land use policies that closely coincide with both public and private interests. In the absence of some such Solomonic solution, however, it is highly unlikely that the conflict between disparate goals—orderly growth and short run profits—can or will be reconciled without considerable controversy. Land use policy, in the words of Haar, is "always an uneasy marriage between the market mechanism and the dictates of public policy [and] many of the conflicts over the ordering of land uses stem from such differing outlooks." Even if there were consensus that land use controls will enhance long run land values more than a myriad of short run decisions, land speculators must essentially operate in the limited time frame of adult life rather than in terms of long run urban growth where the life of a city is measured in centuries. To paraphrase John Maynard Keynes, "In the long run, we are all dead" and even the large corporately owned speculative developments have essentially short run estimated dates of completion. The challenge to public policy is to make the short term interests of speculators coincide with the long range interests of the general public.

After reviewing the very real impact of speculation in raw land on the urban fringe, we consider controls over the spatial impact of speculation a necessity. The alternative of continued inaction—the "do nothing approach"—promises an even more disordered landscape than now exists, higher costs of public services, continued environmental deterioration and the continued exclusion of the poor in general, and the black in particular, from the benefits of urban life. To many, the most serious consequence of sprawl is indeed social and not spatial, for as land prices rise, the cost of housing rises even faster. Snob (large lot) zoning on the periphery further precludes the bulk of America's low income families from enjoying the real benefits of American suburban life.

Yet in England and parts of Canada, for example, the greenbelt "antisprawl" policies in practice have apparently been instrumental in inflating land costs, making even middle income housing quite expensive. The course to be charted must clearly run between the Scylla of unrestrained sprawl and the Charybdis of constriction.

THE GEOGRAPHICAL PERSPECTIVE: A SUMMARY

While the urban fringe may seem but a fortuitous assemblage of unrelated developments, a closer look reveals a rudimentary spatial order to what we call sprawl. Those who would influence that order must of necessity be ready to influence the underlying series of actions or processes if they are to affect beneficially the structure of the city. We know from past studies, for example, that modifications in personal transportation systems influence the range of individual movement, particularly the important journey to work, and play a considerably greater role than physical site features in shaping the city. In fact, transportation can properly be viewed as the primary force behind the creation of an urban frame—a geographical framework within which raw land speculation and ultimate development takes place.

On the other hand, although the changing modes of transportation play a major role in the evolution of urban form and its lateral extent, they ultimately become more *permissive* than *determinative* in the actual land pattern that evolves within the urban frame. The automobile, for example, does not *determine* that there will be sprawl but does *permit* lateral expansion of the city, especially when new roads and freeways are constructed. Other forces become dominant in the determination of where development takes place within the broad area served by transportation. These forces we have discussed as the speculative agents, catalysts and constraints to the land conversion process.

While the entire urban frame provides the setting for raw land speculation, the decisions by agriculturalists and intervening landowners to release raw land to developers determines the timing, the sequence and the location of subdivision and ultimate development on the fringe. In this way many active development zones are created within which residential development takes place. Typically, the number of individual development zones decreases in number and proximity to one another with increasing distance from the city (Figure 2-12).

Suburbanization, or sprawl, is clearly not the result of a relatively aimless or wholly random process. While it is indeed highly doubtful that any single participant in the

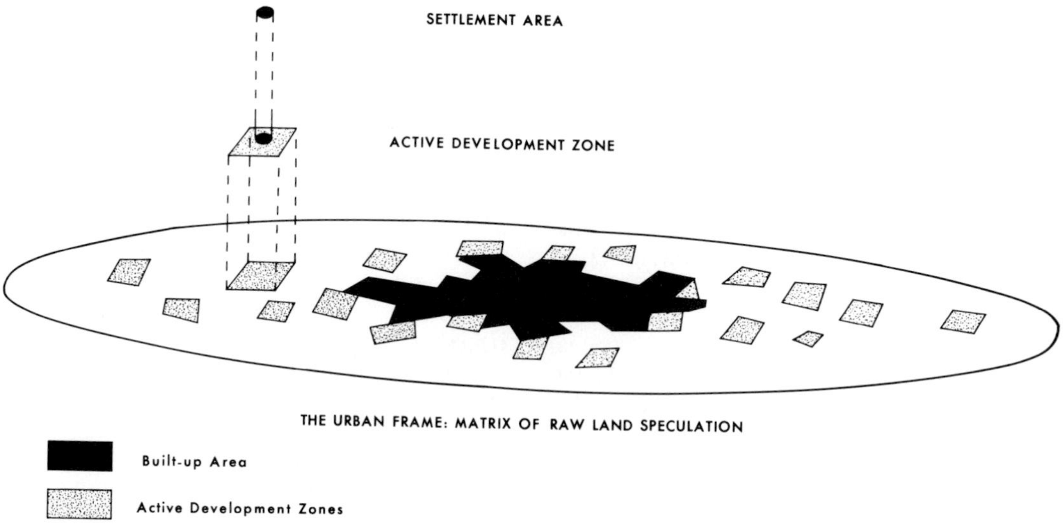

Figure 2-12. The Nesting of Dynamic Processes.

suburban growth process actually chose the pattern which has resulted, the pattern itself can be comprehended. The typical sequence of development seems to run from a nearly random settlement pattern at first to a highly predictable one later on (Figure 2-13). After the first expansion into formerly nonurban zones, development continues not so much by random additions as by clustered growth, a finding that sustains Kaiser's earlier discovery of "a strong positive association between the amount of contiguous recent residential subdivision and whether a parcel of land undergoes subdivision." In terms of the timing of development, Blumenfeld compares it to the slow and powerful groundswell of a wave: first, a period of slow development, followed by one of rapid growth, then a leveling off period and finally a decrease in development.

Nested within the active development zones delineated by speculative decisions and actions are distinct settlement areas—the different socioeconomic neighborhoods that are occupied by individuals in terms of their ability to pay for a certain type of development in a certain location. Here the consumer plays his active role, determining which of the existing developed zones he finds appealing and can afford. It is at this level also that racial restrictions upon mobility operate.

Controls or incentives designed to influence the direction and extent of urban land development must acknowledge the impact of speculation in raw land. Short term or socially undesirable "solutions" such as snob zoning and urban "no-growth" policies are negative policies, in addition to denying a person's aspirations to better his physical and social environment.

In responding to the direct impact of land speculation upon urban form, the best solutions at present seem to lie not with attempts to stop

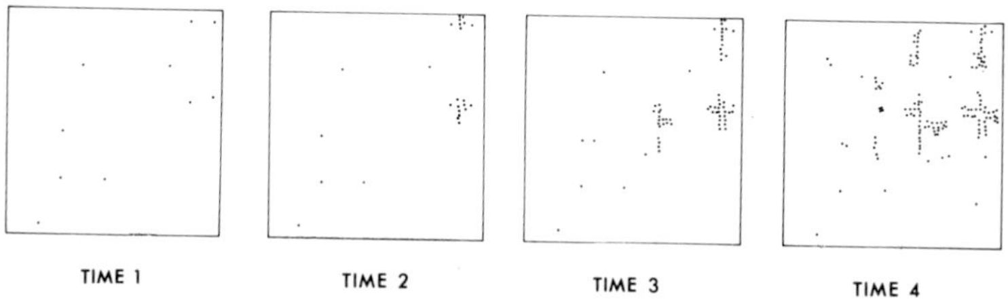

Figure 2-13. Hypothetical Sequence of Suburban Fringe Settlements. (Source: J. Hudson.)

urban growth, but rather with efforts to slow it down and to modify the negative effects of uncontrolled land speculation, yet at the same time providing people with housing at different prices and at diverse locations within the framework of the private enterprise system. The focus of attention should not be so much on sprawl per se as upon the frictions and diseconomies that accompany unfettered land speculation and the consequent sprawl. The need, in short, is to rationalize the man-to-land relationship, not to attempt to halt it; to manipulate in the positive sense of that word the forces that shape our urban areas; and to plan for the rational accommodation of normal residential growth.

The goal of striking some sort of long range symbiotic balance between increasing numbers of urban dwellers and their physical and social milieu is being increasingly stated and supported, if not yet realized. To date, the national, state, regional and local urban growth policies being outlined to attain that goal are of widely divergent form and content. Regardless of their origin, those policies that aim to be legitimate attempts to bring the relationship of man to his environment into something approaching a balance will have to react to the reality of land speculation as one of the major determinants of urban form and the direction of future urban growth.

There are neither instant descriptions and analyses nor instant solutions to persistent social, spatial and economic difficulties. Hence, our examination must be viewed as an interim report of a highly focused and derivative nature. It is also a call for large-scale field studies of the impact of land speculation upon urban form throughout the country, indeed the world. The goal is an inductively derived understanding of all the processes and variables that affect the shape of the city, so that the good can be retained, the bad removed and the ugly transmogrified.

Aristotle felt that "men come together in cities in order to live, but they remain there in order to live the good life." While this good life is still unrealized for millions, and although influencing the impact of speculation in land will not solve all "urban ills," such influences could at least have a measurable positive impact, both spatially and socially, and help assure the attainment of that most basic of underlying urban goals, the persistence of the city as the locus of the "good life."

BIBLIOGRAPHY

Abernathy, Thomas Perkins. *From Frontier to Plantation in Tennessee.* Chapel Hill: University of North Carolina Press, 1932.

Adams, John S. "Directional Bias In Intra-Urban Migration." *Economic Geography* 45, 4 (October 1969): 302-23.

American Institute of Architects. "The First Report of the National Policy Task Force." *Memo,* Special Issue, (January 1972), pp. 1-12.

American Society of Planning Officials. *Problems of Zoning and Land-Use Regulation.* Research Report No. 2. Washington, D.C.: National Commission on Urban Problems, 1968.

Berkman, Herman G. "Decentralization and Blighted Vacant Land." *Land Economics* 32, 3 (August 1956).

Blake, Peter. *God's Own Junkyard.* New York: Holt, Rinehart and Winston, 1964.

Blumenfeld, Hans. "The Tidal Wave of Metropolitan Expansion." *Journal of American Institute of Planners* 20 (Winter 1954): 3-14.

Boal, Frederick W. "Urban Growth and Land Value Patterns: Government Influences." *The Professional Geographer* 22, 2 (March 1970): 79-82.

Borchert, John R. and Frank E. Horton. "Geography and Urban Public Policy." In *Geographical Perspectives and Urban Problems,* pp. 1-24. Washington, D.C.: National Academy of Sciences, 1973.

Bosselman, Fred and David Callies. *The Quiet Revolution in Land Use Control.* Prepared for the Council on Environmental Quality. Washington, D.C.: U.S. Government Printing Office, 1971.

Boyce, Ronald R. "Myth Versus Reality in Urban Planning." *Land Economics* 39 (august 1963): 241-51.

Brodsky, Harold. "Land Development and the Expanding City." *Annals of the Association of American Geographers* 63, 2 (June 1973): 159-66.

Broek, J.O.M. *The Santa Clara Valley, California: A Study in Landscape Changes.* Utrecht: Oosthoek's Vitgebers-Maatig, 1932.

Bucks County Planning Commission. "The Urban Fringe: Techniques for Guiding the

Development of Bucks County." *Land-Use Controls Quarterly* 4, 1 (Winter 1970): 34-42.

Chapin, F. Stuart, Jr. and Shirley F. Weiss. *Factors Influencing Land Development.* An Urban Studies Research Monograph. Chapel Hill: Institute for Research in Social Science, University of North Carolina, in cooperation with the Bureau of Public Roads, U.S. Department of Commerce, 1962.

——. *Urban Growth Dynamics.* New York: John Wiley & Sons, Inc., 1962.

Clawson, Marion. "Suburban Development Districts: A Proposal for Better Urban Growth." *Journal of American Institute of Planners* 26 (May 1960): 69-83.

——. "Urban Sprawl and Speculation in Urban Land." *Land Economics* 28 (1962): 99-111.

——. *Suburban Land Conversion in the United States: An Economic and Governmental Process.* Baltimore: Johns Hopkins Press, 1971.

——. ed. *Modernizing Urban Land Policy.* Baltimore: Johns Hopkins University Press, 1973.

Clawson, Marion and Peter Hall. *Planning and Urban Growth: An Anglo-American Comparison.* Baltimore: Johns Hopkins Press, 1973.

Clawson, Marion; R. Burnell Held; and Charles H. Stoddard. *Land for the Future.* Baltimore: Johns Hopkins Press, 1960.

Cornick, Philip H. *Premature Subdivision and its Consequences.* New York: Columbia University Press, 1938.

Donnelly, Thomas F.; F. Stuart Chapin, Jr.; and Shirley F. Weiss. *A Probabilistic Model for Residential Growth.* Chapel Hill: Center for Urban and Regional Studies, Institute for Research in Social Science, University of North Carolina, in cooperation with Bureau of Public Roads, U.S. Department of Commerce.

Eichler, Edward P. and Marshall Kaplan. *The Community Builders.* Berkeley: University of California Press, 1967.

Elias, C.E., Jr. and James Gillies. "Some Observations on the Role of Speculators and Speculation in Land Development." *UCLA Law Review* 12 (March 1965): 789-99.

Epstein, Bart J. "The Trading Function." In *Metropolis on the Move: Geographers Look at Urban Sprawl,* edited by Jean Gottmann and Robert A. Harper, pp. 93-101. New York: Wiley, 1967.

Faltermeyer, Edmund K. "Controlling the Suburban Explosion." In *Redoing America: A Nationwide Report on How to Make Our Cities and Suburbs Livable.* New York: Harper & Row, Inc., 1968.

Fellman, Jerome D. "Pre-Building Growth Patterns in Chicago." *Annals of the Association of American Geographers* 47 (March 1957): 59-82.

Fellmeth, Robert C., ed. *Power and Land in California.* New York: Grossman, 1973. (Originally published by Center for Study of Responsive Law, Washington, D.C., 1971, as *Power and Land in California: The Ralph Nader Task Force Report on Land Use in the State.)*

Fisher, Ernest M. and Raymond F. Smith. *Land Subdividing and the Rate of Utilization.* Ann Arbor: University of Michigan, School of Business Administration, 1932.

Forstall, Richard L. *Changes in Land Area for Larger Cities, 1950-1970; 1972 Municipal Year Book.* Washington, D.C.: International City Management Association, 1972.

Gaffney, M. Mason. "Urban Expansion—Will It Ever Stop?" In *Land: The Yearbook of Agriculture,* pp. 503-52. Washington, D.C.: U.S. Department of Agriculture, 1958.

Gates, Paul W. *History of Public Land Development.* Washington, D.C.: U.S. Government Printing Office, 1968.

Gold, Niel N. and Paul Davidoff. "The Supply and Availability of Land for Housing for Low- and Moderate-Income Families." In *The Report of the President's Committee on Urban Housing; Technical Studies,* pp. 288-409. Washington, D.C.: U.S. Government Printing Office, 1968.

Griffith, T.L.C. "Evolution and Duplication of a Pattern of Urban Growth." *Economic Geography* 41 (April 1965): 113-56.

Haar, Charles M. *Land-Use Planning: A Casebook on the Use, Misuse, and Re-Use of Urban Land.* Boston: Little, Brown and Co., 1959.

Harvey, R.O. and W.A.V. Clark. "The Nature and Economics of Urban Sprawl." *Land Economics* 41 (1965): 1-9.

Higbee, Edward. "Agricultural Land on the Urban Fringe." In *Metropolis On The Move: Georgraphers Look At Urban Sprawl,* edited by Jean Gottmann and Robert A. Harper, pp. 57-66. New York: Wiley, 1967.

Hoyt, Homer. *One Hundred Years of Land Values in Chicago.* Chicago: University of Chicago Press, 1933.

Hudson, John. "Density and Pattern in Suburban Fringes." *Annals of the Association of American Geographers* 63, 1 (March 1973): 28-39.

Kaiser, Edward J. "Locational Decision Factors in a Producer Model of Residential Development." *Land Economics* 44 (August 1968): 351-62.

Krueger, Ralph R. "The Rural-Urban Fringe Taxation Problem: A Case Study of Louth Township." *Land Economics* 33 (August 1957): 264-69.

Ledermann, Robert C. "The City as a Place to Live." In *Metropolis on the Move: Geographers Look at Urban Sprawl,* edited by Jean Gottmann and Robert A. Harper, pp. 84-92. New York: Wiley, 1967.

Manvel, Allen D. *Trends in Value of Real Estate and Land: 1956 to 1966.* Research Report No. 12. Washington, D.C.: National Commission on Urban Problems, 1968.

Mayer, Harold. "The Pull of Land and Space." In *Metropolis on the Move: Geographers Look at Urban Sprawl,* edited by Jean Gottmann and Robert A. Harper, pp. 23-35. New York: Wiley, 1967.

McBride, George A. and Marion Clawson. "Negotiation and Land Conversion." *Journal of American Institute of Planners* 36 (January 1970): 22-29.

Milgram, Grace. *The City Expands: A Study of the Conversion of Land from Rural to Urban Use, Philadelphia, 1945-62.* Washington, D.C.: U.S. Government Printing Office, 1967.

Morrill, Richard L. "Expansion of the Urban Fringe: A Simulation Experiment." *Papers, Regional Science Association* 15 (1965): 185-99.

Mortimore, M.J. "Landownership and Urban Growth in Bradford and its Environs in the West Riding Conurbation, 1850-1950," *Transactions* (Institute of British Geographers) 46 (March 1969): 105-19.

National Academy of Sciences, National Academy of Engineering. *Urban Growth and Land Development: The Land Conversion Process.* Washington, D.C. National Academy of Sciences, 1972.

Reilly, William K., ed. *The Use of Land: A Citizens' Policy Guide to Urban Growth.* New York: Thomas Y. Crowell, 1973.

Reps, John W. *The Making of Urban America: A History of City Planning in the United States.* Princeton: Princeton University Press, 1965.

Sargent, Charles A. *Urbanization of a Rural County.* Research Bulletin 859. Lafayette, Ind.: Purdue University, 1970.

Schmid, A. Allan. *Converting Land from Rural to Urban Uses.* Baltimore: Johns Hopkins Press, 1968.

Singleton, Gregory H. "The Genesis of Suburbia: A Complex of Historical Trends." In *The Urbanization of the Suburbs,* edited by Louis H. Masotti and Jeffrey K. Hadden, pp. 29-50. Beverly Hills: Sage Publications, 1973.

Stanford Environmental Law Society. *San Jose: Sprawling City. A Report on Land Use Policies and Practices in San Jose, California.* Stanford: Stanford Law School, 1971.

Thompson, K. "Location and Relocation of a Tree Crop–English Walnuts in California," *Economic Geography* 37 (1961): 133-49.

Time, Inc. "Land–A Special Issue." *House and Home* 18, 2 (August 1960).

Tunnard, Christopher and Boris Pusharev. *Man Made America, Chaos or Control.* New Haven: Yale University Press, 1963.

Vance, James E., Jr. *Georgraphy and Urban Evolution in the San Francisco Bay Area.* Berkeley: Institute of Governmental Studies, 1964.

Ward, David. *Cities and Immigrants: A Geography of Change in Nineteenth Century America.* New York: Oxford University Press, 1971.

Warner, Sam Bass, Jr. *The Urban Wilderness: A History of the American City.* New York: Harper and Row, 1972.

Weiss, Shirley F.; Thomas G. Donnelly; and Edward J. Kaiser. "Land Value and Land Development Influence Factors: An Analytical Approach for Examining Policy Alternatives." *Land Economics* 42 (May 1966): pp. 230-33.

Weiss, Shirley F.; J.E. Smith; E.J. Kaiser; and K.B. Kenney. *Residential Developer Decision–A Focused View of the Urban Growth Process.* Chapel Hill: Center for Urban and Regional Research, University of North Carolina, 1966.

Wheaton, William L.C. "Public and Private Agents of Change in Urban Expansion." In

Melvin M. Webber et al., *Explorations Into Urban Structure,* pp. 154-96. Philadelphia: University of Pennsylvania Press, 1964.

Whyte, William H., Jr. "Urban Sprawl." In Editors of Fortune, *The Exploding Metropolis,* pp. 115-39. Garden City, N.Y.: Doubleday Anchor, 1958.

Yearwood, Richard M. "Accepted Controls of Land Subdivision." *Journal of Urban Law* 45 (1967): 217-57.

——. "Land Subdivision and Development: American Attitudes on Land Subdivision and Its Controls." *American Journal of Economics and Sociology* 29, 2 (April 1970); 113-26.

Chapter 3

Abandoned Housing

Michael J. Dear
McMaster University

INTRODUCTION*

What is happening to our cities? Each year some new trend or problem appears to cloud our understanding of urban growth and change. It has become increasingly difficult, for example, to evaluate the significance of the continuing decentralization of population and employment activities to the suburbs, or to cope with the weakening economic base of the central city, or to control the rise of antisocial behavior in metropolitan regions as a whole. An even more complicated task is to recognize the overall significance of these trends in combination. We may even be witnessing, in slow motion, a major change in the function and structure of the city.

One of the most prominent contemporary symptoms of change in cities is the phenomenon of abandoned housing, but very little seems to be known about it. One report will conclude that it is a sign that the housing market is working efficiently, while a second will argue that it manifests a complete breakdown of the market mechanism. The former study may recommend accelerating the pace of abandonment, while the latter advocates a reversal of the trend. Such confusion derives, in large part at least, from the dearth of information on abandonment. For example, in spite of a number of excellent recent studies, very little is known about what actually happens in a neighborhood which is subject to abandonment. At the other end of the geographic scale, hardly anything is known about the national extent of abandoned housing. And, finally, what is most lacking at present is a comprehensive, yet simple account of why abandonment occurs.

Since its appearance on the urban scene in the late sixties, the topic of abandonment has engendered an intense debate about its significance and interpretation. In this essay abandoned housing is regarded (initially at least) as a "phenomenon." The goal of this essay is to understand the phenomenon of abandoned housing–its characteristics, dimensions, causes and implications. Only after this empirical analysis has been completed will it be possible to adopt a rational "policy attitude" toward abandonment.

The Social Context of Abandonment

An objective understanding of the phenomenon of abandonment can only be achieved if

*This study would not have been possible without outside help. I have borrowed freely from both published and unpublished works in the field, and hopefully, I have made proper acknowledgement of these sources in the text. Other than that, I must particularly thank Frank Tate, formerly of the Philadelphia City Planning Commission, for allowing me to use the results of his survey of abandoned housing, which is an empirical cornerstone of this essay. In addition, Rona Zevin, coordinator of the Philadelphia Abandoned Housing Task Force, provided me with much helpful assistance. William Grigsby and George Sternlieb kindly talked with me about abandonment for hours, as did Julian Wolpert, who also encouraged me to write this essay in the first place. My thanks to them all. Of course, any errors or misconceptions which remain are my responsibility.

full attention is also paid to the social context in which abandonment is occurring. It is becoming increasingly apparent, even to the most casual observer, that the American city is the focus of a series of divisive and potentially destructive social, economic and political pressures. Talk of a "crisis in the cities" is not without foundation.

Socially, cities are faced with a continuing exodus of affluent whites to the suburbs, their places being taken by the poorer members of minority racial groups. Antagonisms based upon class differences are thus aggravated by racial tensions. At the same time, criminal and other antisocial behavior is increasing in the city. The fact that these social trends are occurring in an increasingly obsolescent environment has tended to undermine the traditional economic and fiscal strength of the city. The decentralization of employment activity has reinforced this trend: not only is the city unable to attract new industry, but it is frequently unable to retain its existing industry. The concomitant loss of tax revenue reduces the city's ability to finance redevelopment and renewal programs of the kind which might attract new economic activity. In political terms, it should hardly be surprising that a decline in economic strength has been accompanied by an erosion of political power.

These larger trends provide part of the social context for a study of abandonment. It seems likely that some of the causes of abandonment will have to be sought in the context of these "macrofactors." In addition, however, a whole set of "microfactors" have to be taken into account because, in the final analysis, it is the individual property owner who actually abandons a unit. The perceptions and behavior of individual owners obviously have major implications for the abandonment process. A favorable perception might encourage an owner to stick with the property through a difficult period; an unfavorable perception may lead to immediate abandonment. With this in mind, it ought to be noted that the environment associated with abandonment is largely unfavorable. These are some of the events which occurred in 1973 in various neighborhoods of abandoned houses in Philadelphia:

- in April, a seven year old girl was found accidentally drowned in a pit of water in an abandoned house;
- in May, statistics were released indicating that the incidence of residence fires was spiraling upward in areas where abandoned houses were common; and
- in June, a man with a rifle hid in an abandoned house and fired several shots into the street, wounding at least one passerby.

Of course, accidental death, fires and crime are not the sole prerogatives of neighborhoods with abandoned houses. However, such hazards proliferate in these neighborhoods. They are also areas of extreme resident poverty, an obsolete social and physical fabric, and overcrowded housing conditions.

In summary, the social context of abandonment is composed of a set of macrofactors associated with larger urban processes, and a set of microfactors associated with the individual's perception and behavior. A full understanding of abandoned housing is likely to be achieved only by a balanced consideration of both sets of factors.

Explanations of Abandonment

The existing literature on urbanism seems to offer five alternative explanations for the abandonment process. First, it is possible to view housing blight and housing abandonment as part of a general progress toward improved housing conditions. Abandonment comes to be regarded as a consequence of creating better housing elsewhere in the market. As early as 1963, Grigsby was writing "This process of improvement by 'abandonment' . . . is an integral feature of the market" [p. 232]. Aaron has shown that the federal housing subsidy programs "unambiguously" add up to a *filtering strategy*. The main thrust of the programs is to create new housing, and to provide the financial wherewithal to permit households to move into it. Such a strategy cannot help but create a pool of vacant, obsolete houses at the other end of the market.

A *neighborhood succession* view of abandonment regards increased income, coupled with higher consumer expectations and preferences, as prime forces behind the outmigration of residents from obsolescent neighborhoods. In theory, these neighborhoods then become the residences of lower income households (via filtering), or they become redeveloped or renovated for a different use. The important contribution of the neighborhood succession theory is its concentration upon a particular territory, as distinct from its occupants. Under this theory, it is possible to view abandonment as a manifestation of the decay of the inner city residential area, prior to its invasion by a successor land use or function, under normal market processes.

A *low income household theory* of abandonment emphasizes the poverty of those households which remain behind in the inner city housing market. The outmigration of the relatively affluent usually leaves a residue of fairly good housing into which the remaining families could filter. However, because of their absolute lack of resources, these families cannot afford to purchase the better homes. Neither can they afford to pay higher rents which would provide an incentive for some landlord to purchase the newly vacated properties for conversion to apartments.

It may therefore be insisted that residents of the inner city area are obtaining the best housing they can afford, and that the allocative mechanism of the market is simply not providing them with sufficient income to obtain decent housing. According to this scenario, the problem of abandonment reduces to a question of income distribution. It could be argued that if tenants were given sufficient funds they could afford either to purchase their way into better housing conditions (i.e., filter up), or to pay a "realistic" rental, which would induce landlords to provide suitable rental accommodation. In addition, an infusion of funds would provide owner-occupiers with sufficient resources to maintain their properties. As a result, according to this scenario, the necessity for abandonment would be removed.

An *exploitation theory* of abandonment recognizes that there is a very fine line dividing ethical from unethical market behavior. In fact, there are forces built into the housing market encouraging the exploitation of housing consumers by landlords and the real estate-finance sector. Thus, pursuit of a self-interested profit-maximizing strategy encourages landlords to crowd their properties, to charge monopoly rents and to cut back on maintenance. In the case of realtors and financiers, it can be argued that laws and market institutions create an environment in which exploitation of the poor is inevitable. For example, if profits escalate as turnover increases, is it unethical to promote turnover in the stock by a selective policy of red-lining? Is blockbusting immoral, or is it the only rapid way of expanding the stock of housing available to minorities? It seems likely that truly exploitative, aberrant housing market activity is practised by a small minority of landlords, realtors and financiers. However, its effect upon the overall market climate in neighborhoods of abandonment ought not to be underestimated.

A fifth and final explanation for abandonment derives from the possibility that, while any number of macro- or microforces for urban change may be present, the ultimate abandonment is due to some *adverse event* occurring in the owner's life. Such adverse events include acts of crime and vandalism, some personal tragedy or the impact of a specific public policy. The occurrence of these events appears to cause abandonment only in areas where there has been a loss of confidence in the market's capacity for self-regeneration. In areas where the housing market is healthy, the adverse event is normally absorbed by the property owner.

A Definition of Abandonment

The discussion so far has proceeded without any definition of terms. Hence, terms like *abandonment, abandoned houses,* and *neighborhoods of abandoned houses* have been used as though there exists some common agreement about their definition. This is far from true. The purpose of this section is to provide some standard definitions for use in this chapter.

An *abandoned house* is a housing unit that has been withdrawn from the housing market, and one that its owner has no intention of returning to the market in the same use. *Abandonment* refers to the process through which a housing unit becomes abandoned. The specification of this process will be a central concern of this essay. The notion of a *neighborhood of abandoned houses* is largely self-explanatory, and there is little to be gained from a formal definition at this stage. The concept will, however, have some significance in the subsequent analysis.

While such definitions may find general agreement, they are nonetheless the source of large analytical complexities. These difficulties derive from the definition of an abandoned house. It is very hard, for example, to determine exactly when a unit has been withdrawn from the housing market. It is even more difficult to determine an owner's intentions for that unit. Therefore, as well as the conceptual definition of an abandoned house, it is necessary, for analytical purposes to derive a further operational definition.

Sternlieb has discussed the wide range of alternative definitions available to the analyst. Some studies he cites have stressed the physical characteristics of the housing unit itself, while others concentrate upon indicators drawn from the surrounding environment. Very often, it is a matter of adopting some convenient surrogate for the abandoned house variable. In Newark, for instance, Sternlieb used data from a fire inspector's survey of vacant buildings. In addition, tax delinquent properties are frequently utilized as indicative of the extent of abandoned housing. Needless to say, few of these surrogates provide an entirely satisfactory measure.

In fact, one of the "findings" of this study is the complete lack of a standard definition for the concept of an abandoned house. For most analysts, it is a case of accepting the best available surrogate measure. The most immediate and crucial implication of the absence of a definition is that we have no real idea of the scale of the abandonment phenomenon. Intercity comparisons are rendered almost meaningless when different data sources are utilized, since most sources tend to be peculiar to specific localities. Even when similar data sources are used, a comparative analysis may still be prevented. For example, a roster of vacant buildings compiled by a fire inspector may differ from one compiled by a water meter inspector, because of their different survey purposes and methods.

The lack of a standard definition (and the associated dearth of information) is largely due to the almost intractable practical problem of demonstrating that a unit has, in fact, been withdrawn from the market and that its owner has no intention of returning it there in the same use. The relative newness of the phenomenon also prevents a ready resolution of the definition problem.

In order to circumvent these problems, this present study utilizes two different operational definitions of abandoned housing, each with a specific purpose in mind. First, in order to study the abandonment phenomenon close up, special survey data on abandoned housing in a sample area of Philadelphia were utilized. For the purposes of this survey, an abandoned house was defined operationally as a housing structure which showed visible indication of having been withdrawn from the housing market. Such indications included being vacant and boarded up, or vacant but lacking any "for sale" or "for rent" signs. Such a definition is not entirely satisfactory, but it does have the dual advantage of utilizing a range of indicators for abandonment, together with some attempt to seek out physical manifestations of the owner's intentions for a property. Note that a single abandoned structure may contain a number of abandoned housing units.

A later section of this essay discusses studies of the abandonment phenomenon for a range of US cities. A wide range of alternative operational definitions are utilized in these studies and comparisons among the different sources are hazardous. Some more formal intercity comparison is possible using the US Bureau of the Census definition of "housing units vacant one year or more." This is a somewhat loose definition, as the later discussion will indicate: however, it is one of the few acceptable means of achieving a national comparative analysis of the abandonment phenomenon. Accordingly, it is utilized as a second operational definition of abandoned housing in this present essay.

Research Objectives

The goal of this analysis is to provide the fullest possible understanding of the phenomenon of abandoned housing–its characteristics, scale, causes and implications. The realization of this goal requires a consideration of five specific research objectives.

- *What happens in an area subject to abandonment?* What is the geographical pattern of abandonment? What happens to that pattern over time? Is abandonment a random or ordered process?
- *What is the citywide distribution of abandoned housing?* How widespread is the overall pattern? Is abandonment confined to specific neighborhoods? What market conditions are contributing to its spread?
- *What is the nationwide extent of abandoned housing?* Is it solely confined to the older, Eastern cities? What is the scale of the phenomenon? What are the common factors in

the location of abandoned units in each city?

- *What is the theoretical basis or explanation for abandonment?* What causes abandonment? How far does existing theory explain the incidence of abandonment? What new theories are needed to explain abandoned housing?
- *What are the policy implications of this study?* What are the implications of theory for policy? What are the effects of current housing policies? Are alternative policies preferable?

The remainder of this essay is devoted to a consideration of each of these five objectives.

ABANDONMENT IN CLOSE-UP

What actually happens in an area which is subjected to housing abandonment? So little seems to be known about the spatial ordering of abandoned properties and about how this ordering changes over time that it seems essential to concentrate initial analysis upon these fundamental issues. Accordingly, let us focus sharply on one particular area which is subject to considerable housing abandonment. The area chosen for study is called Tioga, which forms part of central North Philadelphia. The reasons for this choice are compelling. First, a special survey of abandoned housing was conducted there in 1969, and again in 1971, by Mr. Frank Tate of the Philadelphia City Planning Commission. Secondly, Tioga is typical of the "twilight" areas of many American cities and, hopefully, much of general concern may be learned from a consideration of its specific example.

Tioga began its existence as a suburb of the city of Philadelphia in the late nineteenth century. Its period of most rapid growth occurred in the early 1900s, although its population increased steadily to about 46,000 in 1960. Thereafter, it experienced a slight decline, to 43,660 inhabitants in 1970. The southern part of Tioga is mostly comprised of small, two story row houses, often built back to back with a narrow intervening alley. Each property fronts directly onto the street, and, as may be anticipated, the overall density of development is relatively high, rising to about 40 housing units per acre. Further north, properties are generally larger, and a greater diversity in building styles is to be found. Overall densities decline to as low as 25 units per acre, although the row structure still predominates.

Tioga is a community in transition. It has experienced a massive turnabout in terms of the racial composition of its inhabitants. The white population, of predominatly European extraction, has been replaced almost completely by black and Puerto Rican stock, in a changeover which has occurred mainly within the last decade. The new residents are poorer than the former residents, and more mobile. And all these changes are occurring against a backdrop of an increasingly obsolete housing stock and worsening housing conditions. The most recent addition to the list of Tioga's characteristics is the phenomenon of abandoned housing.

Abandoned Housing in Tioga, 1969-1971

For the purposes of this study, Tioga is regarded as a six census tract area (numbers 173, 174, 200, 201, 202 and 203). A survey of abandoned structures was undertaken in this area by the Philadelphia City Planning Commission in 1969, and again in 1971. An abandoned structure was defined as one being boarded up and vacant, or vacant and lacking any "for sale" or "for rent" signs.

In December 1969, the survey revealed that 369 residential structures, out of the area's 12,549 residential units, had been abandoned. This suggests that no less than 2.9 percent of Tioga's housing stock showed signs of having been withdrawn from the active housing market and abandoned. However, this percentage rate is likely to be an underestimate, since the survey counted *structures,* whereas the Tioga stock total (derived from census sources) is given in housing *units.* Now, the number of residential structures in Philadelphia represents 80 percent of the figure for the total number of housing units in the city. Applying this ratio to the Tioga data, we obtain an estimate of the number of residental structures in Tioga—a total of about 10,000. Using this figure, the percentage rate of abandonment of residential structures in Tioga in 1969 is perhaps more accurately given as 3.7 percent, although even this may be a slight underestimate, because of the high proportion of multiple occupancy dwellings in Tioga.

The geographical pattern of abandonments in 1969 exhibits two main structural characteristics (Figure 3-1). At the macrolevel, there appear to be six or seven large "clusters" of abandoned houses. Each cluster typically consists of about 12 blocks. Outside the clusters, there are very few abandonments. By contrast, at the microlevel, there are many tightly knit groups of two to three abandoned units completely contained within the larger cluster. In fact, it is the aggregate of these microgroups which gives definition to the macrocluster.

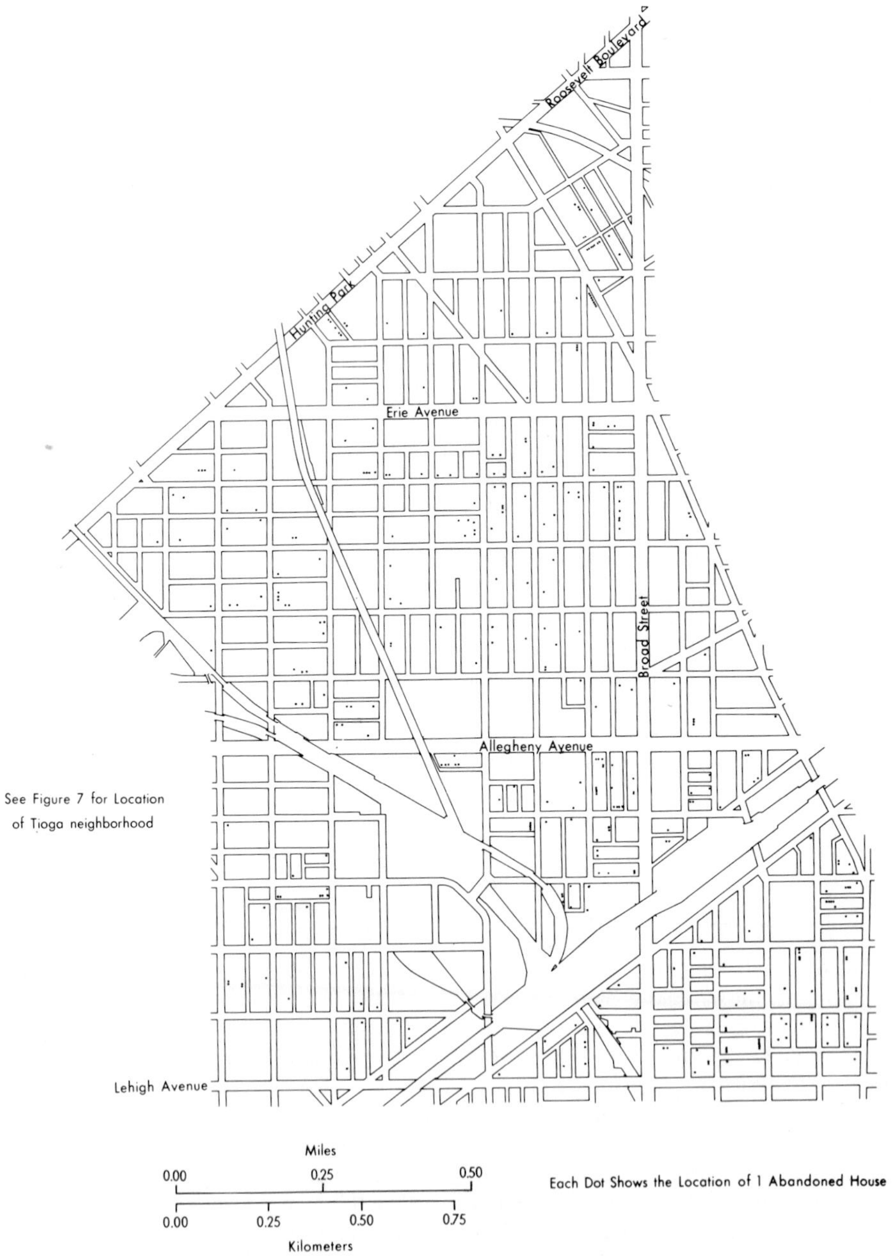

Figure 3-1. The Distribution of Abandoned Housing in Tioga, 1969. See Figure 3-7 for location of Tioga neighborhood.

Between December 1969 and February 1971 a further 155 residential structures were abandoned in Tioga. This represents a 42 percent increase in the number of abandonments. Such a startling increase is, however, tempered by the fact that 61 structures out of the original 369 abandoned in the area were returned to the market by the date of the second survey. Therefore, by February 1971 there was a net addition to the abandonment inventory of 94 residential structures, representing a net increase of about 25 percent on the 1969 figure. The 463 structures abandoned in 1971 represented 3.7 percent of the 12,549 housing units in Tioga, or, more accurately, 4.6 percent of Tioga's estimated 10,000 residential structures.

The spatial distribution of these 463 structures indicates a remarkable resemblance to the 1969 pattern (Figure 3-2). It is evident that the spatial characteristics of the 1969 distribution have been intensified by 1971. The large-scale macroclusters are still very much in evidence. However, the microclusters now typically consist of three to six (or even more) abandoned structures. There is also evidence of a scattering of abandonment outside the major clusters.

The process of abandonment as it operates in space, therefore, suggests an initial broad scattering of abandoned structures, characterized internally by the occurrence of many small groups of abandoned houses. With the passage of time, this pattern is intensified: the broad scatter is maintained, although the small groups now contain a greater number of structures. A two stage process is clearly suggested: the initial abandonments occur, and a later consolidation follows. (This process is illustrated diagramatically in Figure 3-3). It suggests a "leader-follower" sequence which resembles the propagation of plant species or the diffusion of information. It is essentially a contagious sequence.

Contagion has major implications for our understanding of the dynamics of abandonment, and for later policy considerations. For example, the 61 abandoned structures which were returned to the active housing market between 1969 and 1971 in Tioga represented no less than 17 percent of the abandoned inventory. It is impossible, in retrospect, to determine why these units were recovered. However, analysis of map evidence suggests that the reclamation effort was successful largely on the fringes of the abandonment clusters, and mainly in blocks where only one or two structures were abandoned. Only in very rare instances were larger groups of abandoned houses returned to the market.

A Cyclical View of the Abandonment Process

The Tioga evidence suggests that abandonment can be viewed as a *contagious process,* having at least two distinct stages. In this section, an attempt is made to extend and to generalize these specific findings into a more formal cyclical view of the abandonment process. While such a model may not be a perfectly accurate representation of reality, it forms a useful summary of what has so far been discovered about the process, and is a basis for further research.

Given sufficient time, an observer of the abandonment phenomenon might be tempted to conclude that the process of abandonment in space appears to be cyclical in nature (Figure 3-4). The cyclical process of abandonment may be characterized by several distinct stages, as follows.

Stage 0: Neighborhood Deterioration. During this period, the necessary (as yet unspecified) preconditions for abandonment are established. It is likely that these conditions, of themselves, are insufficient to initiate abandonment.

Stage 1: Scattered Abandonment. The first abandonments occur, defining the macrolevel clusters of blight. The most characteristic feature of each cluster is a series of two or three abandoned structures, forming tightly knit groups in themselves but scattered widely throughout the cluster as a whole.

Stage 2: Contagious Abandonment. Abandonment has now firmly taken hold, largely *within* the clusters defined by Stage 1. The microlevel groups of abandoned units are characteristically composed of up to six structures. The process of contagious abandonment is thus one of consolidation and intensification of the existing limits of blight.

Stage 3: Wholesale Abandonment. Some individual blocks in the clusters are now over 50 percent abandoned. At the same time, new areas outside the original cluster boundaries

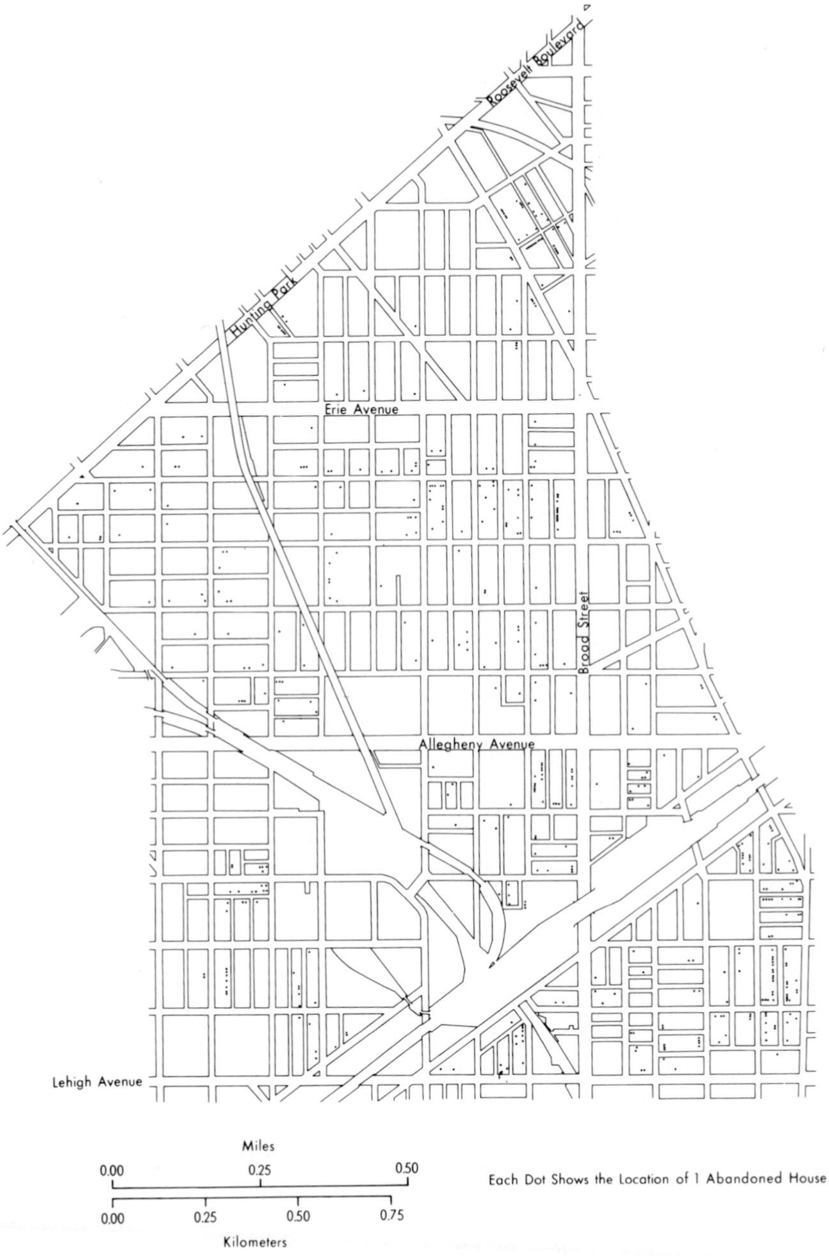

Figure 3-2. The Distribution of Abandoned Housing in Tioga, 1971.

are being subjected to abandonment, typically in a two to three unit cell which characterizes Stage 1 of the cycle. However, something extra now appears, since a spreading and intensification of abandonment is now occurring *beyond* the original core of blight.

Stage 4: Clearance and Renewal or Rehabilitation. Decay is now widespread. As abandoned buildings become public nuisances of one sort or another, someone (usually the city) moves to clear the parcel. Such a move could involve clearance as a prelude to redevelopment, or rehabilitation of the abandoned structures.

Stage 5: Pathological Abandonment. Stage 4 is not necessarily the end of the process. There is sufficient evidence to suggest that a virulent "pathology" of abandonment exists. In clearance-renewal areas this is all to often evident, since such operations are frequently piecemeal and renewal is confined to "holding" operations, such as a parking lot or playground. It is hard to visualize such redevelopment stemming the tide of abandonment: it is more likely, as Figure 3-3 suggests, to aggravate those neighborhood conditions which nurtured the blight originally. Neither is rehabilitation necessarily the answer. The Philadelphia Housing Authority's Scattered Site Rehabilitation Program revamped 3,814 mostly abandoned housing units between 1969 and the present. No less than 148 of these units (i.e., 4 percent) have since been abandoned again, representing an eventual loss of over $2 million. Under such circumstances, the rehabilitation alternative would seem to reexpose the housing stock to the abandonment cycle with haste (cf. Figure 3-3).

Two immediate implications of this cyclical view of abandonment ought to be noted. First, once abandonment has begun it is likely to be very difficult to stop. It may become almost a selfsustaining process under the force of contagion. Second, the cyclical view suggests very strongly that, at different stages of the abandonment process, alternative policy options ought to be developed. A policy option which is appropriate at one level (say, early in the cycle) is unlikely to be effective later in the cycle.

The Tioga Housing Market, 1960-1970

Although the geographic patterns of abandonment over time have now been analyzed, the forces behind those patterns have hardly been touched upon. The only notions of causality so far derived relate to contagion after the process has begun. This section explores further possible causes for abandonment, particularly those which have their roots in the area's housing market over the period 1960-1970. The data used in this section are taken from the relevant US Bureau of the Census volumes, and it should be noted that the equiv-

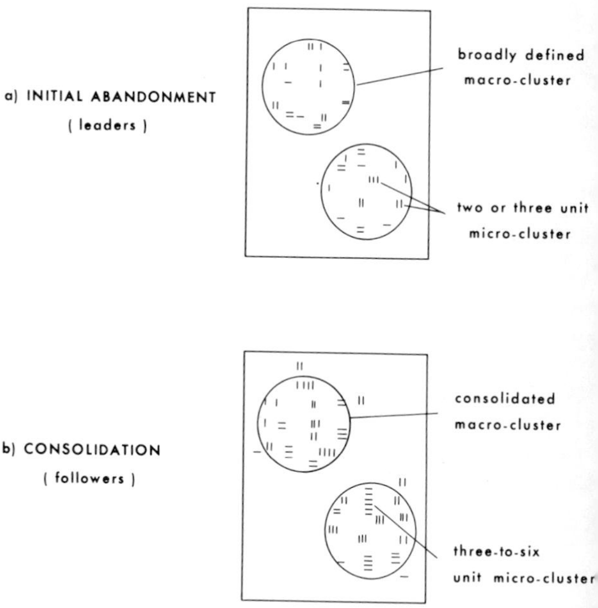

Figure 3-3. Diagrammatic Representation of a Two-Stage Process of Housing Abandonment.

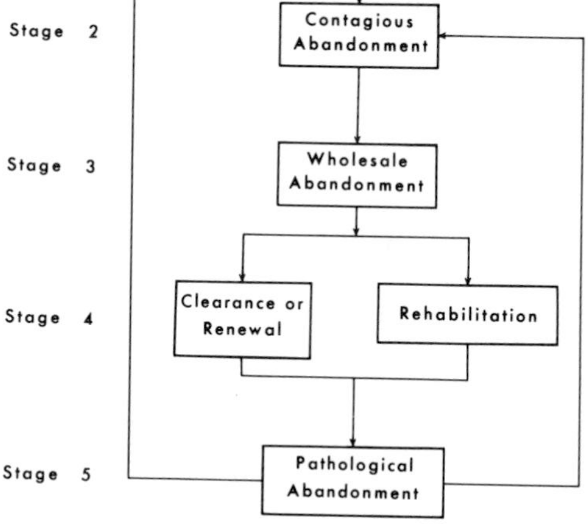

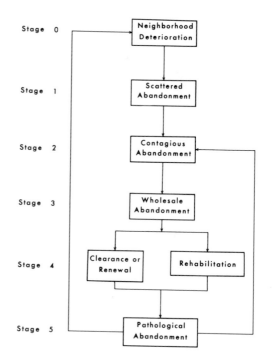

Figure 3-4. A Cyclical Model of Abandonment.

alent 1960 census tracts for Tioga are numbered 37A, 37B, 38G, 38H, 38I and 43C.

Recall that Tioga is predominantly an area of turn-of-the-century row houses, although industrial land uses encroach upon its northern, western and southwestern boundaries to give areas of mixed land uses. Many of the housing structures are approaching the end of their useful lives. Hardly any open space exists in Tioga, and the built-up area is "relieved" only by the swathes of railroad tracks which slice through considerable portions of South Tioga. Public transport is relatively good, although a concomitant volume of through traffic travels daily along the major arteries.

The most prominent change in Tioga over the decade 1960-1970 was the growth in the proportion of nonwhite residents, from 54 percent in 1960 to 84 percent by 1970. This racial transition began as long ago as 1930, but the major "tipping" occurred after 1960. This change occurred while the total population of Tioga remained almost constant at about 46,000 inhabitants. It was accompanied by a significant change in the economic status of the area's residents. During the decade 1960-1970, the city of Philadelphia median income increased by 62 percent from $5,782 to $9,366, while Tioga's median income grew at an equivalent rate, but at a lower level, from $4,761 to $7,627. However, at the same time (by 1970), no less than 21.3 percent of Tioga's families were below the poverty level, compared with a city average of 9.7 percent. Moreover, while the city's unemployment rate dropped from 6.4 percent of the work force in 1960 to 4.6 percent in 1970, Tioga's unemployment rate decreased only from 7.1 percent to 6.3 percent. Not surprisingly, welfare rolls are growing rapidly in Tioga. These changes in the economic status of the area's residents are likely to be a major influence on the local housing market.

The Tioga housing market is, in fact, in a rather depressed state. Very little demolition or new construction of housing units has occurred over the decade, with the result that the total stock has declined in number from 16,352 (in 1960) to 16,048 (in 1970). This was at a time when the city as a whole experienced a 4 percent net increase in its total housing stock. The median value of owner-occupied property grew from $8,700 to $10,700 in the city between 1900 and 1970, but in Tioga the value remained almost constant (i.e., dropped in real terms) at $7,300. Comparative figures for the rental sector support the contention that Tioga's housing market was "softening" over the decade. Median contract rental values for 1960 were $56 for both the city and Tioga; by 1970 the city value stood at $76, while Tioga's had risen only to $68.

The decade 1960-1970 also saw a rise in the number of vacant housing units in Tioga, from 6.6 percent of the stock in 1960 to 8.1 percent in 1970. (Compare the respective city figures of 5.1 percent in 1960, declining to 4.7 percent by 1970.) This loss to vacancy has occurred mainly from the owner-occupied sector, which dropped in share of the housing stock from 45 percent in 1960 to 40 percent by 1970. During this time, the rental sector was a steady 48 percent of the total stock. It might appear paradoxical that while the area's vacancy rate is increasing, the rates of resident overcrowding have also been climbing upward.

One other important housing variable—condition—is notoriously difficult to analyze. According to the 1960 census, 87 percent of the city's housing stock was basically sound: this compares favorably with the 85 percent of Tioga's stock which fell into the same category. Since there were no direct condition questions on the 1970 census, there is no certainty regarding trends in condition since 1960. However, circumstantial evidence—in particular, the increasing age of the housing stock, declining property value and the lack of new demolition and construction activity—suggests that the condition of Tioga's housing stock is likely to have declined over the decade.

By the end of the decade 1960-1970, therefore, the housing market in Tioga was in a rather depressed state. Local demand conditions for owner-occupied properties had definitely declined, but the demand for rented property apparently persists. However, for reasons as yet unclear, the properties released from the owner-occupied sector were not being converted for use in the rental sector. This lack of entrepreneurial response on the supply side is reflected in the almost complete lack of demolition or new construction activity in the area between 1960 and 1970. It seems likely that the absence of response on the supply side is due, in part at least, to the potentially low rate of return on investment (as reflected in the median owner-occupied and rental property values). Whatever the cause, the lack of replacement activity implies that the market is operating with an increasingly obsolete standing stock, which is slowly being allowed to dwindle away. It is also worth special mention that 80 percent of the abandonment in Tioga is occurring in other than the worst housing units.

In summary, the demand side of the Tioga housing market indicates a mixed response, while the supply side is more or less at a standstill. This definite evidence of a "softening" in market conditions by 1970 is likely to be related to the incidence of housing abandonment, since by that date at least 400 of Tioga's structures had been abandoned. In terms of the cyclical model (Figure 3-4), the necessary preconditions for abandonment, in terms of neighborhood deterioration (Stage 0), were laid down during the decade. By the end of the decade, a scattered abandonment (Stage 1) had occurred and contagious abandonment (Stage 2) was in evidence. A question which remains unanswered, however, is what exactly was the force that took Tioga over the brink from neighborhood deterioration and into the active stages of the abandonment cycle? In short, what are the catalysts for abandonment?

In order to answer these questions, it is necessary to consider the housing market at a metropolitan level. There are two reasons for this. First, a consideration of the housing market of metropolitan Philadelphia will put the Tioga market in context, and may highlight other relevant market trends that are not evident at the local level. And second, all evidence suggests that property owners who abandon do not stay in their local neighborhood. In the majority of cases, owners abandon neighborhoods as well as properties. We have to look at conditions outside the neighborhood of abandonment, therefore, in order to understand what is going on inside that neighborhood.

A CITYWIDE VIEW OF ABANDONMENT

In this section, the citywide context of abandonment is considered. First we shall examine the housing market trends of the Philadelphia metropolitan area, in order to consolidate the market analysis of Tioga. Then the extent of the abandonment phenomenon in the city of Philadelphia itself is examined, noticing especially those factors which are common to neighborhoods which are experiencing abandonment. Finally, the dynamics of the housing market are analyzed. This third section is of particular significance, since it will be the first time in the chapter that specific consideration will be given to the microfactors behind abandonment i.e., considerations of individual perceptions and behavior.

Market Trends in Metropolitan Philadelphia

Population. The growth of population within the Philadelphia Standard Metropolitan Statistical Area (SMSA) reflects a pattern typical of metropolitan areas in the United States (Figure 3-5). The city of Philadelphia, which is conterminous with Philadelphia County, has a current (1970) population of 1,948,609: this total has been relatively stable since 1930, although a slow decline has been in evidence since 1950. In fact, the city's net population increase since 1920 has been only 125,000. This is in stark contrast to the suburban counties of the Philadelphia SMSA. These seven counties (Burlington, Camden and Gloucester in New Jersey; Bucks, Chester, Delaware and Montgomery in Pennsylvania) have experienced a growth of almost two million persons since 1920, and now contain 60 percent of the total SMSA population.

While the city's total population has remained numerically constant, some considerable internal readjustments have taken place. First, there has been a considerable intracity migration from the inner to the outer suburbs, where the major sources of virgin building land are to be found. This is a trend which seems likely to continue as long as land is available. And second, there has been a large alteration in the racial composition of the city's population (Figure 3-6). One-third of the city's population is black, a total of 848,300 persons. Since 1930, there has been a continuous migration of whites to the suburbs. For instance, during the decade 1960-1970, roughly 190,000 whites left the city, and 125,000 blacks entered it. The discrepancy between these totals (a loss of 65,000 residents) is bound to have repercussions on the housing market.

Employment. This huge suburbanization of population has proceeded hand in hand

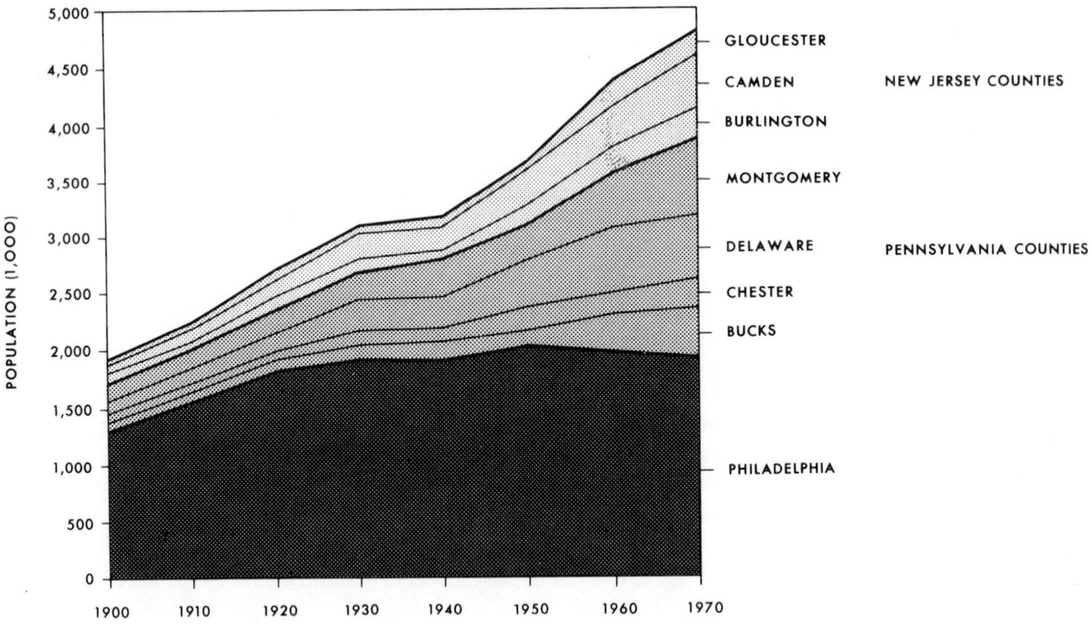

Figure 3-5. Philadelphia Metropolitan Area Population Trends, 1900-70.

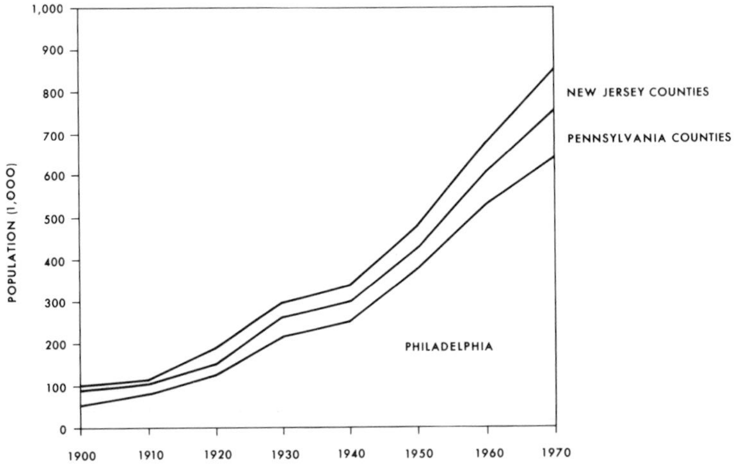

Figure 3-6. Philadelphia Trends in Negro Population, 1900-70.

with a decentralization of employment activities. In this respect, Philadelphia is again typical of many older US cities. The traditional manufacturing-heavy industrial economic base of Philadelphia is slowly being eroded and replaced by tertiary industrial activities. Moreover, the major focus of industrial growth is now the suburban counties surrounding Philadelphia.

Recent statistics released by the US Bureau of Labor Statistics indicate that, while the city of Philadelphia remains the most significant focus of industrial activity and employment in the SMSA, it has recently been surpassed by the suburban counties in terms of the number of jobs provided. Hence, the city provided 898,500 jobs in December 1972, as compared with 936,800 in the seven suburban counties. The Bureau further reports that the city's job opportunities expanded by 5.5 percent during the period 1959-1970, whereas the equivalent figure for the suburban counties was 99.3 percent.

Housing. Taken as a whole, the housing market of the Philadephia SMSA is relatively active. Over the 1960-1970 decade nearly a quarter of a million new housing units were added to the SMSA inventory. However, no less than 88 percent of this net increase accrued to the seven suburban counties of the SMSA, outside Philadelphia. This brought the total number of housing units in the city up to 673,390, as compared with 647,911 in 1960. The equivalent figures for the suburban counties were 861,373 and 677,636, respectively.

It would appear, therefore, that the city's housing market is rather less active than the suburban market. (And it is useful to recall here that Tioga's housing market was much weaker than the city market!) The softness of the city market is further evidenced in figures on housing cost. Between 1960 and 1970, there was a 34 percent increase in the median value of owner-occupied properties in the city of Philadelphia—$8,700 rising to $10,700. The equivalent increase in the suburban counties was 45 percent, however, with values rising from $12,700 to $18,400. Compare this with Tioga's median value, which remained constant over the period at $7,300.

A similar trend is shown in the median contract rental values. For the city, this figure was $56 per month in 1960 and $76 in 1970, representing an increase of 36 percent. The equivalent figures for the suburban counties are $69 and $111 respectively, or a 60 percent increase. Again, it is illuminating to recall Tioga's 21 percent increase from $56 to $68 per month.

Finally, it is particularly interesting to consider the evidence of vacancy rates in the different areas of the SMSA market. The rate of vacant but available housing units (i.e., for sale or for rent) has dropped everywhere within the SMSA. Even in Tioga, this rate has gone down from 5.5 percent in 1960 to 5.4 percent in 1970, although it must be remembered that the size of the stock is declining slowly, However, the city's vacancy rate was 3.4 per cent in 1960, and is now 2.8 percent in a slowly expanding stock. Most significantly, however, the suburban counties' rate dropped from 2.2 percent in 1960 to 1.6 percent in 1970—and in a rapidly expanding market. Once again, therefore, a hierarchy of market softness is demonstrated: the vacancy rates imply that the housing market is weakest in Tioga, less weak in the city as a whole and tightest in the suburban counties.

Summary. The suburbanization of population and employment opportunities, and the developments in the housing market, both point toward a continuing decentralization of social and economic activity within the Philadelphia SMSA. There seems little reason to doubt that the "suburbanization dynamic" is the major force behind most changes in the metropolitan housing market. In particular, it might account for the decline in demand in inner city areas. The precise manner in which this force is translated into action in the housing market at the local level is the subject of our consideration in the remainder of this chapter.

Abandoned Housing in the City of Philadelphia

Philadelphia has a citywide housing shortage. There are nearly 15,000 applicants on the public housing waiting list; there are an estimated 65,000 substandard occupied housing units in the city, and over 6,000 persons will be displaced by public programs between 1972 and 1974. The rehousing responsibilities implied by these figures suggest that it is imperative for the city to be aware of, and understand the reasons for, the steady erosion of its housing stock through abandonment. This is especially important since the net addition to the city's housing inventory over the decade 1960-1970 was only about 20,000 units.

Unfortunately, there is little systematic knowledge about the extent of abandoned housing in Philadelphia. Some indirect attempts at measurement have been made, most notably by the Philadelphia Vacant Property Monitoring System, which identifies structures which have been vacant for a minimum of six months. Structures which are vacant are initially identified by water meter readers and subsequently verified by the city's department of licenses and inspection.

For several reasons the data on long term vacancies are only partially adequate surrogates for abandonment. The monitoring system only covers properties in the private market, for instance, and properties are not automatically removed from the system when they are re-occupied or demolished. Thus, the extent of the long term vacant inventory in the city—an estimated 36,369 structures in 1972—is likely to be overstated. (This represented at least 5 percent of the total city inventory.) Further, since not all long term vacant structures are abandoned, the suitability of the data in estimating the extent of abandonment is further diminished. Recall that the estimates of abandonment in Tioga—a badly blighted area—range from between 3.7 percent and 4.6 percent of the total housing stock.

Using a series of ingenious compromises, the city of Philadelphia's Abandoned Housing Task Force has refined the long term vacancy data in order to provide more accurate information upon housing abandonment in the city. The distribution of tax-delinquent structures in the city (about 7,000, or 1.3 percent of the city-wide total) was compared with the distribution of long term vacant structures, and a compromise definition of the extent of the abandonment phenomenon was derived (Figure 3-7). No specific quantification of the phenomenon was derived, only some specification of its distribution and incidence. Within the city of Philadelphia, abandoned housing is virtually confined to a ring of inner city residential areas in North, West and South Philadelphia. Abandonment appears to be most severe adjacent to the downtown area. The downtown central business district (CBD) is itself unaffected, as are the outer residential suburbs.

The annular pattern of abandoned housing around the city's CBD and its decreasing incidence away from the CBD are observations of major significance for this study. They suggest that (in Philadelphia, at least) *abandonment is confined to specific kinds of neighborhood*—namely, those found in inner city residential areas. They further suggest that the *causes of abandonment may be functionally linked to the macrogeographic structure of the city*, and, hence, to the forces which produce this structure. In the next section, we shall see that the annular pattern of abandonment is common to a large number of cities in the US. It is therefore important to pursue these structural issues further in the present Philadelphia context.

The Philadelphia City Planning Commission has classified the whole city in terms of its housing and neighborhood improvement needs. The taxonomy was based upon several variables, including structural condition, overcrowding rates and the like; the net result is a classification of every census tract in the city according to an eight point scale (ranging from 0 through VII) which is indicative of the need for "improvement," however defined (Figure 3-8). Roughly speaking, Type 0 areas are environmentally sound and require little intervention at present. At the other extreme, Type VII areas are the problem areas, where intervention for improvement has high priority. The remaining points on the scale represent varying degrees of priority between these two extremes.

It is interesting and instructive to compare the distribution of abandoned housing (Figure 3-7) with the classification of neighborhood types (Figure 3-8). The similarity between the distributions of abandonment and the Type IV to Type VII neighborhoods is striking. These are neighborhoods where intervention has high priority. They are areas of relatively low value housing, and above average vacancy rates. They are unstable neighborhoods, with high tax delinquency and long term vacancy rates. They have a high share of poor residents, living in public housing or on welfare. In fact, virtually the same annular structure is apparent on both maps. It appears that abandonment in Philadelphia is associated with neighborhoods in which resident poverty, poor housing conditions and all the other factors generally associated with urban decay are in evidence.

Let us pause briefly to examine the significance of the evidence in the preceding paragraphs. What is being suggested (and it *is* merely a suggestion at this stage) is that abandonment is associated with urban decay and that the macrogeographic forces leading to structural and/or functional change in urban areas are causally linked to abandonment. Now, since all evidence in this essay has led to the acceptance of the "suburbanization dynamic" as the major current force for structural alteration within metropolitan Philadelphia, it

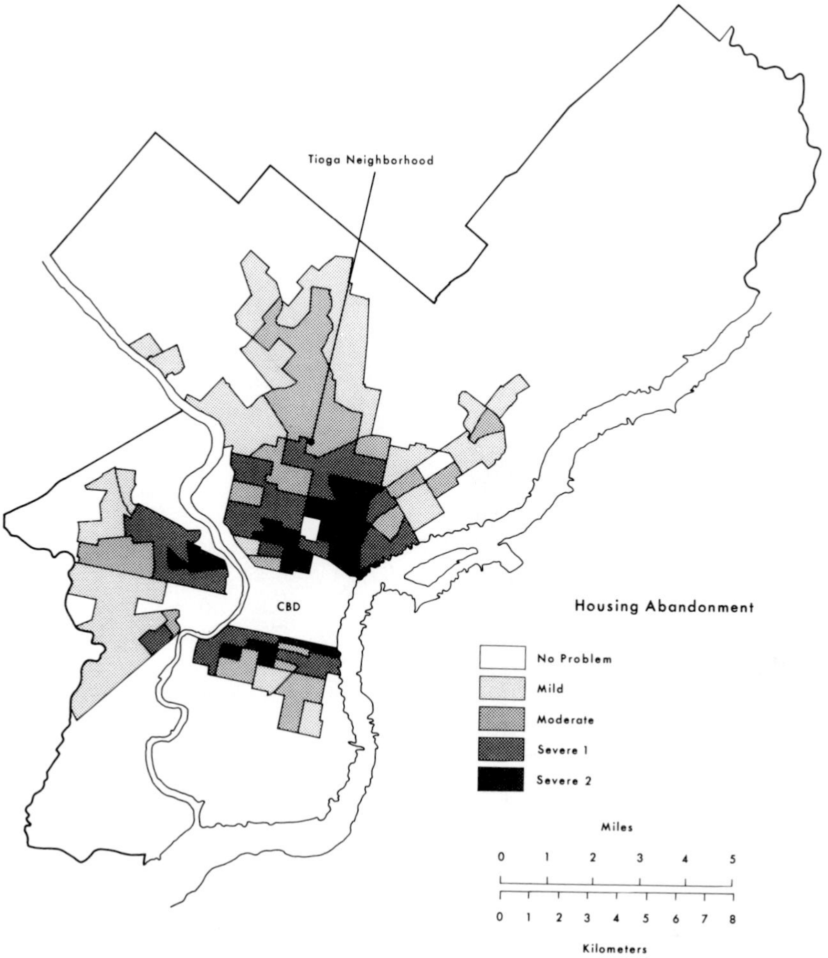

Figure 3-7. Abandoned Housing in Philadelphia, 1972.

seems that we are being drawn toward a theory or hypothesis of abandonment which may be pictured as follows:

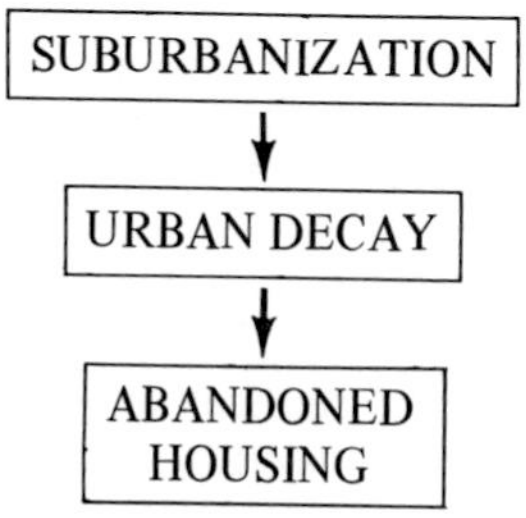

In short, abandoned housing in Philadelphia is the end-state of the process of suburbanization—a process which manifests itself at the local level via the mechanism of urban decay.

It must be emphasized that the above notion merely maintains the status of a hypothesis at the moment. Lest one be carried away by the appealing neatness or the apparent logic of the explanation, it is chastening to consider the evidence of Table 3-1. This is a brief summary of the possible conflicts within the data sources utilized so far in this essay. The contradictions within Table 3-1 suggest the fabric upon which the suburbanization-urban decay-abandonment argument was woven may be a trifle insecure.

For each of the six census tracts in Tioga, Table 3-1 lists all the relevant abandonment data so far utilized. The survey evidence of the percentage of tract housing units which are

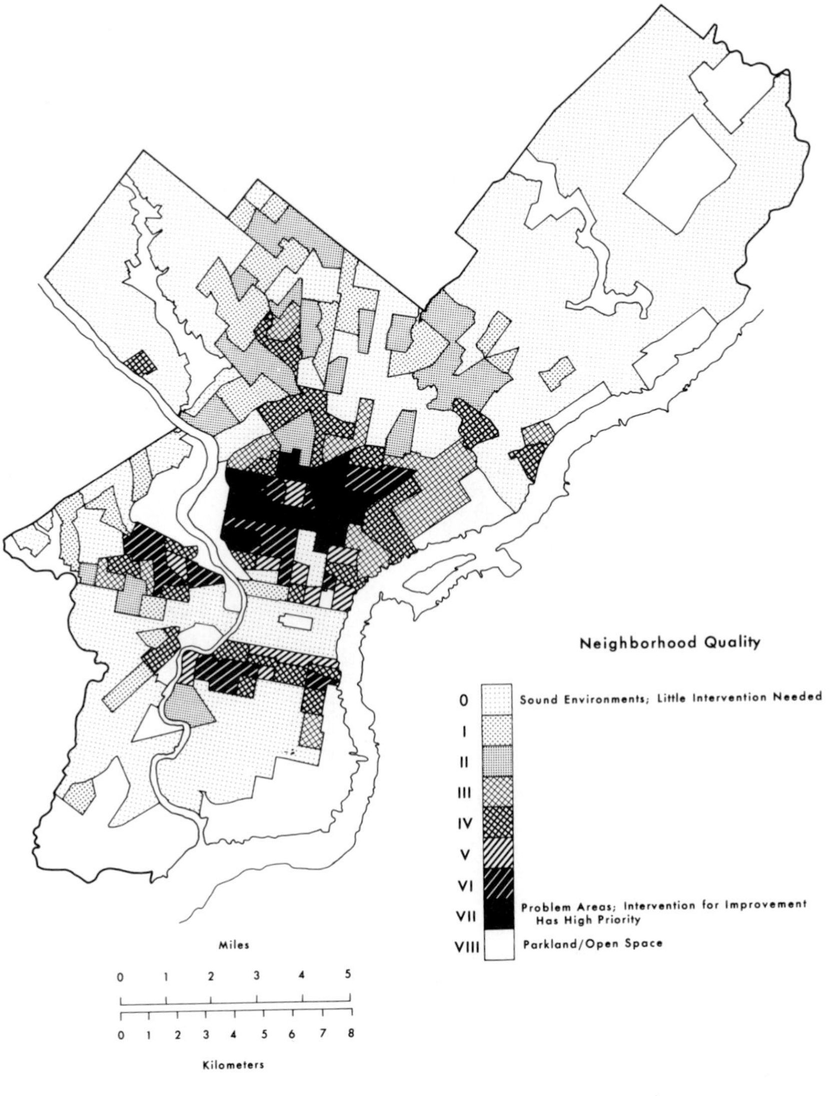

Figure 3–8. Philadelphia Housing and Neighborhood Improvement Strategy Areas.

abandoned is given, along with the Abandoned Housing Task Force's classification of that tract and the planning commission's neighborhood classification.

None of the Tioga census tracts qualifies for a "Severe 2" abandonment classification, although the "Severe 1" classification encompasses one tract with 3.6 percent units abandoned and one with 6.9 percent abandoned. Both these tracts are improvement priority Type VII neighborhoods. At the same time, however, a tract in which 5.8 percent of housing units are abandoned is considered to be a Type IV neighborhood, with only a "Moderate" abandonment classification. Still further contradiction arises for the tract with the least amount of abandoned housing–1.9 percent. This is also classed as a Type IV neighborhood with a "Moderate" problem.

Part of this confusion derives from the fact that it is not just the worst housing units which are being abandoned. As was stated earlier, only 20 percent of Tioga's abandonments have occurred in the worst housing units. This

Table 3-1. Abandoned Housing and Neighborhood Characteristics of the Tioga Census Tracts

	Survey Evidence	*Philadelphia City Planning Commission*	*Abandoned Housing Task Force*
Census Tract Numbers	*Percentage of Tract Housing Units which are Abandoned*	*Tract Classification under Philadelphia Neighborhood Improvement Strategy*	*Housing Abandonment Classification*
200	1.9	IV	Moderate
202	2.1	II	Moderate
201	2.6	II	Moderate
173	3.6	VII	Severe 1
203	5.8	IV	Moderate
174	8.9	VII	Severe 1

Source: data compiled by the author from various sources.

evidence ought to prevent an overhasty acceptance of the suburbanization-urban decay-abandonment (S-UD-A) hypothesis.

However, there now seems every justification for concentrating subsequent analysis upon the housing environment associated with urban decay. In Philadelphia, this is overwhelmingly the inner city residential ring. In the following section, the dynamics of the inner city housing market are examined, and, for the first time in this essay, some examination is made of the importance of individual perceptions and behavior relating to the abandonment phenomenon.

Market Dynamics and Housing Abandonment

The whole process of housing abandonment ultimately reduces to action on the part of the individual owner to abandon a property. The conventional market analyses so far pursued in this essay have failed to come to grips with this fact. Therefore, in this section, the behavior of individual participants in the inner city housing market is considered. The function, motivation and strategies of all major participants and groups of participants are examined, both in theory and in practice. The interdependencies among the conflicting interests of these various groups are likely to have a major impact upon the operation of the inner city housing market and may allow for some preliminary modification of the S-UD-A hypothesis considered in the preceding section.

Housing Market Participants and Behavior: *Real Estate and Financial Institutions.* Financial institutions function to maintain and to regulate the flow of funds in the inner city housing market. They are motivated to make a profit, and hence tend to invest in minimum risk, maximum return projects. They also tend to spread their investments into activities other than residential real estate operations.

Real estate interests utilize the funds made available by financiers in order to realize a profit through buying and selling housing, or through charging transaction costs for their services as intermediary between buyer and seller. Realtors tend to have responsibility for the numerous small-scale transactions which the financial institutions prefer to avoid.

In short, financial institutions operate as facilitators, and real estate interests as coordinators, in the inner city housing market. This seemingly straightforward arrangement has profound consequences. In terms of market strategies, financial institutions clearly have an incentive to support *selectively* different sectors and different geographical areas of a city. For example, it would not pay a bank to invest in a depressed inner city housing area if, by withholding investment funds, the stock in that area would decline to such an extent that it becomes feasible for investors to purchase the land and redevelop it. Under such circumstances, the bank would realize a greater return by a policy of disinvestment, followed by investment in the redevelopment of the area. The market strategies of a realtor are also affected by this "simple" market arrangement. A realtor seeking to maximize profit has an incentive to encourage turnover in the housing stock in order to increase his commissions. There is also a temptation to take the maximum feasible return from each transaction.

It should be noted that "natural" self-interest determines that financier and realtor act in unison in their operations in the market. It is in the interst of both financier and realtor to invest in and to service only those areas of the city where a sufficient profit can be made. A concomitant scarcity of funds exists in high risk-low return areas, where the flow of funds for mortgages, insurance and other purposes soon dries up. Collusion between financier and realtor often results in a "red-lining" of such areas. In Philadelphia, it is generally acknowledged that a red-lining-disinvestment strategy is currently being pursued throughout large sections of the inner city housing market. The city is viewed as a "doughnut" (cf. Figures 3-7 and 3-8). At the center of the doughnut, in the central city, some of the most spectacular increases in housing values have been registered. For instance, one property sold in 1970 for $52,000 was resold in 1973 for $76,500. Outside this core area is a ring of depressed housing conditions, where property values are declining. A typical North Philadelphia house which sold for $7,100 in 1960 fetched $6,900 in 1970. Finally, beyond this ring, is the healthy suburban housing market, where housing values are increasing almost everywhere by 10 percent annually. In the outer and core areas of the city "doughnut" there is a steady demand for housing, plenty of mortgage money and high levels of new construction and renovation. For the inner ring of the "doughnut," however, there is a mere trickle of mortgage money and few buyers.

Landlord. Landlords are the actual providers of shelter: they operate on the interface between the supply side and the demand side of the market. There are many different kinds of landlord, but it is useful here to recognize only the basic distinction between the professional landlord and the part-time landlord. The distinction between these is based on scale and motivation. The part-time landlord generally owns only a few properties and aims to derive a modest, regular income from his or her holdings. When a part-time landlord rents out part of his own residence, motivation in the marketplace may resemble that of an owner-occupier rather than a landlord. In order to avoid these complexities, this essay focusses solely upon the activity of the professional landlord.

The professional landlord normally manages a relatively large number of properties and is motivated to maximize profits. This is generally achieved via the outright purchase of a property, and the realization of an income through renting it to tenants. An alternative strategy is to purchase a property through mortgage financing, and to increase the net wealth of the property through renting it and through the depreciation allowances and tax breaks associated with new investments. Of course, the lack of mortgage money in the inner city housing market prevents the pursuit of this strategy in any red-lined district of the city, as Harvey has explained.

Let us therefore examine the strategies of profit-maximizing available to the typical inner city landlord seeking to maximize income. In order to do this, it is revealing to consider the hypothetical cash flow statement compiled by William Grigsby et al. in their study of the Baltimore housing market (Table 3-2). This statement suggests that the annual net income realized from a typical inner city row house (in 1968) could be as low as $118. This is for a house held free and clear: naturally, if mortgage payments were involved, the return would be further diminished. Assuming that the landlord has paid the equivalent of the assessed value in order to purchase the property (i.e., $2500), the net income from the property would represent a rate of return on investment of under 5 percent. Now, Sternlieb's surveys in Newark reveal that most landlords are looking for a 25 percent return on their capital, and Harvey suggests that even the pessimistic Baltimore landlords would be happy with a 12-18 percent return. It is hardly surprising, therefore, that many landlords "want out" of the market, as Sternlieb has found. The lack of buyers prevents the adoption of this strategy on a large scale. Given that a landlord is locked into the market with a cash flow statement resembling that of Table 3-2, what alternative strategies are available for profit maximizing?

Few strategies are available for increasing effective income. Rents could be cut in order

Table 3-2. Illustrative Cash Flow Statement, Inner City Row House Held Free and Clear, Baltimore, 1968

Gross Income–$76 per month × 12		$912
Less: Vacancies and arrears (13 percent)		120
Effective Income		792
Less: Real estate taxes	$125[a]	
Ground rent	60	
Liability insurance	40	
Fire insurance	40	
Total Fixed Expenses	265	
Operating Income		527
Less: Maintenance and repair	240	
Water and sewer charges	60	
Miscellaneous	30	
Total Operating Expenses	330	
Net Income Before Management		197
Less: Management (10 percent of collected rents)	79	
Net Income From Operations		$118

[a]Assumes assessed value of land and building is $2,500.

Source: W.G. Grigsby, L. Rosenburg, N. Stegman, and J. Taylor, "Housing and Poverty," Institute of Environmental Studies, University of Pennsylvania, 1971.

to bring down vacancy rates, but only at the risk of antagonizing existing tenants. The vacancy rate in inner city areas is typically high in any case. A more vigorous rent collection policy may reduce arrears, but some landlords are fearful for their personal safety under pursuit of this strategy. Further, a too vigorous policy might frighten away existing tenants, as would a policy for crowding tenants into less space.

A reduction in fixed expenses might alternatively be sought. However, real estate taxes and ground rents are certainly immutable in the short term. In the longer term, many Philadelphia landlords could benefit from revised assessments. Citywide assessments are normally about 60 percent of market value, but many landlords are paying taxes based upon assessments which are as much as 200 percent of market value. The cost of insurance–where it can be obtained–is escalating rapidly, so there seems little a landlord can do to increase cash flow via the fixed expense variables.

What about strategies relating to operating expenses? Here the largest and most significant variable costs are maintenance and repair charges, which are spiraling upward in the inner city, due to the increasing obsolescence in the stock, and to inflation of labor and material costs. The rising costs are exaggerated by the difficulty in obtaining maintenance personnel to work in these areas. If, for reasons of personal security, personnel must work in pairs, costs again escalate. However, maintenance and repair outlays are one of the few entries in the cash account statement that the landlord has any control over. Thus, if new gutters are delayed for one year, for example, an extra $100 can be realized from a property.

The other operating expenses are less amenable to landlord manipulation. The problems associated with water and sewer taxes are often especially severe. These taxes vary with degree of usage in Philadelphia, and many landlords have complained that they often get served with massive unscheduled bills as a result of tenant "abuse" of the water system. The matter is complicated by administrative inefficiency: one landlord was billed for water meters which were installed, contrary to her instructions, in vacant buildings which she owned!

A final option on the cash flow statement relates to management costs. In fact, these tend to take an increasing slice from landlord income, as many landlords revert to professional collection agencies as a means of minimizing arrears.

In summary, within this tight budget and low income, savings are only possible by skimping on maintenance and repair costs. This is a strategy which slumlords have been pursuing for some time, and even though their numbers may be small (as surveys by Grigsby and Sternlieb suggest), their impact must be widely felt. It has often been observed that a decision by one landlord not to invest in maintenance tends to produce a similar decision by a neighboring landlord. More importantly, however, even a good landlord, faced with escalating maintenance changes, is forced to pursue management policies which tend to aggravate the decline in the condition of the inner city housing stock.

Government. The many imperfections in the housing and land markets have long been accepted as reasons for government intervention in the housing market. The overall objective of providing a "decent home" for all Americans has given rise to a multitude of policies and programs. Largely under the auspices of the 1965 Housing Act and subsequent legislation, the Department of Housing and Urban Development (HUD) is responsible for the administration of the majority of these programs.

Government has three basic strategies for intervention in the housing market. Direct action, which usually takes the form of public housing, has had only a minor impact upon market conditions. Indirect intervention, by contrast, has had a significant effect upon the characteristics and spatial distribution of housing opportunities in most US cities. Henry Aaron and Anthony Downs have both described this impact in detail. Indirect intervention normally involves investment in the construction of new housing, and (more recently) in rehabilitation of older housing. A third strategy involves several ancillary programs designed to regulate housing development: these include zoning, housing code enforcement, etc. Although the impact of these ancillary strategies upon the housing market is not spectacular, it should not be underestimated. The exclusionary zoning practices of many suburban townships are indicative of the power of this type of strategy.

The involvement of government in the "free" housing market generates powerful internal contradictions which result in conflict. The primary contradiction arises because government, with its own specific motivation, employs a strategy for achieving its aims which involves a different set of actors, with separate—often opposing—motivations and goals. Government has a welfare objective of housing all Americans. However, in order to achieve this goal it underwrites the activities of private financial and real estate interests which have a profit-maximizing objective. Apart from the possible ethical objections to this arrangement, the practical consequences are formidable. The current federal moratorium on housing programs is testimony to the long history of abuse and corruption in the administration and execution of the HUD programs. The evidence presented to the congressional hearing on *Housing Subsidies and Housing Policies* provides a startling account of these scandals.

Aaron has argued convincingly that, at the national level, federal housing policy amounts to a "filtering strategy." By this Aaron means to suggest that the main impetus of federal programs is toward providing a steadily increasing stock of good quality new housing. Government seems to be hoping that families will continue to "filter up" in the housing stock into increasingly better living conditions. Unfortunately, there is evidence to suggest that a large proportion of the poor lack the resources to benefit from this strategy. Such practices as red-lining aggravate their plight. No amount of new housing construction will enable them to filter up into better housing. Thus, the neediest sector of the housing market appears to be largely by-passed by federal housing policies.

A further implication of this troublesome conclusion is that a considerable redistribution of resources is occurring as a result of government intervention in the market. This redistribution is favoring the financial and real estate interests, as well as those groups with sufficient resources to gain access to the housing market in the first place. This is, in essence, the conclusion of the Douglas Commission report on *Building the American City.* The fact that government policy achieves these results ought not to be surprising, as Harvey points out, since government is itself responsive to the constituency which elects it. A *New York Times* article of September 20, 1972 sums up its discussion of the likelihood of federal housing reform with the sobering observation: "What has happened in housing is viewed by many as a classical failure of the Federal Government to make a complex social program work while serving rather well the special interests involved in delivering it." One of the major reasons for this failure is the almost complete lack of "... understanding or public scrutiny of the legislative processes involved" [p. 30].

Owner-occupant. The owner-occupant is one of two major classes of housing consumers, the other being tenants. All participants considered so far in this section have been housing producers. The owner-occupant is in the market for the shelter being provided by these producers. Under present market conditions, there are many advantages to becoming a homeowner, not the least of which are the tax advantages and security of tenure. However, the homeowner in the current inner city market faces many of the problems which beset the landlord in that area—property has little or no resale value, maintenance costs are escalating and general neighborhood conditions are deteriorating. A recent study by Arthur D. Little for HUD also revealed that the property tax burden in the slum and blighted neighborhoods of many US cities (including Philadelphia) is about ten times as high as that of improving neighborhoods. The cause of this bias is unclear. Its effect is to lower the resale value of slum properties even further.

The range of alternative housing strategies available to the owner-occupant in the inner city is strictly limited. Those with sufficient resources can move out. Those lacking the necessary resources (the majority) are "locked into" the local market: they can either remain or abandon their properties.

Tenants. The plight of tenants is somewhat different, although they, too, are in the market for shelter. The tenant moves in anticipation of some increase in housing quality. This is also true of the owner-occupant: the major difference lies in the fact that the tenant's gain is likely to be exceedingly temporary. Especially in the inner city areas, where the housing stock is deteriorating rapidly, it is only a short time before a tenant perceives that some further advance in housing quality is possible through another change of accommodation. The tenant has no incentive and, usually, no resources to maintain the dwelling under these transitory circumstances. Once again, we find that "normal" market processes dictate a continuing neglect of the quality of the housing stock.

One important distinction following from the above is that the tenant, unlike the owner-occupier, does not own a house, and is therefore incapable of "abandoning" it, in the strict sense of our definition. Yet tenant behavior can radically affect the climate of opinion for owner-occupants in their neighborhood. Consider the kinds of changes in the inner city neighborhoods of Philadelphia since the suburbanization dynamic began in the 1930s. The former residents of long standing—owner-occupants and tenants—have slowly been replaced by a transient population. Frequently, the cultural and social institutions which supported the former residents cannot outlast the exodus of their supporters. The new residents often lack commitment to the neighborhood and tend to regard it as a temporary resting place on the road to still better housing. A lack of commitment on the part of slum residents is hardly surprising, since the neighborhood has already been abandoned by real estate and financial intersts, by absentee landlords and by all residents who can afford to leave.

Under these circumstances, commitment to a neighborhood on the part of a tenant is the last thing that should be expected. And, faced with an alienated, nomadic group of neighbors, just how long can an owner-occupant stand to be locked into such a housing market? The situation is aggravated if the newcomers are of a different racial, cultural or economic status.

The Inner City Housing Market in Practice. The Institute of Environmental Studies at the University of Pennsylvania conducted a survey of housing market conditions in Allegheny West, an area immediately adjacent to Tioga, in 1973. Since Allegheny West is similar to Tioga in terms of its history, its socioeconomic characteristics and its housing quality, it may be anticipated that the study findings have some relevance for Tioga. The study certainly provides a very graphic picture of current market conditions in a typical inner city neighborhood of Philadelphia.

Under the direction of William Grigsby, the survey team examined the state of the local housing market and the attitudes of the market participants toward the area. They found that most local real estate and finance agencies had a very negative attitude toward the housing market, which was considered to be "stagnant" at best. Property values are declining, as are levels of maintenance (in both rented and owner-occupied properties). The area has already been lumped in with North Philadelphia, the area of worst blight, in the minds of some realtors. There has been a rapid increase, they perceive, in the incidence of vandalism, crime and board-ups. It is impossible to sell a home to a prospective client without Federal Housing Administration (FHA) backing; and all FHA activity by private lenders has ceased. Currently, the only supplier of mortgage funds is the Federal National Mortgage Association (FNMA).

This cessation of government-financed activity in the area is probably a direct result of the wider experience with federal programs in the city as a whole. In Allegheny West, the Section 235 and Section 221(d)(2) programs were utilized to encourage homeownership during a period of racial transition. However, as the study indicates, the opportunity for low income homeownership appears to have been converted into a problem for the area and its residents. The relative decrease in house prices, the lowered level of maintenance and the high turnover rate can all be attributed in large part to the 235 and 221(d)(2) programs. On the other hand, the opportunity for low income homeownership may have also strengthened the area relative to the decline that might have occurred without the programs. Demand by middle income families dropped throughout the sixties and in the absence of conventional mortgaging, the federal programs at least provided liquidity for sellers and new opportunities for buyers. The unforeseen effects of the programs are arguably the fault of those who conceived and executed them, rather than of the programs themselves.

With regard to owner-occupants and tenants, the study found that 45 percent of the respondents had a generally positive attitude toward the neighborhood and its inhabitants. However, 40 percent thought that the neighborhood was going downhill. While crime was cited as the major social evil in Allegheny West, it is significant that, when asked what could be done to improve the area, the most frequent response related to the physical environment. This included repairing homes, removing abandoned cars, etc. The overall impression of the survey is of a concerned, but powerless, group of residents.

The survey team also sought resident opinions relating to the precise causes of housing abandonment in Allegheny West. These are racial transition and its effect upon house prices; the swift decay of the housing stock, promoted by problem tenants and vandalism; the problems associated with purchase of a house on a low income; and the impossibility of selling a home through FHA mortgaging, because of the stultifying effect of the mass of HUD regulations. Apart from this local wisdom, Grigsby's researchers also tried to trace the owners of abandoned houses in Allegheny West in order to discover the specific reasons for abandonment.

In spite of efforts to find and interview the owners of 65 out of 100 boarded-up properties in Allegheny West, Grigsby was only able to establish owner intentions for about one-quarter of this number. Although this in no way can be regarded as a representative sample, some of Grigsby's findings are thought-provoking, and correspond with findings of researchers in other cities. The most important observation, for current purposes, is as follows:

> None of the abandonments occurred because of a dearth of demand, or because of code enforcement or factors that would suggest a badly obsolete or deteriorated inventory. All of them were in response to events that occur daily throughout the real estate market. In a higher price market, however, all of these dwellings would have soon been re-occupied. And during their period of vacancy they would never have been boarded up. In an area such as Allegheny West, though, where a less expensive asset is at stake and the risks associated with further investment are greater, the tendency to simply do nothing in response to an adverse occurrence is more pronounced. [Pp. iv–18,]

What Grigsby is arguing is that in areas like Allegheny West and Tioga, abandonment is occurring not because of gradually diminishing revenues or rising costs, but because of seemingly random adverse events, such as an act of vandalism, or delayed trash collection, etc. The important point is that *such events occur daily in the real estate market.* What, then, makes the response different in these fringe areas?

Grigsby suggests that abandonment is the response now because the cost of rehabilitation or repair is quite out of line with any anticipated cash flow from the property. Further, owners fear that a property will be vandalized or abused again before it will be possible to return it to the market.

Perhaps more important than either of these factors is the utter loss of confidence in the recuperative power of the inner city housing market. This is nothing less than the psychological abandonment of the inner city by residents, government and real estate-finance interests. This psychological abandonment may ultimately prove to be the major force behind the economic abandonment by realtors and financiers when they follow a strategy of disinvestment or by landlords when they cut back on maintenance. It may also be the force behind physical abandonment, the literal walking away from a property by the landlord or owner-occupier.

We can now begin to understand why abandonment is occurring outside the areas of worst housing, and why the S-UD-A hypothesis is only partially complete. Not only is there a physical contagion in the distribution of abandoned houses; there is also a psychological contagion, which acts as a depressive agent, draining the confidence of inner city market participants. These depressive effects spill over from one neighborhood into another, causing abandonment of sound structures in areas outside the focus of urban decay. Under these circumstances, the phenomenon of housing abandonment begins to take shape as a "problem."

HOUSING ABANDONMENT AS A NATIONAL PHENOMENON

In this section, an attempt is made to estimate the national extent of abandoned housing. The incidence of abandonment nationwide will have important consequences both for our overall understanding of the phenomenon and for the development of a proper policy attitude. For example, if abandoned housing is found only in the cities of one region of the US, then we would wish to inquire further as to the reasons for this confinement. Further, a nationwide campaign to promote or to curtail abandonment would be irrelevant in those regions unaffected by it.

As a first step, the evidence of specific studies of abandonment in ten US cities is examined. In order to gain a truly representative impression, an effort was made to obtain reports from all regions of the country. Thus, three Eastern cites are included, along with four Midwestern cities, two Southern cities and one Western city. The scale and suggested causes of abandonment in all ten cities are examined. In the second part of the section, census evidence of the incidence of abandonment is considered for an even wider range of cities. The section concludes with some summary observations about the extent of the abandonment phenomenon.

Housing Abandonment in Ten US Cities

Two major sources have been used in this summary of the nature and extent of housing abandonment in a sample of ten US cities. The first is a study by Linton, Mields and Coston, Inc., entitled *A Study of the Problems of Abandoned Housing,* which was completed for HUD in 1971. This report examined abandonment in St. Louis, Chicago, New Orleans and Oakland. The second source is the *National Survey of Housing Abandonment,* conducted in 1971 by the Center for Community Change of the National Urban League. This survey covered abandonment in seven cities, although only the evidence for Atlanta, Cleveland, Detroit and New York City will be considered here. The other two cities examined in this survey are Baltimore and Newark, both of which have been the subject of specific abandonment studies.

Atlanta, Georgia. Atlanta does not appear to suffer from abandoned housing. It has an extremely vital economy, which, as in most US cities, is expanding most rapidly in the suburbs. Atlanta's black residential population is concentrated in the inner city, the whites in the outer suburbs. Segregation is virtually complete and racial change occurs quickly in transitional neighborhoods. There is a continuing black immigration to the city from rural areas.

The real estate market in Atlanta is stable and active throughout the city, including the inner areas where there is a wide mix of social classes. There is an extremely low level of mortgage arrears or default and little apparent racial discrimination in the operation of the housing market. There is no evidence of exploitative sales practice (although Bederman would dispute this finding). As a result of these favorable market conditions, little visible evidence of abandonment is found in Atlanta. The occasional vacant dwelling is usually a sign of an investor-speculator who is waiting to acquire neighboring properties prior to some larger redevelopment. An aggressive code enforcement policy promotes good maintenance, as does the speed with which *in rem* proceedings are processed. These usually take only one year in Atlanta, rather than the four to seven years common in the cities of the Northeast. Such supportive public policies generally act to upgrade the housing stock, and to keep vacancies and dereliction down to a minimum.

Baltimore, Maryland. Firm estimates of the extent of abandonment in Baltimore are not available. However, after adjusting the data for the number of vacant structures inventory (compiled by the city's department of housing and community development), William Grigsby and his colleagues suggest that there are about 4,000 abandoned dwelling units in the city. Grigsby further notes that 4.6 percent of all inner city units were boarded up between the winter-spring of 1968 and the summer-fall of 1969. This represents an annual removal of about 4,000 units per annum, or 4 percent. Roughly half of these board-ups could be traced directly to government action—acquisition for urban renewal, for example—and hence could not be regarded as part of the abandonment process. An unquantifiable proportion of the remaining 2,000 units were boarded up because of the imminence of government action. In a separate study, Harvey noted that properties were reverting to the city at the rate of about 1,000 per annum.

Grigsby et al. stress that abandonment of the housing stock in Baltimore, far from measuring any sort of community gain, should be regarded as a problem of increasing severity. Abandonment occurs where maintenance and other operating expenses are rising rapidly at a time when tenant poverty prevents any raising of rents to provide for a reasonable rate of return. The problem is exacerbated by the obsolescence of the inner city housing stock and the lack of managerial capacity of the present inner city landlords, a large proportion of whom are "amateurs" with relatively small holdings. Grigsby's survey suggests that the well-organized slumlord is largely a myth in Baltimore, although where slumlord practices are in evidence their impact is severe. (Similarly, problem tenants are few, but they can often act as catalysts for local decay.) A large number of Baltimore landlords see no way of making money from their holdings other than waiting for public acquisition under some redevelopment program. The proximity of public works or urban renewal projects are a greater spur for abandonment. Vandalism and poor municipal services aggravate the problem.

Chicago, Illinois. Abandonment in Chicago is a serious problem. Although the signs of a "highly concentrated" abandonment—i.e., entire blocks of abandoned structures—are not yet apparent, there is some evidence that a contagious abandonment is underway. Citywide abandonment totals about 5,000 units, or 0.4 percent of the total housing stock. This relatively small percentage figure masks the impact of the phenomenon, however, since the majority of abandoned structures are concentrated in seven inner city neighborhoods. All of these areas have a substantial stock of old, deteriorating housing, and all have a largely black and/or poor population. The greatest concentration of abandonment is to be found just west of the Loop, around Lawndale, and in Chicago's South Side, especially in the Woodlawn-Kenwood area (Figure 3-9). Very few single family homes have been abandoned in any of these areas.

An alternative estimate of the number of abandoned houses in Chicago, by Frank Keller, was derived from a study of the records of the Demolition Court of the Cook County Municipal Court. Keller estimated that 13,671 units were abandoned in Chicago in 1971, displacing 49,216 persons.

Problems with cash flow appear to be a major force behind abandonment in Chicago, although Weissbourd has tended to emphasize the importance of intracity migration patterns as the primary dynamic for change. Between 1960 and 1970, 550,000 white people left the city, to be replaced by only 300,000 blacks. The city as a whole lost 5.2 percent of its population over this period. Some loosening of market conditions is therefore likely to have provided a context for abandonment, although

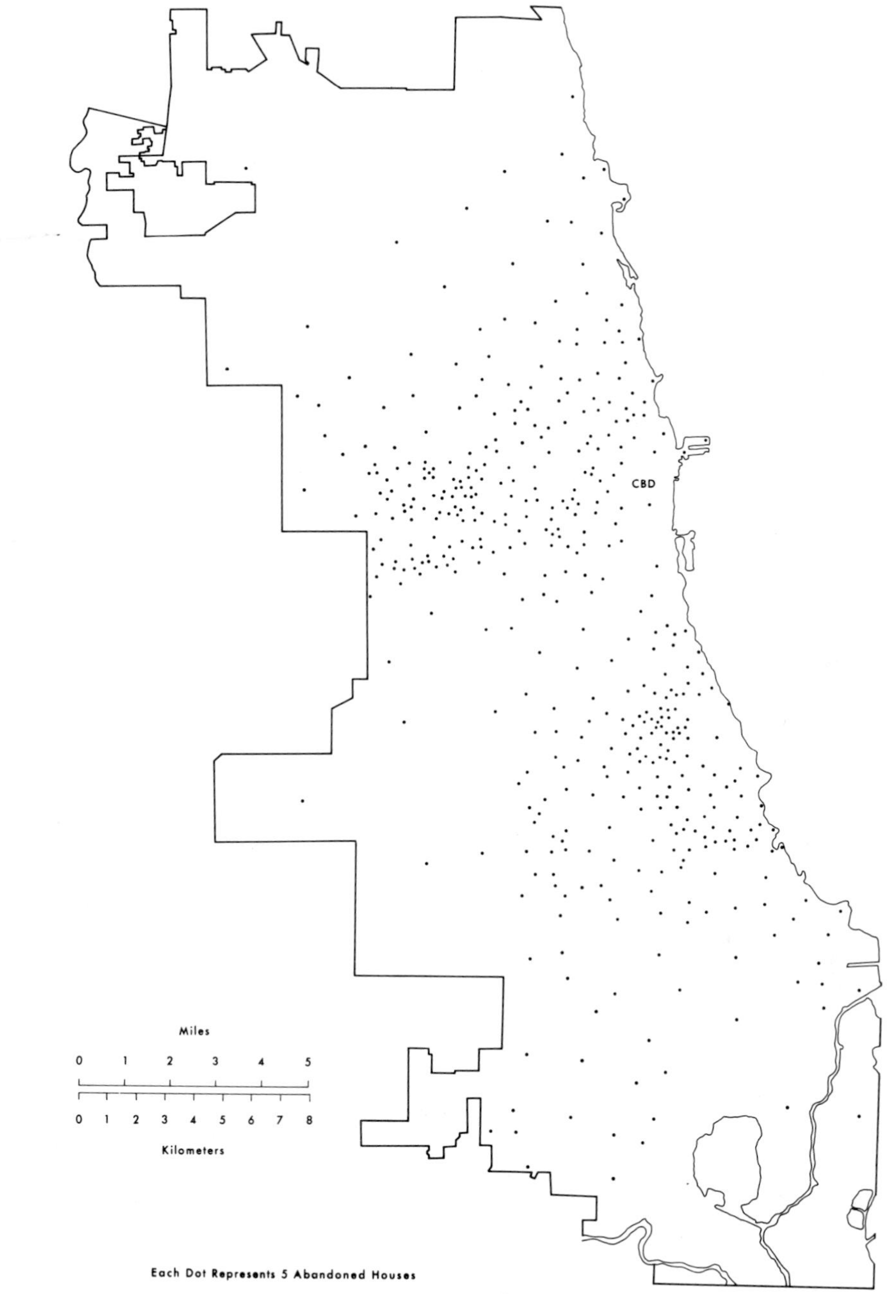

Figure 3-9. Abandoned Housing in Chicago, 1971. After F. Keller, *The Chicago Reporter* (December, 1972, page 3).

the present cash flow problem may appear to stem primarily from increasing maintenance costs, high taxes and insurance costs, increased vacancies, low tenant incomes, and frequent nonpayment of rent.

The general climate of the inner city housing market is impaired by high crime rates, extensive vandalism, lack of recreational and commercial facilities, and overcrowded schools. Moreover, in spite of a decline in overall population, residence overcrowding persists. Perhaps the most significant trend for Chicago is, however, the continuing shift in the income distribution of city families toward an increase in the number of poverty level families. These families are often dependent upon welfare assistance and are highly transient. More importantly, they are becoming increasingly concentrated in areas of population loss, like Lawndale, where abandonment is most prevalent.

Cleveland, Ohio. No reliable estimates exist of the number of vacant and abandoned units in Cleveland. However, a property inventory conducted in 1967 indicated that, of the 271,884 housing units in the city, only 4,920 were vacant. Roughly 25 percent of this total was concentrated in one area, Hough, which contains less than 3 percent of the city's land area and exhibits the highest incidence of overcrowding in the city. By 1969, a second survey had indicated that the total number of vacancies reported in Hough had risen to over 4,000. Rather typically, this vast increase in "abandonments" has occurred primarily during a time of racial transition. From 1910 to 1940, Hough's black population remained at about 1 percent of the area's total. By 1950, the proportion had risen to 4 percent. However, in 1960, it was 74 percent, and nearly 90 percent by 1970.

Abandonment in Cleveland is almost totally absent outside the "poverty area." The concentration of minority group poor in areas vacated by outmigrating, relatively affluent whites follows the pattern which has been detailed for Philadelphia in the preceding section. The decline in the inner city housing market is rooted in the process of suburbanization. The market crisis, however, has been precipitated in Cleveland by institutional disinvestment (red-lining), badly handled public policies (especially relating to code enforcement) and exploitive real estate practices (especially blockbusting and slumlordism). The problem is made worse by a badly worn, obsolescent housing stock which is sadly undermaintained. Under these circumstances, a deepening of Cleveland's inner city housing market problems, including abandonment, seems inevitable.

Detroit, Michigan. In 1970 there were an estimated 6,000 vacant and abandoned housing units in Detroit. This total represents much less of a problem than that of Detroit's neighbor, Chicago. There seem to be three major reasons why abandonment has not reached significant proportions in Detroit. First, there is a relatively high incidence of black homeownership. This is attributable to the general economic prosperity of the city, the predominance of one and two family homes, and the availability of mortgage financing. Second, financial institutions in Detroit have continued to invest in the housing market, presumably because of the historical lack of delinquencies and defaults. And third, the prevailing physical settlement pattern keeps the various economic classes mixed. In particular, those areas which were once white middle class have remained middle class after the process of racial transition. Moreover, in predominantly black areas, high, middle and low income families live in close proximity.

It is important to emphasize the lesson of Detroit. It suggests that where racial transition occurs without a concomitant concentration of poor households, abandonment will tend not to develop. Detroit is a city which is now almost 50 percent black, and both the size of population and of housing stock are declining. The housing market is still fairly tight, however, as the relatively constant vacancy rate over recent years suggests. This market tightness and the relative affluence of the population acts to curb the spread of abandonment.

The observations of the preceding paragraphs were drawn from the relatively optimistic report by the National Urban League in 1971. Of course, since then, there have been some changes in the Detroit housing market. Since 1968, there has been an unprecedented rise in defaults and foreclosures on FHA-insured mortgages in the city. By April 1972, the Detroit HUD area office held nearly 8,000 properties, with many more in default. An additional 2,000 houses have been demolished because their condition was so bad when they came into HUD's possession that they could not be rehabilitated. The mayor of Detroit, in his evidence before a congressional subcommittee on Priorities and Economy in Government, blamed "serious misdirection and mismanagement" of the HUD-FHA programs for posing "a major threat to the health of neighborhood after neighborhood [in Detroit]."

There can be little doubt that the high rate of mortgage foreclosure in Detroit is indicative of a serious "abandonment" problem. This recent trend somewhat contradicts the findings of the National Urban League, although their report does warn that Detroit's future "is far from bright," in view of the rising operational costs faced by landlords and the relative sensitivity of Detroit's economy to national economic trends.

New Orleans, Louisiana. Housing abandonment is not a problem in New Orleans. Moreover, the owners of vacant and derelict structures in that city have not lost their optimism about the future potential of their properties. The factors explaining a lack of abandonment in New Orleans appear to be a mirror image of the reasons causing abandonment in other cities. For example, the city's housing market is fairly tight, and the general scarcity and high cost of developable land have created a market for inner city properties regardless of their condition. Racial discrimination in the housing market has also induced an artificial scarcity in the lower income end of the market. In short, the real estate market is very active where it might normally be expected to be quiescent.

Other conditions in the city have also contributed to a healthy real estate climate. The rates of crime and vandalism, or deficiencies in public services, have not been so great as to promote outmigration or an increase in housing costs. The pressure upon these latter costs has also been alleviated by judicial use of code enforcement and low taxes. The low overall density and preponderance of single and double family units have also encouraged good maintenance practices.

Although the rate of withdrawal of residential properties from the market is low at present, there are indications that this rate could increase in areas where housing costs are rising faster than incomes. This may imply a potential for future abandonment if low income households become concentrated, especially if such a concentration were to occur (as would be likely) in the poor condition, older housing stock. In the Irish Channel area of New Orleans, for example, there has been an increase in the number of tenants not paying rents, and it is generally acknowledged that most buildings would show a loss if the required repair and maintenance expenditures were made. It would appear that the development of an abandoned housing inventory in New Orleans is only being prevented by the continuing, strong demand for housing in the inner city. Alternative evidence, to be considered later in this chapter, suggests that New Orleans does have the beginnings of an abandonment problem.

New York, New York. The true extent of abandonment in New York City is unknown, although Kristof has estimated that about 100,000 housing units had been withdrawn from the market between 1965 and 1968, displacing over 275,000 persons. In a city where there are about two million rental units, this represents an abandonment rate of about 5 percent. This is a considerable scale of abandonment, considering the acute housing shortage in New York City, where the vacancy rate is under 1 percent. Kristof suggests that the system of rent control peculiar to the city was a contributory factor in the abandonment total; and Sternlieb has suggested that, without rent control, the rate of housing loss through abandonment would be lower.

The National Urban League's survey suggests that abandonment has not yet reached crisis proportions as a citywide phenomenon, although as much as 6 percent of the residential structures in certain Brooklyn neighborhoods were abandoned in 1969. One other study of abandonment and urban blight, in the Crown Heights section of Brooklyn, had some interesting observations about the state of the housing market in that area between 1960 and 1970. During that time, over 87,000 whites left the area, but over 98,000 blacks took their places. Even with this excess of demand over supply, abandonment still occurred. The factors associated with abandonment in Crown Heights appear to have been a 164 percent increase in the number of families on welfare and a decrease of 37 percent in the number of retail stores in the area over the period 1958-1967.

Elsewhere in New York City abandonment appears to be associated with several basic socioeconomic conditions that are beginning to form something of a recurrent theme in this chapter. Hence, the factors conducive to abandonment are high operating and maintenance costs; tenant poverty; red-lining and disinvestment practices; vandalism; lack of confidence; and friction between landlord and tenant. In a study for the New York City Rand Institute, Ira Lowry determined that in the rent-controlled sector an owner must counter an annual 6 percent cost increase with only a 2 percent rent increase. With owners faced with a choice between cutting back on maintenance or accepting a rapidly declining net return on investment, a strong current of disinvestment occurred in the rent-controlled sector. In the uncontrolled sector (during the 1968-1969 period), market rents were increasing as much as 25 percent on a two year lease.

Newark, New Jersey. In a thorough study of abandonment in Newark, Sternlieb and Burchell utilized the city's fire department surveys of vacant buildings in order to derive an estimate of the magnitude of abandonment. After making some necessary adjustments to the data, the authors estimated that over the four year period 1967-1971, 7.5 percent of the city's total housing stock was abandoned. The annual loss of residential structures totaled just under 1,500. The study is unequivocal in considering Newark's problem as the "leading edge" of the phenomenon on a national level.

The trends toward suburbanization in Newark are typical of the other cities considered in this essay. The city today has a population of 380,000. In 1950, it was 17 percent black; today (1970), this proportion is 54 percent. Between 1960 and 1970, over 100,000 whites left for the suburbs. Employment totals have declined 25 percent over the decade. Household income, median contract rents and house values have all declined rapidly relative to the suburbs. Only the vacancy rate has increased in the city—to 6.6 percent in the inner core area. In addition, industrial land uses are being abandoned at two and one-half times the rate of commercial and residential abandonments.

As in the case of Philadelphia, the geographic impact of abandonment seems to be synonymous with urban blight in the inner areas of Newark. However, Sternlieb and Burchell have found that other market factors are important, besides those associated with the "normal" process of decay. The authors conclude from a multivariate regression analysis that residential abandonment "seems to be much more a function of tax delinquency, owner-tenant interplay, and neighborhood location than of the physical charactersitics of the building itself." It is interesting to note, however, that they consider that individual abandonments are actually caused by a wide range of specific occurrences, such as an unexpected water tax bill, or personal tragedy. In this respect, Sternlieb and Burchell seem to agree with the essence of Grigsby's "adverse events" approach to abandonment discussed in the previous section. The Newark survey also suggests that a large proportion of the inner city rental market is managed by "amateurs" who cannot cope with the intricacies of a failing market. Most of them "want out"; many of them are leaving through abandonment. The study notes that few entrepreneurs are willing to take their places. There is as yet no adequate replacement for the hard core tenement landlord.

There seems little doubt that the outmigration of wealth and the inmigration of poverty is the major force behind abandonment in Newark. This is compounded by the slow drying-up of the trend for inmigration, resulting in a decline in demand for inner city housing.

Oakland, California. Vacant and derelict units account for about 0.7 percent of the total housing stock of Oakland: the city does not have what could be termed an abandonment problem. Occasional cash flow problems do occur, and there are some foreclosures on owner-occupied structures. However, the resale market is strong, and housing finance is readily available. Although Oakland's population is similar to older Eastern and Midwestern central cities in racial and socioeconomic composition and in its dynamics, the city is not suffering from the same problems as these older cities. This seems to be due primarily to the fact that, although many of Oakland's increasingly large minority population have low incomes, the average income in transitional neighborhoods is substantially higher than that of inner city areas in the East and Midwest.

Other factors strengthening the inner city housing market in Oakland are the prevalence of low density single family homes and the lack of evidence of extreme social disorganization. Crime and vandalism have also not yet reached levels where they begin to have an impact on the housing market climate. Vacancy rates are reasonable and taxes are not placing undue pressure on owners. Public services, such as trash collections, are good, and help to maintain neighborhoods.

In summary, although Oakland is following the typical trend of white outmigration, and a lesser black immigration, together with a concentration of blacks in poorer neighborhoods, the relative affluence of Oakland's black population plus the shortage of low cost housing is acting to prevent abandonment. Further, it seems as though abandonment will not become a serious problem in Oakland as long as financing is available to maintain a high level of homeownership and to facilitate adequate maintenance of rental properties.

St. Louis, Missouri. Abandoned housing in St. Louis is concentrated in the inner city neighborhoods. In 1971 there were over 10,000 abandoned housing units in the city. The majority of this abandonment had occurred since 1966, and in one of the worst areas of the city (Montgomery) over one-fifth of all standing units are abandoned. In some blocks, over 80 percent of the buildings have been abandoned. The negative influence of such areas of concentrated abandonment is already spreading into the surrounding transitional areas. The worst neighborhoods of abandonment in St. Louis are occupied almost solely by very poor people with little hope of upward mobility (Figure 3-10).

Housing abandonment in St. Louis is apparently the result of cash flow problems. Maintenance costs and other operating costs now far exceed rental incomes, which are diminished in any case by high vacancy rates. The problem of cash flow is aggravated by an increasing number of tenants with very low, essentially inelastic, incomes. In addition, the market for residential properties has evaporated, and owners were faced with abandonment or resale at greatly reduced prices. The market climate is depressed by vandalism and crime, and by a generally low level of management ability amongst property owners in the inner city. Code enforcement practices have also been a factor in some abandonments.

The larger market forces causing these conditions are associated with a general inflationary trend in real estate operations, with shifts in consumer preferences and expectations, and with the complex pattern of intracity migration. A rapid influx of low income black tenants has replaced an outmigrating white population. Vacancy rates grew because this outmigration exceeded the inflow and because the larger low income families could not afford to pay for a suitable amount of space in their new neighborhood. All this has led to an excessive wear and tear on the obsolescent stock.

Charles Leven, in his study of the forces behind urban decay in St. Louis, essentially agrees with this interpretation. He has suggested that the prime factor behind the city's housing crisis is the intensity of the population shift, which has also been associated with a decentralization of employment and retailing activities. In his view, the "basic triggering cause [of blight] . . . was a coincidence of forces in the ordinary mechanism of the housing market" [p. 42]. Blight was therefore caused by a severe dislocation in the housing market, rather than vice versa. The most important of these forces for dislocation was the net outmigration of 400,000 whites from the city between 1950 and 1970: these were "replaced" by a net inmigration of about 16,000 blacks. Consequently, a large amount of older, deteriorating middle class housing became available during 1950-1970. It is not surprising that, in spite of demolition of over 20,000 dwellings, the city's vacancy rate rose from 4,426 dwellings to 22,962 over the period. In the meantime, the

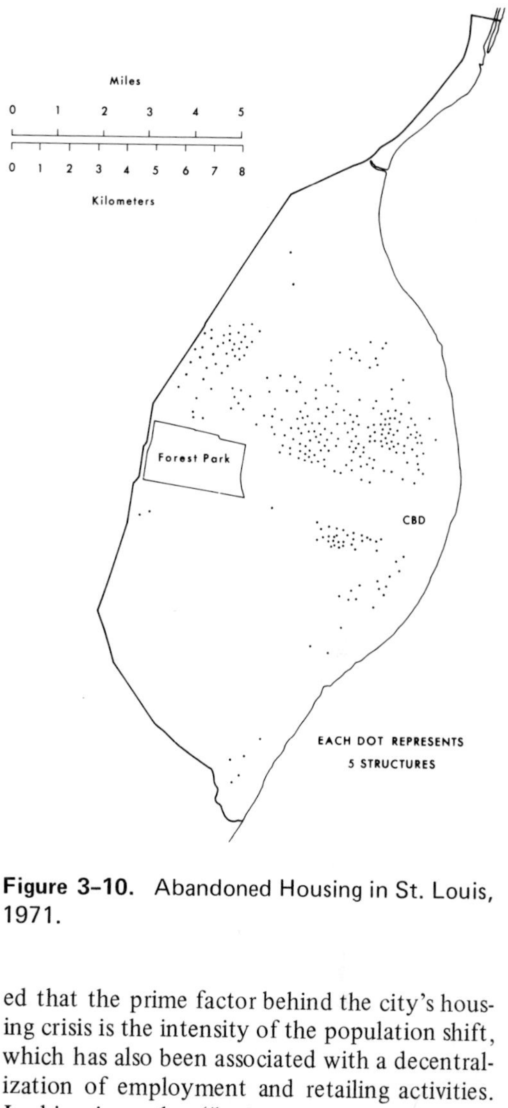

Figure 3-10. Abandoned Housing in St. Louis, 1971.

stock of devalued housing was subject to a cumulative process of "economic exploitation," under a "solely economic" cycle of depletion. The process was intensified by vandalism, crime and deteriorating city services.

Present housing policies toward abandonment in St. Louis appear to concentrate upon acquisition, clearance and renewal. However, since the program is not matched by ancillary policies for dealing with the socioeconomic problems of low income residents, the abandonment phenomenon is not being treated, but rather transplanted elsewhere.

Census Evidence on Abandoned Housing

Some impression of the nationwide extent of housing abandonment may be derived from the US Bureau of the Census data on the number of housing units vacant one year or more. It is unlikely that this variable can be used to provide a reliable estimate of the numerical magnitude of the abandonment phenomenon for the obvious reasons that vacant units are not necessarily abandoned units.

In spite of these drawbacks, it may be possible to regard the distribution of such vacant units as an *indicator* of the abandonment phenomenon, especially if the rate of vacancies is high and spread throughout wide areas of a city. Tables 3-3 and 3-4 provide vacancy estimates for 20 cities, noting whether or not the census data suggest they are experiencing housing abandonment. A city is considered as having abandoned housing if the vacancy rate in individual census tracts is over 5 percent in numerous instances, and if large contiguous areas of the city have vacancy rates in excess of 2.5 percent.

Table 3-3 suggests that all eastern cities of the United States have experience of the abandonment phenomenon, as well as the older Midwestern cities, with the exception of Minneapolis-St. Paul.

For the South, Dallas, Houston and New Orleans all seem to have extensive areas of vacancy, suggesting an abandonment problem. However, Atlanta and Miami are untouched. None of the West Coast cities seems to have experienced abandonment.

Some confirmation of these impressions may be gained by comparing the census results with the evidence of a Senate study indicating the extent, by city, of "known serious housing abandonment." The Senate data confirms the existence of abandonment in the eastern and midwestern cities. However, the southern and West appear to be untouched by abandonment, except for New Orleans and Oakland.

Reviewing the evidence of the preceding studies of abandonment, we discover that eastern and midwestern cities are again confirmed as locales for abandonment, while the South and West seem unaffected. Note, however, that there is conflicting evidence about New Orleans and Oakland. It is possible that the housing market has experienced recent changes (recall the examples of Detroit), and abandonment may now be appearing in these cities.

Some notion about the causes for this apparent regional variation in the incidence of abandonment may be gained from a study of the regional population characteristics for the decade 1960-1970. These trends are reported in the excellent Senate study of the central city problem referred to above. In comparing central city population growth with suburban growth, the study notes that three important trends which began in the 1950s were continued into the 1960s. First, population growth in metropolitan areas continued to be overwhelmingly located in the suburbs. Second, white people continued to migrate in substantial numbers from the central city. And third, central cities continued to have a substantially larger concentration of residents with high need for public services than did the surrounding suburbs.

Several interesting regional dimensions in these population changes ought to be noted. Central City population in the northeastern and midwestern regions declined, while it increased in the southern and western regions, where the younger, less densely developed central cities are located. Where it occurred, central city growth was due largely to annexation or consolidation. Migration of retired people also played a part in central city growth in the South and to a lesser extent, in the West. This migration has a different economic characteristic from migration to the northern and midwestern central cities which was associated with the search for economic opportunity.

Central cities also lost white population during the decade 1960-1970. The rate of loss was greatest within the larger SMSAs and in the Northeast and Midwest regions. Cities in smaller SMSAs and in the South and West had a moderate gain in white population. The black

Table 3-3. National Incidence of Housing Abandonment

Region and City	*Existence of Housing Abandonment* Census Evidence[a]	Senate Evidence[b]	Other Evidence[c]
Northeast			
Baltimore	*	*	*
Boston	*	*	–
Philadelphia	*	*	*
Pittsburgh	*	–	–
New York City	*	*	*
Washington D.C.	*	*	–
Midwest			
Chicago	*	*	*
Cleveland	*	*	*
Detroit	*	*	*
Minneapolis-St. Paul	0	0	–
St. Louis	*	*	*
South			
Atlanta	0	0	0
Dallas	*	–	–
Houston	*	–	–
Miami	0	0	–
New Orleans	*	*	0
West			
Los Angeles	0	–	–
Oakland	0	*	0
San Francisco	0	0	–
Seattle	0	–	–

* = confirmed abandonment
0 = no abandonment
– = no evidence

[a]U.S. Bureau of the Census. *Census of Population and Housing 1970. Census Tracts.*

[b]U.S. Congress, Senate Committee on Banking, Housing and Urban Affairs, Subcommittee on Housing and Urban Affairs, *The Central City Problem and Urban Renewal Policy* (Washington, D.C.: US Government Printing Office, 1973), p. 89.

[c]Preceding city studies in this chapter.

gain in population was greatest in those regions and cities which experienced the greatest white loss—namely, cities located in large SMSAs and in the northeastern and midwestern sections of the country. The black share of suburban population remained relatively unchanged everywhere.

Income disparities between central city and suburb increased between 1960 and 1970. The rate of increase in median family income was about one-third higher in the suburbs than in the central city. Since median incomes in the central city were already lower than the suburbs in absolute terms, the central city's relative position has worsened considerably. Moreover, the income disparity between central city and suburb was greatest in cities from the Northeast and the Midwest, tending to lessen in the South and West.

Finally, it might also be noted that housing construction activity in the suburbs was almost three times as great as in the central cities of the country.

Summary

On a national scale, housing abandonment is currently confined to the cities of the Northeast and Midwest regions of the US. Potential for abandonment exists in the larger cities of the South and the West, notably Dallas, Houston, New Orleans and Oakland.

Where it is occurring, abandonment seems to be universally associated with a large net *loss of population* from the inner city. Since the out-

Table 3-4. Census Evidence of Housing Abandonment

Central City	*Number of Housing Units*	*Number of Housing Units Vacant one year or more*	*Percentage of Housing Units Vacant one year or more*
Northeast			
Baltimore	305,161	2,636	0.86
Boston	232,449	2,112	0.90
Philadelphia			
Pittsburgh			
New York	2,924,483	9,938	0.35
Washington, D.C.	278,439	1,696	0.06
Midwest			
Chicago	1,207,365	7,491	0.62
Cleveland	264,217	2,394	0.90
Detroit	529,115	3,778	0.71
Minneapolis-St. Paul	274,907	777	0.28
St. Louis	238,485	2,851	1.19
South			
Atlanta	170,890	499	0.05
Dallas	317,885	1,870	0.58
Houston	462,932	4,203	0.90
Miami	125,305	238	0.19
New Orleans	208,524	1,750	0.84
West			
Los Angeles	1,183,282	3,101	0.27
Oakland	146,610	518	0.35
San Francisco	310,406	981	0.31
Seattle	221,980	983	0.44

Source: 1970 Census of Population and Housing. See the *1970 Census Users' Guide, Part II*, pp. 115–117, for definition of the term "vacant."

migration is affecting mainly affluent whites, and the lesser immigration is by poor blacks, the inner city is becoming a ghetto, both in racial and economic terms. Above all else, however, the *concentration of poverty* in the inner city area seems to have been the major force behind the disruption of the housing market in the inner city. From a realtor-financier viewpoint, poverty has been compounded by the *reduction in effective demand* for inner city housing resulting from the net loss of population.

Several features are testimony to the depressed state of the inner city housing market. The *cash flow problem* is most basic, since it summarizes many problems, including the huge rise in maintenance costs, the relative inflexibility of landlord budget, etc. In addition to these strictly market factors are a host of *environmental factors,* like poor municipal services, crime and vandalism, and so on.

In a large number of instances, *government intervention* in the housing market has made the climate of depression worse. To meet this must be added the inept "performance" of many other participants in the housing market. For example, *problem tenants* can often act as a catalyst for decay, as can the unethical behavior of a realtor or *slumlord.* The studies in this chapter have steadily underlined the *need for good management* of the housing stock: unfortunately most managers of the inner city market are just waiting for the chance to escape the market, and no one seems prepared to step into the vacuum left by their departure.

AN EXPLANATION OF HOUSING ABANDONMENT

A theory, or at least an explanation, of abandoned housing is necessary for two reasons: first, in order to provide a cohesive understanding of the process of abandonment from the welter of empirical evidence considered in the last three sections of this study, and second, in order to inform policy decisions relating to the appropriate type and level of intervention in the market. This section concentrates upon deriving an orderly explanation for abandonment, while policy issues are taken up mainly in the concluding section.

An Explanation for Abandonment

The broad facts which need to be encompassed within an explanation of abandoned housing are those relating to the suburbanization–urban decay–abandonment (S-UD-A) hypothesis, modified by consideration of the collapse of confidence in the inner city market and the implications of the cyclical view of abandonment. The five explanations for abandonment go part of the way toward explaining these facts. Hence, suburbanization could be viewed as a process of *neighborhood succession* occurring in the suburbs and in the inner city. Urban decay becomes a consequence of this succession process, via the *filtering* mechanism. This improvement by abandonment causes a depressed inner city market, a condition aggravated by the *low income* of residents and exploitative behavior of local realtors and financiers. Abandonment is ultimately caused by some *adverse event.*

Although this composite explanation provides a plausible account of the abandonment process, it also leaves many questions unanswered. For example, the annular-sectoral distribution of abandonment, and its functional implications, are imperfectly considered. Further, the extension of abandonment outside the area of urban decay is ignored; and, even more importantly, the whole contagion issue is left untouched. Quite clearly, a fuller explanation is needed.

It would appear that a comprehensive account of abandonment must be sought on four separate levels. First, on the most general level, an explanation of the major *force* behind abandonment is required. Then, at a second level, it must be shown how the *localization* of this force occurs and is manifest as abandonment in specific neighborhoods. At a third level, the precise *cause* of abandonment within these neighborhoods has to be specified. And finally, at a fourth level, the individual *dynamics* of abandonment require an explanation. In the following paragraphs, each of these four levels is considered in detail (Figure 3-11).

Level 1: Force. Historically, the suburbanization of population and economic activity has occurred as a natural response to internal pres-

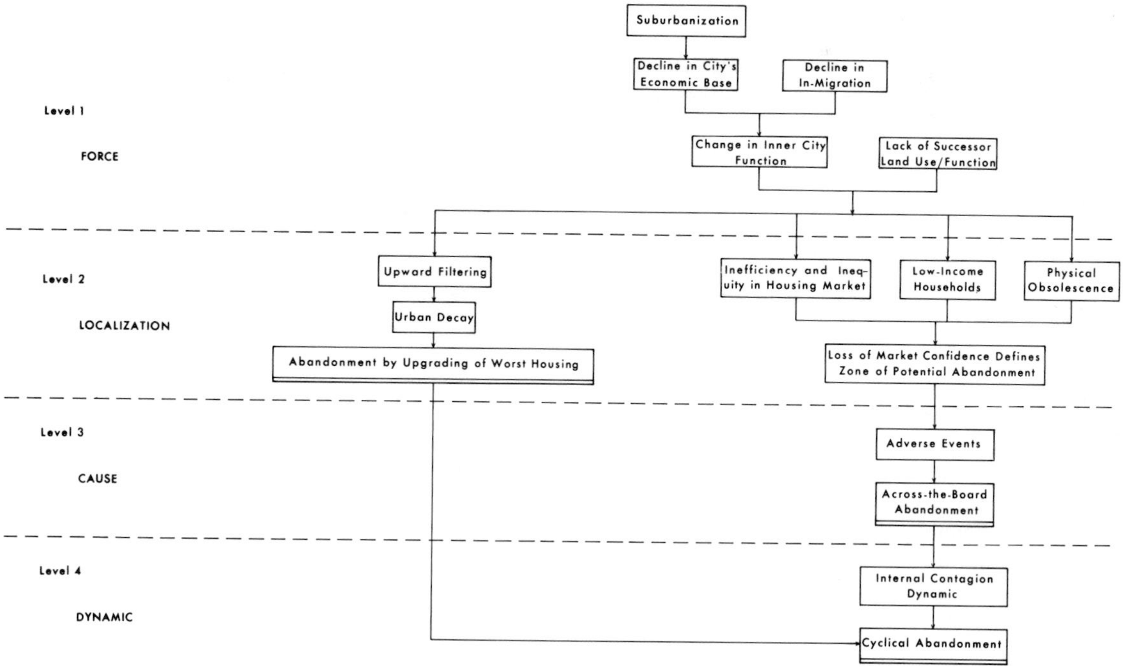

Figure 3–11. An Explanation for Abandoned Housing.

sures for growth within the city. These pressures for "organic" expansion were heightened by a considerable immigration from rural areas. Two more recent trends have, however, caused us to view the continuing process of suburbanization with alarm. First, the steady outmigration of city-based industry is beginning to have a serious impact upon the economic and fiscal stability of the city. And second, the flow of migrants into the city has begun to slow down, and has even stopped in some cities. The consequence of these trends is a change in the traditional functions of the inner city. Their role as the source of a wide range of blue collar jobs is being increasingly challenged by the expanding suburban industrial parks. Moreover, the inner city can no longer claim to be the traditional residence of the city-based blue collar and service workers. There has been a large decline in the demand for housing in these areas.

Under normal circumstances, a change in land use function would not be cause for concern. Market processes would ensure that the new, invading land use would rapidly subvert the existing one, and a land use succession will have taken place. Normally, the issue of abandonment would probably not have arisen. However, the current situation does not appear to involve a "normal" succession. No land user of equivalent magnitude appears to be in the market for the land which is being released from the inner city housing market. The housing function is not being invaded or usurped by an invading function: it is simply abdicating its position with no invader in sight! A "functional vacuum" remains behind in the inner city, and abandonment is the result.

It may, of course, be countered that the natural process of succession is a slow one, and is being hindered in this specific case by artificial or institutional constraints. For example, the difficulties involved in assembling large tracts of land in inner cities is a notorious brake upon redevelopment. Archaic zoning laws also act against an easy succession. Under such circumstances, it could be argued that the demand for inner city land could be artificially diminished. However, one is tempted to believe that if the demand was there, it would somehow surface. Institutional land uses (like universities and hospitals) seem to manage to acquire large tracts of inner city land without too much trouble, for example.

Level 2: Localization. Our understanding of the macrogeographic force behind abandonment does not explain how abandonment comes to be concentrated in specific neighborhoods. There seem to be two aspects to this process of localization. First, one sort of abandonment may occur in association with the normal processes of urban decay (cf. the lefthand side of Figure 3-11). Hence, given a continuous upward filtering of households and a decline in demand for inner city housing, it is natural to assume that the worst housing is going to be abandoned at the end of the filtering chain. Ingram and Kain refer to this as the "scrapping" of the worst units.

The second form of abandonment is more virulent: it spreads beyond the bounds of urban decay in a contagious manner. The overwhelming cause of the localization of this kind of abandonment is poverty. The low income household is outside the filtering process–it is locked into the inner city housing market. The plight of these households is aggravated by the inefficient and inequitable operation of the inner city housing market, and the acute obsolescence of the physical fabric. The coincidence of these three factors leads to a collapse of confidence in the regenerative capacity of the housing market, as manifest in the lack of property resale value. Wherever this value is low, or nonexistent, a *zone of potential abandonment* has been defined (cf. the righthand side of Figure 3-11).

Level 3: Cause. The actual abandonment of a given property is the personal decision of the individual property owner. The ultimate cause of abandonment is an apparently random adverse event occurring within the zone of potential abandonment. Inside this zone, there has been a complete collapse of confidence in the housing market. Outside this zone, such adverse events would probably have been absorbed by the property owner, and would not have caused abandonment. Abandonment associated with an adverse event occurs across the board in terms of housing condition, affecting good and bad condition properties alike.

The random adverse event is acceptable only as an explanation of the initial abandonments in an area. After the first abandonments have occurred, a very different explanation is required to account for the continuation of abandonment. The adverse event explanation then becomes almost irrelevant.

Level 4: Dynamic. At this fourth level of explanation, the abandonment process has acquired an internal impetus largely independent of the forces which led to the initial abandonments. The necessity for recourse to an adverse events explanation of abandonment is now removed. Once begun, abandonment spreads like a disease away from its source in a contagious manner. An entire neighborhood is, in this manner, plunged almost inevitably into a form of cyclical abandonment–an internal dynamic of decay (cf. Figure 3-4).

The reasons for the existence of this apparently internal dynamic of abandonment are unclear. The element of contagion is obviously a critical variable. It seems to operate via the property owner's perception of the housing market. Hence, abandonment is viewed negatively as physical evidence of the psychological and economic abandonment of an area. The presence of abandoned properties in a neighborhood is therefore likely to encourage a policy of disinvestment and undermaintenance on the part of the observer. Such a policy only accelerates further decay in the area.

Another very important factor in the cycle of abandonment is the incidence of crime and vandalism in neighborhoods where abandonment has taken hold. A property vacant for over a week will subsequently be stripped of all salable materials, and later vandalized. It is impossible to quantify the contribution of these processes to the rate of urban decay, but it is surely quite considerable.

A Theory of Abandonment

The explanation of abandoned housing just outlined is suggestive of a larger theory of abandonment, which could be utilized to account for phenomena occurring at several different levels, and in several different sectors, of the urban system. Simple observation suggests that many things are being abandoned–the houses of this essay, for example, together with a large number of retail establishments, industrial structures, port faciliites, office buildings and so on. The same thing is happening to many institutional structures, like cinemas and churches.

A major factor in the abandonment of all these phenomena is *functional obsolescence* (Figure 3-12). The structure simply cannot cope with the new functional demands being placed upon it. Of course, functional obsolescence is inextricably associated with physical and economic obsolescence. Before a structure can be functionally obsolete, it has to be either too old and derelict to operate efficiently, or be too costly to renovate for efficient operation.

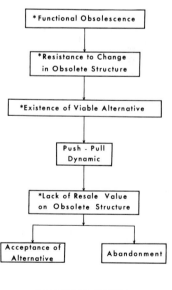

Functional obsolescence is the major necessary condition for abandonment; however, it is not sufficient in itself to cause abandonment. Among the other conditions necessary for abandonment are a *resistance to change* within the phenomenon and the *existence of viable alternatives* to the functionally obsolete (Figure 3-12). Resistance to change can derive from numerous sources: for example, an industrial site may lack sufficient space for expansion, or institutional constraints may not permit such expansion. The existence of viable alterna-

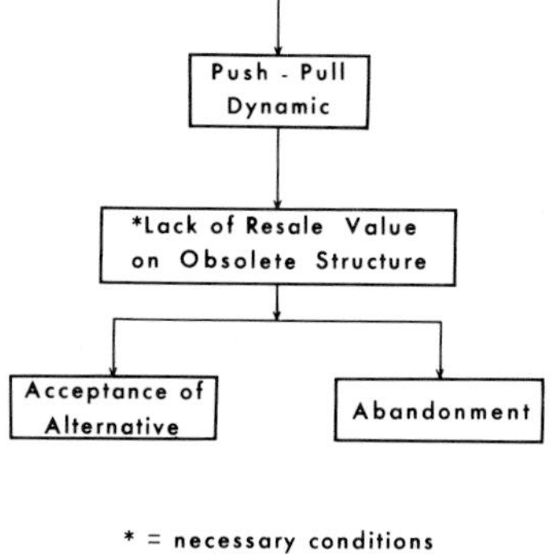

Figure 3-12. A Theory of Abandonment.

tives is obviously essential to the development of a *push-pull dynamic*. The owner of the obsolete structure is now subject to pressure from two sides: the push to leave the obsolete structure and the pull to adopt the alternative structure.

A critical necessary condition at this stage is that the obsolete structure must *lack a resale value* in its present form. If an obsolete structure can be traded for a reasonable sum, then an acceptable market solution to the obsolescence problem has been found. However, if the resale potential is nil or unbearably low, and a large loss has to be borne by the owner in adopting the alternative structure, the obsolete structure may be abandoned by the owner. This situation probably implies that the transaction costs associated with the disposal of the obsolete structure exceed any possible return on the sale of that structure.

In summary, the necessary preconditions for abandonment of any given phenomenon are functional obsolescence, resistance to change, the existence of viable alternatives and the lack of resale value. For abandonment to occur, however, one further catalyst condition is required. In the case of housing, it was the adverse event. For other phenomena, it might be changes in consumption habits, or a revised property tax structure, for example. It might also be that the general process of abandonment, once begun, takes on an internal dynamic independent of the forces leading to the original abandonment. One analogy for contagion in the housing example could be the spatial rearrangement of agglomeration economies which, being irrevocably altered after the first abandonment, could generate an internal force of itself for further abandonment.

ABANDONED HOUSING AND PUBLIC POLICY

A complete and proper treatment of the question of public policy toward housing abandonment would require a separate essay. In this short space, therefore, the emphasis will fall upon the principles of public policy. In any event, this is an appropriate emphasis, since the question of public policy toward abandonment is truly an issue of principle.

The first task is to consider the implications for policy of the explanation of housing abandonment. Appropriate types and levels of policy intervention may be suggested from such an examination. In the light of these observations, current housing policies are reviewed briefly, including certain policies designed specifically to cope with abandonment. Finally, an alternative set of public policies toward abandoned housing is discussed.

A Policy Attitude Toward Abandoned Housing

Abandoned housing is a serious problem in many American cities today. It represents a process of decay which is out of control. A rational policy attitude toward abandonment has to be developed with regard for two particular characteristics of the abandonment process. First, abandoned housing represents the "end-state" of a deep-seated functional change within the inner city; and second, abandonment is an extremely complicated process, and different policy approaches will be necessary at the various stages of the abandonment cycle. The implications of both these characteristics are explored briefly in the following paragraphs.

One of the major dimensions of abandoned housing is the suburbanization–urban decay–abandonment (S-UD-A) hypothesis. Although this hypothesis provided only a partial "explanation" of the process of abandonment, it is nevertheless properly considered as the major dynamic influencing the process. Abandoned housing may thus be regarded as the "end-state" of the suburbanization process. It is important to realize that suburbanization is not a transitory phenomenon, and abandonment by upgrading (under the normal process of urban decay) has been going on for some time. However, the more virulent form of contagious abandonment is a more recent development. It is this latter form of destructive abandonment that aggravates the loss of confidence in the inner city housing market. Nevertheless, the root cause of all abandoned housing is a force which has been present for many decades. Public policies which do not recognize this fundamental characteristic can only have a minor impact upon the abandonment problem.

Public policy also has to come to grips with the fact that different policy approaches will be required at the various stages of the abandonment cycle (Figure 3-4). For example, a minimally funded program for rehabilitation in an area of wholesale abandonment would be futile. On the other hand, such a program in an area of scattered abandonment could be instrumental in reversing the process of decay. Clearly, a suitable hierarchy of intervention policies needs to be developed.

The policy attitude toward abandoned housing (derived from the foregoing analysis) concentrates specifically upon only three levels of the explanation for abandonment. Hence, policies which attack the root causes of abandonment intervene at Levels 1 and 2 of the process (i.e., force and localization). And policies which intervene at the level of individual abandonments are designed mainly to cope with Level 4 of the process (the internal dynamic). It seems that little can, or ought, to be done about the incidence of random adverse events in the housing market (Level 3 of the abandonment process).

Alternative Strategies for Housing Abandonment

Government intervention in the housing market is necessary to reverse the trend toward abandonment in the inner city housing market. There are three major arguments which together constitute an overwhelming case for intervention.

First, on *humanitarian* grounds, government has a responsibility to house the low income inner city households. If nothing is done about abandonment, substantial numbers of these households will be condemned to living in increasingly derelict conditions, through no fault of their own. Government has a social obligation to help these people, since part of their plight is directly attributable to government policy.

Second, there is a wide range of *social and economic reasons* for investing in the continued well-being of our inner cities. A study prepared by the Congressional Research Service for the US Senate Committee on Banking, Housing and Urban Affairs in 1973 has summarized the issues involved in central city problem. Among the many reasons it cites for not lightly writing off the nation's economic and social stake in the central city are the following:

> Financial institutions hold tens of billions of dollars of mortgages and bonds secured by central city residential and business properties and private and public utilities. Continued central city deterioration would lead to the devaluation of these assets, with *serious repercussions within the national financial structure.* Society would bear a *sizable economic burden if infrastructure which is unused or underutilized is duplicated elsewhere*—a situation clearly occurring with the flight of middle-class families to suburbs. [P. 7, emphasis added]

Third, there are sound *theoretical reasons* for not abandoning the inner city. Prime among these is the possibility that the inner city housing market is functionally obsolete and that no invading land use is seeking to succeed it. The inner city may be dying, and even though its fate is uncertain, steps ought to be taken to ensure that it does not collapse. It is too much to expect the highly imperfect land and property market to do the job of reclamation.

The evidence of this essay amounts to an almost unanswerable case for government intervention to reverse the trend toward abandonment of the inner city housing market. The only real case against intervention must rely upon belief in the principle of nonintervention. While such a principle might be appropriate in certain instances, it would appear that this is not one of them. If the rationale for intervention is accepted, then six specific policy approaches may be recommended.

1. The reclamation and rehabilitation of the inner city housing market is a public responsibility. This obligation ought to be recognized by the *establishment of a public or quasi-public corporation* charged specifically with this task. The prime responsibility of this corporation is to fill the vacuum left in the inner city by the departing landlord and real estate interests. It might be appropriate to delegate responsibility for the local operation of the corporation to the neighborhood level. Other responsibilities of this body would include the acquisition of land and property for redevelopment and the administration of federal and local finances in the relevant areas. The corporation should take care that the abuses of earlier programs are not repeated: a *rigid system of public accountability* is required for all future real estate operations in the city.

2. One way of ensuring accountability is via a community-agreed *plan for inner city rehabilitation.* The aim of this plan would be to control change in land use and function, in

order to prevent inefficiencies and inequities in the market from turning the inner city into a wasteland. Such an approach would also imply some plan for control of land use development in the suburbs, since strict control in one area of the market and not in another might encourage the flight of real estate interests from the controlled sector. This suggestion for the control of metropolitan land use seems a logical extension of Downs' call for a national housing strategy, and the Urban Land Institute's advocacy of a national growth policy (providing a framework for direction and coordination of a wide variety of federal programs, including housing).

3. One of the corporation's tasks ought to be to establish a *public works labor force.* This would be a work force capable of operating an on-going program of rehabilitation of obsolescent inner city housing stock. The corporation would ensure that a rolling program of rehabilitation is scheduled, so that work can be guaranteed for personnel. Such rehabilitation would be at public expense, except where private property was involved: some of the outlay could then be recouped. The main advantage of this public works force is that it could act fast to prevent further decay in the housing stock. It would also show that the government—both federal and local—was committed to revitalizing the inner city.

4. As well as broad policies for dealing with the functional basis of abandonment, there is a need for *specific antiabandonment policies.* These policies almost suggest themselves. In areas of scattered abandonment, a small investment in public and private rehabilitation may prove sufficient to restore an area. Where abandonment has taken hold, a neighborhoodwide strategy for improvement seems necessary. This might include public finance of acquisition and redevelopment, extensive rehabilitation and the funding of community support services. Finally, in an area which is far gone into the abandonment cycle, the only realistic policy alternative seems to be to speed abandonment in order to facilitate redevelopment.

5. An important concomitant of the preceding policy is that *redevelopment plans for areas which have already been abandoned* are required. The same may be said for areas which are designated for accelerated abandonment. These cannot be simply left as vacant lots. They should be used positively in inner city areas where public parks are generally very scarce, as are community facilities of any kind.

6. Finally, some form of *direct housing allowance* ought to be made to low income families. This will return to the consumer some semblance of choice in housing and may even begin to redress the power balance in the inner city housing market, so heavily biased toward the supply side at present. It might also improve the profit margins of landlords in the inner city.

These six policies are best considered as elements in a single policy package designed to save the inner city housing market from abandonment. It is likely that a partial approach to the problem will fail, since nothing less than total commitment will reverse the powerful forces currently at work in the inner city. The costs of such a package will, of course, be enormous. Aaron estimated that the cost of his version of a housing allowance scheme would be anywhere between $3.2 billion and $6.2 billion (assuming no welfare reform). To this must be added the cost of the public works labor force and its operations, plus the other operating costs of the corporation.

The antiabandonment policy package obviously need only be applied in cities where abandoned housing is a problem. However, the first signs of abandonment in other cities ought to bring a swift public response, since any delay will increase the cost of preventing abandonment.

Concluding Remarks

One is acutely aware of the gaps which remain in this treatment of the problem of abandoned housing. For example, little or no consideration has been given to the potential cost of the public policies being recommended for adoption. In particular, the very important issue of whether the money would come from an expanded federal budget or from a reallocation of existing resources was left untouched. In addition, few of the program details for the recommended policies were spelled out. Neither was there a proper evaluation of the impact of federal housing policy upon abandonment, nor of the full range of adverse events promoting abandonment.

In defense it may be noted that many of these specific issues are dealt with elsewhere, notably in the studies of Aaron; Downs; Linton, Mields and Coston Inc.; Grigsby et al.; and

Sternlieb and Burchell. However, the major reason for these omissions has been the concentration upon principles which has characterized this inquiry. We have sought to explain the principles of abandonment at local, city and national levels; a general explanation of abandonment has been offered, and the basic principles behind the choice of public policies have been highlighted.

There seems little reason to doubt that abandoned housing is a problem of major significance and that it is likely only to deepen unless prompt action is taken to reverse the trend. Speedy public intervention is especially necessary in those areas only now beginning to be affected by abandonment, since these are the areas which hold out most hope for reclamation. It is too much to expect the inner city housing market to recover "naturally" in those areas where abandonment is occurring. The inner city residents are too poor to do much about their predicament. Most power resides on the supply side of the market. In fact, the provision of shelter in the inner city market may almost be regarded as an externality of the process of redistributing government funds among supply side participants. Under such circumstances, it ought not to be surprising that the sum of individual actions does *not* add up to the community good in the inner city market.

The need, clearly, is for a metropolitanwide housing development strategy. The rationale for this recommendation is simply that a tightening up on suburban housing development is likely to promote a more efficient and equitable use of the housing stock throughout the metropolitan area, but especially in the inner city areas. This essay gives full support for Downs' suggestion of a national housing strategy and for the Urban Land Institute's recommendation for a national growth policy (to direct and coordinate a wide variety of federal programs, including housing).

Any future research should, of course, be directed toward informing the decisions of policymakers. The most outstanding gap in our current knowledge seems to concern the actual magnitude of the abandonment problem. Some concerted federally coordinated effort ought to be made to discover the extent of the problem. It is certainly an issue which ought to be pursued in the next decennial census survey. In addition, a coordinated effort is needed to develop an alternative housing strategy based upon priorities other than the current filtering strategy. This present essay has suggested direct government intervention in the opposite end of the housing market. The detailed programming implications of this reversal of priorities still need to be resolved.

Finally, scholarly interest in abandoned housing ought to consider the whole issue of functional change in metropolitan regions more closely. Traditional theories of land rent suggest that density of development and demand for space are both greatest in the central area, and decline with increasing distance from the center. This essay suggests that perhaps there is a discontinuity in this rent surface, around the inner city area, where the bottom has dropped out of the property market. The reasons for such a functional change may usefully be pursued within a neighborhood succession context. In this chapter, we have argued that the function of the inner city is changing, but that there is as yet no "successor" function to take the place of the traditional function. This apparent absence of an invading land use to replace the existing could, in fact, signal a radical change in the functional structure of metropolitan regions—a change comparable with the process of suburbanization.

BIBLIOGRAPHY

Aaron, H.J. *Shelter and Subsidies: Who Benefts from Federal Housing Policies?* Washington, D.C.: The Brookings Institution, 1972.

Anscombe, F.J. "Sampling Theory of the Negative Binomial and Logarithmic Series Distributions." *Biometrika* 37 (1950): 358–82.

City of Philadelphia. "Philadelphia's Abandonment Demonstration Program; A Proposal." Mimeographed. Philadelphia: Abandoned Housing Task Force, 1973.

Bederman, S.H. "Black Residential Neighborhoods and Job Opportunity Centers in Atlanta, Georgia." Ph.D dissertation, University of Minnesota, 1973.

Downs, A. "Federal Housing Subsidies: Their nature and effectiveness and what we should do about them: Summary Report." Washington, D.C.: National Association of Homebuilders, 1972.

"Federal Housing Reform Unlikely Despite Scandal." *New York Times,* September 20, 1972. p. 1.

Greig-Smith, P. *Quantitative Plant Ecology.* 2nd. ed. London: Butterworths, 1964.

Grigsby, W.G. *Housing Markets and Public Policy.* Philadelphia: University of Pennsylvania, 1963.

Grigsby, W.G.; L. Rosenburg; M. Stegman; and J. Taylor. "Housing and Poverty." Institute of Environmental Studies, University of Pennsylvania, 1971.

Harvey, D. "Geographical Processes and the Analysis of Point Patterns: Testing Models of Diffusion by Quadrat Sampling." *Transactions of the Institute of British Geographers* 40 (1966): 81-95.

——. "Society, The City, and the Space-Economy of Urbanism." Commission on College Geography, Resource Paper No. 18. Washington, D.C.: Association of American Geographers, 1972.

Ingram, G.K. and J.F. Kain. "A Simple Model of Housing Production and the Abandonment Problem." Paper presented at the Joint Session of the American Economics Association and the American Real Estate Urban Economics Association, Toronto, Ontario, 1972.

Institute for Environmental Studies. "The Allegheny West Community Development Project: An experiment in privately-financed neighborhood conservation." Philadelphia University of Pennsylvania, 1973.

Keller, F. "Housing Abandonment in Chicago–The Cancer of The Inner City." *The Chicago Reporter* 1, 6, (December 1972): 1-4.

Kristof, F.S. "Economic Facets of New York City's Housing Problems." In L. Fitch and A. Walsh, *Agenda for a City.* New York: Institute for Public Administration, 1970.

Leven, C.L. and M.L. Weidenbaum. *Urban Decay in St. Louis.* Report PB 209-947. Springfield, Va.: National Technical Information Service, 1972.

Linton, Mields and Coston, Inc. *A Study of the Problems of Abandoned Housing.* Report PB 212-198. Springfield, Va.: National Technical Information Service, 1971.

Lowry, I.S., ed. *Rental Housing in New York: Volume II–The Demand for Shelter.* New York: Rand Corporation R-649-NYC, 1971.

National Commission on Urban Problems (The Douglas Commission). *Building the American City.* Washington, D.C.: US Government Printing Office, 1969.

National Urban League. *National Survey of Housing Abandonment.* New York: The Center for Community Change, 1971.

New York Department of City Planning. "Crown Heights Area Maintenance Program." City of New York, Document NYDCP 72-04, 1972.

Peterson, G.E.; A.P. Solomon; H. Madjid; W.C. Apgar, Jr. *Property Taxes, Housing and the Cities.* Lexington, Mass.: D.C. Heath and Co., 1973.

Philadelphia City Planning Commission. "Population and Housing Trends 1970 Census: Philadelphia and its Metropolitan Area." Public Information Release, 1973.

Sternlieb, G. "Abandoned Housing: What is to be done?" *Urban Land* 36 (March 1972): 3-17.

——. *The Urban Housing Dilemma.* New York: New York City Housing Development Administration, 1972.

Sternlieb, G. and R.W. Burchell. *Residential Abandonment: The Tenement Landlord Revisited.* New Brunswick, N.J. Center for Urban Policy Research, Rutgers–The State University, 1973.

US Bureau of the Census. *Census of Population and Housing 1960. Census Tracts.* Final Report PHC (1)-116, Philadelphia, Pa. - N.J. SMSA. Washington, D.C.: US Government Printing Office, 1962.

US Bureau of the Census. *Census of Population and Housing 1970. Census Tracts.* Final Report PHC (1)-159, Philadelphia, Pa. - N.J. SMSA. Washington, D.C.: US Government Printing Office, 1972.

US Congress, Joint Economic Committee. "The Economics of Federal Subsidy Programs: A Compendium of Papers, Part 5, Housing Subsidies." Washington D.C., US Government Printing Office, 1972.

US Congress, Joint Economic Committee. Subcommittee on Priorities and Economy in Government. *Housing Subsidies and Housing Policies.* Washington, D.C.: US Government Printing Office, 1973.

US Congress, Senate Committee on Banking, Housing and Urban Affairs, Subcommittee on Housing and Urban Affairs. *The Central*

City Problem and Urban Renewal Policy. Washington, D.C.: US Government Printing Office, 1973.

US Department of Labor, Bureau of Labor Statistics. "Employment Structure and Trends: Philadelphia Mideast Region, Report No. 2." Philadelphia, 1971.

Urban Land Institute. "Federal Government in Housing." *Urban Land* 37, 7 (July-August 1973): 3-8.

Weissbourd, B. Letter to *The Chicago Reporter* 2, 2 (February 1973) p. 1.

Williamson, E. and M.H. Bretherton. *Tables of the Negative Binomial Probability Distribution*. New York: John Wiley, 1963.

Zevin, R. "An Analysis of Long-Term Vacancy and Tax Delinquency of Residential Structures in Philadelphia." Philadelphia: Community Research Program, 1972.

Chapter 4

National Progress Toward Housing and Urban Renewal Goals

John Mercer
University of British Columbia

John Hultquist
University of Idaho

INTRODUCTION*

A debate on the desirable geographical consequences of national housing policy and programs should start with awareness of the fundamental geographical facts concerning publicly assisted housing. Three metropolitan areas are chosen for detailed study—Atlanta, Chicago and Seattle—providing contrasting regional coverage and a variety of urban conditions such as stage of urban development, economic base, racial mix and so forth. We begin with a description of the evolution of federal legislation and programs. The next section examines each area's mix of federal housing programs and their geographical consequences. A third section compares patterns of subsidized housing and recent local policy initiatives in the three regions and concludes with recommendations and reflections on the directions of American housing policy.

There do not exist objectives or criteria for future residential environments; therefore, the geographical consequences of federal programs are basically unintentional and frequently unknown. In the few instances where locational issues have been specifically addressed in housing policy, their effect has limited the flexibility of the programs. For example, early policy decisions forbade the use of public housing to change the racial composition of neighborhoods, thereby perpetrating and reinforcing segregation.

This is an essay on housing and national public policy; on housing built or purchased through federal assistance; and on the residential environment of American metropolitan areas. Housing issues were first codified and brought into the public arena with the Housing Act of 1937. However, the emphasis here is on the impact of housing programs developed after that initial legislation. We focus specifically on housing legislation and the related programs, and neglect the influence on housing of federal policies in such fields as transportation, education, health care and civil rights.

UNITED STATES HOUSING PROGRAMS: THE NATIONAL SCENE

In this section, the evolution of federal legislation and related programs concerning publicly

*A study such as this depends on the cooperation and assistance of those working in local public agencies and organizations. There are many people whose help has been most valuable. While we cannot list them all, the following deserve a special note of thanks: Judy Ball, Seattle Housing Department; Gil Till, Department of Housing and Urban Development, Seattle; Morton Kaplan, Department of Housing and Urban Development, Chicago; Piero Faraci and Deborah Washington, Northeastern Illinois Planning Commission, Chicago; Frank Keller, Department of Planning, City of Atlanta; and Margaret Ross, Atlanta Housing Authority. We would also like to thank Frank E. Horton and Kenneth J. Dueker for assistance and encouragement during the initial stages of this study while the authors were associated with the Institute for Urban and Regional Research at the University of Iowa.

assisted housing is reviewed. The legislative review covers four decades—1933 to 1973. The record with respect to the amount of housing produced under selected programs is then examined. Finally, consideration is given to some conceptual and empirical problems of assessing the impact of such programs in terms of national goals and the local urban environment.

Legislation and Programs: An Overview

The legislation stems in part from the belief of policymakers and housing reformers that significant numbers of Americans need help in obtaining decent housing. Despite initial opposition from key elements in American society, an array of legislation has developed.

The initial legislation of the 1930s is a product of depression conditions and the political context of the "New Deal"—the government must act. Its importance lies in the establishment of a federal presence in the housing market—the Public Works Administration built dwelling units for rent and the Federal Housing Administration (FHA) was created to administer a mortgage insurance program. A Low Rent Public Housing program was established in 1937 to enable low income households to obtain "adequate shelter," as was a slum clearance program which would result in an improvement in the quality of the housing stock.

World War II not only diverted attention from the problems of that one-third of the nation which President Roosevelt claimed were "ill-housed," but also brought a decline in housing construction. Following the war years, the problems were intensified by the lack of new housing starts in the face of pent-up and rising demands for accommodation.

The government again responded with legislation and greater appropriations for the Low Rent Public Housing program, while, by 1950, the home construction industry was producing new units at a rapid rate (Figure 4-1). The Housing Act of 1949 contains the first general statement concerning the housing of American families and this is widely referred to as *the national housing goal.* Congress called for "... the realization as soon as feasible of the goal of a decent home and a suitable living environment for every American family." The people, through Congress, thus expressed an ambitious

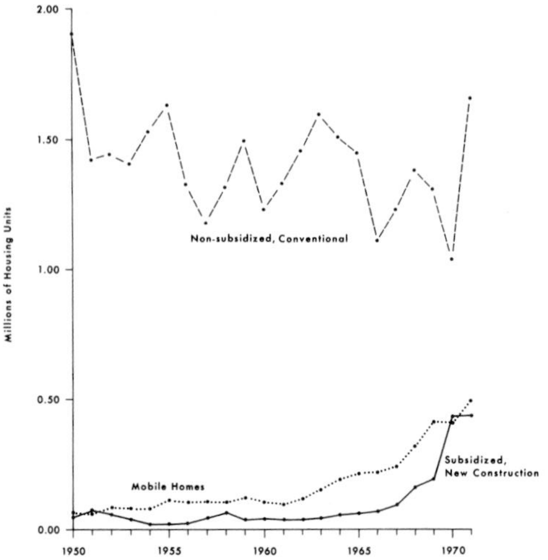

Figure 4-1. United States Annual Housing Starts, 1950-1971. Source: Downs.

and equally ambiguous intent to set about the task of providing appropriate shelter for millions who somehow missed out on America's riches. Yet the statement raises difficult questions. What is a decent home? What is a suitable living environment? Does "as soon as feasible" mean ten years, 25 years or never? Without precise answers to such questions, how can the number of families in need be determined or the yearly effort proposed? Although such questions have never been answered, federal programs to assist people in purchasing or renting dwelling units have been continually conceived and carried out with mixed results. These programs are based on a federal and perhaps public concern for the cost and quality of housing occupied by the people since it is popularly believed that there is a direct relationship between these factors and the general health, morals and well-being of the occupants. The programs are aimed primarily at low income households since they are often unable to obtain decent housing at a reasonable cost to the household, given the price of housing as determined by market conditions in certain locations. They evidently are the ones who need help most.

This twin concern with cost and quality is reflected in the 1949 legislation which (1) created an urban renewal program, the purpose of which was to eliminate substandard units from the housing stock (appealingly referred to as slum clearance) and reverse the processes of housing deterioration, and (2) continued the low rent public housing program designed to construct new and standard units for low income households. These programs were the long-standing basis for governmental efforts to deal with America's housing problems, although more recent legislative action has created other programs (Figure 4-2). What is the basic structure of these fundamental programs?

Low Rent Public Housing (Housing Act of 1949 and Subsequent Amendments). This is a rental housing subsidy program for low income households. In the case of *conventional* public housing, the federal agency, by making loan commitments to local public housing authorities, provides security for bonds which pay for the construction of low rent multifamily units. The federal agency also assists the local public housing authorities in meeting their annual operating costs. There are two variations in the supply of low rent public housing. Where a private builder finds a site and builds units according to locally approved plans and these units are subsequently purchased by the authority for use as low rent multifamily units, this is referred to as *turnkey* public housing. (Housing and Urban Development Act, 1968) The *leased* public housing program (Section 23, Housing and Urban Development Act of 1965) comprises units which are leased by the housing authorities from private owners and rented to those eligible for public housing. The private owner receives market rental rates while these units are then rented by the housing authority at lower rates. Annual federal contributions to the housing authority cover the difference in rental rates. This program has resulted in scattered individual housing units being utilized in the low rent public housing program in contrast to the concentrated nature of those conventional projects.

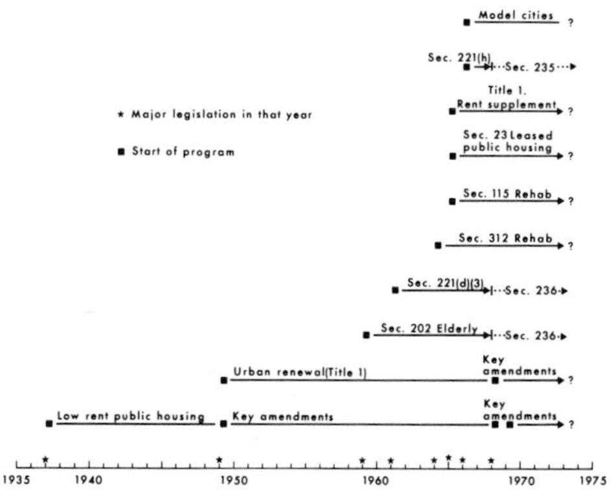

Figure 4-2. Forty Years of Housing Programs.

Urban Renewal (Housing Act of 1949). The urban renewal program has a long and complex history. In its basic form, local governments buy and clear land which is then resold cheaply to private developers or public agencies, with the federal and local governments absorbing the difference between the sale price and what it cost the city to buy and clear the land for redevelopment.

The plans of developers must meet with local government approval. In many instances, substandard and standard residential units were purchased and cleared and sites redeveloped with (1) nonresidential activities such as parks, offices, parking spaces; (2) upper and middle income housing beyond the reach of many citizens; and (3) low income housing, representing a meagre share of the total output from urban renewal programs. For every ten low income units demolished, only one on the average nationwide has been replaced.

The Development of New Programs. With the low rent public housing program receiving limited appropriations from Congress, and few new low income units being generated by urban renewal activities, attention turned to alternative and innovative programs. The first was a program for the elderly. Authorized under Section 202 of the 1959 Housing Act, it encouraged the construction, rehabilitation or improvement of rental or cooperative housing for the lower middle income elderly. Loans were made directly from a revolving loan fund with a below market interest rate (BMIR) of 3 percent to nonprofit or limited profit sponsors, consumer cooperatives and public agencies. This was followed shortly by a subsidized rental program under Section 221(d)(3) of the 1961 Housing Act, focusing on the construction or rehabilitation of structures with five or more dwelling units for low and moderate income households. The lower rents are possible since loans are provided from Government National Mortgage Association (GNMA) special assistance funds with a BMIR of 3 percent to sponsors of low and moderate income rental housing. This association is the source of mortgage financing for the subsidy programs and is somewhat independent from the private market.

Increasingly, the goals of specific programs called for preserving existing housing through rehabilitation. Under Section 115 of the 1965 law, grants of up to $3,500 are provided to property owners in urban renewal and housing code enforcement areas for the rehabilitation of their housing units. Under Section 312 of the 1964 law, homeowners and some nonresident landlords can obtain direct 3 percent BMIR loans for the rehabilitation of properties in urban renewal areas, code enforcement areas or areas which potentially could be so designated.

Other new programs were the rent supplement program, a program to encourage low income homeownership and the Model Cities program. Authorized under Title 1 of the 1965 Housing Act, rent supplements take the form of payments to sponsors who construct new units or rehabilitate existing ones which they then rent to low income, low asset households. The payments represent the difference between 25 percent of the occupant's income and market rentals. Eligibility is, however, quite restricted and only applies to those low income, low asset households who are also either displaced by government action, elderly, living in substandard housing, in homes damaged by natural disaster or on active duty in the armed forces. Rent supplements are used in conjunction with other subsidy programs to permit low income households to occupy units in moderate income multifamily structures. The homeownership program is set out in Section 221(h) of the 1966 Housing Act. Direct loans with a standard 3 percent BMIR are made for purchase and rehabilitation of dwellings for sale to low income families. The interest rate may be as low as 1 percent in certain cases.

Model Cities, both in the creation of the program and its implementation, has sparked considerable public interest and, ultimately, concern. Created by the Demonstration Cities and Metropolitan Development Act of 1966, this program was, as the title suggests, largely of a demonstration or pilot nature. The basic premise was that various ills, such as poverty, disease, hunger and substandard housing, could be overcome (possibly even eliminated) if there were effective coordination and concentration of a range of "helping" programs in neighborhoods or communities where existing programs were either piecemeal or working at cross-purposes.

In addition to the normal federal share of financing in certain housing, education and social service programs, the act authorized the federal government to contribute up to 80 percent of the share usually contributed to such programs by the cities themselves. The federal government could also finance up to 80 percent of the cost of creating and managing comprehensive programs to be implemented with "widespread citizen participation."

These financial inducements were to encourage local governments to concentrate in a comprehensive, planned way on some of the worst or most deprived neighborhoods in a city. In conjunction with local needs and desires, the whole range of program expertise in a host of fields was to be brought to bear on the "model neighborhoods" and their problems. It should be remembered that these programs were created by Democratic administrations in the context of the War on Poverty and Great Society concepts—the federal government was determined and politically committed to redress urban ills. The 1968 reports and supporting technical documents of two commissions created by President Johnson to advise on housing and related urban problems provided a key benchmark. The National Commission on Urban Problems, chaired by former Senator Paul Douglas of Illinois reported on building and zoning laws and taxation policies at all levels of government and their impact on the quality and supply of housing. National progress in the housing field was also reviewed and criticized. The President's Committee on Urban Housing, chaired by industrialist Edgar Kaiser, reported on the means of involving the skills and abilities of the private sector of the economy in the task of overcoming the nation's housing problems. Largely in response to these two important reports, new programs were instituted. Not only were new procedures called for, but these programs were also to replace existing subsidy programs in both the rental and homeownership sector.

One program authorized under Section 235 of the 1968 Housing Act is designed to encourage home ownership among lower middle income households. Loans with subsidized interest rates are made available for the purchase of new, existing or substantially rehabilitated housing; in some instances, the effective interest rate is 1 percent. Households must pay at least 20 percent of their adjusted income toward mortgage amortization. The *amount* of the interest reduction subsidy is thus tied to the occupant's income.

Another key program, which draws its authority from Section 236 of the same act, seeks to stimulate the production of rental units for lower middle income households. In this program, the interest subsidies are made to the sponsors of rental units and loan coverage is extensive. Effectively, HUD pays the difference between fair market rents and 25 percent of the tenant's adjusted income, or the difference between amortization over 40 years and amortization at 1 percent, whichever is less. Again, as household income rises, the rent paid by the tenant increases and the subsidy declines until a market rental is paid.

Federal Housing Programs: Another Perspective. To this point, we have described the principal federal programs in terms of what they can produce for the low and moderate income purchaser or renter—the "clients." Housing construction and rehabilitation require money and housing policy must relate to those who have capital—lending institutions and depositors. What can the programs do for investors?

The government's intervention into the housing market was initially designed during the Depression of the 1930s. Many buyers could not make payments during this period and lost their homes; lending institutions foreclosed on the mortgages, acquiring the houses.

The federal response was a mortgage insurance program which guaranteed, in effect, that the mortgage loan carried no risk. If the borrower defaulted, the lending institution could collect from a special government fund accumulated from fees charged to buyers. Thus, buyers pay to protect the lenders, not themselves. More recently, the 1968 legislation introduced a multifamily apartment rental program which offers investors considerable incentive to put their money into housing production. An investor could theoretically invest as little as \$20,000 in a \$1,000,000 project and claim the entire million dollars in depreciation against ordinary income, in less than the life of the 40 year mortgage. Provisions of the program give investors a nine-to-one depreciation for every dollar invested, while other kinds of buildings have only a three-to-one tax advantage. Investors can use this program to extraordinary advantage by buying inexpensive land, obtaining a higher reappraisal, and, using the new higher values, apply the land value as their investment in the project. Their actual cash outlay could be 2 percent, while the reappraisal makes it look like 10 percent—compared with the 25 percent or more required of the investor in a conventional project. If such apartment investments are worked on existing buildings—that is, in rehabilitation projects—the entire cost of repairs can be written off over five years, up to \$15,000 per living unit. Additionally, if an apartment is sold to tenants or a tenant-oriented nonprofit group, the investor owes no capital gains tax if the proceeds are invested in another similar project. There are other advantages to investors, but from these few it is clear that the federal policy has an impact which does much more than help the poor to live in "a decent home." This is done in the name of stimulating housing production, and it has worked in that respect (Figure 4-1).

However, investigations have revealed scandalous and often criminal actions to which these investment incentive schemes contributed. Indictments against real estate speculators, mortgage companies and HUD employees began after the House Committee on Banking and Currency issued a report (January 6, 1971) detailing over 100 cases of FHA crimes. Two years later, as the extent of the abuses became clearer, the Nixon administration suspended much of the federal housing apparatus. The causes and results of this situation are discussed in the final section of the chapter.

The Record

The achievements under the federal programs outlined above have been disappointing to the advocates of direct federal intervention in the housing market. For example, the 1949 Housing Act contained authorization for 810,000 units of low rent public housing to be built by 1955. Yet by 1969, there were still only 740,580 publicly owned units under management. The urban renewal projects removed low income units from the housing stock—one estimate is that by 1968 there was a net loss of 400,000 such units. Often, middle and high income housing and nonresidential uses were the products of urban renewal projects. When the substantial number of units lost by other public development schemes, such as urban freeway construction, are also taken into account, then it is clear that the 750,000 units under public management in 1969 represented only a small addition to the low income housing stock. Significant numbers of households still had to seek and hopefully obtain low cost housing in the private market.

This record was considered as evidence of failure in the public housing sector by the critics, including the Kaiser and Douglas commissions, despite other evidence which suggested improvements in the quality of the national housing stock. Greater efforts were demanded. The national housing goal as stated in 1949 was reaffirmed and a new production target of six million new subsidized units by 1978 was set. This corresponds to an average annual production of 600,000 units through the 1968–1978 decade. But halfway through the decade the shortfall is clear (Table 4-1) and the target an impossible one to achieve. Nevertheless, the amount of subsidized housing has increased substantially in comparison to previous years (Figure 4-1).

Prior to the new directions of 1968, low rent public housing was the dominant component in terms of national production, even though, as has been noted, it had not even reached its 1955 target by 1969. Rehabilitation has always played a relatively minor role (Table 4-1). The importance of these programs declined markedly in favor of the more recently authorized (1968) rental and homeownership subsidy programs (Table 4-2). Despite this shift in the pattern of production, the low rent public housing program remains important in the national picture since it represents 58 percent of completions through July 1970 (Table 4-3).

Low rent public housing projects can be grim places in which to live, and many projects have acquired poor reputations. Pruitt-Igoe, a public housing project in St. Louis, parts of which were recently blown up by the housing authority, has come to be a symbol of all that is wrong with public housing. Most major central cities in America have their own equivalent(s) of Pruitt-Igoe. Many housing authorities are also in desperate financial circumstances as their increasing expenses outstrip increases in revenue. HUD, as of 1969, now makes direct contributions to housing authorities to cover the difference between annual operating costs of public housing and 25 percent of tenants' incomes. This is generally referred to as the Brooke Amendment after its sponsor, Senator Brooke of Massachusetts.

In terms of their operation, some housing authorities are turning to the less controversial provision of elderly and leased housing, and the ability of federal policy to serve low income families and problem households must be ques-

Table 4-1. Production versus Targets, 1968-1972

	US–All Directly Subsidized Units					
	New Construction		*Rehabilitation*			*Average Annual Units to Achieve 1968 Goal*
Year	*Numbers*	*Percent*	*Numbers*	*Percent*	*Total*	
1968	163,359	85.2	28,417	14.8	191,776	600,000
1969	196,931	87.0	29,432	13.0	226,363	600,000
1970	430,990	91.5	40,093	8.5	471,083	600,000
1971	433,504	91.9	38,043	8.1	471,547	600,000
1972	Not available		Not available		380,000[a]	600,000
5 year cumulative total					1,740,772	3,000,000
1973 estimate[a]					250,000	
1974 estimate[a]					250,000	

[a]Data from a 1973 report to Joint Congressional Economic Subcommittee entitled *Housing Subsidies and Housing Policy* (quoted in *New Republic*, April 7, 1973).

Source: Anthony Downs. *Federal Housing Subsidies: How Are They Working?* (Lexington, Mass.: D. C. Heath and Co., 1973).

Table 4-2. Percentage of all Newly Built Directly Subsidized Units in Key Programs, 1968–April 1972

Calendar Year	*Homeowner Program*	*Rental Program*	*Total*	*All Low Rent Public Housing Programs*	*Other Programs*
1968	0.4	0.0	0.4	41.7	57.9
1969	14.3	5.2	19.5	34.1	46.4
1970	26.9	24.4	51.3	22.9	25.8
1971	32.5	25.1	57.6	15.7	26.7
1972 (4 months)	45.8	18.2	64.0	10.6	25.4

Source: Anthony Downs, *Federal Housing Subsidies: How Are They Working* (Lexington, Mass.: D.C. Heath and Co., 1973).

Table 4-3. Production Under Federal Low and Moderate Income Housing Programs, through July 31, 1970

Program	*Completions (percent)*	*Starts (percent)*
Low Rent Public Housing	58.0	54.0
Section 221(d)(3)–Rental	9.0	10.0
Section 236–Rental and Co-op	1.0	4.0
Rent Supplements	2.0	3.0
Section 235–Home Ownership	5.0	6.0
Other HUD Programs	4.0	4.0
Farmers Home Adminstration Programs	22.0	20.0

Source: Joseph P. Fried, *Housing Crisis–U.S.A.* (New York: Praeger, 1971).

tioned. Other housing authorities, such as Chicago and Atlanta, have become embroiled in controversy as courts have ordered them to disperse their new units and avoid overconcentration within existing black residential areas.

A recent study of federal housing subsidies by Anthony Downs reviews the problems and scandals that have beset the moderate income rental and homeownership programs. He asserts that these specific programs (Sections 235 and 236) are not the major problem area and that there is a grave risk of overreaction on the part of political and administrative leaders. Another writer, Brian Boyer in *Cities Destroyed for Cash,* claims the shift in federal policy in the mid- and late 1960s is responsible for a national tragedy the dimensions of which are extraordinary. Whatever the actual extent of the problems, the future of the moderate income homeownerships and rental programs is uncertain and recent reports suggest they will be stopped. New and alternative strategies are once again under consideration by the Congress.

Problems in Evaluating Housing Policy and Programs

A major problem exists in interpreting the meaning of the data presented thus far. These are the aggregate results of 40 years of public action, but what relationship do they bear to the national housing goal? Is progress being made toward achieving this goal?

The 1968 commissions concluded that only limited progress was being made. The 1968 Housing Act and Fair Housing Act also directed that "highest priority and emphasis should be given to meeting the housing needs of those families for whom the national goal has not become a reality." In 1972 a Comptroller General's report to Congress noted that "the Nation's housing goal . . . remains unachieved." Also, local officials interviewed in connection with this study were of the opinion that the national housing goal had not been achieved, and that in their locality, publicly assisted housing programs were inadequate for the task as they saw it. A body of opinion exists that the national housing goal has not been met, and some of the apparatus designed to meet it is now in limbo.

Yet it is extremely difficult to assess the impact and effectiveness of housing programs in relation to the national purpose. Numerous studies, ranging from reports to Congress by the General Accounting Office to reports on programs in individual cities or metropolitan areas, make this point. If the problem being addressed, the kinds of program activities intended, and the anticipated immediate and long range impacts are not spelled out in measurable terms, then evaluation may be impossible. To carry out effective evaluation it is necessary to specify how expenditures are related to program activities to produce desired results. This is not always done.

The confusing battery of housing programs that has been served up following intensive lobbying by housing reformers and professionals, financial and building interests, big city mayors, welfare groups, and others comes perilously close to this condition of not being evaluable.

There are a number of major difficulties. First, there is almost a complete absence of goal statements at any level other than the national making it almost impossible to assess whether progress is being made in specified localities. We have already commented on the ambiguity of the national goal. Furthermore, the goals of specific federal programs are not related in any systematic way either to each other or the general national goal. Some programs have the stated goal of encouraging homeownership among low and middle income groups, it being assumed that this somehow contributes to the achievement of the general national goal as stated in 1949 and again in 1968. Again, a goal of recent programs has been to involve the expertise of the private sector to a greater degree in the supply of subsidized housing. This emphasis and the related incentives have undoubtedly contributed to the marked rise in production, but some programs have also acquired tarnished reputations as a result of "quick-buck" artists and real estate speculators. It was hoped that the application of private expertise would lead to greater progress toward the production targets set in 1968 and, by implication, the national housing goal. Since the national goal is ill-defined and very general in character, the production targets have emerged as the focus of public action. Needs are sadly neglected in goal formulation and numbers may be politically expedient.

There are other national goals which are both housing goals and civil rights goals. The Department of Housing and Urban Development was directed to take affirmative action in providing equal opportunity in housing. The locational consequences of achieving the general goal have not been spelled out, nor is this goal related explicitly to other program goals.

Secondly, most analysts face problems in determining housing needs to which goals must be related. For example, the General Accounting Office of Congress has roundly criticized HUD's inability to identify the housing needs of the low and moderate income families that the agency seeks to serve. There is considerable difficulty in obtaining accurate reliable data to permit both national and local evaluation. In addition, analyses such as this, which seek to make comparisons between metropolitan regions, are seriously handicapped because of gaps in data coverage and the incompatibility from city to city of data that do exist. Finally, given that the principal thrust of federal housing programs is to deal with the issues of the cost and quality of housing obtained by American households, there are important questions that are at the root of the difficulties in housing needs and goal specification. For example, what proportion of a household's resources should be allocated to obtain decent or adequate housing, and what do we mean by *adequate shelter* or *a decent home* or *standard housing?* These phrases are illustrative of the range of terms that have been employed in discussing housing quality. These questions remain unanswered.

We will next briefly consider three important problems that bear directly on our study: data availability and reliability, housing cost to income ratios, and the measurement of housing quality.

Data Problems. These brief comments are only illustrative of what continues to be a serious problem in the effective evaluation of federal housing programs. As one might expect, there is significant variability in the amount, quality and reliability of data on all aspects of housing programs at the local level. However, this is natural, given the absence of complete urban information systems which produce spatially coded data which are comparable across cities and metropolitan regions.

Equally, or perhaps more, disturbing are the problems that arise in national data with respect to coverage and quality.

As an example of the problems, we find the Real Estate Research Corporation of Chicago stating, "we were unable to obtain accurate information concerning the location of Section 235 units nationwide" [Downs, pp. 50-51]. These data were being sought by one of the nation's leading consulting firms in a study sponsored by the National Association of Home Builders, the National Association of Mutual Savings Banks and the United States Savings and Loan League. Discrepancies in data are also disturbing. Consider the discrepancies in output of selected programs as reported by different sources in Table 4-4. There does not appear to be a simple definitional explanation for these startling differences. That precise data on public programs are not readily available is surely little short of scandalous. As Senator Mondale of Minnesota recently observed, this is important because so much of wise government comes from having the right data.

Methodological Problems. The two major problems that federal housing programs attempt to deal with are (1) households paying too much of their income for decent housing, and (2) households living in what is considered to be substandard or inadequate housing. If it can be established that there is some critical proportion of income which should not normally be exceeded for the purchase of housing services, then a reduction in the number of households whose expenditures exceed this breakpoint could be considered as progress toward "a suitable living environment." An informal rule of thumb that somehow gained acceptance is that no household should allocate more than 25 percent of its income for housing. The percentage has become enshrined in legislation, as noted previously. Thus, the reduction in the number of households whose housing expenditures exceed 25 percent becomes a quantitative goal for some.

However, to link housing policies to the goal of reducing the proportion of income spent for housing is fraught with danger. Do we know "the popular norm" concerning how much people should have to pay for housing, asks Henry Aaron, a prominent housing economist. Is it in fact 25 percent? We do not really know.

Some additional difficulties might be mentioned. The differences in expenditures for housing at various income levels may result from differences in taste. The selection of a dwelling unit, be it an apartment or house, results in the consumption of neighborhood amenities. Since it is difficult to separate the two for measurement purposes, the question arises as to how much of the expenditure is for housing and how much for amenities such as neighborhood characteristics and locational convenience.

Another difficulty is that the relationship between housing expenditures and current family income may be weak. This is because of the variability in incomes and the relative stability of housing expenditures; thus, the proportion of current income spent for residential services will not be constant. Yet this

Table 4-4. US—Housing Unit Production by Selected Programs, Data Discrepancies

	Home Ownership		*Rental*	
Year	*Real Estate Research Corp.*	*President's Annual Reports to Congress on Housing*	*Real Estate Research Corp.*	*President's Annual Reports to Congress on Housing*
1969	28,127	8,000	10,168	1,000
1970	116,073	70,000	105,160	51,000
1971	140,728	138,000	108,681	107,000
1972	124,458 (est.)	141,000 (est.)	49,467 (est.)	147,000 (est.)

Note: The RERC data (Downs 1973) are for new units and do not include rehabilitation units. RERC comments on their data as follows: "[T]he quantiative data used in this analysis represent the joint findings of RERC and HUD, and have been agreed on as substantially accurate by both ourselves and HUD". The data for the President's Annual Report on National Housing Goals are also provided by the Department of Housing and Urban Development.

is the nature of the data reported in the census which are used to establish rent-income ratios. Furthermore, it is extremely difficult to determine what housing costs are for homeowners, especially through the census questionnaire which obtains information only on the perceived market value of homes. Thus, there is a tendency to focus on excessive rent burdens. Weighting of the housing cost-income ratio to take account of family size and demographic structure is also necessary when using such statistics.

This issue of housing cost and proportionate allocation of income has led to discussion of the concept of financial housing needs. These needs arise in the following manner. Suppose the allocation by a household of a "normal" percentage of annual income (say, for example, 25 percent) fails to secure standard housing in a given city or neighborhood (this statement assumes consensus on what is standard housing). In such cases, the need might be met either (1) by reducing the cost of decent quality units so that our imaginary household can occupy such units and not exceed the dollar expenditure represented by 25 percent of household income, or (2) by raising the household income through some form of income transfer so that the 25 percent allocation (now of course a larger absolute amount of dollars) will obtain that "standard" unit under current local market conditions.

This perspective is also found in arguments that households are "housing-poor" in part because of excessive rent burdens. Clearly, it is less of a problem—perhaps not even a problem—if a high income household is spending a sizable percentage of its income for rent. Thus, for example, a Harvard-MIT study which seeks to measure housing needs attempts to control for income and family size. A household with an excessive rent burden is defined as a renter household with an income of less than $10,000 and which falls into one of the following categories:

- a two or more person household with its head less than age 65, paying more than 25 percent of its income for rent;
- a single person household, with its head less than age 65, paying more than 25 percent of its income for rent;
- A household with its head older than 65, paying more than 35 percent of its income for rent.

Following this classification and using national census data, there were some 6.8 million households with a high rent burden in the US in 1970.

Thus, despite the conceptual and measurement difficulties, some analysts are willing to use the ratios as an indication of the numbers of households who require financial assistance to lift them from the "housing-poor" category, regardless of the quality of their current dwelling unit.

Housing Quality. The quality of the dwelling unit is another key element in the assessment of housing needs. The congressional statement of the national goal and other statements over the years have emphasized that the quality of the housing units occupied by households is of basic concern in and of itself.

Is there any consensus on the meaning of the terms *a decent home,* or *adequate housing* or *substandard?* Little work has been done on popular images of housing quality, yet an understanding of housing quality is necesary for both need and goal specification. Progress toward achieving the national housing goal would presumably mean that "indecent" or "below an acceptable level of quality" housing would represent a declining share of the housing stock occupied by American households. However, to show and assess such progress there must be agreement on an acceptable level of housing quality and how it can be measured and recorded.

The concept of housing unit quality is basic to an understanding of physical housing needs. Some argue that such needs exist when there are insufficient decent quality units in existence, and at appropriate locations, so that potentially every household can occupy one (the issue of cost is theoretically set aside for the moment). Another view considers a household as "housing-poor" if it occupies an inadequate unit. The inadequacy may derive from a number of features such as:

- the structural condition of the unit;
- the degree to which there is a complete range of plumbing facilities;
- the degree to which basic toilet facilities exist and are for the exclusive use of the household;
- the degree to which a complete range of kitchen facilities exist and are for the exclusive use of the household;

- the existence of access to a dwelling unit only through another household's living quarters;
- the total absence of heating, or heating which is unreliable and ineffective;
- crowding within the dwelling unit because of its size;
- inadequate lighting and ventilation in the unit.

Again, according to the Harvard-MIT study of housing needs, there are 10.3 million US households whose housing is inadequate (national data, 1970). This estimate does not include all of the above aspects and may be somewhat of an underestimate. The approach taken in the housing needs study indicates that there are more households in need than if one considers the more traditional and restrictive concept of "substandard housing."

Substandard housing, as this concept has commonly been used, represents housing which has both structural and plumbing facility deficiencies, but does not include what would appear to be other relevant aspects of housing quality. Nevertheless, the concept of substandard housing has been employed by HUD and by many housing analysts, including urban geographers who were seeking answers to such questions as: Where are areas of residential blight in the city? and, How can we explain the pattern of residential blight? The data concerning the internal and external structural condition of dwelling units were derived from ratings done by the census enumerators themselves. Despite some training, the part-time enumerators reported information which is widely regarded as unreliable, thus limiting greatly the usefulness of the data. The result was that such data were no longer collected in the 1970 Census of Housing. Thus, the notion of substandard housing, as defined on the basis of certain census variables, is no longer a useful one, if indeed it ever was.

It is clear, therefore, that depending upon the approach taken with regard to the definition of housing quality, different estimates of physical housing needs will be obtained. Thus, if goals are to be related to needs, they will also be likely to vary according to the approach employed. Some analysts suggest that if different concepts of housing quality are used, the nation's housing needs are far greater than we have previously realized, and that there may therefore be even greater demands made for government assistance.

This last point touches on a larger and more complex issue. With unreliable data and vulnerable definitions, we run the risk of false optimism. The conclusion that substantial improvements in housing quality are being achieved is sustained by utilizing census statistics which show continued declines in the substandard component in the housing inventory (Table 4-5).

The principal difficulty here is that the notion of substandard is being applied across 20 years, and no recognition is given to the fact that the level of aspirations has probably changed. And perhaps it has changed more dramatically in recent years than ever before. Thus, what may have been considered standard or adequate in 1949 is not considered satisfactory by 1974. Casual examination of such periodicals as *Architectural Forum, House and Home* and *Better Homes and Gardens* provides a qualitative impression that there has been a substantial change in the housing expectations of the mythical "man in the street." This standard today substantially exceeds that embodied in the current concept of substandard housing which is too narrowly based.

This issue of changing standards is troublesome for the philosophical underpinnings of goal formulation. As we have noted, changes in standards will result in changes in the substandard component of the housing stock. Thus, if needs are reflective of a desire to reduce this component, they, too, will change, as will the quantitative targets which are set as part of goal formulation.

There will always be a "housing aspirations gap" as tastes are defined by what exists; whether or not such housing is attainable is

Table 4-5. Percentage of US Housing Units Substandard

1950	*1960*	*1970*
37.0	19.6	9.2

Source: Census data from Components of Inventory Change Survey. 1950 and 1960 data are from F. Kristof, *Urban Housing Needs Through the 1980's*, Research Report No. 10, (Washington, D.C.: US Government Printing Office, 1968). 1970 data are from D. Birch et al., *Towards Housing Goals for the United States* (Cambridge, Mass.: Joint Center for Urban Studies, Harvard-MIT, 1973).

another question. This can mean that people may express dissatisfaction with their current housing or may perceive other existing housing to be substandard. Thus, if aspirations increase rapidly, the proportion of the housing stock that is perceived as substandard may also rise. The popular conception of a decent home ordinarily can change. What implications does this have for evaluating progress toward the national goal? From one perspective, employing a dated conception of standards and using suspect census data, it can be shown that considerable progress in improving the quality of the housing stock has been achieved. The slum clearance and rehabilitation programs might appear to be effective. However, if we attempt to estimate the amount of substandard housing using a current popular conception of a decent home, the picture is more sobering.

A recent study identifies "seven levels of housing in the public imagery" [Birch, Part 6, pp. 96-103]. These are based on 900 in depth at home interviews with a cross-section of homeowners and renters in the Boston and Kansas City metropolitan regions. The two lowest levels of housing are identified in terms of their quality, nature of occupants, market value and national share of metropolitan housing stock. The *slum level* is, in the public image, "housing that has already been abandoned . . . or, if not, it is so awful that it should be!" The *substandard level* contains housing which, in the view of the respondents, is "below generally accepted standards of decency in size, condition, or appearance, but is definitely above the *Slum Level* in reputation." Together, these levels are estimated to contain 28-30 percent of the US metropolitan stock of 46,083,000 units (1970), or between 13,056,850 and 13,978,510 units. This represents one-fifth (21 or 19 percent) of the total national housing stock. Even without the poor quality rural component (which we know to be substantial) this percentage exceeds that of most current estimates. Even allowing for errors in the estimation procedures, these data support the general point—with changing aspirations, greater proportions of the stock may be considered substandard. If the national housing goal is partly to remove such units from the stock, then it may be a self-defeating task.

There is no easy answer to the question of rising standards and their relationship with policies that seek to eliminate substandard housing. On the one hand, by ignoring the changes in standards, the data may persuade us that the quality of the housing stock is improving. But, at the very best, this is essentially a backward-looking position, and, at its worst, it is pure "head-in-the-sandism." On the other hand, to lay too much stress on changing standards might lead one to deny that any tangible progress is being made when real improvements in living conditions have, in fact, been achieved for many Americans.

FEDERAL HOUSING SUBSIDY PROGRAMS: THEIR USE IN THREE CITIES

What has been the historical development of the principal subsidy programs in each of the three areas? What has been the level of production under each program? Where are the various types of dwelling units located? What has been the impact of these programs in terms of (1) meeting the housing needs of low and moderate income groups, and (2) neighborhood conditions in areas where new subsidized units were built or rehabilitation undertaken? As we noted in the introduction, this kind of basic information is not readily available, and rarely has anyone sought to examine such questions for more than one city in a comparative manner. The unevenness in the degree to which these questions are answerable in each of the metropolitan regions reflects the availability of data and local evaluation studies. Since we were completely dependent on local data sources, exact comparability and an even treatment is not possible at this time.

Seattle

In the Seattle area—as across the nation—the majority of households obtain their housing services from the private sector. The total stock of housing created under the four most important subsidized housing programs amounts to only 4.8 percent of the 1970 King County housing stock or 5.3 percent in the city of Seattle (Table 4-6).

As with the national experience, the economic health of the region is reflected in the housing market. Befitting Seattle's image as a frontier city and Gateway to Alaska, the 1960-1970 decade was a boom and bust era. The economy is dominated by the aerospace

Table 4-6. Housing Units Produced by Major Subsidy Program, as of 1973, Seattle

	Seattle		*Remainder of King County*		
Programs	*Number*	*Percent*	*Number*	*Percent*	*Total*
Section 221(d)(3)–Rental Section 236 –Rental	3,007	67	1,481	33	4,488
Section 235–Home Ownership	1,234	30	2,918	70	4,152
Low Rent Public Housing	7,564	64	4,225	35	11,789
Totals	11,805	58	8,624	42	20,429

Sources: Seattle Housing Authority; Seattle Housing Development.

industry, although there is a diversified nonmanufacturing sector with trade being the most important single source of employment. In response to national conditions, the aerospace industry expanded rapidly in the early part of the past decade. Employment almost doubled between 1960 and 1968. By 1968, this industry represented 60 percent of total manufacturing employment and 19 percent of all wage and salary nonagricultural employment in the metropolitan area. In 1969, as a result of federal restraints and subsequent cancellations of programs such as the SST, the industry underwent a severe contraction. The Boeing Corporation cut its work force by 63 percent between July 1968 and October 1971. Such drastic action by the biggest single employer sent a shock wave through the entire system. Unemployment, which had fallen to a low of 2.9 in 1968, rose sharply to 13.1 percent in 1971. The county welfare rolls climbed and the community had to take direct action to feed hungry families. Some households left the region.

The impact of these economic convulsions is clearly reflected in housing market data (Figure 4-3). By late 1971, the worst was over and the shock absorbed; the economy regained its composure, and recent increases in employment, including the aerospace industry, reflect a more confident mood.

These startling events are masked in the 1970 census data which, when compared to those of 1960, indicate an expansionary situation. Population growth was considerable (28.4 percent for the SMSA) although it was the suburban areas that gained the new population. The city of Seattle's population declined by 4.7 percent, reflecting an internal geographical redistribution common to most large metropolitan areas. However, there was a slight increase in the number of households in the central city and also a small increase in the number of housing units. A substantial number of units were removed in Seattle during the decade; the census data show that almost 36,000 units were added to the stock by new construction, but the number of units in 1970 had increased by only 6,000, indicating the removal of some 30,000 units as a result of both private and public action. It is clear that many of these so removed were older units, as the percentage of the stock built in 1939 or earlier dropped from 63 percent in 1960 to 48 percent in 1970.

Seattle is a low density city with a preponderance of one unit structures (60.4 percent), many of which are owner-occupied. While the local perception is that housing conditions are not as bad as in other metropolitan areas, there is no denying that there are housing problems and, as in other metropolitan areas, that these occur in certain districts of the city. In 1960, 19 percent of all housing units were in poor condition. There was not, however, a great deal of overcrowding (5 percent). The areas of poorest housing conditions were to be found in and around the downtown area (including Seattle's Skid Road area) and in tracts bordering the Duwamish Waterway, a major industrial area to the south of the downtown area (Figure 4-4). Poor housing conditions (25-50 percent blighted) were also found in predominantly black residential areas. Seattle has a small black population (4.8 percent in 1960; 7.1 percent in 1970), but it is nonetheless areally concentrated, and these areas exhibited some of the highest proportions of overcrowding in the city. Some overcrowding also occurred in West Seattle, especially in two

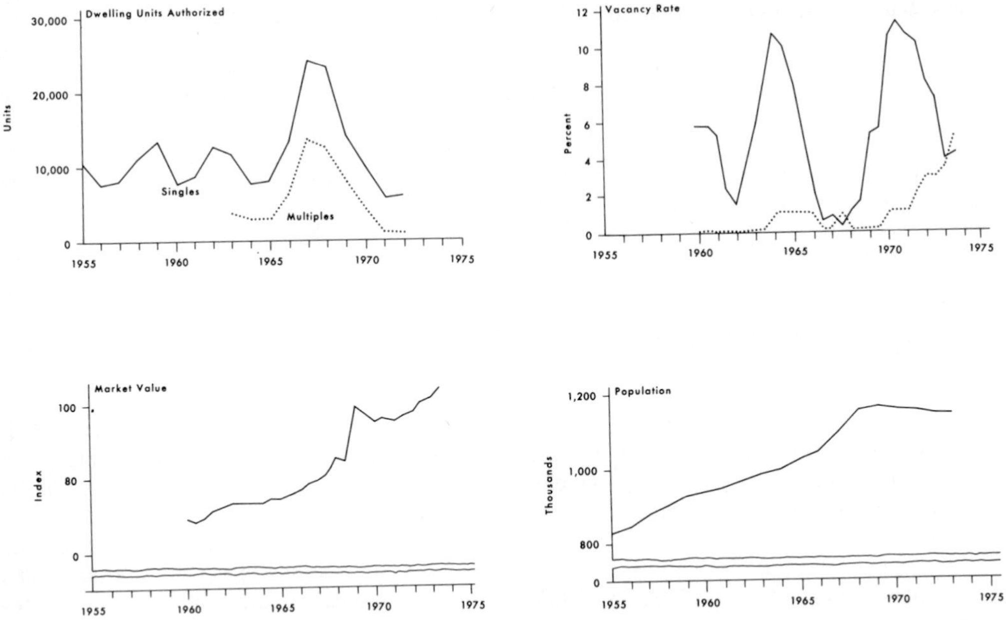

Figure 4-3. The Housing Market in the Seattle Area.

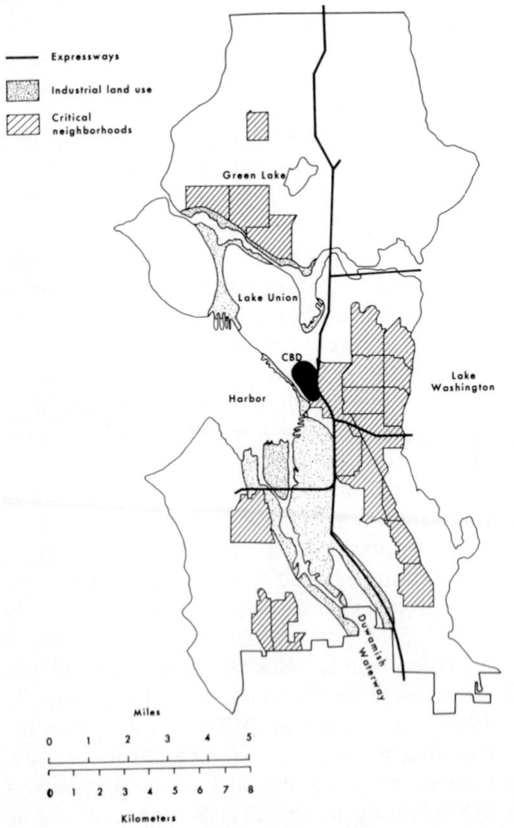

Figure 4-4. Critical Neighborhoods in Seattle.

census tracts which contained large public housing projects.

It was essentially this pattern of housing deficiencies that faced public decisionmakers as they sought to tackle "the housing problem," utilizing various federally supported programs that were available. Only the low rent public housing program and the urban renewal program were available in 1960, although Sector 202–rental housing for the elderly–had just been initiated.

These venerable elders of the national scene are both to be found in the Seattle area, but their impact has been quite limited; for example, under Section 202 only three rental projects, totaling 567 units, were developed from 1964-1967.

Low Rent Public Housing Programs in the Seattle Area. Various forms of public housing units are produced and managed by the Seattle Housing Authority (SHA), which serves only the city of Seattle, and the King County Housing Authority (KCHA), which serves the unincorporated area of King County and various King County municipalities (Figure 4-5).

Seattle. The first project–Yesler Terrace–was constructed in 1939-1940 and was located

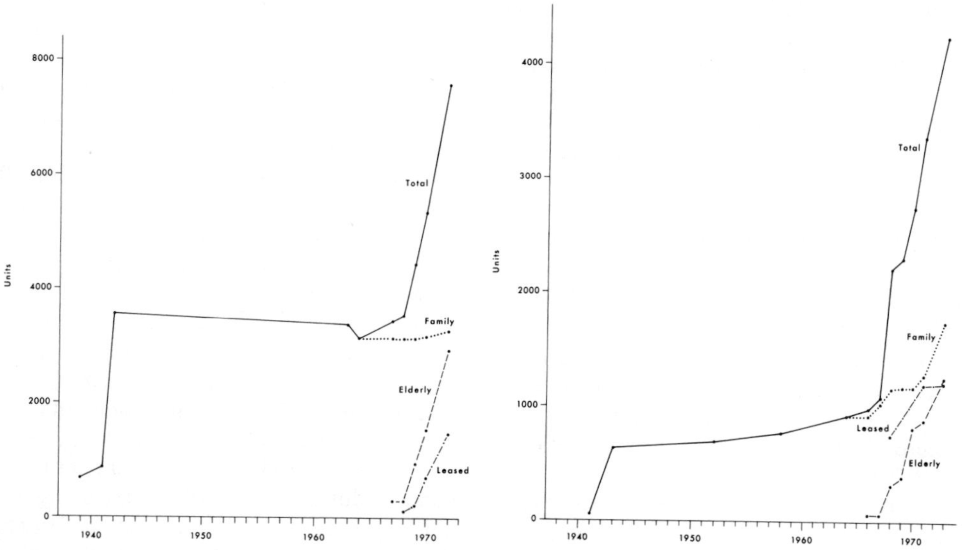

Figure 4-5. Low Rent Public Housing, Units by Year, 1937-1973 in (a) Seattle, and (b) King County.

in the core of the city, close to the downtown area (Figure 4-6). This project was essentially a slum clearance project located in an area of very poor housing conditions. There was a dramatic increase in the number of units during the years of World War II, with three new projects, or "garden communities," being added: High Point, Holly Park and Rainier Vista, all in the southern part of the city. These three projects were wartime housing and their location can be explained largely in terms of access to the industrial areas and availability of large parcels of land. However, after the war years the SHA did not build any new units, and with conversions to nonresidential uses and loss of property for freeway construction there was actually a decline in the number of units available to households.

A 300 unit centrally located development for elderly only marked the beginning of an expansionary period in 1967. The next year, a turnkey program for elderly only housing began, as did the leased housing program. There is now a greater diversity of types of low rent public housing. It was these developments that contributed to the overall increase in the public housing stock since only a small amount of new family housing was constructed (Figure 4-5).

The medium-sized elderly only projects (around 100 units) are generally clustered in

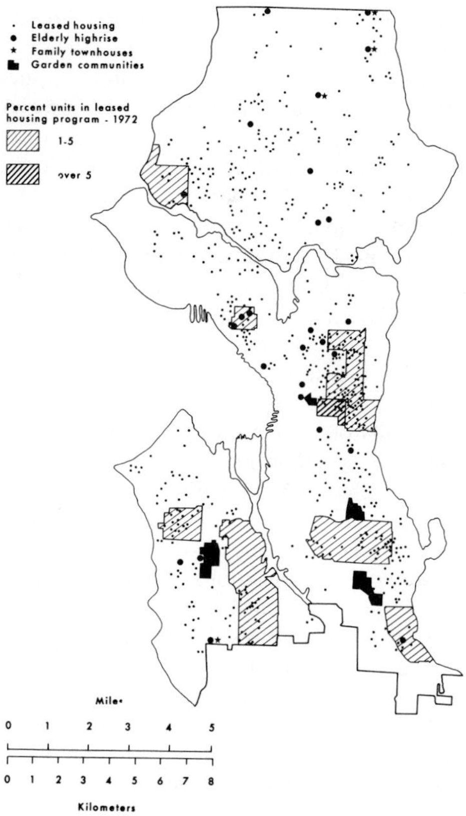

Figure 4-6. Public Housing in Seattle, 1972.

the central part of the city within two miles of the CBD core or are scattered almost at random throughout the city; there are somewhat fewer units in the southern part of the city. Since the turnkey system is dependent on private developer initiatives, the specific site choice is an entrepreneurial one. However, the housing authority used the findings of a planning study on housing needs of the elderly by the United Way organization as a basis for evaluating developer proposals by neighborhood. The spatial distribution of the elderly population with housing needs revealed a strong central component and small pockets scattered elsewhere in the city and the pattern of elderly high rise units effectively reflects this distribution of need.

The leased housing units are located throughout the city, but there is somewhat of a concentration especially in the black residential areas (see Figure 4-6). The location of these units is a consequence of private landlords' decisions to enter into the leasing program and, under certain market conditions, there may be few units entering the program. According to local sources, the economic recession and housing market depression encouraged the growth of the leased housing program as landlords turned to the authority and its waiting list. However, as a consequence of community group pressure, there was a moratorium on additional leased housing units in the southeastern part of the city. The community groups felt that there was too much subsidized housing being developed in this area under a variety of programs.

The SHA does not anticipate any further expansion at this time. Current plans are to redevelop the four family projects, now 30 years old, where there are serious design and project environment problems, such as the high occurrence of crime in the areas immediately around these four projects. These projects, which contain percentages of minority group population considerably above the corresponding citywide proportions, characteristically have vacancy rates on the order of 10 percent, and high turnover rates. While the attempt to improve the environment is desirable, 769 units will be eliminated (almost 10 percent of the total SHA stock). Hopefully, the improvements will result in a reduction in the vacancy rates, thereby offsetting the loss in units, but this is not known. The recent increases in the leased housing program have also been slowed, since the 1971-1972 HUD authorization was 14 percent short of the request.

The SHA exhibits a common paradox shared by many central city housing authorities—high vacancy rates in certain projects and substantial waiting lists for others. At the end of 1972, over 1,000 families were waiting for units in the leased housing program and the total SHA waiting list was 3,800 eligible families.

While the low rent public housing program is aimed at a specific income segment of our society, the SHA is increasingly providing units for elderly low income citizens. In the recent 1968-1972 expansion, only 141 family units were constructed as against 2,378 units for the elderly and these units represent the net family addition since 1942 (excluding leased units). Thus, by 1972, almost two-thirds of the households in SHA units were elderly, with significant proportions of elderly households also to be found in the garden communities and leased housing units).

With no new units proposed, there are many eligible low income families who can expect little help from the SHA at present. Thus, the program might be said to be failing for this group. One estimate (April 1973) by the Seattle office of HUD indicated 10,300 families and 15,150 elderly households eligible for low rent public housing programs, given current income limitations. Of course, many of these households may already have housing that meets their needs; but it is also likely that some proportion live in housing with physical deficiencies, while others may be strained by paying a large share of their income for housing. The blunt truth is that no one knows how many of this eligible group have either physical or financial housing needs which are not met by their present units.

While the authority seeks to serve the low income group, it has by its own admission been unable to do so because of "monetary constraints and the magnitude of the needs." These needs, however, have not yet been precisely specified. There is also no overall policy statement as to where new units should be located.

A stated objective of the housing authority is "to provide decent housing for that portion of the population which cannot afford decent housing without subsidy." Another local agency—the Puget Sound Governmental Conference (PSGC)—estimates an annual income of $8,500 as a critical threshold for this metropolitan region. Families with incomes below this level, they suggest, will be least likely to be satisfied by the private housing delivery system without some form of government subsidy. Some 44,048, or almost one-third, of the families in the city of Seattle fall into this category (1970 data). Clearly, the SHA cannot, and is not expected to, meet the needs of these families, many of whom must seek alternatives provided by other subsidy programs or take their chances in the private market, which of course many do.

King County. The King County Housing Authority exhibits a growth pattern resembling that of the SHA (Figure 4-5). The initial starts were in the war years, followed by a lengthy period of only limited growth. The rapid growth of the late sixties is again due primarily to a new program of housing for the elderly and leased housing; however, unlike the SHA, the KCHA has been adding to its stock of family units in more than token numbers.

There are a number of factors which appear to influence the location of KCHA projects (Figure 4-7). In terms of the general location in a municipality or unincorporated area, one of the key variables is the proportion of the area's households that are eligible for low rent public housing. Community acceptability is another important factor. In suburban Seattle there is little or no racial overtone in respect of this factor, but differences in social status are probably important.

On a more local scale, the availability of vacant land is often important, while, as is common with many public housing projects, land costs are an important constraint. HUD also has developed a set of criteria which housing authorities must use in order to secure HUD approval. While the HUD procedure includes an extensive listing of factors, some broad classes of variables can be identified: cost-related variables, feasibility of relocation of present occupants (should this be necessary), avoidance of potentially discriminatory situations, site suitability in relation to the neigh-

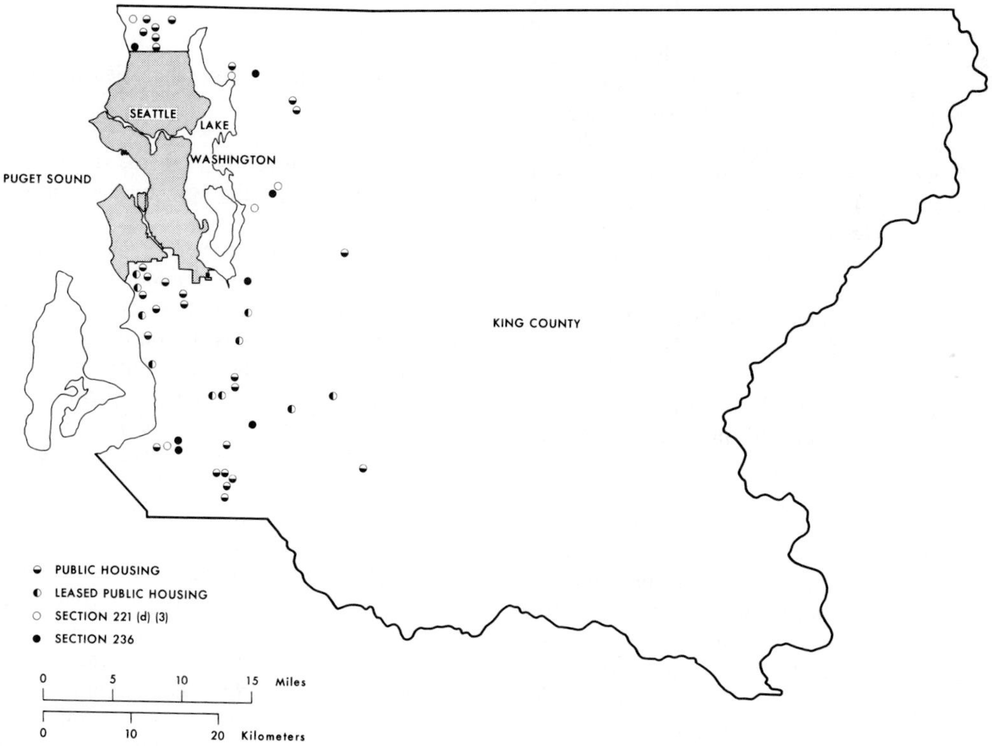

Figure 4-7. Subsidized Housing in King County.

borhood and existing local plans, and benefits of dispersed sites. No site can possibly meet all the suggested criteria, and there are a number of "escape clauses." However, these criteria are nominally used and have influenced the KCHA locational decisions. In terms of the leased housing program, the locational decisions for the projects are effectively private entrepreneurial ones.

Urban Renewal. Although the national authorizing legislation was passed in 1949, in depth studies of potential urban renewal areas in the city of Seattle did not occur until 1958–1960, because the necessary state enabling legislation allowing Washington cities to participate in the federal program was not passed until 1957. The project areas were selected on the basis of a 1954 city planning commission study which identified "substandard dwelling areas" and indicated that some 220 acres could be potential clearance and redevelopment areas.

The Yesler-Atlantic project, located near the CBD (Figure 4-8) was first proposed in 1958 but failed to materialize. The Northlake project was begun in 1964, but since it was undertaken in conjunction with Universty of Washington expansion, it did little to meet nonstudent housing needs. This project, delayed for many years by litigation and described to us as a university land grab, was scheduled for completion in 1974. A less controversial project was the redevelopment of an area in South Seattle for industrial uses; the work, begun in 1966, was more or less completed by 1970. This resulted in the loss of only a few residential units and the development of the site for nonresidential purposes.

The Yesler-Atlantic project was revived in 1966, receiving federal approval in 1968, but litigation again hindered project development until 1971. This project, as is common with other urban renewal projects of the late 1960s, is oriented to low and middle income housing. The Housing and Urban Development Act of 1968 stipulated that, in the future, a majority of housing units created in renewal areas would have to be for low and moderate income households, with at least 20 percent for low income families unless that amount of low income housing was found not to be needed in a community. Some 418 new and rehabilitated dwelling units had been created by 1972.

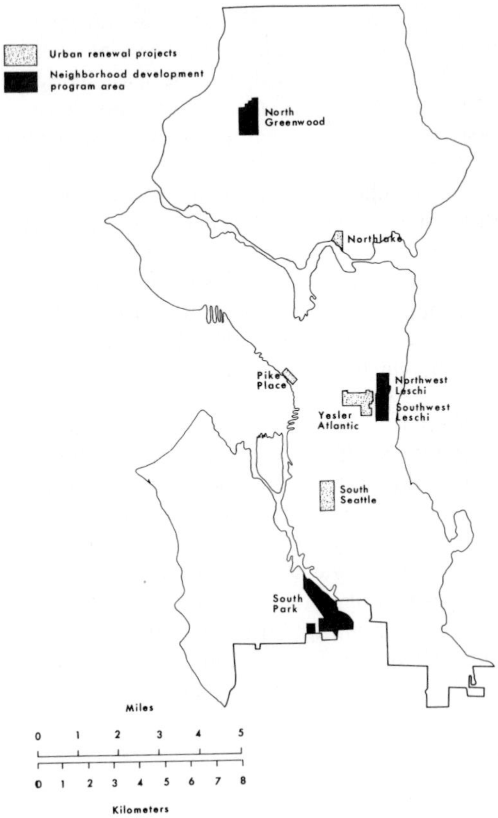

Figure 4-8. Urban Renewal in Seattle, 1973.

No estimate is currently available on the number of residential units lost in the course of this project.

The latest urban renewal project concerns the Pike Place Market, immediately adjacent to the CBD, an area of considerable historic importance since it was the farmer's first marketplace in the young community. As a result of public concern, and a subsequent referendum, the project comes under a historical district ordinance and this delay, together with subsequent litigation, has kept the project very much in the formative stages. The emphasis is now on preservation and a more modest development which includes housing for all income levels, parks and pedestrian areas, parking, and new office-retail space. What finally does occur remains to be seen.

Following the 1968 amendments to the urban renewal program which permitted the establishment of neighborhood development programs supported by annual funding, the city of Seattle moved quickly and by 1973 had designated four neighborhood development program areas–Leschi, Southwest Leschi, North Greenwood and South Park (Figure 4-8). The Leschi, Southwest Leschi and North Greenwood areas are included in Seattle's 20 critical neighborhoods–neighborhoods identified as in a critical state due to decay, poor housing conditions and rapid population change. The remaining area, South Park, is sandwiched between two critical neighborhoods and the industrial area along the Duwamish. These programs primarily emphasize rehabilitation and preservation of existing adequate housing units.

In summary, the urban renewal program has had relatively little impact on Seattle, partly as a result of the late starts and delayed litigation. A negligible amount of low income housing has been created as a result of the projects to date. The neighborhood development program appears to offer greater potential since it may be able to assist in maintaining housing quality in the project areas. However, this program will be eliminated by the federal government if current proposals are implemented.

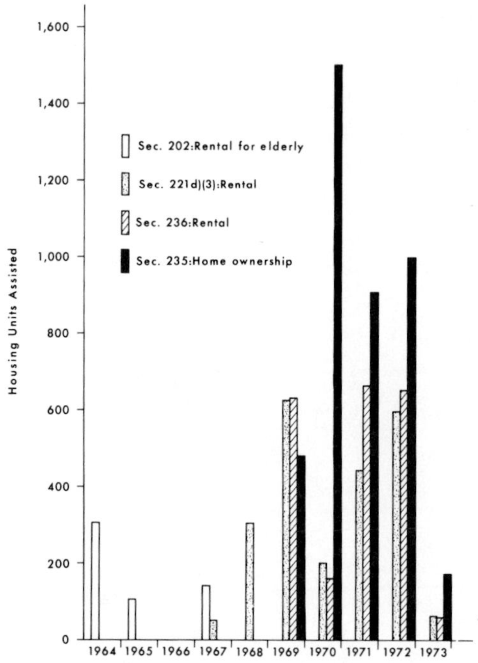

Figure 4-9. Growth of Housing Subsidy Programs in King County.

Section 235: Home Ownership Subsidy, and Section 236: Rental Subsidy Housing. These programs, designed to encourage the private sector to take a more active role in the production of subsidized housing, were created by the 1968 legislation. They had an immediate national impact and quickly grew to represent a considerable percentage of the overall package of assisted housing. The same pattern is evident in Seattle.

The rental subsidy program (Section 236) has effectively replaced both Section 202–rental housing for the elderly–and Section 221(d)(3)–Low and Moderate Income Rental Housing (Figure 4-9). By 1973, 4,488 units had been produced in King County under these programs, with 3,007 units (67 percent) located in the central city and the remaining 1,481 (33 percent) in suburban King County. In late 1971, the HUD office in Seattle began to examine much more stringently the applications for units under the new rental and homeownership subsidy programs on the criteria of market feasibility and location. It was felt that there had been an overproduction of units and these more stringent procedures resulted in a considerable cutback on production, as the 1973 figures show.

The homeownership subsidy program (Section 235) has also had an immediate impact in terms of production, although there is a substantial decline in units produced in 1973. As might be expected with a homeownership program, a greater proportion of the units are located outside the central city than is the case with the rental program (Seattle, 30 percent; suburban King County, 70 percent).

Studies by the Seattle Housing Development (SHD), a local housing agency, provide data on the location and impact of both these programs, and together with data from HUD, these permit some major conclusions.

Consider the housing assisted under the low and moderate income rental programs. The majority of these units are located in Seattle. Within Seattle, almost half the units (47 percent) are in the central section which is predominantly black, or low income, or both. Outside of this extreme concentration, there is a separate cluster in the southeast section of the city. Other projects are dispersed (Figure 4-10).

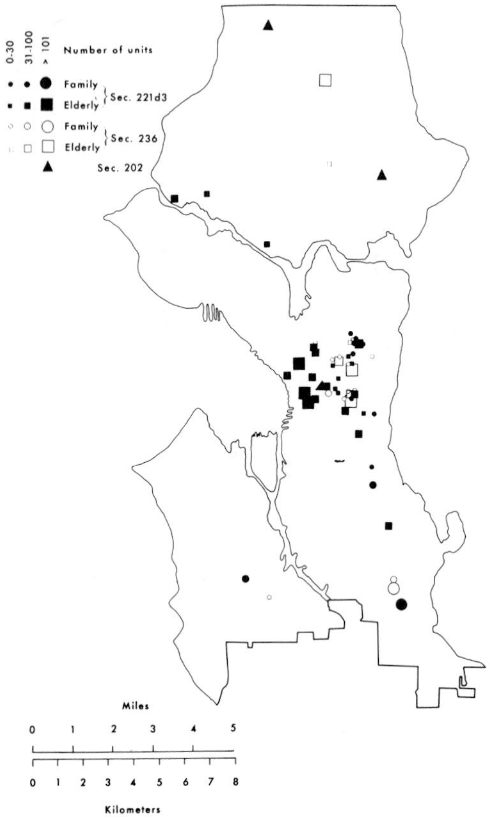

Figure 4-10. Subsidized Rental Housing in Seattle.

Almost 70 percent of the total production of these programs is for elderly occupance. A number of the elderly occupancy projects are located in and around the CBD core. Two large former hotels contribute a significant share. In the remainder of the central area, there are almost equal numbers of elderly and family projects. The latter are, however, small to medium-sized. Outside of the major central cluster there is a marked spatial distinction. In the northern part of the city the three projects are for elderly occupance, while in the southeast and West Seattle areas they are for family occupance. The cluster in the southeast section is immediately adjacent to the large Holly Park public housing family project.

There is a striking contrast concerning the suburban King County projects. Only 60 units (4 percent) are for the elderly, and the projects are dispersed throughout the area with some local grouping (Figure 4-7).

Reflecting the national experience, these rental projects in the Seattle area are experiencing financial difficulty. Over 30 percent of the projects in the city and 46 percent in King County were either in default or had been assigned to HUD as of January 15, 1973. Also, the vacancy rates are disturbingly high, particularly in family projects. Within the city, problem projects (11 of 24) have an average occupancy rate of 66 percent. Similarly, in the remainder of the county the average occupancy rate is 81 percent in five of the ten family projects. The highest individual project vacancy rates occur in the black residential area in the central part of the city.

Four areas of concern are thus identifiable: location, financial difficulty, overconcentration on elderly occupancy and vacancy rates.

The locational pattern of the rental units is the result of HUD operational policies, and of those economic forces affecting the decisions of private builders and developers. HUD operational policies had the most impact in the central city—"rehabilitation" was restricted to Seattle, with the emphasis on the core neighborhoods. Even in the absence of such a policy, it is likely that rehabilitation would have occurred in such areas, since there is greater potential here (see Figure 4-4 for the location of the critical neighborhoods).

Decisions on the location of new construction have been made by private developers. HUD had no locational policy and projects were approved on the basis of economic feasibility and market conditions. The key variables have been cost and availability of land. This has led to small-scale variations in the pattern of the units. In the area of greatest concentration in the city land was cheaper, but land assembly problems have kept project sizes small. In the southern part of the city projects are larger as assembly was less difficult. The average project size increases as distance away from the core increases, largely because of lower land costs and ease of land assembly. Many neighborhoods, however, cannot be considered for these projects because of lack of suitable sites at a feasible cost.

The financial difficulties are largely a result of high vacancy rates, high maintenance costs, and inadequate property development and management. The vacancy rates naturally reflect the local economic slump, which resulted in outmigration from the metropolitan area and a lowering of rents for apartments in the private sector; thus, these units were effectively competing with the subsidized units.

Other contributing factors were location of projects in areas already offering low cost rental units or inadequate public facilities, or both; overproduction of small units with insufficient provision of units to meet the needs of larger families; and poor property management with little attention being given to the special problems facing those who require or obtain subsidized rental units. Resident dissatisfaction thus followed.

The high percentage (68 percent) of units in projects intended for elderly occupance raises doubts about the current ability of the rental programs to meet the needs of families, especially larger ones. The proportion of rental units for elderly only occupance has declined as the emphasis shifted to the newer program (Section 221(d)(3), 78.3 percent; Section 236, 56.8 percent). Rent supplements have been used extensively to assist households in obtaining Section 221(d)(3) housing, especially for elderly households. While rent supplements have also been used with Section 236 units, the extent is much less (17 percent as against 76 percent) and there is no substantial difference in use between elderly and family occupance.

It is difficult, however, to estimate what proportion of the program production should be intended for elderly occupance. A prior question that must be answered is: What proportion of households in need are elderly and eligible? According to HUD estimates in 1973 there were 21,200 households in Seattle eligible for assisted rental housing (58 percent families and 42 percent elderly). From an equity viewpoint, there has been too much emphasis on elderly occupance, doubtless because of their less controversial and less troublesome nature.

Turning to the homeownership subsidy program, it must be noted that the total production figures are somewhat misleading in that they do not represent solely new units. New units comprise about 60 percent, while the remainder were either sold to families "as is" or were rehabilitated before occupancy. Most of the new units are located in suburban King County, where there are four major clusters: Kent, Auburn, Bothell and Kirkland. The general pattern of houses in the city reveals some concentration (Figure 4-11). The concentration occurs in areas which are predominantly black or lower middle income areas into which the black population is moving.

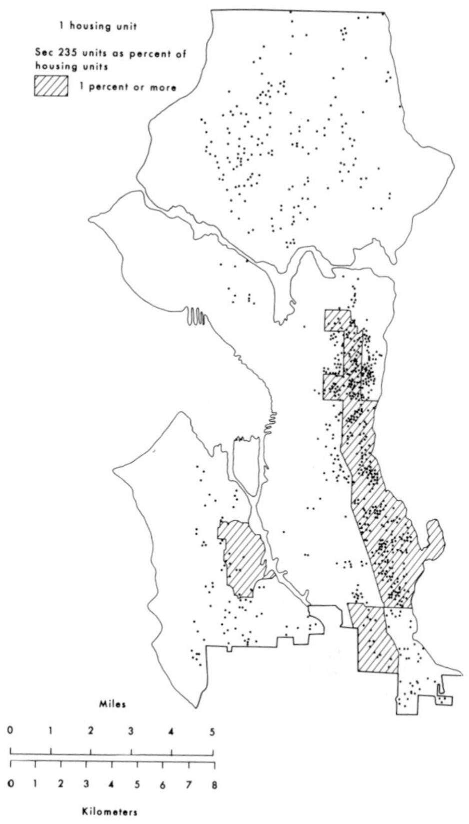

Figure 4-11. Section 235 Subsidized Homeownership Units in Seattle, 1972, Excluding Rehabilitation Units.

There are three major concerns with the homeownership program in Seattle: location, quality of the housing and purchaser problems. There is no HUD locational policy for Section 235 program units, either nationally or locally. Thus, other nonspatial HUD policies and economic and social forces have interacted to create the patterns in the city of Seattle and the concentration in the four suburban districts.

One of the key factors in location is the housing unit price limitations. The existence of limitations means that many neighborhoods of a city are effectively excluded as potential locations, since land costs drive the price beyond the limits. As with the rental programs, the availability of low cost land encouraged construction in the central area and in the southeast where larger parcels of land could be utilized to build several homes at once. This was also a factor in southern King County. HUD actions were also significant. Subsidized units were allocated both to the Seattle Model City program and the housing arm of the Seattle Urban League. Thus, the Model City Neighborhood (MCN) and the area of operations for the Urban League (which included the MCN and the southeast part of the city) received more units than might otherwise be expected. The basic concern of Seattle critics is that this program has not achieved a satisfactory degree of dispersal and that it has contributed to the concentration of low cost housing in certain critical areas in the city and created low income "ghettos" in the suburban areas.

Many families unwittingly obtained existing housing which was in poor condition or found themselves unable to maintain their homes when the need arose. Some families have subsequently abandoned these homes. The new housing is criticized by Seattle Housing Development as being of poor quality, possibly as a result of HUD's regulations limiting construction costs. For example, a California developer has noted that with "today's land costs and costs of quality materials," and given the HUD imposed price limitations on Section 235 units, "you could produce nothing but instant slums" [Detman p. 58]. There is substantial evidence that this has happened. Quality and concern for those who would buy and live in these new units has taken a back seat to achieving production and the creation of profitable business opportunities for the private sector. The poor quality of the new units has also caused ill-feeling among those living in adjacent private homes, as they feared a loss in value of their own homes from being next to shoddy or poorly maintained houses. Very few units have been produced by rehabilitation procedures under this program, yet this may potentially offer the best chance of a good quality home for the low and moderate income purchaser. Due in part to a lack of experience and certain cost and profit constraints, few contractors have thus been willing or able to risk participation in scattered site rehabilitation.

The problems faced by the purchasers fall into three principal categories. The low income of the purchasers makes it difficult to maintain low quality units. The slumping area economy helped accelerate foreclosures as it hit hard at those who are eligible home buyers. Many families were poorly equipped to take on the responsibility of a home, and, despite efforts by the SHD and others, counselling was minimal. For example, families believed a Federal Housing Administration inspection to be a seal of approval. They were also sometimes pressured into purchasing unsuitable or inadequate housing.

The assessment by Seattle Housing Development of the program is that, despite its ability to make homeownership a reality for many families, it has fallen short of its goals, these being: to provide homeownership opportunities for low and moderate income families; to give these families greater freedom of choice as to type and location of housing; to add quality low cost housing to the existing stock; and to improve existing housing through rehabilitation.

A related problem must be noted. The inability of owners to meet their mortgage payments has resulted in considerable acquisition by HUD of new, existing or rehabilitated homes originally purchased under the subsidy program. Acquisitions in 1973 totaled 120 of 1,234 units in Seattle and 444 of 2,918 units in the remainder of King County. It is acquisition rates such as these, the difficulties in attaining the program goals and high program expenditures that have generated much criticism of subsidy programs. It is necessary, however, to consider such programs in their context. HUD has acquired a substantial number of properties in the Seattle area, but much of this can be attributed to the slump in the regional economy. A Seattle Housing Development report on acquired properties also found that 93 percent of all acquired properties in the city and 75 percent in the balance of the county were sold under non-subsidized programs. Many low and middle income homeowners could not easily absorb the economic depression. These Seattle data support general findings concerning the incidence of mortgage defaults and HUD acquisition by the various subsidy programs.

Seattle Summary. The various comments by local agency representatives indicate that, in their view, there remains a need for subsidized housing in the Seattle region. The format for providing this is a matter for debate, as is the question of location. The record to date reveals the spatial concentration of subsidized housing in certain areas in the city (Figure 4-12). Subsidized housing includes low rent public housing and the units produced under the rental and homeownership subsidy programs. Only in a few instances are there very high degrees of concentration, and in two cases this reflects the large public housing projects together with other subsidized housing. Two major areas of concentration exist: the central area and the "finger" reaching into the neighborhoods in the southeast of Seattle. In the latter case, these developments have provoked community reaction over the fear of subsidized housing "ghettos" with an attendant atmosphere. Concentrations are also evident in certain suburban areas, although it is less easy to comment on these because of noncorrespondence of data recording units. Clearly, Auburn in southern King County has a high degree of subsidized housing relative to other suburban communities and some central city neighborhoods.

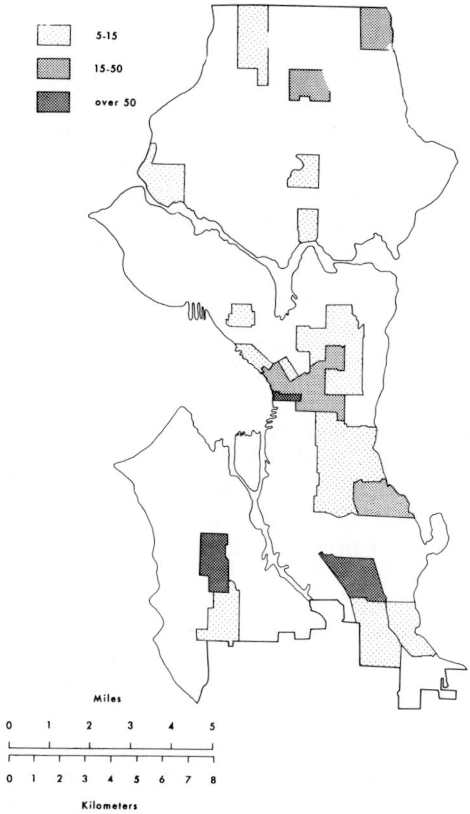

Figure 4-12. Subsidized Housing as a Percentage of All Units, 1973.

If the existing locational practices that have been described for Seattle continue, then this pattern may well be reinforced. Perhaps alternatives such as regional housing plans are viable; more on these in the fourth section of this chapter. It is difficult to measure the local impact of these programs, but they are sometimes clear features of the urban landscape. They may create serious negative side effects for adjacent residents who thus bear added social and economic costs, and there is a clear expression of concern over the quality of the residential environment in areas of concentrated subsidized housing in Seattle.

Chicago

The Chicago case provides further evidence that subsidized housing is a relatively insignificant proportion of the total housing stock, despite the efforts made in this region since 1938 (Table 4-7). The new housing has been built by the private sector. Almost a half-million new units were built in the 1960-1970 decade, while the number of households increased by only 260,000, or 15 percent. Much of this new construction occurred in the suburbs (Figure 4-13). These opportunities encouraged white households to continue to move out of the central city, while in Chicago itself, black households moved into those areas recently vacated by whites. The net effect of this was the steady abandonment and demolition of housing units, many in deplorable condition, such that the occupied housing units in the city of Chicago fell by 20,000.

There were very real improvements in housing conditions as many white households obtained new units in growing suburbs, far from the disruptions of central city life, while black households moved out of difficult inner city areas and increasingly became homeowners. Black households, however, did not penetrate suburbia to any significant extent. There were only 13,000 new black families in the six county suburban area (compared to a net increase of 287,000 white families) and the great majority of these moved to areas of existing black residence in industrial satellite com-

Table 4-7. Production of Subsidized Housing by Program, Northeastern Illinois, 1938–1972

Program	*Northeastern Illinois*	*Percent*	*City of Chicago*	*Percent*
Low Rent Public Housing	45,712	59.5	41,191	67.1
Section 221(d)(3)–Rental	14,512	18.9	12,488	20.4
Section 236–Rental	9,018	11.7	5,516	9.0
Section 235–Home Ownership	7,649	9.9	2,160	3.5
Totals	76,891	100.0	61,355	100.0

Source: Northeastern Illinois Planning Commission.

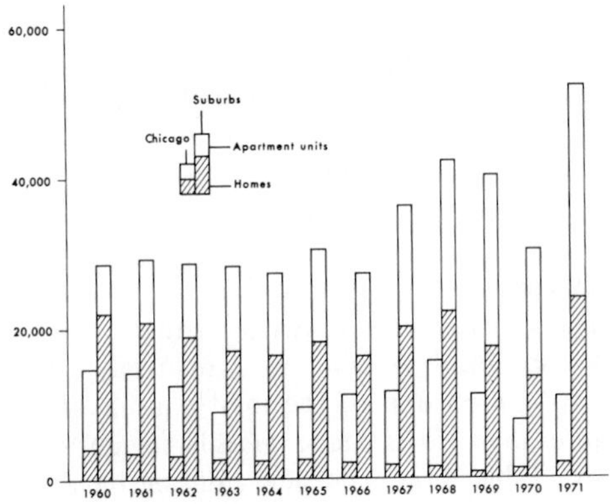

Figure 4-13. New Housing Permits for Chicago and the Suburban Balance of the Metropolitan Area, 1960 to 1971. Source: DeVise.

munities. Segregation in housing remains as great as ever.

While the city of Chicago is losing its white population, its black population is increasing steadily; the black share of total population rose from 23 percent in 1960 to 33 percent in 1970. The city also saw the number of subsidized housing units double from 1962 to 1972, while the private stock declined. Both blacks and subsidized housing are highly concentrated in the city of Chicago and relatively unimportant in suburbia. In 1960, 91 percent of the black population in the metropolitan area lived in Chicago; by 1970, the corresponding percentage was 90 percent. Similarly, 80 percent of all the subsidized units in the metropolitan area are located in Chicago (Table 4-7).

Chicago is primarily a city of apartments and, consequently, a city of renters. Over 40 percent of the housing units are in structures with more than five units and almost two-thirds of the 1970 population are renters; this is a characteristic which seems likely to increase, even in the suburban areas (Figure 4-13). This tendency will be offset, however, by the increasing development of condominiums and the conversion of rental units into condominiums. In this situation, the maintenance and pricing decisions of the landlords and property management professionals are especially critical with respect to the issues of cost of housing and quality of housing.

In 1960, 21.5 percent of all housing units were in poor condition and 11.6 percent of all occupied units were overcrowded. The worst housing occurred in a broad but discontinuous arc around the core of the city. There was a close geographical coincidence between black and low income residential areas. Overcrowding also occurred in areas containing public housing projects.

By 1970, the proportion that were overcrowded had declined somewhat to 9.9 percent. Data are not available to permit comparison with 1960 on structural condition and plumbing facilities. However, 4.3 percent of units lacked some or all plumbing facilities in 1970. An estimated 2.8 percent were dilapidated, yet with all plumbing facilities. Thus, approximately 7 percent of units were deficient in some manner. The 1972 Annual Housing Report of the Northeastern Illinois Planning Commission noted that "there had been a considerable improvement in the overall condition of the housing inventory stock over the past two decades."

The initial public attack on the poor housing conditions was spearheaded by the construction of new units under the low rent public housing program and slum clearance under urban renewal and public works programs. New subsidy programs were only employed after the mid-1960s.

Low Rent Public Housing Programs in the Chicago Area. Various forms of public housing units are provided and managed by the Chicago Housing Authority (CHA) serving the city of Chicago only, and a scattering of minor housing authorities serving Cook County and various suburban municipalities such as Aurora and Elgin, Joliet and Waukegan, for example. The overwhelming bulk of public housing units are located in the city under the jurisdiction of the CHA (Table 4-7).

The growth of the Chicago Housing Authority stock has been steady, although the late 1950s and early 1960s provided the dramatic growth—almost half the nonelderly units were constructed between 1957-1962 (Figure 4-14). More recently family units have increased, but slowly, and the emphasis has been on the elderly and leased housing programs. The authority is one of America's best known and it has had a controversial history. Created in the Depression era, its first projects were essentially unemployment relief projects in blighted areas. The need for housing for war workers further stimulated production in 1943-1947 and, as in Seattle, access to industrial areas and vacant sites were the important locating factors.

The attempt to expand the CHA's program after the passage of the 1949 Housing Act generated considerable conflict, as there was strong opposition to the location of public housing in certain Chicago neighborhoods. A compromise ensured the continuation of production and in the 1950s the authority was active in clearing slum areas as defined by the Chicago Plan Commission; 642 acres of central city slums were cleared and more than 10,000 families were relocated, many going into the low rent public housing which was being built in these same areas. The clearance activities determined the location of the projects. An attempt to maintain a racial balance in the housing projects soon collapsed, and they are now overwhelmingly occupied by black Chicagoans, although some all-white projects remain, particularly those for elderly occupance only. Almost all the family projects are occupied by blacks, and only nine of 37 elderly only projects had any appreciable degree of racial mixture. The leased housing program serves mostly the elderly white population. The growth of this program and emphasis on housing for elderly occupance, along with the cutback of family housing programs has thus led to an increase in the proportion of white tenants from 8 percent in 1963 to 17 percent in 1972.

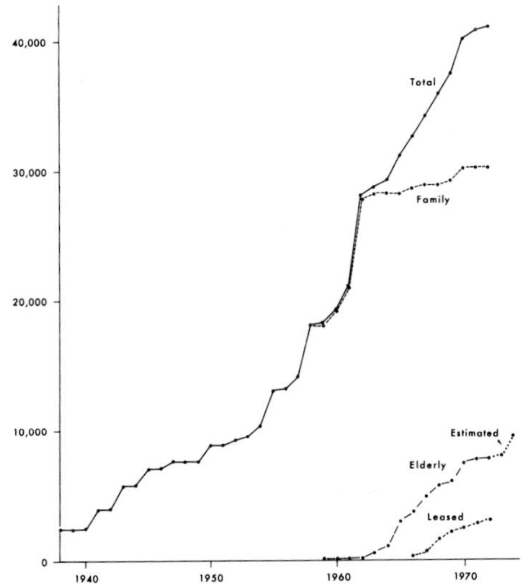

Figure 4-14. Chicago Housing Authority Low Rent Public Housing Units, 1938-1972. Source: Chicago Housing Authority Annual Reports.

The housing authority's various projects fan outward in three "fingers" from the downtown "Loop" (Figure 4-15). The nonelderly projects are located almost entirely within black neighborhoods, 92 percent according to the CHA annual report. This was a direct consequence of the compromise policy of the early fifties. Under Illinois law, the responsibility for approving sites for public housing rests with the Chicago City Council. For years, the council has operated on the principle that public housing can be utilized in slum clearance activities in the central blighted areas and that public housing should be located where it is needed and wanted. The elderly only projects show a marked concentration in the northern "finger" along the lakeshore and these are almost totally white. Some of the family projects in the black areas are massive in size; for example, Taylor Homes contains 4,311 units with a population in 1972 of 25,250, with 75 percent of the families classed as "broken families." Such projects exhibit some of the classic high-rise public housing project characteristics of crime, vandalism, alcohol and other abuse, and the like that have resulted in their being labeled "federal slums."

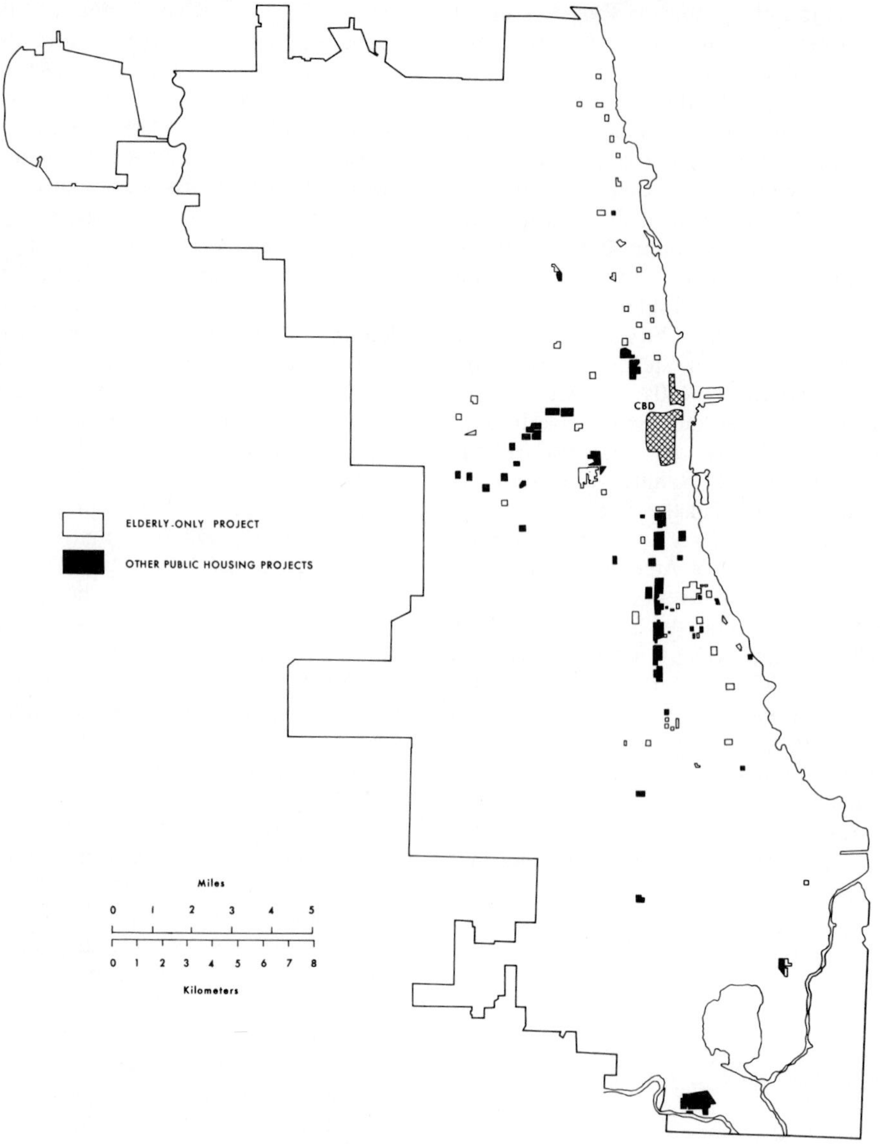

Figure 4-15. Chicago Housing Authority Public Housing Projects, 1972.

In common with other housing authorities, the CHA has moved away from such classic projects and has achieved a greater dispersal of units through the use of housing for elderly occupance—often the only developments which are acceptable to a local community—and by utilizing the leased housing program. One of the objectives of leased housing is to provide housing opportunities in dispersed locations, and to avoid the overconcentration of units in areas already containing public housing. In Chicago, the leased housing units are highly concentrated in three areas: in the predominantly white districts of Rogers Park and Uptown in the north of the city, and in two major black residential areas, Garfield Park and Lawndale on the West Side of the city, and the Woodlawn-Englewood district on the south side (Figure 4-16). The authority claims that only in these areas are landlords willing to

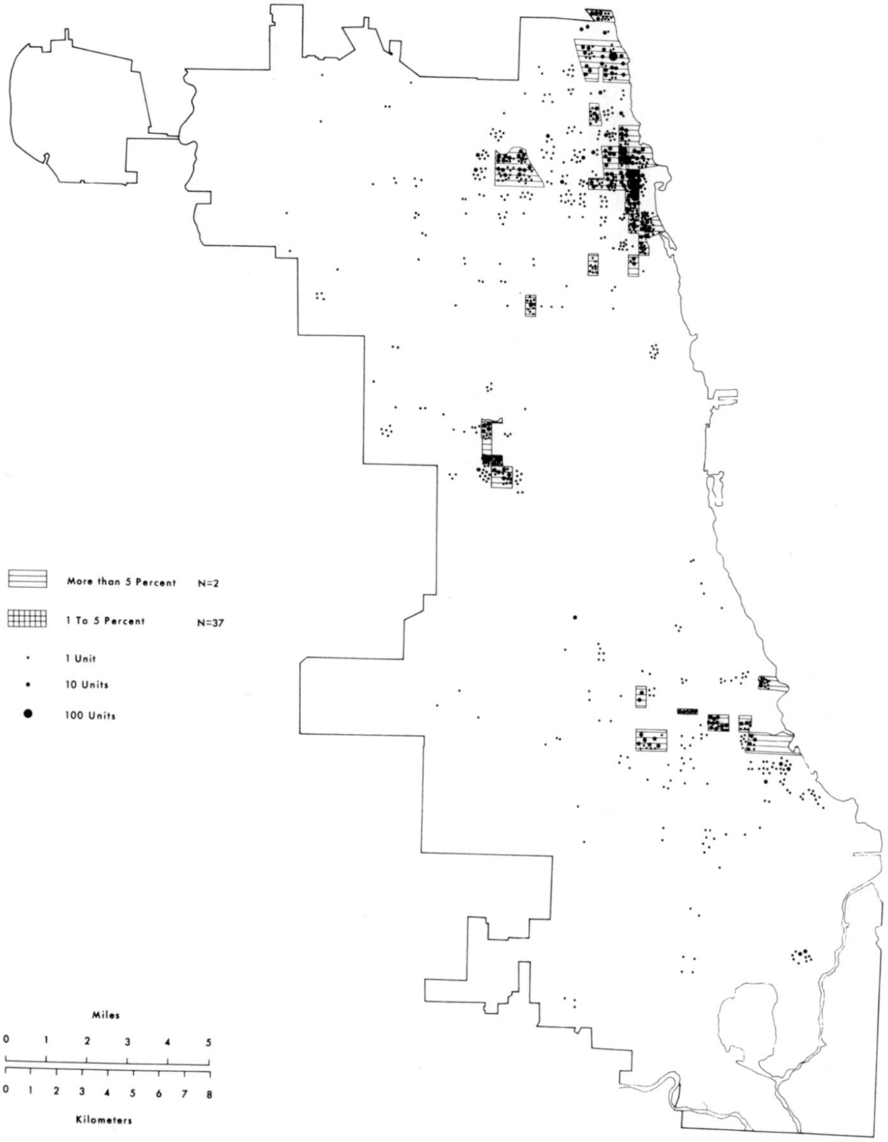

Figure 4–16. Chicago Housing Authority Leased Housing, 1972.

enter into a leasing arrangement with the CHA, since in other areas landlords can readily rent their units on the open market.

This extreme geographical concentration of the various CHA program units, especially within black residential areas, brought about a court action by the American Civil Liberties Union. The decision by Judge Richard Austin ordered the authority to build 700 public housing units immediately in white residential areas and thereafter to build three units in white neighborhoods for every one built in nonwhite areas. One-third of the "white area" homes could be located in suburban Cook County. He also ordered that 600 units in the leased housing program be reserved for nonelderly households. The authority was now faced with the difficult task of finding suitable locations, a problem reminiscent of the conflicts over locations in the early 1950s. The search proceeded extremely slowly, and in 1971, two years after the initial ruling, the court forced the CHA to submit its list of designated sites to the city council, thereby making them public. The proposed sites, containing 1,700 units, were mostly located in areas outside neighborhoods which are 30 percent or more nonwhite—that is, in the general housing area. A buffer zone of one mile surrounding the nonwhite areas was established as the limited housing area (Figure 4-17).

This list was released in the middle of a civic election campaign and uproar followed. The initial proposals were unacceptable politically and a second partial list of sites (including some on the original list) was submitted for council approval in June 1971. The contrast in the location of the two sets of proposed sites is extreme (Figure 4-17). Many of the initial sites were eliminated, and a good deal of "shrinkage" occurred, with a much more clustered pattern being evident. From the original 275 sites, the number of sites in the June 1971 proposal was reduced to 100, 44 of which were in the general housing area and 56 in the limited housing area, and the number of units proposed was 732. HUD subsequently authorized a development program on 40 sites in the general housing area. A specific project, *Illinois 2-85,* with 36 scattered sites comprising 267 family units, was then approved by the CHA in November 1971, and by HUD in February 1972 (Figure 4-17). Fifty units were scheduled for completion in 1974. The project sites are concentrated in areas with numerous elderly and leased housing units.

After the Austin ruling, the authority entered into a cooperative agreement with the Cook County Housing Authority to construct 500 units in Cook County over a three year period, but no units yet have been built. Other suburban governments are not interested in cooperating, according to authority sources.

Perhaps the most striking aspect of the "Austin affair" is that it has taken five years to create a fraction of the units required by the court ruling, and there has been a remark-

Figure 4-17. Sites selected by Chicago Housing Authority in Response to Court Orders, 1971.

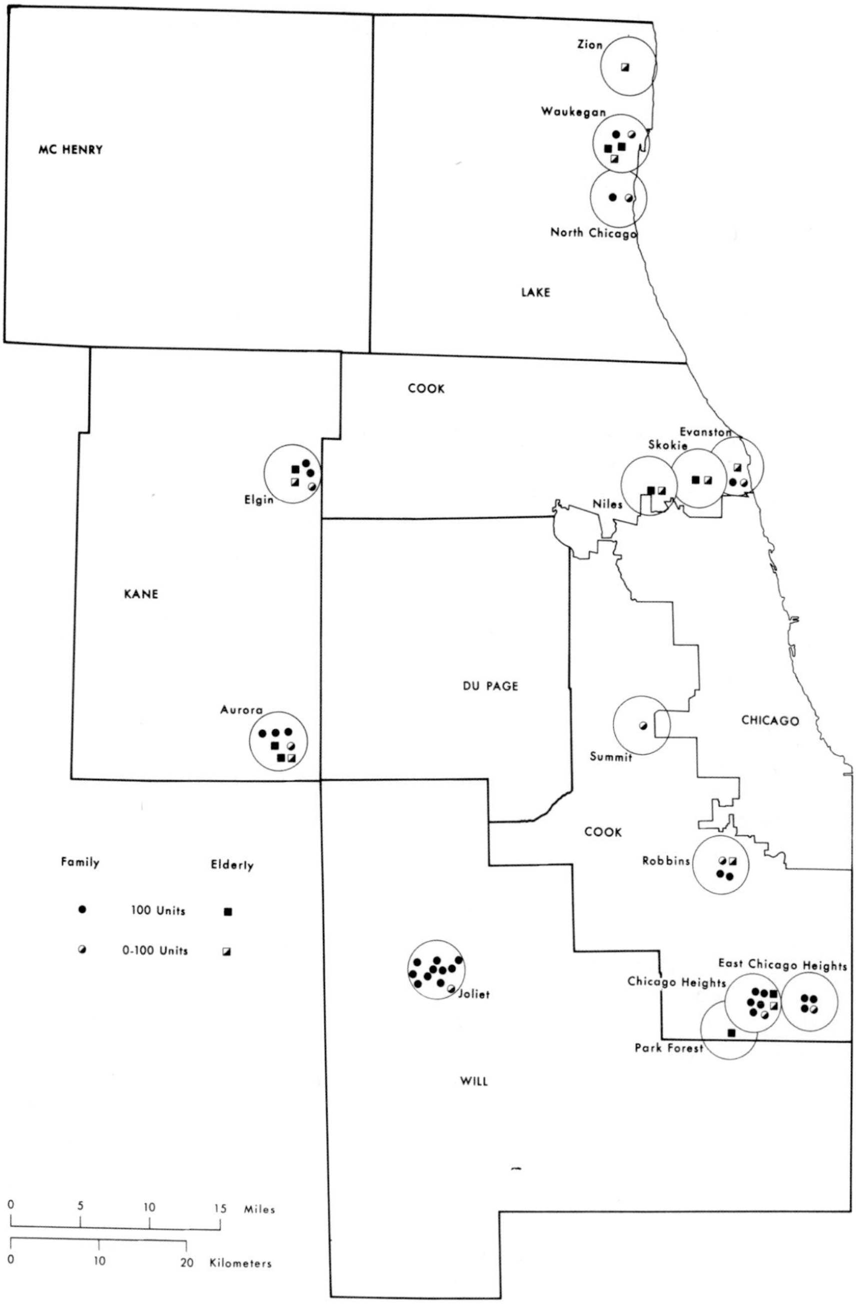

Figure 4-18. Public Housing in Suburban Chicago, 1972.

able spatial contraction in the range of locations of proposed projects during that time. Additional efforts to meet the court ruling have been severely affected by the 1973 federal moratorium, which froze two additional projects with 1,033 units on 407 scattered sites. This situation is a testament to the difficulty of achieving geographical dispersion under such a volatile and politicized program as low rent public housing.

Only 10 percent of the Chicago SMSA's public housing is located outside the central city (Figure 4-18). Many of the 4,500 units are in the four industrial satellite communities:

Waukegan-North Chicago, Elgin, Aurora and Joliet. The balance between elderly and non-elderly occupance in the suburbs is 44 to 56 percent. However, certain communities such as Skokie, Niles and Park Forest–have no family public housing, whereas other municipalities–Joliet, Summit, and East Chicago Heights for example–contain only family housing. There is a major difference in socio-economic status between these groups of municipalities, with that of the latter being generally lower. Again, the point of community acceptability of various forms of public housing must be raised. In general, however, low rent public housing is at present an insignificant housing opportunity in suburban Chicago.

Urban Renewal. This long-standing program has had a considerable impact in Chicago, although the direct impact and consequences have been limited to the central city. The department of urban renewal has expended \$378.5 million in the ten year period 1962–1971, and in that period has received \$170.5 million in federal grants. City authorities claim that the urban renewal program is a catalyst for stimulating private investment, a claim that does not seem unreasonable, given the profitable opportunities created by urban renewal, although it might be difficult to specify the linkages in some instances. The program has resulted in the clearance of large areas of inner city land, the demolition of many housing units and the construction of new housing units and the new industrial, commercial and institutional structures on the cleared sites. Some would argue that it has meant the destruction of neighborhoods, echoing a claim made in other cities. One Chicago example is the Harrison-Halsted project (Figure 4-19) where the Chicago campus of the University of Illinois was developed in an ethnic neighborhood on the Near West Side.

The Northeastern Illinois Planning Commission estimated that in the period 1948-1963 and 1969-1971, 21,462 residential units were removed by urban renewal action. Extrapolating over the missing data period, the total is probably around 28,000 residential units. Some proportion of these was certainly substandard (by then current census definitions), but many standard units undoubtedly were also lost in the project assembly and clearance process. Additions to the city's housing stock on urban renewal sites total around 13,000 (1958-1971), with about 2,500 units under construction in 1971 and 3,500 units in the "pipeline" in various stages of preconstruction processing. The first major residential projects came on the market in the early 1960s and did little to assist those who needed low and moderate income housing. By the middle 1960s the urban renewal program was receiving considerable criticism in Chicago and elsewhere, and activity levels declined (Figure 4-20). The 1968 Federal Legislation which attempted to link urban renewal much more closely with the various housing subsidy programs in order to general more low and moderate income housing as against luxury and high income townhouses and apartment units had direct consequences in Chicago.

From the geographic perspective, the impact of the Urban Renewal program is clearly in the inner city (Figure 4-19). In most cases, the neighborhood development program areas encompass areas in which the emphasis has been on conservation through code enforcement, rehabilitation, and spot clearance and redevelopment. The projects have almost invariably involved large-scale site clearance and redevelopment with new structures, and Chicago's urban renewal activity has emphasized these redevelopment projects in terms of expenditures and new residential units produced. Only about 15 percent of the new residential units have been created in NDP areas and, while one would expect the emphasis to be on rehabilitation and code enforcement in such areas, only 2.2 percent of total program expenditures since inception (1962) have been on rehabilitation and a further 2.5 percent on the neighborhood service program (code enforcement) areas. Furthermore, in March 1973, the city commission for urban renewal noted that rehabilitation efforts under Section 312 (long term loans) and Section 115 (direct grants up to \$3,500) were at a standstill, including "Project Rehab" totaling some 2,700 units. As in other cities, the Chicago experience with rehabilitation efforts has been that it is a costly, complicated and time-consuming procedure.

It is difficult to summarize the impact of a large, complex program such as urban renewal in Chicago where there are numerous individual projects and spatial settings involved. Areas of

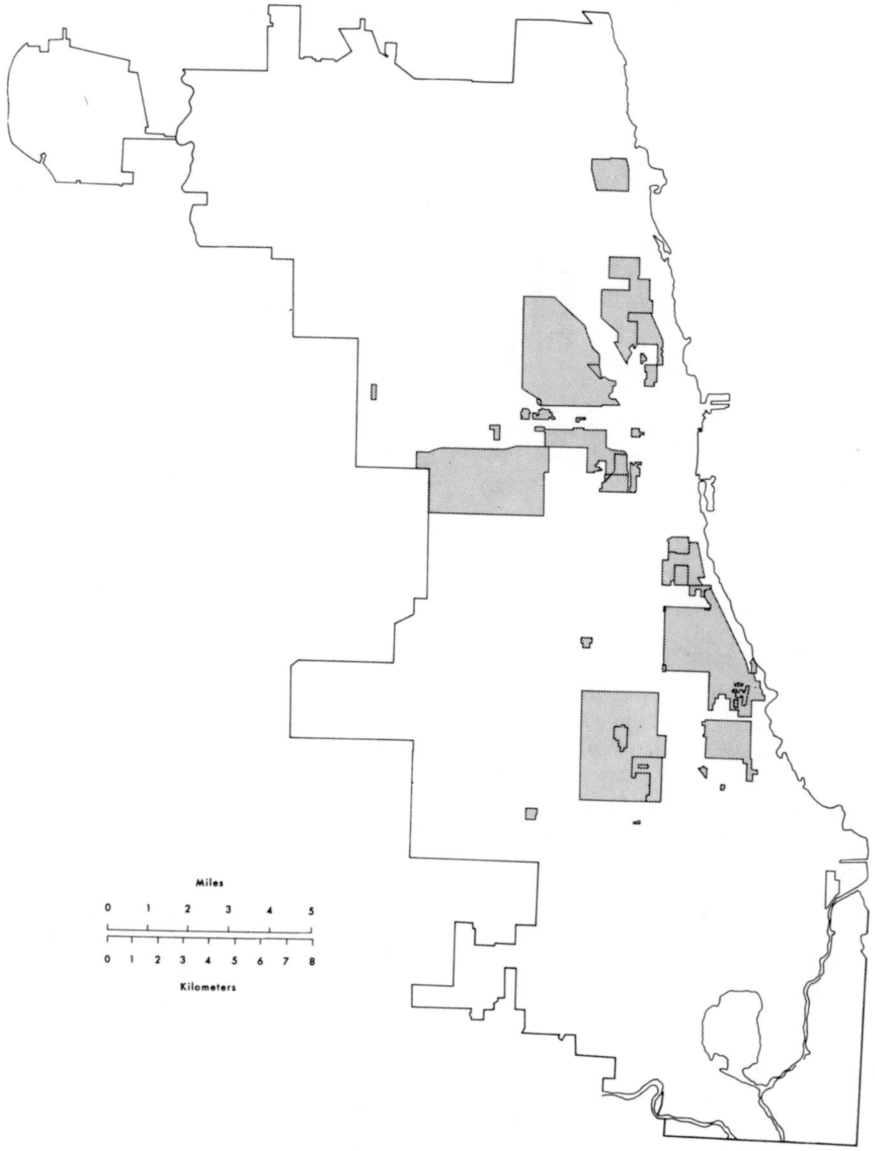

Figure 4-19. Urban Renewal in Chicago, 1971.

greatest activity are roughly conterminous with the areas of residential blight in the inner city. Some prime locations in terms of accessibility to downtown and the lakefront have been "recaptured" for an upper income population. The North-LaSalle project is a good example. Central city institutions have also used urban renewal as a protective device to upgrade and protect their neighborhood environment—for example, the Michael Reese Hospital, the University of Chicago and the Illinois Institute of Technology. The urban renewal program has helped considerably in eliminating blighted housing, but as Herbert Gans and others have noted, it has also eliminated low cost housing, some of it adequate by current standards. Only recently has there been a significant effort to redress this situation. A recent planning study concluded that in Chicago this program has helped improve the quality of the housing stock, but at the expense of further reducing the amount of housing for low and moderate

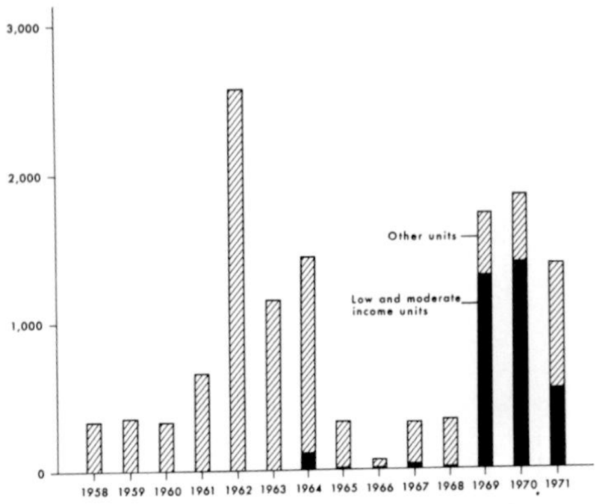

Figure 4-20. Housing Units Constructed on Urban Renewal Project Sites in Chicago, 1958-1971.

income families. Whether or not households displaced by urban renewal activity are adequately relocated in standard housing has always been a contentious issue. One point that most analysts do agree on is that for the majority of relocatees, housing expenditures are significantly higher. Thus, with the use of housing expenditure-income ratios as an indicator of housing need, a substantial proportion of relocatees may be classed as "housing-poor." Greater emphasis on conservation and rehabilitation could reduce some of these kinds of impacts, but the procedure is lengthy and costly and the Chicago record in this area is relatively disappointing.

Sections 221(d)(3) and 236: Subsidized Rental Housing. After the dominant low rent public housing program, the rental subsidy programs have been of considerable importance both in terms of numbers produced and location. In both the SMSA and the city, these rental assistance programs represent about 30 percent of the directly subsidized housing stock. The more recent Section 236 program has been employed to provide low and middle income rental housing outside of the central city and this reflects the policy shift embodied in the 1968 legislation.

Within each program, however, there is still evidence of marked geographical concentration (Figure 4-21). The Section 221(d)(3) units, produced largely in the 1965-1970 period (Figure 4-22), comprise the bulk of the city's rental subsidy units (12,488 as against 5,516 Section 236 units). Geographically, the same pattern that exists for low rent public housing exists for these units. The area of greatest concentration is in the Uptown and Lakeview areas, which are white neighborhoods with a significant elderly population. Other areas with subsidized rental units are predominantly black. The more recently built Section 236 units, brought onto the market in a very brief interval (Figure 4-22), are located on the West Side and on the South Side, especially in areas of newer black residence such as Englewood, West Englewood and South Shore. This is not a surprising finding, given that it is usually middle income blacks who are the first to penetrate all-white residential areas, and that this program is geared to the middle income population, many of whom incur high rent-income ratios under conditions of neighborhood change. The newer rental units in Chicago are almost wholly for family occupance, and this partly explains their absence from the cluster in the white neighborhoods in the north of the city.

The characteristic concentration of rental units is maintained on the suburban scene. The opportunities represented by units produced under these subsidy programs are available in but a few locations and in small numbers relative to the total housing stock (Figure 4-23). As with public housing, the industrial satellite cities are a major component of the pattern. The few Section 221(d)(3) units in the inner suburbs are located in such communities as Robbins and Chicago Heights which have significant degrees of nonwhite population. There is a greater degree of spatial dispersion achieved under the newer Section 236 program; for example, units have been constructed in the western suburbs of DuPage County where such federally assisted housing had not previously existed. A middle income household with an automobile may improve its accessibility to the growing suburban job opportunities if more such units were available.

Section 235: Subsidized Home Ownership. Given the single family dwelling unit character of the program, the units produced are more dispersed throughout the region. However, over half the units in the city are located in six community areas on the southwest side (Figure 4-24). This part of the city was one of

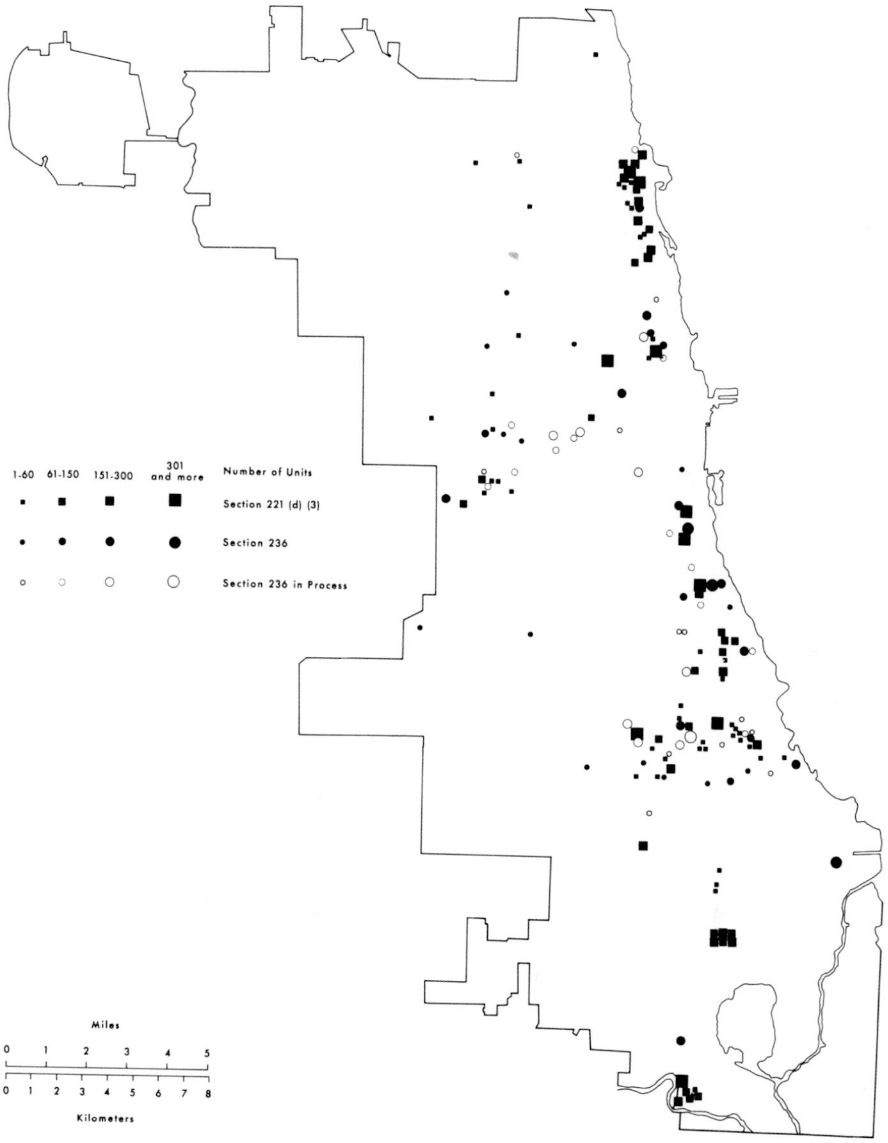

Figure 4-21. Subsidized (Section 221(d)(3) and Section 236) Rental Housing in Chicago.

the few areas where vacant land was available, and this has no doubt contributed to this concentration, as has land cost, given the program's cost limitations. It is difficult from the available data to make statements about the impact of new or rehabilitated Section 235 units on racial change in these areas. We might guess that there is an increasing proportion of blacks, since three of these areas (West Englewood, 48 percent black; Roseland, 55 percent; Morgan Park, 48 percent) show a roughly 50-50 split between blacks and whites, a situation often indicating that an area is experiencing racial change. The suspected relationship here requires more detailed examination.

Again in the suburban areas, a distinct pattern is clear, with significant concentrations of units in the lower socioeconomic status municipalities of southern Cook County, in the Fox River Vally towns such as Aurora and

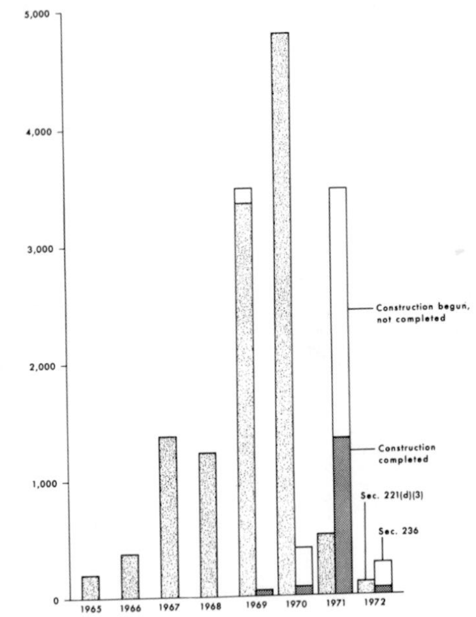

Figure 4-22. Subsidized Rental Housing in Chicago, 1965-1972.

Carpentersville and, in a few instances, in the small new suburbs, for example, Westhaven, Richton Park, Round Lake Beach, Sunnyside, Romeoville (Figure 4-25). The absence of subsidized homes from the western and northern inner suburban areas is again strikingly clear.

Chicago Summary. Given the marked geographical clustering of many of the units produced under the principal subsidy programs, it is not surprising to find neighborhoods in Chicago and some suburban communities which, in addition to being nonwhite ghettos, are also public housing "ghettos," in the sense of significant concentrations (Figures 4-26 and 4-27). The various components of these summary maps have already been described in detail, so that only a few points need to be made here.

In the city, the infamous "wall" of high-rise public housing along the Dan Ryan Expressway on the South Side emerges clearly. The Section 235 subsidized homeownership program has contributed significantly to the spread of subsidized housing into many South Side census tracts, but the relative impact is still limited. The highest percentages are still associated with the concentrations of public housing in the inner city.

In the suburban context, the salient features are the discontinuous ring comprising the satellites and Fox River Valley towns, the southern Cook County suburbs and the small suburbs with recent subsidized construction.

Unlike our study of Seattle, no studies were available from local agencies or other sources which evaluate and assess the impact of these various programs in the Chicago region. Another problem is simply the sheer magnitude of the Chicago case and its bureaucratic complexities.

The situation in Chicago with respect to some programs is probably not significantly different from that documented in Seattle. Thus, for example, the poor quality of newly built subsidized homes in Seattle suburban communities and the related impact on adjacent homes and their occupants has been recorded. In one development in a suburban Chicago municipality, a HUD inspector general's report documents 1,900 variations from FHA minimum property standards. The project, built by Kaufmann and Board (one of the nation's largest builders with 1971 annual sales of $284 million), contained 220 homes selling in the $18,000-25,000 range. The residents complained bitterly about defects which they claimed were rampant in the project.

Recent work by geographers in Chicago has clearly indicated the existence of a dual housing market in the private sector. The data presented here indicate that segregation by race is equally prevalent in the public sector. The various types of subsidized housing in the city of Chicago are overwhelmingly occupied by black households. Where this is not the case, the households are usually elderly whites. In the industrial satellites, the subsidized units are located in white neighborhoods and are occupied by whites. In the major area of concentration, southern suburban Cook County, an interesting racial contrast is evident: the multifamily rental units occur primarily in black residential neighborhoods or municipalities, whereas the homes created under the homeownership subsidy program are located in white communities. Equality of opportunity is a myth in public housing in Chicago and it was this situation that prompted the American Civil Liberties suit discussed previously.

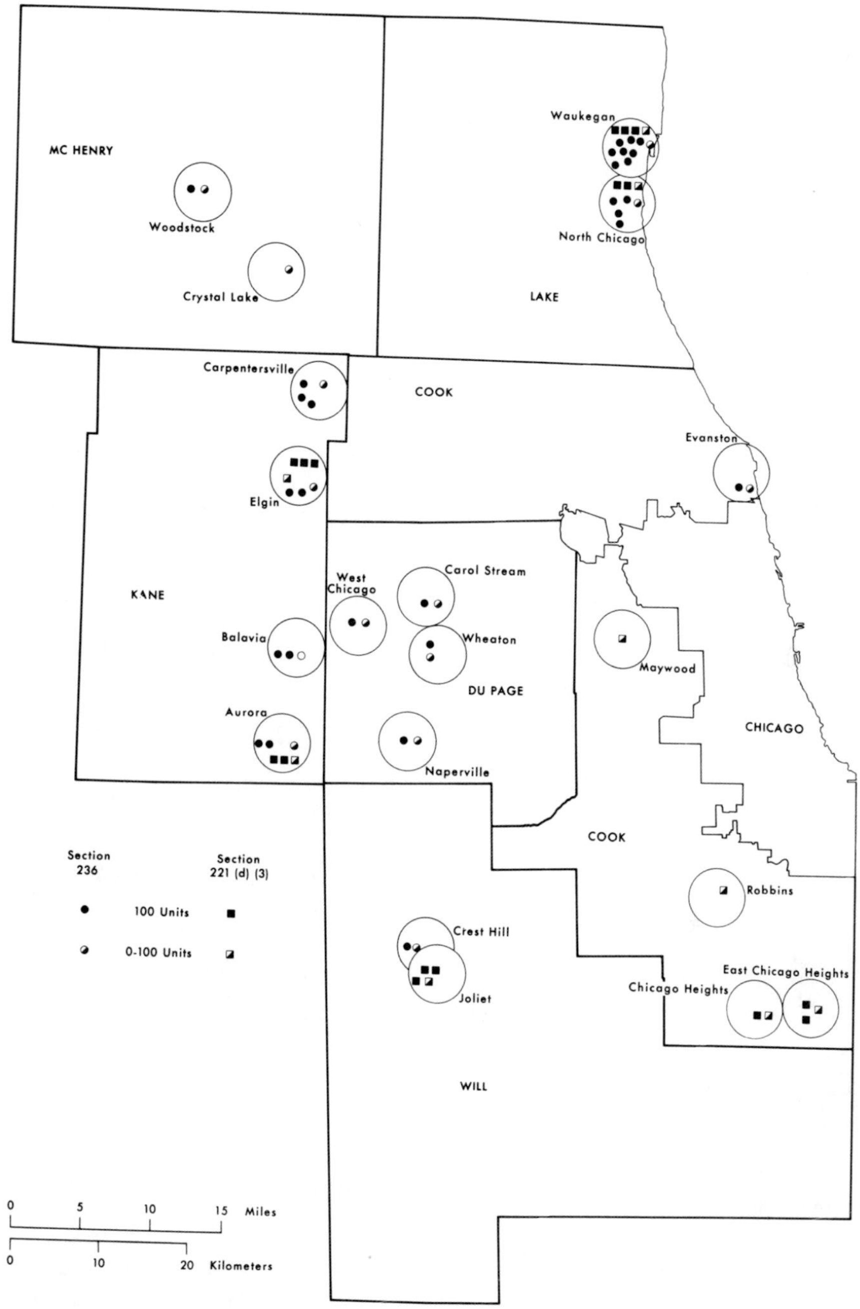

Figure 4-23. Subsidized Rental Housing in Suburban Chicago, 1972.

The existing subsidized housing opportunities in the city of Chicago are in neighborhoods which offer a difficult and precarious residential environment. With the move to the suburbs being made possible through the massive construction of new units, abandonment of the decaying inner city neighborhoods is occurring. Even though subsidized housing has the potential of providing a standard quality dwelling unit at a low cost to the households, the local

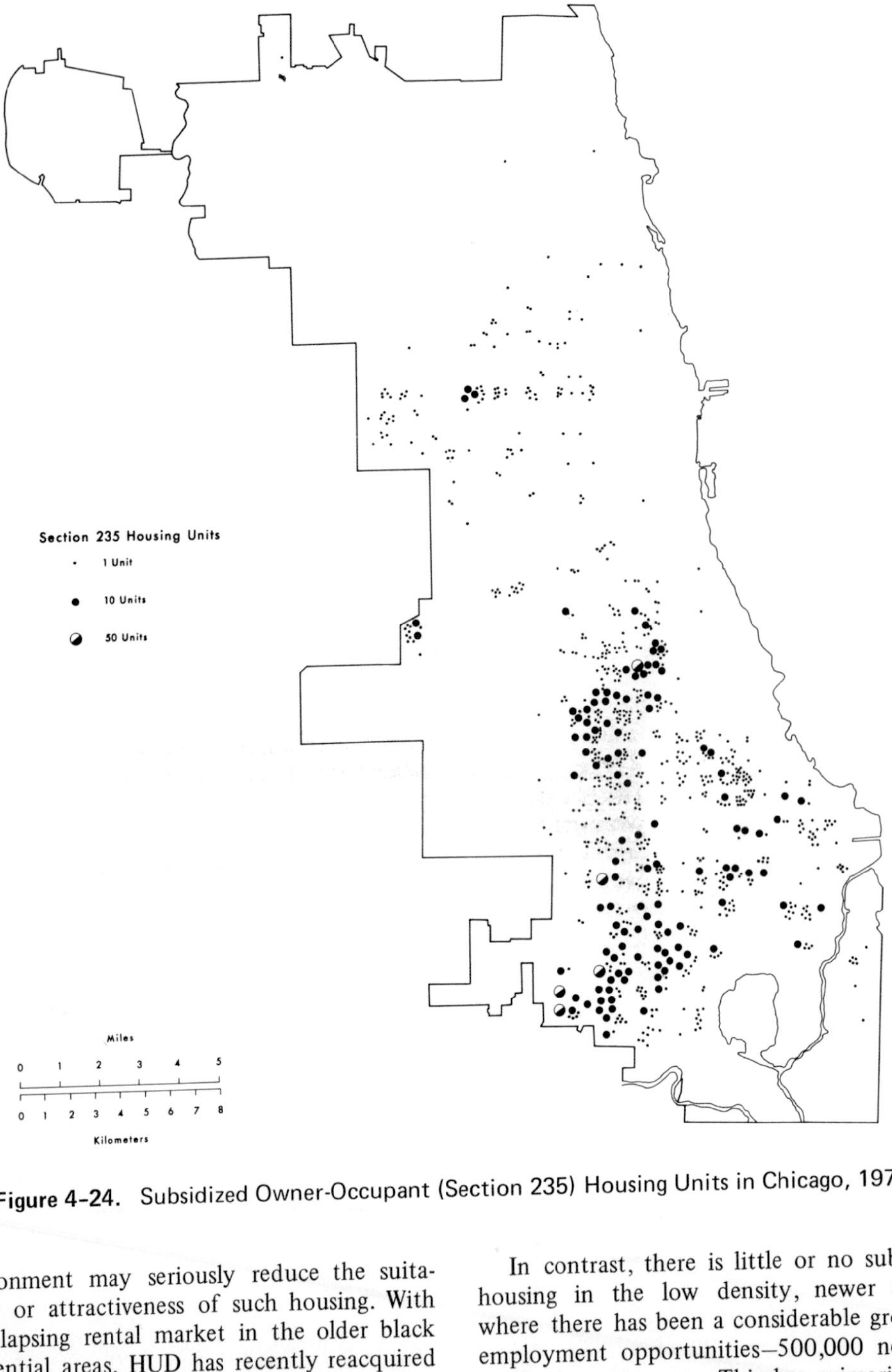

Figure 4-24. Subsidized Owner-Occupant (Section 235) Housing Units in Chicago, 1972.

environment may seriously reduce the suitability or attractiveness of such housing. With a collapsing rental market in the older black residential areas, HUD has recently reacquired 4,500 units of Section 221(d)(3) multifamily rental housing as the owners default on their below interest mortgages. Despite the low dollar costs, vacancy rates have also increased in massive high-rise low rent public housing projects, the environment being a difficult and dangerous one.

In contrast, there is little or no subsidized housing in the low density, newer suburbs where there has been a considerable growth in employment opportunities–500,000 new jobs in the last ten years. This has primarily been in the inner suburbs of the northwest sector, with O'Hare Airport, the expressway network and available land being the major catalysts for growth.

While a case can be made for increasing subsidized housing opportunities to provide im-

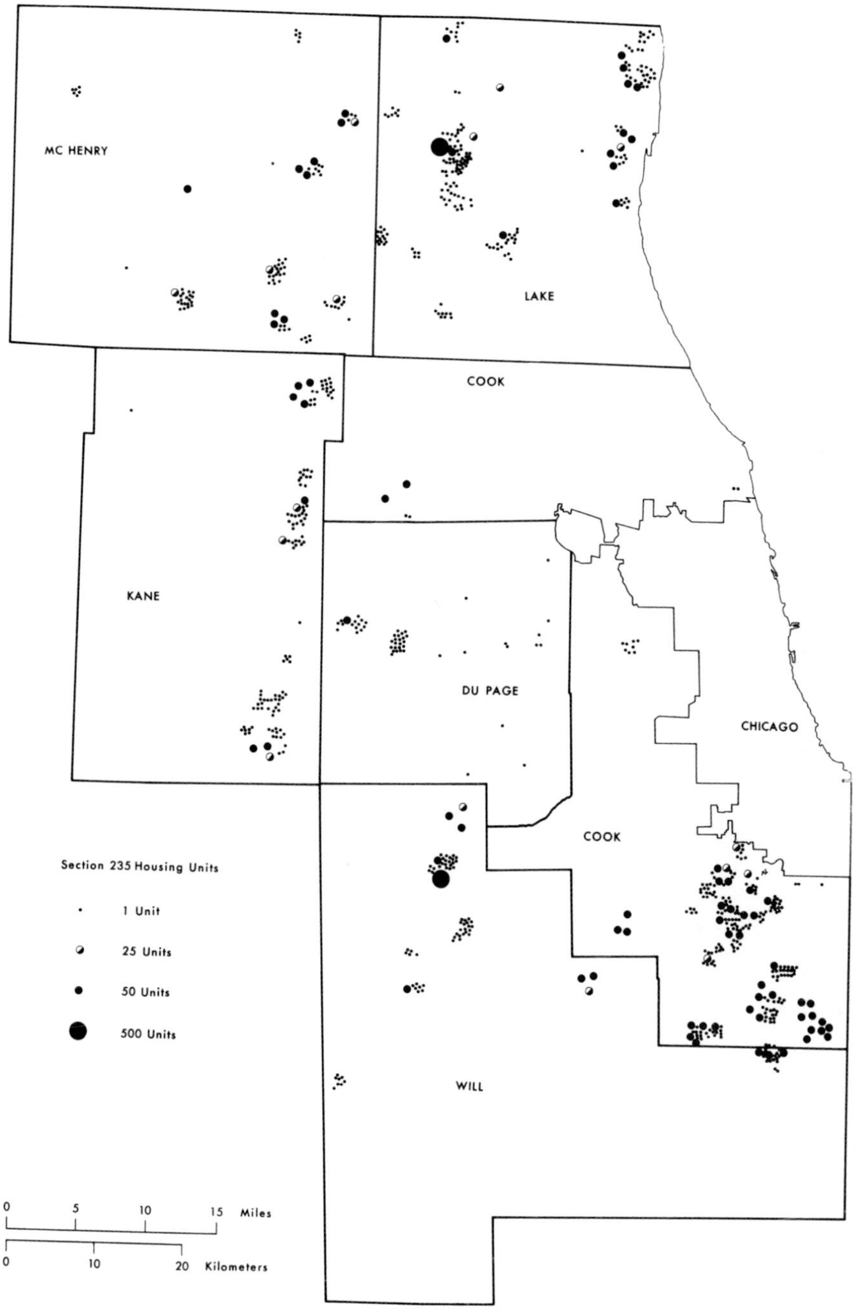

Figure 4-25. Section 235 Subsidized Owner-Occupant Units in Suburban Chicago, 1972.

proved accessibility to jobs and a more desirable neighborhood environment, the inescapable fact is that many households, unable to compete effectively in the housing market, are at present living in the central city and have turned to central city institutions for help. Thus, the demands on the Chicago Housing Authority are severe. In the absence of agency estimates of housing needs, the waiting list often serves as such, though it is likely an underestimate. At the end of 1971, the CHA had almost 20,000 households on its waiting lists.

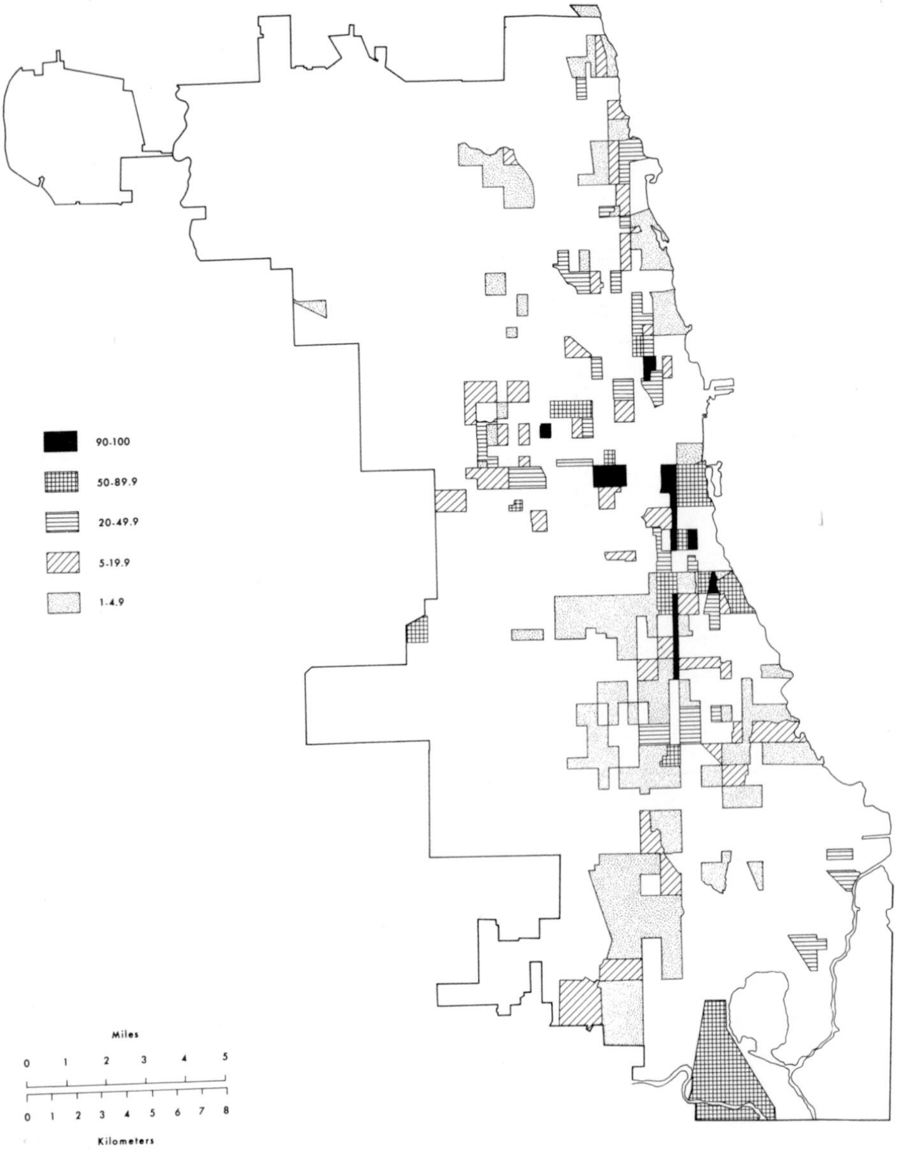

Figure 4-26. Subsidized Housing as a Share of All Housing Units, Chicago, 1972.

Since the "great push forward" began in 1968, the authority has averaged 1,700 new units a year under its various programs until 1973. But even with no new additions, it would take 12 years at the premoratorium level of activity to house those on the waiting list. Unless they find alternative housing, many of the 11,461 elderly households on the list will live out their lives in poor housing. The authority cannot house them under present circumstances.

Try as it might, the CHA cannot deliver in relation to these minimal needs. Most of the 8,000 nonelderly households are seeking one, two or three bedroom apartments in low-rise developments, anxious to avoid the high-rise projects with their grim reputation; or four and five bedroom apartments, of which there are relatively few in any development. Given the rate at which family housing is being produced recently (350 new units a year),

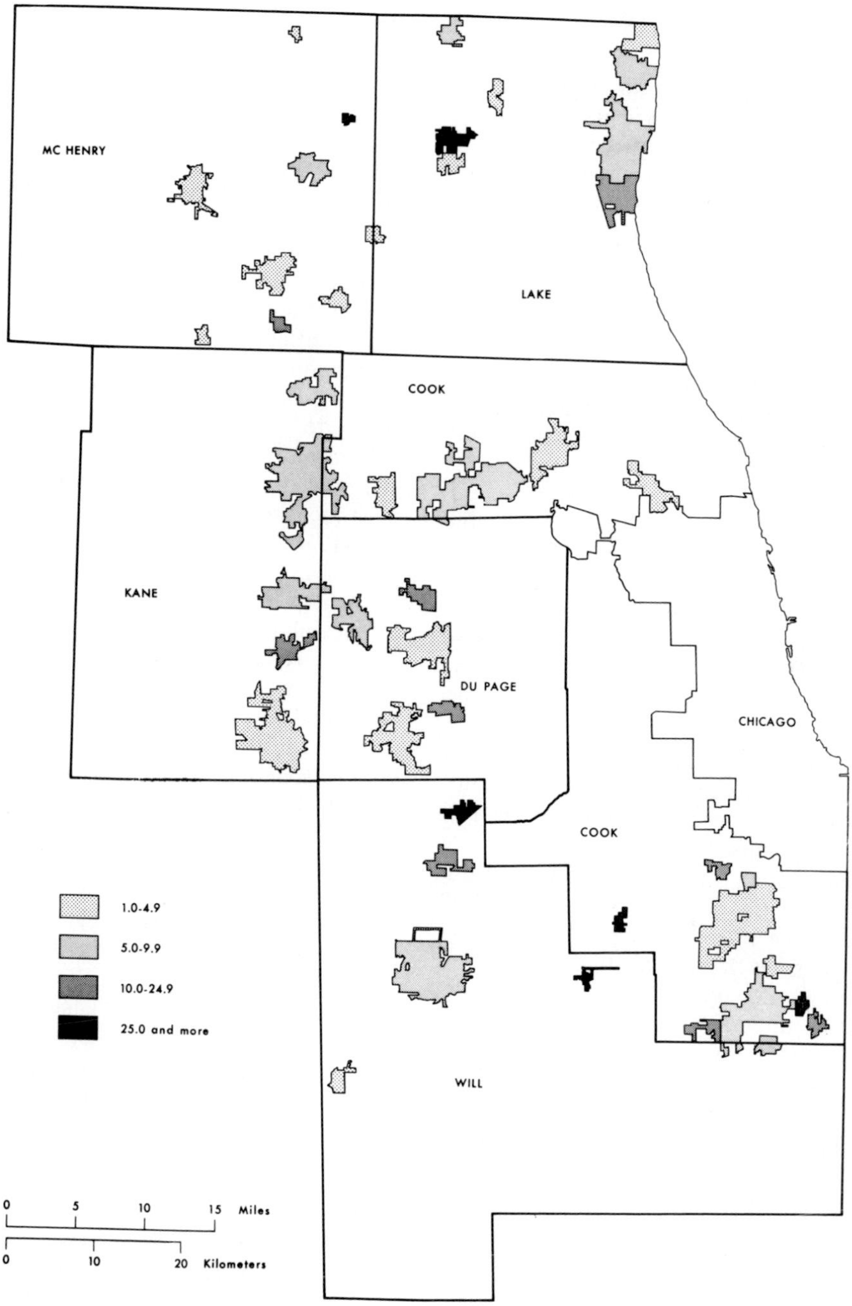

Figure 4-27. Subsidized Housing as a Share of All Housing Units in Suburban Chicago, 1972.

and the cutting back in the scattered site program, the future is bleak.

The elderly only housing program has expanded rapidly recently, but its high demand and small supply mean low turnover, a vacancy rate of almost zero and a three year wait between registration and housing. The housing authority is aware of the demand. In 1969 a program authorization of 5,000 units was sought from HUD and the need for an additional 3,000 units was indicated. The actual number granted was a mere 1,600 units. Under these circumstances, the outlook is grim for those elderly people on fixed incomes facing increasing housing costs in the private sector.

While the leased housing program has expanded rapidly of late, it is not without its problems. Given the white neighborhood location of units presently available under this program, it is not serving black households very effectively, although a need is clearly being met for other households. Furthermore, the CHA claims it is difficult to find landlords with suitable accommodation who wish to enter into the leasing program and whose units are located in the general housing area as designated by the court order. Given the popular perception of CHA tenants as black, low income and problem families, this is a believable claim.

Thus, the agency which has played the major role in the supply of subsidized housing in the region faces very serious problems in meeting the heavy demands placed upon it and suburban governments (understandably) show little inclination to assist in the dispersal of low rent public housing units and their potential tenants.

The CHA is, however, only one element of a complex system whose function is to create subsidized housing units. The demands on this system in the Chicago metropolitan area will continue to be severe. A recent HUD market analysis estimates that an SMSA total of 36,860 subsidized units for 1973-1975 could be occupied by those families who are eligible for direct assistance. Subsidized housing production in northeastern Illinois between 1938 and 1972 totaled only 80,000 units, including 67,000 family units and 13,000 units for the elderly. The Northeastern Illinois Planning Commission estimated in 1973 that the region would need during the 1970s 229,000 additional units of low and moderate income housing units—100,000 for elderly households and the rest for families. While not all of these units will necessarily come from the public sector, it seems unlikely that the private sector can assist substantially without government subsidies, given current trends. The recorded performance over 34 years suggests that it is not only a "long, long road to Tipperary," but that it is a long, long road to anywhere on the Chicago housing front. Admittedly, regional production has increased in recent years prior to the January 1973 moratorium. But even at the average annual rate of 10,000 new units for all programs (1971 and 1972) the goals would not be reached in ten or even 20 years if the need were to be met wholly by subsidized housing. The disparity between estimated need and production in certain subregions is also critically high. Whether or not such subregions will be accepting of housing for low and moderate income groups is another major issue in goal achievement. Despite the lack of detailed impact studies, the conclusion can be drawn that continued locational emphasis on those neighborhoods or municipalities with high proportions of subsidized housing will only serve to accelerate the "ghettoization" of subsidized housing (and more importantly, the residents) and do little to serve the need for such housing in other parts of the Chicago region.

Atlanta

Metaphorically, Atlanta has been billed as a phoenix—a city risen from the ashes of a cathartic war. However, the forces which fueled Atlanta's growth in the latter part of the nineteenth century were not mythological, but rather economic—and these forces have sustained the region's growth ever since. Home to Coca Cola and Delta Airlines, and southeastern headquarters of many national firms, the city of dogwood and azaleas is the focus of a metropolitan area that grew by 36 percent between 1960 and 1970. In fact, the city of Atlanta grew by 2 percent during this period, an uncommon trend for large central cities. Having a diverse economic base with a strong service component and fulfilling its role as the regional capital of the Southeast, Atlanta's prospects for continued growth appear strong.

The Atlanta area is rapidly increasing in population, both white and black, though white has consistently grown faster than black. The ratio of blacks to whites is increasing in the city of Atlanta and decreasing in the surrounding areas and in the SMSA as a whole. There are now more blacks in the city of Atlanta than there were in the five county SMSA in 1960. Housing units in the city of Atlanta increased from 154,097 in 1960 to 170,898 in 1970, an increase of 10.9 percent. This increase occurred in the outer city areas of the Fulton County section of Atlanta and resulted from new residential construction along Interstates 75 and 85 and the South Expressway, and in areas west of the center of

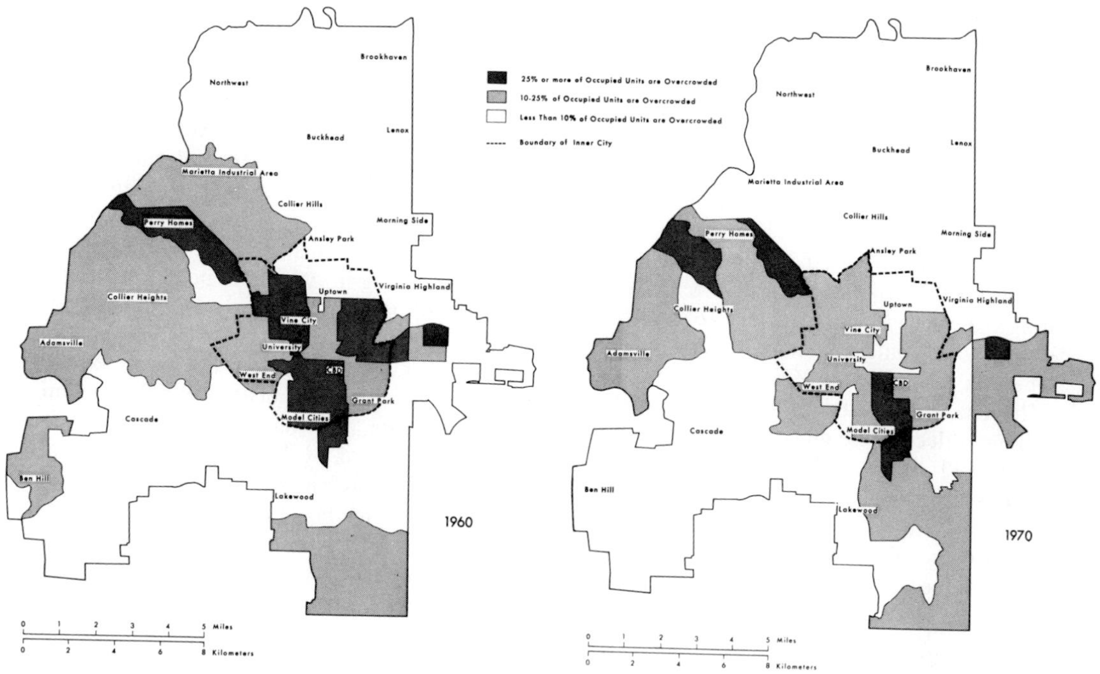

Figure 4-28. Overcrowded Housing in Atlanta, 1960-1970.

the city. A 20 percent decrease in the number of housing units in the inner city occurred (Figure 4-28). Here some neighborhoods lost more than 50 percent of the housing units available in 1960. City records show this decline in inner city housing units to be reversed in the years since the 1970 census, although the increase in absolute terms is small.

Population and Housing Distribution. The housing stock in the Atlanta area is typical of many large metropolitan areas, although perhaps having relatively more single family homes. The bulk of the stock is in single family dwelling units, 66 percent in the SMSA and 49 percent in the city. Almost a third of the city units are in apartment buildings, but just over half of the households are renters, in contrast to Chicago's two-thirds, which suggests considerable renting of single family units, duplexes, triplexes and the like. Many of the units are relatively new, reflecting recent economic activity and population growth. About 25 percent of the city's stock was built in the 1960-1970 decade, compared to Chicago's 11 percent and Seattle's 16 percent.

Atlanta's residential densities are relatively low compared with many cities of the United States, especially industrial cities in the Northeast. Densities are highest in the central area of the city, in keeping with the normal pattern of urban development, and some sections reach 40 dwelling units per acre. The Nash-Bans, University, Butler Street-Glen Iris and Uptown areas are in the 16-40 dwelling units per acre range (about 50 to 125 persons). Most of the remaining residential land in the central area has seven to 16 units per acre. Over half of the residential land of the city lies outside this core area, and at a density of six units or less per acre, much of it is hardly discernible from the adjacent suburbs. Major transportation routes attract a few ridges of higher density beyond the core area. Such areas are found to the west along the Proctor Creek-Perry Boulevard-Bankhead Highway connectors, to the east in DeKalb County along Boulevard Drive and along Peachtree Road north of Brookwood (Figure 4-28).

The Struggles Against Poor Housing. A major element in Atlanta's attempts to reduce substandard housing has been demolitions. This activity has had a major impact on inner city housing in the recent past. In absolute terms the number of housing units destroyed in recent years is significant. One study estimates that over 22,500 low income housing units were destroyed by government action between 1960 and 1970. About 8,400 of these resulted from urban renewal, 12,000 through housing code enforcement and the remainder (2,100 units) for reasons of highway, school and airport expansion. Demolitions are continuing under housing code enforcement—approximately 1,700 units in 1970, 850 in 1971 and 890 in 1972. Other reasons for demolitions during these recent years account for relatively few additional units, generally under 5 percent of the total.

The decline in total number of inner city dwellings reflects these demolitions, which were not required to be replaced by new housing until the 1968 federal housing legislation took effect. But the more recent period shows a reversal of the trends established in the 1960s. The city appears now to be directing its housing code enforcement efforts at less deteriorated areas, emphasizing rehabilitation rather than demolition. Still, the number of units now classed as inadequate is large. Disregarding definitional problems, it has been estimated that nearly 36,000 substandard units existed in Atlanta in 1960. In 1972, just over 1 percent of the dwelling units were classed as dilapidated, nearly 80 percent were standard and the remainder were substandard. The inner city area (Figure 4-28) still contains the greatest concentration of poor quality housing. Here 35.3 percent of the residential units are substandard and 2.9 percent are dilapidated. There are many duplexes in this area, and this type of unit shows a higher rate of poor quality. Most of these were constructed before the mid-1950s, and their older age is a significant factor contributing to their current status, but is by no means the deciding one.

In Atlanta during the 1960s the number of overcrowded units with 1.01 or more persons per room declined from 16.1 percent to 11.1 percent of the total. Although the number of all housing units increased, the actual number of units overcrowded also decreased by about 5,600 units (Figure 4-28). Atlanta's inner city areas generally exhibit sharp declines in overcrowded units, especially the CBD, Vine City–University and Uptown areas. But the city's eastern protrusion—east on Memorial Drive—exhibited an opposite effect. The DeKalb section of the city showed a 56 percent increase in the number of units classed as overcrowded. The inner city decrease, coupled with this increase and that in other adjacent parts of DeKalb County, suggest the problem of overcrowding has been removed and reestablished rather than alleviated. However, there has been substantial immigration and the rate of overcrowding also reflects the accommodation of new families by others, as well as the internal relocation of problem areas.

Overcrowding in Atlanta is predominantly a problem of the black population, as is poor quality housing. In 1970, with a black population of 51.3 percent, only 8 percent of the census tracts whose population was 95 percent or more white experienced substantial overcrowding (defined as 10 percent or more of the housing units being overcrowded). Substantial overcrowding occurred in 91 percent of the census tracts with a 95 percent or greater black population (Figures 4-28 and 4-29).

Considering the supply side, steady and continuous reductions have occurred since 1960 in both the homeowner and renter vacancy ratios in the Atlanta Housing Market Area (or SMSA). In March 1970, the available sales and rental units represented vacancy ratios of 1.2 percent and 3.1 percent respectively, while in 1960 the corresponding ratios were 2.4 percent and 5.2 percent. These ratios are apt to have decreased further, and they represent a tight market.

Assisted Housing in the Atlanta Area. The provision of housing to the Atlanta metropolitan population has essentially remained a private sector task. Major public activity and public-assisted housing are relatively recent (compared to Chicago, for example). Although the Housing Act of 1937 provided the first housing assistance programs with which the Atlanta Housing Authority operated, the first program for private developers was not authorized until 1959. In the Atlanta area, it was late 1964 before the first private subsidized housing was built. Between 1964 and 1970, the programs for public housing and private housing sponsors had produced housing, or plans for housing, totaling about 13,000 dwelling units; thus, by 1970, federally assisted dwelling units totaled more than 27,000 units (including conventional low rent public housing) or about 6 percent of the region's housing inventory. The relative proportion of various

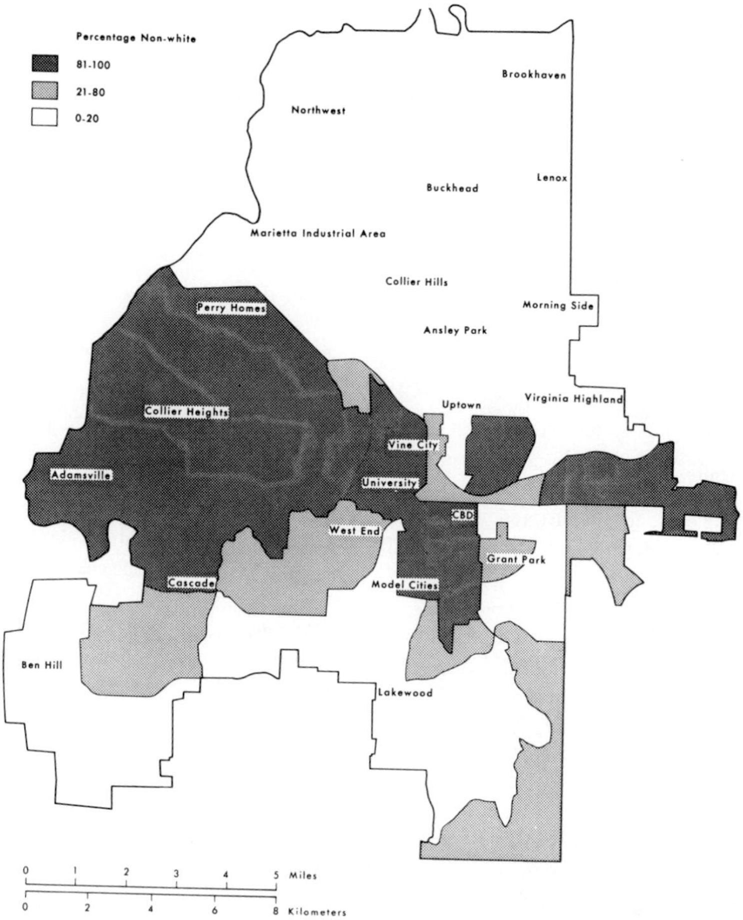

Figure 4-29. Nonwhite Areas in Atlanta, 1970.

programs and type of occupancy is shown in Table 4-8.

While housing for the elderly has received much attention in many areas, Altanta figures show relatively few units completed for this group. However, in terms of those units in planning as of 1970 under public housing (including rent supplement), over 80 percent of the units are for elderly people. Of the 1,104 designated elderly units constructed between 1960 and 1970, 864 (or 78 percent) were in four high-rises in the central city. Since 1970 a number of units have been built in noncentral locations—such as Atlanta's East Lake Meadows—for occupancy by elderly only.

Two trends seem to be evident in the Atlanta region. First, the ratio of elderly to total units seems low relative to the other study areas, but it is on an upward trend. Second, while there is a concentration of elderly units in the central city, new projects are weakening this pattern. As elderly projects are "more acceptable," there are strong forces operating to have such units satisfy court-ordered dispersal of public housing rather than standard projects. Such an order was issued in Atlanta in September of 1971 by U.S. District Court Judge Newell Edenfield.

Geographic Distribution of Public Housing. Public housing in the Atlanta area is concentrated in the inner city area (Figure 4-30), with almost 80 percent of the metropolitan units in Atlanta-Central, Atlanta-South and the Tri-Cities areas. A second but much smaller concentration exists in Cobb-East, or essentially

Table 4-8. Housing Units by Program and Type of Family, Metropolitan Atlanta[a]

Program	Number of Units	Percent of Total
Low Rent Public Housing (including Rent Supplement)		
Families	16,516	60.21
Elderly	2,141	7.81
	18,657	68.02
Other Rental/Cooperative Housing:		
Sections 202, 221(d)(3) and 236		
Families	6,610	24.10
Elderly	1,279	4.66
	7,889	28.76
Homeownership: Section 235		
Families	883	3.22
Total Number of Units	27,429	

[a]Includes units completed, under construction and in planning by 1970.

Source: Atlanta Regional Metropolitan Planning Commission, *Housing All Atlantans* (Atlanta, June 1970).

Marietta. Other projects are dispersed to a few of the smaller communities in the SMSA.

While the inner city has been the area of problem housing and remains so, it has a disproportionate share of public housing units. The Atlanta-Central area with nearly 56 percent of the public housing units has only about 22 percent of the region's population. In contrast, DeKalb-North has about 15 percent of the region's population but only 1 percent of the public housing. The three areas of Atlanta-North, Sandy Springs and Clayton-North have over 12 percent of the population but no public housing.

While most housing authorities in the United States can build only within the boundaries of the jurisdictions which established them, this is not the case in Georgia. The state's enabling legislation permits a city's housing authority to construct up to ten miles beyond the city's boundaries. Restrictions include the need to obtain consent by resolution if the project is to be in an area where another housing authority is already operating. The Atlanta Housing Authority (AHA) has just recently completed two noncity projects in South Fulton County (Figure 4-30). The southernmost project, Campbell Drive, is to have 196 units, and the Boat Rock Road project is to have 268 units. These units are condominium apartments available for purchase by tenants under a turnkey procedure.

As do most authorities, the AHA has a problem in matching unit size to family size. About one-half of the households in public housing have only or or two persons, but only about one-third of the units are one bedroom or efficiency type. Families of seven or more members are underhoused by contrast, but current authority guidelines are designed to ameliorate this problem.

Rental and Cooperative Housing: Sections 221(d)(3) and 236. In the category of rental and cooperative housing, the Atlanta area now contains about 7,000 units, plus two high-rises restricted to elderly occupancy with 442 units. Of 6,868 units, the Atlanta-Central region contains 35.6 percent of these units and the Atlanta-South area contains 36.2 percent.

Because the Atlanta portions of the region have been the major housing problem areas, there is a concentration of subsidized units in these subregions (Figure 4-31). Seven nonprofit housing sponsors are central-city-based black organizations. One is the Butler Street YMCA and the others are church-related. These sponsors are responsible for over 2,000 subsidized units, or about 30 percent of the total. An eighth nonprofit sponsor operates in Marietta. Not included in the data being considered are the four metropolitan Atlanta area elderly high-rises (Section 202), with 837 units. Two of these—of 196 and 199 units—are at the same

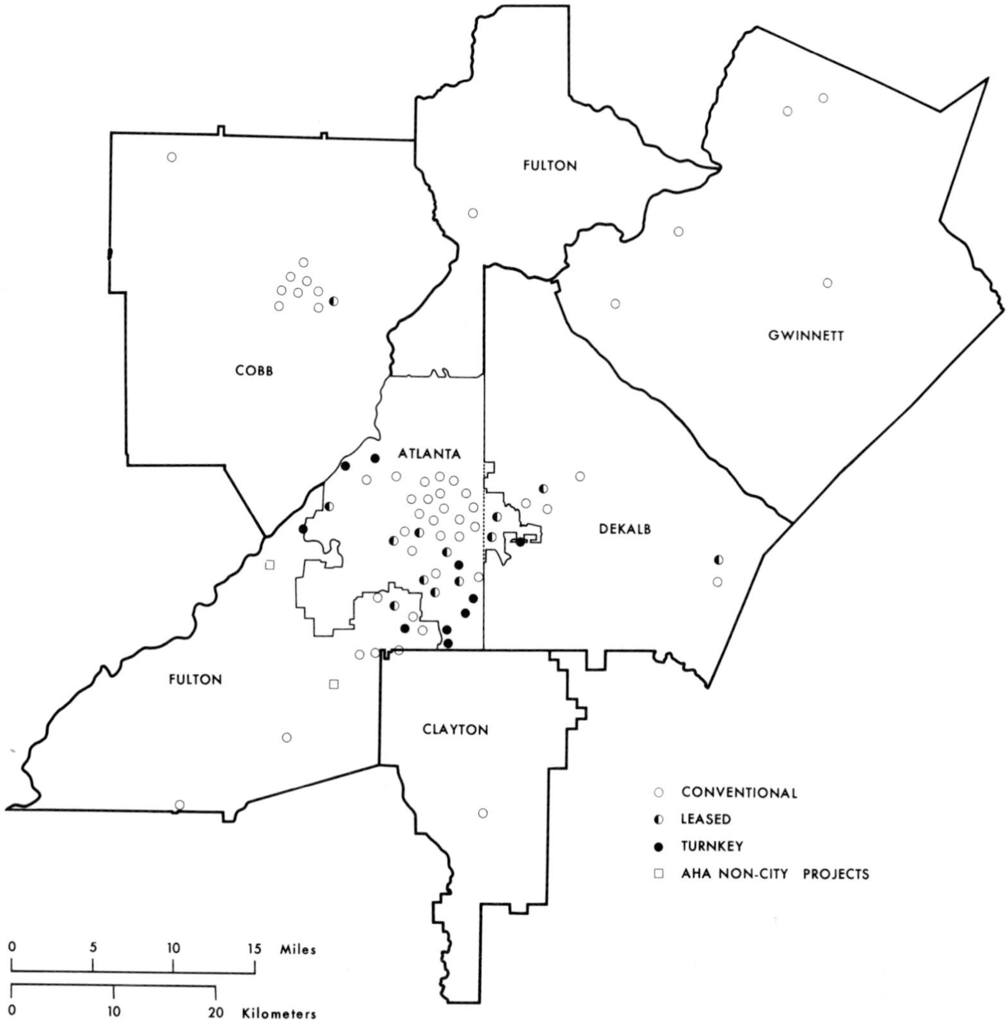

Figure 4–30. Public Housing Projects in the Atlanta Area, 1970.

site in the Buckhead section of the Atlanta-North subareas, and a third 240 unit structure is nearby. The remaining project is located near Emory University in the DeKalb-North subarea.

Under the rental provisions of Section 236, 442 units are in progress or recently completed. One project of 216 high-rise units is near Greenbriar Shopping Center in the Atlanta-South subarea. The second, a 226 unit high-rise, is just off the city of Decatur square in the DeKalb-Central subarea.

Subsidized Home Ownership: Section 235. A General Accounting Office study of housing programs reports that between August 1968 and December 1971, the Atlanta SMSA produced 1,877 subsidized homes under Section 235. Locational information is available from a planning commission report of June 1970; however, only about 900 units are included. About 62 percent of these were located in the city of Atlanta, about 13 percent in Decatur (DeKalb-Central) and 21 percent in the Clayton-North subarea. Nearly 70 percent of these nearly 900 units were existing housing rather than new construction. Such housing was to become ineligible for Section 235 financing after July 1, 1971, and it is expected that this would focus the effects of this program outside

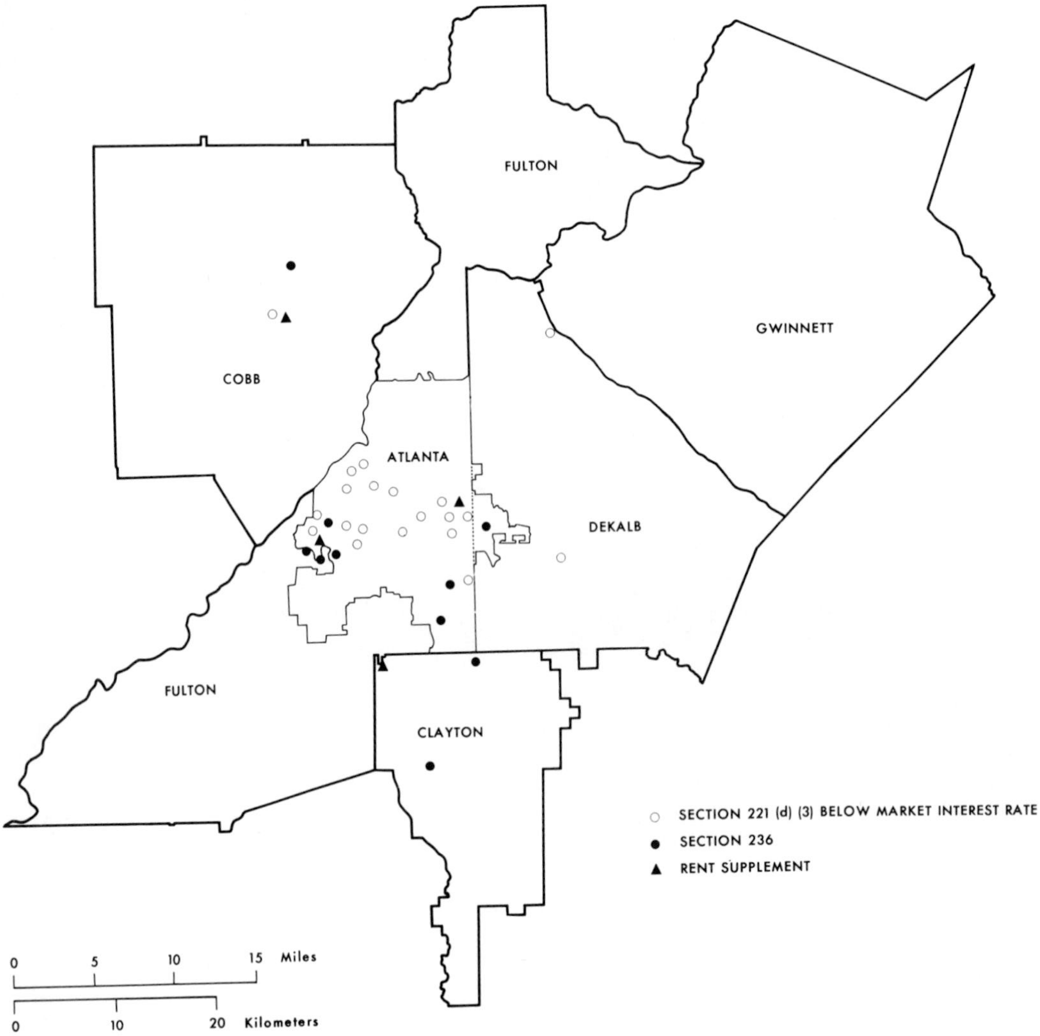

Figure 4–31. Subsidized Rental Housing in the Atlanta Area, 1970.

the city, especially since new housing within the city of Atlanta exceeds the cost limits of this mortgage program. The pattern in Atlanta contrasts sharply with those of Seattle and Chicago for these reasons.

Urban Renewal. There has been a reasonably active urban renewal program in Atlanta, but, in contrast to Chicago, the Atlanta activity has not been geared to the production of a range of housing for various income groups. Much of the renewal activity has been associated with commercial, institutional and transportation redevelopment. Atlanta's urban renewal program began in 1956 and now involves 5,700 acres of land. The program required the acquisition of 5,300 parcels of land and the relocation of 6,300 families and individuals. The Atlanta Stadium is part of the Rawson-Washington project; the Butler Street project includes a Holiday Inn Motel, Marriott Motor Hotel, four high-rise office buildings and other buildings which include about 1,200 new living units. Another area now contains the Atlanta Civic Center.

Use has also been made of federal housing programs aimed at rehabilitation (Section 312 loans and Section 115 grants), but they do not involve large numbers of units. Grants totaling about $634,000 have been accumulated in the Atlanta-Central housing subarea. A total of 406 grants covering about 427 units in the Model Cities, Bedford Pine, West End and University areas of the city of Atlanta have taken up the grant funds. The loan sum is allocated to approximately 800 units through 143 separate loans. Of these, 106 loans (769 units) are in the West End section of the subarea. More recently, the grant program has been used in Edgewood, Vine City, Bedford Pine and Model Cities areas. This additional rehabilitation involved about 420 units. Other rehabilitation programs, such as Sections 221(h) and 235 (j), are almost nonexistent in the Atlanta area. As of 1970, no Section 235(j) projects had been initiated and only one Section 221(h) project of six units had been approved.

"Foreclosures" in Atlanta. The concern that developed in some cities about foreclosures involving subsidized housing was greater than that which surfaced in Atlanta. An explanation is suggested by a report on housing foreclosures in Atlanta by the Atlanta Department of Planning. A survey was conducted during June and July 1973 to determine the nature of the problem, to measure its extent and to aid in formulating recommendations as to the possible use of these units as a resource for families displaced by governmental action.

A total of 402 units were found to be in the foreclosed category during the period of the survey. All were purchases insured by the Veterans Administration (VA) or the Federal Housing Administration (FHA). Nonwhites were buyers in 85 percent of the cases. The report indicates that most units were in standard condition, even though 31 percent were constructed between 1940–1949 and 38 percent were constructed prior to 1940. The average assessed value was $17,291, although 80 percent of the units were valued under $15,000. The foreclosed units appear clustered in two primary areas of nonwhite occupancy: the southwest sector between Fort McPherson and Interstate 20, and the DeKalb portion of Atlanta. The Thomasville area to the southeast appears as a less clustered area of concentration. However, the clustering is of little significance, as it simply reflects the pattern of subsidized homeownership throughout the city.

The chief causes of foreclosures were sought, and, contrary to the expectations of some, abandonment was not considered to be a major cause of foreclosures in Atlanta. Officials of the FHA and VA, and loan officers of private mortgage firms cited excessive obligations and marital difficulties as the main reason for nonpayment and subsequent foreclosure. Moreover, while foreclosures were on the increase in absolute terms, the relative rate of foreclosures was not much different from previous years.

Various recommendations are offered by the Atlanta report with emphasis on improving the buyers' awareness of the meaning and responsibility of homeownership and the need for sound budgeting. A counseling service with such a purpose could also help young couples and/or first-time buyers through the difficult tasks of evaluating and purchasing a home. These recommendations are similar to those advocated by Seattle Housing Development as they considered the same issue.

Atlanta Summary. The Atlanta metropolitan area is a rapidly growing urban system with a complex history and an even more complex spatial organization. The patterns visible in the 1970s are the result of market forces, federal intervention and overt policy decisions by local lenders many years ago. One early "gentlemen's agreement" to facilitate the entrepreneurial development of parts of Atlanta for blacks was documented in *House and Home* (May 1959, p. 91). Because of this agreement, the national emergence of a significant black middle class has been accompanied in Atlanta by the development of black "suburbs" in sections of west and southwest Atlanta, characterized by high quality housing and a high proportion of owner-occupancy.

A healthy economy and significant population increases with concomitant new construction has stimulated the development of the residential pattern now strikingly entrenched in Atlanta. Federally subsidized units are perhaps both stimuli and responses to these distinctive patterns. More precisely, subsidized units and conventionally financed nonwhite developments have proceeded under similar spatially restricting processes.

Urban renewal, transportation developments and other governmental activities have removed many of the very inadequate units in the metropolitan area. Overall, housing quality has improved, even though low rent public housing environments have subsequently been criticized, as elsewhere, on both physical and social grounds. Despite controversy and some setbacks, federal programs have served useful functions, but even these were interrupted in the early 1970s. While providing shelter for some and work for others, the various federal programs have neither served an overriding social goal—say, integration, equity or security—nor have they basically altered the processes which lead to housing deterioration and neighborhood decline. This conclusion, if correct, is disheartening, for it means that what has gone before has been little more than a holding action. The real problem, that of altering processes, has yet to be faced.

Conclusion

This section has provided an introductory description of the geography of public housing in three cities. Where possible, some attempt has been made to assess the impact of the outputs of the principal housing subsidy programs and offer some explanation of the patterns observed. This description is as comprehensive as data permit, and lack of data and suitable secondary resource material contributes to the uneven coverage across the three metropolitan areas. Nevertheless, a sense of development, spatial pattern and problems is achieved for each of the case studies. The salient features of the geography of public housing as they compare and contrast among the three areas will be further discussed in the next section. Contrasts and comparisons in the development of regional housing plans will also be presented.

INTER CITY COMPARISONS AND CONTRASTS

Let us now draw together some of the contrasts and similarities that have emerged from the examination of the utilization and impact of the principal federally subsidized housing programs in the three study areas. Having considered the outputs of these programs in a comparative fashion, another useful intercity comparison can be made concerning the degree to which, and the manner in which, regional housing plans have been developed in the study areas. The development of these plans and related statements of metropolitan housing goals has been actively supported by HUD, although there is no national legislation authorizing such plans.

Comparison of the Use of Existing Programs and Their Outputs

A major problem in making comparisons between cities or metropolitan areas is obtaining data that have similar coverage in terms of area, time periods, program breakdown and so on. To overcome this, data were obtained from the HUD national office to ensure comparability, but this means that the comparison is constrained by that data (Table 4-9). Data from regional sources are employed to make more general and less rigorous comparisons.

The low rent public housing program has generated almost half the total units in each

Table 4-9. Distribution of Units by Program for Which HUD Has Written Insurance, Cumulative as of 1973

Program	*Atlanta (Percent)*	*Chicago (Percent)*	*Seattle-Everett (Percent)*
Section 202—Rental housing for the elderly	1.9	0.2	2.3
Section 221—Subsidized rental housing	20.3	30.1	13.8
Section 236—Subsidized rental housing	20.4	9.8	11.9
Section 235—Subsidized home ownership	7.9	9.3	24.4
Low Rent Public Housing[a]	49.5	50.6	47.7
	100.0	100.0	100.1

[a]Housing Authority Annual Reports

Source: HUD Division of Research and Statistics, personal communication.

case; if the central cities alone are considered, this percentage rises to around two-thirds. This proportion is almost the same for each city, yet as the case studies have shown, the programs in Chicago and Seattle, for example, have had a quite different history. Section 202 rental housing for the elderly is relatively insignificant in all of the SMSAs. The major area of contrast comes in the moderate income programs. In the Seattle area, substantially more use has been made of the homeownership program, and this may reflect the essentially single family nature of the housing stock in this particular metropolitan area. Developers in Chicago and Atlanta have, in contrast, utilized the rental programs to a greater degree and to almost the same extent; but in Chicago the effort has come earlier with the use of longer-established rental programs. Again, the strong apartment-rental nature of the Chicago SMSA housing stock may be an explanatory factor. Another factor which is also operative is the cost limits associated with each program. It is very difficult to build subsidized homes for ownership in the city of Chicago, given land prices and other costs, and given program cost limitations. Atlanta occupies a somewhat intermediate position, with more apartments and a greater renter population than Seattle; the nature of the stock is such that Atlanta is more similar to Chicago, but with a greater proportion of homeowning. Thus, it is perhaps not surprising to find that Atlanta has more rental subsidy units than subsidized owner-occupied units. The reason that Atlanta shows greater use of the newer Section 236 rental subsidy program than Chicago may be related to the recent rapid growth which has placed considerable demands upon the housing supply sector. Of the three central cities, Atlanta actually gained population, while its SMSA population growth (1960-1970) was also the highest—Atlanta: 36 percent; Seattle: 28 percent; Chicago: 12 percent.

The mix of subsidy programs, other than the low rent public housing program, is related to the existing housing stock. In other words, developers who are operating in, and are familiar with, certain types of markets are likely to be active in those subsidy programs which reflect their experience and skills. This relationship clearly requires further examination as it is based on only three cases.

In terms of the overall amount of subsidized housing, the proportion of such housing relative to the total housing stock is quite similar in the metropolitan areas. The respective percentages are Atlanta, 5 percent; Chicago, 3.4 percent; and Seattle, 4.8 percent. The proportions naturally rise if only the central city is considered, but given the overwhelming concentration of such housing in the central city, this is only to be expected. The proportions are still, however, roughly the same. This occurs despite there having been quite different program evolutions in the three metro areas. Evidence for other cities, such as Minneapolis-St. Paul, supports these points of a small proportion relative to total stock and a significant spatial concentration in the central city.

The geography of public housing in the three metropolitan areas is also quite similar in its broad outlines. The principal concentration in the central cities is clear, and within the central city the black residential areas contain considerable numbers of units, especially low rent public housing units and multifamily rental housing. The leased housing program units are more widely dispersed, but even here, some degree of concentration is evident in Chicago and Seattle; no data were available to us for Atlanta. In the suburban areas, a pattern of concentration in certain areas for both subsidized single family homes and the rental units is clear. A broad dispersal of units does not occur, and in some cases, such as Chicago, areas of higher socioeconomic status and areas with fast growing employment opportunities have almost no subsidized housing opportunities. The suburban areas have almost no low rent public housing in Chicago, somewhat more in Atlanta, while Seattle has the most. Given the racial makeup of the metropolitan areas and the degree of racial segregation and tension, low rent public housing may be more acceptable in suburban Seattle, where it is serving a largely white population in a more homogeneous racial setting.

Another important aspect of the low rent public housing programs in all areas is the increasing emphasis on serving the elderly. This is more significant in Chicago and Seattle than in Atlanta. But in all three cases, there has been greater emphasis on "elderly only" housing in recent years, while family housing has received little or a declining emphasis.

The factor of community acceptability and ease with which a more dispersed spatial pattern can be achieved would appear to be the key factors here. Few people oppose the idea of assisted housing for senior citizens, and they are probably regarded as no major threat to a community.

In attempting to achieve the national housing goal, a range of urban renewal, redevelopment and rehabilitation procedures have been created through national action and utilized by local authorities. In our three study areas, rehabilitation programs have been relatively insignificant so far, while the urban renewal program has had a variable impact (Table 4-10). The cities can be ranked as to their degree of rehabilitation activity with Atlanta showing by far the most activity, followed by Chicago and Seattle. In terms of urban renewal, there has been little impact in Seattle. Urban renewal has been important in Chicago with many large residential projects having been completed. Atlanta has also had a number of important projects, and again, a high level of demolition activity. Thus, Seattle again shows some significant contrasts to the other two cities which are somewhat more alike, although there are also important points of difference between Atlanta and Chicago. Where the urban renewal activity has occurred in the cities, it has primarily been located in the older inner city areas. The major exceptions are in the case of institutional urban renewal and renewal for purely industrial purposes.

Comparison of Regional Housing Plan Development

Many housing specialists have come to realize that in order to assess whether or not progress is being made with respect to "housing problems" at the metropolitan and local municipal level, more work is urgently required on obtaining information on housing needs, specifying goals, developing a locational policy for housing, and fostering cooperative and receptive attitudes among the constituent municipalities.

At the national level, HUD is seeking to develop appropriate methodologies for the estimation of housing needs at the metropolitan level. The present situation, as reported to congressional investigators, is a disgrace. For example, in recently preparing estimates of need for subsidized homeownership and rental units, the HUD regional offices were given little time to respond. They noted that their estimates were little more than educated guesses. Nevertheless, these numbers were used by HUD's Washington office together with their own estimates. Differences were resolved by taking the average of the two numbers. The resultant, possibly meaningless, figure was used for the allocation of program resources. Hopefully, HUD will respond to congressional de-

Table 4-10. Rehabilitation and Urban Renewal in Atlanta, Chicago and Seattle, Cumulative, June 30, 1972

	Atlanta	*Chicago*	*Seattle*
Sections 312, 115–Rehabilitation			
Number of loans and grants	986	707	237
Dwelling units involved as percent of year round housing stock	0.7	0.02	0.01
Dollar Value of loans or grants per capita	9.0	2.60	1.60
Urban Renewal			
Workload as percent of year round housing stock[a]	3.8	4.50	0.03
Units demolished as percent of year round housing stock	5.4	2.80	0.04

[a]The workload expresses the number of new housing units developed on urban renewal project sites as a percentage of the 1970 housing stock.

Source: HUD Division of Research and Statistics, personal communication; Census of Population and Housing, 1970.

mands for improved housing need specifications.

At the metropolitan level, the major innovators with respect to the formulation of housing goals and plans have been metropolitan councils of government, many of which were established in the late 1960s. These councils vary from place to place in their specific functions, but a common function is to serve as a forum for the discussion of regional issues and to act as a regional review authority on proposed developments involving federal aid. These councils of government have been encouraged by HUD to develop regional housing plans, sometimes referred to as "balanced" or "fair share" plans. Simply, the concept is that lower income housing, including subsidized housing, not be concentrated exclusively in the central city, but be dispersed throughout the suburbs. To avoid overconcentration in certain suburbs (an established fact in cities like Chicago), each suburb is to take its fair share based on an allocation plan.

As of July 1973 only five metropolitan agencies had adopted some form of fair share plan (this represents 2 percent of the nation's metropolitan areas). The first plan was adopted in Dayton, Ohio, in September 1970. Twenty-five agencies had plans under development in the fall of 1973. Despite HUD's encouragement, there is clearly no rush to formulate these plans with all of their political and socioeconomic implications. If people regard adjacent low income and subsidized housing (and the occupants) as a threat to their well-being, or as leading to a reduction in their own social status, then they will likely oppose the location of such housing near them, or even in the municipality. There is considerable evidence from a number of cities that this has occurred. Yet without some kind of public intervention, HUD officials felt that there would be continued socioeconomic and racial segregation between central cities and suburban areas.

What has been the pattern of response in our study areas? A Seattle agency is in the process of developing a balanced community housing plan. In Chicago, this process is very much in the formative stages, and we were unable to obtain any data for Atlanta. To add another dimension, the Minneapolis-St. Paul situation with a well-developed plan is discussed. Thus, contrasts and similarities in approach can be observed.

Seattle. The staff of the council of government—the Puget Sound Governmental Conference—have formulated a draft fair share plan at the request of the elected officials who represent the area's municipalities. The focus is on housing for low and moderate income households (below \$4,000 and \$4,000–\$8,500 being the two income groups), housing which will be provided with various forms of assistance from HUD or the Farmers' Home Administration. The purposes of the plan are: (1) to provide a conceptualization of the housing 'problem' on the regional scale so that local elected officials can come to grips with it, and (2) to provide general guidelines to HUD about what to do with their subsidized housing. The report assumed that HUD would be doing *something* after the federal moratorium was lifted. It is observed that the private sector cannot produce housing at a low enough cost to meet the needs of the income groups under consideration. Little assistance is expected from the Washington state government, and other sources for plan implementation, such as revenue-sharing and/or general bond issues, offer only a little hope. The "feds" must carry the burden; the potential for a significant state contribution does exist, however, as evidenced by active state housing finance agencies in Minnesota, New York and elsewhere.

The plan comprises a housing needs study, a housing allocation formula and a statement on policy. The fundamental goal is to provide a better balance of housing opportunities for people of all incomes in the central Puget Sound region—particularly in relation to the distribution of job opportunities.

A specific goal of the plan is to increase the supply of decent, safe and sanitary housing for low and moderate income people. The number of units needed for low and moderate income households in the region is 38,500, according to staff estimates. The region's housing stock increased by around 150,000 units in the 1960–1970 decade, but many of these units are likely beyond the economic reach of the low and moderate income households. A more relevant and disturbing fact is that the cumulative total of federal subsidy programs has not reached this figure in almost 35 years. Although the third part of this chapter provided data only on King County, that is where the bulk of the need is concentrated; 27,700 units is the current need estimate, and our estimate of total production to 1973 is just over 20,000.

The estimate of need is derived in the following manner (Table 4-11). The $8,500 income figure approximates an upper eligibility limit for many federal housing programs. It is assumed that all households with incomes less than this have housing needs. Low and moderate income households show a tendency to doubling up so that the pooling of resources allows the acquisition of a dwelling unit. It is assumed that such "doubled" households have needs. The percentage of low income elderly homeowners is based on HUD experience that between 10 and 15 percent of this group seek rental housing. Otherwise, elderly homeowning households with low income (under $5,000) are excluded from the need category as a result of their lack of activity in the homebuying market. A vacancy rate is built in, and the percentages are "widely accepted standards." Thus, the estimate of need is derived.

It is then argued that a certain supply exists which would meet and is meeting the needs of these owner and renter groups. The number of units which are affordable is listed first. An affordable unit is one within the reach

Table 4-11. PSGC Procedure for Estimating Housing Needs, King County Example

King County Renters		
Need		
Renter households with incomes under $8500		85,365
Units needed for undoubling households		2,683
12 percent of low income elderly homeowners		2,443
Vacancy allowance at 5 percent		4,763
Total Units Needed		95,254
Supply		
Occupied units renting under $150 per month		93,230
Less: Deficient lacking plumbing	6,758	
Dilapidated with plumbing	2,508	
		(9,266)
Plus: Vacant for rent with all plumbing and asking rent under $150 per month	15,270	
Less: Dilapidated	(458)	
		14,812
Usable Supply		98,776
Less: Units renting for under $150 per month occupied by households with incomes over $10,000		(17,222)
Net Effective Supply		81,554
Total units needed		95,254
Net Effective Supply		(81,554)
Need		13,700

King County Owners		
Need		
Owner households with incomes under $8500		61,113
Less: Owners 65 years or over with incomes under $5000		(20,358)
Units needed for undoubling households		4,567
Vacancy allowance at 1.5 percent		690
Total units needed		46,012
Supply		
Occupied units valued under $17,500		60,483
Less: Deficient lacking plumbing	699	
Dilapidated with plumbing	538	
		(1,237)
Plus: Vacant for sale with all plumbing and asking price under $17,500	1,148	
Less: Dilapidated	(10)	
		1,138
Usable Supply		60,384
Less: Units valued under $17,500 occupied by households with incomes over $10,000		(28,375)
Net Effective Supply		32,009
Total units needed		46,012
Net Effective Supply		(32,009)
Need		14,003
Rounded to		14,000

of a household with the maximum income of $8,500 spending approximately 25 percent of their income for housing. Units which are deemed to be deficient (irrespective of cost) are removed from consideration. Those units which are affordable, vacant and not deficient are considered usable by the low and moderate income households. Some of the affordable units are occupied by those with incomes well in excess of the $8,500 break point—these are removed since they are neither available nor currently occupied by the "needy" group. The difference between the Net Effective Supply and Total Units Needed yields the figures noted above.

After determining the region's low and moderate income housing needs at about 38,500, the issue of spatial allocation follows, given the requirement of a fair share approach on a regional municipal basis. The agency has identified seven criteria which when taken together indicate what proportion of the need should be met by publicly assisted housing activity in particular jurisdictions. The criteria are:

- The number of families with incomes of less than $8,500. This is taken as a measure of economic need.
- The number of deficient housing units (those lacking plumbing facilities and those which are overcrowded, using the 1.01 persons per room cutoff).
- Renter households with incomes of less than $8,500 who are paying more than 25 percent of their income for rent.
- The number of families with incomes of more than $10,000. This identifies higher income areas which should absorb some low and moderate income households, thereby reducing the concentration of such households.
- Assessed valuation and revenue-sharing funds (in both absolute and per capita terms) are used as indication of a municipality's ability to absorb the costs of residential growth and to provide needed services.
- Since housing opportunities are to be created near employment opportunities, the amount of employment growth predicted for 1970–1980 is used as a criterion.
- The new developments will require space and an areal measure of available land suitable for development is utilized here.

The procedure is to determine what percentage of the regional totals occur in a given municipality for each criterion. Thus, if the regional total for families with incomes under $8,500 is 147,778, and Auburn has 1,818 such families, then Auburn's "share" is 1.2 percent. The seven percentages are then averaged for each jurisdictional area, and the regional housing need of 38,500 units is divided up among the municipalities on the basis of the overall average of the seven criterion percentages. Since these are 1970 data, allowance is made for the 13,000 units of government-assisted housing produced in the period 1970–1973 (hardly any units have been produced in 1973). Therefore, about 25,000 units are allocated across the member municipalities. Interestingly, Seattle's "share" is almost 25 percent, whereas existing data show Seattle to have a greater concentration than this "equitable" or "balanced" approach would warrant.

The plan as developed by the Seattle agency is currently in a state of limbo. Reaction from the elected representatives was cautiously favorable, though there was explicit opposition from one or two suburbs once the data were available for examination. However, both the agency staff and the representatives are at a loss to know where the funds to implement this plan will come from.

The plan itself provides a statement of needs that is still primitive and based on crude assumptions. It also uses criteria whose validity requires further testing; it could be argued, however, that local experience is the touchstone for locally relevant criteria. Where this particular plan is fatally flawed is in the spatial allocation procedure. It is entirely inappropriate to simply average the seven locational criteria, as they are defined. Thus, the "share" of each municipality has no real meaning.

Chicago. The Chicago metropolitan area does not have an areawide council of governments structure which might take a leading role in the statement of local or regional housing goals and the development of a regional fair share or balanced housing plan. Thus the metropolitan area has been less innovative in this field as compared to Seattle and Minneapolis-St. Paul, for example.

Recently, however, the first steps in this direction have been taken by the Regional Housing Coalition. The RHC represents and is supported by the Northeastern Illinois Planning

Commission and various public interest groups concerned with housing. The strategy has been to develop a cautious interim plan which has now been placed in the public arena for discussion. The intent is to develop and incorporate this into a more comprehensive housing plan.

In bare outline, the interim plan documents the necessity for housing to meet presently unmet needs, the location of such needs, and the goals and policies required for a balanced response which takes into account the magnitude of the need, the location of the need and the standards which are to be maintained in the provison of such housing.

Despite its conceptual limitations and purposefully bland, low key approach, two points can be made. One is that this is the first pragmatic and possibly attainable plan to deal with housing needs of low and moderate income households on the regional or metropolitan scale in Chicago. Secondly and predictably, it will either be disregarded or attacked by some important elements in the metropolitan community. Whether this will damage the concept and the plan beyond repair remains to be seen.

It should be noted, however, that some suburban communities are already independently moving in the direction of increasing their stock of low income housing, albeit in a limited way and despite the federal moratorium. In Du Page County, four municipalities have sought a total of 250 units of low income housing under the Section 23 leased housing program. This particular program is also receiving consideration from other Du Page County communities. What the regional housing plans such as the Regional Housing Coalition's proposal must do if its goals are to be achieved is mobilize this kind of initiative on a much wider basis and with some increase in proposed numbers of units. The task will not be easy, for there are numerous examples of strategies adopted by Chicago suburbs (for example, Deerfield and Glencoe, among others) to exclude the various forms of low and moderate income housing.

Space precludes a detailed discussion of the Chicago proposal. It follows the Seattle model with a statement of regional goals, and estimates of housing needs and the supply of low and moderate income units. The methodology for estimating needs is even less sensitive than that of the Seattle agency. The proposed spatial allocation procedure is simply to locate housing on the basis of the spatial distribution of need; no allowance is made for municipal capability to absorb the new housing, nor is there any hint of accessibility to employment opportunities as a locational criterion.

If the interim plan were implemented with subsidy resources flowing to areas with needs, then the suburban areas would receive 70 percent of new subsidized units. In an effort to avoid overconcentration at the community level, it is argued that no community with 25 percent or more of its present stock in the form of low and moderate housing should be expected to add more such housing to the stock. However, there is no discussion of what happens if such a municipality still has unmet needs.

Minneapolis-St. Paul. Although this is not one of the originally selected study areas, some information is provided here to illustrate further the variability in approach to the question of fair share or balanced regional housing plans. The metropolitan council of Minneapolis-St. Paul is an active metropolitan government with an extensive range of powers and programs. It has prepared a *Metropolitan Development Guide* that includes a section on housing in which a metropolitan allocation plan for subsidized housing is described.

Given the estimated level of housing need in the metropolitan area, and given that approximately 40 percent of this is to serve low and moderate income households, the question is raised as to the appropriate location of the needed subsidized housing. The specific purpose of the allocation plan is to broaden the housing choice for low and moderate income people by encouraging the development of publicly assisted housing in areas where opportunities for this group are limited. To achieve this, the metropolitan area is divided into priority areas. The key variable for classification purposes is the extent and degree of urban development in a municipality. This variable is employed essentially as a surrogate for the availability of such services and facilities as sewer and water supplies, major highways, public transit, employment opportunities and retail facilities. Thus, the developed core of the metropolitan area receives the highest priority, while the rural and undeveloped periphery is given the lowest priority. Proposals for funding subsidized housing will be assessed in terms of location by priority area. Where projects are proposed within the same broad priority area, the key variable is the percentage of existing low and moderate income housing in a municipality. Other things being equal, communities with lower percentages will receive priority funding so as to increase the diversity of locational choice. These general criteria do not preclude further consideration of individual projects with respect to such factors as environmental impact, family-elderly occupance proportions, proposed use of rent supplements and so forth.

Modifications to the general guidelines occur in only two instances. First, in the case of the central cities of Minneapolis and St. Paul, the priority rankings indicate that these would be primary areas to receive subsidized housing. The council's purpose in classifying the central cities as conditional first priority is to ensure that they have sufficient funds to meet their commitments, while the balance of regional subsidy funds is provided to priority areas beyond the central cities. However, as was found in our other study cities, existing subsidized housing is already heavily concentrated in these central cities. Thus the metropolitan council's goal of increasing locational choice would be counteracted by giving this area top priority for approval, since this would simply continue present trends. Second, special consideration is also given to such developments as planned unit developments or new towns, especially where these occur in what would otherwise be low priority areas. To ensure a balanced mix in such developments, changes in the general priority rankings are possible.

In addition to the two geographic areas of the central cities, seven subsectors are created to provide small geographic units specific enough for monitoring purposes. Six of these cover the urbanized portion of the area while the seventh is essentially the largely rural section of the council's ten county jurisdiction. The priority areas cut across these subsectors in some cases.

Given a specified amount of federal funding for new subsidized housing, how many units should be built in each subsector? In order to estimate this number, the assumption is made that by allocating these units in direct proportion to the share of present population, expected new residential growth, present jobs and expected new jobs, subsidized housing will be located in relation to urban services, present and anticipated. These numbers are again only guides, and may be exceeded where, for example, one sector contains more proposed units, while others contain less than expected. Rather than hold rigidly to the guidelines and return allocations unused, the council would recommend that the guidelines be set aside; numbers are still important.

In the case of the Twin Cities, therefore, both in setting priorities to judge proposals from developers and in deciding how a given number of units should be allocated by subsector, the amount of urban services and facilities as reflected by existing and future development plays a key role. Other factors do enter into the process, especially in the case of funding approval where individual projects are reviewed on their merits, but within the framework of the more general priorities.

Summary

This section of the essay briefly highlights some of the contrasts and similarities between the three study areas. It is clear that each area has relied heavily on the low rent public housing program, but that with regard to the moderate income subsidy programs, there are striking contrasts in utilization. These contrasts also emerge in the examination of rehabilitation and urban renewal practices.

With respect to regional housing plan devlopment, further contrasts are evident. Seattle would appear to be the farthest ahead, utilizing the council of governments' structure, while Chicago has just initiated a discussion in a potentially hostile arena. Atlanta has apparently made little progress in this area, and information on Minneapolis-St. Paul is therefore included to supplement the two other study cities; this latter area has a well-established program, and is clearly a leader in the field.

A range of procedures indicates how local agencies attempt to measure needs. Certain common denominators emerge, although they are not always expressed in precisely the same terms. Among the variables that are considered are new household formation, demolition of existing units through public and private action, the amount of substandard housing that should be replaced, the number of households that are sharing accommodation, the number of elderly households in certain income categories, the existing supply of housing within certain price ranges and not already occupied by high income groups, and an "acceptable" vacancy rate. In the Seattle and Chicago cases, these are employed and combined in somewhat different manners to yield an estimate of housing need for certain income groups.

When it comes to the allocation of new subsidized units, the contrasts are even more apparent. In the Chicago case, the proposed allocation effectively mirrors the pattern of need; in Seattle, both elements that indicate need and capacity to absorb new units are utilized to indicate allocations; in Minneapolis-St. Paul, the primary variable is the amount of urban services and facilities.

Thus, there is no common procedure, and indeed, there may not exist a "correct," universally applicable procedure. As one would naturally expect, there is also variability in goal statements, but this could be regarded as a healthy sign. However, there is now an additional urgent need. If these metropolitan housing program developments continue and become characteristic of urban America's attempts to grapple with housing issues on a more sensitive, localized basis, then there is a need to critically assess the merits of the methodologies employed if the plans are to be both realistic and useful, and less specious than those currently available. This is a role that the urban educational institutions could well play, and, given the strong locational implications, urban geographers should be actively involved.

REFLECTIONS ON THE GEOGRAPHY OF PUBLIC HOUSING IN AMERICAN CITIES

We have now described and discussed some prominent features of the nation's subsidized housing programs in relation to the residential geography of the metropolitan areas of Atlanta, Chicago and Seattle. We have tried to provide as balanced a picture as the data available to us allow. In these final pages, we will reflect on our topic from three interrelated perspectives, drawing upon works of several others. We will comment on what the nation has accomplished, on how that accomplishment is perceived by various groups and, finally, on the issues we believe housing policymakers must now face.

Accomplishments

One of the most significant aspects of federal activities with respect to our housing (and economic) problems has been the FHA-insured mortgage. Since 1935, this program has assisted in the construction of over seven million houses and apartments, or approximately one-fifth of all privately financed nonfarm units in the country. Furthermore, production under federal low and moderate income housing programs amounted to 1.5 million units during this period, with a majority (57 percent) of completions under the low rent public housing program. Simultaneous with this production of 8.5 million units, roughly a half million units were demolished by urban renewal activities, for a net gain of about eight million units between 1935 and 1970 as a result of federal housing programs. To offset this gain, however, we must recognize that many more units, certainly over one million, were demolished in public works programs—for example, in the construction of transportation facilities, especially highways.

As we entered the 1970s, federally sponsored housing activity was expanding rapidly, but serious problems quickly developed, and these contributed to the federal moratorium of January 1973. The full story of these years is yet to be told. Some allege it was a national disaster in housing, while others suggest that too much is being made of the problems. Now that there has been a period for major policy evaluation, Congress faces the task of developing a new offensive against the housing problems that beset Americans. This task has been greatly complicated and expanded in scope by a slump which hit the housing industry as a whole. While public housing programs were suspended, private housing starts fell dramatically throughout 1973 and into 1974 from a level of about 2.5 million units a year to around one million, far short of the two million units needed each year to house the newly formed households and those displaced from demolished units. As construction dried up, companies were bankrupted and unemployment soared. Federal fiscal policies designed to combat inflation resulted in a severe credit squeeze, so that mortgage money was in very short supply in 1974. Given a rapid increase in the price of both new and existing housing, and the demands of lenders for large downpayments, some households simply did not move, and delayed the purchase of a new house or condominium. This type of situation affects millions more Americans than does any "crisis" in the subsidized housing sector that we have considered in this essay. Late in 1974, Congress acted to inject almost $8 billion into the residential mortgage market. The problems of public housing receded in the face of the collapsing private market.

Yet inevitably, Congress will have to come back to the issues of housing for the poor and other disadvantaged groups. Equally inevitably, the much maligned low rent public housing program will command attention. As has been shown, more than half of all subsidized housing units have been constructed under this program, the oldest and most established of all the federal programs. Low rent public housing projects have usually been built as high-rise buildings of several hundred to a thousand or more units per project, and the projects are often clustered near the central cores of our cities. These low rent units, either by intention or through historical development, have become occupied by nonwhites to a considerable extent. Core area clustering and nonwhite occupancy are also characteristics common to the moderate income, privately sponsored rental housing programs such as the Section 221(d)(3) program. Units occupied either exclusively or primarily by elderly households and units made available under the leased housing program are exceptions to this general pattern, although even here some would argue that not enough spatial dispersion has been achieved.

From a national perspective on housing and location, there is a greater need for improvements in housing quality in America's rural regions than in the urban centers. From a practical point of view, however, the urban areas contain poor and inadequately housed Americans in tightly packed pockets of poverty. Even though the majority of ill-housed families in the United States are white, the cities have served to collect low income nonwhite families, to concentrate them in the oldest and poorest housing and to compound the locational disadvantages by providing large multifamily high-rise units which greatly increased net population density. During these same years, other policies and activities of the federal government worked to reduce population densities for great numbers of urban dwellers. The emphasis on highway development—almost to the exclusion of other means of moving people—has stimulated development of the suburbs. Homeownership also offers considerable tax advantages; the revenue not collected on incomes because of homebuying tax privileges far exceeds that spent on housing subsidy programs. In the past and at present, homeownership generally means single family dwelling units, and the new units are most often found at the periphery of the physically expanding city. Neither the infilling of areas by-passed by urban growth, nor the use of smaller lots, nor the move to cluster development with a higher amenity value, will fundamentally alter this process.

At the risk of oversimplifying, we can say that in the last 30 years urban areas have expanded rapidly, thereby providing many more new, and relatively sound, housing units. Federally-funded programs have removed much of the worst inner city housing, rehabilitated some housing, and provided a considerable number of low rent units in these same central areas. A direct result of all this is that relatively fewer units are in seriously deteriorated condition than was the case 25 years ago. Yet, in the opinion of many, the need for adequate housing has not been satisfactorily met, despite these attempts. In fact, over one-fourth of the nation's households face some type of serious housing problem; they may occupy dwelling units in poor structural condition; or they may be "housing-poor," with housing absorbing an uncomfortably high proportion of their income; or they may be handicapped locationally in that their unit provides poor accessibility to job, educational opportunities, and health and other important services in the urban area.

Perception

As outlined above, the national effort to provide housing for those in need has been both substantial and inadequate at the same time. Analyzing the nation's housing situation is difficult because of the variety of perspectives and interpretations which exist. The situation is like that of a great square rug with a different group at each corner, each regularly peering under the edge and probing with instruments of their own design. From one corner we hear of the great accomplishments and how much better we are than before, and from another we hear a protest that enough is enough—we will not stand for our tax dollars being used to ruin the neighborhood with a public housing project, or to provide homes as good as my own to other middle income families. The third corner provides a paper suggesting that inept government and "big money" are responsible for subverting what is only a half-hearted effort in the first place. From the remaining corner comes a growing concern over water in the basement and rotten porch steps, and why won't the "government man" with the American flag and golden eagle emblem see to it that the house is fixed. He insured it, didn't he? These various groups fail to probe under the rug very deeply, and fail to communicate besides, for the rug is firmly pressed to the floor by a heaping pile of debris that spills to the very edge. There are indications that this pile is composed of ignorance, prejudice and self-interest. A massive effort is needed to sweep off the rug, shake it out and polish the floor underneath.

There is no lack of rhetoric from government officials at both the federal and municipal level, but much of this is political window-dressing to show "action." There is a lack of commitment which explains why so little has been accomplished. President Johnson proclaimed the Housing and Urban Development Act of 1968 as the most farsighted, most comprehensive, most massive housing program in all of American history. The same Congress which adopted the act failed to provide sufficient funding for it. Similar appropriation battles handicapped earlier, equally fine-sounding legislation. This contrasts markedly with the stimulation provided to the drive for middle income homeownership, contributing to the dramatic growth of suburbia.

The suburban residential environment occupied by many Americans has provided relative security, prosperity and a sense of well-being. Despite problems, opinion surveys confirm that the great majority of residents have a high degree of satisfaction with their housing situations. This scene contrasts sharply with the housing conditions of a minority of urban Americans—there is a housing gap. No one really knows how large the gap is, or how many constitute the ill-housed in our cities. But the gap does exist qualitatively, and is felt and experienced by those in the minority. Those in the majority may also be aware of such a gap. However, for the majority, whether middle or low income, who experienced the pre-World War II years, their residential living seems not one of personal retrogression, but one of steady improvement.

Even though the country as a whole may have "troubles," many individuals see themselves as being better off—though a continuing inflationary spiral and economic recession may well change this perception. That most people may be better off, in their housing for example, does not make an exciting message for any medium, least of all the prime purveyor of information for America, television. On the other hand, the ills of society have been vigorously presented to us, and rightly so, for we should not become smug or complacent. But it may well be that individual Americans in relating such information to their own experience do not see any relationship and become immune to statements of "crises," although some situations can cause widespread hardship—for example, the energy shortage. There is no widespread popular support for dealing with a "housing crisis" that does not affect the majority—other matters receive a higher priority.

When the discrepancy between the living standards of the majority and the poor—as typified by the housing gap—actually generates protest, things do happen. The first step is to dampen the fires and channel the protestors toward participation. This was the case in the urban riots of the late 1960s when the country responded with a range of housing legislation and programs such as Model Cities. This legislation was based in part on the work of the President's Committee on Urban Housing. Although it seemed of little significance at the time, this committee, composed mostly of executives from the corporate and financial worlds, assumed the nation's housing problems could be ameliorated by subsidy programs and a fuller participation in them by the private sector. If this assumption were to prove unwarranted, they declared, "*we would then foresee the necessity for massive federal intervention with the federal government becoming the nation's houser of last resort*" [Kaiser, 1969, p. 5, emphasis added.].

Housing Crisis U.S.A., by Joseph P. Fried, real estate analyst for the New York Times, was published in 1971 and provides a chronicle of the nation's efforts in housing the poor. He indicts us and society for a basic failure. On

January 6, 1971, the House Committee on Banking and Currency issued the first formal report on possible criminal abuses of certain subsidy programs. More recently, Brian D. Boyer has given us *Cities Destroyed for Cash: The FHA Scandal at HUD*, a somewhat loosely documented report on the often illegal tactics of real estate speculators, contract dealers, mortgage bankers and FHA inspectors in relation to those programs initiated under the 1968 legislation. There have also been television documentaries and newspaper and magazine commentaries on these scandals. These revelations, which strongly suggest that the programs failed those they supposedly sought to serve but benefited others not in need, have not provoked any violent protest. There have been no demands for the massive federal intervention suggested by the President's Committee on Urban Housing. In fact, the legacy of public housing has made many wary of such intervention. The situation is not perceived by our society as a crisis, and, in truth, it is not by most standards. What we have is the chronic persistence of an unacceptable situation for a minority. Our efforts in scientific research received an enormous challenge from the Soviet *Sputnik*. Perhaps some such external stimulus is needed before we can break through the myth of a major national effort to deal with housing for all Americans to the reality of an overdose of rhetoric and lack of effort.

Policy Considerations

As we view the housing scene, there are some primary concerns for policy which we group under the headings of need determination and approach. We conclude with a brief discussion of each.

Need Determination. HUD should aggressively pursue the development of locally oriented housing needs and housing goal studies in conjunction with the appropriate governmental agencies and community groups. A key element of this approach must be (1) to improve the quality of data on all aspects of housing at the regional and local level, and (2) to improve greatly the degree and quality of interaction between those concerned with the supply, administration and consumption of housing. The Seattle area shows some hopeful signs in this regard, and the council of governments in Minneapolis-St. Paul could well be copied in terms of its data collection and monitoring procedures. Another important aspect here is that HUD must provide assistance, either directly or indirectly, to local groups engaged in this task. At present, there are a number of approaches being adopted and, while diversity is healthy, the questions of competence, reliability and ease of comparison are critical if HUD is to make allocations based on local needs. The continuing debate on the number of families in America that live in intolerable housing or that are housing-poor (or both) is critical testimony of the lack of sophistication of housing analysis in our society. The first order of business then, with regard to the nation's housing problem, is to find out what is where, how fast it is changing and who needs what kind of help. As we have shown in this chapter, the task is not an easy one.

Approach. Simultaneously, we must progress to an integrated, comprehensive approach to the housing gap problem. A thorough examination of welfare systems, income tax laws, transportation planning, energy development and housing policy must be initiated with the intent of developing coherent efforts toward a better-housed citizenry. These efforts must face up to locational and racial issues. This requires that we make a commitment to the type of urban areas we wish to have within most of our own lifetimes. We would suggest as priority item one that the present dual housing market, both in the location of publicly subsidized units and private market matching of buyer and seller, be immediately and vigorously attacked. This might be accomplished by requiring mortgage lenders to show a locationally integrated portfolio. Such an affirmative lending plan would contribute to the elimination of the practice of "blockbusting" and the need for school busing, among other benefits. This, we suspect, would have to be demonstrated before such a plan would be politically acceptable.

We also suggest transit subsidies, via reduced fares, to needy individuals and major expansion of transit services. The 1974 federal initiatives to expand and support mass transit are favorable steps in our opinion. Zoning practices should be made more flexible, or even replaced by performance standards, so as to allow more interspersion of employment sites and residences. This would cut travel costs and reduce energy use in addition to providing greater locational advantages (accessibility) to the many services offered in a major urban complex. We doubt the usefulness of a massive new town program, although experimental projects can provide useful demonstrations. The investment in American cities is colossal and represents one of the country's major resources. It would be a mistake to abandon this structure.

Under the existing sociopolitical order in America it is unlikely that housing will be thought of as a good to be collectively provided in a manner consistent with some overarching social goal. While this may be regretted by some, this seems to be a realistic appraisal, and thus we would recommend second strategy—the aggressive pursuit of regional dispersal of assisted housing opportunities in an attempt to create more diverse and balanced communities that will hopefully be characterized by the tolerance and friendliness characteristic of so many individual Americans. We would support an increased emphasis on the leased housing program, with greater incentives for landlords to participate in this program. The degree of dispersal of housing units achieved by the homeownership subsidy program should be encouraged. However, there are serious problems of quality control and issues of equitable treatment for middle income households that must be resolved if this program is to receive popular support.

We are also in favor of a great degree of public commitment by leaders in our communities toward the regional housing plans. Under such schemes, the perceived threat of low rent public housing projects can be openly discussed, and some fears partially allayed. Better attention to project design standards, with fewer financial constraints, and a range of supporting family services could make smaller public housing projects a worthwhile residential environment in some suburban areas, thus contributing to this regional dispersal which we advocate.

This will all require a major financial commitment and considerable reeducation of both the people and political leaders—not an indoctrination as to the "rightness" of this strategy, but rather the dispelling of myths and half-truths that sustain fears and prejudice, and the best possible prediction of the consequences of public action in this area that social scientists can provide. The challenge to us all is enormous, but hopefully the reservoir of goodwill is large—the goal is a better America for all our people.

If, on the other hand, we jealously seek to hold what we have in terms of status and possessions, if we exhibit a callous disregard for the well-being of others in terms of housing conditions and costs, then the racist housing markets, the spatial and social inequities, the fear and distrust will persist, and words like *tolerance* and *understanding* and *cooperation* will have no meaning for the ill-housed when they hear them from those who are not in need.

BIBLIOGRAPHY

Aaron, Henry J. *Shelter and Subsidies.* Washington, D.C.: The Brookings Institution, 1972.

Atlanta Department of Planning. *Changing Atlanta: Population and Housing.* Atlanta, 1973.

——. *Foreclosures in Atlanta.* Atlanta, 1974.

Atlanta Housing Authority. *Annual Reports.* Atlanta, 1971–1972.

Atlanta Regional Metropolitan Planning Commission. *Housing All Atlantans.* Atlanta, 1970.

"Back from Aerospace Slump: Seattle and the Northwest." *U.S. News and World Report,* October 9, 1972. 41–43.

Berry, Brian J.L., et al. "Attitudes to Integration: The Role of Status in Community Response to Racial Change." Mimeographed. Chicago, 1974.

Birch, David, et al. *Towards Housing Goals for the United States: Concepts, Methods and Measures:* Cambridge, Mass.: Joint Center for Urban Studies of MIT and Harvard University, 1973.

Boyer, Brian D. *Cities Destroyed for Cash: The FHA Scandal at HUD.* Chicago: Follett, 1973.

Chicago Housing Authority. *Annual Reports.* Chicago, 1971.

——. *Annual Statistical Report on Tenant Characteristics.* Chicago, 1972.

Detman, Art, Jr. "Lessons from the National Housing Act." *Saturday Review of Society,* March 17, 1973. 57–58.

Devise, Pierre. "Integration in the Suburbs—Who Needs It?" Working Paper II. 17. Mimeographed. Chicago: Chicago Regional Hospital Study, 1973.

——. "Federal Housing is Packed in Housing Surplus Areas. . . ." Statement to U.S. Senate Subcommittee on Housing and Urban Affairs. Mimeographed. Chicago, March 31, 1973.

Dietsch, Richard. "Housing Slowdown." *New Republic,* April 7, 1973. 11–12.

Douglas, Paul, et. al. *Building the American City: Report of National Commission on Urban Problems to the Congress and to the President of the United States.* Washington, D.C.: US Government Printing Office, 1968.

Downs, Anthony. *Federal Housing Subsidies: How Are They Working?* Lexington, Mass.: D.C. Heath and Co., 1973.

Fried, Joseph P. "Housing Allowances–The Latest Panacea." *Nation,* March 5th, 1973. 304–308.

——. *Housing Crisis U.S.A.* New York: Praeger, 1971.

Gans, Herbert J. *The Urban Villagers.* New York: Free Press of Glencoe, 1962.

Gruen, Nina J. and Claude Gruen. *Low and Moderate Income Housing in the Suburbs: An Analysis for the Dayton, Ohio Region.* New York: Praeger, 1972.

Harney, Kenneth R. "Massive HUD report Hits Hard at Subsidies." *The Washington Post,* October 27, 1973. pp. F-1, F-16.

Hartshorn, Truman. "Comment in Reply." *Annals of the Association of American Geographers* 62, 1 (March 1972): 139–42.

Hill, Lewis. "Statement before the U.S. Senate Subcommittee on Housing and Urban Affairs." Mimeographed. Chicago, March 30, 1973.

Kaiser, Edgar, et al. *A Decent Home: The Report of the President's Committee on Urban Housing.* Washington, D.C.: US Government Printing Office, 1969.

Kristof, Frank S. *Urban Housing Needs Through the 1980's: An Analysis and Projection: Prepared for the Consideration of the National Commission on Urban Problems.* Rsearch Report No. 10. Washington, D.C.: US Government Printing Office, 1968.

——. "Federal Housing Policies: Subsidized Production, Filtration and Objectives." *Land Economics* 68, 4 (November 1972): 309–20; and 69, 2 (May 1973): 163–74.

Mercer, John. "Spatial Pattern of Urban Residential Blight." Ph.D. dissertation, McMaster University, 1971.

Metropolitan Council of the Twin Cities Area. *Distribution and Types of Subsidized Housing in the Twin Cities Metropolitan Area.* Housing Report No. 1. Minneapolis, 1971.

——. *Metropolitan Development Guide.* Minneapolis, 1973.

Northeastern Illinois Planning Commission. *Moderate and Low Income Housing: A Ten Year Estimate of Regional Housing Needs.* Chicago, 1973.

Peel, Norman, et. al. "Racial Discrimination in Public Housing Site Selection." *Stanford Law Review* 23, (1971): 63–147.

Puget Sound Governmental Conference. *Inner City Housing,* Seattle, 1972.

Rainwater, Lee. *Behind Ghetto Walls: Black Family Life in a Federal Slum.* Chicago: Aldine, 1970.

Regional Housing Coalition. *An Interim Plan for Balanced Distribution of Housing Opportunities for Northeastern Illinois.* Chicago, 1973.

"Romney's Broadside at Kaufman and Board." *Business Week,* December 23, 1972.

Seattle Department of Community Development. "Seattle Urban Renewal–Overview." Mimeographed. Seattle, 1973.

Seattle Housing Authority. *Annual Reports.* Seattle, 1969–70, 1971–72.

Seattle Housing Development. *Section 235 Acquired Properties in the Seattle Area.* Seattle, 1973.

Seattle Housing Development. *235 Housing in the Seattle Area.* Seattle, 1973.

Seattle Housing Development. *221(d)3 and 236 Housing in the Seattle Area.* Seattle, 1973.

Seattle Real Estate Research Committee. *Real Estate Research Report* 24, 2 (Fall 1973).

Taggart, Robert. *Low-Income Housing: A Critique of Federal Aid.* Baltimore: The Johns Hopkins Press, 1970.

"The Year That the Building Stopped." *Time,* October 28, 1974. 88–90.

US Bureau of the Cenus. *Measuring the Quality of Housing: An Appraisal of Census Statistics and Methods.* Working Paper No. 25. Washington, D.C.: US Government Printing Office, 1967.

US Comptroller General. *Enforcement of Housing Codes: How It Can Help to Achieve Nations Housing Goal.* Washington, D.C.: US Government Printing Office, 1972.

——. *Opportunities to Improve Effectiveness and Reduce Costs of Homeownership Assistance Housing Program.* Washington, D.C.: US Government Printing Office, 1972.

——. *Opportunities to Improve Effectiveness and Reduce Costs of Rental Assistance Housing Program.* Washington, D.C.: US Government Printing Office, 1973.

US Congress, House Committee on Banking and Currency. *Investigation and Hearings on Abuses in Federal Low and Moderate Income Housing Programs.* Washington, D.C.: US Government Printing Office, December, 1970.

——. *Interim Report on HUD Investigation of Low and Moderate Income Housing Programs.* Washington, D.C.: US Government Printing Office, March, 1971.

US Department of Housing and Urban Development. "Analysis of the Chicago, Illinois Housing Market, as of March 1, 1973." Mimeographed. Chicago, 1974.

US, Office of the President. *Annual Report on National Housing Goals.* Washington, D.C.: US Government Printing Office, 1969–1972.

Washington, Deborah. "Changes in Housing Quality Characteristics, Chicago, Illinois SMSA, 1950–1970." Mimeographed. Chicago, 1974.

Wellar, Barry S. "Residential Structure and Housing Quality." *Annals of the Association of American Geographers* 62, 1 (March 1972): 134–139.

Chapter 5

Progress Toward Environmental Goals for Metropolitan America

Brian J.L. Berry
Harvard University

INTRODUCTION

To ask whether national policy has contributed to an improvement in the quality of metropolitan environments in the last decade is to ask a seemingly straightforward but analytically complex question. Does the question refer to the quality of life, *sensu lato,* embracing both the quality of the human environment and of the natural environment, if indeed these can ever be distinguished analytically (Figure 5-1), or does it refer to the programmatic purview of the Environmental Protection Agency (EPA), *sensu stricto*? This essay proceeds from the latter more restricted view.

In proceeding in this more limited fashion, it is not intended to deny the importance of the larger idea, about which an immense literature has been accumulating in the past decade. As this literature reveals, the quality of life is an elusive concept, compounded of the individual's perceptions of his own well-being and self-worth and his satisfactions with his environment, broadly conceived. One investigation has concluded that factors entering into individual self-perceptions embrace as a minimum those grouped into the 13 categories listed in Table 5-1. Any definition of the environment is similarly multiplex. On the human side, Joyce has proposed a complex battery of measures of the quality of life in an urban area (Table 5-2); separate attitudinal, societal, political, economic and physical indicators are proposed of the quality of accessibility, law enforcement, fire protection, health care, recreation, education, housing and neighborhood, and incomes. Some of the 40 measures listed by Joyce have, in turn, been used by Flax (1973) to rate the relative quality of life in the nation's 18 largest metropolitan areas and to assess the nature and direction of change. His final ratings are presented in Table 5-3 for the reader who may be interested in the present crude state of the art.

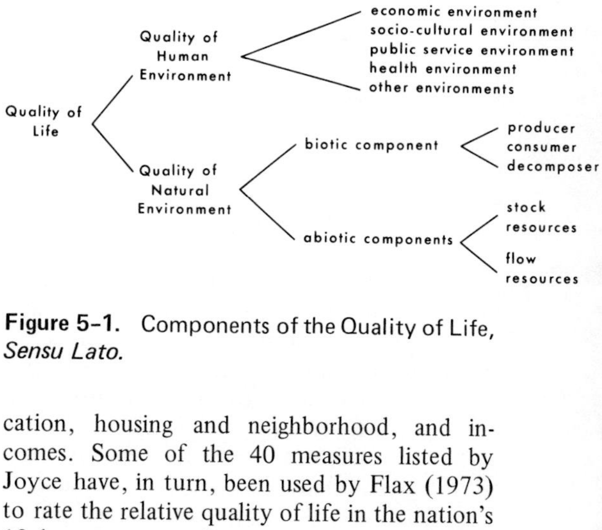

Figure 5-1. Components of the Quality of Life, *Sensu Lato.*

Coming closer to the questions to be addressed in this essay, on the physical side, the Battelle Research Institute has argued that completeness in studying environmental impacts requires comprehension of the elaborate hierarchy of environmental categories, components, parameters and measurements illustrated in Figure 5-2 and detailed in Table 5-4. To complicate matters, the question of environmental impacts involves an escalating scale of effects involving both the health and welfare of individuals, as suggested by Figure 5-3. To

Table 5-1. Factors in Individual Perceptions of Well-Being, After Dalkey

1. Love, caring, affection, communication, interpersonal understanding; friendship, companionship; honesty, sincerity, truthfulness; tolerance, acceptance of others; faith, religious awareness.
2. Self-respect, self-acceptance, self-satisfaction; self-confidence, egoism; security; stability, familiarity, sense of permanence; self-knowledge, self-awareness, growth.
3. Peace of mind, emotional stability, lack of conflict; fear, anxiety; suffering, pain; humiliation, belittlement; escape, fantasy.
4. Sex, sexual satisfaction, sexual pleasure.
5. Challenge, stimulation; competition, competitiveness; ambition; opportunity, social mobility, luck; education, intellectual stimulation.
6. Social acceptance, popularity; needed, feeling of being wanted; loneliness, impersonality; flattering positive feedback, reinforcement.
7. Achievement, accomplishment, job satisfaction; success; failure, defeat, losing; money, acquisitiveness, material greed; status, reputation, recognition, prestige.
8. Individuality; conformity; spontaneity, impulsive, uninhibited; freedom.
9. Involvement, participation; concern, altruism, consideration.
10. Comfort, economic well-being, relaxation, leisure; good health.
11. Novelty, change, newness, variety, surprise; boredom; humorous, amusing, witty.
12. Dominance, superiority; dependence, impotence, helplessness; aggression, violence, hostility; power, control, independence.
13. Privacy.

Source: Norman C. Dalkey, *Studies in the Quality of Life* (Lexington, Mass.: D.C. Health and Co., 1972).

illustrate in an actual case, a study of the effects of poisoning of Iraqi farmers by methylmercury-polluted wheat in 1970, an incident which produced 6,530 cases of hospitalization and 459 hospital deaths, a clear sequence of thresholds for the onset of paresthesia (abnormal prickling or itching), ataxia (loss of muscle coordination), dysarthria (speech disorder following nerve damage), deafness and death was discovered (Figure 5-4).

Two questions are raised: What are the environmental indicators to be examined? and, What are the standards against which environmental quality is to be assessed? The selection of standards indicates a choice by society of an acceptable level of environmental quality and an attendant set of risks that society is willing to tolerate with respect to a specific set of environmental factors. It is because of such choices that we can limit our task in this chapter, for the discussion is restricted to those factors and standards that have been set as part of the nation's attack on environmental pollution in the last decade.

By restricting the focus in this manner, it is possible to begin to ask whether progress is in fact being made toward achieving environmental goals. One way is to compute the ratio of measured levels of environmental pollution to environmental quality standards. A ratio of greater than 1.0 would indicate a substandard environment, whereas a ratio of less than 1.0 indicates that environmental quality standards are being met. The Council on Environmental Quality, in examining trends in air quality, has prepared one set of such ratios for American cities for the years 1967-1972, as Table 5-5 indicates. The improvements in sulfur dioxide (SO_2) and suspended particulate (TSP) levels noted are in part due to the affirmative national policies set in motion by a succession of legislative enactments during the 1960s.

By so limiting the discussion, the first questions that arise are: What are these policies? and, What are the standards that have been set? It is to these questions that the first part of this chapter is devoted. Once the legislative background has been outlined, the balance of the chapter reviews the evidence relating to the nature, intensity and spatial distribution of environmental pollution in American metropolitan areas. We conclude by asking whether progress is in fact being made toward achieving the nation's goals for high quality metropolitan environments.

LEGISLATIVE AND ADMINISTRATIVE BACKGROUND

The key enactment in the attempt to secure pollution-free environments is the National Environmental Policy Act of 1969 which

Table 5-2. Measures Proposed by Joyce as Indicators of Urban Environmental Quality

Manifestations or Aspects	*Accessibility*	*Law Enforcement*	*Fire Protection*	*Health Care*	*Recreation*	*Education*	*Housing and Neighborhood*	*Income Production*
Attitudinal	Model Preference of Transportation	Juvenile Probations per population age 20–21	Malicious False Alarms	Inoculable Diseases (under 13)	Vandalism $ per Park Acre	High School Dropout Rates	Elementary School Enrollment	Percentage White Collar Employment
Societal	Traffic Arrests/ Total Street Miles	Juvenile Dependencies per population age 20–21	Arsons per 100 population	Suicides per 100,000 population	Percentage Population in Different Age Groups	Largest Ehtnic percentage; Percentage Nonwhite Enrollment	Elementary School Transiency Rates	Percent of Households with Wives Working
Political	Deficient Select System/Total Select System Streets	Total Arrests per 100 population	Fire Engine Companies per 1000 population	Percentage Public Hospital Care	Five Year Proposed Capital Improvement Program for Parks and Recreation	Voter Participation Rates	Nonresidential Uses on Residential Parcels	Percentage of Children 4–5 Years of Age on Welfare
Economic	Percentage By-passed Employment Due to Lack of Transportation	Losses Due to Burglary and Robbery	Number of Fires Greater than $1000. Loss	Deaths in 25–44 age Group	Private Recreation Investment per 100 population	Percentage of People 25+ Years Completed College	Median Imputed Rent per Median Income	Unemployment Rate
Physical	Median Work Trip Time by Private Transportation	Part I Felonies per 100 population	Structural Fires per 100 Structures	Infant Mortality Rate	Number of Types of Facilities	Median Sixth Grade Crude Reading Achievement	Percentage Standard Housing; Percentage Lacking Facilities	Number of Householders under $1,000 per Capita Income

Source: Robert E. Joyce, "Systematic Measurement of the Quality of Urban Life, Prerequisite to Management," from Seminar on Management of the City, Research Analysis Corporation, May 1971, pp. 69–86.

Table 5-3. The Nation's 18 Largest Metropolitan Areas Ranked on 14 Environmental Quality Indicators, with Directions of Change Indicated

	A. Quality Levels[a]														
	Unemployment	*Poverty*	*Income Level*	*Housing*	*Health*	*Mental Health*	*Public Order*	*Racial Equality*[c]	*Community Concern*	*Citizen Participation*	*Educational Attainment*	*Transportation*			*Social Disintegration*[e]
													Air Quality[d] *Levels of Three Pollutants (1969)*[b]		
Metropolitan Area	*Percentage Unemployed (1970)*[b]	*Percentage Low Income Households (1970)*[b]	*Adjusted Per Capita Income (1969)*[b]	*Cost for Moderate Income Family (1969)*[b]	*Infant Mortality Rate (1968)*[b]	*Reported Suicide Rate (1968)*[b]	*Reported Robbery Rate (1970)*[b]	*Nonwhite-White Unemployment Ratio (1970)*[b]	*Per Capita United Fund Contribution (1970)*[b]	*Percentage Eligible to Vote for President (1968)*[b]	*Median School Years of Adults (1969)*[b]	*Cost for Moderate Income Family (1969)*[b]	*Particulates*	*SO_2*	*NO_2*	*Estimates of Narcotics Addiction (1969)*[b]
New York	9	9*	4	17	9	1	18	1	18	14*	9*	1	10	18	8	7
Los Angeles/Long Beach	18	15	3	10	2*	17	11	3	17	11*	3*	7	8	10	18	3
Chicago	2	5*	5	13	18	3	14	6	15	2*	7*	13	16	17	5	1
Philadelphia	7*	9*	14	9	17	13	6	9	10	8	13*	2	15	13	1	f
Detroit	17	3	1	5	12	15	17	8	7	5*	13*	8	14	9	16	f
Boston	4	1	17	18	6	10	3	f	12	2*	6	15	5*	14*	4	4
San Francisco/Oakland	16	17*	2	14	2*	18	13	2	13	7	2	16	1	4	10	5
Washington	1	2	8	11	5	7	15	7	16	18	1	10	3*	7*	3	6
Pittsburgh	14*	12	13	3	11	11	5	5	2	2*	13*	3	17	16	15	f
St. Louis	10*	13	12	8	10	4	9	11	6	11*	17	14	18	14*	17	2
Cleveland	12*	7	9	15	8	16	10	12	1	9	9*	6	13	12	13	f
Baltimore	5*	11	16	4	15	14	16	4	14	14*	18	9	11*	11	11*	f
Houston	5*	17*	11	1	16	12	12	10	11	16*	9*	17	5*	2*	14	f
Minneapolis/St. Paul	14*	4	6	6	1	5	7	f	5	1	3*	11	2	7*	7	f
Dallas	3	16	7	2	14	6	8	f	9	16*	3*	4*	3*	1	6	f
Cincinnati	7*	14	10	7	7	9	2	f	3	11*	13*	12	9	6	11*	f
Milwaukee	10*	5*	15	16	4	8	1	f	8	5*	7*	4*	11*	5	9	f
Buffalo	12*	8	18	12	13	2	4	f	4	10	9*	18	5*	2*	2	f

[a]The lowest rankings are assigned to the most favorable conditions

[b]Latest year available

[c]Data available for only 12 metropolitan areas

[d]Pollutants are: Particulate Matter, Sulfur Dioxide and Nitrogen Dioxide

[e]Data available for only seven central cities

[f]No data available

Tie ranking (the lowest rank in the tie is listed). For example, Baltimore and Houston are tied for ranks 5–6 in percentage unemployed and are both listed "5" in this table.

B. Directions of Change

Metropolitan Area	Unemployment	Poverty	Income Level	Housing	Health	Mental Health	Public Order	Racial Equality[c]	Community Concern	Citizen Participation	Educational Attainment	Transportation	Air Quality			Social Disintegration[e]
	Percentage Unemployed (1970)[b]	Percentage Low Income Households (1970)[b]	Adjusted Per Capita Income (1969)[b]	Cost for Moderate Income Family (1969)[b]	Infant Mortality Rate (1968)[b]	Reported Suicide Rate (1968)[b]	Reported Robbery Rate (1970)[b]	Nonwhite-White Unemployment Ratio (1970)[b]	Per Capita United Fund Contribution (1970)[b]	Percentage Eligible to Vote for President (1968)[b]	Median School Years of Adults (1969)[b]	Cost for Moderate Income Family (1969)[b]	Suspended Particulate Concentration (1969)[a]	Levels of Two Pollutants (69)[c] SO_2	Levels of Two Pollutants (69)[c] NO_2	Estimates of Narcotics Addiction (1969)[a]
New York	- 0 +	+ 0 +	+ + -	- - -	+ 0 +	+ + +	- - -	+ + -	+ - +	- - -	+ 0 0	- + 0	+ 0 +	-	0	e - e
Los Angeles/Long Beach	- - 0	0 - -	+ + +	- 0 -	+ + +	0 - +	- 0 +	+ + -	+ - 0	- 0 -	+ + 0	0 0 +	e 0 e	0	-	e + e
Chicago	0 + +	+ + 0	+ + -	- - +	0 - -	+ + +	- 0 +	+ + +	+ - +	- + 0	+ 0 0	- - -	+ 0 -	-	+	e + e
Philadelphia	- + +	+ 0 0	+ - -	- + -	+ - 0	- - 0	- + +	+ 0 0	+ 0 0	- 0 0	0 0 -	- + -	+ - +	0	+	e e e
Detroit	- - -	+ + +	+ + +	- + +	+ - 0	- - 0	- - -	+ 0 +	+ + -	- + 0	+ 0 0	- 0 0	+ - +	0	-	e e e
Boston	- + 0	+ + +	+ - 0	- - -	+ + 0	- 0 -	- + -	d d d	+ - -	- + 0	0 + -	- - -	+ + +	0	+	e + e
San Francisco/Oakland	- - 0	- - -	+ + +	- - -	+ + +	0 - +	- 0 -	+ + +	+ - 0	- + 0	+ + 0	0 - +	+ + 0	+	0	e 0 e
Washington	- 0 0	+ + +	+ 0 -	- 0 +	+ + +	+ 0 +	- - -	- + -	+ - -	0 - +	+ + 0	- 0 0	+ + -	+	+	e 0 e
Pittsburgh	0 - +	+ - +	+ - +	- + -	+ - -	- - 0	- + -	+ + +	+ + 0	- + +	+ 0 0	- + +	+ - 0	0	-	e e e
St. Louis	0 0 +	0 - -	+ - -	- + +	+ 0 0	+ + +	- 0 +	+ - +	+ + -	- 0 0	+ - +	- - 0	- - -	+	-	e + e
Cleveland	- 0 0	+ + 0	+ 0 0	- - 0	+ 0 0	0 - 0	- 0 -	- - -	+ + -	- 0 -	+ 0 0	- 0 0	+ 0 -	0	0	e e e
Baltimore	0 + +	0 - -	+ - 0	- + 0	+ - +	- - 0	- - -	+ + +	+ - +	- - 0	+ - 0	- 0 -	+ 0 +	0	0	e e e
Houston	- + 0	+ - 0	+ - 0	- + 0	+ - 0	- - -	- 0 -	+ 0 -	+ 0 -	+ - +	- 0 -	- - +	+ + -	+	-	e e e
Minneapolis/St. Paul	- - -	+ + -	+ + +	0 + +	+ + 0	+ + +	- + +	d d d	+ + 0	- + +	+ + 0	- 0 +	+ + 0	+	0	e e e
Dallas	- + -	+ - 0	+ + +	- + 0	+ - -	+ 0 +	- + -	d d d	+ 0 +	+ - +	+ + 0	- 0 +	+ + 0	+	0	e e e
Cincinnati	- + -	+ - 0	+ - +	- + +	+ + -	0 0 +	- + 0	d d d	+ + 0	- 0 0	+ 0 +	- 0 -	+ 0 +	+	0	e e e
Milwaukee	- 0 -	0 + -	+ - -	- - -	+ + 0	+ 0 +	- + 0	d d d	+ + -	- + -	+ 0 +	0 0 +	+ 0 0	+	0	e e e
Buffalo	0 0 +	+ 0 0	+ - +	- - 0	0 - -	0 + +	- + -	d d d	+ + 0	- 0 -	+ 0 +	- - 0	e + e	+	+	e e e

[a]Latest year data available
[b]Data available for only 12 metropolitan areas
[c]Each of the two characters represents the level of one of the pollutants. (Each character is equivalent to the "2nd character" described on page 000.)
[d]Data available for only seven central cities
[e]Data not available

Codes used in part B are:
1. The *first character* indicates the *Direction of Change* comparing the recent annual average rate of change with a zero baseline. (+) Conditions Improved (–) Conditions Worsened (0) Conditions Unchanged*
2. The *second character* indicates the *Latest Level* of quality of the particular metropolitan area with respect to the average (mean) level of all 18 metropolitan areas. (+) Better than Average (–) Worse than Average (0) About Average*
3. The *third character* indicates the particular metropolitan area's average annual *Rate of Change* with respect to the average (mean) change of the 18 metropolitan areas. (+) Rate of Change Favorable (–) Rate of Change Unfavorable (0) Rate of Change Average*

For Example: + 0 – means that the metropolitan area is improving, its latest level of quality is about average and its rate of change is less favorable than average.

*Conditions are defined as "unchanged" or "average" if the particular metropolitan area's performance varied by less than ± 10 percent of the range of values of the other metropolitan areas.

Source: Michael J. Flax

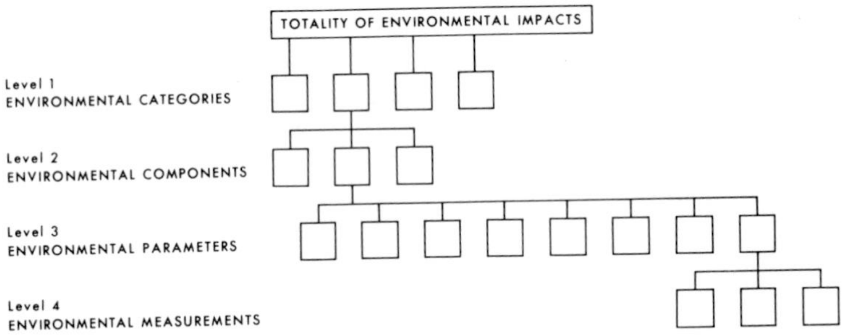

Figure 5-2. A Hierarchical Scheme for Measuring Environmental Impacts

Table 5-4. The Battelle Environmental Impact Assessment System

Environmental Categories

I. Ecology
II. Environmental Pollution
III. Esthetics
IV. Human Interest

Environmental Components

I. *Ecology*
  (A) Species and Populations
  (B) Habitats and Communities
  (C) Ecosystems

II. *Environmental Pollution*
  (D) Water Pollution
  (E) Air Pollution
  (F) Land Pollution
  (G) Noise Pollution

III. *Esthetics*
  (H) Land
  (I) Air
  (J) Water
  (K) Biota
  (L) Manmade Objects
  (M) Composition

IV. *Human Interest*
  (N) Educational-Scientific Significance
  (O) Historical Significance
  (P) Cultural Significance
  (Q) Mood-Atmosphere Significance

Environmental Parameters

I. Ecology

(A) *Species and Populations*
  (1) Rare and endangered plant and animal species
  (2) Productive plant species
  (3) Game animals
  (4) Other animals
  (5) Resident and migratory birds
  (6) Sport fisheries
  (7) Commercial fisheries
  (8) Pestilent plant and animal species
  (9) Parasites

(B) *Habitats and Communities*
  (10) Species diversity
  (11) Food chains
  (12) Land use for habitats and communities

(C) *Ecosystems*
  (13) Productivity rate
  (14) Hydrologic budget
  (15) Nutrient budget

II. Environmental Pollution

(D) *Water Pollution*
  (16) Algal blooms
  (17) Dissolved oxygen
  (18) Evaporation
  (19) Fecal coliforms
  (20) Nutrients
  (21) Pesticides, herbicides, defoliants
  (22) pH
  (23) Physical river characteristics
  (24) Sediment load
  (25) Stream flow
  (26) Temperature

(E) *Air Pollution*
  (30) Carbon monoxide
  (31) Hydrocarbons
  (32) Particulate matter
  (33) Photochemical oxidants
  (34) Sulfur oxides

(F) *Land Pollution*
  (35) Land use and misuse
  (36) Soil erosion
  (37) Soil pollution

continued

Table 5-4 continued

Environmental Parameters

II. Environmental Pollution

(D) *Water Pollution*
- (27) Total dissolved solids
- (28) Toxic substances
- (29) Turbidity

(G) *Noise Pollution*
- (38) Noise

III. Esthetics

(H) *Land*
- (39) Land forms
- (40) Geologic surface material

(I) *Air*
- (41) Pleasantness of sounds

(J) *Water*
- (42) Surface characteristics
- (43) Water-land interface characteristics

(K) *Biota*
- (44) Vegetation
- (45) Fauna

(L) *Manmade Objects*
- (46) Visual
- (47) Condition
- (48) Consonance with environment

(M) *Composition*
- (49) Interaction of land, air, water and manmade objects
- (50) Color

IV. Human Interest

(N) *Educational-Scientific Significance*
- (51) Geological significance
- (52) Ecological significance
- (53) Archeological significance
- (54) Unusual water phenomenon

(O) *Historical Significance*
- (55) Related to persons
- (56) Related to events
- (57) Related to religions and cultures
- (58) Related to architecture and styles
- (59) Related to the "western frontier"

(P) *Cultural Significance*
- (60) Related to Indians
- (61) Related to religious groups
- (62) Related to ethnic groups

(Q) *Mood-Atmosphere Significance*
- (63) Isolation-solitude
- (64) Awe-inspiration
- (65) "Oneness" with nature
- (66) Mystery

Source: US Environmental Protection Agency. *The Quality of Life Concept.* Washington, D.C.: US Government Printing Office, 1973. pp. 145-6.

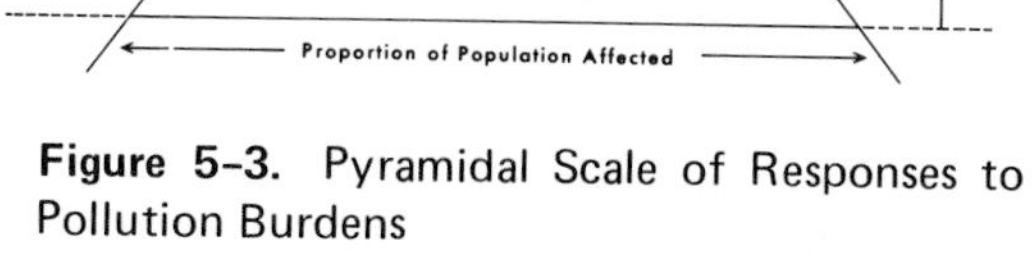

Figure 5-3. Pyramidal Scale of Responses to Pollution Burdens

mandated the federal government to take action "in protecting and enhancing the quality of the Nation's environment to sustain and enrich human life," declaring the purposes of national environmental policy to be "to foster and promote the general welfare, to create and maintain conditions under which man and nature can exist in harmony, and to fulfill the social, economic, and other requirements of present and future generations of Americans." The act requires the President's Council on Environmental Quality to report at least once a year on the state of the environment and efforts to improve it.

To aid in achieving the purposes of the act, the Environmental Protection Agency was created in 1970. The principal functions that were transferred to EPA were the Federal Water Quality Administration; pesticides research authority from the Department of Interior; the National Air Pollution Control Administration; elements of the Environmental Control Administration of the Department of Health, Education and Welfare; pesticide research and standard-setting from the Food and

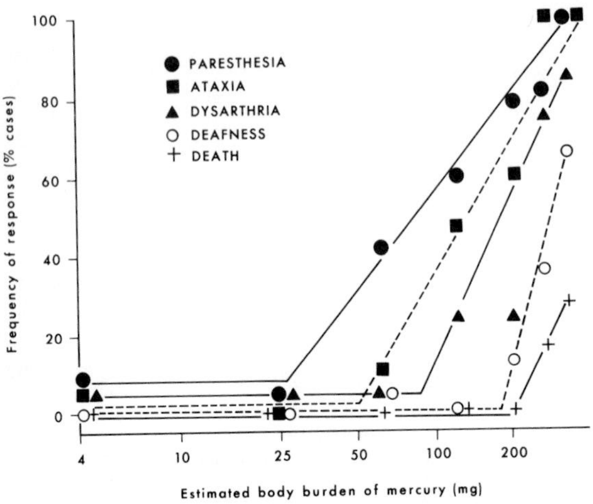

Figure 5-4. The Relationship Between Frequency of Signs and Symptoms and the Estimated Body Burden of Methylmercury at the Time of Cessation of Ingestion of Methylmercury in Bread (After Bakir et al., 1973).

Drug Administration; general ecological research from the Council on Environmental Quality; environmental radiation standards programs from the Atomic Energy Commission; and the pesticides registration program of the Agricultural Research Service. A new federal force was thereby created to accomplish positive environmental improvement on a consistent and uniform national basis—something which it was generally agreed had been lacking when prime responsibility was left to the states and individual location.

Since EPA is a new initiative in guaranteeing environmental quality on a uniform nationwide basis, it is worthwhile to review the efforts of the federal government which culminated in the establishment of this agency. The beginnings were in water pollution control, followed by enactments directed toward control of air pollution, hazardous substances, noise and solid wastes.

Water Pollution Control

Federal involvement in water control began with Section 13 of the Rivers and Harbors Act of 1899 which prohibited the discharge of wastes other than liquids from sewers into the navigable waters of the United States. The Public Health Service Act of 1912 directed that organization to conduct research into the health effects of water pollution. In the process of virtually eliminating major health threats from waterborne diseases, the work of the Public Health Service over the years has provided a solid base of knowledge for the establishment of quality standards. In 1924 the Oil Pollution Act prohibited the dumping of oil into navigable waters except in the cases of emergency threatening life or property, unavoidable accident or as permitted by regulations.

Recent legislative history begins with the Water Pollution Control Act of 1948 which was an experimental measure designed to expire after five years. This act marked the first in a series of acts building the present body of laws. It specifically recognized the primacy of the states in the field of water pollution control, provided for federal research, and funded technical and planning assistance through the Public Health Service and Federal Works Agency.

In 1956, the Water Pollution Control Act was amended, and these changes set up the basic structure of federal water pollution enforcement procedures for the next ten years. The 1956 amendment provided for an enforcement conference to be called by the federal government and to include all interested parties, especially the states. In six months, if no action was taken to abate the problem under study, a hearing could be held. The hearing was to be followed by another six month waiting period, after which the case could be taken to court. This procedure required an accusation that a state had failed to act before the federal government could go to court. However, until the creation of EPA, only one case had appeared in court.

The Water Quality Act of 1965 made far-reaching changes in the federal role. It provided for the setting, by the states, of water quality standards, subject to the approval of the secretary of HEW (now EPA). It also provided for the creation of a federal Water Pollution Control Administration, which would assume adminstrative control for these programs from the Public Health Service.

In 1966, with the signing of the Clean Water Restoration Act, federal involvement again increased. This act provided for another increase in federal construction grants.

The Water Quality Improvement Act of 1970 changed the name of the federal authority designed to deal with water pollution to the

Table 5-5. Air Quality Data for Selected Cities, Ratios of Annual Mean to EPA Primary Standards for Sulfur Dioxide and Suspended Particulates

Pollutant	*1967*	*1968*	*1969*	*1970*	*1971*	*1972*
			Los Angeles			
SO_2				0.14[a]	0.26	0.30
TSP	1.22	1.72	1.24	1.67	1.77	1.57
			Denver			
SO_2			0.22	0.17	0.10	0.09
TSP	1.24	1.42	1.51	1.63	1.57	2.03
			Washington, D.C.			
SO_2			0.36	0.34[a]	0.26[a]	0.50
TSP	1.13	1.14	0.98	1.01[a]	0.97	1.11
			Chicago			
SO_2		2.18	2.30	1.50	0.91	0.59
TSP		1.49	1.80	1.49	1.53	1.30
			Boston			
SO_2	0.23[a]	0.85	0.80[a]	0.59[a]	0.22[a]	0.16
TSP		1.23	1.14	1.07[a]	1.13[a]	1.07
			St. Louis			
SO_2	1.04	1.14	0.91	0.72[a]	0.12	0.24
TSP	1.49		2.48	2.04[a]	1.17	1.24
			Cincinnati			
SO_2		0.36	0.33	0.14	0.21	0.29
TSP	1.48	1.32	1.39	1.34	1.29	1.16
			Philadelphia			
SO_2		1.13	0.87	1.06	0.46	0.55
TSP	2.00	1.49	1.69	1.80	1.33	1.03
			Pittsburgh			
SO_2	0.89	0.94	0.95	0.72	0.62	0.79
TSP	1.78	2.15	1.92	1.69	1.48[a]	1.80
			New York City			
SO_2	4.35	3.03[a]	1.69[a]	0.91[a]	0.87[a]	0.60
TSP	2.18		1.41	1.64	1.41[a]	1.27

[a]These readings do not meet EPA criteria for statistical validity in most cases because an insufficient number of samples were collected during the year.

Source: Based on EPA data from the National Air Sampling Network.

Federal Water Quality Administration. This new act contained tighter regulations related to oil and vessel pollution, a program to solve the acid mine drainage problems and several other functions.

This progressive legislative development culminated in the federal Water Pollution Control Act Amendments of 1972, which mandated a sweeping federal-state campaign to prevent, reduce and eliminate water pollution. Two general goals were proclaimed for the United States:

- To achieve, wherever possible, by July 1, 1983, water that is clean enough for swimming and other recreational uses, and clean enough for the propagation of fish, shellfish and wildlife.
- By 1985, to have no discharges of pollutants into the nation's waters.

The goals were set within the framework of a series of specific actions that must be taken, with strict deadlines and enforcement provisions, by federal, state and local governments and by industries. While most responsibility for eliminating water pollution still resides in the states, the framework of a new national program was provided, with supervision of the states by the Environmental Protection Agency, and the federal control responsibility was extended from interstate waters to all US waters. The federal government was granted power to seek court injunctions against polluters creating health hazards or endangering livelihood, and federal aid to local governments to build sewage treatment facilities was provided.

The specifics of the 1972 amendments relate to industrial and municipal pollution, to the setting of water quality standards, to licensing discharges into the nation's waters and to the enforcement provisions.

The law set deadlines for actions to control water pollution from industrial sources:

1. Industries discharging pollutants into the nation's waters must use the "best practicable" water pollution control technology by July 1, 1977, and the "best available" technology by July 1, 1983.

2. EPA had to issue guidelines for "best practicable" and "best available" technologies for various industries by October 1973. The guidelines can be adjusted by several factors, including the cost for pollution control, the age of the industrial facility, the process used and the environmental impact (other than on water quality) of the controls. EPA also has to identify pollution control measures for completely eliminating industrial discharges.

3. After May 1974, all new sources of industrial pollution are required to use the "best available demonstrated control technology." This is defined by EPA in the form of "standards of performance" for various industries. Where practicable, EPA may require no discharge at all of pollutants from new industrial facilities.

4. Discharges of toxic pollutants are controlled by effluent standards issued by EPA in January 1974. EPA was required to provide an ample margin of safety in setting effluent standards for toxic pollutants. EPA was also empowered to prohibit discharges of toxic pollutants, in any amount, if deemed necessary. EPA had already established, under earlier water pollution control legislation, strict limits on the discharge of such toxic pollutants as lead and mercury. The new law strengthened control of toxic pollutant discharges.

5. Discharge into the nation's waters of any radiological, chemical or biological warfare materials, or high level radioactive waste was prohibited.

6. Any industry that discharges its wastes into a municipal treatment plant was required to pretreat its effluent so that the industrial pollutants do not interfere with the operation of the plant or pass through the plant without adequate treatment. This requirement was to take effect no later than May 1974 for new industrial sources of pollution, and no later than July 1976 for existing industrial facilities.

7. The law also authorized loans to help small businesses meet water pollution control requirements. The loan program is designed for firms that would be likely to suffer "substantial economic injury" unless they receive financial assistance to comply with the law. EPA was required to issue regulations for the loan program by April 1973.

The law also provided for more federal aid to local governments and set deadlines for stronger control measures:

1. Federal construction grants were authorized to reimburse local governments for treatment plants built earlier in anticipation of federal aid.

2. Federal grants were authorized to reimburse local governments for treatment plants built earlier in anticipation of federal aid.

3. In order to quality for a federal construction grant, sewage treatment plants approved before June 30, 1974, must provide a minimum of secondary treatment. After that date, federal grants may be made only to plants that will use "best practicable" treatment.

4. All sewage treatment plants in operation on July 1, 1977—whether or not built with the aid of a federal grant, and no matter when built—must provide a minimum of secondary treatment. Exception: A plant being built with the help of a federal grant that was approved before June 30, 1974, must comply with the secondary treatment requirement within four years, but no later than June 30, 1978.

5. Also by July 1, 1977, all sewage treatment plants must apply whatever additional, more stringent, effluent limitations that may be established by EPA or a state to meet water quality standards, treatment standards or compliance schedules.

6. All publicly owned waste treatment plants—whether or not built with the aid of a federal grant, and no matter when built—will have to use "best practicable" treatment by July 1, 1983.

7. Areawide waste treatment management plans are to be established by July 1976 in urban industrial areas with substantial water pollution problems. Federal grants are authorized to help areawide agencies develop and operate integrated water pollution control programs.

8. In order to be eligible for a federal construction grant after July 1976 a waste treatment plant in one of these urban industrial areas must be part of, and in conformity with, the areawide plan.

The law continued and expanded the water quality standards program initiated under earlier legislation. Water quality standards define the uses to which specific bodies of water are to be devoted—such as public water supply, propagation of fish and wildlife, recreation, and agricultural and industrial water supply—and the maximum permissible pollution levels (called "criteria") to ensure that those uses can be undertaken without damage. The standards are written so as to protect public health and welfare and to enhance water quality. The new standards program thus was established to operate as follows:

1. Water quality standards previously established by states for interstate waters, subject to EPA approval, remained in effect unless they were not consistent with the objectives of the law.

2. The states also were required to adopt water quality standards for intrastate waters and submit them to EPA for approval by April 1973. EPA was required to set standards for intrastate waters if the states failed to do so.

3. If a state found that the use of "best practicable" or "best available" controls would not be adequate to meet water quality standards, more stringent controls were to be imposed. To this end, the states were to establish the total maximum daily load of pollutants, including heat, that will not impair propagation of fish and wildlife. EPA was to identify by October 1973 pollutants for which maximum daily loads might be set.

4. EPA was required to submit a report to Congress by January 1, 1974, on the quality of the nation's waters. The report must identify bodies that, in 1973, met the standards for 1983 or any later date. The report also was to include an inventory of sources of water pollution.

5. The states were required to submit to EPA similar reports each year on the quality of bodies of water within their borders. The first report was due by January 1, 1975.

6. EPA also is required to submit the state water quality reports to Congress each year, along with its own analyses, beginning no later than October 1, 1975.

7. At least once every three years, the states must hold public hearings to review their water quality standards and, if necessary, update the standards subject to EPA approval.

The 1972 law also established a new system of permits for discharges into the nation's waters, replacing the 1899 Refuse Act permit program. No discharge of a pollutant from any point or source is permitted without a permit, and publicly owned sewage treatment plants and municipally controlled discharge points as well as industrial discharges must obtain permits. The permit program operates as follows:

1. Until March 1973, EPA, or a state with an existing permit program deemed adequate by EPA, could issue permits for discharges. State permits issued during this period were subject to EPA veto.

2. EPA had to issue guidelines for state permit programs by the end of 1972 and approve by March 1973 state permit programs that meet those guidelines.

3. After a state permit program goes into effect, EPA will retain the right, unless waived, to review and approve any permit that affects another state. EPA will also have authority, unless waived, to review proposed permits to determine if they meet the requirements of the new federal legislation.

4. A state's permit program is subject to revocation by EPA, after a public hearing, if the state fails to implement the law adequately.

5. The Army Corps of Engineers retains authority to issue permits for the disposal of dredge-and-fill material in specified disposal sites, subject to EPA veto of disposal sites if the discharge will have an adverse effect on municipal water supplies, fishery resources or recreation.

6. Disposal of sludge from sewage treatment plants into water bodies or on land where it affects water quality is prohibited except under a permit issued by EPA. After EPA establishes regulations for issuing sludge disposal permits,

a state may take over the permit program if it meets EPA requirements.

7. Anyone applying for a federal license or permit for any activity that might produce discharge into the nation's waters must obtain certification from the state involved that the discharge will be in complaince with the new law. States must give public notice of all applications for certification and may hold public hearings on certification applications.

8. If a certification by one state will result in a discharge that may affect water quality in another state, a public hearing must be held by the federal agency that issues the license or permit, if requested by the second state. If the permit or license will result in discharges that are not in compliance with water quality requirements, the license or permit cannot be issued.

The law eliminated the earlier system of abatement conferences and hearings to compel compliance with water pollution control regulations. Stringent enforcement machinery, with heavy penalties, now exists to speed compliance with the law. For example:

1. EPA has emergency power to seek an immediate court injunction to stop water pollution that poses "an imminent and substantial endangerment" to public health or that endangers someone's livelihood.

2. Polluters must keep proper records, install and use monitoring equipment, and sample their discharges.

3. EPA has the power to enter and inspect any polluting facility, to check its records and monitoring equipment, and to sample its discharges. A state may assume this authority if approved by EPA.

4. Except for trade secrets, any information obtained by EPA or a state about a polluter's discharges must be made available to the public.

5. EPA may enforce permit conditions and other requirements of the law by issuing administrative orders that are enforceable in courts, or by seeking court action.

6. The 1972 law extended the oil pollution control, liability and enforcement provisions of earlier legislation to other "hazardous substances." These are defined as substances that "present an imminent and substantial danger to the public health or welfare, including, but not limited to, fish, shellfish, wildlife, shorelines, and beaches."

7. Finally, to assist in enforcement, as well as to measure the effectiveness of the water pollution control program, a national surveillance system to monitor water quality was established by EPA in cooperation with other federal agencies and state and local governments to extend the present 20 percent coverage of the nation's streams provided in the past by the Federal Water Quality Administration, the US Geological Survey and the states into a complete monitoring and surveillance network.

Clean Air Programs

Legislative development to ensure abatement and control of air pollution lagged behind that for water but had a similar history. Despite the Donora disaster of 1948, and the emergence of the smog problem in Los Angeles in the early 1950s, federal air pollution legislation was not enacted until 1955. Prior to that date, such controls as were imposed took the form of local "smoke ordinances."

Finally in 1963, following the London "Killer Smog" of 1962 in which 700 died, Congress passed the Clean Air Act. Essentially, its enforcement procedures were the same as those developed for water pollution: a conference, hearings and court action if no abatement took place. The act also provided funds for further research into the problems of air pollution and its control and provided grants for the development of state and local air pollution control agencies.

In 1965, with the passage of the Motor Vehicle Air Pollution Control Act, the federal government recognized the need to control the procedures which resulted in the first vehicular controls in 1968.

The major thrust of federal concern for air pollution came with the passage of the Clean Air Act of 1967 which allowed for the designation of air quality control regions, either within a state or interstate. This act acuthorized the secretary of HEW (now EPA) to set air quality criteria for specified air pollutants within specific regions. The state or states set air quality standards, subject to the secretary's approval, and then provided an implementation plan, also subject to approval.

The Clean Air Amendments of 1970 instructed EPA to set air quality standards nationwide, not just within specific regions. The act also provided stricter regulations on auto exhaust emissions and stronger enforcement procedures which permit EPA, as the successor to HEW, to move with more flexibility and authority.

Pursuant to this act, primary and secondary air quality standards for ambient air in the United States were published in the April 30, 1971, *Federal Register.* These are summarized in Table 5-6. By ambient air is meant that portion of the atmosphere external to buildings, to which the general public has access. The *national primary ambient air quality standards* are the levels of air quality which the administrator of EPA judges are necessary, with an adequate margin of safety, to protect the *public health,* and they are to be achieved by 1975. The national *secondary ambient air quality standards* are the levels of air quality which the administrator judges necessary to protect the *public welfare* from any known or anticipated adverse effects of a pollutant.

Thus, the national primary standard for carbon monoxide was based on evidence that low levels of carboxyhemoglobin in human blood may be associated with impairment of ability to discriminate time intervals. Similarly, the national standards for photochemical oxidants are based upon evidence of increased frequency of asthma attacks in some asthmatic persons on days when estimated hourly concentrations of photochemical oxidant reach 200 $\mu g/m^3$ (0.10 ppm).

The act also specified that major reductions in new car emissions of hydrocarbons (HC) and carbon monoxide (CO) be achieved by 1975 and nitrogen oxides (NO_x) by 1976—subject to a one year extension by EPA if

Table 5-6. National Air Quality Standards

Pollutant	*Primary Standards*	*Secondary Standards*
Sulfur Oxides	a. 80 micrograms per cubic meter (0.03 ppm)–annual arithmetic mean. b. 365 micrograms per cubic meter (0.14 ppm)–maximum 24 hour concentration not to be exceeded more than once per year.	a. 60 micrograms per cubic meter (0.02 ppm)–annual arithmetic mean. b. 260 micrograms per cubic meter (0.1 ppm)–maximum 24 hour concentration not to be exceeded more than once per year, as a guide to be used in assessing implementation plans to achieve the annual standard. c. 1,300 micrograms per cubic meter (0.5 ppm)–maximum three hour concentration not be exceeded more than once per year.
Particulate Matter	a. 75 micrograms per cubic meter–annual geometric mean. b. 260 micrograms per cubic meter–maximum 24 hour concentration not to be exceeded more than once per year.	a. 60 micrograms per cubic meter–annual geometric mean, as a guide to be used in assessing implementation plans to achieve the 24 hour standard. b. 150 micrograms per cubic meter–maximum 24 hour concentration not to be exceeded more than once per year.
Carbon Monoxide	a. 10 milligrams per cubic meter (9 ppm)–maximum 8 hour concentration not to be exceeded more than once per year. b. 40 milligrams per cubic meter (35 ppm)–maximum one hour concentration not to be exceeded more than once per year.	
Photochemical Oxidants	160 micrograms per cubic meter (0.08 ppm) maximum one hour concentration not to be exceeded more than once per year.	
Hydrocarbons	160 micrograms per cubic meter (0.24 ppm)–maximum three hour concentration (6 to 9 A.M.) not to be exceeded more than once per year.	
Nitrogen Dioxide	100 micrograms per cubic meter (0.05 ppm)–annual arithmetic mean.	

Source: *Federal Register*, April 30, 1971.

technology is not available. The reductions in emissions were to be to the level that the Congress estimated to be necessary to achieve the health-based ambient standards even in the most heavily polluted areas of the nation (Table 5-7). There are major implications for urban transportation, particularly commuter driving habits. For 37 metropolitan areas of the United States that are especially hard hit by automotive pollution, state controls on on stationary source emissions and federal emission limits on new motor vehicles will not by themselves reduce total emissions sufficiently to meet the air quality standards for carbon monoxide, hydrocarbons and photochemical oxidants–pollutants largely attributable to motor vehicle emissions–by the statutory 1975 deadline. The affected states were therefore required to include transportation controls in their plans for achieving national air quality standards.

On June 15, 1973, pursuant to a federal court order, EPA announced its approvals and disapprovals of the 43 plans submitted by 23 states for the 37 metropolitan areas. EPA fully approved five plans–for the New York City, Rochester and Syracuse, New York; and Mobile and Birmingham, Alabama, areas. Three other plans–for Kansas City (Kansas and Missouri) and Baton Rouge, Louisiana–were approved after the period for public comment on them had expired. Ten other plans, for seven states and the District of Columbia, were generally approved but had various deficiencies, some only procedural. EPA is working with these jurisdictions–Phoenix-Tucson; Washington, D.C.; Chicago; Portland, Oregon; Philadelphia and Pittsburgh; Salt Lake City; Seattle and Spokane; and the Virginia suburbs of Washington, D.C.–to develop fully approvable plans.

To remedy more serious deficiencies, EPA intends to promulgate considerable portions of plans for nine regions in the states of Maryland–Baltimore and the suburbs of Washington, D.C.–and Texas–El Paso, Austin-Waco, Corpus Christi, Houston-Galveston, San Antonio, Beaumont and Dallas-Fort Worth. Plans for 15 regions in seven states were disapproved because the states did not submit transportation plans. These regions are Fairbanks, Alaska; Indianapolis, Indiana; Boston and Springfield, Massachusetts; Minneapolis-St. Paul; New Jersey suburbs of New York City and Philadelphia; Cincinnati, Dayton and Toledo, Ohio; and San Francisco, San Diego, Sacramento, Fresno and El Centro, California. In some of these areas, states are still working to develop and submit plans. The Denver plan was received too late to evaluate before June 15.

As required by the Clean Air Act, EPA proposed full or partial plans for 19 areas, including five of the seven states that failed to submit plans and seven of the nine regions where substantial EPA promulgation is expected.

In addition, EPA proposed a revised plan for the sprawling, smog-ridden Los Angeles

Table 5-7. Emissions Standards for Motor Vehicles 1974, 1975 and 1976 Model Years

		Exhaust Emissions			*Fuel Evaporative Emission Hydrocarbons*[1] *(HC)*	*Crankcase Emission Hydrocarbons*[1] *(HC)*
		Hydrocarbons[1] *(HC)*	*Nitrogen Oxides*[1] *(NO_x)*	*Carbon Monoxide*[1] *(CO)*		
Light Duty Gasoline-fueled	1974	3.40	3.0	39.0	2.0	0.0
	1975	1.50	3.1	15.0	2.0	0.0
	1976	0.41	2.0	3.4	2.0	0.0
Heavy Duty	1974	sum of HC and NO_X for all 3 years		40 g/BHP hours[2]		0.0
	1975	= 16 g/BHP hour		40 g/BHP hours		0.0
	1976			40 g/BHP hours		0.0

1. Grams per vehicle mile
2. BHP = braking horse power

Source: *Federal Register*, August 7, 1973, and subsequent revisions.

area in California. Responding to a court order, EPA initially proposed in January 1973 a plan that would have curtailed gasoline sales—and thus automobile use—by up to 82 percent from May to October, when the atmospheric inversions that trap pollutants in the Los Angeles basin are most prevalent. The revised proposal, adopted after extensive public hearings held by EPA, emphasizes alternatives such as mass transit and car-pooling.

There are two basic types of transportation control strategies—those which reduce miles driven, such as expanded mass transit and car-pooling; and those which reduce emissions per mile, such as inspection and maintenance programs, retrofit devices for older vehicles and changes in traffic patterns. In most cases EPA and the states have required inspection and maintenance. EPA has also emphasized changes in driving habits, particularly expanded use of public transportation. Retrofits have generally been required only as a last resort.

Buses, and particularly rapid rail transit, generate fewer emissions per passenger mile than automobiles. Thus, air quality objectives are a major stimulus for reducing automobile use in favor of mass transit. This shift also reduces urban congestion and conserves energy.

Under the law, EPA was to promulgate transportation control plans by August 15, 1973, for areas with unacceptable or inadequate state plans. However, in order to meet the 1975 statutory deadline for the Los Angeles and northern New Jersey areas, the EPA plans were forced to require such drastic curtailment of auto use by 1977 as to pose major problems for maintaining the existing way of life in these regions. The administrator of EPA therefore has announced his intention to explore with the Congress the desirability of extending the deadlines for these areas.

Control of Hazardous Substances

From the diverse spectrum of contaminants to man and the environment, environmental protection laws designate some as "hazardous" or "toxic" and set them apart from "ordinary" pollutants for special regulatory treatment. Although precise distinctions are impossible—for example, ordinary oxygen-demanding organic matter can kill fish by robbing them of oxygen—a "hazardous" pollutant is generally defined as one which can directly cause death or serious irreversible or incapacitating disease or behavioral abnormalities or carcinogenic (tending to produce cancer), teratogenic (producing monstrous growths), mutagenic (causing genetic damage), or other long term effects in man.

The federal pesticide control laws dating back to 1910 and the Atomic Energy Act of 1954 show early recognition of the need to regulate the sale or use of hazardous materials in order to protect the environment from contamination. But despite widely reported problems involving environmental exposure to hazardous substances in recent years—including mercury and lead—comprehensive legislation to regulate the many toxic substances whose manufacture and use are not covered by law still await final action.

Pesticides. More than 32,000 pesticide products, containing nearly 1,000 chemicals, are now registered for use in the United States. Of these, EPA has determined that eight residuals demand the most concerted control actions:

Organochlorines

- DDT
- Dieldrin
- Heptachlor
- Heptachlor Epoxide
- Toxaphene

Organo Phosphorus

- Parathion/Paroxon

Herbicides

- Dioxin
- Picloram

In 1972 the administrator of EPA virtually banned DDT. EPA also limited use of other persistent pesticides.

With DDT sales now prohibited, new priorities have emerged for minimizing the adverse environmental effects of pest control. The Federal Environmental Pesticide Control Act (FEPCA) became law in 1972. FEPCA substantially amended the Federal Insecticide, Fungicide and Rodenticide Act of 1947 (FIFRA). It strengthened and expanded the authorities provided by FIFRA in several respects. Most notably, it extended regulatory authorities from labeling to the use of products, authorized classification of chemicals for restricted use only, streamlined administrative procedures and extended controls to products sold only in intrastate commerce.

The old FIFRA controlled only the labeling of pesticides and restricted the registration of any chemical which, when used in conformity with label instructions, would be hazardous to man or the environment. FEPCA, in contrast, makes it unlawful for anyone (including the federal government) to use a pesticide contrary to label instructions.

Under the new act, pesticide products may be classified for "general" or "restricted" use. A restricted use pesticide may be applied only by a certified pesticide applicator—an individual trained in the application and potential effects of pesticides in an EPA-approved state program. The administrator of EPA is empowered to place whatever other constraints on restricted use pesticides he deems necessary. A general use pesticide may be applied by anyone provided the use conforms with label requirements.

Radiation. In the case of radiation, the National Academy of Sciences has recommended four bases for assessment of genetic and other risks:

- *The risk relative to the natural background radiation.* If the genetically significant exposure is kept well below this amount, we are assured that the additional consequences will be less in quantity and no different in kind from what we have experienced throughout human history. This base, although not quantitative, has the great merit that it is not necessary to make any quantitative assumptions about human radiation genetics.
- *The risk of specific genetic conditions.* Using the relative risk (or doubling dose), an estimate of the increase in diseases caused by dominant and X-chromosome-lined recessive mutations can be made for the generation following radiation and for the equilibrium increase under continuous radiation. Estimates of cytogenetic effects can be made directly from mouse data. Numerical values are given in Tables 5-8 and 5-9.
- *The risk relative to the current incidence of serious disabilities.* Diseases caused by dominant and by X-chromosome-lined recessive mutations will eventually increase in proportion to the mutation rate increase. For congenital anomalies and constitutional diseases, NAS suggested that the mutational component (or the fraction of the incidence that is proportional to the mutuation rate) is between 5 and 50 percent.
- *The risk in terms of overall ill health.* The contribution of the mutational component to ill health is arbitrarily taken as 20 percent. With this and a doubling dose between 20 and 200 rem, a dose of 5 rem per generation would eventually lead to an increase of between 0.5 and 5.0 percent in all illness.

Given these conclusions, there is now a renewed effort to reevaluate the adequacy of public protection from the effects of ionizing radiation, particularly involving the potential consequences of release of plutonium into the environment.

The NAS study estimated that in 1970 the US population was exposed to an average of approximately 182 millirems per year from all sources of radiation. The sources of this exposure were: 102 millirems from the natural background (cosmic rays from space, natural radiation in rocks and soil, etc.), 73 millirems from medical exposure (x-rays, etc.), and 4 millirems from fallout caused by atmospheric tests of nuclear weapons. Of the remaining 3 millirems, most was from miscellaneous sources (television, air travel, etc.). Occupational exposures (0.8 millirems) and exposures from nuclear powerplants (0.003 millirems) amounted to a very small fraction of the total.

The current EPA guideline for maximum acceptable whole-body exposure of average population groups to manmade sources of ionizing radiation (excluding medical and occupational exposures) is 170 millirems per year. The guideline for an individual is 500 millirems per year. The actual annual whole-body exposure experienced by average population groups from manmade sources—i.e., from fall out, nuclear power plants and certain miscellaneous sources—is less than 6 millirems, or about 3.5 percent of the 170 millirem limit.

The NAS report estimates that if over a 30 year period the population were to receive annually additional radiation up to the full 170 millirem limit permitted by current guidelines, an estimated additional 3,000 to 15,000 cancer deaths would occur annually. The most likely figure is 6,000—an increase of about 2 percent in the spontaneous cancer death rate.

Table 5-8. Estimated Effects of Radiation for Specific Genetic Damage*

	Current Incidence per Million Live Births	*Number that are New Mutants*	*Effect of 5 Rem per Generation*	
			First Generation	*Equilibrium*
Autosomal dominant traits[a]	10,000	2,000	50–5,000	250–2,500
X-chromosome-linked traits	400	65	0–15	10–100
Recessive traits	1,500	7	very few	very slow increase

Estimates of cytogenetic effects from 5 rem per generation.
Values are based on a population of one million live births.
Unbalanced rearrangements are based on male radiation only.

	Current Incidence	*Effect of 5 Rem per Generation*	
		First Generation	*Equilibrium*
Congenital anomalies			
Unbalanced rearrangements	1,000	60	75
Aneuploidy[b]	4,000	5	5
Recognized abortions			
Aneuploidy and Polyploidy[c]	35,000	55	55
XO[d]	9,000	15	15
Unbalanced rearrangements	11,000	360	450

*The range of estimates is based on doubling doses of 20 and 200 rem. The values given are the expected numbers per million live births.

[a]Autosomal dominant traits are prevailing chromosomally based traits that are not sex-related.

[b]Aneuploidy is having or being a chromosome number that is not a multiple of the monoploid number.

[c]Polyploidy is the condition of having or being a chromosome number that is a multiple greater than two of the monoploid number.

[d]XO is an X-chromosome loss.

Source: National Academy of Sciences, *The Effects on Populations of Exposure to Low Levels of Ionizing Radiation* (Washington, D.C., 1972), pp. 54, 55.

Table 5-9. Estimated Effects of 5 REM per Generation on a Population of One Million*

Disease Classification	*Current Incidence*	*Effect of 5 Rem per Generation*	
		First Generation	*Equilibrium*
Dominant diseases	10,000	50–500	250–2,500
Chromosomal and recessive diseases	10,000	Relatively slight	Very slow increase
Congenital anomalies	15,000	5–500	50–5,000
Anomalies expressed later	10,000		
Constitutional and degenerative diseases	15,000		
Total	60,000	60–1,000	100–7,500

*This includes conditions for which there is some evidence of a genetic component.

Source: National Academy of Sciences, *The Effects on Populations of Exposure to Low Levels of Ionizing Radiation* (Washington, D.C., 1972), p. 57.

The 1972 NAS study recognized that the guideline was based on "an effort to balance societal needs against genetic risks" but concluded that "it appears that these needs can be met with far lower average exposures and lower genetic and somatic risks," and thus "the current guide is unnecessarily high." EPA is reviewing the NAS recommendations and will use them as the basis for an expected revision of environmental standards.

Noise Control

Noise affects all urban residents—in factories, in offices, near construction sites, at places of recreation and even at home. It was long accepted as a necessary though sometimes unpleasant part of living. Now it is regarded as a controllable pollutant which should be regulated. Early municipal ordinances prohibited noise considered excessively or unreasonably loud. They focused on auto horns, steamboat whistles, radio loudspeakers and sound trucks. In more recent years, as instruments for quantitative measurement of noise have been developed, precise numerical limits have replaced general restrictions in noise control regulations.

The first federal legislation expressly aimed at controlling noise was the 1968 amendment to the 1958 Federal Aviation Act. It gave the administrator of the Federal Aviation Adminstration authority to prescribe standards for measuring and controlling civilian aircraft noise and sonic boom. Pursuant to this authority, the FAA established noise emission standards for all new types of nonmilitary subsonic jet aircraft.

A broader base for control was provided by the Noise Control Act of 1972. This act called for extensive federal regulation of major noise sources, pre-empting to some extent state and local controls. The resulting interplay among the levels of government will be an important feature in the success of noise control efforts in future years. The Noise Control Act directed the Environmental Protection Agency to conduct a thorough study and report to the Congress by July 27, 1973, on the aircraft and airport noise problem, including assessment of current FAA flight and operational noise controls; noise emission controls and possibilities for retrofitting or phasing out existing aircraft; possibilities for establishing cumulative noise level limits around airports; and control measures available to airport operators, who were directed to propose for adoption by the FAA any regulations on aircraft noise and sonic boom necessary to protect public health and welfare.

The act also contained special provisions requiring EPA to establish noise emission limits for the operation of railroads and motor carriers engaged in interstate commerce and directing the Department of Transportation to issue regulations ensuring compliance. The EPA regulations will supplement those which may be adopted for new trucks, buses and railroad equipment. The act prohibited state and local regulation of noise from these sources unless it is identical to federal standards, unless there are special local conditions which are determed by EPA not to conflict with its regulations.

The EPA-DOT/FAA authorities for regulating transportation noise sources are part of a broader mandate under the Noise Control Act to set emission standards for new products which are major noise sources and for which standards are feasible—construction equipment; transportation equipment, including any in which an engine or motor is an integral part; and electric or electronic equipment. The administrator of EPA was to promulgate initial noise limits for products in these categories by October 1974. He has discretionary authority to regulate any other product whose noise may endanger public health or welfare.

Solid Wastes Disposal

The solid waste problem is really a series of problems related to the staggering volume of products and other objects discarded after use. Solid wastes range from newspapers and grapefruit rinds to abandoned automobiles and demolition debris. Solid wastes pose potential pollution problems such as ground water leachate from land dumps and air emissions from incinerators. They create aesthetic eyesores such as litter on roads and in parks and the blight of open dumps. They can create resource depletion problems because of the failure to recover waste materials whose reuse can perpetuate reserves of such virgin resources as timber and iron ore. And for municipalities that spend about $5 billion each year for collection, processing and disposal, solid wastes are a major financial problem.

Since the Solid Waste Disposal Act of 1965, the federal government has helped communities find new solutions for their solid waste problems through research, analysis, demonstration of new technology and technical assistance. Although the solid waste problem remains significant, the impact of EPA's efforts over the past few years is now being felt and can be expected to increase as more communities and states adopt new techniques.

The Resources Recovery Act of 1970 added new facets to the earlier Solid Waste Disposal Act of 1965, including not only solid waste "disposal" but also solid waste "recovery" and "recycling." This addition stipulated that special studies and demonstration projects be undertaken to determine means of recovering materials and energy from solid wastes. The act also provided for grants to promote areawide solid waste planning by cities and states, including methods for collecting, separating and disposing of trash; to train personnel of all kinds; and to build new, state-of-the-art, solid waste facilities for recycling or recovering energy or material resources.

For the most part, urban solid waste has been viewed as a local or regional problem, however, and the federal role has been to identify and test possible solutions, with implementation generally resting with state and local governments. Accordingly, the administration has proposed to reduce federal spending for solid wastes.

POLLUTION: NATURE, INTENSITY AND INCIDENCE

With this elaborate legislative and administrative arsenal now available, what exactly is the nature of the pollution problem that federal, state and local governments are combating in metropolitan America? The concerns of EPA—air, water, noise, solid wastes, pesticides and radiation—will be addressed turn and salient features of their spatial variations both between and within metropolitan regions will be indicated.

Air Pollution

Air pollutants consist of gases, liquids or solid particulates. The following list covers all the pollutants currently measured in some way by the Environmental Protection Agency:

Gases: carbon monoxide, methane, nitric oxide, nitrogen oxide, pesticides, reactive hydrocarbons, sulfur oxides, total hydrocarbons, total oxidants.

Elements: antimony, arsenic, barium, beryllium, bismuth, boron, cadmium, chromium, cobalt, copper, iron, lead, manganese, mercury, molybdenum, nickel, selenium, tin, titanium, vanadium, zinc.

Radicals: ammonium, fluoride, nitrate, sulfate.

Others: aeroallergens, asbestos, β-radioactivity, benzene-soluble organic compounds, benzo [a] pyrene, pesticides, respirable particulates, total suspended particulates.

In 1973, EPA selected ten from this array as being of special concern because of their adverse health effects, widespread use, production in large quantities or their toxicity. These ten, to be the objects of the most concerted attack of EPA in the years ahead, are arsenic, asbestos, beryllium, cadmium, fluorides, lead, mercury, carbon monoxide, nitrogen oxides and sulfur oxides.

The principal sources of these pollutants—whose locational patterns are the basis of the spatial distribution of air pollution—are noted in Table 5-10: *stationary point sources* such as power stations and factories; *mobile line sources* such as the automobile; and *areawide sources* such as domestic space heating. Little wonder, then, that pollution increases with city size, as is shown by the regression analyses summarized in Table 5-11, or that the nature and size of industrial concentrations loom large in emissions inventories, as indicated by the data for Philadelphia presented in Figures 5-5 and 5-6.

The broad spatial pattern of pollution within metropolitan regions is one of distance-decay with respect to the city center (Figures 5-7 to 5-9); however, detailed analysis of ambient air quality levels reveals substantial local variability related to local industrial concentrations. For example, Figures 5-10 and 5-11 show that the Gary (Indiana) heavy industrial complex alone is a major polluter in the metropolitan Chicago region.

To what extent are the urban environments illustrated in these maps substandard? Refer back to Table 5-6. Eighty micrograms of sulfur oxides per cubic meter (0.03 ppm annual geometric mean) has been set as the federal primary standard to protect the public health. For particulate matter the primary standard is 75 $\mu g/m^3$ (annual geometric mean). Table 5-5 records ratios of actual pollution levels to the primary standards for ten of the nation's largest metropolitan regions for 1967-1972, using information provided by the newly instituted National Air Sampling Network. Improvements are being made (as Figures 5-5 and 5-6 show for Philadelphia, too), but many serious health hazards still remain in many cities.

The citywide ratios of Table 5-5 should not be taken too literally, however, because they tend to mask important intraurban differences even in metropolitan areas where the index suggests that primary standards have been

Table 5-10. Estimated Emissions of Air Pollutants, by Weight Nationwide 1971 (in million tons per year)[1 2]

Source	*CO*	*Particulates*	SO_2	*HC*	NO_x
Transportation	77.5	1.0	1.0	14.7	11.2
Fuel combustion in stationary sources	1.0	6.5	26.3	.3	10.2
Industrial processes	11.4	13.6	5.1	5.6	.2
Solid waste disposal	3.8	.7	.1	1.0	.2
Miscellaneous	6.5	5.2	.1	5.0	.2
Total	100.2	27.0	32.6	26.6	22.0
Percent change 1970 to 1971[1]	-.5	+5.9	-2.4	-2.3	0

[1]Figures for 1971 are not comparable to those for 1970 published in the 1970 report because of changed methods of calculation. Percent change 1970 to 1971 was calculated using 1970 figures computed on the 1971 basis. The most significant difference from the previous calculations was the use of automobile emission factors based on the 1975 federal test procedures, as opposed to the previously used 1972 test procedures. The new method results in much lower estimates of automobile emissions.

[2]The table does not include data on photochemical oxidants because they are secondary pollutants formed by the action of sunlight on nitrogen oxides and hydrocarbons and thus are not emitted from sources on the ground.

Source: Environmental Protection Agency

Table 5-11. Regression Relationships Between Pollutant Concentrations and City Size, 1969-1970

Class Number and Population Class	*Concentration* TSP^a	SO^2	NO^2	*Number of Sites*
1. Nonurban	25	10	33	5
2. Urban < 10,000	57	35	116	2
3. 10,000	81	18	64	2
4. 25,000	87	14	63	2
5. 50,000	118	29	127	9
6. 100,000	95	26	114	37
7. 400,000	100	28	127	17
8. 700,000	101	29	146	9
9. 1,000,000	134	69	163	2
10. 3,000,000	120	85	153	2
Slope	9.152	6.103	12.109	
Intercept	41.467	0.733	44.000	
r^2	0.748	0.590	0.719	
t statistic	4.874	3.392	4.526	

[a]TSP: Total suspended particulates.

Source: The Mitre Corp., MTR-6013, p. 70. Time span—second half of 1969, first half of 1970. Cited in Council on Environmental Quality, *Environmental Quality, Second Annual Report*, Washington, D.C., 1971, pp. 215 and 243.

Regressions: Pollutant concentration on population class number (1 through 10).

met. Inspection of Figures 5-10 and 5-11 reveals, for example, that substantial parts of the Chicago region failed to meet the primary health standards in 1970, exposing much of the region's population to substantial health hazards, as well as imposing economic costs.

What is the nature of these health hazards and welfare losses? Sulfur dioxide can irritate the upper respiratory tract. If it is absorbed on particulate matter, or if it is converted into sulfuric acid, it can be carried deep into the lungs, where it can injure delicate tissue. Pro-

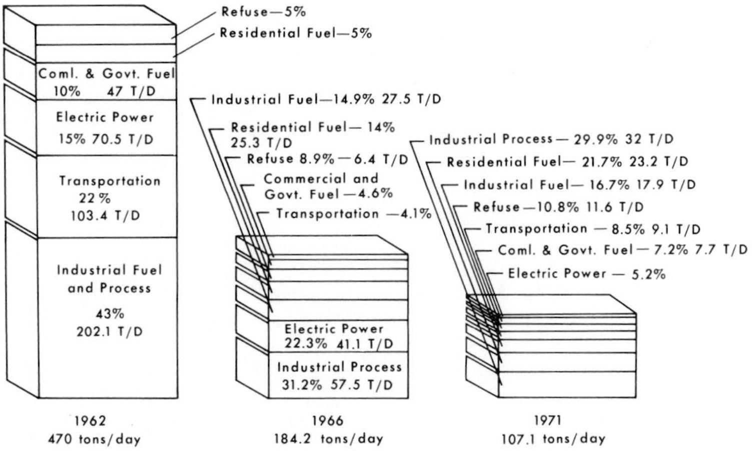

Figure 5-5. Emissions of Particulates in Philadelphia, 1962-1971

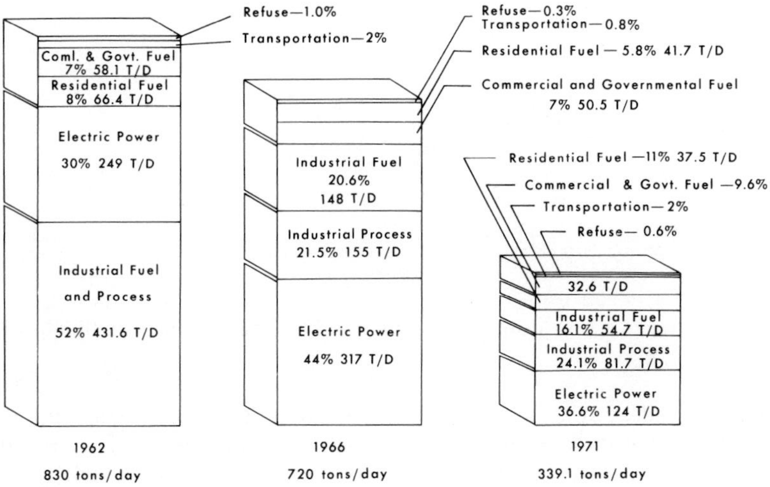

Figure 5-6. Emissions of Sulfur Dioxide in Philadelphia, 1962-1971

longed exposure to relatively low levels of sulfur dioxide has been associated with an increase in the number of deaths from cardiovascular disease in older persons. Prolonged exposure to higher concentrations has been associated with an increase in respiratory death rates and an increase in complaints by schoolchildren of cough, mucous membrane irritation and mucous secretion. Very heavy concentrations of sulfur oxides—as in the four day October 1948 air disaster in Donora, Pennsylvania—cause cough, sore throat, chest constriction, headache, a burning sensation of the eyes, nasal discharge and vomiting. During the year following the disaster, 20 people died in Donora, where the normal mortality would have been two.

Sulfur oxides attack and destroy even the most durable of materials. Steel corrodes two to four times faster in urban and industrial areas than it does in rural areas, where much less sulfur-bearing coal and oil are burned. Sulfur pollution also destroys zinc, silver and palladium (used in electrical contacts), paint pigments and fresh paint (thus delaying drying), nylon hose (which can be destroyed during a

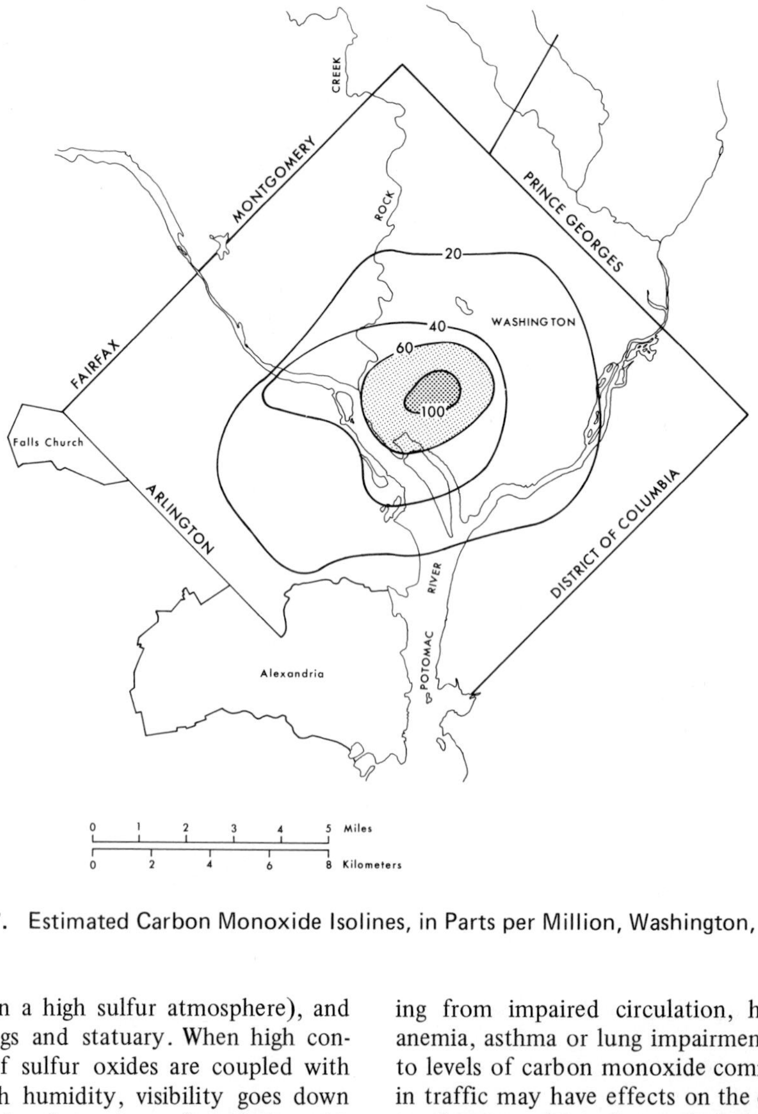

Figure 5-7. Estimated Carbon Monoxide Isolines, in Parts per Million, Washington, D.C., 1964

lunch hour in a high sulfur atmosphere), and stone buildings and statuary. When high concentrations of sulfur oxides are coupled with relatively high humidity, visibility goes down because of the formation of sulfuric acid, which scatters light. Reduced visibility is a hazard to land, water and air transportation.

Similarly, when carbon monoxide enters the bloodstream, it interferes with the ability of the blood to transport oxygen, thus impairing the functioning of the central nervous system. At high concentrations it kills quickly. If CO concentrations reach 100 parts per million parts of air (100 ppm), most people experience dizziness, headache, lassitude and other symptoms of poisoning. Concentrations higher than this occasionally occur in garages, in tunnels or behind automobiles in heavy traffic. Exposure to 30 ppm for eight hours or 120 ppm for one hour may be a serious risk to the health of sensitive people (those suffering from impaired circulation, heart disease, anemia, asthma or lung impairment). Exposure to levels of carbon monoxide commonly found in traffic may have effects on the driver similar to those resulting from alcohol or fatigue—reduced alertness and a decrease in the ability to respond properly in a complex situation, with resultant impairment of driving ability. Susceptibility to carbon monoxide poisoning is increased by high temperature, high altitude, high humidity and the use of alcoholic beverages or certain drugs, such as tranquilizers.

Long term low concentration levels of exposure to chemicals which cause relatively little irritation, discomfort or odor also involve serious health hazards. Certain environmental chemicals, for example, affect DNA by causing alterations in the sequence of purine and pyrimidine bases along the DNA strand or helix. Such alterations in the genetic code involve alterations in the cell genotype which often result

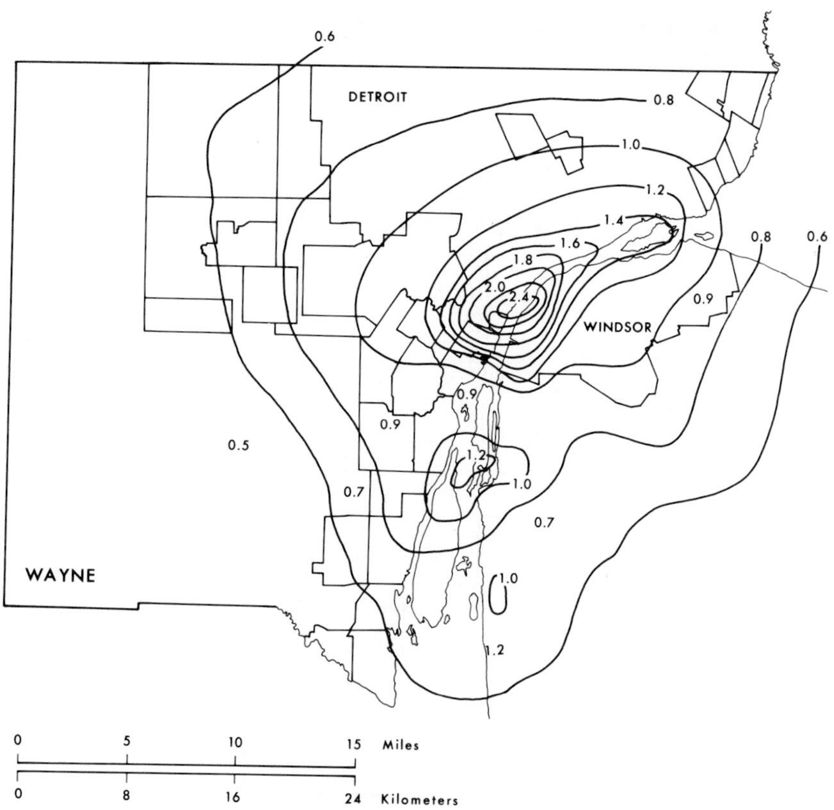

Figure 5-8. Average Annual SO_3 Rates (in Parts per Million) in the Detroit-Windsor Region

in changes in cell phenotype. Little wonder, then, that statistical studies reveal significant statistical relationships between concentrations of a number of environmental chemicals—mostly atmospheric—and mortality rates for several categories of cancer, heart disease and certain congenital malformations in the US. These significant relationships remain when effects of age, sex and race are taken into account.

Beyond these health effects, there are also the welfare effects recognized by the promulgation of the secondary standards noted in Table 5-6. Theoretically, these effects should be reflected in property values. Given well-functioning markets, the price of any capital asset should be the present value of the anticipated stream of net benefits over the asset's useful life. If air pollution reduces the benefits or utility derived from a property, or if it increases the costs associated with it (e.g., cleaning, maintenance), the market price should reflect these changes in capitalized value.

Empirical studies do indeed show that air quality differentials are associated with property value differentials, holding other factors that influence property values—primarily char-

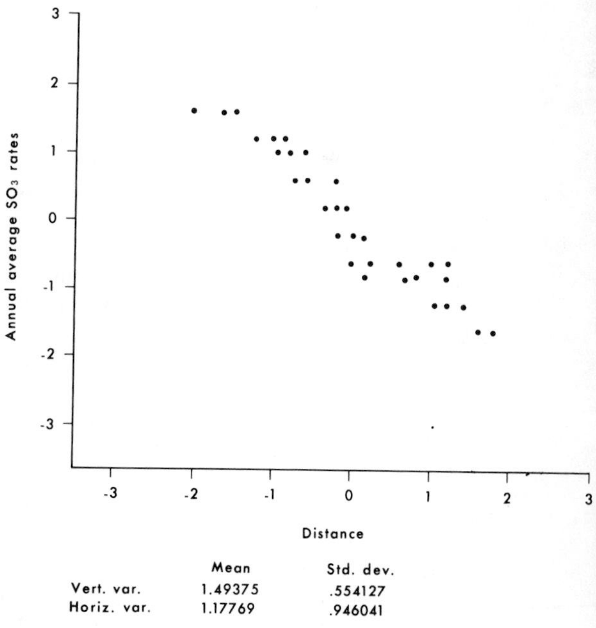

Figure 5-9. Standardized Distribution of Average Annual SO_3 Rates in Detroit on Log of Distance from CBD

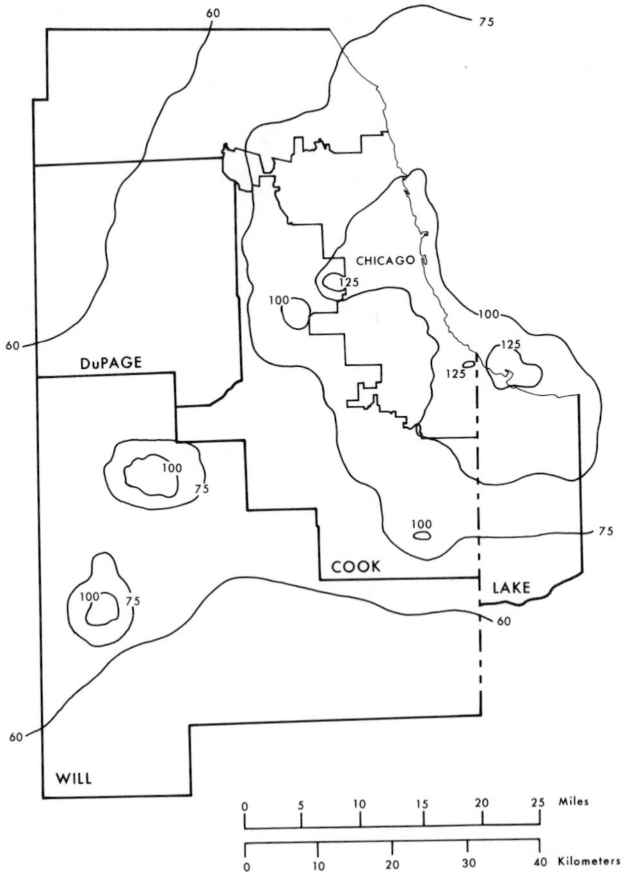

Figure 5-10. Particulate Air Quality Levels in 1970, in Total Suspended Particulates

acteristics of the property, improvements to it, its location and the nature of the surrounding neighborhood—constant. Roughly, a doubling of particulate or sulfation levels results in a 10 to 12 percent decrease in property values. Thus, air quality improvements should produce substantial net benefits.

Who bears the greatest health and welfare burden today, and who is this most likely to benefit from any improvements made? Data from selected cities indicate that the urban poor are subjected to somewhat higher than average pollution levels. Figure 5-12 shows this relationship for three cities. But these data refer only to ambient air pollution levels at the place of residence and thus do not take into account two important factors affecting the real incidence of the pollution. The first factor is that the more wealthy, living in their air-conditioned homes, cars and offices, avoid some of the pollution. The second, which partially offsets the first, is that medium and higher income people commonly commute from their suburban homes to their jobs in the more polluted central city and therefore are exposed to more pollution than these data, which refer only to location of residence, would indicate. We must also remember that the more wealthy have to pay for their efforts to avoid pollution. Air-conditioning and commuting from the suburbs both cost something. The wealthy may on the average be exposed to less severe pollution but at higher avoidance costs. Thus, while the poor may benefit most from the health effects of better quality urban air, the more affluent may receive the greater welfare effects because their avoidance expenditures will be reduced.

Achievement of these benefits will require continued efforts and vigilance. For example, EPA has estimated that only if 1975 vehicular standards are achieved on schedule will it be

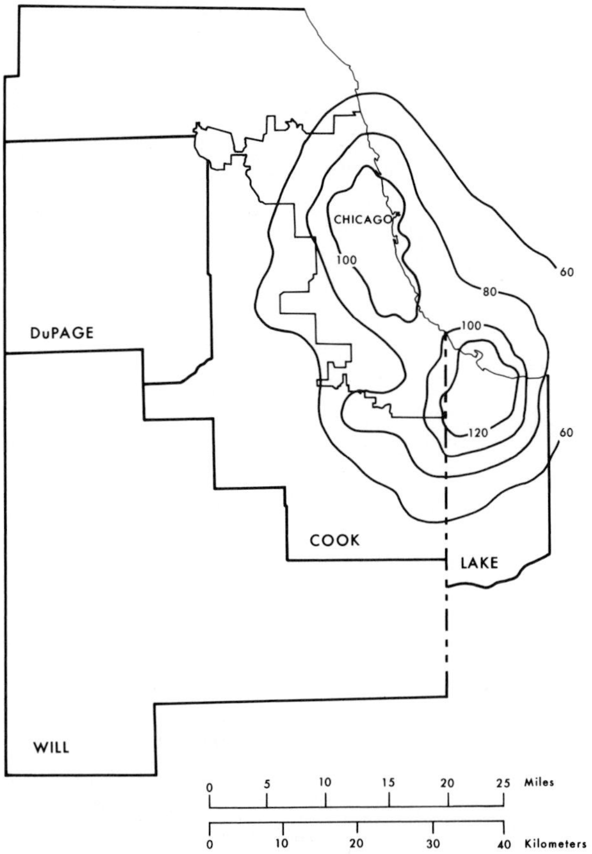

Figure 5-11. Sulfur Dioxide Air Quality Levels in 1970, in Parts per Million

possible to control the growth of pollution from transportation sources (Figures 5-13 and 5-14). Likewise, very strict control of sulfur in fuels will be necessary to achieve primary sulfur dioxide standards by 1975 in the Chicago region (Figure 5-15); a simple ban on burning coal would leave a significantly substandard condition around the steel mills in Northern Indiana (Figure 5-16). Yet it is exactly with respect to such required strategies that plans to improve environmental quality run headlong into the nation's energy crisis, with trade-offs that have yet to be negotiated.

Water Pollution

The committee on pollution of the National Academy of Sciences has classified water pollutants into eight categories:

- domestic sewage and other oxygen-demanding wastes;
- infectious agents;
- plant nutrients, particularly nitrogen and phosphorus;
- organic chemical exotics, particularly insecticides, pesticides and detergents;
- other mineral and chemical substances from industrial, mining and agricultural operations;
- sediments from land erosion;
- radioactive substances; and
- heat.

Table 5-12 gives more details regarding each. In the committee's words, "all these with the possible exception of the fifth and sixth on the list, are being produced largely within the large metropolitan complexes that generally are located along the coasts or the main stems of the rivers," thus confirming a publication of the US Geological Survey that summarized water data for United States metropolitan areas

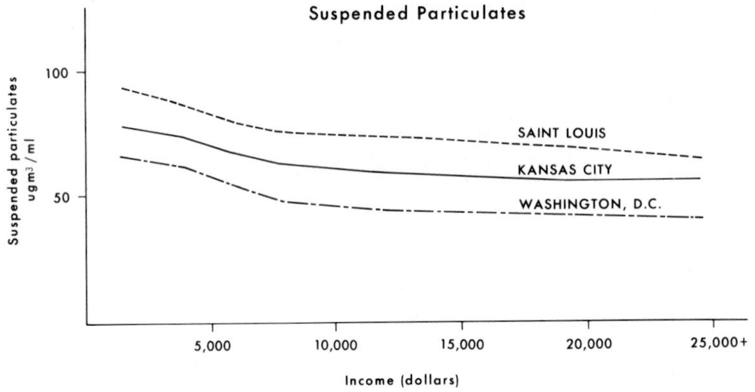

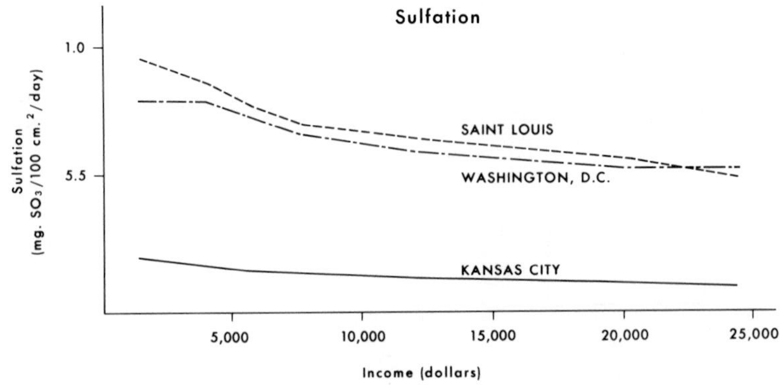

Figure 5-12. Incidence of Air Pollution in Three Cities

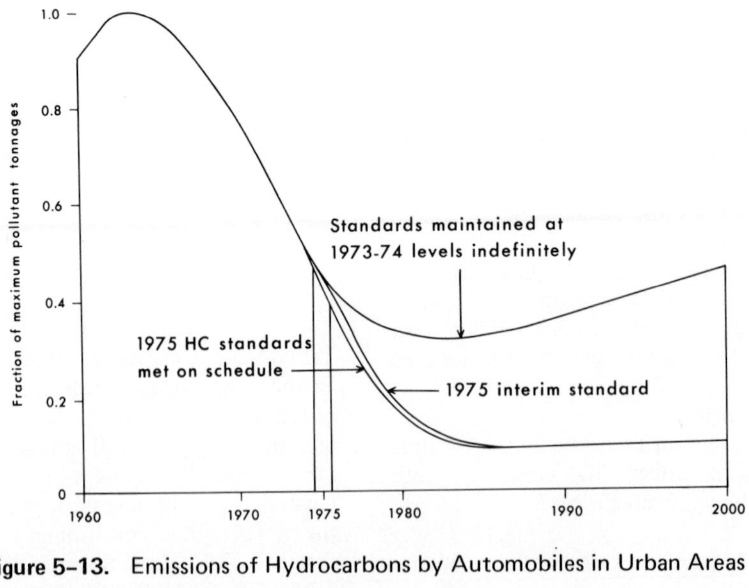

Figure 5-13. Emissions of Hydrocarbons by Automobiles in Urban Areas

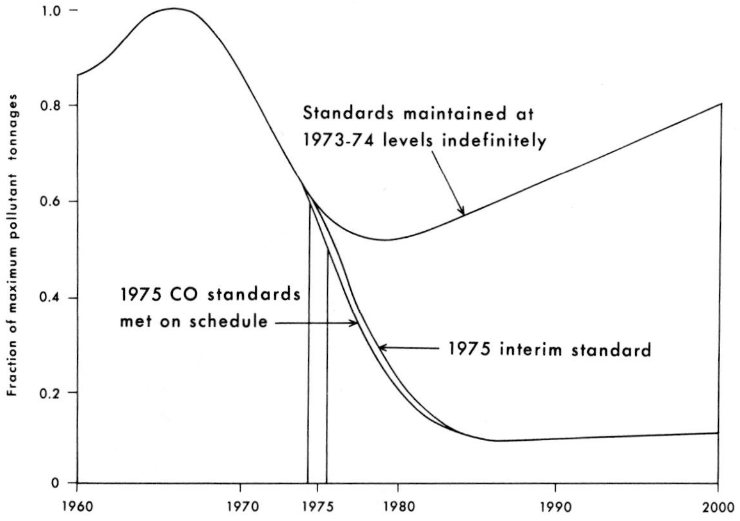

Figure 5-14. Emissions of Carbon Monoxide by Automobiles in Urban Areas

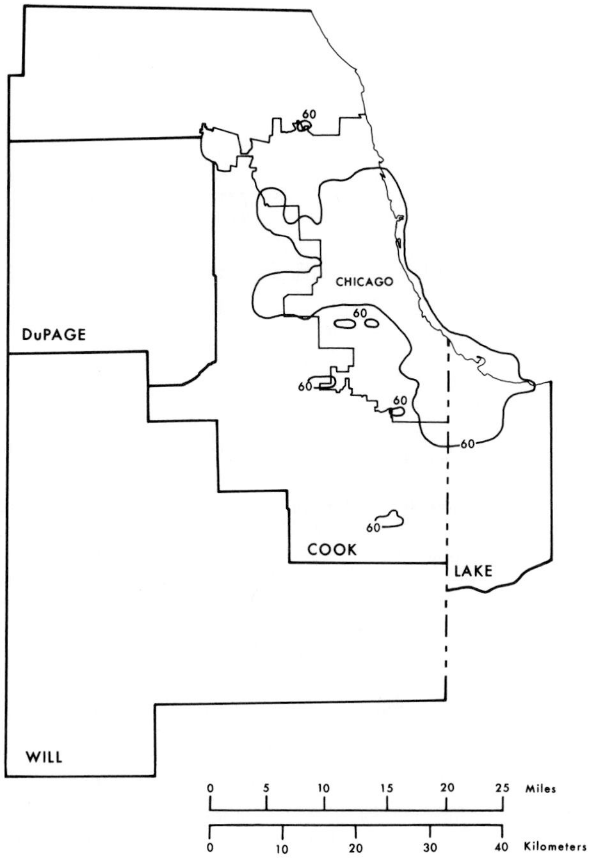

Figure 5-15. Forecasted Particulate Air Quality Levels in 1975 with a 1 percent Sulfur Law for Residential and Commercial Sources

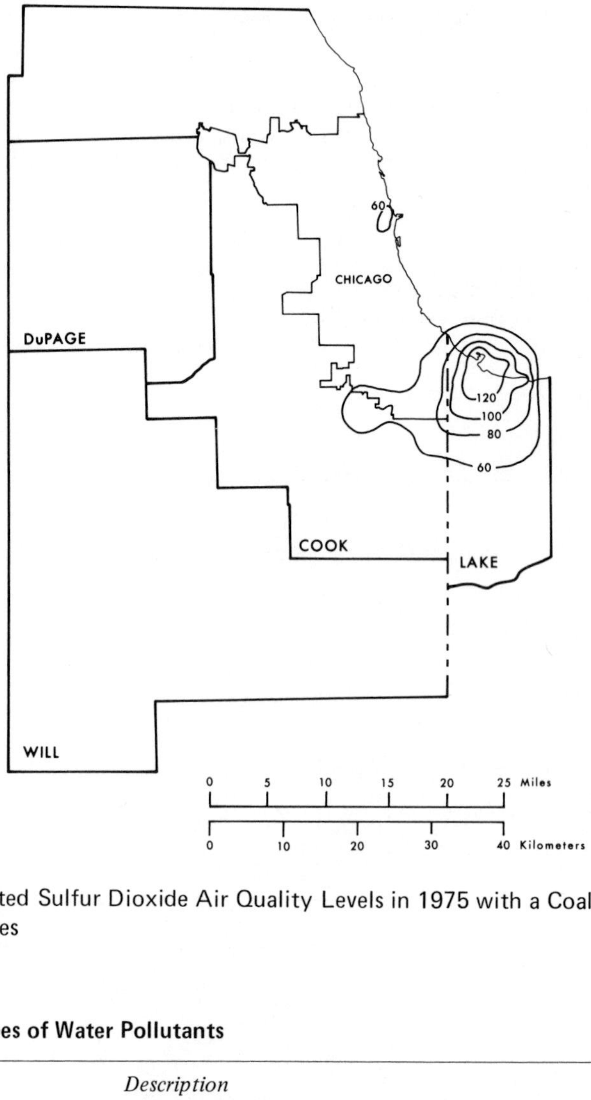

Figure 5-16. Forecasted Sulfur Dioxide Air Quality Levels in 1975 with a Coal Ban for Residential and Commercial Sources

Table 5-12. Types of Water Pollutants

Pollutant	*Description*
Oxygen-Demanding Wastes	These are the traditional organic wastes and ammonia contributed by domestic sewage and industrial wastes of plant and animal origin. Besides human sewage, such wastes result from food processing, paper mill production, tanning, and other manufacturing processes. These wastes are usually destroyed by bacteria if there is sufficient oxygen present in the water. Since fish and other aquatic life depend on oxygen for life, the oxygen-demanding wastes must be controlled, or the fish die.
Disease-Causing Agents	This category includes infectious organisms which are carried into surface and ground water by sewage from cities and institutions, and by certain kinds of industrial wastes, such as tanning and meat packing plants. Man or animals come in contact with these microbes either by drinking the water or through swimming, fishing, or other activities.
Plant Nutrients	These are the substances in the food chain of aquatic life, such as algae and water weeds, which support and stimulate their growth. Carbon, nitrogen and phosphorus are the three chief nutrients present in natural water. Large amounts of these nutrients are produced by sewage, certain industrial wastes, and drainage from fertilized lands. Biological waste treatment processes do not remove the phosphorus and nitrogen to any substantial

continued

Table 5-12 continued

Pollutant	*Description*
Plant nutrients, continued	extent–in fact, they convert the organic forms of these substances into mineral form, making them more usable by plant life. The problem starts when an excess of these nutrients over-stimulates the growth of water plants which cause unsightly conditions, interferes with treatment processes, and causes unpleasant and disagreeable tastes and odors in the water.
Synthetic Organic Chemicals	Included in this category are detergents and other household aids, all the new synthetic organic pesticides, synthetic industrial chemicals, and the wastes from their manufacture. Many of these substances are toxic to fish and aquatic life and possibly harmful to humans. They cause taste and other problems, and resist conventional waste treatment. Some are known to be highly poisonous at very low concentrations. What the long-term effects of small doses of toxic substances may be is not yet known.
Inorganic Chemicans and Mineral Substances	A vast array of metal salts, acids, solid matter, and many other chemical compounds are included in this group. They reach our waters from mining and manufacturing processes, oil field operations, agricultural practices, and natural sources. Water used for irrigation picks up large amounts of minerals as it filters down through the soil on its way to the nearest stream. Acids of a wide variety are discharged as wastes by industry, but the largest single source of acid in our water comes from mining operations and mines that have been abandoned. Many of these types of chemicals are being created each year. They interfere with natural stream purification; destroy fish and other aquatic life; cause excessive hardness of water supplies; corrode expensive water treatment equipment; increase commercial and recreational boat maintenance costs; and boost the cost of waste treatment.
Sediments	These are the particles of soils, sands, and minerals washed from the land and paved areas of communities into the water. Construction projects are often large sediment producers. While not as insidious as some other types of pollution, sediments are a major problem because of the sheer magnitude of the amount reaching our waterways. Sediments fill stream channels and harbors, requiring expensive dredgings, and they fill reservoirs, reducing their capacities and useful life. They erode power turbines and pumping equipment, and reduce fish and shellfish populations by blanketing fish nests and food supplies. More importantly, sediments reduce the amount of sunlight penetrating the water. The sunlight is required by green aquatic plants which produce the oxygen necessary to normal stream balance. Sediments greatly increase the treatment costs for municipal and industrial water supply and for sewage treatment where combined sewers are in use.
Radioactive Substances	Radioactive pollution results from the mining and processing of radioactive areas; from the use of refined radioactive materials in power reactors and for industrial, medical, and research purposes; and from fallout following nuclear weapons testing. Increased use of these substances poses a potential public health problem. Since radiation accumulates in humans, control of this type of pollution must take into consideration total exposure in the human environment–water, air, food, occupation, and medical treatment.
Heat	Heat reduces the capacity of water to absorb oxygen. Tremendous volumes of water are used by power plants and industry for cooling. Most of the water, with the added heat, is returned to streams, raising their temperatures. With less oxygen, the water is not as efficient in assimilating oxygen-consuming wastes and in supporting fish and aquatic life. Unchecked waste heat discharges can seriously alter the ecology of a lake, a stream, or even part of the sea. Water in lakes or stored in impoundments can be greatly affected by heat. Summer temperatures heat up the surfaces, causing the water to form into layers, with the cooler water forming the deeper layers. Decomposing vegetative matter from natural and man-made pollutants depicts the oxygen from these cooler lower layers with harmful effects on the aquatic life. When the oxygen-deficient water is discharged from the lower gates of a dam, it may have serious effects on downstream fish life and reduce the ability of the stream to assimilate downstream pollution.

Source: National Academy of Sciences, National Research Council. *Waste Management and Control.* Washington, D.C., 1966.

Table 5-13. The Incidence of Water Pollution Problems for Metropolitan Areas, 1965

Metropolitan Area Population Size in 000	*Total Number of Areas in Group*	*Areas with Pollution Problem*	*Fraction with Pollution Problem*
< 100	21	8	0.381
100-< 250	78	46	0.590
250-< 500	56	35	0.625
500-< 1000	35	25	0.714
1000-< 2500	22	17	0.773
> 2500	7	6	0.857

Source: William J. Schneider, *Water Data for Metropolitan Areas*, Paper 1871 (U.S. Geological Survey, 1968). A metropolitan area was counted as having a pollution problem whenever the source stated there was a problem with municipal-industrial waste disposal, or that waters were polluted.

as of 1965. This report contained a discussion of water problems for each area including water pollution where this was a problem. Counting the number of instances of a water pollution problem and classifying by population size indicates that the problem becomes more serious with size of metropolitan area, as shown in Table 5-13.

The principal sources of water pollutants are industrial and municipal waste discharges. More than 300,000 domestic water-using factories discharge three to four times as much oxygen-demanding wastes—many toxic—as all the sewered population of the United States (Table 5-14), with the regional distribution shown in Table 5-15. To add to this volume of effluents, less than one-third of the nation's population is served by a system of sewers and an adequate treatment system. The greatest municipal waste problems exist in the areas with the heaviest concentrations of population, particularly in the Northeast.

Availability of a municipal sewage treatment plant does not guarantee that pollutant discharges be eliminated. Treatment of sewage is classified as primary, secondary or tertiary. In primary treatment, the most common form, sewage is stored temporarily in tanks and heavier suspended solids settle into sludge. The liquid is poured off into waterways and the sludge is carted away. Approximately 50 percent of suspended solids and 35 percent of associated biochemical oxygen demand (BOD) are removed by this process. Secondary treatment is biological: bacteria feed on the organic wastes in the effluent from the primary treatment. The effluent here is again allowed to settle. About 85 to 90 percent of suspended solids and BOD are removed. Tertiary treatment is a generic term applied to more advanced processes which are used to obtain a still greater percentage of suspended solid and BOD removal or to obtain improved removal of nutrients (nitrogen and phosphorus), which

Table 5-14. Industrial Wastewater Discharge by Type of Industry

Industry	*Total Industrial Wastewater Discharges, 1968 (Billions of Gallons)*	*Waste Concentration of Process Water (in ppm)—Where Available*		
		BOD	*COD*	*Suspended Solids*
Food and Kindred Products	752.8	87	114	703
Textile Mill Products	136.0	804	327	70
Lumber	92.7	–	–	–
Paper	2077.6	336	3565	388
Chemicals	4175.1	130	378	225
Petroleum and Coal	1217.0	52	210	76
Rubber	128.4	17	57	30
Leather	14.9	–	–	–
Stone, Clay and Glass	218.4	–	–	–
Primary Metals	4695.5	18	80	259
Fabricated Metals	65.0	–	–	–
Machinery	180.8	–	–	–
Electrical Equipment	118.4	–	–	–
Transportation Equipment	293.1	–	–	–

Source: Conference Board Survey of 800 manufacturing establishments.

are not handled well by the standard primary plus secondary treatment. Tertiary treatment is expensive and thus is rare. The addition of tertiary treatment can increase costs to two or three times the average. On all levels, national sewage treatment needs remain high. As Table 5-16 shows, the per capita dollar costs of bringing sewage treatment to secondary levels on a national basis remain substantial, while tertiary treatment costs are very high.

When do waterborne effluents constitute pollution? The determining factor is the use to which the water is to be put, and the standards that have to be met to ensure that use. In 1968 the Federal Water Pollution Control Administration issued a set of standards for public water supplies (Table 5-17). Using these standards, EPA determined that in 1970, of 678 cities (with 81 million population) surveyed, 81 had some public water supply problem (Table 5-18). The occurrence of only 19 cities under Problem III, with 12 of those having a population less than 25,000, lends support to the argument that health problems with public water supplies in the United States are relatively minor. Such trouble as occurs arises most frequently in small cities.

As noted earlier, the Clean Water Amendments of 1972 set as national goals the elimination of pollutant discharges into the nation's waters and the achievement by 1983 of water that is clean enough for swimming and other recreational uses and for the propagation of fish, shellfish and wildlife. Yet, in contrast to air pollution, the setting of water quality standards to ensure achievement of these goals remains a responsibility of the states. Table 5-19 is an attempt to draw together the standards of the state of Washington for three different use groupings for both fresh and marine waters.

Using standards such as these for the state of Washington, EPA has attempted to assess the prevalence, duration and intensity of water pollution in each of the nation's major drainage areas, correcting for natural background pollutant levels and taking into account the flow characteristics of the water sources for which it is computed. Table 5-20 summarizes the EPA data. Unfortunately, of the four apparently significant shifts in reported water pollution that took place—in the Ohio, Gulf, Missouri and Northeastern basins—three are so obscured by variations in procedure that it is impossible to evaluate the degree of real change. Both the Gulf and Missouri basins reported an enormous improvement in compliance with state water quality standards, but the apparent improvement between 1970 and 1971 is almost certainly due to more accurate reporting, not to better water. In the case of the Ohio River Basin, the 1970 assessment overlooked a large number of smaller tributaries which were polluted. The last column of Table 5-20 shows a duration-intensity factor for the 1971 figures. Whereas the prior columns simply indicate what portion of the stream was polluted, the duration-intensity factor indicates how badly polluted it was and for how long during the year it was in violation of the standards. To obtain a prevalence duration-intensity index, the number of polluted stream miles is multiplied by the duration-intensity factor. Thus the higher the factor is, the worse the pollution.

Effluent discharges occur at points on a hydrologic network (Figure 5-17). If a detailed network of monitoring sites is available (the US Geological Survey, in cooperation with EPA, has established a national stream quality accounting network for periodic assessment of stream quality based on continuing measurements), it is possible to pinpoint both local and widespread pollution concentrations and to study their spatial pattern. In its January 1974 report to Congress required under the terms of the Clean Water Amendments of 1972, EPA has analyzed ten of the 20 major rivers in the US in this way, after testing the technique on a short stretch of the Detroit River, where water samples were taken regularly at 41 sites between 1967 and 1969. These are more data than are likely to be available on most rivers, because the Detroit River has been intensely monitored as part of a cooperative effort with Canada to control pollution entering Lake Erie. The data are obviously somewhat out of date, but they were used because the analytical technique could be readily applied. Although quite crude, the analysis shows that over the distance of just a few miles there can be large differences in pollution levels.

The major waste sources in the area are clustered along the banks of the Detroit River. They include steel and chemical manufacturers, a large municipal sewage discharge on the lower river and a large number of combined sewer overflows from Detroit. Smaller concentrations

Table 5-15. Regional Incidence of Industrial Waste Discharge, by Major Industrial Sectors, 1968; Percentage of Discharge of Industry's Wastewater, by Industrial Water Use Region

	Regionally Assignable Discharge	*New Eng.*	*Del. & Hud.*	*Chesa. Bay*	*East. Gr. Lak. St. Law.*	*Ohio Riv.*	*Tenn. Cum.*
Meat Products	99.0	.5	4.2	2.7	1.0	8.6	1.5
Dairy Products	98.8	7.5	4.3	4.9	8.9	5.1	.6
Canned & Frozen Foods	93.1	1.4	3.2	2.5	3.9	2.3	D
All Other Food Products	84.4	3.7	5.9	.7	1.0	4.0	.2
Textile Mill Products	98.5	13.5	4.7	2.9	.5	2.4	6.3
Paper & Allied Products	98.7	11.9	3.3	4.9	3.2	2.4	3.1
Chemical & Allied Products	99.0	1.2	7.3	5.7	6.4	16.6	9.3
Petroleum & Coal	92.0	.1	26.4	D	5.8	2.3	–
Rubber & Plastic, n.e.c.	92.9	15.8	7.4	2.5	35.7	6.8	D
Primary Metals	96.6	.7	6.1	6.9	17.5	29.4	.5
Machinery except Electrical	99.9	14.9	34.0	1.2	4.8	9.0	.8
Electrical Machinery	96.9	9.6	18.	10.8	8.5	25.6	1.0
Transportation Equipment	97.0	31.4	3.	5.1	33.3	4.6	.6
Assignable Discharge	96.5	93.2	96.7	82.6	95.9	98.1	91.5
Percent of Industrial Discharge, 1966	100.0	3.9	8.3	5.3	10.2	16.1	3.8
Percent of Industrial Discharge, 1959	100.0	4.3	10.7	5.0	11.5	18.1	2.5

1. Includes Hawaii

2. Includes Alaska

D = Publication withheld to prevent disclosure of information about individual firms.

n.e.c. = not elsewhere classified.

Source: Adapted from US Environmental Protection Agency. *The Economics of Clean Water.* Washington, D.C.: US Government Printing Office, 1972.

Table 5-16. Sewage Treatment Needs per Capita, by Region and City Size, 1971-1976

		Per Capita Costs (Average)			
Region and City Size (in thousands)	*Number of Cities in Sample*	*Primary and Secondary*	*Tertiary Treatment*	*Interceptor and Storm Sewer Improvements*	*Total*
South					
10–< 50	19	$ 76.01	$ 40.29	$128.56	$244.86
50–< 100	15	45.34	38.44	57.83	141.61
100–< 250	14	65.91	28.44	35.60	129.95
250–< 1000	9	58.26	22.87	60.06	141.19
Northeast					
10–< 50	29	209.86	29.67	167.72	407.25
50–< 100	22	124.36	23.68	122.24	270.28
100–< 250	9	230.19	52.23	170.03	452.45
250–< 1000	2	167.33	201.58	296.44	665.35
New York City	1	165.23	241.49	38.13	444.85
North Central					
10–< 50	36	98.02	42.54	170.82	311.38
50–< 100	16	97.40	32.52	174.50	304.42
100–< 250	17	55.22	16.76	171.40	243.38
250–< 1000	3	161.17	15.58	255.34	432.09
West					
10–< 50	23	79.94	10.82	14.30	105.06
50–< 100	20	45.10	58.56	83.21	186.87
100–< 250	8	28.64	25.06	94.26	147.96
250–< 1000	2	95.87	6.18	205.44	307.49

Source: Calculated from data appearing in National League of Cities, "Statement of Donald G. Alexander before the House Appropriations Committee, May 5, 1971," Appendix A, 1971.

Table 5-15 continued

S.E.	*West Gr. Lak.*	*Upper Miss.*	*Lower Miss.*	*Mo.*	*Ark. W & R*	*West. Gulf*	*Colo. Basin*	*Gr. Basin*	*Cal.*	*Pacf. N.W.*
11.6	2.8	30.9	1.7	17.9	6.7	2.8	D	D	3.5	2.6
2.3	12.5	24.7	2.8	4.3	4.7	1.	D	1.3	7.0	6.4
29.0	5.3	2.9	1.9	.9	1.8	.8	D	D	20.5	16.7
3.4	9.8	14.0	11.7	6.7	.3	1.5	D	D	20.3	1.2
65.7	D	.5	1.4	–	D	D	D	D	.6	D
28.9	7.8	6.0	2.7	1.0	3.8	2.5	.1	D	2.1	15.0
4.7	2.7	2.1	8.0	.4	.9	31.5	D	D	.6	1.6
2.0	12.0	1.2	10.2	1.6	1.1	27.5	D	.1	8.4	.2
6.9	8.4	4.3	3.3	D	.9	D	D	D	.9	D
1.7	25.2	2.6	D	.4	.6	3.4	.2	D	.2	1.2
.7	12.5	19.8	.3	.2	.3	.7	D	D	.7	D
4.1	9.0	5.	.5	.8	.9	D	D	D	3.0	D
1.7	7.1	2.1	D	D	.5	5.0	D	D	2.2	D
97.8	96.1	88.7	78.7	81.3	95.7	99.3	61.7	8.2	81.6	87.6
7.7	12.7	4.1	5.2	1.0	1.3	13.3	0.1	0.2	2.8	4.0
6.9	12.1	3.5	3.7	1.2	1.4	12.3	0.1	0.2	2.5	3.9

Table 5-17. Surface Water Criteria for Public Water Supplies

Constituent or Characteristic	*Permissible Criteria*	*Desirable Criteria*
Physical:		
Color (color units)	75	< 10
Odor	Narrative	Virtually absent
Temperature	Narrative	Narrative
Turbidity	Narrative	Virtually absent
Microbiological:		
Coliform organisms	10,000/100ml	< 100/100ml
Fecal coliforms	2,000/100ml	< 20/100ml
Inorganic Chemicals:		
	(mg/1)	(mg/1)
Alkalinity	Narrative	Narrative
Ammonia	0.5 (as N)	< 0.01
Arsenic	0.05	Absent
Barium	1.0	Absent
Boron	1.0	Absent
Cadmium	0.01	Absent
Chloride	250	< 25
Chromium, hexavalent	0.5	Absent
Copper	1.0	Virtually absent
Dissolved oxygen	⩾ 4 (monthly mean) ⩾ 3 (individual sample)	Near saturation
Fluoride	Narrative	Narrative
Hardness	Narrative	Narrative
Iron (filterable)	0.3	Virtually absent
Lead	0.05	Absent
Manganese (filterable)	0.05	Absent
Nitrates plus nitrites	10 (as N)	Virtually absent
pH (range)	6.0–8.5	Narrative
Phosphorus	Narrative	Narrative
Selenium	0.01	Absent
Silver	0.05	Absent
Sulfate	250	< 50

continued

Table 5-17 continued

Constituent or Characteristic	*Permissible Criteria*	*Desirable Criteria*
Inorganic Chemicals:		
Total dissolved solids (filterable residue)	500	< 200
Uranyl ion	5	Absent
Zinc	5	Virtually absent
Organic Chemicals:		
Carbon chloroform extract (CCE)	0.15	< 0.04
Cyanide	0.20	Absent
Methylene blue active substances	0.5	Virtually absent
Oil and grease	Virtually absent	Absent
Pesticides:		
Aldrin	0.017	Absent
Chlordane	0.003	Absent
DDT	0.042	Absent
Dieldrin	0.017	Absent
Endrin	0.001	Absent
Heptachlor	0.018	Absent
Heptachlor epoxide	0.018	Absent
Lindane	0.056	Absent
Methoxychlor	0.035	Absent
Organic phosphate plus carbamates	0.1	Absent
Toxaphene	0.005	Absent
Herbicides:		
2, 4-D, plus 2, 4, 5-T, plus 2, 4, 5-TP	0.1	Absent
Phenols	0.001	Absent
Radioactivity:	(pc/1)	(pc/1)
Gross beta	1,000	< 100
Radium-226	3	< 1
Strontium-90	10	< 2

Source: U.S. Department of the Interior, Federal Water Pollution Control Administration. *The Cost of Clean Water.* Washington, D.C.: US Government Printing Office, 1968.

of industrial and municipal discharges are spread throughout the seven small drainage areas in Southeast Michigan—the Raisin, Huron, Rouge, Clinton, Belle, Pine and Black rivers. The main rivers, St. Clair and Detroit, are divided almost in half by the international boundary. Only stations in US waters were analyzed because wastes discharged from the Detroit area tend to hug the US shoreline of the rivers.

Figure 5-18 shows three measurements which illustrate the results: total coliform bacteria organisms per 100 milliliters (a measure of pollution from urban runoff and domestic wastes), chlorides and phenols (components of industrial wastes in the area). The graphs depict annual mean measurements for stations close to the US shore, arranged according to their distance upstream from the mouth of the river (at Lake Erie). They show that during the 1967-1969 period:

- The river was relatively clean upstream of Detroit.
- Overflows from combined sewers caused the geometric mean coliform levels to exceed proposed EPA guidelines (10,000 per 100 milliliters) for about ten to 15 miles downstream.
- Industrial sources caused elevated chloride and phenol concentrations in the lower river area.
- Although the year-to-year trends were somewhat mixed, the pollutant levels associated with industry were gradually lessening during the period, while municipal pollutant levels were generally worsening.

Table 5-18. Number of Cities with Water Supply Problem, March, 1970 (of cities serving interstate carriers)

	Water Supply Problem			
	I	*II*	*III*	
1970 Population in 000	*Number of Cities with Problem*[a]			*Estimated Total of US Cities in Class*[b]
< 25	20	12	12	5,000+
25–< 100	8	12	4	600
100–< 500	5	3	3	110
500+	1	1	0	25

Water supply problems are listed in order of increasing severity:
I. Inadequate monitoring program *or* failure to send sampling reports to Public Health Service and/or failure to meet PHS chemical standards *or* provide adequate data. Note that group I includes reporting failure.
II. Low pressure in distribution system and/or inadequate cross-connection code or inspection.
III. Samples do not meet PHS bacteriological requirements and/or inadequate disinfection.

[a]Coverage here limited to 678 municipal water supplies serving interstate carriers, with total population of 81 million. Cities with problems received only "provisional approval."

[b]Estimated number in each class based on 1960 distribution. In 1960, the census listed 4,680 urban places as having populations of 2,500 to 25,000; and 596 urban places with populations under 2,500. In the sample of cities with problems, the "under 25,000" category includes 30 cities above 2,500 and 14 below 2,500.

Sources: Water problem data from US Environmental Protection Agency, Bureau of Water Hygiene, reported in Sally Lindsay "How Safe is the Nation's Drinking Water?" *Saturday Review*, May 2, 1970, pp. 54-55. City size distribution based on U.S. Bureau of the Census, *US Census of Population: 1960*, Vol. 1, Part A, Table 7, pp. 1-13.

Increases in phosphates and organic nitrogen (not shown) also reflected problems due to municipal wastes and nonpoint sources. These trends are consistent with EPA's findings that Detroit's industries were generally meeting abatement schedules while municipalities were lagging. But these trends could be modified after year-to-year variations in temperature, rainfall, stream flow or other conditions are taken into account.

This study demonstrates that although pollution problems may be widespread, local variations in pollutant levels make monitoring and the interpretation of water quality data a difficult and complex task.

Noise Pollution

Noise is unwanted sound. Acceptable community noise levels have yet to be determined and thus standards set in municipal ordinances vary greatly across the country where such standards exist. Most current research focuses upon source delineation and source emission measurement, yet because no agreement has been reached upon measurement systems for community noise levels, different types of noise emissions are measured by different agencies on different measurement scales. There is a total absence of detailed surveillance systems or workable data in the majority of cases. It is thus impossible at this time to talk about progress towards national goals for elimination of noise pollution.

What of noise incidence? The most widely used measure for noise loudness is decibels on the A scale (dBA) which weighs sound intensity according to the presumed pattern of human hearing. Studies of noise perception indicate that an increase of ten decibels for a given tone is perceived as a doubling of noise level—that is, 100 decibels seems twice as loud as 90 decibels.

In decibel measurement, the zero decibel level is set at the threshold of audibility for the normal ear. The threshold of hearing at zero dBA is very low indeed, for if man's ears were any keener they would respond to the molecular motions of air particles. The sound of a whisper is around 25 dBA, ordinary conversation is 60 dBA, and a shout around 80 dBA. Automobile traffic ranges from 50 to 80 dBA, a subway train from 90 to 100 dBA and a jet plane at 1000 feet is over 100 dBA. Construction noise often reaches 110 dBA, the proverbial boiler factory can reach 125 dBA and the decks of aircraft carriers reach 155 dBA. The threshold of noise-induced pain for humans has been estimated variously at 120 to 140 dBA (see Figure 5-19). Compare Figure 5-19 with Figure 5-20, which shows the extent of local disagreement on acceptable community noise levels.

The major noise emission sources of noise pollution in urban places can be classified into two groups: (1) stationary sources and (2) corridor sources. Stationary sources include

Table 5-19. Multiple Use Groupings for Fresh and Marine Waters

Use Grouping	*Human Consumption and Direct Contact Uses*	*Wildlife Habitat and Indirect Contact Use*	*Recreational and Industrial Remote Contact Uses*
Fresh Waters:	Drinking use Swimming and water skiing (direct recreational use) Beverage manufacturing[1] Industrial food preparation[1]	Fish and shellfish rereproduction, rearing and harvest Agricultural use (irrigation and stock watering) Wildlife habitat	Aesthetic and recreational (picnicking, hiking, fishing, boating and palinvisitation) Commerce and navigation Power production Fish passage Industrial cooling water Industrial process use Log storage and rafting Liquid waste transport
Parameters:			
1 Temperature (°C)	18.5	21.0	24.0
2 Color (Platinum-Cobalt Units)	5	10	10
3 Turbidity (Jackson Turbidity Units)	5	10	10
4 pH (Standard Units)	6.5–8.5	6.5–8.5	6.0–9.0
5 Total Coliform Bacteria (/100 ml)	240	1000	1000
6 Total Dissolved Solids (mg/1)	500	500	500
7 Suspended Solids (mg/1)	5	10	10
8 Total Nitrogen (mg/1)	10	10	45
9 Total Alkalinity (mg/1)	150	150	75
10 Total Hardness (mg/1)	100	125	100
11 Chloride	250	250	250
12 Total Iron and Manganese (mg/1)	0.35	0.35	0.11
13 Sulfate (mg/1)	250	250	250
14 Dissolved Oxygen (mg/1)	8.0	6.5	5.0
Marine Waters:	Human water contact use–swimming and water skiing Food fish canning and preparation	Salmon rearing Other food fish Shellfish Wildlife Habitat	Fish Passage Aesthetics (environmental) Recreational (boating, picnicking, hiking and plain visitation) Commercial fishing and fish passage Industrial water use Navigation Log storage and rafting Liquid waste transport
Parameters:			
1 Temperature (°C)	16.0	19.0	24.0
3 Turbidity (Jackson Turbidity Units)	5	10	10
4 pH (Standard Units)	7.8–8.5	7.8–8.5	6.0–9.0
5 Total Coliform Bacteria (/100 ml)	70	1000	1000
14 Dissolved Oxygen (mg/1)	6.8	5.0	4.0

1. Eventual Human Consumption

Source: Water Pollution Control Commission, State of Washington, "A Regulation Relating to Water Quality Standards for Interstate and Coastal Waters of the State of Washington and a Plan for Implementation and Enforcement of Such Standards, 1967; American Water Works Association, "Water Quality and Treatment," 1950; Eugene Brown, M.W. Skougstad and M.J. Fishman, "Methods for Collection and Analysis of Water Samples for Dissolved Minerals and Gases," *U.S. Geological Survey Techniques of Water-Resources Investigation, 1970;* California State Water Pollution Control Board, 1952; California State Water Quality Control Board, *Water Quality Criteria,* 1963; John D. Hem, "Study and Interpretation of the Chemical Characteristics of Natural Water," 1970; R.O. Sylvester and Carl A. Ranbow, *Methodology in Establishing Water-Quality Standards in Water Resources Management and Public Policy, 1968*; US Federal Water Pollution Control Administration, Committee on Water Quality Criteria, 1968; US Public Health Service, "Drinking Water Standards," 1962.

Table 5-20. Water Pollution Index Summarized for Major Drainage Areas, 1970 and 1971

Major Watershed	*Stream Miles*	*Polluted Miles 1970*	*Polluted Miles 1971*	*Polluted Miles Change*	*1971 Duration-Intensity Factor*
Ohio	28,992	9,869	24,031	+13,746	0.42
Southeast	11,726	3,109	4,490	+1,381	0.74
Great Lakes	21,374	6,580	8,771	+2,191	0.45
Northeast	32,431	11,895	5,823	-6,072	0.61
Middle Atlantic	31,914	4,620	5,627	+869	0.47
California	28,277	5,359	8,429	+2,499	0.27
Gulf	64,719	16,605	11,604	-5,001	0.35
Missouri	10,448	4,259	1,839	-2,420	0.31
Columbia	30,443	7,443	5,685	-1,758	0.12
United States	260,324	69,739	76,299	+5,435	0.41

Source: US Department of the Interior, Federal Water Pollution Control Administration, *The Cost of Clean Water*, 1972.

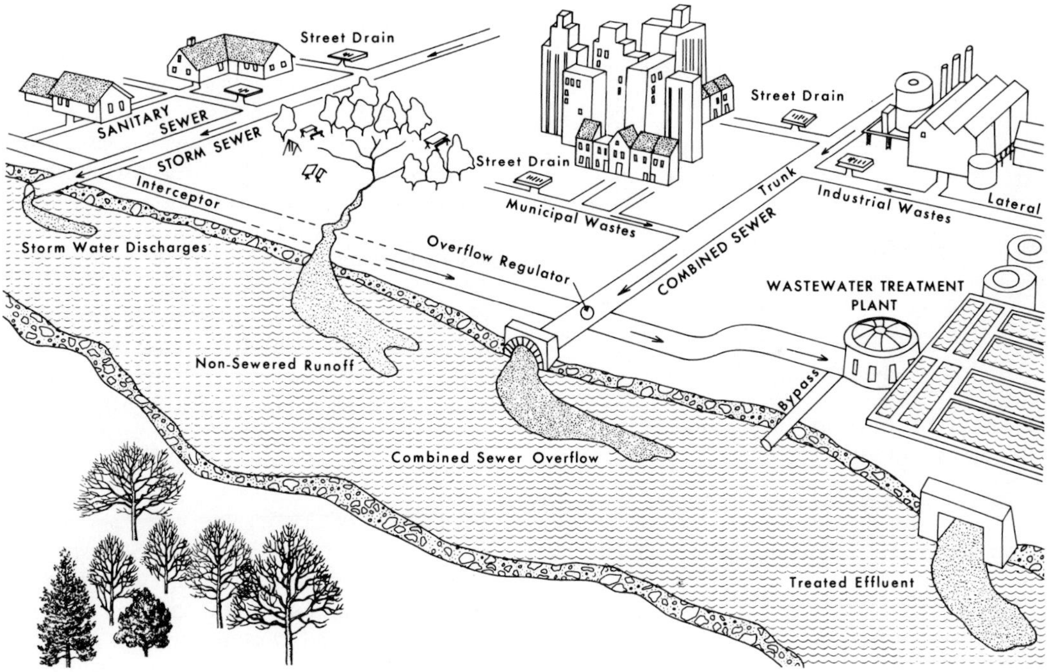

Figure 5-17. Types of Effluent Discharges

industrial noise, construction and demolition noise, and domestic noise (air conditioners, lawnmowers, appliances, etc.) Corridor sources involve urban transportation networks and aircraft flight patterns.

The most frequently cited source of noise intrusions is automobile noise (Table 5-21). Likewise, airport landing patterns lay down bands of extreme and objectionable noise (Figure 5-21). Figure 5-22 shows the range of daytime outdoor noise readings for 18 different locations, while Figure 5-23 relates expected changes in sound levels to population densities through 1985.

Whether a given noise should be considered "dangerous" and the amount of damage a

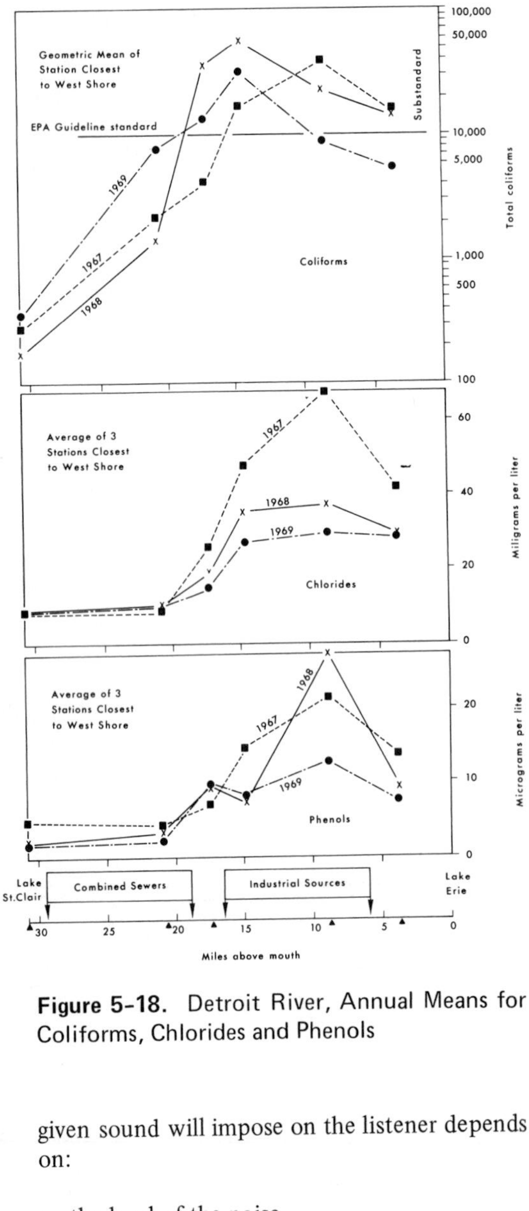

Figure 5-18. Detroit River, Annual Means for Coliforms, Chlorides and Phenols

given sound will impose on the listener depends on:

- the level of the noise,
- how long it lasts,
- how many times it occurs daily,
- over how many years daily exposure is repeated,
- the effect on hearing considered to constitute damage, and
- individual susceptibility to this type of injury.

Table 5-22 provides guidelines for the relations between hearing threshold levels and the degree of hearing handicap. In a similar manner, general damage criteria have been established for prolonged exposure to noise of different levels (Table 5-23). It is difficult to specify allowable exposures for brief and intensive transportation noise exposures. A maximum tolerable limit can be set at 120-130 dBA. Some investigators feel that a ten second exposure is the maximum tolerable level. Other effects of noise include disruption of sleep, difficulties in auditory communication (Figure 5-24), and decremental influences on learning and task performance.

One adjustment to high noise levels is in land and property values. For example, according to McClure a case can be made on the basis of insulation and easement costs that property exposed to jet noise is worth 10 to 20 percent less than it would be if it were not exposed to jet noise. In the case of expressway noise, Colony concluded that a residential property contiguous to a highway might be expected to decrease in value 20 to 30 percent as compared with otherwise identical property not so located. This percentage tends to decrease from the higher to the lower end of the range as the price of the property increases from $10,000 to $30,000. And if a distance-decay gradient of price decrease exists it is a steep one; no detrimental influence of the expressway was detected outside of a narrow band about 50 feet wide along the right of way line. It thus appeared that traffic noise has a noticeable effect on the market value of a residential property immediately adjacent to the right of way—but that such influence decreases rapidly for parcels more distant from that right of way.

Solid Wastes

At present, there exists no systematic measurement system for solid wastes in the United States, nor, given the federal withdrawal from solid wastes activities, is such a measurement system likely to be developed in the near future. Likewise no national goals are likely to be formulated. One is left with local data. But while private haulers may estimate numbers of truck loads, and some municipal landfills measure in cubic yards and tons, the vast majority of disposal agencies and sites do not measure or weigh quantities of solid wastes received. Part of the problem lies in the diversity of the types of solid wastes which are produced. Part also lies in the variety of sources and the diverse methods of disposal that have been institutionalized.

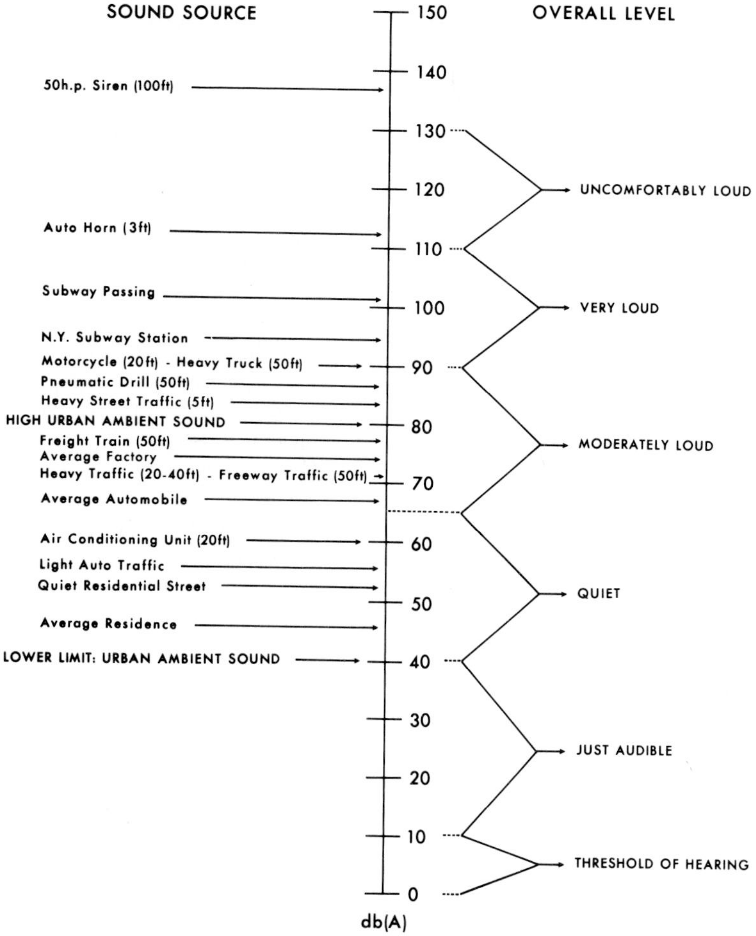

Figure 5-19. Comparison of Sound Sources and Overall Noise Levels

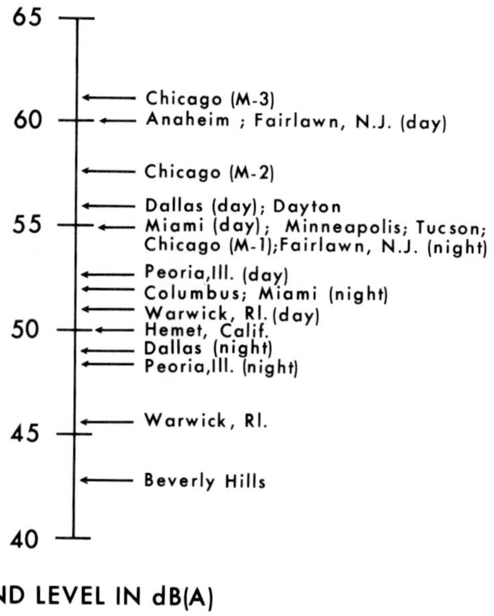

Figure 5-20. Municipal Noise Ordinances for Non-Motor Vehicle Sources: Maximum Noise Limits at Residential Boundary

Table 5-21. Noise Climate as Percentage of Time

Location	*Daytime*	*Nighttime*	*Level of Intermittent Peaks [dB(A)]*
Main Streets with heavy vehicles	68–80	50–70	85–92
Secondary Streets	60–70	44–55	up to 92
Residential Streets with local traffic only	51–60	43–49	occasionally up to 92

Source: Adapted from data supplied by US Environmental Protection Agency.

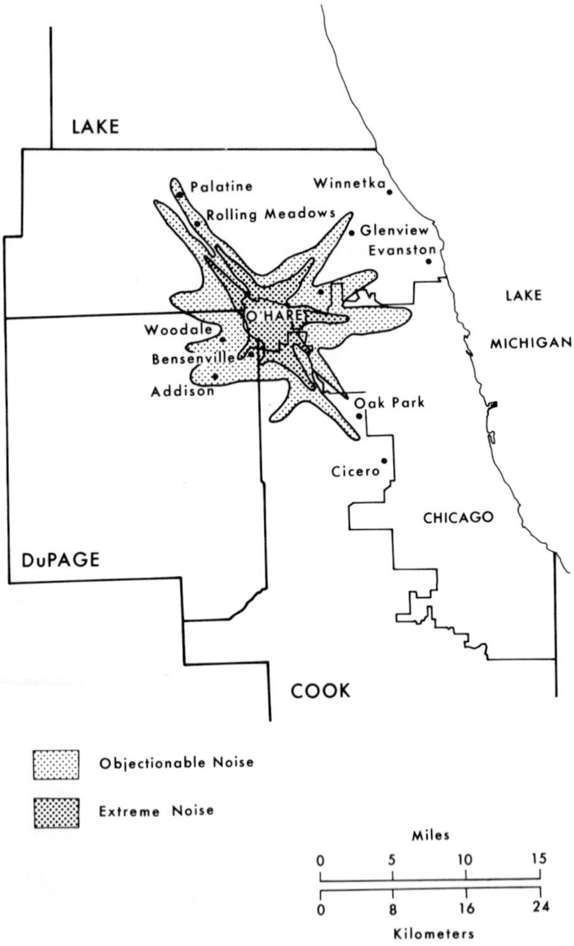

Figure 5-21. 1970 Noise Exposure Contours For Areas Surrounding Chicago's O'Hare International Airport

There are four municipal sources of solid wastes:

Domestic Refuse includes all those types which normally originate in the residential household or apartment house.

Municipal Refuse embraces all the types which originate on municipally owned property. These include street sweepings and litter; catch-basin dirt; refuse from parks, playgrounds, zoos, schools and other institutional buildings; solid wastes from sewerage systems.

Commercial Refuse includes all solid wastes which originate in businesses operated for profit such as office buildings, stores, markets, theaters and privately owned clinics, hospitals and other institutional buildings.

Industrial Refuse includes all solid wastes which result from industrial processes and manufacturing operations such as factories, processing plants, repair and cleaning establishments, refineries, and rendering plants.

Because of this diversity by type and source, no one disposal site handles all solid wastes for any bounded area, contributing to the lack of measurement by any agency or agencies.

One must therefore rely upon local studies for an understanding of solid waste generation and disposal. The most comprehensive state analysis of solid wastes has been conducted by the State of California and published by EPA as *California Solid Waste Management Study 1968 and Plan 1970.* In this study, a complete county and city analysis of sources, total wastes generated and generation factors was undertaken. An important consequence of the study was the calculation of solid waste multipliers for households and industries. Using these, the amount of solid wastes generated can be estimated for other areas. Individual industrial multipliers are shown in Table 5-24. Tables 5-25 to 5-27 provide the California multipliers for municipal and commercial wastes, and for construction and demolition activities. Similar multipliers developed in a New York State study are shown in Table 5-28 and Figure 5-25. Apparently solid waste generation increases with city size and with population densities.

Given the Californian data, an equation of the following form can be used to estimate

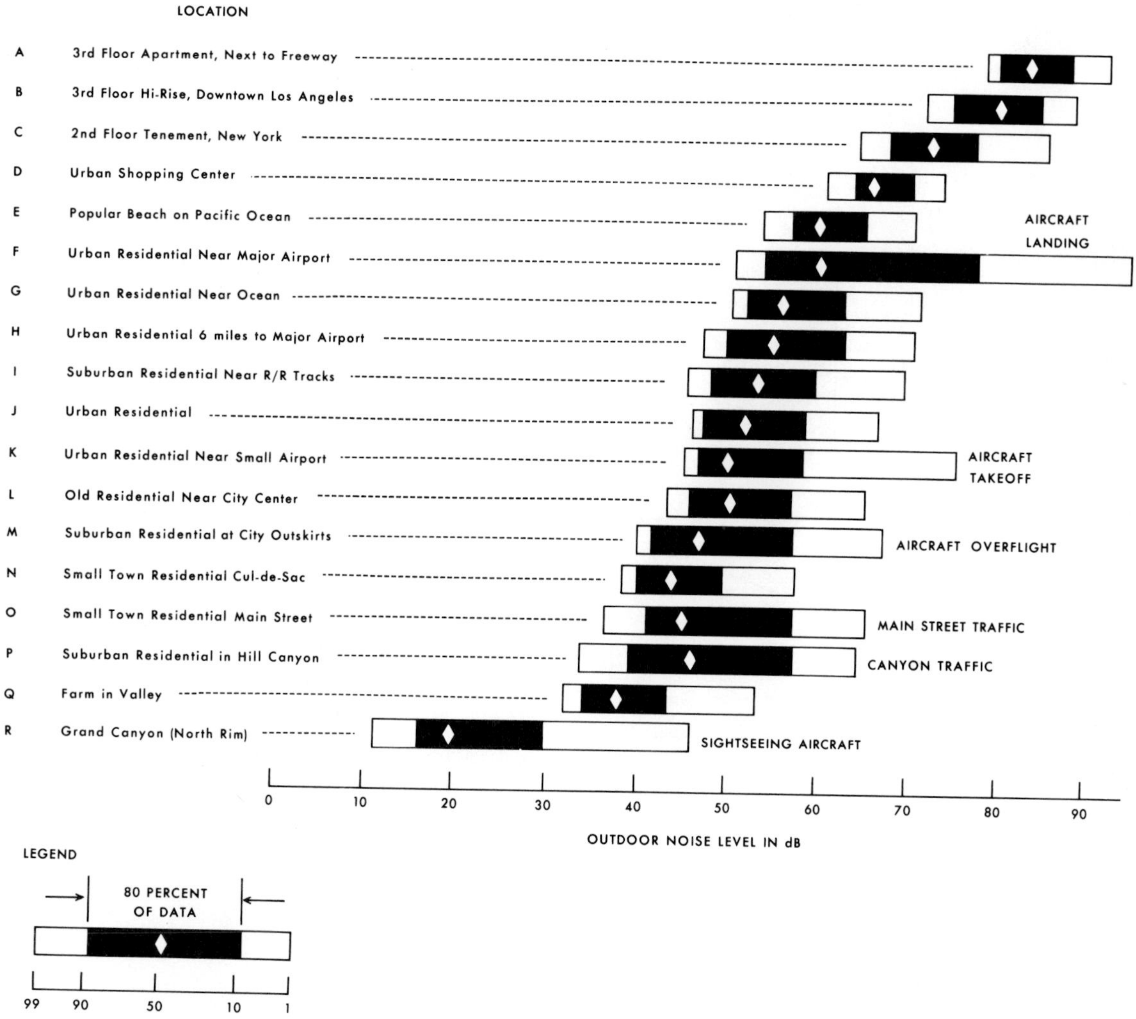

Figure 5-22. The Range of Daytime Outdoor Noise Readings for 18 Locations

quantities of solid wastes generated in other places:

$$w = \sum_i a_i \chi_i$$

where w = the total waste generated
a_i = a waste multiplier for source i
χ_i = the number of source units for source i

Simplifying, the average Californian waste multipliers are as follows:

Single Family Residence	2858.0 lb/unit/yr
Multiple Family Residence	1315.0 lb/unit/yr
Commercial	3.5 lb/cap/yr
Manufacturers	7.6 tons/emp/yr
Demolition and Construction	500.0 lb/cap/yr
Sewage	87.1 lb/cap/yr

Applying these to each major metropolitan area in the US produces the results recorded in Table 5-29.

To the extent that standards exist relating to solid wastes, they focus on their proper storage, handling and disposal, seeking to interdict the many pathways between wastes and

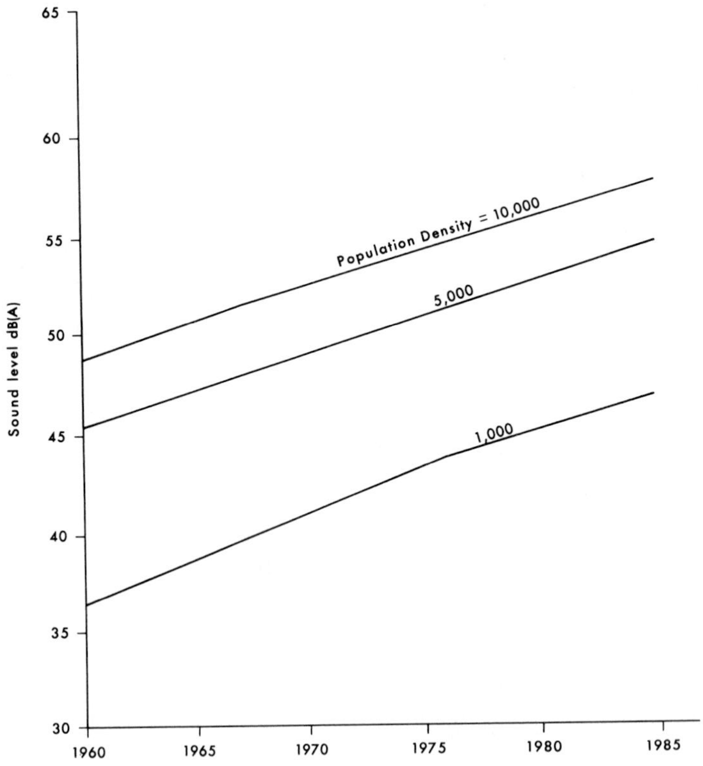

Figure 5-23. Ambient Noise Level for Three Different Population Densities

Table 5-22. Hearing Handicaps Related to Threshold Hearing Levels

		Average Hearing Threshold Level for 500, 1000 and 2000 Hz in the Better Ear		
Class	*Degree of Handicap*	*More Than*	*Not More Than*	*Ability to Understand Speech*
A	Not Significant		25dB	No significant difficulty with faint speech
B	Slight Handicap	25dB	40dB	Difficulty only with faint speech
C	Mild Handicap	40dB	55dB	Frequent difficulty with normal speech
D	Marked Handicap	55dB	70dB	Frequent difficulty with loud speech
E	Severe Handicap	70dB	90dB	Can understand only shouted or amplified speech
F	Extreme Handicap	90dB		Usually cannot understand even amplified speech

Source: US Environmental Protection Agency, *Effect of Noise on People* (Washington, D.C.: US Government Printing Office, 1971), p. 36.

Table 5-23. Critical Sound Exposure Levels

Sound Level	*Effect**
70–80 dB (A)	safe
85 dB (A)	hearing losses begin
90 dB (A)	serious losses begin
95 dB (A)	50 percent probability of a hearing impairment
105 dB (A)	losses in all exposed individuals

*Damage risk for prolonged exposures to noise over a period of several years.

Source: D.O. Dickeson et al., *Transportation Noise Pollution: Control and Abatement* (Springfield, Va.: National Technical Information Service, N71–15557, 1970), p. 22.

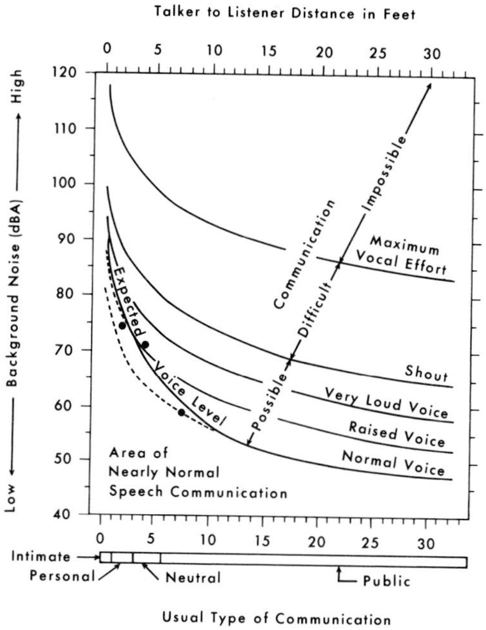

Figure 5-24. Quality of Speech Communication as Dependent on the A-Weighted Sound Level (dBA) of Background Noise and Distance Between Talker and Listener

disease (Figure 5-26). For example, the regulations for the state of Washington specify that "the purpose of this regulation is to set minimum functional standards for the proper *handling* of all solid wastes originating from residences, commercial, agricultural, and industrial operations, and other sources . . ." in order to ". . . prevent land, air and water pollution, breeding of flies, harboring of rodents, fire hazards; and to prevent damage to recreational values, to conserve resources, and to maintain esthetic values, and prevent damage to the environment, and to prevent nuisances" [p. 1]. Yet despite local regulations with stated goals such as these, solid waste is presently disposed as follows in the United States:

On land		
Open dumps	85	90 percent
Sanitary landfill	5	
Burned in municipal incinerators	8 percent	
Other	2 percent	

The last category includes wastes composted, dumped at sea, fed to hogs and burned in on-site incinerators (apartment buildings, conical burners at dumps, etc.).

In a sanitary landfill, refuse is spread in thin layers, each compacted by a bulldozer before the next is spread. The landfill is sealed with a layer of compacted earth at the end of each working day, and the complete fill is sealed with two or three feet of earth. The sanitary landfill eliminates a number of negative externalities associated with open dumps, which can serve as breeding grounds for flies, rats and mosquitoes, and which may well pollute ground water. Available data indicate that substitution of sanitary landfills for dumps increases cost per ton of refuse handled by 33 to 50 percent. The Council on Environmental Quality estimates that site disposal costs can range from \$1 to \$3 per ton for sanitary landfill, and from \$3 to \$10 per ton for incineration. Collection costs average roughly \$15 per ton, though there is marked variation. In particular, collection costs in large urban areas can go substantially higher; New York City costs were \$32 per ton in 1969, not including many employee benefits and depreciation (Table 5-30). The estimated total cost of upgrading open dumps to acceptable sanitary levels nationwide is \$4.2 billion.

When completed, sanitary landfills can be used for parking, some types of construction and recreation facilities—parks, golf courses, even ski slopes. Use for buildings is constrained because of land subsidence and possible emission of methane gases due to anaerobic decom-

Table 5-24. Industrial Waste Multipliers in California

Standard Industrial Classification		Small Firms		Large Firms		Annual Waste: All Firms			
No.	Title	Total Employment 1	Annual Waste Volume per Employee (cu yd) 2	Total Employment 3	Annual Waste Volume per Employee (cu yd) 4	Volume per Employee (cu yd) 5	Densities lb/cu yd 6	Pounds per Employee 7	Tons per Employee 8
19	Ordnance and Accessories	h	h	29,499	4.476	4.476	294.4	1,317.7	0.65885
203	Canning and Preserving	–	–	–	8.977	8.977	1,240.0	11,131.4	5.5657
20	Other Food Processing (Except 203)	920	20.961	4,306	8.720	10.875	885.8	9,633.1	4.81655
21	Tobacco	–	–	–	–	–	–	–	2.49365[i]
22	Textiles	–	–	–	–	–	–	–	0.52575[j]
23	Apparel	98	35.360	623	2.877	6.601	159.3	1,051.5	0.52575
24	Lumber and Wood Products	455	48.492	217		48.492	894.5	43,376.1	21.68805
25	Furniture and Fixtures	385	86.877			86.877	464.0	40,310.9	20.15545
26	Paper and Allied Products	570	65.442	1,535	37.440	45.022	357.0	25,077.3	12.53865
27	Printing, Publishing and Allied	1,744	25.230	1,923	7.252	15.802	1,671.0	26,405.1	13.20255
28	Chemicals and Allied	701	18.348	937		18.348	895.0	16,421.1	3.21075
29	Petroleum Refining	k	k	k	k	k	k	k	k
30	Rubber and Plastics	173	28.583	653	18.854	20.892	148.2	3,096.2	1.54810
31	Leather	–	–	–	–	–	–	–	2.49365[i]
32	Stone, Clay, Glass and Concrete	960	29.235	1,696	5.260	13.926	2,601.5	36,228.5	18.11425
33	Primary Metals	h	4.443	–	–	–	–	–	6.7300[l]
34	Fabricated Metal Products	1,259	21.214	1,304	13.206	17.140	785.3	13,460.0	6.7300
35	Nonelectrical Machinery	2.838	17.909	9,805	11.401	12.862	650.3	8,364.2	4.18210
36	Electrical Machinery	2,337	16.645	37,814	7.333	7.875	756.5	5,957.4	2.97870
37	Transportation Equipment	557	14.348	4,183	24.580	23.378	290.3	6,786.6	3.39330
38	Instruments	825	8.943	926	NA	8.943	562.9	5,034.0	2.51700
39	Miscellaneous Manufacturing Industries	517	5.946	149	NA	10.493	475.3	4,987.3	2.49365[i]

Source: US Environmental Protection Agency. Solid Waste Management Office. *California Solid Waste Management Study.*
h: data not available; i: data missing, SIC 39 multiplier used; j: same as SIC 23, Apparel; k: omitted from calculations; l: same as SIC 34, Fabricated Metals.

Table 5-25. Generation in California Municipal Waste

Waste Source	*Multipliers*	*Source Units*	*Tons/year*
Household Garbage and Rubbish			
Single Family Units	1.42910 tons/unit/year	173,819	248,405
Multiple Family Unit	0.62755 tons/unit/year	106,984	70,347
City Streets: Leaves, Litter, Sweepings, and Tree Trimmings	42.9 lb/capita/year	758,230	16,264
Refuse Collected Along Highway Right-of-Way			
Freeway Refuse	8.0 tons/mile/year	62	496
County Roads Refuse	3.3 tons/mile/year	200	660
Sewage Treatment Residue	87.1 lb/capita/year	805,930	35,098
Local Parks and Playgrounds	5.4 lb/capita/year	805.930	2,176
Regional Parks			415
Total Waste			373,861

Source: US Environmental Protection Agency. Solid Waste Management Office. *California Solid Waste Management Study.*

Table 5-26. Wastes Generated by Commercial Organizations and Services in California

Size of City Population	*Waste Multiplier lb/cap/day*	*Applicable Population*	*Waste tons/yr*
> 100,000	3.5	635,100	405,670
(1) 10,001–100,000	2.5	167,980	76,641
1,001–10,000	2.0	2,850	1,040
		805,930	483,351

(2) 3.81011 tons/employee/year × 265,401 employment = 1,011,207 tons

Source: US Environmental Protection Agency. Solid Waste Management Office. *California Solid Waste Management Study.*

Table 5-27. Wastes Generated by Construction and Demolition in California

Size of City Population	*Waste Multiplier lbs/capita/yr*	*Applicable Population*	*Waste tons/yr*
> 100,000	500	635,100	158,775
(1) 10,001–100,000	250	167,980	20,997
1,001–10,000	100	2,850	142
			179,914
			(rounded)
		805,930	180,000

(2) 41.25205 ton/employee/year × (19,262) employment = 794,597 tons

Source: US Environmental Protection Agency. Solid Waste Management Office. *California Solid Waste Management Study.*

Table 5-28. Municipal Solid Wastes Collection Rates[1] pounds/capita/day

	Waste Collection by Population Density Ranges (Persons Per Square Miles)		
Population Range	*0-3,999*	*4,000-6,999*	*7,000+*
0- 4,999	3.3	–	–
5,000-19,999	3.6	5.0	4.6
20,000-99,999	4.1	4.1	4.6
100,000 +	4.6	5.1	5.6

1. Consultant's Analysis

Source: *New York Solid Waste Management Plan, Status Report 1970* (Washington, D.C.: Environmental Protection Agency, 1971), ch. 13, p. 11.

position; buildings can trap methane, creating an explosion hazard. Despite these constraints, about 11 percent of the present land area of New York City (for example) was created by solid waste fill, including some of the most valuable recreational and commercial sites. Positive externalities can occur in the filling of ravines and gullies, for such can stabilize surrounding terrain.

The other facet of solid wastes disposal is the possibility of resource recovery and recycling. Much experimentation is now being undertaken, but the critical factor is price; as raw materials prices increase, recycling becomes more profitable and the solid waste "problem" is converted into market "opportunity."

Pesticides and Radiation

For pesticides and radiation, little can be said about incidence and impact, and even less about goals. The only pesticides data available for US metropolitan areas are for 1970 and then only for the five cities included in the national food monitoring program reports published in *The Pesticides Monitoring Journal.* The nine pesticide residues reported in Table 5-31 were chosen for their presence in each of the 12 classes of foodstuffs of the market basket survey.

Available radiation data are for 1971 and are presented in Table 5-32. They are derived from Radiation Alert Network figures as reported in *Radiological Health Data and Reports* and *Radiation Data and Reports.* This data set gives the best national coverage of radiation levels and includes the two significant factors of ambient atmospheric levels of beta radioactivity and the beta radioactivity deposited with precipitation.

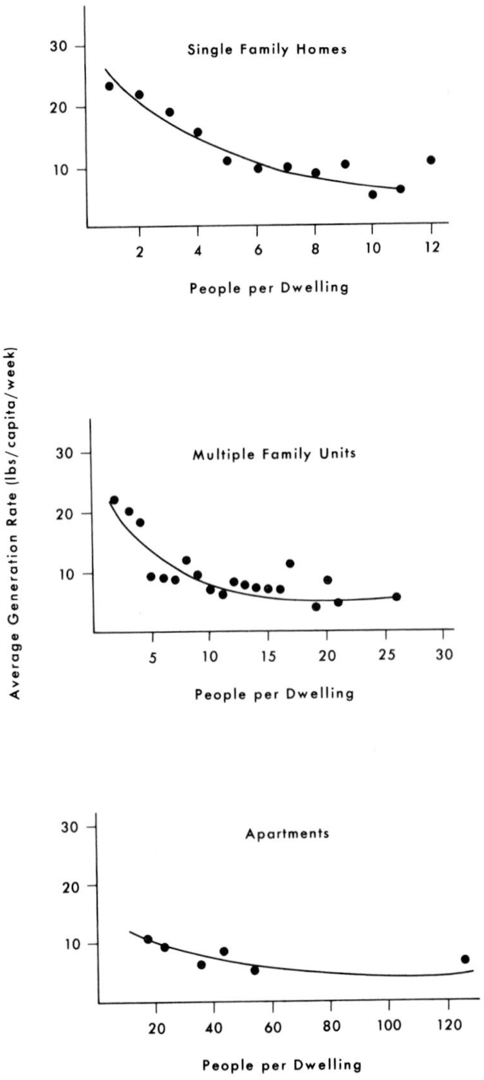

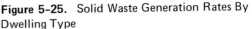

Figure 5-25. Solid Waste Generation Rates By Dwelling Type

IS PROGRESS BEING MADE?

To what extent is progress being made toward achievement of the nation's environmental goals? With a few notable exceptions—such as the elimination of significant water pollution

Table 5-29. Estimated Solid Wastes Generated by US Metropolitan Areas (in 1,000 tons/year)

		Total Wastes	*Total, Excluding Manufacturing*
1	Akron	1670	901
2	Albuquerque	480	421
3	Allentown-Bethlehem-Easton	1512	732
4	Atlanta	2711	1820
5	Baltimore	4310	2717
6	Birmingham	1521	1004
7	Boston	5858	3455
8	Bridgeport	1104	500
9	Buffalo	3067	1728
10	Canton	972	497
11	Charleston	475	316
12	Chattanooga	786	394
13	Chicago	16312	8841
14	Cincinnati	2958	1690
15	Cleveland	5011	2680
16	Columbus	1835	1204
17	Dallas	3223	2091
18	Dayton	2090	1131
19	Denver	2198	1635
20	Des Moines	581	388
21	Detroit	9951	5509
22	El Paso	602	458
23	Flint	*****	659
24	Fort Worth	1634	1038
25	Gary-Hammond-East Chicago	1621	823
26	Grand Rapids	1292	716
27	Hartford	1692	851
28	Honolulu	927	779
29	Houston	3728	2678
30	Indianapolis	2511	1487
31	Jacksonville	890	714
32	Jersey City	1547	732
33	Johnstown	541	350
34	Kansas City	2651	1668
35	Los Angeles-Long Beach	15948	9447
36	Louisville	1881	1045
37	Memphis	1421	985
38	Miami	2123	1680
39	Milwaukee	3438	1793
40	Minneapolis-St. Paul	3904	2355
41	Nashville-Davidson	1133	722
42	New Haven	806	456
43	New Orleans	1782	1360
44	New York	22989	14269
45	Newark	4343	2344
46	Norfolk-Portsmouth	1017	873
47	Oklahoma City	1111	888
48	Omaha	819	540
49	Peterson-Clifton-Passaic	3182	1738
50	Philadelphia	10720	6365
51	Phoenix	1757	1306
52	Pittsburgh	5470	3193
53	Portland	1938	1332
54	Providence-Pawtucket	1941	892
55	Reading	832	403
56	Richmond	1085	694
57	Rochester	2258	1151
58	St. Louis	5373	3128

continued

Table 5-29 continued

	Total Wastes	Total, Excluding Manufacturing
59 Salt Lake City	930	721
60 San Antonio	1345	1137
61 San Bernadino	1964	1611
62 San Diego	2295	1813
63 San Francisco	5662	4159
64 San Jose	2315	1401
65 Seattle-Everett	3181	1949
66 Syracuse	1345	826
67 Tampa-St. Petersburg	1803	1448
68 Toledo	1467	876
69 Tulsa	984	666
70 Utica-Rome	767	441
71 Washington DC	4099	3677
72 Wichita	972	533
73 Wilmington	1176	659
74 Worchester	823	437
75 York	880	447
76 Youngstown-Warren	1347	717

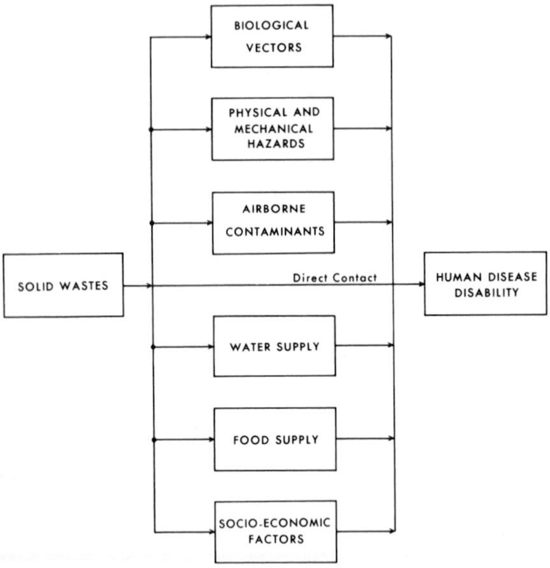

Figure 5-26. Solid Waste/Human Disease Pathways

in Lake Washington and at other sites in the Puget Sound region—it is too early to tell about results. However, the environmental legislation that culminated in the enactments of the period 1965-1972 has produced a new and remarkably powerful and effective administrative machinery. In the case of air and water, standard-setting is well advanced and both new and better surveillance networks now exist. The preconditions for progress, and for measuring it when it occurs, have been provided.

The problem is that as more is learned about the nature and intensity of environmental pollution, the clearer it becomes that pollution is a fundamental accompaniment of the American way of life. Hence, neither cosmetic nor curative programs can have much impact on the problem; nothing less than a fundamental transformation of American lifestyles may be called for.

To illustrate, air, water and noise pollution and solid wastes generation all increase with city size and with the scale of industrial concentrations. Holding constant these relationships, Berry et al. tell us that the more dispersed metropolitan region with a greater degree of automobile usage and of urban sprawl has greater pollution levels than its core-oriented counterpart. Yet increasing size and progressively greater dispersion have been the accompaniments—indeed, the characteristic signs—of growing American affluence and mobility. To the extent that these trends continue, environmental policy will be forced to swim against the American mainstream, continually reacting to pollution problems, responding to crises and trying to ameliorate hazards using the battery of policy directions described by the large arrows in Figure 5-27. We could wish for

Table 5-30. Annual Solid Waste Tonnage and Collection Costs (166 Cities)

Population (000s)	*Tons (per annum)*	*Collection Cost ($ per annum)*	*Average Cost per Ton ($)*	*Cost per Ton for Median City ($)*
10–100	2,813,819	26,757,188	9.50	9.90
100–500	2,803,700	28,605,200	10.20	10.64
500 and over	6,734,800	161,677,900	24.05	12.78
Total	12,352,319	217,040,288	17.66	

Source: US Environmental Protection Agency, Bureau of Solid Waste Management, *A Study of Solid Waste Collection Systems Comparing One-Man with Multi-Man Crews, Final Report*, by Ralph Stone and Co., Engineers, Los Angeles, Calif. (Contract No. PH86–67–248), 1969, Table XVIII, p. 61.

Table 5-31. Pesticides Data Set

City	*DDT*	*DDE*	*TDE*	*Dieldrin*	*Hepta-chlor Epoxide*	*BHC*	*Total Bromides*	*Lindane*	*Kelthane*
Baltimore	0.031	0.018	0.017	0.018	0.010		12.200	0.003	0.200
Boston	0.067	0.063	0.066	0.027	0.041	0.032	8.700	0.007	0.121
Kansas City	0.048	0.023	0.027	0.044	0.015	0.025	6.300	0.055	0.067
Los Angeles	0.050	0.067	0.022	0.011	0.022	0.013	5.100	0.012	0.046
Minneapolis	0.047	0.020	0.017	0.023	0.012	0.019	4.900	0.009	0.068

Source: Federal Committee on Pest Control. *Pesticides Monitoring Journal.* Various issues.

Table 5-32. Radiation Data Set

City	*Gross Beta Radioactivity Maximum*	*Radioactivity Average*	*Rainfall*	*Beta Radioactivity Deposition*
Albuquerque	5	1	65	
Atlanta	2	1	254	13
Baltimore	2		548	4
Birmingham	3	1	906	353
Boston	1		1041	
Buffalo	2	1		
Charleston	3	1	1031	148
Cleveland	2	1	911	256
Columbus	1	1		
Denver	8	2	195	
Detroit	1	1	505	62
El Paso	5	1		
Flint	1	1	505	62
Hartford	1		971	1
Honolulu	2		448	
Indianapolis	2	1		
Jacksonville	1		917	192
Kansas City	5	2	568	133
Los Angeles	3	1		
Miami			853	
Milwaukee	2	1	644	72

continued

Table 5-32 continued

City	*Gross Beta Radioactivity Maximum*	*Radioactivity Average*	*Rainfall*	*Beta Radioactivity Deposition*
Minneapolis	2	1	691	128
Nashville	3	1	983	168
New Orleans			1517	
Oklahoma City	5	1	126	79
Philadelphia	2		1368	51
Phoenix	9	4		
Portland	1		1179	178
Providence	2		142	
Richmond	1		522	141
St. Louis	4	1	564	11
Salt Lake City	4	1	268	92
San Antonio	8	2	316	
San Bernadino	3	1		
San Francisco	1		242	1
San Jose	1		242	1
Seattle Everett			648	
Utica Rome	1			
Washington, D.C.	1			
Worchester	2	1	1199	
York	2		121	28

Compiled by the author from Radiation Alert Network reports.

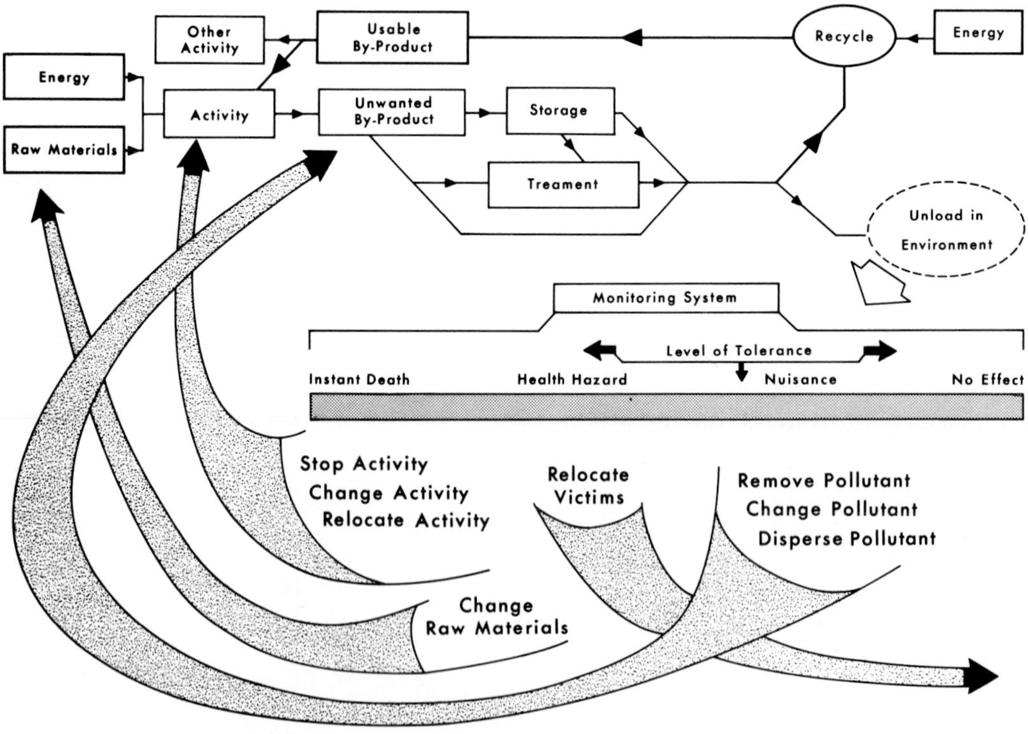

Figure 5-27. Alternative Environmental Policies

more policies that preserve high quality environments rather than having to "cure" polluted ones. It is ironic that if fundamental change in the American lifestyle is forthcoming, it is likely to be the product of another crisis, as growing energy and raw material shortages constrain the outward urge while simultaneously increasing the rewards for recycling and resource recovery rather than unloading effluents in the environment. If this proves to be the case, the more rewarding environmental policy will be to follow the feedback route emphasized by the heavy black lines in Figure 5-27. Whichever transpires in the future, however, one thing is clear: environmental goals are with us to stay, to be set alongside the traditional goal of economic growth and rising pressures for greater equity and social justice.

BIBLIOGRAPHY

The Quality of Life

Bakir, F., et al. "Methylmercury Poisoning in Iraq." *Science* 181 (20 July, 1973): 237.

Dalkey, Norman C.; Ralph Lewis; and David Snyder. "Measurement and Analysis of the Quality of Life. "Prepared for U.S. Department of Transportation, Rand, August 1970.

Dalkey, Norman C. *Studies in the Quality of Life–Delphi & Decision-making.* Lexington, Mass.: D.C. Heath & Co., 1972.

Flax, Michael J. *The Quality of Life in Metropolitan Washington, D.C.–Some Statistical Benchmarks.* Washington, D.C.: The Urban Institute, March 1970.

Joyce, Robert E. "Systematic Measurement of the Quality of Urban Life, Prerequisite to Management." Seminar on Management of the City, pp. 69-86. Research Analysis Corporation, May 1971.

US Environmental Protection Agency, *The Quality of Life Concept.* Washington, D.C., 1973.

Whitman, Ira L., et al. "A Design of an Environmental Evaluation System." In US Environmental Protection Agency, *The Quality of Life Concept.* Washington, D.C., 1973, pp. 7-10.

Air Pollution

Anderson, R.J. and T.D. Crocker. "Air Pollution and Residential Property Values." *Urban Studies* 8, 2 (October 1971): 171-80.

Council on Environmental Quality. *National Environmental Indices: Air Quality and Outdoor Recreation.* The MITRE Corporation MTR-6159. Washington, D.C., 1972.

Croke, E.J. and J.J. Roberts. *Chicago Air Pollution Systems Analysis Program Final Report.* Chicago: Argonne National Laboratory, 1971.

Eisenbud, M. "Environmental Protection in the City of New York." *Science* 170 (November 1970): 706-12.

Freeman, A.M., III. "Air Pollution and Property Values: A Methodological Comment." *Review of Economics and Statistics* 53, 4 (November 1971): 415-6.

Hagevik G., ed. *The Relationship of Land Use and Transportation Planning to Air Quality Management.* New Brunswick, N.J.: Center for Urban Policy Research and Conferences, Rutgers University, 1972.

Lave, L. and E. Seskin. "Air Pollution and Human Health." *Science* 169, 3947 (August 1970): 723-33.

McMullen, T.B. "Comparison of Urban and Nonurban Air Quality." 9th Annual Indiana Air Pollution Control Conference, Purdue University, October 1970.

Ridker, R.G. *Economic Costs of Air Pollution, Studies in Measurement.* New York: Frederick A. Praeger, 1967.

—— and J.A. Henning. "The Determinants of Residential Property Values with Special Reference to Air Pollution." *Review of Economics and Statistics* 49, 2 (May 1967): 246-57.

Stern, A.C., ed. *Air Pollution.* Vol. I. New York: Academic Press, 1968.

US Environmental Protection Agency. "National Primary and Secondary Ambient Air Quality Standards." *Federal Register* 36, 84 (April 30, 1971): PE II.

——. Office of Air Programs. *A Guide for Reducing Air Pollution Through Urban Planning.* Alan M. Voorhees & Associates, Inc. and Ryckman, Edgerley, Tomlinson & Associates. Washington, D.C., December 1971.

——. *Guide for Air Pollution Episode Avoidance.* Washington, D.C.: US Government Printing Office, 1971.

Water Pollution

Carey, G.W., et al. *Urbanization, Water Pollution, and Public Policy.* New Brunswick, N.J.: Center for Urban Policy Research, Rutgers University, 1972.

Grava, Sigurd. *Urban Planning Aspects of Water Pollution Control.* New York: Columbia University Press, 1969.

Greenberg, M.R.; G.W. Carey; L. Zobler; and R.M. Hordon. "A Statistical Dissolved Oxygen Model for a Free-flowing River System." *Journal of the American Statistical Association* 69 (1973): 279–83.

Leopold, L.B. "Hydrology for Urban Land Planning–A Guidebook on the Hydrologic Effects of Urban Land Use." *U.S. Geological Survey Circular* 554 (1968).

Sylvester, R.O. and C.A. Rambow. "Methodology in Establishing Water Quality Standards." In T.H. Campbell and R.O. Sylvester, *Water Resource Management and Public Policy.* Seattle: Washington University Press, 1969.

US Department of Health, Education and Welfare. Public Health Service. *Effects of Land Disposal of Solid Wastes on Water Quality.* Rodney L. Cummins. Washington, D.C.: US Government Printing Office, 1968.

——. *Drinking Water Standards.* Publication No. 956. Washington, D.C.: US Government Printing Office, 1962.

US Department of the Interior. Federal Water Pollution Control Administration. *Interim Report of the National Technical Advisory Commission on Water Quality Criteria.* Washington, D.C.: US Government Printing Office, 1967.

——. *The Cost of Clean Water.* Vol. I and II. Washington, D.C.: US Government Printing Office, 1968.

——. *1968 Inventory of Municipal Waste Facilities.* Three Vols. Washington, D.C.: US Government Printing Office, 1969.

——. *Water Pollution Aspects of Urban Runoff.* The American Public Works Association, Report No. WP-20-15. Washington, D.C.: US Government Printing Office, January 1969.

US Environmental Protection Agency. *Benefits of Water Quality Enhancement.* Syracuse, N.Y.: Department of Civil Engineering. Syracuse University, 1970.

——. *Water Quality Criteria Data Book* Vol. I, II, III, IV. Washington, D.C.: US Government Printing Office, 1970.

——. *The Economics of Clean Water.* Two Vols. Washington, D.C.: US Government Printing Office, 1972.

U.S. Geological Survey. *Methods for Collection and Analysis of Water Samples for Dissolved Minerals and Gases.* Washington, D.C.: US Government Printing Office, 1970.

——. *Techniques of Natural Resources Investigations of the U.S. Geological Survey, Book 5, Laboratory Analysis.* Washington, D.C.: US Government Printing Office, 1970.

——. *Quality of Surface Waters of the United States, 1968.* US Geological Survey Water-Supply Paper 2099. Washington, D.C.: US Government Printing Office, 1972.

Solid Wastes

National Academy of Sciences. National Research Council. *Waste Management and Control.* Washington, D.C., 1966.

State of California. Department of Public Health. *Status of Solid Waste Management in California.* Sacramento: 1968.

US Department of Health, Education and Welfare. *Solid Waste/Disease Relationships.* T.G. Hanks. Washington, D.C.: US Government Printing Office, 1967.

US Environmental Protection Agency. Bureau of Solid Waste Management. *Systems Analysis for Solid Waste Disposal by Incineration.* FMC Corp., Santa Clara Study. Washington, D.C.: US Government Printing Office, 1968.

——. "National Solid Wastes Survey Report Summary and Interpretations." In Richard D. Vaughan, *An Interim Report.* Washington, D.C.: US Government Printing Office, 1970.

——. Solid Waste Management Office. Report SW–2tsg. *California Solid Waste Management Study (1968) and Plan (1970).* Washington, D.C.: US Government Printing Office, 1971.

——. New York State Department of Health. *New York Solid Waste Management Plan, Status Report 1970.* Roy Weston, Environmental Scientists and Engineers. Washington, D.C.: US Government Printing Office, 1971.

Washington State University. Department of Ecology. *Regulations Relating to Minimum Functional Standards for Solid Wastes Handling.* Pullman: 1972. Draft Manuscript.

Noise

Bolt, Beranek and Newman, Inc. *Noise in Urban and Suburban Areas: Results of Field Studies.* Washington, D.C.: US Government Printing Office, January 1967.

——. *Chicago Urban Noise Study.* Report

No. 1411–1413. Downers Grove, Ill.: November 1970.

Colony, D.C. *Expressway Traffic Noise and Residential Properties.* Toledo, Ohio: Research Foundation, University of Toledo, July 1967.

Dickerson, D.O., et al. *Transportation Noise Pollution: Control and Abatement.* Springfield, Va.: National Technical Information Service, N71–15557, 1970.

Greater London Council. *Traffic Noise.* London: Greater London Council, February 1966.

Jacoby, L.R. *Perception of Air, Noise, and Water Pollution in Detroit.* Ann Arbor: Michigan Geographical Publication No. 7, 1972.

Lyon, R.H. "Propagation of Environmental Noise." *Science* 179, 4078 (March 1973): 1083–90.

McClure, P.T. *Indications of the Effect of Jet Noise on the Value of Real Estate.* Santa Monica: The Rand Corporation, 1969.

Shih, H.H. *A Literature Survey of Noise Pollution.* Washington, D.C.: Institute of Ocean Science and Engineering, Catholic University of America, March 1971.

Towne, Robin and Associates, Inc. *An Investigation of the Effect of Freeway Traffic Noise on Apartment Rents.* Springfield, Va.: Clearinghouse for Federal Scientific and Technical Information, October 1966.

U.S. Environmental Protection Agency, *Community Noise.* Report No. NT1D300.3 Washington, D.C.: US Government Printing Office, December 1971.

——. *The Economic Impact of Noise.* Report No. NT1D300.14. Washington, D.C.: US Government Printing Office, December 1971.

——. *Effects of Noise on People.* Report No. NT1D300.7. Washington, D.C.: US Government Printing Office, December 1971.

——. *Fundamentals of Noise: Measurement, Rating Schemes, and Standards.* Report No. NT1D300.15. Washington, D.C.: US Government Printing Office, December 1971.

——. *The Social Impact of Noise.* Report No. NT1D300.11. Washington, D.C.: US Government Printing Office, December 1971.

Pesticides

Federal Committee on Pest Control. *Pesticides Monitoring Journal,* vol. 1, no. 1 (June 1967) through vol. 5, no. 3 (December 1971).

State of New York. New York State Joint Legislative Committee on Natural Resources. *The Use and Effect of Pesticides.* Albany, N.Y., 1963.

US Federal Committee on Pest Control. *Catalog of Federal Pesticide Monitoring Activities in Effect July 1967.* Washington, D.C., 1967.

Radiation

Howells, H. and H.J. Dunster. "Environmental Monitoring in Emergencies." In *Environmental Surveillance in the Vicinity of Nuclear Facilities.* Springfield, Ill.: Charles C. Thomas, 1970.

National Academy of Sciences. Advisory Committee on the Biological Effect of Ionizing Radiations. *The Effects on Populations of Exposure to Low Levels of Ionizing Radiation.* Washington, D.C., 1972.

Sternglass, E.J. "Environmental Radiation and Human Health." *Proceedings of the 6th Berkeley Symposium on Mathematical Statistics and Probability.* Berkeley: The University of California Press, 1971.

Other

Berry, Brian J.L. and Frank E. Horton, eds. *Urban Environmental Management: Planning for Pollution Control.* Englewood Cliffs, N.J.: Prentice-Hall Inc., 1974.

Berry, Brian J.L., et al. *Land Use, Urban Form and Environmental Quality.* Chicago: Department of Geography Research Paper No. 155, University of Chicago, 1974.

Part 3

The Nature and Problems of Urban Programs

Chapter 6

Public School Goals and Parochial School Attendance in Twenty American Cities

John S. Adams
University of Minnesota

Kathleen Molnar Brown
University of Michigan

INTRODUCTION*

Policy discussions in the field of public school education during the past decade have centered on how to raise more money and spend it more effectively and equitably, and on how to integrate public school classrooms to promote equality of educational opportunity. To a lesser degree the spotlight has been shared by questions of job protection for teachers, pay levels, work rules, neighborhood control of schools, and the needs of children with special learning difficulties. There has been comparatively less public discussion of the nature of general academic programs, their breadth or their effectiveness.

As new funding programs and integration schemes get underway, sharply lower birth rates forecast drastically curtailed enrollments in the years ahead. Meanwhile, young households get older and relocate, emptying out school buildings in older high density inner city neighborhoods.

The major debates over school funding and school integration, and the public programs that followed have usually been pursued without much attention to the nonpublic schools—mainly Catholic parish elementary schools—that operate over wide areas of many American cities, enrolling a significant fraction of elementary and secondary school children. The use of these schools raises a question whether they prevent or promote the achievement of public goals for education. To be sure, the nonpublic schools help provide a pluralistic alternative in one important facet of child rearing. They also provide competition to public school systems, although the consequences of this competition are hard to assess.

From one point of view school-age children are clients to be served. From another, they provide the vital foundation needed to keep a school system in business. Thus, when nonpublic schools are available and used, they can help alleviate the budget crunch in public school districts where total enrollments are rising. Conversely, competition from nonpublic schools can threaten job security and upward mobility of public school personnel in districts with declining enrollments. In either case, the interests of the children are but one of several sets of interests considered in the public debate.

From one point of view nonpublic schools, when available, provide an alternative to forced race-class integration of classrooms. On the other hand, the use of nonpublic schools may retard the outmigration of young white households from racially mixed neighborhoods. Perhaps. No one knows for sure.

This study reviews the major school finance and integration questions of the last decade, assessing national progress toward various goals. It concludes by describing patterns of nonpublic school attendance in 20 of the nation's largest cities, exposing some of the essential conflicts between short term public

*The comments and suggestions of John R. Gilbert, Douglas R. McManis, Dana Noonan and James E. Vance, Jr. are gratefully acknowledged.

goals and longer term questions about the role of nonpublic schools in American urban neighborhoods.

PROGRESS AND PROBLEMS DURING THE 1960s

In 1943 the president of Harvard University, James B. Conant, wrote: "The primary concern of American education today is not the development of the appreciation of the 'good life' in young gentlemen born to the purple.... Our purpose is to cultivate in the largest possible number of future citizens an appreciation of both the responsibilities and the benefits which come to them because they are Americans and are free" [quoted in U.S. Bureau of the Census. *We the Americans: Our Educations* p. 1].

In the 30 years since those words were written, the United States has moved rapidly toward realizing that ideal. The median number of school years completed–showing the average American now has graduated from high school–is a decade ahead of projections published as recently as 1965. If rates of school enrollment continue to increase as they did in the last ten to 15 years, there may be 84 million Americans going to school in 1990. If rates of educational attainment continue to increase as they have, the average adult in 1990 will have finished 12.6 years of school. Some 75 percent will be at least high school graduates, including more than one-third who will have some college experience. Education has come a long way since Governor William Berkeley observed in Virginia Colony in 1677: "Thank God there are no free schools or printing; . . . for learning has brought disobedience and heresy into the world, and printing has divulged them. . . . God keep us from both" [*Ibid.* pp. 1-2].

The 1970 census reported great strides in American education during the previous decade. At census time 54 percent of all Americans from three to 34 years old were enrolled in school. For the first time in the nation's history more than half the adult population–52 percent–had finished high school, a substantial increase over the 42 percent of 1960. By census time men had finally caught up to women in median years of school completed, 12.1 years. For the previous 30 years, women's average educational attainment had exceeded men's. Although a higher percentage of whites finish high school than blacks or persons of Spanish ancestry, these minorities are quickly closing the gap.

All states enforce compulsory education laws keeping students in school between the ages of about six and 16 years. Beyond age 15 high school dropout rates were a serious problem up through 1960, but substantial progress was made during the decade in keeping persons in school (Table 6-1). Both whites and nonwhites increasingly stay in school through their seventeenth year. Nonwhites made the biggest gains as the difference between the white and nonwhite dropout rates was virtually eliminated by 1971. The share of enrolled students who attend school regularly is unknown, but in all school systems excessive truancy means expulsion.

Yet despite these improvements, 15 percent of young men between 16 and 21 in 1970 had not finished high school and were not going to school–1.3 million whites, 345,000 blacks and 139,000 of Spanish descent. The dropout rate was 16 percent in central cities, but the suburbs were close behind with 11 percent.

Despite the educational strides, the nation's urban school systems entered the 1970s facing unresolved problems. Some school districts face severe financial difficulties as expenses outrun fiscal resources. A second major concern about elementary and secondary education is the inequality of education offered to children who live in different locations. Part of the location-based inequality depends on wide variations between states and within states in per pupil expenditures on schools and part results from the social class segregation of school children. Related to the segregation of children by social class problem is the persistent

Table 6-1. Percentage of Persons Enrolled in School

	1960		*1971*	
Ages	*White*	*Non-White*	*White*	*Non-White*
14-15	98	96	99	98
16-17	83	77	90	89

Source: US Bureau of the Census. *Statistical Abstract of the U.S. 1972*, Washington, D.C.: US Government Printing Office, 1972 p. 110.

racial segregation of school children. Elimination of racially segregated classrooms remains a major national goal, perhaps the major goal in American elementary and secondary education today.

The simply stated national integration goal for the nation's elementary and secondary schools usually ignores the existence of nonpublic schools and their important role in the nation's largest cities. It also ignores the possibility that nonpublic schools in racially integrated neighborhoods may slow down the exodus of white middle class families. In the plural society of a racially changing neighborhood, the presence of nonpublic schools may intensify classroom segregation, but one payoff may be longer term neighborhood integration.

On a nationwide scale, nonpublic schools are of minor interest, but national figures hide neighborhood instances where they form an important and, occassionally the predominant, educational system. Places like New York, Boston, Philadelphia, Chicago, Detroit and several other large urban areas maintain a disproportionate share of the nation's nonpublic schools. Inside these cities, variations between neighborhoods in the importance of nonpublic schools are much sharper than variations between cities.

Nonpublic schools persist because of a national tradition much older than the public school system that reserves to parents some freedom of choice in the education of their children. This freedom accompanies a general freedom of housing choice except where restricted (within the law) by differences in family income or restricted (outside the law) by racial or ethnic bias. Yet as people exercise their freedom of choice in schooling and in housing, a conflict unfolds in the nation's progress toward socially and racially integrated classrooms.

Against a background of nonpublic schools and goals in conflict, this chapter examines five issues:

- progress toward eliminating funding deficiencies for public education;
- reduction of economic and social segregation and progress toward equal educational opportunity;
- progress toward racial integration of classrooms;
- the role of nonpublic and especially parochial elementary schools in the central cities of the nation's 20 largest urban regions; and
- the role of nonpublic schools in stabilizing racially integrated neighborhoods.

SOLVING THE FUNDING PROBLEM

Public education money comes mainly from state and local taxes, especially from the painful property tax. The recent financial bind developed because the cost of providing education is rising rapidly and because property tax yields fail to increase automatically in proportion to general economic expansion and the need for more money.

The total outlays for public elementary and secondary education tripled during the 1960s, partly because enrollments rose from 33 million in 1957-1958 to 46 million in the 1970-1971 school year. Only about a fourth of the expenditure rise was due to more pupils. The rest came about from increase in expenditures per pupil from $335 per year in 1957-1959 to $867 in 1970-1971. The student-teacher ratio dropped from 26 to 22 and the number of pupils per "other instructional" employee dropped from 325 to 160, but 80 percent of the rise in per pupil costs went for higher salaries and benefits.

The sources of money reflect the sources of control of public education: 53 percent comes from local revenues, 41 percent comes from the states and the tiny remainder is federal money. The shares from each source changed little during the decade, but wide variations exist from state to state. On one extreme, the state of Hawaii supplies 89 percent of the money for public education. It is followed by Delaware (71 percent), Alaska (70 percent) and North Carolina (66 percent). At the other extreme the states emphasizing local autonomy by supplying the lowest proportion of state financing include New Hampshire (10 percent), South Dakota (15 percent), Nebraska (18 percent) and Oregon (20 percent).

Recent resistence to greater local contributions to education has led to rejection of bond issues and negative votes on property tax hikes. The exuberant expansionism of the mid-1960s was giving way in the early 1970s to shortened school years, curtailed academic offerings, teacher layoffs, and reduction of athletic and other programs. Some taxpayers revolt because they feel school expenditures have been rising too fast, producing larger staffs and higher salaries without measurable improvements in educational quality. The single, the childless and the elderly increasingly object to higher outlays. Without children in school they lack a direct and personal stake in the school system.

Finally, voters dislike property taxes, the source of 84 percent of locally raised school funds. Unlike sales tax or income tax withheld, property taxes are paid in large lumps, reassessments come infrequently and produce abrupt tax increases, and again unlike sales and income taxes, property levies often rise as incomes stabilize or drop, the situation commonly experienced by retired persons. Additional discontent with property taxes stems from inequitable administration. One study of Boston showed 1962 ratios of assessed value to market value for single family homes ranged from 0.28 in East Boston to 0.54 in the Roxbury ghetto, while assessment ratios on commercial property varied from 0.59 in Hyde Park to 1.11 in South Boston.

If excessive reliance on property tax is a problem, then progress is measured by a movement toward reliance on nonproperty tax sources (Figure 6-1). Southern and certain western cities rank far below the big city average in property tax reliance. Northern and eastern cities lie well above average, a reflection of local control of public education coupled with long-standing antiurban sentiment in rural dominated legislatures. Property tax reliance in Boston, Baltimore, Hartford, New York and Washington, D.C. cannot be com-

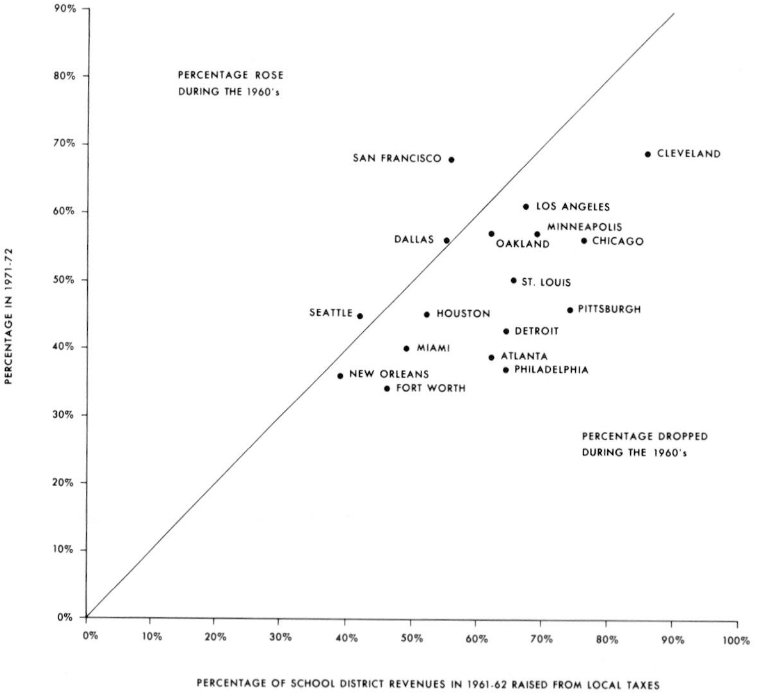

Figure 6-1. Progress Toward Relieving the Property Tax Burden. Taxes are limited to those imposed by school districts and collected by them or by other local governments on their behalf. Data unavailable for St. Paul. Baltimore, Boston, Hartford, New York, and Washington are not served by independent school districts. Source: US Bureau of the Census. *Census of Governments: 1962 and 1967*. Table 8, "Financial Statistics for Individual School Districts.

pared directly with other large cities. In these five cities the city and the school district share identical boundaries, with city councils exercising some jurisdiction over school budgets. In the other cities, school districts and cities are legally separate entities, often with different boundaries so there is no possibility of city council (or town meeting) jurisdiction or budget review. In the absence of such review there are usually fairly strict statutory controls over increases in the school operating budgets. These are maxima in terms of property tax assessments. Bond-financed capital improvements must be approved by voters at an election. During the early 1960s most of the large independent school districts reduced the share of revenues coming from property taxes, but San Francisco and Seattle on the West Coast and Dallas in the South raised the property-based share of their school district revenues.

In only a few states do school districts impose any taxes other than on property. Amounts are small except in Pennsylvania where school districts rely heavily on local gross earnings and occupational taxes.

The past decade was a difficult one for school finance but fiscal problems of school districts should decrease in the 1970s. In the first place, the enrollment boom which clogged the system has all but ended. State legislatures have been reapportioned to give cities and suburbs better representation than many of them enjoyed in 1960. The number of births has dropped each year since 1961 and currently the total number of children aged five to 17 is declining each year. As enrollment pressures decline nationally, the market for teachers has become glutted, dampening if not eliminating relative wage increases for instructional personnel. At the local level, certain suburban districts continue expanding apace while other systems stabilize or decline. Within large systems, schools in young neighborhoods remain full and vigorous, while schools in older neighborhoods experience declines, consolidations and permanent abandonment of obsolete facilities no longer needed.

CLASS SEGREGATION AND EXPENDITURE DISPARITIES

The inequality of education offered children who live at different locations has prompted a reevaluation of the federal role in elementary and secondary education. Inequalities exist at every geographical scale, among regions, states, districts and schools. If the data existed, we probably could document expenditure disparities from room to room and from student to student.

New York spends about three times as much per child on education as does Alabama, but disparities within states are at least as great as disparities among them (Figure 6-2). In most states the highest outlays per pupil are made in the wealthiest suburbs. Central cities spend more than the state averages. They often support the most comprehensive programs in expensive special education, typically have an older teaching staff in the upper ranks of the pay schedule, and always have some old and inefficient school plant.

Suburban areas spend at levels slightly below those of central cities. The younger teachers in the suburbs generally offer more recent training but their salaries average less than those of older central city personnel. At the bottom ranks are school districts outside metropolitan areas which spend considerably less per pupil than those in urban areas.

Variations in per pupil expenditures among states depend on the different capacities of states to raise money and their willingness to do so. Poor states usually spend less per pupil on education but there is a wide variation among states in the proportion of personal income devoted to public education. In states with a high fraction of pupils in nonpublic schools, public resources can be spread over fewer public school students, but public support for public education may be weaker there than in states with insignificant nonpublic enrollments.

State aid to local education is substantial, but it is normally distributed on a per pupil basis or some other basis that does little to offset differences in local fiscal capacity, which usually means taxable property per pupil. Within any state there is a great range between districts in their fiscal capacity. In California the taxable property per public school pupil ranges from \$103 in one rural district to \$952,156 in a district of great industrial wealth but few students. In Los Angeles County the tax base of Beverly Hills is \$50,885 per pupil, while nearby Baldwin Park has only \$3,706. This means that Beverly Hills can tax itself at less than one-fourth the rate of Baldwin Park and still collect more than three times as much taxes per pupil as the poorer district. Through-

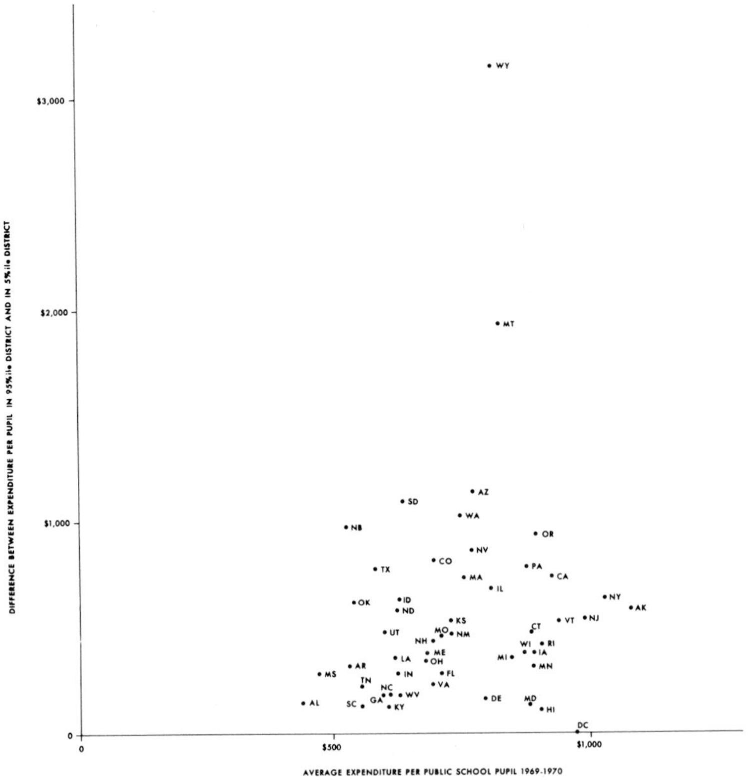

Figure 6-2. Expenditure Disparities Between and Within States, 1969-1970 School Year. Source: *Review of Existing State School Finance Programs*, Vol. 2., *Documentation of Disparities in the Financing of Public Elementary and Secondary School Systems—by State.*

out the country a similar pattern occurs. Wealthy school districts tax themselves at lower rates than poor districts and still raise more revenue per student.

Variations in expenditure patterns resulting from the interplay of ability and willingness to pay for public education have been challenged in the courts in California, Minnesota, Texas and New Jersey. In each case the judges ruled that the existing systems of school finances violated the equal protection clause of the Fourteenth Amendment. The courts decided that access to public education is a "fundamental interest" and that quality education should not be contingent upon local wealth any more than it should be conditioned on race. Since state aid does little to equalize the disparities between amounts raised locally, and since these sums mainly reflect wealth rather than the willingness of residents to tax themselves to pay for quality education, the California Supreme Court, and other courts subsequently, found that the school finance system invidiously discriminates against the poor because it makes the quality of a child's education a function of the wealth of his parents and neighbors.

But what does equality mean? How is it to be measured to suit the courts?

Budgets provide the most readily available resource measures for individual schools but they fail to distinguish quality variations from quantity variations. Some schools spend less on science laboratories per pupil than others but the former may be more efficient, or have lower quality laboratories. Whenever possible, using the per pupil size of the laboratories or the number of library books per pupil clearly is preferable. Dollar and physical measures both suffer, of course, because resources such as the effectiveness of teachers are excluded, but measuring these objectively is often difficult or impossible.

In Philadelphia public schools, the distribution of resources was examined in relation to three groups of pupils generally regarded as disadvantaged—blacks, Spanish-speaking and low income. The dollars or physical units for each resource for each school were measured against the proportions of the disadvantaged groups. This procedure helps explain what proportion of the differences from one elementary school to another in federal funds per pupil, for example, is related to differences in the proportion of low income pupils. If differences in these expenditures are unrelated to the proportion of low income students in the schools, then the explanation might lie in the relative strength of different parent groups. If a substantial proportion is explained, then the differences in federal funds expenditures per pupil might be caused by the proportion of low income students in the school. If a higher proportion of low income students occurs with larger amounts of federal funds per student, the latter might have caused the former. Whether or not the relationship is the desired one depends upon whether the school administration seeks compensatory or neutral objectives in the use of the different resources. If the objective is compensatory, then the disadvantaged should get relatively more resources as compensation for their handicaps. Federally funded expenditures are intended to be compensatory.

If the objective is neutrality in resource use, then blacks, whites, poor and rich should receive equally from the school system. Most school resources are intended to be neutral in allocation. But are they? Are there more pupils per teacher in schools with high proportions of disadvantaged? Are expenditures per pupil on libraries higher, lower or the same among schools with different proportions of disadvantaged students?

In Philadelphia's public schools in 1970–1971, the net effect of the distribution of resources for black students—intended to be neutral—appears to have been neutral. Some neutrally intended items were distributed in a significantly compensatory direction—there were fewer pupils per teacher in schools with high proportions of blacks, for example. Some neutrally intended items were distributed in a significantly countercompensatory direction—there were, for example, higher proportions of teacher vacancies in schools with higher proportions of blacks. The variation in neutrally intended resource outlay from school to school was not greatly attributable to the proportion of blacks in the school. Variability from school to school did exist, but not much was attributable to a larger or smaller proportion of blacks in the school.

Some resource allocations were made to be compensatory. Federal funds and expenditures for remedial reading were distributed such that schools with high proportions of blacks received more than other schools. Variability from school to school for these compensatory resources was intentional, but most of the variation was attributable to factors other than the proportion of blacks.

For Spanish-speaking students, the net effect of resources intended to be neutral appears to have been neutral. No items emerged where school-to-school variations had a compensatory or noncompensatory direction which was explainable by the proportion of Spanish-speaking students. Schools with higher proportions of Spanish-speaking students had significantly less experienced teachers (as measured by longevity salary per teacher), but the Spanish-speaking density accounted for little of the variation in experience from school to school. Resources intended to be distributed in a compensatory fashion went to the Spanish-speaking students in a compensatory way, but barely so.

For low income students, the neutrally intended items were close to being neutrally distributed, but some compensatory bias showed up. Schools with high proportions of low income pupils had fewer pupils per teacher and fewer pupils per other professional staff. They also had high proportions of teacher vacancies and higher capacity utilization.

For the low income students, the analysis of the distributions of compensatory funds revealed that only 3.2 percent of the variation in school-to-school use of federal funds designed to be allocated to the poor were explainable by school-to-school variations in the proportion of low income pupils. On balance then, neutrally intended resources in Philadelphia's public elementary schools were distributed neutrally in 1970–1971, even when earmarked for specific pupil groups. This is one approach to the equality issue.

In 1954, the US Supreme Court in the famous *Brown* v. *Board of Education of Topeka* case, in which racial segregation was the central issue, ruled: "Today, education is perhaps the most important function of state and local government. . . . Such an opportunity, where the state has undertaken to provide it, is a right which must be made available to all on equal terms."

Not until February 1968, however, was this basic philosophy related to school finance reform. Parents of poor children in Detroit complained that they were receiving education of a quality inferior to that in the more affluent suburbs and demanded correction through reforms in educational finance. In June 1968, a few months later, a similar complant was filed in the courts in Illinois. Students and parents argued that a school finance system that failed to compensate educationally the disadvantaged—a system that did not allocate money according to "educational needs"—was unconstitutional. The next year, students and taxpayers in Virginia sued their state's public school and finance officials because per pupil expenditures varied widely over the school districts in the state. None of these cases produced changes in educational financing procedures. The absence of a "judicially manageable standard" and the confusion surrounding educational needs criteria produced many dismissed cases and many others voluntarily withdrawn.

Only when plaintiffs moved away from the issue of equal educational quality to the issue of taxpayer equity did the courts begin rendering affirmative decisions. The difficulties the courts faced in developing manageable criteria for determining what constitutes equal educational quality are the same that educators face when evaluating various educational programs: What quantitative measures should be employed in determining whether programs have achieved their objectives?

Equity for the Taxpayer

There are two sides to an education budget—revenues and expenditures. Debates about equity in school financing move loosely between the two sides. If equity for the child, the school or the school district is the goal, then the expenditures side is emphasized and the question is whether public education funds are being *spent* "fairly." Court cases with this leaning emphasize the inferior education received by children of the poor or children in minority groups. If equity for the taxpayer is the objective, then revenue is stressed and the question is whether public education funds are being *raised* "fairly." Court cases here emphasize the limited funds raised in poor areas with equal tax effort. The child and the taxpayer are seldom different entities—the taxpayer is often the parent of the pupil. But when measuring equity it is useful to emphasize the different hats they are wearing, and taxpayer equity is easier to measure than pupil equity.

Lawyers specializing in school finance reform have recognized a taxpayer equity standard in the eyes of the courts. Their "fiscal neutrality" standard sidesteps the issue of equity in output or educational quality and focuses on the issue of equity in dollar availability. They argue that educational funding should be unbiased in the sense that equal tax effort (equal millage rates on the value of property) should yield equal dollars per child. All states except Hawaii have some form of equalization, but unequal amounts per pupil still are raised from equal millage rates because property values vary so widely.

The landmark decision of *Serrano* v. *Priest* in California was the first in a series of cases successfully argued using this principle of fiscal neutrality. School children and their taxpaying parents from a number of Los Angeles County school districts sued county and state officials on the grounds that the method of financing education in the state of California violated the equal protection clauses of the state and US constitutions. They contended that the state-mandated tax structure resulted in their paying higher tax rates to receive the same or less revenue for education as those in other school districts in the state. The outcome, they argued, was lower educational quality despite high tax efforts for many school districts. On August 30, 1971, the California Supreme Court ruled that:

> We have determined that this funding scheme invidiously discriminates against the poor because it makes the quality of a child's education a function of the wealth of his parents and neighbors. Recognizing as we must that the right to an education in our public schools is a fundamental interest which cannot be conditioned on wealth, we can discern no compelling state purpose necessitating the present method of financing. We have concluded, therefore, that such a system cannot withstand constitutional challenge and must fall before the equal protection clause.

The post-*Serrano* period has seen a steady flow of successfully and similarly argued cases in a number of states. In Minnesota the "fiscal neutrality" argument was used with success. The United States District Court found that the state had organized a tax system yielding less education revenue for some school districts. The state legislature revised its school aid formula and the plaintiffs withdrew their case. Similar decisions were reached in cases in New Jersey, Arizona, Kansas and Michigan in 1972.

Local property taxes have not been declared unconstitutional, and the level of educational spending in any school district has not been mandated. What has been strongly affirmed is the concept of fiscal neutrality. The definition of equity in education mandated by the courts is taxpayer-oriented, measuring education in terms of dollars available to spend and defining equity in terms of equal dollars per child from equal tax rates. It skips over the question of whether a difference in educational expenditures results in a difference in educational quality. It says, simply, that each child should have an equal amount available to be spent on education with the same tax effort on the part the school district.

Equity for the Child

Impressive as these equalizing recommendations and decisions may be, disregard for equity for the child is deplored. In perhaps five recent court cases involving school finance reform, no case stands which ruled in favor of requiring equal educational quality for the children in different school districts in a state. Judge J. Skelley Wright ruled in *Hobson* v. *Hansen* in 1971, in Washington, D.C., that per pupil expenditures on teachers' salaries and benefits in the district schools should not deviate more than 5 percent from the mean, that this covers "only inputs which do have a direct bearing on the quality of a child's education," and this is a "judicially manageable standard." Equal per pupil expenditure may make things equal, but not necessarily fair. One school system might be more effectively organized than another and children's needs might be different. Younger children are cheaper to teach than older ones. The education of a physically handicapped child costs more than that of a normal child. Currently, most financing schemes allot extra funds for such a child, and the costs and results are readily ascertainable. The more subtle question arises with the less visible handicaps related to poverty or race. Children from low income or deprived homes learn less from their families that will help them in school. If the schools are to compensate such children by teaching them in school what middle class children learn at home, extra resources will be needed by districts serving large concentrations of deprived children.

Should heavier allotments be made to overcome these socioeconomic differences? To answer yes, one needs more in the argument than "help the disadvantaged." If more is spent for such a child, is he helped in his school achievements? The much-publicized Coleman Report concluded that when schools with economically and racially similar students were compared, differences in school policies and resources were rarely associated with pedagogically significant or statistically reliable differences in verbal achievement. Does that mean that money does not matter—that spending more on the disadvantaged will not help, because socioeconomic and genetic characteristics matter more? Perhaps, but the issue is far from settled.

Some cost differences are traceable to price differences from place to place. The same dollar buys different amounts of goods or services in New York City, in rural Alabama or in urban Montana. For example, the asking wage for similarly trained teachers is higher in the Northeast and West than in the Midwest or South. It is higher in central cities than in suburbs or rural areas. The salary differential between the Detroit area and the Upper Michigan peninsula is about \$4,000, or about \$160 in per pupil expenditures. Differences in living costs, wage levels in alternative occupations, union strength and working conditions that require hazardous duty pay in some districts and boredom pay elsewhere all contribute to salary disparities.

Other cost differences between school districts reflect environmental differences. Northern and northeastern cities require heating and snow removal. Busing is a major expense for school districts on the Great Plains and for many in the South where consolidated school districts typically serve entire counties. Inner city schools must protect themselves from vandals. Newark in 1970 spent \$2 million—\$25.90 per pupil—to guard its buildings.

City systems also must pay higher salaries to older teachers who have been on the job longer.

Districts full of older buildings pay more for plant operation and maintenance. New facilities are often more efficient to run and cheaper to maintain. Interstate and urban-rural expenditure disparities probably exaggerate differences in real resources for education between the North and the South. On the other hand, the same kinds of comparisons between city and suburb probably hide important differences because the high central city outlays reflect the higher costs of running a school system in the city center.

After accounting for differences in facilities, climate, fiscal outlays, location and other conditions affecting the equity of education received by different children, some difficult issues remain. Conventional wisdom about the impact of schools has been challenged recently from three sources: (1) the discovery that pupil performance is inconsistently related to resources invested; (2) the renewed emphasis on family background and IQ as the main bases for pupil achievement; and (3) the uncertainties surrounding compensatory education and mandatory busing to assist racial integration efforts. Adding to the turmoil, Jencks and his associates after careful study concluded that:

- family background and IQ are the most important determinants of school achievement, although they are not sufficient by themselves to explain differences in performance.
- however measured (by teacher quality, money, facilities, programs, etc.) the equality of schools is far from a reality;
- regardless of inequalities in the schools, school-related factors are trivial in accounting for different pupil achievement; and
- whatever minor effects schools have on pupils are further vitiated by the miniscule correlations between education and later success, measured by occupational status, income and job satisfaction.

If equality is a desirable social goal, Jencks argues that with today's school systems there are better ways to achieve it than through school reform.

PROGRESS TOWARD INTEGRATING THE CLASSROOMS

Even if the nation solved its educational finance problems and eliminated disparities in resources devoted to education, the race and poverty problems would remain. Racial segregation and economic segregation are different but related issues. Schools have never been legally segregated on an income basis as they have along racial lines, although de facto segregation of the poor is common. Despite the frequent correspondence between poverty status and minority status, members of minority groups are not all poor and a large fraction of America's poor are white.

It is hard to sort out the fraction of inadequate school performance of minority and poor children that comes from inferior schools; from poorly trained, hostile or unsympathetic teachers; from the cumulative effects of racial and economic segregation; and from the inability of the home and neighborhood to transmit the attitudes, skills, language and folk wisdom that equip a person to succeed in a complex urban society. Since there has been little educational experimentation for poor and minority students, and only sporadic increases in educational resources devoted to their special needs, it is difficult to know the possible solutions or their cost.

Expensive compensatory education experiments under Title I of the Elementary and Secondary Education Act of 1965 were disappointing. When $1.6 billion per year for compensatory programs failed to produce clear breaks in the cycle of poverty, Congress and the administration became cautious about additional programs. Some began to argue that integration of the schools across racial and economic lines promised better educational performance for poor and minority children than did compensatory programs. But the national effort to integrate the schools moved along a rocky road during the 1960s and by the 1970s had yielded only mixed results.

School Integration and the Courts

The Supreme Court in its unanimous landmark decision (*Brown*) declared in 1954 that dual school systems based on race were unconstitutional and "that such segregation is a denial of the equal protection of the laws guaranteed by the Fourteenth Amendment."

The Court argued:

> We come to the question presented: Does segregation of children in public schools solely on the basis of race, even though the physical facilities and other 'tangible' factors may be equal, deprive the children of the minority group of equal educational opportunities? We believe that it does. . . .
>
> . . . We conclude that in the field of public education the doctrine of 'separate but equal' has no place. Separate educational facilities are inherently unequal.

Although 20 years have passed since *Brown* v. *Board of Education of Topeka,* it has been only recently that real progress was made toward disestablishing state and locally imposed school segregation. In the case of *Green* v. *County School Board of New Kent County (Va.),* heard in 1968, the question was whether a "freedom of choice" plan adopted by the county school board and allowing a pupil to select his or her own school was adequate to abolish the dual segregated system and to convert it to a unitary system. The ineffective "freedom of choice" plan had maintained the dual segregated system so the Court ordered the New Kent County School Board "to come forward with a plan that promises realistically to work, and promises realistically to work *now.*"

The order to adopt effective school desegregation plans resulted in an increased number of cases in which zoning plans as well as "freedom of choice" plans were rejected for school systems which had a long history of segregation. School attendance zones which followed natural or historical boundary lines and which maintained segregated schools met with sharp disapproval from the circuit courts. The neighborhood basis of school attendance zones also met resistance by the Court (*Brewer*) in areas where there was housing discrimination:

> If residential racial discrimination exists it is immaterial that it results from private action. The school board cannot build its exclusionary attendance areas upon private racial discrimination. Assignment of pupils to neighborhood schools is a sound concept but it cannot be approved if residence in a neighborhood is denied to Negro pupils solely on the ground of color.

The geographical problems present in school district desegregation were outlined in 1971 in *Swann* v. *Charlotte-Mecklenburg Board of Education* and include the assignment of pupils to schools based on racial quotas, the elimination of one race schools, the delineation of attendance zones, the transportation of students, and school location and its impact on residential patterns.

The central issues in *Swann* were whether all schools must reflect the racial composition of the system as a whole and whether one race schools had to be eliminated totally. The Court ruled that the elimination of one race schools was desirable but not essential and that racial balance in each school need not reflect the entire system.

Attendance area rezoning and busing were also important points of deliberation. With respect to attendance area rezoning the Court stated (*Swann*):

> Absent a constitutional violation, there would be no basis for judicially ordering assignment of students on a racial basis. All things being equal, with no history of discrimination, it might well be desirable to assign pupils to schools nearest their homes. But all things are not equal in a system that has been deliberately constructed and maintained to enforce racial segregation. The remedy for such segregation may be administratively awkward, inconvenient and even bizarre. . . .

The Court also upheld school busing as a valid means of achieving racial balance in schools and dismantling the dual school system.

The impact of school location on residential patterns was examined (*Swann*) and in the words of the district court:

> The result of this [construction of new schools] will be a decision which, when combined with one technique or another of student assignment, will determine the racial composition of the student body in each school in the system. . . . People gravitate toward school facilities just as schools are located in response to needs of the people. The location of schools may thus influence the patterns of residential development of

> a metropolitan area and have important impact on composition of inner-city neighborhoods.
>
> . . . Since *Brown,* authorities sometimes closed schools which appeared likely to become racially mixed through changes in neighborhood residential patterns.

The court found evidence that while residential segregation in the city was a result of the actions of many government agencies, the school board made use of such housing disparities to maintain a dual system by constructing schools in segregated residential areas and by building them just large enough to serve the immediate neighborhood. The Supreme Court ruled that such construction (and abandonment) of schools to maintain segregation was unconstitutional.

Metropolitan Desegregation

Until the *Swann* decision in 1971 litigation on school desegregation involved single school districts in the South with long histories of dual school systems based on race. *Wright* v. *Council of the City of Emporia (Va.)* marked the beginning of "metropolitan desegregation" litigation on the consolidation or subdivision of school districts. Although the early examples are two southern cities, much of the litigation in this area will probably involve northern and western cities beginning with Indianapolis and Detroit.

The issue in *Wright* was whether the city of Emporia could form a new school district and withdraw from the existing Greenville County School District which was in the process of dismantling its dual school system under court order. The case was one of creating two school districts where previously there had been one. The effect of the proposed district was an increase in the percentage of whites from 34 to 48 percent in the proposed district and a decrease from 34 to 28 percent in the county district. The Court suspected that this racial disparity would increase if white students left the county public schools for private white academies.

In addition to the question of racial disparity, the timing was such that the plan was proposed only two weeks after the district court ordered the desegregation of the Greenville County school system.

The Supreme Court maintained that the creation of a new school district for the city would impede school desegregation, but that the enjoinder was not for all time. Once a unitary school system was achieved, a separate school district could be formed.

It should be noted that *Wright* was the first split decision by the Supreme Court for a school desegregation case since before *Brown* v. *Board of Education of Topeka* in 1954. It was the opinion of the four dissenting justices in *Wright* that the creation of a new school district for the city of Emporia would not increase racial isolation as blacks would still be in the majority in both districts and that the district court was "reaching for some hypothetical perfection in racial balance, rather than the elimination of a dual school system." This last standing was explicitly rejected in *Swann.*

The first Supreme Court case on metropolitan school district consolidation was *Bradley* v. *the School Board of the City of Richmond,* which had a 12 year history of litigation. Although *Brown* had outlawed racial segregation in the nation's schools, the city of Richmond maintained a dual system until 1961 when 11 black children were admitted to white schools under district court orders. In 1963, again under court pressure, the school board adopted a "freedom of choice" plan. With the decision in *Green* v. *County School Board of New Kent County,* a speedier, more effective plan was called for and in 1970 the "freedom of choice" plan was declared unacceptable by US District Judge Robert Merhige, the same district judge who ruled against school district division in *Wright* v. *Council of the City of Emporia.*

However, by 1970 demographic trends had made effective racial integration in the Richmond School District an impossible task. Back in 1954 the city of Richmond school enrollments were 44 percent black and 56 percent white. By 1969 blacks accounted for 70 percent of the public school population while white enrollment had dropped to 30 percent. The racial composition for the Richmond metropolitan area (city of Richmond, and Henrico and Chesterfield counties) remained at constant proportions of 67 percent white and 33 percent black in the face of expanding enrollments. Thus, in November 1970 the city of Richmond asked that the state board of education and the school boards of Henrico and Chesterfield counties be joined as additional defendants. Judge Merhige granted the joinder motion.

The central issues before the district court were (1) the maintenance of racially discriminating school district boundary lines which divided a single heterogeneous metropolitan community into systems of racially identifiable schools, and (2) the equality of education available to black and to white students.

In January 1971, the district court ordered the state board of education to consolidate the school systems of Richmond and Henrico and Chesterfield counties as the only promising solution to achieving a unitary school system.

In June 1972 the decision was reversed by the Fourth Circuit Court of Appeals which ruled that Judge Merhige had overstepped his authority in ordering the three school districts to merge. Despite extensive findings on the governmental role in metropolitan racial segregation, the majority opinion stated that:

> Neither the record nor the opinion of the District Court even suggests that there was ever a joint interaction between any two of the units involved (or by higher state officers) for the purpose of keeping one unit relatively white by confining blacks to another. [*Bradley v. The School Board of the City of Richmond*, Civil Action No. 3353 (E.D. Va. 1972), 4th Cir. (1972).]

The Court concluded:

> We think that the root causes of the concentration of blacks in the inner cities of America are simply not known, and that the District Court could not realistically place on the counties the responsibility for the effect that inner city decay has had on the public schools of Richmond. . . .
>
> Indeed, the record warrants no other conclusion than that the forces influencing demographic patterns in New York, Chicago, Detroit, Los Angeles, Atlanta and other metropolitan areas have operated in the same way in the Richmond metropolitan area to produce the same results.
>
> Typical of all these cities is a growing black population in the central city and a growing white population in the surrounding suburban and rural areas. Whatever the basic causes, it has not been school assignments, and school assignments cannot reverse the trend. [*Bradley v. The School Board of the City of Richmond.*]

In a deadlocked four-to-four decision (with Justice Powell disqualifying himself) the Supreme Court in May 1973 upheld the decision of the court of appeals denying the city-county consolidation. The constitutional question of whether school desegregation orders could ignore boundaries of state political subdivisions was left undecided.

Additional metropolitan desegregation cases pending decisions before the Supreme Court involve northern cities in which there has been no history of dual school systems based on race as were those of Emporia and Richmond. Civil rights lawyers had hoped that the question of the consolidation of suburban and central city school districts left unanswered in *Bradley* v. *Richmond* would be resolved in *Bradley* v. *Milliken.* The plaintiffs brought suit in August 1970 against the Detroit Board of Education and the Michigan State Board of Education accusing them of maintaining de jure racial segregation through official policies and actions of public officials. In September 1971, the district court observed (*Bradley* v. *Milliken*) that:

> . . . [R]esidential segregation within the city and throughout the larger metropolitan area is substantial, pervasive and of long standing. Black citizens are located in separate and distinct areas within the city and are not generally to be found in the suburbs . . . which is, in the main, the result of past and present practices and customs of racial discrimination, both public and private, which have and do restrict the housing opportunities of black people.

The court concluded that:

> . . . While it would be unfair to charge the present defendants with what other governmental officers or agencies have done, it can be said that the actions or the failure to act by the responsible school authorities, both city and state, were linked to those of other governmental units.

Thus the court found that de jure racial segregation existed in the Detroit school system and was maintained by the city school board and the state board of education. Consequently, any school desegregation plan must include the state as a party.

In June 1972, the federal district court ordered the Detroit school system to merge with surrounding school districts on the basis that disparities between city and suburbs were not solely a product of individual private actions but the policies and actions of the state. *Bradley* v. *Milliken* reached the Supreme Court in 1974. The Court rejected the metropolitan remedy. The Court observed that the lower courts had viewed school district boundaries as political conveniences, and in its decision ruled that boundaries cannot be "casually ignored or treated as a mere administrative convenience."

Besides clearing up the constitutional issue of the consolidation of black central city school districts with white suburban school districts, *Bradley* v. *Milliken* helped to bring some order to the confusion on de facto segregation created by *Keyes* v. *School District No. 1, Denver.* Although the Denver school system had never operated under a dual school system, it was found that by using various methods of attendance zoning, school location and a neighborhood school policy, the school board had maintained ethnic and racially segregated schools in one section of the city. The Supreme Court contended (*Keyes*) that segregation even in a portion of the school system "shifts to those authorities the burden of proving that other segregated schools within the system are not also the result of *intentionally* segregative actions."

The intent or purpose to integrate was emphasized as the differentiating factor between de jure and de facto segregation. There is, however, the problem of how "intent to segregate" is to be established.

The confusion between de jure and de facto segregation is emphasized in Mr. Justice Powell's dissenting opinion on the majority's failure to rule on the "neutral" neighborhood school policy of the Denver School Board:

> We have no occasion to consider in this case whether a "neighborhood school policy" of itself will justify racial or ethnic concentrations in the absence of a finding that school authorities have committed acts constituting *de jure* segregation.

Mr. Powell's opinion expresses concern that the "intent" distinction between de factor and de jure segregation establishes one law for the North and another for the South:

> The net result of the Court's language however, is the application of an effect test to the actions of southern school districts and an intent test to those in other sections. . . . It is true that segregated schools, even in the cities of the South, are in large part the product of social and economic factors—and the resulting residential patterns. But there is also not a school district in the United States, with any signficant minority school population, in which the school authorities—in one way or another—have not contributed in some measure to the degree of segregation which still prevails. Instead of recognizing the reality of similar, multiple causes in school districts throughout the country, the Court persists in a distinction whose duality operates unfairly on local communities in one section of the country and on minority children in the others. . . . *Keyes*

Mr. Justice Rehnquist concurred with Mr. Powell's observations in *Keyes*: "The 'intent' with which a public body performs an official act is difficult enough to ascertain under the most favorable circumstances."

Amidst the confusion at the Supreme Court level, the distinction between de facto and de jure segregation in the lower courts is becoming theoretical. The Court's ruling on *Bradley* v. *Milliken* (1974) rejected the metropolitan consolidation remedy, yet in late 1975 the Supreme Court upheld a metropolitan school desegregation plan for the city and suburbs of Wilmington, Delaware. Thus, the central issues remain far from clarified.

Two decades after the *Brown* decision, where do we stand? The debate continues to rage over how far it is necessary to go to wipe out racial segregation in the public schools, but progress is being made (Table 6-2). The Court rulings have produced a dramatic reduction in the proportion of southern blacks attending racially isolated schools. Before the desegregation decisions, many southern cities combined rigid segregation traditions and dual school systems that permitted residential neighborhoods that were racially integrated by northern standards (Figure 6-3). The well-defined class system within southern urban areas obviated the need for residential segregation of the races at the neighborhood level. In some places today, the implementation of desegregration has meant an increase in busing—although sometimes for shorter distances than in the past, and to integrated rather than segregated schools.

Table 6-2. Progress in School Desegregation, 1968 to 1971

	Number (millions)	*Black Public School Percentage in Predominantly White Suburbs*	*Percentage in Schools with 80-100 Percent Minority*
North and West			
1968	2.7	28	57
1971	2.9	28	57
South			
1968	2.9	18	79
1971	3.1	44	32
Border States and District of Columbia			
1968	0.6	28	64
1971	0.7	30	61

Source: US Department of Health, Education and Welfare, "HEW News," January 13, 1972, p. 5.

Outside the South, segregation in schools corresponds to geographical segregation of housing patterns. Whites and blacks often simply live in different school districts. As the courts continue to participate in the school integration process, the northern metropolitan areas organized into numerous subcounty school districts will present greater financial and administrative difficulties than the South, which has large consolidated county school systems. A smaller fraction of northern pupils have been bused, so northern integration within districts could mean much higher transportation outlays. Attempts at racial balance are further constrained by the fact that minority public school children live in the central city while the suburban school districts are almost all white (Table 6-3). Unless school district lines are redrawn there may be little chance for substantial school integration in northern public schools. Little progress was made between 1968 and 1971.

Goals in Conflict

The three major problems discussed so far require:

- easing financial pressure on the schools by reducing dependence on property taxes;
- equalizing resources devoted to education in different jurisdictions; and,
- improving educational opportunities for minorities and the poor by eliminating classroom segregation.

But reliance on the property tax is generally higher in high spending districts, so efforts to relieve the property tax conflict with efforts to equalize resources among jurisdictions.

Second, the poor and the minorities live in central cities which currently spend more per pupil. Their costs are higher and there is more competition for their limited tax resources. If expenditures were equalized with the suburbs, it would be more difficult for central cities to make improvements for poor and minority students. Moreover, abrupt reductions in central city parochial and private school enrollments in favor of public schools would lead to the same unsettling consequences.

Finally, the huge concentrations of poor and minority persons in central cities increase the cost and the difficulty of improving educational opportunities by busing or by school district consolidation. The adoption of such measures would mean exorbitant transportation outlays. Some people expect that massive two way busing following city-suburban school district consolidation would increase the attractiveness of nonpublic schools, especially parochial schools serving local neighborhoods. Any major exodus from public schools to nonpublic schools would reduce somewhat the willingness of communities to finance the public schools. On the other hand, such a movement might speed up acceptance of greater federal support for local schools.

Potential conflicts between national education goals and local performance are easier to

Table 6-3. Racial and Ethnic Composition of Selected Public School Systems, Fall 1968*

	*Percentage Minority***	
New York City (five counties)	56	
Nassau County		6
Westchester County		15
Chicago	62	
Rest of Cook County		8
Detroit	61	
Rest of Wayne County		8
San Francisco (county)	59	
San Mateo County		17
Marin County		5
Oakland	69	
Rest of Alameda County		20
Baltimore City	65	
Baltimore County***		4
Anne Arundel County		13
District of Columbia	94	
Prince Georges County, Md.		15
Montgomery County, Md.		6
Arlington County, Va.		14
Cleveland	58	
Rest of Cuyahoga County		5
St. Louis City	64	
St Louis County***		5

*Ignores central city and suburban enrollments in nonpublic schools.

**Includes American Indians, blacks, Orientals, and Spanish surname persons.

***The city is not in the county.

Source: US Department of Health, Education and Welfare, Office for Civil Rights, *Directory of Public Elementary and Secondary Schools in Selected Districts: Enrollments and Staff by Racial/Ethnic Group,* Fall 1968, OCR-101-70 (Washington, D.C.: US Government Printing Office 1970).

highlight when attention turns to the local arenas where national policies are carried out. The following discussions examine birth rates and school enrollment trends, and the geographical relationships between public and nonpublic schools in the nation's 20 largest urban areas. We conclude with a discussion of the role of nonpublic schools in maintaining stability in racially integrated neighborhoods.

BIRTH RATES AND SCHOOL ENROLLMENT TRENDS

A typical child in the United States enters school at age five and remains until high school graduation at about age 18. Enrollments drop sharply after secondary school. Only about half the 18 and 19 year olds in 1971 remained enrolled, either finishing high school, attending technical or vocational schools, or starting college. Back in 1960 the fraction was closer to a third.

Attendance rates measure the fraction of the population that go to schools but the birth rate determines the number of persons in each age cohort. Today's birth rate controls the demand for schools in the decades ahead just as births in the last few decades provided today's students. Economic dislocations and uncertainties during the Great Depression contributed to a decline in live births to the celebrated 1933 trough of 2.3 million (Figure 6-4). A reduced number of births during the 1930s diminished the demand for education during the 1940s and 1950s, and shrank the number of women of child-bearing age during the 1950s and early 1960s.

Birth peaks reverberate through the schools and through society in a direction opposite from birth troughs. Except for a brief downturn during World War II, the annual number of births rose steadily after the Depression trough, to reach an all-time peak in 1961. Persons born in the late 1930s and 1940s reached family-forming ages during an era of optimism and prosperity and produced a record number of children. These children began entering school during the 1960s, with the largest group—the 13 year olds in 1974—scheduled to leave elementary school and enter high school in about 1975. For the remainder of the 1970s total elementary enrollments will continue downward. Economic pessimism, preferences for smaller families and the continued use of effective birth control measures will keep the birth rate low.

The number of births during the late 1970s and subsequent elementary school enrollment levels starting in the early 1980s will depend on family formation preferences of the boom babies of the late 1950s who will be reaching adulthood. They comprise a record number of potential parents but their future behavior

Figure 6-3. Residential Segregation in New Orleans. Data Source: U.S. Bureau of the Census, 1970 Census of Population.

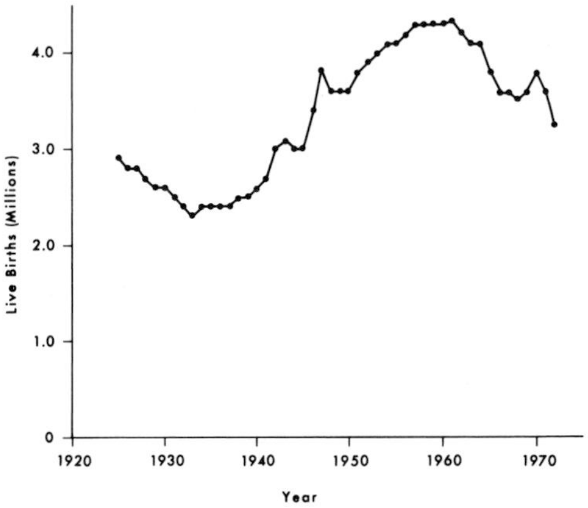

Figure 6-4. Live Births in the United States, 1925-1972. Source: U.S. Bureau of the Census, *Statistical Abstract of the United States: 1972*, page 10; *Historical Statistics of the United States: Colonial Times to 1957*, Washington: 1960, page 214.

seems impossible to forecast. Who would dare forecast the reproductive behavior of a generation of Americans that grew up in crowded classrooms and swollen little league teams only to discover that their hard-won college degrees commanded little if any market premium? Who would blame this anonymous generation for turning its back on an unpleasant childhood and dropping out to seek an identity different from a statistic in a clogged pipeline?

Public and Nonpublic Schools

Virtually all the noninstitutionalized elementary and secondary school age persons in the United States attend three kinds of schools: public schools operated by local school boards and supported by taxes; private, nonsectarian schools supported by tuition and gifts from benefactors; and parochial schools maintained, operated and partially supported by religious organizations.

Across the country public schools predominate at all levels of education—primary, secondary and tertiary. Although public dominance increased abruptly during the 1960s, it varied sharply between levels and continues to differ significantly from one region of the country to another.

At the start of the decade, 84 percent of all students were in public schools. By 1971 the share had risen to 88 percent (Table 6–4). The nonpublic enrollment shares dropped most sharply in kindergarten and elementary schools. Pupils passing through these primary schools were not being replaced at the end of the decade by newly entering pupils. Tuition costs were burdensome to be sure, and doctrinal motives for parochial schooling had doubtless become less compelling by the decade's end. But a better explanation lies in the increasing geographical separation between the locations of the established parochial schools in urban areas and the homes of prospective parochial school pupils. Primary pupils attend school close to home.

Nonpublic high school enrollments (70 percent parochial; 30 percent private) fared relatively better than their primary counterparts. Students will travel farther to get secondary schooling so nonpublic high schools located near the center of an urban area can still be reached by middle class students living near the edge of the city or in the suburbs. Since they currently tap a shrinking pool of parochial grade school graduates, the parochial high school share of the enrollments will continue to drift downward except where they provide an alternative high school that students or their parents find more attractive on grounds of academic standards, social or religious climate, or personal safety.

The type of college attended depends in part on a student's willingness to leave home. College students from families with little tertiary education are likely to select a nearby school at a handy location, obviating the need to cut home ties. Children of college-educated parents are less hesitant about going away to school if a variety of high quality opportunities is unavailable locally.

About a third of the nation's college enrollments are drawn from private schools but the average hides important local variations. For example, 51 percent of the enrollments in New England colleges and universities were in private schools in the fall of 1971. The Middle Atlantic states followed with 40 percent. At the other extreme were the Mountain and Pacific states with 13 and 10 percent. The prestigious and well-endowed private colleges and universities in the Northeast were established during colonial times and the nineteenth century. The prominent ones draw students from all over the world. Meanwhile, recently settled states rely almost exclusively on public schools, or else send their college students out of state.

Private college and university enrollments expanded 50 percent during the 1960s. Their share of total college enrollments shrank only because public enrollments expanded even faster. Despite their high prices, private schools continue to attract students who feel (or whose parents feel) the academic quality, philosophy, reputation, location, size, programs or personal attention are worth the price.

IMPORTANCE OF NONPUBLIC SCHOOLS

The vast majority of nonpublic schools are Catholic parochial elementary schools. The stronghold of these schools is in the large

Table 6–4. School Enrollments, Public and Nonpublic, 1960 and 1971

	1960			*1971*		
	Enrollment (millions)	*Public (Percentage)*	*Nonpublic (Percentage)*	*Enrollment (millions)*	*Public (Percentage)*	*Nonpublic (Percentage)*
Kindergarten	2.1	81	19	2.8	86	14
Elementary	30.3	85	15	33.5	89	11
High School	10.2	90	10	15.2	93	7
College	3.6	65	35	8.1	68	32
Total	46.3	84	16	59.6	88	12

Source: U.S. Bureau of the Census *Statistical Abstract of the U.S. 1972*, Washington, D.C.: US Government Printing Office, 1972 p. 106.

metropolitan regions of the Northeast and Midwest (Figure 6-5). Among the central cities of the 20 largest daily urban systems in 1970, parochial schools were relatively unimportant in the Protestant South except for Catholic New Orleans; in the new cities on the West Coast that grew more from domestic than foreign immigration; and in Hartford where despite large foreign immigration parochial schools never prospered. Perhaps Hartford's unusual prosperity and middle class mobility out of the city meant that immigrants melted faster, or perhaps because Catholics comprise a majority of Connecticut's population there has been less pressure to develop and support a vigorous alternative to the public schools.

In most urban areas the parochial schools serve a larger share of central city than suburban students. Among the cities of the nation's historic past (Boston, New York, Hartford, Philadelphia) and the nineteenth century port cities (New Orleans, San Francisco-Oakland, Baltimore), only in New Orleans and Baltimore is the fraction of elementary pupils in parochial schools higher in the suburbs than in the city. Both are southern cities and both had large middle class Catholic populations in the nineteenth century. The role of race is ambiguous because large numbers of black Catholic pupils in New Orleans attend parochial schools.

Among the large nineteenth century urban centers (St. Louis, Cleveland, Pittsburgh, Detroit, Chicago, Minneapolis-St. Paul, Seattle), middle class central city neighborhoods of high parochial school usage have spilled vigorously out into the suburbs. In St. Louis, Cleveland, Pittsburgh and Chicago the fraction of elementary pupils in parochial schools is higher in the suburbs than in the central city, perhaps because of the unusually rapid social and geographical mobility of Catholics in these areas or because of the early establishment of suburban parishes in the years shortly after World War II when the normal policy was to begin a parish with a school and build the church later. In all other major metropolitan regions of the country, the parochial schools are more important in the central city if they are important at all. Parishes established in the 1960s tended to emphasize religious education apart from parochial schools.

Between 1960 and 1970 the percentage of most cities' elementary pupils attending nonpublic schools dropped sharply. Some of the drop followed migration of upwardly mobile

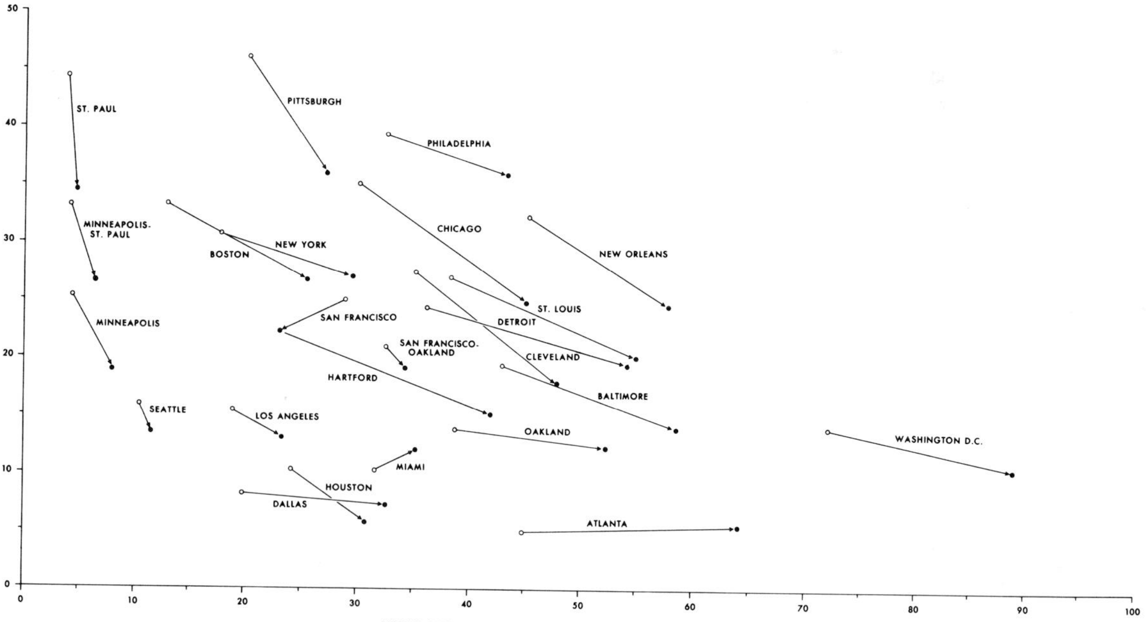

Figure 6-5. Changes in Enrollment Patterns and Racial Composition of Elementary School Children in 22 Cities, 1960 (open circle) to 1970 (solid circle).

Catholic families out of the older neighborhoods where the parochial schools are concentrated. Some of the decline was due to higher tuition costs of running parochial schools with lay faculties increasingly unwilling to contribute instructional services at the level that was common when most teachers were nuns. Still other declines have been interpreted as evidence of a decline in religiosity on the part of Catholic parents or at least a loosening of the separatist outlook of the immigrant church. Others argue that parochial school choice is less a religious observance than a social class phenomenon. Many upwardly mobile parents prefer the more exclusive atmosphere of a nonpublic school, but only Catholic parents have had a nonpublic school option available to them in most areas. Institutional financial support came from the church and from orders of religious nuns, brothers and priests, but use of the parochial schools has been mainly by middle class families.

In neighborhoods where private nonsectarian schools receive institutional support instead of relying solely on tuition, the schools are popular. They also seem to perform a neighborhood stabilization function in addition to their educational role. These mixed motives and outcomes were highlighted when Teachers College of Columbia University decided in 1973 to close an innovative private elementary school it had operated for 25 years in Morningside Heights in New York City. The Agnes Russell School served 148 pupils from the racially and economically mixed residential neighborhood around Columbia University. The school had 19 staff members and charged $1,500 per year tuition and $80 for materials, but fewer than half the students paid the full cost. In the 1972-1973 school year tuition charges covered only $133,500 of the total operating costs of $347,000. Teachers College, suffering the same financial pressures that beset all institutions of higher learning, made up the balance of the Russell School budget.

The school is typical of private schools near many major colleges and universities. It was the most recent of several run by Teachers College since the nineteenth century for children of faculty members and university students. In recent years enrollment has been open to families not connected with the college, and there has been some attempt to use it as a laboratory school serving Teachers College.

Parents anxious to keep the school open proposed a tuition increase with part of the increase set aside for scholarships for perhaps a third of the pupils. Parents felt that the Russell School, although expensive, provided quality education in an area where the public schools are poor. Yet the president of Teachers College argued that the Russell School was just another private school, whereas the teachers being trained there would be teaching mainly in public schools, and that the Russell School students despite their racial and economic diversity were not truly representative of the community. The Russell School closing illustrates the survival difficulties faced by private and parochial schools once they lose their base of institutional support.

NONPUBLIC SCHOOL ENROLLMENT TRENDS

The 1960 census reported nonpublic school attendance patterns for nonwhite pupils and the 1970 census reported the same data for black pupils. Except in certain cities with major concentrations of American Indians or Asian Americans, the vast majority of nonwhites are black.

The proportion of central city elementary school children who are nonwhite rose during the 1960s, while the share of pupils in nonpublic schools declined (Figure 6-5). There are vast differences from city to city in the percentage of black pupils in 1970. On the low side are Seattle, Minneapolis and St. Paul. Boston was low in 1960 but rose to over 25 percent by 1970. The cities with high percentages of nonwhite pupils in 1960—Atlanta, New Orleans and Washington—moved higher at unusually rapid rates during the decade. New Orleans, St. Louis, Detroit, Baltimore, Oakland, Atlanta and Washington ended the decade with black elementary school children in the majority.

The percentage of elementary enrollments in nonpublic schools in 1960 varied from highs in Pittsburgh, St. Paul, Philadelphia and Chicago, to lows in the southern cities of Atlanta, Houston and Dallas. The nonpublic percentage declined in all 22 central cities except in Miami following the Cuban influx and in Atlanta following an influx of migrants from northern cities and perhaps a temporary reaction to court decisions on school desegregation.

Nonpublic Schools and Racial Isolation

Are nonpublic schools associated with racial isolation? The answer appears to be a qualified yes for most of the historic metropolitan centers, the nineteenth century ports and the older inland centers, but not for the others. One measure of racial isolation is the difference between the percentage of *all* elementary school children who are black, and the percentage of the *public* school children who are black. The smaller the difference, the more the racial composition of the public school reflects that of the community (Table 6-5). If the difference is large, it means the nonpublic schools are more white than the community and that the public schools are more black than the community. We will postpone to later in the chapter a discussion of the location of public and nonpublic schools, the role of residential segregation in racial isolation in the schools, and differences in the age structure of the white and black population of cities.

Eleven of the 22 cities showed a difference greater than 5 percent in 1970, with Philadelphia's 18 percent disclosing the greatest difference. In that city, 57 percent of the elementary age children are white but because so many of them attend nonpublic schools 61 percent of the public elementary school pupils were black in 1970. In cities where the difference is small the public school enrollments resemble the racial composition of total city elementary enrollments either because nonpublic schools are unimportant—as in Dallas, Houston and Atlanta—or because nonpublic schools enroll a proportionate share of minority students—as in Minneapolis, St. Paul and Seattle.

The general drift in the largest cities, especially those in the northeastern quarter of

Table 6-5. Racial Isolation in Central City Schools, 1970

	Percent Elementary Pupils Black in 1970		
	All Pupils	*Public School Pupils*	*Difference**
Historic Cities			
Boston	25	32	7
New York	29	37	8
Hartford	42	48	7
Philadelphia	43	61	18
Nineteenth Century Ports			
New Orleans	58	68	11
Baltimore	59	67	8
San Francisco	23	28	5
Oakland	53	57	4
Inland Centers			
Pittsburgh	28	42	14
Detroit	54	64	10
Chicago	45	56	11
Cleveland	48	57	9
St. Louis	55	65	10
Minneapolis	7	8	1
St. Paul	5	6	2
Seattle	12	13	1
Twentieth Century Cities			
Dallas	32	34	2
Houston	31	32	1
Atlanta	64	65	2
Miami	34	38	4
Washington, D.C.	89	93	4
Los Angeles	23	26	3

*Some detail lost in rounding.

Source: U.S. Bureau of the Census, Census of Population, 1970, Vol. 1. Characteristics of the Population, Washington, D.C.: U.S. Government Printing Office, 1972.

the country, has been toward a white elementary school age population with a large nonpublic component and toward a population that is increasingly public-school-oriented and black. Normal aging of older white Catholic populations, selective outmigration to the suburbs of upwardly mobile white families, immigration of lower class black families, plus natural change by the younger black population yields the same picture. The mechanism of change has not been "white flight," but rather a steady process of population turnover by migration and natural change but without replacement in kind.

Religion, Ethnicity and Social Class

But what of the nonpublic school clientele? Who attends nonpublic schools? What makes a family select a private or parochial school as an educational alternative when free public education is available? Do nonpublic schools perform other, noneducational functions?

It is a popular misconception that religious and financial constraints keep nonwhite children out of nonpublic schools. Most black families are non-Catholic and therefore would be unlikely prospects as parochial school clientele. But religious and financial requirements are often eased for black families in order to achieve a better racial balance in the parochial schools. Nationally, a little more than one out of every nine children in Catholic parochial schools is nonwhite and half of the nonwhite enrollment in Catholic schools is non-Catholic. Nonpublic school systems in northeastern cities and in Cleveland, Houston, Dallas, Minneapolis-St. Paul, Pittsburgh, Seattle, Los Angeles and Miami have relatively few black enrollments while in a city such as New Orleans, where there is a large Catholic black population, nearly one-fourth of the nonpublic elementary school population is nonwhite. The percentages are even higher for Oakland (27 percent), Atlanta (35 percent) and Washington, D.C. (54 percent), probably due to their large middle and upper middle class black populations.

As already suggested, racial isolation increases when a disproportionate number of white students attend nonpublic schools. An extreme example is Philadelphia in which 11 percent of the black and 56 percent of the white elementary school children attend nonpublic schools. The result is a public school population almost two-thirds black in a city in which only 43 percent of all elementary school children are black. The point, then, is that racial isolation exists in urban public schools not because nonpublic schools serve only a white clientele, but rather because a large portion of a diminishing white population have chosen nonpublic schools for their children.

Why black families elect to send their children to nonpublic schools remains to be established, although it is suspected that middle class black families prefer this option. Attendance in Catholic parochial schools by white clientele seems to be linked with parental religiousness, the availability of parochial schools, ethnicity, generation and social class.

Catholic parochial schools are more available in some regions of the country than in others. Because of the religious climate in the old country, some ethnic groups have stronger bonds with the church than others. Tuition costs may prohibit poor families from sending their children to parochial schools, while the prestige of attending a nonpublic school may be the attraction for middle and upper middle income families. Finally, devout parents may feel a serious responsibility, indeed a religious obligation to send their children to parochial schools.

However, despite these obvious speculations, the associations are not clear-cut when attributes and correlations are measured. It is suspected that in the United States participation in religious activity, including sending one's child to parochial school, is closely related to social class aspirations. Parochial schools are nonpublic schools, set apart and distinctive. One can imagine the rising young business executive dutifully accompanying his family to Sunday services not because of any deep religious piety but because it is what a rising young business executive is expected to do.

The length of time since immigration also seems to affect religious behavior. In the sociology of religion literature some writers maintain that religiosity among first generation immigrants was high due to a close association of the ethnic form of religion with their own social identity. This need for a "communal" type religion as contrasted to "associational" forms of observance was fostered by the impersonal conditions which European immigrants had to confront in the urban ghettos. As the second generation discarded ethnic traits in order to become more Americanized, participation in the traditional form of the religion of their parents declined. An increase in third generation participation seems to accompany the security of being fully acculturated and a renewed interest in the religion of the grandparents though not necessarily in the traditional, ethnic form.

On the other hand, others feel that religious participation increases generation by generation, as the melting pot mechanisms in American society break down the bonds between ethnicity and religion and produce a threefold division of society into Protestant, Catholic and Jew.

Because of the time differences between the arrival of the various immigrant groups, a high degree of ethnic diversity remains in American society today. Accounting for the length of time an ethnic group has been in the United States, the third generation is more likely than preceding generations to have some parochial school education. The participation in Catholic education by some groups (such as Italian, German and Spanish-speaking) has increased from generation to generation. Participation by some remains the same (Poles) and the attendance of others declines (Irish and French). However, the most important factor associated with Catholic school attendance is still parental religiousness. A strong connection between ethnic background and family religiosity suggests the use of religion as an enforcer of cultural heritage.

The decision to participate in the Catholic school system depends only in part upon values and preferences that are generated and reinforced by factors of ethnic identification such as generation and past religious fervor. The effects of ethnic identification on patterns of school choice are most apparent in the tradition of the ethnic parochial school in which children were educated in both the American and ethnic traditions. The degree to which ethnic groups have used the parochial school system as a source of group solidarity varies from the Irish, French and Polish who have made substantial use of parochial schools, to the Italians and Spanish-speaking who in the past collectively have preferred to attend public schools.

PAROCHIAL SCHOOL ATTENDANCE PATTERNS

Each city has a unique parochial school attendance pattern which reflects the collective behavior of a clientele that has a cultural and religious heritage as well as social and economic position in the urban community. Racial relations and the comparative quality of education in the public schools also determine the attendance pattern. So, to a certain extent, a map of parochial school attendance not only indicates patterns of educational choice, but several underlying facets of a city's social structure as well.

Some cities are more alike than others due to general similarities in their settlement histories and in their social structure. Parochial school attendance exhibits two types of geographical patterns in large American cities: the first pattern resembles an island of high parochial school attendance and is most often associated with a white, ethnic enclave in Eastern and Midwestern cities (such as the Dorchester section of Boston) or large and successful parochial schools in middle class neighborhoods (scattered examples in Minneapolis are typical). In some Eastern cities these islands are quite large and resemble belts of school attendance rather than islands. But these belts are white, middle class and to an extent ethnic neighborhoods the cohesiveness of which is reinforced as black ghettos approach on one or more sides. In this case, the white population is usually prevented from shifting steadily out toward the suburbs by some natural barrier. The belt of high attendance rates between Queens and Brooklyn is a fine example (Figure 6-6). Bounded by poor blacks (Bedford-Stuyvesant) to the west and upper income blacks (St. Albans-Jamaica and Jackson Heights) to the east, white Catholic families are prevented from shifting to outer Long Island since they must also by-pass Flushing Meadows. Short moves to better housing in familiar surroundings are not possible. If families wish to move, then the move must be over a considerable distance. The alternative is to remain in the same neighborhood and attempt to maintain a cohesive community. In many instances social disrup-

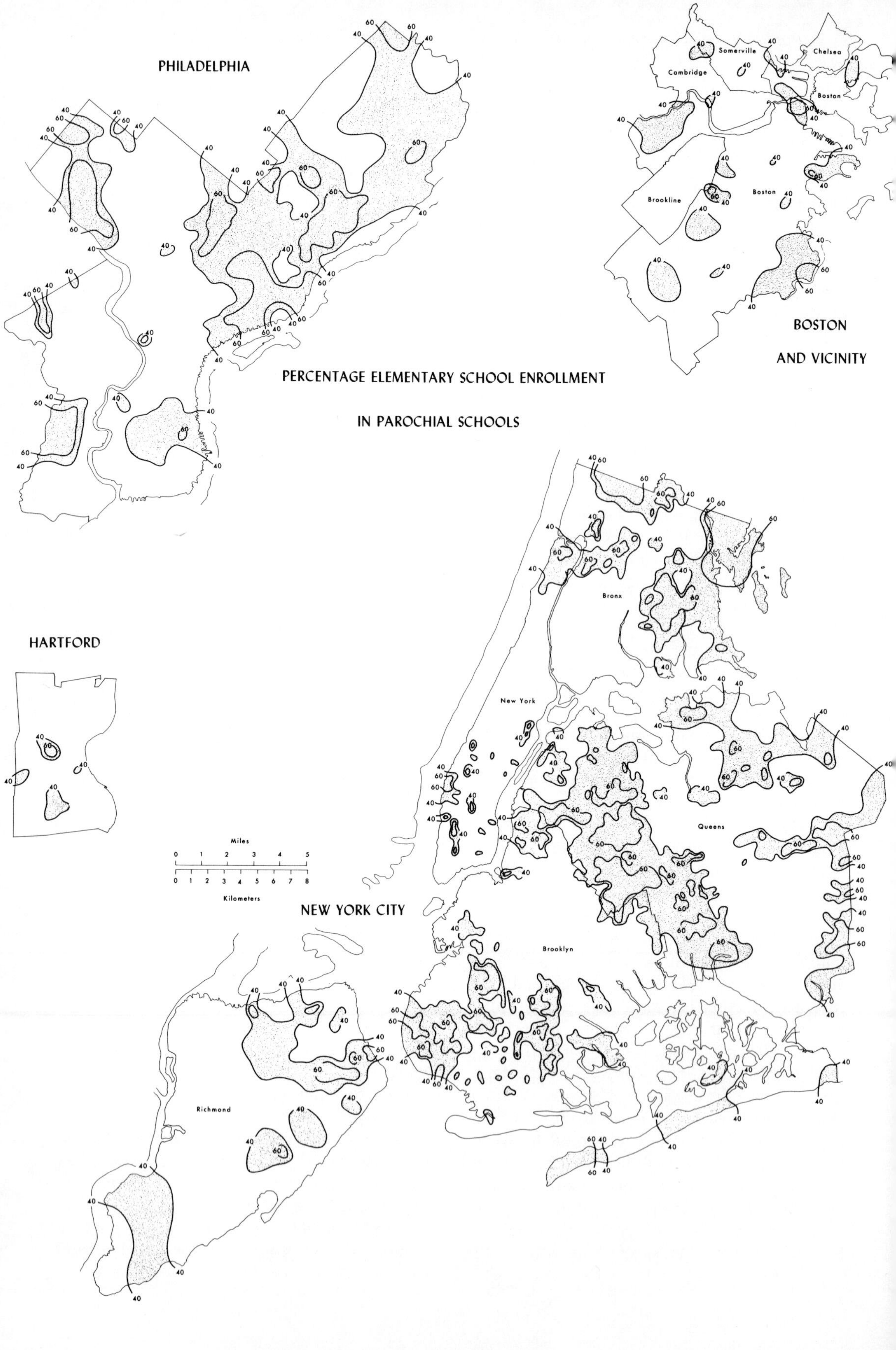

PERCENTAGE ELEMENTARY SCHOOL ENROLLMENT IN PAROCHIAL SCHOOLS tion occurs in the public schools and parents who can afford to do so transfer their children to parochial and private schools in the area.

While the ethnic islands and belts of attendance seem characteristic of Eastern cities, Midwestern cities also display wedges or sectors of school attendance which begin in the central city and which usually extend into the suburbs, unconstrained by natural barriers formed by rivers, bays, marshlands, peninsulas and parks such as those found in Boston, New York and Philadelphia.

Three groups of cities can be identified in terms of patterns of intensity of school choice. The first group includes the old European immigrant cores of the Northeast and Midwest states: Boston, New York, Philadelphia, Hartford, Chicago, Pittsburgh, Detroit and St. Louis. The high percentages of parochial enrollments emphasize a century of commitment by the Catholic Church to the European immigrants who settled in the ghettos of these cities.

Both northeastern and midwestern cities display the two types of attendance areas of island and wedge. However, enclaves show up as cul-de-sacs in transport and migration systems as metropolitan systems unfold on the complex river estuaries and drowned coast lines which seem to dominate in eastern cities. while sectors spill out smoothly into the suburbs in Cleveland, Chicago and St. Louis. The reasons for this, other than the absence of physical obstacles, are not known but may indicate underlying differences in the social or political structure of eastern and midwestern cities. We can hypothesize two attendance patterns for the old immigrant cities: one characteristic of eastern cities in which enclaves are predominant and the other characteristic of midwestern cities in which both islands and wedges occur, the latter being the more prevalent pattern.

Islands of parochial school attendance are most apparent in Boston and include South Boston (on a peninsula); Dorchester, which is bounded by the Roxbury ghetto to the west and by Dorchester Bay to the east; Jamaica Plain, bounded on the west by heavily Jewish Brookline and on the east by Roxbury; Brighton-Allston between Brookline and Cambridge; Somerville; the North End; Charlestown; and Old Boston. Dorchester and Jamaica Plain have a high incidence of first and second generation Irish, while Somerville, the North End and Old Boston are areas of Italian settlement. The presence of a Catholic seminary and the proximity to Boston College and Harvard of Brighton-Allston may attract and retain Catholic and professional families who are more likely to send their children to parochial schools.

Figure 6-6. Percentage Elementary School Enrollment in Parochial Schools: Philadelphia, Boston, Hartford and New York City.

Parochial elementary school attendance patterns in New York also take on an island-like appearance, but large belts also occur. Pockets of parochial school attendance occur on the west side of Manhattan and in Brooklyn, especially in Bay Ridge, Flatbush and Borough Park. These are also areas of Italian, Irish and Polish populations. The extensive belt of parochial school attendance in the Bronx and Queens shows similarities in that both are bounded by an expanding black ghetto. The Bronx attendance area centers in the Fordham University area and is bounded by Harlem to the south. Residents in this area are isolated from the suburbs by Van Cortland Park and Pelham Bay Park. Similarly, residents in Queens are wedged between Bedford-Stuyvesant in Brooklyn, Jamaica-St. Albans to the southeast and Jackson Heights to the northeast. Flushing Meadows and the East River complete the circle of isolation.

Islands of parochial school attendance are also visible in Hartford. Once again parochial school enrollments are high in the vicinty of a religiously affiliated institution of higher education, in this case Trinity College (Episcopalian) located in the south central part of the city.

Philadelphia nonpublic schools serve a larger portion of elementary school population than any of the other 22 central cities, and unlike most other cities the parochial school system is recognized as having an important role in urban education. Contributing to the high parochial school attendance may be the difficulties faced by Philadelphia's public school system. The early seventies were years of great financial stress for the public schools accompanied by long teacher strikes, budget cuts and the elimination of many programs. A wedge of high parochial school attendance extends from downtown northward paralleling the

Delaware River into Bucks and Montgomery counties. Much of Philadelphia's Italian population lives here, as well as in South Philadelphia between the Schuylkill and Delaware rivers. A third area of high parochial attendance is wedged between the Schuylkill and Fairmont Park in Northwest Philadelphia. The influence of the upper middle income and Irish-Catholic suburbs in Delaware County shows up in parochial enrollments in the Morris Park and Paschall portions of West Philadelphia.

The second group of old immigrant cities which have a high proportion of private and parochial school enrollments are Chicago, St. Louis, Pittsburgh, Cleveland and Detroit (Figure 6-7). Three of these cities are located on relatively flat lake plains, one on river bluffs and one on a river junction in a highly dissected portion of the Appalachian Plateau.

Next to Philadelphia, Pittsburgh accounts for the greatest proportion of elementary students who are enrolled in nonpublic schools. However, as was noted earlier, the suburban nonpublic schools enroll a larger percentage of students than the central city private and parochial schools. Attendance in the city is high in Mount Washington, overlooking the downtown Golden Triangle district; the West End; the Riverview Park area in the northwest sector; Lawrenceville and Highland Park along the Allegheny; and along the Monongahela near Hazelwood extending north to Carnegie Mellon University and south along the edge of the city (Mount Oliver, Overbrook, West Liberty and Banksville). A small island of enrollments is located near the University of Pittsburgh in the center of the city. Otherwise black neighborhoods, such as East Liberty and Homewood; Squirrel Hill which has high private, nonsectarian enrollments; and the commercial and industrial districts on the flatter lands account for most of those neighborhoods having low parochial elementary enrollments.

Detroit and Cleveland are both lake plain cities, with a cluster of parochial enrollments near their downtowns and large black ghettos in the core of the city, which have lower parochial school attendance. Whereas Cleveland's parochial school system is stronger in the suburbs than in the central city, Detroit's northeast neighborhoods, which extend from Hamtramck east to Harper Woods and Grosse Pointe Park, show remarkably high parochial school attendance. As in the case of the eastern cities, the boundary of the parochial attendance area closely parallels the boundary between the black neighborhoods of central Detroit and the white neighborhoods of the Northeast. High enrollments along the western edge of Detroit are limited to islands in high income white residential neighborhoods and near Mercy College of Detroit. High enrollments are also found near the University of Detroit, an important Catholic institution at the northwest corner of Highland Park.

Parochial enrollments in Cleveland are highest in a band stretching from Rocky River to Lakewood. Larger populations of Eastern Europeans—especially Poles and Czechs in the southern suburbs of Parma, Brooklyn and Garfield Heights—explain the high parochial concentrations along the southern boundary of Cleveland. Enrollment areas in Euclid, east of Bratenahl, extend into the wealthy white suburbs of Wickcliffe and Willoughby Hills. As with Detroit, enrollments are low in predominantly black neighborhoods. However, this does not mean black children do not attend parochial schools. Maps of the percentage of parochial students who are black show that there are neighborhoods where black students are enrolled in parochial schools, and that in most neighborhoods the parochial enrollments are either all black or all white.

St. Louis, like Cleveland, has a higher fraction of parochial elementary students enrolled in the suburban schools than in the central city parochial schools. The major attendance areas are to the north and south of the black neighborhoods of central St. Louis and extend into the wealthier suburbs.

Although proportionately the nonpublic system is larger in several other cities, Chicago's Catholic school system is the largest nonpublic system and the fourth largest of all school sytems in the United States. Two wedges of parochial enrollments which begin in the central city and expand outward into the suburbs dominate the attendance pattern for Chicago. The first wedge in southwest Chicago is bounded roughly by the Stevenson Expressway to the north and Ashland Avenue to the east, and extends beyond the city limits into Bur-

Figure 6-7. Percentage Elementary School Enrollment in Parochial Schools: Pittsburgh, Detroit, Chicago, Cleveland and St. Louis.

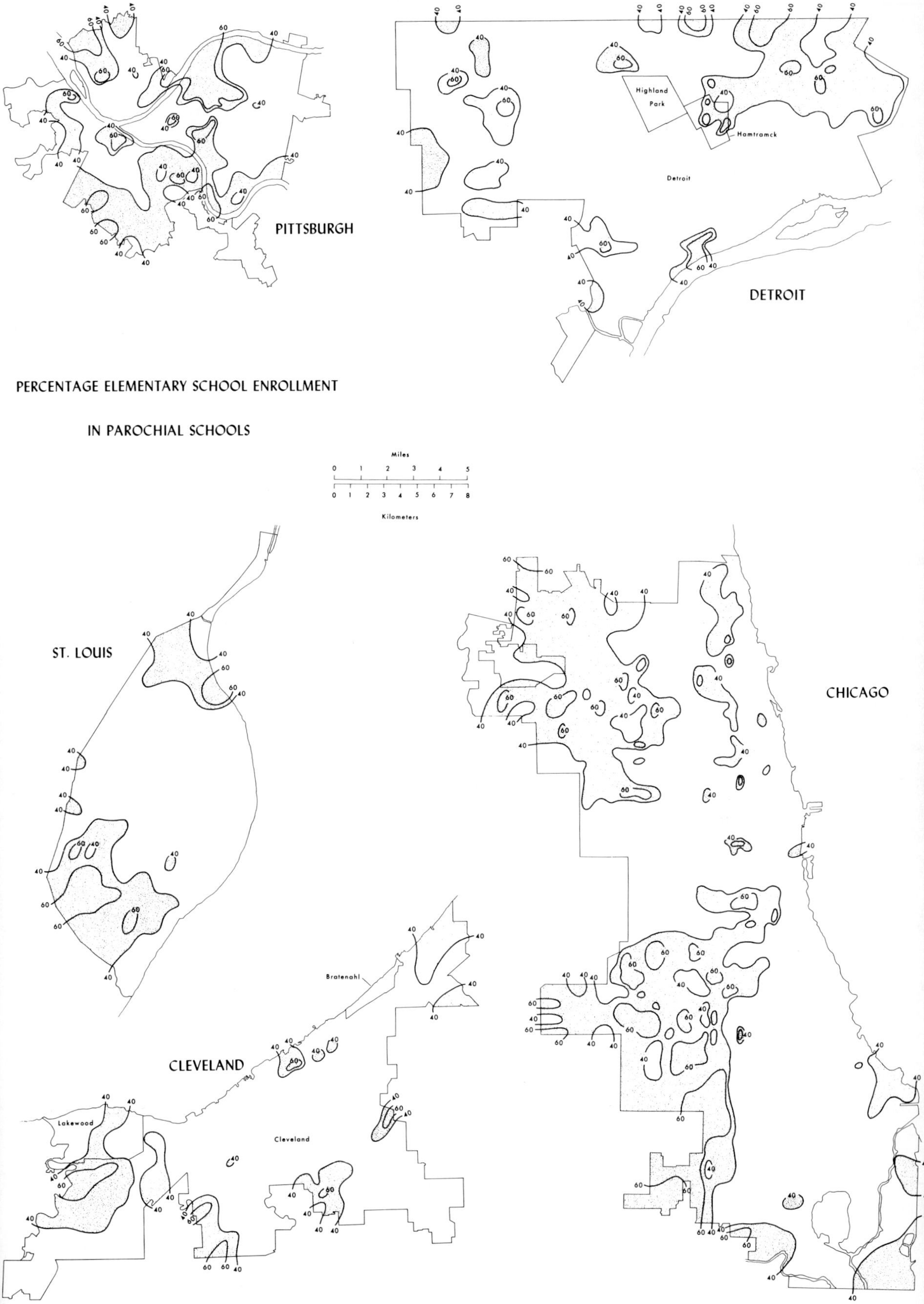

PERCENTAGE ELEMENTARY SCHOOL ENROLLMENT

IN PARROCHIAL SCHOOLS

bank and Oak Lawn. The second wedge is bounded by Chicago and Pulaski Avenues and includes parks named for Chopin and Koscuisko, attesting to the ethnic heritage of the residents. Paralleling the north shore are islands of parochial attendance in an area of a mostly white, non-Catholic population.

The second group of cities which show similarities in parochial attendance patterns are the early Catholic southern cities of Baltimore and New Orleans, and the city pairs of Minneapolis-St. Paul and San Francisco-Oakland (Figures 6-8 and 6-9). These cities are cities of contrast not only because of their attendance patterns but because of the similarities in their historical development.

Baltimore and New Orleans have the largest proportional nonpublic school enrollments for the major Southern cities. However, unlike most of their Northern counterparts, these nonpublic school systems have their greater strength in the suburbs. Both were cities of early Catholic settlement, by the French in New Orleans and by the English, and later

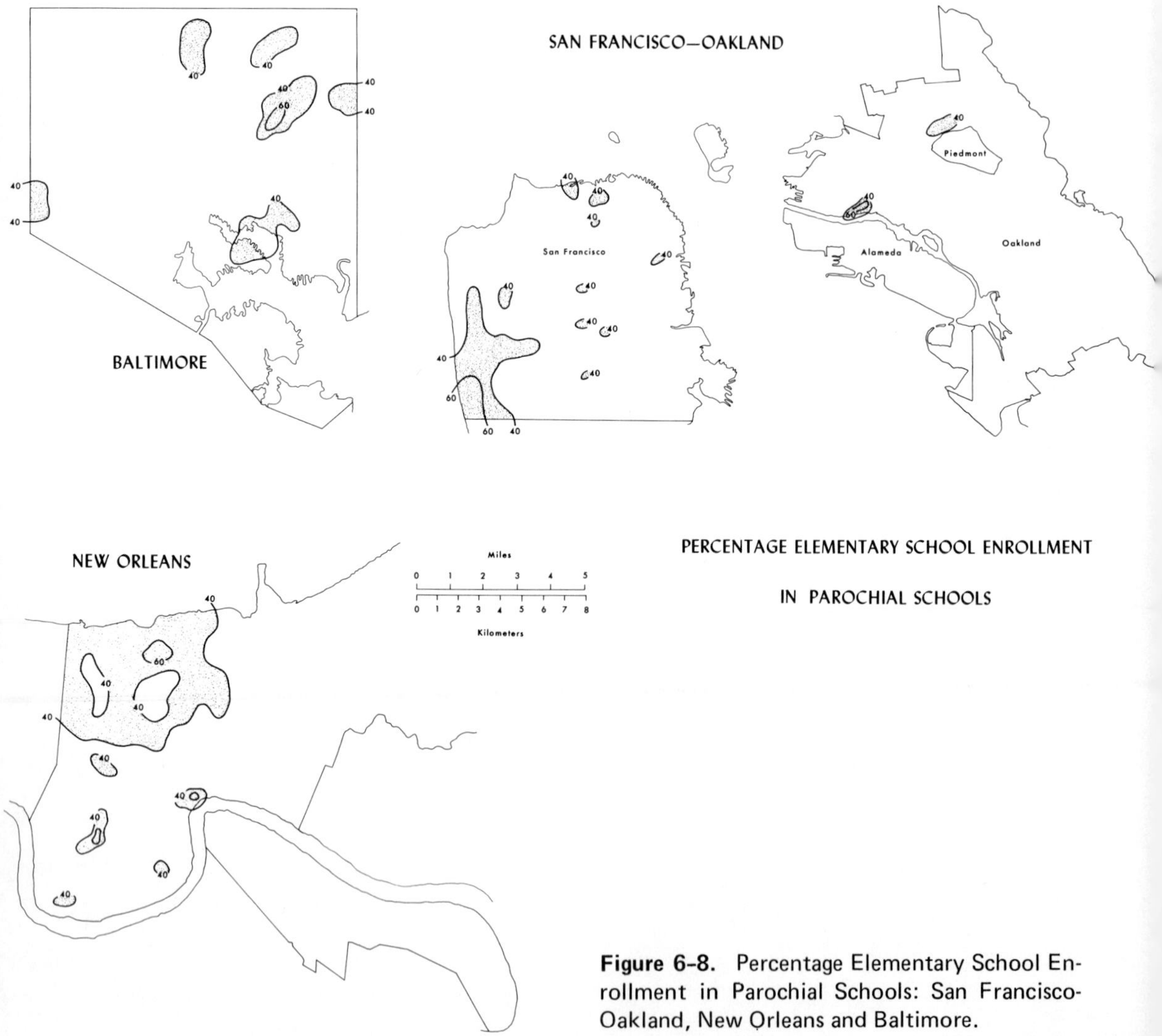

Figure 6-8. Percentage Elementary School Enrollment in Parochial Schools: San Francisco-Oakland, New Orleans and Baltimore.

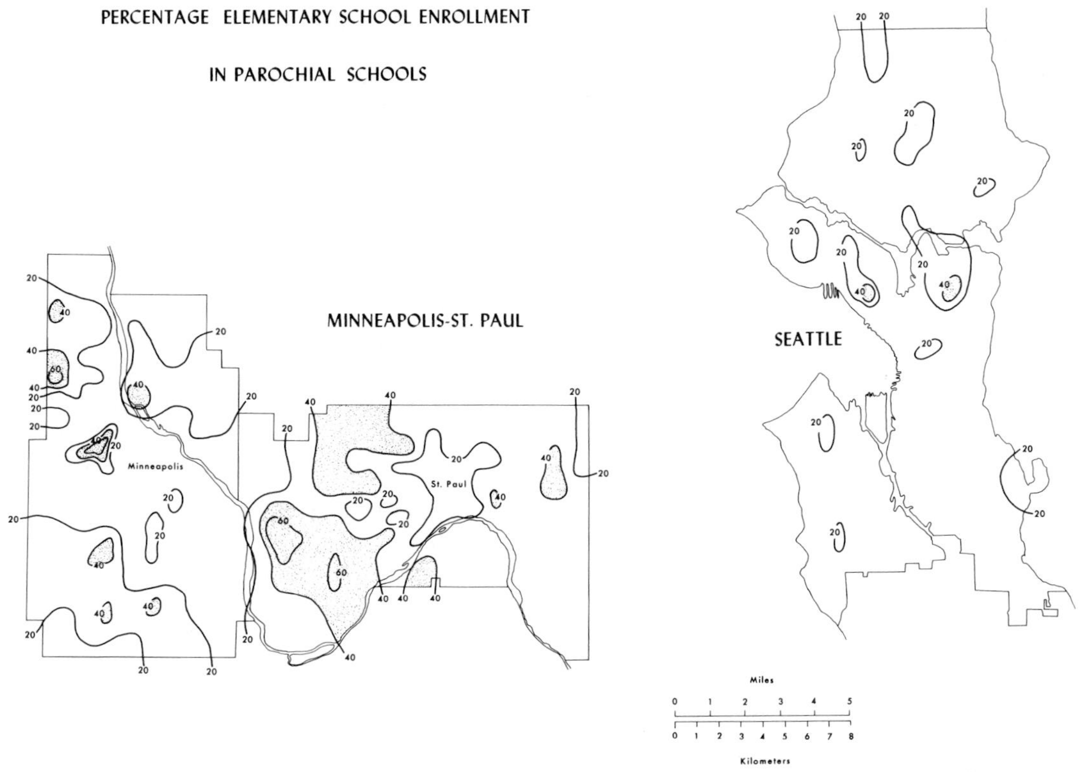

Figure 6-9. Percentage Elementary School Enrollment in Parochial Schools: Minneapolis-St. Paul and Seattle.

Irish, in Baltimore. American Catholicism has its roots in Baltimore, going back to the naming of John Carroll as first American archbishop shortly after the Revolution. Parochial schools were always important in French New Orleans and continue to serve their descendants and the large black population. Most of Baltimore's parochial school enrollments are in the northeast, north of Henney Run Park in an area of numerous religious-associated institutions. The parochial school enrollments in New Orleans concentrate in the northwest corner of the city, with a few enclaves of enrollment around the old established parochial schools of the French Quarter.

Minneapolis-St. Paul and San Francisco-Oakland reveal how two cities within the same metropolitan area can differ. Compare the extensive attendance areas of St. Paul's Irish, German and Austrian Catholic neighborhoods in the western part of the city near Como Park and Highland Park with the small localized islands in Scandanavian Lutheran Minneapolis. Pockets of high attendance in Minneapolis surround large popular parochial schools in middle class sections of the city. Exceptions are in northeast Minneapolis which has the highest concentration of ethnic churches and schools in the city and a small area near downtown Minneapolis which simultaneously serves upper income families in the Loring Park and Kenwood areas with Catholic and Episcopal schools, and lower income downtown families who are relatively isolated from public schools.

Although San Francisco is hardly a bastion of parochial education, it does present a marked contrast to Oakland. Much of San Francisco's parochial enrollments is in islands in the immediate vicinity of the schools. Outside of these islands parochial school attendance is more closely associated with Catholic ethnicity (Park Merced) and middle income neighborhoods to the southwest, and with areas just off government military bases such as Marina Park. To a considerably lesser extent, the same is true for Oakland whose only two areas of high parochial school attendance are next to the Naval Air Station and Supply Depot, and next to the higher income area of Piedmont.

There may be some military personnel who have children in the parochial schools near the Presidio, but as likely an explanation is the heavily Irish and Italian middle class population in the area. The same may well be the case near the Alameda Air Station, where the main center of the Spanish- and Portuguese-American settlement in Oakland predates the founding of the air station. Piedmont is high income and less clearly ethnic, though with a school system separate from Oakland. The black upper class clustered on Piedmont's border might provide some support for the parochial schools.

In drawing comparisons between Minneapolis-St. Paul and San Francisco-Oakland, it is worth mentioning that the role of ethnicity in parochial school attendance is becoming less important, while social class and proximity to military bases or universities is increasingly a more important factor. We have moved from the old immigrant cores of the East and Midwest to the more mixed, younger cities of the nineteenth century. The parochial school system is not as important in this group of cities and neighborhoods of 40 and 60 percent attendance rates occur less frequently.

Seattle marks the transition from the cities of the nineteenth century to those of the twentieth. Only two neighborhoods have parochial school enrollments greater than 40 percent, and these are in a high social class area west of Lake Union and in an area between the US Naval Depot and the University of Washington.

The absence of extensive parochial school attendance areas in twentieth century cities discloses a difference in the social structures of these cities and a failure of the American parochial school system to address its offerings to the tastes and needs of these populations. The maps show a lower intensity of attendance, plus the localized attendance areas of Seattle and Minneapolis. There are no extensive belts or wedges of attendance. In Los Angeles pockets of attendance cluster along an axis running from the San Fernando Valley in the north through West Hollywood to Culver City in the southwest and just south of downtown in the east (Figure 6-10). Highest parochial attendance once again occurs just outside of a military base—the Long Beach Naval Station. Other neighborhoods with high parochial enrollments are found just to the south of downtown and on the periphery of West Hollywood and Culver City.

Parochial school attendance patterns for Dallas, Houston and Atlanta show the small role that nonpublic education has in the educational systems of these cities (Figures 6-11 and 6-12). Attendance areas in Dallas border on the periphery of University Park and Highland Park, while for Atlanta and Houston enrollment areas reflect northern enclaves and institutional areas.

Parochial school enrollments in Washington, D.C., are limited to the wealthy northwest portion of the city, and an area near the Washington Naval Yard and the Naval Research Laboratory along the southern Potomac.

Miami is the last twentieth century city and also shows a low percentage of parochial school enrollments. However Miami was the only city of the 22 which realized an increase from 1960 to 1970 in the fraction of elementary school children enrolled in nonpublic schools. This is probably due to the influx during the 1960s of northern migrants and Cuban refugee families into western Miami. Other relatively high enrollments are in Miami Beach, Surfside to the north of Miami Beach, North Miami and in the university community of Coral Gables.

In summary, then, parochial school attendance patterns reflect the settlement history and settlement geography of the cities studied. Extensive areas of steady and strong enrollment in eastern and midwestern cities develop in highly stable, white ethnic neighborhoods. Very often these neighborhoods border on expanding black and Puerto Rican ghettos and seem to use parochial schools to preserve their identity. Perhaps this reflects an unevenness in the quality of base schools, but it could also reflect an expectation by mobile military families that Catholic schools will usually provide for their children a more stable and predictable educational setting than is available in public schools near military bases. Finally, parochial attendance remains high near institutions such as hospitals, colleges, universities and religious

Figure 6-10. Percentage Elementary School Enrollment in Parochial Schools: Los Angeles-Long Beach.

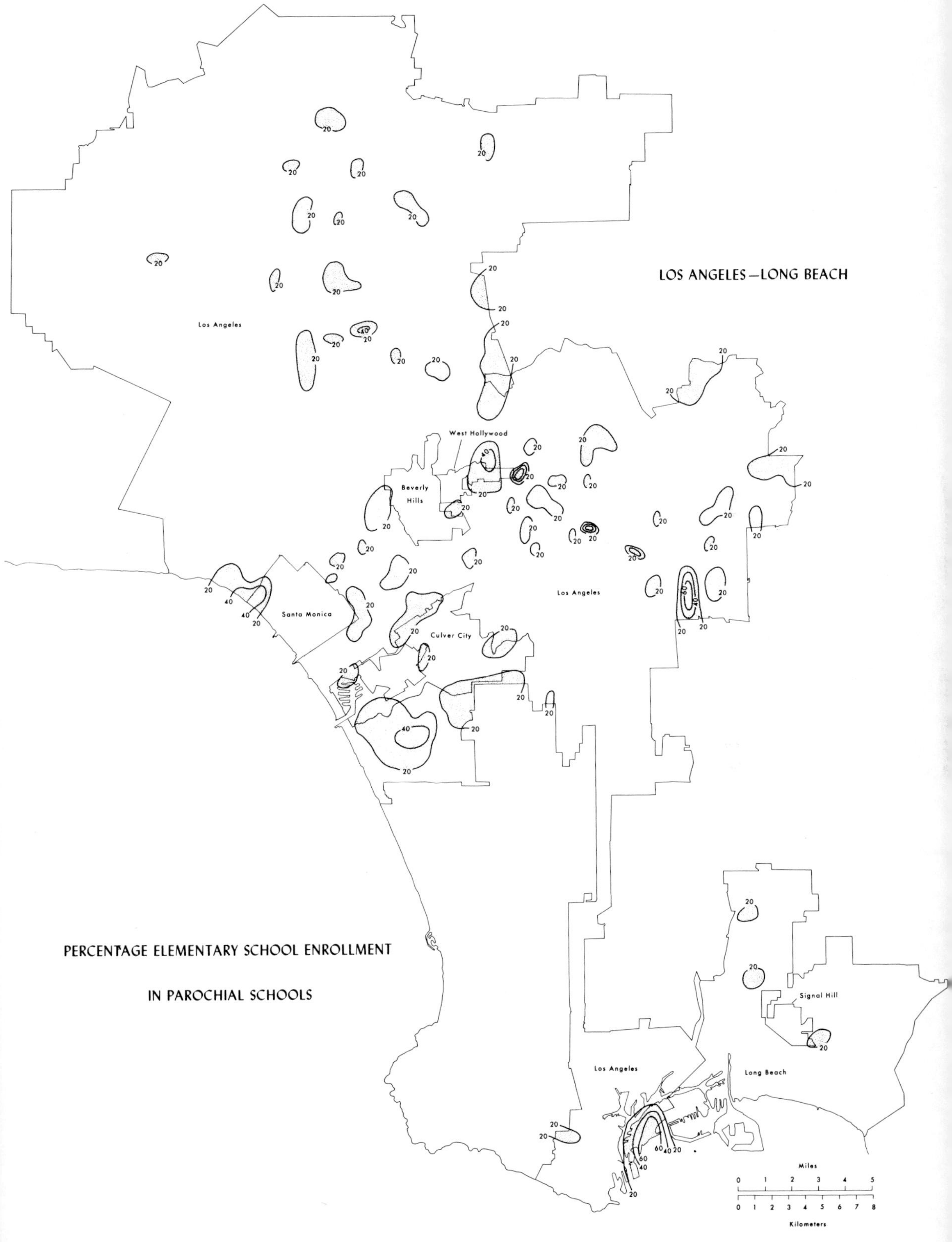
LOS ANGELES—LONG BEACH
PERCENTAGE ELEMENTARY SCHOOL ENROLLMENT
IN PAROCHIAL SCHOOLS
Los Angeles
West Hollywood
Beverly Hills
Santa Monica
Culver City
Signal Hill
Long Beach
Miles
Kilometers

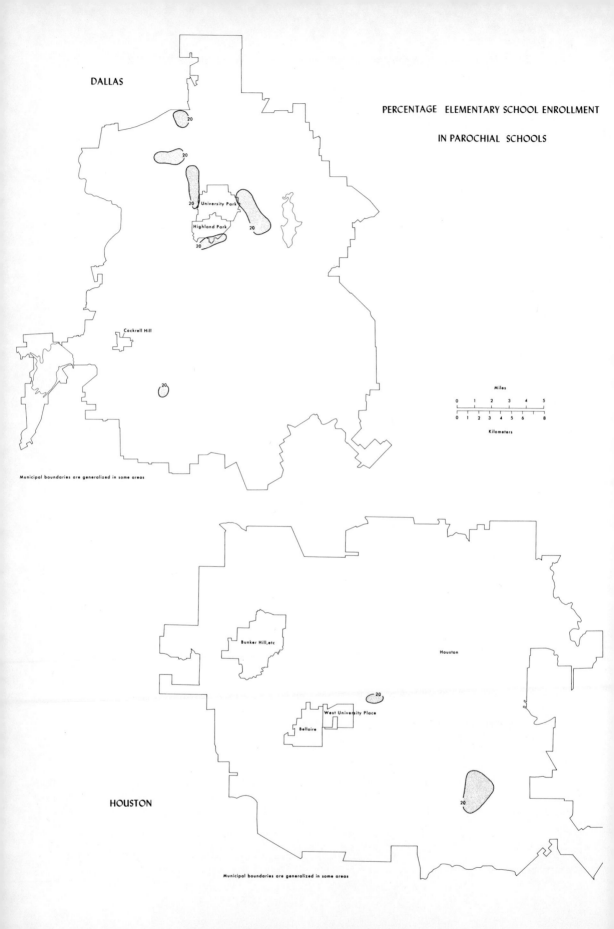

PERCENTAGE ELEMENTARY SCHOOL ENROLLMENT IN PAROCHIAL SCHOOLS

DALLAS

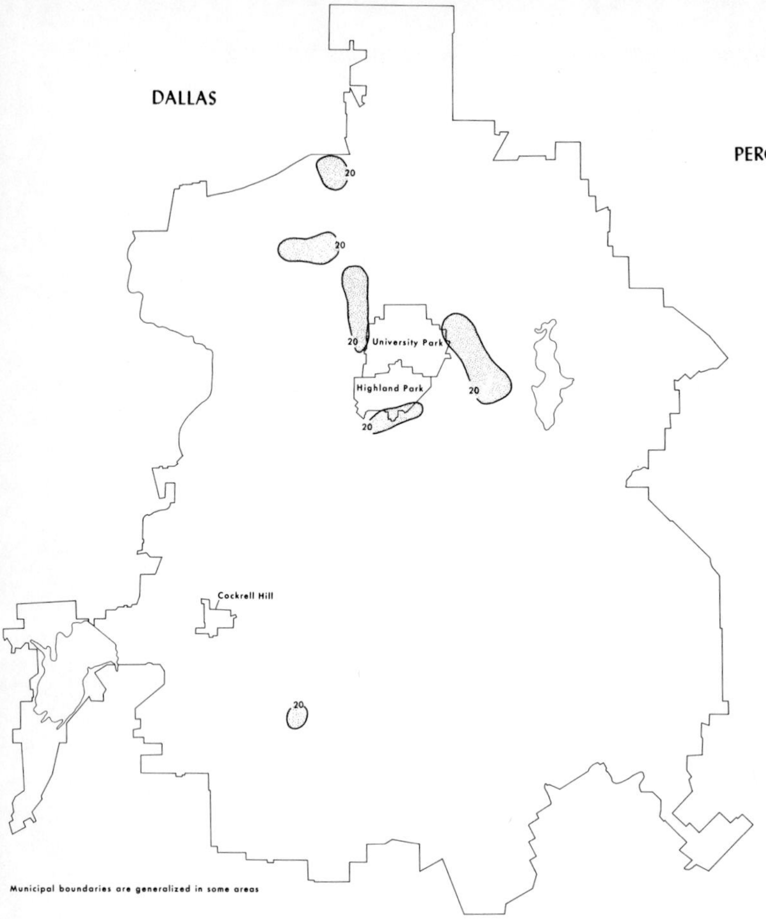

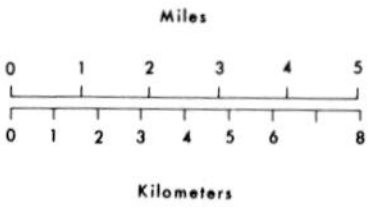

Municipal boundaries are generalized in some areas

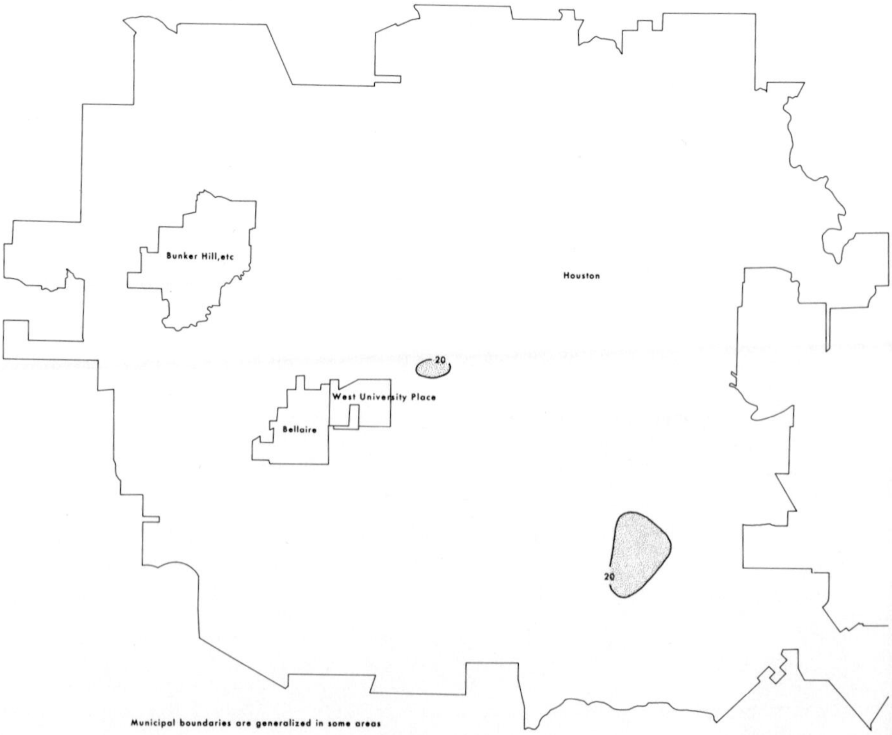

HOUSTON

Municipal boundaries are generalized in some areas

communities, as middle- and upper-middle class parents use parochial schools as a neighborhood-controlled alternative to inner city public schools.

NONPUBLIC SCHOOLS AND NEIGHBORHOOD STABILITY

While adding to the racial imbalance of metropolitan school systems, nonpublic schools may also be the stabilizing force behind the decision of many households to remain in the central city, and in particular in racially changing neighborhoods. The theory is that in the wave of racial change, and the social disruption in public schools that usually follows, white families find that the advantages of city living such as accessibility to work and social activities are often insufficient attractions for remaining in the city. However, in neighborhoods of high nonpublic school enrollment, the communal function of the school and the parish church to which it is attached may mitigate the immediate social consequences of neighborhood racial change and act as a deterrent to panic selling and rapid racial turnover. In instances where parents transfer their children from public to nonpublic schools in order to avoid racial integration, nonpublic school attendance may afford time for those parents gradually to accept neighborhood integration.

In a series of studies prepared for a report to the President's Commission on School Finance, the conditions in the public schools and the general attitude of the white residents were also important determinants of neighborhood stability. The first case studied a nonsectarian private school in a racially changing area in Chicago's South Side. Fifty percent of those households interviewed indicated that they would leave the community if a nonpublic school were unavailable to their children. This particular community had a long history of attempts to stem panic selling in the wake of black movement into the area. The public schools went from 1 percent black in 1950 to almost 75 percent black in 1970. The private school in this case was integrated but remained predominantly white.

Figure 6-11. Percentage Elementary School Enrollment in Parochial Schools: Dallas and Houston.

In Chicago's Italian West Humboldt district, the public schools were 90 percent black in 1971 as compared to 100 percent white in 1963. The all-white Catholic elementary school was surrounded by neighborhoods that have undergone rapid racial change. Panic peddling by realtors was counterbalanced by the efforts of strong community organizations to maintain neighborhood stability. Almost 90 percent of those parents interviewed and whose children attended the parochial school indicated that they would move if this or any other nonpublic school were inaccessible. The overwhelming response for their reasons to move was their refusal to allow their children to attend school with blacks or Puerto Ricans.

Another set of studies was carried out in the Dorchester section of Boston for which three Catholic parochial schools were selected. The first case was a predominantly Jewish-Irish neighborhood before black movement into the area. When questioned about their reaction to a closing of the 15 percent black parochial school, 36 percent of those interviewed said that they would move, while 33 percent would seek out another nonpublic school.

The findings for the two other parochial schools were not as marked. One, in the direct path of black migration and in an area of plummeting land values, had little effect on the retention of clientele. Two-thirds of the parents in the third parochial school said they would send their children to the predominantly black public schools and only two out of 21 respondents said that they would move.

Although the findings are inconclusive, it is likely that many middle and upper income families would move to the suburbs if these institutions were not available, thereby weakening the city's tax base. Catholic schools have helped to maintain many ethnic neighborhoods in Chicago, Milwaukee, Philadelphia and Boston. In racially changing neighborhoods, attendance at a nonpublic school may lessen the perceived impact of social change, affording the white households time to readjust. In these ways, whether well-intentioned or not, nonpublic schools may maintain some racial and socioeconomic balance in the nation's cities. But the important question remains, how major is the role of nonpublic schools in neighborhood stability, or are nonpublic schools as neighborhood services overshadowed by greater social and economic forces within the city?

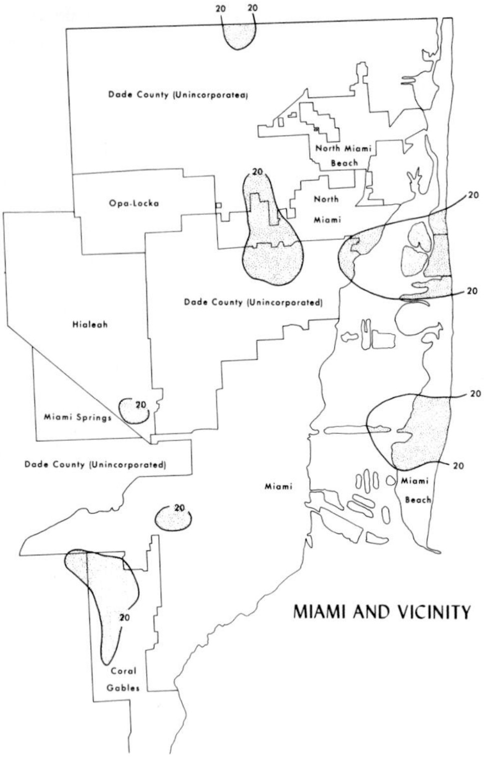

PERCENTAGE ELEMENTARY SCHOOL ENROLLMENT

IN PAROCHIAL SCHOOLS

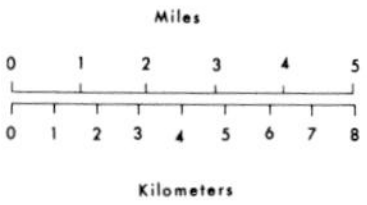

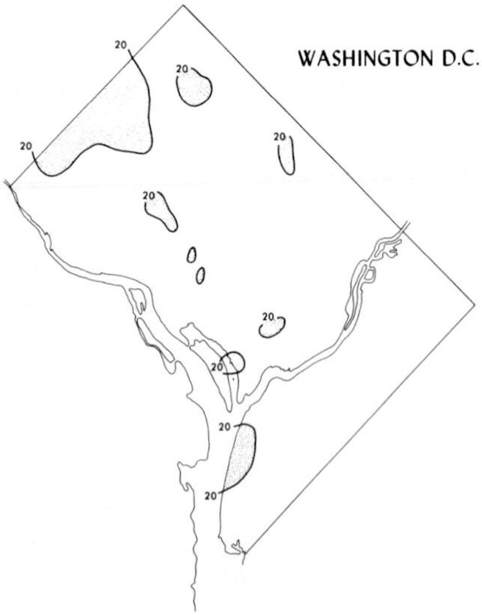

CONCLUSIONS

After a decade of progress in education a variety of issues remain unresolved. Professional educators feel the sting of limited financial resources, yet the vast majority of Americans report satisfaction with the schools. Public education's support by the property tax means that education does not automatically capture an ever-increasing share of national resources as do government activities funded by sales taxes or progressively structured income taxes. Thus, any decision to increase education's share of gross national product becomes a hotly contested issue in every local school district attempting to float a bond issue or increase its property tax mill levy. Perhaps other classes of government expenditure should be subject to more political debate, rather than yielding to occasional pressure to make public education budgets less political. As enrollments decline, and as the share of the population without a direct stake in the school systems rises, political and electoral processes are the appropriate mechanisms for working out local conflicts with due sensitivity to the special needs of local settings.

While a controversy rages over the best ways to measure equality of educational opportunity, what really seems to matter is native intelligence and a family background that prepares a pupil to do well in school. Greater strides have been made in defining a judicially manageable standard of equity for the taxpayer who supports the schools. Attempts at fairness for the pupil must continue, but first must come equity within school districts. Differences between districts and between cities in teachers, students, plant, facilities and curriculum escape remedy because they currently defy analysis.

The South made progress during the 1960s in racial integration of schools. Yet as neighborhood public schools in the South have recently become more integrated, residential neighborhoods have simultaneously become steadily more segregated. If southern residential trends continue, southern cities, like their northern counterparts, will rely increasingly on busing to achieve school integration goals.

Figure 6-12. Percentage Elementary School Enrollment in Parochial Schools: Atlanta, Miami and Washington, D.C.

Busing options are simpler in most southern cities because consolidated school districts usually cover entire counties. Balkanization of school districts in northern metropolitan areas prevents simple busing solutions to school segregation problems. District consolidation or cooperation based on court action or legislative bribe or mandate may speed up northern school integration. A permanent and fundamental solution based on residential integration of all minority groups appears substantially more remote than simple school integration.

Critics sometimes blame nonpublic schools for the racial isolation in many big city school systems. This is usually an oversimplification that ignores the geographical patterns of race, class and residence inside large cities. Within most cities, blacks live in one set of neighborhoods and whites live elsewhere. In white neighborhoods, nonpublic schools thrive mainly in middle class Catholic areas, near major colleges and universities, and near military installations.

Nonpublic schools seem to persist and even thrive temporarily in certain racially mixed neighborhoods but the patterns of cause and effect are obscure. In racially changing neighborhoods the parochial schools are more white than the community and the public schools are more black. The parochial school is only a part of a many sided community center focused on the parish community—church, school, social center and, often, political base. Catholic parishes will remain vigorous only if middle class families able and willing to exercise community leadership want to live in the neighborhood. On balance, it is probably untrue that in the long run young Catholic families move into or remain in a neighborhood because of the parish life it offers. But in the short run, policies that (1) helps make central city neighborhoods relatively more attractive for middle and upper middle class Catholic families compared to urban and suburban competitors may have the indirect effect of (2) stabilizing neighborhood and parish institutions and the viability of parochial schools.

BIBLIOGRAPHY

Abramson, Harold. *Ethnic Diversity in Catholic America.* New York: Wiley-Interscience, 1973.

Bradley v. *The School Board of the City of Richmond.* Civil Action No. 3353 (E.D. Va. 1972), Fourth Circuit (1972).

Bradley v. *Milliken.* 338 F. Supp. 582 (E.D. Mich. 1971), 345 F. Supp. 914 (E.D. Mich. 1972), aff'd, 484 F. 2d 215 (6th Cir. 1973), rev'd, 418 U.S. 717 (1974).

Brewer v. *School Board of Norfolk (Va.).* 397 F. 2d 37, 41–42 (Fourth Cir. 1968).

Brown v. *Board of Education of Topeka.* 347 U.S. 483 (1954).

Coleman, James S., et al. *Equality of Educational Opportunity.* 2 vols. Washington, D.C.: US Government Printing Office, 1966.

Cooper, Joseph H. "The Dollars and Sense of Public Education." *The Urban Lawyer* 6, 1 (Winter 1974): 138–63.

Dorsen, Norman; Norman Chachlin; and Sylvia Law. *Emerson, Haber and Dorsen's Political and Civil Rights in the United States.* 3rd ed. (1967). 1973 Supplement to vol. II. Boston: Little, Brown and Co., 1973.

Erickson, Donald A. and George F. Madaus. *Issues of Aid to Nonpublic Schools.* Vol. I. *Economic and Social Issues of Educational Pluralism.* Report submitted to the President's Commission on School Finance. Boston: Boston College, Center for Field Research and School Services, 1971.

Greeley, Andrew M. *The Denominational Society.* Glenview, Ill.: Scott, Foresman and Co., 1972.

Greeley, Andrew M. and Peter H. Rossi. *The Education of Catholic Americans.* Chicago: Aldine, 1966.

Green v. *County School Board of New Kent County (Va.).* 391 U.S. 430 (1968).

Hartman, Robert W. and Robert D. Reischauer. "Financing Elementary and Secondary Education." In Charles L. Schultze et al., *Setting National Priorities: the 1973 Budget,* pp. 318–366. Washington, D.C.: The Brookings Institution, 1972.

Havighurst, Robert J. "Educational Development in a Metropolitan Area." *Yearbook of Education* (1970), p. 158.

Hobson v. *Hansen,* 269 F. Supp. 401 (D.D.C. 1967).

Jencks, Christopher, et al. *Inequality: A Reassessment of the Effect of Family and Schooling in America.* New York: Basic Books, 1972.

Keyes v. *School District No. 1, Denver,* 413 U.S. 189, 93 S. Ct. 2686, 37 L. Ed. 2d 548 (1973), rehearing denied, 414 U.S. 883 (1973).

Kirp, David L. and David K. Cohen. "Education and Metropolitanism." In *Metropolitanism and Public Services,* edited by Lowdon Wingo. Washington, D.C.: Resources for the Future, Inc., 1972. pp. 29–42.

Kottmeyer, William. *A Tale of Two Cities: A Blueprint for Equality of Educational Opportunity in the St. Louis Public Schools.* St. Louis: St. Louis Public Schools, 1968.

Krashaar, Otto. *American Nonpublic Schools: Patterns of Diversity.* Baltimore: The Johns Hopkins University Press, 1972.

Lineberry, Robert A. and Ira Sharkansky. "Education and Public Policy." In *Urban Politics and Public Policy,* pp. 223–240. 2nd ed. New York: Harper and Row, 1974.

National Catholic Education Association. *U.S. Catholic Schools 1971–1972.* Washington, D.C.: NCEA, 1972.

——. *A Report on U.S. Catholic Schools 1970–71.* Washington, D.C.: NCEA, 1971.

——. *A Statistical Report on the Catholic Elementary and Secondary Schools for the Years 1967–68 to 1969–70.* Washington, D.C.: NCEA, 1970.

The President's Commission on School Finance. *Schools, People and Money: The Need for Educational Reform.* Final Report. Washington: US Government Printing Office, 1972.

Reischauer, R.D. and R.W. Hartman. *Reforming School Finance.* Washington, D.C.: The Brookings Institution, 1973.

Rose, Harold. *The Black Ghetto.* New York: McGraw-Hill, 1971.

The School of Education, University of Michigan. *The Financial Implications of Changing Patterns of Nonpublic School Operations in Chicago, Detroit, Milwaukee, and Philadelphia.* Washington, D.C.: US Government Printing Office, 1971.

Serrano v. *Priest,* 5 Cal. 3d 584, 96 Cal. Rptr. 601, 487 P.2d 1241 (1971).

Summers, Anita A. and Barbara L. Wolfe. "Philadelphia's School Resources and the Disadvantaged." *Business Review* (Federal Reserve Bank of Philadelphia), March 1974, pp. 3–16.

——. "Which School Resources Help Learning? Efficiency and Equity in Philadelphia Public Schools." *Business Review* (Federal Reserve Bank of Philadelphia), 1975 (Special Issue), pp. 4–28.

Swann v. *Charlotte-Mecklenburg Board of Education*. 402 U.S. 1 (1971).

US Bureau of the Census. *We the Americans: Our Education*. Washington, D.C.: US Government Printing Office, 1973.

US Civil Rights Commission. *Racial Isolation in the Public Schools*. Washington, D.C.: US Government Printing Office, 1967.

Wright v. *Council of the City of Emporia (Va.)*. 407 U.S. 451 (1972).

Chapter 7

Geographic Perspectives on Crime and the Impact of Anticrime Legislation

Gerald F. Pyle
University of Akron

> Since the passage of the Safe Streets Act, the rampaging annual increase in crime has been halted and reversed. *For the first time in seventeen years, crime has actually decreased. Moreover, during 1973, 94 of 154 cities (61 percent) with over 100,000 population reported actual crime decreases. In four years, therefore, crime in the United States has been reduced from an 11 percent increase to a 3 percent decrease, and the number of large cities reporting actual crime decreases has gone from under twenty to almost one hundred.* [P. 1]

In these words the 1973 National Conference of State Criminal Justice Planning Administrators reflected current feelings of optimism held by many criminal justice planners. Major crimes during 1972 and 1973 showed a decrease from 1971, thus supporting the Federal Bureau of Investigation's contentions that the meteoric rise in crime during the 1960s was a "wave of crime" which would eventually crest and subsequently decline. The types of crime referred to are those most frequently reported by local police departments to the FBI. They are violent crimes of homicide, rape, aggravated assault and robbery, and property crimes of burglary, automobile theft and larceny.

Scholars writing 200 years from now might easily use the statistics provided in Figures 7-1 and 7-2 for documentary proof that the 1960s was one of the more violent and disruptive decades of United States history. The reporting of both violent and property crimes more than doubled from 1960 to 1970. During 1971, property crimes and robbery peaked to all-time high rates. However, while there was a 3 percent drop from 1971 to 1972 in the overall crime index–i.e., violent and property crimes combined–violent crimes of homicide, rape and aggravated assault continued to rise. Still, in light of the rapid increases in reporting during the 1960s, the decreases in most property-related crimes hearten law enforcement professionals. It is too soon to determine if these decreases in reporting herald a major national decline in index crime rates. The decreases may only indicate a minor lull similar to that reflected by statistics from the mid-1950s. Such a comparison, however, must be approached cautiously. The decrease during the 1950s was not preceded by an exponential increase. Furthermore, at that time there was no comprehensive national strategy such as now exists to reverse a monumental "crime wave." In fact, the very nature of the current concerted national effort to reduce crime may have contributed to increases in the 1960s by improving reporting procedures and by raising

At the time this study was originally written, certain crime statistics appeared to show a decrease. Unfortunately, since that time, violent and property crime rates have again escalated. The author is convinced that part of this escalation is due to the inability of certain law enforcement officials to fully comprehend the meaning of police community relations and preventive programs in the area of juvenile delinquency. Furthermore, many police departments have failed to integrate racially even under court order and these racial unbalances are indirectly contributing to increased crime rates.

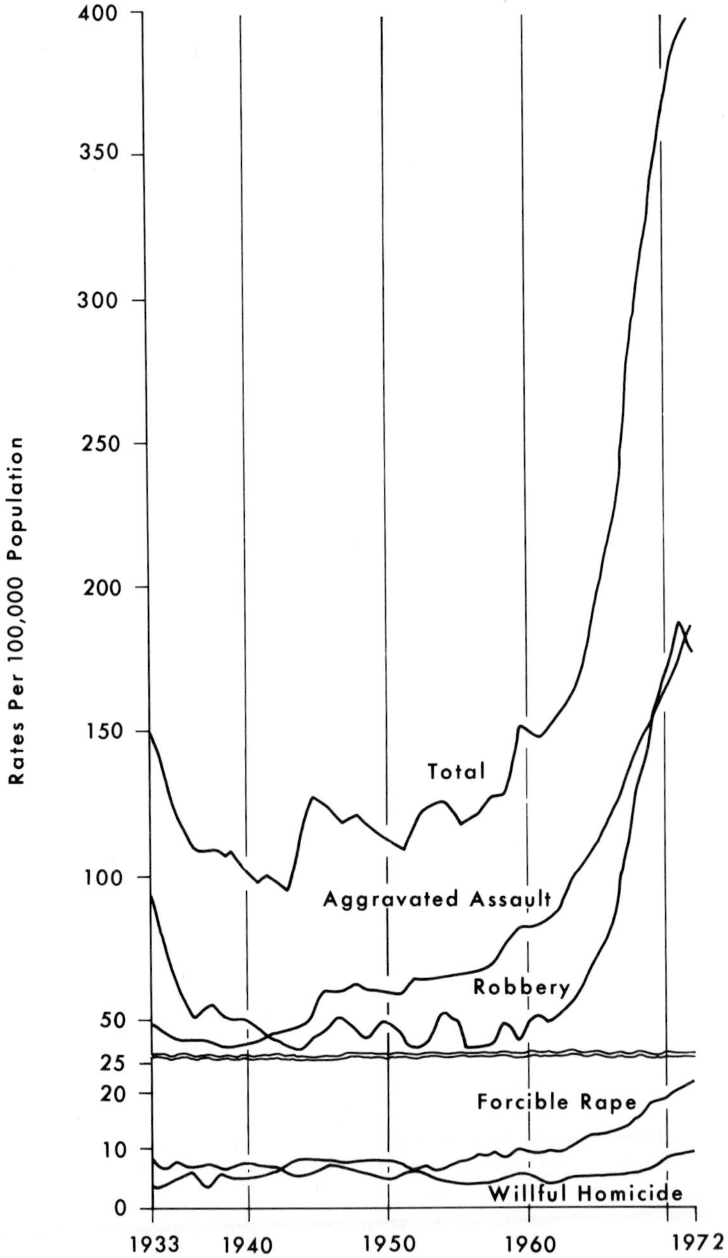

Figure 7-1. Index Crime Trends, 1933-1972. Reported Crimes Against the Person. Note that the scale for willful homicide and forcible rape is enlarged to show the trend. Source: FBI, Uniform Crime Reports Section, unpublished data.

public awareness of the problem and the increasing diligence made possible by greater police resources.

Public awareness of the rapid increases of crime promoted passage of national legislation to combat crime. The national fight against crime began officially with Executive Order 11236, wherein President Lyndon Johnson established the Commission on Law Enforcement and Administration of Justice. Soon after, Congress enacted Public Law 89-197, the Law Enforcement Assistance Act (September

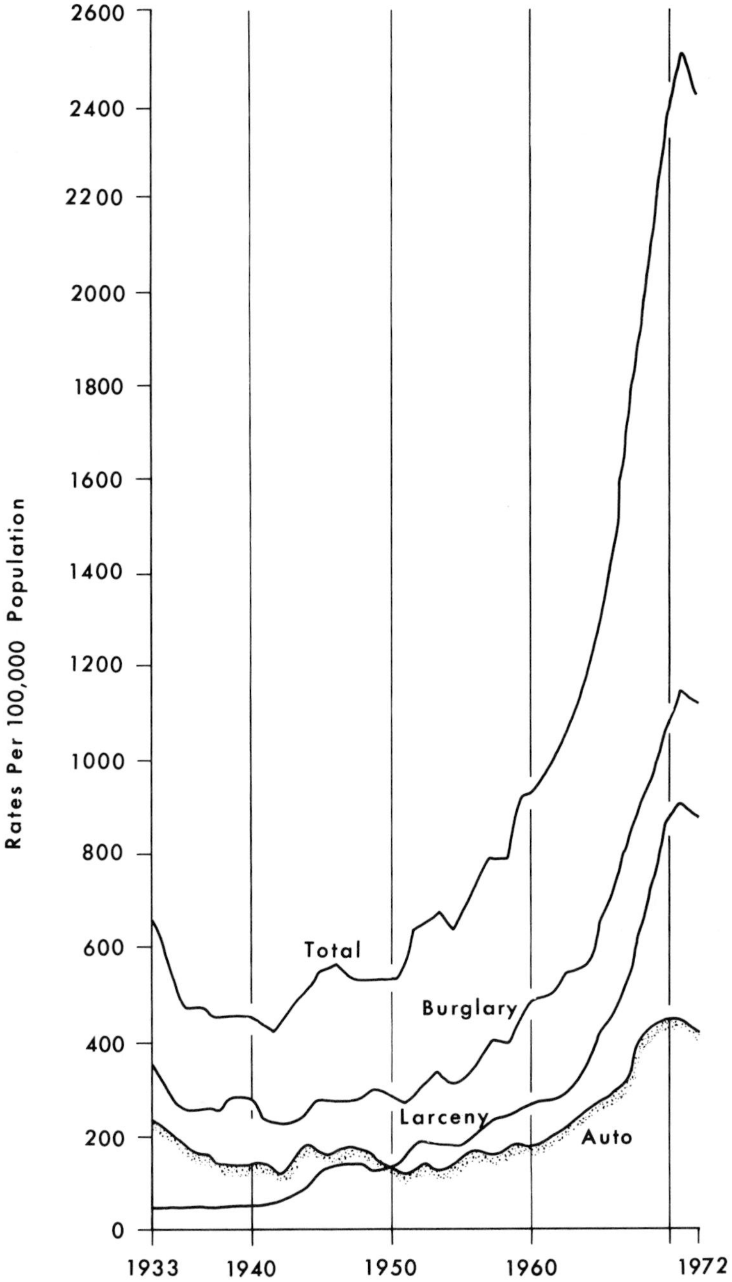

Figure 7-2. Index Crime Trends, 1933-1972. Reported Crimes Against Property. Note that the scale of this figure is not comparable with the scale of Figure 1. Source: FBI, Uniform Crime Reports Section, unpublished data.

22, 1965). This legislation authorized the attorney general to conduct a wide range of programs including the provision of technical assistance and development of research projects. The OLEA (Office of Law Enforcement Assistance) was established and an initial staff of about two dozen government employees assisted in the administration of grants. During the fiscal years 1966, 1967 and 1968, expenditures under the act of approximately $20 million were matched by $10 million in local and state funds in the development of anticrime programs. More than two-thirds of the funds went directly to police departments, and mostly increased expenditures made for "hardware" items such as patrol cars, helicopters, radios, etc.

The above measures also authorized the preparation of *The Challenge of Crime in a Free Society*, the actual report of the president's commission. The commission was to develop a better understanding of the entire criminal justice system and recommend improvements (over 200 recommendations were made). Almost two years elapsed before the report was released to the public in the spring of 1967. Meanwhile, crime rates continued to accelerate, urban ghettos exploded, students protested the Vietnam War and drug abuse became almost commonplace.

Large cities became the focal points of public reactions to increasing crime rates, social unrest, the general cultural revolution of young people and major judicial changes resulting from landmark Supreme Court decisions. Public pressures for "law and order" resulted in the colossal Omnibus Crime Control and Safe Streets Act of 1968 (PL90-351). Although the report of the president's commission helped support the need for such legislation, it also indicated the presence of gross public misconception of crime definitions and the criminal justice system.

The Safe Streets Act has been amended several times since 1968, most recently during June of 1973. The Law Enforcement Assistance Administration (LEAA) now allocates funds to state agencies for further distribution (85 percent) mostly to regional metropolitan criminal justice planning agencies. Discretionary grants are also awarded directly to local governments in high crime areas (15 percent of the LEAA budget). The 1968 legislation, with subsequent amendments, calls for the development of state planning agencies (SPAs), and these have usually been developed as parts of existing state agencies or in some instances new ones. Recent legislative changes call for all states to develop comprehensive plans for crime reduction if funding is to continue. In addition, a special impact cities program has been geared to providing assistance to eight urban centers (Atlanta, Baltimore, Cleveland, Dallas, Denver, Newark, Portland and St. Louis) for reducing stranger-to-stranger street crime and burglary.

While this system of funding may seem awkward, it must be remembered that within the United States there has been no history of a national police force per se. Historically, our system has called for law enforcement administration at state and local levels. The Federal Bureau of Investigation has been concerned with the enforcement of specialized national laws such as customs violations, illegal interstate activities and similar problems. However, the FBI has functioned in many ways to assist local law enforcement agencies. One example is the publication since the early 1930s of the *Uniform Crime Reports.* Since the 1930s, the number of cities reporting to the FBI has grown. With the advent of computer technology, information systems have improved vastly, and many more serious crimes can be accounted for. Thus, part of the increased reporting during the 1960s can be attributed to better and more rapid dissemination of crime data. Clearly, however, major increases during the early 1960s were noted, and many of the computerized information systems were developed during the late 1960s and early 1970s with the support of LEAA funding.

Since the passage of the Safe Streets Act both LEAA and overall criminal justice expenditures have increased. Table 7-1 contains information showing this trend. By June of 1973 (end of fiscal year 1972), almost $12 billion annually was being spent by national, state and local agencies to combat crime. Assuming the downward trend continues (Figures 7-1 and 7-2), it is assumed that the LEAA programs and other forms of increased spending are having a definite impact. Despite their small share of total funding, it seems LEAA programs have promoted improvements within many states' criminal justice systems through state master plans for the coordination of law enforcement. LEAA programs call for supervisory boards of citizens, police, elected officials, and representatives from both courts and corrections working in a cooperative manner as opposed to former isolation.

Crime in the United States occurs disproportionately within large cities. Rates for FBI index crimes in 1972 were almost twice the national rate in cities over 250,000 (Table 7-2). Crime rates for rural areas were about half the national rate and one-quarter the rate

Table 7-1. National Anticrime Expenditures, Fiscal Years 1969 to 1972 (millions of dollars)

Fiscal Year	*LEAA Appropriations*	*Total Direct Criminal Justice System Expenditures*	*LEAA Percent of Total*
1969	63	7,340	0.7
1970	268	8,571	3.1
1971	529	10,165	5.2
1972	698	11,750	6.0
Total	1,559	37,827	4.1

Source: National Conference of State Criminal Justice Planning Administrators, "State of the States on Crime and Justice" (Frankfort, Ky. June 1973).

Table 7-2. Crime Rate by Area, 1972 (rate per 100,000 inhabitants)

	Area			
Crime Index Offense	*Total US*	*Cities Over 250,000*	*Suburban*	*Rural*
Total	2,829.5	4,947.9	2,363.6	1,084.4
Violent	397.7	988.6	221.7	143.6
Property	2,431.8	3,949.3	2,141.9	940.8
Murder	8.9	19.7	4.6	7.4
Forcible Rape	22.3	47.1	17.1	11.2
Robbery	179.9	578.8	72.3	16.1
Aggravated Assault	186.6	353.0	127.8	109.0
Burglary	1,126.1	1,877.5	963.1	507.5
Larceny $50 and Over	882.6	1,104.6	890.5	363.6
Automobile Theft	423.1	967.2	288.3	69.7

Source: Federal Bureau of Investigation, *Uniform Crime Reports,* 1972.

for cities over 250,000. As already indicated, 1972 was the first year in a decade reporting decreasing crime rates. Crimes reported in 1972 (Table 7-2) are taken as *indicators* of crime rates, and obviously do not account for all crime. By the same token, these national totals do not address either variations from one city to another or variations of crime rates within cities. Policy changes have had an impact on national rates because *the public has demanded less crime.* But gross national totals do not tell us where the impact has been the greatest. The primary purposes of this study are first, to explain how variations among and within cities can be identified and second, to show how various cities and different parts of the country have been affected by the policy change as manifested by decreased crime rates. However, the problems inherent with crime statistics must be explained first to add the background required to understand the geographical analysis.

THE MEANING OF INDEX CRIME STATISTICS

Law enforcement is one of the most demanding of all professions. Many necessary police functions are routine procedures such as traffic control and so-called "nuisance calls,"–e.g., controlling marital quarrels and drunkenness. Attempts to control narcotics abuse are a current source of controversy and police actions along these lines combined with those mentioned above have led many critics to denounce "victimless crimes" as unnecessary police functions. However alcoholism, marital strife and heavy use of drugs can all lead to more serious crimes, including murder. It would be an impossible task to formulate a meaningful analysis of the geographical distribution of all such known criminal offenses because of the sheer volume of information required. Normally, the indicator offenses comprising the FBI crime index are used for such studies because they are published annually by a single national agency and the assumption is made that general crime rates tend to parallel specific index crime rates.

It should be understood that FBI crime index information is only as reliable as that furnished to the agency by many local police departments. Studies have shown that crime information varies in terms of reliability from one location to another. For example, Beattie has indicated that the very nature of our system of local police autonomy presents statistical problems. Laws differ from one state to another, and while there are certain common procedures, each state is, in effect, a sovereign entity with its own special criminal justice system. Every decade the US Bureau of the Census enumerates the population of the country and with continuing urbanization the Standard Metropolitan Statistical Area (SMSA) has become the cornerstone for comparative metropolitan analyses. However, it is virtually impossible to obtain uniform and accurate crime data at the SMSA level. Police departments within metropolitan areas, *voluntarily* submit annual reports to the FBI. Because SMSAs are fragmented politically, the number of police departments can range from two dozen to several hundred. Many smaller suburban police departments simply do not report anything to the FBI. Therefore, any SMSA crime totals published are in fact estimates.

Even within cities cooperating with the FBI in reporting crimes, many crimes are missed because they are simply not reported. These crimes range from sex offenses to illegal medical practices. They include embezzlement, theft from employers and consumer fraud. According to Shulman, fairly serious crimes committed by affluent suburban juveniles often are "station adjusted," thus contributing to concealment of information and nonreporting. The best source of information available is in the form of the *Uniform Crime Reports,* but these data are constrained by those local practices mentioned above.

Also, police departments, as distinguished from courts and corrections, are only one part of the overall criminal justice system. All of the offenses analyzed here are based upon police investigations and charges and not on decisions made by courts, coroners, juries or any other judicial body. Final resolution through the criminal justice system is not traced. The crimes under investigation here consist of the seven categories which have been used in the establishment of the index intended to measure trends and distributions of crime within the United States. These seven crimes—homicide, rape, robbery, aggravated assault, burglary, grand larceny ($50 and over) and automobile theft—are considered by most law enforcement agencies as those most frequently reported to them. They have therefore been aggregated over time and used in inclusion of the development of the crime index. They are considered to be the most common local crime problems within the United States.

Homicide is defined to include willful killings. Deaths caused by negligence are counted as manslaughter by negligence and are not included within this category. Also, attempts to kill or assault to kill are considered as aggravated assault and not homicide. Aggravated assault is specifically defined as an unlawful attack by one person upon another for the purpose of inflicting severe bodily injury, usually accompanied by the use of some weapon or other means likely to produce bodily harm or even death. Attempts are also included within this category, because is it not necessary that an actual assault take place when a gun, knife or other weapon is used which would result in serious personal injury if the crime were successfully completed.

The *Uniform Crime Reports* define forcible rape as "carnal knowledge of a female" through the use of threat of force. Assaults to commit rape are included, but statutory rape without force is excluded from this category.

Robbery takes place in the presence of a victim, and it by definition must be intended to obtain some property or object of value from the victim by the use or threat of force. Assaults and attempts to rob are also considered robbery. For reporting purposes, data are collected for armed robbery where any kind of a weapon is used and unarmed robbery where no weapon is used. The latter category thus includes such things as mugging.

Burglary is defined by the *Uniform Crime Reports* (Kelly 1973) as the unlawful entry into a structure by a felon or thief to commit some theft. This category is still considered burglary even if force is not used to gain entrance. Actually, there are three subcategories: forcible entry, unlawful entry without the use of force and attempted forcible entry.

Grand larceny is the unlawful taking or stealing of property or some article or articles of more than $50 value without the use of force, violence or fraud. While this category includes such items as shoplifting, pocketpicking, purse snatching and thefts from autos, it does not include embezzlements, such as forgery and writing worthless checks. Also, automobile theft is not included within this category; it is considered a separate crime index offense by the FBI. The actual definition of automobile theft is the unlawful stealing or driving away of a motor vehicle belonging to someone else and this includes attempts. This definition, however, excludes the taking for temporary use when the vehicle is returned and prior knowledge of this use on the part of the owner has either been granted or at least assumed.

VARIATIONS IN CRIME RATES AMONG UNITED STATES' CITIES, 1960 TO 1970

Landmark nationwide studies of regional variations in reported crimes began in 1938 when Lottier identified certain US "crime regions" on the basis of data taken from the 1934 and 1935 *Uniform Crime Reports.* In general, Lottier concluded that the southeast United States had the highest reporting of homicide, that the pattern formed by robbery was a "central axis" extending west to east with highest reporting and that the heaviest reporting of larceny was in the western part of the country. Lottier also analyzed other index offenses, but felt that on the basis of intercorrelations those mentioned above were independently representative crimes. In brief, Lottier suggested that differences among various parts of the country in the reporting of crime could be traced to different cultural mores which had evolved historically.

Using information gathered from 1946 to 1952, Shannon tested some of Lottier's findings. Shannon found homicide still concentrated in the Southeast. Assault rates were also highest in the Southeast. However, the highest reporting of robbery was in the western states and the Northeast without any apparent west-east axis. Shannon also found that the pattern of larceny reporting also matched that of Lottier. In addition, Shannon came to the following conclusions:

- Burglary rates were highest in the states of Texas, Washington, California, Oregon, Colorado, Arizona, Florida and Nevada.
- High automobile theft rates were found in the Pacific and Mountain states and in some of the East North Central and South Atlantic states.
- Regionally, low crime rates per 100,000 are found in the New England and Middle Atlantic states.
- The Mountain and Pacific states showed higher rates for crimes against property, while the South Atlantic, East South Central and West South Central states recorded consistently high rates for crimes against the person.

In a more recent contribution, Harries completed a study of crime during 1968. Separating his data into violent and property crime, Harries compared his results with the past work of Lottier and Shannon. High rates for murder were clearly concentrated in the Southeast, as had been noted by Shannon and Lottier. High reporting of rape was distributed among a group of western states, including California, Arizona, New Mexico and Colorado. Extremely high rape reporting rates for Los Angeles, Detroit, Denver and Baltimore presumably accounted for the concentration within California, Michigan, Colorado and Maryland. When Harries examined robbery patterns by state, he discovered that two western states—California and Nevada—had high rates, but that the eastern states dominated robbery reporting with New York, Maryland, Illinois, Michigan, Florida and Missouri showing the highest rates. Harries, concurring with Shannon, saw no central axis running east to west as described by Lottier. In relation to aggravated assault, Lottier found a heavy concentration of high rates in the Southeast: North Carolina, Virginia, Tennessee, Kentucky and Florida. Shannon had observed a similar pattern, but Harries discovered that only North Carolina remained in Shannon's top five.

Most such studies not only demonstrate how crime varies by regions within the United States, they also strongly imply that crime is more of an urban phenomenon than it is rural (see Table 7-2). In a 1941 study of Minnesota,

Vold demonstrated marked differences between urban and rural areas. Lottier had arrived at similar conclusions during the 1930s when he showed how crime rates decreased with distance away from central Detroit. Lentz, in a 1956 study, also showed that if only state crime information is used for comparisons, higher urban rates within states are hard to identify.

Another problem is encountered with the statistical analysis of crime reporting among metropolitan areas. Given the larger numbers of crimes committed within larger cities, many have assumed a monotonic relationship between crime and city size. However, there is apparently no such clear-cut distinction. Haynes, using 1960 US metropolitan data, postulated that crime is a function of the "density" of urban opportunities, particularly for the crime of burglary and automobile theft. For example, Haynes showed that New York City demonstrated fewer crimes than would be expected for a city so large in size. In another recent study of violent crimes, Harries (1973) found that only robbery correlated strongly with SMSA size, thus adding support to the contention that violent crime cannot be examined either exclusively or basically as a large city problem. Furthermore, when Harries produced regional clusters, some of the "cultural" differences already mentioned again stood out.

As indicated earlier, one of the primary purposes of this study is to test the impact of public policy changes, presumably as manifested by the LEAA programs, on the distribution of urban crime. Before this is accomplished, however, it is first necessary to examine patterns of interurban and intraurban crime variation. The discussion below is concerned with the latter, and the former problem is examined later within this study. Because of the problems inherent with SMSA-based crime data, only central cities of over 100,000 have been selected for comparison over time. Only those cities (127) which reported major crimes to the FBI for both 1960 and 1970 have been selected. For consistency of comparison, the proportionate circles showing city size categories on the following US maps are based upon 1970 populations.

The Intermetropolitan Distribution of Violent Crimes, 1960 to 1970

The distribution of crimes of passion (violent crimes) for the 127 cities being studied for 1960 is shown within Figure 7-3a. Eight cities—Los Angeles, St. Louis, Chicago, Detroit, Newark, Washington, Jacksonville and Miami—had extremely high crime rates at that time. With the exception of Newark, these cities are all major metropolitan centers. Three southeastern cities (Birmingham, Charlotte and Winston-Salem) had high rates and many larger and some medium-sized cities throughout the country reported violent crimes above the average for the 127 cities. Some of the cities included within the latter category were New York, Boston, Philadelphia, Baltimore, New Orleans, Houston, Denver and San Francisco.

In general, those cities with violent crime rates in excess of the average during 1960 were located within some of the more urbanized parts of the country and the South. This pattern had been essentially the same for several decades, the implications being that larger, more industrialized cities and southern places traditionally were characterized by more individual acts of violence. There are many reasons for this, but the most apparent are easier access to firearms and the stress-producing conditions of poverty. Also, many Great Plains cities and medium-sized northeastern cities with less complex patterns of urbanization reported lower numbers of crime per 100,000 persons. At the other end of the scale, cities with rates below the average showed in 1960 some common geographical characteristics. For example, the four Pacific Northwest cities being examined within this study reported lower than average rates.

During 1970, the average rate of violent crimes jumped from the 1960 average of 192.6 to 600.6 per 100,000 persons for the sample of 127 cities (Table 7-3). Also, one standard deviation in 1970 was more than twice that of 1960. Some of the smaller cities with lower violent crime rates during 1960 showed substantial increases by 1970, but some of the larger cities showed even higher increases. For example, Baltimore, Cleveland, New York, Jacksonville, New Orleans and San Francisco all reported violent crime rates that place those cities in the higher than average class. Urban centers which continued to show the highest relative rates when 1960 and 1970 distributions are compared (Figure 7-3b) were Newark, Miami, Washington, Chicago and St. Louis. Some cities, Chicago and Los Angeles for example, showed categorical decreases, but it must be remembered that overall rates were

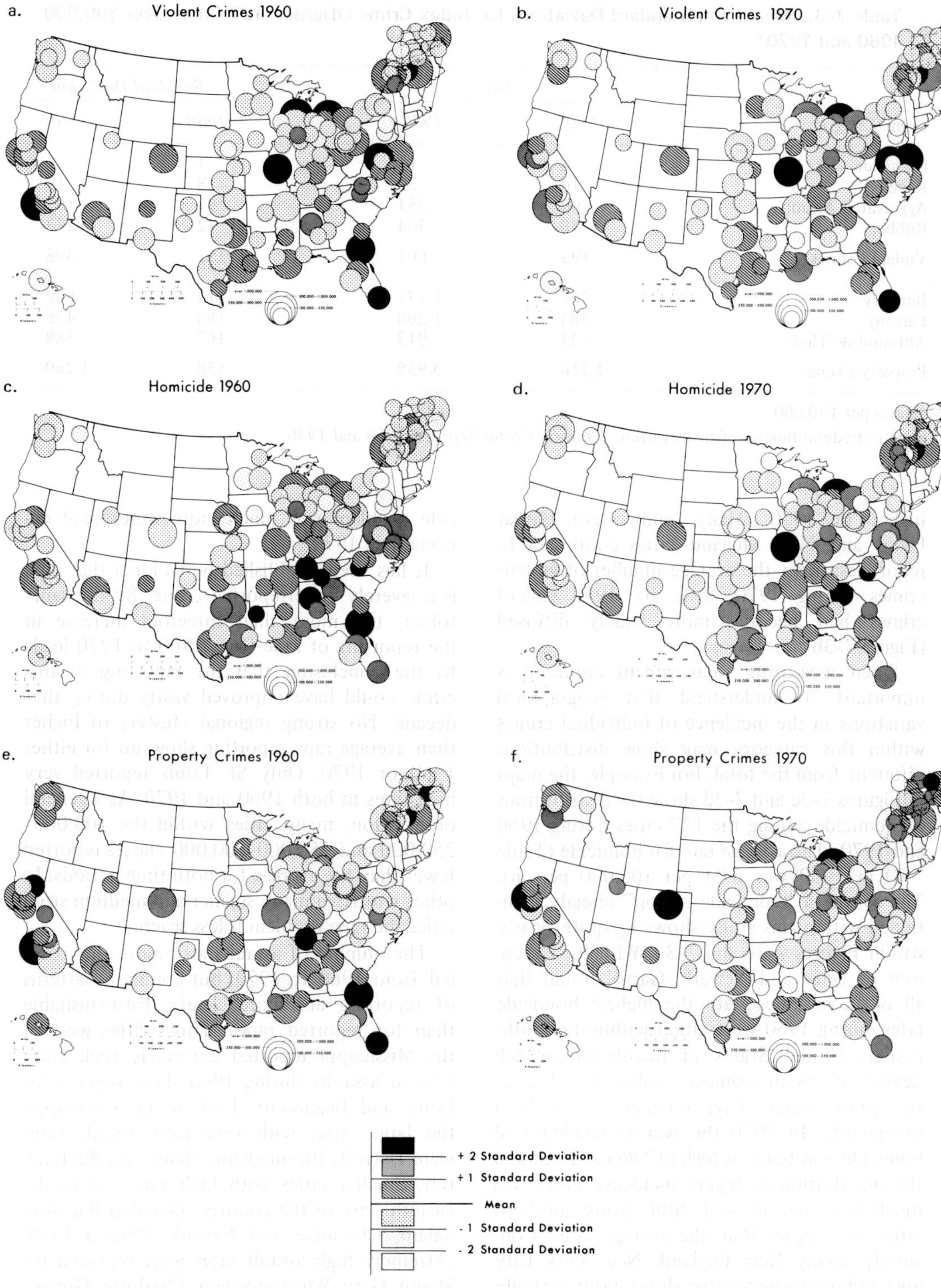

Figure 7-3. Violent Crimes, Homicide and Property Crimes, 1960 and 1970.

Table 7-3. Means and Standard Deviations for Index Crime Offenses, 127 Cities Over 100,000, 1960 and 1970*

	Mean		*Standard Deviation*	
Crime Category	*1960*	*1970*	*1960*	*1970*
Homicide	6	13	4	9
Rape	10	30	8	19
Aggravated Assault	99	254	91	165
Robbery	78	304	72	273
Violent Crimes	193	601	151	398
Burglary	709	1,777	312	669
Larceny	383	1,268	188	476
Automobile Theft	324	913	167	588
Property Crimes	1,416	3,958	558	1,260

*Rates per 100,000

Source: Federal Bureau of Investigation, *Uniform Crime Reports*, 1960 and 1970.

higher in 1970. Many midwestern, Great Plains and New England cities continued to report less than the average number of violent crimes during 1970. Still, by 1970 violent crimes had become more widely diffused (Figure 7-3b).

When measuring total violent crimes it is important to understand that geographical variations in the incidence of individual crimes within this category may show distributions different from the total. For example, the maps in Figures 7-3c and 7-3d show the distributions of homicide among the 127 cities during 1960 and 1970. The average rate for homicide (Table 7-3) in 1960 was 6.04 per 100,000 persons. The southern "homicide region" already mentioned within this study shows up quite clearly within Figures 7-3c and 7-3d. With the exception of Gary and Newark, Gastril found that all of those cities with the highest homicide rates during 1960 were either within the southeastern United States or manifested a high degree of "Southernness" culturally—that is, the cities contain large numbers of southern immigrants. In 1970 the average incidence of homicide was twice as high (12.85) as 1960 and the distribution of higher incidence cities was much less concentrated. Still, many southern cities had higher than the average rates. Conversely, many New England, New York City area and midwestern cities showed substantially inflated homicide rates. As with total violent crime, patterns of geographical concentration in 1960 were less evident in 1970. The homicide problem was much more widespread nationally in 1970.

It has been established by Goldner that rape is a severely underreported crime. By the same token, the more than threefold increase in the reporting of rape from 1960 to 1970 leads to the conclusion that the reporting of this crime could have improved vastly during that decade. No strong regional clusters of higher than average rape reporting show up for either 1960 or 1970. Only St. Louis reported very high rates in both 1960 and 1970. As a general observation, many cities within the 100,000–250,000 and 250,000–500,000 classes reported fewer than the average for both time periods. In other words, in many smaller and medium-sized cities the rape problem is less severe.

The number of assaults also more than tripled from 1960 to 1970, but common patterns of reporting are more clearly distinguishable than for reported rapes. Three cities west of the Mississippi reported extremely high numbers of assaults during 1960—Los Angeles, St. Louis and Beaumont. East of the Mississippi, the large cities with very high assault rates were Detroit, Birmingham, Miami and Washington. Smaller cities with high rates, all in the eastern part of the country, included Winston-Salem, Charlotte and Newark. During 1970, extremely high assault rates were reported for Miami, Gary, Winston-Salem, Charlotte, Greensboro and Baltimore. Fairly high rates were much more dispersed in 1970 than during 1960, and many medium- to smaller-sized cities in the lower Midwest, New England and the Great Plains area reported greatly increased rates. The upper Midwest and Pacific Northwest consistently reported assaults lower than the mean rates for both years. Aggravated assault, much more so than rape, is a crime wherein reporting has improved.

Considered a violent crime, robbery as a criminal offense is often motivated by kinds of behavior different from homicide, rape and assault. This category includes armed robberies at banks, commercial establishments and related opportunities presented as well as such unarmed robberies as muggings. Many robberies are premeditated to varying degrees, while some of the other violent crimes are more related to living conditions and the often unpredictable caprices of human behavior, especially when prior knowledge of a victim is involved. These associations are explained in more detail in this chapter when crimes within cities are examined. All robberies showed a marked increase from 1960 to 1970 (Table 7-3) but the general patterns of distribution did not vary from one period to the next so much as for assault and rape. During 1960 those cities with rates above the average included San Francisco, Sacramento, Los Angeles, Long Beach, Denver, New Orleans, St. Louis, Chicago, Detroit, Gary, New Orleans, Jacksonville, Miami and Newark. By 1970 Oakland, Dayton, Cleveland, Washington, Baltimore, Trenton, Camden and New York City could be added to the 1960 list of high incidence cities, but Sacramento, Denver and Jacksonville could be dropped due to rates under one standard deviation above the mean. Clearly, the value of Haynes' city size opportunities formulation can be supported. Many medium-sized to smaller cities throughout the United States reported rates for both periods lower than the mean.

The Intermetropolitan Distribution of Property Crimes, 1960 and 1970

Once again, as indicated by Figure 7-2 and Table 7-3, property crime rates increased by approximately two and one-half times from 1960 to 1970. The actual rate of increase was in fact less than that of violent crimes, but overall rates per 100,000 persons were greater. During 1960 (Figure 7-3e) Sacramento, Los Angeles, Nashville, Jacksonville, Miami, Newark and Providence reported property crimes much higher than the average of 1,416 per 100,000 persons. Cities reporting fairly high rates included Fresno, Long Beach, Torrence, Denver, St. Louis, Chicago, Baton Rouge, Tampa and Richmond. During 1970 (Figure 7-3f), the pattern of cities with fairly high rates shifted: Pasadena, San Francisco and Oakland reported the highest property crime rates in California, while Portland, Salt Lake City and Denver all reported marked increases. Proportionately, lower 1970 rates showed up for Chicago, Nashville and Baton Rouge, but St. Louis remained high. Detroit showed a marked increase in property crimes, and many New York City area and New England cities reported increases as well. Rates increased in the Washington-Baltimore area, but relatively lower departures from the 1970 average were reported for most Florida cities. (Again, the 1970 average of 3,958 per 100,000 persons was much higher than that of 1960.)

Table 7-3 shows that burglaries more than doubled from 1960 to 1970. Furthermore, the distribution of high incidence cities was quite different from one period to the next (Figures 7-4a and 7-4b). In 1960 only Newark had an extremely high rate of burglaries, but by 1970 Trenton, Camden, Newark, New Haven and Worcester all had high rates. Also, the extremely high rates reported for the Southwest in 1960 were not nearly so apparent during 1970, and higher rates had suffused to the lower Midwest. West of the Mississippi, Denver was high for both periods. High 1960 rates in southern California cities apparently shifted to the San Francisco area, and Portland and Seattle showed marked increases over the decade.

Larceny is defined quite clearly in local statutes; however, local interpretations vary considerably. Whereas shoplifting of items valued at more than $50 is quite common as a larceny charge, in many instances there is a thin line of interpretation between larceny and some types of nonresidential burglary. Furthermore, interurban analysis indicates that this crime is a common charge for juveniles, particularly middle income, during summer vacation months. It should be expected because of the demographic structure of smaller to medium-sized cities that when viewing the distribution of reported larcenies during 1960 and 1970, these places would have higher rates than some larger cities. Such a pattern, while

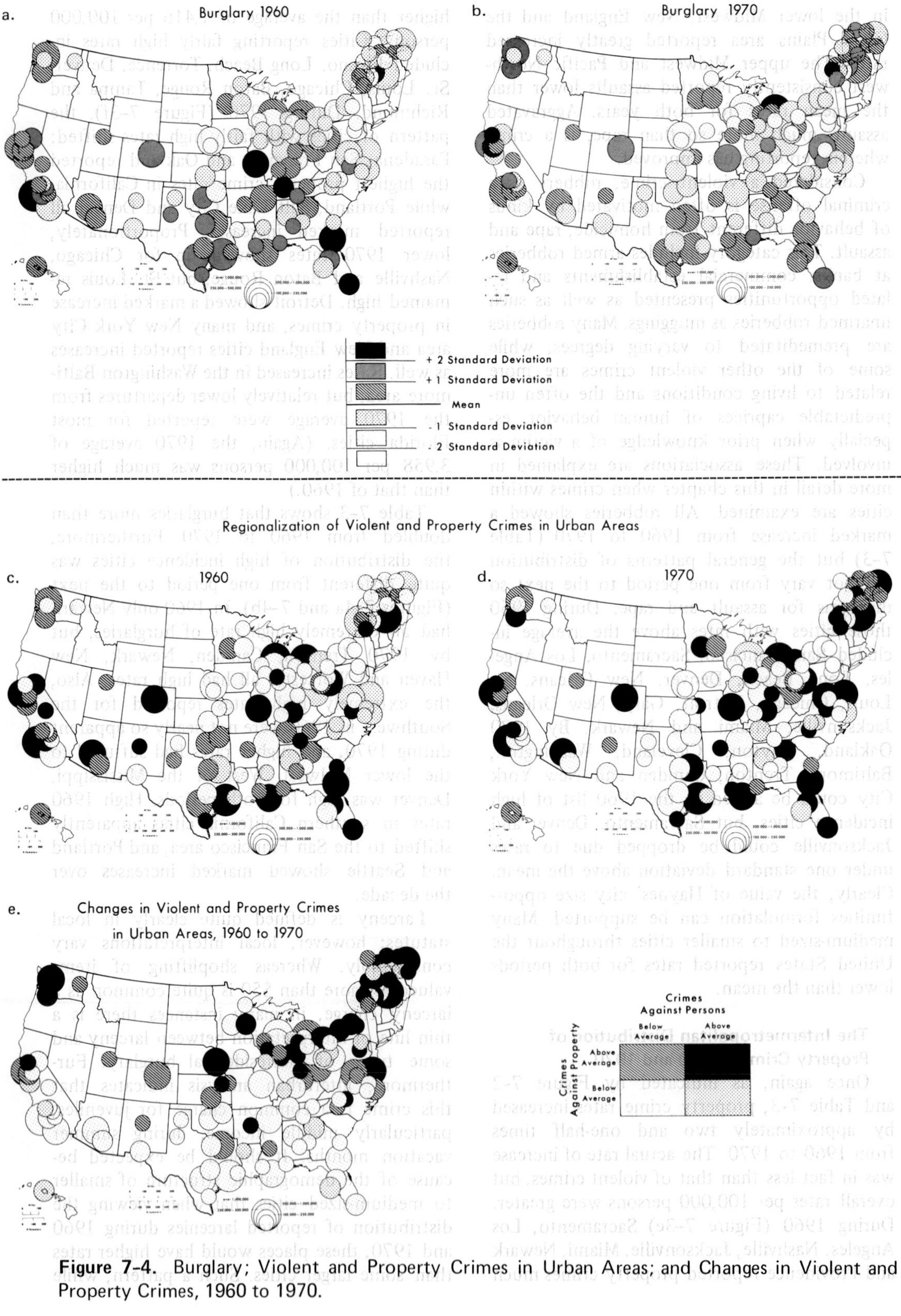

Figure 7-4. Burglary; Violent and Property Crimes in Urban Areas; and Changes in Violent and Property Crimes, 1960 to 1970.

somewhat clouded by variable interpretation of the offense, does show up during both periods. However, such a distribution is more apparent during 1970 than 1960. Los Angeles, Fresno, Sacramento and Jacksonville reported the highest rates during 1960, and other cities with fairly high reporting included New York, Pittsburgh, Chicago and several other smaller cities throughout the country. During 1970, cities with the highest reporting included Salt Lake City, Lansing, Philadelphia and Jersey City. In addition, many medium-sized to smaller cities throughout the country had fairly high reporting of this crime.

Unlike some of the other property crimes, automobile theft is clearly defined. Still, it is difficult to distinguish from the data presented here the differences among those thefts explained as either juvenile "joyrides," automobiles stolen for purposes of committing other serious crimes or professional thefts for purposes of alteration and resale elsewhere. Harries, in his 1973 analysis, found a strong correlation between stolen automobiles and number of registered vehicles. While fairly obvious, this association augments the theories of opportunities offered in relation to property crimes and robberies. An analysis of the distributions of automobile thefts reported from our sample of 127 cities during 1960 and 1970 shows that the only regional concentration during either period was in the northeastern United States in 1970. During 1960 the four largest cities with highest reporting were New Orleans, San Francisco, Chicago and Pittsburgh. By 1970, the only cities outside of the Northeast reporting extremely high rates were Cleveland and St. Louis. Again, reference to Table 7-3 shows that automobile thefts tripled from 1960 to 1970. However, the extremely high northeastern rate somewhat detracted from actual increases sustained elsewhere. In general, this crime is more widespread than most others.

The Regionalization of Crime, 1960 and 1970

The preceding discussion of violent and property crimes helps explain that the utility of these major categorical indexes is somewhat constrained by the differing spatial distributions of individual crimes. Conversely, these two primary categories of the total crime index are the measures more frequently used in criminal justice planning decisions. Some shifts in the distribution of violent and property crimes have been noted. For purposes of comparison, the violent and property crimes can be explained simultaneously. This is accomplished by constructing two-by-two tables classifying the 127 cities into one of four possible categories. Thus, for 1960 the following example of selected cities can be compared:

VIOLENT CRIMES	PROPERTY CRIMES: Below Average Rates	PROPERTY CRIMES: Above Average Rates
Above Average Rates	Atlanta Akron San Antonio Seattle Nashville Tulsa Salt Lake City	New York Miami Pittsburgh Houston St. Louis Denver Los Angeles
Below Average Rates	San Diego El Paso Omaha Memphis Milwaukee Buffalo Albany	Philadelphia Baltimore Washington, D.C. Dallas Cleveland Cincinnati Boston

Figure 7-4c shows 1960 regionalization of crimes in the manner mentioned above for all 127 cities. Most, but not all, of the larger cities in the nation had higher than average rates for both violent and property crimes. However, many large urban centers—e.g. Boston, Philadelphia, Cleveland, Washington and Baltimore—showed up as having higher than average rates for violent crime and lower than average rates for property crimes Many medium-sized to smaller cities had rates of reporting below the average for both crime categories. Notable exceptions to the latter aspect, however, were Savannah, Richmond, Chattanooga, Corpus Christi, Newark, Camden, Flint, Albuquerque and Fresno which all reported rates for both crime categories higher than average for the 127 cities. Also many medium-sized cities within proximity of larger cities reported violent crimes lower than average and property crimes above the mean.

By comparing the two major crime categories simultaneously, a fairly accurate impression of total crime index severity is obtained. Larger cities did have higher overall crime rates in 1960, and the fact that medium-sized cities adjacent to many of these larger centers had higher rates than their counterparts in more isolated locations suggest a sort of "spill-over" due to distance proximity. The latter aspect is more true of areas west of the Great Plains, however. In the West, more extremely high and low combinations showed up. For example, Denver, Phoenix and Albuquerque, in relatively isolated locations compared to the East, had severe crime problems in 1960.

The 1970 "regionalization" (Figure 7-4d) map shows that once again many larger cities demonstrated rates above the average for that year for both violent and property crimes. The two maps (Figures 7-4c and 7-4d) have somewhat similar patterns of distribution of the four classes, but there are some exceptions. For example, many of the Great Plains cities showed rates below the average for both crimes. Conversely, many medium-sized New England cities reported more property crimes than in 1960, and property crimes increased in Baltimore, Washington and Cleveland, thus placing these cities in the same class with New York and Los Angeles in 1970.

There is a more specific method of measuring actual change over the decade. From 1960 to 1970 the average annual increase in property crimes for the 127 cities was 30.35 percent; for violent crimes the comparable rate of change was 40.69 percent. Clearly, rates of increase varied by city. When these rates of change are compared simultaneously, as was accomplished for the individual base years, strong patterns of regional differences stand out. Figure 7-4e shows that the largest Pacific Northwest and many Midwestern and Northeastern cities showed average annual increases over the decade exceeding the average increases for both violent and property crimes. On the other hand, most cities in southern California, the Southwest and the Southeast demonstrated ten year average rates of increase below the averages for both crime types. Los Angeles, New Orleans, St. Louis, Chicago, Miami, Jacksonville and Philadelphia, all cities which demonstrated higher than average rates for many of the crime index offenses in either 1960 or 1970, had rates of increase below the average for the entire decade. On the other hand, many cities with generally lower than average rates for many crimes had higher than average rates of increase—e.g., Topeka, Lincoln, St. Paul, Ft. Wayne, Allentown and New Bedford.

The rate of crime increase continued after 1970, and during 1971 all property crimes and robbery peaked (Figures 7-1 and 7-2) and then started to decrease in the United States, but homicide, rape and assault continued to rise. By mid-1973, for the largest actual number of crimes, 1971 was the turning point which will hopefully continue to develop into a substantial decrease during the 1970s. While possible causes for the presumed decreasing rates are addressed in the final part of this chapter, it should be understood that causality of crime has not been given much consideration at the intraurban scale of analysis because of substantial variations of crime rates within various parts of the 127 cities. In other words, it cannot be assumed that crimes reported to the FBI annually are uniformly distributed within any given city.

SOME EXAMPLES OF VARIABLE CRIME DISTRIBUTIONS WITHIN CITIES DURING 1971

Conclusions about the distribution of crime within cities are often easier to understand than those developed when interregional and intermetropolitan comparisons are made. As already mentioned, variable reporting procedures cause the greatest difficulties to those attempting to find common patterns of crime occurrence. These difficulties are also encountered when analyses of the variable distribution of crime within metropolitan areas are accomplished. However, inconsistency in reporting can be minimized by utilizing crime data generated by either single police departments or related information systems within metropolitan counties. For purposes of intraurban comparisons of crime index offenses, two SMSA central cities—Akron and Cleveland—are used as examples within this study. Cleveland is a larger city with higher rates of change for violent and property crimes from 1960 to 1970 comparable to those of New York, Washington and Boston (Figure 7-4e). On the other hand, Akron is used to exemplify many medium-sized cities (and some larger ones) with lower than average rates of crime change for the same time period.

Crime index offenses for 1971, the currently known peak year for crime in the United States, are mapped and statistically analyzed for both central cities. The Akron analysis is more detailed than that of Cleveland for two important reasons. The first reason is that the Akron study draws from the Summit County Criminal Justice Information System recently developed with support of LEAA funding, and data pertaining to addresses of suspects cleared by arrest are available. Second, because of the importance of "structural" or land use ingredients in analyses of urban crime, an attempt was made to determine percentages of land area within the cities in various types of nonresidential use. These data were obtained for Akron, but no similar recent inventory has been accomplished for Cleveland. However, it is possible to accomplish a traditional cartographic analysis of crime in relation to land use within Cleveland, and this simple visual comparison is quite revealing.

Aspects of Crime in Cleveland, 1971

Cleveland, with 751,000 persons in 1970, is one of the ten largest cities in the United States. As already mentioned, during the decade of the 1960s, both violent and property crimes reported in Cleveland increased at rates greater than the average for most US central cities over 100,000. As with many large US cities, Cleveland's population dropped from 876,050 in 1960 to the 1970 figure above. For the same period of time, the Negro percentage of Cleveland's population increased from 29 to 38 percent. As recently pointed out by Berry, this combination of changes during the 1960s was not uncommon.

The fact that Cleveland is an industrial city is evident when Figure 7-5, the map depicting generalized land use features, is examined. The Cuyahoga River flows sluggishly through the middle of Cleveland and forms the industrialized "flats" area of that city. In addition, much of the Lake Erie shoreline of Cleveland, particularly at the mouth of the river and to the northeast, is comprised of industrial structures, rail yards, docking facilities and a wide variety of industry-related uses. There are also large tracts of industrial land radiating outward from Cleveland along older railway lines and some newer limited access highways. The latter aspect is particularly true of some industrial locations on the fringes of Cleveland's suburban boundaries.

Land parcels allocated to commercial use in Cleveland display the spiderlike appearance of similar uses in many other cities. The commercial core, close to the Cuyahoga River and Lake Erie, forms the nucleus of commercial ribbons radiating outward along arterial roads which had much more importance prior to the construction of limited access highways. Smaller community and neighborhood shopping districts are interspersed throughout the city and surrounded by residential areas.

One of the more striking features of Figure 7-5 is the axis of urban settlement density extending from the commercial core east to the large area of "institutional" land use (which contains the Case Western Reserve University complex). This corridor of intense land use is concentrated along several urban thoroughfares which link some of Cleveland's more affluent suburbs—Shaker Heights for example—to the commercial cores. One of Cleveland's major public transportation rail lines, the Shaker Rapid, also passes through this area. The housing surrounding and to the north of these transportation lines is the most dense in Cleveland. The area is in effect one large urban ghetto and many of the commercial establishments along the major streets display barred windows and gates which can be locked when establishments are closed. This part of Cleve-

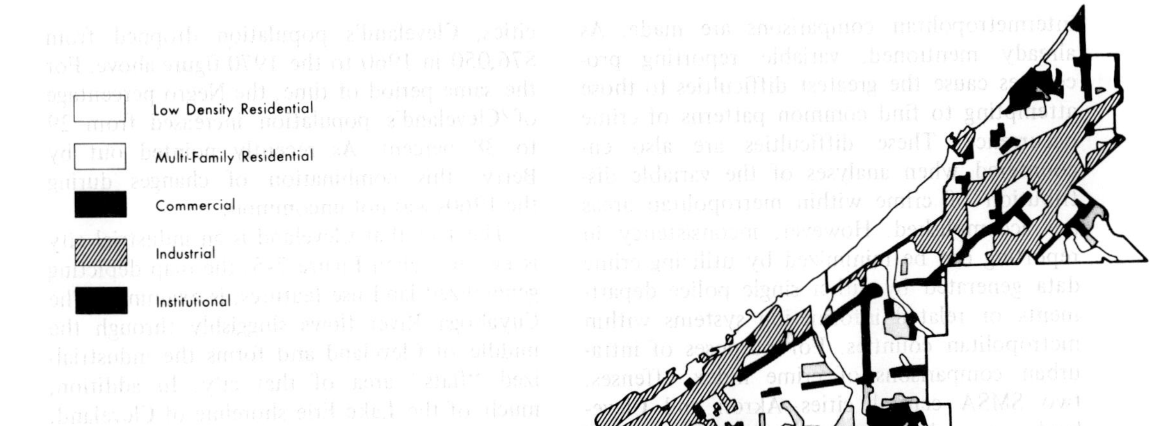

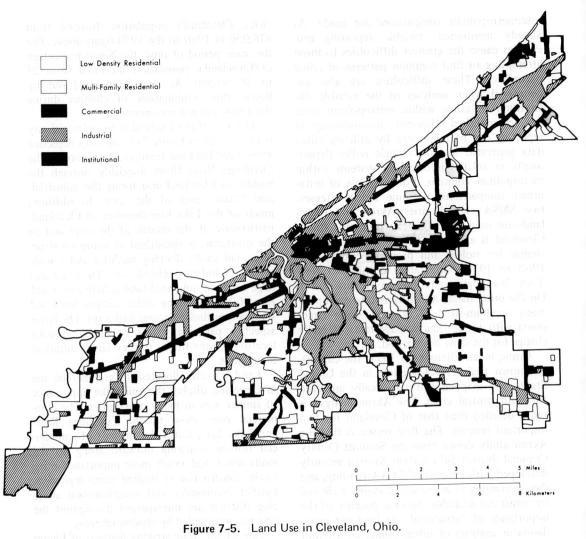

Figure 7-5. Land Use in Cleveland, Ohio.

land also includes the Hough district which exploded into a riot situation during the late 1960s. Charred commercial establishments can still be seen north of the major commercial streets.

All index crime offenses either reported to or by the Cleveland Police Department during 1971 have been aggregated into census tracts and Figures 7-6 to 7-10 describe the geographical distribution of these crimes. For these maps, proportionate circles are used to depict categories of actual raw numbers of crimes reported. It is most useful to view the distribution of three violent crimes—homicide, rape and assault—simultaneously (Figure 7-6). The largest reported numbers of all of these crimes were from Cleveland's well demarcated East Side, with some of the heaviest concentrations within the eastern corridor previously mentioned. However, all of these crimes were not restricted to eastern Cleveland, and while the reporting of homicide was reliable, it is difficult to assess the number of unreported rapes which may have occurred on the city's West Side, or on the East Side for that matter. While still concentrated in and around the Hough area, reported assaults were more dispersed than the other two crimes. The distribution of

Figure 7-6. Cleveland: Reported Murders (top), Rapes (middle), and Assaults (bottom), in 1971, by Census Tract.

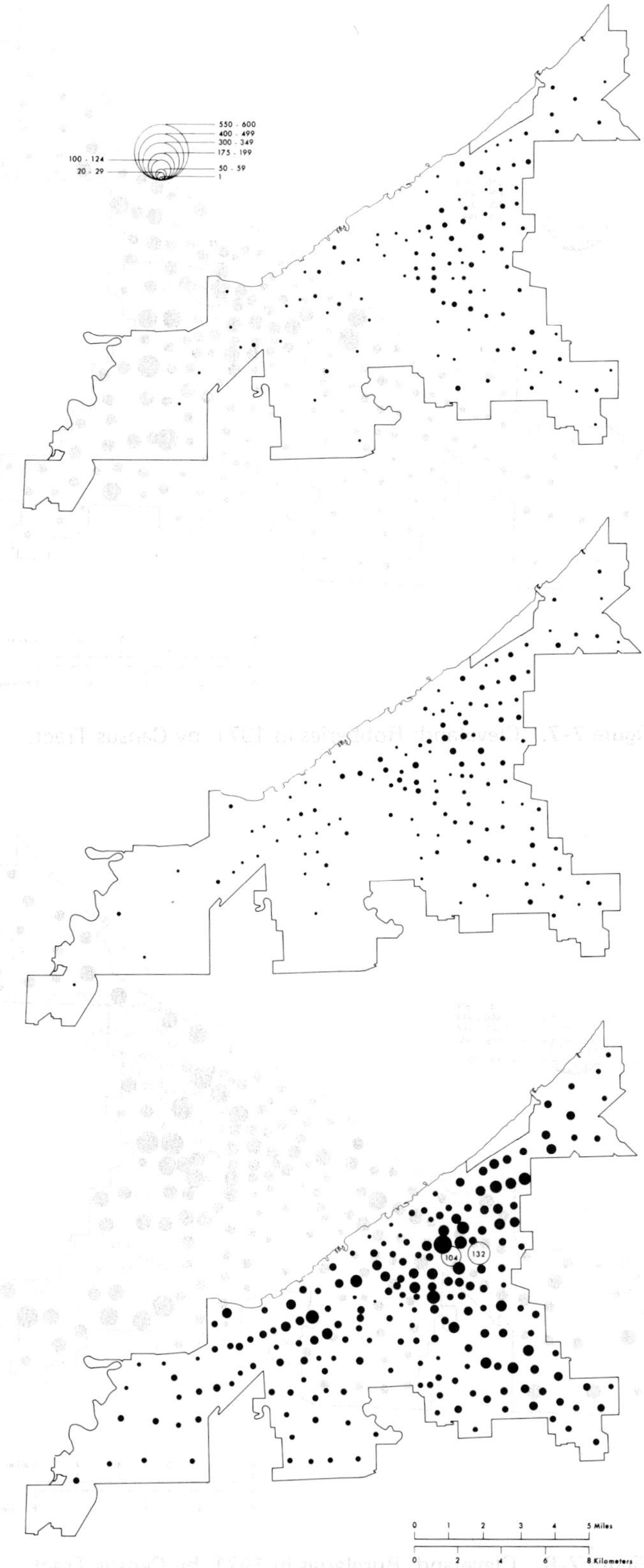
550 - 600
400 - 499
300 - 349
175 - 199
100 - 124
50 - 59
20 - 29
1
104
132
0 1 2 3 4 5 Miles
0 2 4 6 8 Kilometers

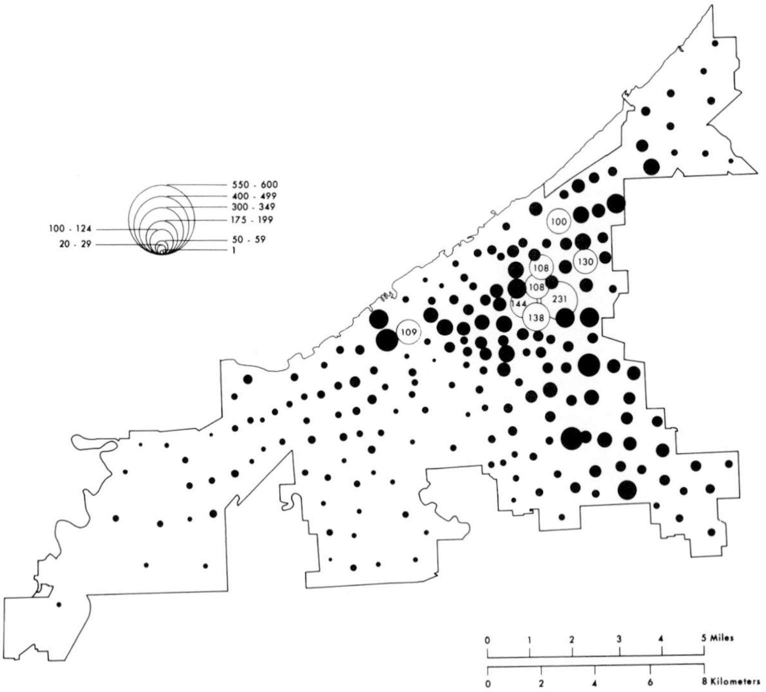

Figure 7-7. Cleveland: Robberies in 1971, by Census Tract.

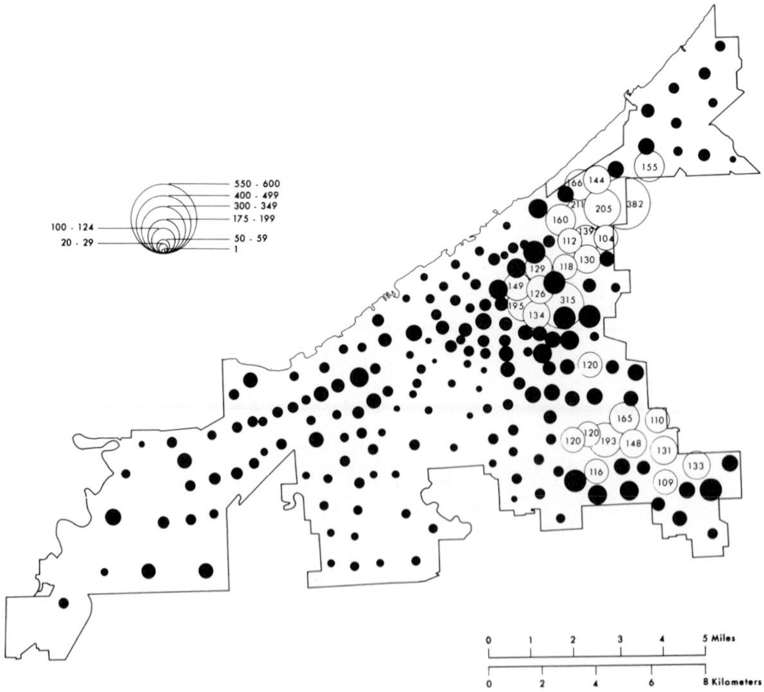

Figure 7-8. Cleveland: Burglaries in 1971, by Census Tract.

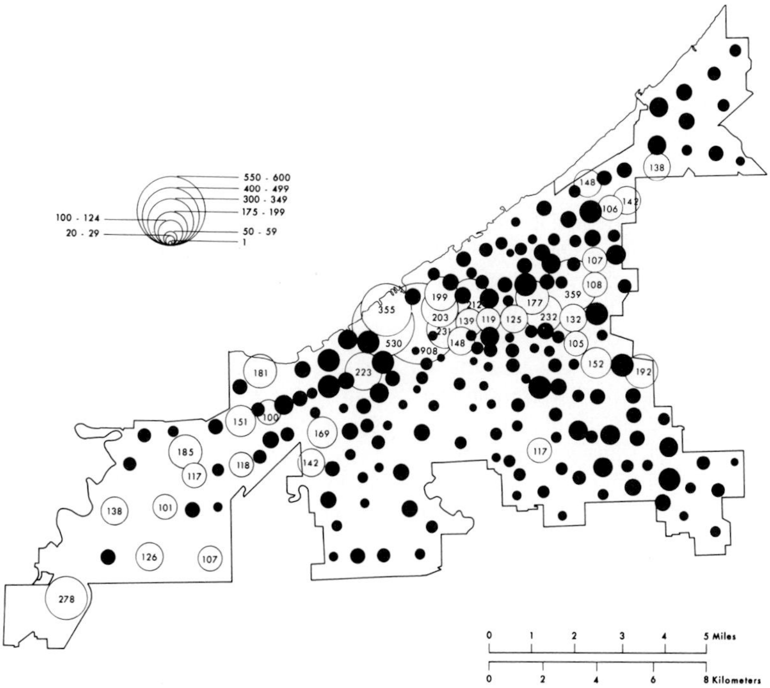

Figure 7-9. Cleveland: Larcenies in 1971, by Census Tract.

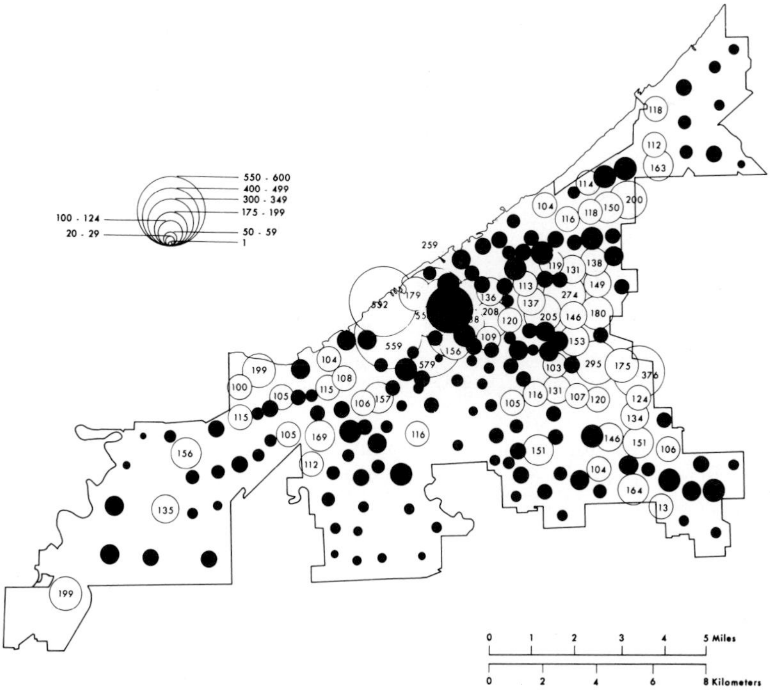

Figure 7-10. Cleveland: Stolen Automobiles in 1971, by Census Tract.

assaults is closely tied to many of the commercial ribbons within Cleveland, and many taverns are, in fact, located within these areas.

Robbery is considered a violent crime because person-to-person confrontations are normally involved. However, the opportunities presented to the armed robber are often in the form of commercial and financial establishments, and unarmed robberies occur in a wide variety of places. The distribution of all robberies taking place during 1971 is contained within Figure 7-7. When compared with the three other violent crimes, robbery is a much more serious crime in Cleveland's commercial core than homicide, rape or assault. However, the East Side corridor of Cleveland accounted for far more robberies during 1971 than any other single part of the city. There was also higher reporting of this crime in northeastern and southeastern Cleveland. The latter areas are at this time in various states of general physical and social urban transition.

The spatial distribution of burglaries within Cleveland once again indicates heavy reporting in 1971 from the East Side. Still, the actual number of burglaries exceeded the number of the individual violent crimes. Thus, in relation to those crimes, burglary was widespread. In comparison to the remainder of the city, however, there were three heavy concentrations of this crime: the East Side "corridor," Northeast Cleveland and Southeast Cleveland.

While larceny is clearly defined legally, ths crime is to some extent ambiguously defined by police reports. It incorporates a wide variety of thefts including shoplifting and simply stealing from attended or unattended buildings and establishments. In many respects this crime is closely related to nonresidential burglary. More whites are arrested for this crime than any other index crime offense except automobile theft. There is reason to believe that in some instances a white and a black can be apprehended for an identical crime of this nature, and the white will be charged with larceny while the black must face the more serious charge of breaking and entering. The map depicting larcenies in 1971 attests to the nature of such reporting. Cleveland's commercial core and the dense corridor to the east had by far the highest reporting of larceny. Because industrial as well as commercial establishments are susceptible to this kind of theft, many other census tracts within Cleveland containing industrial as well as commercial land uses reported substantial numbers of burglaries (Figure 7-5).

During 1971, several thousand automobiles were stolen from downtown Cleveland. There were also heavy concentrations of this crime east of the commercial core and in northeastern and southeastern Cleveland. Many cars were also stolen from Cleveland's West Side. As a general rule, parking lots in commercial areas, industrial sites and apartment complexes are prime target areas for automobile thefts. The spatial pattern of this crime—as well as larceny and to some extent robbery—helps to explain some of the difficulties which might be encountered by applying an urban analysis using socioeconomic census data without considering aspects of land use.

Statistical testing using such information does, in fact, explain the maps in more detail as well as uncover aspects of crime in Cleveland not revealed by the maps alone analysis. On the basis of experiments with crime data from other studies, the statistical method selected as most appropriate is canonical factor analysis. For Cleveland, the seven kinds of crime are considered the information to be explained and the 25 variables obtained for 199 Cleveland census tracts as reported in 1970 are considered the explaining information. Due to the varying distributions of the violent and property crimes, rates per 1,000 census tract inhabitants are used for homicide, rape, assault and robbery, and numbers actually reported are used for burglary, larceny and automobile theft.

The statistical analysis shows, by reading down the columns within Table 7-4, four "clusters" of explanation. The numbers termed "loadings" for each column represent the strength of association for each variable from both sets when compared to all others. Loadings can theoretically range from -1.0 to +1.0, but these limits are rarely reached. Thus, the lower the above measures, the lower the numerical level of importance of each variable. Overall, each column explains crimes which occurred in statistical associations with explaining variables.

For example, Factor I contains significant high negative loadings for homicide, rape, robbery, assault and burglary. These high negative loadings are matched by specific socioeconomic and demographic variables with-

Table 7-4. Canonical Factor Structure, Crime in Cleveland, 1971

Variable	*Canonical Factor Loadings* *I*	*II*	*III*	*IV*
Criterion Set: Crime Variables				
Homicide	-.67	0.49	0.27	0.19
Rape	-.59	0.12	-.32	0.03
Assault	-.63	0.56	-0.30	0.24
Robbery	-.52	0.80	0.10	0.15
Burglary	-.60	-.47	0.42	-.14
Larceny	-.07	0.33	-.11	-.02
Automobile Theft	-.30	0.28	-.19	-.45
Predictor Set: Socioeconomic and Demographic Variables				
Percent Population Change 1960–1970	0.44	-.28	0.19	-.10
Percent Residential Structures Built Before 1950	-.10	0.03	-.13	0.06
Percent Housing Units Without Sound Plumbing	-.29	0.63	0.06	-.12
Percent Dwelling Units Vacant	-.28	0.09	-.14	-.09
Percent Dwelling Units Owner-Occupied	0.52	-.32	0.19	0.25
Percent Same House as in 1965	0.34	-.09	0.30	0.45
Percent Population in High School	0.00	-.44	0.37	0.17
Percent Population 16–25 Years Old Not High School Graduates or Not Enrolled	-.13	0.35	-.35	0.43
Median School Years	0.20	-.27	0.05	-.04
Percent Male Work Force Unemployed	-.41	-.12	0.02	0.03
Percent Female Work Force Unemployed	-.37	0.28	0.24	0.18
Percent Male Blue Collar Workers	-.27	-.04	0.31	0.18
Percent Female Blue Collar Workers	-.58	0.07	0.15	0.14
Percent of Families with Incomes Less Than $5,000	-.58	-.05	-.12	0.12
Percent of Families with Income Between $5,000 and $9,999	-.08	0.44	0.36	-.26
Percent of Families with Income Between $10,000 and $14,999	0.61	-.26	-.07	0.01
Percent of Families with Income Between $15,000 and $25,000	0.54	-.09	0.05	0.07
Percent of Families with Income Over $25,000	-.01	0.15	-.24	-.09
Percent of Families Below Poverty Level	-.56	-.09	0.04	0.11
Median Family Income	0.60	-.09	-.02	-.11
Percent of Population Under 5 Years	0.11	-.19	0.12	0.08
Percent of Population Between 15–19 Years	-.15	-.13	0.26	0.02
Percent of Population Over 65 Years	0.05	0.51	-.30	-.28
Percent of Population 45–64 Years	0.16	0.32	-.20	0.20
Percent Negro	-.76	-.40	0.27	0.07
R^2	0.72	0.61	0.55	0.33
Criterion Set				
Variance Extracted	0.28	0.23	0.07	0.05
Redundancy	0.20	0.14	0.04	0.02
Predictor Set				
Variance Extracted	0.15	0.08	0.05	0.03
Redundancy	0.11	0.05	0.03	0.01

Source: Computed by author.

in the first column of Table 7-4 which help explain conditions in urban neighborhoods with high crime rates or numbers for the above crimes. For this example, five census-related variables indicating the strong influence of poverty and violent crime stand out. These indicators are: the unemployment rate, the number of female blue collar workers, the percentages of low income and poverty families, and the percentage Negro. Such a syndrome of violent crime and poverty has been apparent to those writing about the topic for several decades. There are those who argue that poverty is, in fact, the sole cause of crime; however, others feel that additional factors can also lead to crime.

The second and fourth columns of matched associations (Canonical Factors II and IV) point to the possible contribution of some of these additional crime-producing elements within Cleveland. For example, within the second column the violent crimes of homicide, assault and robbery and the property crimes of larceny and automobile theft share relatively high loadings—or statistical associations—with conditions indicating urban transition. In other words, explaining variables such as a large percentage of housing units without sound plumbing, a high percentage of families with marginal incomes ($5,000 to $9,999) and a high proportion of families over 65 years of age all are indicators of the aging of people and structures. These locations are within the more central portions of most cities—including Cleveland—and there is frequently a great deal of transition as neighborhoods deteriorate. New residential construction rarely takes the form of past building trends. The style of life associated with this form of urban transition can, according to Merton and other authors, lead to a form of psychological despair, or "normlessness." This condition can lead to higher crime rates.

Also, because not all crimes wtihin neighborhoods are actually committed by residents living within the same area, such zones of urban transition can become target areas for criminals. The fourth column of associations implies such an association. Automobile theft is statistically associated with the percentage of families with annual incomes between $5,000 and $9,999 and the percentage of the population over 65 years of age. This association can be tied to at least two known conditions. The first and most apparent is the map in this report showing stolen automobiles (Figure 7-10). Those areas with high reporting of stolen cars are, in fact, in a state of physical transition. The second element is a less direct association, taking the form of the age of those most likely to steal automobiles. For example, studies by Shaw and McKay and by Reckless have shown that more youthful offenders are most often involved in such a crime. While the age structure of the specific neighborhoods in question does not reflect this, areas fringing this target zone are characterized by higher percentages of more youthful persons. Still, this assumption does not imply that all youths are automatically suspect; it does, however, help explain the geographical distribution of stolen automobiles.

This known association between certain crimes and the proximity of higher percentages of younger urban dwellers is more clearly indicated by the third column (Canonical Factor III) within Table 7-4. In this example, burglary has a strong statistical association with the percentage of the population in high school, those of high school age but not enrolled in school and families with annual incomes of from $5,000 to $9,999 annually. This association is more direct than the earlier contention regarding areas fringing the transition zone supplying offenders. While specific data are not available for Cleveland, the analysis of Akron which follows shows that many burglaries are committed by younger persons in marginal income areas *and* close to their place of residence. It is assumed that such a condition also exists within Cleveland. However, Figure 7-8, the map showing the distribution of burglaries within Cleveland, leads to the conclusion that certainly not all burglaries can be explained in the above manner. Again, the Akron analysis, with more specific data, helps identify elements of urban burglary and the other crime index offenses in more detail.

Violent and Property Crimes in Akron, 1971

It is possible to learn even more about crime within cities when this topic is explored for the city of Akron during 1971. Fortunately, the recent development, with LEAA funding, of a computerized crime information system for the Summit County Criminal Justice Commission allows a much more detailed analysis. Unlike the information made available for Cleveland, the Akron crime data include details about suspects including age, sex, race and place of residence when arrested. It is possible to test in more departments some of the earlier findings by those writing about other cities, thus adding to our knowledge of urban crime. The Akron analysis is also different from that of Cleveland because data pertaining to land use characteristics were available. The land use data, in turn, help clarify contentions made about areas of urban transition.

Akron, with a 1970 population of 275,000 ranks fifty-second nationally when compared to other central city SMSAs. As with many of these other cities, the 1970 population of Akron had decreased from the 1960 figure of 290,000. Conversely, the median family income in Akron in 1970 was $8,198 as compared to $7,435 for all Ohio cities and $7,129 for Cleveland. There is substantially less poverty in Akron than in many other larger cities. Part of the reason for this is the egalitarian effect of the strong labor unions operated by workers from the companies forming the rubber oligopoly headquartered in Akron.

As with Cleveland, Akron is a manufacturing city. The city is basically symmetrical, with a central commercial core and commercial ribbons radiating outward in most directions (Figure 7-11). There are, in addition, major and minor commercial outliers. Most of the industrial establishments are either adjacent to the commercial core or on Akron's South Side. The residential pattern is somewhat interrupted in the northwest section of the valley of the Little Cuyahoga River, but some of the city's most dense housing, comprising Akron's older

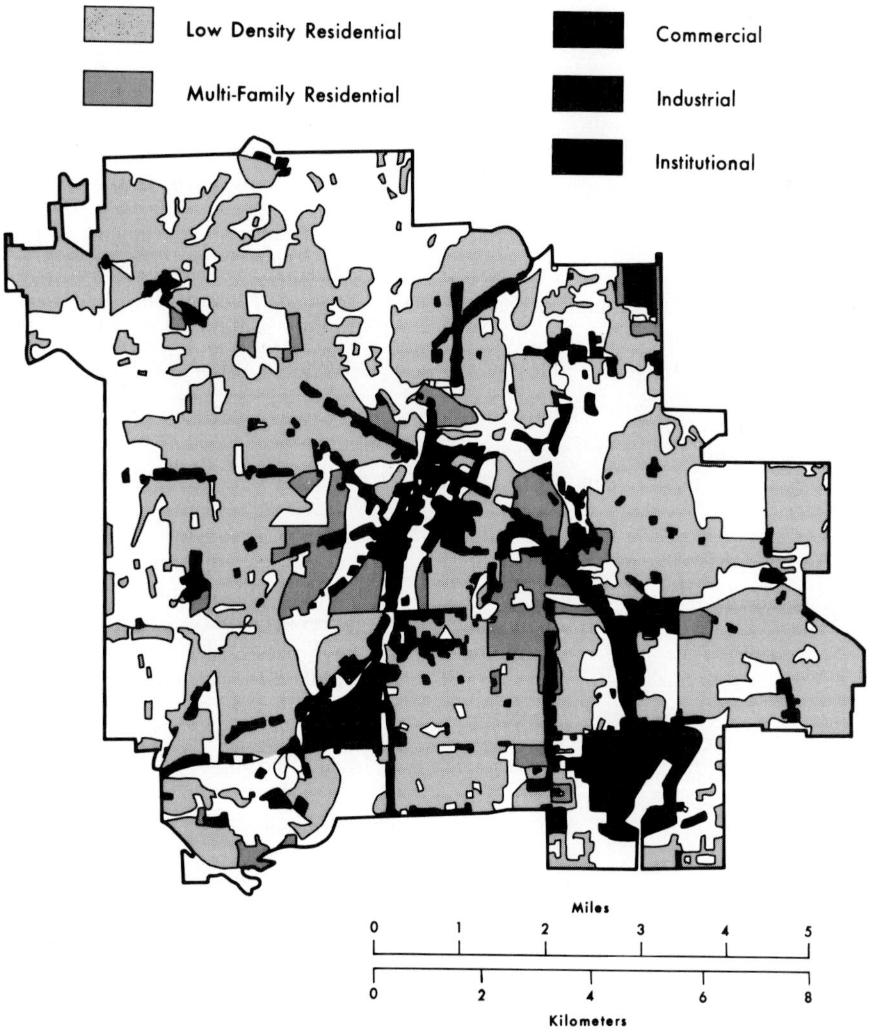

Figure 7-11. Generalized Land Use in Akron.

ghetto area, is within the valley just to the north of the commercial core. Other significant areas of dense housing are to be found within Akron's Lower West Side and to the east and south of the commercial core. Even these areas of more dense housing do not compare to the crowded conditions found within Cleveland and many other larger cities. Still, these somewhat more favorable conditions—higher income levels and generally better housing conditions—do not imply that the crime problem in Akron is not serious. Despite Akron's increase from 1960 to 1970 for both violent and property crimes, the actual rate was lower than the average of the 127 cities over 100,000 during 1971.

The distributions of reported homicide, rape and assault within Akron during 1971 are contained within Figure 7-12. Most of the murders which took place during that time were in some of the more densely populated neighborhoods west, south and southeast of the commercial core. Most of these areas are in some form of urban transition and, as with Cleveland, many contain some of the older housing units within the city. Also, it has been established that there is often a high degree of familiarity between a murder victim and the offender, and this would appear true for Akron also. For example, of all the Akron murders committed in 1971, 66 percent of the arrested suspects resided within the same census tract where the murder took place and 57 percent resided within the same block group. In this instance, it is contended that closer geographical proximity implies a higher degree of familiarity.

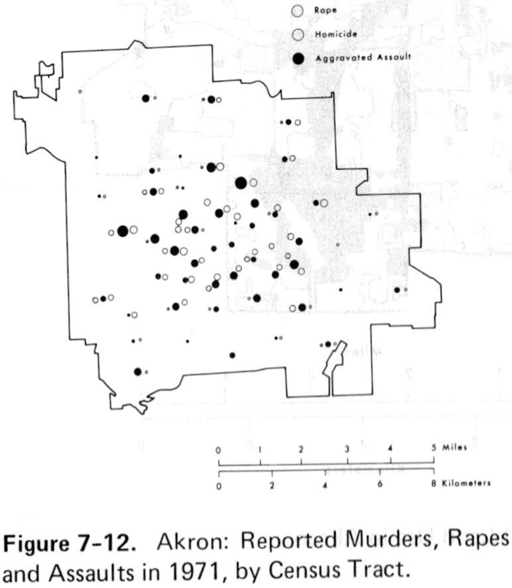

Figure 7-12. Akron: Reported Murders, Rapes and Assaults in 1971, by Census Tract.

The spatial distribution of reported cases of rape in Akron is somewhat different from homicide because the highest reporting is from different census tracts. However, many of the neighborhood characteristics are similar to those areas in which the highest incidence of murder was reported—i.e., they are all areas of urban transition and degrees of housing deterioration. Akron's Lower West Side had the highest reporting of rape in 1971. This is a prime example of an area of racial transition with significant instability. In addition, 70 percent of all rape suspects arrested in Akron in 1971 were nonwhite, yet the victims were about evenly divided between white and nonwhite. Forty-four percent of all known rape victims lived in the census tract wherein the crime took place, but only 35 percent of the arrested suspects lived in the tract where the crime occurred.

The distribution of the incidence of aggravated assault in Akron during 1971 had a spatial pattern similar to that of rape. Both crimes can thus be termed "inner city" offenses. The two sections with highest reporting include the area immediately north of the business district and the Lower West Side. Again, these are areas undergoing a form of transition which can be attributed to earlier urban renewal and highway construction programs within the near central part of Akron. It is thus not surprising to witness higher crime rates in these areas due to recent population movements and known tensions between youths and the police.

The distribution of robberies within Akron is shown within Figure 7-13. As with other violent crimes, the heaviest concentration of reporting of robberies was for the city center, but there is a striking difference in that the highest number of these crimes was reported for the commercial core of Akron (census tract 5013.01). Other census tracts adjacent to the commercial core with high reporting of robbery include 5011 and 5074. In general, the pattern for reported robberies, while somewhat centralized, is still more dispersed than that demonstrated for other violent crimes. This pattern can be attributed to the fact that armed robberies occurred at commercial establishments located along corridors radiating outward from

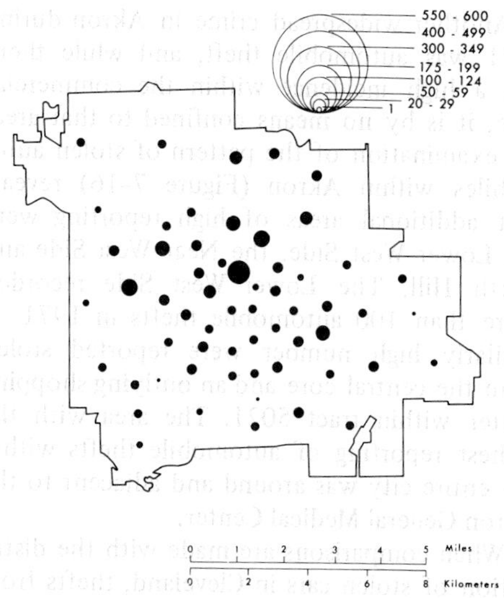

Figure 7-13. Akron: Robberies in 1971, by Census Tract.

the commercial core and the dispersed shopping plazas.

However, the distribution of reported unarmed robberies was much more dispersed throughout the city than armed robberies. While the commercial core was still the highest in terms of reporting, Akron's Lower West Side, a larger residential area, contained almost as many of these crimes as the downtown section of Akron in 1971. Also, Northwest Akron, composed primarily of higher income families and larger homes, showed a fairly high rate of reporting for unarmed robberies. In other words, armed and unarmed robberies did not take place within the same parts of Akron during 1971. Most such studies do not separate robberies into these two categories, and this can result in some misleading conclusions. It can be safely assumed, however, that commercial areas will attract more armed robberies.

Many of those writing in the area of race and crime have developed diverging views. However, some aspects of life are rather obvious: low income areas tend to have a higher incidence of violent crime than do more affluent areas. Akron's version of this rather complex inner city violent crime syndrome consists of the following facts:

- Less than 20 percent of the violent crimes committed in Akron in 1971 were cleared by arrest.
- Seventy-two percent of those arrested for violent crimes were nonwhite.
- Eighty-seven percent of those arrested for violent crimes were male.
- Twenty-three percent of those arrested for violent crimes resided within the same tract where the crime was committed.

Statistics pertaining to property crimes are much less racially biased. During 1971, burglaries represented the greatest proportion of all the crimes presently being studied in Akron (Figure 7-14). Akron's Lower West Side experienced more than 200 burglaries in one census tract alone (5063.01) during 1971. Also, several areas in Northwest Akron also had significant burglaries reported. As already indicated, these tracts in Northwest Akron are comprised largely of older, larger single family dwellings and are presently considered the highest status area of the city. Actually, many of the census tracts with more than 100 reported burglaries contain single family dwellings. These reported burglaries include nonresidential as well as residential breaking and entering, and the areas of Akron with the highest reporting of nonresidential burglary in 1971 were the commercial core, the older developed areas adjacent to the core, and North Hill, in Northeast Akron. In general, the latter areas consist of either commercial and light industrial land

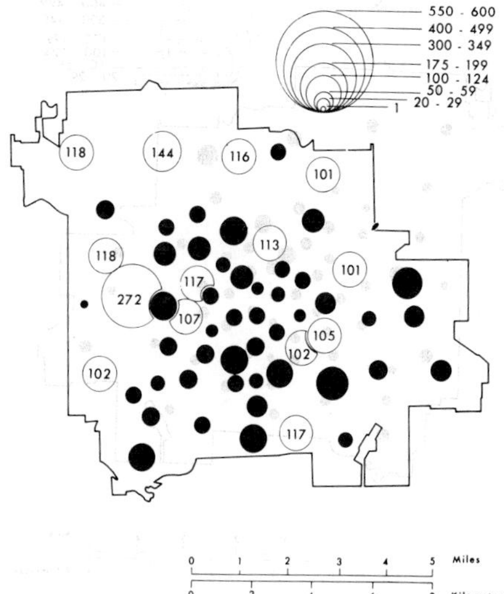

Figure 7-14. Akron: Burglaries in 1971, by Census Tract.

uses or poor quality housing. Furthermore, only 14 percent of all those arrested for non-residential burglary in Akron lived within the same census tract in which the crime was committed and only 7 percent lived within the same block group. On the other hand, 76 percent of those arrested for residential burglary resided within the same census tract and 11 percent lived within the same block group of the crime location.

Larcenies reported within Akron during 1971 were much more dispersed (Figure 7-15) than similar reporting for Cleveland (Figure 7-9). The distributional pattern of this crime shows that the highest reporting was from the North Hill section, the Lower West Side, the commercial core and Akron's older black ghetto areas. In effect, this crime is closely associated with the distribution of commercial land and some of Akron's poverty pockets. However, the reporting of larceny was also more widely distributed among middle and upper income neighborhoods than some of the other crimes being analyzed here. During 1971, 73 percent of those arrested for larceny were juvenile, 93 percent were male and 58 percent were white. When all arrests for crime index offenses reported for 1971 are considered, larceny ranked highest in the percentage of whites arrested.

Another widespread crime in Akron during 1971 was automobile theft, and while there was a high incidence within the commercial core, it is by no means confined to that area. An examination of the pattern of stolen automobiles within Akron (Figure 7-16) reveals that additional areas of high reporting were the Lower West Side, the Near West Side and North Hill. The Lower West Side recorded more than 100 automobile thefts in 1971. A similarly high number were reported stolen from the central core and an outlying shopping center within tract 5021. The area with the highest reporting of automobile thefts within the entire city was around and adjacent to the Akron General Medical Center.

When comparisons are made with the distribution of stolen cars in Cleveland, thefts from the commercial core are a far less serious problem. In terms of arrest statistics, the characteristics of those arrested during 1971 were almost identical to those arrested for larceny. For example, 71 percent of those arrested for automobile theft were juvenile, 92 percent were male and 56 percent were white. However, even with the information pertaining to arrested suspects augmenting our knowledge of crime in Akron—as opposed to the Cleveland analysis—statistical testing with the same method (canonical factor analysis) still helps develop

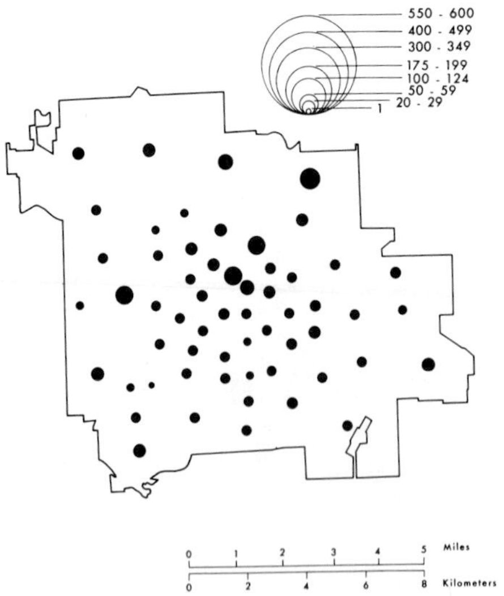

Figure 7-15. Akron: Larcenies in 1971, by Census Tract.

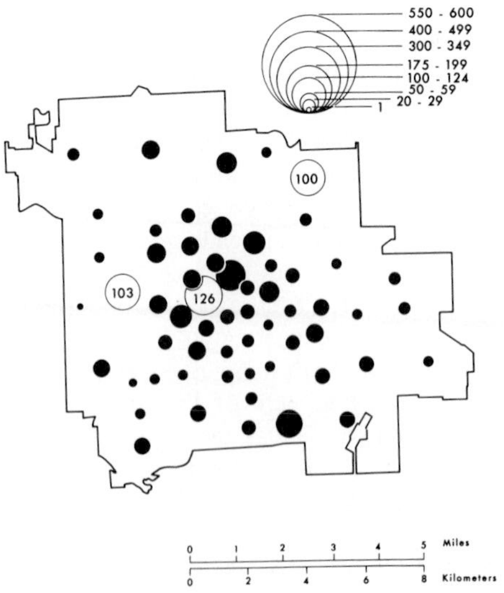

Figure 7-16. Akron: Stolen Automobiles in 1971, by Census Tract.

an understanding of crime in relation to social conditions.

The results of this testing are contained within Table 7-5. As with the Cleveland data, violent crimes within Akron are tested as rates per 1,000 persons and property crimes are maintained as actual numbers reported. In addition, three land use variables are included due to the availability of a recent inventory completed by the city of Akron. These variables are: percentage of census tract in commercial use; percentage of tract in streets, expressways

Table 7-5. Canonical Factor Structure, Crime in Akron, 1971

	Canonical Factor Loadings			
Variable	*I*	*II*	*III*	*IV*
Criterion Set: Crime Variables				
Homicide	-.28	0.54	0.19	-.32
Rape	-.53	0.35	-.10	-.40
Assault	-.63	0.56	0.19	-.20
Robbery	-.95	-.13	-.21	-.01
Burglary	-.21	-.10	0.73	0.17
Larceny	-.45	0.07	-.11	0.24
Automobile Theft	-.52	0.38	0.13	0.65
Predictor Set: Socioeconomic and Demographic Variables				
Percent Population Change 1960–1970	0.44	-.51	0.11	0.15
Percent Residential Structures Built Before 1950	0.02	0.04	-.19	-.24
Percent Housing Units Without Sound Plumbing	-.83	-.13	-.40	-.13
Percent Dwelling Units Vacant	-.34	0.45	-.12	0.39
Percent Dwelling Units Owner-Occupied	0.53	-.54	0.40	-.06
Percent Same House as in 1965	0.34	-.27	0.47	-.30
Percent Population in High School	-.25	-.45	0.34	-.30
Percent Population 16–25 Years Old Not High School Graduates or Not Enrolled	-.39	0.52	-.15	-.17
Median School Years	-.14	0.18	-.06	0.60
Percent Male Work Force Unemployed	-.40	0.38	-.00	0.48
Percent Female Work Force Unemployed	-.29	0.43	0.19	-.28
Percent Male Blue Collar Workers	-.08	0.21	0.03	-.47
Percent Female Blue Collar Workers	-.37	0.64	0.23	-.15
Percent of Families with Income Less Than $5,000	-.63	0.43	-.05	-.45
Percent of Families with Income Between $5,000 and $9,999	0.03	0.27	-.26	-.24
Percent of Families with Income Between $10,000 and $14,999	0.52	-.27	0.06	0.44
Percent of Families with Income Between $15,000 and $25,000	0.40	-.50	0.20	0.24
Percent of Families with Income Over $25,000	-.12	-.08	0.13	0.38
Percent of Families Below Poverty Level	-.66	0.48	0.11	-.39
Median Family Income	0.50	-.55	0.21	0.23
Percent of Population Under 5 Years	0.05	0.15	0.35	-.03
Percent of Population Between 15–19 Years	0.12	0.14	-.31	-.15
Percent of Population Over 65 Years	-.30	-.03	-.24	-.01
Percent of Population 45–64 Years	-.03	-.27	0.00	-.12
Percent Negro	-.44	0.54	0.59	-.13
Percent Commercial Land	-.71	0.16	-.38	0.44
Percent Land in Wholesale and Manufacturing Use	-.30	0.49	-.13	-.01
Percent of Tract in Expressways, Streets and Alleys	-.48	0.17	-.05	-.05

continued

Table 7-5 continued

Variable	I	II	III	IV
R^2	0.96	0.92	0.82	0.64
Criterion Set:				
Variance Extracted	0.31	0.13	0.10	0.12
Redundancy	0.30	0.12	0.08	0.07
Predictor Set:				
Variance Extracted	0.17	0.16	0.07	0.09
Redundancy	0.14	0.13	0.05	0.06

Source: Computed by author.

and alleys; and percentage of tract in manufacturing and wholesale use. The results of the canonical factor analysis indicate findings similar to the Cleveland findings, but they are more readily interpretable.

The four columns of numbers within Table 7-5 under the general heading *Canonical Factor Loadings* show similar associations of crime variables and those data intended to assist in explaining the distribution of the seven crimes in relation to socioeconomic, demographic and land use features of Akron's 59 census tracts. The crime variables indicated within the first column—or canonical factor—consist of three crimes of violence—rape, assault and robbery—and one propery crime—larceny—all with high negative numbers. The explaining variables with the highest negative numbers are: (1) percentage of housing units without sound plumbing, (2) percentage of families with average annual incomes less than $5,000, (3) percentage of families below the poverty level, (4) percentage of land area in commercial use, and (5) percentage of land area comprised by streets, alleys and expressways.

Two explanations are given by the above statistical associations. The first is the identification of a poverty syndrome similar to that explained wtihin Cleveland. There are more violent crimes within poverty areas of Akron than other parts of the city; however, inclusion of the land use variables is a testimony to the fact that more crime opportunities also exist adjacent to poverty areas. In other words, areas with poor housing also contain many commercial areas and more land in transportation uses.

The second factor shows that violence can be produced within urban neighborhoods in the process of various forms of transition and decay. Homicide and assault are strongly associated with a number of variables suggesting these conditions of urban transition. For example, the variable percentage of work force female blue collar workers demonstrates the highest loading among the explaining variables within this dimension. Other important variables to this dimension are percentage of population 16-25 years of age not high school graduates and not enrolled in school, percentage Negro, percentage of families below poverty level and percentage of dwelling units vacant. Percentage of land in wholesale and manufacturing use demonstrates a moderately important association. As will be explained in more detail later in the chapter, the relatively short distance traveled to commit these crimes indicates that many of the victims as well as offenders are subjected to various forms of stress resulting from or associated with conditions of urban blight and decay.

As with the first dimension of the canonical analysis, multiple associations are suggested by the third factor. The crime of burglary demonstrates a very high loading (0.73) with a mixture of predictor variables indicating the nature of those census tracts which are the most victimized. These important indicators are: (1) percentage of dwelling units owner-occupied, (2) percentage of 1970 population residing in the same household as 1965, (3) percentage of population high school graduates, (4) percentage population less than five years of age, and (5) percentage Negro. In other words, many of the census tracts with a high number of burglaries are fairly stable and middle to upper income. However, there are also high burglary rates within lower income areas of Akron, as was indicated by Figure 7-14.

The fourth factor contains a similarly complex statistical association in terms of explaining variables, but much can be learned about the pattern of stolen cars from this combination. Automobile theft is the only crime variable with a fairly high loading of 0.65 on this factor. However, several sets of predictor variables are important. One suggested combination consists of important loadings for percentage of dwelling units vacant and percentage of work force unemployed. Another set of high loading variables is median school years, percentage of families with annual incomes from $10,000 to $15,000 and percentage of families with incomes over $25,000. A fairly high loading also shows up for percentage of land in commercial use. These associations attest to the ubiquity of this crime within Akron during 1971. Such a combination as is found within this factor, and the other three as well, does not imply that the crimes were all committed by residents of census tracts with high reporting. In some instances social conditions led to crimes, and in others, particularly burglary and automobile theft, certain urban subareas presented more opportunities.

The statistical testing of the Akron and Cleveland crime statistics describes how the reporting of offenses can co-vary with certain population and neighborhood attributes within cities. While many such concentrations and associations are intuitively known by law enforcement officials and inhabitants of cities, geographic analysis adds to this knowledge by developing more precise, measurable analyses of distributions. The largest single shortcoming of such measurement of crime information is that the immediate assumption can be made that most crimes are committed by persons living within neighborhoods with high crime rates. Such occurrences are more true for violent crimes, with the exception of robbery, but this is not necessarily the case where property crimes are concerned.

For example, Figure 7-17 shows linkages (lines) established between places of residence of those arrested during 1971 for residential burglaries and actual crime locations (open circles with numbers). Past studies by Phillips, Boggs and others have shown that there are often marked "travel" differences not only among various types of crime but also within different cities.

These generalities regarding the differences traveled to commit different kinds of crimes are important to the development of an understanding of the internal dynamics of urban crimes, but a constraining factor regarding the data used to generate such studies should be realized.

This constraint is that not all crimes are "cleared by arrest" during any given calendar year. Some crimes take months and even years to solve, and others are never solved. In some instances, as is often the case with residential burglaries, many crimes may be committed by a few persons, and details are not known without actual apprehension of the criminals involved. During 1971, more than 4,000 burglaries were reported within Akron, thus making this crime the largest in volume (more than half) of all index crime offenses. More than three-quarters of these were residential burglaries, but only 6 percent were cleared by arrest. Also, in 1971 suspects traveled on the average farther to commit residential burglaries than any other single type of crime (Table 7-6). In addition, the parts of the city with the largest number of "imports" for this crime were census tracts 5063.01 and 5072 (Figure 7-17). Still, there were more suspects arrested for committing burglaries in census tracts 5072 and 5071, higher income parts of Akron than in 5063.01, an area undergoing urban transition. However, part of this circumstance is related to the apprehension of a number of burglars from suburban areas to the north of Akron. Aside from the suburban-based arrests, nearly half of those arrested gave addresses within poverty areas.

In spite of the constraining effect of the low "cleared by arrest" percentage, the movements of suspects depicted within Figure 7-17 help explain further the statistical matching of crime and socioeconomic variables contained within Table 7-6. Part of the statistical association indicates that higher income parts of Akron are target areas for residential burglaries and this finding is supported by analysis of Figure 7-17. In addition, the statistical testing showed that lower income parts of Akron also have higher burglary rates. Reference to Figure 7-17 also shows this. However, one major difference in travel patterns stands out.

The higher income parts of Akron attracted suspects from many parts of Akron and suburbs throughout Summit County. In part, this is an indication of a higher degree of premeditated

Table 7-6. Arrest Statistics and Average Travel Distances, Major Crimes within Akron, 1971

Crime	*Percent Cleared by Arrest*	*Percent of Juvenile Arrests*	*Percent Negro*	*Average Distance From Suspect's Residence to Crime Location (Miles)*
Homicide	51	0	80	1.8
Rape	18	28	71	1.3
Assault	30	9	69	1.3
Robbery	16	38	73	2.2
Burglary	9	57	43	2.4
Larceny	4	73	37	1.8
Automobile Theft	8	71	26	(No Data)

Source: "The Crime Analysis and Information System" (A study by the Center for Urban Studies of The University of Akron, 1973).

"professionalism." On the other hand, those arrested for committing burglaries within the lower income area did not travel so far. It is assumed that these crimes were more spontaneous, and they represented, in effect, the poor stealing from the poor. It should be noted that the lower income area supplied very few of those arrested for committing burglaries within the higher income area.

However, when arrest statistics for all census tracts are statistically tested against actual reporting for all seven types of crime under investigation here, there is no correlation between reporting and arrests for any of the crimes. In other words, arrests are not evenly distributed throughout the city in proportion with actual reported crimes. For the most part, an analysis of all known suspect movements during 1971 shows that the police are quite effective in arresting those committing crimes within higher income areas, particularly if the suspects come from lower income and transitional areas. There are many arrests within lower income areas, but the rate is lower in relation to the number of crimes. Also, arrests within transitional areas correspond more closely to crimes reported within these areas than most other parts of the city. In other words, a form of culture conflict within transitional areas is manifested by the crime rate, and citizens with vested interests within these neighborhoods will tend to cooperate with the police. Conversely, there is reason to believe tensions exist between the police and many inhabitants of transitional areas, thus creating a situation antagonistic toward good police-community relations.

On the other hand, the assumption cannot be made that police are not involved to some degree with various social problems. The report of the president's commission in the mid-1960s explained in detail the amount of police time spent on simple "nuisance calls." In fact, the most recently published *Uniform Crime Reports* indicates that in 1972, 1,724,400 arrests were made for crime index offenses, and almost as many, 1,676,800, were made for the charge of drunkenness alone. In addition, because of the very nature of the profession of law enforcement, a certain authoritarian police personality can develop. Also, Niederhoffer, when writing about attitudes of police in urban areas, contends that certain degrees of police cynicism develop, particularly with regard to social problems of ghetto inhabitants. Police officers often become disenchanted and increasingly pessimistic and misanthropic. Not only are divorce rates high, but there is also the possibility of suicide. Niederhoffer reports that within New York City for the period 1950–1965 the overall male suicide rate was 15 per 100,000, but the police rate was 22.7 per 100,000. Clearly, almost as with a psychological defense mechanism, there is a greater tendency for police to concentrate not on such "software" items as personal problems of poor people, but rather on such tangible "hardware" items as new cruisers, radios and even helicopters in some cities. What impact, then, has this overall authoritarian hardware-oriented attitude had on the apparent trend toward decreased crime rates? One aspect does stand out. The police in Akron have been more effective in middle and upper income areas than in lower income areas.

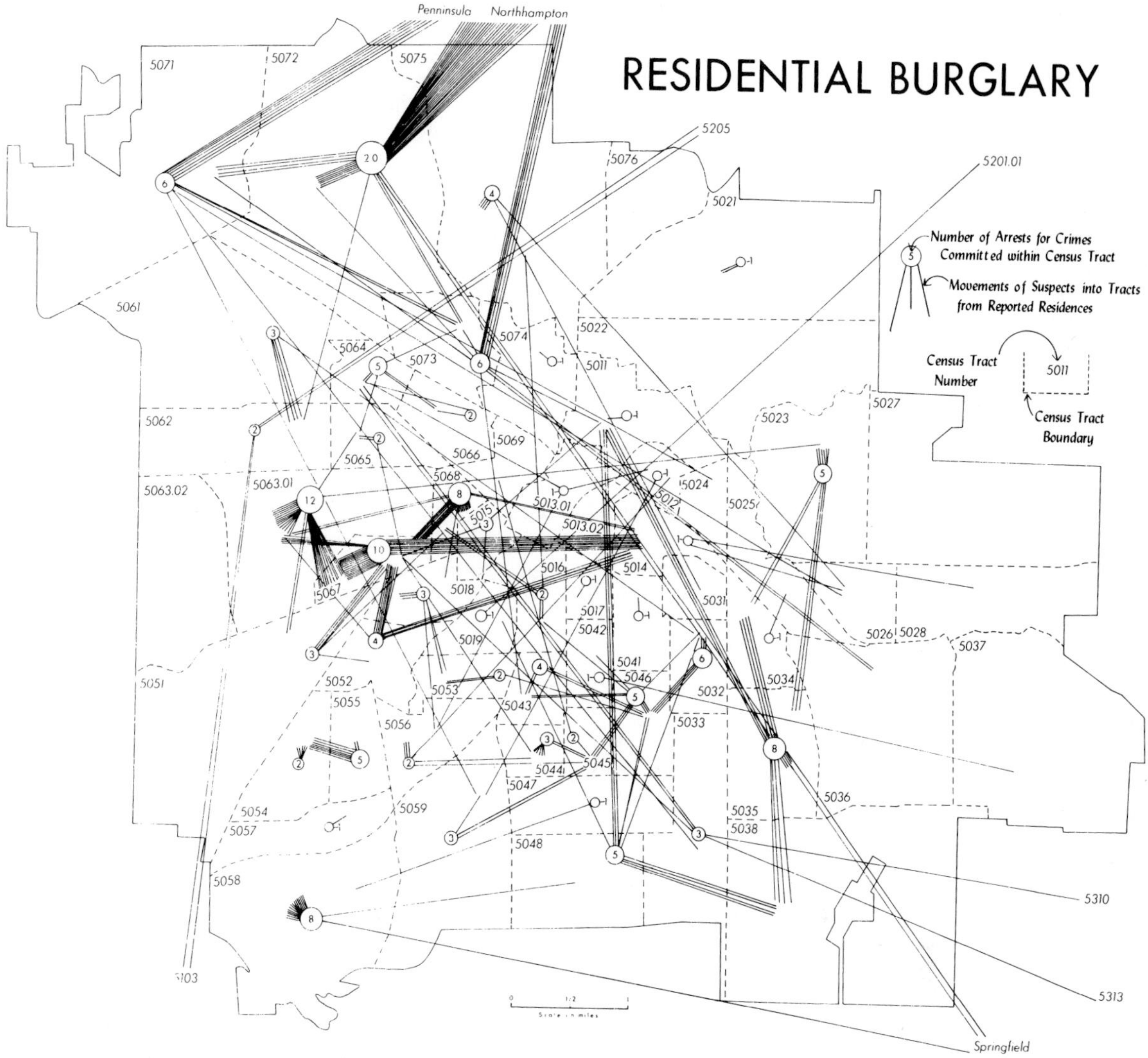

Figure 7-17. Akron: Linkages Between Suspect Residences and the Locations of Residential Burglaries.

Clearly, such an observation does not imply that the police should simply arrest more poor people, fill up the jails and back up the already crowded court dockets. One solution to this problem is the development and/or implementation of already existing crime prevention programs—police-community relations, for example. One of the original purposes of the 1968 crime legislation was the development of many such programs. Such efforts have now begun within Akron, but at this time little has yet been accomplished. One of the largest impediments is the fact that Akron's population is 17 percent Negro, but the police force is only about 3 percent Negro. Many black poverty neighborhoods have higher crime rates, and it is the contention of this study that many crimes could be prevented through racial integration of Akron's police force.

While the full impact of LEAA funding has not yet been felt within Akron, such a statement may be less true for other cities. Fortunately, the apparent national crime decreases reported after 1971 afford an opportunity to explore this possibility. Again, geographic analysis is extremely useful, because differences in changing crime rates can be measured and compared for different parts of the country. Thus, while overall national crime rates appear to be decreasing, these decreases are not evenly distributed nationally.

GEOGRAPHIC ASPECTS OF CHANGING CRIME RATES WITHIN THE UNITED STATES

By the end of 1971, violent and property crime reporting within the United States reached an all time high. During 1972, the reporting of all property crimes and robbery decreased. As indicated by the quotation opening of this chapter, these overall reductions were interpreted as a promise of success by law enforcement planners directly involved with LEAA programs. If many programs have indeed been successful, it is important to know where they are located. One method of identifying such places is to map decreases in crime rates.

In general, many cities in the northeastern US reported decreases. Furthermore, these decreased rates are for some of the largest cities in that region. For example, New York City reported a 5.1 percent reduction in violent crimes and a 22 percent reduction in property crimes. Detroit reported 10.4 percent fewer violent crimes than 1971, and 17.2 percent fewer property crimes. Washington, D.C. reported approximately 25 percent fewer of both classes of crime during the same period. This trend was not restricted to larger cities, for many medium-sized to smaller cities, including Newark, reported similar kinds of change. However, some smaller cities–Canton, Youngstown, Camden and Worchester, for example–reported increases above average for both types of crime index offenses.

Conversely, large cities in many parts of the country demonstrated below average rates of change for both violent and property crimes. Some of these cities include St. Louis, Los Angeles, San Francisco and New Orleans. Many of the cities which showed a below average annual rate of change from 1960 to 1970 actually showed increases for at least one and quite often both classes of crime. The most notable examples of this kind of change are the Pacific Northwest cities and many urban centers within the Great Plains. Many southeastern cities continued to report more than average increases in crime rates, but exceptions to this trend were Miami, Jacksonville and Nashville. Also many smaller cities throughout the country demonstrated some combination of increased rates.

In fact, the general distribution of change from 1971 to 1972 is almost in direct opposition to the 1960 to 1970 trend. This difference partially suggests that a certain time lag may exist for measurement of crime change within the United States, and larger and more industrialized cities may change first. This could result in the higher relative rates of change in many smaller or service-oriented centers. Alternatively, it can be argued that changes in violent and property crime rates are some function of changes in the amounts of funds allocated to crime control. However, this assumption is difficult to document for several reasons. One reason for this difficulty is due to the fact that most LEAA funding is channeled through the state planning agencies already mentioned. Recent changes also call for comprehensive urban anticrime plans before all funding can be allocated. Varying percentages of the funds are absorbed by both state and local administrators' (regional planning units, or RPUs) costs. State planning agencies make decisions regarding the funding of programs submitted by local RPUs on the basis of priorities established by the state agencies. In addition, counties are used as the basic building blocks for RPUs, and the problem of metropolitan fragmentation of government makes statistical comparisons difficult. On the other hand, the latter aspect could serve in a positive manner eventually because petty jealousies and other problems of cooperation among local police agencies must be set aside if cooperative programs are to be funded.

A second problem in terms of national interurban comparison arises because each state exercises virtual autonomy when categorical funding program decisions are made. In accordance with the recommendations of the earlier president's commission report, 11 major program categories can be funded: upgrading personnel; prevention of crime; juvenile delinquency; detection and apprehension of criminals; prosecution, court and law reform; correction and rehabilitation; organized crime; community relations; riots and civil disorders; construction; and research and development. Each state has the option to allocate variable amounts to all of these programs, but some states have not done so. With the exception of specially funded programs, funds are made available to each state on a per capita basis. Thus, instead of most funds being allocated on the basis of crime rates, they are allocated on the basis of population.

The logic underlying per capita funding is not totally fallacious. Many of the heavily populated states do contain larger cities which showed marked increases in crime rates during the 1960s. However, the specific impact of various categorical funding on changing crime rates is somewhat difficult to assess. Percentages allocated to various programs differ widely among the states. When the actual funding amounts are compared to rates of change by state from 1971 to 1972 those states which follow the national trend of increasing violent crimes and decreasing property crimes appear to be receiving larger total amounts of funding. However, within the states, interurban crime change rates can vary substantially.

There is no significant correlation between total funding by states and changes in crime rates. When each of the 11 categories is examined separately, however, some degree of statistical association does show up. And two of these correlations are of particular interest because they offer some degree of support to contentions made by the president's commission with regard to areas requiring attention if the crime problem is to be solved. Table 7-7 shows that three of the specific funding categories show moderate but statistically significant correlations with percentage changes for both violent and property crimes. Interestingly, negative correlations indicating decreased crime with increased funding show up best when violent crime is compared to funds allocated to combating organized crime. A moderate but significant association also shows up when the same funding category is compared to decreases in property crime. The juvenile delinquency and community relations categories are of particular interest because of the emphasis placed upon these approaches by the president's commission. While significant, the correlations are moderate. However, none of the other eight categories of funding showed any sort of correlation.

In spite of the rather modest amounts of LEAA funding in comparison to all the money now being spent nationally to decrease crime, it appears that some of the specific programs may be contributing to this goal. In many respects, it is simply too soon to measure accurately the full impact of the general anticrime movement on our urban centers. It would appear that some of the specialized LEAA programs are having a positive effect, but we must monitor the various programs through the 1970s and hope for a rate decrease comparable at least to the rate of increase of the 1960s. The methods employed within this study offer some means whereby analyses can be accomplished in such a manner that interurban and intraurban variations and forms of criminal behavior in space often buried within gross national totals and trends can be better understood. Clearly, these and other more sophisticated tools offered by professional geographers in the analysis of the spatial variability of crime should be given serious consideration for future studies within and among cities.

Table 7-7. Significant Pairwise Correlations, Crime Change and LEAA Funding Categories

	LEAA Funding Categories		
Changes in Crime Rates	*Juvenile Delinquency*	*Organized Crime*	*Community Relations*
Violent Crime	−0.285 (0.022)*	−0.537 (0.001)	−0.302 (0.017)
Property Crime	−0.361 (0.005)	−0.341 (0.008)	−0.245 (0.043)

*Significance level
Source: Computed by author.

BIBLIOGRAPHY

Amir, Menachem. *Patterns of Forcible Rape.* Chicago: University of Chicago Press, 1971.

Beattie, Ronald H. "Problems of Criminal Statistics in the United States." *Journal of Criminal Law, Criminology, and Police Science* 46 (1955): 178–186.

Berry, Brian J.L. "Contemporary Urbanization Processess." In *Geographical Perspectives and Urban Problems.* Washington, D.C.: National Academy of Sciences, 1971.

Bloch, Herbert and Arthur Niederhoffer. *The Gang.* New York: Philosophical Press, 1958.

Boggs, Sarah. "Urban Crime Patterns." *American Sociological Review* 30 (1966): 899–908.

Bonger, William A. *Criminality and Economic Conditions.* Boston: Little Brown and Co., 1916.

Cohen, Albert. *Delinquent Boys: The Culture of the Gang.* New York: Free Press, 1955.

Doyle, J. Gary and Kwamie Kwofie. "Crime Statistics and the Statistical Analysis of Crime Data." In Gerald F. Pyle et al., *The Spatial Dynamics of Crime,* ch. 4. Chicago: University of Chicago, Department of Geography Research, Monograph No. 159, 1974.

Gastil, Raymond D. "Homicide and a Regional Culture of Violence." *American Sociological Review* 36 (1971): 412–427.

Goldner, Norman S. "Rape as a Heinous but Understudied Offense." *Journal of Criminal Law, Criminology, and Police Science* 63 (1972): 402–406.

Harries, Keith D. "The Geography of American Crime, 1968." *Journal of Geography* 70 (1971): 204–218.

——. "Spatial Aspects of Violence and Metropolitan Population." *The Professional Geographer* 25 (1973): 1–6.

Haskell, Martin R. and Lewis Yablonsky. *Chicago.* Chicago: Rand McNally & Co., 1970.

Haynes, Robin M. "Crime Rates and City Size in America." *Area* (Institute of British Geographers) 3 (1973: 165.

Kelley, Clarence M. *Crime in the United States, 1972 Uniform Crime Reports.* Washington, D.C.: US Department of Justice, Federal Bureau of Investigation, 1973.

Lentz, William P. "Rural-Urban Differences and Juvenile Delinquency." *Journal of Criminal Law, Criminology, and Police Science* 47 (1956): 331–339.

Lottier, Stuart. "The Distribution of Criminal Offenses in Metropolitan Regions." *Journal of Criminal Law, Criminology, and Police Science* 29 (1938): 37–50.

Merton, Robert K. "Social Structure and Anomie." *American Sociological Review* 3 (1938): 672–682.

National Advisory Commission on Criminal Justice Standards and Goals. "A National Strategy to Reduce Crime." Washington, D.C.: US Department of Justice, Law Enforcement Assistance Administration, January 1973.

National Conference of State Criminal Justice Planning Administrators. "State of the States on Crime and Justice, An Analysis of State Administration of the Safe Streets Act." Frankfort, Ky., June 1973.

Niederhoffer, Arthur. *Behind the Shield: The Police in Urban Society.* Garden City: Doubleday & Company, 1969.

Office of Law Enforcement Assistance. "The Law Enforcement Assistance Act of 1965." Washington, D.C.: US Department of Justice, 1968.

Phillips, Phillip D. "A Prologue to the Geography of Crime." In *Proceedings.* Washington, D.C.: Association of American Geographers, 1974.

Poveda, Tony G. "The Image of the Criminal, a Critique of Crime and Delinquency Theories." *Issues in Criminology* 5 (1970): 59–83.

President's Commisson on Law Enforcement and Administration of Justice. *The Challenge of Crime in a Free Society.* New York: Avon, 1968.

Pyle, Gerald F., et al. *The Spatial Dynamics of Crime.* Chicago: University of Chicago, Department of Geography Research Monograph No. 159, 1974.

Radzinowicz, Leon. "Economic Pressures." In *Crime and Justice: The Criminal in Society,* vol. 1, edited by Leon Radzinowicz and Marvin Wolfgang. New York: Basic Books, 1971.

Reckless, Walter. *The Crime Problem.* New York: Appleton-Century-Crofts, 1967.

Reiss, Albert J. and Albert Lewis Rhodes. "An Empirical Test of Differential Association Theory." *Journal of Research in Crime and Delinquency* 1 (1964): 5–18.

Shannon, Lyle W. "The Spatial Distribution

of Criminal Offenses." *Journal of Criminal Law, Criminology, and Police Science* 45 (1954-55): 264-273.

Shaw, Clifford R. and Henry D. McKay. *Juvenile Delinquency and Urban Areas.* Chicago: University of Chicago Press, 1942.

Shulman, Harry Manuel. "The Measurement of Crime in the United States." *Journal of Criminal Law, Criminology, and Police Science* 57 (1966): 483-492.

Vold, George B. "Crime in City and Country Areas." *Annals of the American Academy of Political and Social Sciences* 217 (1941): 38-45.

White, Clyde R. "The Relation of Felonies to Environmental Factors in Indianapolis." *Social Forces* 10 (1932): 498-509.

Wolfgang, Marvin E. "International Criminal Statistics: A Proposal." *Journal of Criminal Law, Criminology, and Police Science* 59 (1967): 65-69.

Chapter 8

Restructuring the Health Care Delivery System in the United States

Dr. Mary Megee
Joplin, Missouri

INTRODUCTION

The health care delivery system of the United States is one of the best in the world. Spectacular advances have been made in the control of numerous diseases. No less than 4.4 million people are employed in the various health occupations. There are some three million beds in hospitals and other inpatient facilities. In recent years there have been notable decreases in mortality rates (9.4 per 1,000 in 1972), and corresponding extensions in the expectation of life, even though by these indexes the nation now lags behind some other developed countries. Yet services have developed unevenly, resulting in extremes of technical sophistication in research and equipment to inadequacies in the delivery of minimum essential care. Many people and entire areas of this richest nation in the world lack adequate medical attention. Equally serious is the severe financial hardship that can and often does result from serious illness.

While those most adversely affected are the poor and otherwise disadvantaged, many middle income families also pay a heavy human price because health services are unavailable or overstrained, and because a long or expensive illness reduces them to poverty. At the same time, the cost of care escalates. Between 1965 and 1972, national health expenditures rose from $39 billion to $83 billion, or from 5.9 percent to 7.6 percent of the Gross National Product (GNP). Total expenses per patient day have also been rising rapidly, increasing from $13.68 in 1965 to $102.73 in 1972, at the rate of 9.4 percent to 15 percent per annum. Per capita health expenditures, meanwhile, increased enormously, from $29.16 in 1929 to $394.16 in 1972. Public health expenditures increased from 13.3 percent of total government expenditures in 1929 to 39.4 percent in 1972. The federal government's increasing participation in the health field gave rise to a plan for testing Public Health Service hospitals in several locations throughout the country. Rising consumer and facility costs brought federal government increasingly into the health area in fields of funding facilities and health insurance, as well as areas to help relieve a major national problem.

For inner city dwellers, the inadequacies frequently result from a decline in medical resources, decrepit buildings, overburdened staffs and reduced service. People generally—whether they are affluent, poor, suburban or rural—experience difficulties in securing adequate primary care. Rural to urban migration also continues to exert more pressure on all existing facilities in cities, while the more recent urban to urban migration movement produces problems related to change in residence which affect the entire health delivery system.

The nation's health services have retained the organization—or lack of it—that may have been adequate for the health needs of an earlier era. As the major health problems shifted from acute to chronic diseases and toward conditions requiring more extended attention, the system failed to develop a continuous form of care to replace that based on episodic treatment. It also failed to shift from the concept of sick care to well care, or curative treatment to preventative treatment.

Involvement of the Federal Government

After nearly a decade of increasing debate, the nation took decisive action in January 1974 with the passage of the HMO bill, which was aimed at remedying many of the inadequacies in its health care system. The main question now remaining is whether or not this will be the most effective and practical vehicle for restructuring the health care delivery system, as well as being the most economic, without producing substantial inflationary effect.

Federal concern with health care actually dates back to the late eighteenth century when Thomas Jefferson wrote in 1787 that "[w]ithout health there is no happiness. An attention to health, then, should take the place over every other object" [Message from the President, p. 1]. This priority has remained in both the private and public values of the United States, though it was not until 1965 that the federal government showed significant interest in the health care delivery system. In a message to Congress in 1965, President Johnson initiated this interest, stating that we must "give first attention to our opportunities—and our obligations—for advancing the Nation's health . . . as it is inescapably the foundation for fulfillment of all our aspirations" [*Ibid*]. The Nixon administration continued this interest and expanded the federal government's role in the field.

Legislation has emanated from this interest in less than ten years in the form of comprehensive health planning (CHP), health maintenance organizations (HMOs), the Hill-Burton program for facility construction and modernization, and the regional medical program (RMP), and health systems agencies (HSAs)—all designed to improve health delivery, providing federal money to maximize both health care services and consumer satisfaction and at the same time minimizing costs, waste, duplication and time.

Goals and Objectives of this Study

The chief goal and a recommendation regarding the health care delivery system with which this study is concerned is as follows:

> To restructure the health care delivery sytem of the United States in such a way as to expand its benefits, to reorganize the entire health system, to minimize the price of health care services, and to achieve greater uniformity and effectiveness of coverage.

The analysis presented in the ensuing pages is based on three conclusions derived from the study of the present health care delivery system in the United States. These conclusions have been translated into the objectives of the analyses of each of the sections which follow. These conclusion-objectives are:

- Faulty allocation of resources is a major cause of inadequacies in US health services that result today in poor or substandard care for large segments of the population.
- The task of assuring all people the ability to cope financially with the costs of health care has been made realizable by the substantial base of coverage now provided by both private and public insurance plans.
- Unless alterations are made in the means of delivering services and paying providers, closing the gaps in financing would overburden an inadequate system and offer little prospect of materially improving the quality and quantity of medical services for the health of the American people.

DIMENSIONS OF THE HEALTH CARE PROGRAM

There is an uneven incidence of morbidity and mortality by types geographically throughout the United States as well as within metropolitan areas. Much of the variation can be explained simply in terms of population distribution and population age structure, but additional variations are brought about by variations from place to place in incomes and racial distribution, as well as the availability of health maintenance programs. In the succeeding pages some efforts will be made to analyze and attempt to show relationships, if they exist, between distributions of income, race, disease and death on both inter- and intrametropolitan levels.

Intermetropolitan Variations in Mortality

There exists a continuum from perfect health to death consisting of several intermediate levels, one of which is morbidity. The most complete information, particularly for metropolitan areas, is in the form of number of deaths by cause. Data for stages of better health on the continuum are difficult to obtain and to measure. They are usually fragmented, difficult to collect and, therefore, generally not amenable to analysis. Consequently, in this phase of the study, number of deaths by selected causes for each of the 20 SMSAs was used as an indicator of the demand for the major health care facilities. Also, from the data it is possible to infer the importance of certain types of diseases, injuries and other illnesses found in those metropolitan areas.

More advances have been made in the twentieth century than in all of previously recorded history in overcoming those diseases which take the heaviest toll of human life. Influenza and pneumonia—the chief causes of death in the United States at the turn of the century—today have been largely eradicated. The three major causes of seven out of ten deaths in the United States annually are heart disease, cancer and stroke. The scene of death in the United States has shifted from causes due to infectious disease at the turn of the century to organic disorders by 1965. Nearly 55 percent of all deaths are due to cardiovascular-renal diseases. Future success in reduction of the general death rate and extension of life expectancy depends upon success in dealing with these causes of death.

Malignant Neoplasms. Malignant neoplasms include malignant neoplasms of the buccal cavity and pharynx, the digestive organs and peritoneum, the respiratory system, breast and genital organs, urinary organs, and all other unspecified sites, as well as leukemia and neoplasms of lymphatic and hematopoietic tissues. In 1968, total deaths due to this disease in the 20 metropolitan areas were 100,326 representing 48 percent of the more than 209,229 deaths in the United States due to this cause.

The average number of deaths in the sample of 20 metropolitan areas was 4,835, varying from a low of 1,404 for Hartford to a high of 23,246 for New York. Death rates varied considerably from a low of 98.7 deaths per 100,000 for Houston to a high of 208.9 for Hartford, which was followed by 201.6 for New York and 200.6 for Pittsburgh (Figure 8-1).

Those cities with higher than expected numbers of deaths include Boston, San Francisco-Oakland, Cleveland, Miami, Seattle and Hartford, while those with significantly fewer deaths due to this disease include Chicago, Washington, D.C., Dallas-Fort Worth, Atlanta and Houston. These findings, as well as others of this nature, point toward the need for further research in determining the factors which might contribute to this disease and to policies with regard to the allocation of facilities, equipment, manpower, money and the like for treating it. Those cities with lower than expected numbers of deaths all suggest the need for studies to determine what conditions in those cities contribute to retardation of this disease, if this be the case. Distributions such as these always suggest the need for planning and policies regarding more judicious allocations of scarce resources to handle the problems related to this disease. Similar statements can be made about each of the other causes of death in this study. No close relationship can be detected between concentration of this disease and high or low deviations from the expected with respect to concentrations of low income and certain racial concentrations for the metropolitan areas in this study.

Certain Causes of Mortality in Early Infancy. Certain causes of mortality in early infancy include birth injury, difficult labor, and other anoxic and hypoxic conditions, as well as other causes of early infant mortality, accounting for more than 25,000 deaths per annum in the United States. This is a comparatively small total compared to other causes of death in the country. In 1968 there were 13,580 deaths from these causes reported by the 20 SMSAs in the study, or 47.5 percent of

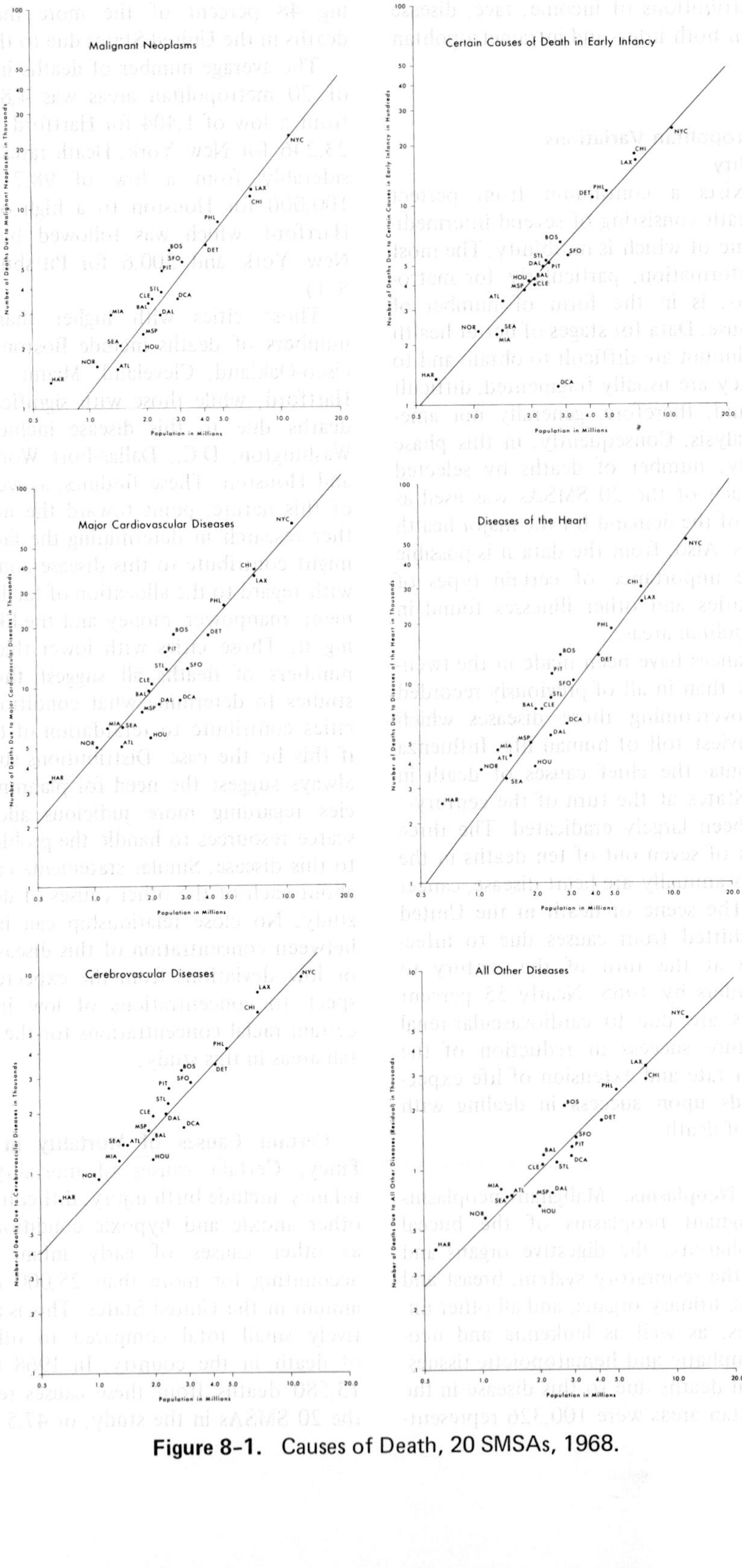

Figure 8-1. Causes of Death, 20 SMSAs, 1968.

the total 28,578 deaths in the United States. The United States has one of the highest infant mortality rates in the world, which should call attention to the need for serious study of both the reasons behind and the methods for rectifying the situation.

The number of infant deaths ranged from a low for Hartford of 143 to a high of 2,391 for New York, making a mean of 679 deaths for the 20 observations. Death rates (per 100,000 population) ranged from a low of 4.3 for Washington, D.C. to a high of 25.3 for Chicago and Detroit. Deaths due to this cause are rather evenly distributed throughout the country as represented by the sample of 20 SMSAs, indicating probably a more or less uniform distribution, as well as a problem of uniform concern throughout the country. These death rates, however, are not only uniform but high, indicating the severity of the problem and calling for more medical research.

Those cities with significantly higher than expected number of deaths due to this cause include Detroit, Philadelphia, New Orleans and Atlanta. Those with fewer than expected numbers of deaths include Washington, D.C., Dallas-Fort Worth, Seattle and Miami. Dispersion from expected levels is depicted in Figure 8-1. Similar inferences can be made regarding the dispersion of each of the SMSAs with respect to the expected number of deaths due to other causes. The distribution of this disease did not seem to be closely related to the concentrations of large numbers of persons of minority races or with low income. In fact, some of the SMSAs with the largest concentrations of blacks and people of Spanish heritage—for example, New York, Washington, D.C. and San Francisco-Oakland—showed substantial departures from the expected. They recorded much lower numbers of deaths due to this cause than was expected for their population sizes.

Major Cardiovascular Diseases. Those ICD (International Classification of Diseases) diseases classed as cardiovascular include diseases of the heart; active rheumatic fever and chronic rheumatic heart disease; hypertensive heart disease; hypertensive heart and renal disease; ischemic heart disease; acute myocardial infarction; other acute and subacute forms of ischemic heart disease; chronic ischemic heart disease; angina pectoris; chronic diseases of endocardium and other myocardial insufficiency; all other forms of heart disease; hypertension; cerebrovascular diseases; cerebral hemorrhage; cerebral thrombosis; cerebral embolism; all other cerebrovascular diseases; arteriosclerosis; and other diseases of arteries, arterioles and capillaries.

In 1968 more deaths resulted from cardiovascular diseases than any other cause—629,767. Analysis showed that the 20 metropolitan areas in the study accounted for 316,699 deaths, or 50.3 percent of the total. The mean number of deaths in the sample was 15,835, ranging from a low of 3,648 for Hartford to a high of 65,279 for New York. Death rates, however, ranged from a low of 277.1 per 100,000 for Houston to a high of 631.8 for Pittsburgh.

Figure 8-1 describes the dispersion from the expected number of deaths due to cardiovascular causes. Pittsburgh, Cleveland, Miami, New Orleans, Boston and Hartford SMSAs show substantially higher numbers of deaths due to this cause than expected. In Miami and New Orleans, there are large concentrations of persons of Spanish heritage and blacks, respectively. Those SMSAs showing fewer numbers of deaths than expected include Washington, D.C., Houston, Detroit, Minneapolis-St. Paul, Dallas-Fort Worth, Atlanta and San Francisco-Oakland. Except for Minneapolis-St. Paul, each of these SMSAs had high black populations, while Dallas-Fort Worth has large numbers of persons of Spanish heritage. Again these dispersions and distributions did not indicate either concentration or deficit of expected number of deaths due to this disease as related to race.

Diseases of the Heart. Figure 8-1 shows the dispersion of SMSAs with regard to expected numbers of deaths due to disease of the heart. Those cities which showed larger than expected numbers of deaths due to this disease include Pittsburgh, Boston, St. Louis, Miami, Cleveland and Hartford, while those showing fewer than expected numbers include Washington, D.C., San Francisco-Oakland, Detroit, Minneapolis-St. Paul, Houston, and Dallas-Fort Worth. The distribution did not seem to be related to distribution of blacks or persons of Spanish heritage, unless it showed that many of the SMSAs with the large numbers of persons in these categories show less than expected numbers of deaths due to this cause.

Diseases of the heart account for more than 465,000 deaths in the United States annually. In 1968, there was a total of 240,426 deaths due to this cause in the 20 SMSAs, representing about 51.4 percent of the total 467,490 deaths recorded that year for the nation as a whole. A mean of 14,126 deaths due to this cause was calculated for the 20 metropolitan areas, with values ranging from a low of 2,642 for Hartford to a high of 52,420 for New York. Rates ranged from a low of 218.7 for Washington, D.C., to a high of 482.1 per 100,000 for Pittsburgh.

Cerebrovascular Disease. Cerebrovascular diseases constitute a major subcategory of the large cardiovascular group and include those diseases so classified by the ICD as cerebral hemorrhage, cerebral thrombosis, cerebral embolism and all other cerebrovascular diseases. Cerebrovascular disease annually accounts for more than 100,000 deaths in the United States and was included in this analysis because of its large and widespread occurrence. The 20 metropolitan areas accounted for 58,153 deaths in 1968, or approximately 47.4 percent of the US total of 122,732. A mean of 2,908 deaths was determined from the sample of 20 metropolitan areas, ranging from a low of 764 for Hartford to highs of 8,005 for Los Angeles and 9,572 for New York. Death rates ranged from a low of 59.5 deaths per 100,000 for Seattle to a high of 113.8 for Hartford. Values of these rates, moreover, showed considerable dispersion, as well as geographic differentiation, pinpointing those areas which have the most acute problems and require further identification of problems, causes and needs in the field of health planning.

Those cities showing significantly higher than normal concentration of deaths due to this disease include Boston, Hartford, Atlanta, Cleveland, Pittsburgh and Los Angeles-Long Beach. Those cities with significantly smaller numbers of deaths than expected due to this disease include, in particular, Washington, D.C., followed by Houston, Baltimore, and New York. Figure 8-1 shows the dispersion of the 20 SMSAs. As in the discussion of deaths due to malignant neoplasms, similar conclusions can be made about the necessity of further study and its reasons.

Accidents. Accidents as a cause of death in this study have been divided into two groups, classified by the ICD as Motor Vehicle Accidents (E810-E823) and All Other Accidents (E800-E807, E825-E949), and together comprising the ICD category Accidents (E800-E949). During the last five years, motor vehicle accidents have accounted for between 20,000 and 30,000 deaths per annum, with all other accidents between 25,000 and 40,000 deaths per annum. In the analysis of death due to these two causes, means of 628.7 deaths due to motor vehicle and 850.85 deaths due to all other accidents, respectively, were obtained for the 20 metropolitan observations (Figures 8-1 and 8-2). Total number of deaths due to motor vehicle accidents ranged from a low of 129 for Hartford to highs of 1,763 for New York and 1,782 for Los Angeles-Long Beach. Unlike the cause of deaths due to diseases, deaths due to accidents did not show as high correspondence with population. Deaths due to motor vehicle accidents were highest in Los Angeles-Long Beach. Deaths due to all other accidents also showed a large concentration in Los Angeles-Long Beach—2,327, second to New York's 2,582. Death rates for all other accidents were somewhat higher, ranging from a low of 21.3 for Houston to a high of 33.1 per 100,000 for Los Angeles-Long Beach.

Distribution of number of deaths due to motor vehicle accidents with respect to expected numbers of populations of certain sizes is shown in Figure 8-1. There was some considerable dispersion. Los Angeles-Long Beach, San Francisco-Oakland, Detroit, St. Louis and Dallas-Fort Worth, in particular, showed substantially larger numbers of deaths due to this cause than expected. The occurrence of deaths due to this cause seemed to show some relation to geographic locations (the Far West) as well as to concentrations of persons of Spanish heritage and of blacks. Those SMSAs with lower than expected numbers of deaths due to this cause include Boston, Hartford, Baltimore, New Orleans, Washington, D.C., Cleveland, Minneapolis-St. Paul, Houston and Chicago.

Suicide-Homicide. Total suicides in the United States account for more than 10,000 deaths per annum, while total homicides account for more than 8,000 deaths per annum in the country. In this study, the 20 metropolitan areas analyzed account for 13,844 suicides and 10,778 homicides, or 48.3 percent and 57.5 percent of the United States totals, re-

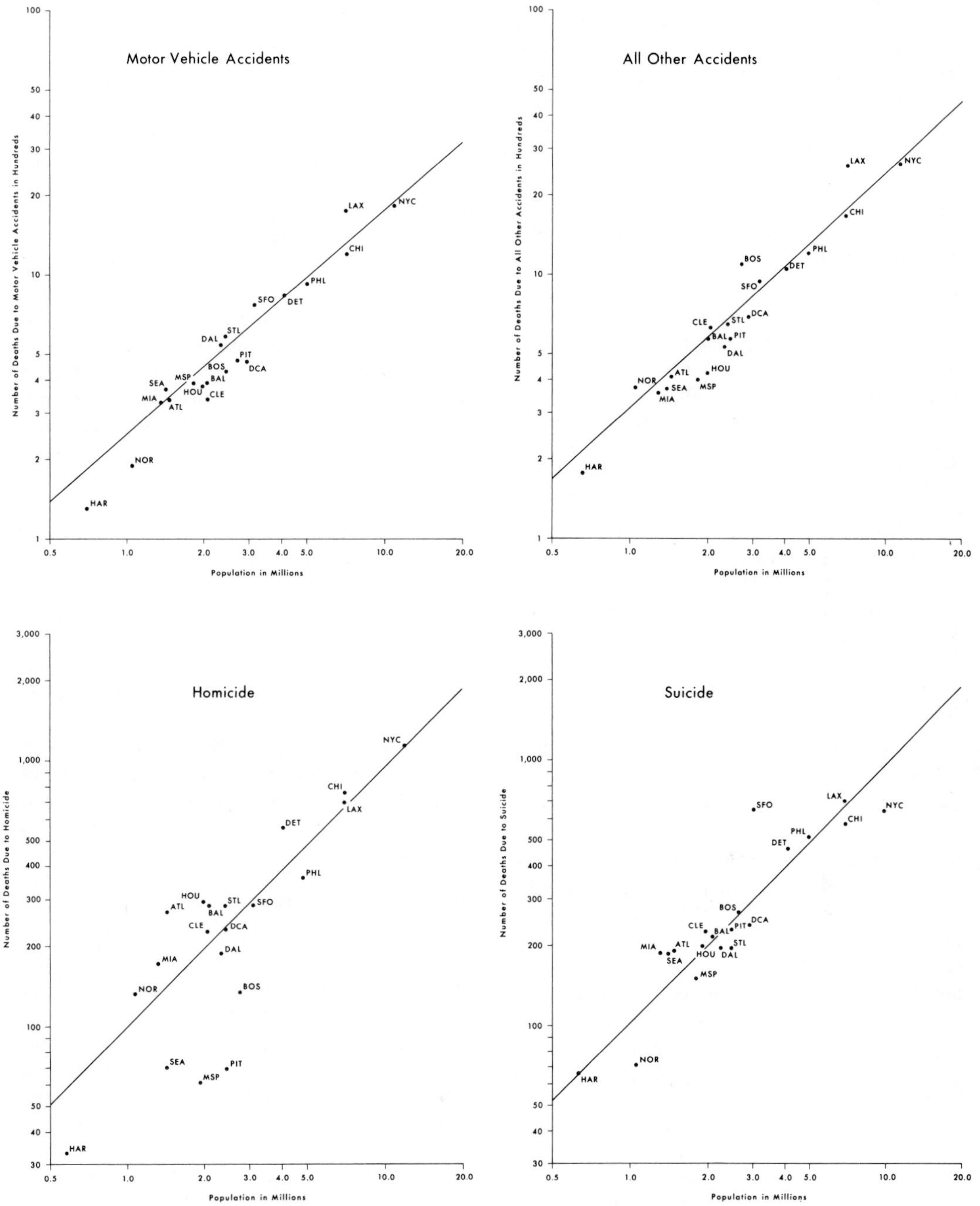

Figure 8-2. Causes of Death, 20 SMSAs, 1968.

spectively, for 1968. Means of 309.9 and 334.2 deaths were obtained for homicides and suicides, respectively, ranging from a low of 33 per 100,000 for Hartford to 1,084 for New York in the case of homicides, and a low of 67 for Hartford to a high of 1,378 for Los Angeles-Long Beach in the case of suicides. There is probably less correlation between population and suicide than between population and any of the other causes of death selected in this analysis. This suggests that factors other than sheer size account for the occurrence of suicide.

Death rates for homicide and suicide show that they are not generally as high as other causes—for example infant deaths—and that there is considerable dispersion and geographic differentiation from other causes of death. In the case of homicides, rates vary from a low of 2.8 per 100,000 for Pittsburgh to a high of 19.2 for Atlanta, while those for suicide range from a low of 5.3 for New York to 20.8 for San Francisco-Oakland, followed closely by 19.6 for Miami.

Figure 8-2 shows that those cities ranking high in suicide include Miami, Atlanta, Detroit and Cleveland. Figure 8-2 also shows that Atlanta, Houston, Seattle, Baltimore, Detroit, Chicago and St. Louis have higher than expected numbers of deaths due to homicide. Those metropolitan areas which have lower than expected numbers of deaths due to homicides include Pittsburgh, Minneapolis-St. Paul, St. Louis, Hartford and Boston. Those cities with lower than expected number of suicides include New Orleans, Dallas-Fort Worth, Minneapolis-St. Paul, New York and Pittsburgh.

All Other Diseases (Residual). All other diseases comprise a residual category of the ICD containing all those diseases insufficiently specified or too insignificant to warrant separate classification. During the past five years, the number of deaths in this category in the United States has exceeded 62,000 per annum. In 1968, some 31,062 deaths in the 20 metropolitan areas fell into the residual category, representing about 49.2 percent of all deaths due to this category in the country that year. This category ranks fourth in the nation in terms of numbers of deaths in any major category. Figure 8-2 shows the dispersion of the 20 SMSAs for these residual causes of death.

Whatever the constitutents of this category, this sizable number of deaths deserves more study and research on a federal level than it has been given. A mean of 1,553 deaths was obtained for the sample, ranging from a low of 413 for Hartford to 5,701 for New York. Death rates ranged from a low of 33.2 per 100,000 for Houston to a high of 63.6 for Minneapolis-St. Paul.

Conclusions and Findings

An analysis of the SMSAs in this study which scored higher or lower than expected in number of deaths by major causes for populations of their sizes revealed the following findings.

Boston, Miami, Atlanta and Detroit ranked first in the study in higher numbers of deaths than expected due to major causes. This large concentration of deaths suggests that these cities are major health problem areas.

Some positive direct relationship also can be inferred between concentration of deaths by major types in the SMSAs and large concentrations of black populations, and, in some cases, relatively low incomes. Some additional explanation for the variations in death rates can be found in the differing population age structures of these metropolitan areas.

Other SMSAs in this study which showed larger than expected numbers of deaths due to several major causes include Cleveland, Los Angeles-Long Beach and St. Louis. All have substantially large black populations, and Los Angeles-Long Beach also includes a large number of persons of Spanish heritage.

Geographically, the areas with relatively high rates of deaths due to several major causes are widely dispersed, occurring in the Ohio River Valley, the South, the Far West, the Mississippi River Valley and New England. For this reason, no inferences of any significance can be made about regional concentrations of death.

It may be inferred, however, that Boston, Miami, Atlanta, Detroit, St. Louis and Los Angeles-Long Beach SMSAs, which, moreover, varied widely in size, geographic location, concentrations of nonwhite populations and median incomes, are the problem metropolises in terms of concentrations of several major types of deaths. These findings have implications for policies aimed at allocating scarce resources of manpower, equipment, facilities, technology, research and other health-oriented services. It is not the purpose here to dictate or formulate these policies for any particular SMSA, but to point out the problem areas as measured by numbers and rates of deaths. The data suggest the need for more in depth studies which aim toward reallocating resources in the health facilities field to meet the special needs of these major population areas which show higher than expected death rates.

In the case of those metropolitan areas which showed substantially fewer deaths than expected for their sizes, Dallas-Fort Worth and Washington, D.C., stand out as the cities with the fewest deaths due to several major causes. At the same time, Washington, D.C., has a large black population, as well as one of the highest per capita median incomes in the study. This finding would seem to negate assumptions of close direct relationship between such variables as number of deaths due to different causes and concentrations of blacks, except to the extent that blacks fail to share fully in the general prosperity of the Washington area. There does seem to be a close relationship between fewer deaths by several types of causes and higher incomes.

Like Washington, D.C., Atlanta also has a large black population and moderately high per capita median income. Minneapolis-St. Paul and Hartford show fewer deaths by the major types than expected for their sizes. These cities are diverse on an intermetropolitan level in their composition and economies. While there seems to be no close relationship between fewer deaths than expected and nonwhite populations in Dallas-Fort Worth and Atlanta, a close inverse relationship seems to exist between number of deaths and high incomes. Minneapolis-St. Paul, on the other hand, does not have a large concentration of blacks or persons of Spanish heritage, but does have a fairly high per capita median income.

The cities which show fewer than expected numbers of deaths due to the several major causes show no significant geographic proximity or relationship, nor any significant relationship between low incidence of death and racial background. If anything, there is more of a relationship between high incidence of nonwhite populations and low incidence of death.

In conclusion, the main findings and relationships which have emerged can be summarized as follows. There seems to exist a rather close relationship between low concentration of deaths due to major types and high incomes—that is, there seems to be a high inverse relationship between number of deaths and income variables. There is less relationship, or a more spurious one, between racial background and incidence of death. There is no regional concentration of death on a broad scale such as the one pursued in this study, and instead death is widely distributed throughout the United States as exhibited by the metropolitan areas used in this analysis and shown in those SMSAs isolated in this summary and conclusions section.

MEASURING DIMENSIONS OF HEALTH ON AN INTRAMETROPOLITAN LEVEL

Emphasis now shifts from measuring dimensions of health on an intermetropolitan level to examining intrametropolitan variation of mortality and morbidity. The distributions of available data for several types of disease, as well as deaths by cause, are analyzed with respect to the distributions of income and race for three metropolitan areas—Philadelphia, St. Louis and Dallas-Fort Worth—in order to determine whether any relationship exists between occurrence of morbidity-mortality and such socioeconomic variables as income and nonwhite populations, notably blacks and persons of Spanish heritage. These socioeconomic variables traditionally have been assumed to be related to large numbers of deaths and diseases. Philadelphia, St. Louis and Dallas-Fort Worth were chosen for several reasons. Data were more readily available for these SMSAs than certain others in the study. Moreover, Philadelphia represented an old SMSA of extremely large size, located in the eastern part of the country. St. Louis and Dallas-Fort Worth represented SMSAs of approximately the same size (2.4 million and 2.3 million), one an older city located in the Midwest, the other a newer city with a rapidly increasing growth rate (19.1 percent compared to 54.2 percent during 1960-1970) located in an area transitional between the South and the West.

Morbidity and Mortality in the City of Philadelphia

In 1970, the Philadelphia SMSA had a population of 4.8 million persons, more than twice the population of either St. Louis or Dallas-Fort Worth. Located in the eastern seaboard megalopolis, it has a long history and today is one of the most important medical centers in the country. In 1972, the Philadelphia SMSA had a total of 77 hospitals, compared to 43 in St. Louis. Dallas-Fort Worth had 53 hospitals, nearly as many as Philadelphia.

Distributions of morbidity and mortality were available by ten health districts for the city of Philadelphia, representing about one-fifth of the total population of the metropolitan area itself. Figures 8-3 through 8-7 show not only the distributions of selected types of active cases of diseases and deaths in the city of Philadelphia but also the distribution of total population and total black population. Total population and total nonwhite population were concentrated largely in sections nine and eight, as well as in districts ten, four and five in the northern one-third of the city. The major active cases of diseases in health districts six, eight and five include bacillary dysentery, rubella, lead poisoning, tuberculosis and viral hepatitis (Figure 8-5). Health district six shows the largest number of diseases by the largest number of major types—rubella, lead poisoning, tuberculosis and viral hepatitis. Both health districts eight and five had large numbers of deaths due to bacillary dysentery, lead poisoning and tuberculosis. All three health districts are physically contiguous and are aligned along an axis which extends westward from the downtown Philadelphia area to the city limits. Elsewhere, active cases of diseases are widely dispersed through the health districts, with the exception of district ten, which while not a major source of active cases of disease, is one of the city's districts with a large number of deaths by major causes.

Figures 8-5 through 8-7 show distributions of numbers of deaths due to several major causes. Analysis of the findings of these data and maps show that health district nine has by far the largest number of deaths by the largest number of major causes (seven), including malignant neoplasms, diseases of the heart, certain causes of death in early infancy, cerebrovascular disease and motor vehicle accidents. It also leads in the total cases category. District nine is an area of dense population, including a large black population and low per capita income.

Ranking next to district nine are districts seven and four. Categories ranking high in death for district seven include malignant neoplasms, diseases of the heart, certain causes of death in early infancy, cerebrovascular diseases, motor vehicle accidents and the total cases category of death. Unlike district nine, district seven does not have a large concentration of blacks or an unusually dense population, but incomes are low. District four also has large numbers of deaths due to six major categories used in this analysis—malignant neoplasms, diseases of the heart, certain causes of death in

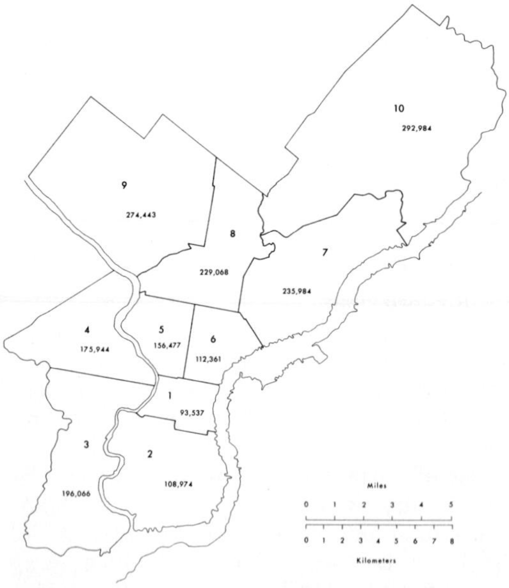

Figure 8-3. Population by Health District, Philadelphia, 1971.

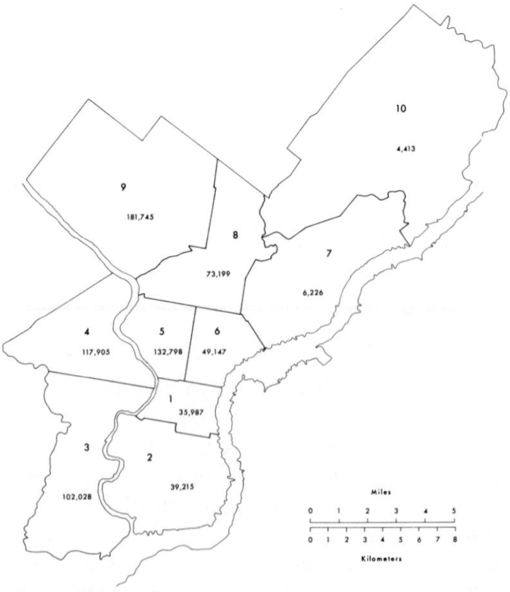

Figure 8-4. Nonwhite population by Health District, Philadelphia, 1971.

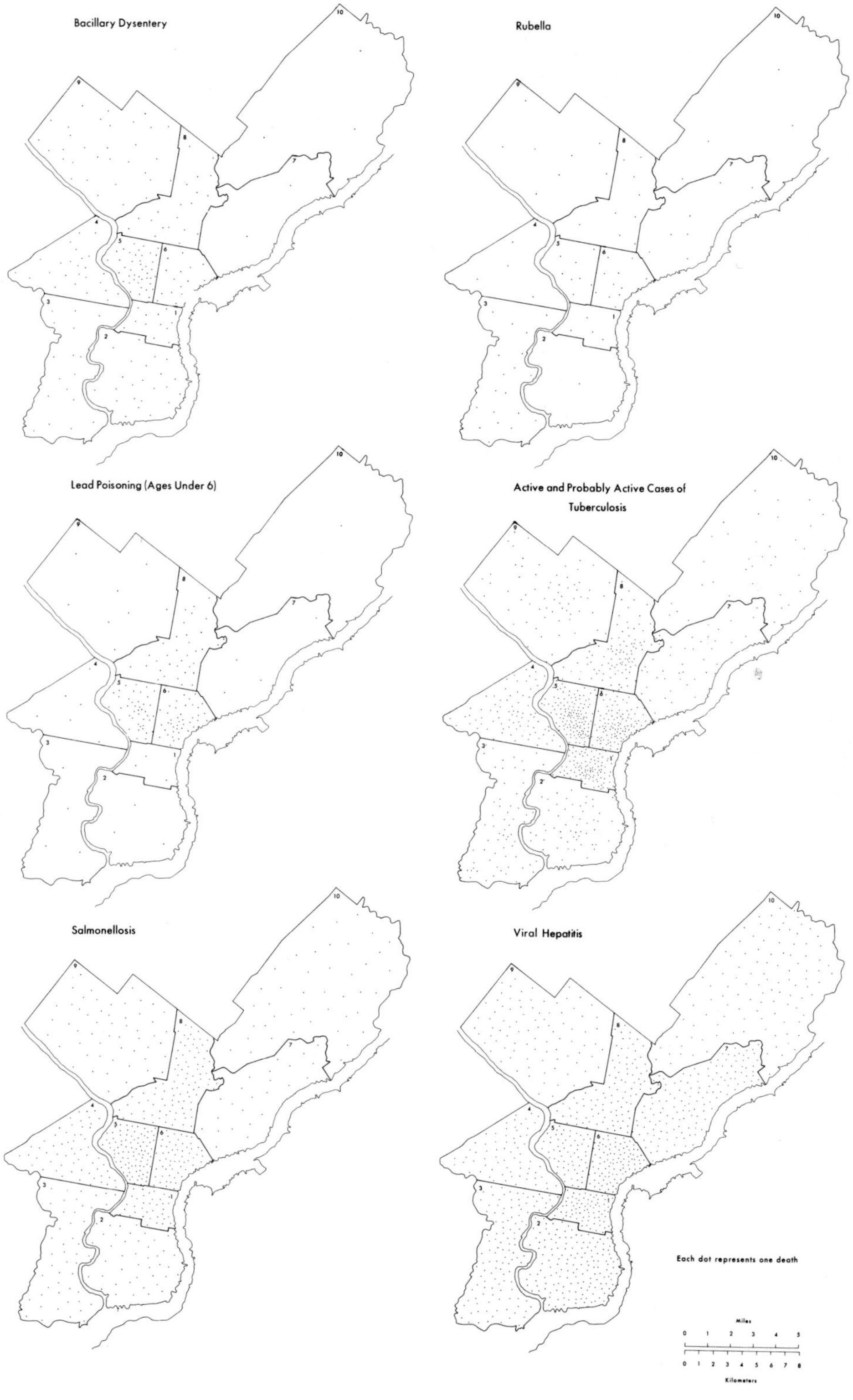

Figure 8-5. Morbidity by Cause, Philadelphia Health Districts, 1971.

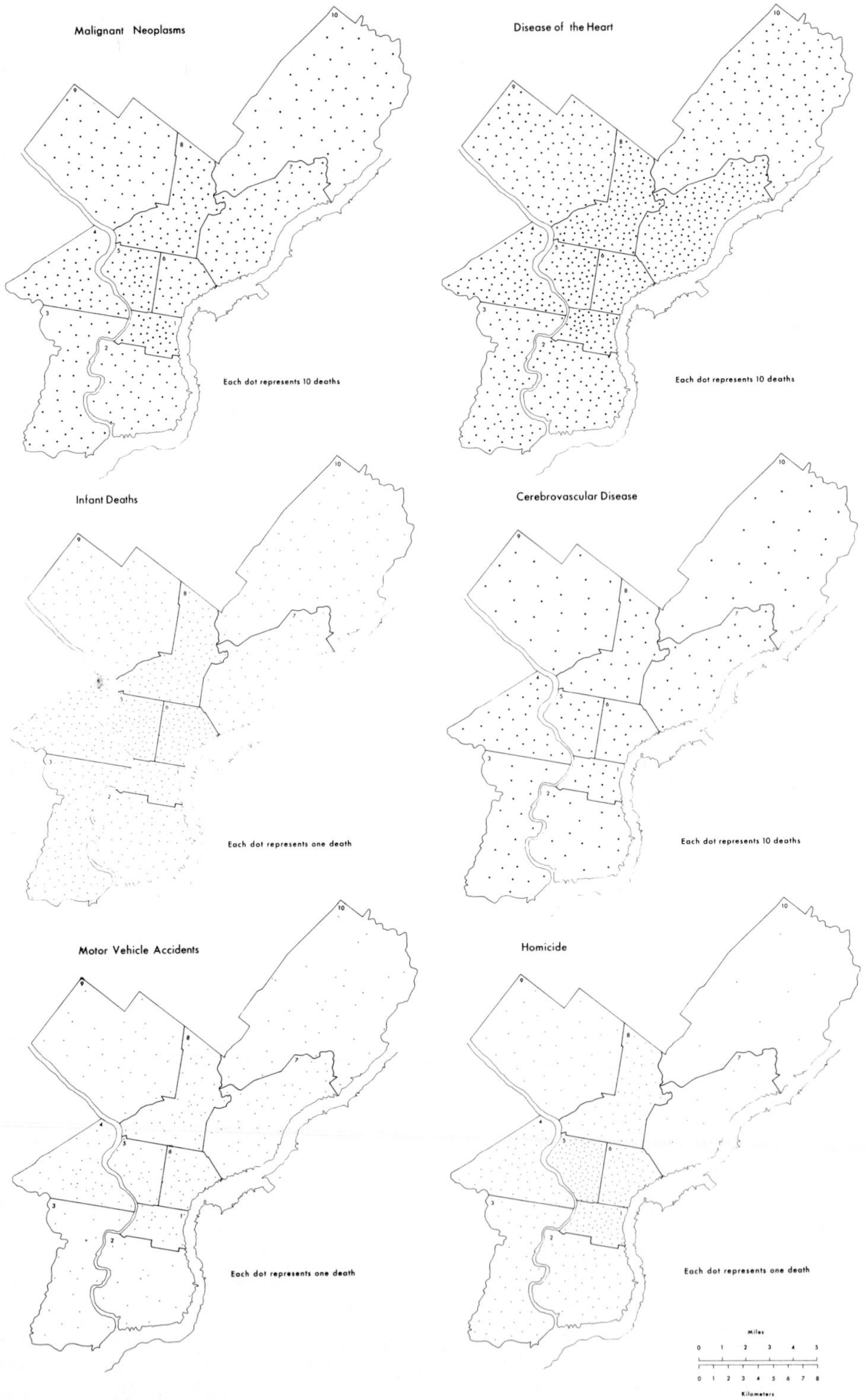

Figure 8-6. Mortality by Cause, Philadelphia Health Districts, 1971.

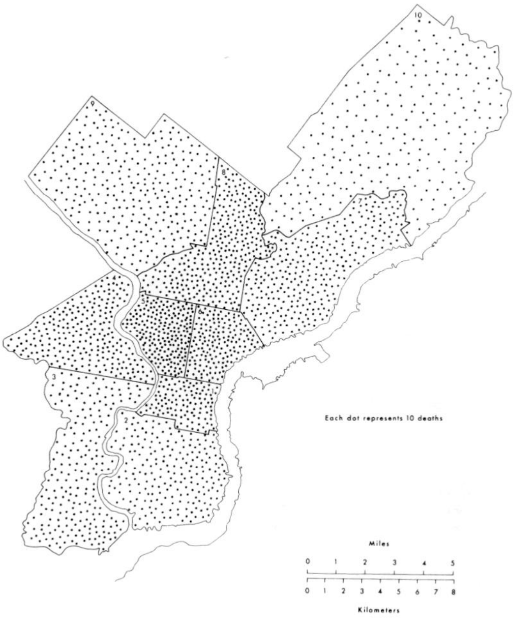

Figure 8-7. Resident Deaths Due to All Causes of Death, by Health District, Philadelphia, 1971.

early infancy, motor vehicle accidents, homicides and especially cerebrovascular disease. This district coincides with areas of high population, especially high black population concentrations, and reflects low incomes. Both districts eight and ten account for a large number of deaths due to five major causes. These two districts coincide also with heavily populated parts of the city, the largest black concentrations of population in the city and low incomes. Each of these districts registers large numbers of deaths due to malignant neoplasms, diseases of the heart, cerebrovascular disease, motor vehicle accidents (district ten) and certain causes of death in early infancy (district eight). District six accounts for a large number of deaths due to four major causes—motor vehicle accidents in particular, homicide and certain causes of death in early infancy. Health district five accounts for a large number of deaths due to certain causes of death in early infancy and homicide.

Non-disease-produced deaths had different distributions generally from those associated with disease-induced deaths. For example, motor vehicle accidents and homicides were concentrated largely in health districts five and six. These districts were neither as heavily populated nor comprised of such large black populations as areas to the north, nor were the incomes as low. Deaths of this type were associated more with proximity to the central business district, the downtown area, and areas of major traffic volume and major thoroughfares, although they did figure importantly in the north where large black populations and total populations are located.

The Dallas-Fort Worth Health Planning Region

The Dallas-Fort Worth SMSA consists of 13 counties in a sprawling yet largely urbanized and rapidly expanding section of north central Texas. It is dominated by the cities of Dallas and Fort Worth, but the largest population and greatest number of health care facilities are located in Dallas. Along with Atlanta, another nontraditional southern city, no other metropolitan area in the South is so widely diversified in the functions it performs. Dallas-Fort Worth ranks high nationally and regionally as a leading financial and market center. It is one of the four largest insurance centers in the nation. As a transport center it now has the potential to become the largest air transport center in the nation. Additionally, it serves as a major transport axis for railroads and highways. On completion of the dredging of the Trinity River, it will serve as a major port 270 miles inland.

The Dallas-Fort Worth economic base is strong and diversified. Manufacturing includes the production of electronics, oil and automotive equipment. cotton gin and air conditioning machinery, chemicals, leather goods, graphic arts, and scientific instruments.

The 1970 population of the Dallas-Fort Worth SMSA was 2.3 million, comparable to that of St. Louis; but the area is projected to have a larger population than St. Louis by 1980—2.6 million compared to 2.5 million.

Health Care Facilities. The location of major medical facilities for the Dallas-Fort Worth SMSA is shown in Figure 8-8, while those for the Dallas Public Health Department are shown in Figure 8-9. In Dallas there has been some decline in use of hospitals since 1969, although a small increase took place in 1972 (Table 8-1). Number of admissions, patient days per hospital bed and hospital use rates showed this pattern.

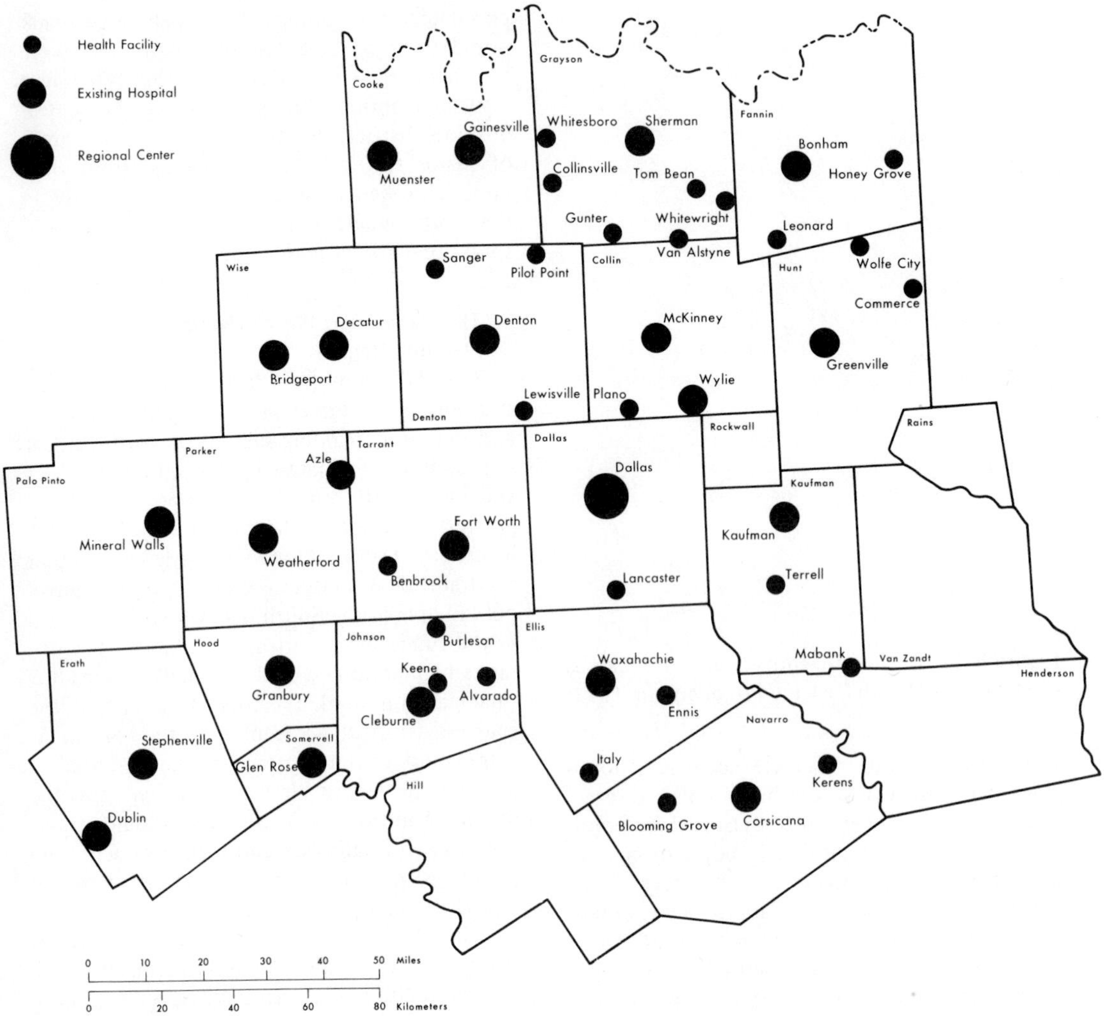

Figure 8-8. Health Care Facilities, Dallas-Fort Worth Health Planning Region, 1973.

Tuberculosis care in Carman Sanatorium, a 25 bed conforming facility, was terminated with its closing in 1972. Although formula-derived methods indicated a need for more beds, occupancy rates in tuberculosis facilities throughout the state are low. The Dallas Society for Crippled Children, which includes the Cerebral Palsy Treatment Center, is programmed for a substantial expansion of its facilities either as an addition to the existing facility or as a total replacement of the existing building. Nineteen outpatient facilities within the service are provided for over 320,000 outpatient visits during the current reporting period. These outpatient facilities are programmed as adequate in number, with modernization scheduled for the six currently nonconforming outpatient units in the city of Dallas.

Areal Distribution of Mortality and Morbidity. Selected mortality and morbidity data by cause were analyzed for census tracts for the city of Dallas (Figures 8-10 to 8-12). The distribution of deaths due to cerebrovascular, cardiovascular and malignant neoplasm diseases, traffic accidents, and deaths of children under one year of age are depicted. Areas of lowest income and concentrations of nonwhites did not necessarily correspond to the distributions

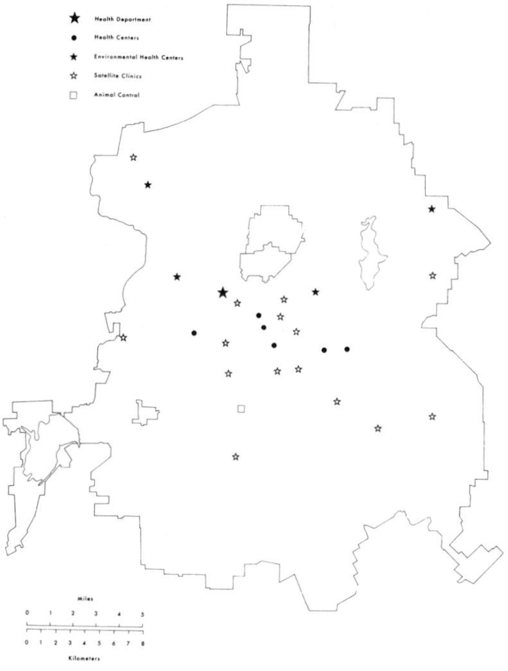

Figure 8-9. Dallas Health Department Facilities, 1973.

of deaths due to any of these selected causes. In other words, there seem to be no significant areal or combinatorial patterns emerging in the distribution of mortality by causes throughout the city of Dallas.

Resident deaths due to cancer in 1972 are widely dispersed across the region (Figure 8-10). Four major areas where numbers of resident deaths exceed 19 per census tract are found, three in the northern part of the city: a physically contiguous area located about 20 miles northwest of the central business district; another relatively physically contiguous area located between 15 and 25 miles northeast of the CBD; a pocket located about 15 miles due north of the CBD; and a small pocket located about 10 miles southeast of the CBD. With the exception of the small pocket area southeast of the CBD, all other areas of concentration of resident deaths due to malignant neoplasms are associated with areas of high income and high value of residences.

The distribution of total resident deaths of infants under the age of one year is plotted in Figure 8-10. Two major areas of concentration of deaths due to this cause stand out: the larger, located between about 15 and 20 miles directly east of the CBD, and the smaller area, a pocket located about 15 miles due south of the downtown area. Less important areas of concentration of mortality due to this cause are located in the southeastern quadrant of the city as well as in a larger sector between about 25 and 35 miles due north of the CBD. The area of largest occurrence of deaths due to this cause, located several miles due east of downtown Dallas, is also an area of high income and residential values.

Distribution of cases of selected types of morbidity are also shown for January, February and March 1972 for cases of infectious hepatitis and for tuberculosis, and a series of maps show monthly occurrence of salmonellosis cases for 1972. The maps show that salmonellosis cases were the most areally restricted in coverage, generally not occurring outside of an inner ring located between 10 to 15 miles from the CBD. Cases of infectious hepatitis were the most numerous, occurring within five to seven miles east of the CBD, in a broad area from 16 to 20 miles northwest of the CBD, in a broad fanshaped area extending southwest from the CBD for a distance of about 15 miles and in an outlying area in the northeast.

Incidence of salmonellosis in 1972 is recorded on a monthly basis. Particularly large concentrations of this disease occurred in 1972 within a radius of ten miles from the CBD. It

Table 8-1. Dallas Area, Selected Health Care Facilities Data

	1969	*1970*	*1971*	*1972*
General Hospital Admissions	141,755	123,374	119,937	122,967
Patient Days/Hospital Bed	293	293	265	268
Hospital Use Rates	1,682	1,286	1,052	1,224
Long Term Care Use Rates	11,241	11,073	14,182	15,667

Source: Data compiled by author.

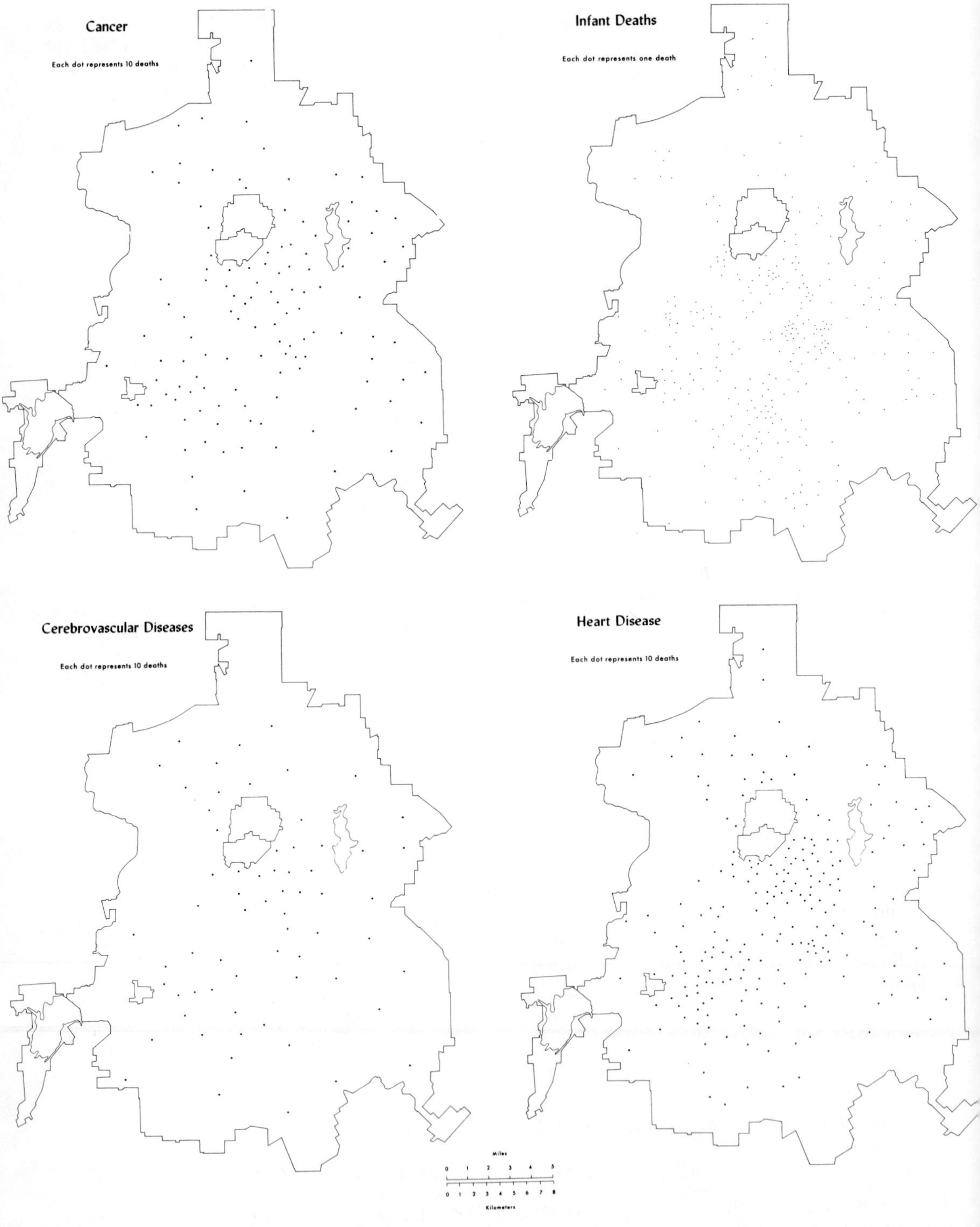

Figure 8-10. Resident Deaths by Cause of Death, Dallas, 1972.

Figure 8-11. Morbidity, Resident Cases, Dallas, 1972.

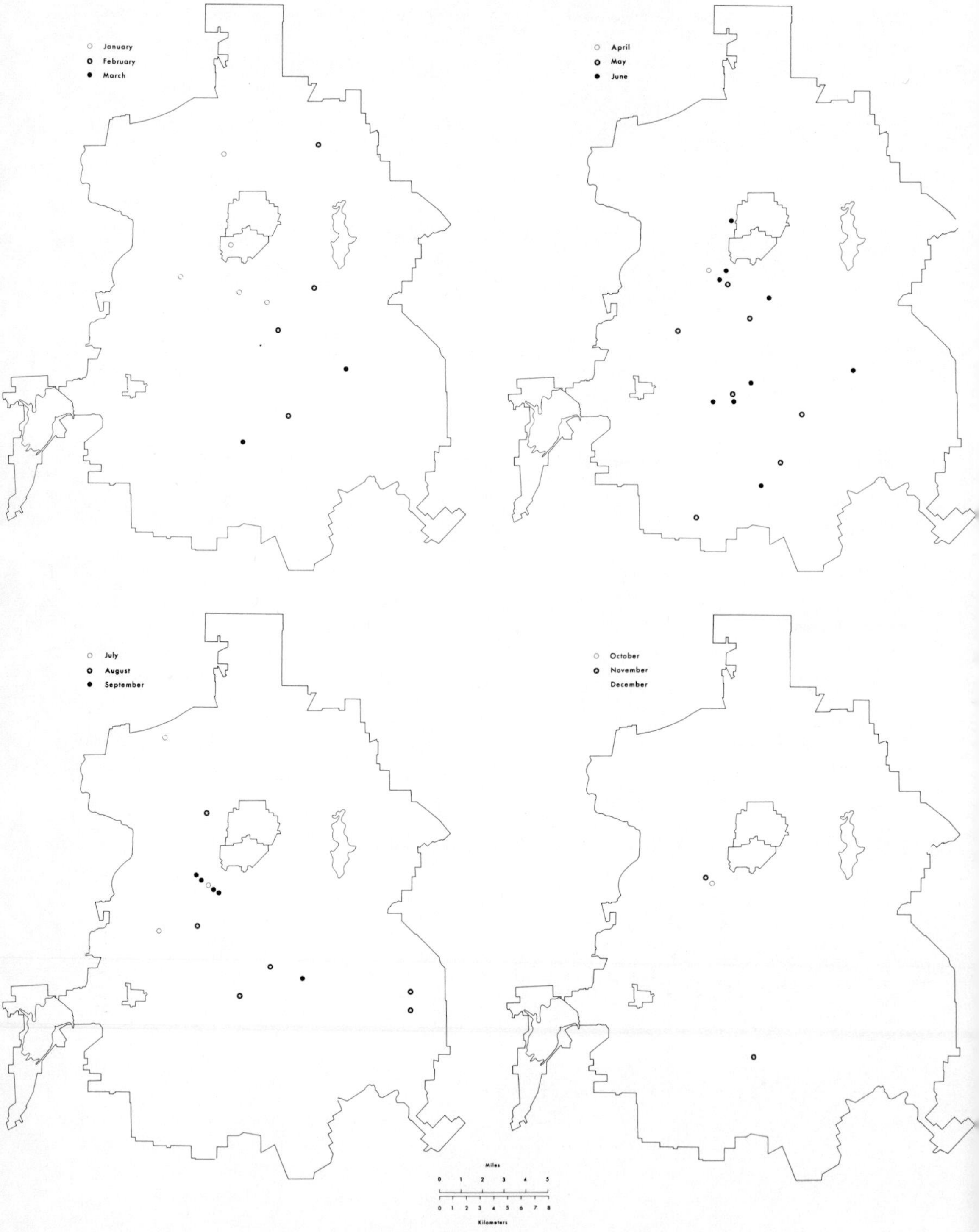

Figure 8-12. Resident Cases of Salmonellosis, Dallas, 1972.

also occurs to a lesser extent between 15 and 20 miles directly north of downtown Dallas. There is no close relationship, however, between occurrence of this disease and income.

St. Louis SMSA

In the city of St. Louis, median incomes exceeding $13,000 per capita were concentrated in only one area–along the Mississippi waterfront in an area of recent urban renewal, high rise luxury apartments and hotel-motel complexes. Median incomes ranging from $10,000 to $13,000 per capita were concentrated in widely separated areas in the western part of the city, in a large area in the southwest, in scattered areas throughout the central western part of the city and in two large areas corresponding with upper middle income class suburbs in the northwest part of the city. None of these areas corresponded with the areas of largest numbers of black population, which followed a large contiguous area extending almost from the Mississippi waterfront on the east throughout the central part of the city and slightly north of the central part of the city to the western edge of the city limits.

The distributions of several major types of death in the city's 26 health districts are described in Figures 8-13 through 8-14. Two physically contiguous health districts (six and 11) located in the northwest central part of the city account for more deaths by more causes (seven) than any of the remaining districts. Both districts have large black populations and relatively low incomes (Figures 8-15 and 8-16) as well as preponderances of deaths due to cerebrovascular disease, accidents, influenza and pneumonia, diabetes mellitus, certain causes of perinatal morbidity and mortality, homicide, arteriosclerosis (district six only), and cirrhosis of the liver (district 11 only).

Districts 12 and 15 follow with the next largest number of deaths from the largest number of major causes (six). District 12 is located physically contiguous to districts six and 11 in the west central portion of the city, while district 15 is located at some distance from the previous one in the southeast part of the city, fronting on the Mississippi River. Districts 12 and 15, like six and 11, are also areas of large black populations and relatively low incomes. These two districts account for large numbers of deaths due to cerebrovascular disease, disease of the heart (district 15 only), malignant neoplasms and arteriosclerosis (district 15 only), accidents, influenza and pneumonia (district 12 only), and cirrhosis of the liver (district 12 only).

Districts 16 and 17, which are physically contiguous to district 15 in the south central part of the city, also accounted for many deaths due to the major types of disease and causes of death, namely disease of the heart and cerebrovascular disease (district 16), diabetes mellitus (districts 16 and 17), and arteriosclerosis and accidents (district 17). Geographically, however, death was widespread and not evenly distributed throughout the city.

Those areas accounting for the largest number of deaths due to diseases of the heart are concentrated in one area–health districts 15 and 16 in the southeastern and south central part of the city. Also concentrated here are malignant neoplasms, cerebrovascular diseases, diabetes mellitus and arteriosclerosis. Concentrated in the northwest central part of the city is another major area of cerebrovascular disease, accidents, influenza and pneumonia, diabetes mellitus, certain causes of perinatal morbidity and mortality, and cirrhosis of the liver.

Accidents are concentrated in three areas, the central part of the city, the west north central area and the east, fronting on the Mississippi River. Concentration of large numbers of accidents is not only related to large concentrations of blacks in the central area but is also associated with major traffic arteries and thoroughfares in the Forest Park, central and Mississippi riverfront areas.

Influenza and pneumonia have only one major area of concentration–the west north central area. Diabetes mellitus has two major areas of concentration, one in the west north central and the other in the central part of the city, the latter in particular associated with a large black population and an area of low income. Arteriosclerosis has the widest geographic distribution. The disease is found in the extreme southern part of the city, the central, the west north central and the eastern riverfront area, and is associated with both black and white populations as well as areas of low to high incomes. Certain causes of perinatal morbidity and mortality are concentrated in only one area of the city–the central area. Homicide

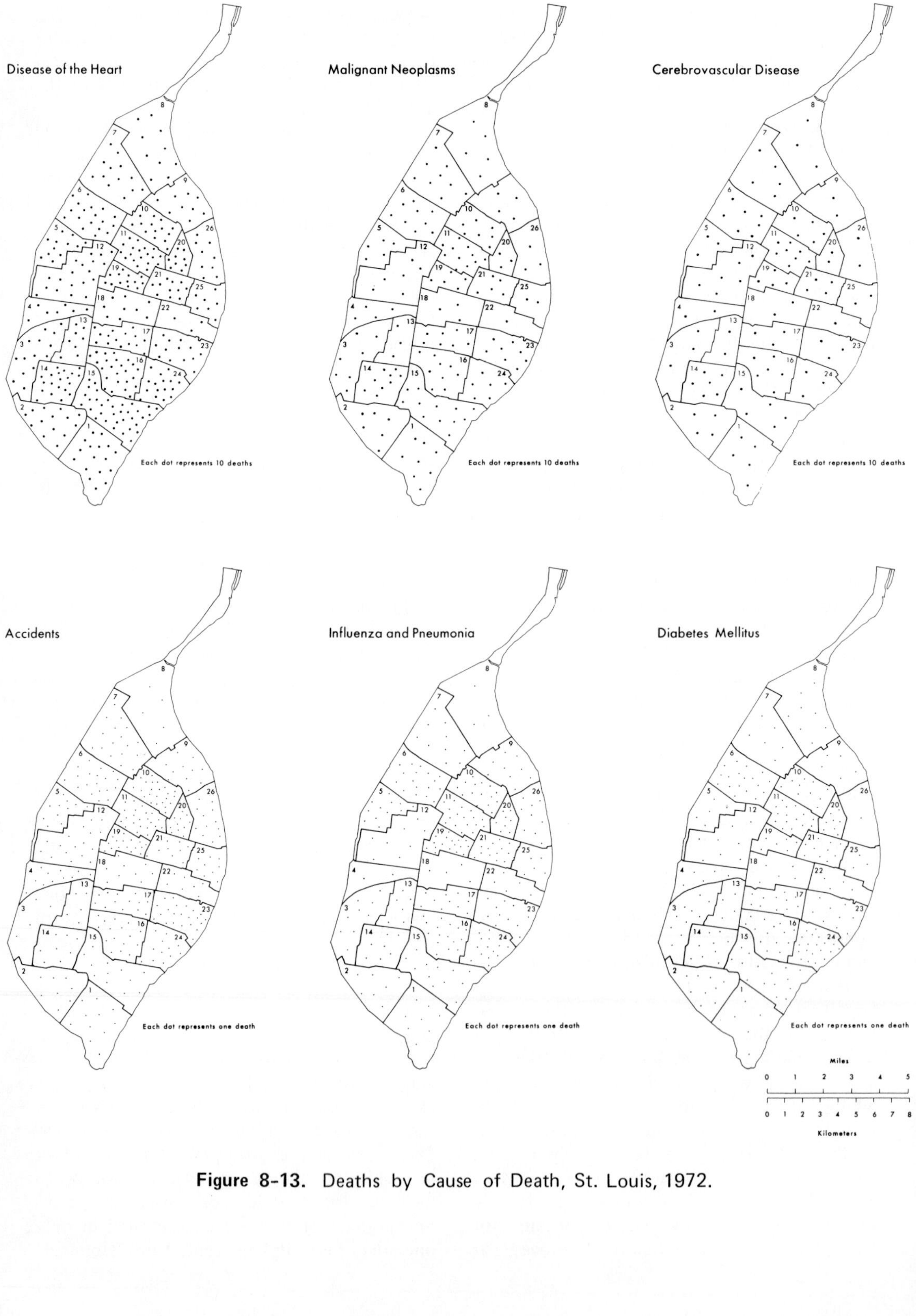

Figure 8-13. Deaths by Cause of Death, St. Louis, 1972.

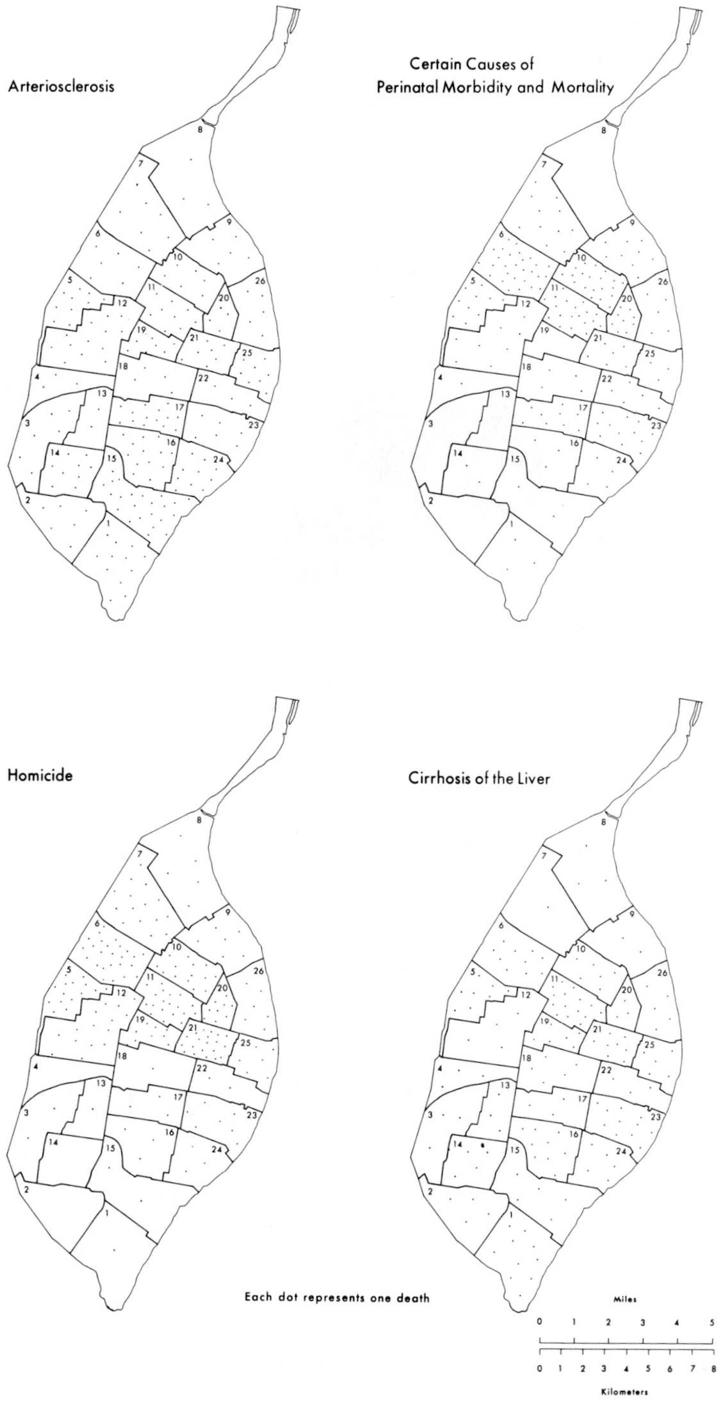

Figure 8-14. Deaths by Cause of Death, St. Louis, 1972.

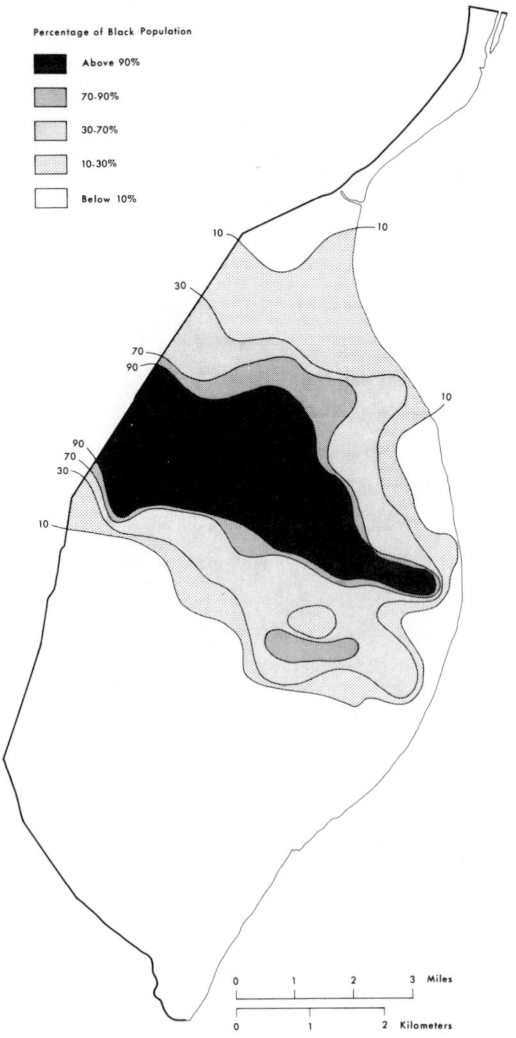

Figure 8-15. Percentage Distribution of Black Population in the City of St. Louis, 1970.

is concentrated in the north along a channel extending from just northwest of the central business district extending almost in a direct line to the west north central area. This cause of death follows an area of large numbers of black populations. Cirrhosis of the liver is concentrated in only one major area of St. Louis—the central part of the city. Again, this is an area of black population and low incomes.

Diseases of the heart is the largest category, accounting for 3,546 deaths during 1971, followed by malignant neoplasms with 1,543 deaths and cerebrovascular disease with 1,042 deaths. Deaths due to accidents, a category which claimed 366 lives, followed these three major causes of death in St. Louis. This category was followed by influenza and pneumonia, which claimed 282 lives.

HEALTH CARE FACILITIES ANALYSIS AND PLANNING

Health facilities and services planning in each state have been accomplished through the cooperative efforts of the health professions, professional organizations, consumers of health services, governmental programs and voluntary health agencies. Planning for such

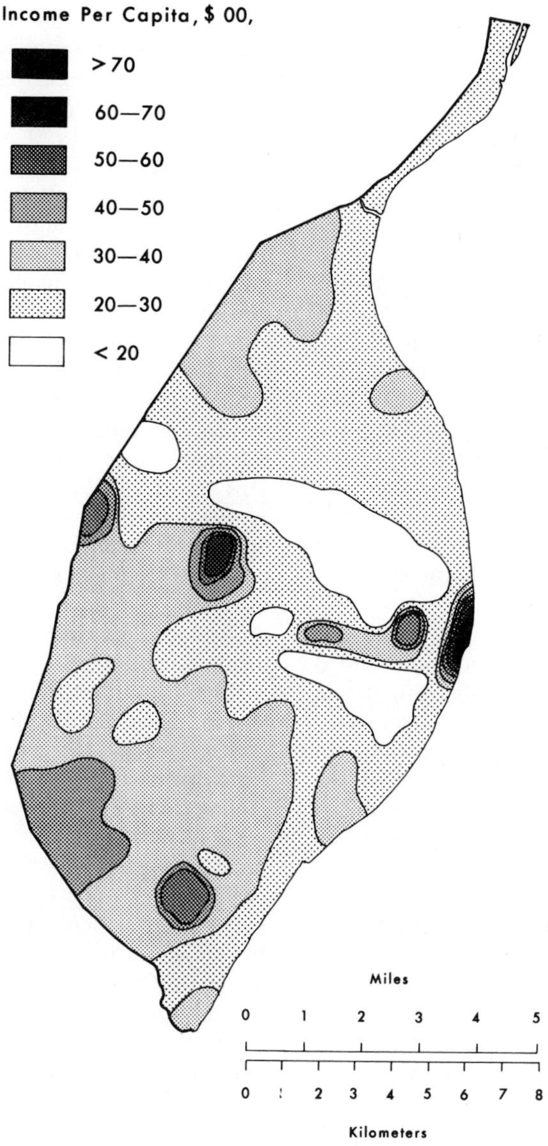

Figure 8-16. Distribution of Annual Per Capita Median Income, City of St. Louis, 1970.

facilities and services must be a process which is flexible, continuing and responsive to advances in medical science and to changing communities in meeting the need for health services. Since 1966, health planning in the United States has evolved from a voluntary movement to one largely based on federal and state legislation enacted for the purpose of enhancing, encouraging and supporting consumers and health professionals in the health planning process. One of the salutary effects has been a voluntary cooperation between consumer and provider which has facilitated the coordination of facilities and services so that capital expenditures, operating funds and manpower utilization for health facilities have been made in the best interest of the public. Second, these laws have set up the legal machinery for a hierarchy to facilitate both the funding and orderly achievement of optimum development of health services and facilities to meet rising needs. Originating in the US Department of

Health, Education and Welfare, particularly in the Hill-Burton and Areawide Comprehensive Health Planning programs, responsibility has been delegated down to the states—in particular to state health planning councils or their equivalent—and thence to areawide comprehensive planning organizations. These organizations, of which there are several in each state, work with health planning agencies and, finally, with both consumers and providers of health services and facilities. Each state heretofore has been more or less autonomous in its organization and management of funds under this hierarchical arrangement. The individual states develop guidelines for optimum planning goals, objectives, needs and policies in order to develop facilities of desirable size, location and commitment to community service. Individual states have also provided final approval or denial to applications for funds for construction and modernization.

During the Depression years and World War II, few hospitals were constructed in the United States. Population increase during this period and physical and technological obsolescence of facilities produced a shortage in number of hospital beds and other health facilities. To meet this new and rapidly increasing problem, Congress enacted the Hospital Survey and Construction Act (PL 725, 70th Congress), which became law on August 13, 1946, and which is popularly known as the Hill-Burton Act. The Hill-Burton legislation originally had two main objectives: to survey the needs of health facilities and to assist local sponsors in each state in the construction of public and other voluntary nonprofit hospitals and public health centers. As a result, each state undertook for the first time an orderly appraisal of its existing hospital and public health center resources and developed comprehensive plans for furnishing adequate hospital, clinic, and similar services to all its people.

Several major amendments have been adopted since the original Hill-Burton legislation was enacted. The most far-reaching change in the program was the establishment of a new grant program (beginning with fiscal year 1966) for modernization of public and voluntary nonprofit hospitals and other health facilities. While modernization had already been possible under Hill-Burton, and in fact more than half of all projects funded prior to fiscal 1966 had involved additions or alterations to existing facilities, this new provision made it possible for the first time to set aside funds exclusively for modernization.

On June 30, 1970, Congress enacted the Medical Facilities Construction and Modernization Amendments (PL 91-296). In addition to extending the program through June 30, 1973, this legislation increased the level of authorization for grants for modernization or construction to record highs of $382.5 million for fiscal year 1971, $402.5 million for fiscal year 1972 and $417.5 million for fiscal 1973. Also, a total of $500 million in loans and loan guarantees was authorized annually for the construction and modernization of health care facilities. This act provided for the assignment of priority areas of relatively small financial resources for outpatient facilities in poverty areas, facilities providing comprehensive health care, facilities providing training in health or allied health professions and facilities providing for treatment of alcoholism.

The Hill-Burton State Plan is set up to guide and influence the development of patient care service through the construction and modernization of hospitals and related medical facilities serving each area of a state, including interstate areas. It presents a coordinated, comprehensive program for the orderly development of needed health services and facilities designed to assure high quality patient care and serves as the basis for the allocation of funds from all sources for modernization and construction purposes as well as public grants in aid for these purposes.

Most states have declared as public policy that hospital and related health care facilities and services of highest quality, efficiently provided and properly utilized at reasonable cost, are of vital concern to the public health. In order to provide for the protection and promotion of the health of inhabitants of the state, the departments of health of each state have been designated as the sole agency for comprehensive health planning under the Comprehensive Health Planning and Public Health Services Amendments of 1966 (Federal Law 89-749), as amended and supplemented. These state departments have the central, comprehensive responsibility for the development and administration of each state's policy with respect to planning hospital and related health care services.

Analysis of Hospital Statistics

In an effort to conform to the framework of the Hill-Burton program and the federal comprehensive health programs, several hospital variables were analyzed for the 20 SMSAs in order to determine which areas of the hospital sector were increasing or declining more than others, and which metropolitan areas showed significant changes absolutely or relatively in health care facilities with respect to each other and with respect to themselves over time (Table 8-2). An analysis of these variables contributes new ideas and supports existing evidence of trends in hospital construction, use of hospital facilities, use of health maintenance organizations (by implication) and the geographic distributions of these and other phenomena.

The findings are useful in interpreting the effects of such programs as Hill-Burton, comprehensive health, health maintenance and proposed social medicine programs. They also provide new output, suggesting new ideas about future trends not only in the health care services sector of the nation but also in terms of the overall economic significance or decline in certain SMSAs. The hospital variables discussed here represent those most readily accessible and comprehensive in coverage in the health field. Data for hospitals are more readily obtainable than data for other types of health care facilities, and indeed persons using hospital facilities are more numerous than those using other types of health care facilities. For this reason the study is justified in using hospital variables and making conclusions based upon the findings of the analyses of these variables with some considerable reliability.

Hospital Beds. Those SMSAs which show a larger than expected number of hospital beds include Miami, St. Louis, Houston, Minneapolis-St. Paul, Boston and New Orleans, while those showing a smaller than expected number of beds include San Francisco-Oakland, Seattle and Washington, D.C. (Figure 8-17). Again, the reason for these extremes can be explained by some of the same factors mentioned previously—that is, more demand, the quality and

Table 8-2. Selected Hospital Statistics for 20 SMSAs, 1972

	1970 SMSA Population (millions)	*Hospitals (per 100,000)*	*Beds (per 1,000)*	*Admissions (per 1,000)*	*Percentage Occupancy*	*Average Stay (days)*	*Outpatient Visits (per capita)*
Atlanta	1.4	1.4	3.8	154	76	6.8	1.1
Baltimore	2.1	1.2	4.1	129	79	9.2	1.0
Boston	2.8	2.3	5.1	163	77	8.8	1.2
Chicago	7.0	1.4	4.3	140	79	9.1	0.9
Cleveland	2.1	1.6	4.4	147	82	9.1	0.9
Dallas-Fort Worth	2.3	2.8	3.8	150	76	7.0	0.6
Detroit	4.2	1.5	3.7	129	89	8.5	0.9
Hartford	0.7	0.9	3.5	129	81	8.1	0.8
Houston	2.0	2.8	5.0	189	74	7.1	0.8
Los Angeles-Long Beach	7.0	2.5	4.0	151	70	6.8	1.3
Miami	1.3	2.1	4.9	175	81	8.5	0.7
Minneapolis-St. Paul	1.8	1.8	5.5	176	74	8.6	0.6
New Orleans	1.0	2.0	5.2	175	75	8.3	1.0
New York	11.6	1.4	4.7	139	83	10.1	1.2
Philadelphia	4.8	1.6	4.2	130	80	9.0	1.3
Pittsburgh	2.4	1.7	5.1	165	83	9.3	1.2
St. Louis	2.4	1.8	5.2	170	82	9.1	0.1
San Francisco-Oakland	3.1	2.0	4.1	144	68	7.3	1.0
Seattle	1.4	1.9	3.2	138	69	5.8	0.6
Washington	2.9	1.1	3.3	122	80	7.5	0.8

Source: Data compiled by author.

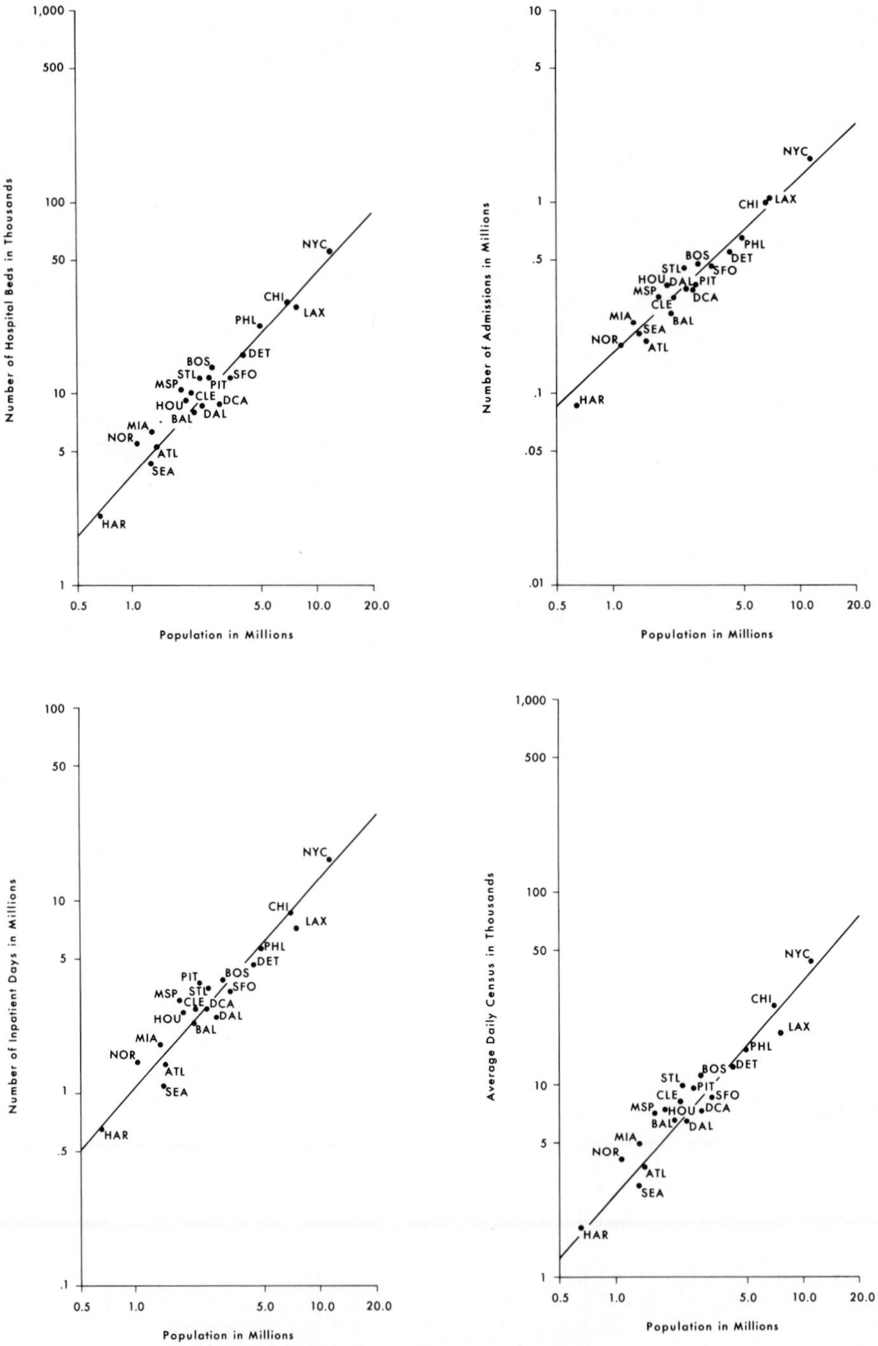

Figure 8-17. Hospital Statistics, 20 SMSAs, 1972.

quantity of health care facilities, healthier or unhealthier urban living conditions, and income differentials. More detailed analyses of these factors for the SMSAs is recommended as a means of determining comparative advantages or disadvantages certain of the SMSAs have with respect to others in the sample. Recommendations can be made for policy and programs related to improvement of health care facilities. It is possible to suggest, again, that there seems to be a relationship between fewer than expected beds and the existence of health maintenance organizations in those cities—for example, in San Francisco-Oakland, Seattle and Washington, D.C. HMOs stress preventive medicine and outpatient treatment in preference to traditional curative and negative forms of long term stays in hospitals.

Admissions. Admissions are the total number of patients admitted to beds or cribs, excluding newborn nursery. The number of admissions for the 20 SMSAs in the study ranged from a low in Hartford to a high in New York. Figure 8-17 shows the distribution of the 20 SMSAs with respect to expected number of admissions for different populations.

There were several major findings with respect to this phase of the analysis. A decline in the number and rate of admissions is expected by 1985. In 1972 there was a larger number of admissions for Minneapolis-St. Paul, New York, St. Louis, Boston, Houston, Miami and Los Angeles-Long Beach than was expected for cities of their sizes, suggesting a need for careful study of health problems related to hospital admissions in these cities. While one possible explanation may be more health problems in these metropolitan areas, further study and analysis is needed to determine other possible factors contributing to this condition before appropriate recommendations can be formulated. In 1972, as well as in forecasts for future years, there is a lower than expected number of admissions for Hartford, Detroit, Atlanta and Baltimore. Detailed studies and analyses are recommended for these SMSAs in order to ascertain the problems and factors producing the deficits and to make recommendations where needed for policies to correct problems. Possible explanations include either better preventive health treatment in those SMSAs or the inability to reach large segments of the population needing hospital treatment. There is a noticeable lack of regionalization or clustering of SMSAs as to actual or expected number of admissions by their major or regional geographic location.

San Francisco-Oakland shows a more rapid rate of increase than many of the other SMSAs. At the same time, Washington, D.C., which now has a smaller number of admissions than San Francisco-Oakland, is expected to exceed San Francisco-Oakland in number of admissions by 1985. Thereafter, the number of hospital admissions in Washington is expected to increase faster than most of the other SMSAs in the study, exceeding the number of admissions expected for San Francisco-Oakland, Detroit and Philadelphia. Washington, D.C., moreover, is expected to exceed the number of admissions for Boston and for Chicago in the twenty-first century, reflecting important future growth of the city.

The Pittsburgh SMSA is expected to experience a steady but rather insignificant decline in number of admissions to hospitals and should be exceeded in number of admissions and other measures by the St. Louis SMSA in 1975, by the Houston SMSA in 1991, and later by Minneapolis-St. Paul, Atlanta and Baltimore. The admissions variable is one of many indicators which point toward the relative and absolute decline of Pittsburgh in medical care facilities, which decline should commence in 1975. These findings indicate both a decline in the relative economic importance of the city and in its health care services. Planners and other persons concerned with the revitalization of Pittsburgh SMSA should be aware of these indicators and trends. Both Atlanta and Minneapolis-St. Paul show rapid rates of increase in admissions, more so than most of the other SMSAs.

Inpatient Days. Chicago showed one of the most rapid rates of increase in number of inpatient days of the 20 SMSAs in the study (Figure 8-17). If trends continue, it will exceed New York by the twenty-first century. The Miami SMSA shows a rapid rate of increase in inpatient days and is expected to exceed Atlanta by 1995. Much of this increase may be explained by the large proportion of population 65 years of age and over in Miami, who presumably require more hospitalization. St. Louis on the other hand shows a declining rate in number of inpatient days.

Those SMSAs which show a greater than expected number of inpatient days with respect to population size include Pittsburgh, St. Louis, Minneapolis-St. Paul, New Orleans, Houston and Miami, while Atlanta, Seattle, Los Angeles, San Francisco-Oakland, Dallas-Fort Worth and Detroit exhibited fewer inpatient days than anticipated. These findings, along with the variations in rates of increase in number of inpatient days, suggest a number of situations which call for federal, state and local action in the area of health care facilities. Those SMSAs with larger numbers of inpatient days than expected for their population sizes may be well supplied with health care facilities, may be capable of handling demand for hospital needs, may provide superior health care facilities and services as demonstrated by the larger than normal demand, or may have reached a critical point in health care services. In the latter case, further investigation could determine what problems if any are contributing to this condition, whether the capacity has been achieved or overattained, whether demand has actually outstripped supply in the health care services sector, whether these cities constitute a comparative advantage in health care services and are serving populations from areas other than the metropolitan area, or whether they are for some determinable reasons not "healthy" cities. The determination of the causes of these conditions for any of these cities through additional studies constitutes the basis for health care planning and policy.

In the case of those cities which registered lower than expected numbers of inpatient days, an excess of supply over demand may exist; medical facilities (hospitals) are either not as superior or they are underused; a sufficient number of hospital facilities is not available to meet rising demand; the populations of those cities are healthier; or hospitals may be receiving more outpatients in lieu of inpatients. Some of these cities have large proportions of their populations enrolled in health maintenance organizations, which may influence the types of treatment given to non-HMO populations as well, since the stress in HMOs is given to preventive rather than curative hospital health care services, so that the number of inpatient days is minimized. Large numbers of persons in Los Angeles, San Francisco-Oakland, Washington, D.C., and Seattle belong to HMOs. This superior outpatient health treatment probably accounts for lower than expected use of hospital facilities in these cities.

Average Daily Census. An analysis of average daily census for each of the 20 SMSAs shows that Washington, D.C., has the most rapid rate of increase of all the SMSAs, increasing faster than San Francisco-Oakland (Figure 8-17). Washington should exceed San Francisco-Oakland in 1980. The Atlanta and Miami SMSAs also showed rapid rates of increase in average daily census. Atlanta is expected to exceed Seattle in 1980, while Miami should exceed Seattle in 1990. Hartford also showed a rapid rate of increase in average daily census. These findings suggest bases for planning for health care facilities in those cities with faster than normal rates of average daily census—for example, Hartford, Washington, D.C., Atlanta and Miami—since they are clearly becoming more important growth centers than many of the other SMSAs in the study. Detailed analysis is needed to explore the reasons for these geographic variations.

Those SMSAs showing the largest deviations in excess of the expected average daily census for their population sizes include Minneapolis-St. Paul, Pittsburgh, New Orleans, St. Louis, Boston, Miami and Houston. SMSAs showing less than expected average daily census include Seattle, Dallas-Fort Worth, Los Angeles-Long Beach and San Francisco-Oakland. While there seemed to be some geographic concentration of SMSAs in the lower than expected group, particularly in the Far West, geography may be less a factor in explaining the variation that the concentration of large populations using health maintenance organizations or being influenced by the presence of such organizations, which are prevalent in the large Far West SMSAs and in the nation's capital.

Outpatient Visits. Although the figures for total outpatient visits do not show significant dispersion from expected number of visits for varying populations, Pittsburgh, New Orleans, Los Angeles-Long Beach, Seattle, Boston, Hartford, Baltimore and Cleveland show somewhat larger numbers of outpatient visits than expected (Figure 8-18). Dallas-Fort Worth, Atlanta, Minneapolis-St. Paul and Chicago show somewhat lower numbers of outpatient visits than expected for populations of their sizes. The findings can be interpreted in a number of ways. Possibly one of the most relevant is that those SMSAs with greater than expected numbers of outpatient visits had either a greater number of health problems or place greater emphasis on preventive types of treatment, which implies a larger number of outpatient visits in preference to curative hospital treat-

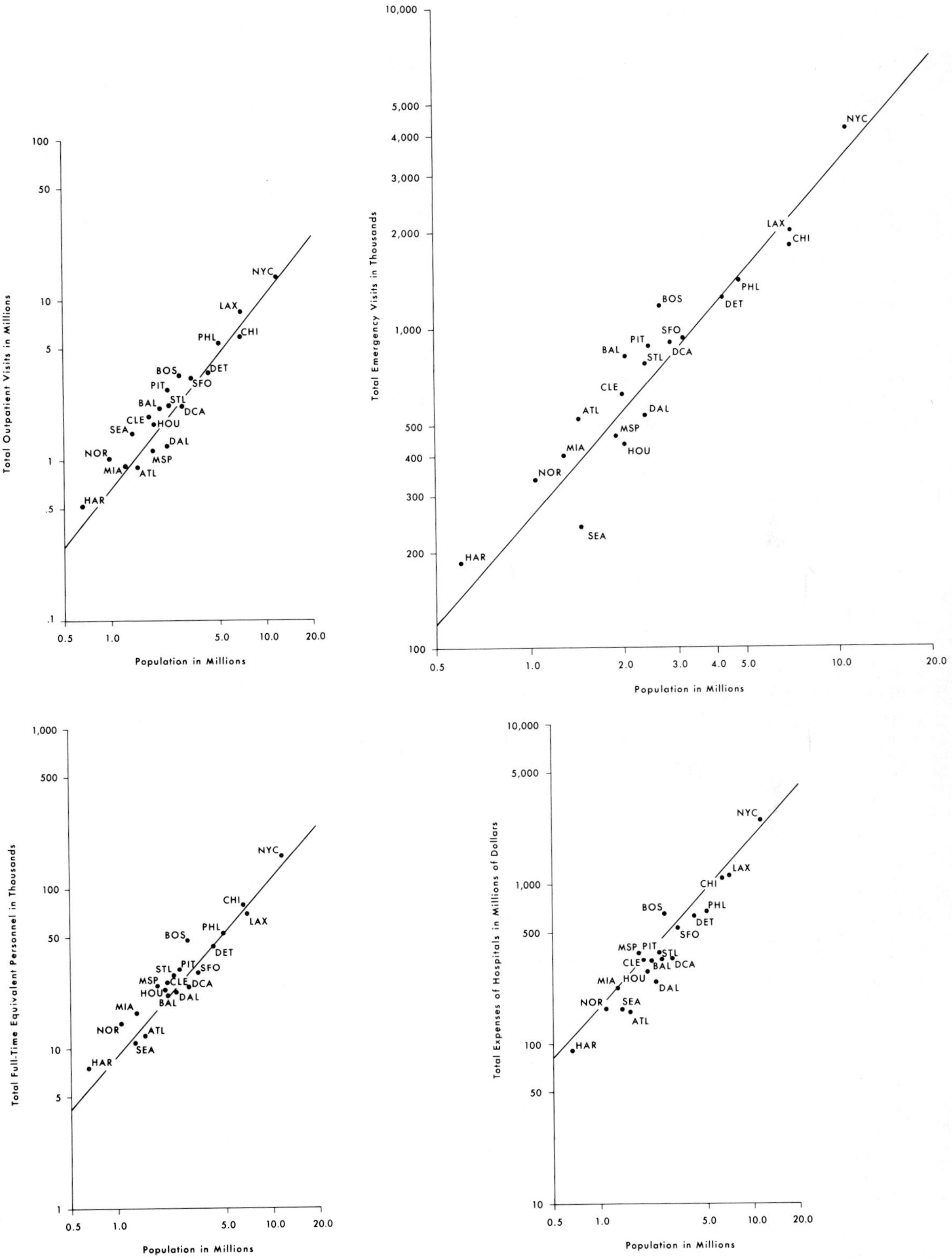

Figure 8-18. Hospital Statistics, 20 SMSAs, 1972.

ment. Outpatient visits thus are an indicator of positive health care, which is to be preferred over the conventional hospitalization method.

Emergency Visits. As one of the four major categories of outpatient visits, emergency visits provide an important indicator of the amount of preventive and nonhospital inpatient care supplied by health care facilities in the 20 SMSAs. In 1972 Baltimore, Boston, Pittsburgh, New York and Atlanta, as well as Miami, New Orleans, Hartford, St. Louis and Cleveland, experienced higher than expected numbers of emergency outpatient visits to hospitals (Figure 8-18). Seattle, Houston, Dallas-Fort Worth, Pittsburgh, Chicago and Los Angeles showed substantially lower numbers of emergency outpatient visits to hospitals than expected for their population sizes. These findings suggest that for the SMSAs with lower than expected numbers of emergency visits, preventive care and increased safety factors may have figured more importantly than in those SMSAs with higher numbers of visits than anticipated.

Full-Time Hospital Personnel. Full-time hospital personnel showed no great amount of dispersion from the expected number in any of the 20 SMSAs in 1972 (Figure 8-18). Minneapolis-St. Paul, followed by Boston, New Orleans, Miami and Hartford, showed a slight excess in the expected number of full-time hospital personnel, thereby indicating either that these SMSAs are better served or that they are overstaffed. Those SMSAs showing some deviation below the expected include Seattle, Atlanta, Washington, D.C., and Los Angeles, suggesting perhaps slight deficits in numbers of hospital personnel. Further study would clarify how to improve the staffing of hospital facilities by medical personnel.

Total Expenses. Dispersion from the expected amount of hospital expenses for the 20 SMSAs is not great (Figure 8-18). Those SMSAs showing some deviation in excess of expected total hospital expenses are Boston, followed by Minneapolis-St. Paul and New York. This finding on the one hand could suggest comparative advantages in the form of well-equipped and well-staffed hospitals, or the finding might suggest diseconomies of operation in these SMSAs all located in the northeast part of the country. Those SMSAs showing lower total expenses than expected for populations of their sizes included Atlanta, Houston, Baltimore, Hartford, St. Louis, Washington, D.C., Detroit, Philadelphia, and especially Seattle and Dallas-Fort Worth. These findings suggest either underdevelopment in hospital equipment, staff and the like; economies of operation; or possibly less demand for hospital facilities due to large segments of the population participating in health maintenance organizations which stress preventive nonhospital treatment as opposed to curative hospital stays. Dallas and Seattle possibly exhibit the most economical operations of the metropolitan areas studied.

Total Assets. The 20 SMSAs show considerable dispersion from the expected amount of total hospital assets in 1972 (Figure 8-19). Hartford, Boston, Miami, New Orleans, New York, Cleveland, Houston and Pittsburgh all register total hospital assets higher than expected for populations of their size, while Dallas-Fort Worth, Washington, D.C., Detroit, Los Angeles-Long Beach and Seattle all exhibit lower than expected total assets. Washington, D.C., seems to be the most deficient in value of

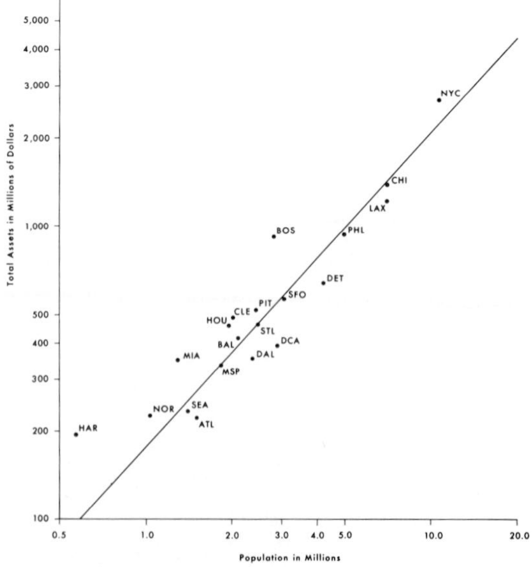

Figure 8-19. Hospital Statistics, Total Assets, 20 SMSAs, 1972.

total assets. Additional studies are needed to determine the causes of these relatively large excesses and deficits in values of total hospital assets, with the idea of making recommendations to remedy the problems. Perhaps in some cases the low deviations from the expected should be recognized as indicators of age or deterioration of hospital facilities, while in others they may represent the shift from demand for curative hospital care to preventive nonhospital treatment and care. A cursory examination of the cities so involved in this category suggests that both causes are operating to produce these deviations.

AN INTEGRATED SYSTEM

Let us turn now to a discussion of one of the three conclusions set forth in the introduction concerning the present system of health care delivery in the United States: the means of delivering services and paying providers; of closing the gaps in financing health care services which already overburden an inadequate system and offer little prospect of materially improving the quality and quantity of health care services; as well as of assuring all people the ability to cope financially with the cost of health care which has been made realizable by the substantial base of coverage now provided by both private and public insurance plans.

Such a system will move more efficiently than any other toward attaining the overall health goal for the nation: a system which is more personal, more comprehensive and continuous, and at the same time dedicated to serving the health needs of consumers and deployed in such a way as to be readily available to them. This type of integrated system provides the incentives, moreover, for efficiency, wherein health care resources to consumers are maximized while rising costs are minimized. At the same time it operates to maximize the satisfaction to providers seeking to practice in close collaboration with their colleagues and to employ more fully the new technologies of medicine. Such a system moves toward the objectives of providing quality care, a network of responsibility and a beneficial merging of the financing and delivery system. The benefits derived from this system will be much greater than those presently offered by the anachronistic hospital-based treatment system and fee payment system currently operating in this country.

Group Practice

The new integrated system of health care delivery which is developing more public and private recognition and participation in the United States is known generally as group practice. Group practice constitutes an alternative framework for health care services, an improvement over the existing hospitals and fee-for-service to physicians system which currently operates in most areas of this country.

After a slow start, the group practice system has finally gained considerable acceptance by both consumers and providers in the United States. The number of such groups has increased from 1,550 in 1959 to 6,200 in 1969, while the number of physicians practicing in in groups increased from 28,400 in 1965 to 40,000 in 1969, representing about one-fifth of all physicians in the United States engaged in patient care. These statistics point toward the growing awareness on the part of both consumers and providers of the advantages to be gained by sharing such resources as laboratories, technology, technicians, nurses, and other personnel and equipment, resulting in maximizing both the effectiveness and the efficiency of the providers' services while simultaneously providing them with the opportunity to practice more contemporary forms of medicine and enjoy a more satisfactory mode of life.

However, while the main benefits thus far in group practice have accrued to the providers and to groups as a whole, the individual consumer probably has not experienced such impressive results. Frequently, the individual consumer has not received the benefits of reduced medical costs. Many groups include only those persons who have organized on the bases of some common professional, economic and intellectual interests, and are not set up to meet the diversified needs of a diversified clientele.

Health Maintenance Organizations

Within the framework of group practice, the most efficient and effective organization in operation today in the United States is probably the health maintenance organization (HMO).

The full advantages to the patient are realized when group practice is linked with prepayment and thus associated with a subscribing population or clientele. Prepaid comprehensive group care is not new. Its beginnings trace back to the Community Hospital of Elk City, Oklahoma, in the late 1920s. Several plans have developed into large-scale operations, in part through the stimulus of consumer groups, labor unions and government employees. In 1970, the Kaiser Foundation Health Plans of Northern and Southern California and Oregon had 962,000, 900,000 and 145,000 members respectively; the Health Insurance Plan of Greater New York 780,000; Group Health Cooperative of Puget Sound 136,000; and Group Health Association of the District of Columbia 75,500. Approximately seven million people are now covered by such prepayment plans (Table 8-3).

Health maintenance organizations provide a distinctive focus for delivering health service. They involve two basic attributes: bringing together a comprehensive range of medical services in a single organization, assuring consumers of convenient access to all of them; and providing needed services for a fixed contract fee which is paid in advance by all subscribers. These organizations can and do take on a variety of forms, names and sponsors, being associated with medical schools, hospitals, groups of physicians' offices and places of employment.

All HMOs have the following principles in common: they are organized systems of health care which accept the responsibility of providing or otherwise assuring the delivery of an agreed-upon set of comprehensive health maintenance and treatment services for a voluntarily controlled group of persons in a geographic area, and they are reimbursed through a prenegotiated and fixed periodic payment made by or on behalf of each person or family unit enrolled in the plan.

Whatever form they take, HMOs all have the following features in common:

- Fees are prepaid, usually set on an annual basis.
- The HMO guarantees to deliver to the subscriber a comprehensive set of medical services.
- The HMO places emphasis on health maintenance (prevention and early detection of disease) and seeks reasonable alternatives to inpatient services.

HMOs differ from traditional health delivery and financing systems in several important ways. Under traditional systems, doctors and hospitals are paid, in effect, on a piecework basis. The more illnesses they treat and the more services they render, the more income they earn. As such, it is alleged that there is no economic incentive for them to concentrate on keeping people healthy. In health maintenance plans, a fixed price contract for comprehensive care covers all costs and reverses this illogical economic incentive so that income grows not with number of days a person is

Table 8-3. HMOs and HMO Enrollments, 1973-1978[a]

	Prototype HMOs		*New HMOs*		*All HMOs*		*Federally Funded HMOs[b]*	
Year	*No.*	*Enrollment (millions)*	*No.*	*Enrollment (millions)*	*No.*	*Enrollment (millions)*	*No.*	*Enrollment (millions)*
1973	33	5.0	27	0.1	60	5.1	–	–
1974		5.4	67	0.4	100	5.8	30	0.3
1975		5.8	134	1.5	167	7.4	50	1.1
1976		6.3	227	3.5	260	9.8	70	2.6
1977		6.8	347	6.5	380	13.3	90	4.8
1978		7.4	493	10.1	526	17.5	110	7.7

[a]Fiscal year data.

[b]Included in "New HMOs."

Source: HSMHA, Excerpts of briefing document on HMO movement prepared by Health Maintenance Organization Service, 1972.

sick but with the number of days he is well. HMOs therefore have a strong financial interest in preventing illness and in treating it in its early stages, thereby promoting a thorough recovery and preventing any reoccurrence. An HMO guarantees to deliver medical services to its subscribers. Most conventional health insurance plans provide patients with money to pay for care and leave them to seek care on their own. When an HMO guarantees to deliver comprehensive medical services, it means that it will provide all the care a family or individual needs, including what doctors call primary care (family doctor care), emergency care, acute inpatient care, and inpatient and outpatient care.

Table 8-4. Estimated Costs and Benefits From Federal Investment in the HMO Demonstration Program

Program Year[a]	*Proposed Direct Federal Support (Cumulative in millions)*	*Projected Savings in National Health Care Expenditures (Cumulative in millions)*
1974	$ 60	$ 12
1975	134	57
1976	239	162
1977	373	357
1978	528	660

[a]Fiscal year data.

Source: HSMHA, Excerpts of briefing document on HMO movement prepared by Health Maintenance Organization Service, 1972.

Conclusions

There is no doubt that the health maintenance organization goes a long way to alleviate problems in the delivery of health services in the United States. Its experience of 40 years demonstrates this. Its positive focus on preventive care rather than negative treatment of illness, moreover, reverses what was heretofore an illogical goal of medicine. Economic incentive on the part of providers based on maintaining good health in consumers provides a more positive approach and better reinforces professional goals and ethics than does crisis-oriented treatment of the sick, where profit increases with severity of illness.

Because HMOs efficiently organize family physicians, specialists and supporting personnel on an integrated team, and because medical care is prepaid, they are able to provide covered families with comprehensive medical services—preventive and therapeutic—of uniformly high quality. At the same time, they have succeeded in keeping rising costs of family medical care within reasonable limits (Table 8-4). A recent actuarial study found the premium a patient would pay for a commercial health insurance plan which encompassed all of an HMOs benefits would cost an average 27 percent more for individuals and 54 percent more for families than what was paid by the HMO subscribers. Other research findings point out that people are receiving high quality care for approximately 25 to 33 percent less cost than traditional systems and that patients in the HMO system are hospitalized for shorter periods of time.

Although originally regarded with suspicion by conservative members of the medical profession, it is becoming increasingly apparent that group practice represents a practical and desirable approach to health care needs.

With all their advantages, however, HMOs represent only a bold first step in the direction of social medicine, offering a compromise to consumers and providers which is apparently more acceptable, at least to the providers, than a complete national insurance program, or socialized medicine. The HMO, like socialized medicine, performs the following major function which represents an improvement over the status quo—it brings together a comprehensive range of medical services in a single organization, thereby assuring patients of convenient access to all of them. Unlike socialized medicine, the HMO provides needed services for a fixed contract fee which is paid in advance by all subscribers. However, fees vary somewhat, and benefits, services and facilities are not uniform from one HMO to another. The primary advantage of the HMO is in terms of increased value of services a consumer receives for the health dollar through incentives for providing better preventive care and greater efficiency.

The growth in numbers and enrollments in HMOs has been appreciable, but total enrollment is expected to be less than 18 million of the more than 225 million population forecast for 1978 (Table 8-3).

HMOs represent a milestone in health care in the United States, and will remain important. They offer the public an alternative to national health insurance rather than just a compromise step between the two extremes—the traditional fee-for-service system and socialized medicine. Socialized medicine, however, would not only provide all the benefits of HMOs but would provide more of them, more rapidly, in both the short and long terms. Moreover, these benefits, services and facilities would be guaranteed to all consumers at less cost, or possibly no cost. Still more advantageously, such a system would provide the full range of facilities and services to all consumers throughout the country in a uniformly available and accessible manner, a goal which multistructural and multiform HMOs probably could never attain. In these and other matters, a national health insurance system would come closest to providing the most efficient method of delivery of health care services, more rapidly, than would the HMO system. By the mid-1970s, in fact, many health professionals saw HMOs as a stop-gap solution until the passage of a comprehensive national health insurance system.

Summary and Recommendations

From the preceding discussion of integrated systems and from surveys made of the development of these systems in the United States, the following conclusions and recommendations have been derived. First, group practice generally facilitates the provision of better quality medical care. Second, group practice can be a mechanism for quality control in the health care delivery system. And third, the federal government's present system of payment for medical care with little or no regard for its quality—especially under Medicare and Medicaid—constitutes a deterrent to the development and use of group practice.

In this respect, the following recommendations are made. To achieve a national health care system that stresses prevention as well as cure, financing should be based on prepayment for an essential set of benefits. Health insurance programs that require a basic level of protection should be made available to all Americans regardless of their income, age or other conditions. This protection should be continuous, so that treatment and care will not be delayed, foregone or deferred because of inability to pay. Priority should be assigned to making insurance available to all, so that upon inauguration of the program all benefits can be provided promptly within the resource limits available. The health care delivery system should be restructured to achieve a national system that stresses prevention as well as cure, so that financing is based on prepayment for an essential set of benefits. To the maximum extent feasible, providers of care should be paid in accordance with fees and charges fixed in advance by agreements and related to a budget that reflects efficient organization and procedures. In this regard, the application of the concept of the health maintenance organization represents an efficient response to such a prepayment system. Provision should be made for diverse sponsorship by both profit and nonprofit groups providing quality care. Inducements and incentives should encourage participation in health maintenance organizations by subscribers and staff, but participation should be entirely voluntary. HMOs should develop broad benefits and serve a cross section, both socioeconomic and racial, of all people in their areas wishing to join. Impediments to the formation of new comprehensive delivery systems by archaic legislation and rulings must be eliminated.

Wherever they exist, the presently authorized comprehensive health planning organizations should be converted by order of the Secretary of Health, Education and Welfare into regional health service agencies. Such agencies should be established for all health service regions which lack them. Their governing boards should be appointed initially by the secretary. Their powers should be augmented to include responsibility for planning facilities and resources, conducting reviews of those presently existing and developing priorities for improvements. They should have authority to delegate tasks to other planning agencies and to assume the planning functions of agencies that are performing inadequately. They should be empowered to encourage, support and authorize organizations to develop comprehensive health maintenance programs according to approved guidelines and standards for better service and lower costs.

The health maintenance organization is based on prepayment and undertakes relatively complete and continuous care for a subscribing clientele or population. Among the many accomplishments of existing health maintenance organizations are striking reductions in the utilization of inpatient care, as well as improved use of manpower and more complete care at an economical cost to subscribers. Comprehensive prepaid plans have brought more competition into health services. These new organizations should operate side by side and compete with conventional practice in the interest of improving the operations of both systems. The health maintenance organization can thus serve a vital role in strengthening the present delivery system and stimulating its reform.

While health maintenance organizations go a long way toward restructuring an archaic health care delivery system in the United States to maximize benefits to all consumers and providers, the writer feels that these organizations and related attempts are only stop-gap methods. The obvious solution seems to be a system of national health insurance or social medicine comparable to that of other countries. The writer looks on the effort of HMOs and HMO-type programs as acceptable substitutes to the providers and to insurance companies, who accrue more advantages from them than do the consumers in the continuum toward a national health insurance program. In the United States it is the providers, not the consumers, who are unable to accept the social medicine concept. HMOs have been set up by the federal government, which bears an increasing burden of the costs of health care in this country and justifiably has an interest in the restructuring of the health care delivery system, as an acceptable substitute to social medicine. It comes at a time when the public is not yet ready to accept what seems to be so radical a move, but which ultimately must be the outcome of all this interest, debate, legislation and appropriation.

BIBLIOGRAPHY

American Hospital Association. *The 1972 AHA Guide to the Health Care Field.* Chicago: American Hospital Association, 1972.

American Medical Association. *Guidelines for Community Health Programs.* Chicago: American Medical Association, 1972.

——, Center for Health Services, Research and Development. "Distribution of Physicians in the U.S., 1971." Chicago: American Medical Association, 1971.

——, Council on Health Manpower. *Expanding the Supply of Health Services in the 1970s.* Report of the National Congress on Health Manpower. Chicago: American Medical Association, 1970.

——, Department of Community Health. "Statement on Health Planning." Chicago: American Medical Association, 1971.

——, Division of Medical Practice. "Contract Practice: Health Maintenance Organizations; HMOs as Seen by the AMA: An Analysis." Chicago: American Medical Association, 1972.

Collen, Morris F. *A Ten Year Progress Report: Medical Methods Research.* Oakland: The Permanente Medical Group and the Kaiser Foundation Research Institute, 1970.

deVise, Pierre. "Consumers Revolt Against Medical Dictatorship." *Hospitals Journal of the American Medical Association,"* February 1, 1971, pp. 51–55.

——. "Health Maintenance Organizations: New Cures for Our Failing National Health?" Working Paper IV–19. Chicago: Chicago Regional Hospital Study, November 1972.

——. *Misused and Misplaced Hospitals and Doctors: A Locational Analysis of the Urban Health Care Crisis.* Commission on College Geography, Resource Paper No. 22. Washington D.C.: Association of American Geographers, 1973.

Earickson, Robert A. *The Spatial Behavior of Hospital Patients: A Behavioral Approach to Spatial Interaction in Metropolitan Chicago.* University of Chicago, Department of Geography Research Paper No. 124. Chicago: University of Chicago, Department of Geography, 1970.

Faltermayer, Edmund K. "Better Care at Less Cost Without Miracles." *Fortune,* January 1970, Reprint.

Feldstein, Martin S. "The Rising Cost of Hospital Care." Published for the National Center for Health Services Research and Development. Washington, D.C.: Information Resources Press, 1971.

Green, J. "Marketing Prepaid Group Practice." Alternative Delivery Systems Conference.

Chicago: Blue Cross Association, October 1, 1971.

"HMOs: New Contender for the Prescription Dollar." *Drug Topics* Volume 117, Number 18 (September 17, 1973), pp. 22-23.

Kaiser, Edgar F. "One Industry's Involvement in Health Care." *Proceedings.* The 80th Annual Meeting of the Association of American Medical Colleges, October 31, 1969. *Journal of Medical Education,* Volume 45 (February 1970), pp. 88-95.

Keene, Clifford H. "Responsibilities in a System of Health Care." *The University of Michigan Medical Center Journal* Volume 37, Number 4 (1971), pp. 172-177.

MacLeod, Gordon K. and Jeffrey A. Prussin. "The Continuing Evolution of Heath Maintenance Organizations." *New England Journal of Medicine* Volume 288 (March 11, 1973), pp. 439-443.

"Message from the President of the United States Transmitting the State of the Union Message."—The Address of the President of the United States, 91st Congress, 1st Session. Washington, D.C.: 1965.

Meyers, Beverlee A. "Health Maintenance Organizations: Objectives and Issues." US Department of Health, Education and Welfare Publication No. (HSM) 73-13002. Washington, D.C.: US Government Printing Office, 1973.

Morrill, Richard L. and Robert A. Earickson. "Locational Efficiency of Chicago Hospitals: An Experimental Model." *Health Services Research* Volume 4, Number 2 (Summer 1969).

National Advisory Commission on Health Manpower. *Report.* Washington, D.C.: National Advisory Commission on Health Manpower, November 1967.

Palmer, Walter K. "How the Kaiser Foundation Medical Care Program Works." Oakland: Kaiser Research Foundation, n.d.

—— "Projecting Capital and Manpower Needs as Related to Enrollments Projects." In *Health Maintenance Organizations: Proceedings of a Conference 1972.* Medical Group Management Association, 1972. pp. 42-48.

Phelen, Jerry, Robert Erickson, and Scott Fleming. "Group Practice Prepayment: An Approach to Delivering Organized Health Services." *Law and Contemporary Problems* Volume 35, Number 4 (Autumn 1970), pp. 797-816.

Pyle, Gerald. *Heart Disease, Cancer and Stroke in Chicago: A Geographical Analysis with Facilities Plan for 1980.* University of Chicago, Department of Geography Research Paper No. 134. Chicago: University of Chicago, Department of Geography, 1969.

Roemer, Milton I. et al. "Health Insurance Plans." In *Studies in Organization Diversity.* Los Angeles: University of California School of Public Health, 1970.

Saward, Ernest W. "The Relevance of the Kaiser-Permanente Experience to the Health Services of the Eastern United States." *Bulletin,* New York Academy of Medicine, Volume 46, Number 9 (September 1970), pp. 707-717.

Somers, Anne R. "What Price Comprehensive Care." *Architecture and Environmental Health* Volume 17 (July 1968), pp. 6-20.

Spivak, Jonathan. "Medical Care—A Personal Experience." *The Wall Street Journal* (September 26, 1973), p. 1.

Tunley, Raul. "Better Medical Care at Less Cost is Possible." *The American Legion Magazine,* August 1970. Reprint.

US Department of Health, Education and Welfare. "Cohort Mortality and Survivorship: United States Death Registration States, 1900-1968." Series 3, Number 16, DHEW Publication No. (HSM) 73-1400. Washington, D.C.: US Government Printing Office, November 1972.

——. "Computer Simulation of Hospital Discharges." Series 2, Number 13. Washington, D.C.: US Government Printing Office, February 1966.

——. "Current Estimates from the Health Interview Survey: United States - 1972." Series 10, Number 85. DHEW Publication Number (HRA) 74-1512. Washington, D.C.: US Government Printing Office, September 1973.

——. "Expenditures for Personal Health Services: National Trends and Variations: 1953-1970. DHEW Publication Number (HRA) 74-3105. Washington, D.C.: US Government Printing Office, October 1973.

——. "Health Characteristics by Geographic Region: Large Metropolitan Areas and Other Places of Residence, United States 1969-1970." Series 10, Number 86. DHEW Publication Number (HRA) 74-1513. Washington, D.C.: US Government Printing Office, January 1974.

——. "Health Manpower in the United

States, 1965–1967." Series 14, Number 1. Washington, D.C.: US Government Printing Office, November 1968.

——. "Health Service Use: National Trends and Variations, 1953-1971." DHEW Publication Number (HSM) 73–3004. Washington, D.C.: October 1972.

——. "Infant Mortality Rates: Socioeconomic Factors, United States." Series 22, Number 14. DHEW Publication Number (HSM) 72-1045. Washington, D.C.: US Government Printing Office, March 1972.

——. "Mortality Trends: Age, Color, and Sex: United States, 1950–1969." Series 20, Number 15. DHEW Publication Number (HRA) 74–1852. Washington, D.C.: US Government Printing Office, November 1973.

——. "Mortality Trends for Leading Causes of Death: United States, 1950–1969." Series 20, Number 16. DHEW Publication Number (HRA) 74–1853. Washington, D.C.: US Government Printing Office, March 1974.

——. "Patient Charges in Short-Stay Hospitals in the United States, 1968–1970." Series 13, Number 15. DHEW Publication Number (HRA) 74–1766. Washington, D.C.: US Government Printing Office, May 1974.

——. "Personal Out-of-Pocket Health Expenses, United States, 1970." Series 10, Number 91. DHEW Publication Number (HRA) 74–1518. Washington, D.C.: US Government Printing Office, June 1974.

——. "Utilization of Short-Stay Hospitals, Summary of Nonmedical Statistics, United States, 1972." Series 13, Number 19. DHEW Publication Number (HRA) 75–1770. Washington, D.C.: US Government Printing Office, June 1975.

Vohs, James A., Richard V. Anderson and Ruth Strauss. "Critical Issues in HMO Strategy." *New England Journal of Medicine* Volume 286 (May 18, 1972), pp. 1-7.

Williams, Josephine J. *Family Medical Care Under Three Types of Health Insurance.* New York: Foundation on Employee Health, Medical Care, and Welfare Inc., 1962.

Chapter 9

The Federal Open Space Programs: Impacts and Imperatives

Rutherford H. Platt
University of Massachusetts (Amherst)

THE HISTORICAL SETTING: US LAND POLICIES IN REVIEW

The Federal Role

The role of the federal government of the United States with respect to the planning and usage of the nation's land surface is anomalous. On the one hand, of the approximately 2.2 billion acres of land and water within the territory of the United States, Congress exercises direct jurisdiction as to the planning and regulation of land use over only 43,148 acres—the District of Columbia. Since authority over other land is not explicitly granted to Congress under the US Constitution, the Tenth Amendment has long been considered to reserve such jurisdiction for the sovereign states. And by virtue of the nearly unanimous delegation of this power by each state, the effective power to plan and regulate the use of land in the United States lies within the lowest level of government—either municipal or county.

On the other hand, such a description of the federal role is obviously inadequate to characterize the actual importance of Congress in the determination of land use in the United States. For instance, the United States government through its various departments and agencies owns outright approximately 700 million acres or one-third of the nation's surface area. As to this empire of largely undeveloped and remote land, state and local policies fade into legal fictions; the undisputed sovereign of the public domain is the federal government which theoretically represents the interests of the people of the United States.

As to the other two-thirds of the nation's territory which the federal government does not own, the influence of Congress and more recently the executive branch in the determination of land use is far more profound and pervasive than the doctrine of state sovereignty would seem to admit. Much of this influence historically has been exerted in the disposition of land once included in the public domain. In 1850 the nation owned 1.4 billion acres, twice the size of its present holdings. In the past 120 years an area equal in size to the entire public domain of today has been transferred from federal ownership to the states, to railroads, to settlers, to speculators, to colleges and most recently to local governments. The statutes and directives which implemented these dispositions, needless to say, substantially determined the eventual usage of lands so affected.

Beyond the disposition of lands "with strings attached," the federal government today through its myriad programs of domestic public works and subsidies exerts influence over both public and private land use decisions in ways which mock the idea of absolute ownership of private property itself. Far from the eighteenth century notion of a "bundle of intrinsic rights" which the landowner holds sacred against all but the most dire of public demands, property in the United States today possesses or lacks value as a direct function of public decisions. And of the latter, the local regulatory function is often eclipsed by the role of federal programs having a direct and massive impact upon the value and utility of land, such as the reclamation program, the Tennessee Valley Authority and its analogues, the rural electrification program, and the federal highway trust fund. In the metropolitan context, perhaps no more profound determinants of urban land use patterns could be cited than the Federal Housing Administration home mortgage insurance program and the interstate highway system.

To recognize the omnipresence of the federal government in the contemporary land use decision process is scarcely to discern any consistent policy or objective towards which federal authority has been directed, whether for good or evil. Indeed, for 200 years the only consistency in federal policies and actions with respect to land may be found in their inconsistency. To cite a familiar example, between 1944 and 1964, roughly 22.5 million acres were brought into production through federally assisted reclamation programs. During much of the same period, the Department of Agriculture spent about $4 billion each year to *remove* agricultural land from production. In 1968 President Johnson declared a national goal to build or renovate 26 million dwelling units during the succeeding decade. In the three years following 1968 the urban renewal program displaced 55,000 families eligible for public housing–i.e., too poor for private housing–yet only 12,000 new units of public housing were completed in connection with urban renewal projects.

The promulgation of conflicting policies and programs is, of course, not merely a question of governmental ineptitude. As a pluralistic entity representing a highly variegated society, Congress must weigh mutually inconsistent interests, viewpoints and pressures. Occasionally, it manages to decide in favor of one side or the other. Frequently, however, it attempts to accommodate both interests at the price of satisfying neither. An example of the latter was the approval given in 1966 by Congress to *both* a federal port *and* a national park, each seeking exclusive dominance of the remaining Indiana Dunes shoreline on Lake Michigan. A historical review of some of the landmarks in federal land use policy reveals the chronic nature of this process of selection and accommodation, from the origins of the nation down to and including the open space programs which are the subject of this monograph.

Policies and Counterpolicies: A Mixed Legacy

Perhaps the greatest accomplishment of the confederation and the most significant event in the history of US public land law was the Land Ordinance of 1785. If for no other reason, the ordinance is renowned for establishing the federal land survey system under which most of the nation's territory west of the original colonies was measured into townships and square mile sections. This pre-eminent feature has obscured the importance of the ordinance as a declaration of national policy, toward the accomplishment of which the land survey system was merely an accessory. The ordinance was precipitated by the cession to the nation of claims by several colonies to land lying west of their settled territories. The issue was thus presented as to what to do with this incipient public domain.

Between the two polar alternatives–retention or disposition–the Land Ordinance of 1785 and its immediate successor, the Northwest Ordinance of 1787, clearly favored the latter. According to Carstenson, revulsion against a feudal lord-tenant system and sentiment in favor of Jefferson's "nation of farmers" apparently was persuasive.

While disposal was a generally agreed-upon public land policy during the first century of the Republic, the subsidiary questions of "disposal to whom and for what purpose?" were to complicate matters from the 1785 ordinance onward. The debate, as crystallized in the deliberations of the Continental Congress and of Washington's administration, focused upon two alternative philosophies: revenue and settlement. According to proponents of the former, such as Alexander Hamilton, public land should be viewed as an economic asset to be sold for valuable consideration so as to replenish the depleted national treasury. Proponents of settlement, naturally including Jefferson, argued that the actual value of the land would be realized not through its initial selling price but instead through its contribution to the national wealth from its productivity and opportunity provided to the common man to farm his own land. The settlement advocates therefore urged selling at a minimal price pursuant to a precise survey with the stipulation that the purchaser record his title, occupy and improve the land. (The "settlement school" was further divided, according to Treat, between advocates of the New England pattern whereby towns were settled incrementally on the edge of the already consolidated territory versus the more expansive southern practice of loosely claiming to occupy large tracts of land with only the crudest of surveys and allocation of land for schools and churches.)

The Land Ordinance of 1785 reflected a compromise between these conflicting proposals. The settlement objective, particularly on the New England pattern, was served by the requirement that land be precisely surveyed prior to sale; that it be available in parcels of 640 acres, reasonably suited to settlement by a family or group of families; and that the sixteenth section be reserved for school purposes. On the other hand, the revenue objective was served in the requirement that land be sold at public auction with a "substantial" minimum price of $1 per acre plus survey costs (raised in 1796 to $2 per acre).

The policy of selling public lands prevailed generally until the Civil War. Free grants of land were occasionally made in special circumstances such as to veterans of the War of 1812. Beginning in 1850, however, vast grants were authorized to railroads and canal companies in the interest of "opening the West". Conveyed in a checkerboard plan, the grant of alternate sections to private companies was intended to render the retained sections more valuable for future sale by the government.

In 1862, the free soil movement accomplished the final overturn of the policy established in 1785. The Homestead Act of that year authorized the granting of fee simple title to 160 acres free of cost to settlers who occupied the land for five years. In the same year, Congress passed the Morrill Act establishing the "land grant college" concept and authorizing disposal of additional land for the purpose of education.

By the late nineteenth century land was moving out of the public domain at an incredible pace. According to Paul Wallace Gates, approximate dispositions of land for specific purposes between the Civil War and the present included:

- 125 million acres to railroads
- 140 million acres to the states
- 100 million acres of Indian lands sold publicly
- 100 million acres of other lands sold publicly
- 300 million acres granted under the Homestead Act

The legal transfer of 700 million acres from federal to other hands was accompanied by a concomitant "policy" of laissez faire toward the exploitation of natural resources on both conveyed and retained lands—the notorious "barbecue" of the nation's animal, vegetable and mineral wealth. As recounted in Stewart Udall's book *The Quiet Crisis,* the excessive and self-defeating practices of the midnineteenth century inspired the intellectual foundation for what later would be the assertion of a counter-policy to disposal and exploitation—namely, retention and conservation. The works of Thoreau, Marsh, Emerson, Parkman, Bartram and Audubon were, and remain today, profoundly influention in this regard.

The period of the Civil War, a watershed in public land law as in other respects, witnessed the first overt federal act in recognition of the conservation ethic. This was the transfer of the site of Yosemite Park to the state of California to be maintained for public enjoyment in accordance with the recommendations of Frederick Law Olmsted. Yosemite was later recovered from California to become a national park in 1905. In 1869, Ulysses S. Grant signed a bill designating the site of Yellowstone Park to be "dedicated and set aside as a public park or pleasuring ground for the benefit and enjoyment of the people . . .", the first national park to be created directly out of the public domain.

In 1891 Congress enacted its most significant antidisposal measure in terms of acreage affected, authorizing the president to "withdraw" certain forests from active lumbering and to retain them as "forest reservations." Under this statute, Presidents Harrison, Cleveland and Roosevelt set aside 132 million acres, the bulk of the 168 million acres which existed in national forests as of 1968.

While of fundamental importance in the history of federal policy respecting the use of land, the 1891 act did not represent a thorough-going departure of a "swing of the pendulum" from prior practices. Rather, as incisively characterized by Gates, the old and the new policies were to co-exist unhappily thenceforward.

> [The Act of 1891] was the first fundamental break with the underlying philosophy of our land system—the desire to dispose of the lands and hasten their settlement. The conservationists had now convinced the country that a part of our natural resources must be retained in public ownership and preserved for the future. Unfortunately, conservation, when first adopted, was embedded in an outworn *laissez faire* land system of a previous age, just as the free homestead plan had been superimposed upon a land system designed to produce revenue. In both cases the old and the new clashed with disastrous results. [P. 340]

The accuracy of this analysis is amply borne out in the introduction to the 1968 Report of the Public Land Law Review Commission where the following "forked tongue" statement summarizes the commission's conclusions:

> . . . [we] urge reversal of the policy that the United States should dispose of the so-called unappropriated public domain lands. But we also reject the idea that merely because these lands are owned by the Federal Government, they should all remain forever in Federal ownership. [P. 1]

Just as the disposal philosophy has been internally in disagreement over the question of revenue versus free land for settlement, so too the retention or conservation school of thought rapidly developed its opposing wings—preservation versus recreation. Following closely upon the establishment of the national forest system, the National Park Service Act of 1916 provided impetus to the latter debate. The national park system, which today includes some 33 million acres (as compared with 700 million acres in the total public domain), was clearly intended to provide benefits to the general public in terms of accessibility, recreation and general use, which were not foremost purposes of the national forest concept. At the same time, national parks were deliberately carved out of the public domain, and sometimes out of national forests, on a basis of superior natural qualities or scenic magnificence. Fundamental precepts of resource management and the National Park Service Act itself dictate that the qualities for which each park site was selected must be zealously preserved, or the nation will have squandered the very choicest of its natural treasures in the process of appreciating them. As stated in a 1972 article in *The New York Times*:

> From the beginning of the park system just a century ago, there has been a classic built-in dichotomy—faced by parks all over the work—between the objectives of preserving the parks intact and making them available for public enjoyment. [Hill, P. 3]

One response to the dilemma has been the establishment, particularly during the last decade, of new categories of national outdoor recreation facilities. On the one extreme, the Wilderness Act of 1964 authorized a national widerness preservation system to consist of tracts selected from the public domain to be managed for maintenance of natural conditions and minimizing of public access and use. Akin to this concept is the national wildlife refuge system, comprising over 26 million acres in all states. Somewhat less austere in purpose, the Wild and Scenic Rivers Act of 1968 authorized acquisition and regulation of appropriate stretches of undisturbed streams for peservation and limited access recreation.

On the other end of the spectrum, emphasizing mass usage over preservation per se, a national trails system has been inaugurated including both urban and remote area pathways. National recreation areas have been authorized to provide regional recreation opportunities on public domain lands. Finally, new national parks are being created within metropolitan areas, as at the "gateways" to New York and San Francisco harbors, and the Indiana Dunes National Lakeshore.

Urban Parks: The Nonfederal Sector

The "gateway" national parks represent a sharp break with tradition in recreation planning and management; until the decade of the 1960s the provision of open space and recreation within urban and metropolitan areas was entirely a nonfederal matter. In the absence of even state involvement in metropolitan recreation, local governments until recently were on their own.

Before the Civil War, urban parks in American cities were virtually nonexistent, as were legal mechanisms with which to achieve them. According to Allison Dunham: "If land use was important in the early 19th Century the only significant questions were those of the law of waste by a life tenant and the law of emblements." Even where specific provision was made for the retention of urban park space—as in the 1811 plan for Manhattan Island which included seven squares and a parade ground—most of the proposed open space was soon usurped by buildings. In Cincinnati, Louisville and St. Louis, according to Richard C. Wade, early attempts to retain parks through planning were likewise unsuccessful. Even the town greens and commons in New England were gradually encroached upon until protected by law for public recreation in the midnineteenth century.

The problem, then as now, was the failure to anticipate the future growth of cities, both spatially and in population. By the time the need for retaining certain tracts as open space was perceived, they were already engulfed in city development and consequently were too expensive to purchase for public use. The classic exceptions to this dreary rule have been Central Park in New York and the Olmsted-inspired regional park systems surrounding such cities as Boston, Cleveland and Chicago. Central Park, established in 1856, represented a degree of public foresight and level of municipal investment probably unparalleled before or since. Consisting of 770 acres of "wasteland" lying well beyond the existing built-up area of New York, Central Park required the literary skills of William Cullen Bryant and the landscaping genius of Frederick Law Olmsted for its achievement. By 1884, according to Chadwick, its entire cost to New York City of $44 million, including land, improvements and interest, had been exceeded by the rise in value of surrounding building sites.

The neglect of the first half of the nineteenth century was succeeded by the "golden age" of urban park development in the second half. As influenced by the English landscape plans of Olmsted and the "city beautiful" motif of the Chicago Exposition of 1893, public support for the creation of urban parks had perhaps never been greater. To a considerable extent, the metropolitan open space resources of today are the products of that era. According to Clawson, Held, and Stoddard, of 103 cities having a population of more than 100,000 in 1950, 66 had gained at least one park by 1880.

The late nineteenth century provided not only many of today's urban park facilities but also the legal mechanisms for the provision of open space on a wider geographical basis than the boundaries of the central city. In 1893, the Massachusetts General Court created the Metropolitan Parks Commission (later merged into the Metropolitan District Commission) with authority to establish a regional park system for Greater Boston. Two years later, New Jersey enacted legislation which permitted Essex County to establish the nation's first county park commission. The "special district" approach and the county geographical unit were then combined in a 1913 Illinois statute authorizing the creation of "county forest preserve districts."

Both local and county park efforts flourished between 1925 and 1940, as indicated in Table 9-1. The Depression was a period of expansion for park systems at all levels (including state parks for the first time). Declining land values evidently encouraged acquisition and public works programs supplied unlimited manpower for construction of facilities.

The high-water mark for metropolitan outdoor recreation was perhaps 1940. In that year city and county parks reached an average of 8.5 acres per thousand urban residents, with 25 percent of cities exceeding the National Recreation Association standard of ten acres per 1000 persons. More recent national averages are not available, but a 1968 National League of Cities sample of 15 cities yielded an average of 7.3 acres per thousand.

World War II curtailed both the usage of existing parks and the creation of new ones. Table 9-1 indicates that local park acreage actually declined for the decade 1940-1950 even as postwar suburban developments swelled metropolitan population by more than 20 percent during the decade. Central cities, facing little further growth, rested on their laurels; new bedroom suburbs, occupied with other concerns, looked to the central cities, to the hinterland and to private country clubs to satisfy their recreational needs.

It is axiomatic that the automobile dominated the recreation habits of the decade of the 1950s. The impact of the private car together with construction of new turnpikes and interstate highways is illustrated in Figure 9-1.

Table 9-1. Municipal and County Parks, 1925–1965

Year	*Agencies Reporting*	*Areas (cumulative)*	*Acreage (cumulative)*
Municipal Agencies (including local special districts)			
1925[a]	1,112	NA	248,627
1930	900	11,686	308,804
1935	1,200	15,105	381,496
1940	1,465.	19,336	444,120
1950[b]	NA	NA	431,000
1960[c]	2,371	22,835[d]	690,636[d]
1965	2,371	26,360	805,336
County and Regional Agencies			
1925[a]	32	135	67,464
1930	73	415	108,484
1935	77	526	159,261
1940	152	779	197,349
1950[b]	NA	NA	313,000
1960[c]	325	3,049[d]	470,366[d]
1965	325	4,149	691,042
Total (municipal plus county)			
1965	2,696	4,625	1,496,378

[a]Years 1925 through 1940 derived from: *Municipal and County Parks in the United States, 1940* (New York: National Recreation Association, 1940), Graphs I and VIII.

[b]Estimate by Marion Clawson in Clawson, Held and Stoddard, *Land for the Future* (Baltimore: The Johns Hopkins Press for Resources for the Future, 1960), p. 154.

[c]Years 1960 and 1965 derived from: *Recreation and Park Yearbook, 1966* (Washington, D.C.: National Recreation and Park Association, 1967), Tables 25 and 26 (1960 computed by subtracting Table 26 from Table 25).

[d]This figure in part reflects more inclusive scope of 1960–1965 NRPA survey than earlier inventories.

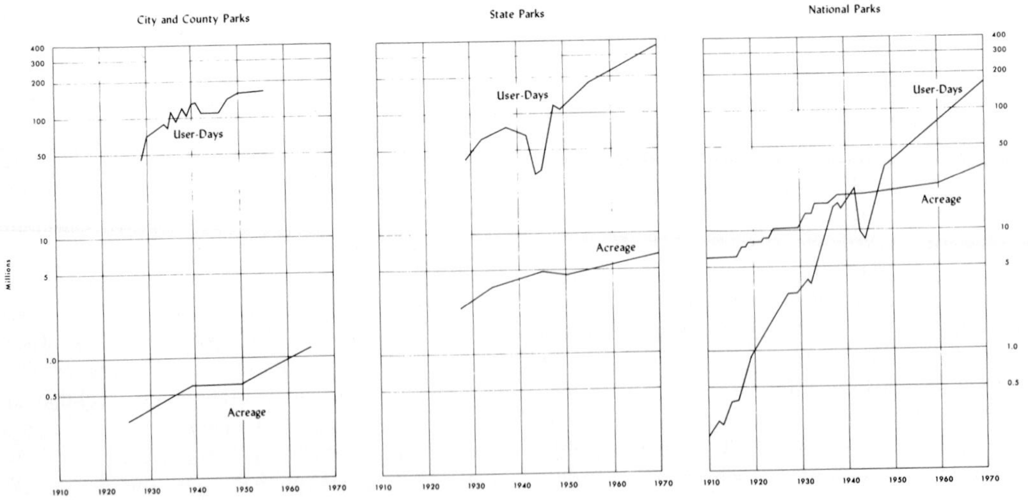

Figure 9-1. National, State and Local Parks: Acreage and Attendance, 1910–1970 (After Clawson, 1963, Figures 4 and 6)

Visits to national parks rose from 33 million user days in 1950 to 79 million in 1960 (and doubled again by 1970); state park attendence rose from 114 million in 1950 to 259 million in 1960. While comparable data for local and county parks is notoriously unreliable due to the difficulty of counting users, it appears that attendence at such facilities leveled off as the popularity of more distant locations increased.

At first glance, Table 9-1 and Figure 9-1 appear to indicate a major increase in metropolitan acreage during the decade 1950-1960. Much of the difference, however, is explained by the inclusion of more management units and kinds of facilities in the 1960-1965 surveys by the National Recreation and Parks Association. As Clawson wrote in 1960:

> To assemble accurate data on the recreation area available for metropolitan areas is a task of no mean size; from general observations, however, it is clear that expansion of park areas in suburbs has been much less rapid than in central cities; the total situation, therefore, has worsened more than the data indicate. [P. 156.]

Furthermore, many key urban parks have been encroached upon or even eliminated by highways and other public projects; the 1971 report of the federal Council on Environmental Quality cites the loss of 22,000 acres of urban parks between 1964 and 1970.

To a significant extent, therefore, the rising demand for outdoor recreation after 1950 was met through public policies encouraging greater use of nonmetropolitan state and national parks in preference to intrametropolitan facilities. This phenomenon undoubtedly has brought joy to those who can afford it and properity to those who cater to it, but many drawbacks can be cited. One problem previously mentioned is overuse of areas primarily treasured in their unspoiled condition. Another objection of extreme current importance is that of conservation of energy.

Unquestionably, a major objection to the national policy favoring nonmetropolitan recreation is that it is inherently discriminatory. The cost of a national park visit in terms of travel, equipment and time away from work is obviously considerable. Moreover, until the 1964 US Supreme Court decision in *Heart of Atlanta Motel* v. *US,* nonwhites were not constitutionally guaranteed a right to be accommodated by restaurants and motels even if they could afford to travel. It is hardly surprising therefore that a Conservation Foundation study of national park users in 1968 found them to be predominantly white, middle income and suburban in residence.

However, the decision to embark upon a counterpolicy—namely, that the federal government deliberately seek to promote the preservation of open space in metropolitan areas—was not the result of the "wilderness ethic," energy concerns or the civil rights movement. Instead, the programs which are the subject of the remainder of this chapter arose out of intense public anguish in the late 1950s and early 1960s concerning the physical pattern of land use or misuse which characterizes our evolving metropolitan regions.

THE FEDERAL OPEN SPACE ASSISTANCE PROGRAMS

Introduction

The ambivalent nature of federal policies toward land use in the United States is well demonstrated in the creation of the Open Space Land Program of the Department of Housing and Urban Development (HUD) and to a lesser extent the Bureau of Outdoor Recreation (BOR) Land and Water Conservation Program. Both programs originated during the 1960s in response to a widespread perception of "urban sprawl," itself a direct result of other federal programs such as housing, taxation and highways. Instead of removing the source of the "evil" by modifying the latter efforts, Congress instead launched the open space programs to counteract them. By thus pitting antidevelopment measures against prodevelopment policies, the objectives of each are mutually thwarted, or at least made more expensive to accomplish.

The HUD program particularly has been conceived, administered and finally interred amid contradiction, confusion and paradox. Originally established under the auspices of urban renewal, the program has been largely effective in suburban areas. Justified simultaneously in terms of mitigating slum conditions and "shaping urban sprawl," the program has done neither. Projected for a threefold increase in funding in President Nixon's 1971

"Legacy of Parks" message to Congress, the HUD Open Space Program was frozen into oblivion in late 1972. Just as the regulations for the program were rewritten to tie open space assistance to other metropolitan goals, the program was effectively abolished.

The BOR Land and Water Conservation Program, administered by an agency specially created for the purpose and having a more specific orientation to outdoor recreation, has functioned more smoothly. However, it shares with the HUD program the unenviable role of makeweight to an overwhelming, if understated, national commitment to urban growth.

The HUD Open Space Program

Origins. The HUD Open Space Program was an outgrowth, ironically enough, of the federal government's effort to promote housing construction and community development. The National Housing Act of 1934, the organic law to which the open space program was eventually grafted, was intended to advance the national goal of "a decent home" for everyone as well as to provide jobs through encouragement of the construction industry. A corollary to this goal, expressed only in the labyrinthine regulations of the Federal Housing Administration (FHA), was that "a decent home" meant preferably a detached, single family, privately owned dwelling outside the central city. Thus, between 1934 and 1971, mortgages insured by FHA for residential construction totaled \$164 billion, representing some 10.5 million single family homes and 1.8 million apartments. The overwhelming majority of these have been located outside of central cities on land not previously used for urban purposes.

Between 1950 and 1960, the fact, if not the meaning, of urban sprawl was unmistakable. Metropolitan population of the United States increased by 26 percent, from 89 to 112 million. Of this total increase, the population of metropolitan areas living outside of the central cities (which in most cases had already ceased to grow through annexation) increased from 41 to 49 percent. By 1966 the suburban population was to exceed the central city population of the nation.

In land use terms, the impact of this redistribution of people was highly visible but difficult to quantify. The 1970 Council on Environmental Quality Report contains the estimate that one-half million acres per year are converted to urban purposes. While not enormous in relation to the total land area of the United States, the resulting "loss of open space" occurred where it would be most acutely felt—namely, in the midst of where people lived.

The years 1958-1961 produced a virtual avalanche of professional and popular literature dealing with the subject of urban growth. Major publications by Resources for the Future, the Urban Land Institute, The Editors of Fortune, The Committee for Economic Development, the Twentieth Century Fund and the New York Regional Plan Association all drew attention to the situation with varying levels of consternation.

This prologue to the "environmental awakening" of a decade later was to inspire much political rhetoric and some significant legislation. A speech by President John F. Kennedy, October 10, 1960, exemplifies the former:

> In every plan for urban redevelopment, parks and recreation must have their place. We must act to protect open spaces along our rivers, lakes and seashores and on the edges of our expanding metropolitan areas. And we must act quickly—for with every passing day, the available open spaces shrink and their cost increases. [Bureau of the Budget, 1961, p. 1.]

Pursuant to presidential suggestion, the Bureau of the Budget prepared a 1961 staff report which recommended:

> In every category of open space—recreational, conservational, residential and structural—public action to acquire or otherwise preserve increasing amounts of properly located land as needed. The pressures of increasing population and intensified use of land for recreation and other purposes will lead to more forms of urban sprawl, more urban claustrophobia and blight, and more transportation chaos, unless pressures for additional open space are met. A very rough estimate of the incremental cost of meeting the nation's needs is about *\$5 billion* at 1960 prices over and above presently projected programs. [P. 1, emphasis added]

Congress took the hint and enacted Title VII of the Housing Act of 1961. The initial authorization for open space grants was $50 million, or 1 percent of the total estimated to be needed to solve the problem.

Statutory Purposes. The Open Space Land Program (hereinafter referred to as simply the "open space program") was a functional and administrative anomaly from the very outset. Until the formation of HUD in 1965, the open space program was housed in the Urban Renewal Authority of the Housing and Home Finance Agency. Yet the statutory and administrative restraints which surrounded the program for most of its existence could scarcely have defined an instrument less useful to urban renewal. Indeed its statement of findings and purposes and its legislative history reveal a total confusion of objectives:

> (b) It is the purpose of this title to help curb urban sprawl and prevent the spread of urban blight and deterioration, to encourage more economic and desirable urban development, and to help provide necessary recreational, conservation, and scenic areas. areas . . . [Sec. 701]

The legislative history, however, makes no mention of "urban blight and deterioration" but stresses the amorphous concept of "urban shaping":

> Open space reservation is essential for healthy urban growth. Its extent and location will profoundly affect the quality of the environment of most of our people and the *shape of direction or [sic] urban development.* These in turn are principal factors in determining the economic productivity of our urban areas and also the cost of essential community facilities and services. [*U.S. Code Cong. and Admin. News*, 1961, (P.L. 87-70), p. 1973. Emphasis added]

Thus the HHFA-HUD open space program from the very outset lacked a particular mission or focus. Functionally, it was addressed to all areas of need from the inner city to the suburban fringe and beyond, and from basketball courts to "green belts." Geographically, even its supposed orientation to "urban areas" was loosely defined by statute to include:

> [Any] area which is urban in character, including those surrounding areas which in the judgment of the Administrator for an economic and socially related region, taking into consideration such factors as present and future population trends and patterns or urban growth. . . . [P.L. 87-70, Sec. 706(1).]

While vagueness as to purpose and geographical scope may be desirable from the standpoint of flexibility, enormous difficulty is presented in trying to measure the relative progress or success of the program toward achievement of its objectives. In trying to be "jack of all trades," the program may conspicuously succeed in none. Politically, this may be interpreted as failure, and therefore grounds for terminating the program. As this study will indicate, however, the real "failure" of the HUD open space program has been the unwillingness of Congress to define realizable objectives and to provide sufficient resources to achieve them. Within the statutory and fiscal context imposed upon it, the HUD program has performed as well as could be expected.

Not only were its goals vague to begin with, but they were changed frequently with passing fancy or sober reappraisal. In the 1965 amendments to the act, for instance, Mrs. Lyndon Johnson's concern with "urban beautification" found its way into the program, only to be deleted again in 1970. "Historic preservation" and "urban parks" were other 1965 additions; together with "undeveloped land," these comprised four distinct subprograms until merged in 1970.

Two years after the 1968 riots, Congress "discovered" the inner city: "(b) The Congress further finds that there is a need for the additional provision of parks and other open space in the built-up portions of urban areas *especially in low income neighborhoods and communities*" [P.L. 91-609, Sec. 401(b). emphasis added]. The statutory purpose thus came full circle to "urban blight" once again.

Administration. Four years under the Urban Renewal Administration did not orient the program to the inner city but did cast it in the urban renewal mode of operation. Unlike its BOR counterpart, the HUD program was based upon direct contact between the federal government and the applicant, be it local government, special district, county or state. In every case the burden lies with the applicant to establish eligibility for each project under the existing HUD regulations. (Ensuing discussion will use the present tense despite the "freezing" of the HUD open space program as of January 5, 1973.)

Two years is considered average time for an application to traverse the obstacle course shown in Figure 9-2. Given the precarious ecology and escalating cost of open land in urban areas, the applicant naturally wants to acquire its site as early as possible. Yet a parcel acquired before a HUD "letter of intent" is issued is not eligible for a grant. A further rule which has bedeviled many applicants is that a "letter of intent" is necessary but not sufficient: ultimate grant approval may occur many months later on the basis of available funds.

In all cases, grants are made on a reimbursement basis only. The applicant must bear the entire cost subject to eventual repayment of

DEPARTMENT OF HOUSING & URBAN DEVELOPMENT
METROPOLITAN DEVELOPMENT
OPEN SPACE LAND PROGRAM & URBAN BEAUTIFICATION PROGRAM
Project Control Card

MP-6

Date of Application

PROJECT LOCATION & DESCRIPTION

Park and recreational purposes

FISCAL YEAR
COUNTY Bristol
CONG. DIST.
S.M.S.A.
RELATED PROJ. NO.

ACTION	DATE	ACTION	DATE
Application received in R.O.		Planning review received	
Acknowledgement letter sent		Application to Relocation	
Application returned for revision		Relocation review received	
Application resubmitted		Application to Legal	
Letter of consent sent		Legal review received	
		Appraisals received	
To PFSD for site inspection		Fair market value established	
Site Inspection report received			
Application to Planning Branch		Recommendation to Washington	

NOTES
FMV-$
Program Output GP:
Acreage:
PROJECT NO.

AUTHORIZED REPRESENTATIVE
Name & Address (Zip Code)

Tel. No.
A/C

	PROJECT FUNDS					
	Federal Grant	Applicant Funds	Est. Total Proj. Costs	Reloc. Costs	Admin. Costs	NOTES
Per Application						
Per Initial Alloc. Order						
Release Date						
Alloc. Order Sgd.						
Notified Applicant						
Rec'd from Washington						
Rev. Appl. Rec'd						
Per Rev. Alloc. Order						
Rev. Alloc. Order Sgd.						
Notif. to Applicant						
Rec'd from Washington						

	Date		Date
Acquisition Info.		Extension	
Due Date		Extension	
Extension		Completed	

ACTION	DATE	ACTION	DATE	NOTES
Grant Contract to Applicant		Executed cpy to Applicant		
Returned by Applicant		Audit Requested & Rept.Rec'd		
Contract executed by ARA		Findings cleared		

REQUISITION FORMS	DATE		AMOUNT				
	TO	FROM	PARTIAL	PARTIAL	FINAL	ATTRITION ACTION	DATE
To Applicant						Ret. "Ineligible"	
Rec'd from Applicant						Ret."Without Prejudice"	
						Disapproved	
To FRAD						Withdrawn	
PAYMENTS							
Letter to Applicant							
Payment Made							

Project No.	Name, Address of Applicant

Figure 9-2. HUD Project Control Card

the "federal share" by HUD. Originally, the federal share was only 20 percent with a 20 percent bonus as an incentive toward regionalization. Since 1965 the federal share has been 50 percent in both the HUD and BOR programs. A 90 percent federal share for "demonstration projects" was briefly authorized but apparently never used.

The inflexible 50 percent local share is still difficult for many local governments to achieve. Certain states, including Massachusetts and Connecticut, in some cases provide half the local share out of state funds. Furthermore, a 1970 amendment to the HUD act allows contributions of land or services to comprise up to half the local share. In all cases, however, the applicant must provide at least 25 percent of the total cost at its own expense.

Originally, HUD funds could only be used to acquire land—specifically "undeveloped or predominantly undeveloped land." This was especially silly from the inner city standpoint since urban renewal was providing plenty of vacant public land. The need was for money to *develop* the open space for recreation and other purposes. The 1965 amendments permitted grants to be made for development of sites acquired under the program. Finally, in 1970, development grants could be made for improvement of any publicly owned open land, regardless of how acquired.

Project Selection Criteria. Allocation of scarce funds in accordance with the apparent intent of Congress is performed through internal project selection procedures. Until drastic modification of the funding analysis process in 1972, project selection occurred in three steps:

- classification of each open space application into a "program output group";
- ranking of sites within each group according to specific criteria established for each group; and
- decision on funding each program output group within the budget available.

The all-important "project output groups" followed, as closely as possible, the various applications of the program outlined by Congress:

Group A—Encouragement of Better Urban Form; Tracts that will demonstrably help

guide urban development or redevelopment. (SMSA only)
Group B–1–Areas Providing Needed Space Opportunity in Low-Income Neighborhood. (SMSA only)
Group B–2–Neighborhood Parks. (SMSA only)
Group C–Historic Sites. (Including non-SMSA)
Group D–Scenic and Conservation Areas. (SMSA only)
Group E–Small Towns, Except Historical Sites. (Non-SMSA only)
Group F–Development. (Including non-SMSA) [*Federal Register,* V. 36, No. 246 (December 22, 1971), pp. 24723–24724.]

Once a project was assigned to one of these groups, its prospects for funding depended upon (1) its ranking within the groups on the basis of specific criteria established for each group and (2) the proportion of the total open space budget allocated to each group. When money for a particular group was exhausted, applications not funded in that group were left stranded.

Under the pre-1972 selection system, therefore, the assignment of a project to a particular output group was a crucial determination. Since funds were allocated to each group by HUD's Washington office, considerable disparity between groups as to supply and demand for funds might arise regionally, where the selection process was performed. For example, low-ranked projects in one group might be funded while middle-ranked projects in a more crowded group might be passed over. Despite its importance, however, HUD treated this initial determination as merely a staff decision, with detailed criteria provided only for the ranking of projects *within* a particular group.

A 1972 report to Congress by the General Accounting Office (GAO) noted several deficiencies in the allocation of both HUD and BOR funds, with particular criticism of selection procedures. As a result of this report and the 1970 legislative amendments, HUD in 1972 revised its entire selection procedure. The output groups were abolished in favor of a weighted ranking system to be applied equally to all applications. The new criteria evaluate:

- local effort and coordination;
- project's ability to meet open space needs;
- local equal employment and entrepreneurial efforts;
- local needs;
- commitment of local, county, state and federal entities to project or program;
- expansion of housing for low and moderate income families; and
- community development.

In the allocation process, an application receives a score and is ranked accordingly. As compared with the old "output group" system, the new procedure gives unprecedented weight to social rather than physical considerations. For example:

- Provision by the local political jurisdiction for low and moderate income housing, incidence of poverty, adequacy of parks and availability of economic opportunities to minorities collectively account for 45-50 points out of a possible 100.
- By contrast, environmental objectives rate a possible 11 points, of which "ecological significance" counts for only two.
- "Jurisdiction of applicant" is distinguished from the local government jurisdiction in which the proposed site is located. Thus the policies of the local government as to factors listed above are taken into account even if the applicant is a special district or regional entity not responsible for such policies.
- Functional "service area" is distinguished from either of these legal jurisdictions and is taken into account in the scoring process.

Unfortunately, the HUD open space program was "frozen" before this new allocation procedure could be effectively tested in practice. The results of the program to be considered in this study were almost entirely the product of the earlier, less sophisticated, fund allocation system.

The BOR Matching Grant Program

The ORRRC Report. The Eisenhower administration's chief contribution to the public deliberations concerning open space was the establishment in 1958 of the Outdoor Recreation Resources Review Commission (ORRRC). The statute which created the commission gave it a sweeping mandate:

> That in order to preserve, develop, and assure accessibility to all American people of present and future generations such quality and quantity of outdoor recreation re-

> sources as will be necessary and desirable for individual enjoyment and to assure the spiritual, cultural, and physical benefits that such outdoor recreation provides; in order to inventory and evaluate the outdoor recreation resources and opportunities of the nation, to determine the types and location of such resources and opportunities which will be required by present and future generations; and in order to make comprehensive information and recommendations leading to these goals available to the President, the Congress, and the individual States and Territories, there is hereby authorized and created a bipartisan Outdoor Recreation Resources Review Commission. [P.L. 85–470, Sec. 1]

Conspicuously missing from this catalogue of purposes is any reference to land use planning, urban growth or, for that matter, open space. In contrast to the HHFA-HUD program just described, ORRRC and its progeny were concerned with function rather than form and specifically the quite tangible function of outdoor recreation. Furthermore, the ORRRC mission was predominantly nonurban. "Outdoor recreation," for instance, was defined in the statute to include:

> . . . the land and water areas and associated resources of such areas in the United States . . . [but it] *shall not mean nor include recreation facilities, programs, and opportunities usually associated with urban development* such as playgrounds, stadia, golf courses, city parks, and zoos. [P.L. 85–470, Sec. 2 emphasis added]

The 15 member commission, under the chairmanship of Laurence S. Rockefeller, performed its work with excellence. The commission's 1962 report, *Outdoor Recreation for America,* and 27 supplementary staff studies and reports, have become one of the most cited and influential products of its kind. The ORRRC report discusses statistically, graphically and in prose the existing and the anticipated state of outdoor recreation opportunities in the United States. Predicting that as the nation's population doubles by the year 2000 demand for outdoor recreation will triple, the report recommended specific federal measures to help meet the impending recreational shortage. Foremost among these recommendations were proposals to create a Bureau of Outdoor Recreation within the Department of the Interior and a grant-in-aid program to assist states and local governments in the acquisition of land.

The Bureau of Outdoor Recreation. Seldom has a national commission report been so quickly acted upon. On April 2, 1962, three months after the formal publication of the ORRRC report, Secretary of the Interior Stewart Udall signed Secretarial Order 497 which created the Bureau of Outdoor Recreation (BOR). A year later, Congress in effect ratified this executive action in passing the Outdoor Recreation Act of 1963 which required the secretary of the interior to implement the general functions for which BOR was created:

- inventory of open space needs and resources;
- classification of outdoor recreation resources;
- preparation of a nationwide recreation plan;
- technical assistance to states, local governments and private interests;
- encouragement of interstate and regional cooperation;
- research and education;
- interdepartmental cooperation;
- acceptance of donations of land, services or money.

Not included in this list is the grant-in-aid program, which had to wait two more years for its authorization. On the other hand, a specific requirement of the act—the preparation of a nationwide recreation plan—has never been implemented.

The decision to concentrate outdoor recreation activities in a new bureau rather than in the existing National Park Service or some other agency was a deliberate choice, made in accordance with the ORRRC report. BOR was to have no operating responsibilities for any land or facilities, and therefore, hopefully, no vested interests in competition with line agencies actually having such responsibilities—the National Park Service, Bureau of Land Management, Bureau of Reclamation, Corps of Engineers, and the Forest Service of the Department of Agriculture. Rivalry with the last named agency was forestalled by the appointment of one of its officials, Edward C. Crafts, to be the first director of BOR. (Fitch and Shanklin).

As an organization BOR has remained small, with approximately 700 employees at the present time. It functions through a Washington headquarters and seven regional offices. Its coordination and technical advisory functions are performed through a variety of channels within and outside the federal government, through an exhaustive array of technical publications and studies, and through conferences for the general public.

The Land and Water Conservation Fund. BOR's program of direct assistance in the acquisition of land for recreational purposes was established by the Land and Water Conservation Fund Act of 1965 (LWCF). Its direct lineage from the ORRRC Act of 1958 is revealed in its substantially similar statement of purposes. No prohibitions as to urban areas are included, however. Instead, a specific fund allocation formula is established under which the setting of policies and priorities is delegated to federal agencies other than BOR and to the states, as described below.

The Land and Water Conservation Fund itself consists of certain designated federal revenues, excluding general tax revenues, which are earmarked by the act for the fund. The 1965 act named the following sources:

- proceeds from the sale of surplus federal property;
- motorboat fuel tax revenue;
- entrance fees to federal recreation facilities.

A 1968 amendment to the act added:

- revenue received under the Outer Continental Shelf Act sufficient to yield a total annual income to the LWCF of $200 million.

Amounts accruing to the LWCF under these provisions are not automatically available to be spent in the form of grants. Congress must separately appropriate funds from the LWCF for actual use by BOR. Sixty percent of the BOR appropriation is available for matching grants to states; the balance goes to other federal agencies for land acquisition.

In order to receive matching grants from BOR, states must prepare a State Comprehensive Outdoor Recreation Plan (SCORP). BOR considers the SCORP to be the vanguard of state land use planning. Its approval process, however, is not especially rigorous. At this writing all states and territories have had their SCORPs approved and are receiving money from BOR.

State grant funds may be used for three purposes: planning (meaning preparation of the SCORP), acquisition and development. Project selection is largely the responsibility of the "state liaison officer" rather than BOR. Processing is a matter of months rather than years and nearly all applications are funded.

The BOR program thus differs drastically from the HUD program administratively. Under BOR, available funds are allotted to each state; HUD funds are distributed according to HUD regions. The BOR program delegates maximum responsibility for allocating each state's share to the state itself; HUD gives the state no function except as a potential applicant for funds for state projects. BOR requires preparation and approval of the SCORP; HUD only requires conformity with comprehensive planning for the area.

THE OPEN SPACE PLANNING PROCESS

The creation of the two open space grant programs obviously could not produce an automatic improvement in the land use consumption pattern or the quality of life in metropolitan areas. Fundamental to the operation of the programs, as recognized in the implementing legislation for each, is the necessity that open space grant funds be allocated pursuant to some sort of comprehensive planning process. Furthermore, like all requests for federal funds, applications for open space grants must be channelled through a regional planning agency pursuant to Office of Management and Budget (OMB) Circular A-95.

Statutory Requirements

"Comprehensive planning" is an amorphous term whose content is not defined in the statutory requirements that it be utilized. Section 703(a) of the original 1961 act establishing the HHFA-HUD program simply required that there be comprehensive planning for the area in which an open space grant is being sought, and that such open space be "important to the execution of" such comprehensive plan. It was left to HHFA to set criteria as to what the comprehensive plan should include or strive for.

The 1970 amendments modified the planning requirement to the effect that open space assisted under the program must be "a part of, or . . . consistent with, the comprehensively planned development of the urban area." In the murkiest of "clarifying" explanation, the legislative history to the 1970 amendments states:

> Adding this alternative standard of consistency with comprehensive planning would help make it clear that the unified or officially coordinated open space program should be closely related to the nature of the individual projects being assisted. [*U.S. Code Cong. and Admin. News,* 1970, (P.L. 91-609), p. 5602]

On the BOR side, Section 5(d) of the 1965 Land and Water Conservation Fund Act provides a more definite statement on planning: "A comprehensive statewide outdoor recreation plan shall be required prior to the consideration by the Secretary of financial assistance for acquisition or development projects." The plan is required to contain the name of the state liaison agency, an evaluation of the supply of and demand for outdoor recreation, and an implementation program. It is sensibly required that the outdoor recreation plan should be cross-referenced with any other state comprehensive plan and should be based on the same population growth projections.

The "statewide comprehensive outdoor recreation plan" is, of course, an activity plan, not a land use plan; the use of the term "comprehensive" with respect to both kinds of plans is perhaps misleading. In neither case is it clear whether "comprehensive" should be construed geographically, substantively or otherwise.

Both HUD and BOR grant applications are subject to still another planning requirement—namely, that expressed in Office of Management and Budget Circular A-95 (based on Section 204 of the Demonstration Cities and Metropolitan Development Act of 1966). The A-95 procedure requires the designation of a "clearinghouse" for each state or region to which all applications for federal aid originating within such jurisdiction will be referred. The clearinghouse is required to evaluate the significance of the proposed grant to "state, areawide, or local plans and programs, as appropriate." As to open space grants, the clearinghouse must consider the impact of the proposal upon:

> • Wise development and conservation of natural resources, including land, water, minerals, Wildlife, and others; . . .
> • Adequate outdoor recreation and open space;
> • Protection of areas of unique beauty, historical, and scientific interest; . . .

The A-95 clearinghouse therefore is theoretically an additional level of scrutiny to ensure that the use of federal funds is related to the implementation of a comprehensive plan. Theory breaks down, however, in the case of HUD applications where the clearinghouse and the comprehensive planning agency are usually one and the same. In the case of BOR, a statewide clearinghouse is normally a different agency from the "BOR state liaison agency" and therefore may perform a more probing review.

Analysis of Comprehensive Plans

Statutory requirements define in sweeping terms the need to relate open space grant applications to comprehensive planning goals and programs. It follows that the "success" of the federal grant programs depends in large measure upon the extent to which regional plans do in fact provide guidance in the allocation of funds. Analysis of the plans for the metropolitan areas of interest to this study therefore follows.

Chicago. Of the three metropolitan areas studied—Chicago, Boston and Hartford—the most recent and elaborate open space plan is that of the Northeastern Illinois Planning Commission (NIPC). Since all three plans have a general conceptual similarity, many of the more detailed comments to be made about the NIPC plan will also be applicable to the other cases. (A statistical comparison of the three regions and their planning agencies is found in Table 9-2).

NIPC is the agency established by state law to perform regional planning for the Chicago metropolitan area defined to include six counties: Cook, DuPage, Lake, Will, Kane and McHenry. Unlike its counterparts in Boston and Hartford, NIPC's territory is conveniently

Table 9-2. Comparison of Chicago, Boston and Hartford SMSAs and Planning Agencies

SMSA Data	*Chicago*	*Boston*	*Hartford*
Area (sq. Miles)	3,720	986	672
Population (1970)	6,978,947	2,753,700	660,559
Rank Among All SMSAs	3	8	49
Percent of State's Land Area	7	12	13
Percent of State's Population (1970)	63	48	21
Percent Change in Population (1960-70)	12	6	21
Percent Nonwhite (SMSA)	18	5	8
Central City	32	16	28
Suburban	4	1	1
Planning Agency Data			
Area (sq. miles)	3,720	1,400+	765
Population (1970)	6,978,947	3,000,000+	669,907
Budget Per Capita (1970)	11 cents	23 cents	31 cents
Municipalities	255	101	30

Source: Compiled by the author.

coincident with the boundaries of the Chicago Standard Metropolitan Statistical Area.

In addition to its comprehensive planning function, NIPC serves as the A-95 clearinghouse for its region. This anomalous situation, which is common around the country, has the deficiency that neither the plan itself nor its application to a given set of circumstances is subject to outside scrutiny. The agency naturally wishes to appear to be competent, thorough and omniscient. Furthermore, it wants to facilitate, not impede, the flow of federal money into its jurisdiction. And finally, it may rely heavily on the political and financial support of its constitutent local governments. For all these reasons, an impartial and critical weighing of proposals by the regional planning agency is perhaps unlikely.

Assuming for the sake of discussion that the review process is not merely pro forma, it is appropriate to consider how useful an actual comprehensive plan may be for this purpose. In other words, aside from the diligence of the planning agency in performing its review function, what is the objective utility of the comprehensive plan for this purpose.

The NIPC comprehensive plan is actually a statement of general objectives set forth in a document entitled "Diversity Within Order" adopted by the commission in 1968. Details of the plan are described more specifically in a series of plan "elements" or reports dealing with topics such as wastewater management, solid waste, housing and open space. (Transportation planning is largely the province of a parallel agency, the Chicago Area Transportation Study, whose recommendations NIPC adopts.) The open space "element" of the comprehensive plan was developed over a two year period and adopted by the commission on March 3, 1971. Experience in the application of the finished product is therefore limited, but the general outlines of the document were promulgated in several preceding plans and reports.

The overall land use pattern envisioned in the NIPC comprehensive plan, to which the open space element is related, is referred to as the "finger plan." Existing development (at least as of the beginning of the NIPC studies) tends to comprise a compact mass or "hand"—including Chicago and the inner suburbs—with "fingers" of built-up suburbs extending along the spokes of various commuter rail lines. The essence of the "finger plan" thus is to concentrate future development close to the already developed corridors and to preserve the "green wedges" between the fingers through public acquisition and encouragement of low density private uses such as farms, institutions, golf courses and cemeteries. In reality, federal grants to local governments in the NIPC area have followed exactly the opposite policy—i.e., they are largely for projects within the fingers.

A major flaw in the NIPC "finger plan" is that it is obviously already 20 years out of date. Scarcely mentioned in the comprehensive plan (except in its reference to the Chicago Area Transportation Study Plan) is the fact that nearly all new radial highway construction has occurred in the "green wedges" as the routes of least cost and resistance. Concomitantly, most new suburban development has been oriented to the interchanges of these highways rather than railway stations, and the filling in of the interstitial wedges is manifest. This has occurred in spite of a valiant delaying effort by NIPC to discourage wastewater sewerage in the wedges so as to keep the opportunities for open space acquisition alive.

NIPC's land inventory itself was a major exercise in data gathering and correlation funded by a HUD "701 grant." Lasting three years, the study involved the comparison of aerial photographs; field checks; and topographic, soils and floodplain maps to rate every undeveloped quarter-section according to its potential as preserved open space. Anticipated benefits were grouped into three categories—recreation, natural resource protection and contribution to urban form.

Criteria were applied to each quarter-section to provide quantitative weights to the three principal functions. These criteria are specific as to natural resource qualities, but remain vague as to both recreation potential and urban form (Table 9-3). Conspicuously absent are

Table 9-3. NIPC Regional Open Space Evaluation Criteria as Applied to Each Quarter-Section

Criterion	*Score Range*
I *Recreational Criteria*	
1. 1975 Demand Index for	
a. All Land-Oriented Recreation except Golf	0–10
b. Golf	0–1
c. Fishing[2]	0–2
d. Saling and Boating[2]	0–3
2. 1995 Demand Index for	
a. All Land-Oriented Recreation except Golf	0–10
b. Golf	0–1
c. Fishing[2]	0–2
d. Sailing and Boating[2]	0–2
Total Recreational Score	0–30
II *Natural Resource Criteria*	
1. Soils with Severe Limitations to Urbanization	0 or 5
2. Soils with Severe Limitations to Septic Filter Field Construction[1]	0 or 2
3. Geological Conditions Least Likely to Protect Ground Water	0 or 2
4. Flood Plains	0 or 5
5. Prime Ground Water Recharge Areas	0 or 5
6. Water Bodies[2]	0, 1
7. Potential Reservoirs	0, 6
8. Sites of Scientific Interest	
a. Sites of Ecological Interest	0, 4
b. Sites of Historical Interest	0, 4
c. Sites of Geological Interest	0, 4
Total Natural Resource Score	0–40
III *Urban Form Criteria*	
1. Located Outside Urban Development Corridors	0 or 5
2. Scenic Areas	0, 8, 10
3. Linkage to Existing Regional Open Space	0 or 2
4. Not to be Served by Sewers	0 or 5
5. Imminence of Loss	0 or 8
Total Urban Form Score	0–30
Total Score	0–100

1. Applicable only if the area is not served by sewer networks.

2. Only quarter-sections with the appropriate water bodies receive a score for water-oriented recreation.

Source: Northeastern Illinois Planning Commission.

factors concerning accessibility, socioeconomic character of the community or the proportion of land area in the area to be served already devoted to public or private open space. Furthermore, the urban form criteria—particularly "location outside urban development corridors" and "linkage to existing regional open space"—emphasize areas remote from the urban public or mass transportation lines and favor the accumulation of open space in areas already well served.

The final product of the open space inventory may be considered a major step forward from the crude diagrams of earlier reports. As a guide to the allocation of federal funds, however, the map (Figure 9-3) and its accom-

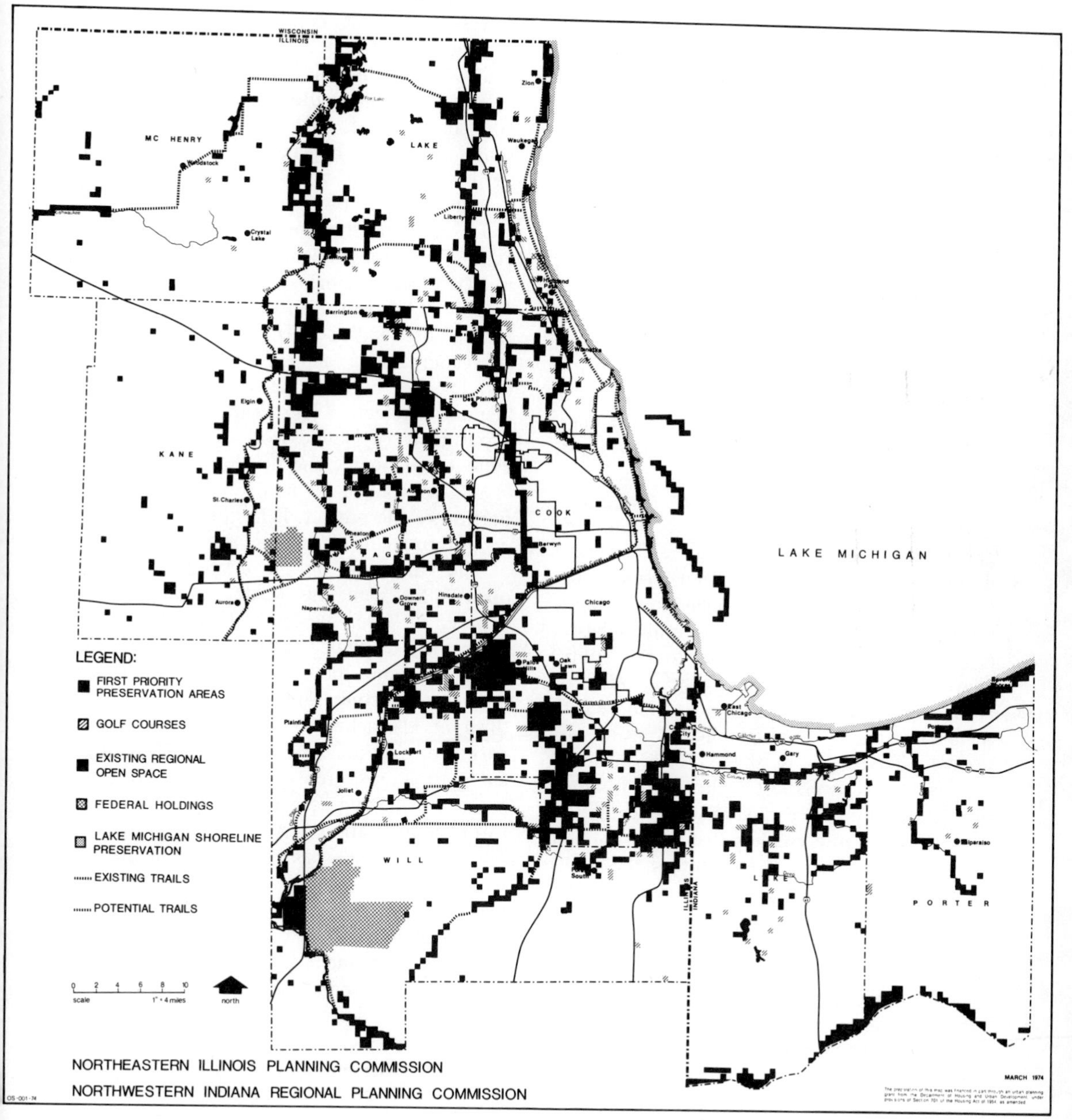

Figure 9-3. Northeastern Illinois Planning Commission Open Space Map

panying report are disappointingly noncommittal. Rather than accepting the logic of its inventory as a basis for setting priorities, NIPC falls back on the old formula of "acres per thousand." Arbitrary adherence to the ratio of 30 acres per thousand population yields a projected total of *340,000* acres of regional open space needed by 1995, or nearly three times the total inventory of public open space acquired in the Chicago SMSA to date!

Figure 9-3 thus represents the results of applying a *deductive* estimation of projected deficit (220,000 acres) to an *inductive* inventory of available land resources. The "first priority" areas shown are therefore simply the "best 220,000 acres" of open land presently in private ownership. Second priority areas are the next best quarter-sections in case first priority tracts are used up.

Among the 220,000 acres recommended to be acquired, no differentiation is made in the published materials, although individual tract scores may be obtained from NIPC. No key areas are identified by geographical location or community name: political geography is graphically almost extinguished from the map.

Boldly consistent with its acquisition objectives, the plan recommends that "until the 1995 needs for open space are met, the emphasis of the open space programs should be placed on land acquisition rather than land development. . . . " As a general precept for the allocation of federal open space funds outside of central cities, this recommendation is reaffirmed in the conclusion to this study. However, like the "green wedge" policy of NIPC's plan, it has been more honored in the breach than in the observance.

A final criticism of the NIPC open space plan is that it overstresses the need for outright acquisition as compared with regulation or purchase of interests less than fee. Although the report document does mention the desirability of nonfee acquisition techniques, the emphasis of NIPC's proposal and funding analysis is directed to outright acquisition. Even if such a monumental land purchasing program could be accomplished, the costs of public management and the complete loss of tax revenue would probably make such a solution unduly extravagant.

Boston. The Boston Metropolitan Area Planning Council (MAPC) performs functions for its region equivalent to those NIPC does for Chicago. Its region comprises 101 towns and cities, including the entire Boston SMSA plus 22 additional municipalities located around its perimeter. Its territory extends approximately from Cape Ann to the northeast to Framingham on the west to Duxbury on the southeast. Like Hartford, but unlike Chicago, MAPC's central city is the state capital.

Planning for land use in New England involves a different municipal geography than in the rest of the nation. In Massachusetts and Connecticut, all land lies within an incorporated municipality, either a town or a city, and counties have no land use regulation functions. New England planners therefore need not contend with evershifting municipal boundaries and the juxtaposition of county and local authority over adjoining land. Whether this improves the land use planning situation in New England remains to be seen.

The MAPC open space plan consists of a report published in April 1969, together with an accompanying map (Figure 9-4). Its origins lay in the Eastern Massachusetts Regional Planning Project, a joint venture by the state department of public works and the department of commerce and development. In 1965, MAPC contracted to prepare the open space portion of the project. It has been in the process of refining its plans ever since.

The first stage in the development of an open space plan was MAPC's "initial plan" adopted in December 1965. This rather jargon-laden proposal called for the long range acquisition of some 200,000 acres within the 152 municipality study area (roughly the eastern third of Massachusetts). Acquisitions were to be made in two systems: "primary"—oriented to natural resource protection; and "secondary"—oriented to recreation and urban form considerations. After considering four schematic diagrams as potential land use patterns—"web-dispersed," "wedge-radial," "greenbelt-circumferential" and "matrix-satellite"—the initial plan called for the achievement of a "composite" of the best feature of each.

Following from the initial plan, MAPC proceeded to define more specifically certain geographical areas which required particular attention. This phase of its effort, culminating in the 1969 plan, was limited to its own 79 municipality jurisdiction (later expanded to 101 municipalities). Comparing various esti-

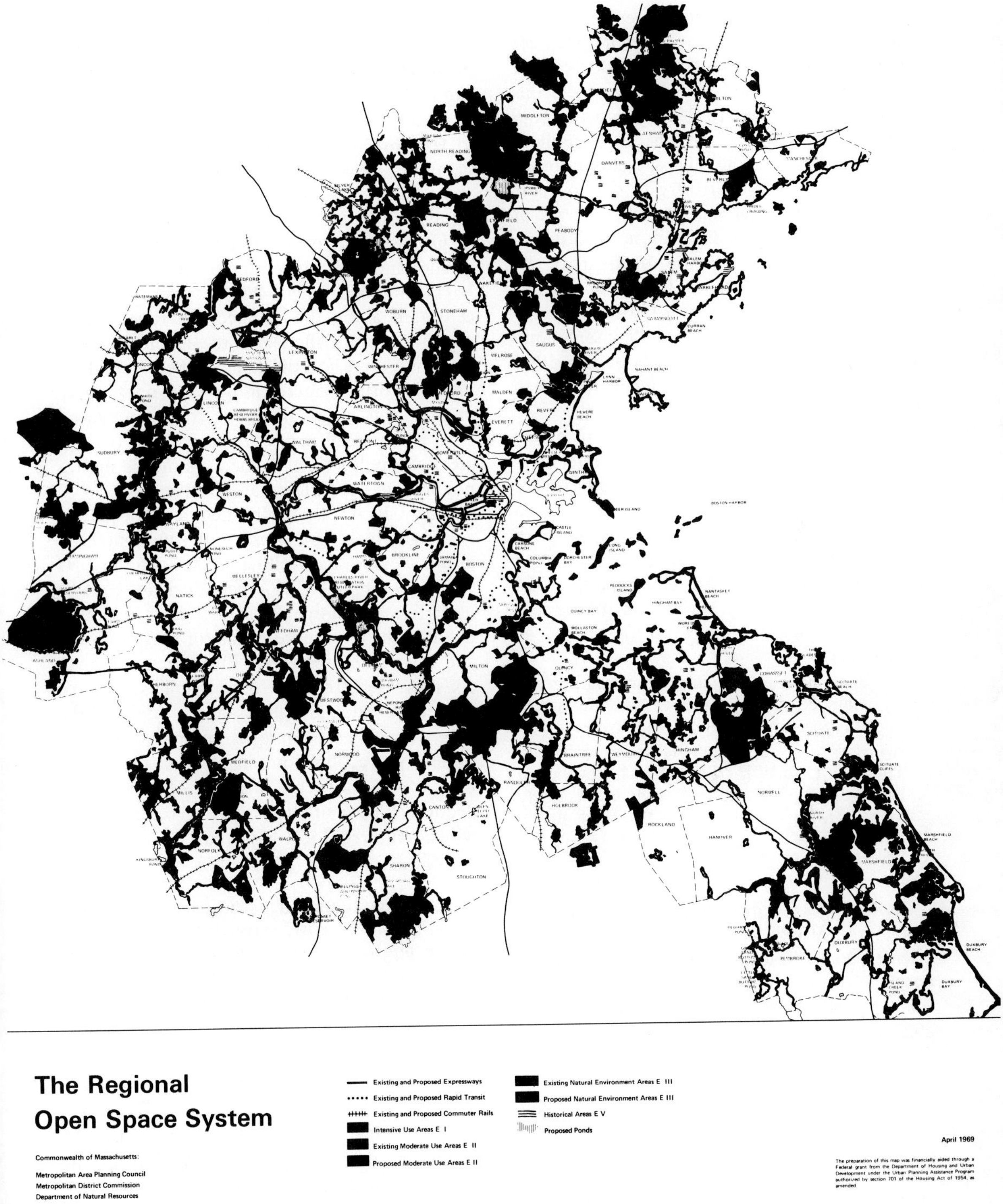

Figure 9–4. Boston Metropolitan Area Planning Council Open Space Map

mates of recommended "acres per thousand," including that of NIPCs, the council concludes that its region is deficient by 22,000 acres of "recreation areas and facilities." By 1990 this deficit will have risen to 45,000 acres as population rises from 2.7 million to 3.4 million. It is interesting to note that the closer correspondence of MAPC's territory to the contours of *existing* development than in the cases of Chicago or Hartford yields a more modest projected increase in recreation open space deficiency. However, in its final plan MAPC recommends approximately 145,000 acres for eventual acquisition to meet "conservation" as well as recreation needs. (After the 1965 initial plan, little reference is made to "urban shaping" in the MAPC reports.)

The recommendations of the 1969 plan take the form of specific geographical references starting at the coast and moving inland. Unlike NIPC, the MAPC plan does not rely upon an "objective" or systematic inventory of each tract of undeveloped land. Instead it refers by name and location to specific features and areas which it suggests are needed to augment public holdings, *viz.*:

> Duxbury Beach–The single most important regional recreation resource on the South Shore is the three-mile sand spit from Marshfield to Plymouth known as Duxbury Beach. The major portion of the beach lies within the Town of Duxbury, and is privately owned and operated by the Duxbury Beach Association for use by town residents. [P. 45]

Reflecting the prevailing terrain of the region, the MAPC open space plan is largely oriented to hydrologic features of one kind or another. In addition to lengthy discussion of the coastline, it deals with riverine systems, great ponds, and inland marshes and wetlands. Its recommendations therefore are mostly regional in scale and suburban in location. The basic plan, however, is supplemented by a separate volume on the planning of athletic facilities for metropolitan Boston.

The subject of preserving open space through the use of techniques other than fee simple acquisition is the subject of another supplementary volume to the basic plan. However, as with NIPC, there appears to be no policy criterion concerning when outright acquisition should or should not be used. The hydrologic orientation of many of MAPC's areas recommended for preservation implies, however, that noncompensatory techniques should be sufficient in many cases.

Hartford. The Hartford Capitol Region Planning Agency (CRPA) exercises planning and A-95 review responsibilities over 30 municipalities in North Central Connecticut, including the city of Hartford. Its region is smaller and much less populous than either the NIPC or MAPC areas. With development concentrated along the Connecticut River Valley which bisects it, the Hartford region is currently about three-fourths undeveloped. Its inland location offers opportunities for open space preservation in all directions from the central city, presumably at lower average cost (due to greater supply) than in the asymmetric metropolitan areas of Chicago and Boston.

The CRPA plan, published in 1966, is accordingly more grandiose, but simultaneously more specific than either of its counterparts (Figure 9-5). The CRPA plan does not confine itself to regional open space but deals in minute detail with open space needs for neighborhood and townwide use as well. Furthermore, it gives considerable attention to nonpublic sources of open space such as utilities, institutions and the like, as well as techniques for public control other than acquisition. In essence, the CRPA plan conforms better than the other plans to Section 703(b) of the original 1961 legislation which required local governing bodies to preserve:

> . . . a maximum of open-space land with a minimum of cost, through the use of existing public land; the use of special tax, zoning, and subdivision provisions; and the continuation of appropriate private use of open-space land through acquisition and leaseback, the acquisition of restrictive easements, and other available means. [Deleted in 1970]

The CRPA employs "acres per thousand" accounting extensively. Starting with a current total of 50 acres per thousand of publicly owned regional open space (as compared with 13.5 in the Chicago region), the plan looks toward a goal of 140 acres per thousand (although confusingly the introduction to the plan calls for a goal for *regional* public open space of 50 acres per thousand). As to town

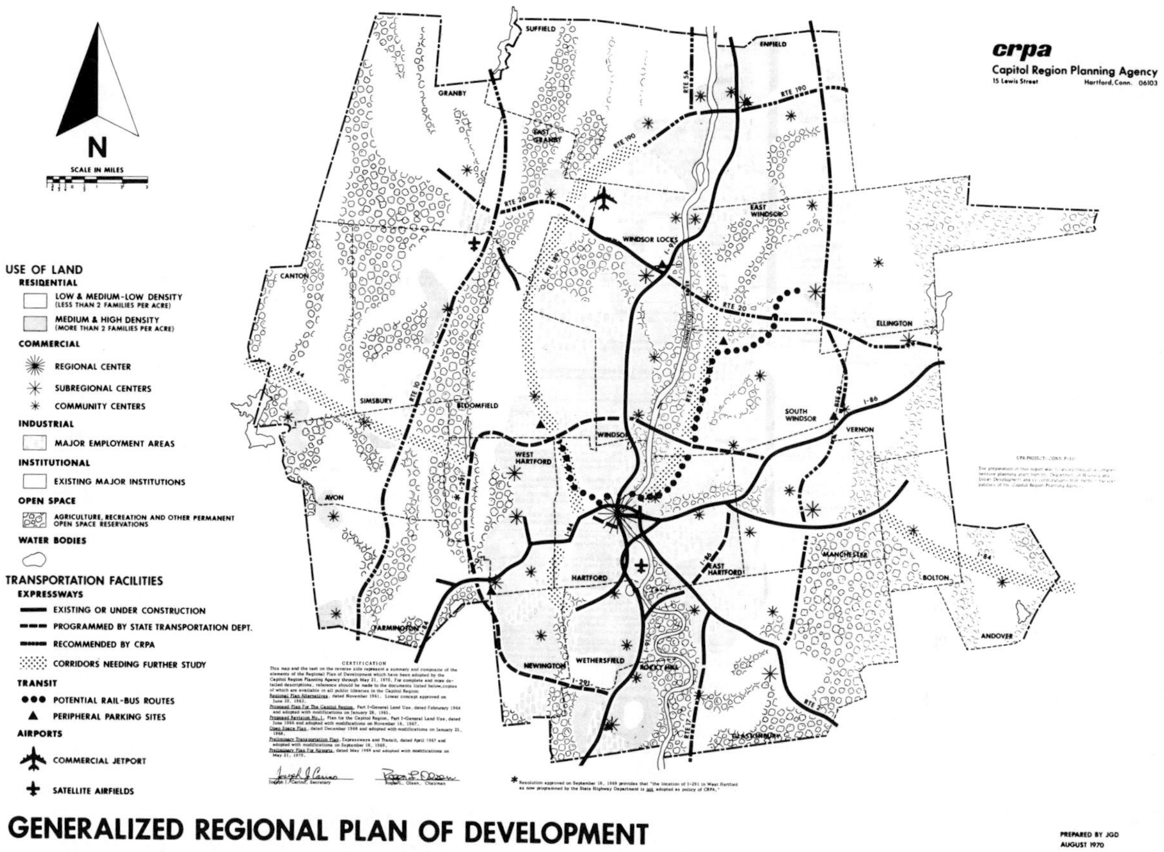

Figure 9-5. Hartford Capital Region Planning Agency Open Space Map

level open space, CRPA recommends a goal of 15 acres per thousand, entailing the acquisition and development of an additional 13,000 acres by 1990.

These plans illuminate a serious problem with the use of "acres per thousand" formulae, namely, that there is no objective norm established to ensure uniformity among metropolitan areas. While Chicago postulates a staggering acquisition program to attain 30 acres per thousand, Hartford begins with 50 acres per thousand and seeks 140 acres per thousand. This is not to suggest that equality of goal would produce equality of access: the formula says nothing about location, parcel size or quality. However, within the scope of its extremely limited usefulness, it would seem that the acres per thousand concept should at least be applied uniformly or according to a rational basis for differentiation.

Aside from these criticisms, the CRPA plan possesses considerable specificity in its recommendations on a town-by-town basis. Areas to be acquired are identified by geographic location, size and political jurisdiction. And as stated earlier, opportunities for the control of open space not requiring acquisition are indicated. Indeed at the time of the plan's preparation some 19,000 acres were already controlled in the Hartford region under floodplain regulations.

Conclusion

The open space components of the comprehensive plans for the three regions under consideration are found to be similar in conceptual framework but quite inconsistent in their emphases, goals, methodology and candor. They tend to deal in the long term (if 1990 is long term) and eschew tough-minded recommendations concerning immediate land use problem areas. All three treat the preservation of open space as something abstract and divorced from the development process which makes it necessary. No plan, for instance, gives significant attention to planned unit development, subdivision controls, performance standards or reduction of visual blight along highways. This tendency to reify open space apart from the conditions which create the need for it is a direct reflection of the congressional tendency to create "open space programs" rather than to modify federal programs which contribute to urban sprawl.

Of course, this discussion has considered only the open space portions of the regional plans; in the case of NIPC at least the most significant open space implications have actually arisen from its wastewater plan and controversy ensuing therefrom. Nevertheless, to the extent that the open space plans serve as the primary guide for the allocation of federal open space funds in metropolitan areas, their major contribution is found not in the specificity of their contents, but in the fact that they exist.

The SCORPs for Illinois, Massachusetts and Connecticut will not be considered in detail. The preparation of these plans is financed out of the Land and Water Conservation Fund and they are approved by BOR. Thus the SCORPs tend to resemble one another rather closely in format if not in detail. As activity plans rather than land use plans, they bear only a tangential relationship to the subject of metropolitan growth.

THE IMPACT OF THE FEDERAL OPEN SPACE PROGRAMS

• I will put forward the most extensive program ever proposed by a President of the United States to expand the nation's parks, recreation areas, and open spaces in a way that truly brings parks to the people.

President Richard M. Nixon
State of the Union Message, Janaury 22, 1971

• MR. BOLAND. Turn to page I–1, open space land program. Again, this program was terminated on January 5. No appropriation is proposed for fiscal year 1974.

Representative Edward P. Boland
Hearings Before the Subcommittee on HUD House Appropriations Committee, 93rd Congress, 1st Session, May 2, 1973, p. 730.

• MRS HANSEN. You have $50 million budgeted for assistance to States and no funds are requested for Federal programs, as you noted.

This is a reduction of $131,800,000 and $112,957,000, respectively, from fiscal year 1973.

. . . .

MR. WATT . . . We are going into a tight budget year. It did not seem justifiable to continue to ask Congress to appropriate additional funds when we already were not spending the monies that you had appropriated to us in years gone by.

Representative Julia Butler Hansen
James D. Watt, Director, Bureau of Outdoor Recreation, Department of the Interior. Hearings before the Subcommittee on Department of the Interior and Related Agencies, House Committee on Appropriations, 93rd Cong., 1st sess., March 6, 1973, p. 127.

• Federal funding will increase for environmental protection and enhancement activities such as providing recreational areas, parks, historic sites, and fish and wildlife protection.

The Budget for Fiscal Year, 1974, Special Analyses, p. 274

The National Results

The foremost obstacle to the success of the federal open space programs has been the precarious nature of their very existence. Unlike national defense, highway construction, social security or FHA mortgage insurance, the federal open space programs have never enjoyed the luxury of permanence. Conceived in public uproar, the programs' subsequent fortunes have fluctuated drastically with political whim, culminating in the demise of the HUD program in 1974.

Fiscal History. The best evidence of the level of priority ascribed to each program is to be found in their respective histories of funding and fiscal activity. Although somewhat foreign to the geographical orientation of this volume, analysis of this kind is crucial to the interpretation of the actual results of the programs in the field. Unraveling the knot of fiscal history is complex, with a tendency for official sources to obfuscate rather than clarify the truth (for example, compare the second and third quotations above with the first and last ones).

The spending of public funds is a multiple stage process–authorization, appropriation, obligation and outlay. Dollar amounts established at each stage effectively set an upper limit for succeeding steps in the process. However, the expenditure of funds is also subject to many independent factors, such as presidential impoundment.

The level of funding "authorized" by Congress constitutes the upper limit theoretically intended to be spent on a particular program. Authorization may be stated to be effective over a period of years and may be enlarged (or diminished if not utilized) by Congress from time to time.

Despite gradual increase over time, the cumulative totals seem trivial in comparison with other federal activities (Tables 9-4 and 9-5). HUD's total *cumulative* authorization for open space has been $683 million as compared with *annual* outlays since 1970 for defense of $80 billion, for agriculture of over $8 billion, for space of over $3 billion, and so forth. BOR's aggregate authorization is somewhat more respectable, but still far short of the $5 billion estimated by the Bureau of the Budget to be required for open space acquisition as of 1960, to say nothing of open space development. Congress has authorized $300 million per year through 1989 for BOR while continuing to limit HUD to a series of last minute extensions which finally expired in 1973.

The programs are parallel in their appropriations histories. Both began hesitantly, underwent review and expansion after three years, "took off" with the 1971-1972 "legacy of parks" and then suffered precipitous budgetary cutbacks in 1973. In the case of the HUD program the reversal took the form of nonexpansion of authorization which had been substantially used up by the end of 1972 (second quotation above). With BOR, the reversal occurred through a vastly reduced request for appropriation. (third quotation, above) even though the Land and Water Conservation Fund Act continues to authorize $300 million a year to be allocated to the fund.

Neither authorization nor appropriation is the final measure of the level of effort of a

Table 9-4. HUD Open Space Program, Fiscal History, 1961-1974 (Millions of Dollars)

Fiscal Year	*Authorizations*[1] *(cumulative)*	*Appropriations*[2]	*Obligations*[3]	*Acreages*[4]
1961	50		16	57,783 (1961-63)
1962		35		
1963		15		
1964	75	15	18	58,000
1965	310 by 6/1/69	15	11	33,700
1966		49	31	52,700
1967		54	69	33,526
1968	410 by 6/1/70	75	77	44,943
1969		75	75	19,280
1970	560 by 6/1/72	75	75	23,923
1971	660 by 6/1/72, extension to 9/30/72, etc.	75	75	25,506
1972		100	52	
1973		100	72	
1974	expired	none		
Totals		$683	$571	349,361 (through January 1, 1972)

1. Title VII, Housing Act of 1961, Sec. 705(b), as amended.

2. Department of Housing and Urban Development, unpublished data.

3. *1961–1965, 1971 HUD Statistical Yearbook*, Table 12 (calendar year data). 1966–1971, Justification material submitted to Subcommittee on the Department of Housing and Urban Development, House Appropriations Committee, 1968–1973 (fiscal year data). 1972–1973, Hearings, Subcommittee on the Department of Housing and Urban Development, House Appropriations Committee, 1974, pp. 664 and 730.

4. *1971 HUD Statistical Yearbook*, Table 12 (calendar year data).

Table 9-5. BOR Matching Grants to States, Fiscal History, 1965–1974 (Millions of Dollars)

Fiscal Year	*Authorizations*[1]	*Appropriations*[2]	*Obligations*[2]	*Acreage*[2]
1965	\$100[3]	\$ 10		
1966	100[3]	82	\$ 14	33,400
1967	100[3]	57	81	197,900
1968	200	61	72	112,004
1969	200	45	72	133,002
1970	200	62	49	29,007
1971	300	185	110	113,300
1972	300	255	192	163,200
1973	300	182	140 (est.)	134,000 (est.)
1974		73		
Totals		\$1012	\$730	915,813

1. Land and Water Conservation Fund Act of 1965, as amended. Includes federal and state allocations.

2. Bureau of Outdoor Recreation, unpublished data. Appropriations represent only the state matching grant portion–i.e., 60 percent of total annual LWCF appropriation.

3. Amount anticipated to accrue from earmarked revenues. No dollar amount stated in 1965 act.

grant program. Appropriations cannot be expended until they are obligated. Nonobligation of appropriated funds may occur due to (1) failure of states to fully utilize their allotted share or (2) withholding of appropriated funds by the Office of Management and Budget pursuant to a "fund freeze." Funds available under the HUD program were readily obligated, with applications for assistance far exceeding the funds available. The deviation between appropriations and obligations in 1972-1973 represents executive impoundment.

No BOR funds have been directly impounded. The fiscal 1974 appropriation, however, was drastically curtailed. In defense of this cutback, the administration cited the existence of an accrued "carry-over" of \$128 million consisting of past appropriations that had not yet been obligated by individual states (third quotation).

BOR officials interviewed in connection with this study, however, conceded that no state has failed to obligate its LWCF allotment within the prescribed three years from the time of appropriation. Furthermore, the expectations generated by the "legacy of parks" rhetoric (first quotation) led many states and local governments to "gear up" for much larger efforts only to be disappointed (Fiscal 1975, however, brought a substantial increase in appropriation to about \$200 million.)

A fourth stage in the fiscal process—outlay—has not been considered separately. Monies obligated on a contract may never be spent, due perhaps to change of plans by the nonfederal party or legal impediment to the performance of the contract. Data on outlays, however, are difficult to assemble.

The Nixon and Ford administrations insist that the HUD program was not abandoned but instead "folded" into "special revenue sharing." This was finally accomplished in the Housing and Community Development Act of 1974 (PL 93-383). Experience under the revenue-sharing approach is of course limited at this writing. But it was predicted by LeGates and Morgan that the result would be a diminished level of assistance to many communities, as well as a reduction of pressure upon local governments to tax themselves to meet the "local share" requirement of the categorical programs.

The summary of "fiscal history" has indicated the uncertainties which have afflicted both the HUD and BOR programs. Public expectations have been raised by loose rhetoric only to be dashed on the realities of inadequate funding. The HUD program has been virtually "hand to mouth," with the two year processing time for applications frequently exceeding the foreseeable lifetime of the program. BOR with its long term authorization and earmarked revenue sources has enjoyed greater continuity, yet it also has fluctuated substantially. The actual field results of the two programs therefore must be viewed in the light of this perplexing funding context.

Acreage. Acreage totals, as shown in the last columns of Tables 9-4 and 9-5, are inherently misleading. The Bureau of Outdoor Recreation estimates that the market price of land suitable for recreation purposes rises by 5-10 percent each year. This means that the same number of acres acquired in 1972 as in 1965 may represent a much greater public investment. Furthermore, the cost of land obviously varies with location. Reorientation of the programs toward the central cities in 1970 would have yielded fewer but more expensive acres than if the same amounts were spent in nonurban areas.

Strictly from the standpoint of acreage, BOR had assisted in the acquisition of more than twice as much land as HUD by July 1, 1972, with roughly the same total obligations. Assuming the same proportion of obligations devoted to acquisition in both programs, this would suggest that BOR has dealt more with larger tracts of cheaper land located farther from urban centers than HUD. This, it will be shown, has been true.

The two programs collectively have assisted in the acquisition of about 1.2 million acres or about 1,875 square miles of new state and local open space—slightly less than the area of Delaware. This compares with a national total of 36 million acres in state and local park systems, and 33 million acres in national parks, monuments, seashores, scenic and wild rivers, and wilderness areas as of 1970. The combined output of the two programs in terms of acquisition has thus increased the state and local holdings by four percent and the nation's total stock of public recreation land by slightly under two percent.

Location. On a national scale, the two programs display very different spatial distribution in their grant activity, reflecting their statutory emphases (Table 9-6 and Table 9-16). Among the ten most populous states both programs display coincidentally similar totals; in the ten least populous states they are vastly different. The former group, with 55 percent of the US population, received 60 percent of HUD's total allocations and 43 percent of BOR's. These represented half of HUD's project load but only one-fifth of BOR projects. The fifth quintile, with only 2 percent of the nation's population, received negligible assistance from HUD but accounted for 9 percent of BOR obligations and 16 percent of its project load.

Noting that BOR continues as HUD withers on the vine, one is tempted to observe that political survival may lie in the "slice of the pie for everyone" approach mandated by the Land and Water Conservation Fund Act. The vague geographical goals of the HUD statute may promote greater equity in terms of "putting the bucks where the people are" but clearly alienates the nonurban spokesmen in Congress.

Another way to characterize the comparative national impacts of the two programs is according to urban versus nonurban location

Table 9-6. Federal Open Space Grant Activity, by Quintiles of States in Descending Order of Population (Dollars in Millions)

	1st	*2nd*	*3rd*	*4th*	*5th*	*Total*
Percentage of US Population	55	27	11	5	2	100
HUD						
Grants	2115	958	697	274	73	4,117
Amount	$326	$111	$76	$22	$5	$540
BOR						
Grants	2122	2789	2006	1806	1741	10,464
Amount	$314	$152	$95	$90	$65	$716

Source: Computed by the author from HUD data through June 30, 1972 and BOR data through March 31, 1973.

of activity. Table 9-7 indicates that 90 percent of HUD's obligations under the "undeveloped land subprogram" fell within Standard Metropolitan Statistical Areas (SMSAs) whereas only 32 percent of BOR's funds were spent in cities of more than 25,000. Strict comparability is impeded by the different methods of recording program activity used by each agency: some projects in SMSAs are not in "cities of more than 25,000," and vice versa. Nevertheless, it is clear that metropolitan areas have received much more attention from HUD than from BOR over the lives of the programs. Since 1972, BOR has increased its metropolitan activities to fill some of the vacuum created by the demise of the HUD Program.

HUD's more sophisticated data-processing system permits classification of that agency's open space activity by still another locational variable—population size of grant recipient Cumulation of amounts shown in Table 9-8 reveals the coincidence that 83.9 percent of both total dollars and acreage related to applicant bodies of more than 25,000 population. If all these "applicant bodies" were cities, it would appear that HUD was devoting three times the effort of BOR (Table 9-7) to such communities.

"Applicant bodies" in Table 9-8, however, include not only municipalities but counties, special districts and states as well. This accounts for the unexpectedly high acreage for appli-

Table 9-7. Urban-Rural Distribution of Department of Housing and Urban Development and Bureau of Outdoor Recreation Open Space Funds, As of January 1, 1972

HUD	*Percentage of HUD*	*BOR*	*Percentage of BOR*
Inside SMSA			
2132 Projects	82		
$287,516,000	90	$191,800,000	32
302,554 Acres	87		
Outside SMSA		*Rural*	
482 Projects	18		
$30,472,000	10	$399,700,000	68
46,507 Acres	13		
Total		*Total*	
2614 Projects	100		
$317,988,000	100	$591,500,000	100
349,361 Acres	100		

Sources: *1971 HUD Statistical Yearbook*, Table 15 (Data is for Undeveloped Land Subprogram only); BOR unpublished data ("Urban" is defined as city of more than 25,000).

Table 9-8. HUD Open Space Grant Program, Totals for US Through June 30, 1972, by Population Size of Applicant Body

	Projects		*Amounts*		*Acres*	
Population	*Number*	*Percent of Total*	*$000s*	*Percent of Total*	*Number*	*Percent of Totals*
1,000,000 and over	229	5.5	92,057	11.0	108,390	26.0
500,000–999,999	425	10.3	105,931	19.6	64,576	15.4
250,000–499,999	434	10.5	76,487	14.1	47,636	11.4
50,000–249,999	1015	24.6	134,239	24.8	100,589	25.8
25,000– 49,999	541	13.1	45,585	8.4	70,131	5.3
5,000– 24,999	1061	25.7	64,062	11.8	37,952	9.8
4,999 and under	424	10.3	23,311	4.3	25,153	6.3
	4129	100.0	541,672	100.0	404,147	100.0

Source: Justification Material Submitted to Subcommittee on the Department of Housing and Urban Development, House Appropriations Committee, *Hearings, 1974*, p. 666.

cants of "over one million." This kind of statistical legerdemain can mislead the unwary.

Purpose. Having roughly characterized *where* open space funds have been used by state, by metropolitan or urban location, and by size of applicant body, it is appropriate to turn to the question of *how* such funds have been employed.

The mainstream of the HUD effort from the inception of the program has been the acquisition, and in later years the development, of "undeveloped land" (see Table 9-17). As explained below, this function by its very nature has been predominantly a suburban rather than a central city activity. In 1965, the alternatives of "historical preservation," "urban beautification" and "urban parks" were created to ameliorate this bias. Their combined dollar output by July 1, 1972, however, has amounted to only 29 percent of the total program. Even during 1971 and its "legacy of parks" HUD still devoted two-thirds of its open space budget to "undeveloped land," and only 8 percent to "urban parks."

The number of development projects assisted by BOR surprisingly is almost twice its total of acquisition projects (Table 9-9). Furthermore, 59 percent of its matching grant funds have been used for development as compared with 40 percent for acquisition. As following discussion will indicate, BOR has been extremely active in the provision of swimming pools and other active recreation facilities in central cities, a fact masked by the nonurban bias of the location data. Further explanation for the large outlays for development is that many states have used BOR funds to improve or develop facilities that they already owned, a practice not permitted under the HUD program until 1970.

Table 9-9. Bureau of Outdoor Recreation Matching Grant Program, Number and Amount of Grants, by Purpose, as of March 31, 1973

	Percent
Planning	
156 Grants	2
$8,957,364	1
Acquisition	
3,514 Grants	33
$288,548,655	40
Development	
6,836 Grants	65
$432,573,080	59
Total	
10,506 Grants	100
$730,079,099	100

Source: Bureau of Outdoor Recreation.

Intrastate results

Analysis now turns from tabulations prepared by the sponsoring agencies to more detailed breakdowns prepared from original grant data for the purposes of this study. The objective from here on is to define with increasing specificity the impact of the open space programs upon particular states and metropolitan areas.

Available data on every open space grant made by HUD and BOR in the states of Illinois, Massachusetts and Connecticut through mid-1973 were obtained, HUD data include: dollar amount of grant, identity of recipient body, community of site location, purpose, and acreage where relevant. BOR data include all of the above except acreage, perhaps reflecting its bias toward "activity" rather than "land use" planning. BOR acreages in some cases were obtained individually from the state liaison officer (typically a penciled notation somewhere in each project file).

Location. Before discussing how federal open space funds *have* been spatially distributed within the three states under consideration, it is appropriate to consider how they *should* be allocated. The regional open space plans described in the second section of this chapter are of little help since they are not statewide. The State Comprehensive Outdoor Recreation Plans should provide guidance as to BOR funds, but they do not contain geographical criteria. Instead they allocate funds by level of management authority, to wit:

- Massachusetts 70 percent state 30 percent local
- Connecticut 75 percent state 25 percent local
- Illinois 50 percent state 30 percent local 20 percent contingency

The real competition for federal resources however, is not between different levels of management authority, but between the mutually competitive subareas of the state: central city versus suburb, large versus small SMSAs and SMSAs versus non-SMSA. How should the resources be apportioned among these claimants on a basis other than "first come first served?"

Several standards come to mind. One would be to allocate funds in proportion to land area: this however would violate HUD's mandate to serve "urban areas" and lead to pernicious results. Second, funds might be distributed in proportion to subarea or community contribution to federal tax revenue. This would amount to a revenue-sharing device and would be unrelated to need. Third, funds might be distributed according to existing open space deficiency, but this would penalize those areas which have done well in the past. One might devise a "cost-benefit" criterion whereby funds would be spent where they would generate the most public benefits. This would be controversial to administer and might result in all funds going to the central city which would be politically inexpedient. In the absence of any better criterion, allocation in accordance with population seems preferable. Of course the location of a project in one subarea does not preclude benefits to population elsewhere. A rural state park may attract users from suburbs and central cities, just as a central park—like New York City's—attracts visitors from out of town. Furthermore, nonrecreational open spaces such as watershed protection areas generate benefits according to hydrological or other physical criteria which may cut across political boundaries. As a general proposition, however, it seems reasonable to assume that each subarea is self-sufficient and that need is proportional to population.

The distinction at the national scale between HUD and BOR as to geographic emphasis reappears at the state scale, but to quite different degrees among the states examined (Figure 9-6). Half or nearly half of BOR funds in each case have been spent in nonmetropolitan areas, representing only 15 to 19 percent of their respective state populations. Curiously, the imbalance toward rural areas is least in Illinois where nonmetropolitan territory is propor-

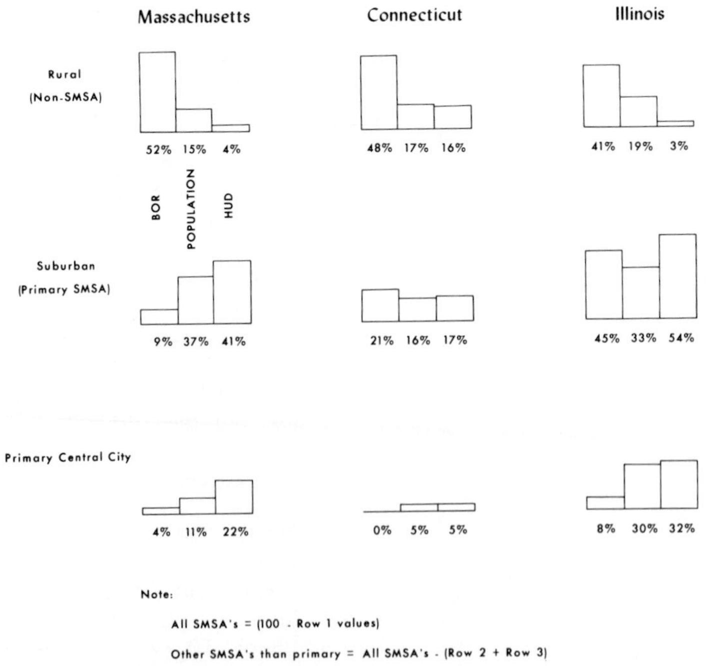

Figure 9-6. Bureau of Outdoor Recreation (BOR) and Department of Housing and Urban Development (HUD) Open Space Allocations. Percentage of state totals in relation to population for selected state subareas.

tionally much greater than in the two New England states. A possible explanation may lie in the differing state formulae for allocation between state and local agencies cited above. The greater the state agency share, apparently the greater the nonmetropolitan distribution of results.

The states differ markedly in their allocation of BOR funds to the suburban areas of their "primary SMSAs." Massachusetts vastly understresses the Boston SMSA, with only nine percent of funds serving a suburban area which has 37 percent of the state's population. Adding the city of Boston, 13 percent of funds serves half the state's population. Connecticut and Illinois both favor the Hartford and Chicago suburbs respectively, with BOR funds exceeding population share in each case.

As for BOR treatment of central cities, Row 3 of Figure 9-6 discloses consistent underallotment: Boston and Chicago have received about one-third what their population would indicate and Hartford has received nothing.

HUD expenditures display the expected low activity in rural areas except for Connecticut where HUD funds have been used for state parks. The latter reflect the greater share of HUD funds pre-empted by state agencies in Connecticut in contrast to Illinois and Massachusetts.

Close correspondence appears between HUD outlays and population in two of the three central cities. Primary SMSAs—both central cities and suburbs—are well treated by HUD, perhaps reflecting the presence of HUD field offices in those cities.

Complementarity of the two programs is depicted in Table 9-10. Comparing the percentage of combined federal activity with share of population for each subarea, it is noted that "other SMSAs" in each state failed to receive their equitable share while "non-SMSAs" in each case were favored. Boston received exactly its fair share, but Hartford and Chicago both fell short, substantially in the latter case. Connecticut achieved the best statewide level of fairness (least average deviation from the norm). This may reflect the urban geography of that state in which no single city or SMSA is dominant (see Table 9-2).

From a public policy standpoint, it might be reasonable for distinct geographical areas to be served by separate programs. Criteria for allocation could then be designed for the particular needs and opportunities of each area, provided equity in funding were maintained between the areas. The HUD and BOR statutes hint at different geographical emphases without spelling out territorial responsibilities for each. Thus both programs have been stretched across the entire spectrum of open space needs—rural, suburban and central city—yielding a net nonurban bias.

Level of Governmental Recipient. Classification of the statewide data according to level of governmental recipient suggests approximate allocation of funds to different kinds of open space facilities (Table 9-11). State agencies generally deal with large tracts of land outside of metropolitan areas. Regional or county entities tend to operate medium-sized facilities in the outer portions of metropolitan areas. Local park boards and special districts provide neighborhood and community parks within their respective jurisdictions. (The National

Table 9-10. Combined HUD and BOR Open Space Allocations, Percentage of State Totals in Relation to Population for Selected State Subareas (Percent of Population in Parentheses)

	Massachusetts		*Connecticut*		*Illinois*	
Rural (Non-SMSA)	(15)	33	(17)	26	(19)	22
Suburbs (Primary SMSA)	(37)[a]	31	(16)[b]	18	(33)[c]	49
Primary Central City	(11)[a]	11	(5)[b]	3	(30)[c]	18
Other SMSAs	(37)	27	(62)	53	(18)	11
	100	100	100	100	100	100

[a]Boston
[b]Hartford
[c]Chicago
Source: Generated by the author from federal grant data.

Recreation and Parks Association has compiled recommended standards for the size, spacing and design of each of these classes of facilities).

Consistent with earlier discussion, Table 9-11 indicates that most of HUD's activity is at the local scale while BOR grants favor state agencies. This reflects the respective statutory schemes for fund allocation: HUD works directly with local governments while all BOR funds are channelled through the states. The latter, as mentioned above, retain as much as 75 percent of these funds for state purposes.

The HUD state level grants deserve special comment. The only state grant in Massachusetts—$46,500—was made in the first year of the program; Illinois' only state grant was for $2,000,000, comprising half of a joint effort with BOR toward acquisition of the Edgewater Golf Course in Chicago. By contrast, Connecticut has received 12 HUD grants for state facilities, nine of which are outside metropolitan areas. The allocation of HUD funds among levels of government is apparently determined more by demand than by federal policy.

The missing link in Connecticut and Massachusetts is the county-regional scale. Neither has a counterpart to the famous county forest preserve districts in Illinois, three of which (Cook, DuPage and Lake Counties) collectively received $10 million under both programs.

The Illinois Forest Preserve District has not been widely imitated. The regional open space plans for Boston and Hartford do not even contemplate such a vehicle; the county unit being virtually abolished in New England. The Metropolitan District Commission in Massachusetts is the only regional entity to receive open space grants in that state, but its level of activity as shown in Table 9-10 is slight as compared with the Illinois Forest Preserve Districts. Despite their alleged dependence upon "regional open space plans," the sponsoring federal agencies have not tried to promote the use of regional mechanisms.

Purpose. A further dimension is the question as to how federal funds have been used. Massachusetts has struck a balance between acquisition and development while the other states incline sharply toward acquisition in both programs (Table 9-12). Within the principal SMSAs, acquisition is again favored decisively except in Massachusetts. Central cities use federal funds largely for development of parks and recreation facilities. In the case of Chicago, more than half the city's acquisition funds were used for the 90 acre Edgewater Golf Course site.

The general picture is haphazard. While states apply formulae for the allocation of BOR funds among levels of government, they evidently do not do so with respect to acquisition versus development. Likewise, in the case of HUD, the preferences of applicant communities rather than state or federal priorities appear to set the pattern. Trade-offs between acquisition and development opportunities are not a matter of explicit policy.

Data as to purpose are limited at the state level as it is nationally. Specific function—for example, floodplain protection, ecological study area, and so forth—is obtainable only from circumstantial evidence. BOR records grants as "acquisition" or "development"; HUD designates grants as one or the other or "combined," but does not aggregate its totals. Table 9-12 assumes all HUD grants which involved the purchase of more than one acre to be "acquisition," whether or not the grant also included development.

Inside Metropolitan Areas

We now turn to consideration of the impact of the federal open space programs upon metropolitan areas and within the study SMSAs—Boston, Hartford and Chicago. However measured, effectiveness at the metropolitan scale is critical to the success of the programs generally. At this scale, the conversion of land from rural to urban uses is perceptually and actually most intense, the opportunities for "saving" open land are most imminent and the impending need for nondeveloped land for many purposes is most acute. Furthermore, the "regional open space plans" discussed earlier deal with the metropolitan scale and therefore should be most influential at that scale.

Data on individual grants made by each program in the three metropolitan areas were organized by municipality to facilitate both

Table 9-11. Federal Open Space Grants by State and Level of Recipient (Thousands of Dollars)

	State	*County-Regional*	*Local*	*Total*
HUD				
Massachusetts				
Grants	1	2	97	100
Amount	$47	$290	$8,807	$9,144
Acreage	647	153	3,567	4,367
Connecticut				
Grants	12	–	154	166
Amount	$1,287	–	$13,694	$14,981
Acreage	1,704	–	8696	10,400
Illinois				
Grants	1	33	190	224
Amount	$2,000	$7,125	$19,337	$28,462
Acreage	90	9,443	9,811	19,344
*BOR**				
Massachusetts				
Grants	42	5	59	106
Amount	$8,802	$806	$5,323	$14,931
Connecticut				
Grants	66	–	29	95
Amount	$4,424	–	$2,154	$6,578
Illinois				
Grants	53	18	90	161
Amount	$17,269	$6,587	$9,992	$33,848

*BOR does not record acreage for individual projects.
Source: Generated by the author from original grant data.

Table 9-12. Percentage Allocation by Purpose of Federal Open Space Funds, by State and Subarea, Through June 30, 1972

	HUD			*BOR*		
	Development	*Acquisition**	*Total*	*Development*	*Acquisition*	*Total*
Massachusetts						
State	50	50	100	54	46	100
Boston SMSA	38	25	63	13	16	29
Boston	22	0	22	4	0	4
Connecticut						
State	17	83	100	22	78	100
Hartford SMSA	5	16	21	0	21	21
Hartford	5	0	5	0	0	0
Illinois						
State	22	78	100	8	92	100
Chicago SMSA	19	67	86	1	51	52
Chicago	17	16	33	1	7	8

*Includes all HUD grants involving acquisition of more than one acre regardless of subprogram.
Source: Computed from original grant data, and HUD and BOR unpublished material.

intra- and intermetropolitan comparisons. The results of such data will be considered as follows: (1) extent of municipal participation in the programs; (2) number and size of parcels acquired; (3) location of open space grant activity; and (4) socioeconomic status of recipient communities.

Extent of Municipal Participation. Most open space grants in metropolitan areas are made to local entities, either municipalities or local special districts. But it does not follow that most municipalities have received such grants. Qualification for federal funding is difficult. A municipality must exert a considerable effort in terms of planning, raising the local share, and preparing and filing the application. The number of communities which have surmounted this obstacle course at least once is therefore a preliminary measure of the success of the federal programs in delivering their benefits on a metropolitanwide basis.

Disparity is noted between the three SMSAs as to extent of local government participation: the greater the number of municipalities, the smaller the percentage receiving grants (Table 9-13). In fact, the difference between the New England cases and the Chicago SMSA is even greater than indicated. More than half of the latter's territory does not belong to incorporated municipalities or park districts; no mechanism exists at the local level for the implementation of the NIPC open space in such areas. By contrast, all land in the Boston and Hartford SMSAs lies within incorporated towns at least potentially capable of acting to fulfill a regional plan. (Of course, the local situation in the case of Chicago is remedied partially by the forest preserve districts, a good illustration of why they were created!)

Even among incorporated areas, the political fragmentation of the Chicago SMSA inhibits widespread participation in the federal open space programs. As of 1970 the region contained 255 incorporated municipalities, of which 85 had fewer than 2,500 residents. There were also 134 local park districts whose territories overlay but did not necessarily coincide with the boundaries of many municipalities. Most of these minor civil units were uninvolved with the HUD or BOR open space programs. For communities of more than 10,000 population, Table 9-12 indicates a percentage of involvement close to that of the Boston SMSA.

For purposes of this study, grants made to park districts are assumed to be made to the municipality with which they are most closely identified, either by name or by common territory. This simplification is justified because in most cases the park district acts as surrogate for the municipality whose debt ceiling is the raison d'etre for the creation of the district.

Among the communities that have received at least one grant, Table 9-12 indicates a high degree of interchangeability between the HUD and BOR programs in all three states. HUD has assisted more communities than

Table 9-13. Participation Rate of Local Governments in Federal Open Space Programs, Boston, Hartford and Chicago SMSAs

	Total Municipal Governments	*HUD Recipients Only*	*BOR Recipients Only*	*Recipients from Both*	*Municipalities Receiving at Least 1 Grant*	
					Number	*Percent*
Boston SMSA	78	20	9	9	38	49
Hartford SMSA	27	10	5	6	21	78
Chicago SMSA	170[a]	31	13	12	56	33
	97[b]				45[b]	46

[a]Municipalities of more than 2,500 population.

[b]Municipalities of more than 10,000 population. (Local park districts are considered synonomous with the municipalities of the same name or generally the same territory.)

Source: Compiled by the author from HUD grant data through June 30, 1972 and BOR grant data through March 31, 1973.

BOR in each state but BOR's local government activity is surprisingly extensive in view of the state allocation formulae mentioned earlier. In each state a significant number of municipalities were assisted by both programs, raising a question as to whether on a strict "needs" basis certain communities have played the game of "grantsmanship" more effectively than Congress actually intended.

Number and Size of Metropolitan Acquisitions. Perhaps the acid test as to the performance of the federal programs in metropolitan areas is the number, size and distribution of parcels actually acquired with their assistance. Of course, development is important, as is nonmetropolitan acquisition. But federal aid would seem to be most indispensable, and therefore best used, in the costly and controversial business of safeguarding open spaces lying directly in the path of urbanization.

The four size groupings of Table 9-14 are intended to approximate the criteria expressed in open space literature for "neighborhood," "local," "community" and "regional" open spaces. While relating size to service area may be risky, it is normally assumed that parcels of less than five acres serve a strictly immediate public, while 80 acres is the threshold for "regional open space" as used in the NIPC open space plan.

Except for the forest preserve districts in Illinois, the results of both open space programs in metropolitan suburbs has been to acquire predominantly small parcels of "local" or "community" significance. This is not surprising since the recipients generally are either local municipalities or local park districts. Bearing out this distinction, the forest preserve grants are skewed toward much larger parcel sizes.

The point therefore can be repeated that in order to deal in acreages of regional significance, whether for recreation, conservation or "urban shaping," regional conduits for federal funds are required. To the extent that the federal programs have been used to provide suburban communities with open space facilities beneficial primarily to themselves, the overall intent of Congress to promote equality of access for metropolitan residents to public services, facilities and opportunities may have been thwarted. Further light on this possibility may be shed by examining the location of federal grant activity within metropolitan areas.

Location. Location is not simply a matter of size and distance. In an urban utopia where class, race, terrain and political jurisdiction are undifferentiated, the benefits generated by an open space facility (at least one intended for recreation) might well be predicted by a "gravity model" relating the size or "attractiveness" of the site, the size of population potentially served and the distance relationship between the two. Open space planning would then involve the relatively simple calculus of optimizing potential benefits from the expenditure of a specific budget for land acquisition, given the scale of land values according to distance from the population "center of gravity."

The real metropolitan world, however, permits no such simplistic determinations. Size-

Table 9-14. Number of Federal Open Space Grants for Acquisition, By Size of Parcel, Boston, Hartford and Chicago SMSAs

Number of Acres	*Boston*[1]			*Hartford*			*Chicago*		
	HUD	*BOR*	*Total*	*HUD*	*BOR*	*Total*	*HUD*	*BOR*	*Total*
0–4	9	3	12	1	4	5	29[2]	0[3]	NA
5–24	11	1	12	12	2	14	43	4	NA
25–79	15	5	20	14	4	18	13	5	NA
80 +	6	3	9	12	5	17	13	15	NA

1. Includes Metropolitan District Commission.

2. Municipal or Park District only.

3. County Forest Preserve District only.

Source: Compiled by the author from HUD grant data through June 30, 1972 and BOR grant data through March 31, 1973.

distance data must be qualified physically, by the natural characteristics of the site; politically, by governmental jurisdiction; and socially, by the cultural context of the area. For instance, according to the *Chicago Sun-Times* of July 9, 1973, a black reporter who merely walked through Calumet Park in an all-white neighborhood of Chicago was harassed and threatened with physical harm by white park users and bystanders. The reverse situation has occurred to this author.

Within the scope of this study, however, analysis is confined merely to intermunicipal comparisons.

Boston. The highest goal of the MAPC open space plan–namely, preservation of coastal shoreline–has not visibly been implemented by the federal open space programs. Figure 9-7 indicates very slight acreage acquired with federal assistance among the towns of Boston's North and South shorelines. Even the 377 acres indicated for Duxbury lies inland, rather than along the beach spit strongly recommended by MAPC The only significant effort to acquire coastal land in the Boston SMSA under the programs has been the BOR-funded purchase of several of the Boston Harbor Islands by the Massachusetts Department of Natural Resources (included in the totals for Hull, Weymouth and Quincy).

The apparent lack of attention given to the acquisition of coastal areas may in part be offset by the development of legal mechanisms for regulating the conversions of coastal wetlands to other purposes. By 1972, "protective orders" had been issued by the state with respect to 24,000 acres of coastal wetlands pursuant to authority granted in a 1965 law (Massachusetts General Laws, Chapter 30, section 105). An indirect factor has been the acquisition by the National Park Service of the Cape Cod National Seashore, about 90 miles from Boston.

Again using the criterion of population as a measure of fairness, intermunicipal equity would be indicated by a constant ratio of dollars per capita from one community to another, at least among those communities which participated in the programs. This clearly has not been the case (Figure 9-7). Allocations vary from less than $1 per capita in the near north suburbs to $121 dollars per capita in Lincoln. The total for the city of Boston is $2.79.

Seventeen out of 24 suburbs within ten miles of the State House received at least one grant. Those nine which are north of transect A-D averaged $4.80 per capita. South of this transect, eight participating towns received an average of $10.42. The latter, of course, include areas more recently urbanized and at lower densitites than in the northern sector.

Land values and population density decline with increasing distance from the central city. Accordingly, more land can be acquired with a given allocation than closer in, and the per capita benefits of such land are greater due to the smaller local population served.

It is therefore surprising to note that per capita allocations actually increase with distance in certain directions. Transects A-B and A-D on Figure 9-7 display this trend (Table 9-15). Transect A-F shows values decreasing among the suburbs; all, howerver, are higher than the central city. A dramatic contrast is observed along transect A-C, where dollars per capita jump from $1.36 for Waltham, an older manufacturing town, to $121.52 in neighboring Lincoln, a wealthy bedroom suburb. (Waltham has received two BOR grants totaling $85,000; Lincoln, five grants under both programs amounting to $919,000.)

Hartford. Turning to Figure 9-8 of the Hartford SMSA, the smaller number of communities permits fewer observations. The extent of participation is comparatively high, with 21 out of 27 communities receiving at least one grant. Moreover, the levels of dollars per capita are higher than the Boston SMSA: seven out of 21 recipients received more than $10 per capita in the Hartford region as compared with seven out of 38 recipients in the Boston area.

Lacking a "shoreline anomaly," activity in the Hartford SMSA is seen to be distributed in all directions from the central city, with a noticeable concentration toward the western periphery. Acquisitions in the Talcott Mountain Range (known as "The Western Highlands") in Simsbury and Bloomfield have implemented recommendations of the regional open space plan. Another success for the plan has been preservation of the Farmington River bottom-

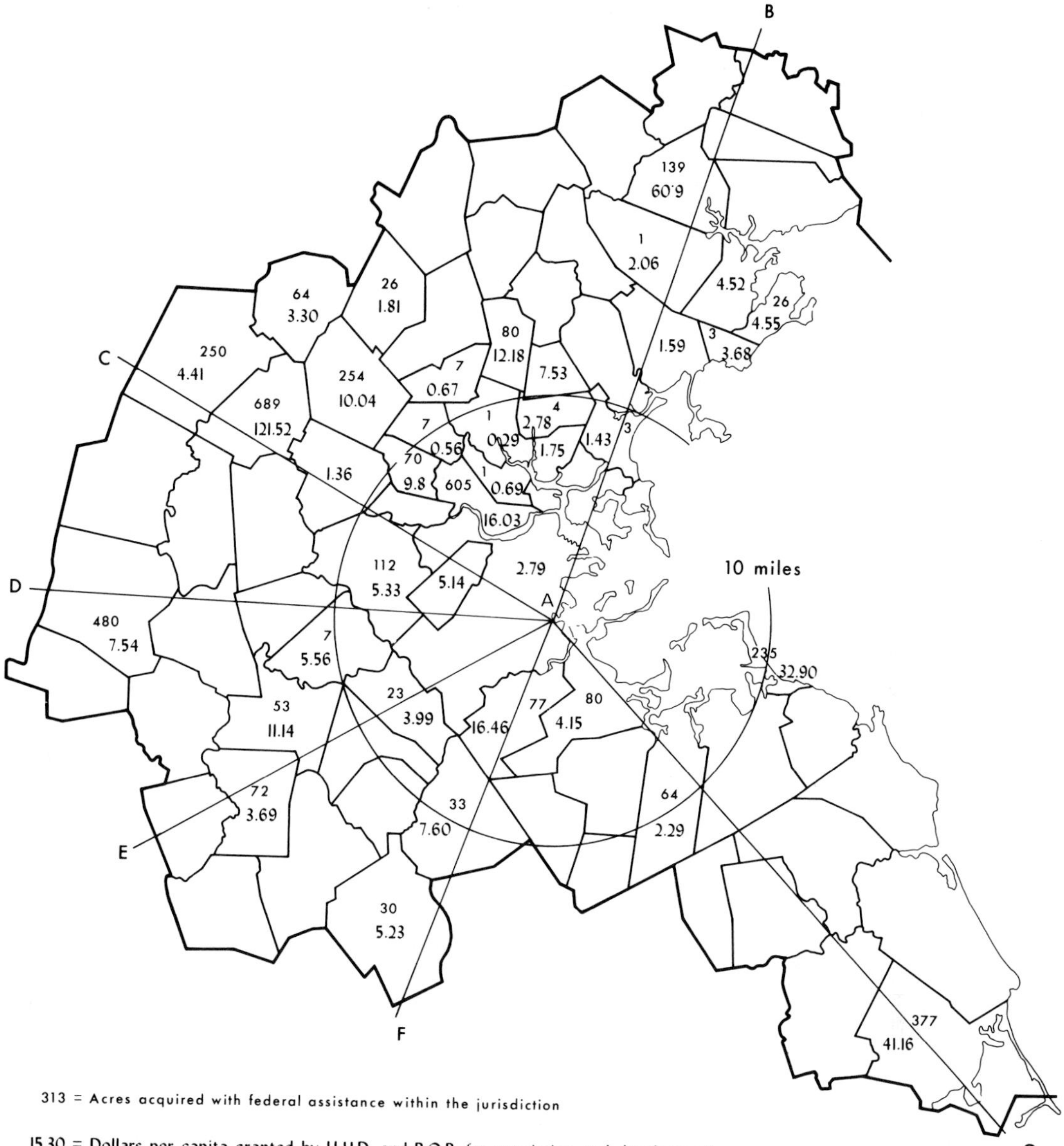

313 = Acres acquired with federal assistance within the jurisdiction

15.30 = Dollars per capita granted by H.U.D. and B.O.R. for acquistion and development.

Figure 9-7. Boston Metropolitan Area: Dollars per Capita and Acres Acquired under BOR and HUD Open Space Programs. Values are zero where no data appear.

land in Windsor. Remaining unaccomplished, however, is hte plan's proposal to set aside 4,000 acres of Connecticut River floodplain known as the "Great Meadows" in Glastonbury and Wethersfield, although local zoning averted a proposed race track in part of this area.

Chicago. Open space grant activity in the Chicago metropolitan area presents a more complex pattern than either of the New England cases. Not only is its political geography more fragmented, but open space activity is proceeding simultaneously at three levels of government—state, county and local. Furthermore, much of this activity is conducted by special districts rather than governmental units of general jurisdiction.

Direct efforts by state agencies to preserve open space in metropolitan areas is unusual in each of the areas studied. The acquisition of

Table 9-15. Total Federal Open Space Grants, Dollars per Capita, by Municipalities Along Selected Transects, Boston SMSA

Scale of Miles	*A–B*	*A–C*	*A–D*	*A–E*	*A–F*	*A–G*
1	Boston $2.79	Boston $2.79	Boston $2.79	Boston $2.79	Boston $2.79	Boston $2.79
4	Chelsea 0	Brookline 5.14	Brookline 5.14		Milton 16.46	Quincy 4.15
				Dedham 3.99		
8	Revere 1.43	Newton 5.33	Needham 5.56	Westwood 0	Canton 7.60	Weymouth 2.29
12	Sangus 0	Waltham 1.36	Wellesley 0	Dover 11.14	Sharon 5.23	Hingham 0
	Lynn 1.59					
16	Peabody 2.06	Lincoln 121.5	Natick 0	Medfield 3.69		Hanover 0
20	Danvers 6.09	Concord 4.41	Framingham 7.54	Millis 0		Pembroke 0
	Wenham 0					
24	Hamilton 0	(Acton)* 9.2				Duxbury 41.16
28						

Source: compiled by the author. *Outside the Boston SMSA.

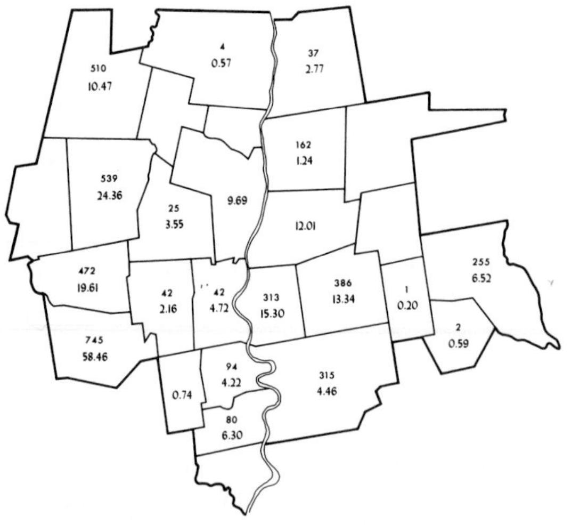

313 = Acres acquired with federal assistance within the jurisdiction

15.30 = Dollars per capita granted by H.U.D. and B.O.R. for acquisition and development.

Figure 9-8. Hartford Metropolitan Area: Dollars per Capita and Acres Acquired under BOR and HUD Open Space Programs. Values are zero where no data appear.

the Boston Harbor Islands was the first federally aided acquisition project undertaken by the Massachusetts Department of Natural Resources in the Boston SMSA. In the Hartford region, the Connecticut State Parks and Forest Commission has received $250,000 in three HUD grants to acquire a total of 707 acres. State activity in the Chicago SMSA, although spotty, is at least more impressive in scale than these examples. Long adhering to the policy of buying extensive acreage at low cost far from population centers, the state of Illinois under Governor Richard E. Ogilvie (1968–1972) placed new stress on metropolitan needs (Figure 9-9). The Illinois Department of Conservation has acted aggressively to protect significant areas of glacial bogs and "knob and kettle" terrain in the northwestern portion of the Chicago region. It is in the process of expanding several state parks near and within the Chicago SMSA, including Chain O'Lakes and Illinois State Beach. And after three years of citizen pressure, it has consented to acquire some 600 acres of south suburban Thorn Creek

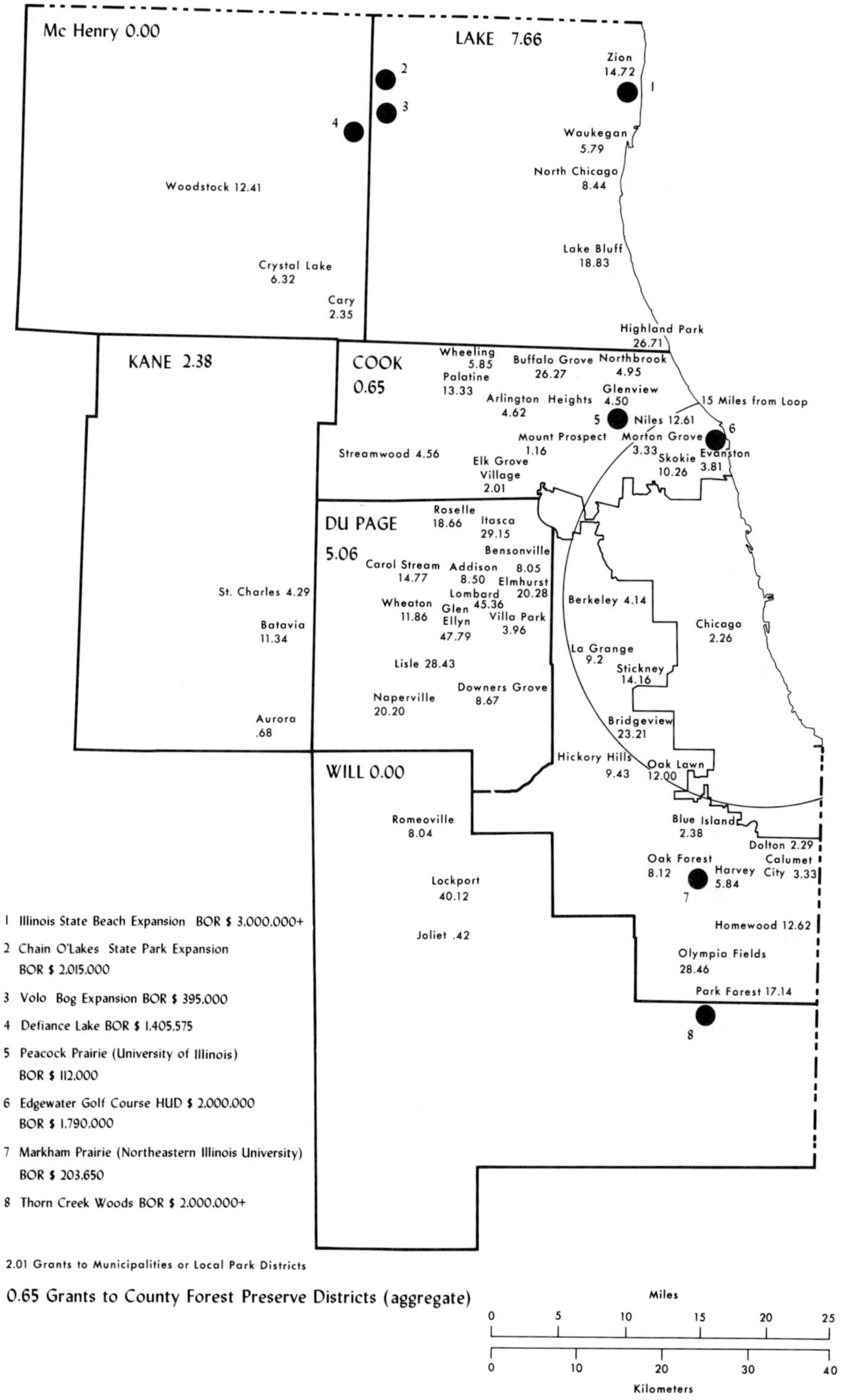

Mc Henry 0.00
LAKE 7.66
Zion
14.72
1
2
3
4
Waukegan
5.79
North Chicago
8.44
Woodstock 12.41
Lake Bluff
18.83
Crystal Lake
6.32
Cary
2.35
Highland Park
26.71
KANE 2.38
COOK
0.65
Wheeling
5.85
Palatine
13.33
Buffalo Grove
26.27
Northbrook
4.95
Glenview
4.50
Arlington Heights
4.62
15 Miles from Loop
5
Niles 12.61
6
Mount Prospect
1.16
Morton Grove
3.33
Skokie
10.26
Evanston
3.81
Streamwood 4.56
Elk Grove
Village
2.01
Roselle
18.66
Itasca
29.15
DU PAGE
5.06
Bensonville
Carol Stream
14.77
Addison
8.50
8.05
Elmhurst
Lombard
20.28
45.36
Wheaton
11.86
Glen
Ellyn
47.79
Villa Park
3.96
St. Charles 4.29
Berkeley 4.14
Batavia
11.34
Chicago
2.26
La Grange
9.2
Stickney
14.16
Lisle 28.43
Downers Grove
8.67
Naperville
20.20
Aurora
.68
Bridgeview
23.21
Hickory Hills
9.43
Oak Lawn
12.00
WILL 0.00
Romeoville
8.04
Blue Island
2.38
Dolton 2.29
Oak Forest
8.12
Calumet
City 3.33
Harvey
5.84
7
Lockport
40.12
Homewood 12.62
Joliet .42
Olympia Fields
28.46
Park Forest 17.14
8
1 Illinois State Beach Expansion BOR $ 3,000,000+
2 Chain O'Lakes State Park Expansion
BOR $ 2,015,000
3 Volo Bog Expansion BOR $ 395,000
4 Defiance Lake BOR $ 1,405,575
5 Peacock Prairie (University of Illinois)
BOR $ 112,000
6 Edgewater Golf Course HUD $ 2,000,000
BOR $ 1,790,000
7 Markham Prairie (Northeastern Illinois University)
BOR $ 203,650
8 Thorn Creek Woods BOR $ 2,000,000+
2.01 Grants to Municipalities or Local Park Districts
0.65 Grants to County Forest Preserve Districts (aggregate)
Miles
0 5 10 15 20 25
0 10 20 30 40
Kilometers

Figure 9-9. State, County and Local Activity; HUD and BOR Open Space Programs in the Chicago Metropolitan Area. Values are zero where no data appear.

Woods in concert with a county forest preserve district, two local municipalities, a university and a private developer.

The state's only federally assisted project in Chicago has been the $8 million purchase of 90 acres of Edgewater Golf Course in the Rogers Park community close to the city's northern boundary. Two state universities have received BOR grants toward the preservation of small fragments of virgin prairie for use as ecological study areas.

Altogether, state efforts have accounted for more than $13 million in federal open space grants received or promised for projects in the Chicago SMSA. From a planning standpoint, the results to date are somewhat haphazard, representing the outcome of citizen pressure rather than deliberate planning. The Illinois example, however, does illustrate the potential role of a state as the "preserver of last resort" for sites threatened by metropolitan growth.

The five county forest preserve districts of the six county Chicago metropolitan area collectively have accounted for more than $10.5 million in total federal grants toward the acquisition of approximately 12,000 acres. As already noted, forest preserve acquisitions comprise most of the larger parcels acquired under the federal programs in the Chicago SMSA, and as such most closely satisfy the criteria for "regional open space" delineated in the NIPC Open Space Plan.

Forest preserve district efforts also display much greater economy than local efforts in terms of dollars per acre acquired. In terms of HUD grants, for which acreage data is available, forest preserve acquisitions averaged about $1,500 per acre total cost while local preservation efforts averaged $12,000 per acre. Those figures do not consider location, nor do they distinguish grants for development versus acquisition which would tend to exaggerate particularly the local figure. Nevertheless, it is undeniable that county-level efforts are more "efficient" from a strict cost per acre standpoint than fragmented local efforts.

As the low cost per acre figure would indicate, forest preserve acquisitions in recent years have tended to be located toward the periphery of the metropolitan area. Most of the federally assisted acquisition in highly developed Cook County is located in the far northwest suburban sector. Much of the acreage acquired is farmland which the forest preserve district, under new enabling authority, plans to reforest.

Due to its early start and visionary leadership, the Cook County Forest Preserve System far excels those of its neighbors except for DuPage County in total holdings and, astonishingly, acres per capita. Lake County to the north and DuPage County to the west are now experiencing severe pressure from development and are trying to remedy their long neglect. Each has received approximately $2.5 million in federal open space grants, or more than ten times the per capita total accruing to Cook County. As with many of Cook County's earlier acquisitions, Lake and DuPage are acquiring extensive floodplain and wooded bottomland. With land values soaring to $15,000 per acre or more, it would appear that more effective use of non-compensatory floodplain zoning might obviate the need to acquire the more frequently flooded portions of a basin.

Kane and Will counties still retain a largely agrarian land use pattern and political outlook, and display correspondingly less forest preserve activity. (Will County's first federal open space grant was recently announced for the purchase of 100 acres in Thorn Creek Woods.) McHenry County, a land of gentlemen farmers, twice rejected the formation of a forest preserve district but in 1971 finally established a countywide "conservation district."

The spatial patterns of benefits generated by county forest preserve would deserve a detailed study of its own. It may be only briefly observed here that forest preserves probably most closely satisfy the three goals for open space preservation listed in the federal statutes–recreation, conservation and "urban shaping."

Local grant activity has occurred predominantly in the outer and less densely populated portion of the region. Approximately 60 percent of the SMSA population lives within 15 miles of the Chicago Loop. This territory, however, contains only ten of the 56 communities (or park districts) which received grants. These ten, including the city of Chicago, together accounted for only 25 percent of the dollars granted by the programs combined and only five percent of HUD-assisted acreage. No forest preserve district or state projects except for Edgewater Golf Course are within this territory.

Outside the 15 mile radius, local grant activity is seen to coincide roughly with the familiar "finger pattern" of older suburbs extending along commuter rail lines. This would appear to be exactly contrary to the NIPC Open Space Plan which, as noted in the third section of this chapter, called for acquisition between, not within, the existing fingers of development.

The overall levels of dollars per capita for these communities which received grants are high: 45 percent received more than $10 per capita (as compared with 33 percent in Hartford and 18 percent in Boston). Due perhaps to the confused municipal geography and the influence of county and state activity, it is not possible to identify a systematic change in per capita level with distance from the central city as in Boston and Hartford.

Two values of less than $1 on the southwestern fringe belong to Aurora and Joliet, old and densely populated industrial centers. High values are otherwise noted among more prosperous communities along the periphery such as Park Forest ($17.14), Naperville $20.20), Woodstock ($12.41) and Zion (14.72). Even higher values are noted along the string of "main line" suburbs including Elmhurst, Villa Park, Lombard, Glen Ellyn and Wheaton: $20.28, $3.96, $45.36, $47.79, $11.86. The "North Shore" suburbs also do well: $26.71, $18.83, $8.44, $5.79, and $14.72. As with Farmington-Avon-Simsbury in the Hartford SMSA and Lexington-Lincoln-Concord in the Boston region, the impression is strong that the open space programs have tended to help most those best able to help themselves.

Socioeconomic Character of Recipients. The US General Accounting Office (GAO) in a report dated October 5, 1972 criticized the tendency for both HUD and BOR open space grants as follows:

> [Densely] populated urban areas with great need for additional recreation facilities have not participated to any significant extent in the BOR and HUD grant programs. We noted that available grant funds often exceeded applications for funds and that most applications for projects which were technically eligible were approved, regardless of their location or apparent value.
>
> Many low-income, densely populated communities have not applied for BOR and HUD grants because they lack matching funds, adequate planning, or public support. In some cases the States received Federal assistance for large projects in rural areas, but because of their locations and the types of recreation offered, they were of little benefit to large segments of the cities' populations. In one case, a large city received BOR and HUD grant funds, but used about half the funds in its more affluent, less densely populated areas which were not readily accessible to many residents of the more densely populated areas of the city. [P. 1]

This study has confirmed the GAO conclusion. We have noted underallocation to central cities and "other SMSAs" (Table 9-9), with most central city grants used for development rather than acquisition (Table 9-12). Also, per capita allocations are observed to increase with distance from the central city, at least in certain sectors (Figures 9-7 to 9-9).

Comparison between per capita grant allocations and two measures of community wealth further corroborates the GAO findings. For each SMSA grant data was correlated with "community mean family income" of socioeconomic status (Figure 9-10). All three SMSAs display nearly identical values for the first, third and fourth quintiles. In each case, the wealthiest communities have by far the highest per capita federal allocations in the region. This is true even though many "first quintile" suburbs did not apply for any grants.

The curves plunge erratically through the second quintile to very low values in the third and fourth quintiles. These represent more densely populated older suburbs or new bedroom communities for the white or black lower middle class. In each case, the fifth quintile displays an upward twist, reflecting the special priority given to development projects in the central city and adjoining areas of poverty or nonwhite population.

Further evidence is gained by comparing grants allocated with another measure of ability of a community to help itself—namely, assessed property value per capita (Figure 9-11). This measure of the wealth of the community places many communities in the same quintile as "mean family income." However, an industrial enclave-tax shelter such as Stickney, Illinois, is found at the bottom of the family income scale and in the top fifth of assessed value ranking: the South Stickney

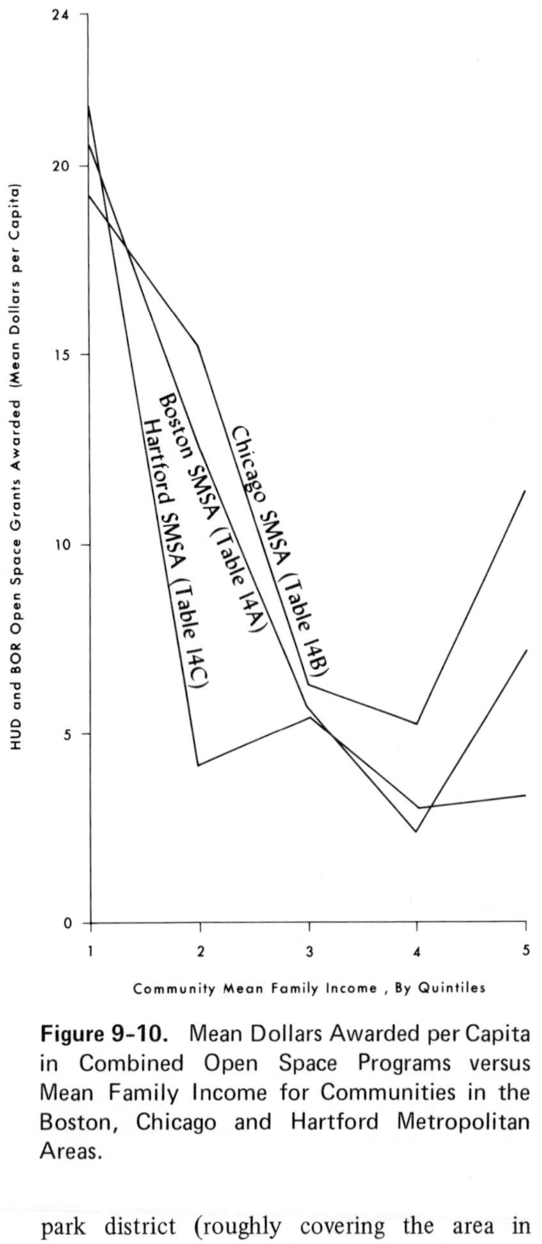

Figure 9-10. Mean Dollars Awarded per Capita in Combined Open Space Programs versus Mean Family Income for Communities in the Boston, Chicago and Hartford Metropolitan Areas.

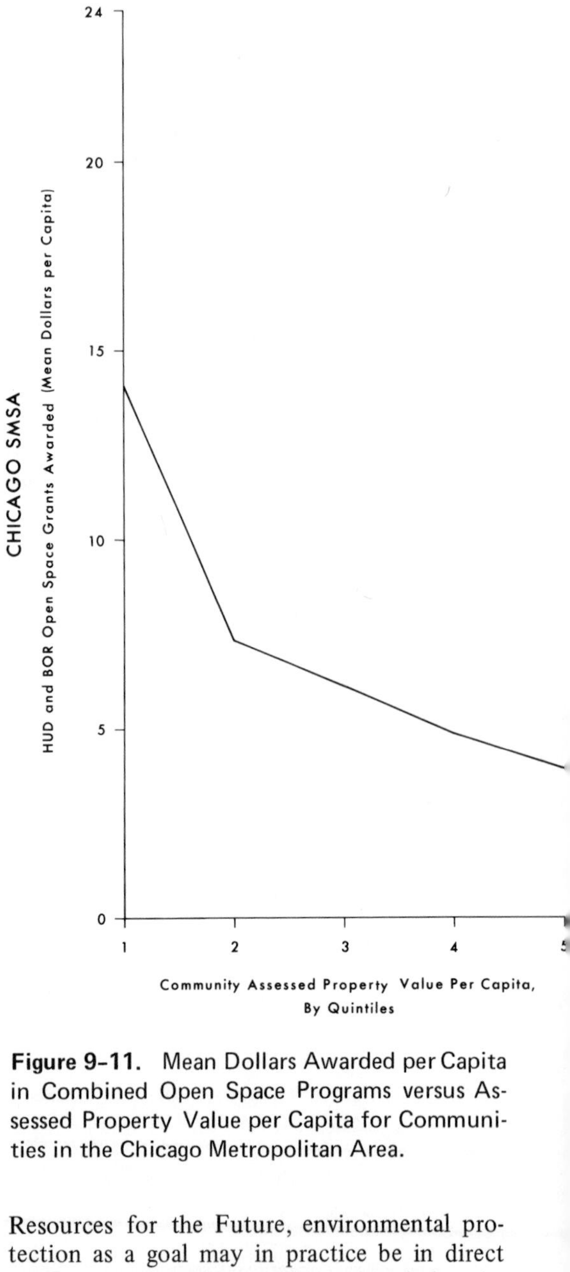

Figure 9-11. Mean Dollars Awarded per Capita in Combined Open Space Programs versus Assessed Property Value per Capita for Communities in the Chicago Metropolitan Area.

park district (roughly covering the area in question) has received nine federal grants totaling nearly one-half million dollars. Again the wealthy gain most from the HUD and BOR open space programs.

The lack of adequate standards over the administration of open space grants not only squanders scarce resources on communities best able to handle their own problems, but also threatens to exacerbate certain other problems on a metropolitan scale. As Richard M. Babcock has observed in an address to Resources for the Future, environmental protection as a goal may in practice be in direct conflict with other goals, particularly the provision of adequate housing and the elimination of exclusionary barriers to residence in any community. To the extent that open space preservation removes land from eligibility for residential or other construction, the temptation to preclude undesirable development in the name of ecology is strong. It would appear that neither HUD nor BOR has avoided the stigma of at least potentially placing the resources of the federal government behind such efforts.

Conclusions and Recommendations

Some favorable conclusions of the study should first be mentioned. More than 1,875 square miles of land are permanently in public ownership as a result of the HUD and BOR efforts. Both programs have been conscientiously administered and available funds have in fact been applied to the acquisition of development of bona fide open space projects with relatively minimum waste or unnecessary overhead. Compared with the acrimony generated by other federal domestic programs such as urban renewal and public lands management, the federal open space efforts have been largely uncontroversial.

The policy of Congress, whatever its wisdom, to spread available funds among all geographic and functional competitors has been followed (Table 9-12). Acquisition and development, recreation and conservation, metropolitan and nonmetropolitan sectors all have shared in the benefits of the programs, albeit not equally.

Perhaps most encouraging is evidence of the willingness of program administrators to learn by experience and to revise allocation procedures and policies accordingly (Table 9-17). This occurred formally in HUD's new regulations of April 14, 1972, and informally in BOR's greater interest in the inner city. These modifications were in part influenced by the October 5, 1972, GAO report.

On the negative side, the most important conclusion of the study is that the combined efforts of the two federal programs have had relatively little impact where they are needed most, namely in acquiring new open space acreage in metropolitan areas. Ten years of effort have produced extremely meager results in terms of the number and size of parcels acquired in the path of urban development (Table 9-14). Moreover, many of these parcels are located in exclusive high income suburbs where they would likely have been preserved anyway.

Each metropolitan area contains substantial voids where no federal grants were received; in Boston and Chicago less than half of suburban municipalities participated in the programs at

Table 9-16. HUD and BOR Open Space Programs, Number of Grants and Total Amounts, By States, in Order of Population (thousands of dollars)

		HUD			BOR		
		Projects	*Amounts*	*Rank*	*Projects*	*Amounts*	*Rank*
1	California	562	$ 75,271	1	258	57,182	1
2	New York	168	42,953	2	233	48,242	2
3	Pennsylvania	249	29,591	5	233	39,019	3
4	Texas	163	18,165	10	276	36,926	4
5	Illinois	236	33,954	4	164	33,691	5
6	Ohio	182	21,057	9	237	24,724	6
7	Michigan	147	26,316	6	389	21,354	7
8	New Jersey	199	36,713	3	160	19,801	9
9	Florida	109	17,931	11	58	19,297	10
10	Massachusetts	100	12,977	15	114	16,009	13
11	Indiana	46	8,095	19	144	14,104	17
12	North Carolina	92	6,695	23	258	13,604	18
13	Missouri	88	10,125	17	390	20,425	8
14	Virginia	111	15,844	12	95	18,503	11
15	Georgia	88	6,899	22	217	16,722	12
16	Wisconsin	102	10,715	16	608	14,788	16
17	Tennessee	121	8,447	18	132	11,233	24
18	Maryland	139	23,437	8	236	15,780	14
19	Minnesota	118	15,145	13	531	12,199	22
20	Louisiana	53	6,078	25	178	15,170	15

(continued)

Table 9-16 continued

		HUD			BOR		
		Projects	*Amounts*	*Rank*	*Projects*	*Amounts*	*Rank*
21	Alabama	102	6,467	24	141	9,757	26
22	Washington	110	25,329	7	140	12,545	20
23	Kentucky	52	5,223	27	187	12,269	21
24	Connecticut	158	14,633	14	99	7,042	42
25	Iowa	79	7,386	21	354	8,530	33
26	South Carolina	35	3,299	33	234	7,534	38
27	Oklahoma	37	2,546	34	167	7,313	40
28	Kansas	34	3,744	30	208	11,286	23
29	Mississippi	32	1,846	38	101	8,112	36
30	Colorado	58	5,677	26	375	10,306	25
31	Oregon	51	3,502	31	415	13,601	19
32	Arkansas	36	2,039	37	107	9,750	27
33	Arizona	27	4,200	28	191	9,428	28
34	West Virginia	4	240	47	130	9,035	30
35	Nebraska	35	2,054	36	255	8,835	31
36	Utah	27	3,447	32	143	9,625	28
37	New Mexico	9	995	40	225	8,365	34
38	Maine	14	1,355	39	178	7,246	41
39	Rhode Island	45	3,780	29	97	5,434	49
40	Hawaii	26	7,395	20	65	8,312	35
41	New Hampshire	12	946	41	76	4,476	50
42	Idaho	7	256	46	145	7,515	39
43	Montana	10	348	44	219	5,652	47
44	South Dakota	6	440	42	292	7,715	37
45	North Dakota	3	153	49	334	6,285	45
46	Delaware	3	173	48	55	6,336	44
47	Nevada	23	2,088	35	46	8,668	32
48	Vermont	3	348	45	147	6,828	43
49	Wyoming	1	4	50	286	5,616	48
50	Alaska	5	6,467	24	141	9,757	26
	Puerto Rico	17	1,341		29	5,072	
	District of Columbia	8	3,475		27	5,099	
	Guam				10	511	
	American Samoa				13	445	
	Virgin Islands				10	472	
		4,218	$541,539		10,506	$730,079	

Sources: US Congress, House Appropriations Committee, Subcommittee on HUD, Hearings on 1974 Budget, p. 667 (includes all HUD open space activity through June 30, 1972); unpublished BOR documents (includes all BOR matching grants to states and their subdivisions through March 31, 1973).

all. Such *lacunae* surely do not signify an absence of suitable land as much as a failure of federal and regional authorities to elicit interest in open space preservation among nonparticipating communities. By the same token, linear "chains" of grant recipients are noted on the Boston and Chicago maps, suggesting the diffusion of interest from one community to the next rather than from higher authority to lower. To accomplish the acquisition of thousands of acres, let alone the hundreds of thousands proposed by regional plans, more direction is needed.

Restructuring Project Selection. With the shift in federal philosophy from matching grants to revenue sharing, the question of how to improve project selection among open space applications may seem beside the point. However, BOR retains the matching grant form and revenue sharing will probably yield even less satisfactory results than the matching grant

Table 9-17. HUD Open Space Program, Projects, Amounts and Acreage, by Year and Subprogram, Through December 31, 1971

Calender Year		*Projects*	*Amounts (in $000s)*	*Acreage*
1961-1965	Undeveloped Land	399	44,185	149,483
1966	Undeveloped Land	328	54,013	52,700
	Urban Beautification	64	9,278	
	Urban Parks	44	10,675	
		436	73,966	
1967	Undeveloped Land	240	23,332	33,526
	Urban Beautification	69	4,847	
		309	28,179	
1968	Undeveloped Land	476	56,971	44,943
	Historic Preservation	11	941	
	Urban Beautification	117	12,850	
	Urban Parks	91	15,285	
		695	86,047	
1969	Undeveloped Land	339	41,147	19,280
	Historic Preservation	22	1,376	
	Urban Beautification	102	12,266	
	Urban Parks	51	11,605	
		514	66,394	
1970	Undeveloped Land	475	48,250	23,923
	Historic Preservation	15	621	
	Urban Beautification	91	12,531	
	Urban Parks	58	13,036	
		639	74,438	
1971	Undeveloped Land	348	50,090	25,506
	Historic Preservation	29	1,569	
	Urban Beautification	112	15,717	
	Urban Parks	44	6,157	
		533	73,533	
Totals	Undeveloped Land	2605	317;988	
	Historic Preservation	77	4,507	
	Urban Beautification	555	67,489	
	Urban Parks	288	56,758	
		3525	446,742	

Source: US Department of Health, Education and Welfare *Statistical Yearbook, 1971* (Washington, D.C.: US Government Printing Office, 1971), tables 10, 12, 16 and 19.

approach. It is therefore appropriate to consider how the administration of federal cost-sharing efforts might be made more efficient and more equitable.

The chief barrier to achievement of regional open space objectives has been the reliance upon local initiative to qualify for federal funds and implement the regional plans. Local governments notoriously serve their own interests, which may be quite different from regional ones. Internal benefits and costs are weighed to the exclusion of external factors. Reduction of internal costs by 50 percent may well facilitate provision of open space that is internally beneficial. But when it comes to sites largely of regional benefit which happen to lie within a given municipality, a matching federal share of acquisition is unlikely to impel the local government to action.

Existing federal grant procedure thus incurs a twofold danger: (1) it subsidizes those efforts which are predominantly of local internal benefit and even counter to regional interests, and (2) it fails to elicit necessary action by local governments as to sites of predominantly extralocal significance. In short, with regard to grants to local authorities, the federal programs may be impeding rather than promoting metropolitan land use goals.

A facile remedy to this impasse might be to preclude grants to local governments in the future under the theory that they are incapable of acting in the regional interest. Such a policy might gain support from the observed propensity of county, regional and state agencies to apply federal funds to the acquisition of larger tracts and to manage their holdings in the interest of the regional public. However, it would disregard the possibility that tracts of purely local significance, if equitably distributed, might in the aggregate constitute a system of regional benefit (in possible analogy to Adam Smith's "invisible hand"). Furthermore, tracts of local benefit may generate incidental benefits to a wider public, particularly in the case of sites visible from a public road or of hydrologic significance.

Therefore, while regional entities should be supported as far as possible, it does not follow that grants to local authorities should be eliminated. Instead, the procedure for allocating such grants should be restructured. In place of existing provisions of federal statutes and the regional plans which provide virtually no guidance with respect to local grants, the following are recommended elements of a revised procedure:

- performance standards for the selection of local open space projects;
- a sliding scale of federal participation according to importance of project as indicated by performance standards;
- federal approval of local land use control regulations as prerequisite to federal assistance. (Analogy is found in the "workable program" requirement of the Urban Renewal Program and the landuse regulations required by the National Flood Insurance Program.)

In place of prosaic descriptions of places "desirable for preservation," the state of the planning art now permits the formulation of objective performance standards on matters such as topography, hydrology, vegetation, soils, socioeconomic character of the jurisdiction and the like. Prospective management policy could likewise be weighed, with covenants to ensure performance. The NIPC Open Space Plan represents a first approach to performance standard planning, although it departs from its own methodology in formulating actual priorities. The HUD revised regulations of April 14, 1972, formulated "performance standards" for the weighting of projects in terms of socioeconomic characteristics of the jurisdiction and service area but did not reach environmental criteria. Merger and refinement of the NIPC and HUD methodologies is recommended.

The scale of federal participation should be capable of adjustment to reflect the results of a more sophisticated project selection procedure. Federal participation might be scaled anywhere between zero and 99 percent depending upon the inherent qualities of the parcel itself, the benefits expected to be generated by it and the socioeconomic status of the jurisdiction containing it. Under current law, a 20 percent bonus in federal participation in various programs—including open space—is authorized in projects relating to a "new community." The 70 percent federal share thereby permitted was of considerable influence, for example, in persuading the Will County (Illinois) Forest Preserve District to apply for its first federal grant.

Finally, a more systematic approach to the funding of local open space projects would entail encouragement of the use of local regulatory powers to set aside land which physically should not be developed and which therefore need not be publicly acquired. Following the precedent of the HUD-administered National Flood Insurance Program, it is feasible for federal agencies to require local governments to adopt and enforce suitable land use regulations as a condition precedent to receiving open space grant assistance. This requirement, however, should be waivable by the federal agency in cases where it would hinder accomplishment of a project of regional significance.

Acquisition versus Development. The tension between use of available funds for acquisition versus development further complicates the existing procedure and underlies the meagerness of the federal contribution to accomplishment of metropolitan goals. Since neither

HUD nor BOR has sole responsibility for all applications of either kind, both are required to make indefinable trade-off choices between acquisition and development. This is no easy process: Table 9-12 indicates the pronounced differences between programs, between states and between subareas of states in the allocation of funds for these purposes.

The preparation of facilities for public use is obviously a necessary phase of the delivery of open space recreation benefits to the public; however, for purposes of federal policy a logical distinction can be drawn between acquisition and development. With land values rising by 5 to 10 percent per year and urbanization an imminent possiblity, time is of the essence in the acquisition of suitable open space in metropolitan locations. With the land safely in public hands, preparation for its eventual use may proceed at any time. Furthermore, acquisition requires that the entire market price be paid at one time, for which effort federal assistance may well be indispensable. Development, however, can be designed and phased as resources permit.

It may thus be argued that acquisition of open space sites should take priority over development in the allocation of federal resources. Special provision is of course required for problem areas such as inner cities where vacant land is abundant but the need for facilities is acute. Assuming that a certain portion of available funds is earmarked for central cities, the acquisition function could elsewhere be given priority over development as a matter of federal policy. Bona fide local commitments to develop sites for recreation could be credited toward the local share, as is done in the urban renewal program with respect to project site improvements. Otherwise grant recipients may be left to their own tax resources and to revenue bond financing for the development of sites.

By funding acquisition ahead of any development projects outside central cities or other designated localities, the project selection process should be both simplified and expedited. The volume of land acquired in terms of projects and acreage should increase significantly and the physical imprint of the federal effort would be more prominent upon the land use pattern of metropolitan areas. Granted that the delivery of open space benefits would not be complete in many cases without site improvements, at least the public would be able to keep its options open. Land not immediately usable could be regarded as a "land bank" whose eventual use and management could be decided later.

Revenue Sharing. The foregoing discussion has assumed the continuation of a categorical grant approach to the allocation of federal open space assistance, hopefully on a sliding scale as outlined above. Current administration intentions are to retain the BOR matching grant program while converting the HUD program to "special revenue sharing." Under the Better Communities Act, all communities receive some federal aid for community development and improvement purposes. Such funds are not earmarked for acquisition.

Pursuant to the argument developed above, as well as to the analysis of LeGates and Morgan, it is suggested that revenue sharing would be counterproductive to the objective of acquiring open land in metropolitan areas. Early indications on the results of revenue sharing to date show that many communities are using such funds to increase municipal salaries and otherwise to alleviate the need for raising local property taxes. It is probable that, given the choice, most communities would prefer to use community development money to subsidize what they are already doing, and perhaps to improve park sites which they already own. The prospects for such funds being used for land acquisition are slight, given the relatively small amounts available and the pressure to alleviate or at least stabilize existing local tax effort.

Toward a (Single) National Land Use Policy. As noted in the first section of this study, the open space programs arose out of intense intellectual and popular hostility to "urban sprawl." The programs were essentially conceived as "antidotes" to the "poison" of uncontrolled and wasteful urban development. Aside from modest and later deleted statements in the Housing Act of 1961 about the need to employ land use controls, no overt attempt was made to alter or "subvert" the basic ground rules of the urban development process which was the source of the problem in the first place. While far mightier efforts of the federal government itself built or facilitated the building of highways, housing developments, reservoirs and sewers, the open space program was cautiously incubated in the Urban Renewal Administration, as though consigned from the outset to the category of hopeless "good works."

The temper of the nation has changed. The National Environmental Policy Act of 1969, the Coastal Zone Management Act of 1972 and the Flood Disaster Protection Act of 1973 all reflect keen national interest in land use policy. A proposed National Land Use Policy Act has attracted strong support, although so far not enough to be adopted. Without waiting for the national law to be passed, several states–including Vermont, Maine, Massachusetts, Florida, Hawaii and California–have passed legislation to subject all or critical portions of their territories to scrutiny by other than local land use decisionmakers.

The objective of "preserving open space" has thus changed during the last decade from a timid federal response to urban scholars and "bird watchers" into "The Quiet Revolution in Land Use Control."

It would, however, be naive to regard this new mood as heralding an abolition of property rights or eliminating the need to compensate owners of land required for public use. The very survival of the new laws in the face of constitutional challenge may well depend upon the capacity of public agencies to purchase outright title or easements to land where an actual development potential is precluded by a state or regional plan. The demand for massive funds for land acquisition may thus be expected to amplify rather than abate as the "quiet revolution" spreads.

Whatever the source, funds will never be adequate to meet all demands, especially in an economy of rising land values. The issue of allocation, therefore, remains paramount, and it is to this issue that the federal experience of the past decade may prove most relevant to meeting the challenges of the next.

BIBLIOGRAPHY

Advisory Committee on Intergovernmental Relations. *Urban and Rural America: Policies for Future Growth.* Washington, D.C.: US Government Printing Office, 1968.

——. *Urban America and the Federal System.* Washington, D.C.: US Government Printing Office, 1969.

Bosselman, Fred and David Callies. *The Quiet Revolution in Land Use Control.* Report of the US Council on Environmental Quality. Washington, D.C.: US Government Printing Office, 1971.

Capitol Region Planning Agency. *Regional Open Space Plan.* Hartford, 1966.

Carstenson, Vernon, ed. *The Public Lands.* Madison: University of Wisconsin Press, 1968.

Chadwick, George F. *The Park and the Town.* New York: Praeger, 1966.

Clawson, Marion. *Land and Water for Recreation.* Chicago: Rand McNally and Co., 1963.

Clawson, Marion; R. Burnell Held; and Charles H. Stoddard. *Land for the Future.* Baltimore: The Johns Hopkins Press for Resources for the Future, 1960.

Committee for Economic Development. *Guiding Metropolitan Growth.* Washington, D.C., August 1960.

The Conservation Foundation. *National Parks for the Future.* Washington, D.C., 1972.

Dunham, Allison. "From Rural Enclosure to Re-Enclosure of Urban Land." *New York University Law Review* XXXV (1060): 1238ff.

Fitch, Edwin M. and John F. Shanklin. *The Bureau of Outdoor Recreation.* New York: Praeger, 1970.

Gates, Paul Wallace. "The Homestead Law in an Incongruous Land System." In *The Public Lands,* edited by Vernon Carstenson, pp. 315-348. Madison: University of Wisconsin Press, 1968.

Gottmann, Jean. *Megalopolis.* Cambridge, Mass.: The MIT Press for The Twentieth Century Fund, 1961.

Herring, Francis W., ed. *Open Space and the Law.* Berkeley: Institute of Governmental Studies, University of California, 1965.

Hill, Gladwin. "A Squeeze in the Nation's Parks." *The New York Times,* December 16, 1972. p. 3.

LeGates, Richard T. and Mary C. Morgan. "The Perils of Special Revenue Sharing for Community Development." *The Journal of the American Institute of Planners* Vol. 39, (July 1973): 254-64.

Little, Charles E. *Challenge of the Land.* New York: Open Space Action Institute, 1968.

Metropolitan Area Planning Council. *Open Space and Recreation Plan and Program.* Boston, 1969.

Milgram, Grace. *The City Expands.* Washington, D.C.: US Government Printing Office, 1967.

Mitchel, Lisle Serles. "Toward a Theory of Public Urban Recreation." *Proceedings of the Association of American Geographers* I (1969): 103-108.

National League of Cities. *Recreation in the Nation's Cities: Problems and Approaches.* A report for the Bureau of Outdoor Recreation. Washington, D.C., 1968.

National Recreation Association. *Municipal and County Parks in the United States, 1940.* New York, 1940.

National Recreation and Parks Association. *Recreation and Park Yearbook, 1966.* Washington, D.C., 1967.

——. "Local Area Survey, 1970." *Parks and Recreation* VL, 8 (August 1971): 20-45.

——. *National Park Recreation and Open Space Standards.* Washingtin, D.C., 1972.

Northeastern Illinois Planning Commission. *Diversity Within Order.* Chicago, 1967.

——. *Regional Open Space Plan.* Chicago, 1971.

——. *Suburban Factbook.* Chicago, 1971.

Outdoor Recreation Resources Review Commission. *Outdoor Recreation for America.* Washington, D.C.: US Government Printing Office, 1962.

Platt, Rutherford H. *Open Land in Urban Illinois: Roles of the Citizen Advocate.* DeKalb: Northern Illinois University Press, 1971.

——. *The Open Space Decision Process.* Research Paper No. 142. Chicago: University of Chicago, Department of Geography Research Series, 1972.

Public Land Law Review Commission, *One Third of the Nation's Land.* Washington, D.C.: US Government Printing Office, 1970.

——. *One Third of the Nation's Land.* Washington, D.C.: US Government Printing Office, 1968.

Regional Plan Association. *The Race for Open Space.* New York, 1960.

Reilly, William K., ed. *The Use of Land.* Washington, D.C.: Citizens Advisory Committee for Environmental Quality, 1973.

Shoup, David and Ruth Mack. *Advance Land Acquisition by Local Governments.* Washington, D.C.: US Government Printing Office, 1969.

Treat, Payson Jackson. "Origin of the National Land System under the Confederation." In *The Public Lands,* edited by Vernon Carstenson, pp. 7-14. Madison: University of Wisconsin Press, 1968.

Trotter, John E. *State Park System in Illinois.* Research Paper No. 74. Chicago: University of Chicago, Department of Geography Research Series, 1962.

Urban Land Institute. *Securing Open Space for Urban America: Conservation Easements.* Technical Bulletin 36. Washington, D.C.: 1959.

US Bureau of the Budget. "Urban Development: The Problem of Open Space." Unpublished Staff Report. Washington, D.C., 1961.

US Council on Environmental Quality. *Environmental Quality, 1970.* Washington, D.C.: US Government Printing Office, 1970.

——. *Environmental Quality, 1971.* Washington, D.C.: US Government Printing Office, 1971.

US Department of Housing and Urban Development. *Statistical Yearbook, 1971.* Washington, D.C.: US Government Printing Office, 1971.

US Department of the Interior, Bureau of Outdoor Recreation. *Federal Outdoor Recreation Programs.* Washington, D.C.: US Government Printing Office, 1967.

——. *Recreation Land Price Escalation.* Washington, D.C.: US Government Printing Office, 1967.

US General Accounting Office. *Greater Benefits to More People Possible by Better Uses of Federal Outdoor Recreation Grants.* Report to Congress, October 5, 1972. Washington, D.C.: Comptroller General of the US, 1972.

Van Doren, Carlton S. "Urban Recreation and Park Standards in the United States." *Proceedings of the Association of American Geographers* V (1973): 266-71.

Wade, Richard C. *The Urban Frontier.* Chicago: University of Chicago Press, Phoenix Books, 1964.

Whyte, William H., Jr. *The Last Landscape.* Garden City, N.Y.: Doubleday, 1968.

Whyte, William H., Jr., et al. *The Exploding Metropolis.* Garden City, N.Y.: Doubleday Anchor Books, 1958.

Chapter 10

Housing and Transportation Problems of the Urban Elderly

Stephen M. Golant
University of Chicago

INTRODUCTION

Rationale of Study*

An analogy can be drawn between the present evolution of federal domestic policies and the potentially traumatic period whereupon the child enters adolescence. Faced with physiological changes the implications of which he does not fully understand and a new normative system of which he is in awe, he sets out in a determined way to adapt constructively, if awkwardly, to life experiences that assuredly must be better than those in the period he has left behind.

In place of adolescence, the administration's recent approach to domestic policy—the New Federalism—can be substituted. Its principal theme is the decentralization of federal programs and the transfer of greater responsibility for the administration and funding of domestic programs to state and local governments. In practice the changing federal orientation has been exemplified by the passage of the State and Local Fiscal Assistance Act of 1972 which authorized permanent funding appropriations for state and local revenue sharing. In the near future Congress will likely pass special revenue-sharing programs such as the Better Communities Act. Among other goals, revenue sharing is to give greater autonomy in decisionmaking to state and local communities to allocate funds. The rationale is that they have a more intimate understanding of existing problems within their political territories and will be more responsive than federal agencies. A complementary program is outlined in the proposed Allied Services Act which is intended to strengthen state and local planning capacities by enabling a wide variety of social and health service programs to be coordinated and administered by a single state agency in conjunction with community participation. Its purpose is to eliminate the existing fragmentation of service delivery. The change in administration policy has hardly proceeded smoothly. The transitional period has witnessed a curb in federal spending, a termination of various community development programs, a moratorium on all new commitments for subsidized housing including Low Rent Public Housing, and an impoundment of funds for various other housing and community development projects.

One result of these decentralization processes giving local and state governments greater administrative and fiscal powers will be their increased responsibility to make decisions regarding the allocation of limited funds to competing human needs. Such decisionmaking will involve two complementary but analytically distinct stages: first, the identification and evaluation of distinctive needs areas, each of which will have its own funding demands; and second, an assessment of the relative importance of each needs area and a determination of priorities for the expenditures of the available funds. The second stage of decision-

*The study was completed before the legislative developments of 1974 and 1975.

making is at least in part a function of the first—that is, cogent arguments for funding a particular program should influence the priority it is given. To that end it is imperative that problems be carefully defined and that strategies for their alleviation or elimination should be capable of being translated into specific legislative programs.

This study, focusing on the urban elderly, identifies housing and transportation as specific needs areas of this population group. It examines the processes that underlie existing problems suggesting strategies for their elimination and looks briefly at past federal policies suggesting reasons for their inadequacy. As findings reported in this chapter will illustrate, it is not possible to assume that the incidence and magnitude of elderly housing and transportation needs will be identical in different urban communities. As a result it is necessary for each urban center to make its own independent analysis of the housing and transportation problems facing its elderly. The primary goal of this study is to provide sufficient understanding of the most relevant variables and relationships in order to undertake these evaluations. It attempts, therefore, to provide a conceptual methodology by which the first stage of community decisionmaking can be effectively carried out.

Scope of Analysis

Theoretical Basis. The chapter examines the aging individual as a resident of a changing urban setting. The emphasis of the analysis is similar to what William Michelson has referred to as an "ego-centered point of view of urban form." The focus is on changes in the needs and goals of the aging individual, and on the changes in his personal resources—e.g., health, income, experience, social status—which influence his ability to realize these needs and goals. This analysis takes place within the context of an urban setting which itself is changing with regard to the opportunities it provides for the gratification of these needs. Housing and transportation problems develop when these two continuing processes—the changing individual and the changing urban setting—are out of phase. The incidence and magnitude of the resulting problems will also vary because different individuals and cities are changing at different rates. An example is illustrative of this approach. An older person because of deteriorating health requires new residential accommodation that has central dining room facilities so that he does not have to provide his own meals. If such accommodation is not available in the urban setting, the older person experiences a problem. He has experienced a change in one of his resources—his health—resulting in his inability to carry out a basic life-maintenance function—the provision of his meals. He has developed a new need that is not provided by the urban setting. In another city a new public housing project provides meals in a central dining room as one of its several congregate facilities. If accommodations are available in the project, a comparable older individual will not experience a similar problem. In this case the changes in the urban setting were in phase with the changing attributes of the aging individual.

Defining the Older Population. The decision to define certain members of the population as "aged" or "old" is frequently based on the criterion of chronological age with age 65 often employed as a convenient metric boundary. This practice is also followed in this paper when it is necessary to provide statistical generalizations concerning the attributes of the older individual and his housing accommodation. Such a procedure can be justified on grounds of analytical convenience but only partly on its theoretical basis. If, for example, a chronologically "old" person is described with respect to his health or the number and complexity of his social roles, on the basis of these variables he may bear little resemblance to other "old" persons or to society's expectations of old age. The imprecision of a chronological age definition is illustrated by the fact that persons ranging in age from 65 to over 100, a period of over 35 years, often are all included in the single category of "old" age.

At least five sets of complementary factors can be defined which collectively give insight into the "oldness" of an individual: (1) the psychological, social and physiological manifestations characterizing an individual's stage of development; (2) society's definition of old age, in particular its age grading system, and its consequential attitudes and responses to the defined group; (3) the significance or importance of this societal definition for the individual; (4) the person's own self-evaluation of his age and the extent to which he desires or is capable of conforming to society's set of behavioral expectations; (5) the extent to which "younger" members accept society's existing definition of old age and how they consequently evaluate and respond to "older" individuals.

A task as difficult as deciding who is "old" or what persons should correctly be called members of an elderly population is providing a justification or rationale for treating "older" persons" as a distinctive consumer subgroup with respect to such needs areas as housing and transportation. It can be argued, for example, that housing problems of old persons that are a consequence of low incomes are also those experienced by members of other low income groups such as the blacks, the young or the young widowed and divorced. This type of argument, however, oversimplifies the implications of the five factors underlying "oldness" which are interrelated and interdependent. While analytically it is often necessary to isolate single variables that contribute to the presence of a housing problem, for older persons it is often not one variable by itself which accounts for the magnitude of the problem. Rather, while the behavior of one variable may be central or dominant, the magnitude of the problem is related to several variables, each with reinforcing and compounding effects. This multiplier effect also results in potential solutions or strategies based on assumptions of a singular cause being ineffectual.

Having made this argument it should be made clear that this chapter will not deal with the thorny issue of whether the housing and transportation problems of older persons are unique to them or whether they are more or less serious than problems faced by other urban population groups. It is accepted a priori that there is a group of individuals who can be identified as "elderly" and, while recognizing the diversity of their "oldness," it is argued that they nevertheless share critical attributes that are a consequence of the natural, irreversible processes of human development in combination with a societal structure which imposes both formal and informal expectations of behavior. Accordingly, the emphasis of this study is on the absolute needs and problems of older persons rather than on their relative deprivation in comparison with other population groups.

Living Arrangements of the Older Population. In 1970 the largest percentage of older persons lived in families either with a spouse or another family member (Table 10-1). This percentage was larger on the fringes of urbanized areas and in those rural areas with under 1,000 populations. In rural places of 1,000 to 2,500 in population, in urban places of under 50,000 in population and in central cities of urbanized areas higher proportions of elderly were either living alone or with a nonrelative. Nationally, 4.8 percent of the 65 and over population live in institutional quarters. The percentage varies considerably among urban and rural places, reflecting the locational decisions of institutions' owners or managers rather than the tendency of "institutional" persons to originate from these areas. This chapter will restrict its attention to older persons living in noninstitutionalized residential accommodations.

Size and Location of the Older Population. In 1970 there were over 20 million persons aged 65 and over, representing 9.9 percent of the total United States population. At the national level, the spatial distribution of the elderly population was very similar to the distribution of the total population. The largest elderly populations were found in New York, California, Pennsylvania and Illinois, each of which had over one million elderly persons, accounting for almost a third of the total United States 65 and over population (Table 10-2). Seventy-two percent of the elderly lived in urban areas with the majority, 55.4 percent, living in urbanized areas, 34.1 percent living in central cities and 21.3 percent living in urban fringe areas. The remainder of the elderly, 27.1 percent, were located in rural areas (Table 10-3).

Several states had particularly high concentrations of older persons. The states of Iowa, Missouri, South Dakota, Nebraska, Florida and Arkansas each had over 12 percent of its population aged 65 years and over. The highest concentrations of elderly were found in very small urban and rural places and the central cities of urbanized areas.

Between 1960 and 1970 the percentage of older persons in the United States increased from 9.2 to 9.9 percent. In particular, higher concentrations of elderly (relative to younger age groups) tended to become more apparent in smaller urban and rural places (Table 10-4). Similar to the changing urban-rural spatial distribution of the total United States population, in terms of absolute numbers the elder-

Table 10-1. Living Arrangements of Urban and Rural Population 65 Years and Over, United States, 1970

(Data in Percentages)			Urbanized Areas			Other Urban Places of		Rural Places of		
Living Arrangement	*Total United States*	*Total Urban*	*Total*	*Central Cities*	*Urban Fringe*	*10,000+*	*2,500–10,000*	*Total*	*1,000–2,500*	*Other Rural*
In Households										
Head of family										
Male	30.2	28.5	28.4	27.3	30.1	28.5	29.3	34.9	30.3	35.8
Female	5.2	5.4	5.4	5.8	4.6	5.5	4.8	4.8	4.9	4.7
Wife of head	19.1	18.2	18.1	17.2	19.4	18.2	19.1	21.5	19.8	21.8
Other family member	12.5	13.0	14.1	12.8	16.2	10.2	9.4	11.1	8.7	11.6
Total in families	67.0	65.1	66.0	63.1	70.3	62.4	63.0	72.3	62.7	73.9
Living alone										
Male	6.1	5.9	6.0	6.9	4.6	5.8	5.8	6.6	6.2	6.7
Female	19.5	21.1	20.4	22.3	17.4	23.4	22.7	15.2	22.2	13.8
Living with nonrelative	1.9	2.0	2.1	2.3	1.8	1.8	1.6	1.5	1.5	1.5
Total unrelated individuals	27.5	29.0	28.5	31.5	23.8	31.0	30.1	23.3	29.9	22.0
In Group Quarters										
Inmates of institutions	4.8	5.1	4.7	4.3	5.2	6.3	6.3	4.1	5.8	3.7
Other in group quarters*	0.7	0.8	0.9	1.0	0.7	0.8	0.7	0.4	0.6	0.4
Total	100.0	100.0	100.0	100.0	100.0	100.0	100.0	100.0	100.0	100.0

*Any house or apartment with five or more occupants unrelated to head of household.

Source: Calculated from U.S. Bureau of the Census, 1970 Census of Population, General Population Characteristics, Vol. 1, Pt. 1 Washington, D.C.: U.S. Government Printing Office 1972.

ly were located to a greater extent in the larger urban centers than in the smaller urban or rural places. The growth rates of older persons also varied unevenly among states. Florida, Arizona and Nevada, for example, experienced percentage increases of elderly as high as 70 percent while Iowa, the District of Columbia and Montana, for example, experienced increases of less than 7 percent.

Urban-rural and interstate variations in the concentration and growth rate of older persons are partly explained by the rate of natural increase of older persons, dependent on earlier birth rates and reflected by the number of persons reaching the age 65 and over cohort less the number of deaths in this cohort. Some of the larger and smaller concentrations and growth rates of elderly persons, however, are a consequence of in- and outmigration flows of both younger and older population groups. For example, in Iowa, Kansas, Missouri, Nebraska, Oklahoma, South Dakota, Maine and Arkansas, which have larger concentrations of elderly, there have been heavy outmigrations of younger age groups. In contrast, the large elderly population growth rates between 1960 and 1970 in Florida, Arizona and Nevada have largely been due to high inmigration rates of older persons (Table 10-2). The factors attracting older persons to these states are many, but include among others a warm year round climate, other older persons with comparable life styles and background, and specially developed retirement communities often containing a complete range of personal, medical and recreational services.

The importance of longer distance elderly migrations as an explanation of residential location should, however, be placed in proper perspective. Compared with the residential migration rates of the total population, the elderly tend to change their place of residence much less frequently. Less than 9 percent of persons aged 65 and over relocated their place of residence over a recent one year period compared with 19 percent of the total population. Of greater relevance is that most moves by older persons were within county boundaries (69.4 percent) and of those outside county boundaries, most of these (61.7 percent) were within state boundaries (Table 10-5).

Because the economic, social and political forces underlying the structure and growth of most urban centers are similar, a number of generalizations can be made with respect to the pattern of intraurban residential concentrations of persons aged 65 and over. Since older persons exhibit a low rate of residential relocation, the majority have lived in their present residential locations for over 15 years. Given that a large percentage of the residential neighborhoods were not newly developed when they were initially occupied, it is not unexpected that the largest concentrations of older persons are presently found in the older or less recently developed parts of the city. Even when residential moves are made by older persons, many of these are of very short distances, which further reinforces this residential pattern. Accordingly, the intraurban pattern of elderly households often reflects the age of the city and the age of its contours of spatial growth. At least three types of intraurban structural change will create deviations from this pattern. First, older residential neighborhoods are often redeveloped and replaced by single detached or attached dwelling units or by condominiums that are less likely to be initially occuped by older persons. If apartments are built on redeveloped land, they may well attract the older resident. Second, in an older neighborhood, an elderly population may be gradually replaced (as a result of deaths or residential relocation) by younger population groups; in many inner cities the change in age compostion of the residential population is also accompanied by a racial change from white to black. Finally, concentrations of older persons may be found in newly developed residential neighborhoods if specially designed elderly public housing projects have recently been constructed.

The Geographic Perspective. An analysis of the location and relative concentration of the elderly population provides a first approximation of where potential housing and transportation problems are likely to exist. However, only very partial conclusions can be made by an analysis of such residential patterns alone. A large variety of factors determine to what extent housing problems exist. A simple example is illustrative. Suppose that two large, equal-sized concentrations of elderly households were identified in two parts of the metropolitan area; one is in an outlying suburban district and the second is very close to the central business district. This information, by

Table 10-2. Location, Relative Concentration and Estimated Net Migration of Population 65 and Over, for States, 1960-1970

	Population (Numbers in thousands)		*Increase*		*Percent Population 65 and Over*		*Estimated Net Migration*	
Region and State	*1970*	*1960*	*Amount*	*Percent*	*1970*	*1960*	*Amount*	*Rate**
United States	20,066	16,560	3,506	21.2	9.9	9.2	123,648	0.4
New England								
Maine	115	107	8	7.6	11.6	11.0	-2,783	-1.4
New Hampshire	78	68	11	15.8	10.6	11.2	2,210	1.8
Vermont	47	44	4	8.6	10.7	11.2	-170	-0.2
Massachusetts	636	572	65	11.3	11.2	11.1	-24,697	-2.3
Rhode Island	104	90	14	16.1	11.0	10.4	-2,501	-1.5
Connecticut	289	213	46	19.1	9.5	9.6	-1,665	-0.4
Middle Atlantic								
New York	1,961	1,688	273	16.2	10.8	10.1	-202,942	-5.9
New Jersey	697	560	137	24.4	9.7	9.2	-12,587	-1.1
Pennsylvania	1,272	1,129	144	12.7	10.8	10.0	-88,470	-4.0
East North Central								
Ohio	998	897	101	11.2	9.4	9.2	-58.753	-3.4
Indiana	494	446	48	10.8	9.5	9.6	-20,245	-2.4
Illinois	1,094	975	119	12.2	9.8	9.7	-105,145	-5.5
Michigan	753	638	115	18.0	8.5	8.2	-50,146	-3.9
Wisconsin	473	403	70	17.4	10.7	10.2	5,163	0.7
West North Central								
Minnesota	409	354	55	15.4	10.7	10.4	6,752	1.0
Iowa	350	328	23	6.9	12.4	11.9	-2,229	-0.4
Missouri	561	503	57	11.4	12.0	11.7	-4,863	-0.5
North Dakota	66	59	8	13.3	10.7	9.3	-338	-0.4
South Dakota	80	72	9	12.5	12.1	10.5	1,099	0.8
Nebraska	184	164	19	11.8	12.4	11.6	4,692	1.6
Kansas	266	240	26	10.8	11.8	11.0	4,160	1.0
South Atlantic								
Delaware	44	36	8	22.6	8.0	8.0	113	0.2
Maryland	300	227	73	32.3	7.6	7.3	3,742	0.8
District of Columbia	71	69	2	2.4	9.4	9.1	-22,814	-15.7
Virginia	366	289	77	26.7	7.9	7.3	1,163	0.2
West Virginia	194	173	22	12.7	11.1	9.3	-10,441	-3.1
North Carolina	414	312	102	32.7	8.1	6.9	9,560	1.5
South Carolina	191	151	40	26.8	7.4	6.3	-2,829	-0.9
Georgia	367	291	77	26.4	8.0	7.4	2,533	0.4
Florida	989	553	436	78.9	14.6	11.2	366,122	36.0

East South Central								
Kentucky	337	292	45	15.4	10.5	9.6	1,236	0.2
Tennessee	384	309	75	24.3	9.8	8.7	9,136	1.5
Alabama	326	261	65	24.8	9.5	8.0	6,603	1.3
Mississippi	222	190	32	17.0	10.0	8.7	-2,396	-0.7
West South Central								
Arkansas	238	194	44	22.3	12.4	10.9	17,750	4.9
Louisiana	307	242	65	26.9	8.4	7.4	-3,765	-0.8
Oklahoma	300	249	51	20.5	11.7	10.7	15,721	3.4
Texas	992	745	247	33.1	8.9	7.8	52,762	3.5
Mountain								
Montana	69	65	3	5.1	9.9	9.7	-1,175	-1.0
Idaho	68	58	10	16.3	9.5	8.7	2,268	2.1
Wyoming	30	26	4	16.6	9.1	7.8	-1,468	-2.9
Colorado	188	158	30	18.8	8.5	9.0	9,512	3.2
New Mexico	71	51	19	37.7	6.9	5.4	2,780	2.6
Arizona	161	90	71	79.0	9.1	6.9	46,176	25.2
Utah	78	60	18	29.4	7.3	6.7	3,695	3.1
Nevada	31	18	13	70.4	6.3	6.4	4,937	12.1
Pacific								
Washington	322	279	43	15.4	9.4	9.8	7,901	1.5
Oregon	227	184	43	23.5	10.8	10.4	17,413	5.1
California	1,801	1,376	425	30.9	9.0	8.8	142,886	5.3
Alaska	7	5	2	27.9	2.3	2.4	-2,669	-18.4
Hawaii	44	29	15	51.3	5.7	4.6	704	1.1

*Rate represents net migration between 1960 and 1970 of the cohort 55 and over in 1960 and 65 and over in 1970 as percent of the population 55 and over in 1960. Computed by use of a preliminary set of national census survival rates.

Source: US Bureau of the Census, *Current Population Reports*, Series P-23, No. 43, "Some Demographic Aspects of Aging in the United States" (Washington, D.C.: US Government Printing Office, 1973).

Table 10-3. Location and Relative Concentration of Elderly and Total Populations in Urban and Rural Areas, United States, 1970

Age	Total United States	Total Urban	Urbanized Areas: Total	Urbanized Areas: Central Cities	Urbanized Areas: Urban Fringe	Other Urban Places: 10,000+	Other Urban Places: 2,500–10,000	Rural Places: Total	Rural Places: 1,000–2,500	Rural Places: Other Rural
				Location of Elderly Persons (Percent of total US population)						
65–74	100.0	72.7	55.9	34.3	21.5	8.6	8.2	27.3	4.2	23.1
75+	100.0	73.3	54.5	33.7	20.8	9.4	9.4	26.7	5.0	21.7
65+	100.0	72.9	55.4	34.1	21.3	8.9	8.7	27.1	4.5	22.6
Total Population	100.0	73.5	58.3	31.5	26.8	8.2	7.0	26.5	3.3	23.2
				Relative Concentration of Elderly Persons (percent of total population)						
65–74	6.1	6.1	5.9	6.7	4.9	6.4	7.2	6.3	7.9	6.1
75+	3.8	3.7	3.5	4.0	2.9	4.3	5.0	3.8	5.7	3.5
65+	9.9	9.8	9.4	10.7	7.8	10.8	12.2	10.1	13.6	9.6

Source: US Bureau of the Census, 1970 Census of Population, General Population Characteristics, vol. 1, pt. 1.

Table 10-4. Location and Relative Concentration of Elderly and Total Populations in Urban and Rural Areas, United States, 1960

Age	Total United States	Total Urban	Urbanized Areas: Total	Urbanized Areas: Central Cities	Urbanized Areas: Urban Fringe	Other Urban Places: 10,000+	Other Urban Places: 2,500–10,000	Rural Places: Total	Rural Places: 1,000–2,500	Rural Places: Other Rural
				Location of Elderly Persons (Percent of total US population)						
65–74	100.0	70.2	52.5	35.5	17.0	9.3	8.4	29.8	4.5	25.3
75+	100.0	68.5	48.6	32.9	15.7	10.2	9.7	31.5	5.4	26.1
65+	100.0	69.6	51.2	34.6	16.6	9.6	8.8	30.4	4.8	25.6
Total Population	100.0	69.9	53.4	32.3	21.1	9.0	7.4	30.1	3.6	26.5
				Relative Concentration of Elderly Persons (percent of total population)						
65–74	6.1	6.2	6.0	6.7	4.9	6.3	7.0	6.1	7.6	5.9
75+	3.1	3.0	2.8	3.2	2.3	3.5	4.1	3.2	4.6	3.1
65+	9.2	9.2	8.8	10.0	7.3	9.8	11.0	9.3	12.2	8.9

Source: US Bureau of the Census, 1960 Census of Population, General Population Charactersitics, vol. 1.

itself, provides little insight as to the potential problems of the occupants in these two locations. If additional variables describing the attributes of these populations and their housing accommodation are provided—for example, knowing that there is a federally subsidized high density housing project occupied by low income elderly widows at the suburban location, and that there is a luxurious high-rise apartment complex occupied by middle and high income elderly couples at the inner city location—then we could *begin* to analyze the differing needs and problems of the two elderly housing populations. In short, any spatial analysis of housing needs must necessarily comprise those variables that sufficiently depict or characterize the factors that underlie potential housing needs and problems.

It is the intent of this chapter to identify and to justify those variables that should be

Table 10-5. Mobility Status of Elderly and Total Populations in United States Living in Private Households—U.S. Residence in March 1970 Compared With March 1969

(Data in Percentages) *Location of Movers*	*Total Population*	*Age* *65–74*	*75+*	*65+*
Total Population	100.0	100.0	100.0	100.0
Total Movers	19.1	8.3	9.1	8.6
Total Movers	100.0	100.0	100.0	100.0
Total Movers within US	95.9	98.5	99.5	99.1
Total Migrants from Abroad	4.1	1.5	0.5	0.9
Total Movers within US	100.0	100.0	100.0	100.0
Within Same County	63.6	70.4	68.0	69.4
From Outside County	36.4	29.6	32.0	30.6
Total Movers from Outside County	100.0	100.0	100.0	100.0
Within a State	46.9	63.2	59.6	61.7
Between States	53.1	36.8	40.4	38.3

Source: US Bureau of the Census, *Current Population Reports*, Population Characteristics, Series P–20, no. 210, 15 January 1971.

considered in any spatial analysis of housing and transportation needs of an older urban population. The variables that are identified are not unique to any geographic unit. That is, they can be evaluated at any spatial level whether the focus is on intracommunity, intraurban or interurban variations in housing and transportation needs. In order to illustrate the complexities of initiating an analysis which incorporates some of these variables, a section of the chapter is devoted to a limited analysis of selected census variables underlying the differentiation of housing needs of elderly in five of the largest central cities in United States.

HOUSING NEEDS AND PROBLEMS OF OLDER AMERICANS

Residential Settings for Older Persons—Basic Goals

The residential setting should be supportive of the needs of the older person, enabling him to engage in a lifestyle of his choice. It should be able to accommodate the changing effectiveness and competency of the older person to realize his needs. The successful adaptation to old age may require him to cope with declining physical energy, poorer general health, smaller financial funds, lower social status, a sudden loss of a spouse or of good friends, or a general decline in his ability to deal with complex situations. The physical attributes and social environment of the residential setting should help facilitate the older person's adjustment to these critical events, allowing him to make a smooth transition from middle age to early old age to late old age. An unsatisfactory living environment will likely contribute to lower morale and life satisfaction.

In general terms it is possible to identify four major goals desired by older persons that attributes of the residential setting can be instrumental in achieving.

Independence. The older person seeks to maintain independent living arrangements as long as possible. This reflects his desire to have maximum personal autonomy and to achieve his needs and wants with minimum dependency on family or friends. He seeks to engage in a lifestyle that neither conflicts with the goals and activities of other members in his residential setting nor subjects him to a variety of regulations and rules.

Security. At least three types of security are important to older persons. The first is economic security, characterized by the possession of sufficient financial resources to occupy a residential setting that is both consistent with existing and future needs and compatible to a lifestyle to which the older person has been accustomed. At the minimum, economic security implies sufficient financial resources to maintain independent living arrangements. The second is physical security, representing a state whereby the older person is not subjected to personal injury whether by accidental causes (e.g., falls, fires) or deliberate attacks (e.g., crime). The third is psychological or emotional security, representing a state whereby the older person is free from worries and anxieties related to his present or future needs.

Environmental Mastery. This refers to the ability of the older person to influence and control his participation and contact with other persons or with activities located in his dwelling unit or neighborhood. Privacy represents one such end of a continuum of personal states whereby the individual can successfully remove himself from other people or activities. The ability of the older person to control his exposure to people and events may decline. To varying degreees the physical design of the dwelling unit and neighborhood setting can enable the older person to compensate for this decline.

Positive Self-Image. The older individual's image of himself will depend on a variety of factors, including his feeling of achievement, his self-confidence in general and his evaluation of how successful his life has been. The dwelling unit and neighborhood setting occupied may be considered as tangible evidence of this success. His judgment will depend on whether his perception of the quality of the residential accommodation is congruous with his evaluation of his status and worth.

The Elderly in Unsatisfactory Residential Settings. When at least one of these goals has not been satisfied, the residential setting can be defined as unsatisfactory. Four groups of elderly persons living in such residential settings can be identified.

The first group of elderly persons live in housing that is dilapidated, deteriorating or lacking some basic plumbing facilities—for example, hot or cold water, inside toilet. While 1970 census statistics did not include a measure of a dwelling unit's physical condition, it did reveal that about 9 percent of households headed by persons 65 years and over occupied dwelling units that lacked one or more basic plumbing facilities. Accommodations with these structural and functional deficiencies may be very uncomfortable, contain safety hazards and in general may be detrimental to good health. Both goals of security and positive self-image may be unfulfilled in these settings.

According to Shanas et al., a second group of elderly persons (about 8 percent of total elderly), who are primarily unmarried (single, divorced, separated or widowed), live in the household of a married daughter or son. The elderly emphatically stress their preference for independent living arrangements. Older unmarried persons who live in these family arrangements very often have few viable residential alternatives because of serious health or income constraints. As many as three goals may be unfulfilled—independence, environmental mastery and positive self-image. These family arrangements should be distinguished, however, from those in which unmarried elderly persons live in the same household with an unmarried child or sibling. In contrast, these living arrangements are far more likely to be satisfactory to both household members.

A third group of elderly are living in institutions or quasi-institutions such as nursing homes or homes for the aged even though they do not require the medical care or fulltime organized supervision provided in such settings. Many elderly persons are found in these establishments because the limited medical services and care supervision they require to maintain independent living quarters are not available in the regular community. The institution as a residential setting can leave unfulfilled as many as three goals—independence, environmental mastery and positive self-image.

The fourth group of older persons is the most difficult to define either conceptually or empirically. These elderly individuals live independently in standard dwelling units and neighborhood settings that are incongruous with their existing needs and resources. Included are a considerable number of elderly homeowners who for reasons to be analyzed later are living in unsatisfactory residential settings. Also included are elderly persons occupying both single and multiple family dwelling units in neighborhood settings that have undergone changes in the socioeconomic and racial composition of their population and in the types and distribution of their land uses and activities so that attributes which were once supportive of the occupants' lifestyles remain no longer. Such elderly persons are "left behind" after the outmigration of the more affluent and socially mobile population. They continue to live in their present residential accommodations because there are few alternatives available to them (except for institutional settings or accommodation with relatives), because of their limited financial resources or because they perceive, however realistically, various difficulties associated with residential relocation. As many as three of the four goals may be unfulfilled for these persons—security, environmental mastery and positive self-image.

Aging Processes Underlying the Housing Needs of the Urban Elderly

Housing needs will vary among elderly persons and will partially be dependent on such individual attributes as socioeconomic status, lifestyle, value or cultural orientations and personality traits. These sources of variation often develop as a consequence of the aging process. Four major associated events can be defined: the departure of grown children, retirement, widowhood and decline in health and/or disablement. Their impact will vary depending on the extent to which they are unexpected or disruptive of a particular lifestyle. They will, however, influence how the older person evaluates and copes with his housing needs.

Departure of Grown Children. In many cases the dwelling unit and neighborhood setting currently occupied were initially selected to accommodate the needs of a large family. With the departure of the last child from the household the dwelling unit may become dysfunctional because of its oversize and because attributes of the neighborhood supportive of the "parent" or "children" roles may now have lost their utility.

The length of the life span that remains following the departure of the last child is tending to increase because, on the average, childrearing is being completed at an earlier age and life expectancy is longer. These two trends have the effect of increasing the length of time in which an inappropriate residential environment may be occupied.

Retirement. The loss of the work role may be accompanied by a change in lifestyle for the male, and if married, his wife. The utility of the present dwelling unit and neighborhood setting may be assessed quite differently. The residential setting takes on new significance if only because the prospects of spending more time in it are greater. The types of activities in which the retired person wants to engage and the services and facilities to which he wants easy access will often not be found in his present community. The preretirement interests and goals which supported some social relationships and the motives for participation in certain neighborhood organizations may be weakened or no longer exist. Retirement will also remove any residential location constraints created by the daily vehicular trip to work. As a result, a residential setting can be selected that is more compatible with a contemplated lifestyle.

The loss of the work role may also be accompanied by a considerable decrease in regular income. The retired individual or couple will be dependent on accumulated savings and social security and pension payments. This change in economic status may influence the potential activity patterns of the retired person. It may restrict the ability of the apartment occupant to budget successfully existing rental payments, and the ability of the homeowner to budget mortgage payments, maintenance costs, operating costs and property taxes.

Longer life expectancy and the earlier age at which increasing numbers of the labor force are likely to retire represent two trends which will create a longer postretirement period and therefore increase the potential length of occupancy of an unfavorable residential setting.

Widowhood. The loss of the spouse may be accompanied by a realization that the present housing accommodation is no longer appropriate. This evaluation will depend on a number of factors. Relocation may be delayed if children are still present in the household and if continuity in their lives (for example, school enrollment) would be disrupted by a change in neighborhood. For a woman, if no children are present, the home-centered activities deriving from the "homemaker" and "wife" roles may have ended. The existing community may also lose its social significance. This will be a function of whether the woman's social relationships and neighborhood organization participation were dependent on the presence of the male spouse or on the husband-wife couple. In order to combat loneliness and to become involved in new activities, a new residential setting may be desired in which opportunities for social relationships are greater.

Widowhood, as in the case of retirement, may result in a significant change of financial status. It has similar consequences for how the economic utility of the residential setting will be assessed.

Declining Health and Disablement. Perhaps the most important consequence of the aging process is changes in the general health and physiological functioning of the older person that restrict his ability to carry out his usual activities independently of others. The residential setting may suddenly become inadequate and dysfunctional. There may be few residential accommodation alternatives. Some design features of the dwelling unit may become barriers preventing maximum utilization. A simple example is the sudden inaccessibility of the second floor of the dwelling unit because the occupant is unable to climb stairs as frequently, if at all. Neighborhood services and facilities also may no longer be accessible by previously used transportation modes. Unattractive attributes of the neighborhood which were previously considered minor may now have far greater significance.

A new set of needs will develop. A residential setting in which the older person has easy transportation access to medical and rehabilitation services will be essential. He may require homemaker, nursing or "meals on wheels" services. If the older person suffers complete disablement, the need for special community services will be accentuated. Given the unavailability of special neighborhood services, these new needs may only be satisfied in an institutional or quasi-institutional setting or within a family member's household.

Associated with declining health will be large medical expenses that may quickly deplete existing savings and make the present residential accommodation too expensive to rent or own.

Specific Housing Needs and Problems of the Urban Elderly

The consequences of these events can be translated into seven major categories of housing needs and problems. The incidence and magnitude of these problems will vary among members of the elderly population. They include spatial accessibility, architectural design, dwelling unit maintenance and cost, availability of facilities and services, availability of special services, the social support system, and the general character of the neighborhood setting.

Spatial Accessibility. Inexpensive, easy and convenient spatial access by automobile, mass transit, or by walking to facilities, services, or persons, is one of the most important attributes of the residential setting. The next section is devoted entirely to an analysis of this need.

Architectural Design of Dwelling Unit:

Size. While older persons generally require a smaller amount of living space than larger, younger families, the smooth transition from late middle age to old age can be facilitated by dwelling unit accommodation that enables the older person to retain a style of living to which he has been accustomed. Thus for the older woman who has recently been widowed and has previously lived in a two or three bedroom house, the one room efficiency apartment offered to her in a lower income public housing project may have little appeal. The older person also requires a dwelling unit of a size sufficiently large to entertain friends and to display or store valued possessions and furniture.

Windows. The decline of vision—specifically the reduction of light admitted by the eye—can be counteracted by insuring that an adequate amount of sunlight is received within the dwelling unit. Windows also enable the older person to observe outside street activity. This capability can be particularly important to elderly persons living alone in an active cultural and shopping area of the city. The potential utility of windows will be greater for the home-bound elderly.

Noise Insulation. High noise levels originating from adjacent apartments or street activities can be stressful to the older person and can accentuate his feelings of helplessness because of his inability to control activities around him. Because some older persons experience hearing difficulties, their radio and television volumes are often much higher than normal. For neighbors of such persons, whether older or younger, these high noise levels may be so disturbing as to create conflicts between their respective households. Adequate standards of sound insulation are therefore required.

Heating and Ventilating Systems. Older persons appear to be more sensitive to both over- and underheating and to draughts than younger age groups. Room temperatures, therefore, should be capable of being regulated. Unfortunately, many low income housing projects, in order to realize savings on capital and operating costs, do not provide central air conditioning for their elderly occupants.

Safety. The design of the dwelling unit can influence the probability of accidents occurring. General declines in agility, physical energy, sense of balance, coordination and vision make the older person more susceptible to home accidents. The risk of danger from falls can be reduced by avoiding the installation of slippery materials and finishes, especially in stairway areas, and by providing railings and grab bars in locations such as bathrooms where falls are likely to occur. The risk of danger from scalds or burns can be minimized by improved kitchen design. There is a direct correlation between the age of the housing structure and the presence of unsafe structural features.

The elderly are also more susceptible to injuries from fire and smoke, since they may have difficulty exiting quickly from a burning building. The risk is increased if they cannot easily negotiate stairs and/or must rely on elevators that can become inoperative. The construction of units with fire resistant materials, automatic sprinkler systems and effective alarm systems can help reduce the risk. Special consideration should be given to the operation of elevators in multifloored apartment buildings. Some older persons are afraid to use elevators. Both for psychological reassurance and physical safety, doors should be timed to open and close more slowly, the rate of acceleration should be slowed, elevators should be programmed to stop level with the floor, handrails should be provided in the cab and communication devices should be available in the elevator.

Social Space. The provision of laundry room, lounge and gardening spaces can facilitate social interaction among tenants in multi-unit apartment buildings. Common balconies or outside hallways can serve a similar purpose. Caution must be taken, however, to avoid threatening the privacy of older persons in the course of providing such design features.

Architectural Barriers. A report edited by Thomas Byerts and Don Conway identified three major types of architectural barriers for the elderly: ". . . those which prevent the old person from passing easily from one area to another, those that keep him from orienting himself to his surroundings, and those which prevent him from using the equipment in his dwelling unit safely and easily." Older persons in wheelchairs have special problems with regard to their indoor movement. Doors in the dwelling unit should be wide enough to accommodate wheelchairs. Control devices should be easily identifiable, reachable and easy to manipulate. For all elderly persons, doors and windows should open easily, without necessitating considerable physical strength. The number of right angle turns should be minimized in designing dwelling units, as the need to change directions when walking makes some older persons more susceptible to falls.

Dwelling Unit Maintenance and Cost. Elderly persons usually occupy older houses. Approximately three-fourths of households headed by older persons occupy dwelling units that are at least 20 years old. The operating and maintenance costs, along with property taxes and any part of an unpaid mortgage, represent the principal expenditures. While these costs could be managed with salary from full-time employment, with retirement and a reduced income these payments can become awesome financial burdens.

Availability of Facilities and Services. The presence of shopping facilities and medical services are frequently identified as important needs by older persons. The presence of parks, libraries, movies and sometimes religious institutions are often given lower priority.

Because elderly persons are diversified with respect to their lifestyles and the resources they have to achieve their needs and goals, there is considerable variation in the community facilities and services that are both preferred and required by different subgroups of elderly.

Some of the more interesting contrasts are those that Tissue has described between older married men, the majority of whom are living in their own homes in suburban areas, and unmarried men, many with a life history of frequent residential moves, living alone in hotels, rooming houses and apartments located in the city's downtown area. Whereas the downtown men emphasized the importance of being able to participate in nearby amusement and recreation facilities, the suburban men emphasized the importance of home-centered activities. In spite of the paucity of studies, it would seem reasonable to conclude that with the exception of life-supporting food and medical needs and adequate transportation facilities, no simple generalization can be made as to the particular facilities and services required by all older persons.

There is considerable variation in the cost, variety and quality of services and facilities that are available to older persons in different parts of the metropolitan area. Because of transportation constraints some older persons often have to buy goods at smaller, neighborhood stores, where they are more expensive and of lower quality and the selection is more limited. This situation often occurs in an aging neighborhood that is undergoing change with respect to its population composition and the number and quality of its services and facilities. As a result, the older person who has lived a long time in his residential setting may now find that the once favorable attributes are no longer present.

Availability of Special Services. The special services required by many elderly persons can be examined under three categories reflecting their potential ease of accessibility to the older person. First, various services are transported to the dwelling unit of the elderly person. Delivered hot meals (meals on wheels programs), mobile dental equipment services, home health services, minor medical services (e.g., periodic checkups, treatment of minor ailments), and homemaker services (e.g., light housecleaning, cooking chores, shopping assistance, special telephone information services) are examples. Second, special services are located on the residential site and are shared by several dwelling units. These congregate facilities are usually found in higher density apartment buildings containing primarily elderly persons and include, for example, central dining room facilities, recreation rooms and lounges, social activity spaces, and physical therapy and gym facilities. Both these categories of services have in common the fact that they are "delivered" to the elderly consumer and transportation facilities are not required to gain access to them. Third, special services useful to the older person can be found in community or senior centers. In some, but not all of these centers, these services have been specially developed for the older person; in others, services are designed to serve all age groups in the community and only some are of use to the elderly. The services provided for the elderly can be quite varied and include, for example, dining room facilities, recreation and social programs, physical and occupational therapy services, medical and dental services, and referral and information services (e.g., counselling on nutrition and money management, advice on health and family matters, information on filling out complex forms or on establishing state or federal program eligibility).

These services enable the person to cope more effectively with the problems of old age. They enable the older person in need of part-time domicilary or medical care to maintain independent living quarters and to be less dependent on the assistance of friends and relatives.

Special services for the elderly in general are poorly developed and insufficient in number. This leaves many elderly with no viable alternatives other than to live with relatives or to enter institutional accommodation. Some elderly persons have insufficient and incorrect information concerning the benefits that can be obtained from existing special services. This leaves open the possibility that older persons who require special services the most are not receiving them.

The Social Support System. Both relatives and friends play an important role in the lives of the majority of older persons. In addition to providing friendship or companionship, they provide various types of assistance including the provision of financial aid, help in periods of illness and emergencies, help with housework and home repairs, and general advice. Greater assistance is usually provided by relatives than by friends. The importance of these relationships for older persons will depend on their previous lifestyle, present living arrangements, recent social losses (e.g., death of spouse) and the newness of the neighborhood setting. Accordingly, while the traditional version of the extended family with three or more generations living under the same roof is no longer an adequate depiction of household and family structure, nevertheless, important intergenerational functional relationships are common. In this sense, the extended family "over space" still is a viable social concept in the modern industrial city.

Very few elderly persons experience extreme social isolation without having human contact, although it has been estimated that about 30 percent of older persons indicate they are lonely. This loneliness is often caused by a recent loss of the spouse or of close friends. Older persons who have lived a considerable length of time in their present residence often find that their neighborhood now contains few if any of their previous friends, who have either died or relocated their place of residence. Even friends who remain may no longer share compatible activities.

An important issue is whether it is more advantageous for older persons living in the regular community to live close to persons in primarily their own age group (proximate housing or age-segregated living arrangements) or whether it is more preferable for them to occupy dwelling units among households containing members of all age groups (dispersed housing or age-integrated living arrangements).

The most influential research by Irving Rosow in his book *Social Integration of the Aged* shows that housing arrangements containing higher concentrations of older persons serve two important functions: first, they maximize the opportunities for new friendships; and second, a normative social system is established in which age peers—by providing and legitimizing role models and supplying psychological support—clarify expectations of appropriate behavior, thereby facilitating a smooth transition and adjustment to old age. Rosow emphasized the need for two important conditions that will be supportive of these functions: first, that residents in age-segregated housing arrangements "be of basically homogeneous social composition, of broadly similar background, social class, and life experience" and second, that segregations "must impinge on residents in socially acceptable terms rather than in terms of devaluation, marginality, and loss of status."

If age-segregated housing is accepted as the most preferable arrangement, there are various ways it can be accomplished. Dwelling units within a high-rise apartment building can be totally occupied by elderly persons but located in a neighborhood with single family housing units occupied by younger families with children. Alternatively, the same elderly occupied apartment building can be located in a neighborhood of single family dwelling units occupied primarily by elderly. These arrangements as well as variations on them accomplish the principal goal of "age-segregation." They also suggest alternatives whereby it is possible for an older person to live independently but close (in the same neighborhood) to (younger) members of his family.

The General Character of Neighborhood Setting. Three general characteristics describing the neighborhood setting have relevance for understanding the satisfaction expressed by older persons toward their residential setting. The importance of living in a "familiar" neighborhood is frequently emphasized. Research has not made clear what aspects of "neighborhood" are being emphasized, but it is reasonable to assume that reference is being made to such elements as streets, stores, buildings, people and merchants.

There is no consensus as to whether older persons prefer a "peaceful" or "active" neighborhood setting. Many elderly experience discomfort from the noise created by children or teenagers. However for some elderly persons an attractive residential location is characterized by intensive urban activity with the continuous noises of people and cars. This may be especially true for persons living alone with few family or community ties.

The third relevant characteristic of the neighborhood is its physical safety. Elderly persons are frequently the victims of such crimes as muggings, robberies, physical assaults and apartment break-ins. Their inability to flee or resist makes them more vulnerable. In addition, it is often common knowledge that their social security checks will arrive on a certain day each month. The crime results not only in needed funds being lost but also in deleterious effects on health and physical well-being. Considerable frustration is felt by the older person because he has little control over these situations. Whether or not they have been victimized, elderly persons' fear for their physical safety often discourages them from leaving their dwelling units. This fear also discourages friends or relatives—especially other older persons—from visiting. The most seriously affected elderly are those living in public housing projects in high crime inner city areas.

There are numerous ways the elderly could be better protected against crime. Improved security hardware, security guards, better locks, greater supervision and control of entrances to buildings represent effective approaches. Generally what is lacking to implement these measures is funding rather than technological know-how.

The Older Homeowner—Advantages and Disadvantages

Nationally 69.5 percent of households headed by persons 65 years and over live in owner-occupied housing. Elderly persons living in central cities of urbanized areas are less likely to be homeowners than those living in fringe areas. Over the last two decades the incidence of homeownership as a form of housing tenure has increased for the older population as it has for the total population.

Advantages of Homeownership. Homeownership offers various advantages to the older person. Under some circumstances the cost of living in an owned home is less than in a rented house or apartment. It represents an important form of economic security and is an asset which can potentially be used as collateral for loans or as a potential annuity source. Since the elderly homeowner is usually living in a familiar residential environment, there is a strong sentimental attachment to both the dwelling unit and the neighborhood reinforced by associated memories and experiences. Moreover, owning a home "free and clear" is part of the American dream and can be interpreted as a measure of individual social status. Finally, given the prospect that after retirement more time will be spent at home, the house may be particularly suited to support a variety of hobby and recreational activities.

Disadvantages of Homeownership. Although the majority of elderly homeowners have completed their mortgage payments, for the minority who have not the monthly payment may be a financial burden representing as much as 75 percent of their reduced retirement incomes. The rent-free house may still represent a drain on savings because of property taxes, operating costs (heating, electricity, water), maintenance and upkeep costs. For the older house, maintenance costs can be particularly high, especially if it is necessary to hire outside labor. Unexpected housing expenses may in addition make it very difficult to maintain a planned budget.

Accordingly, while the net worth of the older homeowner may be substantial given his property and dwelling unit assets, his current spendable income may be insufficient even to fulfill most of his basic needs. Ironically, the full equity of the house may never be realized due to the owner's death. Yung-Ping Chen has outlined a home sale annuity program by which the housing equity could be realized within the lifetime of the older homeowner.

> A housing-annuity program combines home sale and annuity purchase. Assured of lifetime occupancy of the house, an older homeowner would put his home in escrow to convey the property title to a financial intermediary (possibly an insurance company or a pension fund or some other source of funds; referred to as the insurer) at his death or that of his spouse if later, in exchange for monthly annuity income for life. The amount of the annuity would be based on a number of economic, actuarial, and cost accounting considerations, such as rate of interest, rate of appreciation of property value, rate of depreciation of the house, percentage of property value attributable to the lot, the homeowner's sex, age, and marital status, the net equity in the property, and expense loading. [P. 15]

Although there are problems associated with the development of such a program, such as the difficulties of evaluating housing value and the negative or distrustful attitudes of the older homeowner, these would not seem to be insurmountable.

The occupants are often living in a dwelling unit that is quite impractical, if not uncomfortable, in light of their existing needs. In general it will be too large and if it is a two story dwelling and the occupant has difficulty climbing stairs the upper floor may never be used. Often the older house lacks some or all modern conveniences. Much of the mechanical equipment in the house—e.g., plumbing, electrical system—may seriously need replacing. These deficiencies may not only result in discomfort but also create severe safety hazards for the elderly occupant.

The character of the neighborhood setting also may have changed, with previously attractive attributes remaining only in the memory of the older person.

It can also be argued that houses occupied by elderly persons deprive younger, larger families from maximizing the full potential of such dwelling units. Moreover, the extent to which these houses are allowed to physically decline may influence the rate of their neighborhood's physical deterioration.

Special Noninstitutionalized Residential Settings—Group Housing

There are several types of noninstitutionalized group housing for the elderly including retirement hotels, residence clubs or halls and retirement villages. They differ with regard to the number and quality of services offered and the sophistication of their organizational structure. At once extreme is the residential hotel offering only meal facilities and informal social and recreation spaces; at the other is the retirement village providing a complete range of life-maintenance and life-enriching facilities and services.

While the larger, more exclusive retirement villages are located in the year long warm climates of California, Arizona and Florida, other forms of retirement group housing are well dispersed throughout the United States and are located in both large and small urban and rurual centers. The larger retirement villages are restricted to persons with higher income resources, but other group housing facilities are available to older persons with low to moderate income resources. However, the market served by the majority of group housing facilities usually consists of "young," recently retired elderly persons who are in relatively good health. The very old or unhealthy elderly are generally not encouraged to take up occupancy. Evidence from California studies would question the commonly held notion that occupants of retirement housing are usually recent arrivals (following long distance migrations). In fact findings reported by Wilner et al. revealed that the majority of occupants—from 50 to 75 percent depending on type of group accommodations—had lived in the state of California for 20 years or more. More rigorous research is required, however, on the origins of retirement housing occupants.

Because of their diversity it is difficult to make general evaluative judgments as to the success of these various types of retirement housing as forms of residential accommodation. However it would appear from limited research that the major goals and the most specific needs of older persons are being satisfied in many of these settings. Certainly, the most commonly cited criticism that they contribute unwisely to the segregation of the elderly from younger population groups is viewed if anything as a positive rather than a negative attribute by their occupants. From her research on a variety of California retirement housing types, Sherman concluded that in general the following factors were pertinent in the choice of retirement housing: "provision of meals and other services in an urban environment; good value in housing and recreation facilities, with agreeable climate and suburban atmosphere; easy maintenance and recreation facilities; and security." One potential problem that may arise in retirement communities in which dwelling units (including mobile homes) are purchased is the absence of special medical and care facilities for occupants who with aging may become disabled and require special community resources in order to carry out life-maintenance functions. In the event that the older person must find a more supportive residential environment, there is, according to Walkley et al., a question as to the housing resaleability difficulties he might experience.

Difficulties Associated With Residential Relocation by the Elderly

There are a number of reasons why older persons are less likely than members of younger age groups to change their existing accommodations, despite the evidence suggesting that many are living in housing quite incongruous with either their needs or resources. Part of the explanation is simply that many older persons have lived in the same dwelling unit for a long period of time, so that residential inertia itself becomes a reason for not moving. The security and attachments identified with the dwelling unit and neighborhood, and the familiarity with a dwindling number of friends reinforce the decision not to move.

A great deal of stress and physical energy is often perceived to be associated with a potential change in residence. This involves not only the actual moving itself—that is, the transfer of possessions from old to new residence—but in addition the difficulties associated with getting familiar with a new neighborhood, making new friends, and finding and utilizing neighborhood facilities and services. These anxieties can be particularly acute for the older person selling his own home, who is overconcerned with the unavoidable financial and legal procedures to the point that he fears being defrauded.

The lower mobility rates can also be explained by the small economic resources of many elderly in combination with the high cost of available housing. The elderly person selling his house sometimes finds that the price that can be obtained is significantly below what he has perceived to be its market value. It is low enough, in any case, so that the price of a new, smaller house or condominium is beyond his means. This problem is often accentuated by the difficulty experienced in obtaining mortgage insurance. Many apartment alternatives will also be rejected because of the realistic fear that the high rent will result in a rapid and serious drain on savings.

A change in residential location is also prevented because available dwelling units or neighborhood settings are unsuitable. Dwelling units located in attractive neighborhood settings will often be too large or planned uniformly for young families. Alternatively, small houses, condominiums, duplexes or apartments will often be in neighborhood settings that do not satisfy the needs of the older person. Spatial access to health, shopping, and social and recreation services and facilities may be poor. The possibility of being in close proximity to old friends or family may not exist.

Finally, many older persons will not have complete or accurate information about potentially satisfactory housing accommodation. Consequently, they may make an unfounded negative evaluation. Beyer and Nierstrasz have argued, for example, that when older persons are properly informed and advised about the housing opportunities available to them they have a more positive attitude towards relocating.

Given these inherent difficulties associated with the moving decision, it should not be surprising that older persons forced involuntarily from their present residence as a result of urban renewal and redevelopment plans may have a very traumatic, disruptive experience.

Housing Needs and Problems of the Elderly—Interurban Variations

Rationale and Methodology. The purpose of this section is to emphasize that the characteristics of older persons and their residential accommodation vary considerably among urban centers. In order to provide an illustration of these interurban variations, variables describing a select number of these characteristics are examined in five of the largest central cities in the United States.

While it is often analytically convenient to lump the "elderly in United States central cities" into one category, for example when comparing central cities of urbanized areas with their fringe areas, such statistical generalizations can be misleading. This is particularly so when, as will be illustrated, there is considerable variation in the characteristics of the older population and their housing among central cities of comparable size. Moreover, the range of some variable values may well be greater among central cities than between central cities and fringe areas. It should be emphasized that we are not suggesting that central city differences apply only to the elderly and their housing accommodation. It is likely that among central cities there will be comparable differences in the characteristics of housing occupied by younger population groups. Nor are we attempting to explain why these differences occur; this would require an intensive study of the economic, social and political forces that have contributed to the unique characteristics of a central city's infrastructure.

Rather, this limited statistical analysis has three goals: (1) to stimulate research on the systematic differences in elderly housing needs and problems that occur among urban areas of different sizes, economic bases and other typological criteria; (2) to stimulate research on why these variations exist and on their implications for the quality of life of older persons; and (3) to emphasize the need for legislative programs that are sensitive to the unequal needs of elderly living in different urban areas.

Variables as available from the 1970 decennial census describing the older population, their households and their housing accommodation have been tabulated for the central cities of New York, Chicago, Los Angeles, Philadelphia and Detroit (Tables 10-6 to 10-16). As the implications of most of these variables have been discussed, the following analysis will primarily restrict itself to a description of the statistical variations.

Sources of Interurban Variation. The simplest indicator of potential housing need is illustrated by the variation in the absolute and relative sizes of the elderly population (Table 10-6). The number of persons 65 and over ranges from 174,116 in Detroit to 952,637 in New York, reflecting the size variation in the total populations of these cities. The proportion of persons 65 and over ranges from 10.1 percent in Los Angeles to 12.1 percent in New York. Much larger interurban variations are found in the percentage of elderly who are Negro. This value ranges from 9.2 percent in New York to 24.5 percent in Detroit, largely reflecting the racial composition of the total population in these central cities. While racial or ethnic variations in the housing needs of the elderly have not been examined in this study, the evidence from a working paper by Inabel B. Lindsay reveals that "the majority of Negroes over 65 are less well educated, have less adequate income, suffer more illnesses and earlier death, have poorer quality housing and less choice as to where they live and where they work, and in general, have a less satisfying quality of life" [p. 2].

Homeownership as a form of housing tenure ranges from 25.2 percent in New York to 63.2 percent in Philadelphia (Table 10-7). As an example of how misleading national statistics can be, these figures should be compared with the frequently cited United States elderly homeownership rate of 69.5 percent (1970).

There is considerable variation in the living arrangements of older persons who own as opposed to rent their dwelling units (Table 10-8). Among homeowners, the percentage living in husband-wife families ranges from 47.7 in Philadelphia to 56.1 in New York. In rented units, the comparable percentage ranges from 25.6 in Detroit to 38.2 in New York. There are comparable variations in percentages of persons living alone in both owned and rented units. Of particular interest is the percentage of elderly females living alone in

Table 10-6. Residential Concentrations of Elderly Population in Five Largest Central Cities, 1970

Age	*New York*	*Chicago*	*Los Angeles*	*Philadelphia*	*Detroit*
65-74	626,608	228,360	174,706	145,974	109,793
75+	326,029	130,276	109,785	82,091	64,323
65+	952,637	358,636	284,491	228,065	174,116
	Percentage of Total Central City Population				
65-74	8.0	6.7	6.2	7.5	7.3
75+	4.1	3.9	3.9	4.2	4.3
65+	12.1	10.6	10.1	11.7	11.6
	Percentage of Population 65 and over, Negro, in Central City				
Negro persons 65+	9.2	16.9	10.6	20.2	24.5

Source: US Bureau of the Census, 1970 Census of Population, Second Count and Fourth Count, File C, Summary Tapes.

Table 10-7. Tenure Status of Persons 65 Years and Over, 1970

(Data in Percentages)	New York	Chicago	Los Angeles	Philadelphia	Detroit
Owners	25.2	41.0	42.3	63.2	66.0
Renters	74.8	59.0	57.7	36.8	34.0
Total	100.0	100.0	100.0	100.0	100.0

Source: US Bureau of the Census, 1970 Census of Housing, Fourth Count, File C, Summary Tape.

Table 10-8. Living Arrangements of Persons 65 Years and Over Occupying Owned or Rented Dwelling Units, 1970

(Data in Percentages)	New York	Chicago	Los Angeles	Philadelphia	Detroit
Living Arrangements			Owned Units		
Husband-wife family	56.1	52.3	53.0	47.7	52.7
Other family with male head	4.2	4.4	2.3	4.7	3.6
Family with female head	10.2	12.6	8.7	13.9	10.6
Total in families	70.5	69.3	64.0	66.3	66.9
Living Alone					
Male	6.3	7.1	6.7	7.8	7.2
Female	20.9	21.0	25.8	22.4	22.1
Living with nonrelative	2.4	2.6	3.5	3.5	3.7
Total unrelated individuals	29.6	30.7	36.0	33.7	33.0
Total	100.0	100.0	100.0	100.0	100.0
			Rented Units		
Husband-wife family	38.2	31.8	26.0	26.1	25.6
Other family with male head	2.7	2.4	1.4	2.4	2.3
Family with female head	7.6	7.9	5.8	8.6	7.0
Total in families	48.5	42.1	33.2	37.1	34.9
Living Alone					
Male	13.5	17.2	18.5	16.7	23.6
Female	35.5	37.2	45.9	42.9	37.4
Living with nonrelative	2.5	3.4	2.4	3.3	4.3
Total unrelated individuals	51.5	57.8	66.8	62.9	65.3
Total	100.0	100.0	100.0	100.0	100.0

Source: US Bureau of the Census, 1970 Census of Housing, Fourth Count, File C, Summary Tape.

rented units, which ranges from 35.5 in New York to 45.9 in Los Angeles.

There is far greater variation in the incidence of poverty between unrelated elderly persons living alone or with nonrelatives and elderly living in families than there is between cities for these respective groups (Table 10-9). In New York, for example, the percentage of families earning an income below the poverty level is 13.0 compared with 43.5 for unrelated individuals. However, among the five cities the percentage of family heads below the poverty level ranges from 10.9 in Los Angeles to 13.5 in Philadelphia. For unrelated individuals the percentage variation is larger, ranging from 34.1 in Los Angeles to 49.1 in Detroit.

Because of the considerable interurban variation in tenure status and the variation in the incidence of poverty between elderly families and unrelated individuals, subsequent analyses of other variables will control for these two sources of variation. Homeowners and renters will be analyzed separately and only husband-wife elderly families will be examined.

More detailed income statistics reveal that the percentage of elderly homeowners earning an annual income of under $3,000 varies

Table 10-9. Poverty Status of Persons 65 Years and Over, 1970

(Data in Percentages)	*New York*	*Chicago*	*Los Angeles*	*Philadelphia*	*Detroit*
Status			Total Persons		
Above poverty level	77.7	77.2	80.9	75.8	76.5
Below poverty level	22.3	22.8	19.1	24.2	23.5
Total	100.0	100.0	100.0	100.0	100.0
			Family Heads		
Above poverty level	87.0	87.7	89.1	86.5	87.4
Below poverty level	13.0	12.3	10.9	13.5	12.6
Total	100.0	100.0	100.0	100.0	100.0
			Unrelated Individuals		
Above poverty level	56.5	53.9	65.9	49.9	50.9
Below poverty level	43.5	46.1	34.1	50.1	49.1
Total	100.0	100.0	100.0	100.0	100.0

Source: US Bureau of the Census, 1970 Census of Population, Fourth Count, File C, Summary Tape.

Table 10-10. Income of Husband-Wife Families, Head 65 Years and Over, Occupying Owned or Rented Dwelling Units, 1970

(Data in Percentages)	*New York*	*Chicago*	*Los Angeles*	*Philadelphia*	*Detroit*
Income			Owned Units		
Less than $3,000	17.0	17.2	14.4	19.1	16.9
$ 3,000–$4,999	17.1	19.1	19.6	22.4	24.0
$ 5,000–$6,999	13.2	13.6	14.8	15.8	17.1
$ 7,000–$9,999	15.4	16.2	16.4	16.2	14.7
$10,000–$14,999	16.1	16.4	15.8	14.5	14.3
$15,000 or more	21.3	17.5	19.0	12.0	12.9
Total	100.0	100.0	100.0	100.0	100.0
Income			Rented Units		
Less than $3,000	22.3	21.3	20.8	24.7	28.1
$ 3,000–$4,999	19.6	18.4	25.3	21.6	25.4
$ 5,000–$6,999	13.9	14.4	15.4	15.1	15.8
$ 7,000–$9,999	15.0	15.9	15.5	14.2	13.1
$10,000–$14,999	14.0	15.1	12.4	11.1	9.8
$15,000 or more	15.2	14.9	10.5	13.2	7.8
Total	100.0	100.0	100.0	100.0	100.0

Source: US Bureau of the Census, 1970 Census of Housing, Fourth Count, File C, Summary Tape.

from 14.4 in Los Angeles to 19.1 in Philadelphia (Table 10-10). The interurban variation is greater if the percentage of homeowners earning less than $5,000 is considered, ranging from 34.4 in Los Angeles to 41.5 in Philadelphia. The percentage of elderly renters earning less than $3,000 ranges from 20.8 in Los Angeles to 28.1 in Detroit. For renters earning under $5,000 the percentage ranges from 39.7 in Chicago to 53.5 in Detroit. Comparable interurban variations for renters and homeowners occur at the high income levels.

For the elderly person who has voluntarily moved, both the motivation or desire had to be present, and suitable accommodations had to be available. Accordingly, the variability in the elderly rate of recent residential adjustments among the five central cities is related either to the variability in the respective older populations' satisfaction with their present housing and consequently their motivation to move, or in the variability of viable alternative residential accommodations that exist or that they perceive exist in their respective central cities—or some combination of these factors. A much smaller percentage of older persons moved into new owned units than into rented units (Table 10-11). There is little interurban variation in the percentages of elderly who moved into owned units over a one year period. Over a period of five years (implying that persons may have been as young as age 60 when they moved), the interurban variation in relocation is greater, ranging from 5.5 in Philadelphia to 7.8 in New York. There are much greater variations in relocation rates for older persons entering rental units. For persons moving over a one year period the percentage ranges from 6.0 in New York to 18.8 in Los Angeles; for a five year period the percentage ranges from 16.2 in New York to 39.1 in Philadelphia.

The size and/or type of the residential structure containing the rented dwelling units of older persons varies considerably among the five cities (Table 10-12). The percentage of elderly in single family rented residential structures (e.g., single detached, semiattached, row housing) ranges from 1.5 in New York to 27.0 in Philadelphia. Conversely, the percentage of elderly in multifamily apartment houses (20 or more units) ranges from 22.9 in Detroit to 67.6 in New York.

There is very little interurban variation in the unavailability of plumbing facilities in either owned or rented units (Table 10-13). In owned units the percentage ranges from 0.7 in Los Angeles to 1.4 in Chicago. In rented units the percentage ranges from 1.2 in Los Angeles to 2.3 in Chicago.

Interurban variations in the age of rented or owned residential structures at least partially reflect the varying ages of the cities themselves. The age of the structure is positively correlated with the probability that physical repairs are required, or have been undertaken, or that in various other ways (e.g., design, safety, utilities, equipment) the structure is inadequate. The percentage of elderly living in the oldest owned units (over 30 years old) ranges from 49.5 in Los Angeles to 77.4 in Philadelphia (Table 10-14). The percentage of elderly living in the oldest rented units range from 35.5 in Los Angeles to 70.3 in Detroit.

The percentage of elderly living in large owned dwelling units (six or more rooms) ranges from 39.2 in Chicago to 75.6 in Philadelphia (Table 10-15). If owned dwelling units containing five or more rooms are considered, the interurban variation is not as great with percentages ranging from 65.2 in New York to 89.7 in Philadelphia. The percentage of elderly

Table 10-11. Duration of Residence of Husband-Wife Families, Head 65 Years and Older, Occupying Owned or Rented Dwelling Units, 1970

(Data in Percentages)	*New York*	*Chicago*	*Los Angeles*	*Philadelphia*	*Detroit*
Period in Years			Owned Units		
1 or less	3.0	2.7	3.0	2.0	2.7
2–5	4.8	4.4	4.2	3.5	4.4
6–10	4.9	4.8	5.9	4.3	5.1
11–20	13.5	10.1	17.7	9.8	10.1
21–30	26.6	30.8	32.7	25.2	26.4
over 21	47.2	47.1	36.5	55.3	51.5
Total	100.0	100.0	100.0	100.0	100.0
Period in Years			Rented Units		
1 or less	6.0	11.3	18.8	12.9	12.6
2–5	10.2	15.2	19.9	16.2	19.2
6–10	10.8	13.8	16.5	16.6	14.6
11–20	18.9	23.8	21.0	22.1	22.0
21–30	20.3	20.5	17.0	19.0	20.0
over 21	33.7	15.3	6.8	13.3	11.3
Total	100.0	100.0	100.0	100.0	100.0

Source: US Bureau of the Census, 1970 Census of Housing, Fourth Count, File C, Summary Tape.

Table 10-12. Number of Units in Residential Structures Rented by Husband-Wife Families, (Head) 65 Years and Over, 1970

(Data in Percentages)	*New York*	*Chicago*	*Los Angeles*	*Philadelphia*	*Detroit*
Units					
1	1.5	4.5	21.2	27.0	18.3
2	9.0	17.8	7.6	18.6	33.1
3–4	6.5	16.3	13.3	10.9	8.5
5–19	15.4	30.4	32.8	10.6	17.2
20 or more	67.6	30.9	24.7	32.8	22.9
Mobile home or trailer	0.0	0.0	0.3	0.0	0.0
Total	100.0	100.0	100.0	100.0	100.0

Source: US Bureau of the Census, 1970 Census of Housing, Fourth Count, File C, Summary Tape.

Table 10-13. Presence of Plumbing Facilities in Owned and Rented Dwelling Units Occupied by Husband-Wife Families, Head 65 Years and Over, 1970

(Data in Percentages)	*New York*	*Chicago*	*Los Angeles*	*Philadelphia*	*Detroit*
			Owned Units		
All plumbing facilities	98.7	98.6	99.3	98.6	98.8
Lacking one or more plumbing facilities	1.3	1.4	0.7	1.3	1.2
Total	100.0	100.0	100.0	100.0	100.0
			Rented Units		
All plumbing facilities	98.4	97.7	98.8	98.2	98.0
Lacking one or more plumbing facilities	1.6	2.3	1.2	1.7	2.0
Total	100.0	100.0	100.0	100.0	100.0

Source: US Bureau of the Census, 1970 Census of Housing, Second Count, Summary Tape.

Table 10-14. Age of Owned or Rented Residential Structures Occupied by Husband-Wife Families, Head 65 Years and Over, 1970

(Data in Percentages)	*New York*	*Chicago*	*Los Angeles*	*Philadelphia*	*Detroit*
			Owned Units		
Age in Years					
1 or less	0.9	0.5	0.5	0.1	0.1
2–5	3.0	1.7	1.7	1.2	0.5
6–10	8.1	2.2	5.2	2.2	1.0
11–20	11.9	14.6	20.9	10.6	11.0
21–30	9.9	10.0	22.3	8.4	24.2
over 30	66.2	71.0	49.5	77.4	63.2
Total	100.0	100.0	100.0	100.0	100.0
			Rented Units		
Age in Years					
1 or less	0.4	1.1	1.3	1.7	0.2
2–5	2.9	5.4	8.0	6.6	3.1
6–10	7.9	7.3	14.9	12.5	5.0
11–20	11.4	9.4	21.4	14.1	8.4
21–30	12.3	7.6	18.8	8.6	13.0
over 30	65.1	69.3	35.5	56.1	70.3
Total	100.0	100.0	100.0	100.0	100.0

Source: US Bureau of the Census, 1970 Census of Housing, Fourth Count, File C, Summary Tape.

Table 10-15. Number of Rooms in Owned and Rented Dwelling Units Occupied by Husband-Wife Families, Head 65 Years and Over, 1970

(Data in Percentages)	*New York*	*Chicago*	*Los Angeles*	*Philadelphia*	*Detroit*
			Owned Units		
Rooms					
1-2	1.0	0.4	1.3	0.5	0.3
3	13.7	2.1	5.1	2.8	1.3
4	20.1	16.9	17.8	7.0	12.2
5	23.3	41.4	35.5	14.1	40.3
6 or more	41.9	39.2	40.3	75.6	45.8
Total	100.0	100.0	100.0	100.0	100.0
			Rented Units		
Rooms					
1-2	6.6	7.0	8.7	8.4	5.5
3	45.6	21.1	35.5	33.0	21.5
4	30.9	35.9	33.0	27.4	21.3
5	11.6	23.0	17.2	13.8	31.8
6 or more	5.3	13.1	5.7	17.4	19.9
Total	100.0	100.0	100.0	100.0	100.0

Source: US Bureau of the Census, 1970 Census of Housing, Second Count, File C, Summary Tape.

occupying rented units containing six or more rooms ranges from 5.3 in New York to 19.9 in Detroit. The interurban variation is greater if rented units containing five or more rooms are considered, ranging from 16.9 in New York to 51.7 in Detroit.

There is a large interurban variation in the market value of owned dwelling units (Table 10-16). This variation has implications for understanding the financial returns the elderly person expects if and when he sells his dwelling unit. The percentage of owned units valued under $10,000 ranges from 2.5 in Los Angeles to 47.7 in Philadelphia. Conversely, the percentage of owned units valued over $25,000 ranges from 2.9 in Philadelphia to 45.5 in Los Angeles. The interurban variation in rent payments is also considerable. The percentage of elderly paying under $60 monthly rent (excluding elderly paying no cash rent) ranges from 4.4 in Los Angeles to 17.9 in Philadelphia. The percentage paying over $100 monthly rent ranges from 24.8 in Detroit to 63.0 in Chicago.

Societal Response to the Housing Needs of the Elderly

It has been illustrated that the housing problems experienced by older persons are a function of both individual and household attributes associated with life cycle changes, and the extent to which characteristics of the residential environment are supportive of these changes. There would appear to be few, if any, housing problems that are an inevitable or necessary consequence of growing old. If existing and potential housing problems can be identified, and as emphasized their seriousness will likely vary from city to city, constructive programs are capable of alleviating the majority of them.

In the past the major legislative initiative originated at the federal level. Few states have developed housing programs specifically for the elderly. The following sections will examine, therefore, some aspects of the response of the federal government to the housing needs of the elderly.

The Federal Response to the Housing Needs of the Elderly

Principal Strategies. The most important consequence of federal housing legislation has been to increase the supply of housing units for low and moderate income population groups who could not afford comparable units at market prices. Only a few programs have been specifically developed to meet the housing needs of elderly persons. The elderly population has usually qualified for inexpensive

Table 10-16. Value or Rent of Owned or Rented Dwelling Units Occupied by Husband-Wife Families, Head 65 Years and Over, 1970

(Data in Percentages)	*New York*	*Chicago*	*Los Angeles*	*Philadelphia*	*Detroit*
			Owned Units		
Market Value					
Less than $10,000	3.6	5.0	2.5	47.7	18.9
$10,000–$14,999	7.0	14.8	10.1	34.6	31.3
$15,000–$19,999	18.3	28.0	21.0	11.1	31.4
$20,000–$14,999	26.7	25.7	21.0	3.6	12.5
$25,000 or more	44.4	26.6	45.5	2.9	5.9
Total	100.0	100.0	100.0	100.0	100.0
			Rented Units		
Monthly Rent					
No cash rent	1.8	3.0	5.0	4.7	7.9
$ 1–$40	2.3	1.5	0.9	4.8	3.2
$ 40–$59	12.1	6.4	3.5	13.1	14.3
$ 60–$79	23.6	12.0	13.7	23.0	33.0
$ 80–$99	19.7	14.0	17.3	1.4	16.9
$100–$149	22.6	40.2	34.8	18.5	16.4
$150 or more	17.9	22.8	24.8	21.8	8.4
Total	100.0	100.0	100.0	100.0	100.0

Source: US Bureau of the Census, 1970 Census of Housing, Second Count, Summary Tape.

housing under programs intended to provide accommodation for all lower income population groups.

Through a variety of federally subsidized programs the supply of low and moderate cost housing has been increased. Economic incentives have been given to profit, limited profit, and nonprofit sponsors, and local housing authorities to construct, rehabilitate, improve, lease, purchase and operate rental or cooperative housing for low and moderate income groups. This has had the simultaneous effect of increasing the purchasing power of the lower income group and stimulating the private sponsor to supply housing units that qualify for rent or mortgage subsidization. Programs have reduced home financing costs for lower income families by subsidizing the mortgage interest rate. They have designated a maximum percentage of a household's income that could be allocated to the monthly rental or mortgage amortization payment. Other programs have given households displaced by urban renewal a higher priority to enter low rental dwelling units. They have also been provided with moving expenses and assistance to pay initial rent payments or house down payments.

Federal legislation has also provided for the improvement of the physical condition of housing units occupied by persons with low incomes, including the elderly. These programs have made available a combination of grants and loans, partially covering the costs of housing rehabilitation. Only housing in urban renewal and concentrated code enforcement areas or in other areas with a substantial number of structures requiring rehabilitation have qualified, however. Funds have also been allocated on a limited basis for the capital improvement of low rental housing projects.

In programs such as Model Cities supplementary funds have been allocated to deal with inner city problems (the needs of the elderly are often identified as a major problem area) by coordinating the efforts of federal and municipal agencies. There have also been attempts by the Department of Housing and Urban Development to increase the number of administrative and managerial personnel trained to understand and deal with the specific housing needs of elderly residents.

Federal legislation has also provided for special services for the elderly. These are described in the following section.

Specific Housing Programs Affecting the Elderly. Two major groups of programs can be identified that have facilitated the construction of new rental and cooperative housing units and the rehabilitation and leasing of existing older housing for low and moderate income persons, including the elderly. The low rent public housing program, initially created by the United States Housing Act of 1937, has provided various forms of financial assistance for the development, ownership and operation of low rental housing by local housing authorities. The supply of apartment units for occupancy specifically by elderly persons is encouraged by the provision of federal annual subsidy contributions to the local authority and by the establishment of higher construction cost ceilings. A second group of housing assistance programs has been created by several housing legislative acts. A variety of funding schemes have stimulated the construction and rehabilitation of multifamily units for low and moderate income groups–including the elderly–by private profit-oriented sponsors and, to a lesser degree, nonprofit sponsors.

The largest number of units occupied by the elderly have been produced under the public housing program (approximately 70 percent). The remainder have been built under four principal programs, two of which applied specifically to the elderly and handicapped. Section 231 (207) of the Housing Act of 1959 established a program whereby profit and nonprofit sponsors were granted insured (but not interest-subsidized) mortgages to finance new or rehabilitated multifamily dwelling units specifically designed for elderly occupancy (aged 62 years and over). (By 1972 this program was virtually phased out because of many failures and foreclosures.) Section 202 of the 1959 Housing Act established a program of direct government loans over a 50 year period to nonprofit and limited profit sponsors covering 100 percent of the development costs of rental or cooperative housing with 3 percent subsidized below market mortgage interest rates, specifically for occupancy by low and moderate income elderly (aged 62 years and over) and handicapped persons. (Since 1970 Section 202 has not been funded. Previously accepted 202 applications have since been funded under Section 236 and have been referred to as 202-236 conversions.) Beginning in 1961, section 221(d)(3) of the National Housing Act established a program whereby nonprofit or limited profit sponsors were given below market subsidized interest rate 40 year mortgage loans to build or rehabilitate multifamily buildings for moderate income families including the elderly. (In 1972 this program was limited to providing mortgage insurance and did not offer any subsidy.) Section 236 of the Housing Act of 1968 established an interest-subsidy program for rental and cooperative multifamily housing construction with the sponsor paying a mortgage with an interest rate as low as 1 percent, and the federal government contributing the balance of the interest rate charged by the financing agency. All lower income families including the elderly were eligible. (As of 1973 new commitments for all subsidized housing programs were halted.) Complementing these four programs has been Section 101 of the Housing and Urban Development Act of 1965 (rent supplement program). It provided for federal payments to sponsors of any of these four programs in order to subsidize them for the difference between the rent received from tenants (restricted to 25 percent of their income) and the given market rent.

Another major group of federal programs has provided for the funding of special services for the elderly. Several of the housing assistance programs provided funds for the provision of such congregate facilities as community kitchens and central dining rooms. Section 703 of the Housing and Urban Development Act of 1965 has allocated federal funds for up to two-thirds of the development cost of multiservice neighborhood centers offering health, recreational and social services for low and moderate income communities. These centers have served all age groups including the elderly. In more far-reaching legislation special services for the elderly have been authorized under the public assistance titles of the Social Security Act of 1935 as amended in 1962, including Title I, Old Age Assistance; Title X, Aid to the Blind; Title XIV, Aid to the Permanently and Totally Disabled; and Title XVI, Grants to States for Aid to the Aged, Blind, or Disabled or for such Aid and Medical Assistance to the Aged. These service programs have been administered (and initiated) at the state level with 75 percent federal and 25 percent state funding contributions. A report of the Special Senate Subcommittee on Federal, State and

Community Services—*The Rise and Threatened Fall of Service Programs For the Elderly*—has outlined the services that potentially can be provided:

> Mandatory services for the aged, blind, and disabled, include: information and referral without regard to eligibility for assistance; protective services; services to enable persons to remain in or to return to their homes or communities; supportive services that will contribute to a "satisfactory and adequate social adjustment of the individual," and services to meet health needs.
>
> Optional services which states may elect to include in their State plan for the aged, blind, and disabled encompass three broad categories: services to individuals to improve their living arrangements and enhance activities of daily living; services to individuals and groups to improve opportunities for social and community participation; and services to individuals to meet special needs.

Strengthened by the Comprehensive Services Amendments of 1973, the Older Americans Act of 1965 provides for potential funding of various special services for the elderly. The objectives of the act were broadened to provide that community services should include "access to low-cost transportation" (Title I). Under Title III—Grants for State and Community Programs for Aging—funds have been allocated to states in order to initiate a variety of "social services" for the elderly including:

> • health, continuing education, welfare, informational, recreational, homemaker, counseling, or referral services;
> • transportation services where necessary to facilitate access to social services;
> • services designed to encourage and assist older persons to use the facilities and services available to them;
> • services designed to assist older persons to obtain adequate housing;
> • services designed to assist older persons in avoiding institutionalization, including preinstitutionalization evaluation and screening, and home health services; . . .

Under Title V funds have been allocated for the development of multipurpose senior centers and under Title VII nutrition programs are to be better integrated into other social service systems for the elderly.

Evaluating the Federal Response

This paper's conception of "housing" has necessarily been very comprehensive, considering a wide range of variables describing the dwelling unit and the neighborhood setting. Similarly, in its treatment of the older population a wide range of sociological, psychological and biological forces were examined in order to correctly interpret the aging process. The analysis of the housing needs and problems of older persons and the factors that underlie them would suggest that whatever form new federal housing programs assume, the older population should be identified as a distinctive consumer group. This implies that a set of housing goals for the elderly population should be established and legislative programs and funding allocations should be initiated to effectively carry them out. Low and moderate income housing projects and related services, for example, should be administered, developed and operated specifically to meet these goals. This section will argue that because the federal government has not had this special commitment, the housing needs of the older population have not been adequately served.

Low and moderate income housing that has been designed to accommodate older persons has often been underfunded or poorly administered. Housing programs in which the elderly have been one of several eligible lower income groups, have often resulted in residential accommodation that has not adequately served their special needs. With no fixed proportion of government funds allocated to elderly housing, the amount of housing supplied has fallen considerably short of the demand. According to recommendations of the 1971 White House Conference on Aging, housing units for the elderly should be produced at a rate of 120,000 a year. In 1972, one of the highest production years, federal housing programs produced less than 80,000 units specially designed for the elderly. In other years the production rate has been considerably less.

The federal government has not only been unsuccessful in providing a sufficient total supply of housing, but it has also failed to establish controls or incentives insuring an equitable spatial allocation of housing units. Accordingly, the urban and regional distribution of low and moderate rental housing does not appear to bear any relationship to actual need. As Ira Robbins emphasized in his White House conference background paper, the initiative to develop housing exists where local governments have had "...(1) a strong desire to do so, (2) a knowledge of the Federal programs for elderly housing, (3) access to church, foundation, or lender funds, and (4) the expertise to put projects together." However, most states and municipalities have not even undertaken systematic needs assessment studies of their elderly population. While there is much to be said for local governments deciding whether or not to provide housing for their elderly, there is much the federal government could do in the way of requiring evaluation studies and providing supply guidelines or economic incentives to insure minimum urban or regional housing quotas.

One of the more beneficial federal housing programs, Section 202, did in fact provide the specialized housing needed by many elderly. The program was financed through direct loans of the full mortgage to the sponsoring agency. It was unpopular with the Nixon administration because of the large annual financial commitment budgeted for its development. In fact, a report titled "Housing Subsidies and Housing Policy" has suggested that considerable (interest) savings could be realized by "direct loan" (allocated from a separate budgetary capital account) as opposed to "interest subsidy" programs (e.g., Section 236 and Section 235). In contrast to other programs, housing produced under Section 202 was primarily developed by nonprofit or limited profit sponsors such as civic, religious, charitable or other public service organizations. The report of the hearings before the Senate Subcommittee on Housing for the Elderly—*Adequacy of Federal Response to Housing Needs of Older Americans*—produced considerable evidence suggesting that in comparison with the profit-oriented sponsor, the nonprofit sponsor took greater care in initial site selection and had greater commitment to the management and successful operation of the project. However, he often lacked experience in the area of housing development. Given the complexities of bureaucratic procedures—worsened by the general insensitivity of Federal Housing Administration authorities—misunderstandings, long delays and unnecessary increased expenditures often resulted. By establishing education programs and revised, simpler and clearer application procedures, the task of the nonprofit sponsor could be made considerably easier. This is not to suggest that the private developer should be discouraged from assuming his traditional role; only that he should be encouraged to assume higher standards of performance.

The identification of older persons as a particular housing consumer group does not negate the fact that their housing needs are diverse. A variety of dwelling unit types—e.g., high-rise and low-rise apartment buildings, rented houses, small single family houses, condominiums and mobile homes—which to varying degrees contain special architectural design features, extra security devices and congregate facilities or are served by special community services are required. In particular, this implies that older persons with varying levels of disability and social service requirements will have available residential accommodation alternatives that are supportive of their changing needs and which enable them to live as independently as their personal resources permit. Such a variety of housing alternatives have been largely unavailable, particularly to the low and moderate income elderly group.

This also means that greater care must be taken in the location of newly developed or leased dwelling units intended for occupancy by elderly persons, as well as in the relocation of older persons from one housing accommodation to another. Older persons, for example, have been placed in accommodations where needed community services and facilities have not been easily available. They have been located in neighborhoods that have the highest crime rates. Given the evidence regarding the desire of many elderly to live in age-segregated settings, it would also seem inappropriate to place them in apartment complexes with younger families and children who may have little understanding or consideration of the problems of growing old.

In the past, insufficient capital funds have resulted in the inadequate design or in the absence of needed congregate facilities and services in federally subsidized low and moderate income housing projects. It has often been impossible to charge lower rents and still have sufficient funds for even routine maintenance services or for the employment of security personnel who are very much needed in some housing projects. In order to provide suitable housing accommodation for the elderly, larger capital expenditures and larger, more flexible operating budgets are therefore required.

Managerial personnel of housing developments can play a very important role in insuring that the needs of older persons are being satisfied or in identifying developing problems. Housing for the elderly requires management by persons who have received special training—who are knowledgeable of and sensitive to the existing and potential needs of older persons. Again a special commitment is required—there has been in the past an insufficient supply and utilization of such managerial personnel.

Existing eligibility criteria by which an "elderly" person (aged 62 years and over in previous government-sponsored housing programs) qualifies to enter low and moderate income apartment housing are too restrictive and inflexible. We have suggested already that chronological age alone is not an adequate measure of "oldness' and its accompanying problems. Neither is a minimum level of income, which is yet another criterion restricting the eligibility of older persons. The eligibility of "elderly" to receive benefits from low and moderate income housing accommodations should be based not only on economic and chronological age definitions, but also on health and social needs criteria. This implies that persons with higher incomes or of younger chronological ages who might derive benefits from features associated with "elderly" housing should be considered as applicants. Such a policy also necessitates evaluations of housing applicants by a staff specially trained to understand the suitability of potential tenants.

There has been frequent and strong community opposition to the building of public housing, especially in or near white middle class suburban areas. Specifically, many residents of these communities fear that low income black persons will eventually occupy this housing, resulting in an increase in crime and a decline in property values and neighborhood status. In general, communities have been more receptive to housing projects in which they have had assurances that the occupants would be likely to be "elderly" and not comprise population groups they perceive to be undesirable. Because of the unfortunate reputation associated with low rent public housing projects, such apartment housing intended for occupancy by elderly persons has sometimes met with community opposition. While we do not condone racial housing segregation, it would nevertheless appear to be desirable that low or moderate income apartment housing intended for older persons should be carefully identified and distinguished as such so that potential community opposition might be alleviated.

Despite the large proportion of older persons living in their own homes who to varying degrees are living in unsatisfactory accommodations, there has been no systematic federal response to the needs of this group. Given the advantages and disadvantages of homeownership and difficulties sometimes encountered with residential relocation, the formulation of two complementary responses would seem fruitful.

Homeownership for a large number of older persons represents the most preferred form of housing tenure and consequently should be encouraged and maintained as long as possible. Responses are therefore required that increase the ability or competency of the older homeowner to deal with his existing or potential needs and problems. He should be able to avail himself, for example, of homemaker services, part-time nursing care and meals on wheels services and should have access, if necessary through the provision of special transportation services, to health clinics and senior centers. Collectively these responses should enable the older homeowner to live as independently as possible in his own community. Concomitantly, there are at least two potential means of increasing (indirectly) the older homeowner's income resources. The reduction or elimination of the property tax and the implementation of a home sale annuity program represent two alternative strategies. In order to reduce the discomforts resulting from the physical aging of the dwelling unit, low cost loans and/or grants should be made available for home maintenance and rehabilitation.

Other older homeowners, either due to a change in their tenure preferences or because they have experienced disabilities or financial difficulties, will not want or will not be able (irrespective of initiation of responses described above) to remain in their own homes. At least some persons in this category will require assistance in the potentially difficult task of relocating to another residential accommodation. Older persons should be able to avail themselves of services designed to reduce problems associated with the search for new and the selling of old housing accommodations.

In responding to the diverse housing needs of the elderly, within any one level of government a variety of departments and agencies—e.g., health, education and welfare; transportation; housing and urban development—are simultaneously involved in interdependent aspects of program development. Similarly, agencies at federal, state and local levels of government are simultaneously participating in program development. The success of any housing program for older persons will depend on the extent of inter- and intradepartmental communication and cooperation. There is an urgent need for inter- and intradepartmental coordination of programs that are related to the housing needs of older persons. A single agency—perhaps a department of aging—should be given administrative authority at federal, state and local levels to assist in the coordination of other departmental programs that are related to the provision of housing accommodation for the elderly. In the past these relationships have been far from optimum.

TRANSPORTATION NEEDS AND PROBLEMS OF OLDER AMERICANS

Spatial Accessibility of the Elderly—Defining the Problem

Due to the locational distribution of residential and nonresidential land uses in the contemporary urban center, residents are to varying degrees physically separated by space from other persons and from facilities and services. The extent to which space acts as a barrier preventing full utilization of the urban setting is dependent on the relative location of the individual's place of residence with respect to destinations to which he desires access. In evaluating the relative location of the individual's place of residence two major complementary sets of variables must be considered. First, the available means of transportation must be identified and evaluated. Specifically, the number and relative importance of destinations that can be reached by automobile, mass transit or by walking short distances must be determined. These alternatives must then be examined with respect to such parameters as travel cost and time expenditures, comfort, and convenience. Second, given the resources or capabilities of the individual—for example, his general health—the question of how effectively and with what difficulty he can utilize these alternative means of access must be evaluated. A consideration of these two complementary sets of variables represents the major thrust of the analytical inquiry of this section.

A second level of inquiry of this section focuses on the accessibility of services or facilities to older persons after the barrier of distance between residence and destination has been overcome. For the older person in the wheel chair, a service located in a building that can be reached only by ascending a flight of stairs is essentially inaccessible. The degree to which such architectural barriers prevent full utilization of the urban setting will be a function of the seriousness of the physical disabilities of the older person, the number and seriousness of the architectural barriers that characterize selected destinations, and the physical assistance he can expect to receive from other persons in order to surmount these barriers.

There is another level of inquiry that was considered briefly in the previous analysis of special elderly housing services and which can provide considerable insight into potential transportation needs. This is the degree to which the older person can utilize urban services or facilities, or engage in social relationships without physically leaving his dwelling unit. To the extent, for example, that doctors can make housecalls, grocery stores can deliver their goods, eating facilities are located on the premises of the residence, friends and relatives can make visits, and the older resident is satisfied with environmental transactions of this type, then the need for transportation services is correspondingly reduced. There has been, however, virtually no research on the benefits and costs associated with these types of transactions. Accordingly, while identified as potentially important "accessibility" alternatives, they are not considered further in the paper.

Special Importance of Adequate Spatial Accessibility to the Elderly

While adequate spatial access to needed services and facilities is obviously important for all age groups, for the older person the inability to reach required destinations can have a particularly negative impact on the quality of his life. Such difficulties may represent the first concrete signs that he is becoming old and the self-realization that he no longer will be able to carry on an accustomed way of life. For the older person, for example, who has primarily relied on the automobile most of his life and finds that because of a decline in his driver skills or because his driver's license is not renewed he cannot use this mode of transportation, this sudden deprivation and discontinuity can be very stressful. If, in fact, this loss of mobility threatens his ability to maintain his independent living arrangements, the deleterious psychological impact may be even greater.

Growing old necessarily involves adaptation to various types of problems such as a lower income or poorer health. As a result, the impact of losing something as basic as transportation services may in combination with other problems prove to be far more serious for the older person because of its additive or cumulative effect.

The loss of the work role, of old friends or of a spouse represent activities and relationships that the older person may wish to replace. The need for good transportation services may therefore be particularly important, giving him mobility to find substitutes for these losses. Expressed in a more positive sense, retirement is often accompanied by a large increase in leisure time and consequently greater opportunities will exist for the older person who wishes to engage in activities for which previously he did not have time.

The physiological and psychological changes associated with growing old may result in a decline in either physical strength or motivation to engage in new activities. Trips to destinations accessible only by public transportation may be curtailed because of the physical exertion and fatigue experienced in using this transportation mode. The older person may have a fear of leaving his familiar neighborhood to engage in activities located at some distance from his residence irrespective of their potential benefits. It appears reasonable to suggest that the energy or effort that many elderly persons are willing or have the capacity to expend in return for some benefit resulting from some activity may be significantly less than for a younger person. Poor quality service and inconveniences of various kinds may represent to some older persons far more significant barriers than they might for other younger population groups.

Finally, as emphasized in the previous discussion on housing needs, the elderly person often faces considerable difficulties when seeking new residential accommodation with regard to the cost, type and size of dwelling units available. The poor accessibility of some dwelling units to required services and facilities adds yet another restraint preventing the older person from obtaining adequate housing accommodation.

The Major Dimensions of the Problem

The following three sections examine how the aging of the individual and the process of urbanization result in the older individual having difficulty achieving adequate spatial access to services, facilities or persons.

The Impact of Urbanization. Accompanying the successful adoption of the automobile as a major mode of transportation was the rapid spatial expansion of the city with a land use organization reflecting the impact of the new technological innovation. The residential decentralization of the urban population was accompanied by the development of commercial, industrial, recreational, cultural and medical facilities and services in auto-accessible outlying shopping centers and specialized districts dispersed throughout the metropolitan area. Concurrently, there was a decline in the relative and absolute number of services and facilities found in central business districts. As a consequence an increasing proportion of facilities and services have become easily accessible only by automobile transportation. For population groups such as the elderly, who have a low rate of automobile ownership and who are dependent on mass transit, many parts of their metropolis have therefore become inaccessible.

Decline in Urban Mass Transit. A report produced by the Urban Mass Transportation Administration (UMTA) succinctly summarized the manifestations of the transit industry's decline: "... reduced ridership, curtailment of services, increased costs, growing deficits, failure of firms, and the increased public acquisition of systems to prevent the abandonment of service."

Since mass transit represents the most viable alternative to automobile transportation, this decline is particularly serious to groups such as the elderly, the majority of whom are dependent on its service. The most important consequences have been the decline in transit service—especially in off-peak hours, the period in which older persons are most likely to utilize the system for their nonwork trip purposes—and a general upward increase in fare levels reflecting increased salary expenditures of this labor-intensive industry.

Physiological Changes Associated with Aging. The physiological changes that have consequences for the transportation needs of the older person can be discussed under four major categories: vision, hearing, the central nervous system, and the locomotor system.

Vision. Older persons experience a general decline in visual acuity and in particular a loss in peripheral vision. They are more sensitive to daytime glare and may experience a change in color perception. Less light may reach the retina and sight may be diminished in dark settings.

The major consequences for the elderly pedestrian include his having greater difficulty seeing cars approaching from the side, greater difficulty walking at night, possible confusion when interpreting traffic lights, and slower interpretation and response in situations dependent on the receiving and processing of visual information (e.g., the reading of signs or wall maps). The consequences for the elderly driver include an increased probability of error when interpreting signs and signals, increased risk associated with changing lanes and greater difficulty when driving at night.

Hearing. Large numbers of older persons experience a loss of hearing acuity. Such a decrement reduces the older person's sensitivity to auditory signals indicating warnings of danger. It has consequences for him both as a pedestrian and auto driver since auditory warnings can prevent the occurrence of serious accidents.

Central Nervous System. The older person experiences a general decline in many of his sensory and perceptual functions resulting in slower reaction times and increased difficulty in organizing and coordinating complex stimuli. The most important consequences for the older pedestrian or auto driver occur when he is in an unfamiliar or stressful situation that may require rapid processing of information accompanied by an immediate evalution and response.

Locomotor System. The older person experiences a general decline in speed and performance of motor tasks characterized by decreasing agility and muscular strength, difficulty in maintaining balance, and slower and jerkier movements. The consequences for the older pedestrian include his having less endurance for long walks, especially along steep, ascending paths, and reduced capacity to carry heavy packages. The older transit rider has difficulty boarding buses because of the high steps and cannot withstand long periods either waiting for or standing in vehicles. Because of difficulties maintaining balance, he also has greater susceptibility to injuries from falls.

Physiological Changes and Disability. Despite these various physiological changes associated with old age, it has been estimated that 81 percent of older persons not in institutions are ambulatory. Another 8 percent have some trouble getting around but can manage on their own, sometimes using a mechanical aid. Six percent need the help of another person in order to achieve ambulation, while only about 5 percent are home-bound.

The Achievement of Spatial Accessibility by the Elderly—Needs and Problems

It can be hypothesized that the demands for vehicular transportation by elderly persons will vary indirectly as the facilities, services and social relationships they require are accessible by walking or alternatively are located on or transported to the residential site (e.g., congregate facilities, meals on wheels). Except in these latter cases where no mobility is required, the role of alternative transportation modes, at least from the perspective of elderly consumers, becomes minimal. However, only a very small proportion of older persons achieve *all* their needs through such *in situ* arrangements. The mere presence of vehicular transportation services, moreover, whether manifested by the ownership of an automobile or the existence of a transit service, does not insure that these private and public modes will be fully or efficiently used, or how costly in health, psychological or economic terms they will be to their users. Similarly, walking as a mode of transportation has a number of potential limitations. Finally, even when a destination is reached by one of these transportation modes, the facility or service may still remain inaccessible because the building in which it is housed contains architectural barriers. The following sections will examine the types and causes of problems associated with the achievement of spatial accessibility by the older population.

The Use of the Mass Transit System. The major problem areas associated with the use of mass transit are physical design and operating characteristics of the vehicles; frequency, flexibility and complexity of service; completeness and accuracy of elderly consumer's knowledge of mass transit system operation; and cost of service.

Physical Design and Operating Characteristics of System. The problem of waiting for long periods for bus service, especially in bad weather conditions, is often accentuated by the absence of shelters or benches. They are not provided, except on a limited basis, because of cost constraints.

The entrance and departure from buses create a number of difficulties; examples are the necessity of climbing high bus steps, the insufficient time to reach exit doors, the fear and reality of doors closing too soon, and the stopping of vehicles at unsafe points of street exit. The bus driver or preferably other hired personnel could help alleviate some of these difficulties by providing assistance to the older person when he enters or exists from the bus.

Various "moving" characteristics of buses also create problems, including the rapid acceleration and deceleration of stop and go driving, the insufficient time to get seated after the bus is entered, poorly placed or insufficient hand grips, and the stresses resulting from the negotiation of crowded moving vehicles.

Frequency, Flexibility and Complexity of Service. The elderly person using mass transit in major urban centers is disadvantaged because he is using the system at non-rush-hour periods for nonwork purposes. The optimum transit service, however, is available during rush hour periods and for routes oriented to major employment concentrations. He therefore suffers from service which is often very infrequent or absent entirely. Very often posted schedules are not followed with any reliability. He often must transfer several times in order to finally reach his destination. He often experiences a great deal of inconvenience and difficulty in reaching these transfer points.

Completeness and Accuracy of Knowledge of Mass Transit System Operation by Elderly Consumer. Many elderly persons experience difficulty understanding the operation of the mass transit system. Specifically, they have problems interpreting bus and rail schedules, locating transfer points, and finding subway entrance and exit gates. They also have difficulty seeing or hearing information communicated by signs and loudspeaker systems.

Cost of Service. Transportation costs are sufficiently high to represent the third largest item next to housing and food in the household budget of older persons. Rising transit fares, and the need for two or three separate fares on multizonal trips, in combination with low incomes of elderly persons make transit cost one of the most serious barriers.

The Utility of the Mass Transit System. Each of these problem areas can potentially restrict either partially or entirely the utility of an existing transit service to an older population. The extent to which these problems exist will depend on the relationship between on the one hand, the quality of service offered, and on the other, the demands of the elderly transit consumer and his capabilities of utilizing the existing system. Therefore, transit utility cannot be spoken of in absolute terms. While two neighborhoods in a city may offer comparable transit service, their respective elderly populations may differ significantly in their ability to use it effectively. Accordingly, in evaluating the transportation problems of an older population, the degree of congruency between the consumer's need and the transit system's service should be emphasized rather than the characteristics of each analyzed in isolation.

The Use of the Automobile. Two related difficulties are experienced by the older driver. Physiological changes may make driving more hazardous, and institutional barriers involving the renewal of his license and the continuation of his car insurance may prevent him from legally using his automobile.

A number of physiological changes impair his ability to skillfully operate an automobile. This difficulty is accentuated by the use of the automobile in the large urban center. Driving has become more hazardous for the older person because of increased traffic flows, higher speeds related to expressway and freeway driving, and more complex traffic patterns. While he may possess considerable driving experience, declines in his sensory and perceptual processes and his motor skills result in slower reaction times with potentially serious consequences in demanding urban driving situations. It has been shown that accidents by the older driver are more likely to occur when he is involved in such maneuvers as changing lanes, turning, passing or backing up as opposed to simply maintaining his position within the traffic flow of his lane. As a result of poorer vision, the elderly driver has more difficulty interpreting traffic lights and signs and often has to restrict his driving to the daylight hours.

The number of older persons who own automobiles is higher than the number who are licensed to drive. Part of the explanation for this discrepancy is the difficulty the person over age 65 has in renewing his driver's license.

Auto insurance companies also have a discriminatory attitude toward the older driver. Some companies arbitrarily cancel insurance policies of clients over age 65 while others may be relegated to the "assigned risk" category resulting in higher insurance rates and the loss of the premium financing option.

There is some justification for these licensing and insurance policies. While there are conflicts in empirical evidence, it has been shown by Planek, Condon and Fowler that based on an index "accidents per mile travelled," elderly auto drivers are more accident prone than younger age groups. Nevertheless, a general policy applied to all elderly drivers would appear both unfair and unnecessary. A more selective evaluation procedure to identify the high risk elderly driver is required in order to avoid penalizing the competent.

The Utility of the Automobile. There have been no studies which reveal the extent to which the elderly driver is achieving maximum utility from his automobile. That is, to what extent does he restrict his automobile usage because of a realization that his present driving ability is inadequate at certain times or settings (e.g., at night, in hazardous weather conditions, on high speed expressways)? To what extent does he restrict his automobile usage because operating or maintenance costs are too great for a small household budget? Although older persons who own and are licensed to drive an automobile clearly have the greatest potential of fully realizing their mobility needs, it is likely that this potential is not being realized equally by all members of this group. Alternative means of transportation may still be necessary in order to insure that their activities are not being restricted because of mobility difficulties.

Walking As a Mode of Transportation. There is evidence to suggest that older persons in urban areas take more short walking trips than members of younger age groups and may be more dependent on walking as a primary transportation mode.

Walking achieves two distinctive purposes: as the primary means of transportation, when it is utilized to overcome the distance between the residence and the destination; and as a secondary means when it is used in conjunction with vehicular transportation to reach a destination. The latter purpose is exemplified by the walk from the residence to the bus stop or to the automobile or, after departure from the vehicle, the walk to the destination. The inability of the older person to utilize walking as a secondary means of transportation correspondingly limits the utility of vehicular transportation. As Gelwicks has expressed the problem:

> Of what use is it to bring an elderly person . . . to the corner of the shopping center if there is no internal transportation system to assist him in traversing the several acres of parked cars or moving from area to area within the center. [P. 21]

Three general types of problems are associated with walking as a transportation mode:

the older individual's safety, his physical strength and agility, and the quality of walking surfaces.

Safety. As a pedestrian the elderly person is more frequently a victim of automobile accidents than members of other age groups. He also has greater difficulty negotiating slippery or icy sidewalks and his capability of walking is reduced during these hazardous periods because of the likelihood of his falling and sustaining physical injury. The older pedestrian is also frequently the victim of robberies and muggings which may discourage him from walking during the evening or other periods when there is little street activity.

Physical Strength and Agility. The elderly pedestrian is a slower walker. This frequently creates difficulties for him when he crosses busy streets, especially when traffic signals change too quickly. Neibanck has identified a set of critical walking distances between the residence and different types of facilities beyond which dissatisfaction was expressed by a sample of elderly respondents (Table 10-17).

Quality of Walking Surfaces. The following characteristics of walking surfaces restrict their full utilization by the older person: unavailable or poorly surfaced paths; poor separation between vehicular and pedestrian flows creating hazardous walking conditions; the absence of public rest facilities such as benches; and paths that are particularly crowded or occupied by activities—e.g., children playing—which interfere with walking.

Table 10-17. Critical Walking Distances Between Residence and Facility

Facility	*Critical Distance*
Grocery Store	2-3 blocks
Bus Stop	1-2 blocks
House of Worship	1/4-1/2 mile
Drug Store	3 blocks
Clinic or Hospital	1/4-1/2 mile
Bank	1/4 mile
Social Center	indeterminate
Library	1 mile
News-Cigarstore	1/4 mile
Restaurant	1/4-1/2 mile
Movie House	1 mile
Bar	indeterminate

Source: Modified from P.L. Neibanck. *The Elderly in Older Urban Areas* (Philadelphia: Institute for Environmental Studies, University of Pennsylvania, 1965), p. 64.

The Utility of Walking. Because there are potential problems associated with walking as a mode of transportation, an automatic assumption cannot be made that a "short" distance between a dwelling unit and a required facility does not represent a barrier to some older persons. Where walking is assumed to be the primary transportation mode, efforts should be made to assure that problems associated with "safety" and the "quality of walking services" are reduced to a minimum.

Architectural Barriers and the Accessibility of Buildings. An older person confined to a wheelchair, dependent on a mechanical walking device or possessing minor ambulatory difficulties often encounters architectural barriers in buildings containing required facilities or services. For those in wheelchairs, steps in front of or within buildings, or doors of a width insufficient to accommodate a wheelchair, may prevent access if alternative means of entrance such as ramp entrances, or elevators large enough for a wheelchair, are not available. When these architectural barriers prevent access to public transportation facilities (e.g., transit buildings, underground access, vehicles), the impact on the older person is particularly great as he is effectively precluded from utilizing his only mode of transportation.

Societal Response to the Transportation Needs of the Elderly

In the following sections the federal response to the transportation needs of the elderly will be identified and evaluated. While programs have been developed at the state and local levels of government, the major source of legislative direction and funding commitments has been at the federal level.

Federal Legislation and Urban Mass Transit Service. The Housing Act of 1961 represented the first major legislation explicitly providing for federal fiscal assistance—albeit on a modest scale—to urban mass transit in the form of demonstration grants and low cost loans for acquisitions and capital improvements. Under the Urban Mass Transportation Act of 1964 this role was expanded to include grants for capital outlays. It provided for the purchase of new subway and surface rapid transit vehicles and the replacement of obsolete buses. More formal recognition of the distinctive importance of mass transit in the urban system came with the formation of a separate Department of Transportation (DOT) in 1966 and with the creation of the Urban Mass Transportation Administration (UMTA) within DOT in 1968.

The passage of the Urban Mass Transportation Act of 1970 marked an increased fiscal role of the federal government in urban mass transportation. Ten billion dollars is to be provided for urban mass transportation over a 12 year period. Authorization was given for over $3 billion for a five year period beginning in fiscal year 1971 to finance projects of UMTA. Grants were made on a two-thirds federal and one-third local matching basis.

The inclusion of the Biaggi Amendment in the 1970 act marked the first time that legislation provided for the planning, design and operation of urban mass transportation services specifically to meet the needs of the elderly and handicapped. The amendment also authorized the allocation of 1.5 percent of the total funding of the UMTA programs to assist state and local public bodies and agencies in providing loans and grants to modify mass transit systems to the special needs of the elderly and handicapped. DOT, however, has discretionary authority to make use of this amount.

The passage of the Federal Aid Highway Act of 1973 provided $17.9 billion ($16.7 billion from highway trust fund and $1.2 billion from general tax revenues) for continuing and new federal aid highway improvement and construction programs over three fiscal years (1974-1976). In contrast to the Federal Aid Highway Act of 1970, however, states will now be allowed under certain conditions to transfer funds from unwanted urban interstate system routes for an equal amount of public mass transit aid from general funds. For the first time, also, urbanized areas in 1975 and 1976 will be allowed under certain conditions to use revenues from the highway trust fund for rail and bus mass transit capital improvements.

Federal Legislation and Architectural Barriers. The most important legislation dealing with the problems caused by architectural barriers has been the Architectural Barriers Act of 1968. It authorized the Administration of General Services to prescribe standards for the design, construction and alteration of nonresidential and nonmilitary buildings funded by the federal government in order to make them accessible and usable by the handicapped. Subsequent legislation in 1970 made the act applicable to facilities constructed under the authority of the National Transportation Act of 1969 and the National Capital Transportation Act of 1965.

Standards of accessibility were based on the "American Standard Specifications for Making Buildings and Facilities Accessible to and Usable By the Physically Handicapped." Under these standards, if enforced, the majority of building barriers would be effectively eliminated. The wording of the act, however, is vague and nonspecific especially with regard to the definition of buildings which come under the act and the enforcement of its terms. The degree to which these architectural guidelines have been enforced has been a function of initiatives taken by state and municipal level governments to pass more vigorous and effective legislation.

Federal Legislation and the Administration on Aging. The Administration on Aging established by the Older Americans Act of 1965 has supported various state and local programs which have included various types of transportation projects for the elderly. Most of these have been funded under Title III of the act. Research projects investigating various aspects of the transportation needs of the elderly have been supported under Title IV.

Major Types of Response to Transportation Needs of the Elderly

Three major types of response to the transportation needs of the elderly can be identified: reduced fare programs, physical design of the mass transit system, and special transportation services.

Reduced Fare Programs. The rationale behind the reduced fare program is that older persons in the past have had to restrict their use of mass transit facilities because of their lower incomes. This is substantiated by evidence from studies that have assessed the impact of reduced fare programs on elderly ridership. They show consistently that elderly persons increase their transit usage.

While exact statistics are not available, it is estimated that over 100 communities have implemented reduced transit fare schedules on their local transit systems for persons aged 65 years and over. The amount of reduction is generally between 35 and 50 percent of the regular fare and is usually applicable only during the off-peak-nonwork hours of the weekday and during weekends. Recently, Chicago extended its half-fare program to a full 24 hours and Minneapolis-St. Paul eliminated off-peak fares entirely. At present there are significant variations among urban communities in the "income" eligibility requirements of the older persons and the amount of fare reduction.

Physical Design of Mass Transit System. The existing design of mass transit facilities has created barriers restricting elderly persons with ambulatory difficulties, especially those confined to wheelchairs, from fully utilizing the transit system. There have been two types of response. One approach described in the following section has involved the experimentation and development of special purpose transportation systems—such as dial-a-bus—incorporating design features in their vehicles that facilitate use by the elderly and handicapped. The second approach has involved the incorporation of special design features in new mass transit services that are intended for use by the total population.

Several projects involving the design of a prototype bus intended to eventually replace existing buses on regularly scheduled routes have been funded. Design features have included wider doors; extended hand rails; public address systems for waiting passengers; large destination signs in front, side and back of vehicle; fewer steps; a lower floor for bus entry and egress; and driver-operated doors.

Some local transit authorities have also purchased regularly designed buses in order to incorporate such design features. They have had limited use on routes serving housing projects containing elderly and handicapped persons.

The most important example of a specially designed new transit system has been the San Francisco Bay Area Rapid Transit (BART). A similarly designed system is also planned for the Washington Metropolitan Area Transit system. In 1964, BART incorporated the "American Standards Specification for Making Buildings and Facilities Accessible to and Usable by the Physically Handicapped" into all design elements of its system. This required allocation of $10 million by the state government to cover the cost.

Among other design features BART has provided elevators to help nonambulatory or feeble persons move vertically from street to train platform; restrooms with special design features; stairways in stations with handrails on both sides 18 inches beyond top and bottom steps; special parking facilities for handicapped persons that have especially wide stalls and are located close to stations; entrances and exits designed for easy use by wheelchair occupants; a loudspeaker system as well as highly visible signs to assist those with impaired sight or hearing; specially designed service gates and fare collection machines in the stations; closed circuit television communication systems; special directional signs; and low placement of public telephones and elevator buttons.

Special Transportation Services. Because of the inadequacy of regular service provided by a fixed route transit system and the difficulties some older persons find using it, variations of demand-responsive transportation services have been initiated on an experimental basis in several communities throughout the United States. Specially designed passenger vehicles generally carrying fewer than 35 older or handicapped persons have been placed in operation to serve communities containing high concentrations of elderly persons. They have often but not always been intended to provide access to specific destinations such as medical districts or senior centers. Providing door-to-door service, this personalized transportation service has overcome the scheduling and routing difficulties associated with regular bus service. This type of service has also utilized regular transit or school bus vehicles rather than smaller, specially designed vehicles.

This special bus service has been described by various names–minibus, dial-a-ride, dial-a-bus, etc. The general operation is quite simple, involving the older person's telephoning a central office and conveying his trip needs. To varying degrees the scheduling and routing aspects of the system have been computerized, significantly increasing its efficiency. It offers a service comparable to a taxi at significantly lower costs to the passenger.

There have been few formal studies evaluating the benefits and costs of these systems, but in general they appear to be successful in that they have given mobility to those elderly without other viable transportation alternatives. An indirect benefit has been the new social relationships that have been facilitated because of the assemblage of isolated older persons in the vehicles providing the transportation service. Many of these systems have operated, however, only with significant ecnomic deficits, thereby requiring continuing federal or state subsidization. What is not yet clear is whether the benefits achieved by these systems justify their costs, or alternatively whether there are other more optimum means of insuring spatial accessibility.

The formation of the car pool represents another special transportation service, with the drivers being either other older persons or younger volunteers. Generally developed on an informal basis, there has been no systematic evaluation of this transportation alternative.

The Major Issues: Evaluating the Federal Response

Because of the dependence of many elderly on mass transit transportation, any federal legislation that results in the increased availability of funds for the provision of new and improved mass transit service can only be beneficial. However, unless there are significant changes in the physical design and operating characteristics of its vehicles and the frequency and flexibility of its service, mass transit will continue to be inferior to the automobile as a mode of transportation, particularly for trips to non-work destinations. For many elderly persons it will also be a mode of transportation which because of these features will be used only with difficulty, if at all, and consequently may significantly discourage activities that might have been initiated if problems of accessibility had been alleviated. This situation will likely exist as long as mass transit systems are operated as private business firms. As a Carnegie-Mellon University study suggested:

> They [public transportation systems] maintain a profit-oriented outlook, or at least a deficit minimization criterion, which leads to service cutbacks in the face of rising operating costs. If the urban environment is unimaginable without a public transport system, if it is known that consumer behavior is price inelastic, if a large proportion of transit riders are the disenfranchised members of urban society, and if one of the objectives of urban transportation is to increase the range of activity options available to the population, then why not utilize the maximization of service, and not the minimization of deficit, as the prime operating criterion? Perhaps the necessity of public transportation in the urban environment should be viewed as a public good, similar in nature to the necessities of police and fire protection and schools for the children. Instead, urban transportation is operated, advertised, and priced as if the output is a scarce commodity (service) being offered by a private firm. In fact, urban systems are characterized by a large proportion of slack capacity, scarcities being present only at rush hour peaks. [P. 204–205]

Legislation that would earmark special funds for the development of transportation programs for the elderly has either been absent or unenforceable. After the rhetoric of the Biaggi Amendment is filtered out, the 1970 act provided no guarantee that specific funds would be allocated in DOT budgets. There has been, moreover, no formal stipulation guaranteeing that grants or loans approved for the general development of transportation systems would incorporate features making them accessible to the elderly. As in the case of housing programs, the initiative to obtain funding is left to the discretion of state and municipal governments so that even if funds were available, there is no guarantee they will be applied to those cities that require them the most.

A system such as BART, providing at considerable expense special design features intended to eliminate utilization barriers experienced by the elderly, may at least in the short run provide much fewer benefits than expected.

The BART system is chiefly a center city-suburban service and may lack the areal flexibility to serve such groups as the elderly whose origins and/or destinations for nonwork purposes are not located along existing routes. The advantages of such a system may depend on the adequacy of (bus) feeder lines to serve the elderly. If such connecting bus services cannot be utilized by elderly persons, the utility of BART is substantially reduced. Even if there is a commitment by the major urban transit authorities to provide specially designed transit vehicles, the deficiencies of their older systems will prevent maximum mobility of such groups as the elderly since the replacement process will take a considerable time to complete. In economic terms replacement represents the only feasible strategy, since the costs of redesigning an existing system would be far too great.

There is disagreement among professional planners and bureaucrats as to whether such groups as the elderly should be singled out for special treatment with respect to transportation services. Typical are the following comments by Edmond Kanwit:

> Serving the unmet needs of all the people would be a fantastically costly undertaking; it might be cheaper to build more convenient housing near shopping, medical service, and recreation areas than to provide regular public transportation in sparsely populated areas. It might be even more effective to break down the institutional barriers and set up self-help projects.
>
> There must be some determination of priority in relation to per capita cost. We must become more realistic and less sentimental on this issue, because the rising operating costs of transit in relation to passenger revenues are rapidly driving both public and private transit into a narrow area of service restricted largely to that of carrying rush-hour patrons in densely occupied urban corridors. [P. 87–88]

These types of argument are frequently cited in opposition to federal and state funding of special transportation systems for the elderly. However, given the existing operating and service characteristics of urban mass transit systems, even if special design features could be incorporated, it would appear necessary for some form of special vehicular transport system such as dial-a-bus to provide supplementary service. While of particular utility to the elderly, such systems, in order to improve their economic viability, could serve the transportation needs of other population groups. In deciding in what areas in the city to implement such systems, special efforts should be made to identify those elderly who are presently restricting their activities because of transportation user difficulties. As a means to prevent future problems. federal- or state-subsidized housing projects for elderly persons, whether developed by private or nonprivate groups, as a condition for their funding should be required to insure that adequate transportation services are available for their tenants.

Under existing federal policy special transportation services have only been provided on a random basis, usually in the form of demonstration projects, so that continuous funding has always been in doubt. Thre has been little governmental coordination at any level to insure that new services are being initiated where they are needed the most or that existing services are being utilized in the most effective way. Testimony to the existing waste of mass transit capital equipment is the large number of buses that lie idle during daily non-rush-hour periods.

Since the magnitude of transportation difficulties experienced by the elderly is likely to vary in different urban places depending on the transportation alternatives available, the major responsibility for identifying to what extent accessibility is a problem and for responding to these needs will have to be assumed at the city or community level. Only through careful needs assessment studies will those elderly be identified who require special transportation services the most. This implies that funds to initiate such studies and to implement solutions will be available at the federal or state level.

The costs which are cited as necessary to produce special transportation services or better designed vehicles are based on static measurements that do not take into account a variety of direct or indirect benefits that could be achieved with such programs. The consequences of improved transit services, for example, on reducing the need of special housing programs, home delivery sytems, institutional or quasi-institutional accommodations, or on reducing the psychological and economic burden of elderly on their families should be given greater consideration. While younger age groups may support such programs through tax payments, the benefits that will accrue to them when they themselves are old may well exceed their present contributions.

Poor cost evaluation was exemplified by initial criticism of the reduced fare program. The amount of revenue lost to a system was not simply the amount the fare was reduced multiplied by the number of elderly transit trips taken at new fare rate. As Morlok et al. have shown, reduced fares for the elderly generate greater trip activity, thereby partially offsetting the revenue lost.

Since the reduced fare program can be viewed as a means by which the economic resources of the older person are effectively increased, a fundamental issue is whether income maintenance should be provided in such an indirect fashion. Since not all elderly are poor, or dependent on mass transit, the reduced fare program would appear to present a more efficient and less expensive strategy to insure that low income does not deprive older persons from utilizing this essential urban service.

BIBLIOGRAPHY

Aaron, Henry J. *Shelter and Subsidies.* Washington, D.C.: The Brookings Institution, 1972.

Abt Associates, Incorporated. *Travel Barriers: Transportation Needs of the Handicapped.* Springfield, Va.: National Technical Information Service, 1969.

Barg, Sylvia K. and Carl Hirsch. "A Successor Model for Community Support of Low-Income Minority Group Aged." *Aging and Human Development* 3, 3 (August 1972): 243–52.

Barker, Michael B. *California Retirement Communities.* Berkeley: Center for Real Estate and Urban Economics, Institute of Urban and Regional Development, University of California, 1966.

Beattie, Walter M., Jr. "The Design of Supportive Environments for the Life-Span." *The Gerontologist* 10, 3, pt. 1 (Autumn 1970): 190–93.

Bell, John H. "Senior Citizens Mobile Service." In *Transportation and Aging,* edited by Edmund J. Cantilli and June L. Shmelzer, pp. 138–50. Washington, D.C.: US Government Printing Office, 1971.

Beyer, Glenn H. *Housing and Society.* New York: Macmillan Co., 1966.

Beyer, Glenn H. and F.H.J. Nierstrasz. *Housing the Aged in Western Countries.* New York: Elsevier Publishing Co., 1967.

Beyer, Glenn H. and Margaret E. Woods. *Living and Activity Patterns of the Aged.* Research Report No. 6. Ithaca, N.Y.: Center for Housing and Environmental Studies, Cornell University, 1963.

Birren, James E. "The Abuse of the Urban Aged." *Psychology Today* 3, 10 (March 1970): 37–38, 76.

Breslau, Naomi and Marie R. Haug. "The Elderly Aid the Elderly." *Social Security Bulletin* 35, 11 (November 1972): 9–15.

Byerts, Thomas and Don Conway. *Behavioral Requirements for Housing for the Elderly.* Washington, D.C.: American Institute of Architects, 1972.

Cantor, Marjorie H. "The Reduced Fare Program for Older New Yorkers." In *Transportation and Aging,* edited by Edmund J. Cantilli and June L. Shmelzer, pp. 114–22. Washington, D.C.: US Government Printing Office, 1971.

Carnegie-Mellon University, Transportation Research Institute. *Latent Demand for Urban Transportation.* Springfield, Va.: National Technical Information Service, 1968.

Carp, Frances M. "The Mobility of Retired People." In *Transportation and Aging,* edited by Edmund J. Cantilli and June L. Shmelzer, pp. 23–41. Washington, D.C.: US Government Printing Office, 1971.

Carp, Frances M., et al. "Transportation." *The Gerontologist* 12, 2, pt. 2 (Summer 1972): 11–16.

Chen, Yung-Ping. "Making a Theory Work: The Case of Homeownership by the Aged." *Aging and Human Development* 1, 1 (February 1970): 9–19.

Cleland, Courtney B. "Mobility of Older People." In *Older People and Their Social World,* edited by Arnold M. Rose and Warren A. Peterson, pp. 323–39. Philadelphia: F.A. Davis Co., 1965.

Cutler, Stephen J. "The Availability of Personal Transportation, Residential Location, and Life Satisfaction Among the Aged." *Journal of Gerontology* 27, 3 (July 1972): 383–89.

Donahue, Wilma, ed. *Housing the Aged.* Ann Arbor: University of Michigan Press, 1954.

——. "Housing and Community Services." In *Aging in Western Society,* edited by Ernest W. Burgess, pp. 106-55. Chicago: University of Chicago Press, 1960.

Firey, Walter. *Land Use in Central Boston.* Cambridge, Mass.: Harvard University Press, 1946.

Fowler, Floyd J., Jr. "Knowledge, Need, and Use of Services Among the Aged." In *Health Care Services for the Aged,* edited by Carter C. Osterbind. pp. 77-88. Institute of Gerontology Series No. 19. Gainesville: University of Florida Press, 1970.

Freeman, Joseph T. "Elderly Drivers; Growing Numbers and Growing Problems." *Geriatrics* 27, 7 (July 1972): 46-48, 50, 52-53, 56.

Fried, Joseph P. *Housing Crisis U.S.A.* Baltimore: Penguin Books, 1972.

Frieden, Elaine. "Social Differences and Their Consequences for Housing the Aged." *Journal of the American Institute of Planners* 26, 2 (May 1960): 119-24.

Gelwicks, A. Testimony reported in U.S. Senate, Special Committee on Aging. *Older Americans and Transportation: A Crisis in Mobility.* 91st Congress, 2nd Session. Washington, D.C.: US Government Printing Office, 1970, p. 21.

Gerontological Society. "Housing and Environment for the Elderly." A Report of a Working Conference on Behavioral Research Utilization and Environmental Policy, December 16-20, 1971, San Juan, Puerto Rico. Washington, D.C., 1970. Mimeographed.

Golant, Stephen M. *The Residential Location and Spatial Behavior of the Elderly: A Canadian Example.* Research Paper No. 143. Chicago: University of Chicago Department of Geography, 1972.

Goldscheider, Calvin; Maurice D. Van Arsdol; and Georges Sabagh. "Residential Mobility of Older People." In *Patterns of Living and Housing of Middle Aged and Older People,* edited by Frances M. Carp and Wanda M. Burnett, pp. 107-16. Public Health Service Publication No. 1496. Washington, D.C.: US Government Printing Office, 1966.

Grant, Donald P. "An Architect Discovers the Aged." *The Gerontologist* 10, 4, pt. 1 (Winter 1970): 275-81.

Gwynn, David W. "Dial-a-Ride Demonstration Project in Haddonfield." *Traffic Engineering* 42, 12 (September 1972): 68-74.

Hamovitch, Maurice B. and James E. Peterson. "Housing Needs and Satisfaction of the Elderly." *The Gerontologist* 9, 1 (Spring 1969): 30-32.

Havighurst, Robert J. "Research And Development Goals in Social Gerontology." *The Gerontologist* 9, 4, pt. 2 (Winter 1969): 37-54.

Hoel, Lester A. and Ervin S. Roszner. "Impact of Reduced Transit Fares for the Elderly." *Traffic Quarterly* 26, 3 (July 1972): 341-58.

Kanwit, Edmond L. "The Urban Mass Transportation Administration: Its Problems and Promise." In *Urban Transportation Policy: New Perspectives,* edited by David R. Miller, pp. 77-114. Lexington, Mass.: D.C. Heath and Co., 1972.

Kaplan, Jerome, et al. *Transportation of the Aging in Richland County and Ohio.* Columbus: The Ohio State University Research Foundation and Department of Mental Hygiene, Division of Administration on Aging, 1970.

Kassabaum, George E. "Housing for the Elderly—Site Selection." *American Institute of Architects Journal* 38, 2 (August 1962): 65-68.

——. "Housing for the Elderly—Technical Standards of Design." *American Institute of Architects Journal* 38, 3 (September 1962): 61-65.

——. "Housing for the Elderly—Functional Program." *American Institute of Architects Journal* 38, 4 (October 1962): 51-52.

Kisten, Helen and Robert Morris. "Alternatives to Institutional Care for the Elderly and Disabled." *The Gerontologist* 12, 2, pt. 1 (Summer 1972): 139-42.

Kleemeier, Robert W. "Attitudes Toward Special Settings for the Aged." In *Processes of Aging,* vol. 2, edited by Richard H. Williams, Clark Tibbits, Wilma Donahue, pp. 101-21. New York: Atherton Press, 1963.

Kutner, Bernard. *Five Hundred Over Sixty.* New York: Russell Sage Foundation, 1956.

Lamminen, Toivo. *Transportation for the Handicapped.* Springfield, Va.: National Technical Information Service, 1969.

Langford, Marilyn. *Community Aspects of Housing for the Aged.* Research Report No. 5.

Ithaca, N.Y.: Center for Housing and Environmental Studies, Cornell University, 1962.

Lawton, Alfred H. "Sensory and Perceptual Changes That May Influence Housing Needs of the Aging." In *Patterns of Living and Housing of Middle-Aged and Older People,* edited by Frances M. Carp and Wanda M. Burnett, pp. 11–16. Public Health Service Publication No. 1496. Washington, D.C.: US Government Printing Office, 1966.

Lawton, M. Powell. "Supportive Services in the Context of the Housing Environment." *The Gerontologist* 9, 1 (Spring 1969): 15–19.

Lawton, M. Powell and Bonnie Simon. "The Ecology of Social Relationships in Housing for the Elderly." *The Gerontologist* 8, 2 (Summer 1968): 108–15.

Lawton, M. Powell, et al. "Housing." *The Gerontologist* 12, 2, pt. 2 (Summer 1972): 3–10.

Libow, Leslie S. "Older People's Medical and Physiological Characteristics." In *Transportation and Aging,* edited by Edmund J. Cantilli and June L. Shmelzer, pp. 14–18. Washington, D.C.: US Government Printing Office, 1971.

Lindsay, Inabel B. *The Multiple Hazards of Age and Race: The Situation of Aged Blacks in the United States.* A Preliminary Survey for the Special Committee on Aging, United States Senate, 92d Cong., 1st sess. Washington, D.C.: US Government Printing Office, 1971.

Lopata, Helena Z. *Widowhood in the American City.* Cambridge, Mass.: Schenkman Publishing Co., 1973.

Madge, John. "Aging and the Fields of Architecture and Planning." In *Aging and Society,* vol. 2, edited by Matilda W. Riley et al., pp. 229–73. New York: Russell Sage Foundation, 1969.

Messer, Mark. "The Possibility of an Aged-Concentrated Environment Becoming a Normative System." *The Gerontologist* 7, 4 (December 1967): 247–51.

Michelson, William. *Man and His Urban Environment: A Sociological Approach.* Reading, Mass.: Addison-Wesley, 1970.

Montgomery, James E. "The Housing Patterns of Older Families." *Family Coordinator* 21, 1 (January 1972): 37–46.

Morlok, Edward K.; Walter M. Kulash; and Hugo L. Vandersypen. "Reduced Fares for the Elderly, Effects on a Transit System." *Welfare in Review* 9, 5 (September-October 1971): 17–24.

Musson, Noverre and Helen Heusinkveld. *Buildings for the Elderly.* New York: Reinhold Publishing Co., 1963.

Nahemow, Lucille; Constance Shuman; and Leonard S. Kogan. "Findings From a Study of Participants in a Reduced Fare Program." In *Transportation and Aging,* edited by Edmund J. Cantilli and June L. Shmelzer, pp. 42–51. Washington, D.C.: US Government Printing Office, 1971.

National Association of Housing and Redevelopment Officials. *Management of Public Housing for the Elderly.* Washington, D.C., 1965.

Neugarten, Bernice L., ed. *Middle Age and Aging, A Reader in Social Psychology.* Chicago: University of Chicago Press, 1968.

Niebanck, Paul L. *The Elderly in Older Urban Areas.* Philadelphia: Institute for Environmental Studies, University of Pennsylvania, 1965.

——. "Knowledge Gained in Studies of Relocation, A Challenge to Housing Policy." In *Patterns of Living and Housing of Middle Aged and Older People,* edited by Frances M. Carp. and Wanda M. Burnett, pp. 107–16. Public Health Service Publication No. 1496. Washington, D.C.: US Government Printing Office, 1966.

Pastalan, Leon A. and Daniel H. Carson. *Spatial Behavior of Older People.* Ann Arbor: Institute of Gerontology, University of Michigan, 1970.

Pignataro, Louis J. "Recommendations of the Workshop Committees." In *Transportation and Aging,* edited by Edmund J. Cantilli and June L. Shmelzer, pp. 190–95. Washington, D.C.: US Government Printing Office, 1971.

Pincus, Allen and Vivian Wood. "Methodological Issues in Measuring the Environment in Institutions for the Aged and Its Impact on Residents." *Aging and Human Development* 1, 2 (May 1970): 117–26.

Planek, Thomas W.; Margaret C. Condon; and Richard C. Fowler. *An Investigation of the Problems and Opinions of Aged Drivers.* Springfield, Va.: National Technical Information Service, 1968.

Revis, Joseph S. *Transportation.* Background Paper, 1971 White House Conference on Aging. Washington, D.C.: White House Conference on Aging, 1971.

Riley, Matilda W. and Anne Foner. *Aging and Society, An Inventory of Research Findings.* Vol. 1. New York: Russell Sage Foundation, 1968.

Robbins, Ira S. *Housing the Elderly.* Background Paper, 1971 White House Conference on Aging. Washington, D.C.: White House Conference on Aging, 1971.

Rosow, Irving. *Social Integration of the Aged.* New York: Free Press, 1967.

Schooler, Kermit K. "Effect of Environment on Morale." *The Gerontologist* 10, 3, pt. 1 (Autumn 1970): 194–97.

Shanas, Ethel, et al. *Old People in Three Industrial Societies.* New York: Atherton and Routledge Kegan Paul, 1968.

Sheldon, Henry D. *The Older Population of the United States.* New York: John Wiley and Sons, Inc., 1958.

Sherman, Susan R. "The Choice of Retirement Housing Among the Well-Elderly." *Aging and Human Development* 2, 2 (May 1971): 118–38.

Shmelzer, June L. "Elderly Ridership and Reduced Transit Fares: The Chicago Experience." In *Transportation and Aging,* edited by Edmund J. Cantilli and June L. Schmelzer, pp. 123–34. Washington, D.C.: US Government Printing Office, 1971.

Tissue, Thomas. "Old Age, Poverty, and the Central City." *Aging and Human Development* 2, 4 (November 1971): 235–48.

Townsend, Peter. *The Family Life of Old People.* Glencoe, Ill.: Free Press, 1957.

US Congress, Joint Economic Committee. Report of the Subcommittee on Priorities and Economy in Government. *Housing Subsidies and Housing Policy.* Washington, D.C.: US Government Printing Office, 1973.

US, Congress, Senate, Special Committee on Aging. *Usefulness of the Model Cities Programs to the Elderly.* Parts 1–6. 90th Cong., 2d sess. Washington, D.C.: US Government Printing Office, 1968.

——. Subcommitte on Housing for the Elderly. *Economics of Aging: Toward a Full Share in Abundance, Part 4–Homeownership Aspects.* 91st Cong., 1st sess. Washington, D.C.: US Government Printing Office, 1970.

——. *Developments in Aging, 1969.* 91st Cong., 2d sess. Washington, D.C.: US Government Printing Office, 1970.

——. *Older Americans and Transportation: A Crisis in Mobility.* 91st Cong., 2d sess. Washington, D.C.: US Government Printing Office, 1970.

——. Subcommittee on Housing for the Elderly. *Adequacy of Federal Response to Housing Needs of Older Americans.* Parts 1–7. 92nd Cong., 1st sess. Washington, D.C.: US Government Printing Office, 1971.

——. *A Barrier-Free Environment for the Elderly and the Handicapped.* Parts 1–3. 92d Cong., 1st sess. Washington, D.C.: US Government Printing Office, 1971.

——. *Developments in Aging, 1970.* 92d Cong., 1st sess. Washington, D.C.: US Government Printing Office, 1971.

——. *The Multiple Hazards of Age and Race: The Situation of Aged Blacks in the United States.* 92d Cong., 1st sess. Washington, D.C.: US Government Printing Office, 1971.

——. *1971 White House Conference on Aging, A Report to the Delegates from the Conference Sections and Special Concerns Sessions, November 28–December 2.* 92d Cong., 1st sess. Washington, D.C.: US Government Printing Office, 1971.

——. *Developments in Aging, 1971 and January-March, 1972.* 92d Cong., 2d sess. Washington, D.C.: US Government Printing Office, 1972.

——. *Developments in Aging, 1972 and January-March, 1973.* 93d Cong., 1st sess. Washington, D.C.: US Government Printing Office, 1973.

——. *Housing for the Elderly: A Status Report.* 93d Cong., 1st sess. Washington, D.C.: US Government Printing Office, 1973.

——. *Older Americans Comprehensive Services Amendments of 1973.* 93d Cong., 1st sess. Washington, D.C.: US Government Printing Office, 1973.

——. Subcommittee on Federal, State and Community Services. *The Rise and Threatened Fall of Service Programs for the Elderly.* 93d Cong., 1st sess. Washington, D.C.: US Government Printing Office, 1973.

US Department of Health, Education and Welfare, Administration of Aging. "The Older Pedestrian: A Social Gerontological View," by J.L. Shmelzer and M.J. Taves. AoA Position Paper. Washington, D.C., 1969. Mimeographed.

US Urban Mass Transportation Administration. *Feasibility of Federal Assistance for Urban Mass Transportation Operating Costs.* Springfield, Va.: National Technical Information Service, 1971.

Vivrett, Walter K. "Housing and Community Settings for Older People." In *Handbook of Social Gerontology,* edited by Clark Tibbits, pp. 549–623. Chicago: University of Chicago Press, 1960.

Walkley, Rosabelle P. "The California Survey of Retirement Housing." *The Gerontologist* 6, 1 (March 1966): 28–34.

Wendkos, Martin H.; Mollie Soudack; and Grela Fischer. "A Novel Rehabilitation Program for the Non-Institutionalized Disadvantaged Elderly Residing in an Urban Community." *Journal of American Geriatrics Society* 20, 3 (March 1972): 116–20.

Wilner, Daniel M., et al. "Demographic Characteristics of Residents of Planned Retirement Housing." *The Gerontologist* 8, 3 (Autumn 1968): 164–68.

Wilson, Robert L. *Urban Living Qualities From Vantage Point of the Elderly.* Chapel Hill: Institute for Research in Social Science, University of North Carolina, 1960.

Part 4

Metropolitan Governance, Political Systems and Electoral Processes

Chapter 11

Metropolitan Governance

Rex D. Honey
University of Iowa

METROPOLITAN GOVERNANCE

The United States has evolved during this century from an agricultural society to an urban society and now a metropolitan society. By 1970 fully 60 percent of the American people lived in large cities—metropolitan areas of 200,000 or more inhabitants. Over 80 million people, more than the nation's entire turn-of-the-century population, lived in the 33 metropolitan areas with populations exceeding one million.

Economic changes brought people into urban areas and transportation changes spread those areas far beyond their nineteenth century confines. The metropolis replaced the city as the area of concentrated social and economic interplay. As the urban area spread out, its activities spread with it, as did many of its problems. The institutions designed to solve problems, however, did not necessarily follow. Technological and social changes transformed the economic and social geography of the city, but they did not generate corresponding changes in the city's political geography. Typically, metropolitan areas inherited nineteenth century tools for attacking twentieth century problems, some of which call for metropolitan-wide solutions. The old city limits are not wide enough in jurisdiction or resources to manage some urban activities effectively. Management of such activities as transportation planning, water supply, sewage disposal and air pollution control requires jurisdiction over an entire metropolis. Lack of such jurisdiction vitiates attempts to solve many metropolitan problems.

In recognition of these metropolitan problems, the American Congress enacted several bills designed to assure consideration of metropolitan points of view. The executive branch added administrative procedures toward the same end. This volume seeks to gauge the degrees to which this national goal has been met. This chapter asks, To what extent has an areawide approach been achieved in the governance of American metropolitan areas?

The thrust of the Comparative Metropolitan Analysis Project is an examination of national goals for American cities and the extent to which these goals have been reached. Before examining specific programs in actual cities, this chapter must establish the need for a metropolitan approach and the federal government's commitment to fulfill that need. Consequently, the first part of this chapter focuses on the need for a metropolitan approach, discusses alternative ways of satisfying that need and introduces the question of metropolitan size and functions. The second section includes an assessment and recommendations.

The question of metropolitan governance is geographically interesting on two levels. Of primary interest is the level of the individual metropolis. The appropriate jurisdiction for metropolitan governance is in large part a geographic problem—fitting the form of the jurisdiction to the functional needs of the metropolis. The quality of metropolitan governance may also have important geographic side effects, altering the quality of life and, hence, the desirability of specific locations. Also of geographical interest is the pattern of metropolitan governance across the nation, affected as it is by legal, cultural and economic variation.

Need for a Metropolitan Approach

Arguments for a metropolitan approach in governing cities are usually couched in terms of efficiency, effectiveness or equity, or some combination of these. Efficiency is concerned with maximizing public services received for public money spent. Effectiveness is concerned with the adequacy of public services, whether or not they are efficient. Equity is concerned with social welfare, particularly minimizing the plight of the downtrodden. Three major arguments for metropolitan governance are:

- In terms of daily activities, society is organized at a metropolitan scale, and many public services are most effectively and efficiently organized at the scale of societal organization; therefore, a metropolitan jurisdiction is appropriate for managing societal activity.
- A metropolitan approach would minimize externalities and allow fiscal equivalence so that those benefiting or suffering from a public function would have a voice in the operation of that function and responsibility for paying for it, and so that the area affected by a service would match the area paying for the service.
- A metropolitan jurisdiction would make the resources of the entire metropolis available to solve acute problems beyond the fiscal capacity of restricted communities, whether or not the problems were generated by processes operating at the metropolitan scale.

These arguments, which are developed more fully below, make the case for organizing some public services at the metropolitan scale. It is not argued here that all public services should be provided at that level. Rather, it is argued that some—and in most instances some important—public functions would be best handled at the metropolitan scale.*

Commuting patterns, communications and many types of economic activity prove that the metropolis is a major level of societal organization. Metropolitan newspapers, television stations, cultural events and professional sports symbolize the importance of the metropolitan unit. Several governmental functions involve management, if not outright operation, of something organized at the metropolitan scale. How can transportation planning, for instance, be effective unless predicated upon the metropolitan commuting pattern? For effective public services, the best jurisdiction for a public authority charged with responsibility for such a metropolitanwide activity as transportation planning would be the area actually involved—the whole metropolis. Anything short of this would inhibit the effective performance of the public sector.

The externalities argument in support of a metropolitan approach is based on the twin precepts that those benefiting from a governmental activity should share in its support and that those bearing the ill effects of that activity should have a say in its operation. According to this argument, if no metropolitan authority existed and there were a service which would be provided most efficiently from only one source in a metropolitan area, two results are possible. Either each jurisdiction would wait for one of the others to provide this service with none opting to provide it, or one jurisdiction would bear the costs of the service with benefits accruing to external jurisdictions as well as to the jurisdiction paying for the service. In the latter case, only some of the residents of the metropolis would pay for the service even though everyone would benefit. It

*The so-called Tiebout Hypothesis presents another view. It holds that citizens are best served in a political system with many independent municipalities. This allows for a variety of patterns of public services with each individual moving to the municipality which most closely approximates his desired package of public services and costs. A major criticism of the argument is that poorer people cannot as readily move—"vote with their feet"—as their more wealthy neighbors. Consequently, the wealthy congregate in communities with high tax bases and low need for public services, while the poor are left with little tax base and an elephantine need for public services.

is often argued that American central cities subsidize their suburban neighbors this way by providing parks, zoos, museums, stadiums and other facilities enjoyed by people living throughout the metropolis. Similarly, those persons suffering from negative externalities such as living next to refuse dumps or noisy utility stations should not be disenfranchised just because they happen to live across a municipal boundary. Metropolitan decision-making would give such residents a voice in decisions affecting the character of their neighborhoods.

The fiscal equivalence argument overlaps that based on externalities. An authority has fiscal equivalence when the area supplied with a governmental service and the area paying for the service are coincident. This way no one pays for services not received and no one receives services without paying. At the metropolitan scale, the public functions serving the entire metropolis would be paid for by the entire metropolis. As with the externalities argument, such public activities as building stadiums and providing zoos would be supported by all, not just those in the central city.

The metropolitan resources argument has two components. First, it can be argued that some problems result from metropolitanwide processes but only expose themselves in restricted areas. Thus, slums are the residue of a metropolitan housing market, but slums exist in very restricted locales. Since slum problems result from a metropolitan process, so the argument goes, the bill for solving such problems should be shared by persons living throughout the metropolis rather than fall entirely on the municipality which happens to include the slum. This way the burden is shared and no one is unduly penalized by the location of municipal boundaries. The second component of this argument is that the resources necessary to overcome such problems as those occurring in slums are only available on the metropolitan scale (or larger). Most municipalities are unable to raise the necessary revenue, especially when the areas in need are usually the areas with the lowest revenue-producing capabilities. The use of metropolitan resources to solve urban problems would dispel the specter of fiscal disparities plaguing hundreds of American municipalities. It would help poorer communities by providing resources those communities simply cannot raise and it would help more wealthy communities by reducing the severity of problems, such as slum-related violence, which threaten all metropolitan residents.

As is the case with most arguments, that for a metropolitan scale can be carried too far. Not all problems are amenable to metropolitan solution and many that are may be attacked more effectively at a local scale. The metropolitan constituency is only one of several constituencies, and local control remains an important concept in the American system. Whether judged in terms of efficiency, effectiveness or equity, certain functions are fundamentally metropolitan, but others are handled best at the neighborhood level. The argument is that some governmental functions are best organized at the metropolitan scale. If those functions are not organized in that way, the performance of the public sector will fall needlessly low.

One issue in the debate between local and areawide control is which majority is to rule, the metropolitan aggregate or the separate majorities in the individual municipalities? Another question is the proper constituency for each citizen on particular questions. Is it better to have a large voice in a small area so you may affect neighborhood decisions, or is it better to sacrifice neighborhood control over some issues so that you may have a voice in wider affairs? This is a particularly important question when an individual lives and works in different municipalities, as is so often the case in American cities. The American political system is, of course, a hierarchical one, and the question may be translated into one of assigning functions to the appropriate levels in the hierarchy—if the hierarchical levels are appropriate.

Despite the legitimate reasons for organizing some public activity at the metropolitan scale, metropolitan governments are not always designed with legitimate arguments in mind. Some black political leaders argue that metropolitan governments dilute black political power. They suggest that this is why more southern cities have adopted metropolitan governments than northern cities. This argument has credence when a new governmental structure eliminates community control, transferring all power to a geographically larger authority. (Many of the reform governments in the South are of this unitary type.) Such an overreaction does not disprove the need for a metropolitan scale of governance, however. It simply dramatizes the need for jurisdictions at both the community and metropolitan levels.

At all levels, the quality of public services is of critical importance in the contemporary geography of American cities. The metropolitan level is just one in the public service system. It happens to be the level of concern in this chapter. Chapter Twelve, by David R. Reynolds, examines the municipal level.

Alternative Metropolitan Approaches

What form should metropolitan governance take and what functions should be involved? These are difficult questions, and the answers may depend on the specific needs and values of the metropolis in question. Given the special needs of each city, it is not so important to devise a pattern for all cities as it is to array the alternatives so that each city may make the most suitable choice.

Criteria for allocating governmental functions to appropriate jurisdictions include responsiveness to public desire, coordination of metropolitan activities and establishment of metropolitan priorities. Alternative methods of achieving metropolitan governance are discussed with reference to these criteria and other criteria pertinent to each alternative. The alternatives are ways of expanding jurisdiction over at least some governmental activities so that the entire metropolis may be considered as a whole with regard to those activities.

Extraterritorial powers denote the possession of legal rights by a government beyond the scope of its own territory, such as municipal possession of land development control over adjacent unincorporated territory. Through this type of mechanism the city of Houston has been able to dominate its metropolitan area. This solution is limited, however, to metropolitan areas which have central cities unencumbered by incorporated suburbs. Where extraterritorial powers can be employed, they do permit coordination and the establishment of priorities because they allow the concentration of power in one governmental unit. That concentration may also minimize responsiveness, though not responsiveness to metropolitan problems but rather to community problems. This limitation on the responsiveness of the public sector as a unit reduces the appeal of this approach, even where the lack of suburbs makes it feasible.

Intergovernmental agreements are contracts between governmental units whereby one sells a service to another or they jointly perform a function. In some areas, significantly in Los Angeles, intergovernmental agreements are common below the metropolitan level, but they are rarely used to form a functioning unit over an entire metropolis. The voluntary nature of agreements limits their use to noncontroversial issues, and their ability to respond to the public will, to coordinate services and to set priorities is consequently reduced.

Urban counties exist in those states which have authorized one or more counties to exercise functions originally reserved only for municipalities—for example, street lighting or public utilities. If the county is large enough to circumscribe the entire metropolis, this approach may successfully create a metropolitan jurisdiction. In such instances, functions necessitating a metropolitan approach may be assigned to the county. This is attractive where the county effectively contains the metropolis because it requires no radical change. The limitation, of course, is that most large metropolitan areas, and even many small ones, spill out of their central counties. The highly touted metropolitan government of Miami is basically just an urban county. Dade County operates areawide programs and those local programs yielded by the municipalities.

Transfer of functions to state government is the takeover by the state of governmental activities previously performed by local government. This broadens jurisdictions so the metropolis may be dealt with as a whole (unless, of course, the metropolis straddles a state boundary), and this approach may provide access to state resources and expertise. On the other hand, it may reduce responsiveness to the city's residents by removing decisionmaking from the local scene and by giving others in the state a voice in the affairs of the metropolis. It may also inhibit coordination and the establishment of priorities in the metropolitan area because other functions are likely to be left in the hands of local government; hence two sets of officials would be making decisions. Transference of functions is a severe solution.

Transfer of functions to the federal government similarly achieves a view encompassing a whole metropolis–even a multistate metroplis–through the addition of formerly local government functions to the federal repertoire. This approach reduces local control even more drastically than transfer of power to the state. It would certainly make federal resources available, but it would end local or metropolitan government in that decisions would not be made locally or in the metropolis. The Environmental Protection Agency's air quality requirements are a positive example of transferring power.

Annexation and consolidation are methods of enlarging jurisdiction by adding formerly unincorporated territory to a municipality in the case of annexation, and by amalgamating two or more governmental units in the case of consolidation. These approaches certainly enlarge the scope for action, and it is possible to annex or consolidate an entire metropolitan area. Considerable trust and cooperation would be necessary for that unlikely event to happen, however. Metropolitan annexation and consolidation would allow coordination and assessment of priorities by concentrating authority into one jurisdiction. On the other hand, this would eliminate jurisdictions below the metropolitan level, precluding local control over local issues, particularly in large metropolitan areas. Consequently, responsiveness to local issues would be reduced, even if responsiveness to metropolitan issues were increased. Oklahoma City's extensive annexation is an example of this approach.

City-county consolidation turns both county and municipal duties over to a government with jurisdiction over the entire county territory. As a response to metropolitan problems, the advantages and disadvantages are those of annexation-consolidation and the urban county. If the county circumscribes the entire metropolis–a condition not found in larger metropolitan areas–city-county consolidation would transfer functions of an areawide nature to a metropolitan jurisdiction. Unfortunately, consolidation would also transfer functions of a more local nature to that same metropolitan body. City-county consolidation differs from the urban county by eliminating municipalities. The Jacksonville-Duval County and Nashville-Davidson County reforms are examples of this approach.

Metropolitan special districts are limited purpose authorities created to perform one or a few special functions, such as water or sewage treatment. Special purpose districts are attractive because they make it possible to assign functions to authorities created over the area appropriate for those functions and also because they do not disrupt the pre-existing pattern of government. The weaknesses of special purpose districts are that by their very nature they minimize coordination and they make it difficult to establish meaningful priorities between separate functional areas, such as deciding the order of construction of a water purification plant, a library and a new recreation center. If several special purpose districts exist in an area, they also reduce responsiveness to the citizenry either because they fragment citizen attention or because they tend to be run by semiautonomous boards which are virtually immune from the political process. Special districts also reduce the viability of general purpose governmental units by bleeding their power.

Councils of governments are usually voluntary organizations consisting of the elected representatives of local government. If membership is sufficiently wide, or if it is required by the state, COGs can project a strong metropolitan voice. The attraction of this alternative is that, like the special districts, it leaves the basic governmental pattern intact. As a communicative device, the COG may be a positive factor in metropolitan affairs, acting as a focus of areawide attention and a fulcrum for action. A COGs success as a metropolitan agency is partly a question of getting other units of government (municipalities, counties, special districts) to act in concert, and partly a question of its own powers. The powers could range from simple recommendation of policy through control over the planning process to actual provision of areawide services. If a council had no authority to enforce its decisions, it would be unable to attack difficult problems, precluding coordination of metropolitan activities and inhibiting establishment of rational priorities. Even if a COG did have power on paper, that paper might not be exercised, particularly if the council's members perceived their role as protecting the perquisites of their separate municipalities and counties. The representatives could be more interested in representing their separate governments than the people who comprise those governments. If this were to happen the COG might approve all municipal proposals without requiring coordination and the COG members might try to restrict the council's ability to provide services in its own right. All of this could reduce the governmental response to citizen desires in the metropolitan area. On the other hand, if the COG possessed adequate power, especially over planning decisions, and if its members took their responsibilities seriously, it would be possible for councils of governments to achieve high marks with regard to coordination, priorities and responsiveness.

Federation is a governmental structure with two or more levels sharing responsibilities. In a metropolitan context this would include a metropolitan level and one or more lower levels—ideally with each level's duties defined by its position in a hierarchy. For example, a metropolitan government could handle regional parks, refuse disposal and main thoroughfares, while municipal governments administered neighborhood parks, refuse pick-up and residential streets. Federation is appealing because it simultaneously concentrates power into a few units and assigns responsibility to both the metropolitan and community scales. This makes it possible to coordinate metropolitan activities, establish priorities and respond to citizen needs. The fatal flaw of this approach is that it is politically infeasible in most of America's metropolitan areas. Federation requires either the elimination of some pre-existing governmental units or the imposition of an extra governmental layer on an already wary citizenry. Federated metropolitan governments are commonplace in Britain and Canada where metropolitan reform has dashed far ahead of the United States. In the famous case of London the reform was achieved by expanding the size of the county to include the continuously built-up area of the metropolis and enlarging the local government units by amalgamation. The federated government of London reaches a truly metropolitan scale and assures strong community government.

Umbrella governments are regional agencies sanctioned with coordinating powers. They may be refinements of councils of governments, adding to the COG compulsory membership and veto power over the plans of other governments in the area. An umbrella government oversees development programs in its region, molding these to fit the regional plan. The officials of an umbrella government may be appointed by the local governments in the area or they may represent the local citizens directly, or they may be chosen by some combination of means as in the case of the Atlanta Regional Commission. The strengths of this alternative are the limited amount of change it requires and the increased ability to coordinate and set priorities. The strengths are enhanced if the umbrella government is matched by state planning and operations districts covering the same territory. A weakness may be an inability to initiate requisite development programs, depending on the powers granted to the umbrella agency. An umbrella government may be a one step increase in power up from a council of governments, and as such it is a stronger metropolitan authority.

The approaches sketched are not necessarily incompatible, nor is the list absolutely complete. They are some of the ways a metropolitan level could be attained in the governance of an urban region. This still leaves other questions, two of which deserve discussion. One is: How do you define the metropolitan limits? The other is: Which governmental activities should be performed at the metropolitan level? The goal here is not to present a definitive, final solution, but rather to present the issues.

Metropolitan Size and Functions

Defining the areal extent of the jurisdiction of a metropolitan authority presumes a definition of the extent of the metropolis. As Berry, Goheen and Goldstein have noted, geographers are quite familiar with the arbitrary, subjective nature of this task. The influence of a metropolis fades with distance from the city center. A metropolis is not a perfectly discrete entity, all metropolitan on one side of a line and not at all metropolitan on the other. Rather, as with many regional definitions, the edge of the metropolis is a zone. Zones are difficult to administer, however, and authority over territory demands definite divisions of territory—boundary lines. The question is: Where should the metropolitan boundary zone be divided by a boundary line? The answer depends on the reasons for the division. For metropolitan governance the appropriate area depends on the functions to be discharged. Likewise, appropriate functions depend on the area to be served.

Debate rages over which functions are most appropriate for metropolitan governance. One proponent, Melvin Mogulof, proposes three criteria. First are those functions transcending the jurisdictional boundaries of conventional governmental units (cities and counties). Examples of such functions are highway planning, mass transit, open space planning, operation and planning of airports, and planning for the regional job market. Cities and counties are rarely large enough in territory to perform these tasks effectively. Second are those functions where the failure of one jurisdiction to act undercuts the actions of another jurisdiction, as in programs combatting air pollution, upgrading the quality of low cost housing or rationalizing waste disposal. At the minimum, compulsory regional compliance is necessary so that such programs can succeed. A metropolitan authority could assure compliance. Third are those functions subject to economies of scale, even beyond the size of most cities and counties, such as specialized hospitals, water supply and law enforcement training. At the metropolitan level, most urban areas could enjoy these economies. In other words, Mogulof cites those functions of (1) metropolitan breadth, (2) significant metropolitan externalities and (3) metropolitan economies of scale as appropriate for a metropolitan authority.

Others who have studied the question present their own criteria, and one study, by the Advisory Commission on Intergovernmental Relations, ranked several functions on a continuum from most local to most metropolitan: fire protection (most local), refuse disposal and collection, libraries, police, health, urban renewal, housing, parks and recreation, public welfare, hospitals and medical care facilities, transportation, planning, water supply and sewage disposal, and air pollution control (most metropolitan). Others would rank the functions differently. In London, for example, fire protection, ranked most local by ACIR, is provided at the metropolitan level while the basic public welfare functions are performed at the borough, or municipal, level.

Once the appropriate functions are assigned to a metropolitan authority, what areal justification should that authority cover? Peter Hall takes a direct approach:

> A planning region for regional/local planning purposes is, simply, that region which needs to be planned as a whole. One way of defining this is to say that it is that region where there are mutual planning impacts between one part and another. [p. 19]

Despite Hall's confidence, the problem may be difficult. How much mutual impact must there be, especially when the impacts of cities overlap as is the case from Boston to the District of Columbia? The decision must be made in terms of one's objectives and the particular situation in each metropolis.

It may be possible to internalize the metropolis with available units of government—perhaps a county for a small metropolitan area or a group of counties for a larger urban complex. In instances like these it may be appropriate to accept the existing territories as given and to base the assignment of governmental powers on those territories. Thus, a county circumscribing a metropolis, such as Phoenix's Maricopa County, may be adequate for regional governance while smaller Denver County is not.

If the existing governmental units are inappropriate for metropolitan service, it may be wise to work from the service to the territory, delimiting new jurisdictions by functional criteria. Following this logic, a government assigned flood prevention responsibility should encompass the appropriate drainage basins and a government providing public transportation should have authority over the appropriate commuting field.

Whichever pursuit is taken—assigning duties among existing jurisdictions or delimiting new jurisdictions to fulfill functional requirements—compromise is necessary. Each activity may have a unique "best service area," perhaps the drainage basin for one and the commuting area for another. Assignment of governmental obligations cannot be based on individual "best areas," however, because that would create chaos. Many public decisions should be made in concert; highway plans should be coordinated with land use plans, for example, and both should be tied to public utility plans. Also, a plethora of governments would unduly confound voters, giving them too many decisions to make and increasing their information costs. Consequently, an area appropriate for a constellation of roles should be selected. Except where metropolitan areas are growing together (a phenomenon particularly plaguing America's northeast coast), the argument for a metropolitan authority serving several roles is an argument for a large metropolitan authority—Hall's area of mutual planning impacts.*

Regional planning, and therefore pressure for metropolitan governance, is predicated upon a belief that urban development should be channeled by a public authority which views the metropolis as a whole and coordinates its disparate parts. Development occurs, whether coordinated or not, and this view holds that the general welfare is better served if that development is rational and tied together rather than a series of disconnected, individual, profit-seeking decisions. As a metropolis expands, turning countryside into suburb, the area necessary for effective planning expands with it. In recognition of this urban dynamism, the Royal Commission on Local Government in England recommended periodic review of governmental boundaries so that the boundaries do not ossify. The principle applies to the United States as well. Metropolitan boundaries should not be viewed as permanently satisfactory. Metropolitan governance is necessary to make the most of the metropolitan age, but the area involved in that governance must be adjustable so that it applies to changing realities. "Best areas" for public services are only best given specific patterns of social and economic geography. When the behavior producing that geography changes, the "best areas" for public services change too and the political geography of American urban regions should reflect that change.

THE RECORD IN URBAN AMERICA

Over 200 metropolitan areas, according to census definition, exist in the United States. The fact that they can be identified as metropolitan suggests that they are similar. This does not mean they are the same, however, for they do exhibit significant variation. The differences limit the applicability of blueprints for solving urban problems in America, solution in one place not necessarily applying in others. Metropolitan areas are, however, the products of similar processes. The same rules of land economics and regional economics apply, and all American cities share the same culture, though some deviate from the norm more than others. What are the similarities; what are the differences? What is the record of metropolitan governance in urban America? How much can one transfer the lessons learned in one metropolis to the problems of another?

All cities are the products of development decisions and the application of the technology that was available at the time they were being built. Cities and residential areas which grew up in the same era are particularly similar. Technological innovations which shorten distances do so for all cities and as a consequence virtually all cities have spread out, even those not experiencing population growth. The public sector provides essentially the same services in each metropolis. Such similarities permit the development of meaningful models of American cities, especially when the models are based on processes affecting all cities—for example, a private enterprise land development system or the widespread adaptation and use of the private automobile.

Despite the usefulness of our models in advancing the understanding of urban development, the interplay of processes creating cities has resulted in such differences that each city may have to be classified on a basis other than the processes that created them when attempts are made to solve specific problems. Let us consider a few ways in which cities might differ significantly. First, they might differ in physical layout. Richard Forstall and Victor Jones delineated five classes of metropolitan structure in an international study of one hundred metropolitan areas: (1) those based on one center, such as Washington; (2) those with one major center and some minor ones, such as New York; (3) those with dual centers, such as Minneapolis-St. Paul; (4) those with several centers with one dominant, such as San Francisco-Oakland-San Jose; and (5) those with several centers with none dominant, such as Germany's Rhine-Ruhr. Structural differences may nullify the transfer of a solution from one metropolitan area to another. Consequently, San Francisco's rapid transit system, which emphasizes transport corridors connecting the different centers, may be inapplicable to Los Angeles, which has a very diffuse pattern of travel.

*W.I. Carruthers, in studies carried out for the Royal Commission on Local Government in Greater London, showed that it is possible to use a set of interaction and connectivity measures to delimit a metropolitan boundary. Those measures would have to be appropriate for the particular metropolis under study, however. Carruthers's use of commuter train data would be inappropriate for most American cities, for example.

Size is another important variable. The city-county consolidations of Jacksonville, Knoxville and other cities are applicable only when the metropolis does not occupy more than one county. Thus, differences in size may preclude the transference of a solution from one metropolitan area to another of greatly different size. This may be true whether size is measured by the area the metropolis occupies or by the number of inhabitants in the area.

The inherited political system is another important variable. In the United States, government below the level of the state is determined by the state. There is no national system of local government, even though many states do use similar systems. Counties and municipalities are either created by the state or, at minimum, according to state law. In most states the basic local government structure consists of counties and municipalities. Separate from these are likely to be special purpose districts, some of which extend far beyond the built-up urban areas. The rules regulating incorporation, disincorporation, relations among public authorities and the powers of various kinds of public institutions are stipulated by the state and these vary tremendously from state to state. This total package of the political system is an important variable in metropolitan governance. It may make it possible for some metropolitan areas to devise solutions to their problems while for other metropolitan areas the inherited system may compound problems difficult enough in their own right.

Another difference, and it can be an important one, is the physical environment. Arid Los Angeles needs access to outside water in a way unfamiliar to those in humid climates. Many metropolitan governmental functions may involve the management of an environmental system—for example, air pollution control or the provision of safe water. The environmental configurations of individual metropolitan areas may be so different, though, that the solution to the problems of one could be inapplicable to the other. Los Angeles' far reach to the Feather River does little to alleviate New York's shortage of potable water, for instance.

Metropolitan areas may differ in other ways too, such as the trust citizens evince in their chosen leaders. These examples are not meant to be exhaustive, but merely illustrative of the very real differences among metropolitan areas, dramatizing the need to examine the specific local situation when confronting metropolitan problems.

Federal Programs

One factor which does not vary from city to city but is meant to be constant for all cities is the role of the federal government. Through a succession of legislative and executive steps, the federal government has induced the establishment of metropolitan authorities in the United States. This has been accomplished through a carrot-and-stick approach involving federal money—money provided to pay for metropolitan functions or money denied unless specified metropolitan action emerged.

For two decades the federal government has encouraged a metropolitan approach in urban America. While many states have been reluctant to act, the federal government has not. Its first step was the Housing Act of 1954 which authorized expenditure of up to half the funds required to generate metropolitan or regional planning. With the availability of the famous 701 funds, planning blossomed in the United States. This step established a pattern which was to repeat itself several times—use of federal money or an imposition of qualifications for federal money to encourage a metropolitan approach.

The next important step was the emergence of the Advisory Commission on Intergovernmental Relations in 1959. Federally created and supported, ACIR consists of representatives of each level in the American federal system and carries out studies and makes recommendations concerning governmental organization and operation and the effective governance of the nation. ACIR has devoted much of its energies to metropolitan problems, as may be seen from its publications, such as Albert Richter's *Alternative Approaches to Governmental Reorganization in Metropolitan Areas,* or from its model legislation which, among other things, shows states how bills may be written to enable desired changes in local government.

During the 1960s, the federal government took several significant steps to assure a metropolitan viewpoint in the governance of urban America. Important among these steps was the Federal Aid to Highways Act of 1962. With this legislation, the federal government began requiring metropolitan action as a prerequisite for federal money. This legislation requires ". . . a continuing comprehensive transportation planning process carried on cooperatively by state and local governments . . ." as a mandatory qualification for the receipt of federal highway funds in all urban areas with populations of 50,000 or more. Thus, the federal government not only provided funds to support areawide planning (through Section 701 of the Housing Act), it also encouraged such planning by denying funds to those unwilling to plan on a regional basis. Suddenly regional cooperation became much more attractive, attached as it was to the lucrative federal highway treasury.

The federal government embellished the attractiveness of cooperation by amending Section 701 of the Housing Act in 1965. This legislation authorized the federal government to underwrite two-thirds of the expenses of organizations consisting of elected officials from the counties and municipalities in a metropolitan area. Funds were provided so that such organizations, often newly formed councils of governments (COGs), could collect pertinent information and execute the studies necessary before they could develop regional plans. Thus, the federal government added to its offer of money a suggestion on how an area could organize to qualify for that money—and it offered money so that such an organization could operate.

The number of metropolitan areas forming councils of governments jumped dramatically after the 1965 legislation (Figure 11-1). Congress encouraged the formation of COGs even further in 1966 when it passed the Demonstration Cities and Metropolitan Development Act. Section 204 of that legislation required that an areawide agency, designated as the planning authority for its area, review and comment on applications by local governments for federal categorical grants. This legislation did not give regional organizations veto power, but it did give them review authority over many functions. The COG or other designated regional authority was directed to review applications for federal grants and to comment on the extent to which a proposed project complied with plans for the region. This implied the existence of a regional plan—and that the plan should be implemented. (Many regions dragged their feet on their plans, however, because all applications for federal monies could be certified as "not inconsistent with regional plans" as long as no plans existed). The areawide agencies received their "clearinghouse" status June 30, 1967. Consequently, a flood of metropolitan areas established regional agencies—most of which were COGs—in 1967 and 1968 so that they could qualify for federal grants-in-aid.

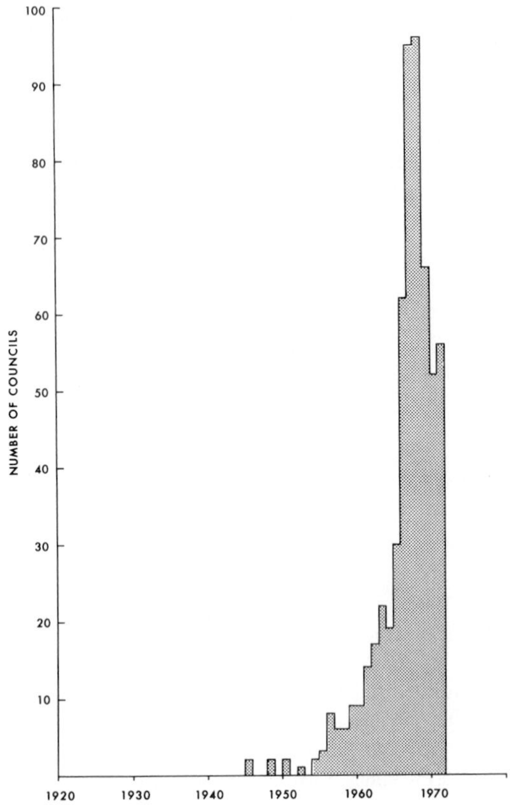

Figure 11-1. Formation of Councils of Government. Source: National Association of Regional Councils

Additional federal legislation clarified, strengthened or otherwise adjusted the areawide review powers. The Intergovernmental Cooperation Act of 1968 authorized a uniform Project Notification and Review System (PNRS) through which regional agencies were to assess local applications for federal funds. This lent form and consistency to the review process. The Housing and Urban Development Act of 1968 required that comprehensive metropolitan land use plans include a housing element. Amendments to the Air Quality Control Act designated 91 urban areas as air quality control regions. This legislation shows that the need for governance at the metropolitan scale was recognized and that problems were at least being reviewed at the metropolitan level across the nation.

The federal Bureau of the Budget—later Office of Management and Budget (OMB)—assumed responsibility for administering and coordinating the areawide review thicket. Through a series of "circulars" OMB has translated the laws into action. OMB has adjusted its requirements to overcome problems, and it has changed to fulfill new legislation. For example, Circular A-80 required coordination of federally assisted areawide programs with local planning in the affected area. Similarly, Circular A-82 implemented Section 204 of the Demonstration Cities and Metropolitan Development Act of 1966 by laying out rules for regional review and comment, and Circular A-85 assured time and assistance for local and state response. These and other circulars were superseded when OMB issued Circular A-95 in July 1969. This circular streamlined administration and clarified procedures by bringing several elements of the federally supported regional review program together, particularly those required by the Intergovernmental Cooperation Act of 1968, the Demonstration Cities and Metropolitan Development Act of 1966 and the National Environmental Policy Act of 1969.

The weight of the federal programs is expressed by the near unanimity with which metropolitan areas have responded to federal inducements. In the spring of 1973, 212 metropolitan area clearinghouses possessed federal certification (Figure 11-2) and they were reviewing applications for over 150 federal programs. (In addition, 200 nonmetropolitan review agencies were reviewing applications in the remainder of the country.) Insofar as revenue-sharing programs eliminate areawide review, they dilute the power of the federal inducements to metropolitan action. Nevertheless, even with the current revenue-sharing programs, the clearinghouses still review many programs and receive operational support from the federal government. Federal leadership has spearheaded the development of metropolitanwide jurisdictions in urban America. Many states have augmented that leadership by creating regional planning requirements and substate planning areas of their own. In many regions local authorities have gone beyond the level of cooperation that is necessary to procure federal aid. This fortunate result probably would not have materialized had the

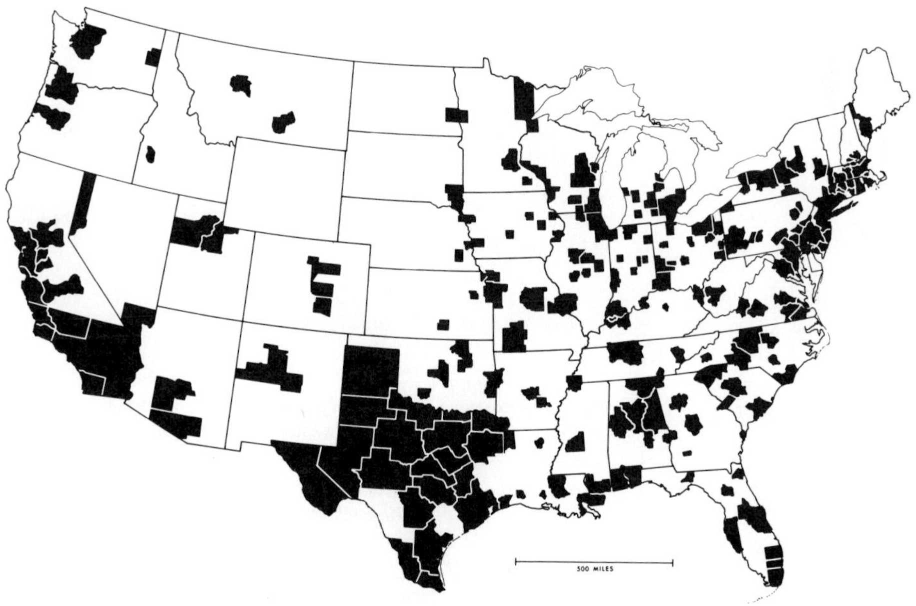

Figure 11-2. Metropolitan Areawide Review Agencies, 1973. Source: Office of Management and the Budget

federal government not led the way, proving that a metropolitan approach is not a monster. Consequently, the political organization of American metropolitan areas has shifted more closely to the patterns of social and economic organization of modern cities. The federal government may induce jurisdictional change but not dictate, so the states and local governments control the extent to which the political map is transformed. The degree of that transformation is the subject of the next section.

The National Pattern

Metropolitan authorities are now partners in the governance of American cities. Table 11-1 identifies the certified clearinghouses in America's largest metropolitan areas and Figure 11-2 illustrates the degree to which the United States is covered by such organizations. The means of attaining a metropolitan jurisdiction vary and most of the existing areawide authorities are weak. Nevertheless, they are now in operation and, given the recency of that phenomenon, that itself is an achievement. In addition, many of these areawide authorities seem to be growing in stature.

Most of the 212 metropolitan clearinghouses certified by the Office of Management and Budget are councils of governments or the closely akin regional planning commissions. Several certified organizations serve more than one Standard Metropolitan Statistical Area, accounting for the discrepancy between the number of clearinghouses and the number of

Table 11-1. Areawide Agencies in America's Largest Metropolitan Areas

Metropolis and Agency	*Jurisdiction*
New York Tri-State Regional Planning Commission	*Connecticut* portion: Central Naugatuck Valley, Greater Bridgeport, Housatonic Valley, South Central and Southwestern State planning districts *New Jersey* portion: Bergen, Essex, Hudson, Middlesex, Monmouth, Morris, Passaic, Somerset and Union counties *New York* portion: New York City, and Dutchess, Nassau, Orange, Putman, Rockland, Suffolk and Westchester counties
Los Angeles Southern California Association of Governments	Imperial, Los Angeles, Orange, Riverside, San Bernardino and Ventura counties, *California*
Chicago Northeastern Illinois Planning Commission	Cook, Dupage, Kane, Lake, McHenry and Will counties, *Illinois*
Philadelphia Delaware Valley Regional Planning Commission	*New Jersey* portion: Burlington, Camden, Gloucester and Mercer counties *Pennsylvania* portion: Bucks, Chester, Delaware, Montgomery and Philadelphia counties
Detroit South East Michigan Council of Governments	Macomb, Oakland, Washtenaw, Wayne, Monroe, St. Clair and Livingston counties, *Michigan*
San Francisco-Oakland Association of Bay Area Governments	Alameda, Contra Costa, Marin, Napa, San Francisco, San Mateo, Santa Clara, Solano and Sonoma counties, *California*
Washington Metropolitan Washington Council of Governments	*District of Columbia* *Maryland* portion: Montgomery and Prince Georges counties *Virginia* portion: Cities of Alexandria, Fairfax and Falls Church, and Fairfax, Loudoun and Prince William counties
Boston Metropolitan Area Planning Council	Suffolk County, and parts of Essex, Middlesex, Norfolk, Plymouth and Worcester counties, *Massachusetts*
Pittsburgh Southwestern Pennsylvania Regional Planning Commission	Allegheny, Armstrong, Beaver, Butler, Washington and Westmoreland counties, *Pennsylvania*

continued

Table 11-1 continued

Metropolis and Agency	*Jurisdiction*
St. Louis East-West Gateway Coordinating Council	*Illinois* portion: Madison, Monroe and St. Clair counties *Missouri* portion: City of St. Louis, and Jefferson, St. Charles, St. Louis and Franklin counties
Baltimore Regional Planning Council	City of Baltimore, and Anne Arundel, Baltimore, Carroll, Harford and Howard counties, *Maryland*
Cleveland Northeast Ohio Areawide Coordinating Agency	Cuyahoga, Geauga, Lake, Lorain, Medina, Portage and Summit counties, *Ohio*
Houston Houston-Galveston Area Council	Austin, Brazoria, Chambers, Colorado, Fort Bend, Galveston, Harris, Liberty, Matagorda, Montgomery, Walker, Waller and Wharton counties, *Texas*
Minneapolis-St. Paul Metropolitan Council of the Twin Cities Area	Anoka, Carver, Dakota, Hennepin, Ramsey, Scott and Washington counties, *Minnesota*
Dallas-Fort Worth North Central Texas Council of Governments	Collin, Dallas, Denton, Ellis, Hood, Hunt, Johnson, Kaufman, Navarro, Palo Pinto, Parker, Rockwell, Somervell, Tarrant and Wise counties, *Texas*
Seattle Puget Sound Governmental Conference	King, Kitsap, Pierce and Snohomish counties, *Washington*
Milwaukee Southeastern Wisconsin Regional Planning Commission	Kenosha, Milwaukee, Ozaukee, Racine, Walworth, Washington and Waukesha counties, *Wisconsin*
Atlanta Atlanta Regional Commission	Clatyon, Cobb, DeKalb, Douglas, Fulton, Gwinnett and Rockdale counties, *Georgia*
Miami Metropolitan Dade County	Dade County, *Florida*
New Orleans Regional Planning Commission	Jefferson, Orleans and St. Bernard parishes, *Louisiana*

Source: Office of Management and Budget

federally defined SMSAs. The Southern California Association of Governments, for instance, covers four SMSAs and Greater New York's clearinghouse, the Tri-State Regional Planning Commission, serves 11. Generally, counties or groups of counties comprise the clearinghouse jurisdictions, the primary exceptions being in New England. Outside New England over one-third of the clearinghouses serve a single county (Table 11-2). These are mostly in metropolitan areas with small populations or large areas. Many of them are county planning commissions or part of a metropolitan government rather than councils of government. For example, Indianapolis and Miami, each of which has a metropolitan government, have county-based clearinghouses rather than COGs. San Diego and Phoenix have one county COGs because their counties are so large, while Asheville and Monroe have one county COGs largely because their metropolitan areas are so small.

At the other extreme are the Texas clearinghouses, especially West Texas, where a combination of state-engendered planning regions, wide open spaces and small counties has produced a series of multicounty organizations. Five of these regional authorities serve 15 or more counties, with Amarillo's 25 county Panhandle Regional Planning Commission leading the way.

The Texas example, though far above the national average of four counties per areawide authority, dramatizes the role of the states

Table 11-2. Jurisdictions of Certified Areawide Review Agencies*

Number of Counties Under Jurisdiction of Areawide Agency	*Number of Clearinghouses with Jurisdiction over that Number of Counties*
1	69
2	19
3	26
4	13
5	9
6	13
7	12
8	8
9	5
10	6
11	2
12	1
13	5
15	1
16	1
17	1
19	1
25	1

*Outside New England.

Source: Office of Management and Budget

in metropolitan governance. The national inducements apply across the country, but some states have added either further encouragement, such as additional funds for metropolitan functions, or mandated regional cooperation, such as state created agencies. Where the state has added to the federal requirements, metropolitan governance is likely to be stronger, as is the case with Georgia's Area Planning and Development Commissions, which have compulsory local government membership, making them more potent than typical COGs.

Most of the changes in metropolitan governance have been fairly superficial, adding an areawide review here, some metropolitan money there. The role of the states has also been important in those instances when the transformation of the political map has been more fundamental by either altering the preexisting structure or granting substantial powers to a metropolitan government. The states, or at least some states, have been involved in the relatively few structural changes in two basic ways. First, many states have enacted enabling legislation so that it is easier to alter the jurisdictional structure of the metropolis. They may have simplified the consolidation procedure, allowed for metropolitan government or granted increased local choice. Second, the states have enacted some changes directly, legislating the change rather than merely legislating permission to change. Examples of the first role are the permissive rules for local change in Tennessee and Florida. Miami, Jacksonville, Nashville and Knoxville have used these opportunities to reform their local governments. Examples of the second role are the creation of the Metropolitan Council of the Twin Cities Area in Minnesota and the consolidation of Indianapolis and Marion County in Indiana, each accomplished in one fell swoop by the state.

Individual state action cannot alleviate the problems of multistate metropolitan areas, however, and many cities do straddle state boundaries, especially when the boundary is a river. Seven areawide authorities certified by the federal government serve three states, and another 20 serve two states. Each of the tristate areas—New York, Washington, Cincinnati, Memphis, Wilmington, Huntington-Ashland and Sioux City—has a river site. Transport functions attract activity from both sides of the river, and a state with jurisdiction on just one side is unable to come to terms with regional problems. Solving problems in these regions requires cooperation at the state level—a difficult proposition at best. The areawide authorities in the multistate metropolitan areas are among the weakest in the nation, most of them being voluntary councils of governments. The divergence between economic and social realities on the one hand and political realities on the other hand are the greatest in these areas, but the roadblocks to the transformation of political space are the most hazardous. Thus the areas with the greatest need for flexibility have the least scope for adjustment.

Since World War II the number of significant structural changes in the political map of American cities is small, despite the rapid transformation of the social and economic patterns during that time. More often than not voters have rejected reform proposals, whether because they prefer different change, distrust change or feel their vested interests will be damaged. One obvious factor affecting the success of a reform proposal is the decision-making structure. The more scope for veto, the less likely change will be enacted. Change requiring approval of the state legislature, governor, local officials and the electorate will be likely to be defeated somewhere along the line, especially if the citizens votes are counted in separate tallies rather than over the metropolis as a whole.

Despite the minimal success at achieving wholesale change, some reformed metropolitan governments are in existence and the less radical federally induced metropolitan review system is operating. What lessons can be learned from these? What approaches can be transferred from one metropolis to another? The next section looks in more detail at five specific cases in the hope that they will help answer these questions.

The Record in Detail

Metropolitan governance in the case study areas—Miami, Minneapolis-St. Paul, Atlanta, Los Angeles and the San Francisco Bay Area—exhibits a variety of situations and responses and some meaningful constants. Only two, Los Angeles and San Francisco, operate under the laws and traditions of the same state. Each differs from the others in urban structure and the inherited mix of counties and municipalities. Miami and the Twin Cities of Minneapolis and St. Paul have developed well-known metropolitan governments. Atlanta has more anonymously experimented with a so-called "umbrella government," a state-backed review and coordination body. The California cities are still limited to voluntary COGs and special purpose districts. In common these cities share a number of traits, so the number of operating variables is held in check. They are among the younger American cities, at least in terms of the periods of their major growth, and each has earned renown for its governmental institutions. The five metropolitan areas comprise this study's laboratory for analysis—with some factors held constant while others vary so the effects may be gauged. They are an imperfect laboratory but hopefully an instructive one.

Miami-Dade County Metropolitan Government. Miami is one of the few American cities with *general purpose* metropolitan government and, with a 1970 census population over 1.25 million, it is easily the largest American city with such a government (Figure 11-3). That government is Metropolitan Dade County which attained metropolitan stature through a home rule charter in 1957. The charter significantly increased the county's independence from the state, freeing county officials to respond to local problems without having to await permission from the legislature. Although it has some of the characteristics of a metropolitan federation—particularly division of duties among separate layers of government—Miami's government is more appropriately labeled an urban county. Through its charter, Dade County is authorized to provide all urban-type governmental functions in its unincorporated territory. It also provides urban services to municipalities asking it to do so. No local level of government serves the unincorporated portions of Dade County, as would be the case in a truly federal system of metropolitan government.

Widely known for its rapid growth and alluring amenities, Miami is the epitome of a twentieth century city. From its incorporation in 1896, Miami has blossomed into the focus of Florida's booming Gold Coast. Dade County's sustaining growth was over 35 percent and 300,000 people in the 1960s. The area's physical environment accounts for its charm, but it is a precarious environment, sandwiched as it is between the Atlantic and the Everglades, and with that location lie many of the region's problems.

It is in this setting that Metropolitan Dade County emerged. The county has 26 municipalities, ranging in population from functionally inert Islandia's eight to over 300,000 in the City of Miami. When Dade County obtained its charter in 1957, it effectively enclosed Miami's urbanized area, but the ensuing years have witnessed the converging growth of Miami northward, toward the southerly expansion of the Fort Lauderdale-Hollywood complex in Broward County.

When the voters approved Dade County's home rule charter in 1975, it culminated a long-time search for a powerful metropolitan authority. That search had been thwarted many times before, and once the charter was established its adherents had to defend it from attempts to erode the newly gained powers. Previous attempts to transform the political map include a 1945 proposal to consolidate Dade County with all its cities, and proposals in 1947 and 1953 to consolidate the county with some of its cities. These measures failed either in the Florida legislature or at the polls

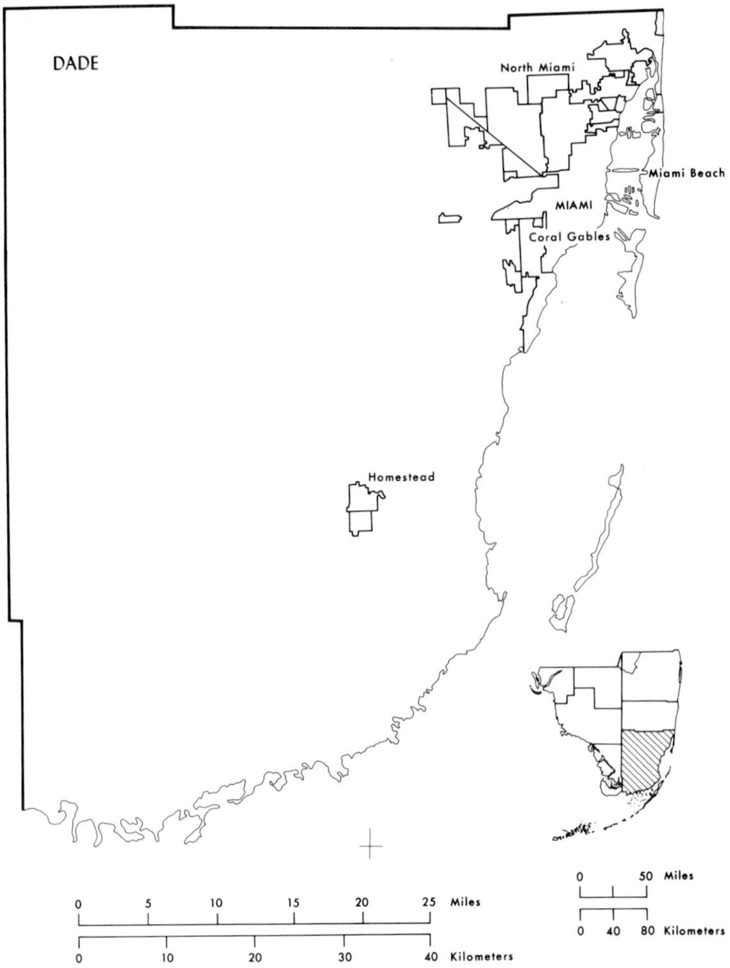

Figure 11-3. Miami Region Political Boundaries.

in the county. After the legislature approved a constitutional amendment authorizing Dade County home rule in 1955, a metropolitan charter board began drafting a charter. Florida voters approved the amendment in 1956, and Dade County voters adopted the completed charter the next year. In 1958 and 1959, however, attempts to reduce the charter's power reached the ballot, only to be denied by the electorate.

As a county, Metro, as the Dade County government has come to be known, possesses substantially more power than the other metropolitan authorities examined in this study. Metro provides urban services in unincorporated areas and to those cities which ask the county to provide services which cities have the jurisdiction to provide. Significantly, the residents of such cities are not levied extra taxes to pay for such services. Most of Dade County's cities have turned some functions over to Metro, either because the city could not provide the service adequately, as is the case with the very small ones, or because the city does not have a large enough income to provide all the services it would like to provide.

Florida municipalities operate under a tax millage ceiling. After that ceiling is reached, a city may only expand a service or add a new one if it reduces or eliminates some other activity. Consequently, many of Dade County's cities have yielded services which they found too expensive or not important enough to keep. Metro then takes over these services. This fiscal incentive is enhanced by the fact that—excepting special assessment districts, such as street lighting districts—Metro taxes all areas at the same millage rate whether an area receives specific services from Metro or not. Thus, people in the city of Miami, which has its own police force, support Metro's Public Safety Department to the same extent as those in the county who are served by that department. In effect, a municipality retaining a service has decided that the utility derived from operating that service *locally* offsets the extra costs of providing duplicate service. For those municipalities providing their own services, it amounts to double taxation.

Metro, of course, possesses the metropolitan powers common in other metropolitan areas in addition to those it has gained as a general purpose metropolitan government. The metropolitan Dade County Planning Commission serves as the federal government's A-95 clearinghouse, so it receives the planning grants for areawide plans and reviews the applications for federal categorical grants. Since there is no level of government between the clearinghouse and the applicant, the planning commission's coordination problems are minimized. No one is able to quit Metro, so it is a significantly more powerful review agency than voluntary organizations. Unlike most other clearinghouses, Metro also has the power to tax, so it is easier for it to raise revenue to implement its plans, either by matching federal or state funds or by developing a project all by itself.

Metro also possesses authority over such countywide organizations as the Library District and the Metropolitan Transit Authority, the latter being particularly important. Florida law allows the use of gasoline taxes for mass transit, and the MTA is planning a mass transit system which will use Metropolitan Dade County's share of the gasoline funds to match federal and state money.

A Dade County traffic study in the early 1960s showed that only 1 percent of Dade County's daily trips crossed into Broward County to the north. Now traffic has increased to the point that Dade, Broward and Palm Beach counties have entered into cooperative planning. The urbanized areas of the three counties have coalesced. They can no longer solve their problems inside their own boundaries, and herein lies the rub for Metropolitan Dade County and its success as a regional entity. Although the county covers 2,000 square miles, which puts it in the largest 10 percent of American counties, much of its area is swamp, and much of that is legally protected swamp. Metro's jurisdiction is not so much too small as merely misplaced. For some problems it simply lacks the requisite jurisdiction, having it where not needed but lacking it where needed. Consequently, multicounty special purpose districts and a multicounty council of governments already exist in South Florida. With more growth likely in the region, the trend toward multicounty involvement is likely to continue.

Two long-standing special purpose districts serve the Gold Coast. The Central and Southern Florida Flood Control District coordinates flood control development in an 18 county area. The Florida Inland Navigation District maintains and improves waterways and bridges in 11 counties from Jacksonville to the Keys. These organizations have jurisdictions defined by the physical geography necessary for the functions they perform. With the existence of these organizations, jurisdictional problems of general purpose governmental units, particularly counties, were minimized, since general government did not have to handle these functions with their unique areal requirements.

The famous case of the Everglades Jetport illustrates the inability of South Florida's general purpose governments to solve regional problems. After environmentalists won a court decision prohibiting construction of a new international airport in the Everglades, Dade County found itself with no satisfactory location within its own borders. Subsequently Dade joined with Monroe and Collier counties to the west to plan the jetport. This led to the formation of the South Florida Everglades Area Planning Council in 1969. Nevertheless, the urbanized counties to Dade's north successfully fought the airport plans. Later, when the issues changed, Broward, Palm Beach, Hendry and Lee counties joined and the organization changed its name to the South Florida Regional Planning Council. A voluntary organization, its membership consists wholly of elected representatives from the seven counties. In other words, it is a council of governments. Since Dade, Broward and Palm Beach counties are recognized by the federal government as both Standard Metropolitan Statistical Areas and A-95 clearinghouses, the counties are powerful and do not relish the relinquishment of their powers to another authority. Add to that the fact that SFRPC has been granted few duties and it is not surprising that its output has been limited.

That output, or output by some wider regional authority, may increase, however. The 1972 Florida legislature created a commission on local government to study the existing system and make recommendations for change. One change which has already been recommended is the implementation of ten regional planning districts in the state. One of these would cover five counties along Florida's Atlantic coast, starting with Dade and running north. The commission recognized two distinct types of planning problems in South Florida—environmental problems based primarily on the drainage network; and development and service provision problems, based primarily on the system of urban settlement. The commission opted to base its regions on the latter. The eventual effect is likely to be multicounty service and planning districts. The state will probably base its service divisions on these districts; federal policy is to match its service areas and planning areas to those of the states. Consequently, Dade County and its neighbors fear this would lead the federal government to seek a geographically wider A-95 clearinghouse to replace the ones now operating in the individual counties. The final result cannot be determined at this time. It can be assumed, however, that the political space of Florida's Gold Coast is likely to be transformed in the near future, adding to the present Metropolitan Dade County a more far-reaching regional authority.

Metro Dade County's success as a metropolitan agency must be assessed in terms of the scope of the problems considered. As long as the problem does not extend beyond the county limits, Metro earns high marks. As a democratically elected institution, it is highly responsive to its citizens. An excellent example of this was an extensive round of hearings in the spring of 1973 to learn how the citizens wished to spend the receipts from an omnibus bond issue which had been approved at the polls. Given its status as a general purpose government, Metro is able to establish priorities among many options and it is also able to coordinate its many activities. Thus, its transportation planning arm knows what its public housing arm is doing, for example.

Unfortunately for Metro, Greater Miami is outgrowing Dade County and Metro's viability as a regional government is waning. For some questions, such as locating and operating the jetport, it has to share responsbility. As the urban area continues to grow, it is likely that Metro will have to share more of its powers or yield them to some South Florida agency. Miami certainly was ahead of the times when it fashioned its metropolitan government in 1957, but this was possible in part because the county was large enough to eliminate externalities. The Miami area is only now being confronted with the obsolescence of its old county boundaries. Like other American metropolitan areas, Greater Miami in the future will have to overcome the static nature of its political organization of space. The South Florida region is learning, like the rest of the nation, that changes in the economic and social organization of space necessitate changes in the political organization of space as well. Metropolitan government boundaries cannot be defined in a permanently satisfactory way as long as the metropolis continues to expand beyond those boundaries. That expansion is now occurring in Greater Miami.

The Twin Cities of Minneapolis and St. Paul. The Minnesota Twin Cities of Minneapolis and St. Paul have a unique metropolitan government—the Metropolitan Council of the Twin Cities Area. Created by the Minnesota legislature in 1967, the Metropolitan Council is appointed by the governor and is essentially a three tier federal system. The antecedent structure of municipalities and counties remains, the Metropolitan Council forming a new level of government superimposed over the others to handle problems of a metropolitan nature. The council has jurisdiction over a seven county area (Figure 11–4).

The dual-centered Twin Cities metropolis is isolated, unencumbered by the coalescence of urban areas that complicates the governance of South Florida and many other urban regions in the United States. The Twin Cities' hinterland is uncontested to the north, west and southwest, and the competition is hundreds of miles away in the other directions. Although St. Paul and Minneapolis are politically separate

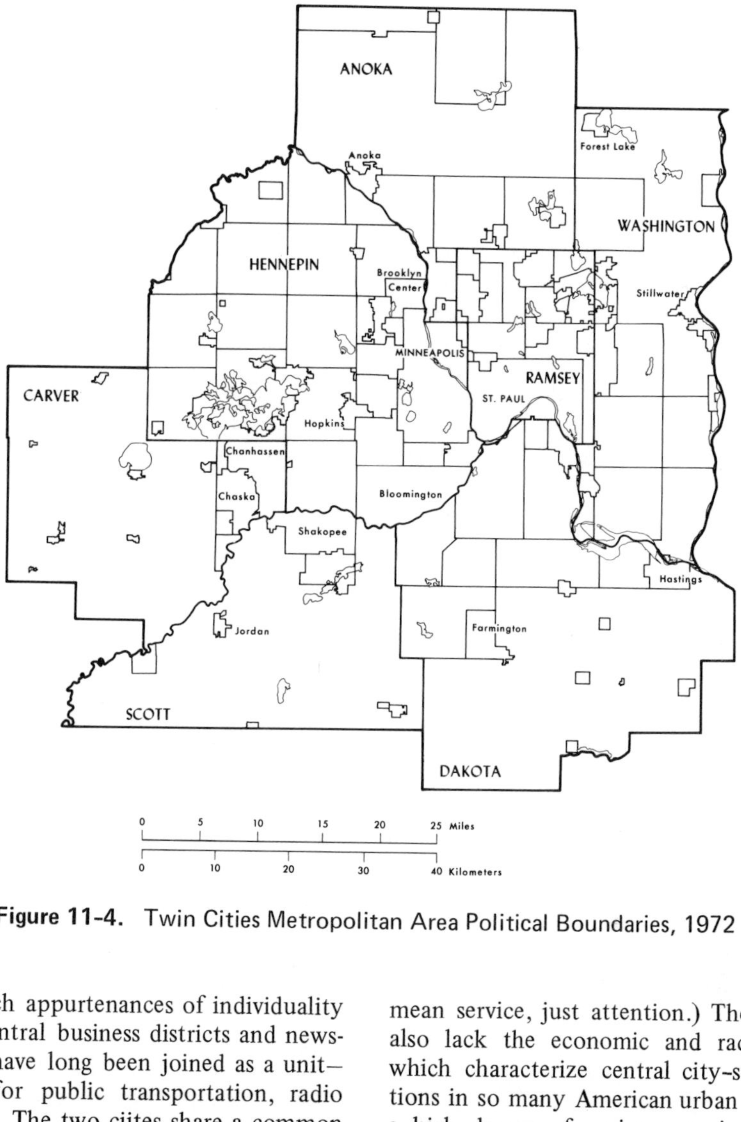

Figure 11-4. Twin Cities Metropolitan Area Political Boundaries, 1972

and retain such appurtenances of individuality as separate central business districts and newspapers, they have long been joined as a unit—significantly for public transportation, radio and television. The two ciites share a common border and the development spreading from each downtown area long ago filled the intervening land. They share a metropolitan airport, and the professional sports enterprises in the area bear a Minnesota identity, neither Minneapolis nor St. Paul. In short, the Twin Cities form a single economic and social unit.

The Twin Cities are not only the cultural and economic center of Minnesota. They account for half the state's population too. Consequently, the state of Minnesota focuses much of its attention on the metropolitan area. (In the past, particularly before reapportionment of the legislature, that did not always mean service, just attention.) The Twin Cities also lack the economic and racial polarities which characterize central city-suburban relations in so many American urban regions. Such a high degree of socioeconomic homogeneity reduces political friction in the area. The cultural homogeneity and the Twin Cities flavor of the legislature both increase the potential for reaching consensus on metropolitan goals and both tend to lower hurdles to metropolitan action.

Intercity rivalry certainly exists in the Twin Cities. In the distant past that rivalry went as far as census tampering. Less obviously, rivalry exists among the many governmental units in the area. Those governmental units are the ones typically found in American cities—counties and municipalities. The seven county Metropolitan Council jurisdiction is divided into more than 100 minor civil divisions (Figure 11-4). Each of these units displays a measure of civic patriotism and this inhibits regional cooperation.

The metropolitan age has changed the Twin Cities, rendering the old governmental structure obsolete just as in other American cities. Problems outgrew political boundaries when the post-World War II Twin Cities grew. Although both central cities have declined in population, the seven county area swelled from its 1950 population of just under 1.2 million to over 1.8 million in 1970, a two decade increase of over 50 percent. As the area grew and the population relocated, the demand for public services likewise grew and shifted. The governmental units kept abreast of some problems through intergovernmental contracts, authorized by Minnesota's Joint Exercise of Powers Act in 1943. Examples of this are extensions of the Minneapolis sewage system to cover several adjacent municipalities and the half dozen mutual assistance pacts which many municipalities joined to assure adequate fire protection. This approach requires amiable relations, however, and joint agreements, even when agreement is achieved, may not be enough of an adjustment.

As the residents began to expect more from local government, and as the fiscal disparities among the units of local government expanded, the old system tarnished. While Minneapolis and St. Paul bore more of the welfare load than the suburbs, the biggest disparities in the ability to pay for public services developed in the suburbs. Some suburban municipalities, particularly in the southwestern part of the metropolis, became very wealthy, attracting such revenue-producing land uses as light industry, regional shopping centers and high income residential areas. Add to this wealth the low need for public services in these areas and the sum is an enviable fiscal situation. Unfortunately, other municipalities found themselves in the opposite stance–few revenue-producing land uses and a lower income population with a high demand for public services, particularly schools. This problem particularly plagued the northern suburbs on the Anoka sandplain. More than anywhere else in the United States, fiscal disparities–differences in the ability to pay for needed public services–surfaced as an issue of metropolitan reform in the Twin Cities. The question became more than just distribution of a metropolitan service; it was also to be the redistribution of metropolitan resources.

The Twin Cities have a long history of metropolitan activity. Edward Bergman credits the University of Minnesota, the main campus of which sits between the downtowns of Minneapolis and St. Paul, for this. The area has had several special purpose districts with wide jurisdiction. Nevertheless, the first important step toward metropolitan power did not come until the creation of the Metropolitan Planning Commission in 1957, three years after the provision of federal funds to assist metropolitan planning. The MPC was a planning and coordinating body with no real power in its own right. When federal programs appeared in the 1960s, the MPC's powers grew accordingly, because it was available to serve as a regional planning agency, and therefore as a funnel for federal funds. It soon became obvious, however, that such a weak organization was insufficient to solve the Twin Cities' growing problems.

An important catalyst for changing the governmental structure of the Twin Cities was the inability of the fragmented, incomplete sewage system to respond to a deterioration in the quality of drinking water in the area. Much of the post-World War II suburban development had depended upon septic tanks and wells rather than integrated municipal disposal and supply systems. Eventually the hydrologic system became overloaded, and in the early 1960s the quality of water in some localities fell so low that it became a health problem. The existing political structure was unable to respond to the problem and the consequence was an increase in the number of adherents to a concerted metropolitan approach. Add to this the long-standing support of metropolitan action by such prestigious local groups as the Citizens League and the sum was action by the Minnesota legislature.

That action finally came in 1967 with passage of the Metropolitan Council Act. The legislation's timing allowed the council to qualify for federal funds under the Demonstration Cities and Metropolitan Development Act of 1966. The Metropolitan Council did not become full-fledged local government in the usual sense, however. First, its members are not elected, but appointed by the governor–14 from districts and a charman appointed at large. The Minnesota senate must approve the nominations, which must be nonpartisan. Second, the council's powers, especially to raise revenue, are tightly restricted. Consequently, the Metropolitan Counil not only has very limited power, but in terms of the selection process it is more like an arm of state government than locally controlled local government.

The primary powers of the Metropolitan Council are the preparation of a comprehensive development guide for the seven county area; power to review plans of the independent commissions, boards and agencies operating in the area; and the power to review the plans of the municipalities in the area, as well as the power to review federal programs in the region. The council is also charged to collect data and instructed to participate in special district and local government activity. After passage of the federal Intergovernmental Cooperation Act of 1968 and issuance of the A-95 Circular in 1969, the Metropolitan Council also became the clearinghouse for applications under federally funded programs.

The year 1969 was a big one for metropolitan relations in the Twin Cities. State legislation that year turned the Metropolitan Council into an umbrella government, giving it jurisdiction over a number of special purpose districts in the region—for example, the Metropolitan Sewer Board and the Metropolitan Park Reserve Board. The Council exerted its political muscle in a substantial way for the first time in 1969 by vetoing the Metropolitan Airports Commission's selection of a new airport site.

That same year the fiscal disparities question was forcefully presented before the state legislature. The eventual result was a program which diverts part of the annual increment to the metropolitan tax base into a metropolitan-wide tax pool. Municipalities which have low revenue-producing abilities and high demand for public services receive disproportionate amounts back from the pool. Affluent, growing communities, on the other hand, yield more than is returned. The metropolitan fiscal disparities program went into effect in 1971 (Figure 11-5). It is based on 40 percent of whatever nonresidential tax base is added to each municipality's tax roll each year. Areas with low property values per person and areas experiencing little or no growth normally receive more money back, offsetting this low revenue-producing situation. Residential property is not subject to the redistribution program.

In many ways the Metropolitan Council of the Twin Cities Area has been a success. Without altering the antecedent structure of counties and municipalities, the council has effectively created a metropolitan constituency in the Twin Cities. In a number of instances it has ensured a metropolitan view in the future development of the area, the consolidation of the area's water and sewage programs being examples. Its ability to coordinate activities and to order metropolitan priorities is limited to negative powers over certain proposals more than the ability to decide affirmatively what will be done. This weakness was exhibited in a controversy over building a domed stadium in central Minneapolis. Although a stadium would require an enormous expenditure with great impact on the metropolis, the Metropolitan Council had virtually no voice in the decision.

Because of its indirect selection, the council does not have the same political necessity to be responsive to citizen demands that duly elected public servants face. That is, since the council need not face the electorate, it might be expected to pay less attention to the "public pulse." Nonetheless, the council has taken its responsibilities to heart and a recent poll of public officials in the Twin Cities area gave the council high marks within its limited powers. The Metropolitan Council, it seems, has very much wanted to be responsive, whether or not politics requires responsiveness.

The Metropolitan Council's limited powers are a problem, and the experiment with the council has been successful enough for moves to have been taken to make it an elective body with increased powers. One house of the 1973 Minnesota legislature passed a bill to do just that—make it elective and give it more power. The measure had substantial community support, but it died in committee in the other house. It is sure to be revived in subsequent sessions of the legislature, and the long term prognosis is that the council, which was preceded by a series of special purpose districts, will itself be succeeded by a more general purpose governmental unit. This will further transform the Twin Cities' political space, bringing it more into line with the economic and social changes of the last several decades. The Metropolitan Council of the Twin Cities Area, it appears, has served its apprenticeship

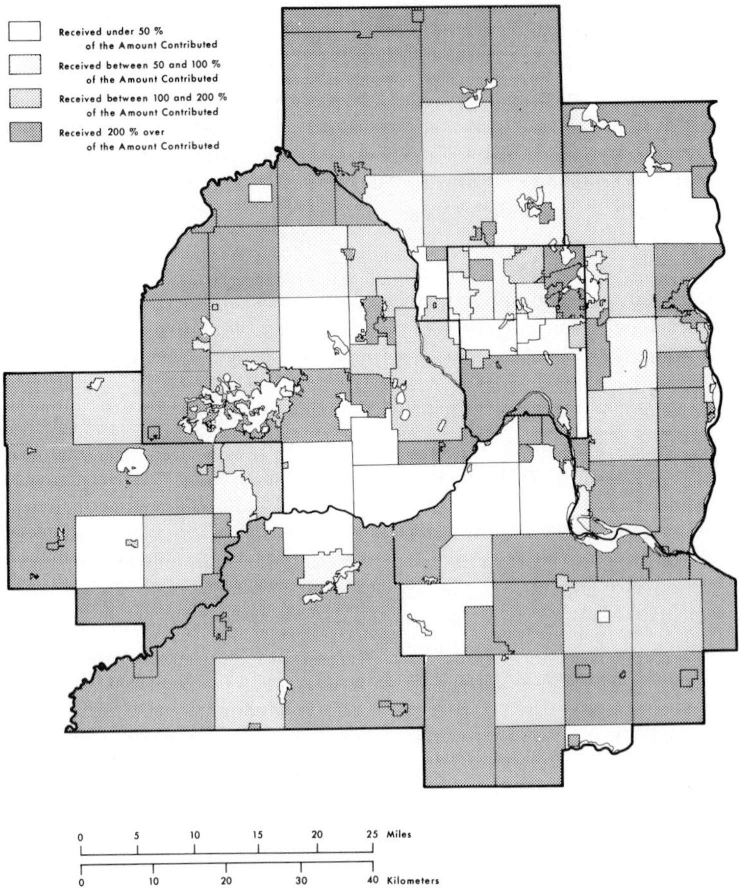

Figure 11-5. Fiscal Redistribution in the Twin Cities, 1972

and will move on to more challenging problems.

When the Minnesota legislature created the Metropolitan Council in 1967, the seven county jurisdiction granted to the council was generously defined. It easily circumscribed the built-up area of the metropolis and it exeeded the five county Standard Metropolitan Statistical Area defined by the federal government. In 1973 the Office of Management and Budget redefined the Twin Cities' SMSA as a ten county area, adding the remaining counties in the Metropolitan Council's area–Carver and Scott–as well as two more Minnesota counties–Chisago and Wright–and St. Croix County, Wisconsin. The addition to the SMSA in part reflects the continual expansion of the metropolis outward. This expansion may eventually require enlargement of the council's jurisdiction. This should not be necessary for years to come, however, thanks to the generous delimitation of the council's boundaries in 1967. The present area is large enough to allow the council to carry out its planning and management functions.

Meanwhile, of the three kinds of activities which Mogulof says require a metropolitan approach, the Twin Cities have effectively achieved that approach in only one–the one in which services must overcome boundary restrictions, as in highway, mass transit and open space planning. The council is less successful at overcoming externality problems, as the stadium example shows, or at achieving economies of scale. Even with these limitations, though, the Twin Cities have come closer than most American cities to transforming their political space to match contemporary social and economic realities.

Greater Atlanta. Metropolitan Atlanta, capital of the Southeast, spreads out of its central city into several surrounding counties. It is one of the nation's more rapidly growing metropolitan areas and, as in the Twin Cities, growth has forced redefinition of Atlanta's metropolitan boundaries. The Atlanta Regional Commission, which is the A-95 clearinghouse for the area, expanded from five to seven counties in 1973. At the same time the federal Office of Management and Budget redefined Atlanta's Standard Metropolitan Statistical Area, enlarging it from five to 15 counties. The population of the seven county ARC area virtually doubled between 1950 and 1970, expanding from three-quarters of a million to over 1.4 million. Although primarily in Fulton County, the city of Atlanta is one of those rare American municipalities spilling into a second county, in this instance DeKalb (Figure 11-6). Greater Atlanta differs from Miami in that its urbanized area is clearly distinct from others in the American system. There is no impending threat of Atlanta coalescing with neighboring metropolitan areas. Like the Twin Cities, Atlanta has no metropolitan neighbors, but unlike the Minnesota metropolis, Atlanta has one unmistakable metropolitan center and growth spreads from it.

Atlanta's governmental structure has undergone substantial change since World War II. First the city of Atlanta, through its plan for improvement in the early 1950s, modernized administrative procedures and tripled its territory. More recently the Georgia legislature created the Atlanta Regional Commission, an areawide authority with some teeth.

The Atlanta Regional Commission is the culmination of a several step process. The last step was an act by the Georgia legislature creating ARC by amalgamating four previously operating organizations. ARC also received additional powers above and beyond those of the units it succeeded. The Georgia legislature also took the first step toward a metropolitan constitu-

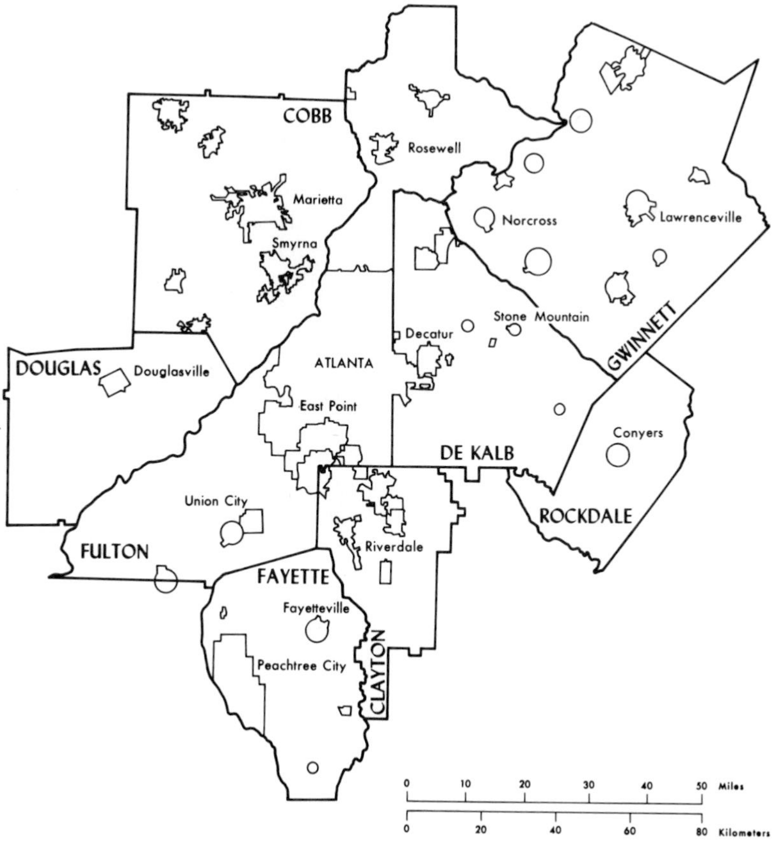

Figure 11-6. Atlanta Region Political Boundaries

ency for Atlanta when it created one of the nation's first planning commissions with authority over more than a single county. It took that step in 1947, giving planning commission jurisdiction over Fulton and DeKalb Counties. That commission—the Atlanta Metropolitan Planning Commission—added three additional counties—Clayton, Cobb and Gwinnett—to its venue in 1960. The commission's importance increased with the availability of federal funds and the imposition of review and comment requirements as qualifications for federal categorical grants.

In the meantime, three other metropolitan organizations developed in Atlanta—the Metropolitan Atlanta Council for Health which coordinated federal hospital grants, the Metropolitan Atlanta Council of Governments which coordinated law enforcement funds and the Atlanta Area Transportation Study which coordinated highway funds. These three, plus the Metropolitan Planning Commission, merged to form ARC in 1971. Douglas and Rockdale Counties joined in 1973, increasing ARC's jurisdiction to seven counties.

ARC has all the powers of its antecedent organizations, as well as some important new ones of its own, significantly, including the evaluation of priorities. ARC is the metropolitan region's Area Planning and Development Commission, one of 19 Georgia created to facilitate planning and coordination among its 159 counties. Because it is an APDC, ARC is more than just a voluntary organization. Its members belong by virtue of state legislation and administrative action. That legislation was supported by local government officials, so it does not represent a diminution of local powers over local objections. In fact, ARC is based on local government and is designed to foster local cooperation. The chairmen of the county boards, the mayor and one alderman from Atlanta, one municipal representative from each county, and several citizen representatives comprise the commission. The citizen representatives, who must make up less than half the commission total, represent districts which cross county boundaries, supposedly to make them less parochial.

As an Area Planning and Development Commission and an A-95 clearinghouse, ARC possesses the power of area plan review and acts as the integrated grant administrator. It is an umbrella government, overseeing the operation of other governments in its area, cajoling those governments when necessary and attempting to achieve what is best for the whole region. ARC lacks zoning powers of its own, but it is responsible for coordinating the region's zoning. In some ways ARC's powers are more negative than positive. It can prevent development but has little power to develop. When ARC objects to a local proposal it sends it back, and the local authority usually accedes to the change. Only rarely does the local agency insist on submitting a grant application bearing negative comment from ARC. Thus far when this has happened, the application has been denied by federal decisionmakers, so ARC's denial has functioned as a veto. This greatly increases the commisson's power to coordinate. ARC receives over 60 percent of its budget from federal grants and contracts. Regional appropriations account for under a quarter of the budget but this is much more than is the case for some clearinghouses.

Atlanta possesses an additional metropolitan authority which, while in some ways subsidiary to ARC, is an autonomous body. This is the Metropolitan Atlanta Rapid Transit Authority (MARTA), which operates public transportation in the region. MARTA operates buses and is developing the rail rapid transit system for the area. It plans transportation in conjunction with ARC, the state and federal agencies. In 1965 the state of Georgia authorized the organization of MARTA subject to a referendum in the then five county metropolitan planning area. The city of Atlanta and Fulton and DeKalb counties voted overwhelmingly to support the organization, and Clayton and Gwinnett counties voted to join by smaller margins. Only Cobb County rejected the measure, so MARTA came into being in a four county area.

MARTA's rapid transit area is even more restricted than the area it serves with regular buses. The four remaining counties held referenda in 1971 to see which were willing to support a proposed 70 mile rapid transit and busway system with a one percent sales and use tax. The way the measure was written, Fulton and DeKalb each had to pass the proposal or the system would not be built. By the smallest of margins—less than one percent in Fulton County—the voters of those counties did vote yes. Those in Clayton and Gwinnett overwhelmingly voted no. Consequently, the *metro-*

politan rapid transit system is limited to the more densely built-up portion of the metropolis, which is where most of the service was to be located anyway.

The transformation of political space in metropolitan Atlanta has produced a significant metropolitan agency, the Atlanta Regional Commission. ARC operates largely as a planning and coordinating agency and does little implementation of its own. Nevertheless, this coordinating and planning power does mean that a metropolitan voice is heard in Atlanta, and this metropolitan voice has the sanction of both state and federal backing. Metropolitan governance in Atlanta deserves respectable ratings for both coordination and the establishment of priorities. As indirect as its representation is, ARC's responsiveness is suspect and has not had much time to prove itself one way or the other. Like the Twin Cities' Metropolitan Council, the Atlanta Regional Commission's duties mainly involve functions whose operation requires more territory than that possessed by conventional governmental units. ARC does not have the redistributive importance of metropolitan governance in the Twin Cities—that is, it does not redistribute funds as Minnesota's fiscal disparity program does. Nor does it have power over functions considered metropolitan because they allow economies of scale or because they are necessary to overcome contradictory policies of local jurisdictions.

The success of the transformation of Atlanta's political space is attested to by the on-going development of a rapid transit system—something the individual governmental units lacked the jurisdiction to build—and by the completion of a number of substantial regional plans—for example, plans lfor rapid transit, criminal justice and the Chattahoochie Corridor, each of which was adopted in 1972. The eventual measure of metropolitan success in Atlanta will be the degree to which such plans are translated into action and change land uses on the ground.

California's Urban Regions. The final two metropolitan areas in this study—Los Angeles and the San Francisco Bay area—exist under the rules and traditions of the same state—California. That state has a progressive reputation for its political institutions. The state itself pioneered the provision of many public services, and its constitution and statutes provide numerous opportunities for citizen participation, including permissive initiative and recall procedures.

Significantly, local government has a strong role in the California legal system. The 1873 Municipal Corporation Act reserved the formation of cities to local volition. Municipalities are not instituted by the state. Local citizens, through mechanisms authorized by the state, must initiate incorporation proceedings. In addition, the larger cities have home rule charters, thanks to state action way back in 1879. This city and county independence from state interference grew with legislation in this century. Most important was a 1935 law sanctioning the use of intergovernmental contracts as counties and cities desired. This environment of local sentiment and local power has shadowed the history of metropolitan activity in the state.

Metropolitan governance has been sufficiently controversial for two state administrations—those of Governor Edmund Brown and Governor Ronald Reagan—to appoint commissions to study the question. Meanwhile, the state role in planning has increased and the voters have created a series of coastal commissions to regulate the development and use of the California coastline. The state has tightened incorporation proceedings by creating local area formation commissions. These commissions, one in each county, assess the impact and viability of incorporation and annexation proposals before the proposals go before the voters. The commissions have reduced the pace of new city formation and systematized battles between competing municipalities over annexation of a lucrative area. California has exhibited its recognition of regional problems by creating regional branches of state services and by creating regional special purpose districts. It has yet to deal with the question of metropolitan governance in a comprehensive way, however. It remains to be seen what will emerge from the blue ribbon commission appointed to study the question.

San Francisco Bay Area. The portion of California with the greatest pressure for jurisdictional change is the San Francisco Bay Area. The Bay Area has transformed its political space to create metropolitan entities and that transformation is likely to continue. The significant regional organizations are a voluntary council of governments, the Association of Bay Area Governments and a myriad of special purpose districts. No general purpose or powerful umbrella government yet exists in the Bay Area, but the Twin Cities model, in which metropolitan special purpose districts paved the way for metropolitan government, may be followed.

The Bay Area is one of the more complex of America's urban regions. Central to the character of the region is San Francisco Bay itself. It simultaneously divides and joins the disparate interests of the region. The bay is both a transportation barrier that limits road development and a transportation avenue allowing marine commerce. The bay divides the communities of the area into distinct entities, but it is also the focus of many economic, esthetic and environmental questions. As a consequence, the urbanized area surrounding San Francisco Bay is the area appropriate for many public functions. More than is typical for American cities, the limits of metropolitan San Francisco can be environmentally defined.

Urbanization of the Bay Area has long been fragmented. Development spread from three main centers—San Francisco, Oakland and San Jose—as well as from many smaller ones. San Francisco has always been the pre-eminent focus of regional activity, as exhibited by its leadership in finance and cultural activities. The dominance seems to have slackened somewhat, however, as the population has spread out, particularly to the east and south. Between 1950 and 1970 the area now under the Association of Bay Area Government's jurisdiction added almost two million people, a 70 percent growth beyond 4.6 million. This was despite a decline in the population of San Francisco proper.

Northern California has fairly small counties, especially in comparison with those to the south. Nine counties border San Francisco Bay, and those counties are divided into close to 100 municipalities (Figure 11-7). The consolidated city and county of San Francisco occupies only a 40 square mile tip of the San Francisco Peninsula at the Golden Gate. Given this severe fragmentation, public bodies in the area have long been forced to cooperate with each other to solve regional problems and this they have done on a number of occasions. The University of California has acted as a catalyst for the cooperation.

Although generally voluntary, this cooperation is also a response to outside pressure in the form of state threats to take over local government functions. Partly as a result of such a threat, elected officials from the region's counties and municipalities organized the Association of Bay Area Governments in 1961. ABAG was not the first areawide organization, nor was it formed solely to solve regional problems. It was preceded by such entities as the Golden Gate Bridge District in 1928 and the Regional Park District in 1934. One spur leading to ABAG's creation was a state proposal to form a regional transit authority. To rally municipal and county power, and to provide a local government alternative to state action, local leaders formed ABAG in January 1961. They sought a discussion group and study organization. Since its inception ABAG has evolved into much more, but its powers still fall far short of what its staunchest proponents advocate.

ABAG's decisionmaking structure is a compromise, taking into consideration the independence of both municipalities and counties, as well as the differences in population among the organization's members. Two bodies—the general assembly and executive committee—rule the organization. Each city and county has one vote in the general assembly and resolutions are subject to approval by a majority of municipal representatives *and* a majority of county representatives. In effect each group possesses veto power, the municipalities' numbers and the counties' population thus balancing. Membership on the executive committee—which makes operating decisions to discharge the general assembly's policies—is proportional to county population. Municipalities within a county split that county's representation on the committee. This structure allows each member organization to have representation and it also gives weight to the populous places which would be dominated by the small municipalities and counties if each authority had equal weight.

Those who created it did not mean ABAG to be a government. They sought a forum for discussion and study, a voluntary association of governments with no power, stressing the voluntary. ABAG was supposed to review

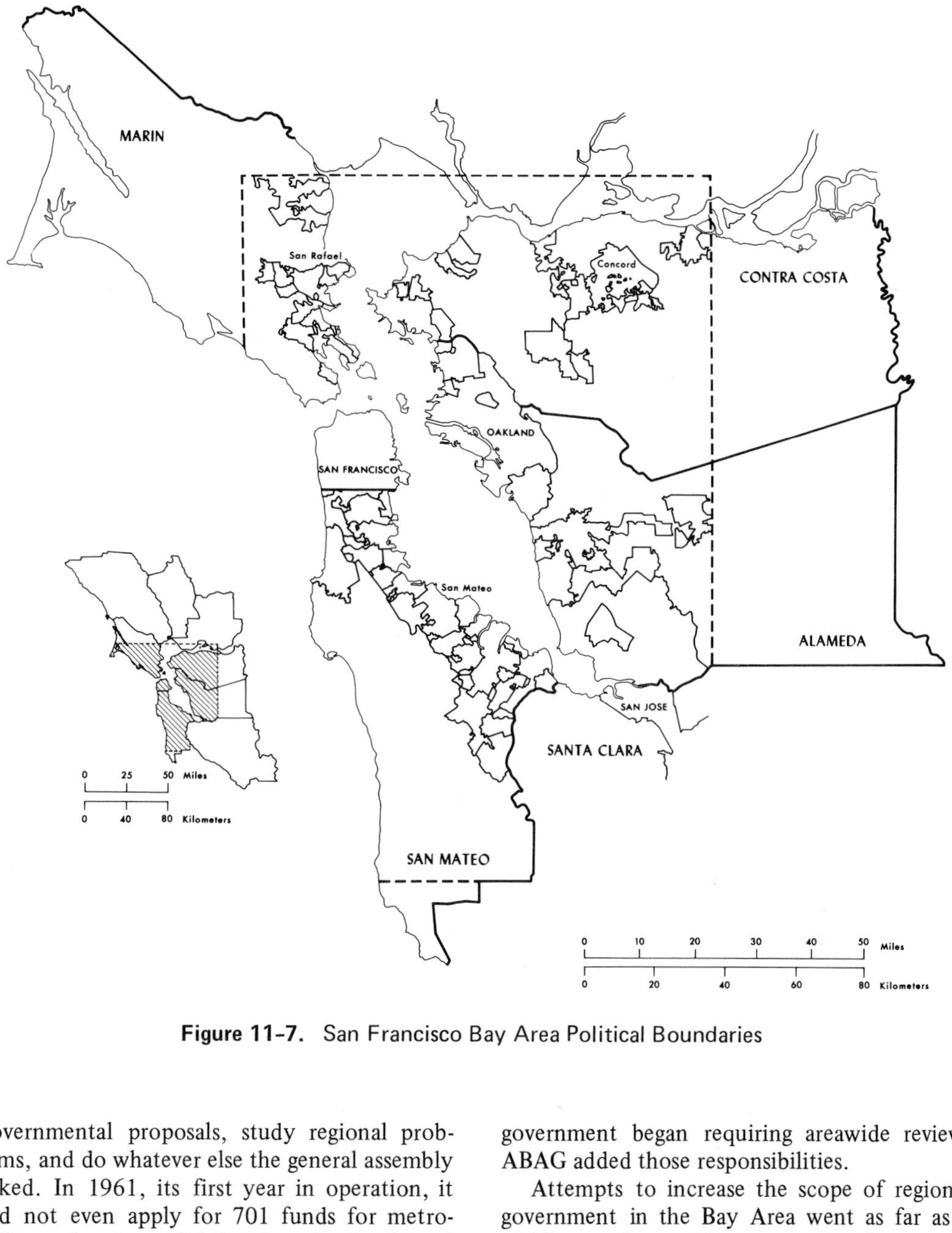

Figure 11-7. San Francisco Bay Area Political Boundaries

governmental proposals, study regional problems, and do whatever else the general assembly asked. In 1961, its first year in operation, it did not even apply for 701 funds for metropolitan planning. ABAG did apply for federal funds to finance the development of a regional open space plan that year, however,

As time passed, those who ran ABAG changed its character. By 1963 ABAG did apply for 701 funds, and soon thereafter the organization embarked on a series of planning ventures for the region, including transportation and solid waste disposal. When the federal government began requiring areawide review, ABAG added those responsibilities.

Attempts to increase the scope of regional government in the Bay Area went as far as a 1966 general assembly request that the state of California consider a limited function, multipurpose regional government for the area. That resolution was by no means unanimous. Santa Clara County and Oakland, among others, opposed it. The request was not fulfilled, and subsequent bills before the state legislature have failed, but sentiment for a stronger authority in the Bay Area was one reason the Governor was able to gain support for his California Council on Governmental Relations. Regional government for the San Francisco Bay Area must be a high priority item for that study group.

As mentioned earlier, ABAG shares regional responsibility with several special purpose districts. One of these is the San Francisco Bay Conservation and Development Commission, known locally as BCDC. Possessing jurisdiction over San Francisco Bay and 100 feet shoreward, BCDC is charged with management of bay shore development. It was created to stop land fill operations and to plan the use of the bay for the benefit of all. Governments bordering the bay, including special purpose districts, are represented on the commission. Funding comes from the state.

Another well-known special purpose authority is the Bay Area Rapid Transit Commission, known as BART, which is developing and operating a rail rapid transit system. Financed by a public bond issue, federal grants, bridge tolls and a sales tax assessment, BART's eventual service area will be limited to Alameda, Contra Cost and San Francisco counties. Marin and San Mateo counties left the organization in 1962, five years after it was established by the legislature. BART's significance is that it has put together a new rapid transit system while other metropolitan areas just talked about needing one. When it opened, BART became the first new operational system in American cities in decades.

The Bay Area Sewage Services Agency—BASSA—is another special purpose authority. It has the responsibility for development and implementation of a sewage disposal plan. Created by the state legislature in 1971, BASSA also reviews local plans affecting water quality.

Other special purpose agencies exist as well (Figure 11-8). The sum is a large number of regional organizations, some of them far removed from voter control. The San Francisco Bay Area earns good marks for the number of its regional programs and the individual success of those programs. It must receive low marks for lack of a strong coordinating and priority-setting body. Since it has no umbrella organization to establish priorities, the Bay Area cannot effectively determine regional goals. Given the structure of government in the region, it is also difficult to measure and respond to citizen demand. Joseph Bodovitz, Executive Director of BCDC, put it this way:

> [C]ontrary to the widespread cliche that we have regional government in the Bay Area, I would like to suggest that we have nothing that remotely resembles regional self-government. We have a great deal of regional administration, a large number of regional agencies—some created by the state and federal government, some local, some regional—all doing things with great efficiency, but if Thomas Jefferson were to . . . hear us describe what we are doing in the Bay Area, it would not be anything that he would remotely recognize as self-government. . . . We've really made technology and efficiency our goals, and maybe that's okay, but we have lost self-government along the way. [p. 68]

In other words, while there is regional governance in the Bay Area in the sense that the regional special districts exist, there is no public institution coordinating, setting priorities and responding to total citizen demand. There is no regional government.

The functions which are organized on a regional basis in the Bay Area are primarily those whose operation requires greater jurisdiction than is possessed by municipalities and counties—transportation and sewage disposal being examples. BCDC might be considered an example of overcoming negative metropolitan spillovers, but the economies of scale argument has not been used to organize regional activities.

The future status of regional governance in the Bay Area depends upon state action, meaning that the decision will be made every bit as much by those out of the Bay Area as by those in it. Early in his administration, when briefed on the problems of administering the region, then Governor Reagan suggested that the situation could be overcome by merging all the counties. Definitely this would create a strong regional authority, and if such an authority acquired the duties now performed by special purpose districts it would be able to coordinate and set priorities. A regional authority like this could also be popularly elected. This flies in the face of residents' identification with their counties, however, and that identification is

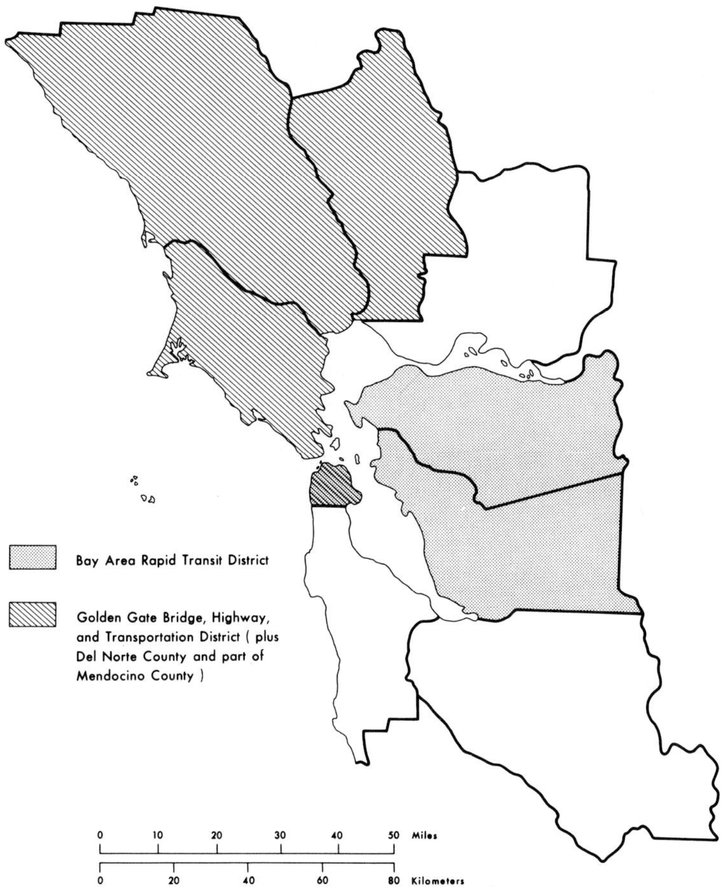

Figure 11-8. Special Districts in the San Francisco Bay Area

one reason why the governor's simple solution has not been used. A more likely way out would be a third level of government above the municipalities and counties, a regional government consolidating the present special purpose districts and ABAG, plus a few additional powers. California Tomorrow, a progressive lobbying organization, proposes such a solution and the Metropolitan Council of the Twin Cities Area is available as a model.

Greater Los Angeles. Second in population among American metropolitan areas, Los Angeles is the archetype twentieth century American city. Developed in the automobile age, it stretches on its skeleton of expressways from the Pacific Ocean to the San Bernardino Mountains. Man has transformed the Southern California landscape, and that transformation has essentially been a twentieth century event. Depending on the definition employed, the area possesses up to 11 million inhabitants, fully double its 1950 population. The main center of activity is downtown Los Angeles, but other important nodes exist as well. These include such long-standing independent cities as Long Beach, Pasadena and San Bernardino, as well as the new skyscraper complexes of Newport Center and Century City.

Politically, Southern California has a long history of strong local control. Municipal home rule charters began in the nineteenth century, and Los Angeles County became the first county in the nation to receive a home rule charter when it was so honored in 1912. This gave Los Angeles County greater freedom for independent action than normally bestowed upon California counties.

The metropolitan authority certified as the A-95 clearinghouse in Greater Los Angeles is the Southern California Association of Governments (Figure 11-9). Its jurisdiction covers six counties, 148 municipalities, over 38,000 square miles and a 1972 population of 10.35 million people. Its area exceeds that of 13 states and it has more inhabitants than 44 states. Significantly, SCAG is a voluntary organization. Over 30 eligible muncipalities do not belong and the vast majority of these are right in Los Angeles County. One Southern California county—San Diego—is out of SCAG's jurisdiction. San Diego County has its own council of governments.

In a region as complex as Southern California, defining an appropriate jurisdiction for a metropolitan authority is a difficult problem. Los Angeles County, with seven million people of its own, is certainly large enough if an agency producing economies of scale is desired. It is not large enough to encircle the whole built-up area, however. Bricks-and-mortar Los Angeles sprawls into all of SCAG's counties except Imperial. The situation is complicated by the fact that each county possesses expanses of undeveloped, and for all practical purposes undevelopable, areas. Mammoth San Bernardino and Riverside counties have their populations concentrated in their western portions adjacent to Los Angeles. The remainder of each of those counties is essentially empty mountains and desert. Imperial County does have development links with the Coachella Valley in eastern Riverside County, but it joined SCAG as much to keep from being dominated by San Diego as from any sense of identity with Los Angeles. In essence, a comprehensive metropolitan Los Angeles need not have the expansive territory SCAG covers. It has that area because counties are its building blocks and Southern California counties are huge. At the same time, Los Angeles County is inappropriate as a metropolitan government, despite its great size, because the urbanized area of greater Los Angeles extends into Ventura, San Bernardino, Riverside and Orange counties.

Local government activity in Southern California centers around two gigantic governmental concerns and this fact has affected SCAG's status. Los Angeles County has more people than any other county in the nation,

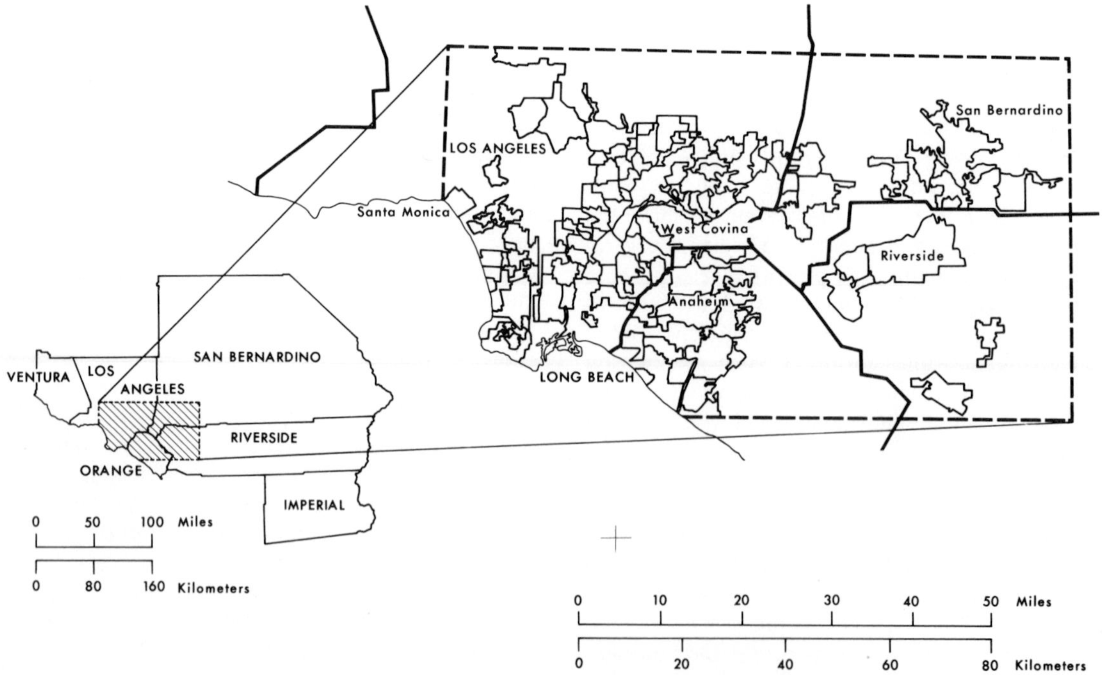

Figure 11-9. Southern California Political Boundaries

and the city of Los Angeles ranks third among American municipalities, behind only New York City and Chicago. Other authorities are respectfully fearful of this pair of giants.

The Los Angeles County Board of Supervisors is jealous of SCAG's advances and lobbies against extending SCAG's powers. This is largely because the supervisors are powerful men who do not relish yielding that power, and because Los Angeles County, in conjunction with its neighbors, does have a record as an innovator in overcoming jurisdictional problems. The board of supervisors consists of only five individuals, each serving over 1.4 million constituents. Not only do these men serve larger constituencies than United States Congressmen and one-third of the United States Senators, they also have responsibility for an enormous budget. In addition, the supervisors act as ex officio commissioners for several key countywide functions such as air pollution control, fire protection and flood control. It is easy to understand the supervisors' reluctance to lose this power to a competing agency, even one in which they have representation.

The supervisors' protective attitude is even more understandable when Los Angeles County's record for solving jurisdictional problems is examined. In the first place, the county is so large that it may effectively internalize the impact of many of its functions. The county is large enough for the benefits of such services as the county park system to accrue primarily to county residents. It is large enough to use sophisticated management techniques and attain economies of scale. It has also been quick to act when the state authorizes new functions. The county was quick to form an air pollution control district, for example.

A second way Los Angeles County has successfully solved jurisdictional difficulties is through the use of its power to offer municipal services and its power to enter into contracts with other governmental units. The consequence is the famous Lakewood Plan, named after the first municipality to purchase most services from the county rather than provide those services itself. Under the Lakewood Plan, a municipality contracts with the county, or another organizaton, for the provision of a service. This allows the purchasing authority to obtain a service without having to develop a supply system all its own. The Lakewood Plan also allows the selling authority to attain economies of scale and fiscal equivalence, and it may minimize problems of service delivery in border areas. Los Angeles County's list of services provided to cities in the county in 1972 included 58 functions and all 77 municipalities. The Lakewood Plan provides local control of an activity by allowing local officials to decide whether or not to purchase a service and, in the event service is purchased, permitting those officials to choose the vendor. The plan also may reduce unit costs to the citizens because the vendor often achieves scale economies.

Largely because of the role of Los Angeles County, Donald Lief was able to conclude that, "[w]hen it comes to decisions of broad community impact, Los Angeles has mastered the art of gradualism." By this he meant that compromise was gradually reached so that a service could be provided, a problem overcome. Thus the governments of Southern California banded together to bring water from the Colorado River, and thus the city of Los Angeles and county of Los Angeles jointly developed two sewage disposal networks based on engineering principles rather than strictly adhering to political boundaries.

All this considered, Los Angeles County naturally regarded itself as the regional government, and when regional planning began receiving federal support, the county renamed its planning arm the Regional Planning Commission. There are many public functions, however, for which Los Angeles County's territory is inappropriate. Like Dade County, Los Angeles County is large enough; however, its boundary simply encloses too much unnecessary mountain and desert and leaves out too much suburb.

Eventually a competitor for regional attention arose in response to the availability of federal funds for councils of governments in metropolitan areas. Officials from muncipalities and counties in Greater Los Angeles formed the Southern California Association of Governments in October 1965. When the federal government sought one metropolitan represenative to review grant applications and develop plans for Greater Los Angeles, it chose SCAG. Los Angeles County was no longer wide enough in jurisdiction to mount a successful attack on regional problems, whether coordinating traffic flows into Orange County and public utilities along the Ventura County line, or preventing the ignominious air pollution Los Angeles daily bestows upon San Bernardino and Riverside. The territory of Los Angeles County no longer matches the territory of Greater Los Angeles. That of SCAG is wide enough, even wider than necessary.

SCAG is a voluntary council of governments and it suffers from all the limitations to which COGs are subject. It has no taxing power of its own. Its members may withdraw simply by presenting a 30 day notice to that effect. It has no development powers of its own. Add to this the fact that many of those local government representatives serving SCAG prefer inaction and the sum is a weak organization, the weakest among the metropolitan areas examined in this study. This weakness was especially true when federal officials were satisfied with SCAG's comment that applications for federal grants were not in conflict with regional plans. Such a statement was automatically true until SCAG developed those regional plans, and this it was hesitant to do. An additional weakness is that federal regulations require that a clearinghouse represent the bulk of the people in an area. Were either the city or county of Los Angeles to exit, SCAG's A-95 certification would be jeopardized.

SCAG's foot-dragging on its development plans has ceased and its status may be changed by the state legislature to a compulsory rather than voluntary organization. These two items raise expectations of more metropolitan impact by SCAG in the future. In part as a result of federal and state prodding, SCAG has now produced a number of comprehensive plans for services in the area and it is working on several others. Among these are plans for housing, transportation and open space. Given its power as an A-95 authority, SCAG could become a strong organ for marshaling metropolitan effort to solve metropolitan problems. It has not really done this in the past, but the future suggests better performance.

SCAG is not the only regional organization serving Southern Califrnia. The federal Environmental Protection Agency has defined a multicounty South Coast Air Basin and legislation is before the state to match that with a state-backed agency. In 1973 the voters of the state passed an initiative creating a system of commissions to manage development of California's coastline, including one for the Greater Los Angeles area. That commission—the South Coast Coastal Commission—consists of representatives of municipal and county governments, as well as citizens appointed from environmental and development interest groups. An additional metropolitan agency of special function nature is the Metropolitan Water District, which brings Colorado River water to Southern California.

Other purportedly regional agencies, such as the Southern California Rapid Transit District, are in actuality limited to a single county, in SCRTD's case to Los Angeles County. This limits their ability to solve regional planning and service delivery problems; hence SCAG's jurisdiction over the development of an area-wide transportation plan.

The political space of Greater Los Angeles is not static, it just does not change as quickly or often as social and economic patterns in the region. Los Angeles' urbanized area is still expanding, especially in those counties adjacent to Los Angeles County. SCAG's minimal influence appears to be increasing and questions about the violability of present boundaries are being asked. If confidence in a regional approach grows and/or satisfaction with the traditional governmental structure decreases, substantial change in the next decade is possible. The immense size of the area lobbies against a general purpose government at the regional level. A restricted multipurpose government is more plausible. Otherwise there would be an enormous gap between the municipal level and the regional level if the latter replaced the counties.

Southern California is complex and possesses strong attachment to local control. The area-wide mechanism of governance now in existence is one of the weaker ones in American metropolitan areas. SCAG is still voluntary and owes its power to the federal A-95 process. Metropolitan governance in Greater Los Angeles contains minimal power to coordinate regional activities and it includes virtually no provision for establishing regional priorities. The indirect rule of those organizations serving the region minimizes the responsiveness to the populace, as does the fragmented nature of those organizations.

Greater Los Angeles is so large that regional entities need not be formed to attain economies of scale. Regional governance is necessary for functions—such as transportation and open space planning—whose requisite breadth crosses county boundaries. This wider approach is also necessary to overcome externalities in some spheres. For this reason Los Angeles County's Air Pollution Control District, which has not controlled air pollution, has been joined by a federal agency dealing with the same problem. Among the five metropolitan areas examined in this monograph, metropolitan governance is easily most weakly developed in Los Angeles, and it is likely to stay that way for the foreseeable future.

The Records Compared. The set of case studies shows that the transformation of the political organization of space is an on-going process in metropolitan America, that the federal inducements encouraging change are indeed leading to change and that both problems and progress vary considerably from city to city. Each of the five regions has strengthened its metropolitan governance substantially over the last couple decades and the trend is in the same direction. Where metropolitan governance existed, federal assistance has strengthened it, and where it had not yet developed, federal nudging helped it come to life. Three of the study areas—Miami, the Twin Ciites and Atlanta—have fairly imposing metropolitan authorities, and the other two have at least some metropolitan planning and special purpose districts. The differences among the cities are in large measure due to state action or inaction.

Perhaps the most important lesson a comparison of the five regions generates is that each area requires a solution tailored to solve its own problems. If problems are similar, the same suit may fit, perhaps with a few alterations. Otherwise, transferring the successes of one region to another may invite disappointment. The more alike two metropolitan areas are in the morphology of development, patterns of circulation, size, legal structure and physcial environment, the easier it will be to transfer a successful system of metropolitan government from one to the other.

Miami's urban county approach would not be useful for the other four areas studied, nor would it be appropriate in most large metropolitan areas. If a county is large enough to encompass the entire built-up area of a metropolis and the closely connected fringe, then the urban county is a very attractive way of achieving a metropolitan scale. But, as Miami itself is learning, the urban county is inadequate if the county fails to enclose the entire metropolis. The county cannot then control metropolitan activity, because part of the metropolis is beyond the county's purview. The urban county is an attractive option for metropolitan governance in that it demands little change in the status quo and allows the retention of municipalities for local problems. Many smaller metropolitan areas would be well advised to employ an urban county form of government to achieve a sound metropolitan scale.

The approaches devised for the Twin Cities and Atlanta provide alternatives for attaining a metropolitan scale in multicounty metropolitan areas. As such, each of these forms would be applicable in a great many metropolitan areas, particularly the larger ones which usually include several counties. Neither of these areas is blessed with the general purpose metropolitan government that Miami has, but each of them has an authority fully encompassing the effective metropolis. In both the Twin Cities and Atlanta, the municipalities and counties survived the creation of the metropolitan authorities intact and this survival reduced the resistance to change.

Both the Twin Cities and Atlanta approaches, or even a stronger multicounty regional government, merit consideration in both the San Francisco Bay Area and Los Angeles. The Bay Area is blessed with a number of excellent special purpose districts, but ordering priorities and coordinating activities is difficult with no strong regional authority. The Atlanta approach, with local government represented, is appealing because it assures local government involvement. The Twin Cities model is stronger, but perhaps not strong enough, as lobbying for increased power for the Metropolitan Council contends.

Greater Los Angeles also needs a multicounty approach, but that region may also need a redefinition of county boundaries. Los Angeles County is a gigantic entity with over seven million people, yet it does not cover much of the built-up area of the metropolis. One solution would be to swap the mountains and desert for the adjacent built-up area. A multicounty regional government for Southern California would be larger than several states both in area and population so it seems prudent to include only those areas really a part of the metropolis, not the desert communities north and east of the mountains. The greatest contribution to the good governance of American cities which Los Angeles has to offer is the Lakewood Plan for providing municipal services. At the metropolitan level, the area has so far outgrown its political institutions that the whole boundary structure and county system should probably be formulated. This would require action by the state of California.

The five areas studied show that there is a need for metropolitan action. Many problems, such as cleaning up the environment and managing the metropolitan transportation system, call for a concerted metropolitan effort. The cities under examination also show that metropolitan governance works. It makes it easier to get areawide problems solved, as in the case of the Twin Cities water quality problems. This is not to say that metropolitan governance in these cities is adequate. It is not, particularly in the California cities. Progress has been made, and that progress can be followed by appropriate transfer of solutions to similar cities and by development of new solutions to unsolved problems.

In the five case study areas, the functions performed at the metropolitan level are primarily those which cannot be effectively performed within the restricted boundaries of municipalities and counties. These are the functions requiring metropolitan breadth—such as regional open space and transportation planning. The transfer of these functions to metropolitan organizations may occur as a result of dissatisfaction with antecedent authorities or as submission to federal or state pressure.

Functions needing a metropolitan scale for other reasons—externalities, economies of scale or fiscal disparity—are less likely to be organized at the metropolitan level. These functions require recognition of a metropolitan community and home rule tendencies lobby against this recognition. Unless the well-being of many constituencies is threatened, as may be the case when water is polluted, control over most functions in these categories is likely to remain splintered. Likewise, low cost public housing tends to remain the burden of central cities and inefficient facilities tend to be maintained at uneconomically small sizes.

Having public activities organized at the metropolitan level is one thing. Coordinating metropolitan activities is another, and this is an additional area in which the case study areas are weak. Special purpose districts abound in American cities, and this dissipates coordination opportunities. Most metropolitan areas—San Francisco and Los Angeles among them—lack a regional overview which effectively ties governmental agencies together. Consequently, cost-cutting opportunities are missed and overhead costs are needlessly boosted.

This criticism holds as well, in most American cities, with regard to establishing priorities for metropolitan development. An agency with the power to set priorities is required before priorities can be rationally assessed and established, and most metropolitan areas lack agencies with that power.

As presently constituted, the governance of metropolitan America can hardly be called responsive to citizen demands. This is partly because there is no unfettered political process for measuring that demand—no metropolitan elections or referenda. It is partly because most metropolitan areas have governmental structures so complex that it is impossible for most citizens to keep abreast of developments. General purpose metropolitan government reduces this complexity, and consequently Miami, with its general purpose metropolitan government, compares favorably.

Taking questions of metropolitan breadth, spillovers, economies of scale, coordination, priorities and responsiveness into consideration, the metropolitan governance of urban America leaves much to be desired when it comes to delivering goods and services. The record of redistribution is even poorer. The only significant redistribution program is that of the Twin Cities, and even there it is only a portion of nonresidential revenues which is shared.

The five urban regions studied in this chapter share youth, rapid growth and federal programs. They differ in area, population, configuration and local government structure. Most important among their differences is action by the states. Georgia and Minnesota legislated change. Florida authorized change in a climate welcoming reform. California has concentrated its activity at the county and municipality level and metropolitan governance in the state has suffered. Improvements in the governance of American cities will doubtlessly require action by the states.

RECOMMENDATIONS

Progress—in many places significant progress—has been made in the achievement of a metropolitan view in the governance of American cities. Still, the political organization of urban America lags behind the constantly changing social and economic organization of the society. A number of steps are available for shortening that lag. Some are steps at the federal level, others are appropriate at the state level and many should be taken at the level of the metropolis itself.

Federal incentives deserve much of the credit for the stength of existing metropolitan authorities, feeble as they may be. Federal funds for specified metropolitan functions coupled with requirements of metropolitan cooperation for the receipt of other funds have induced the formation of a layer of metropolitan agencies across the land. The federal government is in a unique position to further the development of metropolitan cooperation because it alone can affect all cities. If American cities are to be governed effectively in the years to come, that cooperation is essential. The federal government should further metropolitan governance by taking four steps:

- continue and augment the Planning Notification and Review System,
- provide revenue sharing for the metropolitan level,
- establish more powerful regional agencies in the multistate metropolitan areas, and
- implement national land use planning so that discrete metropolitan areas do not coalesce.

The first step should be taken because the clearinghouse review system effectively assures the consolidation of the metropolitan impact of local projects. Weakening the A-95 review process would undermine much of the progress which has been made in metropolitan governance. The review process should be retained and, as they are developed by the federal government, new programs should go under the review procedure.

Revenue sharing for the metropolitan level would reflect the social and economic reality of the metropolis as a major level or organization in the United States. It would ease the burden of the rise in power of this increasingly important level of public activity. It would also assure that revenue sharing would strengthen rather than weaken metropolitan governance. Revenue sharing which is limited to municipalities and counties threatens to reverse the trend toward more metropolitan decisionmaking. That is a reversal the nation can ill afford.

Strengthening multistate metropolitan authorities would help the people in those areas catch up with the rest of the nation. The role of the state is a crucial factor in the strength of metropolitan authorities and states have been reluctant to bestow much power on metropolitan authorities in the multistate urban areas. The federal government should provide supplementary funds in the multistate areas so that no state feels fiscally threatened and the federal government should toughen its requirements for cooperation to assure compliance.

One of the major problems bedeviling metropolitan areas—in the Northeast in particular—is the coalescence of metropolitan areas. This produces complex patterns of interaction and consequently very difficult problems in the provision of metropolitan services. Metropolitan governance is enhanced if coalescence is evaded. Federal land use policy should prevent the coalescence of metropolitan areas. This could be accomplished along the lines of London's green belt or the Rhine-Ruhr's green strips. The result would be the maintenance of each metropolitan area's individuality.

Through these four steps—continuation and augmentation of the Planning Notification and Review System, provision of revenue sharing for metropolitan authorities, addition of power for multistate metropolitan agencies and implementation of land use planning to prevent urban coalescence—the federal government could continue the trend toward sounder, more effective governance of urban America.

The federal role in the strengthening of metropolitan governance is necessary but insufficient. The states are the masters of the governments within their boundaries, whether general purpose cities or counties, or special purpose districts. The continued transformation of political space requires continual participation by the states. The states could strengthen metropolitan governance by:

- providing financial assistance, both in the form of a fiscal disparity formula within the metropolis and funds for a metropolitan government;

- strengthening regional planning, as many states have done, by legislating membership by local municipalities and counties, and by matching the jurisdiction of the regional authority with state planning and service districts over the same territory;
- increasing the fluidity of political space by making amalgamation, incorporation and annexation easier;
- requiring periodic review of governmental activities and areas;
- controlling land development to prevent coalescence of metropolitan areas; and
- cooperating in multistate metropolitan areas.

Financial assistance from the state would remove some roadblocks to the establishment of effective metropolitan governments. State aid could allow the development of metropolitan programs without increasing the tax load on local government sources. A revenue-sharing program within the metropolis could also assist local government and boost awareness of the metropolitan whole.

Strengthened regional planning agencies would be able to accomplish their tasks more readily. If local governments could not opt out they could not deny the regional authority its due attention—and its due financial support. "Piggybacking" regional planning areas and state service districts would increase the coordination among the layers of government within the state and this should have big dividends in both efficiency and effectiveness.

If it were easier to change political boundaries, it would be easier to maintain political units matching social desires. Appropriate areas could be brought within the scope of the metropolitan authority as the metropolis spreads out and municipalities could adjust to changing social geography.

Compulsory review of local government, including metropolitan government, would mean that governmental patterns would not survive merely because of inertia. If adequate, they could be retained. If inadequate, appropriate changes could be made. Governmental boundaries should not be sacrosanct, particularly when they interfere with the performance of governmental duties.

The argument for metropolitan land use control is the same as that for federal land use control. The coalescence of metropolitan areas produces numerous problems and it is a situation to be avoided. State planning should be designed to prevent coalescence, so that those problems are indeed avoided.

The states have the power over local governments within their boundaries, so increased power for multistate authorities presupposes state cooperation. These areas are lagging behind the rest of the nation in the quality of metropolitan governance and the states should act to overcome this. The states should cooperate with one another and the federal government so that the multistate metropolitan areas may have the high quality of governance needed in all metropolitan areas.

That high quality metropolitan governance demands further steps at the level of the metropolis. Of particular importance are, first, searching the alternatives to find the pattern of political organization appropriate for the area and, second, to govern well. The best political organization of space possible counts nil if the quality of public decisions is poor. Each metropolis needs a way of choosing political representatives which will allow the various groups in the area to be heard and which will allow decisions to be made. The spatial organization should consider the patterns of development and movement into and through the metropolis. The division of responsibilities in the metropolis should reflect the social and economic realities of the area. Strong local government should be assured so that no group feels disenfranchised by metropolitan government.

Metropolitan areas which lie totally within a single county should seriously consider an urban county form of government. This approach to the provison of metropolitan goods and services allows the retention of strong municipalities, making it a more desirable choice than city-county consolidation. Except where the counties are unusually large—as in San Diego, Phoenix and Jacksonville—the urban county is applicable only for small metropoltan areas, particularly those below 250,000 people. Most metropolitan areas below that figure contain only one county, so the urban county approach would be a good way of strengthening metropolitan governance.

Metropolitan areas which extend beyond a single county—which include most of the larger ones—need a more encompassing approach than the urban county. The strongest form of metropolitan governance would be a federated system which would divide responsibilities between a territorywide metropolitan authority and municipalities. The metropolitan government could be formed by amalgamating counties if appropriate or by taking parts of adjacent counties if not. Federation would be a radical step if it completely erased longstanding boundaries and such a radical step may be politically unpalatable. If so, the large metropolitan areas should turn to other alternatives.

Most commendable among these "other" alternatives is the establishment of an umbrella government overseeing activity of metropolitan-wide impact and implication. The Twin Cities' and Atlanta's metropolitan authorities are variants of this. Other metropolitan areas would be wise to watch the progress of those two areas, particularly if the Twin Cities Metropolitan Council is strengthened as anticipated.

What is important is not that a blueprint be provided so that all cities share the same perfect solution to their metropolitan problems, but rather, that each urban region find a governmental structure which will enhance the quality of its public sector performance. Each city needs a political organization of space tailored to fit its particular social and economic realities.

CONCLUSION

The political organization of space lags behind the social and economic patterns of a society. Social and economic change are continual and sometimes imperceptible. Changes in political organization are more cumbersome and discrete. As the public sector increases in importance, it is more and more important that government be effective. Political change should follow social and economic change so that a society can be well served. The inertia of political organization often means that reaction to a great problem is required before a system is adjusted. The decisionmaking process should be eased so that it is easier to keep the political organization of space tuned to the ever changing social and economic organization of space. Only in that way will the form of jurisdictions fit the functions of the vibrant metropolis.

Rapid metropolitanization has swept across the United States in this century. The political system has lagged far behind social and economic transformations. The federal programs of the last two decades broke the inertia of governmental boundaries and duties, and some states have added changes of their own. As the case studies, particularly those of the Twin Cities, Miami and Atlanta, have shown, some cities have progressed in the modernization of their political maps. As those cases and, even more so, the cases of San Francisco and Los Angeles show, much more needs to be done before effective, responsive metropolitan governance is assured for America's metropolitan areas.

Given the way power is divided in the American political system, the main agents of continued metropolitan change are likely to be the federal government and the states, the former because it can affect all cities, the latter because they have the power to transform the jurisdictional maps of metropolitan areas and because they should know enough about their metropolitan areas to devise appropriate governmental machinery for those areas.

It has been said of American cities that it is, indeed, impossible to govern them. This impossibility may be, instead, just a lack of imagination and an unwillingness to change. Metropolitan America needs metropolitan governance, and stronger metropolitan governance than it now has. Progress has been made, certainly, but if America's cities are to have governmental structures which will allow the solution of the great problems confronting them, further changes will have to be made. This would not guarantee good government, just make it possible. We cannot afford to be without that possibility.

BIBLIOGRAPHY

Bergman, Edward Fisher. "Metropolitan Political Geography: Achieving Areawide Systems." Doctoral dissertation, University of Washington, 1971.

Berry, Brian J.L. and Frank E. Horton. *Geographic Perspectives on Urban Systems.* Englewood Cliffs, N.J.: Prentice-Hall, 1970.

Berry, Brian J.L.; Peter G. Goheen; and Harold Goldstein. *Metropolitan Area Defini-*

tion: A Re-evaluation of Concept and Statistical Practice. US Bureau of the Census Working Paper. Washington, D.C.: US Bureau of the Census, 1968.

Bodovitz, Joseph E. "Regional Priorities and Resources." In *Adapting Government to Regional Needs,* edited by Stanley Scott and Harriet Nathan, pp. 68–71. Berkeley: Institute of Government Studies, University of California, 1971.

Carruthers, W.I. "Memorandum on the Delimitation of Greater London." In *Report of the Royal Commission on Local Government in Greater London, 1957–60,* pp. 341–53. London: Her Majesty's Stationary Office, 1960.

Forstall, Richard and Victor Jones. "Selected Demographic, Economic, and Governmental Aspects of the Contemporary Metropolis." In *Metropolitan Problems,* edited by Simon R. Miles, pp. 5–69. Toronto: Methuen, 1970.

Frieden, Bernard J. *Metropolitan America: Challenge to Federalism.* Advisory Commission on Intergovernmental Relations, M-31. Washington, D.C.: ACIR, 1966.

Haar, Charles M. "A Federal Role in Metropolitanism." In *Reform of Metropolitan Government,* edited by Lowdon Wingo, pp. 57–88. Baltimore: Resources for the Future, 1972.

Hall, Peter. "The Relationship Between Physical and Economic Planning." *Geographical Journal* 136, 1 (March 1970): 12–15.

Lief, Donald W. "Communities: Lethargy in Los Angeles." *City,* 2, 4: 33–38.

Mogulof, Melvin B. *Governing Metropolitan Areas: A Critical Review of Councils of Governments and the Federal Role.* Washington, D.C.: Urban Institute, 1971.

Olson, Mancur, Jr. "The Principle of 'Fiscal Equivalence': The Division of Responsibilities Among Different Levels of Government." *American Economic Review* 59, 22 (May 1969): 479–87.

Richter, Albert. *Alternative Approaches to Governmental Reorganization in Metropolitan Areas.* Advisory Commission on Intergovernmental Relations, A-11. Washington, D.C.: ACIR, 1963.

Tiebout, C.M. "A Pure Theory of Local Expenditures." *Journal of Political Economy* 64, 5 (October 1956): 416–24.

US Bureau of the Budget. Circular A-95, July 1969 (Revised, Office of Management and Budget, March 1973).

Williams, A. "The Optimum Provision of Public Goods in a System of Local Government." *Journal of Political Economy* 74, 1 (February 1966): 18–33.

Chapter 12

Progress Toward Achieving Efficient and Responsive Spatial-Political Systems in Urban America

David R. Reynolds
University of Iowa

INTRODUCTION

In the United States federal system it should not be surprising that national goals pertaining to governance in urbanized areas, if forthcoming at all, would be highly generalized, flexible and even ambiguous. We commonly think of the US federal system as being comprised of three tiers—federal, state and local. According to the US Constitution, however, this "system" is actually comprised of only two tiers—the federal government and the several state governments. Article X (Bill of Rights) specifies that powers not delegated to the federal government, nor denied it by the states, are specifically reserved to the states or to the people. According to John F. Dillon's famous rule, local governments owe their origin to, and derive their powers and rights wholly from, the respective state legislatures. Although about half the states have written local "home rule" provisions into their constitutions, in general, the state reins on local government remain short and can be tightened upon the whim of their legislatures. Urban political systems are then, at least legally, the creations of the states. This has had the result of introducing a great deal of variation in the structures of local government between states and of acting as a retarding force on the formulation of urban political goals regarding the form and content of local politics.

Prior to the 1950s even generalized national goals pertaining to governance in metropolitan areas were nonexistent. However, in some academic and in "good government" civic circles it was a widely held opinion that a problem of crisis proportions existed in metropolitan America. The dimensions of the problem were thought to be simple: the geography of local government in metropolitan areas was too chaotic for the public interest of the metropolitan community as a whole to be met. The treatment of the metropolitan area as a single community with identifiable interests was rationalized on the grounds that such areas were economic and social wholes bound together by intensive lines of interaction and interdependence. If the dimensions were simple, so, too, was the solution. The "crazy quilt" of independent governmental units should be replaced by an integrated governmental structure in which decisionmaking authority is vested in a single, centralized unit. Only then could the "welfare" of the metropolitan community be maximized. As Scott Greer has emphasized, this "metropolitan problem" was thought to have emerged primarily because the formal boundaries of large cities had failed to keep up with urban growth.

This view of the "metropolitan problem" has its roots, both intellectually and ideologically, in the older, and perhaps better known, municipal reform movement of the late nineteenth and early twentieth centuries. This earlier movement had as its central objectives the destruction of the urban political machines and the "return" of government more directly to the people. The specific structural "reforms" advocated by the reformers included the by now familiar initiative, referendum and recall; the direct primary and proportional representation; at-large municipal elections; the creation of a civil service to eliminate the spoils system; the separation of local issues from state and national influence at the polls by holding nonpartisan elections in "off years"; and the council-manager form of government. In short, the early reformer wished to depoliticize and professionalize municipal politics.

The vitality of the reform movement is attested to by the facts that not a single major city was able to avoid the implementation of at least some of the "reform" proposals and that most middle class Americans have been inculcated with the basic "good government" ethic of these early reformers. As both Greer and Warren suggest, the latter-day reformer, the advocate of metropolitan government, shared both the zeal and the predispositions of his earlier counterpart. Indeed it can be argued that the "new" reformer was an "old" reformer who was frustrated because the traditional administrative and procedural "reforms" could not be implemented on a metropolitan scale until the multiplicity of governmental units in a metropolitan area was eliminated and the governance of the region was reconstituted on a more "rational" basis. In short, the remedies of the old and new reformer were similar, but the "diseases" to which they were to be applied different: the political machine on the one hand and the politically "fractionated" metropolis on the other.

By the early 1950s, the formulation of generalized national urban political goals began to emerge slowly. Academics, the "new" reformers and political leaders were sharply polarized, advocating either increasing centralization or decentralization of governmental control of public service provision in metropolitan areas. However, the advocates of centralization were by far the more numerous and influential. The various centralization arguments tended to rest on geographical complexity, the inappropriateness of Jeffersonian democracy in urban America, "progressive-reform" ideology or inequities in service provision resulting from geographical mismatches between needs and resources. The political economist, Bish, has described the situation as one in which urban political economies and political systems were often described but seldom analyzed. Unfortunately, most descriptions failed to grapple with the complex structure of these systems, degenerating into references to governmental organization as "Balkanized," "fractionated," a "crazy quilt," "chaotic," "absurd," "historical accidents," etc. Such descriptions almost invariably concluded with policy recommendations calling for the consolidation of existing governments into single metropolitanwide governments. Although often filled with overstatement, the early studies of problems of metropolitan governance did serve to point out that most existing systems of government in metropolitan areas were either unable or unwilling to find solutions to public service problems that were metropolitanwide in scope.

In recognition of the need to clarify the roles of state and national governments in helping to secure solutions to such problems the Commission on Intergovernmental Relations (the Kestnbaum Commission) was created by Congress in 1953. The work of this commission culminated in 1956 in a series of recommendations, the essence of which was that the states are the key units for solving areawide problems in metropolitan areas and that they should provide authorizations permitting the creation of general metropolitan units of government. A few states adopted some of the commission's more specific implemental recommendations, particularly those pertaining to annexation, incorporation and interlocal agreements, but none gained widespread acceptance.

With the establishment of the permanent Advisory Commission on Intergovernmental Relations (ACIR) by Congress in 1959, a shift from governmentally supported descriptive to more analytic studies can be noted. A new national policy on metropolitan governmental problems soon began to crystallize. The "reformist" goal of single metropolitan units of government came to be seriously questioned, particularly after the commission analyzed voter reactions to the numerous unsuccessful unification attempts. It was clear that the reform goal of metropolitan government had not struck as vibrant a chord in urban electorates as had earlier reforms. The commission's 1963 report on the optimal performance of local and areawide urban functions by various levels of government signified an important shift in the emphasis of its policy recommendations. Instead of calling for the creation of metropolitan governments, ACIR suggested:

> Many steps can be taken within the present general framework itself by revising arbitrary and outmoded restrictions and making bold use of such tools of intergovernmental relations as metropolitan planning, interlocal contracting, adequate standards to control new incorporations, reasonable annexation laws, and responsible area-wide agencies or contractual arrangements to provide certain services that by nature cannot be handled on a strictly local basis. [p. 24]

In a series of policy studies undertaken between 1963 and 1970, the advisory commission called for strong positive action by state governments (1) to remove constitutional and other legal obstacles that preclude local efforts to meet local demands for public services; (2) to discourage the proliferation of local governments with insufficient resources to meet the service needs of their residents; (3) to limit the growth of single purpose special districts which are not directly accountable to a local electorate; (4) to provide local governments with the authority to cope with problems associated with urban growth; and (5) to foster metropolitan areawide cooperation and coordination through the formation of regional councils of governments (COGs) or other such agencies. In a 1967 policy study of Fiscal Balance in the American Federal System it was also recognized that some local governments were perhaps too large and decisionmaking too centralized to be responsive to the diverse, yet legitimate, service demands of their constitutents. ACIR proposed "model legislation" through which states might authorize large cities and county governments in metropolitan areas *to establish neighborhood subunits of government with limited powers of taxation and local self-government.* Neighborhood subunits of government were seen as an efficacious vehicle by which citizen alienation with large urban governments could be reduced and a sense of community in central cities might be reestablished. The once almost silent voice for decentralization of public policy decisionmaking was to be heard with increasing frequency and voracity after the violent summer of 1967. The demand for a more "participatory democracy" and limited "community control" was, for the first time, clearly designated as an urban political goal equally as valid as the longer-standing goal of facilitating metropolitan areawide cooperation and coordination in certain public services.

By the late 1960s, national goals pertaining to governance in metropolitan areas articulated by the prestigious ACIR can be summarized as: urban governance should become more efficient, effective and accountable. More than two decades of research had reinforced the by then widespread lay impression that many, if not most, urban political systems fared poorly on all three criteria. *Efficiency* refers to technical efficiency in the sense that any government should be expected to deliver public services without wasting resources. *Effectiveness* is a broader concept than efficiency and raises the important issue of priority setting: What does a government do? What services does it provide, at what levels and qualities, to whom, and at what cost to whom? Equity considerations are, therefore, important components of effectiveness. Equity does not necessarily mean that each geographical and/or social group receives equal benefits from government but does imply that the distribution of public services bears some relationship to need. Finally, *accountability* refers to the mechanisms made available by governments for citizens to express their views on government performance and to influence the formulation and enactment of public policy.

The general tone of ACIR's suggestions for achieving the goals of increased efficiency, effectiveness and accountability was one of circumscribed experimentation. Almost any democratically determined change in the geography of local government was to be encouraged if it appeared likely to achieve increases in one or more of these performance criteria without concomitant decreases in the others. The reasons for this are twofold. On the one hand, the federal government is constitutionally prohibited from direct interference with the internal structure of local government in the states. On the other hand, and of equal importance, the fact is that none of these performance criteria is easily measured in any widely accepted and objective manner. In a real sense, therefore, detecting progress in achieving these goals is dependent on arriving at satisfactory measures or indicators of performance on these criteria. Such would need to be relatively easy to obtain and comparable across various governmental units. Quite candidly, at the present time they do not exist. Nonetheless, the question of local government performance is of sufficient importance and urgency to warrant an evaluation of progress even with the crude measures and inferential procedures available. In 1966, 40 percent of all governmental expenditures in the US were accounted for by state and local governments.

Why would a geographer lay any claim to expertise, however partial, in such an evaluation? Surely this is a problem calling for the combined expertise of the economist, the political scientist and the student of public administration. There is truth in this assertion. However, a dominant theme in modern geography is the spatial organization of society. Political systems in metropolitan areas, like all manmade systems in a society, possess spatial organization. Furthermore, although little analyzed by political scientists and others, it is apparent that the spatial organization of a political system is widely perceived to be of import in affecting all three aspects of governmental performance. Witness that almost all postwar proposals for the reorganization of local government in the US have called either for the creation of new geopolitical units, for the consolidation of others, for the reallocation of functional authority between units or for some combination thereof.

There are at least two major ways in which geographic analysis can contribute to the evaluation of local governmental performance. Best developed are analyses of technical efficiency wherein the optimal locational patterns of public facilities for serving a geographically dispersed population with known needs or demands can be specified. Less well developed, but no less important, are analyses more directly concerned with the relationships between the spatial organization of governmental units and the "demand side" of the public service provision question–namely, the interrelated performance dimensions of accountability and effectiveness. In a democracy, assessment of demand and/or need for public services is logically prior to an evaluation of efficiency in service delivery. It clearly makes no sense to deliver the "wrong" or unneeded services, even if delivered efficiently. For this reason an assessment of progress in achieving the goals of increased accountability and effectiveness in the local governance of urban America from the perspective of spatial organization will be the primary theme of this investigation. The issue of technical efficiency will receive attention only in those instances where it seems warranted to presume that questions of public service demand and need are noncontroversial.

This chapter will focus on Los Angeles, St. Louis and Detroit, which are thought to represent a reasonably broad spectrum of metropolitan and local governmental problems. Each contains a large number of local units of government and yet they differ markedly in a number of respects bearing on urban public service provision: (1) they rest wholly or partly within states that differ in the extent to which constitutional change and enabling legislation have made it possible for local governments and their permissible interrelations to change with changing urban environments; (2) they differ in their employment of intergovernmental relations techniques; (3) the geographical and political organizations of their central cities differ; (4) they have quite different patterns of suburban-central city conflict and cooperation. Los Angeles, with its elaborate system of county-city contracting for the delivery of urban services–which some argue should be adopted in other large metropolitan areas–approaches the competitive ideal of some urban economists. St. Louis, with its long history of central city-suburban conflict and numerous unification attempts, is the archetypical "fractionated" metropolitan area of the "reformers." Detroit is a metropolitan area where the hegemony of the municipality as the primary unit of urban public service provision remains unchallenged. Do any of the public service provision systems in these metropolitan areas provide or suggest models that might fruitfully be applied elsewhere in urban America? This is the central policy question to which this chapter seeks an answer.

AN OVERVIEW OF THE SOCIAL, ECONOMIC AND POLITICAL GEOGRAPHIES OF THE THREE METROPOLITAN AREAS

The social, economic and political geographies of the larger metropolitan areas in the United

Table 12-1. Characteristics of Central Cities and Metropolitan Areas

	Los Angeles		*St. Louis*		*Detroit*	
	City	*County*	*City*	*SMSA*[1]	*City*	*SMSA*[2]
Population (1,000s)	2,816	7,032	622	2,363	1,511	4,200
Area (sq. miles)	455	4,083	61	4,118	138	1,952
Population Density, 1970	6,192	1,722	10,163	574	10,949	2,152
Population Change, 1960–1970	13.6	16.4	-17.0	12.3	-9.5	28.5
Nonwhite Population (percent)	22.8	14.6	41.3	16.4	44.5	18.6
Increase in Nonwhite Population, 1960–1970 (Percent)	54.0	75.3	18.6	28.2	38.1	37.6
Change in White Population, 1960–1970 (Percent)	5.4	10.1	-31.6	9.4	-29.1	7.0
Population Under 18 (Percent)	30.2	32.1	3i.8	35.5	32.7	36.4
Population 65 and Over (Percent)	10.1	9.3	14.7	9.8	11.5	8.1
Median Value of Owner-Occupied Housing Units	26,700	24,300	13,200	16,300	15,600	19,600
Median Family Income ($)	10,535	10,972	8,182	10,325	10,045	12,117
Families Below Poverty Line (Percent)	9.9	8.2	14.3	8.1	11.3	6.4

1. The City of St. Louis; St. Louis, Franklin, St. Charles and Jefferson counties in Missouri; and Madison and St. Clair counties in Illinois.

2. Wayne, Oakland and Macomb Counties.

Source: US Bureau of the Census. 1970 Census of Population and Housing.

States are simultaneously similar and dissimilar. Those on which this investigation focuses—Los Angeles, St. Louis and Detroit—are not exceptions. In terms of their generalized social and economic geographies, the metropolitan areas of St. Louis and Detroit conform well to the modern US stereotype (Table 12-1). The poor, black and elderly are concentrated in a densely populated, but declining, central city surrounded by areas of the more affluent, white and young which grade into basically rural, but rapidly "suburbanizing," areas. The Los Angeles metropolitan area, defined here as Los Angeles County, appears to conform less well to this model. Indeed, the popular image of Los Angeles is dominated by two characteristics—its "good life" and "newness." As a result of pursuing a policy of territorial expansion between 1900 and 1930 that is unmatched in US urban history, Los Angeles is, in area, the nation's largest city. By eastern or midwestern standards it is neither "central" to its metropolitan area nor a "city" in the sense of possessing a single core of high density commercial activity. Los Angeles has numerous territorial projections extending out from the old "central" city (Figure 12-1). Indeed, Los Angeles has been aptly described as a cluster of diverse suburbs in search of a central city. However, if one arbitrarily classifies the "central city" to be that areally compact portion of Los Angeles centered on the "original" city, the general social geography of the metropolitan area would much more closely conform with that of Detroit and St. Louis.

Another artifact of Los Angeles' expansiveness is that, by US standards, the city contains a relatively low percentage of blacks—18.4 percent. But the black population is numerically large—over 600,000, is growing rapidly and is highly segregated residentially. The Spanish surname population numbers almost 520,000 and is the largest in North America outside of Mexico City. Both the black and the Mexican-American populations more than doubled in the 1960s. Many of the black newcomers settled in and around Watts, the heart of the black ghetto, in which erupted the first major race riots of the post-World War II period. Many of the Mexican-American immi-

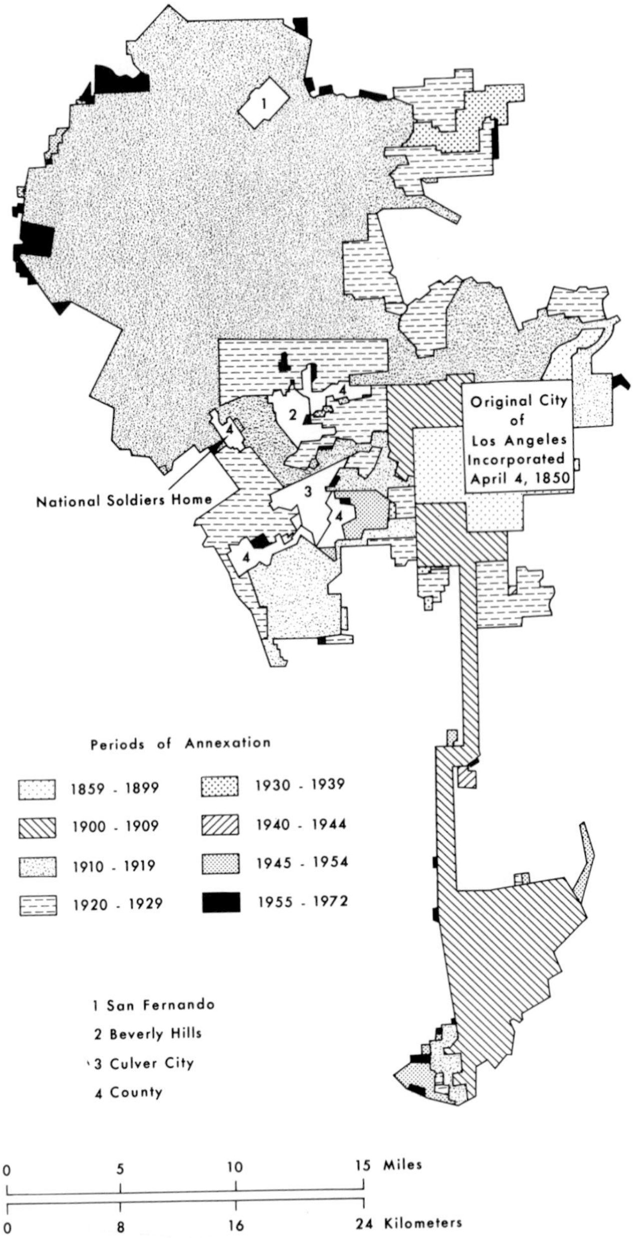

Figure 12-1. Territorial Growth of the city of Los Angeles (adapted from Crouch and Dinerman, p. 161).

grants settled in the *barrios* of East Los Angeles where, in the late 1960s and early 1970s, there have been demonstrations and other signs of increasing frustration. Almost 10 percent of the families in Los Angeles had yearly incomes classified as below the poverty level in 1970. However, as La Noue and Smith phrase it: "Even poverty in Los Angeles has its special quality: the tracts of pastel single-family dwellings in East and Central Los Angeles bake in the sun, dotted with stringy palms, and crisscrossed by freeways." Nevertheless, relative to the "good life" image of the city, the poverty and the segregation are very real and, as a result, Los Angeles, like St. Louis and Detroit, is immersed in its own variety of the "urban crisis."

In many respects the Detroit metropolitan area is a larger, somewhat more affluent version of St. Louis'. The disparities between Detroit and its suburban areas are great and are similar to those in the St. Louis metropolitan area for most of the indicators listed (Table 12-1). Furthermore, they are similar in terms of having central cities with very high concentrations of welfare recipients (approximately 16 percent of the population in each is dependent on some form of public assistance), decreases (in constant dollars) in assessed valuations of taxable property between 1960 and 1970, and high crime rates (60 per 1,000 persons for Detroit in 1968 and 74 per 1,000 persons for St. Louis in 1970). And the list could go on. In some important regards, however, Detroit is quite dissimilar to St. Louis. First, between 1960 and 1970, the nonwhite (essentially black) population of Detroit increased more than twice as rapidly as did that of St. Louis. Second, Detroit has a much larger white ethnic population. Third, it has a much higher incidence of homeownership among both blacks and whites (higher than in Los Angeles or for that matter, in any other major city in the US). Fourth, unlike typical industrial cities in the US, more than half of the housing units in Detroit are single family (Table 12-2). Los Angeles may have its "good life" ethos, but the ethic of individual homeownership was adopted in the Detroit area much earlier than in other US urbanized areas.

All three metropolitan areas have highly segregated housing markets, but the phenomenon of racial invasion and succession in neighborhoods in Detroit has produced considerably more racial antagonism. The high proportion of homeownership is particularly significant since it often means that a home in Detroit represents the lifetime savings of the blue collar Poles, other Eastern Europeans, southern whites and blacks who occupy them—a savings fiercely defended against any loss in value stimulated by the "invasion" of low status blacks. Neighborhood homogeneity is a valued "public good" in urban America, but it is well documented that in Detroit it approaches an obsession.

Unlike both Los Angeles and St. Louis, blacks do not reside in one or two more or less isolated, poverty-ridden ghetto areas. To be sure, large poverty-ridden black ghetto areas exist, but the existence of relatively large and growing black middle class residential areas is a further factor that sharply distinguishes Detroit from St. Louis and, to a lesser extent, from Los Angeles. In the Los Angeles and St. Louis metropolitan areas, black middle class areas are more of a suburban phenomenon.

By implication, St. Louis is archetypical of all that is conjured up by the phrase *urban crisis.* A recent study conducted by Barbara R. Williams for the Rand Corporation analyzed three alternative futures for the city—continued decline, stabilization in a new role as an increasingly black suburb and a return to its former role as the center of economic activity in the metropolitan area. It concluded on the pessimistic note that the most likely prognosis, in the absence of a massive infusion of new revenue from sources outside the city, was con-

Table 12-2. Selected Housing Characteristics, 1970

	Los Angeles		*St. Louis*		*Detroit*	
	City	*County*	*City*	*SMSA*	*City*	*SMSA*
Median Value Owner-Occupied Housing Units ($)	26,700	24,300	13,200	16,300	15,600	19,600
Percentage Single Family Housing Units	52.0	60.9	34.1	66.0	54.4	70.5
Percentage Housing Units Owner-Occupied	40.9	48.5	40.5	64.6	60.0	72.1
Percentage of Households with Black Head Living in Owner-Occupied Housing Units	31.8	37.6	31.3	38.3	51.1	52.3

Source: US Bureau of the Census. 1970 Census of Population and Housing.

tinued decline. Much to the dismay of St. Louis decisionmakers, the Rand report argued that even if new revenue sources do become available, "the analysis suggests that, among the alternatives open to the city, promoting a new role for St. Louis as one of many large suburban centers of economic and residential life holds more promise than reviving the traditional central city functions." There has been no rush to dismantle the Arch—that 630 foot stainless steel monument pathetically attempting to symbolize St. Louis' historical functions as the "gateway to the West"—but it remains one of the few visible expressions of optimism in the City of St. Louis.

The Political Geography of Urban Public Service Provision

In broad purview, the political geographies of the three metropolitan areas are characteristic of the much discussed "metropolitan problem," containing as they do a large number of legally independent, often overlapping, units of local government. Adopting the number of governmental units per 1,000 population as a wide measure of "governmental fragmentation," the St. Louis metropolitan area is roughly two and a half times and four times as fragmented as those of Los Angeles and Detroit, respectively (Table 12-3). In fact, of the SMSAs with 1970 populations exceeding two million, only Pittsburgh has a higher ratio of governments per capita than St. Louis. Since more than two-thirds of the population and one-third of the governmental units in the St. Louis metropolitan area are accounted for by St. Louis County and the city of St. Louis, these two units will be the focus of attention in subsequent discussions of the St. Louis metropolitan area.

There are considerable differences between the three areas in terms of the preponderance of various types of governmental units. St. Louis has by far the largest number of municipalities and on average the "suburban" St. Louis municipalities are much smaller than those in the other two areas. If one considers both villages and cities as municipalities, Los Angeles and Detroit appear, from a spatial-political perspective, to differ primarily in terms of numbers of special districts. However, numbers of various types of units per se fail to convey much information about public service provision in the several metropolitan areas.

The Primacy of the Incorporated Municipality. Historically, the basic provider of urban public services, with the exceptions of elementary and secondary education, in all three metropolitan areas, as elsewhere in the US, has been the municipality. Although municipalities in the three areas derive their legal existence and powers from the constitutional and statute law of the respective states, it is not true in any literal sense that they are the *creations* of state government. Instead, it is more correct to think of state government as providing the legal milieu which *enables* the existence of municipalities or, for that matter, of any unit of local government. The actual creation of municipalities in California, Missouri and Michigan is reserved to the volun-

Table 12-3. Governmental Units in the Three Metropolitan Areas, 1972

	Los Angeles County	*St. Louis SMSA*	*Detroit SMSA*
Total Governmental Units	500	460	224
Counties	1	7	3
Cities	77	173	68
Villages	–	–	17
Townships	–	46	43
Special Districts	341*	131	9
School Districts	81	103	84
Governmental Units per 1,000 Population	0.071	0.195	0.053
Average Population of Suburban Municipalities	37,742	6,692**	24,654
Percentage of Population in Unincorporated Areas	14.6	33.9**	14.6

*Administered by Los Angeles County

**St. Louis County only

Source: US Bureau of the Census. 1970 Census of Population; and 1972 Census of Governments.

tary collective actions of "citizens" in local areas.

In the early 1960s, California and Michigan enacted legislation creating commissions to review proposals for the formation of new municipalities. Such commissions, local in the case of California and statewide in Michigan, have had the effect of discouraging the formation of "tax shelter" industrial cities or other "special purpose" incorporations. Nevertheless, incorporation is still accomplished relatively easily in all three metropolitan areas.

Approximately 85 percent of the populations in the Los Angeles and Detroit metropolitan areas reside in municipalities (Table 12-3). Ironically, the St. Louis metropolitan area, with the highest index of governmental fragmentation and the smallest municipalities, has the lowest proportion of its population residing within municipalities—approximately 66 percent. For the most part, the remaining 34 percent of St. Louis County's population is by no means rural: the population density in the unincorporated portions of St. Louis County in 1970 was a whopping 925 persons per square mile. Clearly, there are options in addition to the municipality for the provision of urban public services in the St. Louis area. In this instance, the options include independent special districts, county governments and local quasi-governmental "improvement associations."

Although the Los Angeles and Detroit metropolitan areas have identical proportions of their populations living in unincorporated areas—14.6 percent—the two areas are quite different in terms of the population characteristics of unincorporated areas. Much of Los Angeles County's 14.6 percent resides in densely populated areas with strong local identities, such as the unincorporated "city" of East Los Angeles. In this respect, Los Angeles and St. Louis counties are quite similar. As in St. Louis County, the residents of densely populated areas also have options for the provision of urban-oriented services in addition to that of municipal incorporation. These are essentially the same as those in St. Louis, but with the important difference that the Los Angeles County government is a much more thoroughgoing municipal service-providing institution than St. Louis County's.

There are very few densely populated unincorporated areas in the Detroit metropolitan area. In 1970, the population density in the unincorporated portions of the SMSA was a relatively low 491 persons per square mile. Of the 43 townships still in existence in the area, only seven had population densities in excess of 1,000 persons per square mile and, of these, only one had a density greater than 2,000. Township governments do not exist in California or Missouri, but in Michigan, as in many states in the eastern United States, townships are locally governed subdivisions of counties organized primarily to serve rural residents with a limited number of services—the assessment and collection of taxes, election administration, and the keeping of vital statistics and records. A few more "urban-oriented" services, such as fire protection and police protection over and above that provided by the county, can, under Michigan law, be provided through township government. However, the taxing authority of townships is so limited that their financing is possible only through special assessments—an instrument impractical for providing services requiring large capital outlays. Whereas the use of independent special districts and authorities has increased dramatically since World War II in the nation as a whole, the Detroit area is notable for their relative absence. Throughout this century, Michigan legislatures have adhered to a philosophy of local government in which the creation of new governmental units is dependent upon the voluntary action of existing units of local government—traditionally cities and townships, but more recently including villages and counties as well. Special districts then have never been a viable alternative to municipal incorporation for meeting the service demands of residents in urbanized areas in Michigan. As will be indicated below, the provision of a wide range of municipal services by counties is not allowed under Michigan law. If a full range of urban services is to be provided publicly, the residents of urbanized areas in Michigan have little choice but to organize themselves into municipalities—either villages or cities. After meeting minimal population and population density requirements, the choice between incorporation as village or city, since the passage of the home rule city and village acts in 1909, has been dictated largely by the expected revenue needs of a community to meet the service demands of its residents and/or a desire for independence from township government. Both home rule villages and cities are subject to the same millage rate ceilings and debt limitations imposed by Michigan law and operate under broad grants of authority in the provision of public services and the exercise of municipal management. They differ primarily in that villages do not have access to as wide a range of nonproperty tax revenues, have less flexibility in their form of government and are not independent of township government for the provision of certain services. In practice, Michigan law differs markedly from that of California or Missouri in its treatment of villages as "half-way" houses between rural-oriented township government and fully urban-oriented city government.

School Districts–Providers of K-12 Public Education. In each of the three metropolitan areas, public education is provided through independent school districts. Districts providing kindergarten through twelfth grade education in the Los Angeles area tend on average to have twice the enrollments of those in the St. Louis and Detroit areas (Table 12-4). The median enrollments in K-12 districts in 1970-1971 were: Los Angeles, 13,231; St. Louis, 6,837; and Detroit, 6,435. Despite large-scale school district consolidation in the post-World War II period, the enrollments of districts vary considerably within each metropolitan area.

In the Los Angeles metropolitan area, the Los Angeles Unified School District dwarfs all other districts both in territorial extent and population. With an enrollment of about 800,000 and a spatial extent well beyond the corporate limits of Los Angeles (to encompass an additional 24 cities), it is the second most populous, and by far geographically the largest school district in the nation. Unlike Los Angeles, the largest districts in the St. Louis and Detroit areas conform perfectly with the boundaries of St. Louis and Detroit. The St. Louis Public School System and the Detroit Public School System, with 1971 enrollments of 300,000 and 110,000 respectively, are also the largest districts in their metropolitan areas. Ironically, outside the Los Angeles Unified School District (and for the enclaves within it), school district boundaries correspond much more closely to municipal boundaries than do those in suburban St. Louis or Detroit. During the 1960s, the number of school districts did not change appreciably in St. Louis County, while in the Detroit area a 20 percent reduction can be accounted for primarily by the consolidation of schools in outlying rural areas. In the Los Angeles area the number of districts has gradually been reduced as the previous pattern of maintaining separate elementary and high school districts has given way to unified K-12 districts.

In all three metropolitan areas, each school district is governed by separately elected boards of education which may levy a property tax and issue bonds with the approval of their constituents. Although direct financial aid from the state governments increased considerably during the 1960s, particularly in Michigan, the property tax remains the mainstay of school district revenues.

Contrasting Roles of County Government. The traditional role for counties in the United States has been that of an administrative sub-

Table 12-4. K-12 School Districts in the Metropolitan Areas by Average Daily Attendance (ADA), 1970-1971

	*Percentage of Districts**		
ADA	*Los Angeles*	*Detroit*	*St. Louis*[1]
Over 50,000	4.8 (2)	1.2 (1)	3.8 (1)
25,000-50,000	11.9 (5)	2.4 (2)	0.0 (0)
15,000-25,000	16.7 (7)	11.9 (10)	11.5 (3)
10,000-15,000	23.8 (10)	7.1 (6)	15.4 (4)
5,000-10,000	26.2 (11)	42.9 (36)	26.9 (7)
2,000-5,000	16.7 (7)	27.4 (23)	26.9 (7)
Less than 2,000	0.0 (0)	7.1 (6)	15.4 (4)

*The number in brackets is the number of districts

1. Includes only St. Louis and St. Louis County

Source: data compiled by the author.

division of the state erected to provide state services at the local level. To varying degrees, this fails to be an adequate description of the functions of county governments in the highly urbanized areas of the United States today. Urban counties have not abandoned their traditional role but most have added a great many more. Some have evolved into genuine units of local government providing service at an areal scale above that of the municipalities. Others have functioned as providers of urban services to residents of newly urbanized or urbanizing areas until such time as residents can organize for their own service provision through municipal incorporation. Still others have evolved into "exporters" of municipal services to other governmental units within their boundaries. When contrasted with the functions of municipalities in urban America, those of counties are incredibly diverse.

Los Angeles County. Beginning in 1912, when, by constitututional amendment, California first authorized counties to provide a wide range of municipal services to unincorporated areas, and in 1914, when they were also authorized to provide certain municipal functions for cities through contractual arrangements, a steady evolution of service provision by Los Angeles County can be traced up through 1954. In that year, Los Angeles County contracted with the newly incorporated city of Lakewood to provide it with a complete set of municipal public services–including law enforcement and fire protection. California state government had aided and abetted this evolution by creating an increasingly flexible legal milieu for units of local government–including counties–to cope with "local" service provision problems. Legislation in the 1920s permitted counties to set up special purpose districts in order to perform almost any type of service for the residents of unincorporated areas. In 1935 legislation also considerably broadened the range of services that counties could provide under contract to cities. Los Angeles County took advantage of practically every authorization available to it, but prior to 1954 concentrated its efforts on providing the residents of unincorporated areas with public services.

The county was serving a population which, after 1920, was increasing more rapidly than that of incorporated areas (Table 12-5). In many areas of the unincorporated portions of Los Angeles County, population distribution and density characteristics were such that they were classified appropriately as de facto cities. Most also had well-defined local identities. It may have been the original intent of county officials to provide these areas with services only until such time as they incorporated. However, the county was so successful in providing public services to unincorporated areas that after 1925 and until 1954 the formation of new cities virtually ceased. Not only did the county provide tangible municipal services to de facto cities but, with the enactment of a 1927 zoning ordinance, it also provided an alternative to incorporation for communities seeking to protect land values and local preferences in land use patterns.

Los Angeles County was also active in expanding its provision of services to municipalities, particularly the smaller ones without already large capital investments in public facilities. By the mid-1920s, not only had it made the County Free Library District available to all municipalities, but it had health service contracts with 19 cities and sewage

Table 12-5. Population of Incorporated and Unincorporated Areas in Los Angeles County, 1900–1950

Year	*Incorporated Areas*	*Percentage Increase*	*Unincorporated Areas*	*Percentage Increase*
1900	129,734	99.7	40,564	6.2
1910	426,274	228.6	77,857	47.9
1920	817,655	91.1	118,800	52.6
1930	1,887,231	130.8	321,261	170.4
1940	2,340,902	24.4	444,741	38.4
1950	3,279,761	40.1	871,926	96.1

Source: data compiled by the author.

service contracts through the various county sanitation districts with at least three cities. Throughout the period 1925 to 1950, the county continuously increased its contracting with cities for land use planning services, the issuance of building permits, building and code inspection services, the enforcement of local animal regulations, and street and highway improvement services. These were all services that were not widely provided by counties—certainly not on a contractual basis—in other metropolitan areas of the United States until the 1960s.

In 1956, after a two year hiatus during which the "city without a payroll," Lakewood, was scrutinized and negotiations entered into with the county by community leaders in the de facto cities, a wave of incorporations occurred (see Figure 12-2). Thirty-two new cities in Los Angeles County have incorporated since 1954, all but two complete or nearly complete contract cities. A contract city, or for that matter any city in Los Angeles County, can choose the level of service provision it desires from the county and then pays the county according to a fee schedule. The schedule purports to cover the full cost of the services provided. A city may contract for as full a range of services and levels as it desires. As Ries and Kirlin have written, "From provider of municipal services in unincorporated areas to encourager of incorporation is both an extraordinary development and a unique role for a county in the United States." By 1970 Los Angeles County was providing municipal services to more than a million residents of unincorporated areas and to the approximately 800 thousand residents of "contract" cities. The importance of the county as a service provider is also reflected in its budget—an expenditure of approximately 2.2 billion dollars in the fiscal year 1970-1971, or roughly four times that of the City of Los Angeles.

St. Louis County. From a spatial-political perspective, one of the more unusual aspects of St. Louis County is that its namesake—St. Louis—is not within its boundaries. The 1875 Missouri Constitution contained two provisions relating to the government of St. Louis. Both were hailed as "advances" in municipal government. The first authorized the city to draft its own charter—the first authorization of municipal home rule in the United States. The second

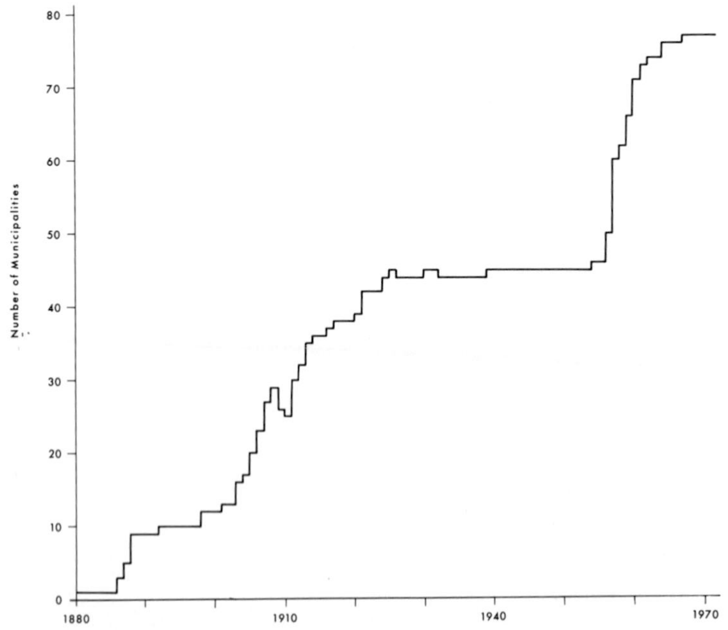

Figure 12-2. Number of Municipalities by Year, Los Angeles County.

permitted St. Louis to withdraw from St. Louis County if majorities in both the city and county were obtained in an election.

In 1876, just prior to the election on city-county separation, St. Louis annexed sufficient rural territory to more than treble its area. The city then had an area of 61 square miles—more than enough, it was thought, to allow for subsequent growth—rendering it then one of the largest cities in geographical extent in the United States. It was already one of the nation's largest cities in population with well over 300,000 inhabitants. In the subsequent election, separation was approved by comfortable margins in both the city and county. In effect, the city of St. Louis became a county in its own right and, as such, was prohibited under the Missouri Constitution from impinging upon the territory of another. The boundaries of St. Louis were "frozen" and it would never annex again.

For the next 75 years, St. Louis County functioned almost exclusively in its traditional role of facilitating the performance of state administrative functions and as a provider of rural-oriented public services, primarily the construction and maintenance of the county road system. Indeed, county officials must have spent much of their time holding elections on municipal incorporation. At the time of city-county separation, the county had a population of approximately 30,000 and contained only three small incorporated places. By 1950 the county had 400,000 inhabitants, almost all of whom resided in one of 88 municipalities. Its politics were typical of the "county courthouse" variety. County provision of urban level police protection, fire protection, sewage disposal and water was unauthorized by law and hence nonexistent. Urban level police protection was provided exclusively by municipalities, whereas fire protection and sewage disposal were provided either by municipalities or by special districts independent of county government. Water was provided largely through private companies.

The present Missouri constitution, adopted in 1945, contains a provision enabling any urbanized county to frame and adopt a home rule charter. It also contains two grants of intergovernment contracting authority to local units of government. The first permits any municipality or political subdivision to contract with other municipalities or units, or with other states or their political subdivisions, or with the national government for the "planning, development, construction, acquisition or operation of any public improvement or facility, or for a common service." The second authorizes a "home rule" county to perform any of the services and functions of any municipality or subdivision of the county, except school districts, when accepted by a majority of the voters in the municipality or other unit. The first grant of contracting authority is ambiguous with regard to counties while the second, with its majority vote in the contracting unit proviso, is less permissive than that which had been granted to home rule counties in California.

In 1950, a home rule charter for St. Louis County was presented to, and passed by, the county's electorate. The charter represented a significant reform in the governmental structure of the county. It gave the county authority to provide municipal level police services, health services, parks and recreation facilities, expanded library services and street maintenance, and to administer county zoning, building and subdivision regulations in all unincorporated areas. It did not grant authority to provide and administer municipal services in incorporated areas. However, the county began to make limited use of the municipal contracting authorization in the state constitution. By the late 1950s the county was providing three types of services to some of the smaller municipalities under contractual arrangements—public health inspection, building inspection and police protection. The extent of county-city contracting was a far cry from the contractual operations of post-1954 Los Angeles County, but it was comparable to the scale of county-city contracting in Los Angeles County in the 1920s.

The more direct effects of county government reorganization were felt in the rapidly urbanizing unincorporated areas of the county. Although the easy incorporation laws of Missouri were essentially unaffected by the 1945 constitution, it was no longer true after 1950 that incorporation was the only practical alternative for residents in many of the newly urbanized or urbanizing areas to be provided with basic levels of public services. A new county police department provided them with protection at a level commensurate with that of most municipalities; the county health department was taking care of their health and sanitation problems; the county department of parks furnished them with recreational facilities and the county libraries with books; the county highway department maintained their streets; and county zoning, building and subdivision regulations helped to preserve their property values. Furthermore, fire protection could be provided by the establishment of a fire district; and the Metropolitan Sewerage District, after its establishment in 1954, was responsible for their sewage disposal (provided they were not in the outlying areas of the county).

By 1970 slightly more than 320,000 persons lived in the unincorporated areas of St. Louis County. This represents more than one-third of the county's population and was an increase of almost 82 percent over the 1960 noncity population. During this time span the population residing in incorporated areas increased by only 20 percent. The creation of new municipalities in St. Louis County did not cease after 1950 (see Figure 12-3), as it had in Los Angeles County from 1925-1954, but county service provision was a sufficiently attractive alternative to have resulted in a diminution in the rate of new incorporations. In 1971 the county, through its various departments and agencies, expended slightly more than $129 million, an increase of more than 300 percent over its expenditures in 1960. On a per capita basis, 1971 expenditures amounted to $136, roughly one-third of those in the City of St. Louis and 45 percent of those in Los Angeles County.

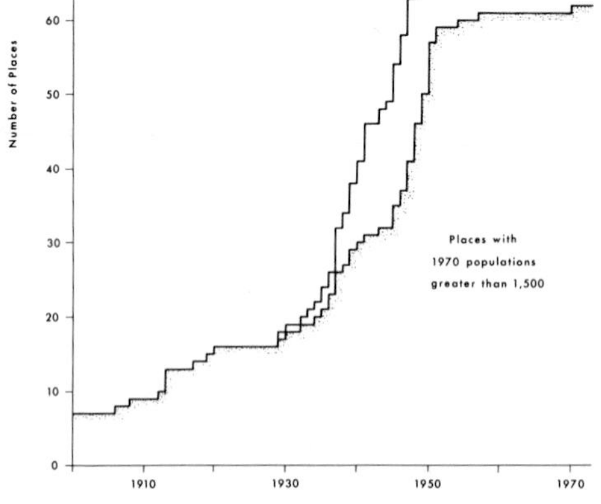

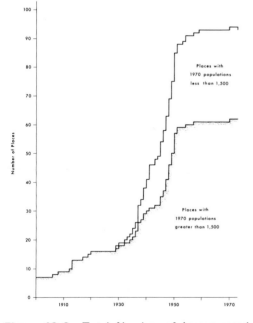

Figure 12-3. Total Number of Incorporated Places in St. Louis County by Year and by Size of Place in 1970.

County Government in the Detroit Area. The philosophy underlying local government in Michigan, as it has evolved under a number of constitutions and under statute law, is paradoxical. While Michigan was one of the earlier states to write into its constitution reasonably broad grants of municipal home rule, Dillon's Rule has been adhered to more steadfastly with regard to county government. Unlike California or Missouri, a Michigan county has no inherent power of self-determination. It has only those powers granted specifically to it by the state constitution and statutes as interpreted by the state supreme court and attorney general. Traditionally, the courts have construed county powers narrowly. In order for a county to exercise a given power, it has been necessary to point to a specific constitutional or statutory authorization.

The question of county government reorganization has been a controversial issue in Michigan politics for at least 40 years. Constitutional amendments proposing county home rule were placed before the voters in 1934, 1936, 1942 and 1944, but were soundly defeated on each occasion. The present Michigan constitution, enacted in 1963, authorizes the people of any county, on a local option basis, to adopt a home rule charter of government. However, this authorization is not self-executing and is dependent upon the enactment of enabling legislation by the state legislature—legislation which has not been forthcoming. The structure and authorities of county government in Michigan have undergone change over the years, but it has been gradual and consistent with the view that the county is an administrative and judicial subdivision of state government.

That the state government and the various municipal governments are the foci of political power in Michigan is attested to by constitutional and statutory provisions which explicitly prohibit a county from enacting legislation superseding state *or* municipal statutes, exercising direct control over planning or zoning, altering any policy set by the state or taking over any function assigned to other units of government. Further evidence of the traditional political "inferiority" of counties is that, prior to 1968, the combined legislative and administrative branch of county government—the board of supervisors—was in effect a "federated" system comprised of one member from each organized township, with representation of cities determined by population size category. Following the 1968 US Supreme Court decision in the case of *Avery* v. *Midland County, Texas,* the Michigan legislature passed an act requiring that each county's governing body be composed of representatives elected, in partisan elections, from districts of approximately equal populations, in accordance with the principle of "one man, one vote." Prior to 1968, the county governing bodies in the Detroit metropolitan area were the largest in the state and were often criticized as unwieldy by public administrators. Wayne County, for example, had 118 "supervisors" in 1965, with a majority of the supervisors appointed by the City of Detroit. In fact, the city government of Detroit literally controlled Wayne County government for the first two-thirds of the twentieth century. In effect, Wayne County undertook only those functions permitted, but not required of it, either at Detroit's suggestion or with its consent.

The number of municipal services that counties in Michigan have been authorized to provide has increased in the past two decades, but remains small when compared with the numbers provided by California counties or even in urbanized Missouri counties. For example, it was not until 1957 that the state legislature authorized urban counties to establish (or acquire) and operate water supply and sewage disposal systems in unincorporated areas. Municipalities can also be included in such systems, but only with their consent unless a majority of the county commissioners determines that the inclusion of a municipality is essential for the protection of health and/or property in an adjacent municipality. In practice, however, and in marked contrast with Los Angeles or St. Louis counties, only *incorporated* areas have been served by county water or sewage disposal systems. In effect, municipalities contract with the county for it to construct *municipal* water and/or sewage systems.

It is not too much of an overgeneralization to state that aside from providing state administrative and traditional rural service functions the three counties in the Detroit area specialize in the provision of services to the residents of municipalities rather than to those in unincorporated areas. Service provision is accomplished primarily through county-city contractual arrangements. There have, however, been some voluntary transfers of responsibility for performing functions from the municipal to county levels. For example, through such voluntary transfers, all three counties in the area have assumed the responsibility of performing public health services in all but a few of the cities within them. The prerogative for municipal service provision, however, remains within the exclusive domain of the individual municipalities. County governments, unlike those of Los Angeles or St. Louis, have made no serious attempts to become providers of municipal services to unincorporated areas. Through the extension of contracting with municipalities for service provision and the voluntary transfer of functions to the county level, the expenditures of the counties in the Detroit metropolitan area have increased dramatically in recent years. In the most highly urbanized county—Wayne—total expenditures in the 1970 fiscal year stood at $630 million, or $236 per capita. This latter figure is intermediate between those of Los Angeles and St. Louis counties but, unlike St. Louis or Los Angeles, the benefits derived from county expenditures were concentrated primarily in cities and villages.

LOCATION, URBAN PUBLIC SERVICE DEMANDS, AND THE GROWTH OF SUBURBS

As noted earlier, state statutes governing incorporation in each of the three metropolitan areas are such that municipalities can be viewed as the voluntary creations of local residents designed primarily for the provision of urban public services. At the turn of the century, urban residents in each of the areas could obtain such services *only* as members of some municipality. Each of the states also provided for the territorial expansion of municipalities into unincorporated areas through annexation and into other incorporated areas through consolidation. Here too, the view of municipalities as voluntary creations has been, and is, dominant. Although annexation and municipal consolidation laws differ in the three states, in all instances the residents of all areas directly affected by a proposed annexation or consolidation are afforded considerable influence in determining whether a merger will take place.

Extension of Service Provision Through Annexation by Central Cities—General Patterns

In the Los Angeles area prior to 1920, in the St. Louis area prior to 1950 and in the Detroit area up to the present time, citizens desirous of receiving urban-type services could move to an incorporated area, they could have their area annexed to an existing city or they could incorporate. In all metropolitan areas, the exercise of one of these options was dependent in part upon the location of residents in the metropolitan area. At the onset of rapid urbanization in each of the three metropolitan areas, when urbanization was focused primarily on the central cities themselves, the extension of service provision through annexation to the central city was dominant. This characterized the St. Louis area until St. Louis's formal separation from St. Louis County in 1876; and the Detroit and, to a lesser extent, Los Angeles areas until the mid-1920s.

Through annexation, Los Angeles and Detroit each grew dramatically in population and in areal extent between 1900 and 1930 (Table 12-6). During this period, the population growth rate of Detroit consistently exceeded that of the remainder of its metropolitan area (see Figure 12-4), indicating that rapid urbanization took place primarily on the immediate periphery of Detroit. In the Los Angeles metropolitan area rapid population growth was much less focused on the periphery of an expanding Los Angeles (Figure 12-5). Instead it was highly decentralized locationally, with secondary foci also in the then outlying cities of Long Beach, Compton, Whittier, Pasadena, Pomona and Santa Monica.

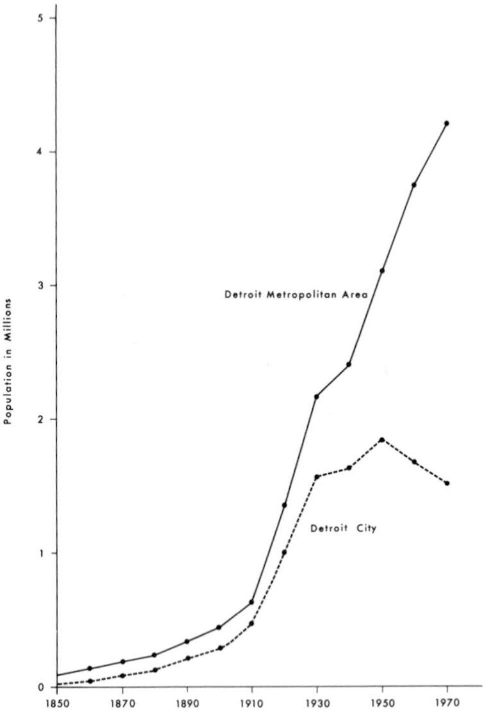

Figure 12-4. Population Growth in Detroit and Its Metropolitan Area: 1850-1970.

Table 12-6. Growth by Annexation in Los Angeles and Detroit

	Area Square Miles		*Population*		*Population per Square Mile*	
Year	*Los Angeles*	*Detroit*	*Los Angeles*	*Detroit*	*Los Angeles*	*Detroit*
1850	28.01	5.85	1,610	21,091	57	3,605
1870	29.21	12.75	5,728	79,577	196	6,241
1880	29.21	16.09	11,183	116,340	383	7,231
1890	29.21	22.19	50,395	205,867	1,725	9,277
1900	43.46	28.35	102,479	285,704	2,358	10,078
1910	100.72	40.79	319,198	465,766	3,169	11,419
1920	364.37	79.62	576,673	993,687	1,583	12,480
1930	441.71	139.02	1,238,048	1,568,662	2,803	11,284

Source: data compiled by the author.

Los Angeles' spectacular territorial expansion failed to keep up with urbanization as well as did the more modest expansion of Detroit.

The expansion of Detroit was accomplished almost exclusively through the annexation of unincorporated areas before they had become highly urbanized. Los Angeles, although also annexing large tracts of essentially rural land, also used its monopoly rights to Los Angeles River water and later those to Owens River water to persuade a number of municipalities and unincorporated communities to consolidate with or be annexed by it. In general, the motivations underlying the use of annexation by Detroit and Los Angeles were strikingly different. In Detroit, the primary use of annexation was to allow for the extension of service provision and the orderly growth of the central city. In Los Angeles, its use was more clearly dominated by territorial imperialism.

The Growth of Los Angeles and Its Suburban Fringe—Territorial Imperialism

Upon the approval in 1905 of the plan by which the City of Los Angeles would construct an aqueduct for the importation of Owens River water, a debate ensued regarding what policy should govern the distribution of "surplus" water in Los Angeles' "water poor" metropolitan area. The issue soon centered on territorial expansion versus increased city revenue. Revenue advocates wanted to market water to extracity communities at the highest price that this "market" would bear, while the "expansion" advocates were determined to utilize the city's monopoly water position to insure the official standing of Los Angeles as *the* metropolis of the West Coast. The expansionist argument held sway and the city adopted the policy (1) that it sell water only to areas that were likely to become a part of the city either by annexation or consolidation; (2) that property owners in the areas desirous of water finance the water distribution systems that would be constructed under the supervision of the city's water engineers; and (3) that each system would become part of the city-owned system once annexation or consolidation was achieved. Under this policy, Los Angeles embarked upon the most ambitious and aggressive program of territorial expansion by annexation and consolidation witnessed in urban America before or since.

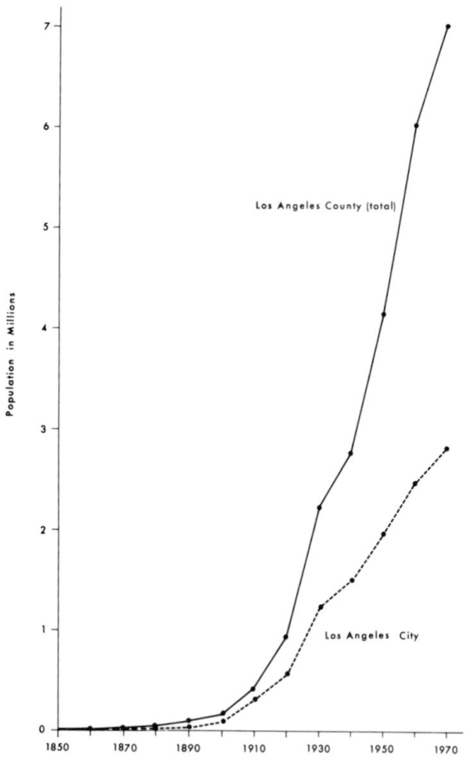

Figure 12-5. Population Growth in Los Angeles County and City: 1850-1970.

Ironically, the territorial expansion of Los Angeles was accompanied by the rapid proliferation of new cities in the area (Figure 12-2). Prior to 1900, 11 cities in addition to Los Angeles had been established. All were geographically distinct, separated from one another by undeveloped land and distant from the corporate limits of Los Angeles. But after 1900 the pattern changed (Figure 12-6). The prime consideration in incorporation proceedings continued to be the desire of local residents for urban services. Increasingly, however, the older and newly established municipalities themselves began to engage in their own annexation drives. It was not uncommon for the residents of an urbanized, unincorporated area to be courted by officials from one or more nearby suburban municipalities as well as by those from Los Angeles. If local identities were strong and an access to a water supply assured, the result was invariably incorporation. Much of the literature on local government has uncharitably and incorrectly referred to such behavior as "defensive" in-

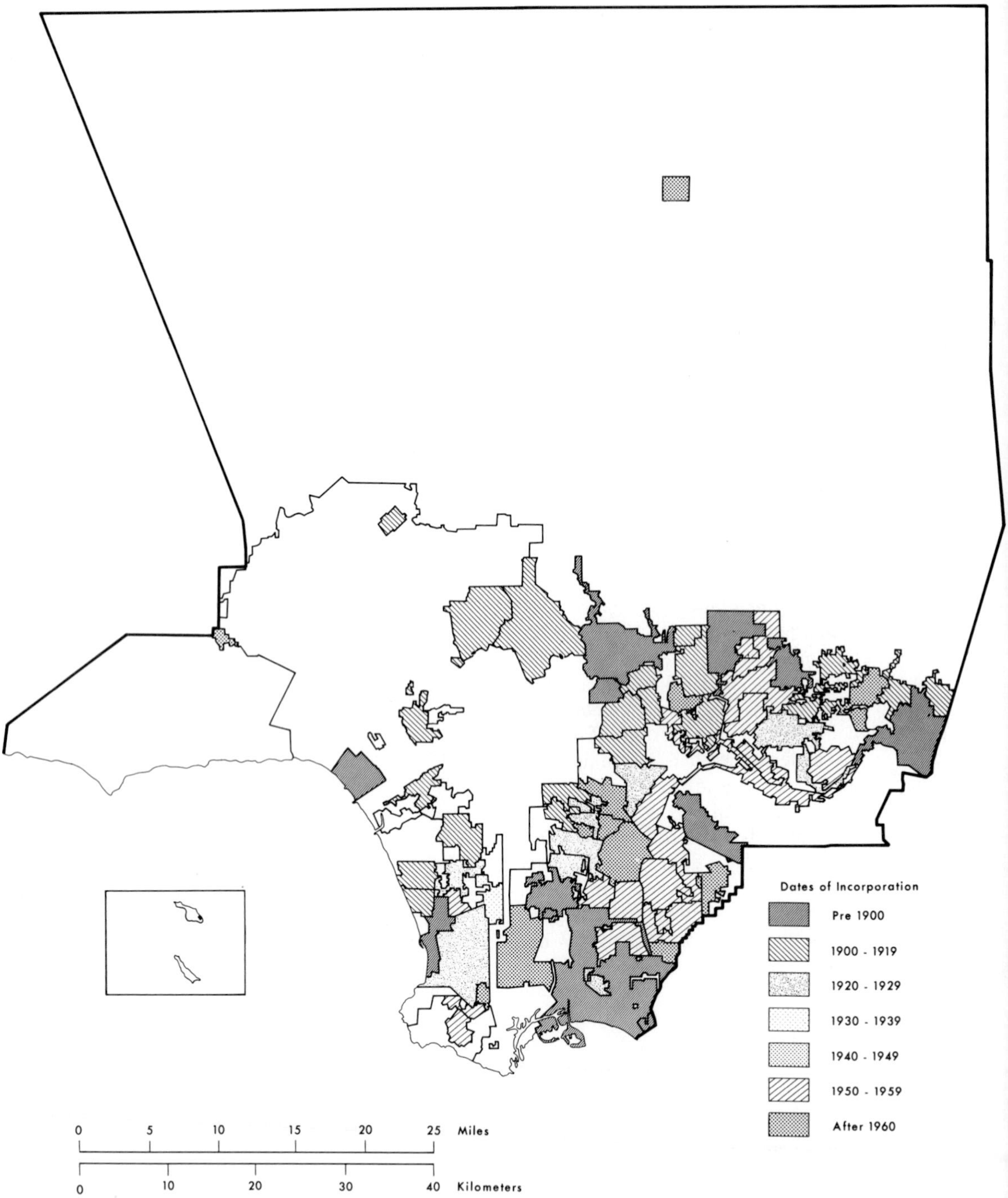

Figure 12-6. The Cities of Los Angeles County, Dates of Incorporation.

corporation. This interpretation is erroneous because it implies that for the residents of such areas remaining unincorporated was a viable choice. It was not, at least prior to the mid-1920s, if they wished to obtain urban public services.

By 1927, the by then gargantuan Los Angeles was cut off from further large scale annexation on the north and northeast by mountains and elsewhere by an almost continuous ring of suburbs. There were a few areas—such as unincorporated East Los Angeles and the present city of Carson—into which Los Angeles might have expanded had it not become increasingly difficult to finance the further expansion of the Los Angeles water system.

In the early 1920s, after repeated warnings from its Public Service Commission that further expansion solely to guarantee a market for water would create shortage problems unless a new supply was obtained, Los Angeles began investigating the feasibility of transporting Colorado River water to Los Angeles—a goal which required both federal and state legislative approval. It was clear that Los Angeles was the only local jurisdiction with sufficient resources to undertake the unilateral development of an aqueduct. However, Los Angeles' use of its water monopoly to force consolidation and annexation had made so few friends in the areas which had been able to maintain their autonomy that it was equally apparent that the suburban municipalities would vigorously fight any proposal which would perpetuate the city's waier monopoly. Thus, to provide water for its own continued population growth, Los Angeles was forced to enter into a cooperative agreement with several counties and other municipalities and form the Metropolitan Water District of Southern California. By 1941, the MWD had brought Colorado River water to the Los Angeles area and had become the wholesaler of water to member counties, special districts and municipalities. The creation of the MWD in 1927 ended Los Angeles' monopoly of the water supply and the threat of involuntary absorption to fringe area cities and unincorporated areas. Large scale annexation by Los Angeles virtually ceased. With the rise of Los Angeles County as a provider of municipal services, the monopoly position of cities also ended. After 1930 and until 1954, only one municipality was established in the metropolitan area.

Detroit and the Growth of Its Suburbs—Peaceful Coexistence

Th completion of the Erie Canal in 1825 opened a cheap water route from New York to the Northwest and made Detroit an important commercial center. The coming of the railroads in the early 1850s further increased the economic importance of Detroit, and by 1880 it had become a major industrial center. However, it was the automobile industry that was responsible for the incredible growth of Detroit between 1900 and 1930.

The early years of the automobile industry—1890-1920—were characterized by mechanical and production experimentation of many small, often short-lived, companies. After World War I, however, with the advent of the assembly line, mass production and the consequent reduction in cost, a large middle class market for the automobile was opened up. The small companies were gradually eliminated or amalgamated into the large, integrated industries known today. The first of the large plants were established in the central part of the city, but just prior to World War I the demand for open space along major rail facilities, so necessary for mass production assembly and distribution, had resulted in the first shift of the auto industry to the periphery of Detroit—specifically to the small villages of Highland Park and Hamtramck. These two "suburbs" soon became centers of the industry and by the mid-1920s had become engulfed by further industrial expansion and consequent residential growth. The next major shift of the growing automobile industry to the periphery occurred in 1919 when the Ford Rouge plant was established in the area between the village of Dearborn and Detroit—an area soon to be annexed by the *city* of Dearborn. This plant, by far the largest of its day, spurred considerable residential and industrial development, particularly in Dearborn, but also in surrounding unincorporated areas. The rapid increases in population in such unincorporated areas throughout the 1920s were accompanied by the demand for municipal services. As noted earlier, the territorial expansion of Detroit through annexation from 1900-1930 had been considerable and had tended to keep pace with the spread of urbanization. However, despite increasing its area by 75 percent in the early 1920s, Detroit was still unable to annex sufficient territory to contain all the new growth areas. The rapidly urbanizing areas surrounding Highland Park and Hamtramck had been annexed. But by the mid- and late 1920s, the voters of Detroit had become increasingly opposed to incurring the additional tax burdens associated with Detroit's obligation to extend city services to annexed, yet largely undeveloped, land. The extension of the boundaries of Detroit to contain all of the urbanizing areas whose growth was stimulated by the Rouge plant was economically and politically impossible. After annexing East Dearborn, the residents of Dearborn showed little enthusiasm for further annexation. The residents of such areas as Inkster, Allen Park, Melvindale and Lincoln Park had little recourse but to incorporate—initially as villages and subsequently as cities (Figure 12-7).

Nevertheless, by 1930 Detroit contained three-fourths of metropolitan area's total population—a ratio that had been increasing each decade for at least 50 years. The population density of Detroit remained fairly constant between 1900 and 1930, evidence that if Detroit had failed to engage in large scale annexation a continuous ring of cities undoubtedly would have developed around it. Between 1910 and 1930 the population of the metropolitan area, although failing to grow as rapidly as that of Detroit, did increase threefold. Accompanying this growth was a rapid proliferation in the number of villages and cities. In the decade 1910-1919 only two new villages were established (Figure 12-8). But the "roaring twenties" marked the beginning of the rapid diffusion of the automobile among middle class families of Detroit and the creation of the first genuine middle class residential sub-

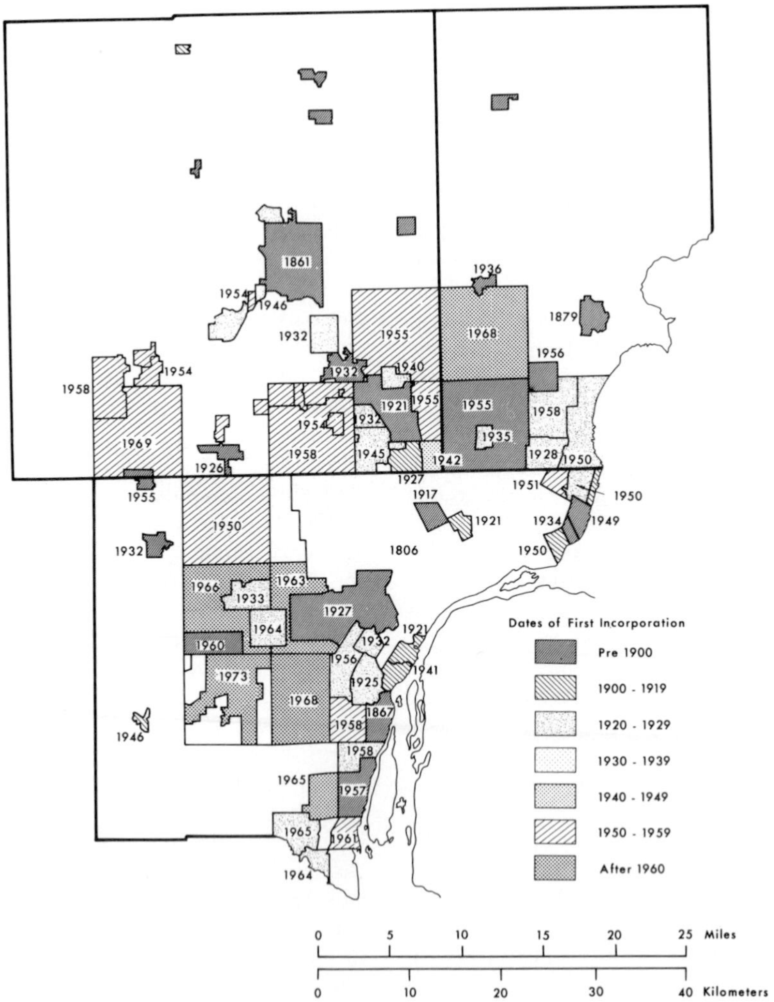

Figure 12-7. Municipalities in the Detroit Metropolitan Area, Dates of Incorporation as Cities.

urbs. A total of 22 new villages and nine cities were established during the decade, primarily along the major highways radiating out from the central business district of Detroit, while Detroit, with its booming automotive industry and acute labor shortage, was attracting a burgeoning population of Eastern European immigrants, southern whites and southern blacks.

The Great Depression hit the automobile industry hard. In 1929 roughly one-fourth of the metropolitan area's population was employed in the automobile plants. Two years later 225,000 workers had lost their jobs and most of the remaining 250,000 were employed only on a part-time basis. The period was a turbulent one, marked by explosive and widespread class tensions. Not surprisingly, the area experienced an abrupt decrease in its population growth rate, particularly in Detroit. Although a large number of villages reincorporated as cities—primarily to avoid the expense of township government and to gain representation on the county board of supervisors—the period 1930 through 1942 witnessed no change in the number of incorporated places in the metropolitan area.

In the 1940s the rate of population increase took an upward turn in both the City of Detroit and in the remainder of the metropolitan area. However, spurred by construction of wartime munitions plants in outlying areas, the most dramatic increases occurred outside Detroit. This growth was confined primarily to areas that had incorporated during the 1920s. As a result, the trend of villages to reincorporate as cities, established in the thirties, continued into the forties. Only one new incorporated place was established and this conformed to the earlier pattern of incorporation along major arterials. After 1950 and continuing through the 1960s, Detroit for the first decade in its history steadily lost population, while the remainder of the metropolitan area grew in population at a rate exceeding that of Detroit itself during the population explosion of 1910-1930. From 1950 through the present, the population exodus from Detroit to the suburban municipalities was comparable to that experienced by St. Louis; but when one considers that Detroit geographically is almost two and a half times as large as St. Louis, the scale of the exodus has been even more dramatic in Detroit.

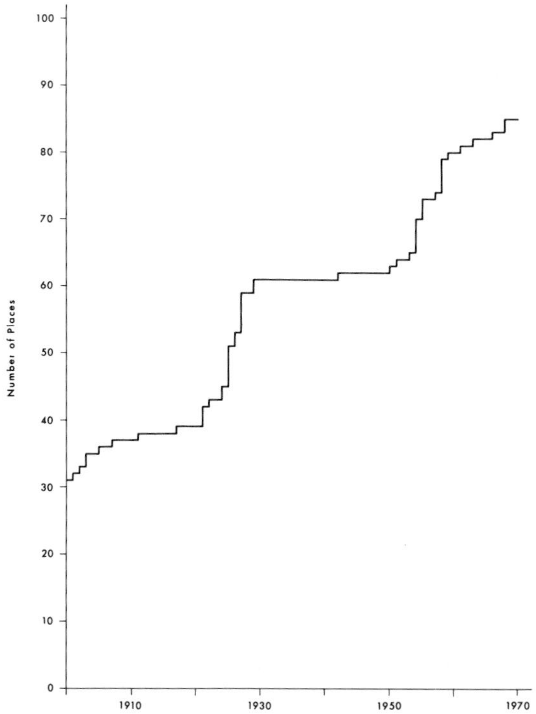

Figure 12-8. Total Number of Incorporated Places by Year, Detroit Metropolitan Area, 1900-1970.

During the 1950s and 1960s a total of 14 new cities and nine new villages (two had changed their status to cities by the late 1960s) were created. Also, two villages reincorporated as cities during this period, but unlike the 1930s, many greatly increased their geographical size in the process. The majority of the new incorporations occurred in the interstitial areas between the major arterials along which most of the incorporation activity had occurred in the 1920s.

As had been true of earlier suburbanization, the locational behavior of the automobile industry and auto-related industries was of crucial significance. After the war, the production of the automobile plants in the Detroit-Dearborn-Highland Park-Hamtramck areas and those in Pontiac simply could not keep up with the demand for automobiles. Since there was little room for expansion in these older areas, new plant construction again took place outward along the major rail lines at locations where large amounts of relatively inexpensive, flat land were available. The growing ancillary metal and special machinery industries, as had long been the case in the Detroit area, located in close proximity to these new plants. Residential growth followed industrial growth.

The availability of GI benefits and the well-entrenched demand for low density residential areas coupled with higher than average levels of automobile ownership and the concept of the "new model" in both automobiles *and* housing also contributed to the exceptionally rapid rates of postwar suburbanization in the Detroit metropolitan area.

Of the 23 cities and villages that were newly incorporated from 1950 to 1970, 15 were to the northwest and north of Detroit, primarily in Oakland and Macomb counties, respectively. Half of these were almost exclusively residential and wealthy. In 1970 all had a median value of housing in excess of $30,000; some were in excess of $50,000. Most of remaining new suburbs in the northwest quadrant can be described as middle and upper middle class and residential. To the west, southwest and south, the newly established suburban communities, although primarily residential, contained a significant amount of industrial land use. These, unlike those to the northwest of Detroit, were and are predominantly blue collar suburbs. The older cities and villages in these parts of the metropolitan area, including villages which reincorporated as cities between 1950 and 1970, also tended to become increasingly industrial and blue collar.

As in the Los Angeles metropolitan area, water played an important role in the development of the spatial patterns of local government in the Detroit area. However, Detroit's use of water in local politics stands in marked contrast to Los Angeles'. The establishment of an *entente cordiale* between Detroit and outlying municipalities on the question of annexation dating effectively from the mid-1920s meant that Detroit, in the post-World War I and II suburban population booms, failed to use the promise of the extension of her water supply system as a bargaining device for territorial expansion. Instead, Detroit's early and consistent willingness to assume the role of wholesaler of water for the metropolitan area set the stage for the development of a metropolitanwide water system based on intergovernmental contracting rather than on special districts or other areawide devices. Indeed, the availability of reasonably cheap Detroit water to suburbanizing areas lacking the resources to justify the construction of independent water systems was important in contributing to the rapid rates of suburbanization noted above. For example, 22 of the areas which are now municipalities had been supplied with Detroit water through township contracts with Detroit prior to their incorporation and another nine which were small villages prior to the receipt of Detroit water incorporated as cities and grew rapidly after becoming connected to the Detroit water system. Detroit has also consistently indicated its willingness to contract with its suburbs for other municipal services.

St. Louis and the Development of Its Suburbs—Spatial Propinquity but Intergovernmental Isolation

In 1876 St. Louis cut itself off from its then nonexistent metropolitan area. By 1920, however, all the area within the city limits had been developed; any further population expansion could come about only through an increase in population density or through residential development in St. Louis County. Both occurred, but the latter more spectacularly (Figure 12-9). The political history of intergovernmental relations in the area has been dominated ever since by unsuccessful attempts to adjust the boundaries of St. Louis. Between 1915 and 1930, city officials in St. Louis must have looked with envy at the spectacular growth of Los Angeles and Detroit through annexation. By the time the legal apparatus by which the boundaries between the city and county of St. Louis could be modified was available, St. Louis County contained a large number of suburban municipalities, the residents of which were sufficiently suspicious of the territorial ambitions of St. Louis to be counted upon to veto any proposed boundary change.

Except for the 1920s, when the previously established municipalities immediately to the west of St. Louis were in the process of "filling up," and until the early 1950s, the continual and rapid increase in population in St. Louis County is closely paralleled by the creation of suburbs (Figure 12-10). Whereas new municipal incorporations were virtually nonexistent in the Los Angeles and Detroit areas during the Depression years, such was not true of the St. Louis area. During these years, two distinct

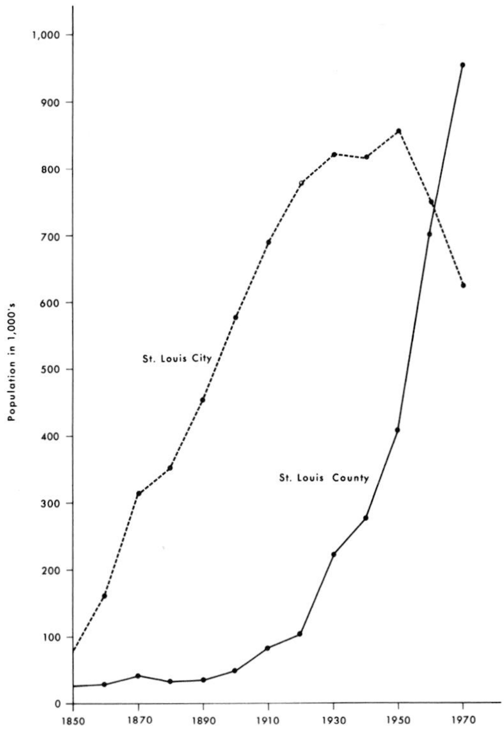

Figure 12-9. Population Growth in St. Louis City and County, 1850-1970.

socioeconomic groups of suburbs were established: a tier of geographically large, "mainline," high income municipalities contiguous to the already existing affluent suburbs west of St. Louis; and two clusters of very small middle income residential suburbs to the city's northwest along the major highways connecting St. Louis with the older, outlying cities of Bridgeton and Florissant. The latter suburbs were the first of the almost exclusively middle income suburbs in the area. The two groups incorporated primarily to provide residents with municipal services, but in the first group the possibility of being annexed by their neighbors and thereby losing control of land use regulations was also important.

The decade of the 1940s was one of rapid incorporation. From 1945 to 1950 alone, 44 municipalities were created—one of the most intense periods of incorporation in US history. The largest concentration was again to the northwest of St. Louis. By 1950, the area between St. Louis, Bridgeton and Florissant was completely filled with small municipalities—most less than one square mile in area. As in the late 1930s, these municipalities were almost exclusively middle class and lower middle class commuter suburbs. Much of the commuting was to St. Louis, but with the expansion of the nearby aircraft and automotive assembly plants, these, too, were becoming increasingly important work sites. As in the 1930s there was a further proliferation—yet another tier of geographically large and affluent suburbs to the west of St. Louis. The establishment in this period of another automobile assembly plant in Fenton, about ten miles from the southwest corner of St. Louis, also stimulated some incorporation activity in its vicinity.

By 1950, the overall spatial pattern of incorporation in St. Louis County could be characterized by a cluster of very wealthy and geographically large suburbs extending west from the boundaries of St. Louis for about ten miles, while to the northwest and southwest of the city, again extending about ten miles, were "wedges" of territory occupied primarily by middle class suburbs, containing former residents of the City of St. Louis. Of the two "wedges," that to the northwest comprised the larger number and, hence, territorially smaller municipalities. A few new municipalities came into existence in widely scattered locations after 1950, but with the growth of St. Louis County as a provider of municipal services and the proliferation of special districts the era of the wavelike proliferation of municipalities had ended.

In total, 89 municipalities had been established after 1900 and only two consolidations involving small cities had occurred, despite repeated urgings by county officials and other advocates of "good government." As in the Detroit area, defensive incorporation to avoid annexation by an expanding central city had been nonexistent. But, unlike the Detroit area, the central city played no role in facilitating the distribution of municipal services through service contracts. Before 1945, it was prohibited, under the Missouri Constitution, from doing so; after 1945, it was preoccupied with its internal problems of economic blight, urban renewal and social change. St. Louis is a small city geographically, and hence "close" to its suburbs, but in terms of intergovernmental relations, it is as if St. Louis were in Illinois. The St. Louis metropolitan area provides one

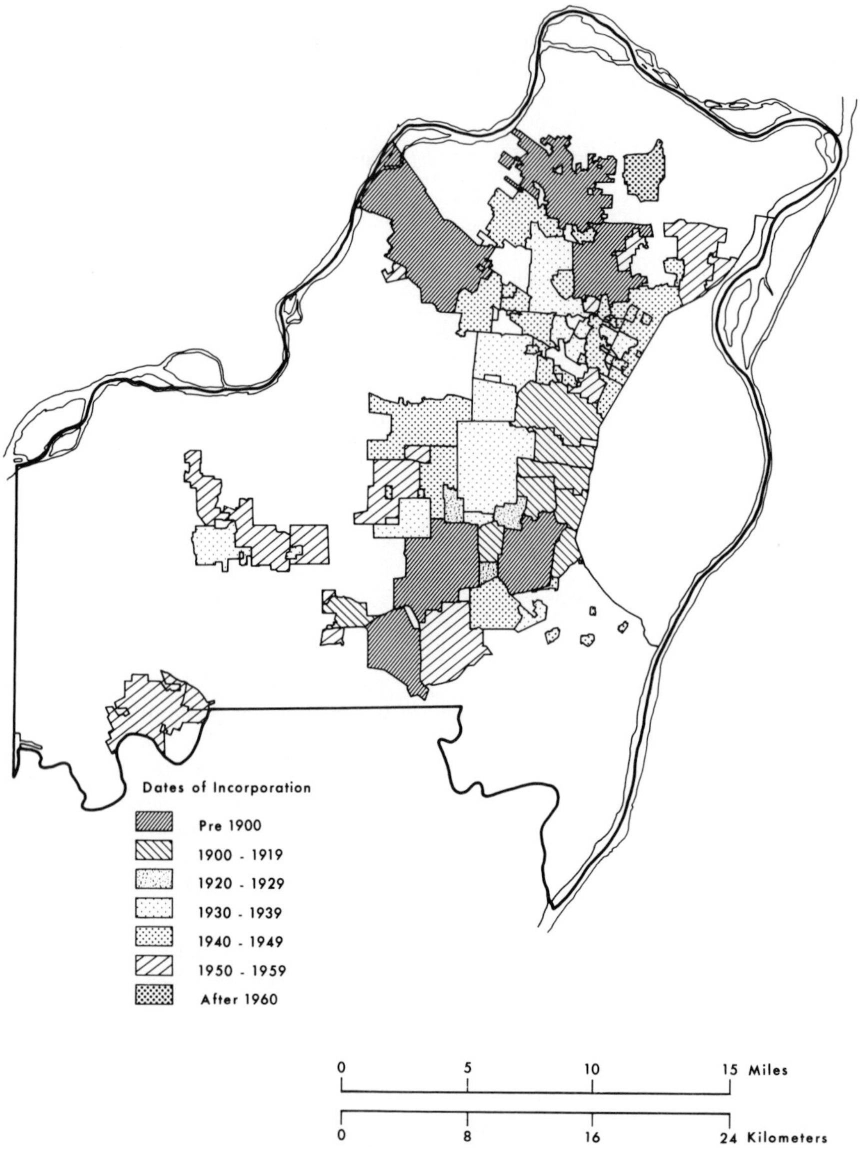

Figure 12-10. The Municipalities of St. Louis County, Dates of Incorporation.

of the best examples of what suburban America would probably look like if city formation were left to the voluntary efforts of local residents.

INTERGOVERNMENTAL RELATIONS AND SERVICE PROVISION

Proposals for the reorganization of service provision in urban America have been many and varied. As mentioned in the opening section of this chapter, most have called for the spatial restructuring of local governance. In most metropolitan areas, however, functional consolidation of service provision within *existing* systems of government has been utilized with much greater frequency than has functional consolidation within spatially *reorganized* systems. Functional consolidation through various forms of voluntary intergovernmental cooperation is by far the most common. The Los Angeles, St. Louis and Detroit areas are no exceptions. Here, as elsewhere, voluntary cooperation between existing governmental units has proved to be an acceptable form of reorganization because it is compatible with the well-entrenched principle of local control.

The utility of voluntary coordination of service provision in a system of local government is obvious. Due to the existence of scale economies in production and the avoidance of high degrees of duplication in public facility capital investment, coordination often enables governments to realize increases in technical efficiency. Coordination can also result in the increased effectiveness of local governments in solving problems that fail to respect boundaries—e.g., air pollution and flood control. And, finally, since the territorial integrity of existing units is preserved, levels of client accountability are unimpaired.

In practice, two general forms of voluntary intergovernmental coordination are common—interunit contracting and joint service provision. The acceptability of one or the other of these forms in a metropolitan area is dependent on the properties of the service in question, the legal milieu provided by the state government, the history of intergovernmental relations in the area, and the geographical distribution of financial resources and service demands across units. For example, for services requiring heavy capital investment in public facilities, increases in technical efficiency through interunit contracting without spatial change in the system of government can only be expected if one or more existing units with sufficient financial resources to undertake the service provision unilaterally are contiguous, or at least geographically accessible, to a large number of other units lacking the financial resources to provide the service themselves. Joint service provision without spatial change will be preferred if the financial resources for initial capital investment can only be obtained through a pooling of those available to a set of contiguous units or if the nature of the service is such that a requisite number and spatial configuration of units is necessary for its provision.

The Los Angeles Area

Throughout the twentieth century, the City of Los Angeles has consistently been the only municipality with sufficient resources to become a major provider of services to other municipalities. By 1927 its geographical shape and expansiveness also made it contiguous to more than half of the 43 then existing suburban municipalities. However, in spite of a flexible legal milieu permitting intermunicipal contracting, Los Angeles failed to become a major provider of services to other municipalities. Its aggressive program of annexation and consolidation had been a deliberate result of using its financial resource base for territorial aggrandizement rather than to achieve efficient service provision through intermunicipal contracting.

While Los Angeles was expanding, the other territorial and fiscal giant in the area—Los Angeles County—had been steadily solidifying its position as a major provider of services to unincorporated areas. Given the spatially fragmented pattern of unincorporated but urbanizing territory served by the county and the consequent physical necessity of adopting a geographically decentralized pattern of investment in public facilities to provide services, the service provision systems of Los Angeles County were also contiguous to a large number of municipalities. This contributed to concomitant growth of Los Angeles County as a provider of services to municipalities.

Since the county's provision of municipal services to "de facto cities" in unincorporated areas was financed in large part through a countywide property tax, the issue of de jure municipalities subsidizing de facto municipalities arose with increasing frequency as more and more "unofficial cities"—as they were called by city politicians—were developed after World War II. By 1952, all the ingredients needed for a chain reaction of incorporations were present in the Los Angeles metropolitan area—relatively easy incorporation procedures; a well-developed precedent for county-city contracting; an already large, urbanized and rapidly growing population in unincorporated areas (the Los Angeles County Regional Planning Commission estimated that the population of unincorporated areas increased by over 200,000 between 1950 and 1954); and a thoroughly urban-oriented county government that was very much on the defensive over the subsidy issue. All it took to set off this reaction were the efforts of the City of Long Beach to annex a rapidly expanding residential area, known locally as Lakewood. Shortly after the leaders of the numerous antiannexation forces within Lakewood were informed by Los Angeles County officials that Lakewood, if unincorporated, could obtain a full range of urban services at levels satisfactory to the community—including police and fire protection—through county contracts and existing county-operated special districts, a campaign for the "city of the future"—one with a minimum number of employees and administrative officers—began. In 1954 Lakewood incorporated and became the first city in the United States to provide its residents with public services completely on a contract basis with a county. By so doing, it was able to avoid the bonded indebtedness which had hitherto been a major obstacle to incorporation in the de facto cities of Los Angeles.

With the passage of a 1 percent countywide sales tax in 1955—whereby the revenue collected in unincorporated areas is retained by the county and that collected in a municipality returned to the municipality—a further incentive for incorporation was provided. By 1967, 31 additional "contract" cities had been created.

The importance of county-city contracting as the primary method of intergovernmental cooperation and coordination in service provision in the Los Angeles metropolitan area is indicated clearly in Table 12-7. Joint service agreements between municipalities are realtively unimportant except for the provision of water. This, as noted earlier, is supplied to most municipalities and unincorporated areas in Los Angeles County through the federation of municipalities and special districts called the Metropolitan Water District. Sewage disposal is provided by Los Angeles under contract to seven of its neighboring municipalities but all other municipalities and urbanized unincorporated areas are provided sewage disposal through 24 county sanitation districts (excluding two single city districts which contract directly with Los Angeles), some of which in turn contract with Los Angeles for sewage treatment. California first authorized the creation of county sanitation districts in 1923. In many parts of the metropolitan area co-inhabited by both small municipalities and urbanized unincorporated areas, special district formation was feasible whereas joint provision, given the unincorporated status of many areas, was not. Small municipalities were able to realize economies through system membership that otherwise were unavailable. Even further economies were achieved when in 1925 the five districts then in existence reached a joint agreement to appoint a single chief engineer and utilize the same county administrative staff. All districts formed subsequently have also entered into this joint agreement. In effect, there are now two major sewage systems in the Los Angeles area—the Los Angeles contract system and the integrated county system based on joint agreements between special districts. Los Angeles County also has extended the offer of membership in its countywide library district and several fire protection districts to all municipalities in the metropolitan area. Most have joined the library district, but only the post-1954 cities are members of county fire protection districts. In part, the lack of appeal of county fire protection delivered through a special district is traceable to the highly developed and successful system of mutual aid that has developed between municipalities over the years.

In brief, there are high levels of intergovernmental cooperation in service provision in the Los Angeles metropolitan area. Cooperation is dominated by a system of county-city contracting, but it is supplemented by county administered special districts, intercity contracting, joint agreements and mutual aid. In the instances of special district formation, some spatial reorganization in the system of local government has occurred. But in Los Angeles few of the many special districts are genuinely independent of municipal government. In almost all instances in which a municipality is within a special district, its mayor is a member of the district's governing board. Municipalities are important in Los Angeles and, due to their apparent success in interacting with one another and with the county so as to achieve increases in the efficiency of service provision without a consequent loss of local accountability, are likely to remain so in the foreseeable future.

St. Louis Metropolitan Area

Prior to the end of World War II, the City of St. Louis was the only political jurisdiction in its metropolitan area with the fiscal resources necessary for instituting a system of coordination in public service provision based on intergovernmental contracting. However, the pre-1945 constitution of Missouri did not per-

Table 12-7. Intergovernmental Cooperation, Selected Services (1970)

	Full Cost County-City Contracting			*Token Fee County-City Contracting*			*Central City–Other City Contracting*			*Other Intercity Contracting*			*Joint Service Provision*			*Mutual Aid Provision*			*Special District Provision*		
	Los Angeles	*St. Louis*	*Detroit*	*Los Angeles*	*St. Louis*	*Detroit*	*Los Angeles*	*St. Louis*	*Detroit*	*Los Angeles*	*St. Louis*	*Detroit*	*Los Angeles*	*St. Louis*	*Detroit*	*Los Angeles*	*St. Louis*	*Detroit*	*Los Angeles*	*St. Louis*	*Detroit*
Animal Control	X	X	*						*			*			*						
Assessment and collection of Taxes	X	X	X																		
Building Inspection	X	*																			
Fire Protection									*		*	X			X	X	X	X	X[1]	X	
Law Enforcement	X	*	*								*	*			*		*				
Police and Fire Commissions		X	X	X			*		*	X	X	*			*		X				
Election Services	X	X																			
Sewage Disposal and/or System Construction or Maintenance	*	*	X				*		*	*		*	*		*				X[1]	X	
Street Maintenance and Construction	X				*				*		*	X			*						
Water Supply			*						X	*		*	X		*					X	
Health Services	X	X				X						*									
Jail Services	X	*	X						*			*									
Parks and Recreation												*			*				*		
Library			X									*							X[1]		
Zoning and Planning	X		*		*										*						

X–Of major importance (involving at least 25 percent of municipalities)
*–Of minor importance (involving less than 25 percent of municipalities)
1–Administered by Los Angeles County
Source: data compiled by the author

mit her to do so. Instead of pressing for constitutional change which would enable intermunicipal contracting across county lines, decisionmakers in St. Louis consistently lobbied for amendments which would permit spatial change in the structure of local government in the St. Louis area: spatial change which would enhance the size or political hegemony of the city. By 1945, when St. Louis was authorized to engage in contracting with its suburban municipalities, the city, due to internal demands, no longer had the financial resource base to do so. Central city-suburban contracting in the St. Louis area remains nonexistent.

In 1945 there were literally no local intergovernmental relations in the St. Louis metropolitan area. With regard to municipal service provision, St. Louis County was impotent, suburban municipalities were on average too small to utilize interunit contracting effectively and joint service agreements between clusters of municipalities were on shaky legal grounds. However, spatial change via the creation of special districts, independent of city or county governments, for the provision of sewage disposal and fire protection had been authorized since the early 1930s. Since only a few of the larger municipalities in the county had the fiscal capacity to finance sewer construction and equip and maintain professional fire departments, the residents of the numerous smaller municipalities increasingly turned to the special district as the device by which their resources could be pooled and such services provided. As in the Los Angeles area, special districts had an additional advantage over joint municipal provision—they could encompass unincorporated areas as well as cities. As a general rule, the voters of the metropolitan area have shown little hesitancy to disband special districts and create new ones when service provision conditions change. For example, in 1954, after a series of studies indicated that the creation of an integrated sewage system covering the city of St. Louis and all the heavily urbanized portions of the county would result in improved health conditions and a tax savings to most residents, voters in both St. Louis and St. Louis County strongly supported the creation of the Metropolitan St. Louis Sewerage District. Formal methods of urban service coordination not involving the spatial reorganization of service provision were almost nonexistent in the St. Louis metropolitan area until after the adoption of the 1945 Missouri Constitution and the implementation of a home rule charter in St. Louis County in 1950.

In 1956-1957 the St. Louis metropolitan area became the subject of the most highly funded social science research project of its day—The St. Louis Metropolitan Survey (Bollens 1961). Political scientists from St. Louis University and Washington University undertook "to prepare . . . alternative proposals for action designed to remedy some or all of the major ills arising out of the present pattern of government in St. Louis City and St. Louis County, and to provide ways and means to meet major metropolitan needs, present and future" [Greer 1972 p. 185]. The ideological orientation of the survey team was one of structural reform. As Scott Greer, one of the political scientists involved in the study, has emphasized, the survey team *assumed* that the existing pattern of government in the city and county "gravely impairs efficiency and dilutes responsibility . . . impedes the orderly and healthy development of the expanding community . . . (while) many major needs of the people . . . which government is expected to meet are not being uniformly met and cannot be met adequately by uncoordinated, piecemeal local action" [also Greer 1972 p. 185].

In the survey's final reports, it was concluded that the residents of St. Louis—city and county—were faced with serious areawide problems that were not and could not be solved adequately within the existing governmental structures. The "problems" created by St. Louis's separation from St. Louis County were singled out for particular attention.

Of the alternatives to adjust city-county relations available under the Missouri Constitution, the survey concluded that only a metropolitan district that would take over areawide service functions, while leaving existing municipal boundaries intact was politically practicable and of great promise. Such a metropolitan district, it was recommended, should be given responsibility for road and highway development, public transportation, areawide planning, economic development, sewage disposal and drainage, civil defense, and property assessment. It was to be a multipurpose metropolitan government of limited functional scope, but with the authority to enact ordinances, levy and collect taxes, issue bonds, and have the specific powers necessary for the performance of its objectives.

Ironically, the results of the survey's large-scale public opinion poll failed to reveal the expected widespread popular dissatisfaction with city and county services. Furthermore, residents of both the city and the county had expressed very high levels of satisfaction with all governments in the area, save the only one that was areawide—the Metropolitan Sewerage District. This was the only governmental unit evaluated as performing poorly by as many as 10 percent of the respondents. The evaluation of county municipalities by their own residents was higher than either the evaluation of the county by county residents or the evaluation of St. Louis government by St. Louisans. The only public service with which even a slight majority of the respondents expressed dissatisfaction was "traffic control and facilities"; while for the usually more controversial services of police protection and the schools, 81 and 30 percent, respectively, expressed that they were "very" or "fairly" satisfied. As for fire protection, a public administrator's prime candidate for areawide provision, a whopping 91 percent expressed satisfaction. To add even further irony, the only variable that seemed to be related consistently to satisfaction-dissatisfaction with service provision was household income; the poorer the household the greater the satisfaction—again counterintuitive to reform ideology. When presented with alternative city-county reorganization proposals, the respondents preferred some form of change to the status quo; however, opinion was widely divided as to what form of reorganization was most desirable. What seemed clear, although not stated in survey reports, was that respondents wanted change in somebody else's government, but not in their own.

Apparently ignoring the opinion poll results, the metropolitan dailies, community leaders and civic organizations accepted the survey recommendations as a blueprint for action and by the spring of 1959 a proposed metropolitan charter had been prepared.

In conformance with the recommendations of the survey, it called for the creation of the "Greater St. Louis City-County District." A strong newspaper and television campaign with the support of various "good government" groups was waged in its support; there was no organized campaign against it. However, in the referendum the charter was overwhelmingly defeated—two to one against in the city; three to one against in the county. It failed in 26 of the 28 wards in the city and in every township in the county.

Comprehensive spatial and functional reorganization of service provision in the entire metropolitan area became a dead issue. One positive effect of the survey, however, was that it sensitized public officials, if not the general public, to the need to work toward solutions to problems that were not being addressed by existing governments. Subsequently, almost all municipalities and fire protection districts in the county have established agreements with one another to provide for mutual aid in police and fire protection emergencies. Intermunicipal contracting for police and fire protection and street maintenance has increased. County-city contracting, although limited to the less controversial services, increased dramatically until the mid-1960s when the greatly increased demand for county-provided municipal services in unincorporated areas forced a curtailment.

From the mid-1960s to the present, St. Louis County officials attempted, without much success, to convince county residents to transfer more service provision responsibilities from the municipal to county level. Consistent with this, further municipal incorporations have been discouraged at almost every turn—even to the extent of refusing to hold an incorporation election. The first real test of the likely success of the county's policy to consolidate service provision at the county level came in 1971. The county council proposed the use of the county's home rule authority to establish and enforce countywide building codes, housing occupancy codes and law enforcement standards. These proposals were opposed by a significant segment of the leadership in the various municipalities and when presented to the voters were rejected by decisive margins. Should subsequent attempts at areawide county control prove unsuccessful, more extensive use of contracting—even to the extent of adopting a "Lakewood type" contracting plan in conjunction with the establishment of minimum service standards—is reputed to be under serious consideration by county officials.

At present, the Missouri Constitution prevents the more ambitious reallocation of service responsibilities from the municipalities to a county on the basis of a countywide vote. Such a reallocation can be made only if the residents of all municipalities and/or districts involved vote their approval. Given the remoteness of this possibility, it would not be surprising if St. Louis County were to "discover California first." In the meanwhile, the importance of special districts as providers of public services is likely to continue (Table 12-7). In 1973, for example, St. Louis and St. Louis County residents' approved a zoological park-art museum district through which all city and county property is taxed to maintain the park and museum, both of which are located in St. Louis and were in severe financial difficulty prior to the district's creation.

Detroit Metropolitan Area

The Detroit metropolitan area offers some of the best examples in the United States of intergovernmental cooperation based on voluntary service agreements between municipalities. Such cooperation has been fostered by the legal milieu provided by state government. First, municipalities have broad grants of authority to engage in service agreements with other municipalities. Second, they must operate within rather stringent millage rate limitations. The result in the Detroit area has been that municipalities have had an added incentive to utilize their intergovernmental service agreement authority in order to minimize their costs and hence their millage rates. Such a policy toward municipal government could have amounted to nothing more than "giving with one hand" and "taking away with the other" had the geography of local government not been conducive to intermunicipal service agreements.

Early in this century, Detroit, like Los Angeles and St. Louis, was the only municipality in its metropolitan area with the fiscal capacity to act as provider to other municipalities of services requiring large capital investments. Detroit's provision of water to outlying municipalities has already been discussed. However, Detroit also indicated its willingness to provide many services on a contract basis—sewage disposal, street construction and maintenance, and fire protection, for example. Although many such contracts were short term in that a contractee often bought Detroit services only until such time as it could develop its own service delivery systems, Detroit's behavior did contribute to a political climate quite unlike the acrimony characterizing those of Los Angeles and St. Louis. The decentralization of the automobile and ancillary industries before and after the two world wars led to the development of other cities in the metropolitan area with fiscal capacities sufficient for them to become providers of services to their neighbors, albeit on a smaller scale than Detroit's. In those portions of the metropolitan area where the resources and demands of any one community were insufficient to justify the provision of a service, subregional delivery systems comprised of several contiguous municipalities have usually been created either to provide the service collectively or to negotiate with Detroit for provision. For example, a subregional approach has been and still is important in instigating the provision of Detroit water to peripheral areas.

The importance of Detroit as a provider of municipal services to other units in the Detroit area has been known for some time. However, it was not until 1965, when the Citizens Research Council of Michigan undertook a study of governmental organization in the area, that the scale and importance of contracting not involving the City of Detroit was fully realized. First, the study revealed that all three counties and all 82 of the then existing cities and villages were utilizing one of more methods of interunit cooperation in performing their service functions; only one of 50 townships was not. Second, the number and variety of such agreements far exceeded that anticipated from traditional thinking on the "metropolitan problem." Fifty-three of the multipurpose units of government had agreements to provide services to other multipurpose units in 953 separate instances. These services included 36 of the 50 governmental service functions identified in the study. All but four of the 137 multipurpose units of government had entered into contracts with other units to receive services. There were 930 of these agreements pertaining to a total of 32 different functions. All but eight of the units (again town-

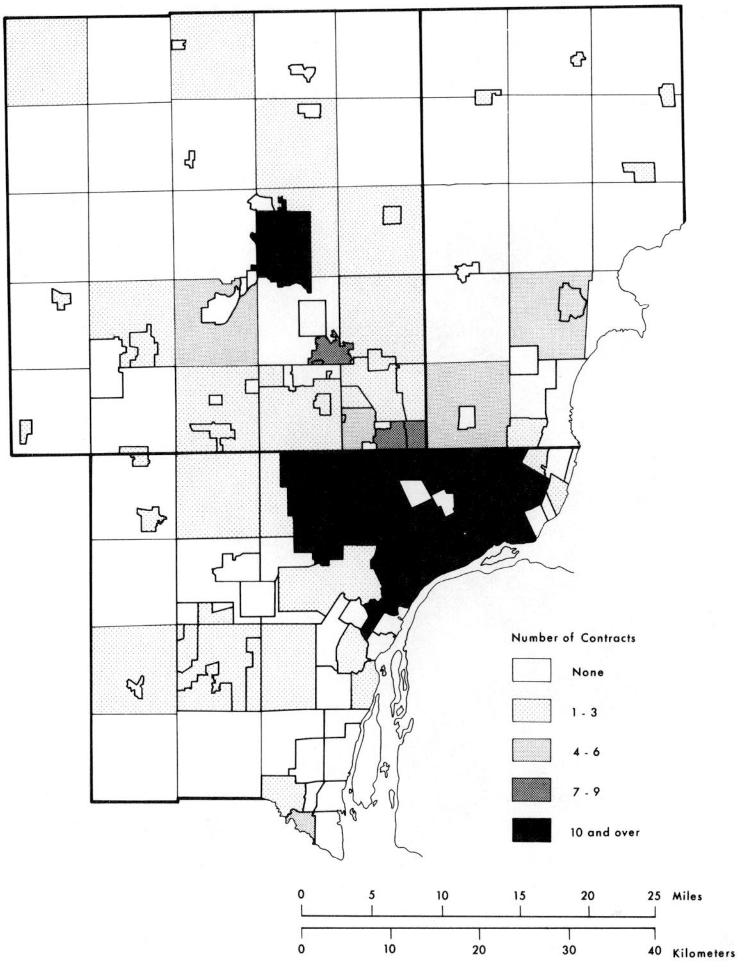

Figure 12-11. Contracts to Provide Services in the Detroit Area, 1965.

ships) had entered into one or more of the 584 existing joint service agreements pertaining to 35 different functions. And finally, it was reported that almost all of the governmental units in the area had at least one informal understanding with other units which would lead to cooperative action under specific circumstances (Figure 12-11 and 12-12).

Police communications; patrol, personnel and other police services; various fire protection services; the reciprocal licensing of building trades; refuse disposal; and park and recreation services are the functional areas in which city, village and township cooperation through contracting and joint agreements is particularly widespread. The suburban ring of municipalities surrounding Detroit has a higher incidence of contracting to receive services than do governmental units more distant from Detroit. The older suburban municipalities to the northwest of Detroit—which tend to be small, but affluent—engage in relatively less contracting to receive services. However, these units are quite highly involved in joint service agreements (Figure 12-13).

In general, governmental units in the area tend to be involved either in bilateral contracts to receive services or in joint service provision with other units rather than in both forms of intergovernmental activity simultaneously. A number of factors account for this, including the age and economic status of a municipality, the service provision activity of the county in which it is located, and, of course, its location

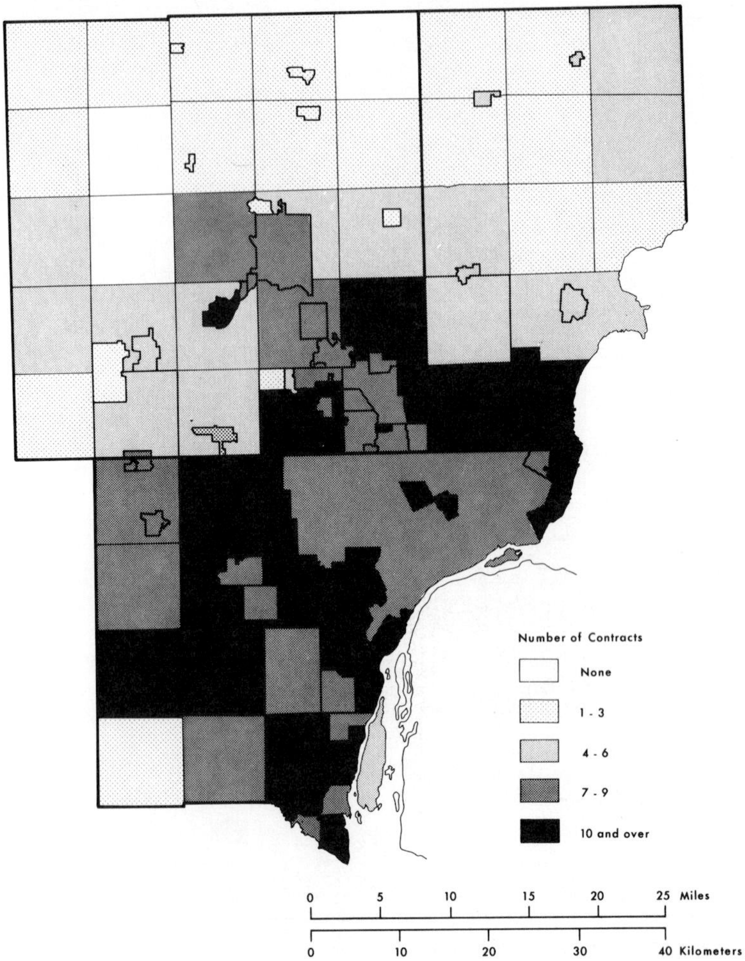

Figure 12-12. Contracts to Receive Services in the Detroit Area, 1965.

relative to Detroit. For example, the relatively low incidence of joint service agreements between the local governmental units in Wayne County can be attributed less to their lack of trust in one another and more to the fact that Detroit and Wayne County, often in collusion, have actively fostered intergovernmental cooperation through their joint service provision hegemony. Units in southeastern Oakland County on the other hand, although largely contracting with Detroit for water, have not, until the late 1950s, had the service provision advantages of location in a thoroughly urban-oriented county. As a result, a number of municipalities and townships at an early stage in their development banded together in a number of joint service provision ventures, including police, fire, library and sewage services. The relative success of these joint ventures can, in part, be attributed to the relative homogeneity of these municipalities as upper middle class residential areas. Finally, the governmental units in southern Macomb County are relatively larger in areal extent and are younger and more industrial than those of southeastern Oakland County; the county government of Macomb County is even more rural-oriented. As a result, joint service agreements are less common between these units, and bilateral service agreements with Detroit more common (but less so than for the Wayne County municipalities contiguous to Detroit).

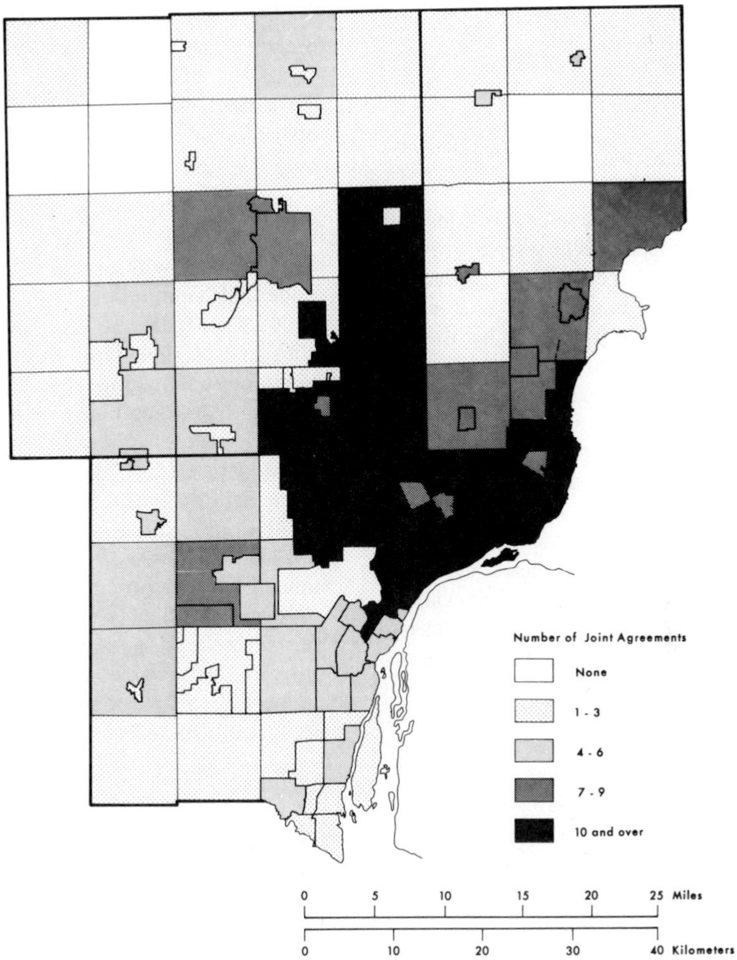

Figure 12-13. Joint Service Agreements in the Detroit Area, 1965.

The Citizens Research Council of Michigan, in a series of case studies conducted as a followup to its 1965 study, found that for the services examined—cooperative data processing, library agreements, fire protection, tax assessment and billing, and the reciprocal licensing of building trades—cooperative agreements between governmental units in the Detroit area have been successful in terms of allowing a high degree of local autonomy while permitting the realization of economies of scale in service provision and the realization of higher service levels or—in the case of reciprocal licensing agreements—in facilitating the operation of the private economy. In the case of fire protection, even the loosely organized mutual aid systems were found to be used actively and effectively as devices for allocating fire protection resources between participating units in such a way that the occasional fire that no single unit could fight with only its own resources could be combated rapidly in a collective manner. In brief, the Detroit area provides ample evidence that the existence of a politically fragmented metropolis need not imply that mutually satisfactory solutions to nonlocal and even areawide service problems cannot be reached. The ethos of collective bargaining, so well entrenched as the vehicle for the resolution of conflict between labor and the automobile industry, seems to carry over into the intergovernmental arena to a much greater extent in the Detroit area than in either the Los Angeles or St. Louis areas.

LOCAL PUBLIC EXPENDITURES IN THE THREE METROPOLITAN AREAS

As we have seen in previous sections, the primary units of local public service provision in each of the three metropolitan areas have traditionally been municipalities and school districts. The latter continue to be the sole providers of public education in all areas, but the functions of municipalities have changed significantly. In the Los Angeles and Detroit areas, the younger municipalities, while retaining traditional city roles as articulators of local public service demands, have increasingly become the purchasers of services produced by other units—in the Los Angeles area, Los Angeles County and "dependent" special districts; and in the Detroit area, other cities and, to a lesser extent, counties. Unlike the Los Angeles and Detroit areas, public service demand articulation, production and delivery functions in the St. Louis area tend to be vested in the same jurisdictions—either municipalities or independent special districts.

Since municipalities in the Los Angeles and Detroit areas and school districts in all three areas remain so important in the provision (if not actual production) of locally demanded public services, analyses of their expenditure patterns, although difficult, are necessary in any comparative study concerned with the formulation of policy recommendations regarding local governance. More specifically, this section attempts to specify the extent to which local expenditures in the three metropolitan areas reflect local need and/or demand or local wealth, or both. Particular attention is directed to comparisons of municipalities in the St. Louis and Detroit areas with the "noncontract" cities of Los Angeles, of "contract" with "noncontract" cities in the Los Angeles area, and of K-12 school districts in all three areas.

Definitions and Data Descriptions

Contract City. A contract city in the Los Angeles area is defined as one that contracts with Los Angeles County for the receipt of at least 20 of the over 50 services made available to cities, two of which must include law enforcement and fire protection. A noncontract city is one that has it own fire and/or police department and contracts for less than 20 services.

Municipalities Included in Analyses. In all analyses involving Los Angeles cities, municipalities without significant amounts of residential landuse or with 1970 populations below 1,500 are excluded whether contract cities or not. This is to ensure that only cities providing goods and services which directly benefit urban households are included.

For revenue and expenditure comparisons recent data are available for only 23 of the 45 municipalities in the St. Louis area with 1970 populations exceeding 3,000. Only these 23 cities are included in the subsequent analyses unless otherwise noted.

Again for data accessibility and compatibility reasons, in all analyses involving expenditures in Detroit area cities, only municipalities in Wayne and Oakland counties with 1960 populations in excess of 10,000 are included.

Expenditure Data. Municipal expenditures refer to all expenditures including interest on capital outlays incurred by a city in a given year with the following exceptions. For the noncontract cities of Los Angeles sewage disposal expenditures are excluded. In the case of contract cities, "municipal expenditures" refers to all expenses incurred through city government *plus* taxes levied on property within the city by Los Angeles County for the provision of fire protection through fire protection districts; but again they exclude sewage disposal expenses. Sewage disposal expenditures were excluded because there is no accurate method to allocate these to cities due to an almost total lack of correspondence between city and county sanitation district boundaries. It was possible to estimate fire protection expenditures in contract cities because each such city was included in one and only one fire protection district. An examination indicated that fire protection tax levies invariably exceeded actual fire protection costs. Therefore, municipal expenditures for contract cities are likely to be somewhat inflated. For the Los Angeles cities, all data are for the 1970-1971 fiscal year.

As in the case of the Los Angeles contract cities, included as a municipal expenditure for nine of the St. Louis County cities in fire protection districts are estimates of the fire protection costs based on fire district tax levies incurred by their residents.

The municipal expenditure data utilized in analyses of Detroit area cities are for 1967 (from the US Census of Governments). Only two of the municipalities included in the Detroit area analyses experienced dramatic population increases between 1960 and 1970, and in these the most rapid growth occurred in the early 1960s. No municipalities, with the exception of Detroit, experienced appreciable population declines between 1960 and 1970. Therefore, there is no reason to presume that the 1967 municipal expenditures when expressed in per capita form (using 1970 populations) are biased to any great extent. Those for Detroit are biased upwardly.

It should be stressed that these data limitations preclude any direct intermetropolitan area comparisons with regard to the levels of expenditure.

Assessed Valuation. Assessed valuation refers to that portion of the total value of real and personal property within a municipality that is subject to local taxation. Within each metropolitan area assessed valuations are computed as a constant proportion of market value. However, they are not comparable between metropolitan areas.

Tax Effort. The property tax effort of a jurisdiction is defined here as the ratio of a jurisdiction's tax rate (in dollars per $100 of assessed valuation) to its per capita assessed valuation. It is an index of the extent to which the assessed valuation of property in a jurisdiction is utilized to finance government and service provision.

Per Pupil Expenditures. Per pupil expenditures include all the current operating, capital outlay and community service expenditures of a K-12 school district in a given year. The number of pupils utilized in calculating this ratio is a district's average daily attendance, unless otherwise noted. They are comparable across all three metropolitan areas.

A Comparison of the Relations Between Municipal Expenditures, Assessed Valuation and Tax Efforts— The Detroit Anomaly

The traditional and still basic source of revenue upon which most cities in urban America rely for service provision is the property tax. The suburban municipalities of St. Louis and Detroit and the noncontract cities in the Los Angeles metropolitan area are not exceptions. Nevertheless, the extent to which cities utilize their property tax bases, measured by tax effort, is highly variable. Although tax efforts are not strictly comparable, in all three cases tax efforts in the central cities are considerably greater than the averages of those in suburbs (Table 12-8). The greatest tax effort differentials between central city and suburbs are in the Detroit area, and the lowest in the Los Angeles area. The variability of tax efforts in the suburbs is in the reverse order—highest in the Los Angeles area and lowest in the Detroit area.

Table 12-8. Tax Efforts in Central Cities and Suburbs

	Tax Effort	*Mean Tax Effort*	*Standard Deviation of Tax Effort*
Los Angeles (1970–1971)	0.000953	–	–
Noncontract Suburbs (1970–1971)	–	0.000543	0.000295
St. Louis (1972)	0.000788	–	–
St. Louis County Municipalities[1] (1972)	–	0.000354	0.000220
Detroit (1971)	0.000700	–	–
Detroit Suburbs[2] (1971–1972)	–	0.000281	0.000161

1. Includes all incorporated places in the county.

2. Includes only incorporated villages and cities in Wayne and Oakland counties, excluding Detroit.

Source: data compilation and calculations by the author.

Table 12-9. Linear Correlation and Regression of Assessed Valuation Per Capita on Per Capita Municipal Expenditures

	Correlation	*Intercept*	*Regression Coefficient*
Noncontract Cities of Los Angeles (N = 46)	0.740	$79	$19.8/1000
St. Louis County Municipalities (N = 23)	0.380	$58	$4.2/1000
Detroit Municipalities (N = 23)	-0.082	$146	-$2.0/1000

Source: Calculations by the author.

Given the importance of property taxation, a reasonable point of departure in an analysis of municipal expenditures is to test for the existence of relationships between per capita expenditures and per capita assessed valuations. The results of these analyses can then be evaluated for their "ability to pay" or equity implications by incorporating measures of income and tax efforts in subsequent analyses. There is a rather strong linear relationship ($r = 0.740$) between per capita expenditures and valuations for the noncontract cities of Los Angeles and a weak linear relationship for St. Louis County municipalities (Table 12-9). But somewhat surprisingly, in the Detroit area there is no linear relationship between per capita municipal expenditures and per capita assessed valuations whatsoever. Examinations of the scatter diagrams of per capita municipal expenditures versus per capita assessed valuations are revealing of further information. For the noncontract Los Angeles cities, variability in per capita expenditures tends to increase with increasing per capita assessed valuation (Figure 12-14). In short, the higher the per capita assessed valuation of a noncontract municipality, the higher its per capita expenditures, but the greater the range of choice of expenditure levels to satisfy local service demands.

Per capita expenditures in St. Louis County municipalities, although tending to increase with increasing per capita assessed valuations, exhibit a great deal more variation than can be accounted for solely by variations in assessed valuations (Figure 12-15). One possibility is that there are two different linear relationships between these two variables: one for municipalities with per capita assessed valuations in excess of $3,500 and another for municipalities with per capita assessed valuations below $3,200. Lending support to these suggestions is that all the municipalities in the first group (with per capita assessed valuations above $3,500) are either the newer of the territorially large and affluent suburbs discussed earlier or post-World War II middle income suburbs containing large amounts of industrial and/or commercial land uses. The municipalities in the second group are almost exclusively old lower middle income residential suburbs. In both groups, expenditures appear equally sensitive to assessed valuations, with an approximately $20-25 increase in per capita expenditures for each $1000 increase in assessed valuation. If so, the sensitivity of per capita expenditures in St. Louis County municipalities to per capita assessed valuation is almost identical to that of noncontract cities in the Los Angeles area. The basic difference between the two groups appears to be that per capita expenditures are considerably higher in the second. These, however, are only suggestions. The unavailability of data for so many municipalities in the area precludes making more definite statements.

The scatter diagram for Detroit area cities suggests a weak, positive, linear relationship between per capita expenditures and assessed valuations, *if* one can explain why the six cities with per capita valuations between $3,700 and $6,400 and expenditures exceeding $170 per capita behave as they do (Figure 12-16). Five of these six cities—in order of expenditures: Highland Park, Detroit, Pontiac, Wyandotte, Hazel Park and Hamtramck—do share at least two common characteristics. First, all are among the oldest cities in the metropolitan area. Second, all are heavy indus-

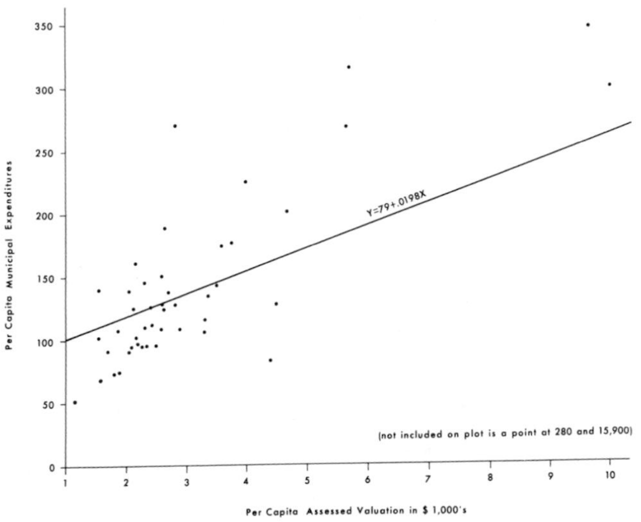

Figure 12-14. Relationship between Per Capita Municipal Expenditures and Per Capita Assessed Valuations, Noncontract Cities of Los Angeles.

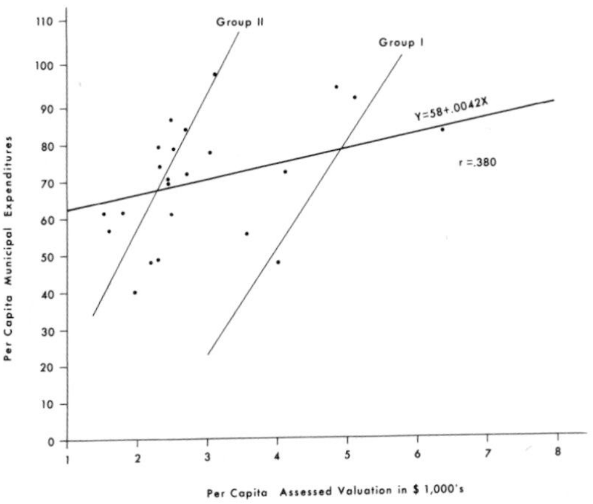

Figure 12-15. Relationship between Per Capita Municipal Expenditures and Per Capita Assessed Valuations, St. Louis County Municipalities.

try cities and not suburbs in the traditional residential sense. They differ from the other old industrial cities—such as Ecorse, River Rouge and Dearborn—in that their property tax bases are considerably lower. Hazel Park, although a younger and more residential city, is contiguous to an old, heavily industrial area. It seems reasonable to suggest that these cities are faced with a set of demands for municipal services that is fundamentally different from those of the other cities in the area. In this regard it is important to note that the older industrial cities with higher property tax bases also have very high per capita expenditures. If one accepts this line of argument, it can be concluded that per capita expenditures in the newer industrial suburbs and in both the new and old residential suburbs of the Detroit area do appear somewhat sensitive to per capita assessed valuations, but less so than in the noncontract cities of Los Angeles. In the older industrial cities, expenditures are relatively independent of assessed valuations.

Turning next to an examination of per capita municipal expenditures and a second indicator of wealth—median family income—only in the Detroit area is there evidence of relationship (Figure 12-17, 12-18 and 12-19). Surprisingly, the relationship here is clearly negative and apparently concave downward rather than linear. Contrary to masking a relationship, as was the case in the previous analysis, the behavior of the high expenditure, older industrial cities of the Detroit area is shaping the relationship between income and expenditures (Figure 12-19). When these cities are ignored, any semblence of relationship between the variables disappears and a disorderly scatter of points similar to that for

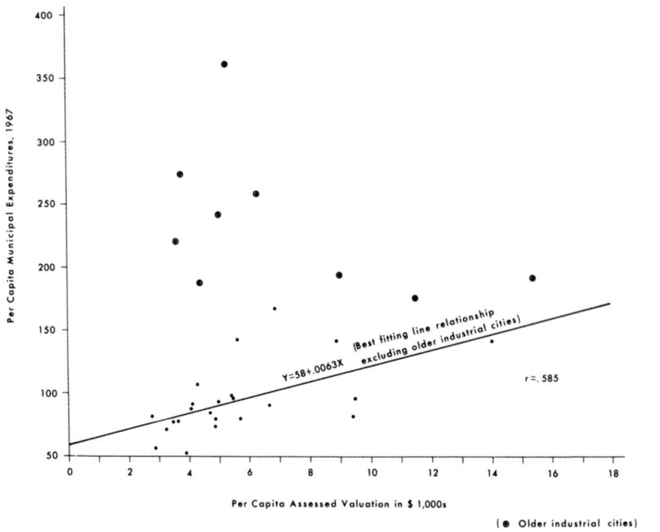

Figure 12-16. Relationship between Per Capita Municipal Expenditures and Per Capita Assessed Valuations, Detroit Area Municipalities.

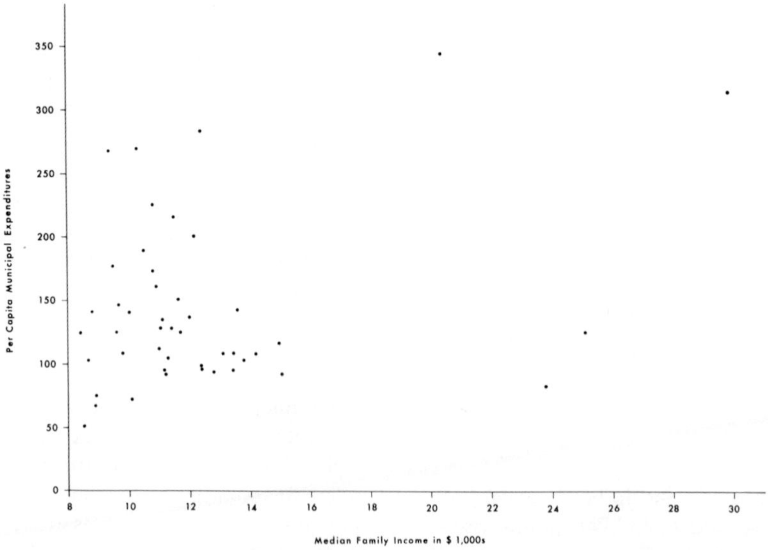

Figure 12-17. Per Capita Municipal Expenditures versus Median Family Income, Noncontract Cities of Los Angeles.

noncontract Los Angeles cities appears. There are, however, two fundamental differences in the per capita expenditure levels of noncontract cities and this "reduced set" of Detroit area cities. First, on the average they are more than twice as high in the noncontract cities. The fact that expenditure levels are for 1966-1967 in the Detroit area and 1970-1971 in the Los Angeles area can perhaps account for some of the difference but not much (Detroit per capita expenditures increased by $25 in this four year period), particularly when one recalls that sewage disposal expenditures are not included in the Los Angeles area expenditures

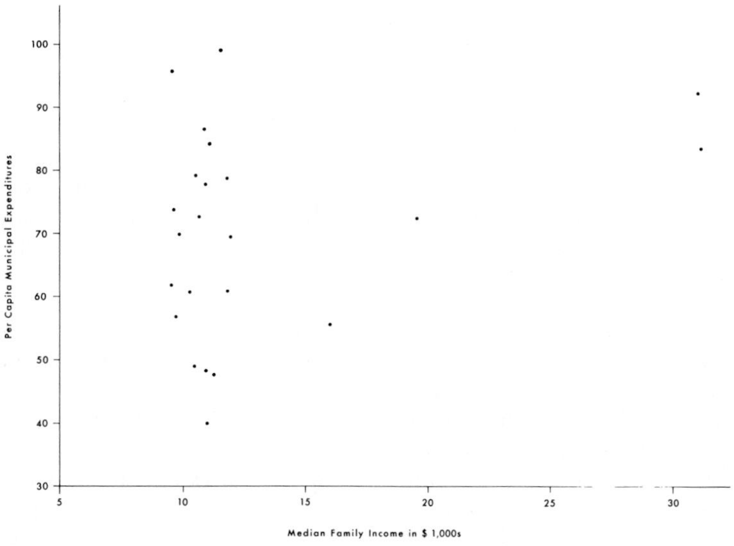

Figure 12-18. Per Capita Municipal Expenditures versus Median Family Income, St. Louis County Municipalities.

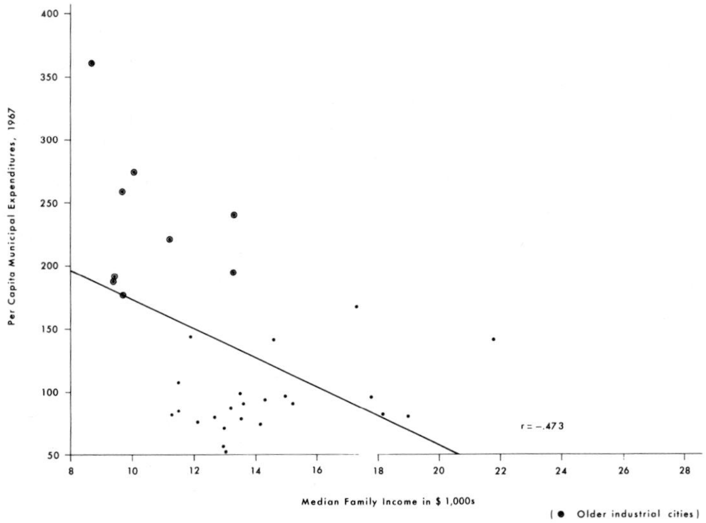

Figure 12-19. Per Capita Municipal Expenditures versus Median Family Income, Detroit Area Municipalities.

but are in those of the Detroit area cities (in Los Angeles cities with municipal sewerage systems the per capita costs averaged approximately $25 in 1970-1971). Second, the variations in expenditures between suburbs is much greater in the Los Angeles area, particularly between the lower income suburbs. A pattern of high variability between the lower income suburbs is also found for St. Louis County municipalities (Figure 12-18).

Since the median income of a municipality is clearly a better, albeit crude, indicator of the need for municipal service expenditures than is per capita assessed valuation, the results of these analyses lead to the hypothesis that expenditures in the Los Angeles noncontract and St. Louis County cities are determined more by fiscal exigencies than by local need or choice. In the Detroit area, by contrast, if one assumes that the benefits of expenditures in the older, industrial cities do not flow primarily to business and industrial firms, it can be hypothesized that the locational incidence of public expenditure is more or less equitable—that is, the highest expenditures occur in municipalities with the greatest need, irrespective of assessed valuation. However, before accepting these hypotheses as facts, it is necessary to be more precise about what distributions of expenditure levels would constitute equitable ones. The income of families in municipalities is clearly important, but so, too, are their tax burdens or efforts. For example, if the low expenditure levels observed for the relatively low median income but nonindustrial suburbs in the Detroit area are achieved only with very high tax efforts, the distribution would probably not be adjudged equitable. Ideally, the quality of public services received in a municipality is also important in making determinations regarding equity. Unfortunately, no generally satisfactory measures of quality exist.

Assume that a metropolitan area contains nine "types" of municipalities based on median family incomes (low, middle, high) and tax efforts (low, moderate, high). If service needs are inversely related to income, *equity with respect to income* at the city scale implies that expenditures will be highest in low income cities, lower in middle income cities and lowest in high income cities. For example, the rank order of per capita expenditures depicted in Figure 12-20 (a), (b) and (c) all manifest such equity. *Equity with respect to tax effort* means that per capita expenditures are positively related to tax efforts within each income class. In Figure 12-20 both (a) and (d) have expenditure distributions that are equitable in terms of tax efforts. A strongly equitable distribution of per capita expenditures is defined here as one that is equitable both with respect to income and tax efforts. In Figure 12-20 only (a) is strongly equitable. The expenditure pattern of Figure 12-20 (d) is clearly inequitable with respect to income. It would be the expected pattern of expenditures if conditions of ability and willingness to pay were paramount in the public expenditure decisions of municipalities.

Utilizing these definitions, it is possible to determine in an aggregative sense the extent to which the expenditure patterns of the noncontract Los Angeles, St. Louis County and Detroit area municipalities are consistent with "strong equity" or "ability and willingness to

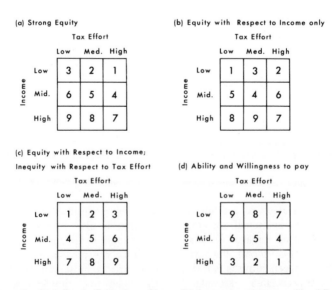

(a) Strong Equity

Income \ Tax Effort	Low	Med.	High
Low	3	2	1
Mid.	6	5	4
High	9	8	7

(b) Equity with Respect to Income only

Income \ Tax Effort	Low	Med.	High
Low	1	3	2
Mid.	5	4	6
High	8	9	7

(c) Equity with Respect to Income; Inequity with Respect to Tax Effort

Income \ Tax Effort	Low	Med.	High
Low	1	2	3
Mid.	4	5	6
High	7	8	9

(d) Ability and Willingness to pay

Income \ Tax Effort	Low	Med.	High
Low	9	8	7
Mid.	6	5	4
High	3	2	1

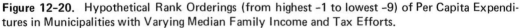

Figure 12-20. Hypothetical Rank Orderings (from highest -1 to lowest -9) of Per Capita Expenditures in Municipalities with Varying Median Family Income and Tax Efforts.

Table 12-10. Mean Values ($) of Per Capita Expenditures in Detroit Area Municipalities with Varying Median Family Incomes (1970) and Tax Efforts*

	Tax Effort (TE)		
Median Family Income (I)	*Low (TE < .000174)*	*Moderate (.000174 ⩽ TE ⩽ .000348)*	*High (TE > .000348)*
Low (I < $12,000)	179 (2)	183 (5)	209 (5)
Middle ($12,000 ⩽ I ⩽ $16,000)	110 (3)	96 (6)	79 (6)
High (I > $16,000)	101 (3)	132 (2)	–

*Based on 1971 and 1972 assessed valuations and tax rates for Wayne and Oakland County municipalities, respectively.

Source: computations by the author.

Table 12-11. Mean Values ($) of Per Capita Expenditures in Non-Contract Cities in Los Angeles County with Varying Median Family Incomes (1970) and Tax Efforts (1970-1971)

	Tax Effort (TE)		
Median Family Income (I)	*Low (TE < .000362)*	*Moderate (.000362 ⩽ TE ⩽ .000724)*	*High (TE > .000724)*
Low (I < $12,000)	168 (6)	134 (14)	128 (8)
Middle ($12,000 ⩽ I ⩽ $16,000)	156 (6)	104 (3)	101 (4)
High (I > $16,000)	215 (2)	222 (2)	–

Source: computations by the author.

Table 12-12. Mean Values ($) of Per Capita Expenditures in St. Louis County Municipalities with Varying Median Family Incomes (1970) and Tax Efforts (1971)

	Tax Effort (TE)		
Median Family Income (I)	*Low (TE < .000236)*	*Moderate (.000236 ⩽ TE ⩽ .000472)*	*High (TE > .000472)*
Low (I < $13,000)	–	72 (2)	60 (2)
Middle ($13,000 ⩽ I ⩽ $19,000)	–	62 (10)	87 (1)
High (I > $19,000)	86 (4)	76 (4)	

Source: computations by the author.

pay" considerations. The average per capita expenditures of municipalities with varying median family incomes and tax efforts for the three sets of cities are indicated in Tables 12-10, 12-11, and 12-12. The designations "low," "middle," etc., with respect to median family income and tax efforts, are relative to the respective metropolitan areas. A "moderate tax effort" is defined as one within 25 percent (plus or minus) of the mean tax effort of the cities in the area in question, a "low tax effort" is less than 25 percent of the mean, and so on. The boundaries of the median family income categories are more subjective but correspond wherever possible to "gaps" in distributions of this variable for each set of cities. All operational definitions are indicated in the tables, as are the numbers of cities included in calculations. Some of the entries are based on small numbers of municipalities; hence they must be interpreted cautiously.

As hypothesized, the mean expenditure pattern of the Detroit area cities most closely approximates that of strong equity. Expenditures are highest in low income cities; equity with respect to income is evident for the low tax effort cities over the three income levels, and for all tax effort levels with respect to low and high income cities. Expenditures in the middle income cities present an anomaly—they decrease with increasing tax efforts and on the average are the lowest in metropolitan areas. This phenomenon can in part be accounted for by recent changes in suburbanization. Middle income cities with high tax efforts are the almost purely residential counterparts of the old industrial cities discussed above. All are pre-World War II white collar suburbs close to Detroit which, in the housing shortage yet economically booming period following the war, became mixed blue-white collar. However, with a relative decline in the value of the housing stock and without industrial tax bases, the only way to maintain prewar levels of service provision in these suburbs was to increase tax effort. The middle income, moderate tax effort cities—with the exception of Dearborn—are also almost exclusively residential but blue collar (all the suburbs whose settlement was stimulated by the establishment of a Ford plant in East Dearborn are in this category). If Dearborn's expenditures are deleted from the calculation of this group's average, it plummets to \$76—a figure comparable to that of the middle income, high tax effort suburbs. Since the higher expenditures of the middle income, low tax effort cities can be attributed to their status as new suburbs with significant concentrations of industrial and commercial land use, the apparent inequity with respect to tax effort in the middle income suburbs of Detroit is probably not real. As we have already seen from the analysis of expenditures and assessed valuations, whatever inequity in municipal expenditures may exist between middle and high income suburbs, it is not great.

The pattern of average expenditure levels in the noncontract cities of Los Angeles (Table 12-11) appears to be equitable with respect to income for low and middle income cities. But it is apparent that the expenditure differentials between the low income cities and the middle income cities are not as great as those in the Detroit area. What is so striking about this pattern is that it manifests inequity with respect to tax efforts. Within these two income levels, expenditures on the average are lowest in those municipalities whose residents assume the highest levels of property taxation. An even sharper contrast is drawn when the city of Los Angeles is deleted from the analysis: the mean expenditure for the low income, high tax effort group of cities decreases from \$128 to \$108. With regard to the noncontract cities of Los Angeles one cannot escape the conclusion that their per capita expenditure levels, although modified by variations in tax efforts, are determined primarily by local property values.

So few St. Louis area cities, particularly those with very low median incomes, are included that the extraction of strong generalizations based upon the data of Table 12-12 would be sheer speculation. There are hints that low tax efforts are confined largely to high income municipalities and that high tax efforts, if they exist, are found almost exclusively in low income cities. The data plot in Figure 12-21, which is based on all 94 municipalities in St. Louis County, confirms these suspicions. In all three metropolitan areas (excepting contract cities in Los Angeles) tax efforts tend to decrease but at a decreasing rate, with increasing per capita assessed valuations (Figures 12-22 and 12-23). However, the Detroit area is the only one in which this form of relationship is characteristic of muncipalities irrespective of their median family income category. Among the noncontract cities of Los Angeles, as well as in St. Louis County, low tax efforts are enjoyed primarily in cities with high median incomes.

Even though expenditure data for the numerous low tax effort, low per capita assessed valuation municipalities in St. Louis are lacking, it is clear, given their heavy dependence on property taxation, that their per capita expenditures must be relatively

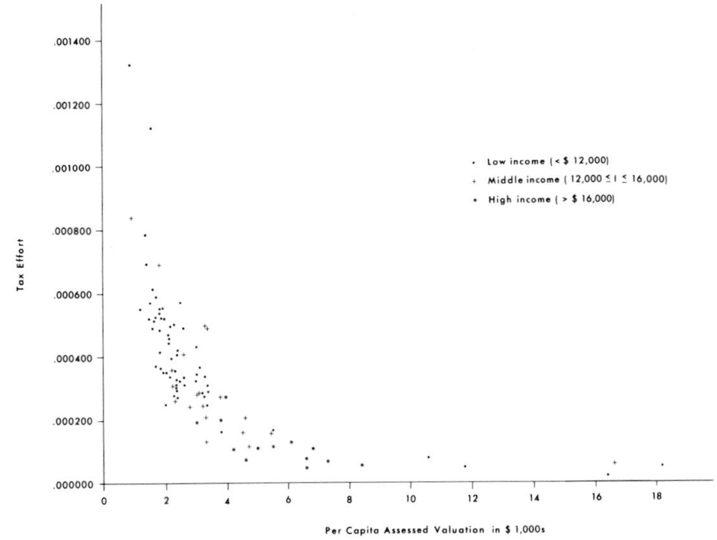

Figure 12-21. Tax Effort versus Per Capita Assessed Valuations, All St. Louis County Municipalities.

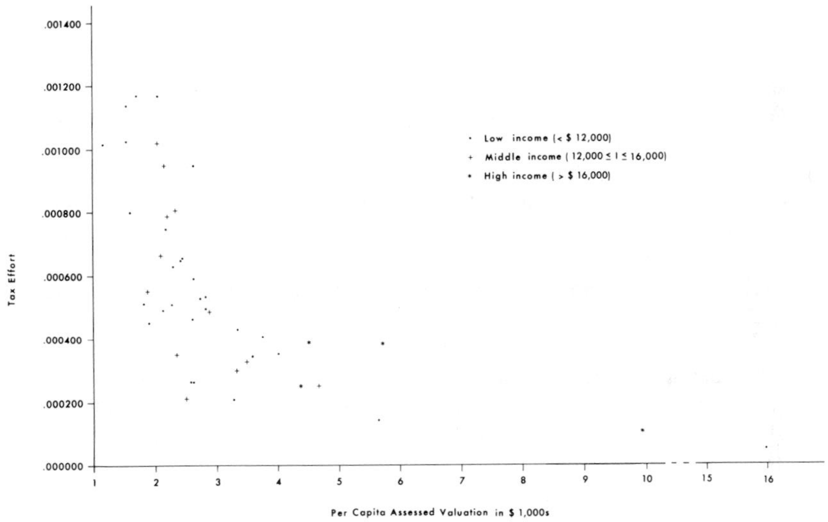

Figure 12-22. Tax Effort versus Per Capita Assessed Valuations, Noncontract Cities of Los Angeles.

low. For example, in 1972 the municipalities with the three highest tax efforts could have generated only $12.38, $28.55 and $7.44 per capita, respectively, from municipal and fire district property taxation. Comparable figures for the three lowest tax effort municipalities are $54.05, $68.76 and $22.98. Although data presented earlier suggest that "municipal" expenditures may be determined more by local property values than by citizen choice, it is also evident that municipal expenditures in St. Louis County are remarkably low when compared with those of the Los Angeles or Detroit area cities. Much of this is attributable to the small size of cities in St. Louis County—43 percent have populations below 1,500, 61 percent have less than 5,000 residents and only one city has as many as 50,000 residents. Ser-

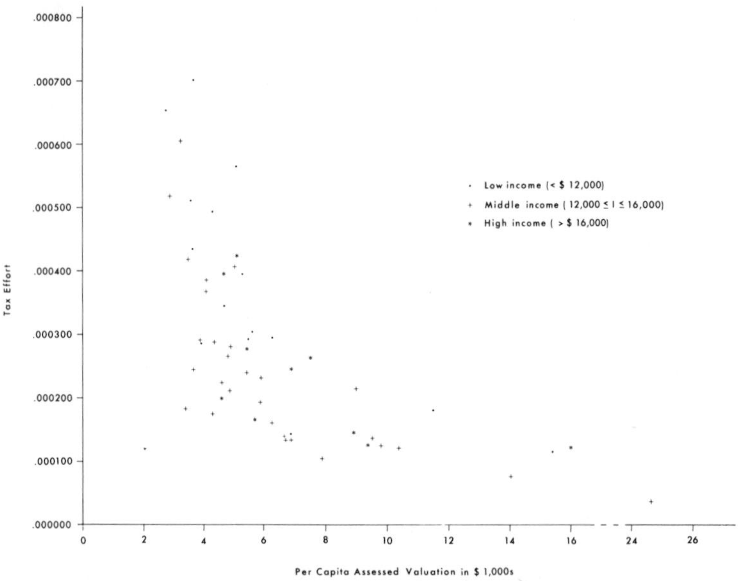

Figure 12-23. Tax Effort versus Per Capita Assessed Valuations, Detroit Area Municipalities.

vices may be "substandard," but at least they do not cost much and the style of government tends to be highly personalized.

To demonstrate that the apparently atypical pattern of expenditures in Detroit area municipalities possesses some of the attributes of equity is not to explain why the pattern occurs. The generalized concave downward shape of the relationship between per capita expenditures and median family income can be accounted for only partially by variations in municipal tax efforts and the locational pattern of industry. The older industrial cities, including Detroit, with their generally low median incomes do indeed have high property tax efforts but their much higher per capita expenditures cannot be accounted for by these alone. Obviously they have other sources of revenue that are not utilized extensively by the other municipalities in the area. Highland Park, for example—the city with the highest per capita expenditures in 1967—had a sizable income from the same source which contributed greatly to its high municipal expenditures—its hospital complex. Perhaps not unexpectedly, Detroit utilizes the widest variety of revenue sources. The city has an income tax levied at the rate of 2.0 percent on city residents and 0.5 percent on all nonresidents employed in the city. In 1970 the tax netted the city three-fourths as much revenue as did the property tax. Also, Detroit obtained slightly less than two-thirds as much revenue in 1970 as through the property tax through shared revenue from the state and grants from both the state and federal governments. On a per capita basis these intergovernmental revenues flowing to Detroit amounted to $114.85 (37.0 percent of this was from the federal government). This was roughly three times as much as was received by any of the other cities in the metropolitan area with populations in excess of 50,000 in 1970. Other municipalities with relatively low assessed valuations per capita and low median incomes, including all of the older industrial suburbs, derive higher per capita revenues from intergovernmental transfers than do the remaining municipalities in the area even though the chief source of this revenue, the state, reallocates state-collected taxes back to municipalities more on the basis of population than of "need."

The generally low per capita expenditures of all other municipalities in the Detroit area is quite unlike the Los Angeles noncontract city pattern: expenditures tending to increase substantially with increases in assessed valuation. The Grosse Pointes and other more exclusive, high income suburbs, which if they were in Los Angeles probably would be "big spenders," are apparently able to sustain the life styles of their residents with quite modest per capita municipal expenditures. No doubt strict enforcement of zoning regulations, relative inaccessibility and a penchant for privateness—private beaches, private tennis courts, etc.—are important in accounting for this. But also important is their extensive utilization of intergovernmental cooperative and service agreements, particularly in the provision of fire protection. More generally, however, the city of Detroit contributes to the low costs of service provision in its suburbs by its longstanding willingness to provide most of them with a low cost water supply, many of them with low cost sewage collection and treatment, others with police training, and so on.

Unfortunately, no data are available to assess precisely the extent to which Detroit has subsidized service provision in suburban areas, or the extent to which economies have been realized through intersuburban cooperative service agreements. However, William Neenan, in his "Suburban-Central City Exploration Thesis," presents a detailed analysis of benefit and revenue flows between Detroit and six suburban municipalities. Considering only conservative estimates for the direct and indirect benefits, Neenan estimated that in 1966 the net subsidy from Detroit to the six suburban municipalities ranged from \$1.73 to \$12.58 on a per suburban resident basis. His estimation of the amount of the subsidy due to Detroit's provision of water was based only on his calculation of the extent to which Detroit failed to charge the full cost of providing water to a municipality. If one were to include in the water subsidy the amount a municipality would probably incur if it had an independent water system, the amount of the subsidy would be considerably greater. Ironically, of the 13 cities with 1970 populations in excess of 50,000 which purchase Detroit water, only one had per capita water supply costs greater than those of Detroit itself. The territorially extensive and high income city of Sterling Heights (area, 36 square miles; population, 61,365) had per capita water costs of \$47.39 in 1970; those for Detroit were \$36.85. The city with the next highest per capita water costs was the geographically distant Pontiac (\$23.06); all the remaining cities incurred per capita water costs between \$8.00 and \$21.00. Eight of the 13 cities incurred per capita water costs of less than one-half of those incurred by Detroit residents.

In conclusion, the atypical municipal expenditure pattern in the Detroit metropolitan area is the result of (1) a locational pattern of industry and income segregation in suburban areas—whereby a number of cities with low residential property values have high *industrial* property values and few have *only* low *residential* property values; (2) relatively large intergovernmental revenue transfers to Detroit and to those suburbs with both low assessed valuations per capita and low median incomes; and (3) a pattern of intergovernmental relations permitting the realization of service provision economies.

An Evaluation of the "Lakewood Plan" of Contracting

The "Lakewood Plan" of county-city contracting in Los Angeles County is a system of public service provision in which the production of most services remains with the county but the articulation of demands pertaining to the range, levels and timing of delivery of services devolves to small units of government—municipalities. Under this system, Los Angeles County sells a "package" of services to a "contract" city, usually for a period of five years. In 1969, for the 30 cities that Los Angeles County considers as "contract" cities, the number of services included in a "package" ranged from a low of 20 to a high of 41. The contracting city selects the package it desires, subject only to the limitation that it cannot contract for a level of provision below that which is provided by the county to unincorporated areas on a countywide basis.

"Contract" cities retain the full legal authority to undertake their own production of public services and to contract with other municipalities or private vendors. In order not to lose "customers," the county has had to keep its prices down, at least to the costs which could be achieved by these alternative methods of provision. The county has also been forced by its clients to minimize some of the less tangible costs associated with service delivery. For example, to assure the continuance of contracts with several cities, the county decentralized road maintenance and police protection services, including the requirement that county policemen reside in the city to which they are assigned. The county has not always proved responsive or efficient enough for some cities and has, on occasion, been underbid by private vendors. In more cases, a city has decided to undertake its own production of a service. Police protection has been a particularly sensitive service area on the issue of community accountability but even here, as of 1969, the county had lost only one police service contract.

From all easily observed outward manifestations, it appears that the county's emphasis on consumer satisfaction as well as on service delivery efficiency has had the more general result of making the internal workings of the county bureaucracy more socially efficient—i.e., more effective and accountable, as well. However, little real effort has gone into evaluating the success of this system of contracting. According to Ries and Kirlin:

> The county considers it a success, primarily because it is working, and cities keep incorporating and contracting. . . . The county—consistent with presumptions for resolving the "problem" of metropolitan government—also sees the program as a step toward achieving economies of scale in appropriate governmental functions. It views the program as a laboratory, where a process similar to natural selection will sort out appropriate roles for county and city. Hence, it is considered an interim step toward a comprehensive reallocation of functions between levels of government. [p. 106].

The purpose of this section is to go beyond county proclamations and anecdotal evidence and attempt a determination, however, preliminary, of the extent to which the Lakewood Plan of contracting represents a real step toward the simultaneous achievement of efficiency, effectiveness and accountability in the provision of municipal services. Since it is likely that the success of a city in articulating the service demands of its residents, even in small units of government, is dependent upon their social and economic homogeneity, the analysis begins with some social and economic contrasts between the contract and more traditional (noncontract) cities in the Los Angeles metropolitan area. It then proceeds to comparisons of their expenditures and revenue patterns. Unless otherwise noted analyses are based on 27 contract cities and 46 noncontract cities.

Homogeneity of Contract Cities. An aggregate profile of the socioeconomic characteristics and per capita governmental expenditures for contract and noncontract cities is presented in Table 12-13. Municipal expenditures have already been defined; *general governmental expenditures* are a measure of the municipal costs not directly related to the delivery of a public service and more related to direct costs of local demand articulation. Operationally, these consist of administration costs, building maintenance costs, the interest and principal on bonds, retirement fund contributions, insurance, community promotion, election expenses, and miscellaneous departmental and nondepartmental costs. As can be seen, contract cities have, on the average, lower percentages of black residents, fewer foreign born residents, less highly educated populations, lower percentages of families with "high" incomes, lower valued housing, lower median family incomes, and lower per capita general and municipal governmental expenditures. Contract cities have, again on the average, a higher proportion of Spanish-speaking residents and/or residents with Spanish surnames and a higher percentage of families with small children. Some of the differences, however, appear small. Table 12-14 is designed to provide rough indexes of the salience of these differences between contract and noncontract cities. It was constructed by determining the grand means—over all Los Angeles area cities—of the several socioeconomic and fiscal characteristics. The percentage of contract cities falling above the grand mean is compared with the percentage of noncontract cities also falling above that value.

All differences between the two types of cities, except for per capita assessed valuation, appear salient. However, the most pronounced differences occur with respect to the two governmental expenditure measures—municipal expenditures on the average being almost twice as high per capita for the noncontract cities, with general governmental expenditures per capita being two and a half times greater in the noncontract cities. In brief, the contract cities have populations that are more homogeneous with respect to non-Mexican-American ethnicity and possibly race, are considerably poorer, are less well educated, are more oriented to the rearing of small children, and are

Table 12-13. Mean Values of Socioeconomic Characteristics and Governmental Expenditures for Contract and Noncontract Cities, 1970

Characteristics	*Contract Cities*	*Noncontract Cities*
Percentage Negro	1.09	3.81
Percentage Spanish Speaking or with Spanish Surname	26.92	16.63
Percentage Foreign Born	7.6	9.7
Median School Years Completed	11.9	12.5
Percentage of Families with own Children under Six Years	33.6	23.6
Percentage of Families with Incomes less than Poverty level	8.1	6.3
Percentage of Families with Incomes more than $15,000 a Year	24.8	31.6
Median Value of Owner-Occupied Housing	$25,511	$26,460
Median Income	$11,176	$12,457
Assessed Valuation Per Capita	2,642	3,353
Municipal Expenditures Per Capita	$73.16	$144.45
General Government Expenditures Per Capita	$14.84	$36.08

Source: data compilation from US Bureau of the Census publications and calculations by the author.

Table 12-14. Socioeconomic Status and Governmental Expenditures Profile of Contract and Noncontract Cities, 1970

		Percent Falling Above Grand Mean	
Characteristic	*Grand Mean*	*Contract*	*Noncontract*
Percentage Negro	2.81	11	24
Percentage Spanish Speaking or with Spanish Surname	20.16	50	21
Percentage Foreign Born	9.0	25	49
Median School Years Completed	12.3	38	63
Percentage of Families with Own Children under Six Years	26.8	80	23
Percentage of Families with Incomes Less than Poverty level	6.9	58	36
Percentage of Families with Incomes more than $15,000 a Year	29.4	20	51
Median Value of Owner-Occupied Housing	$26,187	22	40
Median Income	$12,016	25	37
Assessed Valuation per Capita	$3,090	30	33
Municipal Expenditures Per Capita	$118.08	7	54
General Government Expenditures Per Capita	$28.23	11	48

Source: data compilation by the author.

spending much less in articulating demand and in actually providing public services than are the noncontract cities. Whether the quality of the services received are comparable for the two types of cities cannot be determined with available data. However, if service quality is lower in contract cities, it cannot possibly be as much lower as the differences in expenditure levels might suggest. Further evidence to support this contention is presented below.

Relationships Between Expenditure Levels and Economic Characteristics. As can be seen from Figure 12-24, there is a weak linear rela-

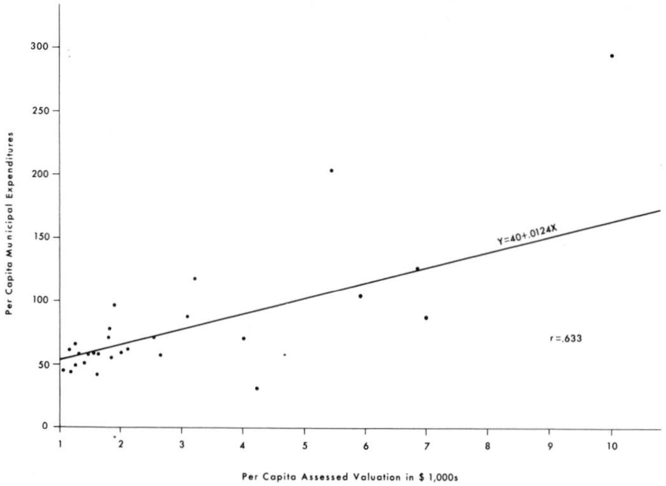

Figure 12-24. Relationship Between Per Capita Municipal Expenditures and Per Capita Assessed Valuations, Contract Cities of Los Angeles.

tionship between per capita municipal expenditures in contract cities and their per capita assessed valuations. However, in contrast to the pattern of noncontract cities (Figure 12-14), expenditures in contract cities increase less rapidly with increasing assessed valuations and contract cities almost invariably have lower per capita expenditures than noncontract cities with the same per capita property values. If the quality of municipal services is lower in contract cities, it is not low enough for their residents to expend more of their relatively underutilized property tax resources.

Service delivery is more technically efficient in the contract cities (Figure 12-25 and 12-26). Per capita service expenditures (municipal minus general governmental expenditures) are weakly but linearly related to per capita property values in both sets of cities. But in contract cities service expenditures are less sensitive to property values and consistently lower.

Since only eight of the contract cities levied any municipal property tax whatsoever in 1970-1971, it might be hypothesized that indicators of wealth, other than assessed valuations, are more influential in determining their per capita service expenditures. Such a hypothesis is not supported for indicators such as the median value of owner-occupied housing and the percentage of families with incomes exceeding $15,000 a year (Figures 12-27 and 12-28). Furthermore, simple physical indicators of potential service demand—such as population density or geographical size—cannot account for the variations in per capita service expenditures simply because there is very little variation in these indicators between contract cities (recall that all those included in the analysis are post-1950 residential communities; also see Figure 12-6 regarding size). The general conclusion reached, then, is that variations in public service expenditures in contract cities appear to be the result of variations in local preferences which, in turn, are related to the value of property within a city. Such also seems to be the case for noncontract cities, with the important exception being that assessed valuation affects not only how much service is preferred but also how much is actually obtained.

Revenue Sources for Contract and Noncontract Cities—The Issue of Equity. Although few of the contract cities have *municipal* property taxes, all incur a property tax administered by the county for the provision of fire protection through one of four fire prevention districts. Even including this tax, property taxes levied in contract cities remain, on the average, less than half of those levied in noncontract cities. Clearly, then, except for fire protection, contract cities rely primarily on other revenue sources for public service provision. One is the

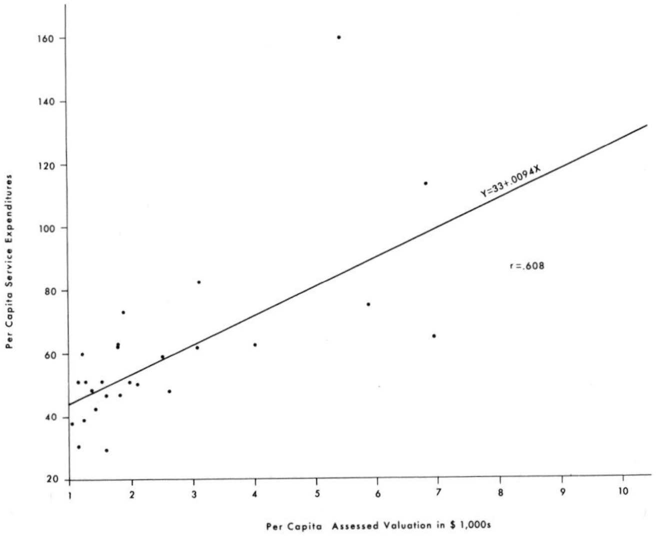

Figure 12-25. Relationship between Per Capita Service Expenditures and Per Capita Assessed Valuations, Contract Cities of Los Angeles.

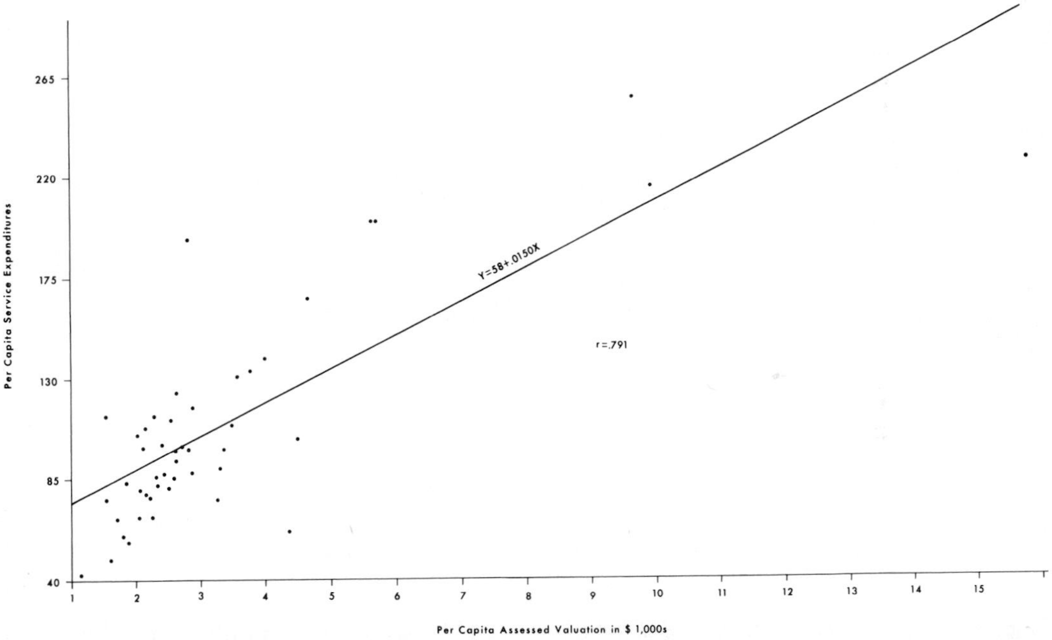

Figure 12-26. Relationship between Per Capita Service Expenditures and Per Capita Assessed Valuations, Noncontract Cities of Los Angeles.

city sales tax. In only four of the contract cities does this source of revenue exceed that obtained through intergovernmental transfers—primarily payments to cities on the basis of population from various state taxes and from a percentage of the county's reimbursement of state taxes on gasoline.

Even though the contract cities contain relatively poorer populations, they tend to receive less intergovernmental revenue on a per

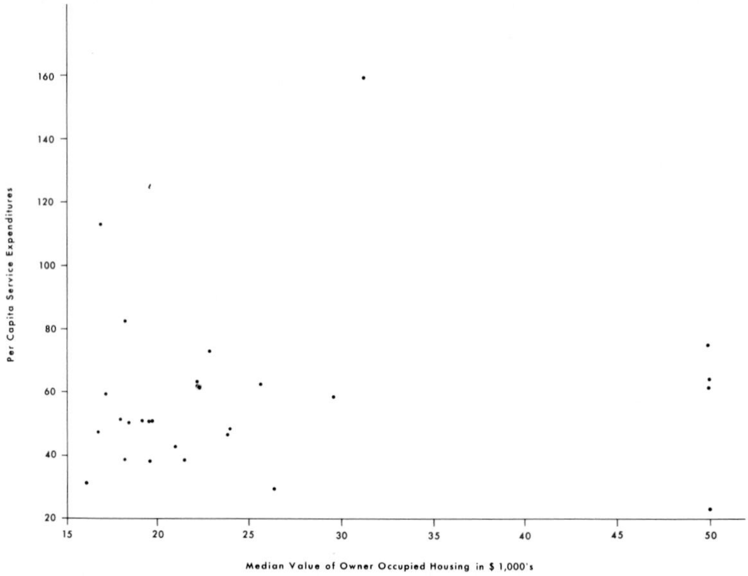

Figure 12-27. Per Capita Service Expenditures versus Median Value of Owner-Occupied Housing, Contract Cities.

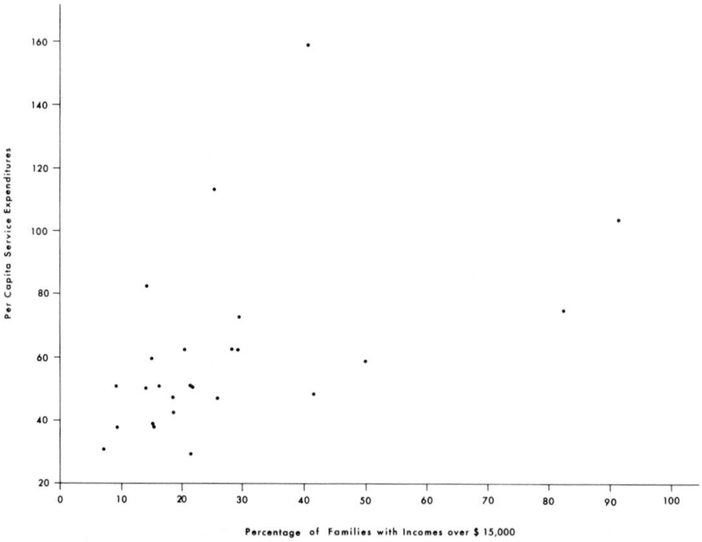

Figure 12-28. Per Capita Service Expenditures versus Percent of Families with Incomes Exceeding $15,000 and Contract Cities.

capita basis than do noncontract cities (Table 12-15). Yet when intergovernmental revenue is expressed as a percentage of municipal revenue, contract cities are seen to be much more reliant on such revenue sources. These differences between the two sets of cities are clearly salient (Table 12-16).

Regarding equity and income redistribution, these findings suggest that on a strict per capita basis there is *no* direct redistribution of income

Table 12-15. Mean Values of Governmental Revenue Attributes of Contract and Noncontract Cities, 1970

Atrribute	*Contract Cities*	*Noncontract Cities*
Intergovernmental Revenue Per Capita	$23.51	$26.33
Intergovernmental Revenue as a Percentage of "Municipal" Revenue*	34.72	21.85

*Includes fire protection property tax levies for contract cities and excludes expenses and outlays incurred for sewage disposal in noncontract cities.

Source: data compilation and calculation by the author.

favoring the contract cities but, instead, one slightly favoring the noncontract cities. However, assuming that the qualities of public service provided in the two types of cities are comparable, it is clear from the much greater reliance of contract cities on intergovernmental sources of revenue that there is an indirect redistribution favoring contract cities. The redistribution attributable to state "revenue sharing," although by no means strongly progressive, is approximately twice as progressive in the contract cities (Figure 12-29 and 30).

Summary and Conclusions Regarding Lakewood Plan. The profile of contract cities that emerges from this analysis is as follows: Contract cities (1) are, for the most part, those incorporated since 1954 and (2) have populations less well educated, more heavily Mexican-American and poorer than those of the other cities. In addition, they (3) make less use of property taxes as a source of revenue and (4) depend more heavily than other cities on sales taxes and on intergovernmental transfers (particularly the latter) for income with which to finance both government and public service provision. Demographically, they (5) are slightly more homogeneous than noncontract cities. Ries and Kirlin also found that contract cities are growing more rapidly and that they offer a broader range of services than noncontract cities. These characteristics—together with the evidence suggesting a progressive redistribution of income to the contract cities and the finding that across contract cities service expenditures per capita increase less rapidly with increases in per capita property values—lead to the conclusion that service provision is, on the average, more efficient and effective in the contract cities of Los Angeles County than in more traditional cities.

In 1970 the average population of the residential contract cities included in this analysis was 28,363; that in the noncontract cities—excluding Los Angeles and Long Beach—was 46,635. Given that the contract cities have slack fiscal resurces to devote to the articulation of the public demands of generally smaller numbers of people, there is every reason to believe that the Lakewood Plan of contracting has, if not in actuality, at least the potential for higher levels of citizen accountability.

A Comparison of School District Expenditures

Standing in marked contrast to the patterns of expenditures in municipalities, those of K-

Table 12-16. Governmental Revenue Profile of Contract and Noncontract Cities, 1970

		Percent Falling Above Grand Mean	
Characteristic	*Grand Mean*	*Contract*	*Noncontract*
Intergovernmental Revenue Per Capita	$26.33	19	54
Intergovernmental Revenue as a Percentage of "Municipal" Revenue	26.37	89	22

Source: data compiled by the author.

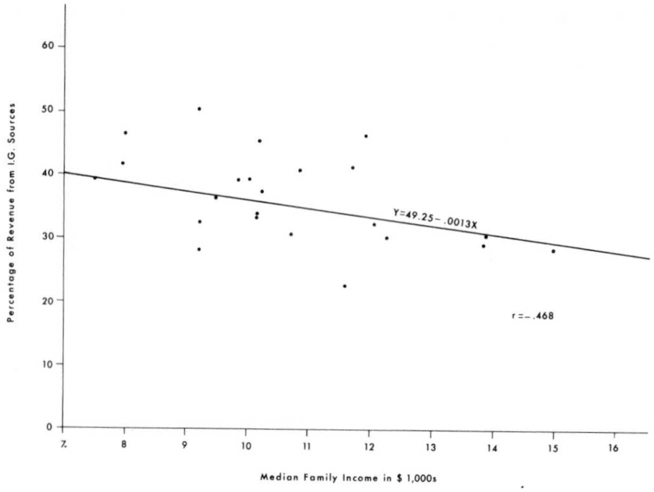

Figure 12-29. Percentage of Revenue from Intergovernmental Sources versus Median Family Income, Contract Cities.

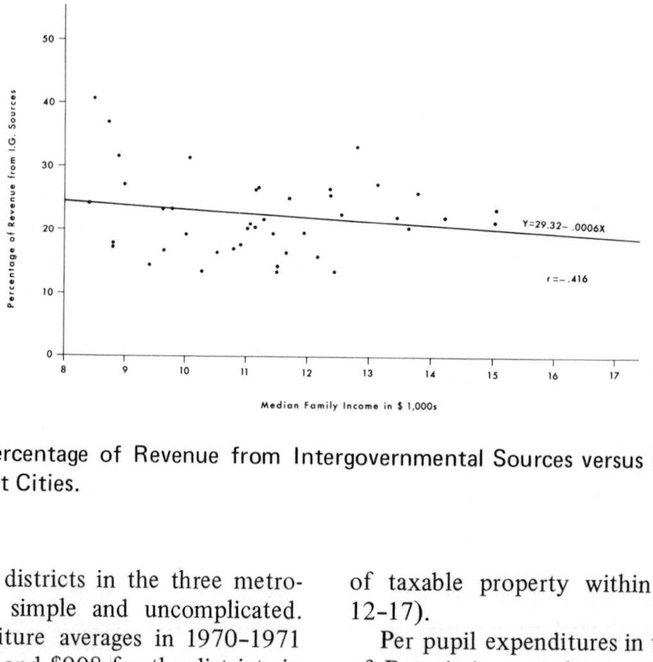

Figure 12-30. Percentage of Revenue from Intergovernmental Sources versus Median Family Income, Noncontract Cities.

12 public school districts in the three metropolitan areas are simple and uncomplicated. Per pupil expenditure averages in 1970-1971 were $881, $923 and $908 for the districts in the Los Angeles, St. Louis and Detroit areas, respectively. Allowing for the lower costs of school building heating in Los Angeles, these averages appear remarkably uniform. However, they belie fantastic variations within each area—in short, there are few "average" school districts. One does not have to search far to find one variable to account for almost all of the variation. It is the per pupil assessed valuation of taxable property within a district (Table 12-17).

Per pupil expenditures in the school districts of Detroit increase least with increases in per pupil taxable property bases ($12.00 per $1,000 in per pupil assessed valuation). The relationship in the Los Angeles area is similar to that of Detroit. But in the school districts of St. Louis County the rate of increase in per pupil expenditures with increasing assessed valuations is slightly more than twice that of those in the Detroit area. In the Detroit area, the difference in per pupil expenditures be-

Table 12-17. Regression Analysis of 1970-1971 Per Pupil Expenditures and Assessed Valuations (Per Pupil) in K-12 School Districts in Los Angeles County, in St. Louis and St. Louis County, and in the Detroit Metropolitan Area

	a	*b*	R^2
Los Angeles	$679	$14.90	0.86
St. Louis	$525	$24.57	0.94
Detroit	$670	$12.00	0.76

Note: a–indicates the expected value of per pupil expenditures when per pupil assessed valuation equals zero. b–indicates the average rate of change in per pupil expenditures for each $1,000 increase in per pupil assessed valuation.

Source: calculations by the author.

tween a school district with a $10,000 value and one with a $25,000 per pupil assessed valuation is approximately $180. The comparable figures for the Los Angeles and St. Louis areas are $224 and $369, respectively. Differences of $15,000 in per pupil assessed valuations are not uncommon in the three areas (Figures 12-31, 12-32 and 12-33).

School districts in all three areas receive some financial aid directly from their respective state governments. In Michigan and California, the amounts of state aid per pupil received by school districts are decreasing functions of their per pupil assessed valuations. For districts with very low assessed valuations per pupil, Michigan is the more generous of the two, with aid in excess of $500 per pupil. For districts in the Los Angeles area of comparable per pupil assessed valuations, aid is approximately $350 per pupil. The Michigan system of school district aid is also considerably more progressive. Districts with very high per pupil assessed valuations receive only token aid $20 to $30 per pupil), whereas in Los Angeles even "property rich" districts–such as Beverley Hills–obtained state aid in excess of $100 per pupil. Missouri, by contrast, is frugal in the extreme. Special grant programs for the more fiscally impoverished districts do exist, but Missouri has yet to discover nonregressive systems of financial aid to education. Instead, "redistribu-

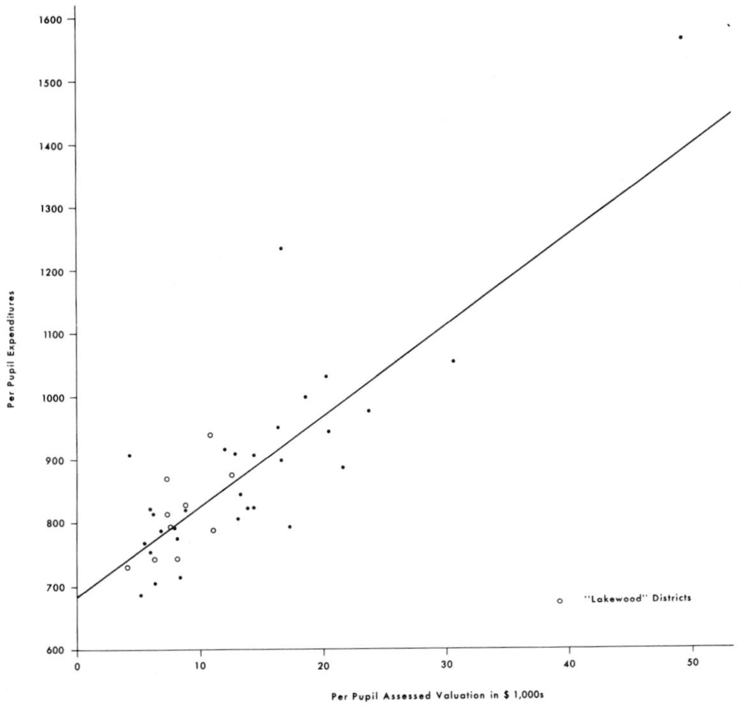

Figure 12-31. Relationship between Per Pupil Expenditures and Per Pupil Assessed Valuations, Unified School Districts in Los Angeles County.

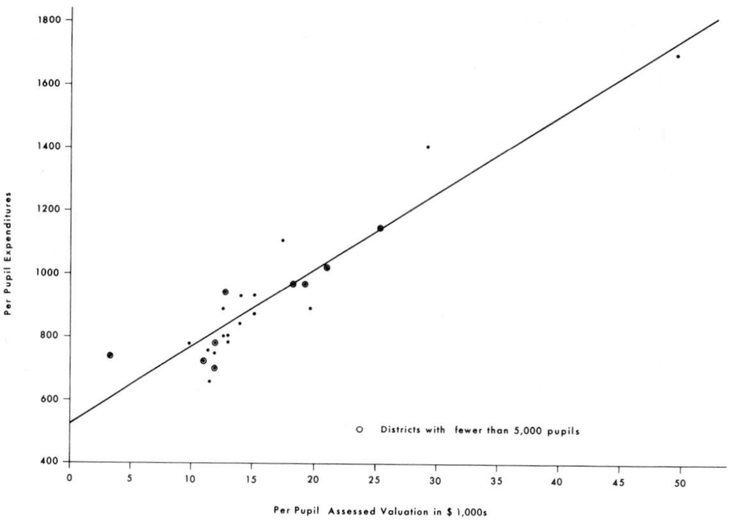

Figure 12-32. Relationship between Per Pupil Expenditures and Per Pupil Assessed Valuations, St. Louis County School Districts.

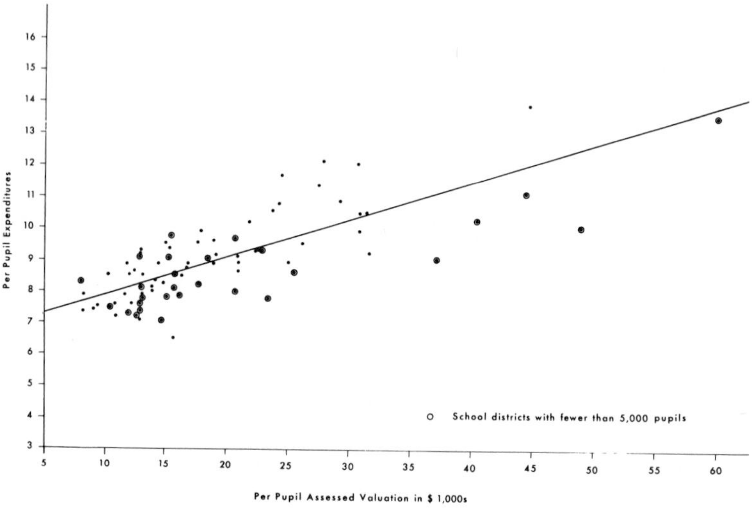

Figure 12-33. Relationship between Per Pupil Expenditures and Per Pupil Assessed Valuations: Detroit Metropolitan Area High School Districts.

tive" formulas based on enrollments predominate.

Largely as a result of the niggardly fiscal attitude of Missouri state government toward public education, the relatively low levels of per pupil expenditures in the property-poor districts of St. Louis County are achieved only through extremely high tax efforts. In fact, in 1970-1971 there was a strong inverse relationship between the rankings of per pupil expenditures and tax efforts (Spearman's ρ = -0.81). In terms of tax efforts and per pupil expenditures, the school districts in the Los Angeles and Detroit areas again are in marked contrast with those in St. Louis County. In neither area is there strong evidence to suggest that the linear relationships between school expenditures and assessed valuations are achieved only through extremely high tax efforts in the "poorest" school districts. Instead, they are more the result of relatively high tax efforts in all districts except for those with very high assessed valuations. Interestingly, tax efforts in the central city school districts are among the lowest in each of the three metropolitan areas.

As noted earlier, the Detroit and St. Louis areas, unlike Los Angeles, contain a relatively large number of school districts with small enrollments (less than 5,000). As can be seen from Figures 12-32 and 12-33, there is no persuasive evidence—except for those with very high assessed valuations in the Detroit areas—that small districts have either higher or lower per pupil expenditures than do larger districts with comparable assessed valuations per pupil.

The K-12 school districts in the Los Angeles area comprised largely or wholly of territory under the jurisdiction of one or more of the contract cities are indicated in Figure 12-31. If the California Court is correct in asserting that the quality of a child's education is dependent on the tax base of his school district (we have already seen that the amount spent on him is), what is somewhat surprising is that the districts comprising Lakewood Plan cities expend relatively low amounts on education, given the relative youth of the contract city populations and their "child orientation." One might hypothesize that tax monies "saved" by contracting with the county for other services would be invested in education. Apparently this is not the case. Do Lakewood Plan residents place a low value on education, is this a function of the "independence" of the school districts from other governmental units, or is it a statistical aberration? Unfortunately, the available data do not permit a determination.

Although the relationship between the input of tax dollars into public education and the output in terms of educational quality is doubtless far less direct than the taxpayer desires, it is obvious that public investment in education is highly variable but predictable from one school district to another in all three metropolitan areas. In the Detroit and Los Angeles areas some of this variability has been reduced in recent years by long overdue, progressive, state financial assistance. Residents of some school districts—most notably in St. Louis County—are able to enjoy the benefits of heavily funded public education with relatively low property tax efforts while others are able to obtain only a less heavily funded, and probably lower quality, education with very high tax efforts. However, one should not draw the perhaps hasty conclusion that the "problem" can be solved by such devices as further school district consolidation or through complete school district consolidation.

First, there is no evidence to suggest that very large school districts deliver a higher quality than do smaller ones. Evidence that does exist suggests quite the opposite. For example, the Los Angeles Unified School District has the supposed fiscal advantages of largeness yet has one of the most uneven internal distributions of "quality education"—as measured by high school dropout rates—in the nation (Figure 12-34). Second, without tax effort increases in the property-poor sections of most metropolitan areas, uniform property taxation in areawide school districts would generate even less per pupil revenues than the existing multiple districts. For example, based on 1970-1971 assessed valuations, enrollments and school tax rates levied in the City of St. Louis, a school district encompassing both St. Louis and St. Louis County would raise revenues sufficient for expenditures of only $377 per pupil—a figure considerably lower than that expended by even the "poorest" of present districts. If the real issue underlying quality in education is money, then accelerated state aid to relatively small districts is certainly a superior alternative to the creation of metropolitan-area-wide school districts reliant almost exclusively on property taxation.

THE ARTICULATION OF DEMAND FOR PUBLIC SERVICES IN CENTRAL CITIES: PROBLEMS OF ACCOUNTABILITY UNDER CONDITIONS OF CLIENT DIVERSITY

In terms of public service provision, the municipal governments and school systems in the cities of Los Angeles, St. Louis and Detroit are paradoxes in their own metropolitan areas. Whereas the concept of home rule is well entrenched in the three metropolitan areas, in their central cities home rule is considerably less "local" than in the suburbs.

In the suburbs, geographical smallness has contributed to their being relatively homogeneous internally both in socioeconomic characteristics and in demands for public services. As a result, suburban home rule tends

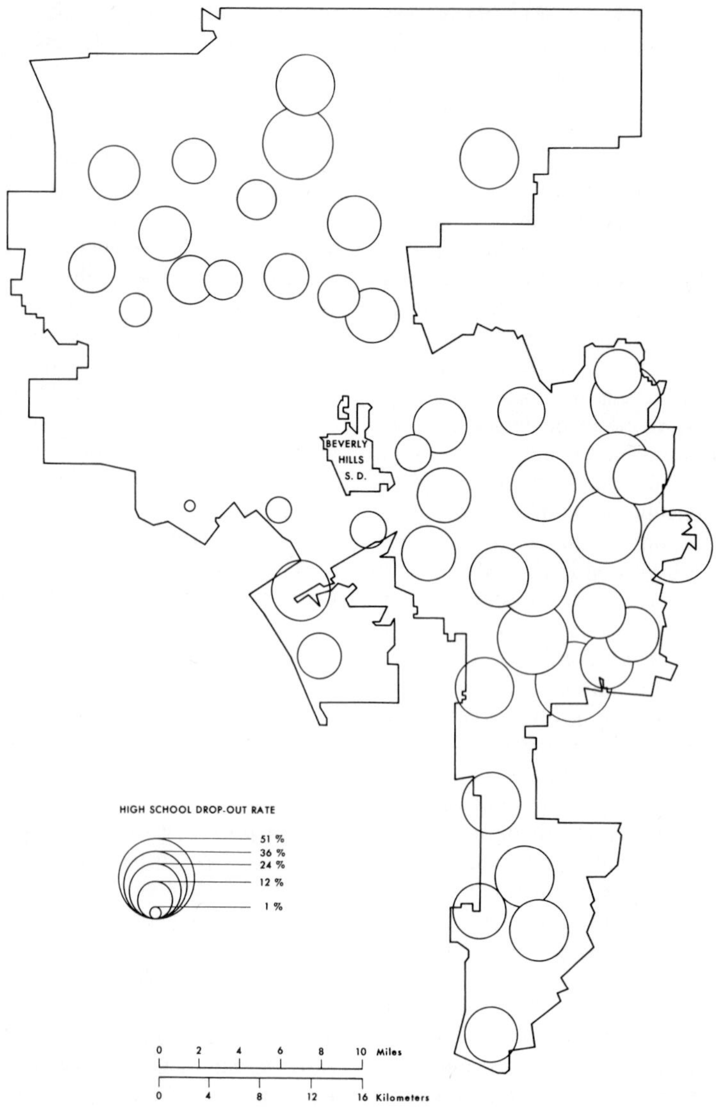

Figure 12-34. Drop Out Rates in High Schools of the Los Angeles Unified School District, 1968.

toward a preoccupation less with the question of what services should be provided and more with that of how they can be provided as inexpensively as possible. In short, problems of achieving efficiency in service delivery and of generating revenue are relatively more important than the problems of demand articulation. The central cities, by contrast, with their large, geographically sprawling, and economically, demographically and culturally diverse populations are confronted with severe problems of demand articulation. These problems are twofold. First, how should public decision-makers determine which services will be provided and at what levels of quality and quantity? Is the city government or school system to provide only the services (and levels) that are needed more or less equally by all city residents? If so, what are these services? Should services for which demand or need is not uniformly distributed in the city be provided also and, if so, which ones? Second, given that location and conditions of economic, social and cultural heterogeneity will produce different orderings of public service priorities between individuals and between geographical subcommunities in the city, by what processes will the resulting conflicts be resolved? As Kenneth Arrow has demonstrated, it will be highly unusual, under such conditions, if a ranking of priorities can be found which will agree with the rankings of even a simple majority of citizens. Should decisionmakers, therefore, not bother to set service delivery priorities for the city as a whole but set different ones for different subareas?

The conflicts engendered by these demand articulation problems, if not resolved, can lead to "crises of legitimacy." To varying degrees the central city municipal governments and school systems of Los Angeles, St. Louis and Detroit are embroiled in such crises.

In the suburban areas, conflict arising from demand articulation tends to be resolved by each municipality attracting households with more or less the same local public investment priorities and repelling those with divergent ones. In effect, the resolution is territorial; to get the level and mix of public services they want, households must move or create jurisdictions containing people of similar tastes or needs. There is, of course, no reason to believe that the results of this process will be equitable in the sense of each suburban government or school district having the financial resources to implement service delivery in conformance with the preferences of its residents. In fact, if preferences are largely determined by income, there is every reason to expect the results to be quite inequitable. At the very least, however, the segregation of suburban residents into small homogeneous jurisdictions leads to a savings of resources—both human and monetary—which otherwise would be devoted to resolving demand articulation problems within jurisdictions—a "savings" that can be invested in preferred patterns of service delivery.

Central city governments are faced with a dilemma. Consider the following courses of action pertaining to service provision. First, the government can behave as it has in the past and provide a fixed bundle of public services intended to be uniform across neighborhoods. Second, for certain basic public services, it can provide some minimum levels across all neighborhoods but emulate its suburbs by allowing the creation of geographical subunits with the responsibility for ensuring the delivery of additional services more in conformance with local needs and desires. Third, it can provide a uniform mix and level of services across all neighborhoods but attempt to be more responsive to the needs of special groups within the city—the poor and aged for example—by establishing city-wide advisory groups and/or formal client advocacy agencies.

The first strategy will clearly be preferred by central city decisionmakers provided the fiscal resources of the city are large and growing and that the uniform mix and levels provided are of higher quality and greater than those available outside the city. If resources are strongly constrained and extracity alternatives are available, the heterogeneity of the city's population itself creates incentives for subgroups of individuals to disperse and regroup in more homogeneous jurisdictions outside the city. The second strategy, from the standpoint of the city officials, has an undesirable and perhaps politically suicidal aspect to it. Allowing the creation of geographical subunits with a modicum of independent decisionmaking authority would necessitate a reduction in the size and probably a restructuring of existing service provision bureaucracies. The costs of reorganization could be sufficiently high in the short run to result in service levels well below those previously delivered uniformly. Since politicians are elected "for the short run" this possibility, however remote, would greatly diminish its attractiveness.

The third course of action is attractive if the number of groups with "special needs" is small and their needs are widely perceived as legitimate by the city's electorate. However, if the number of special agencies or advisory groups is likely to proliferate—as it will if great diversity already exists within the city—this strategy is counterproductive. It would greatly increase the number of groups with which existing officials would need interaction and could lead to a de facto structure of city government far more complicated and inaccessible than exists already. If the fiscal resources available to the city government were stable or shrinking, it would also possess the same disadvantage as the first strategy—an incentive for individuals with divergent preferences for public services to leave the city would still exist. Furthermore, through the politicization of "new" client demands, the disadvantages of service provision in the central city vis-à-vis a suburb would be even more visible to greater numbers of such individuals.

There are, of course, alternative policies which central cities can adopt but the above three illustrate the general dilemma which has confronted most central city municipal and school system governments in recent decades and will likely continue to face them in the foreseeable future unless there are changes in federal, state and local policies. The problem is this: central cities have lost the competitive advantage in service provision they once held over their suburbs and without locating new sources of revenue there appears to be no relatively simple way of restoring it. Central cities may be more efficient in producing more service output per dollar input than most of their suburbs, but the number of services demanded and the associated costs of providing them are increasing more rapidly than city revenues. Central city governments in the past did not need to be as accountable to their clients as they need to be today because the only residential alternatives in their metropolitan areas were suburbs in which the quality and levels of public service tended to be much lower and the costs higher. The tables have turned.

The remainder of this section will be devoted to brief descriptions of the reactions of central city governments—both municipal and school system—to the problem of being accountable under conditions of client diversity.

St. Louis Municipal Government

St. Louis was certainly the first of the three central cities to experience dramatic changes in the social, racial and economic composition of its electorate. During World War II, St. Louis had increasingly become the segregated residence of southern blacks and "mountain" whites. The Mill Creek area between the central business district and the exclusive "midtown" shopping area two miles to the west had been the primary recipient of these immigrants. At the war's end this area was widely and correctly acclaimed one of the worst slums in the United States. Yet in the last quarter century St. Louis public policy seems to have been directed more toward restoring the city to its past glory by attracting business and the middle class back to the central city and less toward satisfying the demands and needs of its "new" residents. Between 1945 and 1960, public officials in St. Louis spent most of their time either engaging in quixotic crusades to adjust the boundaries between the city and St. Louis County or in trying to convince city voters to support massive bond issues earmarked for capital improvements—particularly streets and highways—and for funds to match those from the federal government for land clearance and urban renewal. The latter attempts were successful, but middle class voters were leaving the city with a frequency rivaled only by that of their support for bond issues. This is not to suggest that local policy was necessarily misdirected, but only that it was unbalanced and, with the advantage of hindsight, doomed to failure because of its inability to control what was going on in the St. Louis suburbs. They offered apparently adequate levels and mixes of public services at low costs and environments that certainly appeared controllable relative to ones in St. Louis.

Throughout the 1960s and early 1970s, attempts to restore the economic and residential vitality of St. Louis continued. However, officials in both municipal and school district governments were slow in experimenting with ways to increase the effectiveness and accountability of service delivery. The structure of municipal government—with its small wards and strong aldermen—possessed no clearly visible targets for criticism on grounds of citizen access (Table 12-18). No demands for the establishment of geographically based advisory boards or subunits for the improvement of demand articulation were heard and none created except in Model Cities neighborhoods where federal guidelines demanded them. A few citywide advisory boards were created—such as the Council on Human Relations and various "mayor's coordinating committees"—but, consistent with the government's determination to continue the illusion that St. Louis was a middle class city, most were "blue ribbon" committees containing no, or token, representation of the city's poor and black. The ward organizations were supposedly the vehicles by which local demands for services were articulated and the mayor's office, including the several advisory boards, was the articulator of citywide needs and demands. The former have been highly responsive to local service problems provided their solutions do not require significant financial outlays. In St. Louis, it is no secret that city government is on the verge of bankruptcy; thus, many

Table 12-18. A Summary of the "Demand Articulation" Characteristics of Central City Municipal and School System Governments

	City of Los Angeles	*L.A. Unified School District*	*City of St. Louis*	*St. Louis School System*	*City of Detroit*	*Detroit School System*
Electoral System	NP–D	NP–AL	P–W	NP–AL	NP–AL	NP–AL and NP–D
Average Population Served Per Member of Legislative Branch of Government (in thousands)	188	3,300	22	622	1,511	1,511 and 189
Number of Branch City Halls or Equivalent	11	4	0	6	7	8
Citywide Ombudsman or Equivalent	No	No	No	No	Yes	No
Central Complaint Processing Center	No	No	No	No	Yes	No
Number of Permanent Citywide Advisory Boards	0	3	4	0	2	0
Number of Permanent Geographically Based Advisory Boards[1]	0	0	0	6	4	NA
Number of Geographically Based Subunits of Governments	0	0	0	0	0[2]	8

Legend: NP–nonpartisan; P–partisan; D–districts; W–wards; AL–at large

1. Excluding Model Cities neighborhoods.

2. Their formation is presently being studied.

Source: data compiled by the author.

demands that otherwise would be heard are voluntarily suppressed. As late as the Spring of 1974, the Mayor warned that an actual cutback in the levels of basic services appeared imminent because of decreased city tax revenues.

Indicative of the fact that a significant number of St. Louisans have abandoned hope of city government coping with local service problems is that, since the mid-1960s, a large number of neighborhood and local, territorially based community organizations have been formed, primarily through grassroots organizational efforts. By midsummer 1973 well over 100 such organizations existed in St. Louis. The precise purposes and activities of each organization are unknown. However, from the records and correspondence made available by the city plan commission, it appears that 88 are essentially property maintenance and improvement organizations whose most visible activity is the sponsoring of neighborhood festivals for the purpose of generating revenues for local improvements such as summer recreation and education programs for neighborhood youth, housing improvements and the establishing of community service directories. Five community corporations appear to be federations of smaller neighborhood groups with essentially the same purposes. Five organizations are component units of the city's Human Development Corporation and five are the citizen advisory boards in the Model Cities areas. These organizations offer various social service programs but function primarily as referral agencies in locating jobs and in aiding residents in making their local service demands known to appropriate city authorities. Three organizations have been established in high crime areas by local residents to act as local protection groups which attempt to monitor both police and criminal activities in their respective areas. For the most part, they receive the cooperation of the police department.

Due to the pivotal position of housing and neighborhood rehabilitation in the economic development strategies of the city and the failure of the city-initiated rehabilitation programs of the 1950s and 1960s that lacked local participation, the city plan commission has attempted to establish communication links with each of these organizations on a continuing basis. In formulating the city's future development program in 1972, each of the neighborhood organizations known to exist was contacted and invited to assist the plan commission in formulating short and long term housing, land use, service and development needs for their respective neighborhoods. There is some concern in the plan commission about how representative of "neighborhood interests" these organizations actually are, and about the relative paucity of such organizations in some of the poor and black areas. At least one member of the commission expressed the hope that each neighborhood in the city might eventually have a formally constituted neighborhood government that could act as the basic building block in the demand articulation process. However, he sees this as an eventuality only if the political influence of the "self-initiated" existing organizations increases through local efforts. Several neighborhood organizations already exert considerable political "muscle" in the politics of their ward organizations. However, an attempt to initiate neighborhood government through city charter revision is unlikely until the political organization of the wards is influenced more significantly by neighborhood groups than is currently the case. In the meanwhile, city officials will probably continue to utilize existing neighborhood organizations and encourage their continued proliferation, in part to supplement existing means of neighborhood access to city government, but also in the hope of generating popular support for city policies. Whether this policy, coupled with the city's efforts to provide a relatively uniform bundle of basic public services across all neighborhoods, will be successful in stemming the further deterioration of the quality of life in St. Louis is problematic.

St. Louis Public School System

In contrast to St. Louis city government, that of the St. Louis public school system has no formal and few regularly utilized informal mechanisms by which the residents of subareas in St. Louis can be assured of affecting the local delivery of education. The 12 person board of education, elected at large, has been controlled for at least two decades by a coalition of upper class whites and middle class blacks. Educational policy for all schools in St. Louis is set by the board. In spite of the declines in the assessed valuation of taxable property (in constant dollars) in St. Louis and the rising costs of providing education, the board has been unsuccessful in getting the electorate to pass a single school bond referendum since 1962. (In Missouri, school bond referenda must receive a two-thirds majority.) Rather than attempting to increase citizen support for the system by increasing lay participation in decisionmaking. the board angered both central city black legislators and suburban legislators in 1968 by proposing the merger of the St. Louis and St. Louis County school systems. The proposal was quickly killed in Jefferson City.

At present, the St. Louis school system is divided into five administrative districts, each with a superintendent with some discretionary authority. However, despite the increasing demands of local school activists that district superintendents be responsible to "district boards of education," the role of each district superintendent continues to be that of implementing the policies of the board of education. Each district has two parent congresses comprised of delegates from PTA and similar parent organizations. The congresses, although established by the board of education in the late 1960s and clothed in the rhetoric of community participation, have no decisionmaking authority and function only in advisory capacities. Their effectiveness in articulating local educational needs and demands is entirely dependent on whether the district superintendents choose to assume advocacy stances with the central administration. There is no evidence that any have. Since all district superintendents in 1970 were system veterans over 60 years of age, and since their administrative status is dependent only on the continued confidence of the central administration, this is not surprising.

Both governments of St. Louis have become increasingly dependent upon federal sources of revenue for service delivery; yet, with the advent of revenue sharing and the uncertainty surrounding federal grants-in-aid to cities, even this source is viewed as unreliable. St. Louis officials are hopeful that the state will eventually increase its "aid" to St. Louis. After all, St. Louis residents have always been the principal contributors to state coffers—in 1967 St. Louis produced 25 percent of Missouri's revenue yet got back only 12 percent. Nevertheless, anxious eyes are cast on their growing across the state rival—Kansas City.

Los Angeles Municipal Government

Los Angeles is in a number of ways quite dissimilar to St. Louis and Detroit. Two characteristics—its immense geographical size and relative youth—are important in accounting for the affluence of Los Angeles relative to St. Louis or Detroit. Although the rate of increase in taxable wealth in Los Angeles is lower now than throughout most of its history, it is still positive (in constant dollars). Los Angeles is by no means embroiled in a fiscal crisis on a scale comparable to that of St. Louis. One might presume, then, that in terms of service provision, Los Angeles is in an advantageous or, at least, less disadvantageous position vis-à-vis its suburbs than is St. Louis or Detroit. This would be an accurate presumption if it were not for two factors. First, the service demands and needs that citizens might hope to realize through municipal action in Los Angeles are more diverse than those confronting the cities of St. Louis and Detroit. The latter two have their equivalents of Watts, but they do not include agricultural areas or Hollywoods. In fact, there are at least 65 identifiable (and self-identified) communities within Los Angeles—all of which are political nonentities. Some—including Watts and Hollywood—were formerly independent cities that, through water shortages, were forced to consolidate with Los Angeles. None of these possesses formal mechanisms for making its collective service demands and needs known to the 23 semiindependent boards or commissions administering the 35 service departments and bureaus of city government. Theodore Lowi has referred to Los Angeles's departments of government as "well-run but ungoverned"—the "new machines."

Second, the steady increase in the service provision activity of Los Angeles County and its willingness and ability to tailor service provision to local desires and needs through contractual arrangements with suburban noncontract and contract cities have made the suburbs far more attractive to a greater variety of households than they would have been otherwise. In short, the diversity of Los Angeles provided the incentive for outmigration of some households, or for new immigrants to the metropolitan area not to locate in the city; and the suburbs, with considerable assistance from the county, provided the attraction. In this regard it is interesting to note that the City of Los Angeles, according to 1973 population estimates, decreased in population for the first time in its history.

Geographically, most of Los Angeles' departments and bureaus are decentralized administratively, and have been, at least to some extent, ever since the city embarked on its territorial expansion program over 60 years ago. However, actual decisionmaking regarding service delivery is concentrated at the central administration levels of the various bureaus and departments. Even strictly local policy matters must be referred to department headquarters for consideration and approval. Direct evidence having a bearing on the process or processes by which city officials actually go about determining the number, levels and timing of public service delivery in subareas in Los Angeles is unavailable. What little evidence there is leads to the conclusion that nobody really knows.

One traditional route by which the need for services is articulated is for a citizen with a complaint to contact his councilman. A citizen who utilizes his councilman normally gets prompt results, provided complaints are few and the solutions simple. However, at best, this procedure could be but a small segment of the demand articulation process, particularly when each councilman represents 188,000 residents and only a minor percentage of Los Angeleans ever contact their councilmen. Most councilmen spend little time with citizen groups and open their district offices to citizens only on a part-time basis.

An even more traditional route for "aggregating" consumer demand is through the ballot box. But given Los Angeles' "weak mayor-council-commission" form of government with its independent and semi-independent departmental structure and that, on the average, only about 25 percent of those registered vote in municipal elections, it is very indirect and not particularly representative.

In Los Angeles, formally constituted citizens advisory councils or groups of districtwide representatives are nonexistent. What little citizen participation there is in the demand articulation process is almost entirely confined to the OEO-supported Community Action Program, to non-governmentally sanctioned entities and to informal organizations that are issue-specific and typically transient. Los Angeles fails to have even a central complaint office. Most municipal departments have such offices, but the average citizen is often loath to know which department is the appropriate one to contact. This reinforces the tendency of most citizens either to contact their councilmen or to do nothing. These problems of citizens access prompted a 1969 Charter Study Commission to conclude that alienation toward city government was widespread in all communities in Los Angeles irrespective of race or income.

Alienation is not a recent phenomenon. Since World War II there have been at least a dozen local movements advocating either secession from the city or the establishment of boroughs with independent taxing authority. Borough creation received enough citizen support to secure the backing of the mayor in 1950 and 1952, the city council's own Charter and Administrative Code Committee in 1964 and 1967, and a city councilman in 1968. All proposals were rejected by the city council and hence failed to reach the referendum stage. This was also the fate of the 1969 Charter Study Commission's mild proposal calling for the formation of self-initiating neighborhood advisory boards and the creation of a central ombudsman office with representatives elected from neighborhoods.

The city does have 11 branch administrative centers (BACs). They were created in the early 1960s primarily to reduce the driving time of city employees to their offices. But by the late 1960s they were increasingly touted by city officials as a program to bring city services closer to the people. However, not all residential areas are conveniently located relative to a BAC; the distribution of departments within them is uneven and not easily justified on grounds of rendering the city service departments more accessible to clients (Table 12-19). For example, in 1970 the BAC in Watts, which is about ten miles from the main civic center, had the lowest budget, the least number of employees and only three departments represented —a city clerk's office, a one person human relations department and a part-time councilman's office.

The organizational structure of service production in the City of Los Angeles is very much

Table 12-19. Los Angeles Branch Administrative Centers: Functions, Employees and Expenditures, 1970

	Number of Departments Represented					
Branch Administrative Center	*General Government*	*Public Safety*	*Public Works*	*Human Relations and Social Services*	*Number of Employees*	*Estimated Operating Cost*
San Fernando Valley Region						
Van Nuys	6	3	4	2	435	7,408,920
Reseda	2	1	3	0	120	2,043,840
Sunland-Tujunga	0	1	0	0	15	255,480
Western Region						
West Los Angeles	4	2	3	0	180	3,065,760
Venice	0	1	1	1	61	1,038,952
Westchester	2	1	3	0	39.4	671,061
Downtown Region						
Hollywood	1	1	2	1	111	1,890,552
Eagle Rock	0	1	1	0	6	102,192
Watts	2	0	0	1	3.2	54,502
Wilmington–San Pedro Region						
San Pedro	5	2	4	1	109	1,866,707
Wilmington	0	1	0	0	6	102,192

Source: George J. Washnis. *Municipal Decentralization and Neighborhood Resources.* New York: Praeger, 1972.

like that in Los Angeles County. Both are large and, by business standards, highly efficient. Los Angeles County government, however, has evolved a system of service provision responsive to diversity, while Los Angeles has not.

Los Angeles Public School System

If the City of Los Angeles is a paradox in its metropolitan area, the Los Angeles Unified School District is even more so. Professional educators and administrators in the district are, of course, not unaware of its population diversity and the area's ethos of local control. However, they have long claimed that the disadvantages of the districts' immense size are outweighed by the social costs that could result if it were broken apart into "parochial fiefs," of unequal wealth and educational services—a claim that until very recently was thought sufficient to justify an educational policy that denied the legitimacy of decisional inputs from minority groups and from local communities.

The board of education, which appoints the district's superintendent and exercises ultimate executive authority, consists of seven members elected in nonpartisan elections. The school district is the largest, most densely populated unit of local government in the United States in which all members of government are elected at large. Even further diluting the power of minority groups and communities is that candidates run for numbered seats. Not unexpectedly, the board is almost invariably composed of white, upper middle class individuals. As is typical of Los Angeles politics, the board is executively weak with the superintendent wielding broad administrative powers.

In order to comply with federal guidelines and to meet rising minority group demands, a number of advisory commissions to the board were created after 1965. However, it was not until 1970, when a bill to decentralize certain decisionmaking functions of large school districts to the local level passed in both houses of the state legislature—only to be vetoed by the governor—that the full extent of citizen disaffection finally penetrated official thinking within the system. The response by the superintendent and the board was to conduct a massive campaign including a series of public hearings and polls of all school employees and citizens in the district with the intent of determining popular sentiment regarding "desirable next steps in decentralization." The questionnaire sent to citizens was beset with ambiguity and technical deficiencies. The most serious was that its format made it impossible to measure the intensity of support for the various proposals. It was clear that those responding favored the devolvement of some authority to a more local level, but no one plan emerged with overwhelming grassroots support. Recommendations of the superintendent calling for the division of the district into ten local units and for greater community participation in local school decisions were rejected by the board. What emerged in 1971 was a "local option" plan, permitting school personnel, students and parents at each school to determine the form of school-community advisory committee they wanted. However, the "one shot" type of access to the system afforded by the campaign and the "local option" plan was sufficiently cooptive to have muted demands for further decentralization, but probably only temporarily.

At the present time, the Los Angeles Unified School District is divided into four "regions," each with a field service center to administer certain support services which previously operated from a central headquarters. These are more or less the equivalent of the city's BACs. The district is also divided into eight "maintenance" and 12 "operations" areas, purely for greater administrative efficiency and not for increased citizen participation. If any major advances in the accountability of the system to its clients have occurred, they are not apparent and are unsystematic.

Detroit Municipal Government

Detroit, like Los Angeles, is large and possesses formal systems of public service demand articulation and provision that appear ill-suited for satisfying the diverse tastes and needs of its residents. Like St. Louis, it is in fiscal crisis. Detroit has a strong mayor-council form of government, but the mayor and the nine common council members are all elected from the same constituency—city wide—in nonpartisan off year elections. As numerous studies of Detroit politics have indicated, such a system entails a number of inherent biases in terms of representativeness. Two of the more important are that (1) candidates openly espousing policies to satisfy demands of minorities—whether racial, ethnic, economic or geographical—usually can not be elected and (2) campaigns, particularly for common council, require strong financial backing if citizen information levels are to be high. Throughout the 1960s, for example, the effects of these biases were that most white candidates for council were elected from de facto white middle class "wards" with as little as 40 percent of the total vote while most black candidates needed to more actively pursue city-wide support. Also, given the low informational levels of most campaigns, race had the potential of being a more salient issue than it would have been otherwise.

In spite of its "reformed" system of government, until the mid-1960s there was not a single area of Detroit city government—including its public service departments—that had any formal mechanisms for citizen participation on some collective (including local area) basis. Unlike in Los Angeles, this did not mean that there were no informal, yet effective, mechanisms for local demand articulation. One in particular has been of great importance and has functioned as Detroit's largest de facto political system: the UAW-dominated Wayne County AFL-CIO Committee on Political Education. From its inception COPE has been organized on a small geographical subarea basis. In Detroit, with its high rates of union membership, COPE precinct organizations have traditionally played very important roles in public service demand articulation, providing referral services and local evaluations of the quality of city services. However, the influence and effectiveness of COPE declined considerably throughout the late 1950s and 1960s as union membership rates in Detroit declined due to the increasing suburbanization of the auto industry and its workers. By the mid-1960s, COPE was still effective in some areas of the city but the days when it could be claimed that it provided all city neighborhoods with access to Detroit government and its service departments were gone. No informal local community based organizations with comparable influence could take its place and none did.

Detroit service departments, as a result of the mayor's appointment powers, do not function as self-sustaining and uncontrolled bureaucracies. But, they are not easily influenced except through the mayor's office. In the mid-1960s, faced with steadily mounting demands for community- and poverty-related services, the mayor found it necessary—and, with federal funding, possible—to establish a series of committees and advisory boards, most with citizen input. But the concept of political decentralization, whereby some decisionmaking authority is delegated to, or reserved for, legally sanctioned subunits of city government continued to be alien to the political ethos of Detroit.

By 1970 the council, sensing that citizen confidence in city government had even further deteriorated since the 1967 riot, voted to place on the November ballot the question of whether city voters wished to create a commission to prepare a new city charter. Detroiters, both black and white, voted overwhelmingly "yes." The council, arguing that an appointed study commission would be perceived by Detroit voters as neither representative nor independent of city government influence, called for a specially elected charter commission which would submit a proposed charter directly to the people for approval or rejection.

After over a year and a half of public hearings, meetings with neighborhood organizations, the circulation of drafts, and further rounds of hearings and meetings, the Charter Commission submitted a new charter to Detroit voters in the November 1972 election. From its research, the commission was fully agreed that the service demands and needs of Detroiters in various portions of the city were not being heard with equal clarity. They all agreed that some provision for at least limited neighborhood self-government was necessary, but disagreed on whether the size of the common council should be expanded and a majority of the members elected from districts and on whether partisan elections should be reinstated. As a result, the commission included three proposals on the ballot—the main body of the new charter, one on electing eight of 15 members of the council from districts and one on instituting partisan elections. Most of the pre-election debate centered on the latter two proposals and on a section in the charter calling for the equivalent of a civilian review board to oversee the police department. Black wards voted heavily in favor of the charter and the other proposals, but in the city as a whole the charter was narrowly defeated while the electoral proposals were defeated by two-to-one margins.

The consensus of the commission was that the charter had failed primarily because of the much editorialized-about fear of a return to a "corrupt ward system of government." The Charter Commission, however, did not disband. By law, it had until August 1973 to complete its task. It continued to work with groups which had expressed concern over the inclusion or omission of certain provisions in the proposed charter, and by August had drawn up a new, slightly modified, version of its original proposal minus, of course, partisan elections and the election of council members from districts. In November 1973 the charter passed easily.

Detroit now has an ombudsman to assist residents with problems that arise in dealing with municipal agencies, many departments have citizen advisory boards and the mayor is committed to appointing an independent "decentralization commission" "representative of a cross section of citizens and areas of the city." By August 1975 this commission was to recommend which, if any, functions of city governments should be decentralized to the "community" level and propose an ordinance for the establishment of subarea governments. If community government is recommended, the various "community councils" shall receive appropriations in the city's annual budget. The commission's proposed ordinance will be submitted directly to the electorate on a separate ballot within 180 days of the date the commission files its report. Given that the present mayor is a strong advocate of community government and that the Charter Commission's research suggests widespread popular support for it in all communities of Detroit irrespective of race, Detroit will probably become the first or second (New York may be the first) major central city in the United States to devolve the geographical locus of at least some demand articulation and service delivery functions of municipal government.

The Detroit Public School System

In terms of educational decisionmaking, the Detroit Public School System is also quite different from those in St. Louis or Los Angeles. It is the only one that is decentralized. In the fall of 1971, the Detroit public school system was reorganized into eight regions, each with its own school board and a central board of education comprised of the leading "vote getter" in each region and five additional members elected at large. Previously, the system had been governed by a seven member central board of education elected at large. Throughout the 1960s, a majority of the board members were cognizant of the necessity of increasing citizen input in educational decisionmaking but were fearful that community-based solutions would be incompatible with the goal of an integrated education. Hence, little real decentralization of authority occurred until it was mandated by state government in 1969. In 1967 and 1968, the demand for more community control over the schools was confined largely to a few black organizations whose members had become disillusioned with integration as a practical vehicle to achieve quality education. But by 1969 even the prestigious prointegration Detroit NAACP made a formal request to the school board calling for the creation of elected local and regional boards with almost complete personnel and budgetary power.

The 1969 law was far less radical than that suggested by the NAACP. It merely called for the creation of from seven to 11 regions with elected boards which—subject to central board guidelines—were to be given some discretion in hiring superintendents and teachers, in determining curricula, in testing and in the use of school facilities. However, the board's attempt to implement a seven district plan with an eye more toward integrating the regional school boards than the classrooms drew the ire of community control and integration advocates alike, but particularly the former. After a period of intense conflict, the 1969 law was repealed, a new bill passed and four of the school board members were recalled. The new bill was almost identical to the original except that it specified that boundaries were to be drawn so as "to enable students to attend a school of preference" unless school capacities were insufficient in which case priority was to be given to students residing nearest the preferred school. The actual drawing of the boundaries was left to a governor's commission. The commission members agreed to create four white-controllable and four black-controllable regions, subject to the technical problem of drawing boundaries that remained as close as possible to existing school boundaries while meeting the one man, one vote criterion.

It is not yet possible to evaluate the "success" of school decentralization; it has only been in effect for two and a half years. Some writers were willing to write decentralization off as a failure in community control as soon as the results of the first elections (in November 1971) were known. Only two regions had boards with black majorities; no region had an all black board; three regions had all white boards; and ten of 13 central board members were white. However, these results were largely an artifact of the haste, uncertainty and lack of information that surrounded the pre-election campaign. In the November 1973 elections, however, blacks were in the majority in four districts and were in the majority on the central board.

Much of the past two years can be characterized as a learning experience both for the new school activists and for the members of the regional boards and the members of the central board. Regional board members were quick to learn that decentralization was not to begin with much authority resting with the regional boards: the calendar and budget had, of necessity, been set for the entire academic year 1971-1972, and internal structures of the regional boards and their relationships with the central board were highly ambiguous. Most of the problems encountered can be characterized as "growing pains." Even in the short time that the regional boards have been in existence, there is no doubt that the kind of citizen participation in school affairs has changed dramatically. At least throughout the first year of decentralization, public attendance at each regional board meeting was equal to or greater than that of the old central board meetings—even during the heated community control-integration controversy. More community organizations have begun to establish formal liaisons with the regional boards. Individuals in attendance at regional board meetings are increasingly stating their problems in terms of regional rather than more abstract city needs, particularly in the two predominantly black regions. The three most salient issues in these regions have been classroom size, teacher residency and teacher accountability. The demand for teacher accountability, in part a result of the new school activism engendered by decentralization, was a major issue in the 43 day teachers strike in the fall of 1973.

What the longer run effects of school decentralization will be are unknown. Indeed, much depends on the extent to which decentralization is viewed as a process rather than as a structural condition by central and regional board members, by community organizations, and by individual citizens themselves.

CONCLUSIONS AND POLICY RECOMMENDATIONS

Conclusions

In the first section it was argued that if any national goals pertaining to governance in metropolitan areas emerged in the 1960s they were that political systems in organized areas should become more efficient, effective and accountable in their provision of public services. The means by which these goals were to be implemented were, of constitutional necessity, ambiguous and perhaps best described as democratically circumscribed experimentation. Has progress been made in achieving these goals in the urban America for which the Los Angeles, St. Louis and Detroit metropolitan areas can be viewed as empirical windows? If so, how much and by what means?

First, if any recent progress has been made it has not been the results of any fundamental changes in the spatial organization of local governmental units themselves. Municipalities, counties and special districts still abound in urban America. Second, the continued existence—indeed persistence—of such units nonetheless belies some rather significant changes in the spatial organization of local governance and service provision. Some of these changes must be hailed as signs of progress. As stressed in earlier chapters, the functions of counties and/or municipalities have undergone significant change in all three metropolitan areas. Such has not been the case with school districts. The "Lakewood Plan" of county-city contracting is certainly the most spectacular. Although this system of service provision developed out of a set of conditions specific to the constitutional and statutory milieu of California, an issue of tax subsidy, the prior existence of a thoroughly urban service-oriented county and the geography of settlement in the Los Angeles area, its implementation in the mid-1950s and subsequent perfection through the 1960s have resulted in increases in the technical efficiency and citizen accountability of service delivery in "contract" cities relative to those of traditional cities. Much of the increase in efficiency can be attributed to the fact that the costs of demand articulation formerly borne by the county devolves spatially to the municipal level and that scale economies in service provision can be obtained in small jurisdictions without spatial expansion.

The Lakewood Plan appears in no way to have resulted in the decreased effectiveness of government to cope with areawide problems. In fact, the devolvement of considerable decisionmaking in service provision to the municipal level has permitted elected county officials to more actively pursue solutions to areawide problems. Finally, since services provided by the county to each contract city can be coordinated to take into account external effects that the provision of a public service in one contract city can have on other contract cities, the effectiveness of local government is increased further. In the Detroit metropolitan area there is also evidence that on the average significant increases in service provision efficiency and effectiveness—at least in suburbia—have resulted (1) from Detroit's continued willingness to assume the role of water and sewage disposal wholesaler for other governmental units in the area, (2) from an increase in the contracting activities of counties and (3) from higher levels of cooperation between existing municipalities. Of the metropolitan areas examined, Detroit's spatial fragmentation appears not to have resulted in gross inequities in the ability of municipalities to finance the provision of public services. This has undoubtedly also contributed to the creation of an intergovernmental relations environment conducive to cooperation.

Only in the St. Louis metropolitan area does progress in achieving the goals of increased efficiency, effectiveness and accountability appear meager. But even here the degree of cooperation and coordination between municipalities through informal agreements and special districts is considerably higher than it was two decades, or even a decade ago. In the St. Louis metropolitan area as a whole, the long history of antagonism between the two large units of government—St. Louis and St. Louis County—and its spillovers into the state political arena appear more responsible for the rather sorry condition of intergovernmental relations in the area than anything intrinsic to the number or structure of governmental units themselves. Furthermore, the extent of local community identity and apparent satisfaction with existing units of government in suburban St. Louis is so high that few residents are willing to trade the accountability they enjoy in the currently existing small municipalities for increased efficiency in service delivery. When a service provision problem can be demonstrated to be of areawide concern, the citizens of the area have preferred spatial change, via the formation of special districts, as the method with which to cope with it.

As the analyses of school district expenditures in the three metropolitan areas demonstrated, any increases in equity and effectiveness are traceable to increased state financial aid to school districts based on formulas designed to offset inequalities in abilities to pay. Attempts to affect equity through the creation of very large school districts such as the Los Angeles Unified School District appear to be undesirable expedients, unless educational administrators can evolve more satisfactory systems of client accountability than they have heretofore.

In short, despite the fact that direct quantitative measurements are unavailable, there is, nonetheless, ample indirect evidence to suggest that the existence of a large number of politically independent governmental units is not prima facie evidence that simultaneously efficient, effective and accountable solutions to service provision problems cannot be found. However, as the foregoing sections have made clear, the locational incidence of progress in achieving such solutions is locationally biased: it is primarily a suburban phenomenon. The benefits of the Lakewood Plan, Detroit area contracting, and county "modernization" and special district formation in St. Louis County are suburban benefits.

In the last two decades, as incomes have risen and transportation costs have fallen, more and more central city residents have dispersed and regrouped into relatively homogeneous political jurisdictions where public services tailored to their particular desires and needs can be provided. Increases in the effectiveness and efficiency of suburban governments—engendered by the rise of counties as producers of urban services—in response to suburbanization provided another incentive for outmigration from central cities of those who could marshall the resources and were not otherwise denied (most commonly due to race) entrance to suburbia. As central cities became even more heterogeneous in terms of client demands—with a continued influx of the poor and outmigration of the more affluent—existing forms of taxation and allocation of public services returned a lower proportion of the tax dollar to middle class citizens of central cities in the form of goods especially tailored to their own needs and tastes than could be obtained in the suburbs. The ethic of social responsibility being less strong than that of short term economic rationality, the much heralded exodus of the middle class from US central cities continued unabated throughout the 1960s.

The most common reactions of central city governments were attempts to "redevelop" their cities so as to render them more attractive to industry, commerce and the middle class and, hence, to restore them to their past prominence. Some city officials may have considered it desirable to relegate their city's previous commercial and industrial functions to lesser roles but, due to past investment decisions relative to buildings, transportation arteries and public facilities, more seem compelled to take the opposite tack and promote additional investment to protect what already existed. Few attempted spatial or other structural changes in the organization of city government which offered promise of increasing the accountability and effectiveness of city service provision. Instead officials tended to act as if there had been no change in their social environments. The result was that city service provision appeared accountable to no one—not to the remaining middle class and certainly not to the resident poor.

Central cities were, and are, embroiled in two interrelated crises—one fiscal, the other of legitimacy. Most city officials seem to think that the latter will go away if new sources of revenue can be located. This prognosis represents a fundamental misunderstanding of the underlying causes of the two crises. The ethic of consumer sovereignty in the market place and its collective equivalent in the public economy have always been strong in America and have been fostered at almost every turn by policies of the federal and state governments. It has increasingly been satisfied in suburbs and frustrated in central cities. In the past, central cities, when they were rich and still residentially competitive with the suburbs, did not have to cater to this ethic because the "social costs" of not catering to it were more than offset by the increases in private income central city residents could obtain. Even if central cities are successful in becoming relatively "rich" again—an unlikely possibility given that more voters in urban America now live in the suburbs—there is no assurance that they could become rich enough vis-à-vis suburbs to offset the disadvantages they currently possess in terms of delivering services in neighborhoods that are in conformance with the demands and needs of residents. In short, the internal spatial organization of most central city governments is not conducive to the effective articulation of local needs and demands, let alone to satisfying them.

The popular impression is that the demands for "citizen participation," "accountability" or "community control" are confined to minority groups and the poor. It is true that these demands are "heard" most frequently from minorities and the poor; but that the demand for local control is more widespread is also registered in census statistics which indicate the continued depopulation of most central cities in urban America.

It appears that a more even geographical distribution of progress in achieving the goals of increased efficiency, effectiveness and accountability will necessitate a spatial reorganization of local governance. Continued improvement in the relations between existing governments—including the further functional reorganization of service production and provision responsibilities—without spatial change is insufficient and will continue to accelerate the decay of central cities.

Recommendations

Based on the above conclusions, it is recommended that central city governments in all three metropolitan areas engage in spatial and administrative changes designed to enable groups of urban residents with common interests, tastes and needs to define and receive public goods and services tailored to their collective needs. For this strategy to be developed fully and equitably, it is essential that some mechanism for generating revenues be found that will allow low income residents to live where they want to without requiring the political units they choose to depend primarily on internal sources of funding. Since almost all large central cities have contributed heavily to the economic development of their respective states, it is suggested that states begin to share more state-collected revenues with all local units of government, not on the usual per capita bases currently in use but on a formula based on the ability of residents to pay. This would not really amount to "conscience" money. As was mentioned earlier, even the city most heavily immersed in fiscal crisis, St. Louis, continues to put more revenue into state coffers than it receives back in shared taxes.

The specific spatial and administrative changes would need to be tailored to the particular central city in question. Some suggestions are outlined below.

Los Angeles. The city of Los Angeles would appear well suited administratively, fiscally and geographically to implement its own "Lakewood Plan," even without the massive infusion of state or other "outside" revenues. As in the Lakewood Plan, the city government could set citywide minimum standards of service provision but permit the "incorporation" of neighborhood or community subunits with the legal authority to contract with city service departments, private vendors, other cities or Los Angeles County for the provision of services above such standards and to apply to the state and federal government for special grant monies. Revenue collected by the city government from internal sources that is not budgeted for provision of functions that remained at the city level could be allocated to the neighborhood governments on the basis of population. Shared state and federal revenues could be allocated to subunits on some basis of need arrived at through negotiations between elected city officials and neighborhood government officials. At the outset, it is not recommended that neighborhood governments be permitted independent taxing authority without the approval of the city government. The provision of services in any subareas not electing to form their own neighborhood governments would continue to be the responsibility of the city government. The boundaries of councilmanic districts should be drawn so as to conform as closely as possible to those of the neighborhood units and yet be consistent with the one man, one vote principle. This should lead to the more effective articulation of the demands of Los Angeleans for services provided through citywide programs.

The various city departments would receive appropriations from the city government only for its citywide service provision activity and for that located within "unincorporated" areas in the city. If the departments are as efficient in service delivery as is usually claimed, a system such as this would in no way endanger their continued operation or even growth.

Elected city officials would be responsible for representing the city in labor negotiations, in regional agencies, in resolving external effects problems between neighborhood units and in overseeing the general operation of city government.

These are meant only as suggestions. The more precise contours of government reorganization and the allocation of service provision responsibility should be left to a city charter revision committee with the authority, as in Detroit, of reporting their proposals directly to the voters of Los Angeles for approval or rejection. In the past, governmental reorganization in Los Angeles has been a practical impossibility due to the requirement that the city council approve all charter revision proposals prior to their submission to the electorate.

No doubt the implementation of this proposal could create political problems between Los Angeles County and the city of Los Angeles. For example, the service departments of Los Angeles would probably try to compete with the county service departments by attracting contracts from nearby municipalities in order to increase the size of their "markets." However, such competition in the long run should lead to increased efficiency in service delivery and perhaps to the consolidation of county service departments with city departments and vice versa.

In terms of its school district, it is recommended that, at the very least, the new subunits of city government and the existing suburban municipalities in the school district become basic units from which advisory boards to the board of education are formed. The central school board should also take into advisement the possibility of creating a "lesser" house of representatives comprised of city subunits and suburban representatives to help formulate and pass upon educational policy in the district.

St. Louis. Whereas a system of neighborhood subunits contracting with existing city service departments appears well suited to the peculiarities of Los Angeles' existing city government and social geography and could seemingly be implemented almost as easily as the Lakewood Plan was in 1954, St. Louis poses a set of problems that would decrease the attractiveness of such a system. First, St. Louis is a small city—so small in fact that, for many services, implementation of a contracting plan within St. Louis would probably not be as efficient as one which also included St. Louis County and the other urbanized portions of the metropolitan area. St. Louis County's gradual rise as an efficient producer of urban services to unincorporated areas since 1950 places it in a position at present not dissimilar from that of Los Angeles County on the eve of its implementation of the Lakewood Plan. If a contracting plan were instituted St. Louis County, not St. Louis, would be the logical "contractor."

Second, the history of miserable intergovernmental relations between the city and county, coupled with the fact that for many St. Louis County residents St. Louis is what they are trying to escape from, would not bode well for the political fortunes of county council members who voted their approval of a contract to provide St. Louis with services. The hue and cry of "subsidy" from county residents would be heard as far away as Kansas City if the provision of service involved a significant flow of revenue, primarily because the residents of small municipalities would fear that St. Louis, due to its size, could extract concessions from the county government that were unavailable to them.

In the short run, St. Louis officials would be well advised to pursue a strategy more like Detroit's. They should establish small jurisdictions, perhaps based on the areas presently covered by local improvement associations, and begin experimenting with different modes of service provision whereby at least the administration of some local public services are shifted from the city to the small jurisdictional or neighborhood level. In St. Louis even a small step toward restoring a sense of citizen efficacy such as this would involve revenue already allocated for other purposes. Therefore, what is recommended is that the "new" or "creative" federalism that one heard so much about in the late 1960s and early 1970s be modified to include—probably most suitably under "special revenue sharing"—a federally funded program for underwriting the "set-up" costs of self-initiated subunits of limited local government. Such units should be authorized to make budgetary requests of the legislative branch of city government to carry out local service projects, much like any other existing department or bureau.

Even this limited form of self-government could be counterproductive in St. Louis and other cities unless outside sources of revenue can be secured. Accountability without resources may satisfy certain psychological needs of central city residents but it can do little to satisfy their material and environmental needs.

Some states, and Missouri is one, have been something short of beneficient in their aid to cities and school districts and there is little to indicate that they will change without additional incentives. What is recommended then is (1) that federal funding through grants-in-aid, state matching grants and revenue sharing be reduced or denied to any state failing to institute programs which decrease the dependency of cities and school districts on their internal sources of revenue; (2) that federal revenue sharing with cities be instituted on a more substantial basis and one that is more likely to be perceived as permanent enough to represent a tenable solution to the problems of municipal finance in large cities; and (3) that each city requesting federal funding satisfy federal guidelines that would be the internal equivalent of A-95 review—namely, that the city or school district requesting funds has made a reasonable attempt to assess the social impacts of its proposed expenditure. It is suggested that the implementation of a program authorizing the establishment of geographical subunits of city government be construed as satisfying these review requirements, provided it can be shown that the subunits have been delegated some advisory or decisionmaking authority pertaining to the service function with which the city's or school district's expenditure proposal is concerned.

Once St. Louis becomes a viable political-economic unit of government and has evolved an internal spatial structure of local governance more in conformance with the American ethic of limited home rule, it should not only be better able to cope with its own problems, but would also help create the kind of political climate in which broader regional government, perhaps based on a system of county-city contracting, is possible.

Detroit. Much of what has been recommended in terms of local policy for St. Louis also applies to Detroit. Significantly, Detroit is well on the way to implementing geographical decentralization and would do so even more assuredly if the federal policy proposal to underwrite the set-up costs of subunits of government were enacted. However, despite their similarities, Detroit is not St. Louis. Most significantly, Detroit is far more important to its metropolitan area as a public service producer than is St. Louis. For this reason there are stronger incentives for suburban Detroiters to support state legislation designed to increase the fiscal capacity of Detroit. Suburbanites may not like Detroit, but all they have to do is turn on a water faucet to be reminded of their dependency upon her. Also, Detroit's recent and apparently determined effort to cope with its internal problems in education and municipal government through internal spatial and administrative reform cannot escape suburban attention.

The Detroit metropolitan area is too large and counties within it too small to become effective service producers. If some form of regional governance comes to the Detroit area, the city of Detroit will play an extremely important role in it—it has no political rivals. However, the Detroit city government has evinced little or no interest in creating a regional government. First, Detroit is now a predominantly black central city, and wields more power in the de facto regional governments that currently exist—the Southeast Michigan Council of Governments (SEMCOG) and the Southeast Michigan Transportation Authority (SEMTA)—than it would in a regional government not made up of representatives from existing governmental units. Second, internal problems of citizen accountability and service delivery appear of much more immediate relevance.

The best hope for the Detroit metropolitan area as a whole is that Detroit—through the receipt of increased federal and state revenues, the implementation of its new city charter and the likely creation of neighborhood government—will succeed in emulating its suburbs in terms of the quality and effectiveness of services received in its neighborhoods. In this way, the receipt of relatively low cost service provision in suburbia will be ensured and the quality of life in Detroit enhanced.

Final Notes

None of the above recommendations is designed primarily to restore central cities, their business districts and their industries to positions of economic dominance in their respective metropolitan areas. None, however, is incompatible with such restoration. Redevelopment programs are to be encouraged but, in the decade ahead, first priority should be given to developing more viable and equitable democratic institutions at the local level which are capable of making social diversity a strength, not a weakness.

The recommendations also do not imply any rejection of proposals for the creation of two tiered or multitiered systems of service provision and governance in metropolitan areas. Advocates of such systems devote most of their attention to the "proper" functional and spatial scope of the metropolitanwide tier and assume that existing municipalities can function adequately as the first or lowest tier. Such an assumption, in my opinion, is untenable. A system of metropolitan governance should be built from the bottom up, not from the top down. The problem in urban America today is that some of the existing "bottoms"—particularly central cities—are not only feared by suburban residents but, on the grounds of effectiveness and accountability, are also unacceptable to many, if not most, of their own inhabitants.

BIBLIOGRAPHY

Public Documents

Advisory Commisson on Intergovernmental Relations. *Factors Affecting Voter Reactions to Governmental Reorganization in Metropolitan Areas.* Washington, D.C., 1962.

——. *Alternative Approaches to Governmental Reorganization in Metropolitan Areas.* A-11. Washington, D.C., June 1962.

——. *Performance of Urban Functions: Local and Areawide.* Washington, D.C., 1963.

——. *A Handbook for Interlocal Agreements and Contracts.* M-29. Washington, D.C., March 1967.

——. *Fiscal Balance in the American Federal System.* Vol. 1. Washington, D.C., October 1967.

——. *Fiscal Balance in the American Federal System: Metropolitan Fiscal Disparities.* Vol. 2. Washington, D.C., October 1967.

——. *Urban and Rural America: Policies for Future Growth.* A-32. Washington, D.C., April 1968.

——. *State Aid to Local Government.* A-34. Washington, D.C., April 1969.

——. *The New Grass Roots Government? Decentralization and Citizen Participation in Urban Areas.* M-71. Washington, D.C., January 1972.

——. *City Financial Emergencies: The Intergovernmental Dimension.* A-42. July 1973.

——. *American Federalism into the Third Century: Its Agenda.* M-85. Washington, D.C., May 1974.

California State Controller. *Annual Report of Financial Transactions Concerning Cities of California, Fiscal Year 1970-71.*

——. *Annual Report of Financial Transactions Concerning Counties of California, Fiscal Year 1970-71.* Sacramento, 1971.

——. *Annual Report of Financial Transactions Concerning Counties of California, Fiscal Year 1971-72.* Sacramento, 1972.

——. *Annual Report of Financial Transactions Concerning School Districts of California, Fiscal Year 1970-71.* Sacramento, 1971.

——. *Annual Report of Financial Transactions Concerning Special Districts of California (Other than Water Utility), Fiscal Year 1970-71.* Sacramento, 1971.

California Intergovernmental Council on Urban Growth. *Report on a Statewide Survey of Local Agency Formation Commission.* Sacramento, 1966.

City of Detroit. *Annual Report of the City of Detroit, Michigan by the Auditor General. For the Fiscal Year Ended June 30, 1971.*

——. Mayor's Committee for Community Renewal. *City of Detroit Regional School Board Districts Data Book,* August 1971.

——. City Clerk. *Municipal Manual, 1972.*

City of St. Louis. *Annual Report of the Comptroller,* Fiscal Period Ended April 30, 1971.

Detroit Board of Education. *Guidelines for Regional and Central Boards of Education of the School District of the City of Detroit.* October 26, 1970.

Detroit Charter Revision Commission. *A Report to the People.* Detroit, September 1972.

——. *Discussion Draft of the New Charter for the City of Detroit with Commentary.* Detroit, June 1972.

Detroit City Plan Commission, Social Planning Division. *Urban Incentive Tax Credits: A Self-Correcting Strategy to Rebuild Central Cities.* Detroit, 1972.

——. *Social Purpose Taxation.* Detroit, September 1972.

Detroit Public Schools. *Facts about Detroit Schools.* Detroit, February 1972.

East-West Gateway Coordinating Council. *Regional Management and Intergovernmental Affairs.* St. Louis, 1972.

——. *Regional Housing Plan for St. Louis Metropolitan Area.* St. Louis, 1973.

Los Angeles City Charter Commission. *Report: City Government for the Future.* Los Angeles: City Hall, 1969.

Michigan Department of Administration. *Michigan Manual, 1969-70.* Lansing, 1970.

Oakland County Board of Commissioners, Equalization Committee. *1972 Report on Local Taxes.*

St. Louis Charter Commission of 1967. *New St. Louis County Charter.* Clayton, Mo.: 1968.

St. Louis City Plan Commission. *St. Louis Development Program: A Summary.* St. Louis: January 1973.

St. Louis County. *Financial Report.* Clayton, Mo.: 1972.

——. *1972 Rate Book.* Clayton, Mo.: 1972.

——. Office of the Supervisor. *Directory of County Services to Municipalities.* Clayton, Mo.: January 1972.

——. Department of Planning. *St. Louis County Fact Book.* Clayton, Mo.: April 1973.

Southeast Michigan Council of Governments. *1970 Census Data, 1st Count.* Detroit, February 1972.

——. *Public High School Districts in Southeast Michigan: Selected Financial Data.* Detroit, 1972.

Special Commission on Urban Problems. *Urban Growth and Problems.* Report to Governor George Romney. Lansing, 1965.

US Bureau of the Census. *Census of Governments, 1967.* Vol. 7: *State Reports,* No. 22: *Michigan.*

——. *Census of Housing: 1970.* Vol. 1: *Housing Characteristics for States, Cities, and Counties,* pt. 6, California; pt. 26, Michigan; pt. 27, Missouri. Washington, D.C.: U.S. Government Printing Office, 1973.

——. *Census of Population: 1970.* Vol. 1, *Characteristics of the Population,* pt. 6, California; pt. 26, Michigan; pt. 27, Missouri. Washington, D.C.: U.S. Government Printing Office, 1973.

——. *City Government Finances in 1970-71.* Series 6F71, no. 4.

Wayne County Treasurer. *Wayne County Treasurer's Annual Report, 1971.* Detroit: 1971.

Books and Monographs

Arrow, Kenneth F. *Social Choice and Individual Values.* 2nd ed. New York: John Wiley and Sons, 1963.

Banfield, Edward C. *Big City Politics.* New York: Random House, 1965.

Bebout, John E. *Decentralization and the City Charter.* Detroit: Citizens Research Council of Michigan, 1971.

Bigger, Richard and James D. Kitchen. *How the Cities Grew.* Los Angeles: University of California, Bureau of Governmental Research, 1952.

Bish, Robert L. *The Public Economy of Metropolitan Areas.* Chicago: Markham, 1971.

Bollens, John C., ed. *Exploring the Metropolitan Community.* Berkeley: University of California Press, 1961.

Bollens, John C. and Henry J. Schmandt. *The Metropolis: Its People, Politics and Economic Life.* 2nd ed. revised. New York: Harper and Row, 1970.

Break, George F. *Intergovernmental Fiscal Relations in the United States.* Washington, D.C.: The Brookings Institution, 1967.

Citizens Research Council of Michigan. *Governmental Organization in Metropolitan Southeast Michigan.* Detroit: Metropolitan Fund, 1965.

——. *Five Examples of Governmental Cooperation in the Southeast Michigan Six-County Region.* Detroit: Metropolitan Fund, 1967.

——. *Financial Problems in the Detroit School District.* Detroit: Metropolitan Fund, February 1972.

Committee for Economic Development. *Reshaping Government in Metropolitan Areas.* New York, 1970.

Costikyan, Edward N. and Maxwell Lehman. *Re-structuring the Government of New York City.* New York: Praeger, 1972.

Cox, Kevin R.; David R. Reynolds; and S. Rokkan, eds. *Locational Approaches to Power and Conflict.* Beverly Hills: Sage, 1974.

Crouch, Winston W. and Beatrice Dinerman. *Southern California Metropolis.* Berkeley and Los Angeles: University of California Press, 1964.

Dillon, John F. *Treatise on the Law of Municipal Corporations.* Chicago: James Cockcroft, 1872.

Edgar, Richard E. *Urban Power and Social Welfare.* Beverly Hills: Sage, 1970.

Gittell, Marilyn and T. Edward Hollander. *Six Urban School Districts.* New York: Praeger, 1968.

Gordon, Leonard. *A City in Racial Crisis: The Case of Detroit Pre- and Post- the 1967 Riot.* Dubuque, Iowa: Wm. C. Brown Co., 1971.

Greer, Scott. *The Urbane View.* New York: Oxford University Press, 1972.

Hirsch, Werner Z. *The Economics of State and Local Government.* New York: McGraw-Hill, 1970.

——, ed. *Los Angeles: Viability and Prospects for Metropolitan Leadership.* New York: Praeger, 1971.

La Noue, George R. and Bruce L.R. Smith. *The Politics of School Decentralization.* Lexington, Mass.: D.C. Heath and Co., 1973.

League of Women Voters, Oakland County. *Know Your Oakland County Government.* Lansing, 1972.

Lee, Eugene C. and Willis D. Hawley. *The Challenge of California.* Boston: Little, Brown and Co., 1970.

Leonard, J.M. and Lent D. Upson. *The Government of the Detroit Metropolitan Area.* Detroit: Detroit Bureau of Governmental Research, 1934.

Lineberry, Robert L. and Ira Sharkansky. *Urban Politics and Public Policy.* New York: Harper and Row, 1971.

Manuel, A.D. *Urban America and the Federal System.* Washington, D.C.: Advisory Commission on Intergovernmental Relations, 1969.

Massam, Bryan H. *The Spatial Structure of Administrative Systems.* Commission on College Geography, Resource Paper No. 12. Washington, D.C.: Association of American Geographers, 1972.

Murphy, Thomas P. *Metropolitics and the Urban County.* Washington, D.C.: Washington National Press, 1970.

National Bureau of Economic Research. *City Expenditures in the United States.* New York, 1959.

Neenan, William B. *Political Economy of Urban Areas.* Chicago: Markham, 1972.

Nordlinger, Eric A. *Decentralizing the City: A Study of Boston's Little City Halls.* Cambridge, Mass.: MIT Press, 1972.

St. Louis County Municipal League, *1973-74 Municipal Officials of St. Louis County.* Clayton, Mo.: 1974.

Schmandt, Henry J., et al. *Metropolitan Reform in St. Louis.* New York: Holt, Rinehart and Winston, 1961.

Sinclair, Robert. *The Face of Detroit.* Washington, D.C.: National Council for Geographic Education, 1970.

Soja, Edward W. *The Political Organization*

of Space. Commission on College Geography, Resource Paper No. 8. Washington, D.C.: Association of American Geographers, 1971.

Sturm, Albert Lee. *Constitution-Making in Michigan, 1961-62.* Ann Arbor: Institute of Public Administration, The University of Michigan, 1963.

Syed, Anwar H. *The Political Theory of American Local Government.* New York: Random House, 1966.

Thompson, Wilbur R. *A Preface to Urban Economics.* Baltimore: The Johns Hopkins Press, 1965.

de Torres, Juan. *Government Services in Major Metropolitan Areas.* Conference Board Publications in Economic Policy Research, 1972.

Warren, Robert. *Government in Metropolitan Regions: A Reappraisal of Fractionated Political Organization.* Davis: University of California, 1966.

Washnis, George J. *Municipal Decentralization and Neighborhood Resources.* New York: Praeger, 1972.

Widick, B.J. *Detroit: City of Race and Class Violence.* Chicago: Quadrangle Books, 1972.

Williams, Barbara R. *St. Louis: A City and Its Suburbs.* R–1353–NSF. Santa Monica: Rand Corporation, 1973.

Zimmerman, Joseph F. *The Federated City: Community Control in Large Cities.* New York: St. Martin's Press, 1972.

Articles and Periodicals

Aberbach, Joel D. and Jack L. Walker. "Citizens Desires, Policy Outcomes, and Community Control." *Urban Affairs Quarterly* 8 (September 1972): 55-75.

Bish, Robert L. and Robert Warren. "Scale and Monopoly Problems in Urban Government Services." *Urban Affairs Quarterly* 8 (September 1972): 97–122.

Citizens Research Council of Michigan. "New Directions in the Proposed Detroit Charter." *Council Comments,* no. 855 (August 16, 1972).

Cohen, Jerome and Nathen E. Cohen. "The Social Climate of Metropolitan Los Angeles." In *Los Angeles: Viability and Prospects for Metropolitan Leadership,* edited by Werner Z. Hirsch, pp. 21–50. New York: Praeger, 1971.

Doyle, Patricia Jansen. "St. Louis: City with the Blues." *Saturday Review,* February 15, 1969, pp. 90–93 and 105.

"A First Look at City Use of Revenue Sharing Funds." *Nation's Cities* 11 (August 1973): 8–11, 36.

Fauri, David P. "The Limits on Consumer Participation in Public Social Programs." *Public Welfare* 31 (Summer 1973): 16–24.

Goldbach, John. "Local Formation Commissions: California's Struggle over Municipal Incorporations." *Public Administration Review* 25 (September 1965): 213–20.

Grant, William R. "Community Control vs. School Integration—the Case of Detroit." *Public Interest,* no. 23 (Summer 1971): 62–79.

Gregory, Karl D. "Detroit: Crisis in the Central City." In *Fiscal Issues in the Future of Federalism,* pp. 33–59. New York: Committee for Economic Development, 1968.

Hirsch, Werner Z. "The Fiscal Plight: Causes and Remedies," In *Fiscal Pressures on the Central City: The Impact of Commuters, Nonwhites, and Overlapping Governments,* edited by Werner Z. Hirsch, et al., pp. 3–40. New York: Praeger, 1971.

Kirlin, John J. "The Impact of Increasing Lower-Status Clientele upon City Governmental Structures: A Model from Organization Theory." *Urban Affairs Quarterly* 8 (March 1973): 317–43.

Lowi, Theodore. "Machine Politics—Old and New." *The Public Interest,* no. 9 (Fall 1967): 83–92.

Margolis, Julius. "The Demand for Urban Public Services." In *Issues in Urban Economics,* edited by Harvey S. Perloff and Lowden Wingo, Jr., pp. 527–65. Baltimore: The Johns Hopkins Press, 1968.

Moore, Charles H. and Ray E. Johnston. "S "School Decentralization, Community Control, and the Politics of Public Education." *Urban Affairs Quarterly* 6 (June 1971): 421–45.

Neenan, William B. "Suburban–Central City Exploitation Thesis: One City's Tale." *National Tax Journal* 23 (June 1970): 119–29.

Ostrom, Elinor. "Metropolitan Reform: Propositions Derived from Two Traditions." *Social Science Quarterly* 53 (December 1972): 474–93.

Ostrom, Vincent. "Operational Federalism: Organization for the Provision of Public Services in the American Federal System." *Public Choice* 6 (Spring 1969): 1–17.

Ostrom, Vincent and Elinor Ostrom. "Public Choice: A Different Approach to the Study of

Public Administration." *Public Administration Review* 31 (March-April 1971): 203–16.

Porter, David O. and Teddie Wood Porter. "Social Equity and Fiscal Federalism." *Public Administration Review* 34 (January-February 1974): 36–43.

Ratner, G.M. "Inter-neighborhood Denials of Equal Protection in the Provision of Municipal Services." *Harvard Civil Rights–Civil Liberties Law Review* 4 (Fall 1968): 1–63.

Ries, John C. and John J. Kirlin. "Government in the Los Angeles Area: The Issue of Centralization and Decentralization." In *Los Angeles: Viability and Prospects for Metropolitan Leadership,* edited by Werner Z. Hirsch, pp. 89–116. New York: Praeger, 1971.

Shoup, Donald C. and Arthur Rosett. "Fiscal Exploitation by Overlapping Governments." In *Fiscal Pressures on the Central City: The Impact of Commuters, Non-whites, and Overlapping Governments,* edited by Werner Z. Hirsch et al., pp. 241–301. New York: Praeger, 1971.

Smith, Michael P. "Alienation and Bureaucracy: The Role of Participatory Administration." *Public Administration Review* 31 (November-December 1971): 658–64.

Sonenblum, Sidney. "Evaluating Governance." In *Governing Urban America in the 1970's,* edited by Werner Z. Hirsch and Sidney Sonenblum, pp. 38–54. New York: Praeger, 1973.

Tiebout, Charles M. "A Pure Theory of Local Expenditures." *Journal of Political Economy* 64 (October 1956): 416–24.

Tullock, Gordon. "Federalism: Problems of Scale." *Public Choice* 6 (Spring 1969): 19-29.

Weiler, Conrad J., Jr. "Metropolitan Federation Reconsidered." *Urban Affairs Quarterly* 6 (June 1971): 411–20.

Reports

Cozzolino, Joe. *Citizen Participation in the Detroit Governmental Structure.* A Report to the Detroit Charter Revision Commission. Detroit, June 1971.

Detroit Geographical Expedition and Institute. *A Report to the Parents of Detroit on School Decentralization.* Department of Geography, Michigan State University, East Lansing. 1970.

Dyer, Thomas. "Fiscal Disparity in St. Louis County." St. Louis: Center of Community and Metropolitan Studies, University of Missouri, April 2, 1973.

Robert Gladstone and Associates. *Fiscal Trends and Outlook for St. Louis, Missouri.* A technical report prepared for the St. Louis City Plan Commission. St. Louis, 1969.

Merz, Paul E. *Local Government Finances in the Nation and the St. Louis Metropolitan Area.* A report prepared for the East-West Gateway Coordinating Council. St. Louis, 1969.

New Detroit Committee. *Progress Report.* Detroit, April 1968.

Roos, Lawrence K. *State of the County.* A report delivered to the St. Louis County Council. January 4, 1973.

Unpublished Material

Detroit Charter Revision Commission. "The New Charter for the City of Detroit." Detroit, June 19, 1973. Mimeographed.

Fisk, Donald M. "Output Measurement in Urban Government: Current Status and Likely Prospects." Paper read before the 1973 Annual Meeting of the American Political Science Association at New Orleans, September 4–8, 1973.

Long, John Jeffrey. "Electoral Systems for Common Council in Detroit: An Analysis of the At-Large System and a Proposal for District Elections." Report written for the Detroit Charter Revision Commission. No Date. Typewritten.

Rossi, Peter H. and Richard A. Berk. "Generalized Performance Measures for Urban Political Systems." Paper read before the 1973 Annual Meeting of the American Political Science Association, New Orleans, September 4–8, 1973.

Other Sources

Detroit Charter Revision Commission. Personal Interview with Richard Simmons, Jr., Chairman. July 25, 1973.

Chapter 13

Malapportionment and Gerrymandering in the Ghetto

John O'Loughlin
University of Illinois-Urbana

INTRODUCTION

Between 1962 and 1965, the US Supreme Court handed down a series of decisions setting forth the constitutional requirements for boundary shapes and population sizes of election districts. By these decisions, the Court ended the practice of "silent gerrymandering"—that is, allowing huge populations to build up in some districts, usually urban areas, and allowing tiny populations in rural areas. This chapter is concerned exclusively with the districting situation within US cities. Specifically, the aim is to determine whether the Supreme Court decisions have equalized districts in terms of both population size and shape, between white, black and mixed or integrated neighborhoods.

To make these comparisons, districts in these three types of neighborhoods are examined for their shapes and population sizes in 1958 (before the Supreme Court decisions) and 1968. The electoral districts are categorized by type of election (US congressional, state senatorial, state assembly and city council) and region (Northeast, Midwest, South and West). In this way, the effects of the Supreme Court's decisions over the decade 1958-1968 can be evaluated in more detail. For a smaller sample of districts in 1968, the actual districtings are compared to optimal districtings in order to determine if discrimination has been eliminated from districting procedures. Finally, some consequences of past and present districting plans on black representation are suggested.

The chapter is arranged in the following way. The policy implications of the analysis of malapportionment and gerrymandering for a democratic society are outlined immediately below. A summary of the relevant Supreme Court decisions is given so as to set the stage for the analysis of how the justices' dictates have been met. Since many of the terms used may be unfamiliar, explanations of the most commonly used terms are given. The methodology and operational measurements are explained in part three. The movement toward population equalization of election districts during the 1960s is discussed in part four, with the other requirement of districting—compactness—examined in part five. The final section is devoted to a summary of the results of the study.

Policy Conclusions

The constitutional requirements of districting, as defined by the Supreme Court, should be met. This is most easily achieved by nonpartisan redistricting. Most legislative bodies now recognize the necessity to reapportion the states as soon as possible after the census figures are available, before the courts do it for them. The legislators also recognize that the courts are more likely to accept plans that are drawn by bipartisan bodies. Therefore, most recent redistricting plans minimize disruption to incumbents while meeting the equal population requirement. Because of this and because of changing population distributions, gerrymandered districts are still a feature of the American political scene.

Academics are beginning to enter the redistricting picture as a result of the increasing acceptance of bipartisan redistricting. Washington state courts, for example, appointed a geographer, Richard Morrill, to redistrict the state for the 1972 elections. The availability of many computer algorithms that incorporate the constitutional requirements makes the redistricting task reasonably straightforward. More important, computer redistricting eliminates political bias. However, unless the courts override the legislative body, this body will veto any plan that threatens the reelection of incumbents. But protection of incumbents, within certain limits, can also easily be incorporated into any computer algorithm.

Malapportionment of US congressional, state senatorial and state assembly districts was ended by the Supreme Court by its insistence on almost mathematical precision of equal population size. Recently, the court allowed population deviations as large as 16 percent in Virginia.

Malapportionment continues to exist at the city council level. Deviations as large as 30 percent are common in Chicago, Philadelphia, Atlanta and St. Louis. Unlike the many challenges to redistricting plans at the other three governmental levels, few have been brought against those of city councils. But it seems as if this is changing. For example, the new district alignments of Chicago and Los Angeles were challenged in court. It is not clear yet whether redistricting plans at the council level are subject to the same constitutional requirements as other governmental bodies. Until the Supreme Court decides this issue, it is likely that the present malapportionment and gerrymandering of city council districts will continue.

Gerrymandering of districts at all four levels is a continuing problem. It is almost impossible to prove gerrymandering exists: all that is usually possible is to produce a strong suspicion. Perhaps the most effective method of pinpointing a gerrymander is to overlay a map of the suspected gerrymander on a map of the group suspected of being gerrymandered. The onus is then on the body that produced the plan to explain any strange indentations, or why any one group constitutes a large minority in a number of districts. As the discipline that is most familiar with maps and mapping, geography has an essential role to play in the identification and abolition of gerrymanders.

Because gerrymandering and malapportionment affect the outcome of elections, the problem of nonresponsiveness of the political system for the gerrymandered-malapportioned group is present. If, (as is sometimes the case) this gerrymandered-malapportioned group is an inner city poor group, the problem assumes an even more serious nature. Policies such as rat control and garbage collection, and questions such as the location of noxious facilities or the imposition of a commuter tax, will be decided in favor of the outer city. With the increasing social concern of geographers and the renaissance of political geography, perhaps the discipline will confront one of the most pervasive abuses still extant in the United States today.

COURT DECISIONS ON DISTRICTING REQUIREMENTS

During the period 1946 to 1975, the US Supreme Court handed down ten important decisions on the constitutional requirements for the delimitation of election districts. Based on the interpretation of the "one man, one vote" clause of the Fourteenth Amendment, these decisions have dictated the numerous reapportionments of the 1960s and fundamentally altered the electoral basis of the American democracy.

With the repeated failure of the state legislatures to reapportion and redistrict themselves, it was left to the Supreme Court to do the job for them. By 1946, noncompliance by the state legislatures with the federal requirements for districting and apportionment–compactness, contiguity and equal population–led to the first appeal for relief to the Supreme Court. In *Colgrove* v. *Green,* 328 U.S. 549 (1946), the Court decided that malapportionment was not a judicial issue. That judgment was succeeded by an unsuccessful executive attempt by President Truman and a legislative effort by Congressman Celler to impose guidelines–no deviation greater than 15 percent from the state average–for apportionment. In *Baker* v. *Carr,* 369 U.S. 186 (1962), the Court reversed its 1946 judgment but it was not until *Reynolds* v. *Sims,* 377 U.S. 578 (1964), that the Court asserted that apportionment of both legislative bodies–state senate and state assembly—should be based on population. In the same year, the Court ordered Georgia to reapportion its congressional districts because of the great disparity in population of its districts [*Wesberry* v. *Sanders,* 376 U.S. 1 (1964)].

In two recent decisions, *Kirkpatrick* v. *Preisler,* 394 U.S. 526 (1969), and *Wells* v. *Rockefeller,* 394 U.S. 542 (1969), the Court rejected apportionment plans in Missouri and New York as falling outside the "one man, one vote" requirement of the Fourteenth Amendment to the Constitution. By these two decisions, the Court insisted on absolute equality of populations in each district. A flurry of reapportionment plans followed these Court decisions, resulting in the end of rural bias. For a long time urban areas had been underrepresented but are now slightly overrepresented; it is suburban areas which are now discriminated against.

In *Mahan* v. *Howell,* 93 U.S. 979 (1973), the Supreme Court retreated from the absolute insistence of equal population, allowing a deviation of 16 percent between the largest and smallest state senatorial districts in Virginia.

The Supreme Court effectively eliminated the gross inequalities that existed between electoral regions, but it has been far less effective in reducing the practice of gerrymandering. Early indications were that the Court would be as forceful with respect to the compactness requirement as it was with the equal population requirement. In *Gomillion* v. *Lightfoot,* 364 U.S. 339 (1960), the Court eliminated a racial gerrymander in Tuskegee, Alabama. However, in *Wright* v. *Rockefeller,* 376 U.S. 52 (1964), the Court refused the appeal of plaintiffs that the Manhattan congressional districts were drawn so as to confine the majority of blacks and Puerto Ricans to three districts and exclude them from the seventheenth Congressional District.

Similarly, in the following year, the Court reversed a lower court ruling that multimember districts discriminated against minority groups. However, in this Georgia case, *Fortson* v. *Dorsey,* 379 U.S. 433 (1965), the Court enunciated the principle of "effective representation"—that is, one man, one vote that counts." This principle was used in the Indiana case of *Chavis* v. *Whitcomb,* 205 F. Supp. 1364 (1969), where the court ruled that multimember districting was discriminatory to ghetto citizens, in violation of their right to "effective representation" implicit in the Fourteenth Amendment.

While the requirements of equal population and single member districts have helped to ensure the implementation of "effective representation," boundary delimitation may ultimately decide whether all groups are represented equally. Based on a survey of all congressional elections 1946 through 1964, Sickels concluded that "in larger competitive states during the last two decades, the gerrymander (including all devices active and passive, accidental or deliberate) accounted for an average advantage of three seats to the party favored in the state legislature." Probably because of the lack of an agreed-upon measure of gerrymandering, and the difficulty of demonstrating a gerrymander, the Supreme Court has not yet eliminated this continuing electoral abuse.

Definitions

Malapportionment refers to the unequal population sizes of election districts. The Constitution guarantees that one citizen's vote will be equal to another's. If the population sizes of election districts vary substantially, the citizens of districts with smaller populations are overrepresented—more representation than they should have based on the districts' population size—and those of districts with larger populations underrepresented—less representation than they should have based on the districts' population size.

Gerrymandering is the manipulation of the boundaries of election districts in order to give a political party or interest group an unfair electoral advantage. Not all gerrymanders are deliberate. Some groups, because of their geographical concentration or dispersal, may be victimized politically by any delimitation of electoral boundaries.

The three most common methods of gerrymandering are: (1) *stacked districts,* which usually have a grotesque shape. The districts wander in search of pockets of strength of the gerrymandering party. This type best fits the common view of gerrymandering. (b) *Excess votes,* a method that concentrates the opposition party's votes in as few districts as possible so that the opposition wins these seats with large majorities. It is based on the philosophy that if you are going to lose a district, lose it as big as possible. (c) *Wasted Votes,* a method that arranges districts so that the opposition party's votes are "wasted" on losing candidates. The opposition party constitutes a large minority in many districts.

Gerrymandering is generally equated with lack of compactness. However, while stacked districts are invariably noncompact, the districts produced by gerrymandering of the excess or wasted vote methods may be quite compact. Therefore, indexes of compactness, often used to evaluate gerrymandering, may not be the appropriate measure.

Contiguity, often included in the requirements of districting contiguity (that every part of an election district touch another part of the same district), is very difficult to implement. For example, every island cannot be considered a separate congressional district. Both because of this difficulty and because noncontiguous districts have never been the basis of a Supreme Court case, only the equal population and compactness requirements are considered.

Redistricting and reapportionment, often used interchangeably, mean the redrawing of electoral districts, usually after the decennial census or a court decision. The legislators are "reapportioned" among new election districts.

Optimal districting is the phrase used to denote redistricting done by a nonpartisan, nonpolitcal group. Using only the criteria of equal population size and compactness of districts, a plan of the new districts may be proposed. Numerous computer algorithms—most commonly the Weaver-Hess method—are available for such projects.

Electoral bias is the difference between the proportion of the votes a party receives and the proportion of the seats it wins. In single member contests the difference between these two proportions can be substantial. A negative bias is present when the party receives a lower proportion of seats than it had of votes; positive bias exists when the proportion of seats is higher than the proportion of votes.

Proportional representation means that each group should have representatives in proportion to their size. For example, if blacks comprise one-quarter of a city's population, then blacks should number approximately one-quarter of the city council.

Each of the above electoral manipulations has important implications for a democratic society. The one man, one vote provision of the US Constitution can be a reality only if malapportionment and gerrymandering are no longer realities of the American political scene. Electoral districts should be redrawn and legislators reapportioned every ten years after the national census so as to reflect the changing distribution of the American population. Ideally, because of the rapid relocation of many Americans, redistricting should take place every five years.

The question of electoral bias revolves around the spatial distribution of party support. In Western democracies, uniform spatial support for a party is rarely present. Usually a party has spatial neuclei of support; the party will suffer a negative electoral bias if its candidates consistently receive less than one-half the total vote. This negative electoral bias can also be accomplished by gerrymandering of the "wasted vote" type above. Optimal districting insures that any negative electoral bias that occurs is a result of the varying spatial distribution of party support, not deliberate gerrymandering.

The Supreme Court, the Congress and the executive branch have only given due consideration to population equality, contiguity and compactness as criteria for reapportionment. As Banzaf noted, "the Court appears to have given little weight to the strength and cohesiveness of the political parties, the presence and distribution of major ethnic blocs, the power structure within the legislative body (committes and their chairmen, etc.) and other factors which obviously would affect the ability of a citizen voter to pick a representative of his choice and to have some influence on which bills pass."

In particular, little attention has been given to the proportional representation of racial, economic or cultural groups. Of particular interest here is the black ghetto. If the ghetto is large enough, it constitutes a potential political power base. Integration will dilute this potential, and while segregation of housing may be decried by liberals, it nevertheless produces a massive power block for blacks. In *Wright* vs. *Rockefeller,* 376 U.S. 52 (1964), Congressman Adam Clayton Powell argued for the status quo—blacks and Puerto Ricans confined to three CD's but mostly to the Eighteenth—as it assured one Negro representative. Justice Douglas characterized Powell's statement as "separate but better off" and said that was "no more permissible than the discredited doctrine of separate but equal facilities for Negroes." The issue—homogenous or heterogenous districts—of course, also borders on that of gerrymandering—black areas allocated to many electoral districts to ensure their minority status—and will be discussed further later in the chapter.

METHODOLOGY AND OPERATIONAL DEFINITIONS

Great concern exists that the rural-urban apportionment and districting dichotomy of the pre-1962 period may have been replaced by a racial dichotomy. Specifically, the question arises as to whether blacks are better or worse off since the Supreme Court decisions and what change, if any, occurred with respect to the larger American society? Are there any significant differences in the compactness and population sizes of the electoral districts in black, mixed and white areas? Were differences (or similarities) magnified as a result of the reapportionment revolution?

In order to answer the above questions a series of hypotheses were tested. Also, in an endeavor to shed more light on these questions, two further concepts were introduced—political region and type of electoral district. The United States was divided into four regions: Northeast, Midwest, South and West. This typology is based on the work of Daniel Elazar, who identified political-cultural regions of this country. It is hypothesized that location in different regions will affect the rate and degree of reapportionment. The sample was composed of two cities from each region: in the Northeast, New York and Philadelphia; in the Midwest, Chicago and Milwaukee; in the South, Atlanta and New Orleans; and Los Angeles and Seattle in the West. Among the reasons for the selection of these cities were availability of electoral district maps and/or population figures, and whether they had district rather than at-large council elections. (This criterion eliminated most cities: although Atlanta does have at-large elections, the council candidates must be nominated by district.)

The results of this study are, of course, valid only for these eight particular cities. However, the history of reapportionment and redistricting in these cities was duplicated in other large cities in these four regions. We can generalize from the experience of these eight sample cities to cities in the same regional setting. While the exact reapportionment experience may be slightly different due to the different legislative efforts in the state houses, the overall pattern of reapportionment changes in these four regions was similar.

The sample of election districts was also classified by type of district. Four types were used—US congressional, state senatorial, state assembly and city council. It was hypothesized that significant differences would exist between these types of districts in the rate and degree of reapportionment. Since the major Supreme Court decisions on malapportionment were handed down in the early 1960s, by selecting a sample of districts from before and after these decisions, the effects of the judgments may be discerned. Therefore, 1958 and 1968 were selected as the sample years.

Black neighborhoods are those areas (electoral districts) greater than 50 percent black; changing or mixed areas, those districts between 25 and 50 percent black; and white areas, those with less than 25 percent black population according to the census. These levels have theoretical and practical significance. Rose estimated the critical percentage or "tipping point" in the changeover of an area from white to black to be approximately 30 percent. A percentage level of 50 percent assures that all predominantly black areas, as well as those shortly to become all black (remembering the time lag between the census years and the sample years), are included in the same category.

To facilitate the comparison of the population sizes, the index Percentage Population Deviation (PPD) was chosen from the many available. The index is very easy to construct. For example, the PPD for the first Pennsylvania Congressional District for 1968 was -4.68. The total population for the state was 11,319,366 (1960 figures) and it had 27 congressmen. Therefore, the average population for the 27 districts was 419,236. The population of the first district was 399,628 or 19,608 below the state average. Converting this figure to a percentage of the state's district average, it is 4.68 percent. Districts with a population greater than the state average have a positive index and those with a smaller population have a negative index. By the same method, PPDs were derived for the state senatorial and state representative districts in the eight sample cities. For city councilman districts, the average population for the cities' districts was chosen as the standard. The selection of the operational measure of compactness was much more difficult. The notion of compactness is clear-cut. As pointed out by Orr, "a major rationale for compact districts, of course, is that a noncompact district raises the suspicion of gerrymandering. Also, a compact district usually allows a representative to be more accessible to his constitutents, plus they are more likely to share common interests." However, a gerrymandered district need not necessarily weave and wend all over the map. A compact district may be a gerrymandered one. The most compact shape is a circle in which the perimeter encloses the greatest area, with respect to the length of the perimeter.

Gibbs, describing the shapes of American cities, used an index relating the area of the city to the area of a circle drawn using the long axis. Roeck used a similar index to compare the shapes of congressional districts. The basis of both these methods—as it is for all indexes using a circle as a standard—is that the circle can be used as the ideal of compactness, just as the average district population is used as the ideal of population equality. Schwartzberg used a similar index but instead compared the perimeter of the district to the perimeter of a circle of equal area. Both Roeck's and Schwartzberg's methods are useful for different purposes, Roeck's being particularly sensitive to elongation, whereas Schwartzberg's approach is more influenced by indentations.

Haggett outlined four shape indexes, all of which relate the area of the district under study to the area of a circumscribing circle. Three simple ratios are given in which pairs of measurements—area and perimeter, area and long axis, and the radii of the two circles (circumscribing and inscribing)—are related. In each case, the shape ratio is modified to allow ready comparison with a circle. His fourth index relates the length of the short axis of the district to its long axis.

For these reasons, the index used in this study was selected from Haggett's four choices. A pretest of these four indexes was run for sample districts and the most consistent index, defined by similarity to the average of all four, was picked.

The sample used in the pretest consisted of the proposed state assembly districts for New York City, 1972. Fourteen ADs were chosen at random for analysis and four indexes, measuring the compactness of each AD, were calculated (Table 13-1).

The formulae for the calculation of the four indexes are:

$$S_1 = A[0.282\,P]^{-1}$$

$$S_2 = A[0.866\,L]^{-1}$$

$$S_3 = R_i[R_o]^{-1}$$

$$S_4 = A[(0.5\,L)^2\pi]^{-1}$$

where A = area of circle, whose diameter is axis of the unknown shape,

L = longest axis,

P = perimeter of unknown shape,

R_o = radius of outer circle (circumscribing),

R_i = radius of inner circle (inscribing).

The average of each of the four indexes for each assembly district is given in Table 13-1. S_1 was nearest to the average three times; S_2, four times; S_3, four times; and S_4, six times. S_4—the Roeck method—was chosen for this study. This index does not assign each shape a unique number, but a comparison is made between two shapes, one of which is unknown and the other, a known geometrical figure.

The following questions were answered for both the population sizes and compactness indexes of the electoral districts. (All were examined for both the national sample and the regional breakdown.) First, were all districts more equalized in population and compactness in 1968 than in 1958? Second, for each of the four types of electoral districts, did the population deviations decrease and compactness indexes increase between 1958 and 1968? Third, for districts in black areas, were the malapportionment and compactness indexes more equalized in 1968 than in 1958? Fourth, did districts in white areas experience significant changes between 1958 and 1968 in their population sizes or level of compactness? Fifth, did districts in changing or mixed neighborhoods change significantly in their malapportionment or compactness between 1958 and 1968? Sixth,

Table 13-1. Comparison of Indexes of Compactness, New York City, 1972

Area of City	*Assembly District*	S_1	S_2	S_3	S_4	*Average*
White	37	0.46	0.46	0.29	0.29	0.37
	32	0.28	0.50	0.52	0.49	0.44
	44	0.28	0.26	0.21	0.21	0.24
	52	0.40	0.48	0.40	0.53	0.45
	63	0.44	0.38	0.50	0.68	0.50
	69	0.27	0.27	0.36	0.52	0.35
	79	0.30	0.30	0.27	0.30	0.29
	85	0.32	0.48	0.29	0.38	0.37
Mixed	34	0.52	0.58	0.52	0.62	0.56
	59	0.37	0.32	0.44	0.39	0.38
	86	0.48	0.15	0.29	0.32	0.30
Black	53	0.82	0.08	0.50	0.46	0.46
	70	0.28	0.09	0.50	0.64	0.37
	74	0.26	0.08	0.35	0.28	0.24

Source: computations by the author.

in 1958, were there significant differences in the levels of malapportionment and compactness between white, black and mixed electoral districts? Seventh, in 1968 were there significant differences in the levels of malapportionment and compactness in these types of neighborhoods? The significance of these differences was measured by analysis of variance.

PROGRESS TOWARD EQUITABLE APPORTIONMENT IN AMERICAN CITIES

This section is devoted to an examination of the population sizes of electoral districts in black areas of eight cities. By comparing the size of the districts with those in white and mixed neighborhoods and by analyzing the effects of the "Reapportionment Revolution" after the decisions of the Supreme Court in the early 1960s, we can state the degree to which black areas are over- or underrepresented.

Because of antiquated provisions of state constitutions—for example, no county could have more than one state senator in California—some of the malapportionment indexes for 1958 reached absurd proportions. Illustrative of these indexes are the +622.75 for the New Orleans State Senate District in 1958, the +642.46 for Fulton County (Atlanta) State Senate District in 1958, the +114.5 for Fulton County state representatives in 1958 and, the biggest of all, +1114.5 for the Los Angeles County State Senate District before reapportionment in California in 1965. Such gigantic indexes were not common in the Northeast and Midwest, where the urban bloc had a greater vote in the legislatures. Southern and western legislatures, traditionally rural-dominated, allowed the "silent gerrymander" to run rife, and with the rapid growth of the cities, guaranteed their underrepresentation.

The means and standard deviations for the black areas and the total sample for both 1958 and 1968 are listed in Table 13-2. In all but three instances, the mean PPD is positive, with the largest deviation that of the 1958 black sample. In general, the deviations for the total sample are closer to the optimum—0.0—while those of the black sample vary from -10.83 to +7.44. Reapportionment during the ten year span—1958 to 1968—had a much more beneficial effect in black areas, reducing the mean from +7.44 to +3.81 and the standard deviation from 16.38 to 9.46. On the other hand, the mean actually increased for the total sample, although the standard deviation was more than halved. The regional breakdown shows great overrepresentation for the black areas in Chicago-Milwaukee and slight underrepresentation in the three other regions. For the total sample in 1968, the mean of the PPDs is near the optimum in all four regions. The Midwest displays the greatest variation of

Table 13-2. Means and Standard Deviations of Percentage Population Deviations for Total and Black Samples, 1958 and 1968

	Mean	*Standard Deviation*		*Mean*	*Standard Deviation*
1958 Total	+1.01	25.62	1958 Black	+7.44	16.38
1968 Total	+2.42	11.68	1968 Black	+3.81	9.46
1968 NE Total	+0.94	9.20	1968 NE Black	+2.17	6.58
1968 MW Total	-0.67	15.68	1968 MW Black	-10.83	13.91
1968 S Total	+2.65	8.08	1968 S Black	+2.67	3.82
1968 W Total	-1.98	12.80	1968 W Black	+0.04	0.16

Source: computations by the author.

deviations—15.68 and 13.91—while the West varies from 12.80 for the total sample to 0.16 for the black sample.

In Figure 13-1, the PPDs for black districts are more concentrated around the optimum than those for the total sample, which are more evenly spread across the continuum. For 1968, on the other hand, the two distributions are markably similar, although they are slightly skewed in different directions (Figure 13-2). In Figure 13-3, the two graphs exhibit markedly different attributes. Because of reapportionment and the reduction of the indexes, the 1968 curve is more peaked near the optimum (Figure 13-4).

The PPDs for the total sample in the four regions are plotted in Figure 13-5. The Northeast appears to be the best apportioned, as most of its PPDs cluster near the optimum, with the West relatively malapportioned. The modes

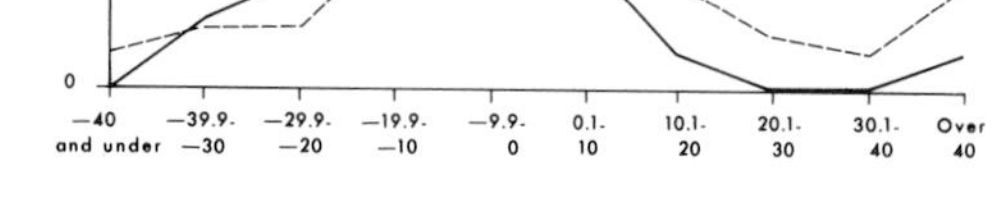

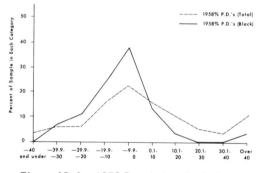

Figure 13-1. 1958 Population Deviations.

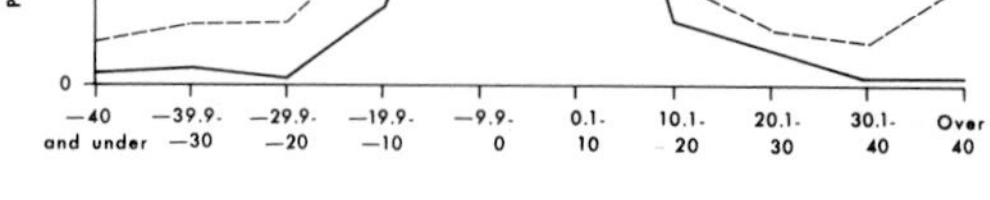

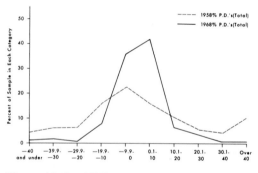

Figure 13-3. 1958 and 1968 Population Deviations (Total).

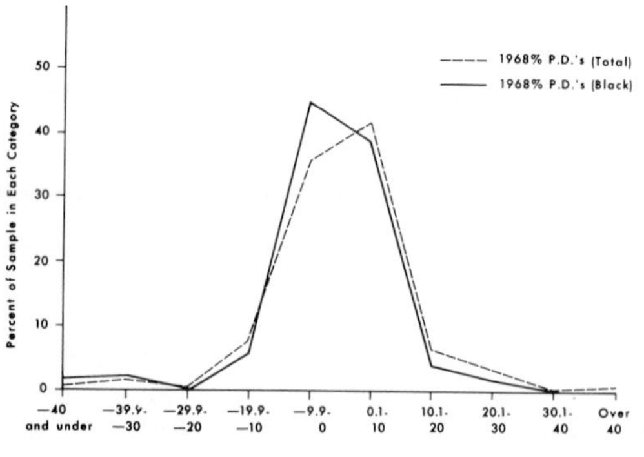

Figure 13-2. 1968 Population Deviations.

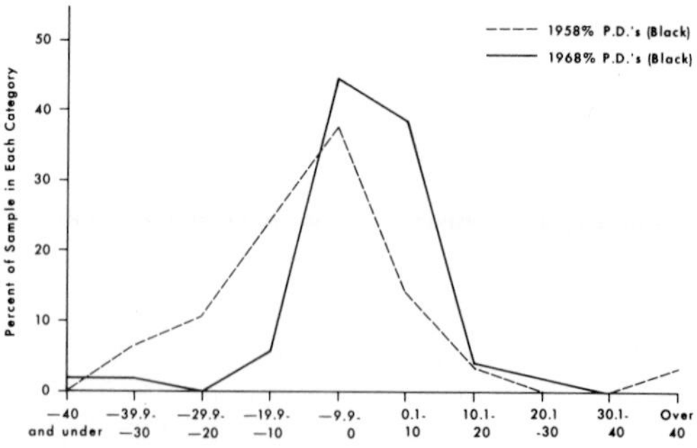

Figure 13-4. 1958 and 1968 Population Deviations (Black).

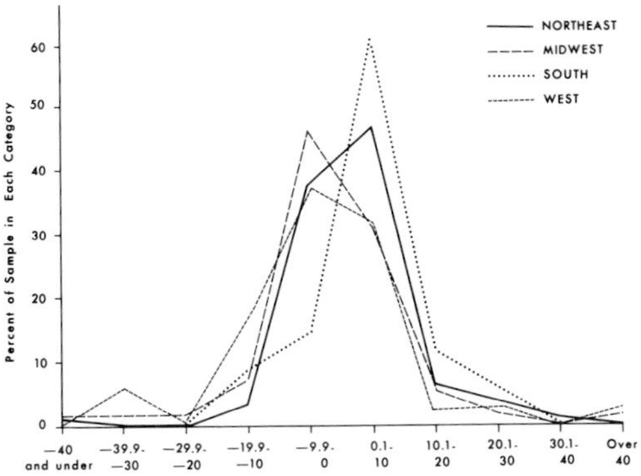

Figure 13-5. Population Deviations for Total Sample, 1968.

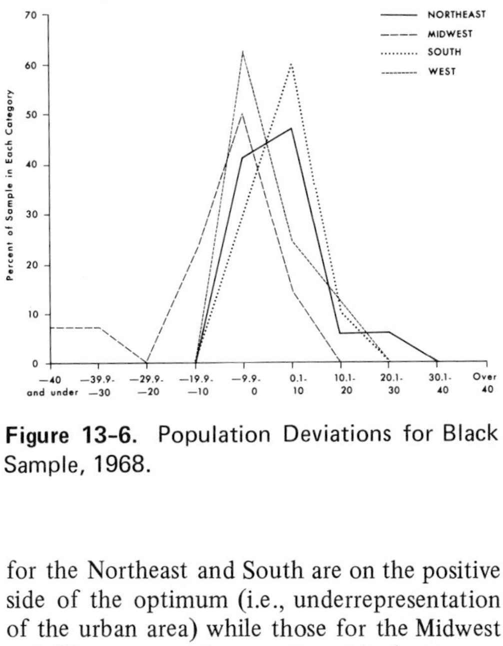

Figure 13-6. Population Deviations for Black Sample, 1968.

for the Northeast and South are on the positive side of the optimum (i.e., underrepresentation of the urban area) while those for the Midwest and West are on the negative side (overrepresentation). For the black sample, the South has the greatest clustering near the optimum (although on the positive side), while the Midwest has only 65 percent of its sample between -10 and +10, due to the overrepresentation of many black districts in Chicago and Milwaukee (Figure 13-6). When comparing the total sample distribution to that of the black sample for each region in 1968, only the West displays a significant difference in the two curves. Whereas only 70 percent of the PPDs of the total sample occur between -10 and +10, 88 percent of the black sample is within 10 points of the optimum. This suggests that the black areas are much better apportioned than the cities as a whole.

The Supreme Court decisions had a great effect on the population sizes of the districts, as confirmed by the analysis of variance. This result is not surprising since all states reapportioned after the Supreme Court decisions. When the data are split by region, the differences of the population sizes of the districts between 1958 and 1968 are significant for the West, the South and the Northeast. However, in Chicago-Milwaukee the districts showed no significant change in population sizes from 1958 to 1968. This is probably due to their relatively better apportionment at the earlier time period.

There were significant differences in the population sizes of the districts for 1958 in the three different areas of the cities (Table 13-3).

Table 13-3. Mean Percentage Population Deviations in Districts in 1958

Region	*White*	*Mixed*	*Black*
West	-13.60	-28.11	+3.46
South	+0.08	+38.25	+47.27
NE	+2.96	+9.29	-9.09
MW	+0.65	-9.63	-14.35
Total	-0.64	+4.32	-6.50

Source: computations by the author.

The average PPD for white areas was -0.64, for black areas -6.50 and for mixed areas +4.32. In this case, blacks are overrepresented and the mixed neighborhoods underrepresented. The representation of the white areas is near the optimum.

In Los Angeles-Seattle, blacks are underrepresented, while the other two areas are adequately represented. In the South, both the black and mixed neighborhoods are grossly underrepresented. For both the Northeast and the Midwest, significant differences existed between the population sizes of the districts in the three areas. However, while white areas are within the normal range, the means for the other areas show that black areas were overrepresented. The mixed neighborhoods are underrepresented in the Northeast and overrepresented in the Midwest. This pattern of apportionment can be explained by the internal migration within the cities. When the legislatures were last apportioned prior to 1958, a large proportion of the cities' populations lived in what were the black and changing areas in 1958. With the movement of the newly affluent whites to the emptier areas within the city limits, these hitherto correctly apportioned neighborhoods became underrepresented, while the black areas, although undergoing a change-over of population rather than a loss, became relatively overrepresented. The pattern is different in the West and South because of the recent growth of cities in those regions. When the cities were apportioned there, the population was more evenly distributed throughout the city than in the older regions of the country. With the postwar influx into the inner city of blacks, these inner city areas became underrepresented. In summary, then, for 1958 a dichotomous classification results. Blacks were overrepresented in the Northeast and Midwest, while the opposite held true for black areas in the South and West.

Extending the analysis to 1968, tests were made to determine whether the differences in the percentage population deviations for the three types of neighborhoods were significant. The data are summarized in Table 13-4. For the country as a whole, the means for each type of city neighborhood were near the optimum, with the black areas being slightly underrepresented. The regional pattern exhibits marked differences. For the Midwest, the differences between the means were significant. In Chicago and Milwaukee the black areas are overrepresented, the deviation from the optimum being 10.83 percent, while the white areas are slightly underrepresented. It is not immediately clear why this should be so. Between 1958 and 1968, the deviation of the mean of the PPDs for white areas actually increased while that for the black areas decreased by a third (from 14.35 to 10.38). The overrepresentation of black districts occurs solely in the councilmanic districts in Chicago, where deviations from the optimum as large as 33 percent occur. Since apportionment of the council's seats is in the hands of the Mayor Daley organization, it is to their advantage to underrepresent the outer districts, which trend Republican, and overrepresent the inner city, which is overwhelmingly Democratic.

Table 13-4. Mean Percentage Population Deviations in Districts in 1968

Region	*White*	*Changing*	*Black*
West	-2.39	-3.00	+0.04
South	+2.99	+1.85	+2.67
NE	+0.18	+1.02	+2.17
MW	+3.75	-0.80	-10.83
Total	+0.68	+0.50	+3.81

Source: computations by the author.

In Los Angeles-Seattle the means for each neighborhood type do not differ appreciably from the optimum, but they do in the South. In New Orleans and Atlanta, all neighborhood types are underrepresented, the remaining vestiges of rural-dominated legislatures. There is no significant difference between the three neighborhood types in the Northeast, although the mean for the PPDs in the black areas is the greatest at +2.17. Summarizing, it can be said that only the Midwest showed a significant difference between the three types of neighborhoods and that this can be attributed to the malapportionment of Chicago's city council districts. The differences between the three types of districts—black, changing and white—that had existed in 1958 had, due to the reapportionment of the sixties, been eliminated by 1968. The overall effect of the Court's decisions was beneficial in equalizing representation for all regardless of the area of the city they live in.

The inflated means for 1958 districts in the West and South in Table 13-5 can be attributed to the great malapportionment between city and rural areas. The fact that Atlanta, New Orleans and Los Angeles each had only one state senatorial district and that Atlanta had only three state representatives in 1958 biased the means considerably. A quick glance at the means indicates that in all but two instances—the house districts for the Northeast and the council districts for the West—the average deviation of the PPDs for each type of electoral district in each region decreased between 1958 and 1968 (Tables 13-5 and 13-6). The decrease was most marked for the state senatorial and state house districts. This was to be expected since it was state legislatures which were most malapportioned in 1958.

At the national scale, the differences between four types of electoral districts were significant in all but the councilmanic case. That the city council districts were not affected by the reapportionment of the early sixties is expected. The Supreme Court's decisions had

Table 13-5. Mean Percentage Population Deviations in Districts 1958 (Region and Type)

Region	*US Congressional*	*State Senate*	*State House*	*City Council*
West	-9.29	+375.18	-20.78	-5.86
South	+33.69	+632.60	+197.13	+8.71
Northeast	+2.25	-3.35	-0.13	+2.17
Midwest	+6.51	+9.63	-3.38	-9.63
Total	+3.94	+112.00	+18.74	-1.97

Source: computations by the author.

Table 13-6. Mean Percentage Population Deviations in Districts 1968 (Region and Type)

Region	*US Congressional*	*State Senate*	*State House*	*City Council*
West	+4.65	+0.81	-2.22	-8.01
South	+10.50	+2.96	+1.63	+4.77
Northeast	-1.67	-0.34	+3.09	+1.33
Midwest	+0.41	-0.67	-1.00	-1.25
Total	+1.67	+1.56	+0.41	-0.60

Source: computations by the author.

the greatest impact at the congressional district and state legislature level. Few challenges to council districts plans in the courts seemed to place this type of districting in a category of its own. Although the cities were reapportioned between 1958 and 1968 for their various councils, the application of the "one man, one vote" proviso was not nearly so rigorous as in the state legislatures. Thus, for example, deviations as great as 34 percent in Los Angeles, 16 percent in Seattle, 21 percent in Atlanta, 33 percent in Philadelphia, 43 percent in Milwaukee and 85 percent in Chicago continued to exist in 1968.

Cities in the Northeast, West and Midwest did not experience any significant change in the population size of their congressional districts between 1958 and 1968. However, significant regional differences emerged from the tests of state senatorial districts. Three of the four cities in the South and the West had only a single senate seat allocated to them in 1958. There was no significant change for the Northeast or Midwest cities at any of the four leads of government between 1958 and 1968. Reapportionment of state senatorial districts effected little change in the Northeast and Midwest, but brought about profound changes in the legislatures of the South and West.

Since no significant reapportionment of city council districts took place on a national scale during the 1960s it was expected that the regional pattern would not be very different. Only in the West was there a significant change in the size of the population districts. In fact, the average deviation from the optimum—0.00—increased from 5.86 to 8.01. Even after many reapportionments (two between 1958 and 1968), great deviations still existed in the Los Angeles council districts. It is evident that the "one man, one vote" requirement was not being enforced at the local level and that malapportionment was getting worse during the 1960s at this level.

The distinction between the older metropolitan areas—Northeast and Midwest—and the South and West did not appear in the analysis of state house changes. House districts in the Northeast and the West experienced a significant change in their population deviations between 1958 and 1968. In the other two regions, house districts did not show significant change. The change in population sizes of state house districts in the West can be explained by the disappearance of the great deviations that had existed prior to reapportionment (see Tables 13-5 and 13-6). In the Northeast, reapportionment led to an increase in the average deviation from the optimum from 0.13 to 3.09, from almost perfect apportionment to slight underrepresentation. The reason undoubtedly lies in the greater representation of the rapidly growing suburban areas around New York and Philadelphia, so that the cities themselves became relatively less heavily represented in the state houses.

The next question concerned is the change between 1958 and 1968 in the population size of the four types of districts, classified by the type of area of the city. A summary of the data is given in Tables 13-7 and 13-8. A cursory inspection of the means reveals, with four exceptions, reductions in the deviations of PPDs from the optimum. Of these four exceptions, only one, that for white US Congressional districts, is not in a black area. The inflated 1958 means for the changing (25 to 50 percent black) state senatorial districts are due to the great deviations from the average in Los Angeles, New Orleans and Atlanta referred to earlier. For state senatorial districts in the white areas, the change was from gross overrepresentation to slight overrepresentation in 1968, because of the fairer representation of Los Angeles County in the California state senate. The mixed neighborhoods became almost optimally apportioned during the decade. Little change was evident in the black areas and it was not significant at any level.

For US congressional districts, the only significant change occurred in white areas, due to the better representation of Fulton County (Atlanta) and Los Angeles. Black state house districts experienced a significant change which proved advantageous for black areas as they are now slightly overrepresented. No changes proved to be significant for the councilmanic districts, bearing out the earlier statement that local districts were least affected by the reapportionments. No attempt was made to analyze further the changes by regions—for example, the changes in black congressional districts in the Northeast—because the sample sizes would not allow tests of significance to be made. No overall pattern emerged when the changes in the population size of districts are analyzed by type of electoral district and area of city simultaneously.

The final series of questions examined the changes between 1958 and 1968 within each type of neighborhood—black, changing and white—both at the national level and by region. In all cases, but two, the means of the PPDs decreased (Tables 13-9 and 13-10). The Midwest white districts increased from 0.65 to 3.74. The reason probably lies in the malapportionment between white and black districts. In 1968 the average deviation for black districts was -10.83, which denotes overrepresentation of black areas. This is most obvious at the councilmanic level, where negative deviations of 14 percent, 34 percent and 44 percent still existed in Chicago and Milwaukee in 1968. The average deviation for white districts in the

Table 13-7. Mean Percentage Population Deviations in 1958 Districts (by Neighborhood and Type)

Type of Neighborhood	*US Congressional*	*State Senate*	*State House*	*City Council*
White	−0.08	+167.00	+1.47	-4.41
Changing	+17.46	−5.10	−1.04	+3.46
Black	+1.43	−0.80	+0.65	−3.84

Source: computations by the author.

Table 13-8. Mean Percentage Population Deviations in 1968 Districts (by Neighborhood and Type)

Type of Neighborhood	*US Congressional*	*State Senate*	*State House*	*City Council*
White	+1.81	+0.29	+0.94	−1.39
Changing	+2.26	+0.31	+0.87	+1.92
Black	+1.31	+1.35	−1.91	−4.74

Source: computations by the author.

Table 13-9. Mean Percentage Population Deviations in 1958 Districts (by Region and Neighborhood)

Region	*White*	*Changing*	*Black*
West	-13.60	-28.11	+3.46
South	+0.08	-38.25	+47.27
Northeast	+2.96	+9.29	-9.09
Midwest	+0.65	-9.63	-14.35
Total	-0.64	+4.32	-6.50

Source: computations by the author.

Table 13-10. Mean Percentage Population Deviations in 1968 Districts (by Region and Neighborhood)

West	-2.39	-3.00	+0.04
South	+2.99	+1.85	+2.67
Northeast	+0.18	+1.02	+2.17
Midwest	+3.74	-0.80	-10.83
Total	+0.63	+0.50	+3.81

Source: computations by the author.

South increased from +0.08 to +2.99 during the 1958-1968 decade. This change may be attributed to a more equitable distribution of districts, both within the states of Georgia and Louisiana, and within the cities of Atlanta and New Orleans. (The average deviation for black districts dropped from +47.27 to +2.67 during the time period.) At the national level in 1968, while both white and changing areas are near the optimum representation, black areas are underrepresented by nearly 4 percent. This is in sharp contrast to 1958, where black areas were overrepresented by 6.5 percent. The change represents an overall net deficit of over 10 percent.

For black areas at the national level, the change in population deviations between 1958 and 1968 was significant. Neither of the other two analyses (total white districts and total changing districts) showed a significant change over this decade. Big reductions in the means of the PPDs in black areas occurred in both the Northeast and Midwest, as reapportionment reduced some of the bias in representation that had existed toward the inner city over the outlying areas.

Comparison of the white electoral districts, by region, showed a significant change between 1958 and 1968 only in the West. This is in accord with previous statements that, since the West was probably the most malapportioned region in 1958, it should be the region most affected by reapportionment. For the mixed areas, the two regions—Midwest and Northeast—both showed significant changes between 1958 and 1968. In this sample, it seems as if the mixed neighborhoods were the ones most profoundly affected by reapportionment.

GERRYMANDERING AND OPTIMAL DISTRICTING

As was mentioned earlier, the other main requirement of redistricting is that of compactness. This section will analyze the districts in black areas and compare them to districts in white and mixed neighborhoods for both 1958 and 1968. An analysis similar to the one performed for the population deviations was undertaken. The sample of districts is the same for the analysis of the PPDs.

Analysis of the Compactness Requirement

Means and standard deviations were calculated for the total and black samples and the results are given in Table 13-11. The means of

Table 13-11. Means and Standard Deviations for Sample of Compactness Index

	Mean	*Standard Deviation*		*Mean*	*Standard Deviation*
1958 Total	0.41	0.15	1958 Black	0.41	0.19
1968 Total	0.41	0.15	1968 Black	0.45	0.15
1968 NE Total	0.42	0.15	1968 NE Black	0.43	0.11
1968 MW Total	0.43	0.15	1968 MW Black	0.53	0.15
1968 S Total	0.34	0.15	1968 S Black	0.39	0.16
1968 W Total	0.43	0.13	1968 W Black	0.44	0.19

Source: computations by the author.

the compactness indexes (CIs) were remarkably similar. Only two—1968 South total and 1968 Midwest black—were not between 0.39 and 0.45. No overall change occurred between 1958 and 1968 but the average of the black CIs did increase from 0.41 to 0.45. The nature of the sample (primarily New Orleans) may explain the low means of the 1968 South total. The shape of the city as a whole determines, to a certain extent, the CIs of its districts. In all cases except one—and then they are identical—the mean of the black CIs was greater than that of the total sample (Table 13-12). This is to be expected, since black districts are inner city in nature and as such are not affected by the irregular boundary of the city. Districts—usually white—at the outer fringe of the city have lower compactness indexes than those further in toward the center. The standard deviations of the total samples were remarkably similar but show a wider range for the black sample.

The compactness indexes for the total and black samples in both 1958 and 1968 were plotted in Figures 13-7 through 13-12. Little difference was seen between the various graphs. A better level of compactness is indicated by greater skewness of the graphs to the right. In Figures 13-7 and 13-8 the black districts were slightly more compact than the corresponding total sample. A comparison of the total sample for 1958 with that for 1968 revealed little change. For the black districts, the 1968 graph displayed a greater skewness to the right, indicating a slight trend towards more compact districts during the 1960s.

The regional breakdown for 1968 showed the West to have the most compact districts, with the South having the least compact. For the black sample, the South also had the least compact districts and the Midwest had slightly more compact districts than the other three

Table 13-12. Means of Compactness Indexes (by Region)

1958 Total	*Mean CI*	*1968 Total Sample*	*Mean CI*
Northeast	0.40	Northeast	0.42
Midwest	0.44	Midwest	0.43
South	0.34	South	0.34
West	0.40	West	0.45
Total	0.41	Total	0.41

Source: computations by the author.

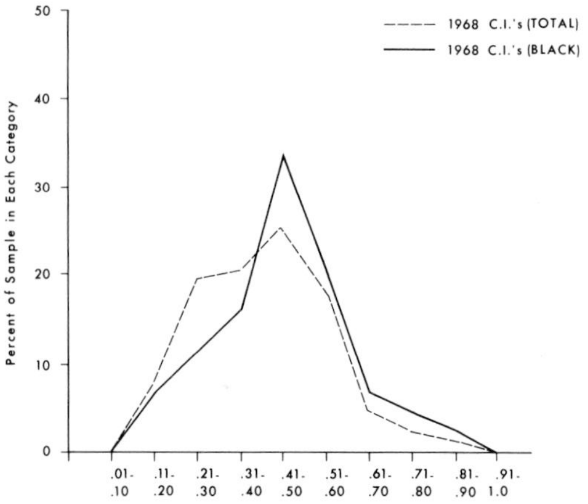

Figure 13-7. 1968 Compactness Index.

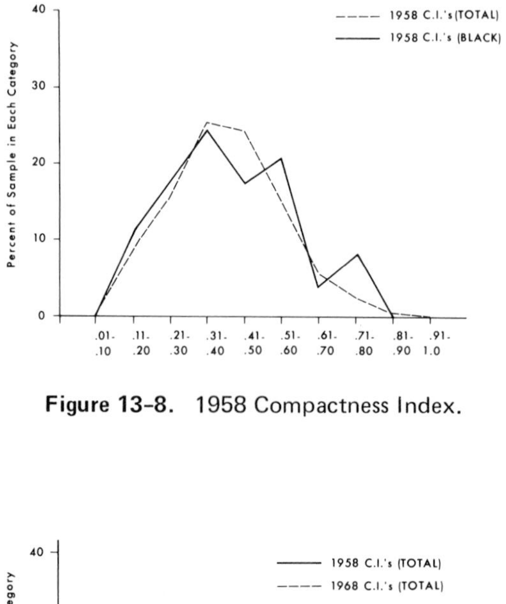

Figure 13-8. 1958 Compactness Index.

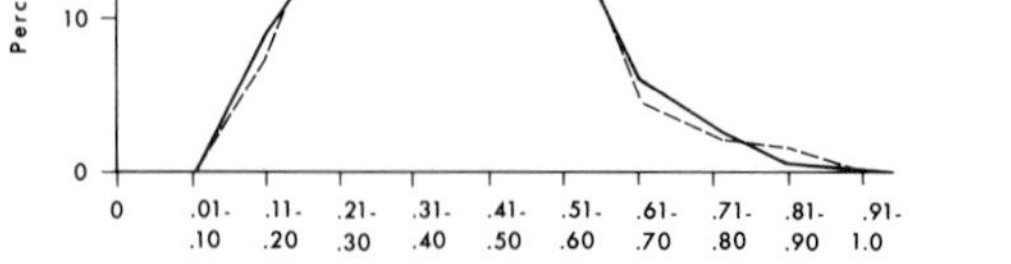

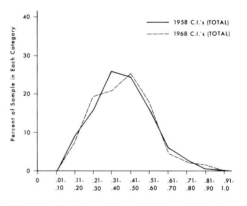

Figure 13-9. Compactness Index for Total Sample, 1958 and 1968.

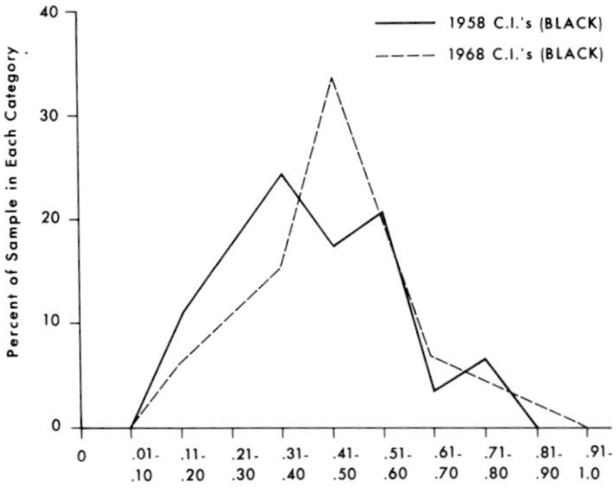

Figure 13-10. Compactness Index for Black Sample, 1958 and 1968.

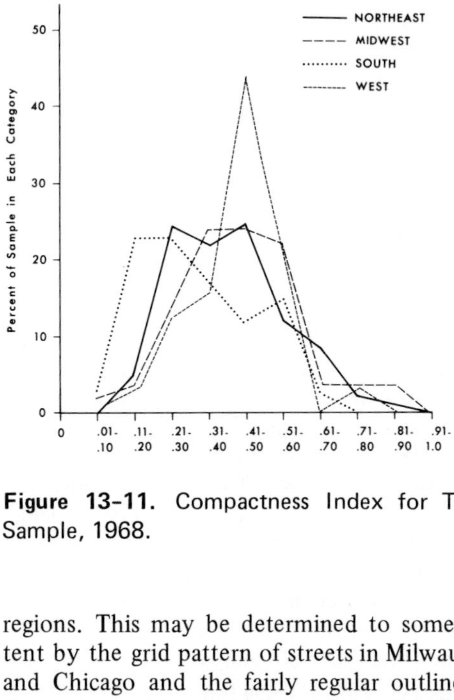

Figure 13-11. Compactness Index for Total Sample, 1968.

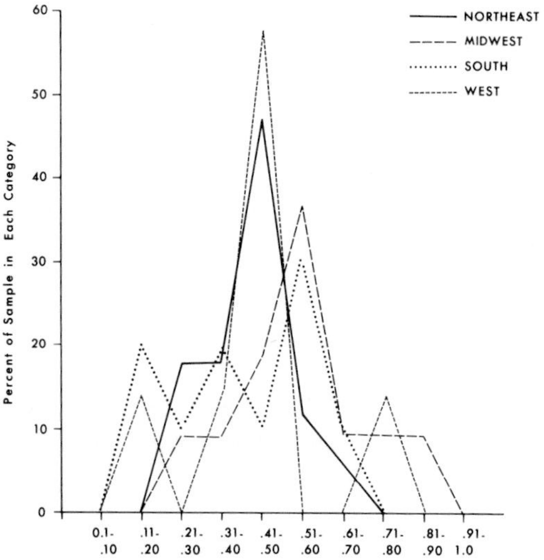

Figure 13-12. Compactness Index for Black Sample, 1968.

regions. This may be determined to some extent by the grid pattern of streets in Milwaukee and Chicago and the fairly regular outline of these two cities, which contrasts markedly with that of cities such as New York, New Orleans and Seattle. The problem is compounded for New Orleans by its ward pattern, on which all districting is based. The traditional strip pattern back from the river has persisted, leading to an elongation of all districts.

With this evidence, not many tests were expected to show significant differences. Out of the 48 analyses of variances undertaken only 14, or 29 percent, were found to be significant at the 5 percent level. That there was no significant change in the compactness of the total sample between 1958 and 1968 was upheld. This is in sharp contrast to the same result for the percentage population deviations, and substantiates statements made earlier that the Supreme Court decisions were effective in reducing malapportionment, but ineffective in reducing gerrymandering. When the sample is split by region, the analysis pointed to significant changes in the Northeast and Midwest in the compactness indexes and to little change in the South and West. This dichotomous regional division of the country also occurred in the analysis of the percentage population deviations. The means of the compactness indexes (CIs) for the Northeast increased slightly, indicating a trend toward greater compactness, while that for the Midwest decreased slightly.

The slight decrease in the overall compactness of the districts in the Midwest (Table 13-12) may be attributed to the realignment of the city council districts (wards) in Chicago, where the average CI dropped from 0.41 to 0.39. When a comparison was made of the compactness indexes in the three types of neighborhoods, it was seen that only in the Midwest was there a significant difference between the indexes (Table 13-13). Here the districts in the mixed neighborhoods were significantly more compact than those in the white or black areas. Whether the arrangement of the electoral boundaries leading to these

Table 13-13. 1958 Means of Compactness Indexes (by Region)

Region	*White*	*Changing*	*Black*
Northeast	0.39	0.38	0.41
Midwest	0.43	0.47	0.41
South	0.40	0.45	0.28
West	0.38	0.32	0.48
Total	0.40	0.42	0.40

Source: computations by the author.

Table 13-14. 1968 Means of Compactness Indexes (by Neighborhood and Region)

Region	*White*	*Mixed*	*Black*
Northeast	0.38	0.45	0.43
Midwest	0.41	0.49	0.53
South	0.30	0.31	0.39
West	0.45	0.34	0.44
Total	0.42	0.45	0.45

Source: computations by the author.

degrees of compactness is a historical accident or deliberate policy is impossible to say without a detailed analysis of the process by which the districts were drawn. Such an analysis is beyond the scope of this study.

For 1968 the significant differences between the three areas of the cities are repeated for the Midwest and, for this time period, also for the Northeast.

The redrawing of the boundaries of the electoral districts, concomitant with the reapportionment following the numerous Supreme Court decisions, led to a dramatic shifting in the relative position of the average of the compactness indexes of the black districts in the South, Midwest and West. (Contrast Tables 13-13 and 13-14).

The means of the compactness indexes of the four types of electoral districts, subdivided by region, are listed in Tables 13-15 and 13-16. A quick glance at the means gives an indication of the relative position of each type of electoral district. For 1958, in all regions except the West (where it is exceeded by the mean of the house districts), the mean of the city council districts was the largest, suggesting that the districts formed by the city councils are more compact than those formed by the state legislatures. By 1968 this statement was no longer true. By redistricting during the 1960s, state legislatures created more compact districts for the US Congress, the state senates and the state houses. (An exception is congressional districts in the Midwest.) Some city council districts remained the same, retaining the old ward lines, and, relative to the other three types of districts, city council districts became less compact.

To gain further insights into factors governing the compactness of the four types of electoral districts, they were split by type of neighborhood (black, changing or white) they were in. The means of the compactness indexes are given in Tables 13-17 and 13-18. The means can be compared either horizontally—for example, in white areas for 1968, which type of district had the highest mean?—or vertically—for example, which area of city had the lowest mean for council districts in 1958? No attempt was made to analyze the difference between the compactness indexes due to the small sample in some of the categories. No pattern emerged from the horizontal comparison. No one type of district had a consistently higher mean than any other. In fact, each type of district was highest twice. However, a clear-cut pattern emerged from the vertical comparison. The mean of the districts in black areas were highest in five of the eight comparisons contrasting with two for the changing districts and one for the white areas. This rather flimsy evidence supports previous statements that black areas are most compact. It appears as if black areas were most affected by the redistrictings at the state legislature level. Little change occurred elsewhere in the cities, with the possible exception of council districts and state senatorial districts in white areas. Mixed neighborhoods were not affected at all.

The final set of analyses dealt with the change in the compactness indexes of all districts within each type of neighborhood between 1958 and 1968. The means for both time periods are listed in Tables 13-19 and 13-20. At the national scale no significant change occurred in the compactness of black areas. Neither did significant change take place in any of the four regions. Similar results were obtained for the analyses of the change between 1958 and 1968 in the mixed districts. With the exception of the West, the results were duplicated for the white districts, emphasizing once more the lack of change in the

Table 13-15. 1958 Means of Compactness Indexes (by Region and Type)

Region	*US Congressional*	*State Senate*	*State House*	*City Council*
NE	0.39	0.39	0.41	0.44
MW	0.40	0.40	0.45	0.46
South	0.39	0.32	0.25	0.42
West	0.33	0.31	0.45	0.35
Total	0.39	0.39	0.40	0.43

Source: computations by the authors.

Table 13-16. 1968 Means of Compactness Indexes (by Region and Type)

Region	*US Congressional*	*State Senate*	*State House*	*City Council*
NE	0.39	0.41	0.42	0.39
MW	0.36	0.44	0.46	0.43
South	0.49	0.32	0.29	0.42
West	0.47	0.47	0.47	0.39
Total	0.40	0.42	0.43	0.42

Source: computations by the author.

Table 13-17. 1958 Means of Compactness Indexes (by Neighborhoods and Type)

Area of City	*US Congressional*	*State Senate*	*State House*	*City Council*
White	0.37	0.38	0.44	0.42
Changing	0.45	0.38	0.38	0.41
Black	0.38	0.45	0.36	0.47

Source: computations by the author.

Table 13-18. 1968 Means of Compactness Indexes (by Neighborhoods and Type)

Area of City	*US Congressional*	*State Senate*	*State House*	*City Council*
White	0.39	0.41	0.40	0.41
Changing	0.44	0.40	0.43	0.37
Black	0.40	0.47	0.47	0.42

Source: computations by the author.

Table 13-19. 1958 Means of Compactness Indexes (by Neighborhood and Region)

Region	*White*	*Changing*	*Black*
Northeast	0.39	0.38	0.41
Midwest	0.43	0.47	0.41
South	0.40	0.45	0.28
West	0.38	0.32	0.48

Source: computations by the author.

Table 13-20. 1968 Means of Compactness Indexes (by Neighborhood and Region)

Region	*White*	*Changing*	*Black*
Northeast	0.38	0.45	0.43
Midwest	0.41	0.49	0.53
South	0.30	0.31	0.39
West	0.45	0.34	0.44

Source: computations by the author.

compactness indexes consequent on the Supreme Court's decisions.

Optimal Districting

The existence of high compactness may not necessarily be an indication that little gerrymandering is present, just as low compactness indexes do not prove gerrymandering. Roeck stated that "on the basis of the districts examined . . . , it seems reasonable to say that every district with a degree of compactness of less than 30 percent should be reexamined carefully. Districts having a degree of compactness below 20 percent should be considered suspect until proven valid." The vast majority of the 400 compactness indexes computed for this study were above 0.35, with every mean computed between 0.35 and 0.45. Clustering of the means around 0.40 was noted in particular. Fewer than ten compactness indexes were below 0.10. These were mostly in New Orleans, New York and Chicago.

However, elongated districts, which give rise to those low CIs, may not be the result of gerrymandering. The uneven boundaries of city limits; indentations, such as river estuaries; and panhandles, such as Western Maryland or Far Rockaway in New York City, all lead to low compactness indexes. For example, it is difficult to draw districts in Manhattan that do not have low compactness indexes. For these reasons, it was decided to broaden the scope of the study and to utilize another method to arrive at a more definitive statement of the relative level of compactness of districts in black areas. The actual districts are compared to "optimal" districts. Specifically, the number of districts with black majorities are compared for both the actual and optimal redistricting plans. By doing this, it is possible to gain some knowledge of gerrymandering of black areas. Finally, the results are compared to two theoretical models based on Bunge's work.

Of the three alternative methods available to produce these "optimal" districts, the Goodchild-Massam technique was selected. A comparison of these methods and a summary of the Goodchild-Massam technique are available in O'Loughlin's doctoral dissertation.

The cities used in the analysis are the same as for the previous analyses. However, only one time period was used in the derivation of the optimal districts because of the vast number of computations in the iterative process: 1968 was chosen because of its recency and relevancy. Because of the time taken to recompute the centers of the wards and the electoral districts, and to measure the distances between them, limitations have to be placed on the number of electoral districts and wards in each city. Table 13-21 lists the data units used as input and the type of electoral districts for which the optimal districts were derived. As far as possible, the input data units are those which are generally recognized as the basis of redistricting. The use of assembly districts in New York and Los Angeles was necessitated by the absence of any other large-scale political unit. Census tracts in Atlanta are related to that city's precincts. Only in Seattle was a nonpolitical unit used. For each of these input units the 1960 population was computed. (The 1960 census figures were used, rather than the 1970 figures, because the districtings that existed in 1968 were based on the earlier census figures. By using similar base figures, comparisons between the optimal and actual districtings can be fairly made.) The constraint of each electoral district was found by dividing the total population of the city by the number of elec-

Table 13-21. Sample for Optimal Districting

City	*Input Districts*	*Number*	*Type of Optimal District*	*Number*
New York City	Assembly Districts	68	US Congressional	19
Philadelphia	Wards	66	State Senatorial	9
Chicago	Wards	50	US Congressional	8 + part of 9
Milwaukee	Wards	19	State Senatorial	7
Atlanta	Census Tracts	111	City Council	8
New Orleans	Wards	17	City Council	5
Los Angeles	Assembly Districts	31	US Congressional	14 + part of 15
Seattle	Census Tracts	110	State Senatorial–Assembly	9

Source: computations by the author.

toral districts to be derived. The number of electoral districts was determined by the allocation by the state legislature or city council of the actual districts in 1968, so facilitating comparison with the actual electoral districts.

Figures 13-13 through 13-20 show the location of black areas, the actual boundaries of the electoral districts and the optimal districts for each city. Table 13-22 summarizes the differences between the two types of districting on the proportion of blacks in each district. A trend was noted toward more districts with black majorities, from 11 to 17, but this trend was not present in every city. Milwaukee and New Orleans exhibited no change while Seattle actually lost its only black majority district. Atlanta, Los Angeles and Philadelphia both added one black majority district, but the greatest change was exhibited in Chicago and New York, both with a gain of two. When the changes are analyzed by region (Table 13-23), major changes were seen in the two older metropolitan regions, with very little or no change in the West and South.

In the Detroit Geographical Expedition report, Bunge outlined two theoretical models of gerrymandering, that by the inner city and that by the outer city or suburbs. It is the latter kind that is of interest here. Two subtypes may be distinguished (Figure 13-21). In the smaller black areas example (Figure 13-21 upper), the four districts each contain sizable minorities of blacks, even though there are enough blacks to justify a black majority district. This type of gerrymandering is quite common in cities with small black neighborhoods. Examples that were included in this study are the city council districts in New Orleans (Figure 13-18). The second subtype of gerrymandering is more common. The black area is large enough to warrant two or more representatives but has only one. The city is districted with one black majority district and the rest of the black area is subdivided into white majority districts (Figure 13-21 lower). Examples of this type of gerrymandering are US congressional districts in New York City (Figure 13-13), state senatorial districts in Philadelphia (Figure 13-14), US congressional districts in Chicago (Figure 13-15), state senatorial districts in Milwaukee (Figure 13-16), and city council districts in Atlanta (Figure 13-17).

As was mentioned earlier, high compactness indexes may not indicate the absence of gerrymandering. In fact, high compactness indexes

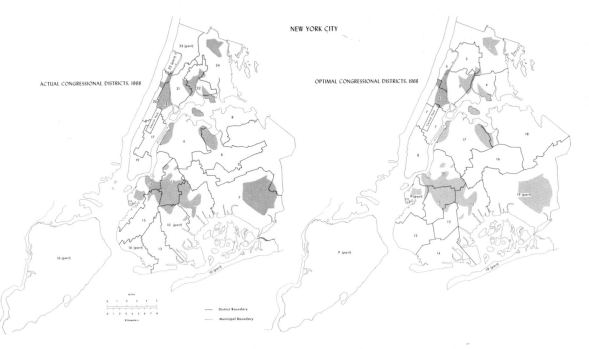

Figure 13-13. Actual and Optimal Congressional Districts, 1968, New York. Shading indicates areas more than 50 percent black in 1970.

PHILADELPHIA

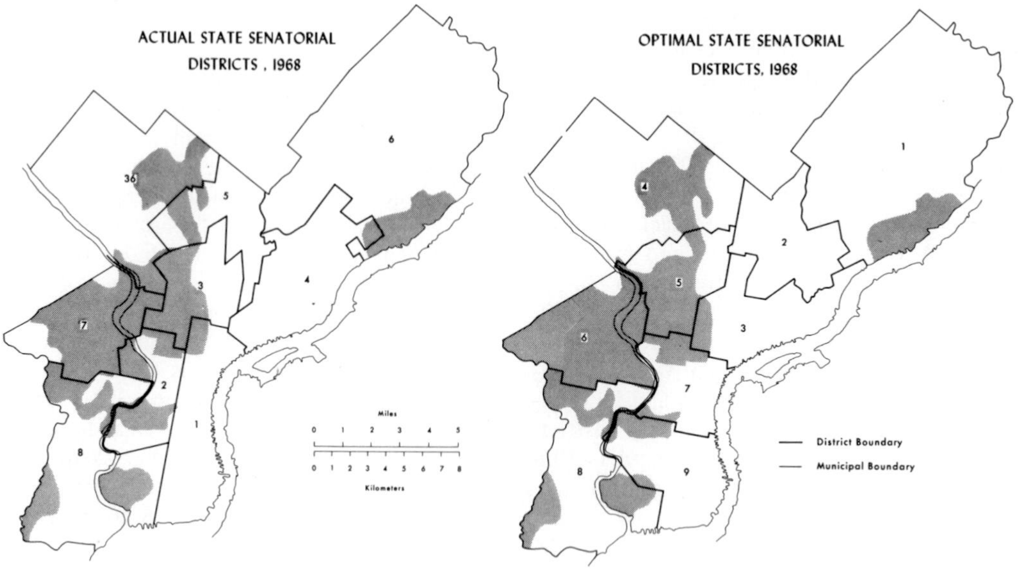

Figure 13-14. Actual and Optimal State Senatorial Districts, 1968, Philadelphia. Shading indicates areas more than 50 percent black in 1970.

may indicate gerrymandering in black areas. The change toward higher compactness between 1958 and 1968 was most pronounced in the older metropolitan areas which, compared to the West and South, have larger black ghettoes. During this decade the ghettoes in the Northeast and Midwest underwent continued expansion. In reality, they shifted in size from the type in Figure 13-21 (upper) to that in Figure 13-21 (lower). Because of this it was no longer possible to deny blacks at least some representatives and the districts drawn were compact (Figure 13-21 (lower). This is, of course, only a tentative explanation of the trend toward higher compactness indexes in black areas, but an extremely plausible one considering the evidence portrayed in Figures 13-13 through 13-20. It casts serious doubts on the use of compactness indexes of any kind to measure gerrymandering. Perhaps the best method remains the ratio of representatives to population. If blacks form 40 percent of the population of a city then, if the political system is equitable, they should form 40 percent of its representatives. Because of the spatial distributions of many black populations, it is usually necessary to engage in deliberate gerrymandering of white areas to ensure black majority districts. Some examples exist of this procedure. Many black inner city districts are losing population rapidly. White areas on the fringes of the ghettos have to be added to bring those districts represented by blacks up to the state average population size. The redistricters have to be very careful how they delimit the new boundaries, so as not to deprive the black representative of his seat. At this time, no legislative body wants to be known as one that deprived blacks of representation by one of their own race. This reasoning was behind the delimitations of the boundaries of the First Missouri and the Thirteenth Michigan Congressional districts in 1970.

A brief example will suffice to illustrate the usefulness of the proportional representation method and to provide further comparison with the compactness method and the optimal districting method (Table 13-24).

The results of this brief analysis point to the size of the black ghetto as being the controlling factor in electing blacks (Table 13-24). A situation analogous to that in Figure 13-21

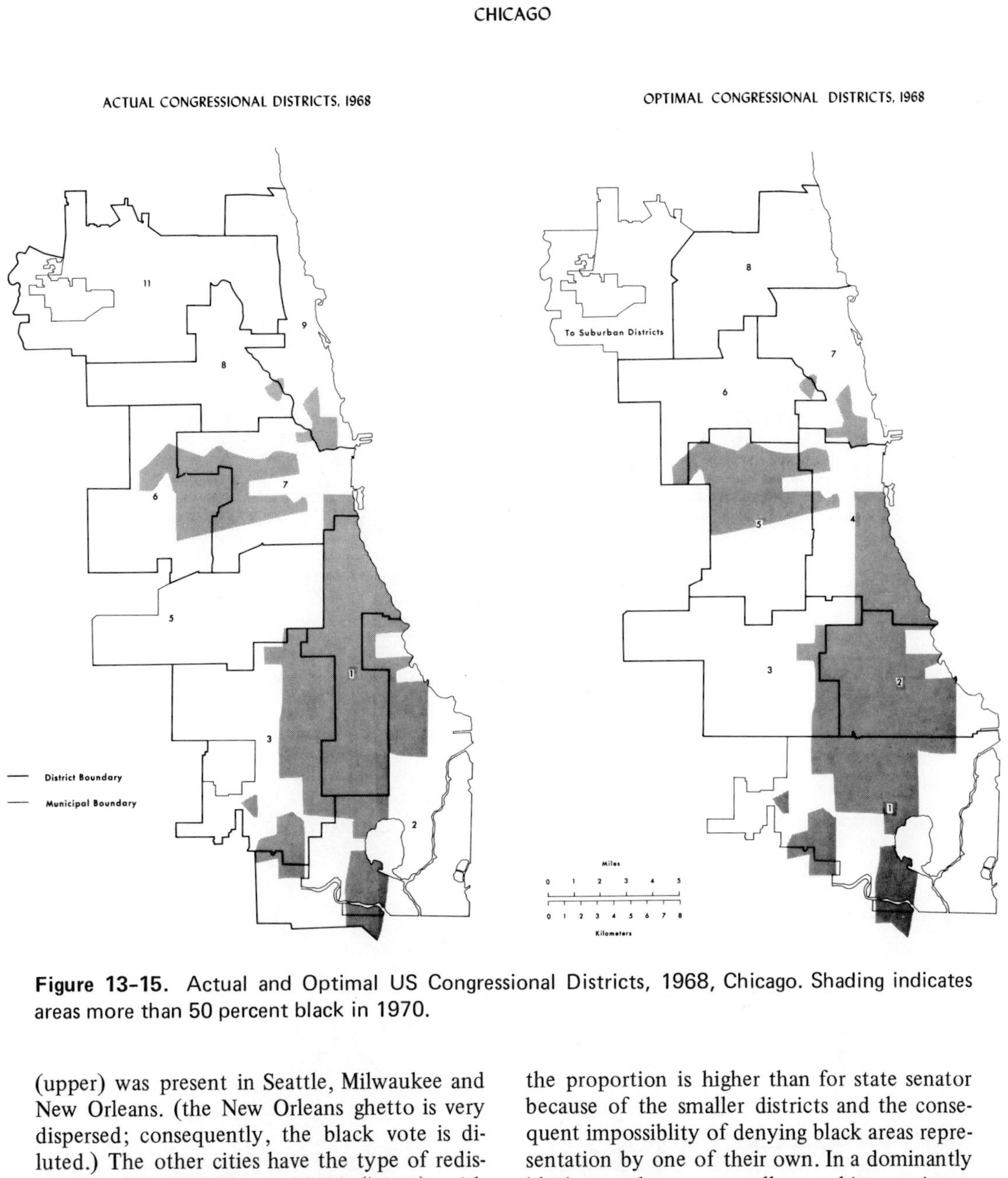

Figure 13-15. Actual and Optimal US Congressional Districts, 1968, Chicago. Shading indicates areas more than 50 percent black in 1970.

(upper) was present in Seattle, Milwaukee and New Orleans. (the New Orleans ghetto is very dispersed; consequently, the black vote is diluted.) The other cities have the type of redistricting shown in Figure 13-21 (lower), with at least one representative. The indexes derived here are highly related to the compactness indexes of black areas for 1968, but not to the results of the comparison of the ideal to the optimal. This method is useful as a check on the results and gives a quick summary measure of how well blacks are represented in each city. Obviously the proportion of the total elected that are black varies with the type of electoral districts. For state representatives, for example, the proportion is higher than for state senator because of the smaller districts and the consequent impossiblity of denying black areas representation by one of their own. In a dominantly black area there are usually no white nominees, but in a mixed area (state senate district) the electorate often has a choice between a white and a black candidate. Blacks and whites vote for either a black or a white, with the white often successful.

CONCLUSIONS

Until 1969, the Supreme Court insisted that all districts have equal population, usually

MILWAUKEE

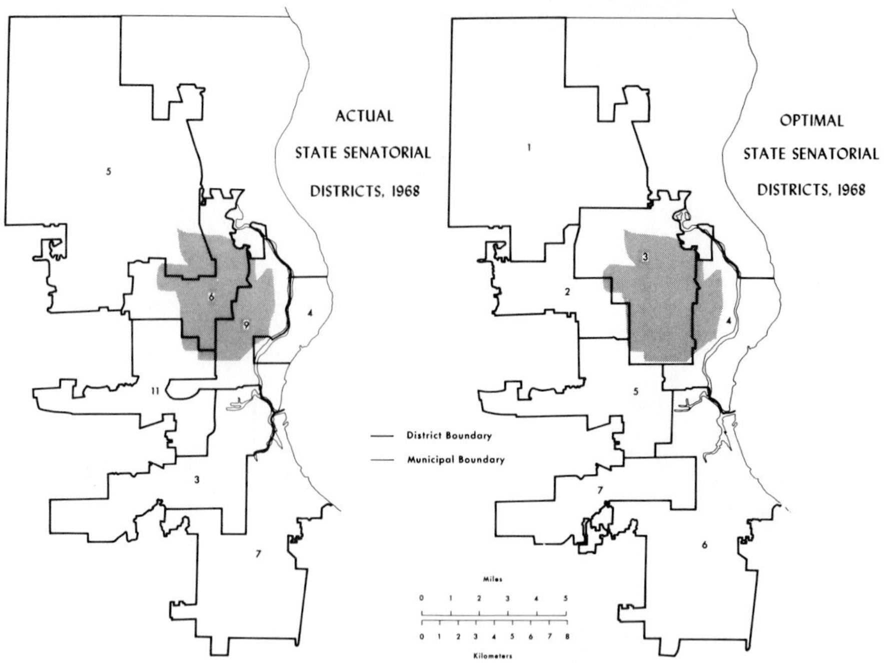

Figure 13-16. Actual and Optimal State Senate Districts, 1968, Milwaukee. Shading indicates areas more than 50 percent black in 1970.

ATLANTA

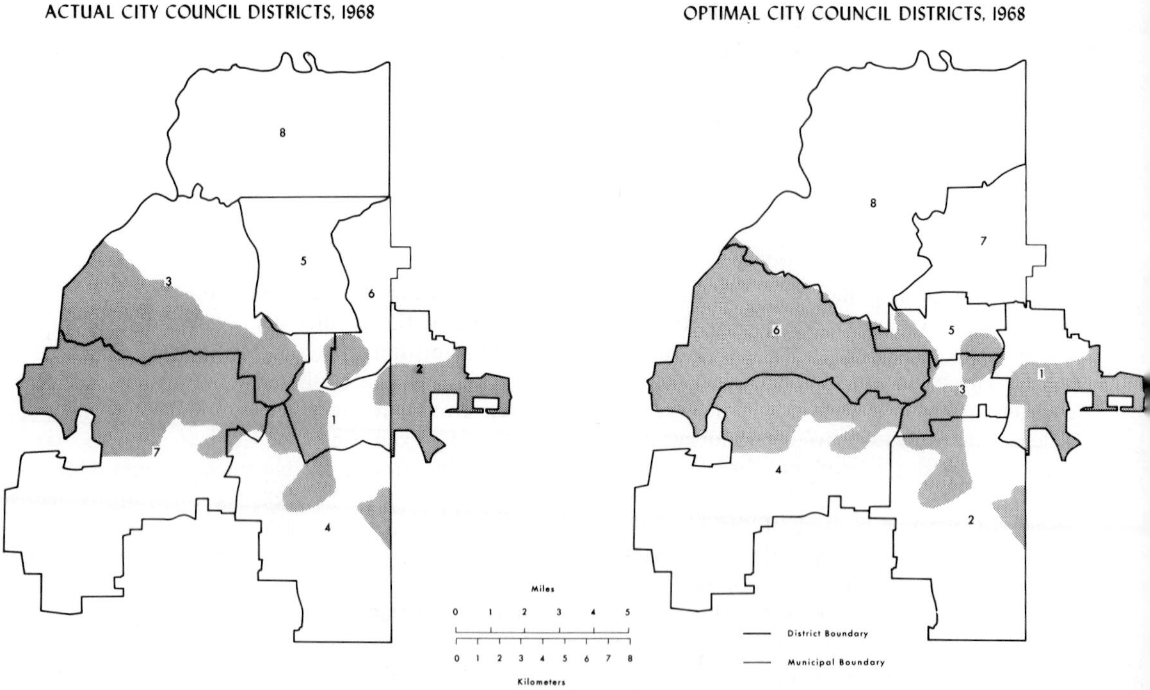

Figure 13-17. Actual and Optimal City Council Districts, 1968, Atlanta. Shading indicates areas more than 50 percent black in 1970.

NEW ORLEANS

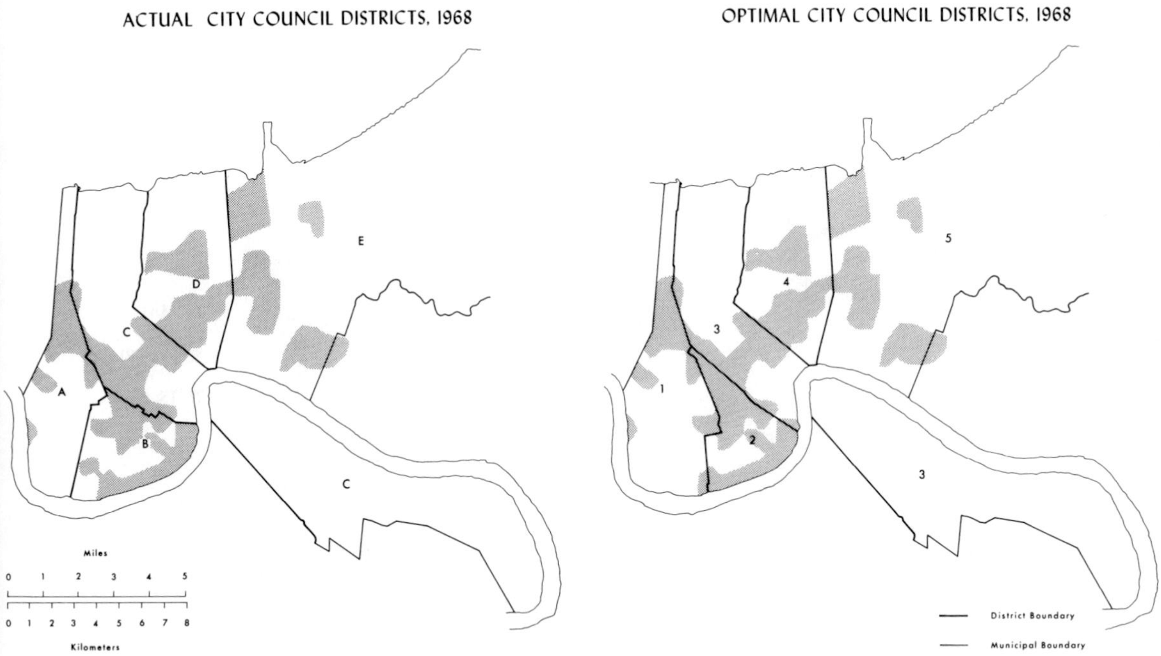

Figure 13-18. Actual and Optimal City Council Districts, 1968, New Orleans. Shading indicates areas more than 50 percent black in 1970.

LOS ANGELES COUNTY

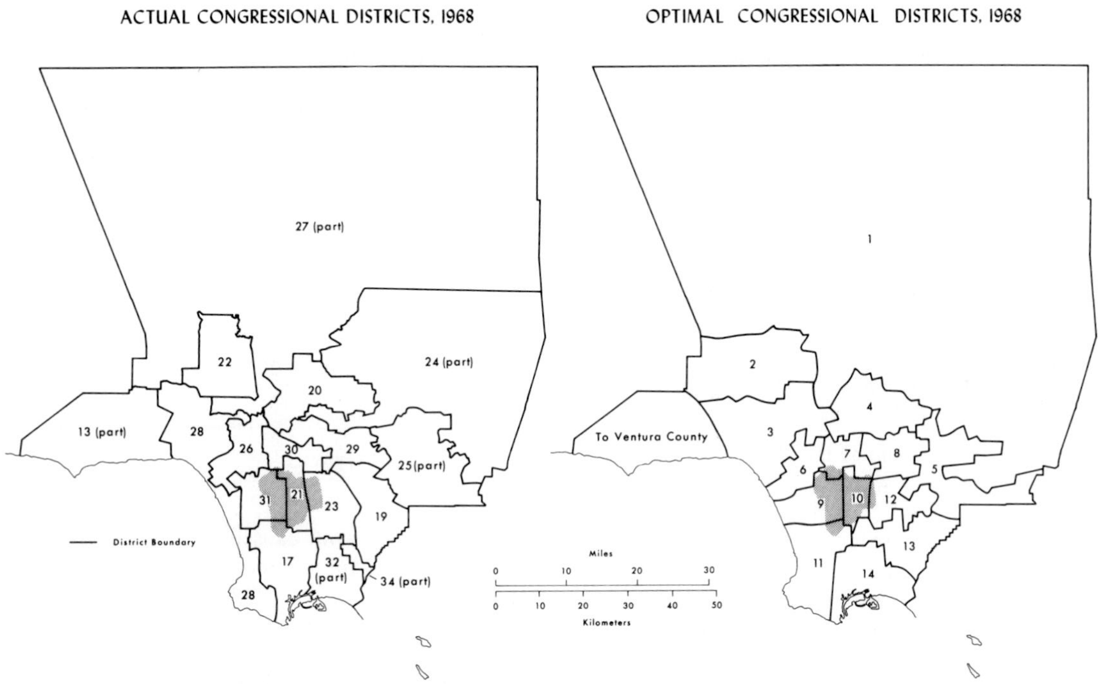

Figure 13-19. Actual and Optimal US Congressional Districts, 1968, Los Angeles. Shading indicates areas more than 50 percent black in 1970.

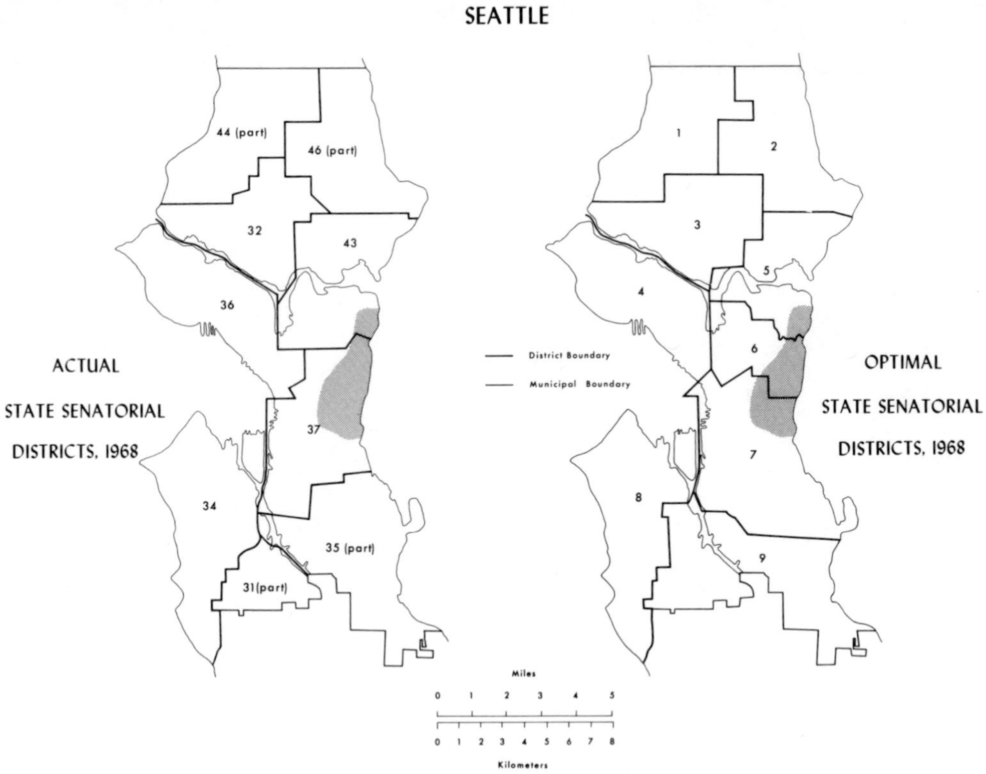

Figure 13-20. Actual and Optimal State Senate Districts, 1968, Seattle. Shading indicates areas more than 50 percent black in 1970.

Table 13-22. Comparison of Districts in Actual and Optimal Redistrictings

	Actual (percent)				*Optimal (percent)*			
City	*< 25*	*25-50*	*50-75*	*75-100*	*< 25*	*25-50*	*50-75*	*75-100*
New York	12	5	2	0	11	4	4	0
Philadelphia	3	4	1	1	4	2	2	1
Chicago	5	3	0	1	4	2	2	1
Milwaukee	4	4	1	0	4	2	0	1
Atlanta	4	2	1	1	3	2	2	1
New Orleans	1	3	1	0	1	3	1	0
Los Angeles	12	1	0	1	11	1	0	2
Seattle	8	0	1	0	7	2	0	0
Total	49	20	7	4	45	18	11	6

Source: computations by the author.

within 3 to 5 percent of the state average. The analysis here shows a consistent reduction of the population deviations (a measure of how far the population of a district varies from the optimum, or state average) between 1958 and 1968.

The reapportionments which followed the Court's decisions reduced underrepresentation in black districts but caused all city districts to become slightly more underrepresented in 1968 than they were in 1958. This may be attributed to a greater allocation of districts to the rapidly growing suburban areas.

For the 1958 national sample, black districts were overrepresented, while the mixed areas were underrepresented. (White districts were

Table 13-23. Regional Comparison of Actual and Optimal Redistrictings

	Actual (percent)				*Optimal (percent)*			
Region	*< 25*	*25-50*	*50-75*	*75-100*	*< 25*	*25-50*	*50-75*	*75-100*
NE	15	9	3	15	15	6	6	1
MW	8	6	1	1	8	4	2	2
South	5	5	2	1	4	5	3	1
West	20	1	1	1	18	3	0	2

Source: computations by the author.

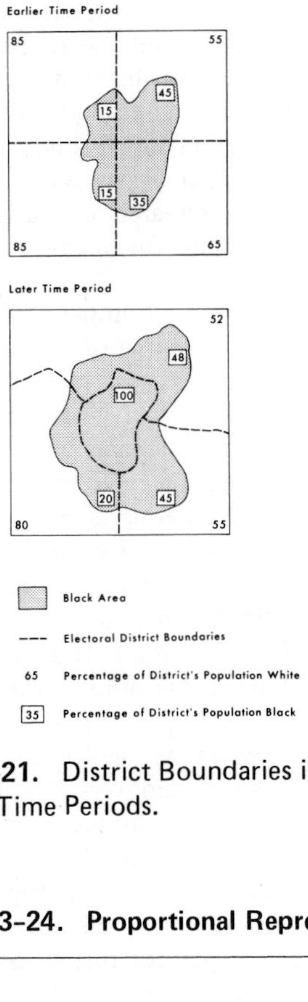

Figure 13-21. District Boundaries in the Ghetto at Two Time Periods.

districted fairly.) Black districts had fewer representatives than their numbers merited in the West and South, but more in the Northeast and Midwest. Mixed districts were near optimally districted in all regions except the South. By 1968, all districts in all types of neighborhoods–(black, changing and white–were fairly districted.

When the changes in the population sizes of the sample districts between 1958 and 1968 were examined by type of election districts (US congressional, state senate, etc.), significant change occurred in state senatorial districts in the West and South. Given the huge population reductions which occurred in some districts in the South and West between 1958 and 1968, this result is not surprising. Significant reductions also took place in state assembly districts in the West and Northeast, but only western city council districts showed any significant reduction. The Supreme Court decisions had their greatest impact at the state legislature level both because of the gross malapportionment of some of these districts in 1958 and

Table 13-24. Proportional Representation of Blacks in Eight Cities, 1968

City	*Type of District*	*Number of Districts*	*Number with Black Representatives*	*Percentage Represented by Blacks*	*Percentage of City Population Black*	*Proportion of Ideal Representation by Blacks*
New York	US Congressional	19	2	10.5	21.2	0.50
Philadelphia	State Senate	9	2	22.0	33.6	0.65
Chicago	US Congressional	9	1	11.1	32.7	0.30
Milwaukee	State Senate	7	0	12.5	14.7	0.00
Atlanta	City Council	8	1	12.5	51.3	0.24
New Orleans	City Council	5	0	00.0	45.0	0.00
Los Angeles	US Congressional	14	1	7.1	17.9	0.39
Seattle	State Senate	9	0	0.0	10.0	0.00

Source: computations by the author.

also because of the low priority placed on equitable districts at the local level (city council districts).

Besides an overall reduction in the population deviations of all districts between 1958 and 1968, no other clear pattern emerged when the population deviations of districts in black, mixed and white neighborhoods are split by type of district. The final series of results showed black areas gaining representatives relative to white and mixed areas between 1958 and 1968. This apparent overrepresentation of black districts is misleading. Because reapportionment decisions and population sizes of districts are based on census figures, which are lower than the actual figures in black areas, the overrepresentation is apparent rather than real.

The second part of the analysis was concerned with the shape of districts. The Supreme Court has dictated that election districts should be as compact as possible. In immediate contrast to their efforts in reducing population deviations, the Court has been remarkably ineffective in producing compact districts. In general, black districts are slightly more compact than either white or changing districts. The reason why black districts are more compact, in all probability, lies in their being inner city in nature. Thus, black districts are not affected by the boundary indentations of the city limits, as are white districts.

Because shape indexes are suspect and may not be the best way of determining gerrymandering, it was decided to compare the districts drawn by legislators with those produced by a computer algorithm. By comparing the number of districts with black majorities in both districting plans, it is possible to determine whether black neighborhoods are gerrymandered. From the results it appeared as if the black vote in New York, Los Angeles and Chicago congressional districts, and in state senatorial districts in Philadelphia, was diluted in 1968. Finally, based on the analysis, a model which relates black intraurban migration and reapportionment changes to gerrymandering of black neighborhoods is presented.

When the results of both sets of analyses are compared, some generalizations may be made. Black districts are more compact and have lower populations than either of the other two types. Changing areas have populations greater than the average and the lowest compactness. Between 1958 and 1968, black areas changed from slight underrepresentation to slight overrepresentation, with a rise in the level of compactness. No such change occurred in the other two types of neighborhoods. Districts which are drawn by state legislatures—US congressional, state house and state senate—were most affected by reapportionment, while city council districts were affected little, either in their average population deviations or compactness levels. Regionally the country showed a consistent division between the South and West on the one hand and the Northeast and Midwest on the other. Many results were not explained, and in these instances the study assumes a descriptive rather than an analytical form. However, since this is an initial study in a largely unexplored field, many gaps will appear in the analysis. Further research on each individual city should account for many of the unexplained patterns.

Although the initial impetus for reapportionment and redistricting of electoral districts came from urban residents in malapportioned states, and although gerrymandering by the two political parties remains a continuing feature of the American political scene, ethnic and racial gerrymandering is perhaps the most invidious of all. A 1972 review by a nonpartisan research group found the implementation of the 1965 Voting Rights Act to be haphazard in the South. This group detailed the gerrymandering of blacks in both the urban and rural South.

A similar review is needed for the urban areas in the North and West. Such a review should study the disenfranchisement of all groups, be they racial, social or economic. As yet, blacks have not had the opportunity to dictate the delimitation of electoral boundaries in large cities. To prevent further gerrymandering, the redistricting process should be taken from legislators and placed in the charge of nonpartisan groups who will redistrict only on the criteria of equal population and compactness. Such a procedure is essential if the constitutional requirements on voting are to be met.

BIBLIOGRAPHY

Banzaf, J.F. "Multi-member Electoral Districts—Do They Violate the 'One Man, One

Vote' Principle?" *Yale Law Journal* 75, 8 (July 1966): 1309-38.

Bunge, William. "Geography, Gerrymandering and Grouping." *Geographical Review* 55, 2 (April 1966): 258-66.

Detroit Geographical Expedition. *Field Notes.* Discussion Paper No. 2. East Lansing: Michigan State University, Department of Geography, 1970.

Elazar, Daniel. *Cities of the Prairie.* New York: Basic Books, Inc., 1970.

Gibbs, Jack P., ed. *Urban Research Methods.* Princeton, N.J.: D. Van Nostrand Company, Inc., 1961.

Haggett, Peter. *Locational Analysis in Human Geography.* London: Edward Arnold (Publishers) Ltd., 1965.

Massam, Bryan H. and Michael F. Goodchild. "Temporal Trends in the Spatial Organization of a Service Agency." *Canadian Geographer* 15, 3 (Fall 1971): 193-206.

O'Loughlin, John. "Spatial Justice for the Black American Voter: The Territorial Dimension in Urban Politics." Ph.D. dissertation, The Pennsylvania State University, 1973.

Orr, Douglas M., Jr. *Congressional Redistricting: The North Carolina Experience.* Chapel Hill: University of North Carolina Department of Geography, 1970.

Roeck, E.C. "Measuring Compactness as a Requirement of Legislative Apportionment." *Midwest Journal of Political Science* 5, 1 (February 1969): 70-74.

Rose, Harold M. "The Development of an Urban Subsystem; The Case of the Negro Ghetto." *Annals,* Association of American Geographers 60 (March 1970): 1-17.

Sharkansky, Ira. "Reapportionment and Roll Call Voting: The Case of the Georgia Legislature." *Social Science Quarterly* 51, 1 (June 1970): 129-38.

Schwartzberg, Joseph J. "Reapportionment, Gerrymandering, and the Notion of Compactness." *Minnesota Law Review* 50 (1966): 443-52.

Sickels, R.J. "Dragons, Bacon Strips and Dumbbells—Who's Afraid of Reapportionment?" *Yale Law Journal* 75, 8 (July 1966): 1300-1308.

Washington Research Project. *The Shameful Blight: The Survival of Racial Discrimination in Voting in the South.* Washington, D.C.: Washington Research Project, 1972.

Index

About the Authors

John S. Adams is Professor of Geography and Public Affairs and Head of the School of Public Affairs at the University of Minnesota, Minneapolis, Minnesota 55455.

Brian J.L. Berry is Williams Professor of City and Regional Planning and Director of the Laboratory for Computer Graphics and Spatial Analysis at Harvard University, Cambridge, Massachusetts 02138.

Kathleen Molnar Brown is Assistant Professor of Geography at the University of Michigan, Ann Arbor, Michigan 48104.

Michael J. Dear Is Assistant Professor of Geography at McMaster University, Hamilton, Ontario L8S 4K1.

Stephen M. Golant is assistant professor in the department of geography and the department of behavioral sciences, University of Chicago, Chicago, Illinois 60637.

Rex D. Honey is Assistant Professor of Geography at the University of Iowa, Iowa City, Iowa 52242.

John F. Hultquist is Associate Professor of Geography at the University of Idaho, Moscow, Idaho 83843.

John O'Loughlin is Assistant Professor of Geography at the University of Illinois at Urbana-Champaign, Urban, Illoinis 61801.

Dr. Mary Megee is a planning consultant in private practice in Joplin, Missour 64801.

John Mercer is Assistant Professor of Geography at the University of British Columbia, Vancouver, British Columbia V6T 1W5.

Rutherford H. Platt, an attorney and geographer, is Assistant Professor of Geography at the University of Massachusetts, Amherst, Massachusetts 01002.

Gerald F. Pyle is Associate Professor and Associate Director of the Center for Urban Studies at the University of Akron, Akron, Ohio 44325.

David R. Reynolds is Professor of Geography at the University of Iowa, Iowa City, Iowa 52242.

Charles S. Sargent, Jr. is Assistant Professor of Geography at Arizona State University, Tempe, Arizona 85281.